the science of good food

The ultimate reference on how cooking works

the science of good food

David Joachim and Andrew Schloss

with A. Philip Handel, Ph.D.

Robert
ROSE

Disclaimers

The recipes in this book have been carefully tested by our kitchen and our tasters. To the best of our knowledge, they are safe and nutritious for ordinary use and users. For those people with food or other allergies, or who have special food requirements or health issues, please read the suggested contents of each recipe carefully and determine whether or not they may create a problem for you. All recipes are used at the risk of the consumer.

We cannot be responsible for any hazards, loss or damage that may occur as a result of any recipe use.

For those with special needs, allergies, requirements or health problems, in the event of any doubt, please contact your medical adviser prior to the use of any recipe.

For complete cataloguing information, see page 605.

Editor: Carol Sherman

Copy Editor: Shaun Oakey

Recipe Editor: Jennifer MacKenzie

Proofreader: Karen Campbell-Sheviak

Indexer: Gillian Watts

Design & Production: PageWave Graphics Inc.

Illustrations: Crowle Art Group

Cover Photography: Colin Erricson

Prop Stylist: Charlene Erricson

Photography Credits: see page 608

We acknowledge the financial support of the Government of Canada through the Book Publishing Industry Development Program (BPIDP) for our publishing activities.

Published by Robert Rose Inc.

120 Eglinton Avenue East, Suite 800, Toronto, Ontario, Canada M4P 1E2

Tel: (416) 322-6552   Fax: (416) 322-6936

Printed and bound in Canada

3994 9770   5/09

1 2 3 4 5 6 7 8 9 TCP 16 15 14 13 12 11 10 09 08

INTRODUCTION:
WHERE FOOD AND SCIENCE MEET

Cuisines change. A new ingredient, cooking technique, nutrition study, piece of kitchen equipment, or the latest dish from a trendsetting chef is enough to evolve the way we think about what we cook and eat. One of the most powerful changes in food in this century has been propelled by the transformative effect of science on haute cuisine. Award-winning chefs and cutting-edge restaurants from Spain to Singapore to the United States have become famous for harnessing the principles of chemistry and physics to create mind-blowing taste sensations. Their early innovations have already filtered down to adventurous home cooks, who are experimenting with foams and using vacuum sealers to cook sous vide ("under vacuum").

The convergence of food and science may seem new, but in fact food and science have always been closely aligned. Candy is a vivid example. The original candies were medicines made by medieval apothecaries. A little honey or other sweetener helped to mask the awful taste of the medicine. By the 1800s, candy makers abandoned any medicinal benefits and focused instead on the pure pleasure of sweetness, developing all manner of sugary confections, from multicolored lollipops to rich-tasting toffee. But you can still see the medicinal origins of candy in throat lozenges and chewable vitamins.

By the mid-1900s, the intersection of food and science was dominated by nutrition. Chefs, home cooks, and consumers became increasingly interested in how food affects our health and in ways to improve food's nutritional benefits. Heavy cream-based sauces gave way to lighter purées of vegetables and fruits. And new cooking technologies such as nonstick pans and microwave ovens allowed cooks to reduce the calories in their cooking.

By the late 1900s, interest in nutritional science led to a deeper awareness of food composition and a hunger among chefs for more information about the chemistry of cooking. Fortunately, the discipline of food science had been developing for centuries. Until that time it had focused on processed foods to improve the packaging, shelf life, safety, flavor, texture, and aroma of packaged food products, as well as the technology and machinery necessary to produce food products. From early-19th-century research on canning to the latest studies on flavor perception and food packaging, food science provided a wealth of scientific information about the chemistry and physics of cooking.

In the new millennium, innovative chefs began to use that knowledge to create more exciting dining experiences. They took industrial ingredients like transglutaminase, an enzyme that binds meat into hot dogs and chicken nuggets, and used the enzyme's capacity as "meat glue" to form shrimp "noodles" and to pull pork shoulder from the bone, glue it back together, and cook it under vacuum to create a single piece of meat, richer and more succulent than any pork raised on a farm. Chefs discovered that they share the same goal as food product scientists: to create pleasurable sensations through food and to discover new ones by combining or juxtaposing flavors, textures, shapes, colors, temperatures, and aromas. Ultimately, home cooks also share the same goal of making great-tasting food. And science can help.

The Science of Good Food simplifies the complex science of food for home cooks and chefs alike. Organized from A to Z, it contains more than 1,600 entries that clearly explain the physical and chemical transformations that govern all food preparation and cooking. Entries touch on a variety of sciences and disciplines, including chemistry, physics, botany, zoology, biology, anatomy, physiology, nutrition, flavor science, psychobiology, agriculture, animal husbandry, food safety, and food product development.

Entries on ingredients discuss the basic molecular makeup of meats, poultry, game, fish, shellfish, vegetables, fruits, grains, cheeses, eggs, doughs, and most other foodstuffs, as well as what happens when these foods react with heat, so that you can cook better with these ingredients. Entries on equipment discuss such topics as why copper bowls make superior egg foams and which kind of grill gives you the best crust on a steak. Entries on chemistry principles unravel the physical and chemical transformations that take place during everyday cooking, explaining things like aeration, caramelization, and gelatinization. Scores of charts and tables, and more than 200 photographs and drawings, help to illustrate the basic principles of food science.

In addition to demystifying the complexities of cooking, *The Science of Good Food* sheds some light on the confounding phenomena of everyday eating, such as why artichokes make certain foods taste sweeter and what causes some people to think cilantro tastes like soap. We also give you the know-how you need to experiment in the kitchen and solve cooking problems that may crop up. We include more than 100 recipes that demonstrate the science of good and innovative cooking, from Perfect French Fries (page 260) to how to caramelize sugar in a microwave oven (page 398). The ultimate goal throughout the book is to provide practical information that you can use to create better-tasting food. The straightforward explanations of the what, how, and why of food and cooking are intended to help you become a more skilled and confident cook. After all, cooking and science are really after the same thing: helping us to enjoy life. We hope this book helps you do just that.

HOW TO USE THIS BOOK

The entries in *The Science of Good Food* are arranged alphabetically and cross-referenced like an index. An extended index also appears at the back of the book to make it easier to find what you're looking for. Entries are listed in strict alphabetical order, even when they consist of more than one word or of a hyphenated word. For example, Aldehyde appears before Al Dente.

Entries are broken into three sections, called What It Is, What It Does, and How It Works. The first section defines the item and may include a bit of historical or other interesting information. The second section discusses the item's significance in food preparation and cooking and offers practical kitchen tips. The third section explains the science behind the item, including flavor chemistry and chemical transformations that occur during cooking. Other practical tips are included in Kitchen Wisdom boxes, while more detailed science information appears in Science Wise boxes. Interesting food trivia is included in a section called Fast Facts.

The A-to-Z organization of this book makes it easy to find individual items but harder to see the connections between those items. For that reason, the entries are extensively cross-referenced. Let's say you want to know how sauces can be thickened by starch. The Sauces entry is a good place to start, but you'll find out even more by going to the Starch entry, which will appear bold within the Sauces entry. Whenever you see a word in **bold**, that means you can find more information about that particular item by turning to its own entry. If you don't find what you're looking for in a particular entry, check out the See Also cross-references at the end of the entry. Hopefully the A-to-Z format, the index at the back, and the extensive cross-referencing throughout the book forge these all-important connections between the individual entries.

A quick word about measurements. We have included both imperial and metric measurements throughout. In some cases (particularly in the recipes) the metric measurements have been rounded for ease of use. We also included ranges of measurements to account for minuscule differences in food products and cooking conditions around the world. There are no absolutes in food because food comes from living, respiring organisms that are subject to innumerable variables such as climate, soil, and genetics. We have tried to be precise without being absolute.

A

ABALONE • See Fish

ABSINTHE • See Liqueur

AÇAI • See Berries

ACEROLA • See Berries

ACETIC ACID • See Vinegar

ACETOBACTER • See Vinegar

ACID

What It Is • Have you ever wondered why acids taste sour? Acids are chemical compounds that are likely to donate positively charged protons, usually hydrogen ions. Since the presence of free hydrogen ions can have a dramatic effect on other molecules around it, our bodies have a specialized taste sensation for estimating the concentration of protons in a solution — sourness. Your taste buds detect the level of hydrogen ions and send a signal to your brain indicating the level of sourness. The acid concentration in the cells in your body is carefully regulated. Since the liquid contents of a cell are a buffer system that resists changes in pH, a common reaction to the taste of acid is to drink water to dilute it.

What It Does • Depending on concentration, acids can titillate the palate, affect the color of cooking vegetables, coagulate milk into cheese, aid in digestion, or corrode metal. Almost every food we eat is acidic to some degree, from meat to orange juice — even milk is slightly acidic — and so the chemistry of acids affects most recipes.

Chemical leaveners depend on the reaction between acids and **alkalis** to produce enough carbon dioxide gas to raise baking batters.

A little lemon juice or vinegar added to the water for a poached egg helps to coagulate albumin **protein**, insuring that the egg white remains firm and compact.

Dried beans cooked with tomato, lemon,

or other acidic ingredients will take longer to soften because acid stabilizes the cell walls of **legumes**. This can be problematic when cooking particularly hard beans, like chickpeas and soybeans, but for cooking less fibrous beans, like lentils, or for long-cooking preparations, like baked beans, a little acid helps beans keep their shape as they soften.

In a seviche (also ceviche), citrus juice and/or vinegar denatures the delicate proteins of fish and shellfish the same way cooking with heat does. The flesh becomes firm, opaque, and dry enough to be eaten without ever being heated.

As the active agent in marinades, acid decreases the number of chemical bonds between proteins, encouraging meat fibers to bond with flavorful components in the marinade, and tenderizing tough meat fibers.

Adding a pinch of acid, usually cream of tartar or lemon juice, to egg whites while beating them brings their pH to a point where the proteins coagulate easily. The resulting albumin foam stays flexible and glossy, and therefore rises higher when baked.

Bacteria used when making fermented dairy feed off sugars in milk, producing lactic acid that coagulates the casein milk proteins, causing the milk to thicken into buttermilk or yogurt and eventually separate into cheese curds.

Acid turns the **chlorophyll** of green

kitchen wisdom

All Acids Act Similarly in a Recipe
Although it is most common to make seviche with lemon or lime juice, orange juice or vinegar would also work. The difference is in the finished flavor, which results from the specific aromatics of each acid. But you must also pay attention to the strength of the acid. The more concentrated the acid, the less of it you will need. Acid strength is measured by pH, which is a logarithmic scale. A decrease of one point in pH indicates 10 times the acid concentration. Orange juice has a pH of 3; lemon juice, with a pH of 2.2, is eight times as concentrated. So if you are substituting orange juice for lemon juice in a seviche recipe, you will need more orange juice to get the same effect.

Technicolor Seviche

Seviche (also ceviche), an ancient technique for "cooking" fish with acid, became popular along the western and northern coastlines of South America, where supplies of long-burning fuels are scarce but where there is an abundance of acidic tropical fruits. Acidity denatures and coagulates the delicate muscle proteins of fish, turning the translucent gelatinous meat opaque and firm in much the same way that heat does, but more gradually and with none of the caramelized flavors that you get from cooking over a fire.

12 oz	skinned and boned flounder fillet (or other flat fish), thinly sliced	375 g
4 oz	skinned and boned salmon fillet, thinly sliced	125 g
½ to 1 tsp	minced chile pepper	2 to 5 mL
1 cup	freshly squeezed lemon or lime juice	250 mL
2	scallions (green onions), trimmed, thinly sliced	2
1 tbsp	finely chopped red onion	15 mL
¼ cup	finely chopped red or yellow bell pepper	50 mL

1. In a nonreactive bowl, combine flounder, salmon, chile, and lemon juice. Cover and marinate in the refrigerator until opaque and firm, 1½ to 2 hours, depending on how thin the fish is cut.

2. Drain, discarding marinade. Add scallions, red onion, and bell pepper and toss gently. Refrigerate for up to 24 hours. Serve chilled.

MAKES 4 APPETIZER SERVINGS

vegetables khaki color, which is why marinated green beans or asparagus lose their bright color, and why an acid, such as lemon juice or tomato, should never be added to a cooking green vegetable until the last minute. Likewise, green vegetables should be cooked in an open pot. Covering them with a lid concentrates the natural acidity of the vegetable and dulls its color. Although adding an alkali like baking soda to the water will neutralize the acid, don't do it. It will brighten the green color but it will also destroy the vegetable's vitamins and degrade its texture to mush.

Acid brightens anthocyanin, the color of red-purple vegetables, which is why red cabbage is usually cooked with vinegar or some acidic fruit.

Enzymatic **browning**, the chemical reaction that causes some cut fruits and vegetables to discolor, proceeds slowly if the food is tossed in a weak acid, such as a solution of lemon juice and water, as soon as it is cut.

Acids catalyze the breakage of **starch** molecules into smaller pieces so they have less thickening power, which is why sauces that contain wine or citrus juice will not thicken as much as nonacidic sauces. Root and tuber starches, such as potato starch, tapioca, and arrowroot, are more sensitive to acids than are grain starches like wheat flour and cornstarch.

Acid in a poaching liquid, marinade, or frying batter helps to dampen volatile aromas in fish. It also breaks down muddy-smelling compounds that farm-raised fish accumulate from algae in their feed.

How It Works • Acidity is measured on a pH scale, a standard measure of hydrogen ion activity that ranges from 1 (extremely acid) to 14 (extremely alkali or basic). Pure water is considered neutral, neither acidic nor alkaline, with a pH of 7. Though H_2O

molecules are fairly stable, at any given moment a small percentage (about 0.0000001%) dissociate, allowing free hydrogen ions to bond with nearby intact water molecules, creating positively charged H_3O molecules. The more this happens, the more acidic a solution becomes. Strong acids like hydrochloric (HCl) fully dissociate into hydrogen ions and chloride ions. Weak acids like the organic acids found in foods (acetic, citric, lactic, etc.) partially dissociate so only part of the total amount of hydrogen is donated.

See Also • Alkali, Cells, Chemical Leavener, Chlorophyll, Eggs, Enzyme, Fermentation, Legumes, Protein, Starch

ACIDOPHILUS • See Fermentation

ACKEE • See Fruit

ACORN • See Nuts

ACORN SQUASH • See Squash

ACRYLAMIDE • See Browning

ADDITIVES • See Food Additives

ADENOSINE TRIPHOSPHATE (ATP) • See Metabolism

ADVOCAAT • See Liqueur

ADZUKI BEAN • See Legumes

AERATION

What It Is • Aeration, the art of harvesting air, has been exploited by cooks since the rising of the first bread. Early breads aerated by accident as wild yeasts falling onto resting dough metabolized the sugar in the flour and released carbon dioxide. In the heat of an oven the CO_2 expanded and a softer, lighter, more flavorful loaf resulted. Since incorporating air by chance proved beneficial, it is no wonder aerating

techniques continued to proliferate. By the mid-17th century all of the techniques we still use for beating **eggs** were known (whipped cream wasn't common for another 200 years).

What It Does • The first challenge in collecting air is to find something to hold it. Any flexible **protein** or **fat** can be aerated. Cakes rise from air beaten into solid shortening, butter or eggs. Meringues inflate because stretchy egg-white proteins can hold up to five times their volume in air. Whipped cream relies on chilled fat in heavy cream to trap air, and milk proteins hold air in the fragile foam that tops a cappuccino.

Cakes

When sugar is beaten into **butter** or shortening its sharp crystalline structure cuts deep into solid fat, drilling it with thousands of air pockets. During baking, that air expands. At the same time, water in the walls of the air bubbles turns to steam, causing the bubbles to inflate further. At 150 to 160°F (66 to 71°C) egg white proteins in the batter coagulate and set and then **starch** granules from the flour absorb water and swell. By then the fat has melted, but it doesn't matter, because the air it once held is now set in a bubbly network of soft, fluffy crumbs. Cakes are usually baked at moderate oven temperatures, around 350°F (180°C). If the oven temperature is too low the fat releases its air before the other elements in the batter set and the cake will not rise.

Butter is preferred in cakes for its flavor, but vegetable shortenings have smaller fat crystals that create a finer network of air bubbles. Small bubbles stay in suspension longer than big bubbles, so cakes made with shortening tend to be lighter than those made with butter. The temperature of the fat is also important. Too cold and the fat crystals will be too hard and not malleable enough; too warm and the fat may not be solid enough to hold air. For maximum aeration the ideal temperature is about 60°F (16°C) for butter, and 70°F (21°C) for vegetable shortening.

kitchen wisdom

Beating Egg Whites: How Stiff Is Too Stiff?

Achieving optimum loft in an egg foam is a matter of creating the maximum number of bubbles with maximum moisture between them. The ultimate lift depends somewhat on what you're lifting (cake, soufflé, mousse, meringue), but it's largely a balance between the foam's volume (number of bubbles) and the ease with which it can be mixed with other ingredients without bursting (amount of moisture). Soufflés and cakes benefit from softer beaten whites, which can be incorporated into the batter more easily. Meringues and mousses need stiffer foam to ensure that they hold their shape.

Egg Foams

Beat an egg white with a wire whisk and magic happens. The clear viscous liquid collapses and then almost immediately starts to solidify. As a whisk passes through egg white, the stress causes the proteins to unfold. Any water bonded to the protein flows out, and the relaxed protein strands start to bond to one another, creating a flexible film that traps and stabilizes the bubbles. Adding a weak acid such as tartaric acid from cream of tartar brings the pH of the solution down to where the proteins unfold more easily. The goal is to create as many small bubbles as possible, so don't beat too vigorously during the initial phase of inflating egg whites. Rapid movement incorporates too much air with each stroke, resulting in a fewer number of larger bubbles and a less stable **foam**.

Once a fine foam forms, the faster you beat, the more air is incorporated and the better the mass expands, but it is possible to go too far, for the same phenomenon that forms foam can break it. As the protein bonds increase in number and become tighter, they squeeze out the water. The bubble walls dry out and burst, and the foam collapses, and a collapsed foam won't rise.

Another cause of failure of egg whites to foam is the presence of fat. Fats are very nonpolar and therefore better competitors than air for the nonpolar parts of proteins. The proteins surround the fat rather than the air, compromising a cook's ability to form a good network of bubbles. Fat can come from yolk that was not separated from the white, from oily utensils, or from using plastic bowls. Fats often adhere to plastic even after cleaning.

Fresh eggs are best for forming foams because they have more of the thick protein (ovomucin) that easily traps air. Ovomucin degrades as eggs age.

Meringues and marshmallows, egg foams reinforced with sugar, are more stable than unsweetened foams. Sugar attaches to the water inside the bubbles and makes the foam more cohesive. This keeps the bubble walls more flexible so they are less likely to dehydrate, break, and drain. However, sugar also inhibits proteins from forming bonds, so it should be added only after the foam initially forms — about halfway through the inflation.

science wise

Soufflés are baked aerated sauces. The base sauce can be something like melted chocolate, a purée of fruit, or a sauce Mornay, into which beaten egg whites are folded to make a mixture thick enough to hold a shape but soft enough to fall easily from an inverted spoon. Too thin and the sauce will not be able to hold on to the air; too thick and the rise will be unimpressive.

Egg yolks don't have nearly the same potential as egg whites for producing high-flying foams — although the yolk is richer in protein than the white, it has those pesky fats that interfere with protein film formation. Eggs yolks will form a fine foam if you beat them at about 160°F (71°C), which thickens the protein just enough to help it overcome the interference of the fat. Another problem is a lack of water. Yolks have less than one-sixth of the moisture of egg whites. Add about 2 teaspoons (10 mL) of water (or any other watery liquid) for every large egg yolk and it will whip as voluminously as any egg white, which is exactly how zabaglione is made. Egg yolk foams are not as stable as egg white foams unless they are heated, but be careful: a temperature just a little higher than 160°F (71°C) will yield scrambled eggs.

Dairy Foams

Per volume there is one-third less protein in **milk** than in egg white, so its foam is more fragile and shorter lived. Milk must be heated, usually with steam, in order to develop foam that will last for any length of time. Until it reaches 160°F (71°C), milk proteins won't solidify enough to trap air. Skim milk foams better than fattier milks because fat interrupts the ability of protein to form a stable network, but whole milk bubbles into a richer, denser head. Always use the freshest milk possible when foaming. Acids that form in old milk can cause it to curdle as it heats.

Because cream and milk are different parts of the same liquid, you might expect whipped cream to behave similarly to foamed milk — not so. Unlike milk and egg foams, whipped cream is not stabilized by protein. It is stabilized by fat. As cream whips, the network of fat must be sufficient to surround the air bubbles and keep the liquid parts of the cream in suspension, which means that in order for cream to whip, it must be at least 30% fat. Whipping, or heavy, cream is 35 to 40% fat; lighter creams, such as table cream and half-and-half, contain less than 20% fat and cannot be whipped.

Because cold fat is firmer than warm fat the fat bubbles are more stable, which is why using chilled cream, a chilled bowl, and chilled beaters makes a big difference.

How It Works • The amount of protein or fat in a liquid determines how long it will stay foamy. The surface tension of **water** (the attraction between its molecules) is too strong to hold on to air. Beat pure water with a whisk and bubbles will form but then instantly burst as the water pulls itself back together. However, the non-water molecules in egg or cream block the water molecules from reattaching, allowing the air to stay in suspension longer. The extra non-water molecules also make the water thicker, giving the air bubbles more time to build into a cohesive mass.

The strength of protein-based foam is stabilized by unfolded and then reassociated proteins. Different parts of a protein have different abilities to bond with polar water and nonpolar air, and so when you beat protein, the unfolded protein strands tend to line up with their water-loving (hydrophilic) ends immersed in liquid and their water-avoiding (hydrophobic) parts in the air, similar to the way an emulsifier keeps oil and water stabilized in mayonnaise. Thus situated, the proteins easily build bonds with one another, forming a very stable network of bubbles that holds water and air in place.

See Also ● Beer, Cake, Eggs, Foams, Milk, Protein, Starch, Water

AFFINAGE • See Cheese

AFLATOXIN • See Fungi, Mushrooms

AGAR • See Seaweed

AGARICUS • See Fungi

AGAROSE • See Gums

AGAVE • See Cactus

AGING • See Beef, Cheese, Fermentation, Fruit, Liquor, Oxygen, Wine

AGRICULTURE

What It Is ● The business of agriculture reinvents itself continuously — from the subsistence farmer who grows just enough food for the needs of his or her family to corporate farms that are after maximum financial gain from the industrial production of crops and livestock. Over millennia changes in machinery, chemistry, breeding techniques, genetics, and government farm subsidization have influenced the types and amount of human food, animal fodder, fuels, fibers, and drugs available to us.

Most agricultural advances have happened in the last 200 years, and along with them has come increased degradation of the environment. Responses to the negative environmental impact of industrial farming practices have engendered a shift in the debate over how the business of agriculture operates. The widening sphere of influence held by large seed and chemical companies, meat packers, and food processors has been of concern both within the food community and to the general public. Increasing consumer awareness of agricultural issues has led to the rise of community-supported agriculture, the local-food movement, the Slow Food movement, and the growth of organic farming.

What It Does ● Domestication of plants over the centuries has increased yield, improved disease resistance and drought tolerance, and enhanced the taste and nutrition of food crops. During the Middle Ages the innovation of three-field crop rotation revolutionized crop yields, just as later experiments with seed selection and breeding techniques changed the characteristics of commercial plants, allowing the plant breeder to manipulate the "natural selection" of plants and animals and to speed up genetic change, generating as many as three generations of plants per year.

Agriculture has always altered natural environments — cutting down forest for fields, depleting and supplementing nutrients in soil, redirecting water resources to improve irrigation. But until the industrial innovations of the 1940s and '50s the environmental consequences were manageable. Before then most farmers raised a variety of crops and livestock, periodically rotating their crops, so that the soil depletion from one crop was relieved by the metabolic by-products of another. Animal manure naturally fertilized the soil, which nurtured higher-quality plants, which in turn made it easier to raise healthier animals.

The term "organic" has surfaced since farming became industrial; before that it was the only way crops were grown and animals were raised. Organic food is produced without using synthetic pesticides, petroleum- or sewage-sludge-based fertilizers, bioengineering, or ionizing radiation. Organic meat, poultry, eggs, and dairy products must come from animals fed 100% organic feed and no antibiotics or growth hormones. Animals producing grass-fed meat must feed solely on foraged pasturage and cannot be fed on grain or grain by-products. They must have continuous access to pasture during their growing season.

How It Works • Starting in the mid-20th century the business of farming became more competitive. Farmers found that to be profitable, they had to isolate crops from livestock and concentrate on just a few high-profit items. By restricting what was planted (mostly to corn, soy, and wheat), farm work was streamlined, labor could be cut, and yields increased. The new approach, called monocropping or monoculture, eliminated crop rotation to enrich the soil. Instead petroleum-based fertilizers, specifically designed to replace the nutrients depleted by a particular crop, and pesticides and fungicides designed to protect that crop, took the place of more labor-intensive sustainable agricultural practices.

Petrochemicals have dramatically increased crop yields, and farmers have become dependent on them to preserve their profit margins. But they have also proven to be harmful to our health and the environment. Many pesticides in current use have been shown to cause brain and nerve damage, birth defects, endocrine- and immune-system malfunctions, and some cancers. Much of the work done with **genetic** engineering of seeds has concentrated on minimizing the use of pesticides and herbicides.

The same economic forces that streamlined farming affected animal husbandry as well. Under monocropping so much grain was produced that the excess was fed to livestock. Because corn and wheat are so much higher in calories than grass, grain-fed animals reached slaughter weight faster. Meat became cheaper to produce, production increased, and the consumption of meat grew.

Livestock producers focused on the most profitable animals (cattle, hogs, chickens, and turkey), raising them in more confined housing, which reduced labor and production costs. But raising animals in close confinement led to the spread of disease, which caused the current practice of routinely including **antibiotics** in animal feed. The typical feedlot operation houses about 32,000 cattle or 100,000 chickens, and contributes significantly to the growth in greenhouse gases and surplus nitrogen and phosphorus in rivers and lakes from waste runoff.

Fish farming (aquaculture), taking its lead from the same intensive production model, has yielded similar results — better supplies of cheaper fish, but more disease and more environmental impact.

In all its guises monoculture has decreased the biodiversity of food crops and livestock. Because the health of any ecosystem is measured partially by the diversity of its gene pool, the narrowing range of agricultural biodiversity can only be seen as detrimental.

fast facts

- In the early 16th century, crop exchanges between the New World and the old one changed agriculture and eating habits around the globe. Crops like tomatoes, chiles, corn, potatoes, cocoa, and tobacco traveled east to Europe, Africa, and Asia, and varieties of wheat, spices, coffee, and sugarcane were planted in the New World by Europeans.
- The amount of cereal grains grown worldwide equals the amount of all other crops combined.
- Monocropping, which is often held responsible for the loss of botanical biodiversity, was first practiced by the Sumerians in 5200 BCE.

A good supply of diverse genetic material is intrinsic to our ability to hybridize crops and livestock against increasingly resistant diseases. The resurgence of heirloom crops — high-quality, open-pollinated cultivars from an earlier period — counters the trend, but presently 80% of our food supply comes from just 20 kinds of plants. Some crops, like bananas, that rely on one or two species for the world supply, could be wiped out by a single bacterial infestation. We should not forget that the Irish potato famine, which reduced the population of Ireland by 25% between 1845 and 1851, was largely caused by monocropping.

See Also • Antibiotics, Beef, Chicken, Fish, Genetics, Hybrid, Meat, Pork, Poultry, specific fruits and vegetables

AGUARDIENTE • See Liquor

AHI • See Fish

AÏOLI • See Emulsion

AIR BUBBLES • See Aeration, Baking, Foams, Protein

AJWAIN • See Spices

AKULE • See Fish

ALBACORE • See Fish

ALBEDO • See Citrus

ALBUMEN • See Eggs

ALBUMIN • See Blood, Eggs

ALCOHOL

What It Is • Some yeasts when denied oxygen produce alcohol as a by-product of breaking down sugar (glucose) for energy. Normally, when oxygen is present, yeasts, like other aerobic organisms (those that live in air and use oxygen), use it to metabolize glucose for energy, releasing just water and carbon dioxide as by-products. But when oxygen is cut off they have to have some other way to get energy from glucose. Even though most yeasts can live on very little oxygen, when they enter an anaerobic (without oxygen) environment they start to produce alcohol as a by-product of **metabolism.** For every **molecule** of sugar that is metabolized without oxygen, two molecules of alcohol and two of carbon dioxide are released. The carbon dioxide is released into the atmosphere and the alcohol collects and so the area surrounding them fills up with alcohol.

Alcohol is toxic to living cells. Even yeasts can't tolerate a high concentration. The euphoric feeling it gives humans results because it disrupts the normal function of our nerve cells. To capture that euphoria, for millennia people have been using yeasts to turn the sugars in fruit juices and starches in grains into alcoholic beverages. **Wine** and brandy come from the alcoholic **fermentation** of fruit, particularly grape juice. **Beer** and distilled spirits are the result of the fermentation of grain.

What It Does • Alcohol has many distinctive properties that are exploited in the kitchen.

One end of an alcohol molecule combines well with fats and oils, while the other end bonds easily with water, making alcohol extremely versatile in infusing flavor into food. Its fat-bonding end helps it carry oily aromatic molecules through cell membranes easily, and its water-loving side makes it especially effective in a **marinade**.

Alcohol is more volatile, or vaporizable, than water, with a lower boiling point (172°F/78°C), so much of the alcohol in a stew, soup, or sauce evaporates during cooking. Long-simmered liquids retain about 25% of the alcohol initially added, but briefly cooked dishes can keep as much as 85%.

Alcohol is flammable, making it possible to flambé (French for "to flame") any distilled alcohol. Because the combustion energy is fully absorbed by the rapid vaporization of the spirits, the food doesn't get scorched.

Alcohol freezes at a much lower temperature than water (−173°F/−114°C), so it can inhibit freezing when added to ice creams or sorbets.

At low concentration, 1% or less, alcohol increases the release of aromatic molecules into the air, so adding a very small amount of alcohol to a dish can enhance flavor perception. At higher levels, above 5%, the effect is diminished by the aroma of the alcohol itself.

How It Works • The higher the level of alcohol in a beverage or food, the more pronounced its effect, but liquors with the highest alcoholic level have distinct properties. Ethanol, the main alcohol produced by yeasts, is composed of two carbon atoms, but yeasts also produce small amounts of long carbon-chain alcohols. These alcohols have one end that resembles a fatty acid chain and therefore behave more like fats. They are more effective at transferring the flavor of aromatic oils into a dish, and they lend an oily, viscous mouth feel to whiskeys and brandies. They also tend to concentrate in the membranes of our cells, where they are more irritating and narcotic than simple ethanol.

Alcohol is a drug that affects the operation of any tissue it contacts. It alters behavior because it slows the higher functioning of the brain, and as more alcohol enters the nervous system it interferes with more basic processes, especially memory, concentration, muscular coordination, speech, and vision.

The degree of intoxication depends on how much alcohol has been absorbed into the cells. Once alcohol passes through the stomach into the bloodstream, it rapidly distributes through all body fluids, penetrating cell membranes throughout the body. Smaller people feel its effects faster because they have less bodily fluid and fewer cells to absorb the alcohol.

Alcohol has a calorie content between carbohydrates and fats, about 7 calories per gram (sugar has 4, fat has 9). Unlike fats and sugars that are metabolized after absorption, some alcohol metabolism happens in the stomach, about 30%

science wise

Nice Legs • The phenomenon known as legs, the film of liquid on the inside of a glass of wine or spirits that seems to move slowly up and down, is created by the volatile interaction between alcohol and water. Alcohol lowers the attraction between water molecules in spirits and wine, but in the filmy residue on a glass the alcohol evaporates rapidly, leaving behind water molecules that bond more tightly together and tighter to the surface of the glass. The resulting liquid thickens into legs. The more alcohol present, the faster it will evaporate, and the more pronounced the legs will be. Contrary to popular opinion the appearance of legs has no bearing on the quality of wine.

in young men and 10% in young women, which is why men experience a slower rise in blood alcohol level than women do. In men, alcohol metabolism in the stomach decreases with age, but in women it increases, so that older women have higher alcohol metabolism in their stomachs than men. Foods, especially fats and oils, slow the passage through the stomach, giving the stomach a longer time to metabolize alcohol before it passes into the bloodstream, and thereby reducing the rise of blood alcohol to half of what it reaches on an empty stomach.

Most of the metabolism of alcohol takes place in the liver, starting with its conversion to acetaldehyde catalyzed by the enzyme alcohol dehydrogenase. The more alcohol you consume, the more enzyme is synthesized, which is why those who drink regularly feel intoxicated more slowly than the uninitiated.

See Also • Beer, Bread, Fermentation, Liquor, Marinade, Molecule, Wine

ALDEHYDE • See Toxin

AL DENTE • See Pasta, Vegetables

ALE • See Beer

ALEPPO PEPPER • See Spices

ALEURONE LAYER • See Grains

ALFALFA • See Legumes

ALGAE • See Seaweed

ALGINATES • See Gums

ALITAME • See Sweeteners

ALKALI

What It Is • Alkalis are bases, compounds that accept protons, and therefore complement **acids** in cooking. Alkaline solutions have a pH greater than 7. Mixed in the right proportion, acids and alkalis neutralize one another, producing reactions that can release CO_2, a phenomenon that is taken advantage of in the working of **chemical leaveners** such as baking soda and baking powder. Baking soda (sodium bicarbonate) and egg white are the only common alkaline foods, and they are fairly weak. The pH of eggs increases with age (from about 7.6 to as high as 9.4) as carbon dioxide is lost through the shell.

What It Does • Strong alkalis have a soapy flavor and slippery texture that limits their usefulness in food preparation. Think of the unpleasant aftertaste of biscuits or muffins that have been raised with too much baking soda, or the slimy mouth feel of raw egg white, and you will understand why cooking with alkalis is not nearly as popular as using acid.

Besides chemical leavening, the transformation of **corn** into hominy or masa is the most common use of alkalis in food processing. Corn kernels have an exceptionally hard hull that pre-Columbian Americans learned to loosen and remove through a process called nixtamalization (from the Aztec), in which dried corn was cooked in water alkalized with potash (the carbonate-rich ashes from a wood fire), lime (calcium carbonate), lye (sodium hydroxide), or washing soda/soda ash (sodium carbonate). Once the hull was loosened it was rubbed off and washed away, leaving behind a plumped-up corn kernel (hominy) that could be easily worked into a pliable dough (masa) for making tortillas.

The tangy blistered skin on pretzels develops from the reaction of a 1% alkaline solution sprayed on the dough right before baking to increase the Maillard reactions, and the bizarre gelatinous textures of both Chinese hundred-year eggs (pidan) and Scandinavian lutefisk come from the denaturing reactions of salt and alkali on protein.

How It Works ● Whereas acids are defined as compounds that release protons, alkalis absorb protons, and therefore have the same tendency to disrupt chemical bonds that acids do. Among other things, they denature **proteins** causing them to unfold, and they catalyze protein hydrolysis, splitting them into shorter chains of amino acids. When corn is slaked into hominy, the amino acid tryptophan breaks off, giving hominy and masa dough a mild sweet meaty aroma.

See Also ● Acid, Chemical Leavener, Corn, Eggs, Protein

ALKALOID ● See Toxin

ALLERGY

What It Is ● For those who suffer with food allergies, food can seem like an enemy. Though scientists have a basic understanding of how allergies work, there is little consensus about their cause. A combination of genetic factors (allergies run in families) and environmental factors clearly plays a role, but new theories like the "hygiene hypothesis," which holds that we have weakened our immune systems by becoming too clean, are gaining credence.

Allergic reactions to food cause the immune system to react to normally benign stimuli as if they were dangerous. There are no cures — only treatment for symptoms — and the prevalence of allergies is on the rise in developed countries. It is estimated that 11 million North Americans have allergic reactions to food that require treatment, and the occurrences of some food allergies are rising at an alarming rate. From 1997 to 2002 the number of North American children under five with peanut allergies doubled, and allergies that most kids outgrow, like those to eggs and dairy, are lingering longer than they did in the past. Although children typically outgrow allergies, adults don't. Almost all allergic reactions are to some form of protein.

What It Does ● When an allergy-prone person comes in contact with a potential allergic food, such as peanuts or shellfish, the body treats it as an attack and launches an offensive that results in all sorts of allergic reactions: congestion, wheezing, stomach distress, itchiness, inflammation, rashes, and hives. Systemic responses involving reactions in many parts of the body, called anaphylaxis, can cause the airways to shut down and blood pressure to drop. Without immediate treatment with epinephrine, a hormone that opens the breathing passages and increases heart function, death can occur.

How our immune systems, elegantly designed to protect us from multiple diseases, can be misdirected to "protect" us from healthful nutrients is baffling. New research into the cause of the rise in allergies leads credence to the hygiene hypothesis. Children who grow up where they are in frequent contact with dirt and animals are less likely to develop allergies. In 2006, researchers at Duke University studying the immune systems of wild rodents and their lab-raised relatives found that cells from the cleaner, less-diseased lab rodents reacted much more virulently to a stimulus of plant pollen than did cells from parasite-ridden wild animals.

Helping the immune system distinguish healthful from harmful substances without error is a goal that has so far eluded immunologists. The main treatment, immunotherapy, involves injecting tolerable amounts of allergen into the body in ever increasing increments until the immune system learns to tolerate an allergen at full strength. Immunotherapy has been most effective in treating airborne allergies. Injections do not help to counteract food allergies. However, in January 2007, a small

fast facts

- The most common food allergens for children are milk, eggs, peanuts, soy, and wheat.
- The most common food allergens for adults are shellfish, peanuts, tree nuts, fish, and eggs.
- The protein fragments responsible for food allergies are not broken down by cooking or by stomach acids or the enzymes that digest food.

study published in the *Journal of Allergy and Clinical Immunology* reported that when children suffering from egg allergies were fed increasing amounts of egg protein over a two-year period, their tolerance built up, allowing them to eat up to two eggs at a time without triggering a reaction. The same approach is being tried on children with peanut allergies. Starting with the equivalent of 1/1,000 of a peanut, kids in the study have been worked up to a peanut a day. It may not be enough to allow them to eat a peanut butter sandwich, but it could protect these kids from anaphylactic shock if they accidentally come into contact with a speck of allergen.

No one knows for sure whether avoidance or exposure is the best way to treat allergies, but in the meantime federal labeling laws in many countries require manufacturers to list all potential allergens in plain language (e.g., "milk" not "casein") on all food product labels. Yellow food coloring and sulfites, which occur naturally in wine, and are added as a preservative to wine and dried fruits, have caused allergic-like reactions in some populations. Asthmatics can be fatally affected by sulfites, and some people get skin reactions from food coloring, but at this time no one knows exactly how these substances are interacting with the immune system, and so they are not typically classified as allergens.

How It Works • The first phase of the allergic defense response starts when the body produces a class of antibodies called immunoglobulin E (IgE) designed to keep a specific allergen at bay. The antibodies attach themselves to receptors on the surface of "mast" cells that line the lungs, intestines, skin, mouth, nose, and sinuses, sensitizing them to the food in question. The next time the person eats the allergen, the mast cells are ready for battle. The allergen gets trapped between pairs of IgE antibodies, causing the mast cell to burst and release powerful chemicals like histamine that attack the offending substance, but also trigger the familiar allergic reactions.

If the mast cells release chemicals in the nose and throat, the allergic person may have an itching tongue or mouth and may have trouble breathing or swallowing. If mast cells in the gastrointestinal tract are triggered, the person may have diarrhea or abdominal pain. Skin mast cells produce hives and itching. Late-phase allergic reactions can occur from four hours to two days after the initial symptoms subside, without further contact with an allergen. It is believed these are caused by lingering mast cell chemicals. Antihistamines, taken orally or by injection, treat allergic reactions by preventing the activation of mast cells.

Many people experience gas, bloating, or other unpleasant reactions to something they eat. This is not an allergic response, because it does not involve the immune system. This far more typical reaction to food is called food intolerance. Food intolerances tend to increase with age.

ALLIGATOR • See Game

ALLIUM

What It Is • *Allium* is one of the largest genera of edible plants in the world. Botanical sources list between 500 and 1,000 species, but just a few dozen are important sources for food, including onion, garlic, and shallot, which are grown primarily for their bulbs, and leek, chive, and scallion, which are grown for their leaves.

What It Does • Allium bulbs are composed of swollen layers of leaf bases that store energy for the next growing season in chains of fructose sugars. The high sugar content is why onions brown easily when cooked at high temperatures and why they develop a pronounced sweetness when simmered long and slow. Garlic cloves, which

Caramelized Onions

Bulb alliums, like onions and garlic, are loaded with fructose, which is sweeter than table sugar, and all you have to do to bring the sweetness out is apply heat. Spanish or yellow onions are the best for caramelizing. Don't use "sweet" onions, like Vidalia or Maui. These have less sugar, less flavor, and a lot more water, which makes them harder to caramelize and much blander.

2 lbs	large Spanish or yellow onions	1 kg
2 tbsp	olive oil	25 mL
½ tsp	kosher salt	2 mL
¼ tsp	ground black pepper	1 mL

1. Preheat oven to 400°F (200°C). Cut onions in half lengthwise without peeling. Lay them on their cut sides and cut off the pointed ends and remove the dry skin layers. Trim the root end so that all the roots and dirt are gone but the core holding the layers of onion together is still attached. Cut each onion half lengthwise into 6 to 8 thin wedges.

2. On a large, rimmed baking sheet, toss together onions, olive oil, salt, and pepper and spread out in an even layer. Roast, tossing onions halfway through to help caramelize evenly, for 30 minutes. When they are done they will be browned on their edges.

3. Remove from oven and sprinkle 2 tbsp (25 mL) water over top. Toss to combine, using the moisture to scrape any brown bits stuck to the bottom of the pan into the onions. Use immediately or transfer to an airtight container and refrigerate, tightly closed, for up to 2 weeks.

MAKES 2 CUPS (500 ML)
OR ABOUT 1 LB (500 G)

each consist of one swollen leaf base surrounding a shoot, are much lower in water and higher in fructose, which is why garlic browns so much more quickly than onions. Leaf alliums, like leeks and scallions or green onions, which don't form bulbs, are much lower in sugar and therefore stay pale during cooking and do not develop much sweetness.

Alliums absorb sulfur from the soil and turn it into a variety of defensive chemicals designed to repel predators; the sulfur compounds also account for the pungency of onions and the powerful fumes emitting from cut raw onions that sting your eyes. So-called sweet onions are grown in sulfur-poor soil, giving them less than half the pungency of regular onions. They are much less aromatic in cooking, and contrary to their name, they have slightly less sugar than traditionally grown onions. Don't waste your time cooking them. They don't add much flavor to a dish and brown poorly. Instead serve them raw in sandwiches or salads. Traditionally grown onions can be made to taste more like sweet onions by being soaked in ice water, which washes away some of their sulfury components.

How you cook an allium changes its flavor. Cooking in water produces milder and sweeter flavors. Cooking in hot fat increases

Common Culinary Alliums

Name	Type	Description	Use
Chive	Leaf	Thin, dark green grass-like leaves that grow in clumps	Raw or briefly cooked as herb
Cipollini onion	Bulb	Small; flattened; white to dark golden; papery flesh; sweet	Roasted, grilled
Elephant garlic	Bulb	Baseball size; multi-large-cloved head; white papery skin	Raw or briefly cooked
Garlic	Bulb	Golf ball size; multi-cloved head; white or purple papery skin	Raw or cooked
Leek	Leaf	Long, sturdy, fibrous green leaves; white moist root end	Simmered, braised, roasted, or grilled
Pearl onion	Bulb	Small (about 1 inch/2.5 cm) in diameter; white papery skin	Boil, braise, or sauté
Ramps or ramson (wild leek)	Leaf	Wild, broad, dark green leaf with purple root end	Cooked
Red onion	Bulb	Red; slightly pungent	Raw or briefly cooked
Scallion (green onion)	Bulb or leaf	Small white bulb with long, tender, dark green leaves	Raw or briefly cooked
Shallot	Bulb	Small; multi-bulbed; dark papery skin; purple tinge to flesh; sweet	Roasted or sautéed
Spring onion	Bulb	Green with white root end; moist; mild	Briefly cooked
Sweet onion (including Maui, Oso Sweet, Vidalia)	Bulb	Large; slightly flattened; yellow papery skin; moist flesh; very mild	Raw
White onion	Bulb	Large; white papery skin; moist	All-purpose
Yellow onion or Spanish onion (large yellow onion)	Bulb	Pungent bulb; golden papery skin; stores well	All-purpose

pungency. Garlic sautéed in butter is milder than garlic cooked in oil, and pickling alliums diminishes their sharpness.

Spring onions, harvested in the spring or early summer when they are still green and immature, never develop the strong flavor of papery-skinned storage onions, which are harvested in the fall and winter. White onions tend to be moister and milder than yellow onions. Red onions, pigmented with water-soluble anthocyanins on the surface of each leaf base, lose much of their color during cooking.

Scallions, or green onions, can be either very young bulb onions, in which case they will taste stronger, or more mature non-bulbing varieties. Shallots, specialized onions that grow in small tight clusters, tend to be milder, sweeter, and drier than larger bulb onions.

Leeks don't form bulbs; rather their leaves grow straight and tall. Although the dark green leaves are completely edible, only the white parts of the leek leaf near the root develop onion-like pungency. In order to increase the length of the white portion, soil is hilled around the leek as it grows to shield it from chlorophyll-developing sunlight. Leeks have fewer sugars and more long-chain carbohydrates than other alliums, giving them a slippery texture when cooked that helps to thicken soups and stews.

Elephant garlic, a bulbing variety of leek, gets its name because it looks like a giant garlic bulb, but don't let the garlic allusion fool you. Elephant garlic has all the mild qualities of leek, with very little of the highly charged pungency of garlic.

How It Works
Allium **cells** are filled with sulfides, sulfur-containing components whose potential for pungency can only be realized if they come in contact with special enzymes called allinases. Each cell contains several storage vacuoles containing allinase that remain separated from the sulfur

kitchen wisdom

No-More-Tears Onion Chopping

To keep tears at bay when you are cutting onions, you can wash away the sulfur chemicals from the onion, neutralize the enzymes that activate the sulfur, or prevent the sulfur gases emitting from the onion from reaching your eyes. Here are a few effective techniques.

- Carefully cutting onions under a few inches (centimeters) of water dilutes the sulfur components.
- Thorough chilling or briefly freezing onions reduces the enzymes.
- Chopping near a lit candle or gas burner draws the onion gases toward the flame, where they burn off with the rest of the flame exhaust.
- Covering the eyes with goggles keeps the gases from the eye surface. Contact lenses act similarly.

compounds as long as the cell stays intact. Cutting into an allium releases the enzymes, causing an explosion of flavor. The finer an allium is chopped, the more pungent the flavor becomes. Chopped garlic is especially strong because it contains a different set of sulfur compounds that are more pungent, but roasting garlic cloves whole keeps them mild and sweet, in part because the garlic's high sugar content caramelizes, and in part because the heat activates sulfur-digesting enzymes and they never get a chance to do their work.

When an onion is chopped, sulfenic acid is released, and breaks down into several compounds, one of which is a volatile chemical (thiopropanal-S-oxide) that acts as a kind of tear gas. It travels through the air into the cutter's eyes and nose, where it attacks the nerve endings, causing the eye to sting. Tears dilute the acid and relieve the stinging, which is why it's helpful to cry when you chop onions or other alliums like shallots, leeks, and chives. Garlic breaks down into different chemical compounds, which do not sting the eye.

See Also • Acid, Cells

ALLSPICE • See Spices

ALMOND • See Extracts, Liqueur, Nuts, Oil

ALTITUDE • See Atmospheric Pressure

ALUM • See Vegetables

ALUMINUM COOKWARE •
See Bakeware, Cookware

AMARANTH • See Grains

AMARETTO • See Liqueur

AMERICAN CHEESE • See Cheese

AMER PICON • See Bitters

AMINES • See Flavor

AMINO ACIDS • See Protein

AMMONIA

What It Is • Ammonia, a chemical compound with the formula NH_3, is caustic and hazardous. When dissolved in water it becomes household ammonia (ammonium hydroxide) and is used as a disinfectant and a glass cleaner.

What It Does • Ammonia cleaning products of 5 to 10% concentration are effective household cleaners but not as popular as they once were. This is largely because their fumes are irritating to the eyes and mucous membranes in the nose and digestive tract, and also because they cannot be combined with other household cleaners containing bleach.

How It Works • Like chlorine, ammonia is antibacterial, and is sometimes added to drinking water in small concentrations along with chlorine to purify it. Ammonia and chlorine should never be mixed for cleaning. In an uncontrolled environment, like a bucket of water, ammonia and chlorine cause a chemical reaction that releases toxic gas and carcinogenic compounds.

See Also • Disinfectant

AMYLASE • See Digestion

AMYLOPECTIN • See Starch

AMYLOPLAST • See Starch

AMYLOSE • See Starch

ANAHEIM CHILE • See Capsicum

ANASAZI BEAN • See Legumes

ANCHO CHILE • See Capsicum

ANCHOVY • See Fish

ANDOUILLE • See Sausage

ANETHOLE • See Flavor

ANGELICA • See Bitters, Herbs

ANGOSTURA • See Bitters

ANIMAL FOODS

What It Is • We get food from animals directly and indirectly. The **meat** we eat, the **bones** and skin we use for making broths and flavorings, the **fats** we fry in, and the entrails and **blood** that go into sausages are direct animal products. Indirect animal products used for food include **milk** from mammals and the products derived from milk, like **cheese**, **butter**, yogurt, and **ice cream**. They include the **eggs** from birds that we scramble and fry for breakfast, and those from fish that we nibble on as **caviar**. Bees produce **honey**, and there would be no bird's nest soup in Chinese cuisine if it were not for the saliva of cave-dwelling swifts that makes up the edible nests.

What It Does • Humans are omnivorous, meaning we can eat, digest, and metabolize food from animals and vegetables equally well. Economics, food availability, our native cuisines, and religious and social constructs all influence which foods we choose. Some people choose to not eat animal products at all (dietary vegans), others draw the line at direct animal products (lacto-ovo vegetarians), and still others pick and choose a combination of animal products they will consume based on personal taste, food intolerances, or their current dietary concerns.

Although eating a balanced diet of animal and vegetable products is the easiest way to ensure proper nutrition, animal products are not necessary for a balanced diet. Strict dietary vegans might have to work harder to get all nutrients. The American Dietetic Association advises those who aren't eating any animal products to take special care in getting enough vitamin B_{12}, vitamin D, calcium, iodine, and omega-3 fatty acids. On the other hand, eating only animal products eliminates many essential vitamins and minerals from the diet, and can provide too many calories in the form of saturated fat.

How It Works • The characteristics and quality of any animal food depend on the type of animal, the resources available to the animal as it grew, its genetics, the conditions under which it was turned into food, and how the food was packaged and stored. For example, all milk contains water, protein, fat, carbohydrates, vitamins, and minerals, but the combination of those components makes cow's milk different from the milk of goat, sheep, camel, yak, reindeer, or water buffalo. Even when we look at one type of milk, the breed of the animal, the vegetation that the animal ate, the amount and type of exercise it experienced on and before the day of milking, and the time of day the milk was taken all affect the milk's composition. The flavor and texture of milk can be changed by its processing — how much of the cream was skimmed off, whether and how the milk was pasteurized and/or homogenized, and how and for how long it was stored before and after purchase.

See Also • Beef. Blood, Bones, Caviar, Cheese, Chicken, Eggs, Fermentation, Honey, Lamb, Meat, Milk, Pork, Protein, Vegetables

ANTIBIOTICS

What It Is • Large-scale meat and chicken production, where animals are raised in close confinement, leads to the spread of disease. To control pathogens many meat producers routinely include antibiotics in animal feed, with the added benefit of increasing growth rate. Routinely giving livestock antibiotics, chemicals that inhibit or stop the growth of microorganisms like **bacteria**, **fungi**, and parasites, has inadvertently led to a rise in antibiotic-resistant strains of *Campylobacter*, *E. coli*, and *Salmonella* bacteria, particularly in poultry, that pose a continued health risk for consumers.

What It Does • Antibiotics inhibit or eliminate the growth of bacteria in humans and animals. They work either by killing the bacteria directly or by preventing them from reproducing. In either case the desired result is the same: to abolish the bacteria from the environment. Although antibiotics are highly effective at targeting their goals, bacteria are also effective at evolving to resist any particular antibiotic.

How It Works • Unless an administration of antibiotic is 100% effective, the small subset of the bacterial population that survives will multiply, and the susceptibility of the new population to the same antibiotic will be much less than the original population's, since they have descended from those few bacteria that survived the original treatment. Their survival often results from an inherited resistance to the antibiotic that was uncommon in the original population but is now part of the genetic makeup of the new generation.

Bacteria also have the ability to transfer antibiotic resistance from one bacterium to another via plasmids, small, circular DNA molecules that are capable of autonomous replication. R-plasmids (resistance plasmids) can transfer from one bacterial cell to another and carry their antibiotic resistance with them. In this way bacteria can become antibiotic resistant without ever being exposed to an antibiotic.

In response to these practices and the consequent problems, several organizations, including the American Society for Microbiology, the American Public Health Association, and the American Medical Association, have called for restrictions on antibiotic use in food animal production and an end to all non-therapeutic antibiotic uses, like increasing growth, in livestock.

The story of how fluoroquinolones were used to fight *E. coli* infection in chickens is an example of how antibiotic-resistant bacteria can flourish inadvertently. The U.S. Food and Drug Administration (FDA) approved the use of fluoroquinolones for poultry in 1995. Immediately the incidence of *E. coli* went down, but at the same time another bacterium, *Campylobacter*, became resistant to fluoroquinolones. By 2000 the Centers for Disease Control and Prevention reported a rise in antibiotic-resistant *Campylobacter*, and now most chickens raised in the U.S. are infected with the bacterium. Even chickens raised organically and with no antibiotics added can be contaminated. According to the FDA, at least 50% of the instances of *Campylobacter* food poisoning come from contaminated chicken. The resistant bacterium also infects farm workers and, because of manure runoff, has been found in lakes, rivers, and drinking water.

See Also • Agriculture, Bacteria

ANTIOXIDANTS

What It Is • The very act of living results in the production of chemicals that put wear and tear on our bodies. Even the function of breathing and the metabolic processes involving oxygen result in the formation of unstable chemical by-products called free radicals that react with and damage our cells. Antioxidant molecules produced by our bodies stave off the damage by reacting harmlessly with free radicals before they get a chance to interact with and do damage to our cells' mechanics.

The same antioxidation occurs when an acidic ingredient like lemon juice is rubbed on the cut surfaces of produce to prevent the produce from browning from exposure to oxygen in the air.

Many plant pigments are natural antioxidants. Carotenoids, including orange beta-carotene, yellow lutein, and red lycopene in roots and fruits, have antioxidant power. Any part of the photosynthesizing system of a plant — those parts that are dark green — fight free radicals. **Vitamins** A, C, and E are antioxidants. Then there are thousands of phenolic compounds, including all of the anthocyanins that give purple vegetables their pigmentation, help protect DNA from degradation, and slow the development of heart disease.

What It Does • Antioxidants help keep human cells healthy by neutralizing the actions of naturally occurring cell-damaging substances like free radicals. Free radicals can affect almost all of our bodily systems. For example, oxidative damage to a cell's DNA can cause the cell

Beta-Carrotene Cake

Many people assume that as far as desserts go carrot cake is good for them, when in truth it's most likely as fatty and sugar-laden as any cake. The one thing it does have is a little vitamin A. In this recipe the beta-carotene (a precursor to vitamin A) has been supercharged with extra carrots, dried apricots, and apricot nectar to pack more than twice the recommended daily amount of vitamin A for adults in each slice.

	Nonstick spray oil	
2 cups	all-purpose flour	500 mL
2 tsp	ground cinnamon	10 mL
1½ tsp	baking soda	7 mL
½ tsp	salt	2 mL
3	large or extra-large eggs	3
1 cup	granulated sugar	250 mL
¾ cup	vegetable oil	175 mL
¾ cup	orange juice	175 mL
1 tsp	vanilla extract	5 mL
3 cups	shredded carrots	750 mL
1 cup	dried apricots, diced	250 mL
¾ cup	nuts, any variety, chopped	175 mL

Icing

4 oz	cream cheese, softened	125 g
2 tbsp	confectioner's (icing) sugar	25 mL
⅓ cup	apricot nectar	75 mL
½ tsp	vanilla extract	2 mL

1. Preheat oven to 350°F (180°C). Coat a 10-inch (25 cm) Bundt pan or tube pan with spray oil. Set aside.

2. In a bowl, combine flour, cinnamon, baking soda, and salt.

3. In a large bowl, beat together eggs and sugar until well combined. Beat in oil, orange juice, and vanilla. Add flour mixture and mix just enough to form a smooth batter. Fold in carrots, apricots, and nuts. Scrape batter into prepared pan. Bake in preheated oven until a tester inserted in the top of the cake comes out clean, 35 to 40 minutes. Let cool in pan for 30 minutes. Loosen sides with a knife, cover with a rack, invert, remove pan, and let cake cool completely.

4. Icing: Meanwhile, in a bowl, beat cream cheese until smooth. Beat in confectioner's sugar, apricot nectar, and vanilla until smooth. Spoon over top of cooled cake, allowing rivulets to run down the sides.

MAKES 12 SERVINGS

Sources for and Benefits of Common Antioxidants

Antioxidant	Common Sources	Benefits
Anthocyanins	Grapes, blueberries, açai	Slow heart disease
Ascorbic acid	Most fruits and vegetables	Reduces DNA damage
Carotenoids	Orange and green vegetables	Reduce DNA damage
Chlorophyll	Green vegetables	Reduces DNA damage
Flavonoids	Most fruits and vegetables	Reduce free-radical production
Glucosinolates	Cabbage and radish families	Reduce DNA damage
Isoflavones	Soybeans	Reduce free-radical production
Lutein	Dark leafy vegetables	Slows macular degeneration
Lycopene	Tomatoes	Reduces DNA damage
Phenolics	Tea, beans, cabbage family	Slow heart disease
Salicylates	Raisins, dates, chiles	Slow heart disease
Terpenes	Citrus	Reduce free-radical production
Tocopherols	Vegetable oils	Reduce DNA damage
Zeaxanthin	Citrus, corn	Slows macular degeneration

to multiply uncontrollably into a tumor. In the bloodstream free radicals can irritate the arterial linings, eventually leading to heart disease, and free-radical damage from ultraviolet sun rays can cause carcinomas to grow in the skin. We need a constant supply of antioxidants to fight the potential damage, and though our bodies manufacture many antioxidant molecules, the more help we give it, the better off we are.

How It Works • Each food source contains its own blend of antioxidants, and each antioxidant protects against a certain type of cellular damage. It is important to eat a variety of fruits and vegetables. Taking supplements of specific antioxidants may not give you the same protective effects because some antioxidants work in concert with each other. Eating whole foods rather than isolated antioxidants offers the most benefits to your health.

See Also • Browning, Chemical Bonding, Nutrition, Pigment, Vegetables, Vitamins

APPALOOSA BEAN • See Legumes

APPENZELLER • See Cheese

APPLE

What It Is • In Western culture apples are to fruit what water is to thirst. We cannot think of the broader category without the specific coming to mind. An apple is our image of the unnamed fruit in the Garden of Eden, and a golden apple started the Trojan War. Snow White was poisoned with a bewitched apple, and Isaac Newton first understood the law that keeps us all down to earth when he watched a Pippin fall from a tree.

Apples are the most cultivated tree fruit in the world, with more than 7,000 cultivars. Yet only about three dozen are considered commercial, and of those a handful count for the bulk of sales.

What It Does • The apple attributes we cherish — large, crisp, sweet, and tangy — are all due to cultivation, and bear little resemblance to the small, sour, seedy fruit that is a wild apple. The natural tendency of apple trees, like their progenitor, the rose, is to produce as many small, seedy fruits as possible, rather than a few choice beauties. It was not easy to manipulate apple trees to evolve into their current form, and because of that most apples will no longer grow true from seed. The flowers of most varieties can be fertilized only by the pollen of other varieties, and there is a tendency for their offspring to revert to the wild state rather than to reproduce desirable cultivated attributes. For that reason most apples are propagated asexually through grafting.

For kitchen purposes apples are divided into four groups.

- *Eating apples (aka dessert apples)* are crisp and juicy, with a balanced sweet and sour taste when eaten raw (pH about 3.5, about 15% sugar). They become bland when cooked. Most eating apples are bestsellers in the U.S., including Red Delicious and Gala.
- *Cooking apples* are tart when raw (pH around 3, about 12% sugar) and well balanced and firm when cooked. They tend to lack juiciness and crispness and are not good eaten out of hand. They include many of the heirloom apples, like Bismark, Pippins, Bramley, and Calville, cultivated for baking, and they have largely been replaced in North America by all-purpose apples. The Rome Beauty is a modern cultivar bred for baking.
- *All-purpose apples* are good eaten raw or cooked. They are usually best for cooking when young, when they tend to be tarter, and better raw once they've matured. They include such varieties as Granny Smith, Golden Delicious, Cortland, Gravenstein, Winesap, and McIntosh. Some varieties, such as Cortland and McIntosh, break down quickly when cooked, while others, such as Northern Spy and Winesap, hold their shape better when cooked.
- *Cider apples* are mainly grown in Europe for pressing into hard cider. They are high in acid, and have an abundance of tannin that helps to control fermentation and clarity. Tannin links proteins to visible particles in the cider causing them to precipitate.

Apples are processed into several popular commercial products.

- *Apple juice* retains a fresh flavor and pale color for about an hour after juicing, after which it darkens in color and develops off metallic flavors. Heating the juice rapidly to destroy its enzymes arrests those changes. Almost all commercial apple juice is pasteurized, a process that kills most of the bacteria in the juice. Unpasteurized apple juice has been connected with *E. coli* outbreaks and should be avoided.
- *Sweet apple cider* is unfiltered apple juice. Hard cider is a fermented product with an alcohol content of about 4%.
- *Applesauce* is a purée of cooked apples. Apples are a good source of **pectin**, which keeps applesauce thick and smooth without the need for starches or gums.
- *Apple butter* is a sweet spread made by reducing applesauce until its sugars caramelize and its pectin thickens. Apple butter is typically seasoned with cinnamon and can include some cider in the reduction.

Apple Varieties

The following chart lists common apple varieties alphabetically and categorizes them by type, description, and use.

Variety	Type	Description	Uses
Braeburn	Eating	Medium; green flecked with red; sweet-tart; crisp; juicy	Raw
Bramley	Cooking	Large; green; acidic; fleshy; juicy	Chutney, applesauce
Cortland	All-purpose	Large; shiny red with green; tart; crisp white flesh	Raw, chunky applesauce, salad
Cox's Orange Pippin	Eating	Medium; brownish-green, russeted; sweet and tart; crisp	Raw, pie
Empire	Eating	Large; matte red; sweet and tart; crisp; juicy; fragrant	Raw, smooth applesauce
Fuji	All-purpose	Medium; red with yellow undertone; tangy; sweet; firm cream-colored flesh; juicy	Raw, pie
Gala	Eating	Medium; red and yellow; sweet; firm; juicy	Raw
Golden Delicious	All-purpose	Medium with five bumps on base; yellow; sweet; firm; aromatic	Raw, tarts, chunky applesauce
Granny Smith	All-purpose	Medium-large; green; tart; crunchy, hard; juicy	Raw, pie, chunky applesauce
Gravenstein	All-purpose	Large; yellow or green with red stripes; tart; crisp; aromatic	Raw, smooth applesauce, pie
Idared	Cooking	Medium; soft; mildly tart; juicy	Pie, sauce, baking
Jonagold	All-purpose	Hybrid of Jonathan and Golden Delicious	Raw, tarts, pie
Jonathan	All-purpose	Small; pale red; crisp; fine-textured white flesh; slightly tart; aromatic	Raw, pie
Lady Apple (Pomme d'api)	Eating	Tiny; yellow or green with red strips; slightly tart; crisp white flesh	Raw, baked/stewed, served with meat or as dessert
Macoun	All-purpose	Medium; shiny red with green; sweet; crisp; fragrant	Raw, smooth applesauce
McIntosh	All-purpose	Medium; shiny red with green; sweet; crisp; fragrant	Raw, smooth applesauce
Mutsu (Crispin)	All-purpose	Large; dull green; acidic; firm	Raw, baking, pie, chunky applesauce
Newton Pippin	Cooking	Medium; green; tart; crisp white flesh	Pie, applesauce
Northern Spy	Cooking	Large; yellow and red; tart; extra-firm and juicy	Pie, chunky applesauce
Red Delicious	Eating	Medium-large, elongated; red; sweet; crisp	Raw
Rome Beauty	Cooking	Large bright red; mildly tart; juicy; firm; aromatic	Baking
Spartan	Eating	Medium; sweet-tart; crisp; fine-textured	Raw
Winesap (Stayman Winesap)	All-purpose	Medium; red and green, russeted; tart; firm; juicy; fragrant	Raw, pie

How It Works • Along with **pears** and quince, apples are pome fruits, which means they are the swollen tip of the flower stem containing the plant's ovary. As pome fruit grow, the flower shrivels, leaving behind a scar on the bottom of the fruit that connects directly into the seed core. Pomes contain starch stores that can be converted into sugar after harvest, so they are best picked green and held in cold storage until ripening is desired.

The qualities we appreciate in apples, tartness with a slight sweetness and intense crispness, tend to be the characteristics of underripe fruit, so most apples are eaten on the green side.

As much as a quarter of an apple's volume is occupied by air lying between the cells. Before ripening, the cell walls are rigid and full of juice that presses against the air pockets, creating a system of intense rigidity. When you bite into a pre-ripe apple your teeth pierce the cells, breaking them open. Juice rushes into your mouth and the escaping air transfers the aroma of the apple toward your olfactory membranes. As apples ripen, their cell walls soften and they lose moisture. When you bite into a fully ripe apple your teeth press the flexible cells together, collapsing the air pockets into an unpleasant mealy mass.

The air pockets are also a consideration when baking whole apples. It is necessary to peel a strip of skin from the top of an apple before you bake it. Otherwise the air in the fruit will expand in the heat of the oven, causing the skin to burst.

All apples turn brown when exposed to air due to enzymatic **browning**. But sweet apples like McIntosh tend to turn brown faster when cut than do tart apples like Granny Smith. To prevent any apple from browning when cut, coat the cut surfaces in lemon juice or soak pieces in acidulated water, a mixture of about 4 cups (1 L) water and 3 tbsp (45 mL) lemon juice.

See Also • Fruit, Horticulture, Pectin

APPLE BRANDY • See Cider, Liquor

APPLEJACK • See Cider, Liquor

APPLE PRODUCTS • See Apple

APPLE SCHNAPPS • See Liquor

APRICOT

What It Is • Native to China and cultivated there for nearly 4,000 years, apricots now grow in mild temperate climates throughout the world, where they are prized for their highly aromatic creamy flesh and vibrant color, which can range from white to red and comes from lycopene. Most apricots are orange because of their high carotene content. Apricot trees flower and fruit early (the name comes from the Latin word *praecocia*, meaning precocious) so they are best suited to climates where mild, short winters are predictable.

What It Does • Apricots have a short growing season and the fresh fruit has a very short shelf life, and for that reason most are processed into preserves or dried fruit. Apricots are high in pectin, which gives them a meaty texture when fully ripe and a toothsome flesh when dried. Apricots are typically sun-dried and treated with sulfur dioxide to preserve their color and nutrition. Unsulfured apricots need to be dried longer to preserve them, which makes them turn dark and gives them a flat baked flavor.

Apricots have been bred with plums in order to lengthen the growing season and storage capabilities of the fresh fruit. Apriums closely resemble apricots; pluots are more like plums.

How It Works • The flavor of apricot comes from a rich blend of citrus, herbal, and floral terpenes, and from peach-like compounds. They are particularly high in beta-carotene, a powerful **antioxidant**, and when dried are a good source of iron.

Apricot pits are toxic in quantity because they contain amygdalin, which when combined with digestive enzymes in the intestine form a type of cyanide. Apricot kernel oil is not poisonous because the amygdalin is not soluble in oil and therefore remains behind when the oil is extracted. Apricot kernel oil is high in polyunsaturated fat and has a nutty flavor similar to almond oil. It's often used as a massage oil but also tastes delicious as a salad oil.

See Also • Antioxidants, Fruit

APRICOT BRANDY • See Liquor

APRICOT LIQUEUR • See Liqueur

APRIUM • See Apricot, Hybrid

AQUACULTURE • See Fish

AQUAVIT • See Liquor

ARAK • See Liquor

ARAME • See Seaweed

ARBORIO RICE • See Rice

ARCTIC CHAR • See Fish

ARDENNES HAM • See Ham

AREPA • See Corn

ARGAN OIL • See Oil

ARMAGNAC • See Liquor

AROMA • See Flavor

ARRACACHA • See Roots

ARROWROOT • See Starch

ARTHROPODS • See Crustacean

ARTICHOKE

What It Is • Globe artichoke is the large bud of a thistle that is harvested before it gets a chance to bloom. It is composed of a hairy purple choke, which is the undeveloped flower head; a fleshy artichoke heart (bottom) that is the flower base and the upper part of the stalk; and an enclosure of bracts, armored leaves shingled around the flower to protect it before it blooms. This diversity of edible and inedible parts poses a unique challenge for a cook.

What It Does • The edible parts of an artichoke include the soft upper part of the stem, the pulpy bases of the bracts, and the heart. The choke is too fibrous to eat, although baby artichokes, which have not yet developed the hairy choke, can be eaten in their entirety. The babies are not immature globe artichokes; rather they are secondary buds that grow lower on the stalk. Baby artichokes grow very slowly and therefore can be enjoyed before the choke develops. They are often sold frozen, canned, or marinated as artichoke hearts.

Mature globe artichokes must be boiled or steamed to soften their tough fibers, and the choke has to be removed before the artichoke is eaten. Mature artichokes are also deep-fried. Baby artichokes are tender enough to be roasted or sautéed.

How It Works • Most of the qualities and limitations of an artichoke come from the abundance of phenolic compounds that react with oxygen, causing artichokes to turn brown as soon as they are cut. Tannic phenols cause an immediate unpleasant astringent reaction when raw artichoke comes in contact with our salivary proteins. Although cooking fixes both problems, it also causes the flesh to change from vibrant green to drab olive. Some of the phenolic compounds have antioxidant effects, and one of them, cynarin, has the unique ability to make food eaten after a bite of artichoke taste sweet. Cynarin inhibits the sweet receptors in taste buds, so when it is replaced by the next bite of food, the receptors reactivate and the new food tastes sweet. Italian liqueur makers have harnessed this effect in Cynar, an aperitif made primarily from artichokes.

See Also • Flavor, Flowers

ARTIFICIAL FLAVORS • See Extracts, Flavor

ARTIFICIAL SWEETENERS • See Sweeteners

ARUGULA • See Leaves

ASADERO • See Cheese

ASAFETIDA • See Spices

ASCORBIC ACID • See Antioxidants, Citrus

ASEPTIC PACKAGING • See Milk, Pasteurizaton

ASH • See Alkali, Fire

ASHANTI PEPPER • See Spices

ASIAN CELERY • See Celery

ASIAN NOODLES • See Pasta

ASIAN PEAR • See Pear

ASPARAGUS

What It Is • Asparagus, the stalk of a member of the lily family, is unusual because it doesn't bear leaves. Small bracts (leaf-like plates that cover a flower bud) traverse the stalk, gathering at the tip in a pointed crown. Cultivated since Roman times, asparagus has always been considered a luxury, and remains expensive even though it is produced commercially because each stalk grows at its own rate and must be harvested by hand.

What It Does • Although most asparagus is green, white asparagus, blanched by mounding the stalk with soil as it grows, has been cultivated since the 1700s. White asparagus has a more subtle flavor than green stalks (which are rich in sulfur volatiles) and a pronounced bitterness toward its thicker end. White asparagus will turn red or gold if exposed to light after harvesting. Purple asparagus turns green during cooking because it is high in anthocyanins, water-soluble purple pigments that dissipate when boiled or steamed.

Harvested young asparagus is noticeably sweet (about 4% sugar), but as the season progresses, or if the asparagus sits after harvesting, the sugar rapidly turns to starch. The stalks become fibrous, the bracts open, and the flavor changes from sweet to mildly acrid. These changes progress rapidly within the first 24 hours after harvest and start at the base of the stem and travel up the stalk toward the tip, so all commercially purchased asparagus has a tough base that must be snapped off before cooking. This is easily done by grasping the end and the center of the stalk and bending the stalk, which will naturally break right at the point where it becomes tender. Because the bases are tougher than the tips, asparagus is often cooked in a tall, covered pot (asparagus cooker) that allows the stalks to stand upright with the bottoms submerged in boiling water and the tips steaming gently above.

How It Works • Asparagus is a well-known diuretic that gives a strong aroma to urine. Our bodies metabolize asparagusic acid into methyl mercaptan, a chemical that closely resembles skunk spray. About 40% of the population claim to be immune to the effect, although it is now believed to be more common. According to recent studies, only a small percentage of the population lacks the genes to detect the odor.

ASPARTAME • See Sweeteners

ASPERGILLUS • See Mold

ASPIC • See Gelatin

ASTAXANTHIN • See Fish

ASTRALAGUS GUM TRAGACANTH •
See Gums

ASTRINGENCY • See Flavor, Wine

ATEMOYA • See Fruit

ATMOSPHERIC PRESSURE

What It Is • All food and cooking are subject to changes in atmospheric pressure, which is the weight of air on the surface of things, but only **baking** and **boiling** are affected to a measurable extent.

We tend to think of the boiling point of water as a constant 212°F (100°C), but that temperature is only the amount of energy it takes to boil water at sea level. As elevation rises, the amount of air pressing down on the surface of the water decreases, and the less energy it takes to make the water boil, with the result that the water boils at a lower temperature.

If you go in the opposite direction, below sea level, there is more air sitting on the surface of the water and the boiling point goes up. Since there is not much dry land that lies below sea level, increasing the boiling point of water by increasing atmospheric pressure most often happens artificially in a pressure cooker. Pressure cookers speed up cooking by trapping the steam escaping from boiling water, thereby building up pressure on the surface, and raising the boiling point.

What It Does • The lower temperature of boiling water at high altitudes causes several changes in how food cooks:

- Boiling pasta, potatoes, beans, and other starchy foods takes about 10% longer for every 1,000 feet (305 m) of elevation.
- Braised meats are more succulent, because less moisture is squeezed from the coagulating proteins at a lower simmering temperature, but they may need slightly more time to cook.
- Roasted meats dry out more before they brown.
- Bread doughs rise faster, which gives less time to develop flavor in the dough, making it advisable to do a second rising.
- Moisture in a baking dough or batter steams earlier, causing baked goods to dry out. Recipes may need a little more liquid, reduced baking time, and increased oven temperature.
- The loss of moisture in a baking cake throws off the ratio of liquid to dry ingredients in a batter. To bring the ratios back in balance you can reduce the amount of sugar and flour and increase the amount of liquid.

High-Altitude Kitchen

The following charts give guidelines for adjusting baking and cooking at various elevations.

Baking

Altitude Above Sea Level	Sugar (for each cup/250 mL add)	Baking Powder (reduce each cup/250 mL by)	Liquid (reduce each cup/250 mL by)	Temperature and Time (increase temperature and reduce time by
3,000 ft (914 m)	½ to 1 tbsp (7 to 15 mL)	⅛ tsp (0.5 mL)	1 to 2 tbsp (15 to 25 mL)	10 to 15°F (5.5 to 8°C); 2 minutes
5,000 ft (1524 m)	½ to 2 tbsp (7 to 25 mL)	⅛ to ¼ tsp (0.5 to 1 mL)	2 to 4 tbsp (25 to 60 mL)	25°F (14°C); 5 minutes
7,000 ft+ (2134 m+)	1 to 3 tbsp (15 to 45 mL)	¼ tsp (1 mL)	3 to 4 tbsp (45 to 60 mL)	25 to 30°F (14 to 17°C); 5 to 10 minutes

Cooking

Altitude Above Sea Level	Boiling Point	Vegetables (increase cooking time by)	Stewing and Braising (increase cooking time by)	Roasting (increase cooking temperature by)
3,000 ft (914 m)	206°F (97°C)	20 to 30%	30 minutes	10 to 25°F (5.5 to 14°C)
5,000 ft (1524 m)	202°F (94°C)	40 to 50%	1 hour	20 to 30°F (11 to 17°C)
7,000 ft+ (2134 m+)	198°F (92°C)	60 to 70%	2 to 3 hours	30 to 50°F (17 to 28°C)

- High-moisture quick bread and cake batters may over-rise because less air pressure is weighing them down. Remedy this by letting the batter sit 10 to 15 minutes before baking to let the leavening gases escape. You can also reduce the chemical leavener in your recipe by about ⅛ tsp (0.5 mL) per 2,000 feet (610 m) above sea level.
- Shortbread and other low-moisture cookies can lose the little moisture they have during baking, which keeps the **gluten** from setting, leading to crumbly results. Increase the liquid slightly (using a larger size egg is a good way to do it) and/or add a little gluten to the dry ingredients.
- At very high elevations most of the air in a rising baked good can be lost before the dough sets enough to trap it. To remedy, increase the oven temperature to set the dough sooner.

In a pressure cooker, the combination of the increased temperature and air pressure forces heat into ingredients faster, thereby reducing cooking times by as much as 70%. Soaked dried beans can take as little as 10 minutes to cook through in a pressure cooker. A pot roast that would braise for 3 hours in conventional cooking will take less than an hour in a pressure cooker. Because there is less evaporation in pressure cooking, the amount of liquid used for a soup, stew, or braised meat should be reduced by about 60%.

How It Works • For every thousand feet (305 m) of elevation, the boiling point reduces by about 2°F (1°C). Even a low-pressure weather front can lower the boiling point, or a high-pressure front could raise the boiling point by a degree or two.

Pressure cookers standardize the temperature inside the cooker at 250°F (120°C) by regulating how much steam gets trapped through the use of vents. The standard pressure in home pressure cookers is 15 pounds per square inch (103 kPa). This is equivalent to boiling water in an open pan on a stove set in the bottom of a pit 19,000 feet (5791 m) below sea level.

See Also • Baking, Boiling, Bread, Cake, Vegetables

ATOM

What It Is • We got our idea for atoms from the ancient Greeks, who believed all matter was made up of invisible indivisible particles. Although we now know that atoms can be divided into subatomic elements, in food chemistry we still talk about atoms as the smallest particle into which an element can be divided without losing its characteristic properties.

What It Does • If there is one motivating force behind all the chemical activity that makes cooking and eating possible, it is the attraction between protons and electrons. Opposite electrical charges attract each other; identical electrical charges repel one another. When an atom has more protons than electrons, it is apt to attract an electron from another atom nearby. If that nearby atom is negatively charged, with an extra electron or two, those electrons may switch orbits, joining the two atoms together in a **chemical bond**. This is how **molecules** form.

How It Works • The electrons orbit around the nucleus in layers. Those close to the nucleus are held tightly, while others traveling farther out have a weak attachment to the atom. The more electrons there are in the outer orbits, the greater the chance that the atom will react with nearby atoms. Metals, for instance, tend to have a lot of electrons in outer orbits, making them bond easily with oxygen (which is why copper discolors and iron rusts), transfer heat (why metals are used for the manufacture of cookware), or interact with living tissue (why too much copper or aluminum in your system is toxic).

Of all the electron-attracting elements the most important in food chemistry is oxygen. The interaction between oxygen and other atoms is so common that scientists have a special term for it, oxidation, which refers to any chemical reaction in which an electron jumps from one atom to another, even if the electron-grabber is not oxygen.

See Also • Antioxidants, Chemical Bonding, Molecule, Oxygen

AURICULARIA • See Fungi

AVIDIN • See Eggs

AVOCADO

What It Is • Thick-skinned and creamy-fleshed, the semitropical avocado is the one fruit that ripens only after it is picked. So the best place to store avocados to keep them from over-ripening is on the tree. Once they are harvested they ripen in about a week.

All commercially grown avocados are hybrids, derived from three geographical varieties: Mexican avocados are small, dark-skinned, and high in fat; lowland Guatemalan avocados are large and pale green-skinned with coarse, watery flesh, and moderate fat; and highland Guatemalan avocados are pale green, moderate in fat, and have small pits. Hass avocados from California, a hybrid from Mexican fruit, with rough dark hides and a rich, creamy flesh, account for most of the avocados sold. The remainder are mostly Fuerte and Booth, both Guatemalan hybrids principally grow in Florida. They are large, smooth skinned, and bright green. Their flesh is mealier than Hass and lower in fat.

What It Does • As with many tropical and subtropical fruits, an avocado's ripening cycle is enhanced by warm temperature and stopped by cold. Avocados ripen best between 65 and 75°F (18 and 24°C), and their cellular machinery grinds to a halt when temperatures drop below 45°F (7°C). Ripe avocados can be refrigerated for several days without damage.

Because they contain **enzymes** that encourage oxidation, avocados are prone to browning from exposure to air. You can stop the degradation by rubbing the cut flesh with citrus juice, which interrupts the enzyme action, or by covering it tightly to prevent contact with air. Coating the surface with oil or placing polyvinyl chloride (such as Saran Wrap) right against the avocado's surface work the best. Polyethylene plastic wrap (such as Glad), which is gas permeable, won't do as good a job.

The most popular avocado preparation, guacamole, takes advantage of the fruit's high fat and low fiber contents to transform it into an unctuous purée without cooking. Hass avocados can be as much as 20% fat, largely monounsaturated, including oleic acid, which has been effective at lowering LDL **cholesterol** in the blood and raising HDL levels. In addition to fats, avocado oil is high in **lecithin**, a powerful emulsifier that keeps sauces and vinaigrettes made with avocado creamy and smooth. The presence of lecithin is why you can load up a guacamole with moisture from tomato and citrus juice without fear of the liquid seeping out. Avocado oil is prized for frying, because it has a high smoke point.

Although avocados are sometimes added to cooked soups or stews at the end to help them thicken, the fruit cannot be heated for long. When fully cooked, avocados become overtly bitter, probably because of the abundance of phenolic compounds in the flesh.

Avocado leaf is used as a seasoning in Mexican cooking. It has a mild licorice flavor and must be toasted to bring out its aroma. When purchasing avocado leaves, make sure they are from a Mexican variety of avocado, such as Hass. Leaves from non-Mexican varieties can be toxic.

How It Works • Avocados are high in the carotenoid lutein, which is beneficial to eye health, and according to a study published in the *Journal of Nutrition*, March 2005, there is some evidence that combining avocados or avocado oil with other carotene-rich foods, like peppers, carrots, or tomatoes, increases the bioavailability of their alpha-carotene, beta-carotene, and lutein by a factor of 7.2, 15.3, and 5.1, respectively.

See Also • Browning, Cholesterol, Enzyme, Fat

AWONORI • See Seaweed

AZUKI BEAN • See Legume

B

BACON

What It Is •

At one time the word "bacon" meant pork of any type, which could be why bacon can come from several parts of the pig (see Types of Bacon, below). Although all bacon is cured with salts, flavoring it with smoke is a matter of cultural preference. North American and northern European bacons tend to be smoked, while Italian, Spanish, and southern French bacons are more often cured just with herbs and spices.

What It Does •

Sliced, or streaky, bacon is between one-half and two-thirds fat, which sounds alarming. However, most of that fat renders out, or melts, during cooking. Cooked bacon loses about 80% of its raw weight (mostly fat, and a small amount of water), which means a slice of crisply cooked bacon has only 35 calories, as opposed to 126 calories in a slice of raw bacon.

The sweet-smoky flavor of bacon fat enhances classic dishes in many cuisines. Bacon was traditionally used to add succulence to lean roasted game meats, either by wrapping small birds in bacon (barding) or inserting lardons of bacon deep into the flesh of a roasting haunch (larding). In contemporary cooking, wrapping grilled seafood in bacon strips adds moisture and fat. Rendered bacon fat contains 85% saturated and monounsaturated fatty acids, which means it will resist rancidity for months if kept cold.

Types of Bacon

Name	Other Names	Where Produced	Description	Processing
Canadian bacon	Back bacon, Middle bacon	North America, United Kingdom	Center-cut or end-cut pork loin, very lean, cylindrical	Brine-cured, smoked
Cottage bacon	Shoulder bacon	North America, United Kingdom	High amount of lean, chop-shaped, swirls of fat	Dry- or brine-cured
Guanciale	Jowl bacon	Italy	Short wide strips of fat and lean, pepper and herbs	Dry-cured
Hock bacon	Smoked ham hock	Southeast U.S., United Kingdom	Lower leg with skin, boil before frying	Brine- or dry-cured, smoked
Lardo	Fat back	Italy	Creamy white fat, salted, rosemary and cloves	Dry-cured
Pancetta	Italian bacon	Italy	Salted rolled seasoned pork belly	Dry-cured, air-dried
Salt pork	White bacon	United States	Fatty parts of belly, little meat, used for flavoring	Dry-cured
Slab bacon	Flitch	North America, United Kingdom	Pork belly with rind	Brine-cured, smoked
Sliced bacon	Streaky bacon, Rasher	North America, United Kingdom	Thin strips of belly, striated fat and lean	Brine-cured, smoked
Speck	Leg (Italy), Belly (Germany)	Italy, Germany	Meaty, like prosciutto, with juniper, rosemary, allspice	Dry-cured, cold-smoked
Tocino	Bacon	Spain	Spanish for bacon or cured pork	Dry-cured
Wiltshire bacon	British bacon	United Kingdom	Made from a secret blend of spices	Dry-cured, lightly smoked

kitchen wisdom

Uncurling Bacon

When bacon is pan-fried, the lean meat proteins contract and the fat melts, causing the strips to curl, making it difficult to fry bacon evenly. Short-order cooks use weights to keep the strips flat, but you can achieve the same result without specialized equipment. Lowering the heat melts the fat and contracts the lean more gradually, which minimizes curling. Microwaving bacon strips between sheets of paper towel (1 sheet per bacon slice) on High keeps the lean parts moister, lessening their tendency to contract, so the strips stay flat. Baking bacon on a rimmed sheet pan in a moderate oven doesn't eliminate curling, but because the heat in an oven comes from all directions, rather than just from the bottom as it does in a skillet, the strips cook evenly.

Imitation bacon bits and strips, which are made from flavored and shaped soy (or other vegetable) protein, are a feeble knockoff of the real thing. Bacon substitutes can also be made from veal, turkey, and/or duck.

How It Works • Dry-**curing** draws about 40% of the moisture out of fresh bacon, concentrating its flavor, setting its color, and softening the fat. Although a few types of artisanal bacon are dry-cured for several weeks, all industrially produced bacon is cured quickly in brine, which is mostly water. Brine is injected into the slab through a set of fine needles, and increases the weight of the bacon by about 10%. That's why the label says "water added." After a few hours of brining, the bacon is smoked and packed. Although brine-cured bacon has a salty, smoky flavor, it is not nearly as deep and concentrated as bacon that is dry-cured.

The bright pink color of bacon develops during curing because nitrite in the curing mixture forms nitric oxide that converts hemoglobin pigment to pink nitrosomyoglobin. Nitrite also flavors the bacon, protects the fat from rancidity, and inhibits the growth of botulinum bacteria. It also has been linked to possible cancer-causing nitrosamines that develop when nitrites combine with proteins during digestion or when bacon is fried at high temperatures. For that reason, U.S. food regulations limit the amount of nitrite in bacon to 0.02%. The addition of ascorbic acid or sodium erythorbate reduces nitrosamine formation. Nitrite-free bacon has become increasingly available. It tastes a bit different from traditional bacon and its lean, or meat, parts are brown rather than pink.

See Also • Brining, Curing, Fat, Pork, Smoking

BACTERIA

What It Is • Bacteria, which are various single-cell microscopic organisms, live everywhere, growing in every habitat on Earth. They fertilize soil, aid in human digestion, and give plants the ability to absorb nitrogen. Their photosynthesis supplied the atmosphere's original oxygen, and the earliest fossils known, nearly 3.5 billion years old, are of single-celled bacteria-like critters that existed long before multicellular plants evolved.

What It Does • Bacteria get a bad rap. Although they may cause problems for humans under specific conditions, most bacteria live their lives without interfering with ours. For instance, *E. coli* bacteria naturally present in our intestines help us digest food, metabolize glucose, and produce

fast facts

- A gram of soil houses 40 million bacterial cells, and there are a million bacterial cells in a milliliter of fresh water, equaling about 5 nonillion (5×10^{30}) bacteria on the planet.
- Your body has about 10 times as many bacterial cells as human cells.
- If you were able to measure the combined biomass of all bacteria the sum would exceed the mass of all other living matter combined — pretty impressive for organisms so small that they are invisible to the naked eye.

and absorb vitamins, but when virulent strains of E. coli cause serious diseases in people with susceptible immune systems, we get the message that all E. coli should be eradicated.

Bacteria in the gut are indispensable for **digestion**. The gastrointestinal tract contains an immensely complex ecology of microorganisms. A typical person has more than 500 distinct species of bacteria in their lower intestinal tract. Specialized bacteria help herbivores and wood-eating insects break down plant cellulose.

For centuries people have eaten particular foods for their healthful bacteria content. Yogurt and other fermented dairy products depend on lactic acid–producing bacteria for a mild tartness and creamy consistency. In the production of prosciutto two specific staphylococcus bacteria replace the nitrite chemistry of other hams, giving nitrite-free Parma ham its sweet character. Fermenting anaerobic bacteria transform fresh pork into salami and cabbage into sauerkraut, just as they add richness in the production of coffee and cocoa.

How It Works • Although most bacteria are benign or beneficial, a handful are dangerous to humans. They can be largely avoided by following these safe food-handling practices:

- store proteins and perishable produce below 40°F (4°C) and hold hot foods above 140°F (60°C) before serving
- cool leftover hot food to below 40°F (4°C) and heat refrigerated ingredients to above 140°F (60°C) as quickly as possible

Common Disease-causing Food-borne Bacteria

Bacterium	Where Found	Transmitted By	To Avoid	Symptoms
Campylobacter jejuni	Intestines, raw milk, untreated water, sewage	Water, raw milk, uncooked animal protein, especially poultry	Use clean water, thorough cooking, proper storage	Fever, headache, diarrhea, pain, within 2 to 5 days
Clostridium botulinum	Intestines, soil, water, plants, anaerobic low acid foods, honey	Inadequately processed low-acid foods, improperly vacuum-packed food, home-canned foods, dense meats, produce in oil	Check vacuum-packaging for damage or bulging	Symptoms of botulism include: Damage to nervous system, trouble breathing, within 4 hours to 8 days
Clostridium perfringens	Intestines, soil, sewage, anaerobic conditions	Inadequate cooking, improper storage and temperature control	Thorough cooking, proper temperature control, reheating to greater than 165°F (74°C)	Diarrhea, gas pain, within 8 to 24 hours
Escherichia coli (E. coli)	Intestines, raw milk, untreated water	People, water, raw milk, ground beef, unpasteurized fruit juice, raw produce	Pasteurization, thorough cooking, use clean water	Diarrhea, cramps, nausea, within 2 to 5 days
Listeria monocytogenes	Intestines, milk, soil, leafy produce	Fresh dairy, soft cheeses, raw vegetables, raw meat, fish and poultry, refrigerated prepared food	Hand washing and proper food handling, thorough cooking	Fever, headache, back ache, within 12 hours to 3 weeks in pregnant women, the elderly, and immunocompromised individuals
Salmonella	Intestines, feces, raw poultry and eggs	Raw or undercooked meat, poultry, eggs, seafood, or dairy	Thorough cooking, separate cutting surfaces, hand washing	Diarrhea, cramps, nausea, fever, headache, within 6 to 48 hours
Staphylococcus aureus	Skin, nose, and throat, infected cuts	Person to person, meat and meat products, cream-filled pastries, egg salad	Hand washing, cover mouth when coughing, proper food handling	Nausea, vomiting, diarrhea, within 1 to 6 hours
Vibrio vulnificus	Oysters, clams, and crabs	Raw and undercooked shellfish	Proper cooking	Vomiting, diarrhea, abdominal pain, within 16 hours; blood infection in those with chronic liver disease

science wise

- use separate cutting surfaces for raw proteins, such as meat, poultry, and fish, to prevent cross-contamination
- use separate utensils, cutting boards, and dishes for raw and cooked food
- keep work surfaces clean with a weak bleach solution, which is much more effective at eradicating bacteria than soap and therefore is less likely to cause antibiotic resistance
- wash hands thoroughly and often
- take special care with potential hazardous ingredients (see chart, left)

See Also • Cheese, Curing, Digestion, Fermentation

BAGELS • See Bread

BAKEWARE

What It Is • Bakeware holds batters and doughs until they are set by the heat of an oven. The size and shape of a baking pan doesn't just influence a baked good's dimensions, it affects baking time, doneness, and how brown and crusty the finished cake, bread, cookie, or pastry will be.

What It Does • Choosing the right pan for a particular baking recipe means juggling a number of factors, including different materials, shapes, sizes, and colors — all these details have an influence on taste, texture, appearance, and cooking times.

Shape

The shape of a baking pan affects the look of the finished baked good and the rate at which the batter or dough bakes. Although there are literally hundreds of novelty-shaped baking pans, the standards are:

- *Round cake pans* for layer cakes.
- *Square cake pans* for brownies, bars, snack cakes, and cornbreads.
- *Rectangular cake pans* for sheet cakes.
- *Loaf pans* for breads and other sweet or savory loaves.
- *Baking sheets* for cookies, thin sheet cakes, and rolled cakes such as jelly rolls. Sheet pans can be flat, one-sided, or rimmed.
- *Tube pans*, round high-sided pans with a hollow cylinder in the center, in one or two pieces, are good for heavy-battered cakes that benefit from heat flowing through the cylinder to bake the center of the cake before the edges burn, and for foamy cakes that benefit from the additional pan walls to give the batter more surfaces to cling to as it rises and support as it cools inverted.
- *Bundt pans* are heavy-gauge deeply fluted tube pans.
- *Springform pans* are round cake pans with a removable bottom and detachable sides for baking cakes that are difficult to unmold, like cheesecakes and tortes.
- *Muffin and mini-muffin pans* for baking muffins and cupcakes are difficult to grease, so nonstick-coated muffin pans have become the norm.

Material

- *Aluminum*: Heavy-gauge aluminum is the best choice for all-purpose baking pans. It transfers heat quickly and evenly and doesn't warp or

Pan Sizes

Pan Dimension Inches (centimeters)	Pan Volume Cups (milliliters or liters)
Round	
6 x 2 (15 x 5)	4 (950 mL)
8 x 1.5 (20 x 4)	4 (950 mL)
8 x 2 (20 x 5)	6 (1.4 L)
9 x 1.5 (23 x 4)	6 (1.4 L)
9 x 2 (23 x 5)	8 (1.9 L)
10 x 2 (25 x 5)	11 (2.6 L)
Springform	
9 x 2.5 (23 x 6.25)	10 (2.4 L)
8 x 3 (20 x 7.5)	11 (2.6 L)
9 x 3 (23 x 7.5)	12 (2.8 L)
10 x 2.5 (25 x 6.25)	12 (2.8 L)
Tube	
8 x 3 (20 x 7.5)	9 (2.1 L)
9 x 3 (23 x 7.5)	12 (2.8 L)
9.5 x 4 (24 x 10)	16 (3.8 L)
10 x 4 (25 x 10)	16 (3.8 L)
Bundt	
7.5 x 3 (19 x 7.5)	6 (1.4 L)
9 x 3 (23 x 7.5)	9 (2.4 L)
10 x 3.5 (25 x 8.75)	12 (2.8 L)
10 x 4 (25 x 10)	12 (2.8 L)
Square	
8 x 8 x 1.5 (20 x 20 x 4)	6 (1.4 L)
8 x 8 x 2 (20 x 20 x 5)	8 (1.9 L)
9 x 9 x 1.5 (23 x 23 x 4)	8 (1.9 L)
9 x 9 x 2 (23 x 23 x 5)	10 (2.4 L)
10 x 10 x 2 (25 x 25 x 5)	12 (2.8 L)
Rectangular	
11 x 7 x 2 (28 x 18 x 5)	6 (1.4 L)
13 x 9 x 2 (33 x 23 x 5)	14 (3.3 L)
Loaf	
8 x 4 x 2.5 (20 x 10 x 6.25)	4 (950 mL)
8.5 x 4.5 x 2.5 (21 x 11 x 6.25)	6 (1.4 L)
9 x 5 x 3 (23 x 13 x 7.5)	8 (1.9 L)

Round

Springform

Tube

Bundt

Square

Rectangular

Loaf

have hot spots like less expensive thin-gauge pans. Insulated baking sheets sandwich a layer of air between two sheets of aluminum, to help keep cookies from burning on the bottom. They also keep cookies from browning and may cause them to spread before the batter sets.

- *Glass:* Ovenproof glass such as Pyrex heats slowly and transfers heat evenly. It is preferred for items that take time to heat through and benefit from crusting, such as casseroles, soufflés, and pies. Glass is transparent to infrared heat so heat goes through rather than being reflected back, encouraging crusting and faster baking times. Its transparency also allows you to judge the color of a pie crust while it bakes.

- *Iron:* Retains heat better than other materials, making it the preferred material for developing a crisp crust and soft interior; think cornbread. To get the best results, preheat the pan in the oven before filling it with batter. Iron rusts and has a tendency to stick if it is not seasoned properly. Lining iron baking pans with enamel eliminates these potential downsides, and gives them similar properties to glass bakeware.

- *Nonstick pans and baking paper:* Metal is more porous than glass, which makes metal pans prone to sticking. To make them nonstick they are coated with enamel (which is glass) or heat-safe plastic (Teflon is the main brand). Any pan can be made nonstick by lining it with paper. Waxed paper and foil are an inexpensive alternative but the wax can melt and foil has sharp edges that can tear into a delicate cake. Specially designed baking paper, called baking parchment or parchment paper, is preferable. Parchment is made by infusing paper pulp with silicone, which creates a very strong, slick, heat-resistant paper. Parchment is sold in sheets and rolls, and can be cut to any size or shape. Cupcake papers are fluted paper rounds designed to fit into the cups of muffin pans.

- *Silicone:* Looks like rubber can stand temperatures from −90°F (−68°C) to 580°F (304°C), allowing you to bake directly from the refrigerator or freezer. Although they are often advertised as nonstick, they are not 100% reliable and should still be greased and floured, especially if they are deeply fluted. Because silicone transfers heat slowly, these pans are best for standard 9- by 2-inch (23 by 5 cm) round cakes or smaller. Large tube cakes may need as much as 20 minutes extra baking time. It is best to allow silicone-baked cakes to cool to room temperature before unmolding them. If used as directed, silicone pans are nontoxic and as nonreactive as glass bakeware. Silicone baking sheets are used to line the bottom of sheet pans. They are also available for muffin pans.

Weight
Heavy-gauge professional-weight baking pans are preferred. Flimsy baking pans can warp in a hot oven and tend to emphasize hot spots, causing foods to bake unevenly. Heavier pans frequently have wide rolled rims, which makes them easier to grip securely with an oven mitt or pot holder.

Color
Dark pans absorb heat, which makes them cook items faster. Shiny pans reflect heat, so they cook more slowly. For some baked goods, such as breads, dark pans are an advantage, delivering a darker, crisper crust. For items such as cakes, however, dark pans can cause crisp edges and uneven rising. Dark cookie sheets brown the bottoms of cookies more than shiny ones. Black iron corn-muffin pans yield a crisp crust and a soft, moist interior.

How It Works • It is important to use pans that are the size called for in the recipe. If you don't have the exact shape pan, substitute a different shape pan of a similar volume. The Pan Sizes chart (see left) shows pans of comparable volume. You can use a pan of slightly larger or smaller volume but baking time will be affected. Note that if the width or length dimensions are very different, even if the volume of the two pans is similar, the baking time will be affected. The more the batter fills the pan, the longer it will take to bake.

To measure the volume of any pan, fill it with water to its rim, then carefully transfer the water to a measuring cup (or measure the water before you pour it into the pan). If calculating the volume of a pan that leaks, such as a springform pan or a tube pan with a removable bottom, pour in sugar or dry rice instead of water.

Just because a pan can hold 12 cups (2.8 L) of liquid doesn't mean that you can bake 12 cups (2.8 L) of batter in it. Because different baked goods rise by different amounts, use the following guidelines for filling pans.

- fill cake pans ½ to ⅔ full
- fill cupcake or muffin tins ⅔ to ¾ full
- fill casserole and soufflé dishes about 1 inch (2.5 cm) below the rim
- fill jelly roll pans ½ full
- fill pie pans to the rim

See Also • Heat

BAKING

What It Is • St. Honorius, help me! If you have ever prayed to the patron saint of bakers for the resurrection of a fallen cake, you know firsthand that baking, the feat of transubstantiating batter or dough into something edible, is a hazardous art. And rightly so, for baking is a complex science, spanning several scientific disciplines, and sidestepping enough potential hazards to make success look more like alchemy than chemistry. Fortunately, understanding the science of baking is not that difficult, since many baked goods contain the same five ingredients.

What It Does •
Flour: The Foundation
Without **flour** baked goods would fall apart. When mixed with liquid, **protein** in flour forms an elastic web of **gluten**. The higher the protein content and the more mixing that is done, the thicker the gluten becomes, which is why recipes for chewy breads call for high-protein bread flour and long periods of kneading. Light, fluffy cakes and quick breads benefit from low-protein high-**starch** cake flour and a minimum of mixing after the flour is added. All-purpose flour falls in-between and is a blend of high- and low-protein flours. (For a listing of the protein content of various flours, see Non-Wheat Flours chart, page 240.)

Sugar: Flavor, Texture, and Color
Sugar (sucrose) isn't just sweet; it makes baked goods tender, moist, and crisp, and yields a rich brown color. Remove sugar from a cake or cookie recipe and the results will be dense, dry, and pale. Add extra sugar and the baked good will become crisper and browner. Add too much and the cake will not set. When heated, sugar melts and caramelizes. When combined with proteins it forms brown colors and roasted flavors. It retains moisture in baking because sugar is hygroscopic, meaning it attracts water from the atmosphere, and hydrophilic, meaning it binds water and holds on to it, causing sweet baked goods to remain moist and tender much longer than sugar-free baked goods. The same phenomenon is the reason excess sugar causes cookies to spread or makes bread dough go slack: the sugar binds up the liquid that would otherwise interact with flour proteins to form gluten. Sugar also interferes with starch gelatinization (thickening on heating) so increases tenderness.

Be careful when substituting brown sugar for white in a recipe. Brown sugar contains molasses (the darker the sugar, the more molasses it has), which is acidic and can throw off the alkali-acid ratio in baking powder. You can correct the imbalance by adding a pinch of baking soda. Also be careful when substituting honey for sugar. Honey is more hygroscopic, which can make the surface sticky, and honey causes more browning than white sugar.

Leavener: The Rise
Whether it's a bulbous boule, a chewy chocolate chip cookie, or an airy ring of angel food cake, all baked goods rely on leaveners to lighten a dough. The most basic leavener is air. Air bubbles get trapped in the web of gluten whenever dough is beaten or kneaded. When heated, the air expands and the baked good rises. In addition, as a dough or batter cooks, water is converted into steam that fills the air bubbles, stretching the gluten even more. The expansion can be intensified by adding yeast or chemical leaveners, such as baking powder and baking soda, which produce **carbon dioxide** gas that increases the volume of bubbles. Leaveners don't produce more bubbles, they just make

existing bubbles larger, so it is vital to incorporate air into a batter or dough, by beating it, kneading it, or adding an aerated substance such as a firmly beaten **egg** white.

Fat: Leavener, Tenderizer, and Flavor Enhancer

Although a little bit of **fat** goes a long way, the amount of fat in a baked good affects almost everything about it. Baked goods made with more fat, such as cakes, cookies, pastries, and shortbreads, are more tender than low-fat yeast breads. Fat prevents water from hydrating the flour proteins that form the fibrous gluten and therefore the gluten strands are shorter, hence the term "shortening." The higher the proportion of fat, the more pronounced that effect will be. Solid saturated fats, such as shortening and lard, which are 100% fat, make a more tender, flakier pie crust than butter or margarine, which are only about 80% fat. Low-fat spreads, in which most of the fat is replaced with water, can be as low as 50% fat, which makes them a poor substitute in baking. Solid fats hold more air bubbles, making them better for aerated cakes. As well, since we depend on fat to transport aromatic components into our olfactory sensors, the addition of fat increases all of the flavors in a baked good. The flavor of the fat itself has an effect. Buttery cookies may not be as tender as those made with shortening, but they sure taste better, and although olive oil is the perfect choice for tenderizing focaccia, a strong-flavored olive oil can ruin the flavor of a carrot cake.

Liquid: The Activator

The liquid (water) in a batter or dough activates all the other elements. It triggers the production of gluten, swells the starch, dissolves the sugar, wakes up the yeast, and sparks the chemical reaction of baking powder and baking soda to produce carbon dioxide. Liquids that contain fat, such as milk, cream, egg yolk, and oil, tenderize, whereas liquids that contain acid, such as buttermilk and sour cream, affect the way a dough rises, and break down the protein in the flour, thereby inhibiting the development of gluten. Adding liquid near the beginning of mixing a dough, as is done in bread baking, encourages gluten formation; waiting until the end, as is done when mixing up cakes or pastry, keeps baked goods tender.

Relative Ingredient Amounts for Basic Baked Goods

Baked Good	Flour	Liquid	Fat	Leavener	Sugar	Salt
Biscuit	10 oz (284 g)	6 oz (170 g)	2 oz (56 g)	0.3 oz (9 g)	0	0.2 oz (7 g)
Cake/Muffin	10 oz (284 g)	8 oz (227 g)	5 oz (142 g)	0.75 oz (21 g)	8 oz (227 g)	0.2 oz (7 g)
Pie crust	7.5 oz (213 g)	2 oz (56 g)	4 oz (114 g)	0	0	0.1 oz (3 g)
Quick bread	12 oz (340 g)	12 oz (340 g)	2 oz (56 g)	0.3 oz (9 g)	5 oz (142 g)	0.2 oz (7 g)
Sugar cookie	1 lb (454 g)	1 oz (28 g)	8 oz (227 g)	0.1 oz (3 g)	10 oz (284 g)	0.05 oz (1.5 g)
Yeast bread	1 lb (454 g)	12 oz (340 g)	0.5 oz (14 g)	0.14 oz (4 g)	0.5 oz (14 g)	0.8 oz (23 g)

How It Works • Although most doughs and batters contain all the ingredients mentioned previously, the way they are combined and the ratio of one ingredient to another results in the differences between breads, cakes, cookies, and pastries. The difference between dough and batter is the ratio of liquid to flour. Batters are fluid: a pour batter has a ratio of 1 part flour to 1 part liquid, a drop batter has 2 parts flour to 1 part liquid. Doughs are stiff enough to hold in your hand. A soft dough has 3 parts flour to 1 part liquid and a stiff dough has greater than 3 parts flour to 1 part liquid.

Here are how various doughs and batters are prepared:

- *Biscuits:* Combine flour, sugar, leavener, and salt. Cut in butter or shortening until finely mixed. Stir in enough liquid to form a soft, pliable dough.
- *Cakes:* Beat fat (usually butter) and sugar until aerated. Stir in eggs and flavorings. Combine flour and leavener in a separate bowl, and beat into batter alternating with liquid. Fold in chunky ingredients, such as dried fruit, nuts, or chocolate chips. Fold in beaten egg whites, if using.
- *Cookies:* Beat fat (usually butter) and sugar until aerated. Stir in eggs, flour, flavorings, and leaveners to form a firm dough.
- *Muffins and quick breads:* Sift together dry ingredients (flour, sugar, salt, and baking soda or powder) in one bowl. Combine liquid ingredients in another bowl. Make a well in the center of the dry ingredients and add liquids all at once. Stir minimally to restrict gluten formation.
- *Pastry:* Combine flour, sugar, and salt. Cut in butter until finely mixed. Stir in enough liquid to form a rough dough. Do not handle the dough too much.
- *Yeast breads (sponge method):* Combine some of the flour, yeast, and liquid and mix until a moist web of gluten forms. Set aside to rise. Stir in salt, fat, and enough flour to form a pliable dough. Knead it to strengthen the gluten and set aside to rise.
- *Yeast breads (straight dough process):* Combine the flour, yeast, salt, sugar, and warm liquid and mix until a thick web of gluten forms. Knead it and set aside to rise.

See Also • Acid, Alkali, Bread, Cake, Carbon Dioxide, Chemical Leavener, Cookies

BAKING POWDER • See Chemical Leavener

BAKING SODA • See Chemical Leavener

BALSAMIC VINEGAR • See Vinegar

BANANA

What It Is • Bananas are technically **berries** that grow on the world's largest tropical herb, *Musa acuminata*. Although there are more than 500 varieties, the industrialized world eats only a few subgroups including the very small Lady Finger, the widely cultivated Gros Michel, and several from the Cavendish group including the Dwarf Cavendish and the Giant Cavendish. Each year the United States imports $1 billion of Cavendish bananas, almost all from Latin America.

Plantains are bananas that are generally intended for cooking as a starchy vegetable before ripening, although they sweeten as they ripen. In India there is no distinction between bananas and plantains other than bananas are eaten for dessert and plantains are used for cooking. Currently bananas and plantains are the largest fruit crop in the world. Bananas are generally propagated from suckers rather than cross-fertilization of seeds and thus with no genetic mixing, bananas can't adapt to invasive disease or extreme changes in climate, so the world's banana crops are relatively vulnerable to devastation.

What It Does • Banana is the only fruit that ripens just as well after picking as it does on the tree. Green bananas store their sugar in the form of **starch**, which is converted back into sugar during post-harvest ripening. For that reason bananas are usually picked and shipped green. Once they arrive at their destination bananas are sprayed with ethylene gas to trigger and accelerate ripening. When there are too many bananas reaching the market, ripening can be slowed by lower temperature storage or prevented for up to three weeks by storage under a modified atmosphere of decreased oxygen and increased carbon dioxide.

How It Works •
The starch-to-sugar ratio in green bananas is 25 to 1, but shifts dramatically as the fruit ripens to 1 to 20, making ripe bananas one of the sweetest fruits, second only to dates. The high sugar content and low moisture of ripe bananas produces a concentration of flavor and aroma that makes the banana an ideal fruit for flavoring baked goods without watering down the batter.

Although plantains develop some sugar as they ripen, their starch-to-sugar ratio never converts to the same degree as in bananas. Ripe plantains remain dry and starchy and, like potatoes, require cooking to become edible.

Although chilling fruit is the primary method for delaying ripening, this is not the case for bananas and plantains. Temperatures below 50°F (10°C) cause their cells to malfunction, and uncontrolled enzymatic browning turns the skins black. Unripe bananas contain phenols in their vascular network that can cause discoloration of the skin under refrigeration, although the color and flavor of the fruit will not be affected much by cold.

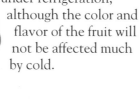

fast facts

- Bananas are older than recorded history. They were cultivated in Southeast Asia long before any other fruit was domesticated.
- Each stem on a banana tree produces a single flower from which an average of 10 clusters (called hands) grow, each with about 12 individual pieces of fruit (called fingers). A stem produces bananas only once, and the entire stem is cut off for harvesting.
- The distinctive curve of bananas happens because the tips grow upward, causing the fruit to bend against the downward force of gravity.

Bananas develop their creamy texture as pectins change during ripening and their distinctive aroma primarily from amyl acetate and other amyl and isoamyl esters of organic acids. As bananas ripen, the development of malic acid in the fruit, which can increase twofold, enhances its flavor markedly.

See Also • Berries, Enzyme, Fruit

BARBECUE

What It Is •
A low fire, billows of wood smoke, and long, slow, steady cooking times of up to 24 hours are the hallmarks of real barbecue. The word can also refer to the cooker used for barbecuing, a social gathering at which barbecued food is served, or the sauce served with barbecued food.

Barbecuing is often confused with **grilling**. Although both involve flames, the similarity stops there. In barbecuing the heat is low and the cooking is slow. Grilling is done directly over flame; the heat is higher and food cooks through relatively quickly. Many people refer to their grills as barbecues, which adds to the confusion.

fast fact

What It Does • Barbecue cookers, or pits, have two or three chambers: an offset firebox, a cooking chamber with a chimney, and sometimes a vertical smoker for cold-smoking fish. The smoke from burning wood flows from the firebox into the cooking chamber through a system of vents that can be opened or closed to control the amount of heat and smoke that contact the food. By positioning the food on racks in the cooking chamber, a pit master can ensure maximum or minimum exposure to smoke moving from the vents on one side of the chamber up through the chimney at the opposite end. Often a pan of water is placed in the cooking chamber to provide steam.

How It Works • Even though the heat in the firebox can exceed 400°F (200°C), the temperature in the cooking chamber should stay between 200°F (93°C) and 225°F (107°C). At this low temperature, foods cook very slowly without burning, which is key to dissolving the thick connective tissue that surrounds the muscle fibers in tougher cuts such as brisket and ribs. It takes time for these connective tissues to soften and add moisture to the meat. The process is helped along by basting, or mopping, the meat with a watery acidic liquid as it barbecues.

See Also • Grilling, Meat, Smoking

kitchen wisdom

Wood Smoke – The Flavor of Barbecue

Even though barbecued meat is seasoned with spice rubs, doused with vinegary basting liquids, and dipped into pungent barbecue sauce, its dominant flavor is smoke. Depending on the wood burned, the smoke can be sweet or acrid, fruity or resinous. The most common woods used for smoking (in alphabetical order) are:

- *Alder:* light, aromatic smoke; preferred for salmon
- *Apple* and *Cherry:* sweet, fruity smoke; great with poultry and pork
- *Hickory:* strong, full-flavored smoke; popular with ribs, pork shoulder, bacon, beef brisket, and turkey
- *Maple:* sweet and fragrant smoke; goes well with chicken and full-flavored fish
- *Mesquite:* heavy smoke, pungent flavor; works best with beef
- *Oak:* good all-purpose smoky flavor, not as strong as hickory, and never bitter
- *Pecan:* rich, fragrant, mellow smoke; won't overpower delicate seafood

BARLEY • See Grains

BASE • See Alkali

BASIL • See Herbs

BASMATI RICE • See Rice

BASS • See Fish

BAY LEAVES • See Herbs

BEANS • See Legumes

BEEF

What It Is • Weighing in at more than half a ton (455 kg), the average beef cattle yields more than 500 pounds (225 kg) of edible meat. Most breeds are hybrids of Hereford, Durham, or Angus combined with drought-tolerant humped cattle from Asia, particularly Brahmans, to create a stock that is resistant to environmental hardships and disease, and possesses the large musculature, good marbling, and tender meat that is the hallmark of great beef.

Tastes have changed since the high point of beef consumption in the 1950s and '60s, and beef producers responded to declining sales and concerns over dietary fat by shortening the amount of time that animals are fatted in feedlots, and by breeding leaner and larger European cattle into the North American hybrid. New breeds such as the Chiangus, a mix of Angus and Chianina, the giant cattle

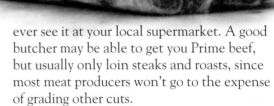

of central Italy, have become premium beef in the U.S., because they are both very lean and very tender, a sensory combination that could not have been attained a generation ago.

What It Does • Beef cattle are sorted by sex and maturity. Male cattle are large and yield more meat per carcass, but the meat tends to be stringier and tougher than the meat from female animals. Female animals have finer-textured, more tender meat, but their muscle groups are smaller and give lower yield per carcass. So neither male nor female cattle have all of the characteristics the beef industry wants: tender, fine-textured meat and large, high-yielding muscles. In order to raise cattle with both maximum yield and maximum tenderness, male cattle are castrated before puberty, which causes the animals to mature in size while their musculature stays soft and tender — everything one wants in cattle designed for the plate.

The best-quality beef comes from younger females and castrated males. Females who have not yet calved are called heifers; after bearing a calf they are referred to as cows. Males are bulls, steers (castrated bulls), or bullocks (young steers). Bulls are not generally sold as fresh meat, and only steers, heifers, and bullocks produce beef of the highest quality. The meat from older animals is ground for processed meats such as canned chili or is used in pet foods.

The U.S. Department of Agriculture (USDA) has eight quality grades for beef: Prime, Choice, Select, Standard, Commercial, Utility, Cutter, and Canner. Canada uses seven grades: Prime, AAA, AA, A, B1-4, D1-4, and E. All beef sold at retail markets falls within the top three grades, based on yield, muscle configuration, and, most important, marbling, the fine threads of fat that striate through lean muscle.

Prime (AAA) beef has the highest degree of marbling, but since only about 2% of the beef produced in North America is graded Prime, and almost all of that is exported or sold to restaurants, it is unlikely that you will ever see it at your local supermarket. A good butcher may be able to get you Prime beef, but usually only loin steaks and roasts, since most meat producers won't go to the expense of grading other cuts.

The richest (and most expensive) beef in the world comes from Japan. It is sometimes sold as Kobe and sometimes wagyu but neither name tells you much. Kobe is the capital of Hyogo prefecture, a main beef-producing region, and "wagyu" simply means Japanese (*wa*) beef (*gyu*). (It is known in Japan as *shimofuri*, meaning highly marbled.) Like all beef the quality of wagyu is communicated by its grade. The best grade, A5, has a velvety texture and a network of fat threaded through its lean muscle that gives it a marbling content close to 40% and a mouth feel closer to foie gras than beef. In comparison, USDA Prime beef contains less than half the marbling of A5 wagyu.

Bison lies at the other end of the fat spectrum. Also known as American buffalo, bison is bred with cattle to create low-fat, reduced-cholesterol beef, sold as beefalo.

How It Works • The amount of exercise a particular muscle gets determines the flavor and tenderness of the meat it produces. So knowing where on the animal your steak or roast comes from tells you a lot about how you should cook it and what results you can expect. A beef carcass is divided into eight primal cuts and more than 30 retail cuts of steaks, chops, roasts, ribs, stewing cubes, and ground beef.

Tender cuts come from the muscle groups that get the least amount of exercise, which run along the back of the cattle — the rib, short loin, and sirloin. Tougher meats are from the areas that move or support the body — the chuck, brisket, plate, flank, and round.

As a muscle is exercised, its fibers take on protein, making the muscle bigger, redder, and more flavorful. At the same time, its connective tissue thickens and becomes more elastic, which makes the muscle harder and tougher. So when meat is taken from an older animal or an exercised muscle group, it will have lots of flavor, a dark red color, and a tendency to be tough.

Grass-Fed, Feedlot, and Organic Beef

Completely grass-fed cattle have stronger-flavored meat than those fed on grain, mostly corn. Almost all beef raised in North America gain at least 30% of their weight in grain feedlots, which meat producers use to standardize flavor (through a consistent diet), maximize tenderness (by discouraging exercise), and minimize the time and expense it takes to bring an animal to market. During this period cattle are kept in the close quarters of feedlots, increasing the likelihood that they will spread disease, which is why most industrially raised cattle get pumped up with antibiotics to keep their meat safe. By law, cattle stop receiving antibiotics before slaughter to insure that antibiotics are not in the meat at the time the beef is butchered and sold. The length of time for antibiotic withdrawal varies by country.

In many countries, raising beef completely on grass is the norm. Pasture-fed Argentinean beef is world famous, and grass feeding has gained popularity in England since the outbreak of **mad cow disease** there.

Grass-fed beef should not be confused with meat labeled "organic." In the United States, certified organic meat must meet the USDA National Organic Program standards, insuring that the animal was:
- fed on 100% organic feed (vitamin and mineral supplements are allowed)
- given access to pasture if it is a ruminant, such as cattle
- not given hormones to promote growth, nor antibiotics

Note that organic beef can be fed on grain in feedlots, but for no more than 200 days, and its feed must be organic.

Aged Beef

Beef benefits from a period of aging. Although most is aged only incidentally during the few days that it takes to ship it from the packing plant to the butcher's counter, a small amount of Prime beef (less than 1% in the U.S.) is dry-aged for three to four weeks. Dry-aging is done under refrigeration (at 34 to 38°F/1 to 3°C) and high humidity (70 to 80%). Under these conditions, muscle enzymes in the meat continue to be active, breaking down large proteins into smaller, more flavorful amino acids and glycogen into sweet sugars. Enzymes also break down fats into aromatic fatty acids and convert adenosine triphosphate (a nucleotide that allows muscle cells to transfer energy) into inosine monophosphate, which has a savory flavor. Other enzymes called calpains and cathepsins attack the connective tissue and contracted muscle fibers, causing them to relax and thus tenderize the meat. The effect of the enzymes is twofold: 1) it makes the connective tissue between the muscles dissolve more quickly during cooking, allowing the meat to be more tender at rarer temperatures, and 2) it decreases the pressure from connective tissue on the muscle fibers, so less juice is lost as the meat cooks.

During dry-aging, a substantial amount of dehydration takes place, which concentrates flavor. Mold also grows on the surface of the meat and must be trimmed off, resulting in a weight loss of up to 20%. This extra work and lower yield explains the higher price of dry-aged beef.

A significant percentage of the remaining meat in the U.S. goes through a process that the meat industry calls wet-aging. Wet-aged meat is vacuum-packed in plastic and kept under refrigeration from four days up to two weeks. During that time the same muscle enzymes activated in dry-aging help to tenderize the meat and improve its flavor, but because the sealed plastic doesn't permit dehydration, the rich concentration of flavor that is the hallmark of dry-aged beef never occurs.

See Also ● Animal Foods, Mad Cow Disease, Meat

Cuts of Beef

Retail Cut	Primal Cut	Other Names	Description	How to Cook
Bottom round	Round	Rump roast, eye roast, gooseneck round, outside round	Oblong; boneless; coarse grain, medium marbling, tough and flavorful; rump and round eye are boneless lean and tender enough to roast if from high grade beef	Braise, slow roast, barbecue, ground
Brisket	Brisket	Brisket flat (first cut), brisket point (second cut)	First cut is flat, rough rectangle; long fibers, medium-coarse grain, leaner than second cut, which is triangular, fattier, and coarse grained; both cuts are tough and flavorful	Braise, barbecue
Cheeks	None	Jowl	Flat and ovular; finely grained; tough and flavorful	Braise
Chuck roast or steak	Chuck	Pot roast, chuck eye roast, bolar roast, blade roast or steak	Large and square; lots of connective tissue; coarse grain running in different directions; tough and flavorful	Braise, stew, barbecue, ground
Coulotte	Sirloin	Knuckle, London broil, sirloin tip, top sirloin cap	Rounded, triangular top cap of top sirloin; well marbled; medium grain; medium tender and flavorful	Grill, roast, braise, kebabs
Flank steak	Plate	London broil	Flat rectangle; long, coarse, regular often parallel grain; lean, tough and flavorful, tenderized by slicing in thin strips	Braise, roast, broil, grill
Ground beef	Chuck, round, sirloin	Hamburger, ground chuck/round/sirloin	Pink to red; uniform texture; sold by proportion of lean to fat	Grill, broil, pan-fry
Hanger steak	Plate	Butcher's steak, hanging tender	Shaped like a long V; dark red; lean; membrane runs down middle	Grill, broil, pan-fry
Knuckle	Round	Ball tip roast or steak, round tip roast or steak, sirloin tip roast or steak, London broil	Large round roast; solid dark lean meat; tough and flavorful; can be cut in steaks, kebabs, London broil	Roast, braise

continued on next page

Bottom round

Brisket

Chuck roast or steak

Coulotte

Flank steak

Ground beef

Hanger steak

Knuckle

Cuts of Beef (continued)

Retail Cut	Primal Cut	Other Names	Description	How to Cook
Oxtail	None		Cylindrical; stringy, coarse textured meat, lots of fat and connective tissue, tough and flavorful, velvety texture when braised	Braise
Rib roast	Rib	Prime rib, rib eye roast	Large fine-grained eye topped by coarse-grained "lifter" section; striated with fat; tender and flavorful; when on arched rib bones called standing rib	Roast
Rib steak	Rib	Delmonico, rib-eye	Large fine-grain lean with fat on one side; tender and flavorful	Grill, broil, pan-fry
Shank	Fore shank	Shin	Crosscut section of leg; lots of tendon and connective tissue; very tough and flavorful	Braise
Short ribs	Chuck, rib, plate	Crosscut ribs	Rectangular, rib bone running lengthwise; medium-coarse grain; striated with fat; medium tough, flavorful	Braise, stew, grill
Skirt steak	Plate	Fajita steak	Rectangular, flat; lean; coarse grain; medium tender, flavorful	Braise, grill
Strip steak	Short loin	New York strip steak, Kansas City steak, club steak	Rectangular; medium grain; layer of fat and gristle on one side, tender	Grill, broil, roast, pan-fry
T-bone / Porterhouse	Short loin		T-shaped bone separates strip (medium-fine grain) from fillet (fine grain); marbled; layer of exterior fat; tender	Grill, broil, roast
Tenderloin	Short loin	Fillet, filet mignon, Châteaubriand	Baseball-bat shape; yields round steaks, velvety texture; lean; very tender	Grill, broil, roast, sauté
Top round	Round	Round roast, round steak, London broil, minute steak	Large round, boneless; lean; medium tender and flavorful	Roast, pot roast, grill, broil, pan-fry
Top sirloin	Sirloin	Sirloin butt, London broil, sirloin steak	Large round; veined with fat; medium tender, flavorful	Roast, grill, broil
Tri-tip	Sirloin	Triangle steak	Triangular; medium-coarse grain, visible fat; valued for balance of flavor and tenderness	Grill, broil, roast

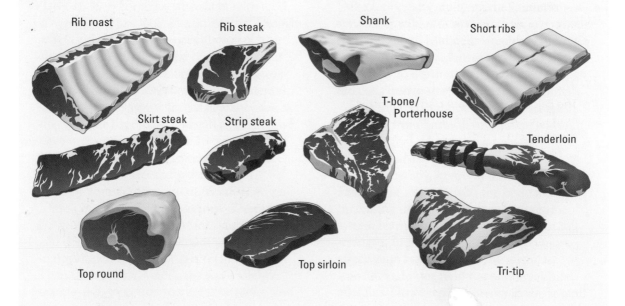

Rib roast   Rib steak   Shank   Short ribs

Skirt steak   Strip steak   T-bone/ Porterhouse   Tenderloin

Top round   Top sirloin   Tri-tip

BEER

What It Is • As early as the 3rd century BCE, Egyptians, Babylonians, and Sumerians malted barley and wheat to make beer. From the Middle East the techniques for brewing from grain traveled into northern Europe, where in a climate too cold for vineyards, beer became the common alcoholic beverage.

What It Does • Beers fall into two broad categories, ales and lagers, which are differentiated by their method of fermentation (see Fermentation, page 53). Ales tend to be dark, robust, fruity, and sweet. Lagers, in comparison, are pale, crisp, and bitter.

The different characteristics of beer are:

- *Color:* Ranging from pale yellow to inky brown-black, color is determined by the kind of malt used (see Malting, page 52). In the U.S., color intensity is measured in Standard Reference Method (SRM).
- *Body:* Mouth feel, from crisp to velvety, comes from the remnants of long-chain starch molecules in the **malt** and from the alcohol content. Body is measured in Finished Gravity (FG).
- *Bitterness:* Comes from the type and amount of hops in the beer. The effect of hops in beer is measured in International Bittering Units (IBU).
- *Overall taste:* The flavor of beer is a complex amalgam of saltiness from minerals in the water, particularly chloride and sulfate, sweetness from unfermented malt sugars, acidity from organic acids produced during yeast fermentation, bitterness from hops and dark roasted malt, and savoriness from amino acids in the malt.
- *Aroma:* Dozens of chemical reactions make up the "nose" of beer. They can be woody, citrusy, malty, floral, caramel, smoky, fruity, buttery, spicy, or an aroma like fermenting hay.
- *Bubbles:* The prickly freshness of carbonation is more pronounced in lagers than in ales.
- *Alcohol:* Measured by ABV (Alcohol Percentage by Volume).

Although most beers are made from barley malt, wheat-malt beers (which are always ales) are increasingly popular. Wheat beers

fast facts

- The calories in beer are derived mostly from residual starches (those that were not converted to sugars) and the alcohol. Light beers contain less alcohol (typically 3.2%) and use special yeasts that convert more of the starch to sugar so less starch remains in the final product.
- India Pale Ale (IPA) has more hops and a higher alcohol content than pale ale (60+ IBU and 7+% ABV), the result of British efforts to create a beer that would not spoil during long voyages to India and other hot climates.

differ from traditional ale in two ways: they use a different yeast, which gives them a spicy, somewhat medicinal or barnyard flavor, and they are always cloudy because of pentosans (nonstarch carbohydrates) in wheat that bind to proteins and form the haze.

Malting and Kilning

Unlike wine grapes, which are full of **sugar**, grains store their energy as **starch**. In order for fermentation to take place, the starch has to be broken down into sugar, which is catalyzed in the mashing step by malting enzymes, usually from barley or wheat. During malting (which goes on for five to nine days) enzymes (amylases) in the germinating grain are activated, and proteins are solubilized. About 10% of the starch is converted to sugars. The longer the malting, the more sugars that are formed and therefore the

Beer Characteristics

Category	Style	Description	Statistics*
Lager	Pilsner	Light-colored; sweet caramel flavors; medium to high bitterness; hoppy aroma; high carbonation; clean, crisp	IBU: 35–45 ABV: 4.0–5.0 FG: 1.014–1.020 SRM: 3–5
	American lager	Pale amber; Pilsner-type beer to which sugars are added; sweet; less hoppy than Pilsner; watery, clean, crisp	IBU: 5–17 ABV: 3.5–4.5 FG: 1.006–1.010 SRM: 2–4
	Bock	Amber; hearty; pronounced malt flavor; light hops; heavy mouth feel	IBU: 35–45 ABV: 4.0–5.0 FG: 1.018–1.024 SRM: 3–5
	Marzen	Amber; malty sweet; low to medium bitterness; heavy mouth feel; high alcohol	IBU: 18–25 ABV: 5.0–6.0 FG: 1.012–1.020 SRM: 15–35
	Helles	Pale color; low hops flavor and aroma; clean; low alcohol	IBU: 18–25 ABV: 4.0–5.0 FG: 1.008–1.012 SRM: 3–5
Ale	English bitter	Three styles – Ordinary, Special, and Extra Special: range from pale through medium gold to dark copper color; low carbonation; low to high hops flavor; medium to strong bitterness; light to full body	IBU: 20–65 ABV: 3.0–6.2 FG: 1.008–2.000 SRM: 6–14
	Pale ale	Pale to amber color; very little malted sweetness; high hoppy bitterness; light to medium body; high alcohol	IBU: 40–60 ABV: 5.0–7.6 FG: 1.012–1.018 SRM: 8–14
	Scottish ale	Dark; malty sweet; mild bitterness; light to medium body; high alcohol; can have smoky character	IBU: 12–20 ABV: 5.0–7.6 FG: 1.010–1.014 SRM: 10–18
	Porter	Very dark; sweet malt balanced by hops; medium body	IBU: 25–40 ABV: 4.5–6.0 FG: 1.008–1.016 SRM: 30+
	Stout	Almost black; strong malt sweetness and hoppy bitterness; medium body; high alcohol	IBU: 50–80 ABV: 7.0–9.0 FG: 1.020–1.030 SRM: 40+

*IBU = International Bittering Units; ABV = Alcohol Percentage by Volume; FG = Finished Gravity (body); SRM = Standard Reference Method (color intensity)

darker the color that is created from the Maillard reaction products that form during malt drying.

Once the barley reaches the desired balance of enzymes and sugar, the maker of the malt, or maltster, "sets" the degree of malting by drying the grain in a kiln. To make mild malt with a lot of active enzymes and little color, the drying takes place at a low temperature. Dark malts are heated to higher temperature to encourage browning and a richer flavor. Brewers have a wide range of malts to choose from, such as pale or lager, ale, crystal, amber, brown, caramel, chocolate, and black. Blending different malts allows brewers to create a particular balance of color, flavor, and enzyme activity.

Hops

Early brewers added herbs and spices to brewing beer to delay the development of off flavors from oxidation and bacterial growth. Hops, the dried oily, resinous flowers (or "cones") of the vine *Humulus lupulus*, were so much more effective at delaying spoilage than other aromatics that by the end of the 14th century they were an essential flavoring ingredient in beer. Hops add bitterness and aroma to a brew. Bland commercial brews use very little hops, about 0.5 grams per liter. Flavorful microbrews and traditional Pilsners add up to 5 grams per liter. Bittering compounds, the phenolic acids humulone and lupulone in the hops' resin, balance the sweetness of the malted grain, while terpenes can lend different varieties of hops their characteristic flavors, ranging from a woody resinous piney scent to more subtle citrus or flowery notes.

Brewing

Beer brewing takes place in four distinct phases:
- *Mashing:* When ground dried barley malt is added to warm water, the enzymes revive and begin to catalyze the conversion of starch into sugars and protein into amino acids. The resulting slush is called the wort. Often adjuncts such as unmalted barley, rice, corn, or wheat are added to the mash to increase its volume and bulk up the amount of starch and

science wise

Lambics • Belgian lambic beer is a whole other story. Instead of adding carefully selected yeasts, the natural flora present in the brewery are allowed to spontaneously ferment the wort. The wort for lambics is aged in wood for months before boiling and aged hops are used that are less bitter. Then it is conditioned in wood for six months to two years, all of which infuses the beer with its characteristic flavor and color. The finished mixture may then be blended with other lambics or some plain ale, or it can be refermented using a lactic acid bacteria and fruit for another six months, which is what is done to make kriek (cherry lambic) or framboise (raspberry lambic).

protein. Rice and corn need to be precooked separately to gelatinize their starch to make it available for conversion to fermentable sugars.
- *Boiling:* Hops are added to the wort and the mixture is boiled, which flavors the beer, inactivates the enzymes, kills any dangerous microbes, denatures proteins, clarifies and deepens the color, and concentrates the flavor.
- *Fermentation:* Yeasts are added to the cooled boiled wort, where they metabolize the sugars and produce alcohol and carbon dioxide. Ales go through rapid fermentation done at high temperatures with ale yeast (called top fermentation because the yeasts tend to float) producing acidic, strong-flavored beers. Slow fermentation at low temperatures with lager yeast (called bottom fermentation because the yeasts stay submerged) produces milder, cleaner-tasting lager beer.
- *Conditioning:* When the desired alcohol level is reached, top-fermented beer is cleared of yeast and run into a tank or cask. At this point the beer (called green beer) is flat, harsh tasting, and cloudy. During conditioning, more yeast and sugar, or some fresh wort, are added, and the tank is closed, trapping the carbon dioxide produced by the yeast, and thereby carbonating the beer. Yeasty odors are released periodically through an escape valve, and some hops or hops extract may be added for flavor. After a few days of cooling, a finishing agent, such as

gelatin, vegetable gum, isinglass, or clay, is added to precipitate proteins and tannins that could make the finished beer hazy. The beer is then centrifuged and filtered to clean it further, bottled or canned, and usually heat pasteurized. Most draft beers are not heat-treated. Bottom-fermented beer goes through a simpler process. Traditionally immediately after fermentation it was packed in ice and aged for several months, but today it is typically chilled quickly to near-freezing temperature and stored for two to three weeks, which helps purge off-odors. Carbon dioxide may be pumped in to accelerate the purging. As in top-fermented beer, it is centrifuged and filtered to clarify the brew.

Packaging and Storage

Unlike wines, beers do not improve by aging (aside from some specialty Belgian beers), and are best consumed as fresh as possible. There are four factors that negatively influence the freshness of beer:

- Exposure to oxygen makes beer taste stale and astringent; for that reason air is kept to a minimum in bottles and kegs. A shot of nitrogen added to the bottle reduces the space for oxygen and improves a beer's head.
- Although the alcohol and hop resins in beer keep harmful microbes at bay, organisms that affect the flavor of beer grow over time so most bottled and canned beer and some draft beers are pasteurized to improve their shelflife. Running the packaged beer through a hot water spray (140°F/60°C) for two to three minutes extends its storage life from two months to nine months. Pasteurization gives beer a slight cooked taste, and to avoid it some beer brewers sterile filter their beer, which goes beyond the standard filtration process, forcing the beer through superfine filters that lift out small microbes. Some body and flavor is lost in the process but the results are fresher tasting than pasteurized beer.
- Heat accelerates oxidation and staling. Unpasteurized beer should be kept at 38°F (3°C), and although pasteurized beer can be stored at room temperature safely, colder temperatures slow its deterioration.
- Exposure to light causes beer to develop sulfurous skunky odors due to hop acids that break down in light that falls within the green to violet range of the spectrum. Brown glass absorbs blue-green light waves before they can get to the beer; clear glass and green bottles don't. Sunlight can turn beer in a few hours; fluorescent light can do it in a few days. It is best to play it safe and store beer in the dark.

See Also • Alcohol, Grains, Liquor, Malt, Starch, Wine

science wise

Beer Foam • Beer is not the only carbonated beverage we enjoy, but it is the only one where we expect the head of bubbles to last for longer than a split second. Here's how it works: The amount and type of protein in beer makes stable bubbles that hold on to water tenaciously, so they are less likely to burst than the bubbles in a soft drink or sparkling wine. In addition, in the last decade or so, beer manufacturers have started to inject small amounts of nitrogen into beer during packaging. Nitrogen is less soluble in water than carbon dioxide so its bubbles are slower to dissolve in the surrounding liquid. The bubbles are also smaller, causing them to form a fine-textured creamy head. Nitrogen can be added by the tap that delivers the beer from a keg.

BEETS • See Roots

BELL PEPPER • See Capsicum

BERRIES

What It Is • Botanically a berry is any **fruit** that has numerous seeds scattered through its pulp. Cranberries, currants, gooseberries, and blueberries fit this definition nicely, but so do watermelons, cucumbers, bananas, papayas, oranges, and kiwifruit. And then there are a lot of berries that don't fit the definition at all. Blackberries and raspberries are clusters of little drupe fruits, each one surrounding a small stone with a hard shell. A mulberry is a composite fruit, each section

Berries

Name	Genus	Description	Season	Grown	Uses
Açai	*Euterpe*	Black purple; small; large pit; flavor of raspberry with aftertaste of chocolate; high in antioxidants, anthocyanins plus other polyphenols	Year-round	Sub-tropical climate, mostly Brazil	Juice, dried, pudding
Acerola	*Malpighia*	Bright red; looks like cherries with three lobes; sweet and tart; high in vitamin C	Year-round	Sub-tropical climate, mostly South America and Caribbean	Preserves, vitamin C products
Barberry	*Berberis*	Bright red; small; tart berry; similar to cranberry	Summer, fall	Temperate climate, Northern Hemisphere	Preserves, dried
Bilberry	*Vaccinium*	European blueberry	Summer	Temperate climate, Europe	Raw, sauces, preserves, pastry, cakes, muffins
Blackberry	*Rubus*	Medium-size; dark purple; made up of 50 or more tiny composite fruits; slightly sweet-tart with red juice	Summer	Temperate climate, worldwide	Raw, sauces, preserves, pastry, cakes, muffins
Blueberry	*Vaccinium*	Small; dark blue skin, coated with silvery film; pale flesh; lots of tiny seeds; highly aromatic; rich in antioxidants and anthocyanins	Summer	Temperate climate, worldwide	Raw, sauces, preserves, pastry, cakes, muffins
Carissa	*Carissa*	Small; deep red to purple; floral, tart, plum-like	Spring, summer	Subtropical climate	Raw, preserves
Cloudberry	*Rubus*	Small wild raspberry; golden; tart	Summer, fall	Subarctic climate, Northern Hemisphere	Preserves, tarts, liqueur
Cranberry	*Vaccinium*	Small; bright red skin; white crisp juicy pulp; many small seeds; highly acidic; high in pectin, antioxidants, and antimicrobials	Summer, fall	Temperate climate, North America	Sauces, relishes, baking
Currants	*Ribes*	Small; many small seeds; white to dark red and black; darker colors are rich in vitamin C, anthocyanins, and antioxidants	Summer, fall	Temperate climate, worldwide	Preserves, dried, liqueur (cassis)
Dewberry	*Rubus*	Small; close relative of blackberry; dark purple; sweet-tart red juice	Summer	Temperate climate, Northern Hemisphere	Raw, preserves, cobbler
Elderberry	*Sambucus*	Small; purple or yellow; tart; must be cooked; rich in anthocyanins	Summer, fall	Temperate climate, Northern Hemisphere	Preserves, wine
Goji berry (aka wolfberry)	*Lycium*	Small; elliptical; orange-red; lots of small seeds; very sweet; high in antioxidants	Summer	Temperate climate, worldwide, especially China	Dried
Gooseberry	*Ribes*	Large green or red currants, sometimes green with red-veins; usually picked unripe and tart; usually cooked	Summer, fall	Temperate climate, worldwide	Preserves, tarts, sauces

continued on next page

Berries (continued)

Name	Genus	Description	Season	Grown	Uses
Grapes	*Vitis*	Pale green to deep purple; sweet, tart and crisp. Wine grapes are small and acidic, raisin grapes sweet and thin skinned, eating grapes are mostly seedless. Dark varieties high in anthocyanins.	Fall	Temperate climate, worldwide	Wine, raw, dried into raisins, baking
Huckleberry	*Vaccinium*	Similar to blueberry with fewer but slightly bigger seeds	Summer	Southern U.S.	Raw, sauces, preserves
Kiwifruit	*Actinidia*	Shape and size of small hen's egg; hairy light brown skin; green to yellow flesh; lots of small black seeds; ripen well off the vine; high in vitamin C and carotenoids	Year-round	Subtropical climate, mostly New Zealand and California	Raw, salads
Lingonberry	*Vaccinium*	Small; bright red skin; white crisp juicy pulp; many small seeds; highly acidic; high in pectin, antioxidants, and antimicrobials	Summer, fall	Northern Europe	Sauces, preserves, relishes, baking
Marionberry	*Rubus*	Cross between Chelahem blackberry and olallieberry with qualities of both	Summer	Temperate climate, worldwide	Raw, sauces, preserves, pastry, cakes,
Mulberry	*Morus*	Similar to blackberry in looks and flavor; dark purple or red; often tart	Summer	Temperate climate, worldwide	Sauces, syrup, preserves
Olallieberry	*Rubus*	Cross between blackberry, raspberry, and dewberry; purple with red juice; tart	Early summer	Northern California	Pie
Raspberry	*Rubus*	Red with violet overtones or white to golden; composite fruits; slightly sweet, decidedly tart and floral, with bright colored juice the color of the berry	Summer	Temperate climate, worldwide	Raw, sauces, preserves, liqueur, pastries, cakes, muffins
Strawberry	*Fragaria*	All sizes (cultivated are larger), red skin covered with "seeds"; sweet-tart, with pineapple notes; rich in vitamin C, anthocyanins, and antioxidants	Summer	Temperate climate, worldwide	Raw, sauces, preserves, pastries, cakes, muffins

springing from its own flower on a short flowering stalk; so is a pineapple. Strawberries, which could be the poster child for all berries, are technically not fruit at all, since their plump red pulp is the swollen receptacle, and the "seeds" on the surface of the strawberry are the actual fruits.

What It Does • The fruits we call berries may be similar superficially — most are small, juicy, and fragile — but they are botanically diverse, covering more than 10 genera, and can look as different as a raspberry does from a kiwi. The berry chart lists them by name alphabetically.

How It Works • True berries are single fruits that derive from a plant's ovaries. These include all of the berries from the genus *Vaccinium*, plus grapes, currants, gooseberries, and kiwifruit. Those from the genus *Rubus*, including blackberries and raspberries, are composite fruits. In composite fruits, each flower has between 50 and 150 ovaries, and each ovary forms its own small fruit with a stony seed. The fruits are held together by the flower base and a web of small hairs that cover the fruit's surface. As they ripen, raspberries separate from the flower base, so they have a hollow center; blackberries stay attached and therefore appear solid.

Strawberries are the strangest specimens because not only are they not a true berry, they are not even fruit. The pulpy flesh of a strawberry is its flower base that has swollen with juice, forming a cushion that protects its numerous ovaries, which nestle all over the surface, appearing as seeds. In fact each "seed" is a tiny fruit that holds a miniature seed inside, similar to buckwheat or sunflower "seeds." During ripening the swollen cells of the flower base separate from one another, filling the interior of a strawberry with hundreds of small air pockets. Its structure is maintained by the pressure of cells pushing against one another. When the cells are weakened by heating, chopping, freezing, or chewing, the air is released and the fruit instantly turns mushy.

Anthocyanins, a group of red-blue pigments in many berries, are phenolic compounds, chemicals that have potent **antioxidant** activity, and give many berries their reputation for preventing DNA damage and fighting heart disease and cancer.

fast fact

- Commercially grown raspberries and strawberries are some of the most heavily sprayed food crops. USDA tests have shown high concentrations of pesticides and fungicides. Since it is difficult to wash these berries without damaging them and impossible to peel them, it is a good idea to buy organic, if you can't pick your own from a source that you know has not been sprayed.

See Also • Antioxidants, Fruit

BETA-CAROTENE • See Antioxidants

BETAINS • See Food Additives

BHA • See Food Additives

BHT • See Food Additives

BIOENGINEERING • See Genetics

BISCUITS

What It Is • "Biscuit" comes from the French, meaning "twice cooked," and originally referred to baked goods that were dry, hard, and stored well. Hardtack is an example. These rock-hard biscuits, with a near perpetual shelf life, were a nutritional mainstay when fresh food was unavailable, like on long sea voyages and during military campaigns. Italian biscotti are true to this tradition, as are the shortbreads that the British call biscuits and Americans call cookies. In France, a biscuit is a dried meringue. American biscuits, also known as tea biscuits, are baked only once, and they tend to be thick, moist, and soft, but with a thick crust that gives them the appearance of old-world biscuits.

What It Does • American biscuits are simple to throw together and bake quickly, making them popular breakfast breads. There are two styles, one wetter than the other, but both are made similarly, with flour, baking powder and/or baking soda, shortening and/or butter, and milk or buttermilk. Drop biscuits have a higher proportion of liquid, and drier kneaded biscuits have more flour and fat.

How It Works • The fine-grained cakey texture of drop biscuits results from cutting the fat into tiny pieces and mixing the dough minimally to limit **gluten** development. When making kneaded biscuits, keep the fat in larger chunks and knead the dough briefly before forming the biscuits. This yields a flaky texture and a slight pull when the biscuit is torn. The addition of buttermilk, like any acid, inhibits gluten formation, and ensures tenderness. It also whitens the flour and reacts with baking soda to leaven the biscuits.

Because there are not many ingredients in a biscuit recipe, and because the baking time is short, the flavor of the flour is important. Most biscuit recipes call for low-protein cake flours or all-purpose flour.

See Also • Baking, Chemical Leavener, Flour, Gluten

BISON • See Beef

BITTERNESS • See Flavor

BITTERS

What It Is • Complex mixtures of barks, flowers, herbs, seeds, roots, and other aromatics steeped and/or distilled in alcohol, bitters originally were prized for their medicinal value. Bitters can have an alcohol content of 45%, but they are normally consumed in small amounts, usually a few drops as a flavoring in a cocktail, so the amount of alcohol they contribute to a mixed drink is negligible.

What It Does • Currently bitters are added to drinks for flavor and color, but they still retain a curative reputation for aiding digestion, stimulating the appetite, and relieving hangover symptoms. Some of the more popular bitters are:

- *Angostura:* an extremely concentrated bitters made of herbs and spices. The exact formula is unknown, but it is known to be based on gentian and always contains angostura bark. It provides the color for pink gin.
- *Amer Picon:* a French bitters, reddish brown in color, made from gentian, bitter orange peel, and quinine.
- *Campari:* the most popular Italian bitters worldwide, made from bitter herbs, rhubarb, pomegranate, ginseng, bergamot, and orange peel.
- *Cynar:* made from artichoke leaves and herbs, popular in Italy.
- *Fernet Branca:* from Italy, reputedly made from 40 ingredients including chamomile, myrrh, saffron, and rhubarb.
- *Gammel Dansk:* a Danish bitters, a complex blend of rowanberry, angelica, star anise, ginger, laurel, gentian, cinnamon, and bitter orange.
- *Peychaud's Bitters:* a gentian-based bitters similar to Angostura, but less concentrated and sweeter.

How It Works • Although the belief in the medical benefit of bitters goes back more than 300 years, and they continue to be an important part of the folk remedy medicine cabinet, hard scientific data on their curative powers is lacking. In their medical defense

Common Ingredients of Bitters and Their Reputed Medicinal Benefits

Ingredient	Used In	Benefit
Angelica	Benedictine, Chartreuse, Dubonnet, Gammel Dansk	Anesthetic, strengthens immune system
Artichoke	Cynar	Aids digestion
Bitter orange	Amer Picon	Appetite suppressant
Cascarilla bark	Campari	Aids digestion
Gentian root	Angostura, Amaro Erbes, Gammel Dansk, Peychaud's Bitters	Aids digestion, strenthens immune system, fights infection
Quinine	Amer Picon, Vermouth	Malaria treatment
Wormwood	Absinthe, Pelinkovac	Antiseptic, relieves gastric pain

bitterness is often a characteristic of medicines, and natural toxins that have antibiotic properties are frequently bitter. So it is not without reason to think that bitters could have some general medical benefit.

The formulas for bitters are closely guarded. Most manufacturers claim that their products contain dozens of ingredients and only a handful of people know the formula, so it is impossible to say exactly what goes into bitters and what the actual benefits are (see Common Ingredients of Bitters and Their Reputed Medicinal Benefits, left).

See Also ● Flavor

BIVALVES • See Mollusks

BLACK TEA • See Tea

BLANCHING • See Boiling

BLOOD

What It Is ● The nourishing fluid that circulates through the veins and arteries of animals provides a secondary food source for many populations. The Masai of Kenya drink cattle blood for both spiritual and physical power, and many cuisines take advantage of the coagulating properties of blood **protein** to thicken sauces and to create smooth mousse-like sausages, such as blood pudding, blutwurst, and boudin noir.

What It Does ● In traditional coq au vin, a French rooster simmers in a sauce flavored with wine and herbs that is thickened with the blood of the animal near the end of cooking. Civets are game stews that are finished similarly.

How It Works ● Blood is about 80% water and about 17% protein. Some of the proteins are found in blood cells (including the red blood cells that contain hemoglobin pigment) that are suspended in plasma, and some are dissolved in plasma. Plasma makes up about two-thirds of the volume of pig and cattle blood (the most common culinary blood sources), and is about 7% protein by weight. Albumin protein in plasma provides most of the blood's thickening power, thickening at around 167°F (75°C). Since water simmers at 190°F (88°C), sauces and sausages thickened with blood must be cooked very gently in order to ensure that they thicken evenly and not coagulate into solid clumps.

See Also ● Protein, Sauces, Sausage

BLOOD CHOLESTEROL • See Cholesterol

BLUEBERRIES • See Berries

BLUE CHEESE • See Cheese

BOAR • See Pork

BOILING

What It Is ● Boil is a four-letter word. Shunned by gourmets and condemned by nutritionists, for years it has been seen as hopelessly old-fashioned, a thoughtless cooking method that ruins food.

Boiling has become a victim of its own success, synonymous with overcooking, mainly because it is so effective at transferring heat. Boiling is heating food submersed in liquid, usually water. Along with its lower-temperature versions, simmering and poaching, the liquid completely surrounds a food, so the food's entire surface is in contact with the cooking medium.

What It Does ● Water molecules are densely packed, so even at low temperatures the molecules constantly collide with food, transferring their heat to it. If you have any doubts about the effectiveness of boiling compared with dry cooking methods, like roasting, baking, or grilling, consider the following:

Case I. You are baking potatoes. The oven is roaring away at 400°F (200°C). You want to check how the spuds are doing by prodding with a finger. The test takes about five seconds, and you pull your hand away just as it begins smarting from the oven heat.

Case II. You are boiling potatoes. The water in the pot is 212°F (100°C), assuming you are at sea level, far less than the oven temperature in the previous example. You want to check how the potatoes are progressing, so you submerge your hand in the boiling water to poke one, and OUCH! (Of course you never get that far.)

Get the picture? Turbulently boiling water transfers heat more efficiently than does air, even at lower temperatures.

Besides being efficient, boiling is also versatile. Slow it to a simmer and it could coax the flavor out of a stone. Ease it down until it barely bubbles and it will melt the delicate flesh of a fish. By simmering rice or boiling noodles in broth, they become instantly infused with meaty richness. Pears simmered with cloves and sticks of cinnamon take on the perfume of their cooking liquid, just as throwing a fistful of crab boil into the pot inflames crabs with a peppery punch. A dash of vinegar added to a bath for poaching eggs helps to keep the egg white firm and intact. A speck of salt enhances the natural flavors of blanched green beans, heightening their color and boosting their sweet vegetable qualities.

Poaching, simmering, boiling and blanching are at heart one cooking method that in practice yield a variety of results. All that distinguishes one from another is that each marks a different temperature stage in the process of bringing water to a boil. The qualities of your ingredients determine which stage you use.

Poaching is appropriate for tender ingredients and is essential for cooking delicate proteins like seafood and white-meat poultry. Because temperatures are kept low, poached foods literally warm to doneness. The exterior of the ingredient does not overcook before the interior is done because the temperature of the poaching liquid is close to the temperature that the ingredient will reach at full doneness. Such slow, gentle cooking encourages an exchange of flavors between the poaching liquid and the poached ingredients. The ingredient absorbs flavor from the liquid as it sacrifices some of its juices to the cooking liquid, so that the leftover fluid from poaching becomes a flavorful broth ready to turn into a sauce.

Simmering is preferred for tough meats, because it not only dissolves the collagen and tenderizes the meat but creates a rich, flavorful broth. Bollito misto, pot au feu, and corned beef and cabbage are all famous simmered meat meals.

Cooking at a full boil is reserved for tough, fibrous vegetables, legumes, and pastas. These are foods that benefit not only from an increase in temperature but from the vigorous turbulence of a rolling boil that forces heat deep into the fibers of the food. When cooking pasta, this constant churning has added benefits. The swirling noodles are kept in motion, so none of them gets a chance to touch another for any length of time, making pasty pasta impossible.

Sometimes ingredients are boiled briefly for a specific preparation. Boiling something without cooking it through is called blanching, and it is used mostly to soften the fibers of tough vegetables like green beans or broccoli stalks before adding them to a salad, a sauté, or a casserole. Sometimes hard-to-peel produce, like tomatoes or peaches, is blanched to blister the skins, which can then be removed without damaging the flesh underneath. The term "blanch" (French for "white") comes from the common Renaissance cooking technique of

Orechiette with Potatoes, Tomatoes and Spinach

In this single dish in a single pot you will witness all forms of cooking in water — boiling, simmering, poaching, and steaming.

1 lb	orechiette	500 g
1 lb	small golden potatoes, peeled and cut into 1-inch (2.5 cm) cubes	500 g
¼ cup	extra virgin olive oil	50 mL
1	medium onion, chopped	1
Pinch	hot red pepper flakes	Pinch
3	cloves garlic, minced	3
	Salt and freshly ground pepper to taste	
12 oz	baby spinach leaves, trimmed	375 g
8 oz	ripe tomatoes, cored and finely chopped	250 g
⅓ cup	freshly grated Parmesan or Romano cheese	75 mL

1. In a large pot of boiling salted water, cook pasta and potatoes, stirring a few times to ensure pasta does not stick. Follow package directions, boiling vigorously for the time recommended or until pasta is tender.

2. Meanwhile, in a large skillet, heat olive oil over medium-high heat. Add onion and cook, stirring occasionally, until lightly browned, about 4 minutes. Add pepper flakes, garlic, salt, and pepper and stir for a few seconds. Add a large ladle of pasta water, cover the pan and simmer until the onions are tender, about 3 minutes. Check periodically to make sure the liquid doesn't completely evaporate. If it starts to look dry, add a little more pasta water.

3. Remove pasta pot from heat and add spinach, stirring, until it wilts, about 1 minute.

4. Remove a few ladles of pasta water and reserve. Drain pasta and toss with onion mixture, tomatoes and cheese in a serving bowl. Add a little of the reserved pasta water if the pasta looks dry.

Pasta tips

- Pasta is boiled vigorously to gelatinize its starch and activate the gluten for a perfect al dente bite. The vigorous movement keeps the pasta jumping, making it less likely that the pieces will get a chance to stick to one another.
- If cut to the same size, potatoes and pasta cook at similar rates. Because the exterior of the potato pieces cook more than the interior they will slough some of their starch into the pasta water, which gives the finished sauce a creamy finish.
- While pasta cooks, sauté onions in a separate pan to bring out their sweetness, then add a ladleful of the pasta water and simmer until they're tender.
- Leafy greens, such as spinach, wilt quickly. A brief poaching in the pasta water during the last seconds of cooking is all they need.

MAKES 4 TO 6 SERVINGS

briefly boiling almonds to remove the bran, thus turning the nuts from dark brown to white, so that they could be ground and used to thicken a pale sauce without discoloring it.

How It Works • As a pot of water heats, the water molecules near the bottom of the pot warm up first. As they get hotter, they move faster and farther apart from each other, creating a lower density. The cooler molecules up above are closer together and more dense and so they fall to the bottom of the pot, where they in turn are heated and begin to rise, setting up convection currents. Eventually the water at the bottom reaches the boiling point (212°F/100°C) and is hot enough to vaporize into steam.

Because the hotter water at the bottom is less dense than the cooler water at the surface, it rises, causing the surface of the water to swirl. This slight movement on the surface of the water is the visual sign that the water is ready for poaching, between 170°F (77°C) and 180°F (82°C).

When bubbles at the edge of the pot begin to break through the surface it is referred to as a simmer, 180 to 190°F (82 to 88°C). When bubbles undulate across the entire surface of the water, it is said to be at a gentle boil, and at 212°F (100°C), when the surface of the water breaks turbulently, cascading with large, vigorous bubbles, it is called a rolling boil.

All of these temperature points depend on the atmospheric pressure weighting down the surface of the water: the greater the pressure, the more heat is required to reach a boil. Every 1,000 feet (305 m) of elevation above sea level lowers the boiling point by about 2°F (1°C). Since food takes longer to cook at lower temperatures, boiling at high elevations can alter the timing or the success of a recipe. Likewise, a pressure cooker speeds up boiling by artificially increasing the atmospheric pressure inside the pot, thereby raising the temperature of boiling water. Most pressure cookers operate at 15 pounds per square inch pressure (psi), yielding a temperature of 250°F (120°C).

See Also • Atmospheric Pressure, Heat

BONES

What It Is • A matrix of protein and connective tissue (collagen) embedded with minerals, bones are a cook's main source of the natural **gelatin** that delivers the elixir-like mouth feel to meat consommés and demi-glace. Bones also add flavor to broths and roasted meat in the form of protein and through bone marrow, a rich mixture of protein and monounsaturated fats that is the main factory in the body for the fabrication of red and white blood cells.

What It Does • Leg bones, roasted for their marrow, are usually served with toast and an elongated spoon for scooping the marrow from the bone's central cavity. Marrow has long been considered highly nutritious because of its concentration of protein and calories, but it is also packed with dietary cholesterol, and nowadays is considered an occasional treat rather than health food.

Moisture is the key for dissolving flavorful proteins and gelatin in bones. When preparing stocks, bones and meat are placed in cold water and gently heated, which gradually extracts flavorful protein and gelatinous collagen into the surrounding liquid. Bones from younger animals are bland, but they are permeated with collagen, which is why veal bones are preferred to tastier beef bones for stock making. If you must use beef bones from older animals get as many limb bones capped with cartilage as you can. Cartilage, which is a deposit of connective tissue that cushions the joint to help it move more smoothly, is a good source of gelatin. Meat is better at delivering flavor than bone, so the best stocks are made from a combination of young animal bones and meat; cheap stocks use less meat and the bones from older animals in an attempt to fill in the flavor gap.

fast fact

- Knowing where your meat comes from is especially important in the case of bone marrow. Spinal marrow, which is the source of mad cow disease, is found in T-bones, ribs, the neck, and tail. Bone marrow from leg bones is safe because it has no contact with brain tissue.

How It Works • Meat roasted on the bone is moister and more flavorful than boneless roasts. Moisture from the meat portion of the roast helps to dissolve the collagen and protein in the bone, lubricating the meat surrounding it. This effect is most pronounced with fish, which have a skeleton of such delicacy that the bones start to dissolve at around 165°F (74°C). Hence the superior flavor of fish roasted whole rather than in fillets, and the higher calcium content of bone-in canned salmon over fresh.

The minerals in bone make it a better heat conductor than the meat surrounding it, but the honeycomb of air permeating most bone tissue slows down the heat transfer, with a net result that bones act more as insulators than heat conductors. This could explain the expression "tender at the bone," since meat touching bone tends to cook through more slowly than the meat farther away from the bone.

See Also • Gelatin, Meat, Soup

BORAGE • See Leaves

BOTULISM • See Bacteria

BOUILLON • See Soup

BOURBON • See Liquor

BOVINE SPONGIFORM ENCEPHALOPATHY • See Mad Cow Disease

BRAINS • See Organ Meats

BRAISING

What It Is • Dry cooking methods like grilling, roasting, and frying are great at **browning**. Wet cooking methods like **boiling** and steaming excel at softening tough fibers. Braising, the primary method for cooking tough, flavorful ingredients, reaps the best from both worlds: ingredients are first browned with dry heat and then liquid is added and the ingredients are simmered to tenderness.

One of the great benefits of braising is that it improves tough budget cuts of meats and gnarly fibrous vegetables. These cheaper foods are loaded with flavor but usually need long cooking to overcome their toughness. The moist heat of braising accomplishes this effortlessly.

What It Does • The first step in braising is usually browning ingredients in a little hot oil, but the browning step can be accomplished in other ways — on a grill, under a broiler, or in a super-hot oven. After the food is browned, enough liquid is added to come at least halfway up its height, and the food is simmered in a covered pot until tender. The liquid can be anything from water to demi-glace, and the amount depends on how long the food will simmer. The objective is to end up with a sauce that is barely thickened at the same moment that the braised ingredient reaches full tenderness.

Sometimes ingredients are dusted or dredged with flour before browning. The flour absorbs surface moisture, which could interfere with browning, and adds starch that helps to thicken the finished sauce. The coating of flour need be no more than a light dusting. In fact, if it is too heavy, the skin of flour will brown rather than the ingredient, and when liquid is added, this browned skin will peel off, leaving behind unattractive naked steamed bits.

You can braise over a low burner or in an oven. Stovetop braising is faster, but the ingredient will need to be turned occasionally, because the heat is only coming from one direction. Braising in an oven takes about 20% longer, but the ingredient cooks evenly with no manipulation.

Though any pot can be used for braising, a deep skillet, Dutch oven, or braiser is best. Because of the two-step process, you need a pot with a wide enough bottom to brown ingredients without crowding, with deep enough sides to hold the necessary liquid, and with a tight-fitting lid to trap in steam so that the exposed parts of the ingredients cook at a similar rate as the submerged parts.

How It Works • Though meat is not always floured for braising, it usually is when the braised dish is a stew. Most stews are nothing more than braised dishes in which the meat is cut into bite-size pieces before it is browned and then cooked in enough liquid to cover it.

Stew meats pose a particular challenge to the browning process. Because the meat is in many smaller pieces, there are far more surfaces that need browning and through which liquid is apt to seep. When meat browns, it always secretes some moisture, even if it has been floured. If the amount isn't great, the droplets of meat juices falling into the hot fat vaporize and dissipate into the air. However, if the pan is crowded and the chunks of meat touch, those droplets will get trapped between the pieces, where they will continue to steam and will prevent the meat from browning. Anyone who has ever tried to speed up searing meat by forcing an extra-large batch into the skillet knows this phenomenon firsthand.

But successful browning isn't enough, for

braising cannot be completed without a period of simmering. While browning produces flavor, only simmering can get fork-tender results. Braised meats reach optimal tenderness at simmering temperatures about 190°F (88°C), where they can cook for hours without toughening, and gradually the tough collagen proteins dissolve into complete tenderness.

By definition, braised meats are always cooked through. There is no such thing as rare stew or medium-rare pot roast. When braising, the only test for doneness is tenderness. So don't bother with a meat thermometer or charts that dictate minutes per pound (kilogram). Your stew or braised meal is ready when you can stick a fork into the meat easily. The exact amount of time needed depends on how much the meat was browned, the level of simmering, and whether the pot was placed over a burner or in the oven. That's why most recipes give a range of cooking times, qualified by the general phrase "until fork-tender."

See Also • Meat, Sauces

BRAN • See Grains

BRANDY • See Liquor

BRASSICA • See Cruciferous Vegetables

BRAZIL NUTS • See Nuts

BREAD

What It Is • Bread is basic. Most likely it was the original baked good, for at heart bread is nothing more than flour and water. Salt goes in for flavor, and if you let the dough lie around before baking, airborne yeasts will take advantage of its nutrients and leave behind a respiration product of carbon dioxide that will make the dough rise. Though modern techniques have streamlined the process, so that a commercial loaf can be ready for baking in about four minutes, the results are bland and puffy, with none of the tang and pull of the real thing. Those who are serious about bread ignore the innovations and make their daily bread the way it's been done since someone pulled the first swollen loaf from a fire, brushed off the ashes, took a bite, and deemed it good.

What It Does • There are four basic steps to making bread:
1. Mix flour, water, salt, and yeast
2. Knead the mixture to develop a network of gluten
3. Give the yeast time to fill the dough with gas
4. Bake to set the structure and flavor

Within this simple process, there are more than a baker's dozen of possible variations. In each step there are several options that will change the finished product. Will the bread be soft or chewy, hearty with whole grain or smooth and pale? Will it be sweet or tangy, crisp or crumbly, flat or bulbous? The following investigates each step and shows how different elements create different breads.

How It Works •
Step 1 - Mixing
Flour influences the texture, flavor, and nutrition of bread. High-**protein** bread flour, milled from high-protein **wheat**, takes time and lots of kneading to produce **gluten** and high-rising loaves with a distinctive flavor and a chewy consistency. Lower protein all-purpose flour produces a dough that is easier to knead but never rises as much; it yields blander, softer loaves. Low-protein soft wheat flour results in a tender cake-like crumb with far fewer air bubbles. Whole-grain flour has stronger flavor and better nutrition, but the germ and bran in these flours decrease the quality of the gluten and can make a loaf leaden. For that reason, even when bread is labeled "whole grain" the bulk of the flour may still be white bread flour.

The chemical composition of the **water** and the amount of water used can have a marked influence on the texture of bread. Acidic water tends to weaken gluten. Alkaline water makes it stronger. And hard, or mineral-rich, water produces a firmer dough because of the strong chemical bonds between gluten proteins and calcium and magnesium. The standard ratio of water to all-purpose flour in bread is 65 to 100. Decreasing the water makes bread firmer and denser; increasing water makes it softer and more aerated. Water composition also influences yeast fermentation.

Salt does more than just flavor bread. It tightens the gluten and improves the volume of the baked loaf. Sea salts, which have more calcium and magnesium, can strengthen the gluten further. In sourdough breads, salt limits the gluten-damaging effects of the acid-producing bacteria, giving the finished loaf better structure. Salt can kill yeast, so it is usually added to a dough after the yeast has had a chance to reproduce enough so that the loss of some yeast will not inhibit the rising.

To rise a standard dough in a few hours you will need about 5 grams of dry yeast, or 10 grams of cake yeast, per 500 grams of flour. Lengthening the rising time allows you to use less yeast. If a dough is left to rise overnight, the amount can be reduced to barely 0.5 grams (an amount that still contains millions of yeast cells). In general the less yeast used and the longer the dough takes to rise, the better the flavor of the finished bread will be. This is partly due to the naturally strong flavors of yeast, but also because delicious flavors develop as dough ferments (see Fermentation, page 66).

Using a starter such as sourdough, which pre-ferments yeast in a small amount of dough or using the sponge method of dough preparation, ensures a long, slow rise and the best flavor.

As soon as flour gets wet its **starch** and protein begin to absorb water, activating enzymes. Enzymes start converting starch molecules from the flour, turning them into sugar. Yeasts feed on the sugar, producing carbon dioxide and alcohol. Protein in the flour absorbs some water and sprawls out into springy strings that bond with their neighboring proteins, and gluten starts to form during kneading.

Step 2 - Kneading

Kneading stretches, folds, and compresses gluten strands. As more connections form among the proteins, the dough takes on a smoother texture and a springy, satiny feel. In addition, during kneading air gets trapped in the dough. The more you knead, the more that air is dispersed. For an even finished texture you want a fine network of tiny air bubbles. In some breads, particularly flatbreads, coarser dough with bigger air bubbles is desirable. These doughs are typically kneaded less. Even though it is possible to over-knead, it is only likely to occur when kneading with a machine; you would get too tired kneading by hand before that happens.

Perfectly Plain Bagels

To insure the chewiest possible texture bagels are made from high-gluten hard spring wheat flour. If you can't find high-gluten flour you can substitute bread flour bulked up with vital wheat gluten, about 1 tablespoon (15 mL) gluten for every cup (250 mL) of bread flour.

2½ cups	hot water, about 110°F (43°C)	625 mL
¼ cup	granulated sugar	50 mL
1 tbsp	dry yeast	15 mL
2 tsp	salt	10 mL
5½ to 6 cups	high-gluten flour	1.375 to 1.5 L
	Vegetable oil	
¼ cup	malt syrup	50 mL
	Yellow cornmeal	
1	egg white mixed with 3 tbsp (45 mL) ice water (optional)	1
¼ cup	sesame seeds or poppy seeds (optional)	50 mL

1. In a large bowl, stir together water and sugar until dissolved. Stir in yeast and set aside until the mixture is foamy, about 10 minutes.

2. Stir in salt and about 3 cups (750 mL) flour to form a stiff dough. Turn out onto a floured board and knead, adding flour, about ½ cup (125 mL) at a time until you have a smooth, highly elastic, very stiff dough. It will be denser than most bread doughs, but it should not be dry.

3. Place the dough in a lightly oiled bowl and turn to coat with oil. Cover with a clean damp kitchen towel. Let rise in a warm, draft-free place until doubled in bulk, about 2 hours. Meanwhile, fill a large pot with water (about 1 gallon/4 L), and bring to a gentle boil. Stir in the malt syrup. Reduce heat to maintain the water at a simmer.

4. Preheat oven to 400°F (200°C). Turn the dough out onto a clean surface and cut into 12 pieces. Roll each piece into a rough ball. Poke a hole through the center of each ball with a finger and work your finger around the hole stretching the dough into a ring. Set aside to rise for about 15 minutes. Drop the bagels into the simmering water, 2 or 3 at a time (don't crowd the pot). After the bagels rise to the surface, simmer for about 3 minutes. Turn them over with a slotted spoon and simmer 3 minutes more. Transfer to a kitchen towel spread out on the counter.

5. Once all the bagels have been boiled sprinkle a large baking sheet with a light dusting of cornmeal. Place the bagels on the pan with as much space between them as possible. Brush the bagels with egg wash and sprinkle with seeds, if desired. Bake until well browned, about 30 minutes. Let cool on a wire rack or on a dry clean towel. Do not attempt to cut them until they are cool (hot bagels slice abominably and you'll end up with a wadded mass of bagel pulp. Don't do it).

MAKES 1 DOZEN BAGELS

Step 3 - Fermentation

As dough ferments, its yeast continues to produce carbon dioxide, which filters into the air pockets formed by kneading, causing them to inflate and raise the dough. The gentle stretching continues to develop the gluten, so even barely kneaded dough will become stretchier and more cohesive during **fermentation**. Yeasts reach their greatest activity at around 95°F (35°C), so at that temperature a dough will rise rapidly, but a fast-rising dough can also develop unpleasant yeasty aromas and an abundance of unwanted by-products of yeast metabolism, like alcohol. Lowering the temperature, by letting the dough rise in a cool room or in the fridge, extends the rise, diminishes off flavors, and encourages more desirable flavors. The longer a dough ferments the more time there is for yeasts and bacteria in the dough to generate flavor compounds. This is most evident in whole wheat breads, in which a slow rising increases the nutty and honey-like flavors in the grain.

At the end of fermentation the dough should have doubled in size and be pliant enough to keep the imprint of a finger when gently poked. Knead the dough a few more times to release built-up carbon dioxide, disperse the air bubbles, and redistribute the yeast and moisture. High-gluten doughs may go through a second fermentation, because it may take longer to develop their tougher gluten.

At this point the dough is formed into a loaf and given a partial rise, or proof, to prepare it for baking. Professional bakers often retard this last rise by refrigerating the dough overnight so that they can bake the bread fresh every morning. A refrigerated rise has the added benefit of generating more good fermentation flavors, and since the bread rests for a longer period, gases from the yeast distribute more evenly through the loaf.

Step 4 - Baking

The oven in which bread bakes adds another dimension. Traditionally breads were baked in stone or brick hearth ovens that were preheated by building a wood fire on the floor of the oven and stoking it until the oven floor and walls radiated heat. When the bread was ready to be baked, the fire was scraped out and the bread was laid directly on the floor of the oven, which was 700 to 900°F (371 to 482°C). The bread rose rapidly and released steam into the confined space, which increased the heat transfer and moistened the surface of the dough, keeping it pliant and giving the bread more time to rise before the crust set. Gradually the heat of the oven subsided, allowing the bread to finish baking gently. This dynamic baking situation — an initial blast of high heat, a dramatic rise (called oven spring), and a gradual finish — became the hallmark of classic bread baking.

Home ovens cannot accomplish the same thing. Serious bakers modify them by placing baking stones on the floor or lowest rack of the oven, and by adding a pan of water to generate steam, but nothing exactly replicates hearth baking. Professional ovens lined with stone and equipped with steam jets do a good job. For home use the best solution is to bake bread in a covered iron Dutch oven that has been preheated at a high temperature for at least an hour. The confines of the closed pot trap steam from the bread and mimic the closed space of a hearth. Likewise, the heat-retention properties of iron are similar to those of stone, giving a quick blast of heat for a dynamic rise and an incredible crust.

As soon as the dough heats up, gases trapped in the loaf expand and the loaf rises. This dramatic oven spring is caused by alcohol and water in the dough vaporizing, filling the gas cells and expanding the dough by as much as 50%. Oven spring is over within the first eight minutes of baking.

Oven spring subsides when the crust hardens enough to resist it and when the interior of the loaf gets hot enough to start coagulating the gluten and gelatinizing the starch, between 155 and 180°F (68 and 82°C). Now the gas cells can no longer stretch to accommodate the expansion of the vapors inside them, and the increasing pressure eventually ruptures the walls of the cells, changing the interior of the bread from a network of separate gas cells into an open arrangement of interconnecting pores resembling the holes in a sponge.

The late stages of baking brown and crisp the crust. Although browning is most dramatic on the surface of a bread, the changes in the crust affect the flavor of the whole loaf as toasted caramelized aromas diffuse toward the center. A light underbaked bread has less flavor throughout than a dark crusty loaf.

Bread is done baking when the crust is brown and crisp and the loaf sounds hollow when rapped on the bottom. The hollow sound is an indication that the open network of air developed throughout the loaf has set.

When a loaf emerges from an oven its crust is dry (about 15% water) and very hot, about 400°F (200°C), but the interior of the bread will be at least 40% water and only 200°F (93°C). At this point it is very difficult to slice. During cooling these differences even out: moisture migrates from the interior into the crust, causing its crispness to diminish. As the bread cools the air pressure in the bubbles decreases and the air pockets shrink, the bread compacts, and it becomes easier to slice.

Types of Bread

Bagels: Made from stiff dough and high-protein flour, bagels are first boiled for a chewy texture and a crisp, blistered crust. Boiling causes the starch on the surface to swell into a thick crust that browns richly during baking. A hole in the center helps the bagel cook evenly, by allowing water to circulate freely through the ring. After boiling, the puffed and lightly scabbed bagels are air dried, brushed with a coating of egg or starch, and baked in a hot oven. The addition of barley **malt** to the dough adds enzymes that break down carbohydrates into simpler sugars and proteins into amino acids, increasing surface browning during baking.

Cake-like breads: Tender and sweet, some breads, for instance, brioche, challah, panettone, and pandoro, are hybrids of cake and bread. Like cakes, they have the gluten-tenderizing additions of egg and fat, and enough sugar to register as sweet on the palate, and like bread they are raised with yeast and are kneaded to give them a subtle chewiness. Because large amounts of sugar slow the growth of yeast, recipes for sweet breads usually call for more yeast than do those for regular breads. And because sugar increases browning reactions, these breads are baked at lower temperatures to prevent burning.

Flatbreads: Flatbreads cook quickly on a hot, flat surface such as a griddle, the floor or wall of an oven, or a stone. They comprise a wide range of bread styles, from pizza to puri, and can be leavened or unleavened. Because flatbreads are thin they do not need a lot of gluten to maintain their structure, so they can be made from a variety of grains and require less kneading. Many flatbreads are baked in direct contact with a hot surface, causing them to rise quickly, often forming bubbles or air pockets in their centers that puff impressively during baking. Puffing happens when the bottom and top crusts of the flatbread set up before the moist dough in the center. Steam inside builds up and tears the soft interior, forcing the two surfaces apart. Flatbreads will stay puffed as long as the steam remains volatile, but they collapse as they cool. The resulting pocket is often stuffed for sandwiches.

Flatbreads are the earliest breads, and they are still the most common style of bread throughout the world. The international flatbread family includes:

- *Baobing and shaobing:* thin, floppy unleavened Chinese flatbreads used as wrappers
- *Carasau (aka pani carasau or music-paper bread):* Sardinian unleavened cracker bread, made with durum semolina
- *Chapati:* soft whole-grain unleavened skillet bread from India; a puffed chapati is a phulka
- *Crumpet (aka English muffins):* griddle-cooked yeasted muffins cooked in rings for standardization
- *Focaccia:* soft, thick leavened flatbread from Italy that is often coated with seasoning
- *Injera:* bubbly sourdough flatbread from Ethiopia, often made from teff flour
- *Lavash:* paper-thin unleavened Armenian flatbread used as a wrapper; can be soft or crisp
- *Matzoh (also matzo, matzah):* an unleavened sacramental cracker-like flatbread produced for the Jewish holiday of Passover. Matzoh must enter the oven no more than 18 minutes after the flour is mixed with water to ensure that no yeast has had a chance to grow in the dough.
- *Naan:* rich leavened flatbread from India, baked on the walls of a ceramic tandoor oven
- *Pita or khubz:* leavened pocketed flatbread that is a Middle Eastern mainstay
- *Pizza:* thin leavened flatbread usually topped with sauce, cheese, and other toppings
- *Pretzel:* yeasted dense dough ropes, often knotted, and glazed with an alkaline solution for a dark brown, crisp, tangy surface; can be soft or crisp
- *Puri:* deep-fried puffed unleavened bread from India; usually bite-size
- *Scandinavian flatbrød:* unleavened, usually crisp, and often made from rye, oats, and/or barley
- *Tortilla:* unleavened skillet flatbreads from Mexico made from wheat or corn

Gluten-free breads: For people who cannot tolerate wheat gluten there are gluten-free breads made with alternative flours, like rice or soy. They usually include a polysaccharide, often xanthan gum, which has a gluten-imitating elasticity.

Layered breads: Layering yeasted dough with butter produces slightly chewy buttery-rich flaky baked goods that are a combination of risen bread and puff pastry. Croissants are made with lightly kneaded white bread dough that is rolled into a sheet and folded with a layer of softened butter

a soft, moist texture that delays staling. Most rye breads will get moldy before they go stale. Classic pumpernickel, which is made with a starter and all rye flour, gets its dark color by being baked long and slow. Over the 16 to 24 hours that pumpernickel bakes, its proteins and sugars turn dark chocolate brown. Modern commercial pumpernickel, which is made mostly from wheat flour, has caramel color added.

Sourdough breads: Sourdough bread begins like yeast-starter bread (see below), but in sourdough the formation of acids in the sponge is encouraged. Although the acid, mostly lactic acid, gives sourdough its distinctive flavor, the trick to working with a sourdough starter is to keep the acid level under control. Bacteria grow faster than yeasts, and their acidic by-products inhibit the yeasts' gas production and weaken gluten. Because browning reactions are slower in acidic conditions, sourdough breads tend to be paler than other breads.

Yeast-starter breads: The most common method for making risen breads, including classic breads like French baguette and Italian ciabatta, begins with a mixture of flour and water called a sponge. Wild yeasts and bacteria that happen to be in the flour and the air, or yeast that is added to the mixture, are encouraged to grow in the sponge, producing carbon dioxide and alcohol from the yeast, and acids from the bacteria. When foamy the starter is bulked up with more flour and water and formed into dough. Usually some starter is retained, periodically refreshed with more flour and water, and kept to raise another dough.

See Also ● Biscuits, Fermentation, Flour, Gluten, Grains, Oven, Starch, Wheat

BREAD CRUMBS • See Bread

BREADFRUIT • See Fruit

mixed with flour. Like puff pastry the dough and butter are rolled and folded multiple times, so care must be taken to keep the dough from developing gluten (which would make it tough) and to keep the butter from melting (which would limit its rise). Indian paratha is made similarly, except ghee is used in place of butter, and the bread is griddle cooked rather than baked.

Quick breads: Biscuits, muffins, scones, and some savory cakes are raised with **chemical leaveners**. They are called quick breads because they do not require rising time.

Rye breads: Rye has a low concentration of gluten-forming proteins and so doesn't form an elastic network the way wheat flour does. Rye breads are usually wheat breads with a small proportion of rye flour added for flavor. What rye does have is a good proportion of arabinoxylan carbohydrates, a group of large aggregate sugars that have the ability to hold up to eight times their weight in water (wheat can hold only two times). They give rye bread

BREADING

What It Is • Kentucky Fried Chicken would be nothing special without its breading. Like other breadings, the Colonel's secret recipe lends the chicken its signature flavor and, more importantly, its crunchy surface texture. The primary role of breading is to help create a tasty crust. Breadings range from plain flour to more complex combinations of eggs, seasoned cornmeal, seasoned bread crumbs, crushed crackers, crushed potato chips, or virtually any other ground or crushed **starch**. Batters are also used to coat foods before cooking, but because batters are just thinned doughs they tend to produce a cake-like coating rather than the crunchy crust that is the mark of a good breading.

What It Does • Breading absorbs moisture from the surface of the food (which cuts down on splattering during **frying**) and forms a barrier between the food and the heat. During cooking, the breading dries out instead of the food itself. It's a win-win situation because the breading becomes deliciously crisp on the surface while helping to keep the food inside nice and moist. If the food is fried at the correct temperature, the protective layer of breading also helps to keep the interior of the food from becoming too greasy.

How It Works • Breaded foods, such as meat, are either dusted to help them brown or coated heavily to create a crust. Either way, the first step is the same: the food is coated in something powdery, such as flour or cornstarch, to absorb surface moisture. When simply flouring meats this is important because any water present on the meat's surface will keep the surface from browning. When a crust is desired, dusting prevents droplets of water from becoming trapped under the breading, where they could turn to steam during cooking and cause the breading to blister off. Only a fine dusting of flour is needed, which is why recipes often instruct you to shake off any excess flour before starting to cook.

For thicker breading the food is coated two more times, first in protein, most often beaten egg, or a fermented milk product like buttermilk or yogurt, and then in a finishing coat of something dry and crisp, such as bread crumbs, cracker crumbs, or crushed cereal. The protein acts as a kind of glue, helping the finishing coat to adhere to the food. When heated, the protein coagulates, causing the breading to seal around the food, trapping its moisture inside, and creating a closed steaming environment that helps to speed up the cooking time. Again, a thin film is all you need. Too much protein and the "glue" layer will be too thick to dry quickly, which can cause the crust to fall off during cooking. For the same reason, a breaded ingredient should rest on a rack for 10 to 20 minutes to help the protein dry before cooking. Just as when drying glue, this resting time will help the breading to stick to the food, guaranteeing that it will stay in place during high-heat cooking.

See Also • Bread, Fermentation, Flour, Frying, Steaming

BREEDING • See Genetics

BRINING

What It Is • A mixture of salt, sugar, water, and other flavors, a brine adds moisture and flavor to meats. Soaking meat in a 5% salt brine for as little as a few hours before cooking can make meats noticeably juicier and preserve tenderness.

What It Does • The best candidates for brining are those meats that are naturally low in fat and/or moisture, and those meats that tend to dry out during cooking. Lean cuts of pork, chicken, and turkey benefit greatly from brining, but so do some fattier cuts. Spareribs, for instance, which have a good amount of fat but tend to toughen when heated, are perceptibly tenderized and made moister through brining.

Since brining works from the outside in, the meat fibers closest to the surface are the ones that reap most of the benefits, and since these are the parts that tend to dry out most during cooking, even a short period of soaking can produce noticeable benefits.

Incomplete brining will give you less than optimum moisture retention, but over-brining can impregnate an ingredient with salt to disastrous effect, especially when the muscle tissue is delicate, like that of fish.

Cider-Brined Ribs Glazed with Cider Syrup

Pork ribs can come from the loin or the belly. The loin runs along the spine, and therefore loin ribs are called "baby back." Belly ribs (side ribs) are from the front of the rib cage. They are larger, less meaty, less expensive, and tastier than back ribs. Their biggest problem is that they tend to dry out unless you boil or steam them first. That is unless you brine them.

1 quart	apple cider, divided	1 L
2 tbsp	kosher salt, divided	25 mL
1½ tbsp	dark brown sugar	22 mL
1¼ tsp	ground allspice, divided	6 mL
½ tsp	freshly ground black pepper	2 mL
¼ tsp	cayenne pepper	1 mL
2	racks pork ribs (about 4 lbs/2 kg), St. Louis-cut spare ribs or baby back ribs	2
	Vegetable oil	
1 tbsp	honey	15 mL
1 tsp	hot pepper sauce	5 mL

1. In a resealable plastic bag, combine 2½ cups (625 mL) apple cider, 1½ tbsp (22 mL) kosher salt, brown sugar, 1 tsp (5 mL) allspice, black pepper, and cayenne pepper, mixing and massaging until salt and sugar dissolve. Cut rib racks in half and place in bag. Seal bag, leaving about 1 inch (2.5 cm) open. Push on the bag to release any trapped air through the opening, and close the bag completely. Massage the liquid gently into the meat and refrigerate for 6 to 12 hours.

2. Preheat grill for indirect heat. If using charcoal, set up a split bed of charcoal, burning the coals until it is covered with a thin film of ash. If using a gas grill with three or four burners turn the middle burner(s) off and set the outside burners to medium; if your grill has two burners, leave one side off.

3. Clean the grill grate with a wire brush and coat the grate with oil. Place ribs on the grill away from the heat, cover the grill and cook until an instant-read thermometer inserted into the thickest part of the ribs registers about 155°F (68°C), about 1 hour. If your grill has a temperature gauge it should stay between 325 and 350°F (160 and 180°C).

4. Meanwhile, in a skillet over medium-high heat, boil remaining 1½ cups (375 mL) cider until lightly thickened and reduced to ⅓ cup (75 mL). Skim off any foam that rises to the surface periodically, and reduce the temperature near the end of cooking to keep the syrup from burning. Stir in remaining salt, allspice, honey, and hot pepper sauce.

5. When the ribs are cooked through, coat the meaty side with glaze, and cook, turning halfway through, for 6 minutes more. Transfer the ribs to cutting board and cut into 1- or 2-rib sections.

MAKES 4 SERVINGS

Brining Timing

Ingredient	Brining Time
Small seafood and thin fish (less than 1 inch/2.5 cm)	about 30 minutes
Thick fish (more than 1 inch/2.5 cm) and boneless poultry	about 1 hour
Bone-in poultry pieces, chops and steaks	2 to 3 hours
Roasts (less than 3 lbs/1.4 kg) and ribs	3 to 6 hours
Large roasts or whole birds (up to 6 lbs/2.7 kg)	4 to 8 hours
Whole large birds, such as turkeys	8 hours to overnight

Optimal brining time depends on a number of factors, including the density of the ingredient, its size, its shape, and the strength of the brine. Use the above chart as a general guideline.

How It Works • Brine works in two ways. Salt dissolves the protein in contracting muscle filaments, making them looser and therefore more tender. It also increases the capacity of muscle cells to bond with water, causing them to absorb water from the brine, increasing their weight by as much as 10%. As the water infuses into the meat, any flavor components from herbs, spices, or flavorful liquids are also absorbed, making brines an effective way to season meats beneath the surface. When meat cooks it naturally loses moisture, about 20%, but by bulking up the moisture in meat through brining, you can effectively cut the net loss of juices by half.

The biggest disadvantage in using brine is that the drippings from the meat will tend to be too salty to use as a base for a sauce. This is only a problem when you are roasting a turkey or other large poultry, for which you might want to prepare gravy.

See Also • Pork, Poultry

BROCCOLI • See Cruciferous Vegetables

BROILING • See Grilling

BROMELAIN • See Enzyme

BROTH • See Soup

BROWNING

What It Is • Brown means more than just color in cooking. Brown means oven-rich flavors and a savory crust surrounding a succulent filling. Brown means the aroma of roasts and toasted grain. It means a steak seared over a live fire and the beefy essence of stew. Without browning, poultry is flabby, pot roast is pallid, and gravy is as gaunt as wallpaper paste. But with it, all our great carnivorous urges are met in a single sensation. Enzymatic browning that happens when you peel an apple, avocado, or eggplant is a completely different reaction involving oxidation, not heat.

What It Does • For food to brown, two criteria must be met: the cooking temperature has to exceed 250°F (120°C) and water content must be not too high or too low. Really, these are two ways of saying the same thing. Because water boils at 212°F (100°C)

fast fact

- **Browning Warning.** Not all browning reactions are beneficial. The cooked flavor and darker color of evaporated and sweetened condensed milk and the brownish color of dried egg are the result of Maillard browning. More serious, acrylamide, a known carcinogen, develops during the Maillard reaction between sugars and the amino acid L-asparagine, and has been shown to cause damage to DNA in rats. The health significance of this in humans is still unclear, but considering that so many food preparations involve browning, and since some browning reactions produce antioxidants that protect against DNA damage, the threat to health seems less than major. Erring on the side of safety, though, it is probably prudent to be conservative in your consumption of heavily browned foods.

and can get no hotter without changing into steam, it is impossible for food to reach high enough temperatures to brown if it is just boiling. Unlike water, oils and other fats can achieve temperatures far hotter than 250°F (120°C) before they vaporize, which is why even a thin film of oil browns effectively. That's why browning only occurs in an oven, under a broiler, over a grill, or in hot oil.

When foods are heated, in an oven or on the grill, the surface gets hot and water evaporates from the surface to create the right concentrations of food components and water for the browning reactions to occur. The higher the temperature and the longer the heat exposure the more browning that takes place.

As food browns, its fibers start to tighten. Like a moist sponge that's being squeezed, any moisture held within is forced to the surface and out into the pan, where it turns into steam. If ingredients are first dusted with flour or a spice rub, any moisture leaching from the fibers during cooking is absorbed at the food's surface and cannot interfere with the browning process.

How It Works • Nonenzymatic browning reactions occur in two distinct ways depending on what is being browned. Caramelization of sugar is the simpler of the two. When sugar (sucrose) is heated it first melts into a thick fluid and then gradually browns, starting at 365°F (185°C), from pale yellow to deep brown. The passage through its various color stages corresponds to changes in taste, texture, and aroma. The chemical reactions involved in this transformation are many and varied, and result in the development of hundreds of reaction products, including organic acids, residual sugar, bitter phenols, fruity esters, and many fragrant volatile molecules and brown-colored polymers. Commercially, sucrose, corn syrup, and other sugars are heated with specific acids, alkalis, or salts to create various caramel colors that are added to colas, syrups, gravies, dark beers, whiskeys, and many other foods.

Meats, breads, cocoa, coffee beans, butter, and other foods that are not primarily sugar brown through a different set of processes called Maillard reactions, named after Louis Camille Maillard, who discovered them in 1910. The process begins with the reaction between a sugar molecule (either from glucose in meat or starch in flour) and an amino acid (free or part of a **protein** chain). At 250°F (120°C) or higher an unstable structure forms which then breaks down through a series of reactions into hundreds of by-products. Maillard flavors are more complex and diverse than caramelized flavors because the involvement of the amino acids adds more reactants to the mix. Molecules from fat oxidation and other compounds are also involved, creating the complex flavors of roasted foods. Maillard flavors include savory peptides, sulfur compounds, green vegetable flavors, cooked potato flavor, fried flavors, toasted flavors, chocolate flavors, and earthy components in addition to the typical caramelized flavors. An egg wash on the surface of bread during baking adds both the sugar and protein ingredients for a richly brown crust. Many Maillard reaction products are good antioxidants too.

See Also • Oxygen, Sugar

BRUSSELS SPROUTS • See Cruciferous Vegetables

BTU • See Heat

BUCKWHEAT • See Grains

BUFFALO • See Beef

BULGUR • See Wheat

BURDOCK • See Roots, Thistles

BUTTER

What It Is • Slosh some cream around for a few minutes, and inevitably the fat will separate from the milk and you will get butter. Butter has been popular since the earliest days of dairying, probably because it keeps longer than fresh milk or cream and can be made from the milk of any lactating

Home-Churned Sweet Butter

It is easier to make butter from pasteurized than it is from ultrapasteurized cream. Ultrapasteurized products are homogenized, which makes it harder to separate the fat from the buttermilk. Unfortunately most of the heavy whipping cream sold commercially is ultrapasteurized. You will probably have to go to a farmers' market or a high-end grocery store to find pasteurized cream.

2 cups	pasteurized heavy (35%) whipping cream, preferably not ultrapasteurized (see Variation, right)	500 mL
½ tsp	salt (optional)	2 mL

1. Let cream stand at room temperature for about 30 minutes. Pour into a food processor fitted with a plastic or metal blade. Process cream until it separates into solid grains of butter and liquid buttermilk, 5 to 8 minutes. When the sound of the processor changes from whirring to sloshing, you will know the butter has formed. Continue to process until butter comes together into a few large grainy globs, about 1 minute more.

2. Drain off buttermilk liquid and add ½ cup (125 mL) of ice cold water to food processor. Process until the water turns cloudy, 1 to 2 seconds. Drain. Add another ½ cup (125 mL) ice cold water and process again. Keep adding water, ½ cup (125 mL) at a time, processing and draining until the water stays clear, an indication that all of the buttermilk has been washed from the butter.

3. Transfer butter to a small bowl, preferably wooden. Add salt, if desired, and mix with a wooden spoon, pressing the butter against the sides of the bowl. As you work the butter more buttermilk will be released. Drain this off as it appears and continue working the butter until smooth and solid, about 3 minutes. (Note: the butter will still be pliable and soft until it is refrigerated.) Store tightly wrapped in the refrigerator for up to 2 weeks.

MAKES ABOUT ¾ CUP (175 ML)
OR 6 OZ (175 G) BUTTER

Variation: *For cultured butter:* Use ½ cup (125 mL) crème fraîche in place of ½ cup (125 mL) cream.

animal. It was the only animal fat allowed in ancient Rome on meat abstention days, and, from the 16th century onward, during Lent. Because water droplets are suspended in the fat it is referred to as a water-in-oil emulsion.

What It Does • In milk, fat is in the form of tiny globules suspended in a mixture of water, milk protein (casein and others), and lactose (milk sugar). For butter making, cream is concentrated by separating fat from liquid until its fat content is between 36 and 44%. When churned, the fat globules break, and the released fat coalesces into larger and larger clumps until it becomes a continuous mass of about 80% fat with about 16% water droplets suspended inside. The remaining 4% is made up of proteins, sugars, and salts.

Butter can be made in several ways and to different concentrations of fat, water, protein, sugar, and salt. Each variation has its own cooking properties and flavor distinctions.

- *Sweet cream butter* is the most basic type. Made from pasteurized cream without added salt, it has a slightly cooked flavor and mild sweetness.
- *Salted sweet cream butter* contains between 1 and 2% salt, which is the equivalent of 1 to 2 teaspoons per pound (5 to 10 mL per 500 g). Originally salt was added as a preservative, and at 2% it does act as an antimicrobial agent.
- *Cultured cream butter* is the standard type in Europe. It is made with pasteurized cream that has been fermented with bacteria that produce lactic acid, giving it a slight tangy taste.
- *European-style butter* is American-made butter that emulates European butter. It is a cultured butter with a higher fat content. Typical American butter is 80% fat. France requires that its butter be at least 82% fat, and most American producers aim slightly higher for their European-style products. These butters

have 10 to 20% less water than typical American butter, which makes them preferable for baking.

- *Raw cream butter,* made from unpasteurized milk, is available only from farms and is not produced commercially. It has a fresh cream flavor, is quite perishable, and may harbor harmful bacteria.
- *Professional bakers' butters* are almost pure butterfat. They are manufactured to melt at specific temperature points depending on the baker's needs. It is also known as anhydrous milk fat.

Butter acts as a tenderizer in baked goods by interrupting the formation of gluten in dough, and as a spread or sauce when softened. Butterfat is soft enough to spread at 60°F (16°C) and doesn't melt until 85°F (30°C), a temperature range that makes it versatile for making composed butters to plop atop a steak, or melt into a rich butter **sauce**. For some classic sauces, notably beurre noisette and beurre noir, butter is heated slowly until its proteins and sugars brown via Maillard reactions, yielding a rich toasted nut flavor and color.

To make clarified butter, melt whole butter slowly until the milk proteins coagulate and the fat and water separate. Skim off the milk solids, and decant the pure butterfat, leaving behind the water and any milk solids that sank to the bottom. Without proteins that can brown and burn, clarified butter can be heated to higher temperatures than whole butter. Also, because the heating process generates some antioxidants via Maillard reactions, clarified butter can be stored for months under refrigeration without spoiling. Ghee, a form of clarified butter used in Indian cooking, is heated until all of the water evaporates and the milk solids toast lightly.

How It Works ● Although there are a variety of butters, butter production is fairly standard. Once the fat content of the cream is standardized and the cream is pasteurized and cooled, it can be cultured or not. Cultured butter is inoculated with bacteria that ferment the lactose into lactic acid and convert the citrates in the cream to diacetyl and acetyl methyl carbinol (acetoin), a major

kitchen wisdom

Storing Butter

With the water being dispersed in microscopic droplets, butter resists contamination by microbes and can be kept at room temperature for several days. But its flavor is easily compromised by exposure to light and oxygen that can break down fat molecules, turning them rancid. For that reason it is best to keep butter cold, frozen if possible, away from light, and tightly wrapped to prevent it from absorbing adjacent aromas. Do not wrap butter in foil, since contact with metal accelerates fat oxidation, particularly in salted butter.

contributor to butter flavor. At the same time aromatic esters are created that give food cooked in butter its distinctive flavor. Sweet cream butter that is not cultured has less of these properties.

The sweet or cultured cream is aged at 40°F (4°C) for at least 8 hours, during which time about half of the fat coalesces into solid crystals. The number and size of the crystals both determines how quickly the cream will be able to be churned into butter and affects the texture of the finished product. The aged cream is then warmed slightly and churned.

Done with a variety of paddles and mechanical devices, churning can take anywhere from a few seconds to 15 minutes to bring together the fat globules in the cream into small grains of butter, about the size of cooked grains of rice. The fat crystals that formed during aging weaken the globule membranes, causing them to rupture more easily. As the cream churns, the proteins in the membrane surrounding the fat globules are drawn into the water phase and the now freed fat flows together into a continuous mass. What started as fat droplets in water in the cream (an oil-in-water emulsion) is now water droplets in oil in the butter (a water-in-oil emulsion) due to phase inversion.

When churning is complete, the water, which is natural buttermilk, is drained away. The solid butter grains are washed with clean water to remove any buttermilk clinging to their surface that could give the butter a sour taste, and the grains are kneaded to consolidate the fat and force out more buttermilk. If the butter is to be salted, finely ground salt or strong brine is added at this point and the butter is shaped and packaged.

The type of milk, the feed of the animal, and the time of day of milking all affect the qualities of butter. Cows fed on fresh pasturage produce milk that makes softer butter than those fed on hay and grain, and the butter has a pale yellow cast from carotene in grasses. Cows that don't eat grass produce paler milk fat and the butter is almost white. Producers often compensate by adding annatto (a natural coloring produced from annatto seeds) or pure carotene for color.

See Also ● Baking, Browning, Emulsion, Fermentation

BUTTER, CLARIFIED ● See Butter

BUTTERCUP SQUASH ● See Squash

BUTTERFISH ● See Fish

BUTTERHEAD LETTUCE ● See Leaves

BUTTERMILK ● See Fermentation

BUTTERNUT SQUASH ● See Squash

BYRRH ● See Liquor

CABBAGE • See Cruciferous Vegetables

CABRALES • See Cheese

CACHAÇA • See Liquor

CACIOCAVALLO • See Cheese

CACTUS

What It Is • Totaling more than 1,500 species, members of the cactus family are succulent plants that retain water, giving them a puffy and swollen appearance. Cactus spines and the waxy coating on the plant's surface help prevent evaporation, allowing the plants to thrive in arid regions such as their native Mexico as well as Australia, India, dry regions of the Mediterranean, and the southwestern U.S.

What It Does • Some varieties of cactus, such as *Opuntia ficus-indica*, have broad, flat stems that resemble a paddle and are edible. Cactus pads (nopales) taste similar to green beans with lemon and are often eaten raw in salads and salsas. They can also be baked, fried, or pickled. When cut, cactus pads ooze a slimy mucilage similar to that of okra. As with many vegetables, smaller pads have a more tender texture and larger ones taste tougher.

kitchen wisdom

Less Goo
To minimize the okra-like sliminess of cactus use quick, high-heat cooking methods like grilling, broiling, frying, and roasting.

Certain cactus species, such as *Opuntia ficus-indica* and *Opuntia megacantha*, bear delicious fruit in the summer and fall. These prickly pears (cactus pears) have a thick green or red skin caused by betain pigments and a melon-like aroma from alcohols and aldehydes that are similar to those in melons. They're slightly sweeter than apples with about 1% more sugar by weight. They can be peeled and eaten raw or used in salsas. The juice is often boiled down to a syrup or paste that's used for candies and cakes.

The Central American cactus *Hylocereus undatus* also bears pink-skinned fruit known as dragon fruit, pitaya, or strawberry pear. Its flesh is white and fragrantly sweet with harmless little black seeds. Like other cactus pears, dragon fruit is often eaten fresh or made into juice or syrup.

How It Works • As with pineapple, cactus pears contain a protein-digesting enzyme that prevents gelatin gels from setting when added raw. If using cactus pears in a gelatin solution, cook the fruit pulp first to denature the enzyme and circumvent the problem.

Cilantro Cream Nopales with Pine Nuts

With a flavor similar to green beans and an unctuous texture, cactus pads (nopales) take well to cream sauces. This one gets aroma from cilantro and crunch from toasted pine nuts. Look for small young cactus pads for the most tender texture.

2 tbsp	pine nuts	25 mL
8 oz	cactus pads	250 g
2 tbsp	Herb Pesto (see recipe, page 307), made with cilantro, dry Jack cheese, pine nuts, and olive oil	25 mL
2 tbsp	whipping (35%) cream	25 mL
⅛ tsp	salt	0.5 mL
⅛ tsp	freshly ground black pepper	0.5 mL

1. In a small skillet over medium-low heat, toast pine nuts, shaking pan occasionally, until fragrant and golden brown, 2 to 4 minutes. Set aside.

2. Using a paring knife, carefully trim off outer edges and short ends of cactus pads then slice off spines from both sides. Slice pads into short strips. Place cactus strips in a steamer basket over simmering water, cover, and steam until tender-crisp, 2 to 3 minutes.

3. In a bowl, combine cilantro pesto, cream, salt, and pepper. Add hot cactus strips and toss. Serve sprinkled with toasted pine nuts.

MAKES 4 SERVINGS

See Also ● Liquor, Sweeteners

CAERPHILLY • See Cheese

CAFFEINE

What It Is ● The world's most widely consumed drug, caffeine is an alkaloid found in the beans, seeds, leaves, and fruit of several dozen plants. This chemical compound, trimethylxanthine ($C_8H_{10}N_4O_2$), tastes mildly bitter at 150 to 200 ppm in water and may go by different names when found in coffee (caffeine), tea (theine), guarana (guaranine), and yerba mate (mateine). But it's all the same thing. You can also find caffeine in chocolate and in kola nuts, which gave rise to colas and other soft drinks that contain caffeine.

Caffeine concentration varies among plants. Guarana seeds pack the biggest jolt (4 to 8% caffeine), followed by black tea leaves (2 to 4%), kola nuts (2 to 3%), coffee beans (1 to 2%), yerba mate leaves (0.5 to 2%), and cacao (cocoa or chocolate) beans (0.25%). However, because of processing, the caffeinated beverages and foods we enjoy contain much different concentrations of caffeine. For instance, even though tea leaves contain more caffeine than coffee beans, a cup of brewed tea has about half as much caffeine as a cup of brewed coffee. That's because we use less tea by weight to brew each cup. Another eye-opener: espresso contains less caffeine than regular brewed coffee. Blame the roasting method for the beans and the brewing method for the coffee. The darkly roasted coffee beans used for espresso contain less caffeine than the lightly roasted beans used for most brewed coffee. That's because the more a coffee bean is roasted, the more caffeine gets burned off. Plus, espresso is brewed more quickly than other styles of coffee, so less caffeine is extracted from the grounds. (See Caffeine in Common Food Products chart, page 80, for a list of popular foods and their caffeine content.)

What It Does ● Caffeine is a psychoactive central nervous system stimulant. It delays drowsiness, speeds reaction time, and improves muscle endurance. After ingesting caffeine, it takes 10 to 15 minutes to start feeling its effects. Blood levels of caffeine peak about 30 minutes after ingestion, are reduced to nearly half in three hours, and disappear in about six hours.

The physical effects of caffeine are most noticeable among infrequent users, as frequent users become accustomed to the sensations. Upwards of 600 mg caffeine a day (more than 6 cups of coffee) will amplify its quickening effects and may result in restlessness, irregular heartbeat, insomnia, and speed the loss of calcium from the bones leading to premature osteoporosis. Taking more than 6,000 mg in a single dose can cause convulsions and death.

Caffeine in Common Food Products

This chart shows the approximate caffeine content of foods, beverages, mints, and alertness aids. Figures come from the U.S. Department of Agriculture and Food and Drug Administration.

Food Product	Amount	Caffeine (milligrams)
Chocolate, bittersweet	1 oz (28 g)	20
Chocolate, semisweet	1 oz (28 g)	13
Chocolate, unsweetened	1 oz (28 g)	30
Cocoa powder, unsweetened	1 tbsp (15 mL)	20
Coffee, brewed/pressed	8 oz (237 mL)	70 to 125
Coffee, decaffeinated	8 oz (237 mL)	2 to 4
Coffee, drip	8 oz (237 mL)	115 to 175
Coffee, espresso	1 oz (30 mL)	30 to 90
Coffee, instant	8 oz (237 mL)	65 to 100
Energy drink, No Name (formerly called Cocaine)	8.4 oz (248 mL)	280
Energy drink, Red Bull	8.3 oz (245 mL)	76
Foosh Energy Mints	1 mint	100
Ice Cream, Häagen-Dazs coffee	1 cup (237 mL)	58
NoDoz Maximum Strength	1 tablet	200
Soft drink, cola (Coke Classic)	12 oz (355 mL)	35
Soft drink, cola (Diet Coke)	12 oz (355 mL)	47
Soft drink, Dr. Pepper	12 oz (355 mL)	41
Soft drink, guarana	12 oz (355 mL)	30 to 50
Soft drink, Mountain Dew	12 oz (355 mL)	55
Soft drink, root beer (Barq's)	12 oz (355 mL)	23
Tea, black (brewed)	8 oz (237 mL)	47
Tea, black (decaffeinated)	8 oz (237 mL)	2
Tea, green (brewed)	8 oz (237 mL)	30 to 50

However, there is no firm evidence that moderate daily caffeine use (200 to 300 mg a day/about two to three cups of brewed coffee) raises blood cholesterol levels, causes heart disease, or increases cancer risk. Health experts conclude this amount of caffeine a day is harmless for most people. Pregnant women are advised to take less.

Experts do warn against caffeine dependence, which may occur when you ingest upwards of 350 mg daily. Withdrawal symptoms include headaches, irritability, fatigue, and depression. These generally subside within a few days of abstaining from caffeine because it doesn't accumulate in the body.

How It Works • Once ingested, caffeine travels through the bloodstream to the brain. There it takes the place of the neurotransmitter adenosine, which would normally bind to receptors in your brain and slow down nerve impulses, causing drowsiness. Caffeine takes adenosine's place and prevents the slowing of nerve impulses, in turn making you more alert and awake. Caffeine also increases your brain's dopamine levels, which gives you a feeling of well-being.

See Also • Chocolate, Coffee, Tea

CAJETA • See Dulce de Leche

CAKE

What It Is • Maybe it's the butter with its rich taste and ability to create tenderness. Or maybe it's the sugar's sweetness and caramelized flavor. Or the tenderness of the flour. Or the rich taste created by the eggs. Whatever it is, cake is a treat. Cakes may be light and airy or heavy and dense. But most of all, when compared with other baked goods, cakes are sweet.

Sweetness wasn't always the defining characteristic of cakes. The first cakes, such as oatcakes, evolved from unleavened breads and crackers. Later cakes, such as panettone, stollen, and fruitcake, evolved from yeast-raised breads. In the 18th century, yeast-raised cakes eventually gave way to sweeter cakes, such as plum cake, pound cake, and sponge cake, raised not by yeast but instead by **aerating** the batter through prolonged beating of sugar and fat or using an egg white foam to incorporate air bubbles. In the mid-1800s, baking soda and other **chemical leaveners** lightened the load of strenuous beating and improved the ability of cake batter to rise.

What It Does • In addition to the usual ingredients of eggs, sugar, flour, and fat, a cake is defined by its leavening, which is the method used to create bubbles in the batter. Some cakes use yeast to generate carbon dioxide bubbles. With most cakes, sugar and fat and/or eggs are beaten together to incorporate air into the batter. And some use chemical leaveners to produce carbon dioxide bubbles. Either way, when heated, those bubbles are what makes the cake batter rise.

The exact ingredients, their proportions, and the aeration methods used result in several different styles of cake. In North America, these styles generally fall into two main categories, foam cakes and shortened cakes.

Foam Cakes

For these light and simple cakes, you beat whole eggs and/or egg whites and sugar at length to incorporate air bubbles in the batter, known as a **foam**. If using only egg whites, the foam should be made in a grease-free glass, stainless steel, or, preferably, copper bowl to ensure maximum aeration. Then you fold in flour gently to avoid deflating the foam and to prevent the formation of **gluten** in the flour, which would make the cake dense and tough instead of light and tender. You can also incorporate a variety of flavorings, from butter and milk to cocoa powder to flavoring extracts. Foam cakes are baked immediately to capture the maximum leavening effect of the air bubbles in the foam. Foam cakes do not use chemical leaveners. This method produces light, airy cakes such as:

Meringue: Fat-free, this cake is leavened only with aerated egg whites. Dacquoise is a type of meringue cake made with ground nuts and little or no flour and then layered with whipped cream or buttercream.

Angel food: Another fat-free cake leavened only with egg whites. It is essentially a meringue with flour and sugar added.

Sponge: These popular foam cakes are leavened with beaten eggs. Typically, the eggs are separated, the whites are beaten with sugar, the yolks are beaten with sugar and flavorings, then the two foams are gently combined and folded with flour.

French biscuit cake: These cakes are essentially sponge cakes with additional egg yolks. Biscuit cake is the classic cake used for roulades and cake rolls such as bûche de Noël.

Génoise: This French sponge cake is leavened by beating warm whole eggs and sugar until the eggs take on so much air that they resemble whipped cream. Génoise makes a great layering cake, as seen in classic petits fours.

Chiffon: These cakes are remarkable because they combine lightness and richness from a high proportion of whipped egg whites and a fair amount of vegetable oil. The oil makes the cake taste moist and more tender

fast fact

- In 1927, Harry Baker, an insurance salesman and part-time Hollywood caterer, invented the chiffon cake, a type of sponge cake made with oil instead of butter. He sold the formula to General Mills in the 1940s.

than, say, a biscuit cake. These hybrid cakes also use chemical leaveners for aeration.

Shortened Cakes

Shortened cakes are made by beating sugar and fat together until the fat is filled with air bubbles, a process known as creaming. Butter aerates best at 67°F (19°C); shortening roughly 77°F (25°C). When you cream the sugar and fat, the sugar's sharp crystalline structure slashes deep pockets in the fat, and those pockets take on air. Then you beat in eggs, one by one, which help to hold even more air. Finally, you fold in flour and usually a chemical leavener such as baking powder or baking soda.

Traditionally the dry ingredients are added with alternate additions of milk, cream, or another liquid so that the flour first gets coated with the beaten fat. This fat coating protects proteins in the flour from being turned into gluten when you stir in the liquid, creating a lower-gluten, more tender cake. An alternative method for making tender shortened cakes, known as the two-stage method, is to combine all of the dry ingredients (flour, baking powder, salt) in one bowl and all of the wet ingredients (eggs, vanilla, milk) in another. You beat the butter and half of the wet ingredients into the dry ingredients to aerate the batter, then beat in the remaining wet ingredients. This method

also improves tenderness for the same reason the creaming method does. However, this method makes the cake more likely to toughen from overmixing. Either way, both methods produce several types of rich, moist cake:

Pound cake: Originally calling for a pound each of butter, sugar, flour, and eggs, this cake has evolved to include sour cream, additional egg yolks, and other flavored liquids.

Butter cakes: Rich and moist like pound cake, butter cakes are lighter and more finely textured because of a lower proportion of eggs and fat and a higher proportion of sugar and liquid.

The basic ingredients play key roles in cake making. For instance, cake flour is finely milled, producing a finer crumb in cake. It's also low in protein, which means it contains less gluten proteins. But some cakes also incorporate almond flour, chestnut flour, other nut flours, or cocoa powder. Cake flour is usually bleached with chlorine, which lowers its pH (makes it more acidic), and causes egg proteins in the batter to coagulate at a lower temperature. It also allows starch in the flour to absorb more moisture, and both of these changes produce a delicate, fine-textured crumb in a very stable structure.

As for the fat, both butter and shortening aerate and tenderize a cake. Fine-textured cakes are created by lots of small gas bubbles. Coarse-textured cakes have fewer, larger gas

Basic Ingredient Proportions in Cakes

Most cakes consist of the same five ingredients: liquid, eggs, flour, sugar, and fat. The chart below shows the approximate percentages (by weight) of each ingredient in various cakes. Cakes that have a higher ratio of sugar than flour are sometimes called "high-ratio cakes" because they make a light-textured cake. Keep in mind that the fat percentages below do not include the butter's milk solids and water.

Cake Type	Liquid	Egg	Flour	Sugar	Fat	Characteristics
Angel food	6%	47%	13%	34%	0%	Light, springy, very sweet
Sponge	4%	45%	20%	31%	0%	Light, spongy, sweet
Biscuit roulade	0%	59%	14%	27%	0%	Light, springy, dry (syrup often added for moisture)
Génoise	0%	46%	23%	23%	8%	Sturdy, springy, dry (syrup often added for moisture)
Chiffon	14%	35%	18%	24%	9%	Light, rich, moist, tender
Pound	12%	22%	22%	22%	22%	Moist, rich, dense
Butter	24%	10%	27%	27%	12%	Moist, soft, finely textured

bubbles. Which type of fat is best? Vegetable shortenings have lots of small fat crystals that can entrap lots of small air bubbles. Butter and lard, on the other hand, have fewer but larger fat crystals that entrap fewer but larger air bubbles. This means that shortenings make lighter, more fine-textured cakes. But butter tastes better. Some bakers use a combination.

Sugars help sweeten cake batter and help it retain moisture. Sugars also tenderize the cake by competing for water and preventing the formation of gluten from the flour. Superfine sugar dissolves more quickly and does a better job of creaming the fat in pound cakes and butter cakes, because it has more fine, sharp edges that pierce more holes in the fat, for a finer texture in the finished cake.

How It Works ● Baking transforms batter

to cake. The heat of the oven triggers many of the chemical processes that create a cake's defining textures and flavors. Each of the key ingredients — fat, sugar, flour, eggs, and chemical leaveners — is affected.

Yeast-raised cakes and those using baking

science wise

Red Chocolate ● Devil's food cake (and, to some extent, red velvet cake) gets its ruddy color from the addition of baking soda, which increases the alkalinity of cocoa to pH 7.5 and turns the cocoa pigments dark red. Too much baking soda can cause a bitter or soapy aftertaste.

powder or other chemical leaveners produce carbon dioxide that migrates to the air bubbles incorporated into the batter. When heated during creaming, the gases expand and make the cake rise. Even cakes with no chemical leaveners, such as angel food cake, have enough air bubbles from the egg white foam to expand in the oven's heat and raise the cake. Water in the batter also changes to steam and expands, contributing to the rise.

In the oven, gas bubbles expand and mature. By this point in the baking, the cake's structure should be set and when cooled creates a solid foam. If the oven is set too low and the batter heats too slowly, the gas bubbles overexpand before the cake sets, creating a large-holed, coarse-grained texture in the finished cake.

Keep in mind that altitude and **atmospheric pressure** also affect the baking, particularly the expanding gas bubbles. As altitude increases, there is increasingly less atmospheric pressure, which allows the leavening gases to expand more rapidly, stretching and weakening the structure of the cake, which can result in a coarse texture or cause the cake to fall. Cakes baked at high altitudes (above 3,000 feet/914 m) use lower oven temperatures and less leavening agent.

The cake batter sets, in part, because eggs and flour contain protein that coagulates, or firms up, when heated (at about 180°F/82°C). The liquid in the batter, such as milk, cream, water, and even eggs (which are about 74% water), also hydrates the starch in the flour when it is heated. As the starch granules absorb moisture and swell, they form a paste, which then stiffens or sets. This process is known as gelatinization and is followed by gelation (forming of a gel) upon cooling.

Troubleshooting Cakes

It's deeply satisfying to turn out a beautiful cake. It's equally saddening to open the oven door and find a fallen mess. If your cake is less than perfect, use the guide below to find out what may have gone wrong and how to fix it for future baking.

Problem	Possible Cause	Solution
Cake doesn't rise	Leavening expired	Buy new baking powder
Cake falls	Oven too hot	Reduce oven temperature
	Too much leavening	Reduce baking powder, baking soda, or aerated egg whites
Cake is lopsided	Uneven heating	Check for oven hotspots with oven thermometer; recalibrate oven
	Oven is not level	Level oven with carpenter's level
	Insufficient pan preparation	For shortened cakes, grease sides of pan to prevent batter from sticking
	Pans crowded in oven	Allow airspace around pans and rotate for even heating
	Flour not fully incorporated	Mix batter thoroughly
Cake breaks	Insufficient cooling	Cool cake in pan on rack for 15 minutes before removing
	Too much leavening	Reduce baking powder, baking soda, or aerated egg whites
	Too much sugar	Reduce sugar
	Oven too cool	Increase oven temperature
Cake bottom burns	Baking pan too thin or dark	Use heavy-gauge bakeware; reduce oven temperature by 25°F (14°C) when using dark pans; check cake during baking
	Poorly prepared pan	Line pan with parchment paper
	Poor pan placement	Place pans equidistant from oven walls. Two pans should be in upper and lower thirds of oven
Cake top burns	Oven too hot	Reduce oven temperature
	Too much sugar	Reduce sugar
	Baking time too long	Reduce baking time
Cake unevenly colored	Insufficient mixing	Mix batter thoroughly
	Too little liquid	Add liquid to help dissolve dry ingredients
	Sugar only partially dissolved	Use superfine sugar
Fruit sinks in batter	Fruit not dusted with flour	Dust fruit with flour to prevent sinking
	Oven too cool	Increase oven temperature so cake sets before fruit sinks
	Too much leavening	Reduce leavening to avoid lightening batter so much that fruit sinks through soft structure
Batter overflows	Pan too small	Fill pans no more than ⅔ full. See Pan Sizes, page 40, when substituting pans
	Too much leavening	Reduce baking soda, baking powder, or aerated egg whites

The fat (shortening, oil, or butter) in the batter tenderizes the cake. When heated, the fat melts, releases the air it once held, and slides into the coagulated and stiffened structure of the cake, tenderizing and moistening it. Shortening contains emulsifiers that do a better job than butter of dispersing fat throughout the batter. Regardless of whether you use butter, shortening, or oil, more fat in a cake weighs it down and makes it heavier. Call to mind the dense texture of fat-rich pound cake. Less fat, on the other hand, allows the gas bubbles to expand more in the oven, creating the more open, airy texture of angel food and sponge cakes.

Sugar delivers the characteristic sweetness of cakes but also tenderizes them by competing for available water that's also necessary for gluten formation and starch gelatinization. Sugars and proteins combine in the Maillard reactions, **browning** the cake's surface and developing hundreds of new flavor compounds that we recognize as delicious.

The heat level is important, too. Most cakes are baked at a moderate 350°F (180°C). If the oven is too low, the fat melts so quickly that it releases its leavening gases before the other elements in the batter set, preventing the cake from rising. If the heat is too high, the crust forms before the center is set, causing a soggy center with gases that continue to expand late in the baking process, which can crack the crust. Keep an oven thermometer in your oven for accurate temperature measurements.

Now that we've discussed ingredients, mixing, and baking, the cake is ready to eat, right? Well, cooling and storing also affect the finished product. Cakes need to cool to allow the flour's gelatinized starch to gel and firm up the cake. If removed too soon, the cake may stick to the pan. If left in the pan too long, the cake will steam so much that it becomes soggy. Shortened cakes should be cooled in the pan on a wire rack for five to 10 minutes to allow cool air to circulate beneath the pan bottom and speed cooling. Then remove the cake from the pan and let it cool completely on a wire rack to allow excess

kitchen wisdom

Three Tips for Better Cakes

- To brighten a cake's flavor, include at least ½ teaspoon (2 mL) salt in a typical 10-serving cake.
- To make fine-textured angel food cake, add cream of tartar to the egg whites, which lowers the pH, stabilizing the egg white foam and whitening the flour pigments.
- To quickly grease cake pans, use nonstick baking spray, a mixture of fat and flour. Or make your own baker's grease by stirring together 1 cup (250 mL) plain vegetable shortening and ½ cup (125 mL) flour. Refrigerate the mixture indefinitely and use in place of butter and flour for greasing pans.

steam to escape into the air. Angel food, chiffon, and sponge cakes should be cooled completely upside down in the tube pan to avoid crushing their delicate foam.

Cakes keep well at room temperature for a few days because of their fat and their sugar, which retain moisture. Refrigerating cakes tends to dry them out, but they freeze well, especially if they are high in fat. Wrap completely cooled cakes tightly in plastic wrap to prevent air from reaching the cake and speeding spoilage.

See Also • Aeration, Bakeware, Baking, Bread, Butter, Candy, Cheesecake, Eggs, Emulsion, Flour, Foams, Gluten, Pancakes, Sugar

CAKE PANS • See Bakeware

CALABAZA • See Squash

CALABRESE SAUSAGE • See Sausage

CALAMARI • See Mollusks

CALAMATA OLIVE • See Olive

CALAMONDIN • See Citrus

CALCIUM • See Minerals

CALENDULA • See Flowers

CALORIE

What It Is • We count calories, burn them, and cut them, but how many of us actually know what a calorie is? A calorie is a measure of heat energy — the amount of heat it takes to raise the temperature of 1,000 grams of water by 1°C (that's about a pint of water by 1.8°F). In fact, Calories are referred to with a capital C, which actually represents 1,000 calories or one kilocalorie (see Science Wise, right).

Most of us think of calories in terms of food, but the measurement can be applied to anything that holds energy or uses it up. For instance, a gallon of gasoline contains about 31,000 calories, and a Quarter Pounder with Cheese has about 530 calories. So, if you could power your car with cheeseburgers it would take 2.75 Quarter Pounders with Cheese to drive 1 mile (1.6 km).

What It Does • Foods that yield more heat energy are higher in calories. Foods that give off less heat energy are lower in calories. For instance, 1 gram of pure **fat** yields about 9 calories, which is fairly high on the calorie spectrum. One gram of pure alcohol gives off a bit less, about 7 calories. The least caloric food groups are **proteins** and **carbohydrates**, each of which gives off about 4 calories per gram. Water and air have no calories.

Most foods include a mix of proteins, carbohydrates, and fat, which can make it

science wise

Measuring Calories • Using the scientific definition of a calorie (the energy needed to raise 1 gram of water 1 degree Celsius), the number of calories in foods is numerically quite high. So food energy is usually given in kilocalories (1000 calories = 1 kilocalorie). However, in common usage the kilocalorie has become the Calorie (with a capital C) that frequently is called a calorie. Internationally, the units of food energy used are joules (J) and kilojoules (kJ). A British Thermal Unit (BTU) is the amount of heat energy needed to raise one pound of water one degree Fahrenheit.

Heat energy potential can be measured in the laboratory using a bomb calorimeter in which food is burned and the heat given off measured. Energy determinations using a bomb calorimeter overestimate the caloric value because fiber components are included.

1 calorie = 4.184 joules
1 kilocalorie (kcal) = 1,000 calories = 1 Calorie
1 kilocalorie = 4.184 kilojoules (kJ)
1 British Thermal Unit (BTU) = 1.055 kJ = 0.252 kcal = 0.252 Calorie

difficult to determine the exact calorie content of a specific food. For instance, a serving of pancake mix has 162 Calories, but if you look closer at the nutritional label you will see that those calories are divided between 1.5 grams fat (14 kcal), 32 grams of carbohydrate (128 kcal), and 5 grams of protein (20 kcal), which adds up to 162 kcal.

Nutritionists often look broadly at diets as a balance of calories in and calories out. The calories come in from food and go out through activity. A 150-pound (68 kg) person burns about 1,600 Calories a day just for normal processes of **metabolism** such as

fast fact

• Although chewing a rib of celery uses up 7 more calories than the amount of calories actually in the celery, the difference is not enough to cause weight loss, making celery a good diet food, but not an effective diet plan.

Low-Calorie Orange Walnut Cookies

These sweet, crunchy meringue cookies have only 13 Calories each. Fat is the most concentrated source of calories and this recipe contains no added fat. The cookies are leavened solely by whipping egg whites, which contain no fat. The only fat comes from walnuts, and most health experts recommend nuts as part of a healthy diet. The recipe contains sugar, of course, but just enough to add sweetness without an overload of calories. Avoid making these cookies on humid days, which can make the cookies less crisp.

½ cup	walnuts	125 mL
3	egg whites, at room temperature	3
Pinch	cream of tartar	Pinch
½ cup	granulated sugar	125 mL
1 tbsp	grated orange zest	15 mL
½ tsp	vanilla extract	2 mL

1. Preheat oven to 350°F (180°C). Place walnuts on a baking sheet and bake, shaking the pan once or twice, until walnuts smell fragrant, about 5 minutes. Let cool and finely chop.

2. Reduce oven temperature to 200°F (100°F). Line the baking sheet used for the walnuts as well as another baking sheet with parchment paper or foil.

3. In a large, clean, dry, and grease-free bowl, preferably copper or glass, combine egg whites and cream of tartar. Using an electric mixer, beat on medium speed until whites form soft peaks when beaters are lifted, 3 to 5 minutes. Gradually add sugar, beating until whites resemble shaving cream and hold stiff peaks when beaters are lifted, 3 to 5 minutes more. Fold in walnuts, orange zest and vanilla.

4. Spoon meringue into a large resealable plastic bag (or into a piping bag without a tip). Cut off a corner of the bag, and squeeze meringue into 1½-inch (4 cm) rounds on prepared sheets.

5. Bake in preheated oven for 1 hour and 15 minutes without opening oven door. Turn off oven and let meringues sit in oven until cool, for at least 1 hour or up to 8 hours. You can bake these at night, turn off the oven, and let them cool in the oven until morning. Serve immediately or store in an airtight container for 1 to 2 days. The meringues will keep longest if the humidity is low.

MAKES ABOUT 60 COOKIES

---

breathing, **digestion**, circulating blood, replacing cells, thinking, and maintaining body temperature. That's a little more than a kilocalorie a minute. Physical activity burns more calories. In 20 minutes of moving around, that same 150-pound (68 kg) person will burn about 110 Calories walking leisurely, 180 Calories playing football, and 260 Calories running quickly (at a pace of 1 mile/1.6 km every nine minutes). When you tally the total calorie output of physical activity and normal metabolism, a mildly active 150-pound (68 kg) male of average height (5 ft 9 in/ 173 cm) will burn about 2,300 Calories a day. Maintaining that 150-pound (68 km) weight is often a matter of consuming the same amount of calories as food that is burned off as activity.

How It Works • Just as ounces and pounds measure the weight of food, calories measure the potential energy of food. Calories reported on food labels are an estimate based on the Atwater system (named for American chemist Wilbur Olin Atwater) that determines energy values on the basis of protein, fat, and carbohydrates, which yield 4, 9, and 4 calories per gram, respectively. However, digestion is not 100% and many factors influence how many calories are derived from a meal. Although only an estimate, the caloric values do provide valuable comparisons of the energy content of foods.

During digestion and the early stages of metabolism, calories are released (or burned) as **enzymes** in your intestines break down carbohydrates into glucose and other simple sugars, fats into glycerol and fatty acids, and proteins into amino acids. These nutrients travel through your bloodstream to individual cells throughout your body and release their stored energy for use by the cells. About 6 to 10% of the energy in food is required to digest, absorb, transport, store, and metabolize it. This energy goes by several names such as the calorigenic effect, the thermal effect, the specific dynamic action and diet-induced thermogenesis.

See Also • Alcohol, Carbohydrate, Fat, Heat, Metabolism, Protein

CALVADOS • See Liquor

CALYPSO BEAN • See Legumes

CAMEMBERT • See Cheese

CAMPARI • See Bitters

CANADIAN BACON • See Bacon

CANDY

What It Is • Candy is manipulated **sugar** or **chocolate**. Sugar candies evolved from medicines. In medieval times, apothecaries used the sweet stuff to deliver all kinds of healing tinctures and extracts in candies, a practice still evident today in cough drops, throat lozenges, and chewable vitamins.

Once sugar became widely available,

fast fact

- Cotton candy debuted at the 1904 World's Fair in St. Louis, Missouri. Like lollipops, the sugar syrup for cotton candy is concentrated to about 99% sucrose at a temperature of 310 to 320°F (154 to 160°C). But instead of being poured onto a surface and shaped into hard lollipops, it is forced through a special machine with "spinnerets" that blow the sugar syrup into thousands of extremely thin filaments that quickly solidify in the air.

confectionery moved far beyond health concerns toward pure hedonism. Hard candies were common in the 1600s, and by the 1800s taffy, toffee, nougat, fondant, and chocolate had become mainstays of candy making.

What It Does • Sugar candies can have any number of textures, from hard, glassy, brittle, grainy, and gritty to chewy, gummy, pasty, pillowy, cottony, and creamy. You can create these textures by heating, cooling, shaping, and adding various ingredients to granulated sugar in controlled ways.

Crystallization

Much of the candy maker's art lies in manipulating sugar crystallization. Sugar (sucrose) molecules naturally bond with one another into orderly patterns that create the solid form of the sugar crystals in your sugar bowl. Salt forms crystals, too. Crystals like sugar and salt form from liquid solutions when the maximum amount of sugar or salt that can possibly dissolve in water at that temperature is exceeded. Common ways to form crystals are to increase the sugar or salt concentration by removing the solvent (such as water, in the case of making sea salt) or to decrease the temperature (sugar is less soluble at lower temperatures). Other solutes in the water (like sugars other than sucrose) will interfere with sugar's attempt to crystallize. With enough of these other solutes, sugar will not crystallize at all. Most candies begin with dissolving sugar in water to make a sugar syrup, along with an "interferent" such as corn syrup, cream, butter, or egg white to control or prevent the crystallization that occurs as the syrup cools, then boiling away water to obtain the appropriate sugar concentration, and finally cooling. Adding acids like lemon juice or cream of tartar causes some of the sucrose to hydrolyze, or break down, into invert sugar (the glucose and fructose components of sucrose) that will interfere with crystallization. Stirring and beating also manipulate the number and size of the sugar crystals that form, creating various textures of candy. When you mix sugar and water, the sugar crystals dissolve into a solution, or sugar syrup. By adjusting the amount of water, you can make a thin, medium, or heavy syrup that would be good for moistening cakes, making candied citrus peel, or sweetening sorbets. The attraction of water to sugar molecules is greater than the attraction of sugar molecules to each other, which keeps the sugar in solution. When the maximum concentration of sugar is dissolved in water at a particular temperature, the solution is said to be saturated. But sugar is one of a few materials that can become supersaturated, meaning that it can contain more than the theoretical maximum concentration of sugar. To attain supersaturation, you concentrate the sugar solution by heating and evaporating water and then cool slowly, undisturbed and without the presence of any seed crystals, which are crystal nuclei that attract other crystals and grow into bigger crystals. Dust particles, scratches on the surface of the container, and agitation of the sugar syrup can cause rapid crystallization from a supersaturated solution. Rapid crystallization is how you get many small crystals that give a crystalline candy its desirable smooth texture.

A supersaturated sugar solution is very sensitive. That's why there are so many precautions for cooking sugar syrups during candy making. To prevent recrystallization:

- use a narrow pan so the flame from your gas burner (if you're cooking with gas) can reach the sides of the pan and dissolve any sugar crystals that may stick there
- oil the inside of the pan to help crystals slip back into the syrup
- clamp a candy thermometer onto the pan then leave it undisturbed
- brush crystals down from the sides of the pan with a damp pastry brush and wash the brush clean of crystals between brushings
- pour the syrup from the pan onto a smooth surface without scraping
- stir only after cooling, using a wooden spoon because metal spoons readily conduct heat and would abruptly change the temperature, encouraging crystallization

Sugar Concentration

As a sugar syrup boils and water evaporates, the concentration of sugar in the solution increases and the solution's boiling point increases. Syrups with a lower sugar concentration (more water) will cool into softer candies like caramels. Syrups with a higher sugar concentration (less water) will cool into harder candies like lollipops.

Before the days of candy thermometers, cooks tested the sugar concentration by pouring a drop of the syrup into ice water and observing it as it cooled (many cooks still use this method). See the chart on page 90 for details on testing sugar concentration using a thermometer or the ice water test.

If you boil off all the water from a sugar syrup, you're left with 100% molten sugar. At this point, the temperature is about 320°F (160°C). If you continue to heat the sugar, it begins to caramelize, starting at about 340°F (171°C) going from light to medium to dark caramel brown and developing hundreds of flavorful compounds in the process. At this stage, the caramel may be used for more advanced "sugar work" like pulled sugar sculptures, spun sugar nests, and molded caramel cages to create fancy desserts. Keep in mind that as sugar caramelizes and develops its delicious flavors, it becomes increasingly less sweet. If you continue cooking sugar above 375°F

(191°C), it will turn from brown to black and from sweet to bitter. Cook it even longer, and it will ignite.

How It Works • Candies are made by controlling sugar crystallization. Sugar (sucrose) is composed of two simple sugars bonded together: fructose and glucose. When you heat sugar syrup with an acid like lemon juice or cream of tartar, it breaks down into these two component parts. Known as invert sugar, this broken-down sugar interferes with

the sugar's tendency to crystallize as it cools. Commercial candy makers sometimes use prepared liquid invert sugar, but most use corn syrup, which performs the same function. Corn syrup is also cheaper, caramelizes less easily, and gives candies more chewiness.

Ingredients like milk, cream, butter, egg whites, and gelatin can also interfere with sugar recrystallization. By altering the proportions of these "interferents," you can create a huge array of textures in candy.

Sugar Syrups and Common Candies

Three key factors influence the type of candy you make: the concentration of sugar in the syrup, added ingredients, and beating or aeration as the syrup cools. This chart shows how various concentrations of sugar and added ingredients are used to create different types of candies. The figures and formulas here are approximate to facilitate the at-a-glance nature of the chart.

Candy or Syrup	Sugar	Water	Corn Syrup	Acid	Milk or Cream	Butter
Thin syrup	1 cup (250 mL)	2 cups (500 mL)				
Medium syrup	1 cup (250 mL)	1½ cups (375 mL)				
Heavy syrup	1 cup (250 mL)	1 cup (250 mL)				
Fudge	1 cup (250 mL)		1 tbsp (15 mL)		½ cup (125 mL)	1 tbsp (15 mL)
Fondant	1 cup (250 mL)	½ cup (125 mL)	1 tbsp (15 mL)			
Pralines	1 cup (250 mL)			1 tsp (5 mL) lemon juice		
Rock candy	1 cup (250 mL)	½ cup (125 mL)				
Caramels	1 cup (250 mL)		1 cup (250 mL)		1 cup (250 mL)	¼ cup (50 mL)
Marshmallows	1 cup (250 mL)	¼ cup (50 mL)	1 tbsp (15 mL)			
Nougat	1 cup (250 mL)	2 tbsp (25 mL)	¾ cup (175 mL)			
Divinity	1 cup (250 mL)	¼ cup (50 mL)	2 tbsp (25 mL)			
Taffy	1 cup (250 mL)	⅓ cup (75 mL)	¼ cup (50 mL)			
Butterscotch	1 cup (250 mL)	1 tbsp (15 mL)	½ cup (125 mL)	1 tbsp (15 mL) vinegar		¼ cup (50 mL)
Brittle	1 cup (250 mL)	2 tbsp (25 mL)	½ cup (125 mL)			⅓ cup (75 mL)
Toffee	1 cup (250 mL)	¼ cup (50 mL)	1 tbsp (15 mL)			¾ cup (175 mL)
Hard candy	1 cup (250 mL)	½ cup (125 mL)	⅓ cup (75 mL)			
Pulled sugar	1 cup (250 mL)	¼ cup (50 mL)	2 tbsp (25 mL)	1 tsp (5 mL) lemon juice		
Spun sugar	1 cup (250 mL)	¼ cup (50 mL)	1 tbsp (15 mL)			
Medium caramel cages	1 cup (250 mL)	¼ cup (50 mL)	1 tbsp (15 mL)			
Dark caramel cages	1 cup (250 mL)	¼ cup (50 mL)	1 tbsp (15 mL)			
Baker's caramel	1 cup (250 mL)	¼ cup (50 mL)				

Textures are also created by allowing the concentrated sugar solution to cool slowly and undisturbed to develop supersaturation and then beating or stirring the syrup as it cools to manipulate the number and size of the sugar crystals that form. For instance, if you beat hot syrup, it will create relatively few crystals that are large in size, resulting in a coarse, grainy texture in the candy. If the syrup is cooled and then beaten, it creates a greater number of fine crystals, giving the candy a smoother, creamier texture.

Prolonged beating or kneading of cooled syrup creates the very fine consistency and creaminess of candies like fudge and fondant. If you beat air into the syrup, you can create the light textures of candies like nougat and marshmallow.

Crystalline and Noncrystalline Candies
Even with all these variables, candies fall into two main categories: crystalline and amorphous (noncrystalline). Crystalline candies generally have a lower sugar

Egg White	Gelatin	Temperature	Sugar (Sucrose) Concentration	Stage	In ice water, sugar syrup forms:	Candy Type
		214°F (101°C)	40%	Thread	Soft thread	
		216°F (102°C)	50%	Thread	Soft thread	
		220°F (104°C)	65%	Thread	Soft thread	
		234°F (112°C)	80%	Soft ball	Soft, flat ball	Crystalline
		237°F (114°C)	85%	Soft ball	Soft, flat ball	Crystalline
		240°F (116°C)	86%	Soft ball	Soft, flat ball	Crystalline
		248°F (120°C)	87%	Firm ball	Firm, pliable ball	Crystalline
		248°F (120°C)	87%	Firm ball	Firm, pliable ball	Noncrystalline
	1 tbsp (15 mL)	248°F (120°C)	87%	Firm ball	Firm, pliable ball	Aerated noncrystalline
1		250°F (121°C)	90%	Hard ball	Hard, pliable ball	Aerated noncrystalline
1		252°F (122°C)	92%	Hard ball	Hard, pliable ball	Aerated noncrystalline
		270°F (132°C)	95%	Soft crack	Hard, pliable thread	Noncrystalline
		290°F (143°C)	97%	Soft crack	Hard, brittle thread	Noncrystalline
		300°F (149°C)	98%	Hard crack	Hard, brittle thread	Noncrystalline
		300°F (149°C)	98%	Hard crack	Hard, brittle thread	Noncrystalline
		310°F (154°C)	99%	Hard crack	Hard, brittle thread	Noncrystalline
		315 to 335°F (157° to 168°C)	99+%	Very pale caramel		
		340 to 350°F (171 to 177°C)	100%	Light caramel		
		355 to 360°F (179 to 182°C)	100%	Medium caramel		
		365 to 380°F (185 to 193°C)	100%	Dark caramel		
		410°F (210°C)	100%	Black caramel		

concentration than amorphous ones. Crystalline candies are so named because crystals are allowed to form once the sugar syrup cools. Rock candy makes a dramatic example. Boil sugar syrup to about 248°F (120°C), insert a stick or string, and the sugar will naturally crystallize on the stick or string and the crystals will grow increasingly larger over several days. Other crystalline candies include pralines, fudge, and fondant.

Fondant is a smooth paste of fine sugar crystals made by extensive beating. Fondant can be rolled into a thin sheet and draped over cakes or it can be flavored and shaped to form the center of filled chocolates, thin mints, and other candies. These centers are often called candy "creams," which are loose fondants diluted with thin sugar syrup or water.

Fudge is fondant with added milk, cream, and/or butter (and often chocolate). These ingredients interfere with the syrup's tendency to crystallize, so fudge doesn't need to be beaten as much as fondant to create fine crystals and a creamy texture.

Amorphous candies have a higher sugar concentration and little to no crystallization (hence the name "noncrystalline"). Amorphous candies include lollipops, sour balls, butterscotch, nut brittles, caramel, dulce de leche, toffee, taffy, marshmallows, and gumdrops. Precise sugar concentrations and added ingredients play a major role in determining the final texture of these candies.

Lollipops and other transparent hard candies are the most recognizable amorphous candies. Sugar syrup is cooked and concentrated to about 99% sugar by weight, leaving only 1 to 2% moisture in the solution. A fairly high proportion of corn syrup (about ⅓ cup/75 mL corn syrup per cup/250 mL of sugar) is usually added for body and to help prevent recrystallization. But, more importantly, the thick, hot syrup cools rapidly. Quickly chilling hot sugar syrup immobilizes the sucrose molecules before they have a chance to bond with each other. Instead of crystallizing, the sucrose molecules harden into an amorphous mass that's transparent like glass. And, voilà, you have the hardness and transparency of a lollipop.

kitchen wisdom

Make Candy When It's Dry

Avoid making candy on rainy or humid days. Sugar pulls moisture from the air, and in damp conditions, evaporating moisture from a sugar syrup may take longer than expected and cooling the candy may be problematic. When the air is moist, even hard candies can remain soft because of all the moisture pulled into the candy by the sugar. To prevent softening, store candies with a desiccant such as pure blue silica gel or those sachets found in vitamin bottles.

To candy nuts with a crystalline coating, stir the nuts and sugar syrup constantly until the syrup crystallizes. To candy them with a smooth, noncrystalline coating, avoid stirring.

When making nut brittle, be sure the nuts are warm so that they don't cool the sugar syrup too quickly and prevent it from spreading easily.

Toffee, butterscotch, and brittle are also cooked to 99% sugar concentration (about 300°F/149°C), but they usually include a fair amount of butter, cream, or milk, so not as much corn syrup is needed to prevent crystallization. The milk proteins and fat enrich the candy and make it opaque instead of clear. As the milk proteins and reducing sugars brown from heat, they create deep, roasty flavors. The butterfat also smooths out the candy and makes it less chewy than, say, taffy. Brittles often include a bit of baking soda to neutralize acids created during browning, a process that generates carbon dioxide that leaves small bubbles in the candy (look closely at peanut brittle to see them).

Taffy, another noncrystalline candy, is cooked to only 95% sugar concentration (about 270°F/132°C). The additional moisture makes the syrup cool into a slightly softer candy, and it's opaque instead of transparent because it is pulled, stretched, and folded over and over to incorporate air bubbles, which make the candy easier to chew.

Caramel candies are usually cooked to about 87% sugar concentration (248°F/120°C), which leaves even more moisture in the candy and makes it softer and chewier. Like toffee and butterscotch, a fair amount of butter is added for richness, along with a generous amount of milk, cream, and/or sweetened condensed milk, which gives the candy body, creaminess, and flavor as the milk proteins and reducing sugars brown via the Maillard reactions. Baking soda is usually included to neutralize acids generated by **browning**. Caramels, taffy, toffee, butterscotch, and brittle don't need to be clear, so other sugars like brown sugar and molasses can be added along with the granulated sugar.

Nougat, torrone, divinity, and marshmallows are amorphous candies made light and chewy by aeration. For the first three, sugar syrup, sometimes including honey, is cooked to about 90% sugar concentration (250°F/121°C), then the hot syrup is beaten into aerated or whipped egg whites. As the syrup cools and begins to solidify, you end up with a cross between meringue and candy. Marshmallows are similar to nougat, except the syrup is cooked to only 87% sugar concentration, so there is more moisture in the final confection. Commercially made marshmallows often use gelatin for the foam instead of egg whites, resulting in a more firm, stable, and elastic foam structure.

Other amorphous candies include jelly beans, gummy worms, Turkish delight, and various Asian gel candies. To make them, cook the syrup to about 92% sugar concentration (252°F/122°C), then mix it with a solution of gelatin, pectin, starch, agar, or plant gums, which makes the candy dense and chewy when it cools. Pasty candies like marzipan and halvah fall into the amorphous family, too. To make them, cook sugar syrup, sometimes with honey, to about 87% sugar concentration (248°F/120°C), then beat it into a mixture of finely ground almonds (for marzipan) or sesame seeds (for halvah) and powdered sugar. Egg white or gelatin are sometimes whipped in to lighten the texture and set the paste.

See Also • Browning, Chocolate, Corn, Sugar

CANNING

What It Is •
A process of preserving food by boiling it in a container, canning was invented in 1809 by Nicolas Appert. Glass bottles were used by Appert, but in 1810, Pierre Durand improved the process by using cheaper, lighter, and more durable wrought-iron canisters (cans). Curiously, the can opener wasn't invented until 30 years later. Wars increased demand for canned food, generating the technologies necessary to mass-produce inexpensive canned goods like baked beans, chili, Spam, and Vienna sausage.

What It Does •
Canning creates a vacuum inside the jar or can, which removes oxygen, prevents the growth of undesirable microorganisms, and creates a hermetic (airtight) seal. Canning also destroys enzymes and changes the nutritional profile of some foods, but not much. Studies have found very few nutritional differences between canned, fresh, and frozen foods. Heat processing

science wise

Clostridium botulinum • Oxygen and acid inhibit the growth of the bacterium *Clostridium botulinum*, which thrives in air-free, low-acid environments. The bacterial spores can survive prolonged boiling at 212°F (100°C) but are killed at the pressure-canner boiling temperature of 240 to 250°F (116 to 120°C) used for most canned foods. However, if a jar or can of low-acid food is improperly processed, it could create an anaerobic, low-acid environment. Under these conditions, *C. botulinum* produces a powerful nerve toxin, botulin, causing botulism, that can be deadly to humans. The toxin blocks nerve function and can lead to respiratory and muscular paralysis. Scientists have capitalized on botulin's muscle-paralyzing ability for cosmetic purposes. Botox (a contraction of "botulinum toxin") may be injected to localized areas of the body in very small doses to block muscle contraction, which in turn inhibits wrinkling.

releases a small amount of the food's vitamin C into the canning liquid, but most other nutrients remain stable. In some cases, heat processing increases the availability of nutrients. Calcium is higher in canned fish, lycopene higher in canned tomatoes, and the fiber in canned beans becomes more soluble and useful to the body. Preservatives are not necessary in canned foods, but many include salt to improve flavor.

fast facts

- The standard "safe" shelf life of commercially canned foods is two years from the date of manufacture.
- The world's first can of beer was sold by Kreuger Beer in Richmond, Virginia, on January 24, 1935. Canning revolutionized the beverage industry. Compared to bottles, cans are lighter, more compact, more stackable, more durable, and quicker to chill.

How It Works • Heat processing turns all canned foods into cooked foods. The boiling temperature and processing time depend mostly on the food's acidity. Low-acid foods (above pH 4.6) like meat, poultry, fish, eggs, dairy, and most vegetables must be boiled in the can in a pressure cooker, which raises the boiling temperature to 240 to 250°F (116 to 120°C) and kills the spores of dangerous *Clostridium botulinum* bacteria. High-acid foods (below pH 4.6) like most tomatoes, fruits, and berries don't need such extreme canning temperatures because the acid itself inhibits the growth of *C. botulinum*. These high-acid foods can be simply hot-filled into containers at water's sea-level boiling point of 212°F (100°C). At higher altitudes, however, water boils at lower temperatures, requiring increased boiling time or a pressure cooker.

Canning may be done in glass jars or tin-coated steel cans. Most modern cans have two parts sealed by a double seam that creates an airtight seal. Jars and cans of food should be stored in a cool, dark, dry place for no more than a year, preferably at 50 to 70°F (10 to 21°C).

See Also • Bacteria, Pasteurization

CANOLA • See Oil

CANTALOUPE • See Melon

CAPE CAPENSIS • See Fish

CAPE GOOSEBERRY • See Fruit

CAPERS • See Flowers

CAPICOLA • See Pork

CAPON • See Chicken

CAPSAICIN • See Capsicum

CAPSICUM

What It Is • A New World discovery made in the 1400s by Columbus and Spanish explorers, capsicums comprise a huge family of at least 50,000 varieties of peppers, ranging from sweet bell peppers to blazing-hot habaneros. Capsicums come in a wide variety of colors (green, red, orange, yellow, and purple) and shapes (from short and blocky like bell peppers, to long and narrow like banana and Anaheim peppers, or tiny and round like tepín peppers). The principal difference between sweet and hot peppers is that sweet peppers have a recessive gene that prevents them from producing capsaicin, the spicy-tasting compound in hot peppers.

What It Does • When fresh, capsicums can be eaten raw in salads or cooked. They are often used in soups, stews, and sauces or hollowed out and stuffed. They can also be roasted, which concentrates their sweetness. Hot varieties are often chopped to create salsas, sambals, chutneys, chow-chows, and other condiments. They're frequently blended with other ingredients to make chile sauces, pastes, and a plethora of hot sauces such as Tabasco and Sriracha.

Once the joy of hot and spicy foods spread around the globe, hot capsicums, or chile peppers, became the most widely cultivated spice in the world. Chiles create signature

fast facts

- Black pepper and chile peppers are the world's two most popular spices, yet consumption of chile peppers outranks that of black pepper by 20 to 1.
- In the late 1980s, salsa surpassed ketchup as the condiment of choice in North America.
- Only mammals are affected by capsaicin. Birds are immune to it.

kitchen wisdom

Glove-Free Chile Chopping
To easily core and seed chile peppers without wearing rubber gloves, hold the uncut chile by its stem, then cut the flesh from the core and seeds. Continue cutting without touching the pepper.

flavors in Mexican, Latin American, Indian, and Asian cuisines.

Dried capsicums are often crushed to make chile flakes or ground into paprika (sweeter varieties) and cayenne pepper (hotter varieties). Ground capsicums are included in dozens of classic spice mixes around the world such as chili powder and curry powder. When smoke-dried, they create the deep flavor of Spanish pimentón and Mexican chipotle. In Mexico, dried chiles are often toasted, rehydrated, and puréed in various combinations to form numerous thick and richly flavored sauces such as mole. In the southwestern U.S., both fresh and dried varieties are cooked into a stew known as chili.

To prolong fresh peppers, it's best to store them at about 50°F (10°C) in the refrigerator in a loose plastic bag. They can also be frozen for a few months, which preserves the flavor fairly well but weakens the cell walls and softens the texture when thawed. As with other spices, the flavor of dried and ground capsicums fades with age, so replace your paprika, cayenne, and chile-containing spice mixes periodically.

Capsicums are high in carotenoids, which give the peppers bright colors. Like other richly colored vegetables, both sweet and hot peppers are high in vitamins A and C. They're also a decent source of folic acid, potassium, and vitamin E.

How It Works • As capsicum peppers mature, they change color from green to various shades of red, orange, yellow, and purple. Their fresh vegetable aroma comes from chemical compounds called pyrazines. Drying a capsicum concentrates its flavor and creates more complex aromas than found in the fresh pepper. When puréed or ground, both fresh and dried peppers have the ability to thicken sauces because their cell walls are composed of about 75% **pectin**, the same

Capsicum and Heat Levels

The massive variety of peppers grown around the world makes chile pepper nomenclature incredibly confusing. Here's a brief look at just a few of the varieties, their most common and alternative names; size, shape, and color; and heat level on the Scoville scale.

Fresh Pepper	Characteristics	Scoville Units
African Bird	½ to 1 inch (1 to 2.5 cm) long; blunt point; red	100,000 to 200,000
Anaheim (green California, red Colorado)	6 to 8 inches (15 to 20 cm) long, 1 to 1½ inches (2.5 to 4 cm) wide; blunt point; green or red	500 to 1,500
Banana (sweet)	5 inches (12.5 cm) long, 1 to 1½ inches (2.5 to 4 cm) wide; blunt point; pale yellow to orange-red	0 to 250
Bell (sweet)	4 to 5 inches (10 to 12.5 cm) long, 3 to 4 inches (7.5 to 10 cm) wide; bell or elongated bell shape; various colors	0
Bhut (Naga) jolokia	2 to 4 inches (5 to 10 cm) long, 1 inch (2.5 cm) wide; pointed; red	800,000 to 1,000,000
Cachucha	2 to 3 inches (5 to 7.5 cm) long, 1½ to 2 inches (4 to 5 cm) wide; bell shape; various colors	0 to 250
Cayenne (ginnie)	4 to 6 inches (10 to 15 cm) long, ½ inch (1 cm) wide; pointed; green or red	10,000 to 40,000
Cherry (Hungarian)	1 inch (2.5 cm) long, 1½ inches (4 cm) wide; cherry shape; green or red	100 to 500
Habanero	1½ inches (4 cm) long, 1 inch (2.5 cm) wide; lantern shape; yellow, orange, red, or green; fruity	100,000 to 500,000
Hontaka (Japones)	1 to 2 inches (2.5 to 5 cm) long, ¼ inch (0.5 cm) wide; pointed; red	15,000 to 30,000
Jalapeño	2 to 4 inches (5 to 10 cm) long, 1 inch (2.5 cm) wide; blunt point; green or red	5,000 to 10,000
Malagueta	1 to 2 inches (2.5 to 5 cm) long, ¾ inch (2 cm) wide; pointed; yellow-orange or green; fruity	8,000 to 30,000
New Mexico (green or red)	6 to 8 inches (15 to 20 cm) long, 1½ to 2 inches (4 to 5 cm) wide; blunt point; green or red	500 to 1,500
Peperoncini	3 inches (7.5 cm) long, ¾ inch (2 cm) wide; pointed; pale green to red	100 to 500
Pimiento	3 to 5 inches (7.5 to 12.5 cm) long, 2 to 3 inches (5 to 7.5 cm) wide; pointed bell shape; red	0 to 500
Poblano	4 to 5 inches (10 to 12.5 cm) long, 2 to 3 inches (5 to 7.5 cm) wide; dimpled pointed bell shape; dark green or red	1,250 to 2,500
Rocoto (manzano, péron)	2 to 3 inches (5 to 7.5 cm) long, 2 to 2½ inches (5 to 6 cm) wide; bell or lantern shaped; yellow-orange or red	20,000 to 50,000
Scotch bonnet	1½ inches (4 cm) long, 1 inch (2.5 cm) wide; lantern shape; yellow-green, orange, or red; fruity	200,000 to 325,000
Serrano	1 to 3 inches (2.5 to 7.5 cm) long, ½ inch (1 cm) wide; blunt point; green or red	10,000 to 25,000
Tabasco	1 to 1½ inches (2.5 to 4 cm) long, ¼ to ½ inch (0.5 to 1 cm) wide; blunt point; yellow-orange or red	30,000 to 50,000
Tepín (chiltepin)	½ inch (1 cm) diameter; round or oval; red	40,000 to 80,000
Thai	1 to 2 inches (2.5 to 5 cm) long, ¼ inch (0.5 cm) wide; pointed; various colors	15,000 to 30,000

gelling substance that allows other fruits to be made into **jam and jelly**.

As noted, hot varieties contain a heat-producing alkylamide compound called capsaicin, which is produced by the pepper's placenta, the white internal membrane or "core" that holds the seeds. From there, it migrates into the seeds and along the inner walls of the pepper in lesser amounts. The concentration of capsaicin in a chile pepper depends on variables in the plant's genetic makeup, growing conditions, and the pepper's ripeness. Hot and dry conditions increase the plant's capsaicin production, which peaks when the green fruit starts to mature and change color. The pungency of any capsicum is

Dried Pepper	Characteristics	Scoville Units
African Bird	½ to 1 inches (1 to 2.5 cm) long; blunt point; red	100,000 to 200,000
Ají Colorado (cuzqueño)	4 inches (10 cm) long, ¾ inch (2 cm) wide; pointed; red; fruity	30,000 to 50,000
Ají Panca (cuzqueño)	3 to 5 inches (7.5 to 12.5 cm) long, 1 inch (2.5 cm) wide; tapered point; ruddy brown; fruity	500 to 1,000
Aleppo (Halaby)	4 to 6 inches (10 to 15 cm) long, ½ inch (1 cm) wide; pointed; red	6,000 to 10,000
Ancho (dried poblano)	4 inches (10 cm) long, 3 inches (7.5 cm) wide; heart-shaped; reddish brown or mahogany; earthy and fruity	1,250 to 2,500
Arbol (de Arbol)	2 to 3 inches (5 to 7.5 cm) long, ¼ inch (0.5 cm) wide; pointed; shiny red; grassy	15,000 to 30,000
Cascabel (bola)	1½ inches (4 cm) diameter; round; reddish brown	1,250 to 2,500
Cayenne (ginnie)	2 to 4 inches (5 to 10 cm) long, ½ inch (1 cm) wide; pointed; shiny red	10,000 to 40,000
Chilcostle	3 to 5 inches (7.5 to 12.5 cm) long, ½ inch (1 cm) wide; pointed; deep red	3,500 to 5,000
Chilhuacle Rojo	2 to 3 inches (5 to 7.5 cm) long, 1½ inches (4 cm) wide; blunt point; reddish brown	1,250 to 2,000
Chipotle (smoked jalapeño)	2 to 4 inches (5 to 10 cm) long, 1 inch (2.5 cm) wide; blunt point; grayish chocolate brown	5,000 to 10,000
Guajillo	4 to 6 inches (10 to 15 cm) long, 1 inch (2.5 cm) wide; blunt point; shiny brownish orange-red	2,000 to 4,500
Habanero	1½ inches (4 cm) long, 1 inch (2.5 cm) wide; lantern shape; yellow, orange, red, or green; fruity	100,000 to 500,000
Mulato (dried poblano)	4 inches (10 cm) long, 2 to 3 inches (5 to 7.5 cm) wide; blunt point; chocolate brown	1,250 to 2,500
New Mexico (Anaheim or roasted green)	5 inches (12.5 cm) long, 1 inch (2.5 cm) wide; blunt point; brownish green	500 to 1,500
(Colorado or red)	6 inches (15 cm) long, 1½ inches (4 cm) wide; blunt point; red	1,000 to 2,500
Onza (rojo)	3 inches (7.5 cm) long, ½ inch (1 cm) wide; pointed; brick red	2,500 to 5,000
Pasilla (negro)	6 inches (15 cm) long, 1½ inches (4 cm) wide; blunt point; raisin brown	1,000 to 1,500
Pasilla de Oaxaca	4 inches (10 cm) long, 1 inch (2.5 cm) wide; blunt point; mahogany red	4,000 to 8,000
Pátzcuaro	5 inches (12.5 cm) long, 1 inch (2.5 cm) wide; blunt point; purplish red	3,000 to 8,000
Pico de Pajaro	1 inch (2.5 cm) long, ¼ inch (0.5 cm) wide; pointed; dark orange-red	40,000 to 80,000
Piquin (pequín)	½ inch (1 cm) long, ¼ inch (0.5 cm) wide; blunt oval point; orange-red	50,000 to 100,000
Piri piri (pili pili)	¼ to ½ inches (0.5 to 1 cm) long, ¼ inch (0.5 cm) wide; blunt point; red	30,000 to 60,000
Puya (pulla)	4 to 5 inches (10 to 12.5 cm) long, ¾ inch (2 cm) wide; pointed; purplish red	5,000 to 15,000
Serrano	1½ inches (4 cm) long, ½ inch (1 cm) wide; blunt point; orange-red	10,000 to 25,000
Tepín (chiltepin)	½ inch (1 cm) diameter; round or oval; red	40,000 to 80,000
Togarashi (ichimi)	½ to 1½ inches (1 to 4 cm) long, ¼ to ½ inch (0.5 to 1 cm) wide; pointed; red	10,000 to 40,000

measured on the Scoville heat scale, a system invented in the early 1900s by Wilbur Scoville, a chemist working for the Parke Davis pharmaceutical company. Today's chemists use high-performance liquid chromatography to analyze capsaicin concentration and express that concentration in terms of Scoville units. One drop of pure capsaicin in one million drops of water (1 ppm) is equal to 15 Scoville units. Sweet bell peppers measure zero on the Scoville scale, jalapeños average 6,000 units, and pure capsaicin clocks in at 16 million Scoville units. (For a list of fresh and dried capsicum and their approximate Scoville units, see Capsicum and Heat Levels chart, left and above.)

carambola

When capsaicin touches sensitive areas of your body, such as the mouth, lips, throat, tongue, eyes, and genitals, it creates a distinct burning sensation. It binds to nerve receptors that register heat and pain, causing those nerves to become hypersensitive and producing the same sensation you would get if you were actually burned. This triggers the release of pain-relieving endorphins in the brain, which produce a mild anesthetized feeling of well-being similar to that of opiates. If the compound is heated above 140°F (60°C), it becomes volatile and may irritate your nose and eyes. When consumed, capsaicin makes us feel warm, increases the body's metabolic rate, and stimulates blood flow and sweat. It also has antibacterial properties.

See Also ● Fruit, Spices, Vegetables

CARAMBOLA ● See Star Fruit

CARAMEL ● See Candy

CARAMELIZATION ● See Browning

CARAWAY ● See Spices

CARBOHYDRATE

What It Is ● Along with **protein**, **fat**, **water**, **vitamins**, and **minerals**, carbohydrates are one of the macronutrients absolutely necessary to sustain all life. Most carbohydrates are produced by plants, in which they comprise a large family of molecules including **sugar, starch**, cellulose (**fiber**), **pectin**, and **gums**. These molecules are "hydrates" of carbon (hence the name), organic compounds containing various arrangements of carbon, hydrogen, and oxygen atoms. In cooking and food production, carbohydrates like sugar, starch, pectin, and gums play various key roles.

What It Does ● The carbohydrates in our food come primarily from plants. Sugars sweeten our desserts and drinks; starches like wheat form the structure of our breads and noodles. In the kitchen, carbohydrates have a role to play in every course of the meal, from appetizer to dessert. For instance, starches gelatinize and thicken **sauces**. Other carbohydrates like sugar form solutions such as sugar syrup used to make **candy** and desserts. Carbohydrates like pectins form gels such as fruit **jams and jellies.** You can also create gels with plant gums like agar, carrageenan, and alginates, which are carbohydrates derived from **seaweed**. In commercial food production, gums such as xanthan gum and locust bean gum help to stabilize emulsions, creating smoother ice creams.

How It Works ● Carbohydrates are synthesized in plants from a complex series of reactions involving photosynthesis and **chlorophyll**. When we eat plant foods, carbohydrates are converted to glucose (blood sugar), our main source of energy. Our bodies convert carbohydrates into glucose at different rates. Whole-grain starches like barley are converted at a much slower rate than refined starches like white rice and white flour. And simple sugars like those found in candy are very rapidly converted to glucose. To rank which carbohydrate foods spike our blood sugar and which cause a more gradual rise, nutrition scientists developed a number system called the glycemic index. Many people, especially those with diabetes or who are overweight, use the index to make smart food choices.

See Also ● Alcohol, Diet, Fat, Fiber, Nutrition, Protein, Starch, Sugar

CARBONATION • See Carbon Dioxide

CARBON BONDING • See Chemical Bonding

CARBON DIOXIDE

What It Is • In its solid form, we know it as dry ice. But in food and cooking, carbon dioxide (CO_2) generally comes in the form of a colorless, odorless gas. Composed of two oxygen atoms bonded to a carbon atom, carbon dioxide is produced by all animals, plants, many fungi, and some bacteria as a result of everyday breathing and cellular respiration. Plants use the gas for photosynthesis in combination with **chlorophyll**.

What It Does • Open a bottle of champagne, beer, or soda and witness carbon dioxide in action. It's the gas that fizzes up and bubbles in our beverages. When yeast microorganisms ferment in bread dough, they produce carbon dioxide, creating thousands of tiny bubbles that cause the dough to rise. **Chemical leaveners** like baking soda and baking powder also release carbon dioxide gas when exposed to acidic ingredients like lemon juice or when heated. You can see the CO_2 at work when you mix baking soda and vinegar to create a "volcano" of bubbles, more commonly known as a **foam**.

Carbonation happens in two basic ways, naturally and artificially. In soft drinks, carbon dioxide gas is injected into liquid under pressure, where it dissolves and some reacts with water to form carbonic acid, which makes the soda taste slightly more sour and fills it with bubbles. Filtered beer and some sparkling wines are also artificially carbonated. Bottle-conditioned and cask-conditioned beer and Champagne, on the other hand, are naturally carbonated by the fermentation of yeast microorganisms, which produce carbon dioxide gas as a result of cellular respiration.

You can carbonate almost any food. In 2005, Fizzy Fruit entered the marketplace in an attempt to get kids more interested in eating healthful foods. The logic is that the fizz enhances the taste sensation of eating fruit, making it more attractive to kids in particular. There's no end to the food that can be fizzed. Sparkling yogurt, anyone?

How It Works • In our environment, carbon dioxide balances the ecology of plants and animals. Animals (and humans) inhale oxygen in the air, then exhale carbon dioxide, which is taken in by plants to help them survive, grow, and manufacture themselves into many of our foods. In turn, plants give off the oxygen necessary to the survival of animals.

See Also • Foams

CARBON STEEL • See Cookware, Knives

CARCINOGEN

What It Is • From the healthy oils in fish to the **antioxidants** in produce, many foods help protect us from cancer. But some substances found naturally in foods, a few by-products of cooking, and certain compounds used in food production may increase the risk of developing cancerous tumors. These carcinogens include mycotoxins such as aflatoxins produced on grains and nuts attacked by **fungi** as well as fruits and vegetables such as the betel nut and safrole from sassafras plants. Other potential carcinogens form primarily in meat or from high-heat cooking and include nitrosamines, heterocyclic amines (HCAs), polycyclic aromatic hydrocarbons (PAHs), and acrylamide.

What It Does

What It Does • Studies on laboratory animals have shown that excessive exposure to carcinogens from the environment (including from food) can damage DNA and may lead to the development of cancerous tumors, particularly those of the stomach and large intestine. Health organizations have set no upper limits for their consumption.

How It Works

How It Works • Nitrosamines develop in cured meats. Nitrites are added during **curing** to delay rancidity, create the pinkish red color of bacon and ham, and to inhibit the growth of dangerous C. *botulinum* bacteria, the cause of botulism (see Science Wise in **Canning**, page 93). Nitrosamines also develop from nitrates found in leafy vegetables.

Potentially carcinogenic nitrosamines are formed when these nitrites and the natural amino acids in meats interact in our stomachs or in high-heat cooking. To limit nitrosamine formation, U.S. food manufacturers are required to keep added nitrites below 120 parts per million. They're also required to add ascorbic acid (vitamin C) or erythorbic acid, which reduce nitrosamine formation. With these safeguards, nitrosamine risk is considered fairly low, but you can reduce nitrosamine risk even further by cooking bacon and other cured meats at low temperatures (below 300°F/150°C or over medium-low heat) and discarding the drippings.

Heterocyclic amines (HCAs) form when proteins in meat, fish, and poultry are exposed to high temperatures (350°F/180°C and above). Near a high flame, in a hot oven, in a skillet, or on the grill, amino acids in the meat react with each other or with creatine or creatinine (compounds found in muscle) and develop HCAs. These potential carcinogens concentrate in the crust and drippings of grilled, broiled, roasted, and fried meats. The American Institute for Cancer Research has shown that you can reduce HCA formation by marinating meats, cooking at lower temperatures, and cutting meats into smaller pieces so they cook faster and spend less time exposed to high heat.

Polycyclic aromatic hydrocarbons (PAHs) consist of more than 100 chemicals formed whenever you see smoke. In cooking, that typically means the smoke generated by wood fires or by dripping fat that incinerates in flare-ups. To reduce PAHs, limit your food's exposure to smoke. Grill over gas instead of wood or let your charcoal or wood fire burn down to glowing coals that emit very little smoke. It also helps to use woods that burn at lower temperatures, such as hickory and apple, instead of dense woods like mesquite, which produce more PAHs. Cook with less fatty cuts of meat and trim surface fat to reduce smoky flare-ups. As with HCAs, using small pieces of food reduces risk. Avoid trapping smoke by grilling with the lid up.

If you like making or eating smoked foods, consider using a smoker with a built-in filter to reduce PAHs. You can also use liquid smoke, a widely available "natural" product containing far fewer PAHs than actual smoke.

Acrylamide, a recently discovered food carcinogen, has less to do with meat and more with high heat. When starchy foods like bread, crackers, chips, and french fries are baked, fried, roasted, grilled, or otherwise cooked at high temperatures (350°F/180°C and above), sugars in the food react with the amino acid asparagine (which is especially high in potatoes) to form acrylamide. Only limited research has been done on acrylamide to date, but health experts see no cause for alarm. Acrylamide is not a new risk, and we've been eating bread and crackers for centuries. Nonetheless, cooks and food manufacturers can reduce acrylamide formation by adding asparaginase (a naturally occurring enzyme) in their starchy food preparations. Research also shows that potato chips and french fries cooked to a lighter color contain less acrylamide than darkly browned chips and fries.

Our gastrointestinal tracts contain several detoxifying enzymes and shed their layers continuously, helping to protect us from cancer. We also eat many foods containing cancer-

fast facts

fast facts

- The sun, the principal source of energy for life and food on Earth, emits ultraviolet radiation that can be carcinogenic to our skin in excessive amounts.
- Irradiated foods and those exposed to microwaves are not considered carcinogenic.

protective antioxidants. If you're concerned about cancer risk, limit your consumption of cured meat and foods cooked at high temperatures, and eat more antioxidant-rich fruits and vegetables. Also keep in mind that consuming excess calories overall increases cancer risk more than any carcinogen in food, according to the U.S. National Research Council.

See Also • Antioxidants, Irradiation

CARDAMOM • See Spices

CARDOON • See Thistles

CARIBOU • See Game

CARISSA • See Berries

CARNATION • See Flowers

CAROB

What It Is • Also known as locust bean and St. John's bread, carob comes from the evergreen carob tree (*Ceratonia siliqua*), which grows in hot, dry climates. The tree grows long green pods with sweet pulp that can be eaten fresh. When dried, the pods darken to a deep brown and resemble a wide vanilla pod. The pulp in the dried pods is often roasted and ground into a powder used in baking and candy making. Seeds in the pods are also used to make locust bean **gum**, a common thickener in commercially prepared dairy products like ice cream and cream cheese.

What It Does • For those allergic to chocolate, carob makes a viable alternative in baked goods and candies. Solid carob chips and bars can easily replace chocolate chips and bars. When replacing cocoa

fast fact

- The word "karat" used by jewelers and goldsmiths originates from the carob tree, which produces seeds of fairly uniform weight that became the standard for weighing diamonds and gold.

powder with carob powder, reduce the sugar in the recipe by 2 tablespoons (25 mL) and increase the fat by 2 tablespoons (25 mL). Because of its lack of fat, carob powder tends to create a slightly grainier texture in baked goods and candies.

How It Works • Carob powder contains more sugar and less fat than cocoa powder (about 40% sugar and 0.7% fat, compared to the 1% sugar and 8% fat in cocoa powder). For people concerned with stimulants like **caffeine** and theobromine (an alkaloid found in chocolate), carob makes a good alternative to chocolate. One hundred grams (about 3.5 ounces) of carob contains zero caffeine and about 3 mg of theobromine, whereas the same amount of chocolate contains 180 mg of caffeine and 2,320 mg of theobromine. Both carob and chocolate contain health-boosting flavonoid antioxidants.

See Also • Chocolate, Gums

CAROTENE • See Antioxidants

CARP • See Fish

CARRAGEENAN • See Seaweed

CARROT

What It Is • The carrot family encompasses a large group of **herbs** such as parsley, cilantro, dill, fennel, and chervil; **spices** such as coriander, cumin, dill, fennel, caraway, celery seeds, and aniseed; and such **roots** as parsnips, arracacha, and the orange vegetable so beloved by Bugs Bunny.

The taproots of annual plants, carrots (*Daucus carota*) come in more than 100 varieties, from 2-inch (5 cm) roots to 3-foot (90 cm) long batons that may be orange, yellow, white, red, purple, or black. Those in the orange-yellow spectrum tend to be grown in the West and contain high levels of carotene **pigments**. Those in the red-purple spectrum tend to be grown in Asia and contain high levels of anthocyanin pigments.

fast facts

- In the early 1600s, feathery wild carrot leaves (Queen Anne's lace) were fashionable hair and headdress decorations.
- In 2005, research showed that falcarinol, a natural fungicide in carrots, may reduce breast cancer risk.

What It Does • Carrots flavor countless stocks, soups, and stews in the form of mirepoix, a mixture of diced onions, carrots, and celery (usually in a ratio of 2:1:1). Crunchy raw carrots are popular in salads, and carrot juice is used in beverages and to flavor the cooking liquid for grains and poaching liquid for fish. With their high sugar content (as much as 5%), carrots are sometimes used to sweeten foods such as carrot cake and muffins. Cooking enhances a carrot's sweetness because heat destroys the root's cell walls, making its sugar more perceptible to our palates. If you like sweet carrots, the sweetest appear in the fall and winter, when cold weather causes plants to convert starches to sugars.

How It Works • A carrot's pine-like perfume and turpentine aromas come from **flavor** components called terpenes. High temperatures and excessive sun exposure can amplify these turpentine aromas. Most of a carrot's flavor concentrates in its storage cells around the center core, which is less flavorful because it merely functions to carry water from the roots to the leaves.

Orange carrots have more **antioxidant** beta-carotene than any other vegetable (28,100 International Units in 100 grams or about 3.5 ounces). Sweet potatoes come in second, with 20,100 IUs. Our bodies convert beta-carotene into the essential nutrient **vitamin** A. According to U.S. Department of Agriculture data, the orange carrots found in today's markets have more than twice as much beta-carotene as they did in 1950. Mature carrots have more beta-carotene than baby carrots. Beta-carotene levels are highest right under the carrot skin, so it helps to scrub but not peel carrots for maximum carotene retention. You'll also get more beta-carotene from cooked carrots than from raw ones. Cooking frees the antioxidant from the carrot's cells, making it easier for us to extract and absorb beta-carotene during chewing. Beta-carotene is very stable, so carrots retain their orange color even when prepared with acids or overcooked. If you consume extraordinary amounts of carrots or carrot juice, excess carotene pigment is stored in fatty tissue beneath your skin and can make your skin look more yellow.

Carrots also contain some anthoxanthin pigments, which are water-soluble and may discolor carrots cooked in cast-iron or aluminum. Anthoxanthins can react with these metals and create a blue color, which mixes with the yellow carotene pigment and results in a green hue.

See Also • Antioxidants

kitchen wisdom

Keep Them Crisp
Trim carrot tops (leaves) to prevent them from robbing the roots of moisture and hastening their deterioration. You can help revive limp carrots by soaking them in ice water for 30 minutes so they reabsorb some lost moisture.

CARTILAGE • See Bones

CASABA MELON • See Melon

CASCABEL CHILE • See Capsicum

CASEIN • See Milk

CASHEW • See Nuts

CASSAVA

What It Is • Most North Americans are familiar with "pearls" of tapioca used to make pudding and thicken pie fillings but are less familiar with the plant from which it comes. Also known as manioc and yuca, the hardy tropical cassava plant was domesticated in South America and migrated to tropical regions of Africa and Asia. Its **roots** can survive underground for up to three years and have become an important staple food in those regions. Two main types of cassava roots are used for food: bitter cassava (*Manihot esculenta*), a highly productive variety that is bitter-tasting and contains cyanogenic glycosides that are converted to toxic cyanide; and sweet cassava (*Manihot dulcis*), a less productive but safer variety found in most North American markets. Bitter cassava is usually leached of its toxins before being made into cassava meal, granules, flakes, or flour. In West African countries, it is fermented, roasted, and ground into flour called gari. Pearl tapioca and quick-cooking tapioca are made by moistening dried cassava, forcing it through sieves into small grains, then rotating the grains in pans until they form little balls, which are steamed until partially gelatinized and then dried. Sweet cassava is sold in its raw root form because it can be eaten safely after peeling and cooking. Cassava roots have a rough brown skin (sometimes with a waxy coating to prevent them from dehydrating) and average about 8 inches long by 2 inches in diameter (20 by 5 cm). The flesh inside is bright white, dense, and starchy.

What It Does • Raw sweet cassava roots can be peeled and cooked like potatoes. In its dried flour form, cassava can be used like wheat flour and often turns up as a thickener. Cassava-thickened mixtures will not break down when frozen like those thickened with wheat flour. In most recipes, about 4 teaspoons (20 mL) of cassava flour are added to 1 cup (250 mL) of liquid, brought to a simmer, then removed from the heat and left undisturbed until thickened (about 15 minutes).

Tapioca "pearls" are the small or large translucent, gelatinous spheres used to make traditional tapioca pudding and Asian bubble

Sweet Cassava Coconut Squares

Popular in Thailand, these gel-like squares are made from coconut milk thickened with freshly shredded cassava root. Most North American markets only sell sweet cassava in its raw root form, which is safe to eat without further preparation.

1	large cassava root (2 to 2½ lbs/ 1 to 1.25 kg)	1
1½ cups	coconut milk	375 mL
1	large egg	1
1	large egg yolk	1
1½ cups	granulated sugar	375 mL
½ tsp	vanilla extract	2 mL
¼ tsp	almond extract	1 mL
¼ tsp	ground allspice	1 mL

1. Preheat oven to 350°F (180°C) and butter a 9-inch (2.5 L) square pan. Peel cassava and shred on fine holes of box grater (you should have 3 to 3½ cups/750 to 875 mL). Transfer to a bowl and stir in coconut milk. Let stand for 10 minutes.

2. Stir in egg, egg yolk, sugar, vanilla extract, almond extract, and allspice. Spread into pan and smooth top.

3. Bake in preheated oven until lightly browned on edges and set yet soft like firm custard, 45 to 50 minutes. Let cool completely in pan on a wire rack. Cut into squares.

MAKES 25 SQUARES

tea. Quick-cooking or instant tapioca, more common in North American markets, is precooked tapioca used to thicken puddings and pie fillings.

How It Works • Cassava is higher in **starch** than many other roots (about 36% carbohydrate). In the ground, the storage cells of these roots swell with starch, eventually converting it to sugar, which allows the plant to survive hot, dry climates for extended periods. Bitter cassava contains another survival mechanism: cyanogenic glycosides that an enzyme converts to toxic hydrogen cyanide when the plant cells are ruptured. The bitter-tasting poison is meant to deter animals from eating the plant. Bitter cassava is made edible by leaching these toxins through soaking, boiling, fermentation, and/or air-drying.

When heated with liquids, cassava starch granules absorb moisture, swell, and thicken, a process known as gelatinization. Cassava starch gelatinizes at about 126 to 150°F (52 to 66°C), which is lower than most other starches, allowing you to thicken mixtures cooked at lower temperatures such as pie fillings that do not reach boiling temperatures in the oven. It also has a more neutral flavor than cornstarch, potato starch, and wheat flour.

See Also • Roots, Starch

CASSIA • See Spices

CASSIS • See Liqueur

CAST IRON • See Cookware

CATECHINS • See Grapes

CATFISH • See Fish

CAUL FAT • See Fat

CAULIFLOWER • See Cruciferous Vegetables

CAVENDISH BANANA • See Banana

CAVIAR

What It Is • Fish roe is available in two basic categories, hard roe (female eggs) and white or soft roe (the milt or seminal fluid of male fish). In North America, only eggs from sturgeon can be labeled simply "caviar." Other fish eggs must specify the fish from which they come, such as "salmon caviar." Traditionally, true caviar comes from wild sturgeon in the Caspian and Black seas. The three varieties include beluga, osetra, and sevruga, ranked in that order from largest size to smallest and highest quality to lowest. See Caviar Types and Characteristics chart, right, for other types of caviar.

The term *malassol* (Russian for "lightly salted") indicates that you're buying only 2.5 to 3.5% salt by weight and often appears on the finest caviar, taken early in the spawning season. "Pressed caviar" refers to ripe eggs taken late in the season, often

Caviar Types and Characteristics

Overfishing of wild sturgeon has led to caviar's dwindling availability, so eggs from other wild and farmed fish have become popular and generally referred to as "caviar." This chart describes each type of fish egg, gives its alternative names in the marketplace, and includes eggs from shellfish such as lobster and sea urchin.

Sources and Names	Characteristics
Bowfin (Cajun caviar, choupique)	Black, shiny, small, firm; turns red when heated
Capelin (masago)	Orange, somewhat translucent, very small; often served with sushi
Carp (tarama)	Light pink, very small; occasionally salted; puréed to make Greek taramasalata spread
Cod (tarako)	Pink, very small; salted and sometimes smoked; available as a paste in tubes
Flying fish (tobiko)	Red-orange (sometimes dyed black), small, crunchy
Grey mullet (Sardinian caviar, bottarga di muggine, tarama, karasumi)	Amber, small; often salted, pressed, and dried; puréed to make Greek taramasalata spread
Herring (kazunoko)	Yellow-pink, medium-size, rubbery; often pickled and sold in a shaped mass
Lobster (coral)	Coral pink when heated; small; often added to sauces
Lumpfish	Green (often dyed red, orange, or black), small, firm; salted and bottled
Paddlefish	Light to dark steel gray or golden, medium-size; lightly salted; rich, buttery taste
Pollock (mentaiko, momijiko, tarako)	Pink to dark red, very small; may be spiced with ground dried chile pepper (mentaiko), dyed red (momijiko), or salted and grilled (tarako)
Salmon (red caviar, ikura)	Red-orange, large, translucent, juicy; lightly salted; may be smoked; known as sujiko when sold as the whole ovary
Sea urchin (uni)	Red-orange to yellow, velvety soft; often served with sushi
Shad	Small roe swaddled in two oblong, translucent membranes
Smelt	Orange, small; somewhat crunchy; sometimes served with sushi
Sturgeon, *Acipenser gueldenstaedti* (osetra caviar)	Gray to brown, small; strong flavor; also includes the rare and superior golden brown grains of "golden," "Imperial," or "sterlet" caviar from the albino sturgeon of this species
Sturgeon, *Acipenser sinensis* (Mandarin caviar)	Grayish green, large; velvety, mildly sweet
Sturgeon, *Acipenser stellatus* (sevruga caviar)	Gray to reddish or greenish black, very small; very strong flavor
Sturgeon, American hackleback (Black pearl caviar)	Black, small, buttery; sweet
Sturgeon, American lake	Light to dark gray, large, soft; mildly sweet
Sturgeon, *Huso huso* (beluga caviar)	Light to dark gray-blue, large, velvety soft; mildly sweet
Trout	Golden brown-orange or yellow, large, firm, sticky; salty
Tuna (bottarga di tonno)	Amber, small; strong flavor; often salted, pressed, and dried
Whitefish (American golden caviar)	Pale orange or iridescent gold, small, crunchy; mild flavor; often smoked

damaged, and pressed together to hang and drain, which compacts them into a spreadable, jam-like consistency. It takes about 5 pounds (2.2 kg) of ripe eggs to make 1 pound (454 g) of pressed caviar, which often contains more salt than other varieties (up to 7%) yet costs about half as much. Pressed caviar is concentrated and has a stronger flavor than loose caviar.

Some fish eggs are pasteurized at 120 to 160°F (50 to 71°C) for one to two hours to improve their shelf life, which creates a slightly firmer, more rubbery texture, and greatly diminished flavor.

fast facts

- In the 1800s, caviar was served like today's salted peanuts — free of charge — to stimulate thirst and beer sales in American saloons.
- In recent years, the United Nations has begun to ban the export of wild-caught sturgeon caviar to help revive the species in the Caspian and Black seas. Farmed sturgeon caviar remains a viable and good-quality alternative.

What It Does • Due to its rarity, high-quality caviar is expensive (upwards of $150 an ounce/28 g) and almost always served simply on its own, perhaps with soft bread and butter or thin pancakes (blini) and sour cream.

Nutritionally, fish eggs are similar to other animal eggs but are richer in fat, cholesterol, and sodium. Three tablespoons (45 mL) of caviar (the volume equivalent of one chicken egg) contains about 120 calories, 9 grams fat, 282 mg cholesterol, and 720 mg sodium. A large chicken egg contains 75 calories, 5 grams fat, 213 mg cholesterol, and 63 mg sodium. Sturgeon and salmon caviar contain the highest levels of fat and cholesterol. Like other eggs (and fish), caviar is highly perishable and best stored on ice in the coldest part of the refrigerator right up until serving time.

How It Works • Brightly colored caviar appears orange, red, or pink from carotenoid **pigments**, while steely gray, brown, and black caviar is colored by melanin pigments. Apart from the richness of lipids in fish eggs, the defining taste of caviar comes from salt. Caviar was originally salted, like other foods, to preserve the eggs. Salting also creates a **brine** that plumps the eggs with moisture, increasing their juiciness. Salt firms up the caviar's surface, too, creating the contrast of a crisp "pop" in the first bite that releases the buttery, mouth-filling interior. Salt further enhances flavor by inducing protein-digesting enzymes in the egg to increase levels of flavorful amino acids in the caviar.

One downside to salt: it can react corrosively with such metals as silver and steel, creating off flavors in the caviar. Avoid metal spoons and dishes when serving fish eggs.

See Also • Eggs, Fish

CAYENNE • See Capsicum

CELERIAC • See Celery

CELERY

What It Is • Native to European wetlands, the wild celery plant (*Apium graveolens*) once tasted bitter and went by the name of smallage. In the 1600s, Italians bred the bitterness out of the plant, creating a cultivar with thicker stalks and a slightly paler green color (the *dulce* variety). The most popular North American variety is known as Pascal, while Europeans often prefer milder-tasting "golden celery" grown underground to prevent chlorophyll development. Asian celery (the *secalinum* variety) is a juicier, stronger-tasting cultivar with slimmer stalks, which produces highly aromatic seeds used as a spice.

Celery root, or celeriac, comes from the *rapaceum* variety, which expends more energy developing its roots than its stalks. Off-white with a crunchy texture, celeriac tastes slightly milder, sweeter, and more parsley-like than its pale green upper stalks.

What It Does • Celery stalks have a distinctive flavor that forms one-third of the Cajun "holy trinity" of aromatic vegetables (onions, celery, and bell peppers) and a part of the French mirepoix (onions, celery, and carrots). You'll also find the stalks filled with cream cheese, swizzled in Bloody Mary cocktails, chopped in Waldorf salad, and served alongside Buffalo chicken wings.

Celery stalks contain mostly water and fiber. The tough cellulose that supports the plant doesn't break down easily, so many cooks remove celery's fibrous "strings" prior to

Celery Root Strata with Chard and Gruyère

Eggs and milk help soften the sharp flavors of celery root. Here they form the basis of a layered brunch dish. For an easy breakfast, assemble the strata the night before, refrigerate it, then pop it in the oven the next morning. Celery root browns like an apple when cut so toss the cut pieces in a bowl of water with a few squeezes of lemon as you work to prevent browning.

1	celery root (about 1 lb/500 g), peeled and thinly sliced	1
4 cups	milk or light (5%) cream, divided	1 L
1 cup	chicken or vegetable stock	250 mL
1	bunch green chard, stems and leaves separated, each chopped	1
1	large clove garlic, minced	1
	A few sprigs fresh thyme	
¾ tsp	salt or to taste	4 mL
¾ tsp	freshly ground black pepper	4 mL
6	large eggs	6
2 tsp	Dijon mustard	10 mL
Pinch	grated nutmeg	Pinch
12	slices sourdough or firm white sandwich bread	12
2 cups	grated Gruyère cheese	500 mL

1. In a deep, wide sauté pan over medium heat, place celery root, 1 cup (250 mL) of the milk, stock, chard stems, garlic, and thyme. Simmer, stirring occasionally, until celery root is fork-tender, about 20 minutes. Remove and discard thyme stems (the leaves will have cooked into the vegetables). Stir in chard leaves and cook until wilted and most of the liquid evaporates, 3 to 5 minutes. Add ¼ tsp (1 mL) of salt and ¼ tsp (1 mL) of pepper. Taste and add more salt, if necessary, depending upon saltiness of stock used.

2. Preheat oven to 350°F (180°C). In large bowl, whisk together eggs, remaining 3 cups (750 mL) milk, remaining ½ tsp (2 mL) salt, remaining ½ tsp (2 mL) pepper, mustard, and nutmeg.

3. Line bottom of a shallow 3-quart (3 L) baking dish (such as a 13- by 9-inch/3 L dish) with 6 of the bread slices. Pour just enough egg mixture over bread to cover, spreading it out to coat bread completely. Spread chard filling evenly over top. Sprinkle with half of the cheese. Layer with remaining 6 slices bread. Pour remaining eggs over top, pushing on bread to thoroughly saturate it. Sprinkle remaining cheese on top. Bake in preheated oven until eggs are set and cheese is slightly browned on top, 45 to 50 minutes.

MAKES 10 TO 12 SERVINGS

cooking. You can also make celery more tender by growing the plant with plenty of water, tying the stalks together, and supporting the stalks with synthetic support structures.

Celeriac's knobby brown skin must be peeled and then the vegetable can be grated, shredded, or julienned and eaten raw, as in the French bistro favorite celery rémoulade (celery root in mustard mayonnaise). It can also be roasted, braised, sautéed, or incorporated into soups and stews. Cooking brings out the vegetable's sweetness. When mashed or puréed, celeriac becomes pleasantly creamy on its own and also makes a great addition to mashed potatoes.

Celery seeds are used in pickling spice mixes, to flavor salads, and ground to make up about one-third to one-half of celery salt.

How It Works • The aromatic celery stalk gets its pine and citrus **flavors** from volatile compounds called terpenes. Its sharp notes come from phthalides, the same compounds found in lovage and walnuts. The seeds of the celery plant taste bitter because of their essential oil (apiol); they also contain limonene (a terpene) and sedanolide

fast facts

- A celery stalk contains about 7 calories. Chewing and digesting fibrous celery may burn slightly more calories than that but not enough to cause significant weight loss.
- *Céleri bâtard,* French for "false celery," refers to lovage, a plant that is similar to celery.
- The flavor of celery is so distinctive that soft drink makers offer celery-flavored sodas such as Dr. Brown's Cel-Ray.

(a phthalide), which give them sharp citrus aromas that are similar to those of the stalk.

Generally, all parts of the celery plant are safe to eat. However, poorly handled celery stalks and celeriac can develop elevated levels of furocoumarins (psoralens), natural chemicals that can damage our DNA, cause dermatitis, and aggravate the skin's sensitivity to light. Psoralens develop when the plant gets extremely cold, is exposed to excess sunlight, or is infected by mold. They are celery's natual defense against insects. Psoralens mostly affect workers who handle celery daily, as they are absorbed through the skin as well as by eating. To avoid any risk, buy good-quality fresh celery stalks and celeriac and use them within a few weeks of purchase.

See Also • Chlorophyll

CELERY SEEDS • See Celery

CELLS

What It Is • Every plant and animal food that we eat consists of microscopic cells or compartments that form its structure and carry out its life-sustaining functions. From the outside in, these compartments consist of a thin, permeable plasma membrane that encloses the cytoplasm that contains the cytosol, a gelatinous fluid holding the cell's organelles, which perform the cell's vital functions such as respiration. The organelles and their **enzymes** include the nucleus (the site of DNA storage and replication); chloroplasts (for photosynthesis), and mitochondria (for respiration and energy generation); the ribosomes and endoplasmic reticulum (where proteins and fats are manufactured); and Golgi apparatus, lysosomes, vesicles, and vacuoles (which package components and regulate the cell's metabolism, development, and waste products). All plant and animal cells include some arrangement of these components in their tissues, but plant cells also have special cell walls outside the membrane that form the plant's structure. Animal cells lack cell walls, which allows the cells to change shape.

What It Does • A food's color, texture, and flavor are determined by its cell structure and substances contained within the cells, particularly in its vesicles and vacuoles. Colors come from various **pigments**. Textural components stem from protein, fat, and carbohydrates like cellulose (**fiber**), **starch**,

pectin, and **gums**. We taste **flavor** in the cell's **sugar**, **salt**, **acids**, savory amino acids (**proteins**), bitter alkaloids (**toxins**), astringent tannins, and other substances that we perceive as pungent. Aroma comes from a massive array of secondary metabolites such as terpenes, phenolics, and sulfurous compounds.

Preparing and cooking food can dramatically change its color, texture, and flavor on a cellular level. For instance, cutting raw beef slashes its cells and exposes its purple myoglobin pigments to oxygen, which changes their color from purple to red. Cutting an apple slashes its cells and exposes the fruit's enzymes to oxygen, which creates melanins that make the apple appear brown instead of white (enzymatic browning). Heat causes multiple cellular changes, too. Sautéing an onion (or any vegetable) damages its cell membranes starting at about 140°F (60°C), causing the vegetable to lose its primary component — water — and go from firm and juicy to increasingly soft and dry. At temperatures above 330°F (166°C), carbohydrates and amino acids released from the cells begin to undergo Maillard **browning** reactions and develop hundreds of savory flavor compounds. Cooking also makes a cell's flavor components more easily perceptible by our taste buds, destroying some nutrients and making others more available to our bodies.

How It Works • Most cells are about 70% water, which fills the cell structure, plumping up plants and animals into the shapes we see.

kitchen wisdom

How to Maintain Firmness
Some fruits and vegetables, such as apples, cherries, tomatoes, beans, beets, potatoes, sweet potatoes, carrots, and cauliflower, can resist the softening of cell walls that occurs during prolonged cooking. To keep these foods from getting too soft during the long cooking of a sauce or stew, start them out at a relatively low temperature (130 to 140°F/54 to 60°C or about medium-low heat) for 20 to 30 minutes, which will activate an enzyme (pectin methylesterase) in the vegetable's cell walls that causes firming of the plant tissue.

fast fact

• The head of a pin is about 2 millimeters in diameter. The average human cell is about 0.0505 millimeters in diameter. The average bacterial cell is about 10 times smaller than the average human cell.

Plant cells tend to have one large vacuole that fills with water, creating 90% of the cell's volume and giving the plant its full shape or "turgidity." Since juicy foods taste better than dry foods, a big part of food preparation and cooking involves managing the flow of water in and out of the cells. For instance, meats dry out during cooking as their muscle cells shrink and squeeze out the water they contain. But muscle cells can also absorb water through **brining**, a process that actually increases a cell's ability to hold water, making meats taste juicier when fully cooked. Plant cells can lose or absorb water, too. Cut and cook an onion and it softens as its cells break down and leak water. But soak a limp flower or celery stalk in ice water and its cells swell with water, regaining some of their former firmness. Various preparation techniques also change a food's cells, altering the food's texture, flavor, and aroma. Puréeing vegetables, for instance, dismantles their cell walls, releasing carbohydrates that bind with water, creating a smooth and fluid form of the original food.

See Also • Browning, Enzyme, Genetics

CELLULOSE • See Fiber

CELSIUS • See Heat

CEPE • See Mushrooms

CEPHALOPOD

What It Is • Cephalopod means "head-foot" and describes how the feet, or tentacles, of these marine **mollusks** are attached to their head. Octopus, squid, and cuttlefish are the most common culinary cephalopods,

fast facts

- Cephalopods are widely considered the most intelligent invertebrates because of their comparatively large brains and well-developed senses.
- Cuttlefish ink was once used to create the color sepia. Squid ink is often used to color pasta.

each of which contains ink sacs that release blue-black or brown-black pigments to befuddle their predators. Cephalopods share some of the same features as mussels, oysters, scallops, clams, and other mollusks, but instead of an outer shell, they have a softer internal shell called a pen, quill, or cuttlebone. Sucker-covered tentacles and arms help the animal move. Octopuses, squid, and cuttlefish also have special skin cells called chromatophores that allow them to change color for camouflage or communication.

What It Does ● The Japanese eat about 60% of the world's octopus catch. Octopus is available fresh or cleaned (eyes, mouth, and viscera discarded) and frozen. Squid may be sold fresh, frozen, canned, dried, or pickled. Squid innards are easily removed, leaving the tubular body that is often stuffed. The body of squid (calamari) can also be cut crosswise into rings and fried or stewed. Cuttlefish are available fresh or seasoned and roasted (sarume). Of the three, cuttlefish are the sweetest and most tender.

All cephalopods move by expanding and contracting their mantle (body tube) and squirting water from their heads, a process that requires extremely strong muscle fibers. This means that octopuses, squid, and cuttlefish consist mostly of tough, finely textured muscle fiber and connective tissue. Octopus has the toughest texture and cuttlefish the most tender. Baby octopus needs no tenderizing, but mature octopus flesh is so tough that it is often tenderized before cooking by pounding or blanching in salted water several times. The general rule for making any cephalopod edible is to keep the cooking very short or to make it very long — but not in between. Quick-cooking methods like grilling and frying as well as slow, moist-heating cooking methods like simmering for one hour or more will render an octopus, squid, or cuttlefish tender. Anywhere in between makes it tough. For tough cephalopods like large octopus, starting with a frozen product rather than fresh helps make it more tender because the water in the animal freezes and forms expanding ice crystals that stretch the tough cell walls, softening them so that they are easier to chew when cooked.

How It Works ● Octopuses, squid, and cuttlefish are pleasantly chewy when quickly cooked to a temperature of about 130°F (54°C). When they reach 140°F (60°C), their connective tissue shrinks and contracts, making the meat tough and chewy. After prolonged cooking of more than an hour, the connective tissue softens and the collagen turns into gelatin, giving the cephalopods a more tender, gelatinous texture similar to that of slow-cooked meats like brisket.

See Also ● Meat, Mollusks

CERAMIC • See Cookware

CHALAZAE • See Eggs

CHALLAH • See Bread

CHAMPAGNE • See Wine

CHANTERELLE • See Mushrooms

CHAPATI • See Bread

CHAR • See Fish

CHARCOAL • See Grilling, Liquor, Stove

CHARD • See Leaves

CHARENTAIS MELON • See Melon

CHAROLI NUTS • See Nuts

CHARRING

What It Is • Food that is slightly charred and just shy of burned can have intense flavors. Charring is essentially the severe **browning** of food, wood, or other biological matter that turns it black. Charring is occasionally used for flavor in cooking, but it's primarily used to make charcoal for **grilling**.

What It Does • Charring food creates a slightly bitter flavor and crunchy texture. Bits of char, or carbonized material, can be pleasant in small amounts on a grilled steak, for instance. Charring also makes it much easier to start a wood fire because charred wood (charcoal) ignites more readily than raw wood.

How It Works • Charring exposes foods or woods to such extreme temperatures or such extended periods of heat that it evaporates moisture and most other compounds in the tissues. The tissues become devoid of hydrogen and oxygen, leaving behind only carbon, ash, and traces of volatile compounds.

See Also • Browning, Carcinogen, Grilling

CHARTREUSE • See Liqueur

CHAURICE • See Sausage

CHAYOTE • See Squash

CHEDDAR • See Cheese

CHEESE

What It Is • If you've never tried Swiss Appenzeller cheese, give it a taste. Humans have been eating it since the Middle Ages. Cheeses like Appenzeller are jewels in our culinary crown, members of a dazzling family of foods made simply by curdling **milk**, draining off the liquid, then controlling the way the solid curds age.

First and foremost, cheese is milk. The kind of milk (cow, sheep, goat, water buffalo, etc.), the animal breed and its feed, and the milk's handling (raw or **pasteurized**, curdled with acid or enzymes) all affect the final flavor, texture, and nutritional composition of cheese. For instance, buffalo milk and sheep's milk are higher in fat and protein than cow's milk and goat's milk. That makes buffalo and sheep milks best for creamy cheeses like *mozzarella di bufala* and Italian ricotta. Goat

Charred Brussels Sprouts

Completely burnt foods taste overly bitter and unpleasant. But small amounts of char can heighten the taste and texture of food. In this recipe, Brussels sprouts are quickly cooked over fairly high heat in a sauté pan, which prevents the sprouts from developing unpleasant sulfurous compounds. It also creates a layer of slightly bitter char on the sprouts that balances the concentrated sweetness of the balsamic vinegar. The recipe is adapted from a more elaborate dish served by chef Marc Vetri at his eponymous restaurant in Philadelphia.

18 to 20	small Brussels sprouts, root ends trimmed	18 to 20
1 tbsp	olive oil	15 mL
1½ tsp	best-quality balsamic vinegar	7 mL
2 tbsp	butter	25 mL
	Kosher salt and freshly ground black pepper	

1. Cut sprouts in half through stem. Heat oil in a large sauté pan over high heat. When hot, add sprouts and shake to coat with oil. Turn sprouts cut-side down and cook undisturbed until deeply browned (almost black) on cut sides, 6 to 8 minutes. Add vinegar and toss to coat sprouts (vinegar will evaporate). Reduce heat to low, turn sprouts cut-side down, and cook until tender when pierced, 3 to 4 minutes more. Stir in butter and season with salt and pepper.

MAKES 4 SERVINGS

milk tends to be lower in fat and protein, making it more suitable for crumbly logs and disks of cheese. Cow's milk occupies the middle ground.

The milk alone shows you why chèvre tastes so different from Swiss cheese. It also explains why cheese made from **soy** milk has a completely different taste than cheese made from the milk of mammals. But before cheese is even made, the way the milk is handled changes the final product. In France, Switzerland, and Italy, government regulations require cheese makers to use raw, unpasteurized milk to guarantee the authenticity and quality of great cheeses like Brie, Camembert, Emmental, Gruyère, and Parmesan. The enzymes and bacteria in raw milk create the flavorful compounds that form the defining tastes of these cheeses. In Canada, the sale of raw milk cheeses has been banned since the 1930s, but they are widely available. The U.S. Food and Drug Administration allows the manufacture and sale of raw milk cheese as long as it is aged for at least 60 days at a temperature not lower than 35°F (2°C) to reduce the number of pathogenic bacteria.

In recent years, the World Health Organization (WHO) has considered a worldwide ban on the production and sale of raw milk cheeses to protect people — at least in theory. Part of the problem is that large-scale industrial cheese-making pools milk from thousands of animals. Pasteurization is the only practical way to prevent a contaminated batch of milk from infecting thousands of pounds of cheese. However, small-scale, nonindustrial cheese producers like many in Europe and the artisanal cheese makers in North America are better equipped to assess the health of their smaller herds. Perhaps artisanal cheese makers deserve alternative measures such as certification that will preserve not only the safety but also the quality of cheeses that have been made with raw milk for hundreds of years.

How Cheese Is Made

It takes about 10 pounds (4.5 kg) of cow's milk or goat's milk to make 1 pound (454 g) of cheese. If you use richer sheep's milk, it only takes about 6 pounds (2.7 kg). The entire cheese-making process isolates the milk proteins and fat and then uses microorganisms to develop flavor and texture in the cheese. The first step is coagulation of the particles (micelles) of the major milk protein, casein, causing them to bond to one another in a matrix, forming a soft yet solid curd trapping fat globules, fat-soluble vitamins, and several minerals. Milk caseins are coagulated by acid or an enzyme or a combination. A bacterial culture containing *Lactococcus*, *Lactobacillus*, or *Streptococcus* may be added to the raw or pasteurized milk to convert lactose in the milk to lactic acid and other metabolic by-products, which help the milk to coagulate. Milk can also be coagulated, or "set," with an enzyme called chymosin (or rennin), which occurs naturally in rennet, the stomach lining of a calf. This natural rennet is required for many traditional semifirm and hard European cheeses like Parmesan, but most North American cheeses are coagulated with chymosin from genetically engineered bacteria. Plants like cardoon thistles, fig tree bark, and mallow, which have a similar coagulating effect on milk, can also be used. **Acids** from lemon juice or vinegar (citric or acetic acid, respectively), which form a finer, softer curd more suitable to soft cheeses like cottage cheese, can be added directly. By whatever means it is formed, the curd floats in liquid whey, a mixture of milk sugar (lactose), whey proteins, and water-soluble vitamins and minerals. At this point in the

fast facts

- Evidence of cheese making has been found in Egyptian tombs dating from 3000 to 2800 BCE.
- Cows milked in the evening generally give milk that's higher in fat content (best for cheese making) than cows milked in the morning.
- In well-ripened cheeses like blue, Cheddar, and Swiss, the milk proteins are broken down into tyramine and histamine, two compounds that cause blood pressure spikes and headaches in some people.

Guide to Cheese Styles

Here's a snapshot of cheese styles based on cheese-making method. Note that some cheeses fall into more than one category. For instance, Cambozola, a hybrid of Camembert and Gorgonzola, is surface-ripened but it's also a blue cheese.

Cheese-making Method	Cheese	Milk
Fresh	Asadero (queso Oaxaca)	Cow
	Boursin	Cow
	Chèvre, unaged	Goat
	Cottage	Cow
	Cream	Cow's milk and cream
	Farmer cheese (hoop cheese)	Cow
	Feta	Sheep, goat, or cow
	Haloumi	Sheep, goat, and/or cow
	Mascarpone	Cow's milk and cream
	Mozzarella	Cow or buffalo
	Myzithra, unaged	Goat or sheep
	Neufchâtel	Cow
	Paneer	Cow or buffalo
	Quark	Cow
	Queso fresco (blanco, Panela)	Cow
	Ricotta	Sheep or cow
	Robiola Piemonte	Cow, goat, and/or sheep
	Yogurt cheese	Cow
Surface-Ripened	Brie	Cow
	Brillat-Savarin	Cow
	Camembert	Cow
	Chèvre (Bucheron)	Goat
	Explorateur	Cow
	Teleme	Cow
Washed Rind	Époisses de Bourgogne	Cow
	Esrom (Danish Port Salut)	Cow
	Handkäse	Cow
	Limburger	Cow
	Livarot	Cow
	Maroilles	Cow
	Muenster	Cow
	Oka	Cow
	Pont-l'Évêque	Cow
	Port Salut	Cow
	Reblochon	Cow
	Taleggio	Cow
Natural Rind	Caerphilly	Cow
	Fourme d'Ambert	Cow
	Gamonedo	Cow, sheep, and goat
	Gloucester	Cow
	Grana Padano	Cow
	Havarti	Cow
	Manchego	Sheep
	Pecorino Romano	Sheep
Blue-Veined	Cabrales	Cow, goat, and sheep
	Danish Blue	Cow
	Gorgonzola	Cow
	Roquefort	Sheep
	Stilton	Cow
Pressed, Uncooked	Cheddar	Cow
	Chihuahua	Cow
	Derby (Sage)	Cow
	Kashkaval	Sheep
	Kasseri	Sheep
	Kefalotyri	Sheep
	Morbier	Cow
	Tomme de Savoie	Cow
Pressed, Cooked	Appenzeller	Cow
	Emmental	Cow
	Fontina Val d'Aosta	Cow
	Gouda	Cow
	Gruyère	Cow
	Idiazábal	Sheep
	Parmesan	Cow
Pasteurized Process	American	Cow

Guide to Cheese Texture

The moisture content of cheese helps to determine its texture. But even a single style of cheese such as provolone can range widely in moisture content depending on how long it is aged. For that reason, the figures below are approximate. They come from the U.S. Food and Drug Administration's maximum moisture and minimum fat percentages for cheese composition. Other countries have different standards, but these figures give you a good idea of how a cheese's moisture content translates into texture.

Moisture (%)	Milk Fat (%)	Texture	Cheese
80	4	Soft	Cottage cheese
80	0.5	Soft	Cottage cheese, dry curd
60	45	Soft	Mozzarella
55	33	Soft	Cream cheese
52	0	Soft	Gammelost
52	30	Soft	Mozzarella, part-skim
50	50	Semisoft	Limburger
46	50	Semisoft	Muenster
45	50	Semisoft	Roquefort
45	45	Semisoft	Provolone
45	40	Semisoft	Edam
44	50	Semisoft	Monterey Jack
43	47	Semisoft	American pasteurized process
42	50	Semisoft	Gorgonzola
41	43	Semifirm	Emmental (Swiss)
40	42	Semifirm	Caciocavallo
39	50	Semifirm	Cheddar
39	45	Semifirm	Gruyère
38	10	Hard	Sapsago
32	32	Hard	Parmesan

process, colorants are sometimes added to the milk to create an orange color in the cheese. Early on, carrot juice and marigold petals were used, but cheeses like Cheddar, Cheshire, and Leicester are now colored with annatto seed (achiote) extract.

Next, the solid curd is concentrated by draining off the liquid whey. Fresh cheese like cottage cheese is simply drained and salted, leaving the moist curd in clumps, perhaps with cream added. For semifirm and hard cheeses, the curd may be repeatedly drained, cut into smaller and smaller grains, drained again, and sometimes pressed to remove even more moisture. The protein-rich curd is used to make the majority of cheeses. However, the liquid whey also contains protein and can be made into soft whey cheeses like Italian ricotta and Norwegian mysost (primost), and gjetost.

For most cheeses, the curd is then heated (up to 135°F/57°C for semifirm and hard cheeses like Emmental and Parmesan). Heating helps to tighten the curd to drain off more whey and develop some flavor among the beneficial bacteria and enzymes in the curd. The cooked curd is poured into perforated forms to shape the cheese and drain it further. Most cheese is then salted, either by dry-salting the surface (as for Cheddar) or by soaking the cheese in brine (as for feta). Salting retards the growth of undesirable microorganisms and concentrates the curd by drawing out moisture and firming up the proteins.

The final step is aging, or ripening, the cheese, known as affinage. At this point, the cheese may have certain strains of bacteria, mold, or yeast added that generate many flavor-producing enzymes. The finest cheese makers, or affineurs, tend the cheese under climate-controlled conditions such as a ripening room or a cave to regulate the temperature and humidity. During aging, the affineur may brush the cheese to keep the surface or rind clean, flip the cheese to redistribute minerals, or wash the rind with wine, brandy, or other flavored liquids to keep it moist.

Cheese Styles

Slight alterations in the basic cheese-making steps create thousands of different cheeses around the world. Ripening is especially important because the particular microorganisms added during aging will affect the final taste and texture of the cheese. As the cheese's surface or rind develops, it may be left alone, exposed to specific organisms, washed with flavored liquid, or covered with leaves, herbs, ash, cloth, wax, fat, foil, or plastic to develop flavors and/or to prevent moisture loss, spoilage, and damage. It's useful to categorize various styles by cheese-making method.

Fresh: Cream cheese and cottage cheese are called fresh because they are uncooked and unripened or only slightly ripened. Fresh cheeses are usually soft and mild (perhaps slightly tart) with no rind. Fresh cheese is usually eaten within a few days.

Pasta filata: For cheeses like mozzarella, provolone, scamorza, caciocavallo, and kashkaval, the curd is dipped in a bath of hot whey (about 140°F/60°C) to soften it so that it can be kneaded, stretched, and pulled into strands by hand or machine. This process creates a "spun paste" or pasta filata that is pliable enough to be shaped.

Surface-ripened or bloomy rind: These cheeses are exposed to various molds or bacteria so that they ripen from the outside in. For instance, Brie and Camembert are exposed to *Penicillium camemberti* mold, and Limburger is exposed to *Bacterium linens* bacteria. Excess organisms are brushed or washed off during ripening. These soft-ripened cheeses are often broadly disk-shaped to maximize surface area for the bacteria to develop. They usually have a thin rind with a white, downy surface and a soft, oozing layer just below the rind. They may be mild and buttery or strong and stinky.

Washed-rind: During ripening, these cheeses are washed or rubbed with brine, cider, wine, beer, grape brandy, or other liquids to create various flavors.

Natural rind: The rinds of these cheeses are not exposed to mold, bacteria, or flavored liquids. Instead, they are allowed to develop naturally. The natural rinds are kept clean and tend to be thin. Natural-rind cheeses are usually well aged, so the cheese becomes rather dense.

Blue-veined: Blue cheese is usually inoculated with *Penicillium* molds and deeply pierced to provide air circulation, which allows the mold to develop throughout the cheese. Gorgonzola is inoculated with *P. glaucom*, while Roquefort, Danish Blue, and Stilton are inoculated with *P. roqueforti*. These cheeses vary widely in tartness, intensity, and creaminess.

Pressed, uncooked: For cheeses like Cheddar and Morbier, the curd is pressed but not heated to create cheeses with a semisoft to semifirm texture.

Pressed, cooked: To make cheeses like Emmental and Parmesan, the curd is heated and then pressed, which greatly concentrates the flavor and texture.

Pasteurized process: Cheeses like American are made from a blend of fresh and aged cheeses that are shredded and mixed with colors, gums, stabilizers, and emulsifiers to create a smooth, easy-melting, or spreadable cheese with a long shelf life. James Kraft patented the method for making process cheese in 1916.

Moisture and Texture

As a cheese ages, it loses moisture and concentrates in flavor and texture. For that reason, moisture content makes a good barometer of whether a cheese will be soft or hard. See Guide to Cheese Texture chart, left, for popular cheeses arranged by moisture content.

Cheese tends to be soft, creamy, crumbly, or chewy, but sometimes a cheese can be crunchy. Hard Parmesan, crumbly Roquefort, and even good melters like Cheddar can develop crunchy-tasting crystals of calcium phosphate or calcium lactate. These crystals remain because the ripening bacteria used to make the cheese reduce either the cheese's acidity or its moisture, leaving the crystals intact.

What It Does • Heat causes most cheeses to melt. When you continue to heat cheese beyond its melting point, it gets increasingly dry, and browning reactions occur in the milk proteins, creating deep caramelized flavors. As the cheese is heated, it begins to soften, and beads of fat form on the surface. Then

the bonds that hold the milk protein together begin to collapse, and the cheese melts into a pool of liquid. How well a cheese melts depends mostly on its moisture and fat content. Dairy fat begins to melt at about 90°F (32°C), but if there isn't much fat in the cheese, it won't melt well. Soft cheeses like Brie that are high in moisture and fat melt easily as soon as they are warm (about 130°F/54°C). Semifirm cheeses like Cheddar and Swiss start to ooze at about 150°F (66°C), and hard, dry grating cheeses such as Parmesan don't soften until temperatures get above 180°F (82°C). Some low-moisture, low-fat cheeses like fresh goat cheese, queso blanco, sheep's milk ricotta, and paneer don't melt at all. Any cheese curdled with acid instead of rennet won't melt because water easily evaporates from the weak curd, the proteins readily bond together, and, in the absence of moisture, the cheese dries out instead of melting.

Most cheeses high in moisture, fat, acid, and/or salt will melt well. A high proportion of these components helps to prevent the milk proteins from bonding to one another and keeps the cheese smooth as it is heated. If cheese gets unpleasantly stringy when heated, it means that the milk proteins are bonding together. To avoid stringy melted cheese, keep the milk proteins from bonding by grating the cheese finely, adding it over low heat or no heat, and stirring gently or not at all just until the cheese is melted. You can also prevent stringiness by adding an acid ingredient such as white wine (tartaric acid), the trick behind classic Swiss fondue. Better yet, add lemon juice (citric acid). Starch works, too. In a cheese sauce, for instance, the starch in the flour, cornstarch, or arrowroot will coat the protein and fat in the cheese, keeping the proteins separate so that the cheese melts smoothly. That's why Gruyère works so well in classic French Mornay sauce and Fontina in Italian fonduta.

Nutrition, Storage, and Serving

As it originates from milk, cheese is mostly protein and fat. The saturated fat in cheese may raise blood cholesterol in certain individuals, but many low-fat and skimmed milk varieties are available. Cheese also tends to be high in beneficial nutrients like calcium, phosphorus, and vitamin A. Lactose-intolerant people can tolerate cheese but not milk, because most of the lactose in milk stays in the whey during cheese making, not in the curd that's used to make cheese. Of course, "whey cheeses" like ricotta can pose problems.

Most cheese should be stored in the warmest part of your refrigerator (usually the door) or in a cool basement, preferably at about 55 to 60°F (13 to 16°C) so it can continue ripening slowly. The less moisture in the cheese, the longer it will last. Hard, low-moisture cheeses (30 to 40% moisture) like Parmesan can last for several months because there is very little moisture for bacteria to proliferate. On the other hand, fresh, high-moisture cheeses (70 to 80% moisture) like cottage cheese provide ample moisture for bacteria to grow and last only a few days. Soft and semisoft cheeses (45 to 55%

moisture) like mozzarella, Roquefort, and Monterey Jack last a few weeks, and semifirm cheeses (40 to 45% moisture) like Emmental, Cheddar, and Gruyère last a few months.

Fully ripened mass-produced cheeses can be tightly wrapped in plastic wrap, aluminum foil, or waxed paper. But still-ripening artisanal cheeses like surface-ripened Brie or blue-veined Cabrales should be left loosely wrapped or unwrapped. As the cheese ages, it may develop some harmless mold that is easily scraped away. But if you notice an unusual mold, fetid odor, or slime, throw the cheese away. Rarely, cheese will develop toxin-bearing *Aspergillus versicolor*, *Penicillium viridicatum*, or *P. cyclopium*, molds that can penetrate about 1 inch (2.5 cm) into cheese and can't simply be scraped off.

For the best flavor, all cheese should be removed from the refrigerator and warmed up in its wrapper before it is eaten. About 40 to 60 minutes at room temperature will bring out its full flavor. Eating the rind is mostly a matter of personal preference. Some cheeses, such as those that are waxed, have inedible rinds.

How It Works • There are more than 400 flavor compounds in Cheddar cheese. Just imagine how many there are in more complex cheeses like Époisses! The flavor compounds in any cheese come from the milk itself as well as from chemical reactions that occur during cheese making and ripening. Cheese scientists have been isolating and examining these compounds for years. We've known for centuries that cow's milk tends to make mild-tasting cheese, sheep's milk makes tangier cheese, and goat's milk even tangier and more earthy-tasting cheese. But now we also know that animals with a more diverse diet produce milk and cheese with more complex flavors. Cows pastured in alpine regions eat a variety of flowers and grasses that contribute pleasant flavors from compounds like carvone and citronellol. Animals grazed on summer's diversity of plants produce more full-flavored milk and cheese than winter animals fed on less diverse silage and hay. We've known for hundreds of years that when the milk is exposed to bacteria, molds, and yeast during cheese making and ripening, it develops

multifaceted flavor. But now we know that during ripening, enzymes break down milk protein (casein) into amino acids such as glutamic acid, which gives cheese its savory or umami flavor. As the cheese ripens, enzymes further break down amino acids into amines like trimethylamine (which contributes a fishy aroma), putrescine (rotting meat aroma), sulfur compounds (onion and garlic aroma), and ammonia (nose-clearing astringent aroma). Cheese scientists call this protein breakdown proteolysis. But milk fat in the cheese is also broken down into fatty acids, creating many of the pungent flavors we taste in cheese. Fats may be broken down into lactones or esters, which lend peachy, coconutty, and other fruity aromas to cheese. Volatile fatty acids like butyric acid create the sharp flavors of goaty, barnyardy, and stinky cheeses.

Even the initial starter used to acidify the milk influences the final flavor of the cheese. For example, to make Swiss Emmental, the bacterial culture *Propionibacter shermanii* is added to cow's milk and it remains in the curd, developing flavor. The bacterium metabolizes the curd's lactic acid during ripening and converts it to propionic acid, acetic acid, and diacetyl; it also gives off carbon dioxide gas in the process. The acids contribute sharp flavors and aromas to the cheese and propionic acid prevents mold growth, while diacetyl contributes butteriness. The carbon dioxide forms the familiar holes or "eyes" of Swiss cheese as the cheese ages under warm conditions and the bacterium is encouraged to grow at a steady rate.

Stinky cheese like Époisses and Limburger make another good example. Cultures of *Bacterium linens* are used to ripen these cheeses. They grow on the cheese surface as the cheese maker washes the rind (which also creates a reddish-orange smear from carotenoids). The bacteria break down the milk proteins into highly aromatic amines, isovaleric acid, and oniony sulfur compounds and hydrolyze milk fat and volatile fatty acids such as butyric, caprioc, and caprylic.

While some bacteria break down milk protein, others break down milk fat. Blue cheeses like Roquefort, Stilton, and Gorgonzola are inoculated with molds such as *Penicillium roqueforti* and *P. glaucom*. These molds metabolize the milk fat, creating methyl ketones such as 2-heptanone, alcohols, and other compounds that give blue cheese its distinct pungent aromas.

The microbial and chemical reactions increase as milk goes from fresh liquid to aged solid. Some reactions produce peptides that break down into their component amino acids such as cysteine and methionine. These chemicals then release compounds such as methanethiol, dimethyl sulfide, and methional or 3-(methylthio)propanal. It may sound like chemistry mumbo jumbo, but these are the very compounds that we find delicious when we taste cheese. For instance, concentrated methional smells like boiled potatoes and lends the Cheddary flavor to Cheddar cheese. During aging, the protein, fat, and carbohydrates in milk are broken down into various compounds that taste sour, nutty, fruity, or barnyardy, for example. Sometimes undesirable bitter compounds form in cheese as when the milk protein is broken down into catabolites of amino acids such as tryptophan and phenylalanine. The microorganisms also change the texture of the cheese during aging.

See Also • Cheesecake, Flavor, Milk, Mold, Pasteurization, Toxin

kitchen wisdom

Cheesecake Won't Set?
When flavoring cheesecakes, avoid mixing in raw pineapple, kiwi, mango, or papaya. These fruits contain enzymes that digest proteins in the cheese and eggs, preventing the filling from setting. You can still use them on top, though, as a decoration.

CHEESECAKE

What It Is • With its cookie crumb or pastry crust and dairy-based filling, cheesecake is more **custard** tart than cake. Pastries have been filled with various cheeses for centuries, and cheesecakes can be sweet or savory. Most are sweet and made around the world with various fresh cheeses. For savory cheesecakes, you can combine ingredients such as cream cheese and smoked salmon or Cheddar cheese and bacon. You can also make cheesecake with other creamy ingredients like silken tofu.

What It Does • Like other custards made with eggs and dairy products, cheesecakes require even, gentle heat to prevent curdling. They are often baked in a water bath to evenly distribute the heat around the cake pan and provide moist steam to keep the baked custard from drying out. To avoid lumps, it helps to bring the cheese and eggs to room temperature before mixing the filling and to add the eggs one at a time. Gradual temperature changes also help prevent cracks. If the pan is too small, the filling will rise too high and will overcook on the

Southern Comfort Cheesecake

Low and slow is best for cheesecake. Instead of using a water bath, this cheesecake gets gentle heat from a low oven temperature and a long cooking time. A small amount of flour helps to absorb moisture and prevent the filling from "weeping" or losing its liquid. Mix gently to incorporate minimal air and help prevent cracking. The long cooking time (6 to 7 hours) allows any air to escape slowly before it can make the cheesecake rise and then fall when cooled. Cooling the cheesecake with the oven door open allows the filling temperature to change gradually, providing more protection against cracks. For flavor, Southern Comfort provides peach aromas that blend well with the almond cookie or gingersnap crust. You could also use amaretto or brandy in the filling and chocolate wafers or graham crackers for the crust.

Crust

1 cup	almond cookie or gingersnap cookie crumbs	250 mL
2 tbsp	granulated sugar	25 mL
3 tbsp	melted butter	45 mL

Filling

2 lbs	cream cheese, at room temperature	1 kg
1 cup	granulated sugar	250 mL
5	eggs, at room temperature	5
¼ cup	Southern Comfort	50 mL
2 tbsp	vanilla extract	25 mL
2 tbsp	all-purpose flour	25 mL
Pinch	salt	Pinch

1. Preheat oven to 190°F (90°C). Line bottom of a 9-inch (23 cm) springform or round cake pan with 3-inch (7.5 cm) sides with parchment paper and coat paper with cooking spray.

2. Crust: Mix cookie crumbs with sugar and melted butter. Press crust evenly into pan bottom and very slightly up sides. Set aside.

3. Filling: In a bowl, stir together cream cheese and sugar. Stir in eggs until combined. Briefly whisk together Southern Comfort, vanilla, flour, and salt until combined. Gently stir into cheese mixture.

4. Scrape mixture into prepared pan and bake in preheated oven until sides are set and center looks jiggly and slightly undercooked (about 170°F/77°C on an instant-read thermometer), about 6 to 7 hours. Turn off oven, open oven door and let cake cool in oven for 1 hour. Transfer to a wire rack and let cool in pan for 1 hour more. Run a knife around cake circumference then remove springform. If using a regular round cake pan, cover it with plastic wrap and an inverted plate. Flip pan and plate together then remove pan and peel off parchment. Cover cake with another inverted cake plate and flip so cake is right side up. Cover with plastic wrap and refrigerate for 1 hour or up to 8 hours.

MAKES 16 SERVINGS.

edges before the center is done. If the pan is too big, the entire filling may quickly overcook and crack.

How It Works ●
As a cheesecake filling heats up, the proteins in the eggs and cheese gradually begin to coagulate, or firm up. The coagulation temperature is higher than it would be for eggs alone because the proteins are surrounded by molecules of sugar. When the proteins firm up, the custard sets, but it is still very delicate because the proteins are diluted by sugars and moisture in the cheese.

Overbaking a cheesecake will make that delicate protein network fall apart, squeezing out the moisture (and creamy texture) that it holds. This process of proteins losing moisture, known as syneresis, causes cheesecakes and other custards to curdle, collapse, and crack, forming fissures that fill with leaked moisture. To help stabilize the filling and prevent curdling and syneresis, add a starch, such as 1 tablespoon (15 mL) of flour or 2 teaspoons (10 mL) of cornstarch or

fast fact

- On February 21, 2004, in Brooklyn, New York, competitive eater Sonya Thomas ate 11 pounds (5 kg) of cheesecake in nine minutes, setting a Guinness World Record.

arrowroot per cup (250 mL) of filling. The starch absorbs water, swells, and prevents the proteins from coagulating too quickly and curdling. The downside is that the starch moves the custard's texture away from silky smooth and toward coarse and grainy. You can also prevent cracking and moisture loss by beating the filling ingredients very gently just until blended, which minimizes the amount of air worked into the batter and reduces its ability to rise (and fall). Baking at a low temperature for a long time allows any air in the batter to gradually escape. Bake cheesecakes only until the center is still jiggly and looks underdone to avoid overcooking the custard and squeezing out precious moisture. Gentle cooling helps prevent cracks, too, because it allows steam in the filling to contract gradually.

See Also • Bakeware, Baking, Cake, Cheese, Custard

CHELATION • See Chemical Bonding

CHEMICAL BONDING

What It Is • All food molecules are held together by chemical bonds. The bonds themselves are formed by the attractive electrical forces between the atoms of a food molecule. For instance, a molecule of water functions as a unit because of the chemical bonds among its atoms of hydrogen and oxygen. Whenever food is prepared and cooked, molecules of water, air, and other food substances interact, and their atoms swap electrons, creating many chemical reactions. When the atoms are rearranged and share electrons in new stable forms, new molecules are created.

The most stable chemical bond occurs when two or more atoms share each other's electrons. Known as covalent bonding, this type of strong chemical bond is what defines the structure of a molecule. In your kitchen, oxygen in the air is an example of a covalent bond. An atom of oxygen equally shares its electrons with another atom of oxygen to form a stable molecule, O_2. Each atom of oxygen has an equal affinity for the other oxygen atom's electrons.

In other chemical compounds, one atom can have a slightly greater affinity for electrons than another atom. Such is the case with water. In a molecule of water (H_2O), two hydrogen atoms are covalently bonded to one oxygen atom. But the oxygen atom has a greater affinity for electrons than the hydrogen atom, so the available electrons spend more time around the oxygen atom, creating a slightly negative charge on the oxygen side and a slightly positive charge on the hydrogen side of the molecule. With a negative side and a positive side, the water molecule is called polar. The water molecules interact with each other, forming weak bonds — called hydrogen bonds — between the positive end of one water molecule and the negative end of another. Although weak, there are many bonds, so the effect is significant. Hydrogen bonds between water and other polar molecules in food are extremely important because all food plants and animals consist primarily of water. Hydrogen bonding explains many changes that occur during food preparation and cooking.

Another type of chemical bond forms when one atom has such a great affinity for electrons that instead of simply sharing another atom's electrons, it assumes complete control of them. When this happens, one atom becomes positively charged and the other atom becomes negatively charged. An atom or molecule with a net electric charge due to the loss or gain of electrons is known as an ion. The attractive force between the positive ion and the negative ion holds the two atoms together in what's known as an ionic bond. Common table salt is a good example of ionic bonding. Salt is a compound of sodium (Na) and chlorine (Cl). The chlorine atom takes an electron from the sodium atom and becomes negatively charged. The sodium atom gives up its electron to the chlorine atom and becomes positively charged. The attractive force between positive and negative creates an ionic bond, holding the atoms together in the compound sodium chloride (NaCl) known as salt. In water, NaC1 molecules separate into ions (called dissociation) and become surrounded by water molecules.

What It Does • Preparing and cooking food is essentially the controlled breaking and forming of chemical bonds. That's how food goes from raw to cooked. The nature of the chemical bonds within any food determines exactly how that food will behave as it interacts with other foods. For instance, the strong covalent bonds that hold together food molecules like the proteins in meat, the carbohydrates in vegetables, and the fats in dairy products are not easily broken. Fair amounts of heat are required to break these bonds. Weaker chemical bonds, like the hydrogen bonds in water and the ionic bonds in salt, are more easily broken. For instance, when you heat starch in water the heat energy breaks the hydrogen bonds between the starch molecules in the starch granule, water enters, and the granule swells. The swollen granules take up more space, causing the mixture to thicken.

How It Works • In food preparation and manufacturing, a special form of chemical bonding is known as chelation. This type of bonding is often an ionic bond that forms when certain ingredients called chelating agents or sequestrants bond to metal ions and chelate or sequester them in a ring structure. Chelation of metal ions, such as ions of copper and iron, prevents those metal ions from interacting with other chemical compounds that could cause the food to oxidize, discolor, or deteriorate. Chelating agents are often used as preservatives in packaged foods. Thousands of packaged foods, particularly those with

fats like ice cream, crackers, and snacks, contain either natural chelating agents like citric acid (found in citrus foods) or synthetic chelating agents like EDTA (ethylenediaminetetraacetic acid). These chelating agents preserve the quality of foods, but they're also used to help retain nutritional minerals such as iron.

See Also • Atom, Molecule

CHEMICAL LEAVENER

What It Is • Cakes, cookies, muffins, and breads are often leavened, or risen, with carbon dioxide gas. Yeast is a natural leavener that produces the gas as it metabolizes sugar. Baking powders (or baking soda plus an acid) are chemical leaveners that produce a carbon dioxide gas from an acid-base reaction with water as the reaction medium.

A white crystalline powder, baking soda is usually refined from mineral deposits, but it can also be made artificially. Baking powder is a crystalline powder that combines baking soda with dry acidic ingredients that react when water is added, plus cornstarch to prevent clumping and to control the amount of gas produced per unit of baking powder.

What It Does • In its natural form, baking soda is an **alkali** (base) and regulates the acidity in all living things. When bakers around the globe discovered that it could be used as a quick leavener instead of more time-consuming yeast, baking soda and the baking powders that include it inspired countless "quick breads."

To take advantage of its leavening power, quick breads made with baking soda should be baked immediately. Otherwise, the carbon dioxide gas gradually escapes from the batter before it reaches the oven. Too little baking

kitchen wisdom

Baking Soda Enhances Crispness
To create a lighter, thinner, crispier crust for tempura or other fried foods, add 1 teaspoon (5 mL) baking soda per cup (250 mL) of flour in the batter.

fast fact

- Most of the world's baking soda is produced by the Solvay process, the reaction of calcium carbonate, sodium chloride, ammonia, and carbon dioxide in water.

soda leaves muffins and soda breads flat because there isn't enough carbon dioxide gas to make them rise. Too much baking soda can cause cake batters to overexpand and collapse, leaving behind a fallen mess with an alkaline (soapy) aftertaste. As a rule of thumb, use just enough baking soda to react with the acids of the other ingredients. For instance, use ½ teaspoon (2 mL) baking soda for every 1 cup (250 mL) buttermilk, yogurt, or sour cream; ¾ cup (175 mL) brown sugar, molasses, or honey; ½ cup (125 mL) natural (not Dutch-process) cocoa powder; 1½ teaspoons (7 mL) cream of tartar; or 1 teaspoon (5 mL) lemon juice or vinegar.

Baking powder is baking soda with the acid already mixed in. That's why baking soda is generally used in recipes that include acidic ingredients, whereas baking powder is used in recipes that contain no acidic ingredients. When both baking soda and powder are used in a recipe, the baking powder usually does the real leavening work. But the recipe may include an additional acidic ingredient such as brown sugar or molasses, so baking soda is added to fully react with the extra acidity of those ingredients.

How It Works • When baking soda comes in contact with acidic ingredients such as lemon juice or sour cream, it produces carbon dioxide gas (CO_2). In baked goods, the gas becomes thousands of air bubbles in the batter or dough. When the batter or dough is heated, those gas bubbles expand, causing the cake or cookies to rise. The bubbles stop expanding only when the dough firms up enough for it to set.

Baking powder produces CO_2 when the dry components are mixed with water. Some baking powders are "double-acting" because CO_2 is released twice — once when the sodium bicarbonate mixes with acidic ingredients in the batter, and again when the

batter is heated in the oven. The "double-acting" baking powder found in most supermarkets usually includes baking soda and dry acid salts such as monocalcium phosphate (MCP) and sodium aluminum sulfate (SAS). When heated, SAS produces sulfuric acid that reacts with the sodium bicarbonate to produce more CO_2. Single-acting baking powder includes only MCP. Commercial baking powders for restaurants and food manufacturers may include various acid salts such as sodium aluminum phosphate (SALP), sodium aluminum pyrophosphate (SAPP), dimagnesium phosphate (DMP), or dicalcium phosphate dihydrate (DCPD). These allow restaurants and manufacturers to formulate baking mixes that won't release their leavening gases too soon or that leaven baked goods at specific oven temperatures. For instance, SAPP delays the release of CO_2 after it is heated; SALP releases the gas between 100 and 104°F (38 and 40°C); DMP releases it between 104 and 111°F (40 and 44°C); and DCPD releases it between 135 and 140°F (57 and 60°C). Refrigerated doughs have water present so use glucono-delta-lactone as a leavening component. It is converted into gluconic acid when heated and then reacts with sodium bicarbonate to produce CO_2.

See Also • Acid, Alkali, Atmospheric Pressure, Baking, Cake, Carbon Dioxide, Cookies

CHERIMOYA • See Fruit

CHERI SUISSE • See Liqueur

CHERRY

What It Is • Like peaches, plums, apricots, and nectarines, cherries are stone fruits with thin skins, soft flesh, and hard pits. They're just smaller than their cousins. Worldwide cherry production includes well over 1,000 varieties that generally fall into two culinary categories: sweet and sour. Sweet cherries (*Prunus avium*), among them the dark red

Bing, yellow-red Royal Ann, Rainier, and Lambert varieties, are the most widely grown around the world. Sour cherries (*Prunus cerasus*) are slightly smaller and softer, are less widely cultivated, and include varieties such as the dark red Morello, used to make cherry brandy (kirsch), and the bright red Early Richmond and Montmorency. Chokecherries, a very tart wild North American type, were one of the berries used by Native Americans to make pemmican, a sort of dried meat jerky.

What It Does • Heat improves cherry flavor, so many cherries are cooked into dishes like cherry pie, cherry cobbler, and classic French clafouti. Sweet cherries are often eaten fresh but can be cooked. Sweet Royal Anns are often bleached with sulfur dioxide, dyed red or green, flavored with bitter almond oil, then bottled in sugar syrup and sold as maraschino cherries. These make a poor substitute for Italian marasca cherries preserved in alcohol.

Sour cherries are typically mixed with sugar and cooked into jams, sauces, or desserts. When dried, both sweet and sour cherries can be used like raisins in cooking. They're high in fiber and help retain moisture in low-fat baked goods.

Cherries don't ripen after they are picked, so they should be stored in the refrigerator.

How It Works • Cherry flavor originates from three different components: benzaldehyde (contributing almond flavor, which is especially concentrated in the pit), linalool (a terpene that provides intense floral aroma), and eugenol (the sharp, spicy flavor of cloves). Cherry red color comes from anthocyanin pigments. These water-soluble pigments will turn cooking liquids and sauces red or, in some cases, blue. Anthocyanins are red in acidic conditions and turn blue in alkaline ones. Cherry muffins and scones can develop a blue ring around the red cherries when the anthocyanins react to the alkaline environment of the quick-bread batter. To prevent the blue ring, make the batter less alkaline by adding an acidic ingredient such as cream of tartar, buttermilk, sour cream, or yogurt.

See Also • Antioxidants, Fruit, Pigment

fast fact

- The "Cherry Capital of the World" is Traverse City, Michigan, home of the world's largest cherry pie and an internationally recognized National Cherry Festival held every year.

CHERRY PEPPER • See Capsicum

CHERRYSTONE CLAM • See Mollusks

CHERRY TOMATOES • See Tomatoes

CHERVIL • See Herbs

CHESTNUT • See Nuts

CHÈVRE • See Cheese

CHEWING GUM • See Gums

CHICKEN

What It Is • Chickens have been bred for food ever since they were domesticated in Southeast Asia around 7500 BCE. In the 1800s, the species of chicken (*Gallus gallus*) now popular in North America and Europe was bred from Chinese imports. The most widely bred type, the American Cobb, is a crossbreed of Britain's Cornish and America's White Plymouth Rock chickens. At four to six weeks old, Cornish Rock game hens weigh 1 to 2 pounds (454 g to 1 kg) and have tender, bland-tasting meat. Broiler-fryers are matured a bit longer, to about two to three months, and weigh 3 to 4 pounds (1.4 to 1.8 kg). Roasters and capons (castrated males) are matured at least twice as long, weigh 4 to 5 pounds (1.8 to 2 kg), and have more well-developed, flavorful meat. They're also slightly higher in fat. Stewing chickens are matured up to 18 months and develop even more flavorful meat, but its toughness makes stewing chickens best for moist-heat cooking methods.

In North America, most chickens are plucked, eviscerated, then water-chilled, causing them to absorb up to 12% of their weight in water, which slightly dilutes the flavor of the meat and bumps up the profit per pound. In Europe, most birds are air-chilled, resulting in slightly more flavorful meat and drier skin that crisps and browns more easily.

After the Second World War, the mass production of chickens in North America greatly reduced their cost and increased their popularity. Because the majority of birds are raised in large flocks in crowded facilities, sanitation becomes difficult, and chickens sold in North American supermarkets are often contaminated with bacteria (see Safe Storage and Preparation, page 126, for more information on bacteria). Other, less-industrialized production methods have led to various alternative labels on chickens, including:

Free-range: Unlike industrially produced chickens, these birds have access to the outdoors, but may spend very little time outside. Credible producers of free-range chickens raise their flocks outdoors for a specified time each day and often feed them a vegetarian diet in addition to their natural forage. In North America, the term "free-range" is not legally defined. The meat of free-range chickens may be slightly firmer and more flavorful than that of cage-raised chickens.

Pastured: Pastured poultry is raised in rotating outdoor pens on a diet with a high percentage of natural forage. The meat tends to be firmer and more flavorful than that of mass-produced chickens.

Red label (label rouge): This French label for free-range chickens requires a particular slow-growing breed that is fed mostly grains and is raised in moderately sized flocks that are given outdoor access. Red-label chickens are matured about twice as long as cage-raised chickens, and the meat tends to be moister, firmer, and more flavorful.

Poulet de Bresse: These free-range birds are raised near the Burgundy village of Bresse, fed on milk, corn, and other grains, and slowly raised in flocks not exceeding 500 birds. Poulet de Bresse (Bresse chickens) have well-developed muscles and full-flavored meat. They are labeled AOC (Appellation d'Origine Contrôlée), the French certificate of origin and authenticity for foods produced in a traditional manner according to strict, time-honored methods.

fast fact

- There are more chickens than people in the world and the U.S. produces more than 7 billion chickens a year, according to the Department of Agriculture.

Organic: In the United States, regulations require organic chickens and feed to be produced without the use of antibiotics, genetic engineering, chemical fertilizers, sewage sludge, or synthetic pesticides. Flock size and outdoor access are not regulated.

Kosher: In accordance with Jewish religious law, kosher chickens are raised humanely with tight bacterial controls, salted for up to an hour after being hand-slaughtered by a certified kosher butcher, then rinsed, making them taste slightly saltier than other chickens. Regulations do not address feed, outdoor access, or antibiotics.

What It Does ●

Domesticated chickens use their muscles very little and consequently their meat develops very little flavor. This mild-flavored meat has become the world's culinary canvas. Nearly every culture prepares chicken in distinctive ways, from India's chicken tikka to Italy's chicken cacciatore to fried chicken in the U.S.

Chicken parts cook at different rates because of the amount of exercise each part gets. As chickens move around, their legs and thighs (dark meat) develop firmer muscles and tough connective tissue that needs to soften to be palatable. When fully cooked, the softened legs and thighs of a whole chicken will move easily when wiggled and release clear or pale gold juices when cut or pierced. The meat temperature is best kept between 165 and 170°F (74 and 77°C) to prevent the meat from drying out. The breasts (white meat) of a chicken get less exercise and are more tender. To be safe, all chicken parts should reach an internal temperature of 165°F (74°C). To resolve the discrepancy in cooking rates between dark meat and white meat, it helps to cut up whole chickens and cook the parts separately. Or, to cook whole birds evenly on a grill or in an oven with bottom heat, cook the bird upright on a vertical roaster, which keeps the more tender breast meat farther away from the heat. Or, in a conventional oven, cook the whole bird breast side down for the first half of the roasting, then turn breast side up. Whichever method you use, it helps to brine chicken and to baste it with liquid to keep the meat moist throughout cooking. Some cooks find that roasting whole chickens quickly at high temperatures (about 500°F/260°C) for about one hour provides the best combination of crisp skin and moist meat. Some of the breast meat will be dry near the skin, but the interior of the breast will stay moist.

About half of the moisture in chicken skin is water. To get crisp, brown skin, you have to evaporate excess moisture, which is the logic behind the exceptionally crisp skin of fan-dried Peking chicken. It helps to air-dry the bird before cooking, use dry-heat cooking methods such as grilling or frying instead of moist-heat cooking such as stewing or steaming, and rub the skin with butter, oil, or another fat to help transfer heat to the skin quickly.

Keep in mind that when fully cooked, young chickens may still appear red near the bone. Don't worry, the meat is done — it's just that the young animals have built up so little calcium in their bones that the bones leak blood.

Safe Storage and Preparation

Chicken skin makes the bird spoil faster because of bacteria and the rapid oxidation of fat in the skin. For these reasons, chicken is best refrigerated at less than 35°F (1.6°C) for only one to two days or frozen for a month or two. Frozen chicken can be safely thawed in its packaging on a plate in the refrigerator or in cold water.

When preparing raw chicken, clean it thoroughly. Industrially produced chickens are regularly given antibiotics in their feed to combat pervasive bacteria like *Escherichia coli* (*E. coli*) and *Salmonella*. U.S. Department of Agriculture studies show that the majority of mass-produced chicken sold in supermarkets is contaminated with *Campylobacter* bacteria. To reduce the risk of food-borne illness, avoid storing or preparing chicken near foods that will be eaten raw. Use hot soapy water to wash everything that has come in contact with raw chicken to prevent cross-contamination.

Nutrition

Chicken has become an inexpensive source of protein around the world. Compared with more expensive meats like beef, pork, and lamb, chicken is also lower in saturated fat and higher in healthful monounsaturated and polyunsaturated fats. Due to a diet high in natural forage, there is some evidence that pasture-raised chicken and some free-range chicken is higher than mass-produced chicken in vitamins A and E, omega-3 fatty acids, and other beneficial nutrients.

To reduce the total calories of chicken by nearly half, remove the skin before serving. Keep chicken fat in perspective, though. Chicken fat itself contains less than half of the saturated fat of butter and almost twice the healthy monosaturated fat, making it a reasonably good cooking fat.

How It Works • Chicken breasts are white because these muscles function in short but intense bursts followed by long periods of rest. The muscles are fueled primarily by a stored starch called glycogen, which is rapidly converted into energy and leaves the breast meat pale in color. By contrast, chicken legs and thighs are dark because these muscles are constantly used to support the weight of domestic chickens as they stand and move around. The leg and thigh muscles work slowly but steadily and burn fat for energy. To do that, they need a constant source of oxygen, which is supplied by an oxygen-binding red pigment called myoglobin. This pigment (and the presence of iron) makes chicken leg and thigh meat appear dark.

See Also • Bacteria, Eggs, Meat, Poultry

CHICKPEA • See Legumes

CHICORY

What It Is • This family of bitter greens (*Cichorium*) includes two main types, the chicories (*Cichorium intybus*) and the endives (*Cichorium endivia*). The chicories include varieties such as:

Belgian endive (witloof): Witloof (literally, "white head") is grown in darkness to prevent photosynthesis (known as blanching), resulting in tightly packed mostly white or pale green leaves, and tends to be less bitter than other chicories.

kitchen wisdom

Reducing Shrinkage

To keep a boneless, skinless chicken breast from shrinking during cooking, cut out the tough white tendon that runs along its length.

fast fact

- According to the UN Food and Agriculture Organization, China, the U.S., and Italy lead the world in chicory production.

Chicory (sugarloaf): These greens have curly ruffled leaves.

Radicchio: An Italian chicory, radicchio tastes more bitter than other varieties. The two most popular North American varieties are verona, which has a small round head with burgundy leaves and white veins, and di Treviso, a more torpedo-shaped tighter head with red to pink leaves and white veins. It is covered to prevent photosynthesis, which would add a green color to the red leaves and make them look brown.

One member of the *Cichorium intybus* family (variety *sativa*) has been cultivated for its large root, known as chicory root.

The related endives include varieties like:

Curly endive (frisée): Frisée is often cultivated with a broad weight on top, which flattens the head and causes the inner leaves to be white and the outer ones green or pink.

Escarole (batavia): Mild in flavor, escarole has broad, coarse green leaves with pointy tips.

What It Does •

Both chicories and endives lend a pleasant bitterness to salads. The long, hollow, canoe-shaped leaves of Belgian endive can be filled with cream cheese, chutney, or other relishes, as the hollow cup shape of radicchio leaves can be filled with grain or vegetable salads. These bitter greens are sometimes braised, grilled, or added to soups.

Chicory root finds its way into beverages, often roasted, ground, and used as a substitute for roasted coffee beans. It's sometimes mixed with coffee to create "Creole coffee."

How It Works • The bitterness comes from the plant's alkaloids, a natural defense mechanism. In addition to bitter-tasting terpenes (lactucin and lactucopicrin), chicories also contain 5% tannins. Chicory root tastes more bitter than coffee and contains no caffeine. Contemporary hybrids are high in health-promoting inulin (see **Fiber**).

See Also • Leaves, Roots

CHIHUAHUA CHEESE • See Cheese

CHILE PEPPERS • See Capsicum

CHINESE ARTICHOKE • See Roots

CHINESE BROCCOLI • See Cruciferous Vegetables

CHINESE GRAPEFRUIT • See Citrus

CHINESE HAM • See Ham

CHIPOLATA • See Sausage

CHIPOTLE • See Capsicum

CHIVES • See Allium

CHLOROPHYLL

What It Is • Everything from limes to lawn grass appears green because of chlorophyll, an antioxidant pigment found within the cell walls of plants. It is the chemical compound that allows plants to synthesize energy from the sun's rays, providing a plentiful source of nutrients for animal and human survival.

kitchen wisdom

Keeping Greens Green

To keep vegetables bright green, cook them briefly. When blanching them, use a large amount of boiling water and keep the lid off. Cook the vegetables only until tender-crisp or tender and bright green (about 30 seconds or up to six minutes), then plunge the vegetables in ice water to stop the cooking. The ample water and lack of a lid dilutes acids in the vegetables (or the water) and allows the acids to escape the liquid, keeping acid from discoloring the chlorophyll. It also helps to salt the cooking liquid, which partially prevents chlorophyll's conversion to a drab grayish green. When blanched like this, vegetables can be chilled then fully cooked at a later time yet still retain their bright green color. While alkali (baking soda) will convert chlorophyll to bright green chlorophyllin, it destroys the vegetable's texture and its vitamins.

The pigment is most noticeable in green leafy vegetables like spinach, but you can also see it in avocados, grapes, lima beans, and green lentils. There are two types. Chlorophyll-a provides the vivid blue-green color seen in dark green leaves such as kale. Chlorophyll-b imparts a more pale yellow-green hue in foods like napa cabbage. Various concentrations of the two types create everything from the light green hue of apples to the dark green color of collards.

What It Does • The green color and flavor decline as plant foods age (especially when exposed to excess sunlight, ironically enough) and when they are prepared and cooked. Chlorophyll is fat soluble before it is heated and becomes water soluble when cooked, easily turning the cooking water green. Heat, acid, and certain metals can also convert bright green chlorophyll to a dull grayish green and eventually to brown.

Chlorophyll's conversion from bright green to olive drab occurs dramatically when vegetables are heated. Brief cooking (five to six minutes) actually makes green vegetables appear brighter. That's because as the vegetable is heated, oxygen escapes from the chloroplasts within its cell walls, revealing more of the green chlorophyll. With continued heat, however, the green color begins to fade. Each chlorophyll molecule contains a magnesium atom that is released when heated and denatures, or transforms, into other compounds called pheophytin and pyropheophytin, which have an unappetizing grayish green or drab brown color. Steaming or stir-frying are good cooking methods because small pieces of vegetables will cook quickly before chlorophyll has a chance to discolor.

Acid also causes green chlorophyll to convert to drab pheophytins. The acid can even come from the vegetable itself. When a green vegetable, especially one high in acid, is cooked above 140°F (60°C), its acids are released from its cells and mix with its own chlorophyll. Low-acid vegetables like green peas look greener when cooked than high-acid vegetables like green beans. Acid from outside sources like lemon juice, cream of tartar, or other acidic ingredients will dull chlorophyll's color, too. If you're dressing some green vegetables with vinaigrette or lemon juice, do it just prior to serving. Raw, uncut vegetables will hold their color better than cut blanched or cooked ones because their cells are intact and not as easily affected by acid.

Iron and tin cookware can cause a similar conversion reaction in chlorophyll. To keep vegetables bright green, avoid cooking them in cast-iron or tin-lined pans.

The bottom line is that whenever a vegetable's cell walls are dismantled by cutting, cooking, pickling, freezing, or other preparation methods, the chlorophyll is headed toward drabsville. See Kitchen Wisdom, left, for more ways to prevent chlorophyll discoloration.

How It Works • Chlorophyll's primary function is photosynthesis. The chloroplast cells of plants absorb sunlight and convert it to energy. Plants combine the chlorophyll and water in their cells with carbon dioxide absorbed from the air to create glucose (sugar). The sugar is either used immediately for growth or stored as starch and used for energy later. During photosynthesis, plants give off oxygen, making this process essential to life on Earth.

As a plant matures, chlorophyll levels decrease (sometimes as a result of increased acidity) and reveal other pigments in the plant's cells. That's why bell peppers and tomatoes ripen from green to red. Ripe green avocados and gooseberries are notable exceptions to this general rule.

See Also • Leaves, Pigment

CHOCOLATE

What It Is • It's been called an aphrodisiac, and the botanical name for the cacao tree, *Theobroma cacao*, translates from the Greek as "food of the gods." Whatever you call it, chocolate is among the world's most popular foods. It is made from the beans of the cacao, a South American tree first cultivated in southern Mexico by the Pre-Columbian Olmecs. The beans are fermented, dried, roasted, and ground to make various types of chocolate.

The vast majority (about 90%) of the world's chocolate comes from one type of cacao tree, the Forastero grown in Africa, Asia, and Brazil. Forastero trees are hardy and produce bold-flavored cacao beans. Criollo trees produce cacao beans with more delicate, complex flavors, but they are less hardy, so Criollo chocolate is more expensive, accounting for less than 5% of the world's supply. Trinitario trees, a natural hybrid of Criollo and Forastero originating in Trinidad, yield beans that range widely in flavor and also account for less than 5% of the chocolate produced worldwide.

Cacao beans are seeds that grow in ridged oval pods that hang from the trees. To

develop chocolate's signature texture and flavor, the beans are removed from the pods and fermented for several days. The beans are then dried (often sun-dried) and roasted at a relatively low temperature (250 to 320°F/121 to 160°C) for less than an hour to preserve their delicate aromas. The inner pieces, or cocoa nibs, are removed from the roasted beans and repeatedly ground, forming a brown paste called chocolate liquor. This alcohol-free "liquor" contains about 30% cocoa solids and 55% cocoa butter, the cream-colored vegetable fat responsible for chocolate's velvety texture. To make most chocolate products, the cocoa solids are filtered from the cocoa butter and then recombined with extra cocoa butter during conching. Invented by Swiss candy maker

fast fact

- Cacao trees grow within 20° north and south of the equator because their survival depends on about a half gallon (2 liters) of annual rainfall and warm temperatures between 70 and 90°F (21 and 32°C). West Africa produces about two-thirds of the world's cacao harvest.

Mocha Bonbons

Mocha-holics beware. These bonbons are addictive. They're a combination of chocolate truffles (essentially melted chocolate and cream) and brigadeiro, a fudgy Brazilian candy made from cocoa powder and sweetened condensed milk. Letting the chocolate mixture stand at room temperature for 6 hours allows the cocoa butter to gradually crystallize, creating a smoother texture in the bonbons. Corn syrup smoothes out the texture, too. To bump up the flavor and texture, the bonbons are rolled in crushed chocolate-covered espresso beans, but you could use crushed nuts, chocolate sprinkles, or Dutch-process cocoa powder.

8 oz	bittersweet chocolate (65 to 72%), broken into small pieces (about 1⅓ cups/325 mL)	250 g
⅓ cup	whipping (35%) cream	75 mL
¼ cup	sweetened condensed milk	50 mL
1 tbsp	butter	15 mL
1 tbsp	instant espresso powder	15 mL
1 tsp	corn syrup	5 mL
2 tsp	coffee-flavored liqueur, such as Kahlúa	10 mL
½ cup	chocolate-covered espresso beans	125 mL
	Butter or oil	

1. Place chocolate pieces into a heatproof bowl.

2. In a saucepan over high heat, combine cream, condensed milk, butter, espresso powder, and corn syrup. Bring to a boil, then reduce heat so mixture simmers, stirring occasionally, until it thickens into a medium-thin syrup, 3 to 5 minutes. Pour over chocolate and stir very gently (preferably not at all) until melted. Stir in liqueur and let cool at cool room temperature (about 65°F/18°C, as in a basement closet) for 6 hours. Cover and refrigerate until stiff, 3 to 4 hours.

3. Line a baking sheet with parchment or wax paper and refrigerate until well chilled, about 20 minutes. Use a melon baller or spoon to scoop out rough 1-inch (2.5 cm) balls of the chocolate mixture and place on cold baking sheet. If mixture is too stiff, let soften at room temperature until it can be rolled, 15 to 20 minutes. Cover with plastic wrap and refrigerate until firm but pliable, about 1 hour.

4. In a food processor fitted with a metal blade, grind chocolate-covered espresso beans until coarsely chopped, then transfer to a bowl. Grease your hands with butter or oil and roll chocolate balls between your palms into smooth 1-inch (2.5 cm) balls. Dip balls in crushed espresso beans until coated all over. Serve at room temperature or cover and refrigerate for up to 3 weeks or freeze between wax paper in an airtight container for 2 months. Thaw overnight in refrigerator and return to room temperature before serving.

MAKES ABOUT 35 BONBONS

Rodolphe Lindt in 1879, conching creates an exceptionally smooth texture by kneading, rolling, and gently heating the chocolate liquor (between 130 and 190°F/54 and 88°C) with additional cocoa butter for several hours or several days. It's essentially controlled friction. Longer conching creates smoother-textured chocolate. During conching, manufacturers also add ingredients like sugar to make bittersweet chocolate, dry milk to make milk chocolate, and flavorings such as vanilla. As a final step, the molten chocolate mixture is tempered, a process of cooling and reheating the chocolate to precise temperatures, which creates glossy, smooth-textured chocolate that snaps when broken.

Chocolate liquor is processed into most of the solid chocolates, candies, and powdered cocoas that we enjoy. Solid chocolate is a suspension of very fine cocoa solids in its own fat, cocoa butter. Cocoa powder is dried chocolate liquor from which 70 to 90% of the cocoa butter has been removed. The more cocoa butter that's left in cocoa powder or added to solid chocolate, the richer the texture of the final product.

Here are the main forms of cocoa powder and solid chocolate:

Natural cocoa powder: This dried form of chocolate liquor has the most concentrated chocolate taste, contains no sugar, and is naturally acidic with a pH slightly higher than 5. In the U.S., low-fat cocoa powder contains less than 10% cocoa butter. High-fat cocoa powder contains at least 22% cocoa butter.

Dutch-process cocoa powder: In the 1830s, Dutch chocolate maker Conrad van Houten began treating cocoa powder with alkaline salts like potassium carbonate to reduce its acidity and allow the powder to mix more easily with water. "Dutched" (also called European-style or alkalized) cocoa powder has a milder flavor, darker color, and higher pH (around 7 or 8) than natural cocoa powder. It contains no sugar.

Instant cocoa powder: This precooked cocoa product is formulated to mix easily with water or milk to create cocoa beverages. It contains about 80% sugar, includes an emulsifier, and generally is not used for baking.

Unsweetened chocolate: When pure chocolate liquor is cooled and solidified, it's known as unsweetened, bitter, or baking chocolate. In the U.S., it must contain 50 to 58% cocoa butter but contain no sugar. In Canada, unsweetened chocolate must contain at least 50% cocoa butter.

Dark chocolate (aka bittersweet, semisweet, and sweet chocolate): Adding vanilla and sugar to chocolate liquor during conching creates dark chocolate that may be bittersweet, semisweet, or sweet. Semisweet and bittersweet chocolates contain at least 35% chocolate liquor by weight. Many fine bittersweet chocolates contain more than 70% chocolate liquor. Sweet chocolate may contain as little as 15% chocolate liquor. In Canada, it must contain at least 30% chocolate liquor.

Mexican chocolate: Flavored with cinnamon, almonds, and vanilla, this chocolate has a more grainy texture than other dark chocolates.

Milk chocolate: Adding vanilla, sugar, and milk to chocolate liquor creates the North American favorite, milk chocolate, with a minimum of 12% milk solids and a relatively low 10% chocolate liquor (in Canada, it must contain at least 25%).

Gianduja: Adding hazelnut or almond paste (about 50% by weight) transforms dark or milk chocolate into gianduja, a popular chocolate in Italy and Switzerland.

Couverture chocolate: These high-quality dark and milk chocolates contain additional cocoa butter (a minimum of 32% in the final product) to create easy melting chocolate suitable for making candy.

White chocolate: Without cocoa solids and their distinct chocolate flavors, white chocolate isn't really chocolate at all. It's a candy made from cocoa butter, lecithin, milk, sugar, and vanilla. The best-quality brands use a relatively high percentage of cocoa butter.

Compound coatings: These faux chocolates contain chocolate liquor but no cocoa butter. Instead, they use less expensive fats like coconut oil, palm kernel oil, cottonseed oil, or soybean oil and are easier to work with because they lack cocoa butter and its sensitivities to heat. They are formulated with fats that coat foods like doughnuts better or melt at a higher temperature, which is required for mass-market candies that will be stored during the warm summer months. These products lack the luxurious texture of real chocolate.

Mass-market chocolates tend to contain only the minimum amounts of chocolate liquor. Some contain no chocolate liquor at all (neither cocoa butter nor cocoa solids). Many manufacturers have lobbied the U.S. government to allow products made without cocoa butter to be labeled "chocolate," but current regulations require all products called "chocolate" to contain at least 10% chocolate liquor, a portion of which must contain cocoa butter. Fine chocolate makers use the best cacao beans and ample amounts of chocolate liquor, and list the percentage of chocolate or cocoa, which refers to the total combined weight of the cocoa solids and cocoa butter. For instance, 72% chocolate contains 72% cocoa butter and cocoa solids and about 28% sugar by weight.

What It Does • In everything from holiday candies and cakes to workaday puddings and ice creams, chocolate brings smiles to faces around the world. Along with cream, it is one of the basic ingredients in ganache, the irresistible filling used for chocolate truffles, cakes, and other desserts. Apart from its use in sweet cookies, pies, tarts, custards, mousses, soufflés, and syrups, chocolate also forms the bitter-astringent flavor component of many savory sauces such as mole and other bitter chocolate sauces served with game meats.

Many bakers prefer unsweetened natural cocoa powder for its concentrated chocolate flavor and so that they can control the addition of fat, sugar, vanilla, and other flavorings. Naturally acidic, cocoa powder is often used to help activate **chemical leaveners** like baking soda. On the other hand, Dutch-process (alkalized) cocoa powder is not acidic, so the two cocoa powders are not interchangeable in baking. An acid ingredient must be added when using Dutch-process cocoa in combination with chemical leaveners. To replace 3 tablespoons (45 mL) natural cocoa powder with the same amount of Dutch-process cocoa in baking, add ⅛ teaspoon (0.5 mL) cream of tartar to the recipe. But many bakers reserve the milder flavor of Dutch-process cocoa for desserts that call for a less intense chocolate flavor, such as when dusting truffles and cakes.

Melting

Solid chocolate is essentially a suspension of cocoa powder in cocoa butter, which is very sensitive to heat. Cocoa butter melts at relatively low temperatures of 87 to 97°F (31 to 36°C), so gentle heating is best, especially for milk chocolate and white chocolates. Even a tiny drop of water can cause melting chocolate to quickly "seize," or harden into a stiff, grainy paste that will not melt. Make sure your pans, bowls, and utensils are bone-dry and avoid using pot lids, which can trap moisture. Adding more warm liquid will saturate the seized paste and eventually make the chocolate fluid again, but it will thin out the texture of the melted chocolate.

To melt chocolate without seizing, chop or break the chocolate into small, fairly uniform pieces so that it melts evenly, then carefully melt:

In a pan over direct low heat: This method requires constant stirring and risks burning the chocolate, but it can be done in a hurry.

In a heatproof bowl over gently simmering water: This method, often done in a double boiler, provides gentle heat and requires less stirring but risks seizing the chocolate because of the presence of water and steam.

In a preheating or low oven: Many cooks prefer this simple method for its even, gentle heat and complete absence of water. If the oven is already preheating for making chocolate desserts, why not simply melt the chocolate there? Just be sure to remove the chocolate from the oven as soon as it is melted enough to be stirred smooth and before the oven gets too hot (no more than 300°F/150°C).

In a microwave oven: Microwave cooking melts chocolate easily but may subject the chocolate to extreme hot spots and requires frequent stirring. Melt dark chocolates at medium (50%) power, and milk and white chocolates at low (30%) power, stopping to stir every minute until the chocolate is melted and smooth. Keep in mind that some chocolates such as chocolate chips may be melted enough to be stirred smooth even though they retain their shape.

On a warming tray or heating pad: If you have a warming tray or heating pad handy, put it on the lowest setting and place the bowl of chocolate on it, stirring occasionally until smooth.

In a pan or bowl with ample warm liquid: When chocolate will be combined with hot cream, melted butter, or other warm liquid (at least ¼ cup/50 mL warm liquid per 6 ounces/175 g of chocolate), you can heat both ingredients in the same pan using any of the methods above, stirring frequently until the ingredients combine. Alternatively, you can heat the liquid first, then add the solid chocolate to the warm liquid, stirring until smooth and combined.

Tempering

Because cocoa butter is heat sensitive, solid chocolate is tempered by manufacturers. This process of cooling the melted chocolate in a controlled way stabilizes the cocoa butter and creates glossy, smooth-textured chocolate that snaps when broken. If melted chocolate is cooled in an uncontrolled way, the fat molecules form loose crystals that will remelt at low temperatures (63 to 83°F/17 to 28°C), creating greasy chocolate that melts too easily. The crystal that melts between 90 and 95°F (32 and 35°C), just a few degrees below our body temperature, is the crystal that creates chocolate's melt-in-your-mouth texture. Tempering is a process of eliminating the other crystals to create the tightly packed, stable crystals that give chocolate its incomparable snappy texture that melts luxuriously after just a second or two on our tongues.

When you are simply melting the chocolate and mixing it with other ingredients to make cookies, brownies, cakes, buttercream, ganache, mousse, or custard, be sure the melted chocolate isn't heated above its tempering range, which tops out at about 90°F (32°C). However, when melted chocolate is being used to "enrobe" or form the surface of a food, as on chocolate-dipped fruit, candies, cookies, or truffles, or when it is molded into various shapes, it will lose its temper and must be retempered to restore its glossy surface sheen and snappy texture.

To easily temper manufactured chocolate for enrobing or molding, use a very accurate thermometer (preferably digital). Finely chop the chocolate, then melt about two-thirds of it to 115 to 120°F (46 to 50°C). Then cool the chocolate to 95 to 100°F (35 to 38°C).

Add the remaining one-third chopped chocolate to the melted chocolate, stirring gently until all the chocolate is smooth and cools to 88 to 90°F (31 to 32°C). Stirring gently encourages stable crystals to form gradually.

If you follow the temperatures meticulously, your well-tempered chocolate should coat the back of a spoon. Drop a bit of the molten chocolate onto a plate and it should dry and set with a glossy sheen in three to five minutes. If it takes longer to set or the surface appears grainy, repeat the tempering process.

To help chocolate keep its temper as you work with it, keep it within the tempering range of 88 to 90°F (31 to 32°C) by resting it in a bowl of water that's a few degrees warmer than the chocolate (92 to 95°F/33 to 35°C) or by setting the bowl of tempered chocolate on a warming tray or heating pad on the lowest setting. Be sure to stir gently and check the temperature often. If the chocolate goes below the tempering range or solidifies, you can store it for later use, and you can retemper it at a later time.

Many foods can simply be dipped in tempered chocolate, then set on parchment or wax paper to cool and harden. For truffles and other foods that may melt when held in your hands, wear latex gloves, and put a large

spoonful of melted tempered chocolate in your palm. Add a chocolate truffle to your palm, roll it around until coated, and set it on wax paper to dry. Once cooled, many truffles are dipped once again (double-dipped) for a thicker coating.

Keep in mind that imitation chocolates (compound or summer coatings) don't require tempering because they are made with fats that are less sensitive to heat than cocoa butter. They can simply be melted to 5 to 10°F (3 to 6°C) above their melting point.

Molding, Modeling, and Curls

Tempered chocolate can be painted or spread onto molds as simple as a leaf, flat sheet, or metal bowl (to create a dome-shaped chocolate shell) or as elaborate as a multipart mold to create candies like hollow Easter bunnies. Chocolate molds should be kept at about 78 to 80°F (26 to 27°C) to prevent the tempered chocolate from cooling too quickly, which could create a less snappy texture. When molded chocolate cools, it will shrink slightly and pull away from the mold, making it easy to unmold.

Tempered chocolate can also be mixed with sugar and/or corn syrup and kneaded into more pliable chocolate used for modeling simple or elaborate chocolate sculptures. To make modeling chocolate, temper about 10 ounces (300 g) dark chocolate, mix it with ⅓ cup (75 mL) corn syrup to form a kind of dough, then cover and chill it for eight hours. Let it warm up until pliable.

To make chocolate curls, warm the chocolate briefly in a microwave oven at Low (30%) power in 10-second increments, set it under a 40- or 60-watt light bulb for a few minutes, or let it rest at about 80°F (27°C) for an hour or two. Then hold the block between paper towels (to avoid melting it with your body heat) and drag a paring knife or vegetable peeler across the surface. You can also drag a putty or bench knife or large metal spoon across the surface of softened chocolate as if you were scooping ice cream. If you don't dig too deeply, the chocolate will scrape off in long, thin "pencil" curls (with a putty or bench knife) or wider curls (with a spoon).

science wise

Magic Candy • Candies like chocolate-covered cherries are marvels of modern confectionery. How do they get the liquid inside a solid chocolate shell? They don't inject it in. In fact, the center starts out firm. The cherries are actually coated in fondant candy, a smooth paste of sugar and water that solidifies as it cools around the cherries in a round mold. The candy is then dipped or enrobed in melted chocolate. Here's the fun part: the fondant is made with an invertase enzyme, which slowly converts sugar (sucrose) to invert sugar as the candy is stored. The invert sugar is more soluble than sucrose, and in the moist environment of the fondant-coated cherry, it transforms the candy's solid center into a creamy liquid during storage.

Storage

When stored in a place that's cool (about 60 to 65°F/16 to 18°C), dark, and not too humid (less than 50% humidity), chocolate should last a year or more. But if the temperature fluctuates wildly or goes above 75°F (24°C) for several months, as in the summer, the chocolate may develop a cloudy, pale-gray "fat bloom" of melted and then recrystallized cocoa butter on the surface. Similarly, if the humidity is high, excess moisture may dissolve some of the sugar in the chocolate and create a similar-looking, blotchy "sugar bloom" on its surface. Regardless of bloom, the chocolate is still usable, although chocolate with sugar bloom may seize more easily when melted because of the presence of moisture.

In the warm summer months, you can refrigerate chocolate, but that may cause condensation to form on the surface as it cools, leaving behind moisture that can create sugar bloom and interfere with smooth melting. Chocolate can also be frozen, but it should be thawed completely in the refrigerator. After refrigerating chocolate, minimize condensation by gradually cooling it to room temperature before melting it. Just remember: cocoa butter prefers gradual temperature changes.

How It Works • The silky-smooth, mouth-filling texture of chocolate comes mostly from cocoa butter. This remarkable fat is solid below 88°F (31°C) but begins to melt above 93°F (34°C). This is the temperature that happens to be just below our body temperature, which creates an incomparably lush sensation as solid chocolate gradually melts into a luscious puddle on our tongues. High-cocoa-butter chocolates feel distinctly more luscious than low- or no-cocoa-butter chocolates, so they cost more. Conching (fine grinding) and, to a lesser extent, the emulsifier lecithin also smooth out the texture of solid chocolate, enhancing its mouth feel. The cacao beans in European chocolates are usually ground finer (less than 80 millionths of an inch) than British and North American chocolates and tend to taste slightly smoother.

Most of the flavors we know as "chocolate" (there are well over 500 of them) develop when cacao beans are fermented and roasted. The primary flavors are astringent and bitter, coming from tannins (accounting for 6% of chocolate liquor by weight) and theobromine, an alkaloid compound in cacao beans. Fermenting cacao beans also produces flavors such as astringent acetic acid, savory amino acids, nutty benzaldehyde, and floral linalool. Roasting the beans creates caramelized flavors from furaneol, browned flavors from pyrazines, and malty flavors from maltol.

Healthfulness

Most of chocolate's healthfulness comes from antioxidants that reduce the everyday oxidative stress on our bodies. Cocoa powder is the most concentrated source of these antioxidant compounds, which account for 8% of cocoa powder's weight. Studies show that hot cocoa beverages contain more antioxidants than wine and tea. However, alkalizing, or Dutch-processing, cocoa powder destroys most of the antioxidants in cocoa powder, so stick with natural cocoa if you're looking for a health benefit.

The health-promoting antioxidants in chocolate are called polyphenols, and they can reduce the risk of heart disease by preventing clots and improving blood flow. Polyphenols like flavonols and procyanidins are most concentrated in high-quality cocoa powder and solid dark chocolates that contain a high percentage of chocolate liquor or cocoa solids. The more bitter the chocolate, the more antioxidants it will deliver to your body. That's one reason why some chocolate manufacturers promote the percentage of cocoa in their bitter chocolate products. However, recent studies show that manufacturers of lesser-quality dark chocolate candies sometimes strip the chocolate of its flavonols during processing because flavonols taste bitter and they think consumers don't want bitter-tasting chocolate. Thus, the percentage of cocoa on a package of chocolate may tell you whether the chocolate is bittersweet or semisweet, but it doesn't necessarily tell you anything about flavonol content. In a perfect world, manufacturers would list flavonol content, but to be sure you're getting a health benefit from dark chocolate, only buy high-quality chocolate with a high percentage of cocoa solids. Better yet, contact the manufacturer and ask them about the flavonol content of their chocolate.

The mild stimulant or mood-enhancing effect of chocolate comes primarily from theobromine, the bitter-tasting alkaloid for which cacao trees get their Greek name, *Theobroma cacao*. Chocolate has a reputation for caffeine content, but it contains 10 times more theobromine than it does caffeine.

The mood-altering effect of chocolate may also be partially attributable to anandamide, another polyphenol and relative of the psychoactive compound in marijuana. Despite these mood-altering and stimulant compounds, chocolate is not thought to have chemically addictive qualities. Most people just can't get enough of its melt-in-your-mouth texture.

Health experts generally agree that moderate chocolate consumption can promote good health. It's true that cocoa butter is rich in saturated fat (about 6 grams in 1 ounce/28 grams of dark chocolate), but the body quickly converts this saturated stearic fatty acid into unsaturated oleic fatty acid. As a result, chocolate's saturated fat hasn't been shown to pose a significant risk for heart disease. Chocolate also contains antioxidants, magnesium, copper, potassium, and calcium (in milk chocolate), all of which improve circulation and heart health. Yes, moderate consumption (1 ounce/28 g a day) of solid chocolate is considered beneficial to your health. So what are you waiting for? Have a little piece!

See Also • Antioxidants, Caffeine, Candy

CHOKECHERRY • See Cherry

CHOLESTEROL

What It Is • A soft, waxy lipid (a type of **fat**), cholesterol comes in two forms: dietary cholesterol, which is found in animal foods, and blood cholesterol, which is produced by the liver to support vital body functions but which, in excess amounts, appears to be linked with the development of heart disease. Eggs and organ meats are the richest sources of dietary cholesterol, while meat, poultry, fish, milk, and dairy products contain varying amounts.

What It Does • In a small subset of individuals, excess dietary cholesterol plays a role in negatively raising blood cholesterol levels. However, most people don't need to closely monitor their intake of dietary cholesterol. It is the quantity of saturated and particularly artificially created trans fatty acids consumed that has the greatest impact on blood cholesterol levels. These fatty acids tend to stimulate the liver to produce more cholesterol, which ends up raising blood cholesterol levels.

Although trans fatty acids that result from the process of partial hydrogenation have no health benefits, our bodies do need saturated fatty acids in moderation and there are some saturated fatty acids that don't appear to negatively affect blood cholesterol levels. For instance, your body easily converts stearic acid, the saturated fatty acid in butter and chocolate, to oleic acid, a monounsaturated fat that has a positive effect on blood cholesterol. What refreshing

news for those of us who love butter and chocolate! (For a list of common fats and their saturated fat content, see Saturation Ratios of Common Culinary Fats chart, page 220.)

How It Works • Our livers produce about 1,000 mg of cholesterol a day, which is all we need for vital body functions like manufacturing cell membranes and steroid hormones, including sex hormones such as estrogen and testosterone. This blood cholesterol also helps us metabolize fat-soluble vitamins like A, D, E, and K. The liver can remove some excess cholesterol from the blood, but the rest may build up in our arteries over time and increase risk of circulation problems and heart disease.

See Also • Fat, Metabolism

CHORIZO • See Sausage

CHRYSANTHEMUM GREENS • See Herbs

CHUFA • See Stems

CHUTNEY • See Sauces

CICELY • See Herbs

CIDER

What It Is • Pressing the juice from apples and sometimes pears creates various types of cider. When the juice is sold unfiltered it is known as sweet cider or apple cider (as opposed to apple juice, which is filtered). Fermented juice is known as hard cider because it contains at least 0.15% ABV (alcohol by volume). Outside North America, the term "cider" generally refers to fermented, alcoholic hard cider.

science wise

Frozen Assets • Applejack is a product of American ingenuity. When New England colonists sought stiffer drinks in the winter but didn't want to fuss with distillation, they turned to "freeze-distillation." They simply left their barrels of cider or apple wine out in the bitter cold. Water freezes at 32°F (0°C), but ethyl alcohol freezes only at the extremely low temperature of −179°F (−117°C). The ice froze on the surface, drawing water from the cider or wine and leaving behind a more concentrated, higher-alcohol beverage. They skimmed off the ice and repeated the process enough to concentrate the alcohol to 25 to 40% (50 to 80 proof).

When cider is carbonated, it becomes sparkling cider. When made with pear juice, popular in France and the U.K., it's called poiré or perry. In Canada, producers have popularized "ice cider" made with frozen, high-sugar apples in a method similar to ice wine. In the U.K., where most of the world's cider is produced and consumed, "real" cider must contain 85 to 90% fresh apple juice with no added or artificial flavors or colors.

What It Does • Made since about 1200, hard cider is popular in regions where grapevines don't grow as well as fruit trees. The flavor of cider ranges from dry to sweet, and its color may be clear, pale gold, or golden brown, depending upon the fruit varieties and degree of fermentation and filtering. Less filtered ciders tend to have a stronger flavor, darker color, and more cloudy appearance. Mass-produced white cider is highly filtered.

The nonalcoholic version, sweet cider, is never filtered. That's the only thing that distinguishes it from apple juice. Sweet cider is popular in North America as a cold and warm beverage (as in mulled cider) and is sometimes used to make sweet or savory sauces. Sweet cider is not required to be pasteurized, but manufacturers usually do it to prevent the cider from fermenting and turning into hard cider and to insure against pathogenic *E. coli* and *Salmonella*. However, unpasteurized cider may retain more complex flavors than the pasteurized product as a result of the heat processing of **pasteurization**. The only precaution with unpasteurized cider is that it should be kept refrigerated. If your sweet cider looks fizzy and tastes astringent, fermentation has probably begun and the cider should be discarded. The bacteria that have fermented the sugars in the juice could be harmful.

fast fact

- The U.K. leads the world in hard cider consumption and production, providing the international market with more than 110 million gallons (4.2 million L) per year.

How It Works • The juice of any apple or pear can be fermented into cider, but certain apples, called cider apples, are preferred for their high acidity and astringent tannins. Cider apples are typically juiced and blended to provide a combination of sweet, sharp, bittersweet, and bitter-sharp flavor characteristics that encourage fermentation, alcohol development, acidity, and tannins in the final beverage.

At the cider mill, whole apples are ground down (scratted) into a pomace, then the juice is pressed out and transferred to vats or casks to ferment. Cider is fermented with yeast at lower temperatures (40 to 60°F/4 to 16°C) than most other alcoholic beverages to preserve the delicate aromas in the fruit juice. Yeasts feed on the fruit sugars and convert them to ethyl alcohol (grain alcohol).

Dry ciders, such as Spanish *sidra*, have had most of their sugars converted into alcohol and they taste as dry as dry white wine. After the initial fermentation, the juice may be filtered or unfiltered, creating a clear or cloudy appearance in the cider. The fermented juice is then "racked," or transferred to clean vats or casks, for secondary fermentation that may last up to three years. Sometimes additional sugar is added to raise the alcohol level and enhance carbonation, as in sparkling cider. The highest quality sparkling ciders are made according to the *méthode champenoise* used for Champagne. Either way, hard cider contains between 3 and 8% alcohol, slightly lower than the alcohol content of **beer**.

Let's suppose you add enough sugar to continue fermentation until the alcohol content reaches 10 to 12%. At that point, you have apple **wine**, which may display flavors as complex as grape wines if it is carefully aged in wooden casks.

Now, let's suppose you distill or concentrate that apple wine. Then you have created apple brandy like Calvados or applejack, both of which have an alcohol content of about 40%.

When hard cider or apple wine is allowed to oxidize (usually with the help of bacteria called *Acetobacter aceti*), the ethyl alcohol in the cider converts into astringent acetic acid and you get sour-tasting cider vinegar.

See Also • Apple, Beer, Carbon Dioxide, Fermentation, Liquor, Vinegar, Wine

CIDER VINEGAR • See Cider, Vinegar

CILANTRO • See Herbs, Spices

CINNAMON • See Spices

CIPOLLINI • See Allium

CITRIC ACID

What It Is • Citric acid is a weak organic **acid** that's found in citrus fruits. It's also the main acid in tomatoes and provides some of the acidity in coffee. When the moisture from foods containing citric acid evaporates, the acid itself appears as a white, odorless crystalline powder, sometimes called sour salt or lemon salt.

Citric acid was first obtained by extracting it from lemons, but today it is made commercially by fermenting sugar (often molasses) using *Aspergillus niger* bacteria. The acid is then isolated by getting rid of the moisture. Produced this way, citric acid is chemically identical to the organic substance found in lemons. Citric acid is available in two forms: a dry, white powder called "anhydrous" or water-free citric acid (used for dry products), and a "monohydrate" citric acid that contains 8 to 9% water as part of the crystals.

What It Does • Lemon juice tastes pretty sour, right? Well, it's only about 5 to 7% citric acid. Multiply that sourness by about 15 times and you'll have the taste of 100% citric acid. It is essentially the pure flavor of sourness and is used in thousands of food products. Citric acid can be added to foods (as a **food additive**) to provide tartness alone without introducing other flavors. Dozens of tart-tasting beverages

science wise

Sequestering and Spherification • Sodium citrate is sometimes confused with citric acid because it is the sodium salt of citric acid. This white, odorless crystal has many of the same capabilities and uses in food as citric acid. It's used as a preservative in some foods and as a sequestering agent in ice creams to prevent fat globules from sticking together. In avant-garde restaurants, such as Heston Blumenthal's The Fat Duck and Wylie Dufresne's WD-50 (along with many others grouped under the term "molecular gastronomy"), sodium citrate is sometimes used to regulate the acidity of high-acid liquids. These liquids are mixed with alginates (extracted from seaweed), then dropped into calcium chloride, which coagulates the liquid into jelled spheres that resemble caviar or small marbles. This process is known as spherification.

include citric acid because it is highly soluble in water. You'll also find citric acid in sour balls and other candies, where it provides tartness and helps to prevent sugar from crystallizing, an essential process of candy making. Look on the label of your favorite jelly. You'll find citric acid there too because its acidity helps to gel foods that contain pectin such as **jams and jellies**.

Citric acid also acts as a preservative in food products by inhibiting the growth of harmful microbes and inhibiting the natural enzymes in food from causing the food to deteriorate. In canned foods, for instance, it helps to maintain texture, color, aroma, and vitamin content. In frozen fruit, it helps to prevent enzymatic browning and discoloration (in the same way that rubbing a cut apple with lemon juice helps to prevent browning). Citric acid even helps prevent discoloration and off flavors in seafood products like fish sticks. In food products containing fat (we're talking thousands of foods here), citric acid acts as an **antioxidant** preservative by delaying the natural process of fats going rancid as a result of oxidation or decay. It's also used in ice creams to prevent fat globules from sticking together.

You'll find citric acid in many foods that

bubble up, too. It's frequently the acid that activates alkaline sodium bicarbonate (baking soda) and releases carbon dioxide bubbles in effervescent products like Alka-Seltzer antacids.

How It Works • In whole foods, citric acid is mostly concentrated in lemons and limes and may constitute up to 8% of the fruit's weight. Citric acid delivers that sharp, clean bite of tartness, but dissipates quickly from the tongue, whereas the tartness of other acids like fumaric acid lingers a little longer on the palate. Food manufacturers and some chefs use citric acid's short-lived tartness to create specific flavor sensations in foods.

When used as an antioxidant preservative in foods, citric acid inhibits the enzymes that cause fruits and vegetables to discolor and deteriorate and sequesters metal ions that catalyze fat rancidity. Citric acid helps to maintain color and flavor in beverages like soft drinks by stabilizing the pH. In this role, it's known as a "buffering" agent because it controls the amount of free hydrogen ions available in the soft drink, preventing those hydrogen ions from forming chemical bonds that could alter the pH and the taste of the drink. Different acids vary in their buffering ability, but citric acid has the widest buffering range, providing pH protection from pH 2.5 to pH 6.5.

When citric acid is used as a preservative in foods containing fat, it's called a sequestrant or chelating agent. The citric acid reacts with metal ions such as ions of copper and iron and sequesters, or chelates, them in a chemical ring structure. Chelation prevents those ions from reacting with other chemicals that could cause the foods to oxidize, discolor (turn brown), degenerate, and decay.

See Also • Acid, Citrus, Food Additives

fast fact

- In a 1% solution with water, the pH of dry anhydrous citric acid is 2.2, while citric acid monohydrate in a 1% solution has a pH of 2.3 (because there was already water in the monohydrate when it was weighed).

CITRON • See Citrus

CITRUS

What It Is • Orange juice is a popular morning refresher around the globe, but North Americans drink more of it than anyone else. Overall, oranges and other citrus fruits are the third most commonly cultivated fruit family in the world (just behind the apple/pear family and the banana/plantain family), not least because citrus trees yield high quantities of fruit. Worldwide citrus production includes about 65% sweet and sour oranges, 15% mandarin oranges (including hybrids like tangelos and tangors), 10% lemons and limes, and 10% grapefruit. Most citrus fruits stem from three main parent species, mandarin orange (*Citrus reticulata*), pomelo (*Citrus grandis*), and citron (*Citrus medica*), all native to China, India, and Southeast Asia.

These citrus granddaddies have produced hundreds of varieties ranging widely in color and flavor (see Families and Flavors of Citrus chart, page 142). But they all have a similar anatomy. The outer colored peel or zest is known as the flavedo, a good term because that's where the intensely flavorful essential oils and vitamin C tend to concentrate. Just beneath the flavedo lies the inner white peel, or albedo (white pith), which supports the flavedo's essential oil glands and is rich in bitter compounds and pectin. The entire peel encases the pulp, with segments consisting of delicate juice sacs (vesicles) held together by a fibrous membrane.

What It Does • The various components of citrus fruits are widely used in cooking and food products around the world. But most of the world's harvest is processed into juice. About 70% of the North American orange crop is processed for the food industry. In the early 1940s, the Florida Department of Citrus began concentrating orange juice in a vacuum and freezing it without significant flavor or vitamin loss. In addition to frozen concentrate, citrus fruit is now processed into frozen ice pops, canned or bottled segments, marmalades, essential oils, pectin, citric acid, and flavor chemicals used by the food, pharmaceutical, cosmetic, and perfume industries.

Citrus peels contain essential oils with wonderfully intense aromas, which are usually pressed or extracted from the peel and used to flavor soft drinks (such as Sprite), candies (lemon drops), and liquors (triple sec). Cooks often strip the outer peel, or zest, from the fruit to lend citrus aromas to baked goods and other dishes. Sometimes the zest is dried and/or candied. Citrus flowers are another source of essential oil, which is extracted from the flowers of bitter oranges to create orange blossom water and is useful for making jams and jellies and other thickened mixtures because it's rich in pectins.

Uses for Citrus Varieties

Sweet oranges, the jack-of-all-trades, are the most widely produced citrus fruit because they can be juiced, used for essential oils, used fresh in salads, or cooked in main dishes and desserts. Seedless navel oranges are best for eating fresh. Milder-tasting Valencia oranges (and similar varieties like Hamlin) are seedy and best for juicing. Blood oranges have a hint of plum or raspberry aroma and lend a pink or burgundy color.

Mandarin oranges (tangerines) tend to be smaller than sweet oranges and have looser skin that is easily peeled. Most varieties are eaten fresh (think of clementines), and seedless satsumas are often separated into segments and canned. Tangelos and tangors are mandarin hybrids, as is yuzu, a favorite in teas, sauces, and other dishes, where it lends a complex mix of citrus, clove, and thyme flavors.

Sour oranges are used mostly for their peels, which are rich in bitter compounds that flavor food products like Angostura and other bitters. Whole sour oranges, such as Seville, have also been made into marmalades since the 1500s, if not earlier. In liqueurs, sour orange peels provide the distinctive citrus aromas in Grand Marnier, Cointreau, curaçao, and triple sec. Bergamot is often classified as a sour orange but it may also have some parentage in the lime. Regardless, it

fast facts

- Grapefruit juice decreases your body's production of enzymes necessary to metabolize some prescription and nonprescription drugs. Consult your physician or pharmacist about taking medications with grapefruit juice.
- Ugli is a registered trademark of Cabel Hall Citrus Ltd., the Jamaican distributor that exports the fruit. It was named when a buyer at a Canadian produce market looked at the fruit's thick, baggy, pale orange skin and called it ugly.
- The fishy aroma of less-than-fresh seafood comes from ammonia and amino acid broken down into amines. The citric acid found in lemon juice and other citrus fruits helps to neutralize those compounds and freshen up the fish. That's one reason why seafood and citrus go so well together.

provides the characteristic citrus perfume in Earl Grey tea and some colognes.

From Morocco to San Diego, lemons are the most common culinary citrus. They deliver a refreshing bite to drinks like lemonade, mayonnaise and other sauces, seafood and poultry dishes, and countless desserts. Sicily produces about 90% of the world's lemons. In North America, Eureka and Lisbon are the most widely used varieties. The Meyer lemon, a hybrid cross between mandarin orange and lemon, has sweeter

juice and a more floral aroma.

Limes are slightly more acidic than lemons. Seedless Tahiti (Persian) limes are the most common North America variety, while seeded Key (Mexican) limes have a slightly more robust flavor. Key limes lend their flavor to Key lime pie and such products as Rose's Lime Juice. They're preferred outside North America, particularly in Mexican and Latin American dishes such as seviche, where their acidity denatures the proteins in fish and shellfish, making the flesh firm and opaque in the same way that cooking with heat does. Makrut or wild lime (formerly called kaffir) is used mostly for its leaves, which have a sort of green-lemon aroma similar to lemongrass. The finger lime, native to Australia and named for its elongated shape, has intensely aromatic juice used to flavor drinks, jams, sauces, and other foods.

Pomelos (Chinese grapefruits) are slightly larger than grapefruit, with a very thick rind. Pomelo juice tends to be slightly sweeter than grapefruit, which itself is a hybrid of pomelo and sweet orange and the only citrus to originate in the New World (in the West Indies in the 1700s). The grapefruit's name comes from the fruit's habit of growing in grape-like clusters. White grapefruit varieties are more aromatic, but red blush grapefruits like Rio Star, developed in Texas, tend to be sweeter.

Kumquats are the runt of the citrus

family. They're actually a different genus (*Fortunella* rather than *Citrus*) and are usually eaten whole because the thin skin is sweet and well balanced by the pleasantly bitter pulp. Calamondins, a related fruit, are a hybrid of kumquat and mandarin orange.

The one citrus that tends to be harvested exclusively for its peel is citron. It contains very little juice, but its wrinkled peel is highly aromatic. Citron peels are traditionally brined, then allowed to ferment with airborne yeasts to bloom their flavor. The same flavor-enhancing technique is at work in preserved lemons that are packed in salt and fermented to soften and deepen flavors. Fermented citron

peel is frequently candied and used in sweet breads like fruitcake.

Citrus fruits don't ripen further after picking. Choose the heaviest fruits, as they tend be the juiciest and least dried out. To more easily extract the juice from citrus, bring the fruit to room temperature and/or roll it on a countertop to break the juice sacs before squeezing.

Citrus is often sprayed with a waxy coating to prevent moisture loss and help the fruit last longer. Before zesting citrus fruit, wash it with hot water to melt off the wax. After removing the zest, the nude fruit can be refrigerated in a plastic bag for about one week. Whole fruits are best kept refrigerated in a plastic bag, where they'll

Families and Flavors of Citrus

Citrus fruits have been naturally hybridizing and mutating for centuries. Even the parent species like mandarin orange (*Citrus reticulata*) and pomelo (*Citrus grandis*) were once hybrids. Cultivation techniques have created hundreds more. Below you'll find just a few of the varieties in each major citrus family, and some common hybrids. Citrus flavor comes primarily from a compound called limonene. Some other flavors in citrus fruit include pine (pinene), fresh lemon (citral), green lemon (citronellal), floral (linalool, geraniol), herbal (terpinene), thyme (thymol), oregano (carvacrol), spicy (myrcene), clove (eugenol), bitter (nootkatone, naringin), rich (decanal, octenol), musk (sulfur compounds), sharp (sinsensal), and green honey (valencene).

Citrus	Varieties	Citrus	Varieties
Sweet orange (*Citrus sinensis*)	Cara Cara, Dream navel, Glen navel, Hamlin, Jaffa (Shamouti), Jincheng, Roble, Valencia, Washington navel	Citron (*Citrus medica*)	Buddha's hand citron, Diamante, Etrog
		Makrut lime (*Citrus hystrix*)	Thai
Blood orange (*Citrus sinensis*)	Moro, Sanguinelli, Tarocco	Yuzu (*Citrus junos*)	Japanese citron
Mandarin orange (*Citrus reticulata*) or tangerine	Clementine, Dancy tangerine, Murcott, Page, Ponkan, satsuma, Willowleaf (Mediterranean)	Kumquat (*Fortunella*)	Hong Kong, Meiwa (neiha kinkan), Nagami
		Calamondin (*Citrus reticulata x Fortunella*)	Variegated Calamondin, Kalamansi
Sour orange (*Citrus aurantium*)	Bittersweet, Chinotto, Seville, Tunis, Bergamot	Oroblanco (*Citrus grandis x C. paradisi*)	Sweetie
Lemon (*Citrus limon*)	Bearss, Eureka, Lisbon, Meyer, Yen Ben	Rangpur (*Citrus reticulata x C. limon*)	Mandarin lime, Kusiae, Otaheite
Lime (*Citrus aurantifolia* and *latifolia*)	*Indian sweet, Key* (Mexican), Tahiti (Persian or Bearss)	Tangelo (*Citrus reticulata x C. grandis or C. paradisi*)	Orlando, Minneola, Nocatee
Grapefruit (*Citrus paradisi*)	Burgundy, Duncan, Foster, Marsh, Rio Red, Ruby, Ruby Red, Star Ruby, Triumph	Tangor (*Citrus reticulata x Citrus sinensis*)	Ortanique, Temple, Ugli
Pomelo (*Citrus grandis*)	Hirado Buntan, Pandan Wangi, pink pomelo, Red Shaddock, Wainright		

Candied Citrus Peel

The bitter compounds in the albedo (white pith) of citrus peels are water-soluble but the highly aromatic essential oils in the colorful outer zest are not. To candy citrus peel, cooks usually blanch the entire peel a few times to leach out the bitterness from the pith, scrape away most of the pith, then candy the aromatic peel in sugar syrup. To easily remove the entire peel from citrus fruit, blanch the whole fruit in simmering water for 30 seconds, then plunge into ice water, and the peel will easily separate from the fruit.

3	oranges or 6 lemons or citrons	3
2 cups	granulated sugar, divided	500 mL
2 tbsp	light (white) corn syrup	25 mL

1. Remove entire peel from citrus (reserve fruit for another use) and place peel in a small saucepan. Cover with water and bring to a boil over high heat. Drain, rinse with cold water, then cover again with water. Repeat boiling and rinsing two more times. Using a spoon or paring knife, scrape away as much white pith from zest as possible. Cut zest into matchstick strips and set aside.

2. In a saucepan over medium heat, combine 1 cup (250 mL) of the sugar, corn syrup and ⅔ cup (150 mL) water, stirring until sugar dissolves. Reduce heat to low. Add citrus zest and cook gently until only a film of syrup remains, 5 to 7 minutes. Transfer to a parchment-lined baking sheet and let cool to room temperature, then cover and let stand for 8 hours to dry (or dry on the parchment-lined baking sheet in a 250°F/120°C oven for 30 minutes).

3. Place remaining sugar in a large bowl. Return citrus zest to saucepan and bring to a simmer over medium-low heat. Drain any excess syrup, then transfer zest to sugar in bowl, shaking until well coated. Transfer to parchment or wax paper and let dry for 1 to 2 hours. Refrigerate in an airtight container for 2 to 3 months.

MAKES ABOUT 2 CUPS (500 ML)

last for about two weeks. If they get soft before you can use them, grate the zest, squeeze the juice, and freeze each separately. Citrus zest and juice both freeze well for about six months.

Anatomy of Citrus

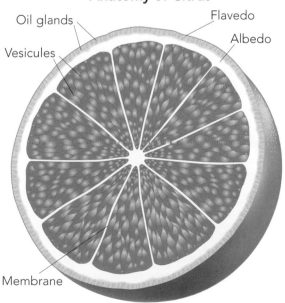

Oil glands

Flavedo

Vesicules

Albedo

Membrane

How It Works • As in other plants, **pigments** produce a rainbow of colors in citrus. Limes and other green-rind citrus get color from chlorophyll. In fact, most citrus peels start out green, but low temperatures (typically at night) destroy the chlorophyll and reveal the yellow-orange carotenoids beneath them. These carotenoids are what give oranges, lemons, and white grapefruit their color. Red oranges are colored by the carotenoids lycopene, beta-carotene, and cryptoxanthin. Pink and red blush grapefruits get their color from the carotenoid lycopene. The blood red color of blood oranges comes from a different set of pigments called anthocyanins, including pelargonidin and delphinidin. The pale white pith of citrus fruit gets some color from anthoxanthin pigments. To eliminate green chlorophyll and bring out other colors, citrus fruits are often treated with natural and harmless ethylene gas.

The tongue-tightening tartness of citrus fruits comes from citric acid. Sweetness comes from sugars like fructose and sucrose.

kitchen wisdom

Use Citrus Zest for Flavor
When perking up green vegetables with citrus, keep them from turning brown by using only the zest and not the juice. Lemon zest contains most of the flavor (that's where the essential oils are) but none of the juice's acid, which is what causes browning in green vegetables.

Citrus varies in sugar and acid content, which is why oranges taste sweeter than limes. For instance, by weight, sweet oranges contain about 10% sugar and 1.2% acid. More tart grapefruits are 6% sugar and 2% acid. In lemons and limes, the acid outweighs the sugar. Lemons are only 2% sugar and 5% acid, and limes are tarter still with 1% sugar and up to 8% acid. Bitterness in citrus comes from phenolic compounds in the albedo (pith) and peel.

The subtle nuances of citrus flavor and aroma come from numerous aromatic compounds, particularly the terpenes. The most distinctive citrus flavor comes from a compound called limonene. You can smell this light, refreshing aroma not only in citrus fruits but also in the herbs mint, dill, and tarragon and the spices caraway, cardamom, and black pepper. Other aromas in citrus fruit come from terpenes like pinene (pine aroma), terpinene (herbal resin aroma), citral (lemon aroma), and linalool (floral aroma). Meyer lemons get a whiff of the herb thyme from a compound called thymol. Makrut lime leaves get their green-lemon aroma from a terpenoid known as citronellal. Oranges and, to a greater extent, grapefruits get a trace of savoriness from glutamic acid (the flavor of MSG). The slightly bitter taste of grapefruits comes from a flavonoid called naringin, which dissipates as grapefruits mature. Ketones give blood oranges their raspberry-like flavor, and most citrus peel gets richness and depth from decanal and octenol. Other citrus flavors come primarily from sulfur compounds. See Families and Flavors of Citrus chart, page 142, for a list of various citrus fruit families and their flavor components.

These color and flavor compounds don't only appeal to our senses of pleasure. Many of them are good for us, too. The limonene found in all citrus has been shown in several studies to help ward off cancer. The carotenoid lycopene in grapefruit may help to reduce risk of heart disease and cancers such as prostate cancer. And the antioxidant polyphenols in blood oranges can help improve circulation and heart health. Citrus is best known for its vitamin C (ascorbic acid) content. But about 75% of the vitamin C in an orange is concentrated in the peel and white pith. The juice contains only about 25%. Cut or squeezed citrus fruits lose about 20% of their vitamin C after eight hours at room temperature or 24 hours in the refrigerator. For the most vitamin C, cut and use fresh citrus right away.

See Also • Acid, Citric Acid, Flavor, Fruit

CLAM • See Mollusks

CLEMENTINE • See Citrus

CLOSTRIDIUM BOTULINUM • See Bacteria, Canning

CLOUD EAR • See Mushrooms

CLOVE • See Spices

CLUB SODA • See Carbon Dioxide

COAGULATION • See Blood, Proteins

COCKLE • See Mollusks

COCOA • See Chocolate

COCONUT

What It Is • Coconuts have become synonymous with the tropics. After all, that's where the coconut palm (*Cocos nucifera*) and its various cultivars thrive, in warm, humid climates, absorbing air through their roots in the sandy coastal soil. In ideal conditions, a tree can produce up to 75 coconuts a year. The coconut is the largest common culinary nut.

It's encased in a thick, woody outer shell (husk). The husk is removed and used for fuel such as coconut charcoal, while the rest of the tree is used in the construction, furniture, and pharmaceutical industries. The hard stone center of the coconut is used mostly as a food.

What It Does • Unripe green coconuts (about four to seven months old) have a jelly-like flesh that can be eaten with a spoon. Most coconuts sold in North American markets are mature coconuts (about one year old) with the outer husk removed, leaving only the shaggy brown "bark" protecting the meat.

When you shake a coconut, you can hear the coconut water sloshing around inside. This water is sweeter and more plentiful in young, tender, green coconuts. As the water firms up into coconut meat, it reduces slightly in volume and becomes less sweet, finally turning sour in old, rotten coconuts.

fast facts

- The word "coconut" stems from the Portuguese *coco*, which means monkey, and refers to the three dark "eyes" on a coconut that make the nut look like a monkey's face.
- Aromatic coconut sugar is made from the sap of various palm trees and may be called palm sugar or gur.

Coconut meat can be grated or sliced and toasted. In North American markets, it is often sold shredded and dried (flaked), sometimes sweetened with sugar. The finest grade of dried, shredded (desiccated) coconut is called macaroon. We have Philadelphian Frank Baker to thank for desiccated coconut. In the 1890s, Baker developed the desiccation method to bring a taste of the tropics to cooks in colder climates, who developed dishes like coconut cake, coconut cream pie, and coconut macaroons.

Coconut milk is extracted from the meat by

Coconut Milk

This recipe makes a medium-density coconut milk. For a thick coconut milk or coconut cream, see Variations, right.

1 cup	packed grated fresh coconut, brown skin removed	250 mL
1 cup	boiling water	250 mL

1. Place coconut in a heatproof bowl and add boiling water. Let stand for 30 minutes.

2. Pour mixture into cheesecloth set over a bowl. Squeeze liquid into bowl. It can be used immediately or refrigerate for up to 1 week or freeze for 6 months.

Variations: *For Thick Coconut Milk:* Use 4 cups (1 L) packed grated fresh coconut and 1 cup (250 mL) water.

For Coconut Cream: To capture the coconut cream make Thick Coconut Milk, refrigerate the milk, then skim off the cream that rises to the top.

MAKES ABOUT 1 CUP (250 ML)

soaking grated coconut in hot water, then squeezing the meat in cheesecloth. Thinner milks can be made by repeating the extraction. Coconut milk's high protein content causes it to coagulate like cow's milk when acidic ingredients are added, making it a good base for coconut custards. It's also useful for thickening sauces. As with cow's milk, coconut milk can be left to sit or refrigerated to allow its fatty coconut cream to rise to the top. Coconut cream tastes wonderfully rich and lends a mouth-filling texture to drinks like piña coladas and to curries and desserts. When sweetened and flavored specifically for drinks, coconut cream is often called "cream of coconut." Don't confuse cream of coconut with creamed coconut, which is coconut cream that has been highly concentrated until it is nearly solid.

Dried coconut meat is known as copra, from which coconut oil is extracted. Refined coconut oil has become an important culinary oil. It's a preferred fat among food manufacturers because it has a high smoke point (450°F/230°C) and its high saturated fat content gives the oil — and the products made with it — a long shelf life. Coconut oil is solid at room temperature and lasts for about two years before going rancid. It's a great frying and baking fat that produces light, crisp results because highly saturated oils are not absorbed into food as much as less saturated oils. (For information on palm oil or another popular frying fat, see **Oil**.)

When buying fresh coconuts, choose heavy ones, which indicates lots of moisture. Store them at room temperature for four to five months, or remove the meat and refrigerate it for up to one week or freeze it for up to eight months. Coconut milk can also be refrigerated or frozen for about the same time.

How It Works • The meat of mature coconuts consists of about 45% water, 35% fat, 10% carbohydrates, and 5% protein. The fat is about 90% saturated and contains lactones that give coconut its rich, milky aroma. Although coconuts have less total fat than nuts such as peanuts, they are one of the few plant sources high in saturated fat (more common among animals). It's also very high in antioxidants and a number of fatty acids. The saturated fat in coconut oil consists of about 45% lauric acid, 17% myristic acid, 10% palmitic acid, 8% caprylic acid, and 7% capric acid. Preliminary research indicates that the lauric acid in coconut oil may help to boost the immune system.

For the health conscious, coconut water remains a sensible choice rich in coconut flavor but low in calories (only 17 calories in a 3½ ounce/100 mL portion). Coconut water is also high in potassium, phosphorus, and zinc.

See Also • Fat, Oil, Sugar

COD • See Fish

COFFEE

What It Is • Picture an Ethiopian goatherder tending his flocks in 850 AD. He notices a few of his goats becoming more active after eating berries from a nearby bush. He decides to sample some berries himself and is thrilled by the sudden jolt of energy. Or so the legend goes — Arabian cooks eventually learned to boil the beans in water, and the earliest cups of coffee were brewed. Since then, coffee has become the world's most popular beverage. We consume more than 400 billion cups of the stuff every year.

Coffee beans come from an estimated 15 billion coffee trees growing worldwide. Global production of coffee beans hovers around 7 million metric ton, and coffee is the most widely traded commodity after oil. The two primary species are *Coffea arabica*, which accounts for 60 to 70% of world's harvest, and *Coffea canephora* (robusta). Arabica trees grow best in high elevations (about 2,000 to 6,000 feet/600 to 1,800 m above sea level) and have a complex aroma owing to their high sugar content. Robusta beans grow in altitudes below 2,000 feet (600 m) and tend to taste more bitter and less complex. (See Regional Coffee Characteristics, page 150.)

Once matured, coffee cherries (which are red) are picked, often by hand, and their green coffee beans are fermented, cleaned, dried, and then roasted, ground, and brewed. Instant, or solubilized, coffee is made by dehydrating brewed coffee (or freeze-drying it). Spray-drying is less expensive but freeze-drying retains more flavor. Instant coffee powder or granules quickly reconstitute into coffee and are useful for adding coffee flavor whenever you don't want the moisture of brewed coffee, as in some cakes, cookies, candies, and frozen desserts. Some brewed coffee is made into low-quality liquid coffee concentrate that is reconstituted to serve hundreds of people at once, such as at

science wise

Coffee Bean Genes • Scientists have recently located the gene in the coffee plant that is responsible for producing sucrose. This is the sugar that undergoes Maillard browning when coffee beans are roasted, creating many of the rich, nutty, toasted aromas that we've come to love in brewed coffee. The enzyme sucrose synthetase produces the sugar and locating this enzyme may allow coffee growers to regulate sucrose content in beans, alter the degree of browning that occurs in the beans, and make better-tasting coffee.

sports arenas and convention centers. The beans and brew are also made into coffee liqueurs (such as Kahlúa) and coffee extract, and can be used as an ingredient in beverages. Coffee adds flavor to pan gravies and stews and sauces. It's also added to rye and pumpernickel breads, cakes, and other desserts.

What It Does ● Roasting, grinding, and brewing dramatically affect the flavor of coffee. Beans are usually roasted at high temperatures until the beans reach 375°F (190°C) for light roasts or up to 425°F (220°C) for dark roasts, a process that takes anywhere from two to 15 minutes. When the beans reach 212°F (100°C), moisture inside them turns into steam and evaporates (taking some caffeine and acids along with it), which reduces the weight but increases the size of the beans as they become more porous. When beans reach about 320°F (160°C), **browning** occurs and develops many of the familiar roasted flavors we associate with coffee. When the beans reach 400°F (200°C) and above, a fair amount of carbon dioxide is produced, and oils in the bean are driven to the surface.

For brewing coffee, roasted coffee beans are ground to varying degrees of fineness according to the brewing method that will be used. In general, the shorter the brewing time, the finer the grind. Espresso is the finest grind because it is brewed in less than 30 seconds. Turkish grind is slightly coarser and used for simmering the coffee in a pot, then serving it unfiltered and allowing the grinds to settle to the bottom of the cup. Drip coffee calls for a medium grind, and percolator and French press are the coarsest grinds. Matching the grind to the brewing method ensures the best-tasting coffee because a coarse grind used to make espresso, for instance, results in a weak, acidic brew, while a fine grind in an automatic drip machine will create bitter-tasting coffee.

Brewing Methods

Brewing uses water to extract flavor from ground coffee beans. Ideally, about 18 to 22% of the weight of the grounds will be extracted to create a rich flavor without a bitter taste. Higher percentages result in "overextraction" and make bitter, astringent coffee. As a starting point, use 2 tablespoons (25 mL) of coffee per 6-ounce serving (55 grams per liter).

Keep in mind that brewed coffee is about 95% water. Hard water (high in calcium and magnesium) can hamper the extraction of flavorful compounds in coffee and make the brew more cloudy. Many coffee machines include water softeners or filters to prevent these minerals from gumming up (calcifying or scaling) the machine's pipes. However, overly softened water can cause overextraction and bitter tastes in coffee. For the most flavorful brewed coffee, use filtered or spring water between 195 and 205°F (90 and 96°C), or just below boiling point. Any higher and the heat of the water will extract more bitter compounds from the coffee than most people want to taste.

French press coffee tends to have a fairly robust taste because the grounds steep in hot water for several minutes. In percolators, the extracted coffee boils over itself in a cycle of high heat and extraction that produces very bitter-tasting coffee. As the old adage goes, "Coffee boiled is coffee spoiled."

Drip coffee makers (invented by the French) do a slightly better job, allowing gravity to slowly pull hot water down through an upper coffee chamber lined with a fine

Spicy Coffee Rub

Dark and rich with roasted coffee aromas, this rub goes best with robust meats like beef, lamb, and duck. Ground chiles give it a kick and a small amount of sugar balances the bitterness of the coffee.

⅓ cup	finely ground espresso or dark roast coffee	75 mL
2 tbsp	pure chile powder (such as ancho)	25 mL
2 tsp	ground cumin	10 mL
2 tsp	granulated sugar	10 mL
2 tsp	salt	10 mL
1 tsp	freshly ground black pepper	5 mL
½ tsp	cayenne pepper, or more to taste	2 mL

1. In a small bowl, combine ground coffee, chile powder, cumin, sugar, salt, black pepper, and cayenne. Use immediately or freeze in an airtight container for up to 4 months.

MAKES ABOUT ⅔ CUP (150 ML)

fast facts

- More than 50% of the world's coffee is purchased and roasted by four companies, Kraft, Nestlé, Smuckers, and Sara Lee.
- Coffee-producing countries tend to be at an economic disadvantage to well-heeled coffee-buying countries. Coffee labeled "fair-trade" is grown and processed under conditions that promote fair payment, a safe and healthy working environment, and gender equality, especially among economically disadvantaged populations.
- Kopi Luwak is the world's most expensive coffee. The coffee cherries are eaten by the luwak and pulp is digested as they go through the animal, but not the beans. The beans are collected, mashed, and roasted. Only 500 pounds (227 kg) are produced annually.

paper or metal filter (metal is preferred for a fuller-bodied brew), resulting in a brew that's less bitter than percolator coffee. However, automatic drip coffee makers rarely heat the water above 185°F (85°C), which isn't hot enough to extract sufficient aromatic compounds from the coffee.

Espresso coffee machines were invented in the mid-1800s to rapidly brew single servings of coffee. In this system, the water is heated to about 200°F (93°C), then pump-driven through a compact cake of fine coffee grounds (about ¼ ounce/7 g) at roughly eight to nine atmospheres of pressure (about 9 bar or units of measure) for approximately 20 seconds. This brewing method uses a higher proportion of coffee to water than other methods and extracts a single, concentrated serving, or "shot," of coffee that's usually about 1½ ounces (40 mL). Espresso brewing results in a stronger flavor than any of the gravity-brewing methods. As a type of pressure cooking, espresso brewing also extracts more of the coffee's oils and emulsifies them with some of the finely powdered coffee solids along with carbon dioxide gas and forms a foam of "crema" on the surface of the brewed espresso.

Brewed coffee should be served within a few minutes. It's best served at about 140 to 150°F (60 to 66°C) but can be held in a thermal carafe. If left on a hot plate, the additional heat will cause it to become increasingly bitter and acidic and less aromatic.

In an ideal world, coffee would be brewed within a few days of roasting. After a week or two, roasted coffee loses much of its flavor because the aromatic compounds are so volatile. If you can, grind the beans just before brewing, as grinding speeds flavor loss from coffee beans (again, because the aromatic compounds easily escape into the air). To store whole bean or ground coffee, avoid air and moisture by using an airtight container that's just big enough to hold the coffee. Coffee sold in a valve-lock bag will last a few weeks longer than loose coffee because the bag keeps oxygen away from the coffee, but it does allow some carbon dioxide and aromatic compounds from the beans to escape. Keep your coffee in its valve-lock bag in an airtight container for the longest storage. You can freeze coffee but it may lose some flavor in the process.

science wise

Decaffeination • Decaf accounts for about 20% of North American sales. Green coffee beans are usually decaffeinated by steaming or soaking them first in hot water, which extracts the caffeine and many flavor components. Then the water extract is exposed to solvents like methylene chloride or ethyl acetate to extract the caffeine, which is often sold to pharmaceutical companies who turn them into caffeine tablets. The label "naturally decaffeinated" usually refers to ethyl acetate because it is an organic solvent found in fruits. The original beans are then resoaked in the decaffeinated water for the flavors to be reabsorbed. But not all of them get added back. A newer method involves extracting the caffeine into compressed carbon dioxide. Decaffeinated coffee has had about 97% of the caffeine removed, resulting in caffeine content of about 2 to 4 mg in a cup of brewed coffee.

Extraction isn't the only method of decaffeination. Recently, Japanese scientists genetically engineered a hybrid *Coffea* plant that produces 70% less caffeine in its beans and brings new meaning to the phrase "naturally decaffeinated" coffee.

Regional Coffee Characteristics

Buying coffee has become as complex as picking a decent wine. Here's a road map to the three major coffee-producing regions around the world. Ask your coffee seller for the best grade available, keeping in mind that the best "high-grown" coffees are grown high in the mountains.

Latin America/Caribbean: Coffees from Latin America are the most popular in the world because they generally have light body, bright acidity, and a clean, simple taste. They're great for coffee blends because no single characteristic dominates. Some popular regional varieties include Antigua, Huehuetenango, Tarrazu, Bourbon Santos, Chanchamayo, Medellin, Bucaramanga, and Jamaican Blue Mountain.

Africa/Arabian Peninsula: On the other side of the globe, the intense, dry heat of Africa and the Arabian Peninsula produces coffee with more distinct, idiosyncratic flavors. African coffees tend to exhibit a pronounced wine-like acidity and dried fruit aromas. Three standouts from this region include light-bodied Ethiopian Yirgacheffe, rich-bodied Kenyan varieties, and chocolatey Yemen Mocha.

Asia/Pacific: Asia and Hawaii produce a more floral cup of coffee. The best known of these coffees are buttery-tasting Hawaiian Kona and musky, earthy Sumatra Mandheling.

How It Works • Carbohydrates in coffee beans create about one-third of the body in brewed coffee. Some body also comes from oils in the beans. Arabica beans contain more oil (about 16%) than robusta (10%) and create a fuller-bodied brew. Lightly roasting coffee beans to about a medium roast retains more oils, while dark roasting drives oils to the surface, where they eventually burn off into the air.

Roasting also creates many of the flavors we've come to love in coffee. Scientists have identified nearly 1,000 flavor chemicals in coffee. Caffeine accounts for about 1 to 2% of the bitterness in coffee beans, and robusta beans contain about twice as much bitter caffeine as arabica beans. Some bitterness also comes from trigonelline, which is about one-fourth as bitter as caffeine. Roasting burns off some caffeine, explaining why lightly roasted beans, such as cinnamon roast, are higher in caffeine than dark Italian (espresso) roasts. Brewing method also affects caffeine content. (See Caffeine in Common Food Products chart, page 80, for the caffeine content of specific coffees.)

The acidity or astringent taste of coffee comes from sugars that are broken down during roasting into citric, malic, acetic, lactic, and chlorogenic acids. Coffee made from arabica beans is more acidic because these beans contain about twice as many sugars as robusta beans. Liveliness in coffee also comes from carbon dioxide created during roasting. The bulk of coffee's aroma comes from roasting, which creates toasted flavors from compounds called furans, a tar-like aroma from guaiacol (more pronounced in robusta beans), slight fishiness from pyridine, and a buttery aroma from diacetyl. Many of the aromatic polyphenol compounds in coffee are antioxidants. In fact, drinking coffee is one of the primary ways that North Americans ingest health-boosting antioxidants. Considering all factors, most health experts agree that three cups of coffee (or 1½ shots of espresso) a day does not have significant health risks and may improve health.

See Also • Browning, Caffeine, Roasting

COFFEE LIQUEUR • See Liqueur

COGNAC • See Liquor

COINTREAU • See Liqueur

COLD-SMOKING • See Smoking

COLLAGEN • See Gelatin

COLLARDS • See Cruciferous Vegetables, Leaves

COLLOID

What It Is • First studied in 1861 by Scottish chemist Thomas Graham, a colloid is a mixture of invisibly small particles of one substance dispersed throughout another. It differs from a solution in that the particles in a solution are dissolved into the dispersing substance, but in a colloid, the particles remain intact. Colloid is the Greek word for "glue."

Emulsions, **foams**, and gels (made with **gelatin**) are common colloids in food. Emulsions are typically colloids of fat and water. For instance, mayonnaise is a colloid of fat (from egg yolks and oil) dispersed in liquid (lemon juice or vinegar). Foams are colloids of gas bubbles dispersed in liquid or solid. An example would be the carbon dioxide bubbles dispersed in the foam on a head of beer. Gels are colloids of water in something solid, such as the water dispersed throughout **pectin** in **jams and jellies**.

What It Does • Most colloids in food are called hydrocolloids because they consist of particles dispersed in water, which makes up about 70% of all cells in food. These colloids are typically liquid in form. But colloids can exist as a liquid, solid, or gas. For example, wood smoke is a colloid of carbon, tar, ash, and other particles suspended in air that exists as a gas. Cheese and butter are colloids of fat that are solids. Egg whites are viscous colloids of protein that are liquids. If you whip air into the egg whites, the colloid becomes a foam. Hydrocolloids may be liquid (as in milk) or solid (as in jelly). Some hydrocolloids can change from liquid to solid and back to liquid by heating and cooling. For instance, heat most cheeses and they melt from a solid into a liquid. Let them cool and they resolidify.

Hydrocolloids are used to thicken, gel, and stabilize many different foods. Hydrocolloids take on various glue-like states. You can find them at work in countless commercial food products such as sauces and ice creams. Avant-garde chefs, such as Britain's Heston Blumenthal and Spain's Ferran Adrià, also use hydrocolloids to create unexpected textures in food, as they have the ability to slow down the flow of liquids and create varying glue-like states of firmness from liquid to gel to solid. Ingredients used to create hydrocolloidal dispersions include gelatin, pectin, methylcellulose and other forms of **fiber**, xanthan and other **gums**, agar and other **seaweed** products, and transglutaminase, affectionately known as "meat glue." Many of these hydrocolloids are familiar in cooking, such as the smooth texture of sauces thickened with cornstarch. Many others are unexpected, such as the gelatinous texture of beer gelled with agar and gelatin, then served in the form of a transparent sheet over beef. With a hydrocolloid, you can firm up almost any flavored liquid into a soft or firm gel and shape it nearly any way you like.

How It Works • Colloids consist of two phases, dispersed and continuous. In the example of a starch-thickened sauce, the starch is the dispersed phase because it is dispersed in tiny particles (less than 1/1,000 of a millimeter) that are evenly distributed throughout the stock, water, or other liquid that makes the mixture continuous, or flowing. Adding lots of starch stops the flow and solidifies the mixture into a gel. Adding a bit less starch may simply slow down the continuous phase and create a thickened yet flowing texture.

Here's what keeps the particles dispersed in a hydrocolloid:

1. Layers of water molecules are bound to the surface of the particles by a "surfactant," often a protein molecule with one end that stays in the dispersed phase and another end that stays in the continuous phase.

2. Particles are often positively or negatively charged, and the repulsion between like charges on the particles keeps them separate. Subtle changes in temperature, acidity, and charge can easily alter the surfactant's behavior or the attraction and repulsion between particles, causing the colloid to collapse and the two phases (or ingredients) to separate.

See Also • Fiber, Foams, Gelatin, Gums, Molecular Gastronomy, Pectin, Sauces, Seaweed

COMBUSTION • See Fire

CONCH • See Mollusks

CONDENSED MILK • See Milk

CONDUCTION • See Heat

CONFECTIONER'S SUGAR • See Sugar

CONFECTIONERY • See Candy, Chocolate, Sugar

CONFIT

What It Is • French for "preserved," confit is a traditional method of preserving meat without refrigeration by slowly poaching the meat in its own rendered fat, then storing it in that fat. It's a specialty of southwestern France and often refers to duck or goose (and sometimes pork and other poultry like turkey) preserved this way. The term has since broadened and may refer loosely to nearly any food poached and preserved in fat or even in sugar, as in the case of fruit "confit."

What It Does • Confit is a verb as much as it is a noun, and to confit a food is to make it rich and succulent by saturating it with fat and flavor. The fatty legs of poultry such as ducks and geese (especially geese fattened for their *foie gras*) are commonly cooked and flavored this way. Traditionally the meat is cured in salt and often a dry rub of herbs and spices for a day or so, poached gently (at about 200°F/93°C) in fat for several hours until almost tender but still somewhat pink, then stored submerged in the cooking fat in a stoneware pot called a grésale.

Duck Confit

Now that meat can be preserved with refrigeration, confit is made for flavor more than to preserve the meat. If you like, add aromatics such as sliced onions and sprigs of fresh rosemary or thyme to the pan along with the duck during poaching. Don't be tempted to eat the confit right after it's done. Wait at least a week. The taste of aged confit is incomparable. Scrape excess fat from the meat, then serve cold in a salad or fry or broil the pieces. Use the fat to roast potatoes or cook other vegetables. If you don't have a local source for duck fat, you can order it online from purveyors like D'Artagnan and DiBruno Brothers.

5 to 6 lbs	duck or goose parts (preferably legs, about 4 to 5 duck legs or 2 to 3 goose legs)	2.5 to 3 kg
3 tbsp	coarse salt	45 mL
2 tsp	dried thyme leaves	10 mL
½ tsp	freshly ground pepper	2 mL
1	bay leaf, crushed	1
Pinch	ground allspice	Pinch
2	garlic cloves, minced	2
5 to 6 cups	rendered duck fat, goose fat, or lard (2.5 to 3 lbs/1.25 to 1.5 kg)	1.25 to 1.5 L

1. Rinse poultry and pat and dry thoroughly. In a small bowl, combine salt, thyme, pepper, bay leaf, allspice, and garlic. Rub over meat. Cover and refrigerate for 2 to 3 days.

2. Brush off most of seasonings from poultry, then place in a relatively shallow, wide pan (such as braising pan) just large enough to hold remaining ingredients. Add enough fat or lard to generously cover meat. Cook, uncovered, over very low heat (use a heat diffuser plate if you have one) for 1½ to 2 hours. The fat should gently bubble like poaching liquid at about 200°F (93°C) but no higher or meat will toughen instead of soften. When done, meat will be just tender and juices will run mostly clear.

3. Pluck meat from poaching liquid and place in a crock, terrine, or a plate (if you'll store the meat in its cooking pot). Pour poaching liquid into a fat separator and pour off juices from fat (save juices to make gravy or for another use). Return fat to pan and boil for 5 minutes. Strain through a sieve and discard any solids. Pour fat over meat in crock, terrine, or the same cooking pot. Let cool, then cover and refrigerate for at least 1 week or for up to 6 weeks.

MAKES ABOUT 4 SERVINGS

fast fact

- Rillettes are similar to confit in that pork or fatty poultry is seasoned and cooked in its own fat until fall-apart tender, then mashed and mixed with the fat. But the French don't have a monopoly on preserving meat in fat. Qawarma is a comparable Lebanese preparation made by salting fatty lamb, then cooking and preserving it in its fat.

The meat of confit may be eaten cold (as in a salad) or hot (fried or grilled with vegetables) and often becomes an ingredient in more elaborate dishes such as the goose confit used to make classic French cassoulet. The flavorful fat can be used for frying or as shortening in pastry for quiche or tarts.

How It Works
● The meat is completely immersed in the fat, which protects it by sealing out air. The traditional stoneware pot is hermetically sealed with additional fat and keeps out light and air that could speed spoilage. The fat may also be skimmed from the meat juices or boiled for five minutes, which prevents the meat juices from spoiling the confit. Generous salting also inhibits bacterial growth. Modern recipes typically call for less salt and specify refrigeration to safeguard against spoilage and to prolong shelf life.

Like other slow-cooking methods, confit gradually softens tough connective tissue in meat, creating a moist and succulent texture. As confit ages, the meat becomes more tender and flavorful as the fat gradually oxidizes over time, hovering on the delicious border of rancidity that often characterizes well-aged cheeses.

See Also
● Boiling, Fat

CONGER • See Fish

CONNECTIVE TISSUE • See Meat

CONSERVES • See Jam and Jelly

CONSOMMÉ • See Soup

CONVECTION • See Heat

COOKIES

What It Is
● Sweet little handheld cakes, cookies are irresistible. The name comes from the medieval Dutch word *koekje*, meaning "little cake," but they're also known as petits fours in France and sweet biscuits in the U.K. The endless potential for flavoring and shaping cookies has led to hundreds of different styles around the world. Most are rich and sweet because of plenty of fat and sugar in the dough. Regardless of how they're flavored, most cookies share the basic ingredients of flour, fat, liquid or eggs, sugar, and baking powder or baking soda. Depending upon the type of ingredients used and their proportions, cookies may be soft like cake or crisp like pastry, including everything from thin, crisp wafers such as tuiles and fortune cookies to chewy almond macaroons with a crisp crust to thick, soft, fudgy brownies and bar cookies.

What It Does
● Cookie dough falls somewhere between pie dough and cake batter. When the dough is crumbly, as for shortbread cookies, it resembles pie dough. But most cookies include eggs, sugar, and leavener, while most pie doughs don't.

Cookies are closer to cakes. The majority of cookies are made, like cakes, by creaming fat and sugar, then stirring in eggs, flour, flavorings, and often baking soda or baking powder. Creaming the fat and sugar together fills the batter with air bubbles (**aeration**), nearly doubling the batter's volume, and lightens the batter's texture and color. Just be sure to avoid overbeating, which can beat the air right out of the batter and cause cookies to come out flat. Overbeaten butter and sugar will look grainy and curdled. (For more on creaming, see Shortened Cakes, page 82.)

In general, it helps to take the chill off the ingredients for cookie dough so that they aerate well and mix evenly. The butter and eggs should be at room temperature or just slightly colder. Beat in the eggs gently (or beat them in a separate bowl, then fold them into the batter) to avoid breaking the air bubbles you created during creaming.

To prevent clumps of dry ingredients, sift together the flour and baking powder before adding them, and add gradually for even distribution. The final mixing can spell the difference between tender and tough cookies. For tender cookies, mix the dough gently. Mixing the fat, flour, and sugar before adding the liquid and/or eggs also creates more tender cookies. Gentle mixing is especially important in reduced-fat cookie doughs because less fat means less tenderness. When making tougher cookies, such as biscotti, use more flour and less fat, mixing more forcefully to help develop gluten in the flour and create a firmer structure.

The amount of spread in a cookie is determined mostly by the type and amount of fat, liquid, and flour and the temperature of the dough. For instance, all-butter cookies tend to spread more than those made with shortening. Soft cookie dough containing more liquid will also spread more than firm cookie dough containing less liquid. Chilling the dough can help keep cookies from spreading because cold fat takes longer to melt and spread in the oven. Chilling the dough for 12 hours or for up to a few days also gives the eggs time to soak into the dry ingredients, leading to a drier dough that resists spreading, browns more evenly, and develops richer flavor. Baking room-temperature dough tends to create thinner, crisper cookies with more spread.

Cookie Shapes and Styles

Cookies are best categorized by the way the dough is shaped. Slight alterations in the proportion of ingredients allow cookies to be shaped almost any way you like. Some cookie doughs can be shaped in multiple ways. For instance, drop cookies like chocolate chip cookies can be formed into slice-and-bake icebox cookies or made into bars by spreading the dough in a pan. Here's an overview of the various shapes and styles.

Drop: These cookies are made by simply dropping balls of dough onto a baking sheet. This shaping method is often used for chunky doughs like oatmeal raisin cookies. For uniform-sized cookies and even baking, use a measuring tablespoon, melon baller, or spring-loaded ice cream scoop.

Icebox: Similar to drop cookie dough, icebox cookie dough usually contains fewer add-ins and is less chunky. It's shaped into a log, chilled, sliced, and baked. Slicing a log of dough creates uniform-sized cookies and allows you the flexibility of holding the cookies in the refrigerator or freezer (hence "icebox"), then baking them whenever you are ready.

Hand-shaped: These cookies are formed into balls, rounds, crescents, or other shapes by hand. Italian biscotti are made with biscuit-like dough that is hand-shaped into a loaf and baked, then sliced and baked again (biscotti means "twice-baked"). When making hand-formed cookies, work quickly and handle the dough as little as possible to avoid warming up the dough and melting the fat, which can cause the cookies to flatten out in the oven.

Pressed and piped: Some hand-shaped cookies, like peanut butter sandies, are flattened slightly with a fork or the bottom of a drinking glass. Others, like shortbread, are pressed into a decorative ceramic mold, then baked like a small cake. Pressed cookies may also be individually stamped with carved wooden embossers. Or the stamp can be a carved wooden rolling pin that's rolled over the cookie dough, as in German springerle. More elaborate pressed cookies are made by filling a tube such as a cookie press (cookie gun) or pastry bag with soft cookie dough and pressing or piping the dough through the decorative tip at the other end to create uniform, intricate shapes such as Scandinavian spritz cookies. In general, pressing dough makes for crisper cookies. The thinner the dough, the crisper the cookies will be.

Rolled cut-outs: These Christmastime favorites are somewhat like pieces of rich, sweetened pie dough. The dough is chilled, rolled out, and cut into various shapes to create sugar cookies or gingerbread cookies that are baked and then sprinkled with sugar or decorated with icing. Rolling the dough between sheets of waxed or parchment paper helps to prevent sticking.

Wafers: Crisp wafer cookies are made with a thin, buttery batter that's poured or spread onto a baking sheet. Sometimes the batter is spread over a stencil to create specific shapes. Wafers are typically removed from the baking

Cookie Ingredients and Characteristics

Most cookies get their texture and color from a combination of flour, fat, liquid or eggs, and sugar. Changing the type and amount of these ingredients alters a cookie's texture and color, yielding thousands of possibilities. For instance, a typical sugar cookie contains about 3 cups (750 mL) flour, 1 cup (250 mL) or 8 ounces (250 g) fat such as butter and/or shortening, 2 tablespoons (25 mL) or 1 ounce (28 mL) liquid or 1 egg, 1¼ cups (300 mL) or 10 ounces (300 g) sugar, and about ½ teaspoon (2 mL) baking powder. It comes out pale white or ever so slightly golden when baked. But replacing 1 to 2 tablespoons (15 to 25 mL) of the granulated sugar with an equal amount of corn syrup creates a more golden brown cookie. That's because corn syrup browns at a lower temperature than granulated sugar. Here's how to get the texture and color you want in a cookie by changing the type and amount of its basic ingredients.

Desired Characteristic	Flour	Fat	Liquid or Eggs	Sugar	Chemical Leavener
Thin	All-purpose flour made from soft wheat (low-protein)	Butter or lard	Add 1 to 2 tbsp (15 to 25 mL) water, milk, or cream	Add 1 to 2 tbsp (15 to 25 mL) granulated sugar or corn syrup	Baking soda
Crisp	Bread or all-purpose flour made from hard wheat (high-protein)	Shortening or lard	Egg whites	Add 1 to 2 tbsp (15 to 25 mL) granulated sugar	Baking soda
Chewy	Bread or all-purpose flour made from hard wheat (high-protein)	Butter or stick margarine	Whole eggs	Replace 1 to 2 tbsp (15 to 25 mL) granulated sugar with brown sugar, honey, or molasses	Baking soda and/or powder
Tender	Cake or all-purpose flour made from soft wheat (low-protein)	Add 1 to 2 tbsp (15 to 25 mL) butter, margarine, reduced-fat spread, or oil	Whole eggs or egg yolks	Add 1 to 2 tbsp (15 to 25 mL) granulated sugar or brown sugar	Baking soda and/or powder
Soft	Cake flour (low-protein)	Reduced-fat spread or oil	Whole eggs	Omit 1 to 2 tbsp (15 to 25 mL) granulated sugar; replace another 1 to 2 tbsp (15 to 25 mL) granulated sugar with brown sugar, honey, or molasses	Baking powder
Puffy	Cake flour (low-protein)	Reduced-fat spread or oil	Whole eggs	Omit 1 to 2 tbsp (15 to 25 mL) granulated sugar; replace another 1 to 4 tbsp (15 to 60 mL) granulated sugar with brown sugar, honey, or molasses	Baking powder
Well browned	Bread or all-purpose flour made from hard wheat (high-protein)	Butter or stick margarine	Whole eggs or egg yolks	Replace 1 to 2 tbsp (15 to 25 mL) granulated sugar with corn syrup	Baking soda and powder

sheet while still hot and pliable and molded into shape over a rolling pin (for tuiles), in muffin cups (for tulipe cookies), or by tightly rolling the cookie into a cigarette.

Filled and sandwich: These are the most popular commercially made cookies, but homemade thumbprints filled with jam are another type of filled cookie.

Bars and brownies: Baking cookie dough in a pan eliminates endless batches of individual cookies. This shaping method brings cookies even closer to cake. Many bar cookies are nothing more than a soft drop cookie dough pressed into a shallow baking pan or rimmed baking sheet. Almost any cookie dough can be made into bars. If a looser cake-like batter is used, the bars fall somewhere between cookie and cake. Such is the case with brownies.

Baking and Cooling

For evenly baked cookies, invest in a couple of heavy-gauge (at least 1/16-inch/1.5 mm thick) aluminum cookie sheets. Thicker cookie sheets transfer heat more evenly and don't buckle as easily. Flat sheets, and those rimmed on one or two sides, allow you to easily slide the baked cookies off the sheet. To prevent sticking, use a silicone baking mat, parchment paper, or greased foil (note that greasing may increase spread in cookies). Some bakers use nonstick cookie sheets, but many avoid them because nonstick dark surfaces retain more heat than light, uncoated surfaces and often burn the bottoms of cookies before the tops are baked through. Using insulated cookie sheets (two sheets of aluminum with a layer of air between them) or stacking two sheets together will prevent burnt bottoms but often won't transfer heat fast enough to crisp the cookies, resulting in underbaked, overly spread out cookies with a doughy texture.

To avoid spreading, cool the baking sheets between batches (under cold water if necessary). Or have balls of chilled dough ready on a baking mat or parchment, then transfer the whole mat or parchment to the hot baking sheet and pop it in the oven.

For the most even heating, adjust your oven racks to the top third and bottom third of the oven. All ovens have hot spots, so rotate sheets from the top to the bottom rack and from back to front halfway through baking. To avoid overbaking cookies, keep an oven thermometer in your oven for accurate temperature readings. If the oven temperature is too low cookies may spread more, while higher temperatures will encourage more crispness. As for timing, check the cookies early and, in general, err on the side of underbaking. You can always bake them a little longer, but you can't rescue a burnt cookie. For softer, chewier cookies, slightly underbake. For crisper cookies, bake until the edges are well browned and the surface appears dry.

Cool cookies on their baking sheet just long enough for them to firm up so they can be moved (usually two to four minutes). If you wait too long, the cookies may stick to the pan, especially if you're making thin wafer cookies. Generally, the longer they're on the hot sheet, the crisper they'll get. To finish cooling, transfer cookies to racks, which allow for good air circulation.

Storage

Cookie doughs, especially those containing lots of butter or other fat, freeze well. You can freeze the dough for up to six months, then thaw briefly (and slice if using a log) and bake. To prevent air from oxidizing the fat in the dough and speeding spoilage (and to prevent the fat from absorbing other flavors from your freezer), wrap dough tightly in plastic wrap, then in foil, or put in a freezer-grade resealable plastic bag. Layer unbaked cut-out shapes or balls between parchment paper in an airtight container. Baked cookies, especially those with lots of butter, such as shortbread, can also be frozen. Cool them completely, then layer between parchment and freeze in an airtight container for up to four months. Thaw frozen cookies at room temperature or warm them up for a few minutes in a 300°F (150°C) oven. Store baked cookies at room temperature in an airtight container for one to two weeks. Avoid storing crisp and soft cookies together

because crisp cookies will absorb moisture from the soft ones and they'll all become soft.

How It Works • Cookies are so small that even slight changes to the ingredients and their proportions create noticeable differences in the baked cookie. Here's how each ingredient functions to create the textures, colors, and tastes of various cookies.

Flour: Cookies get much of their structure from flour. Proteins in the flour create a web of gluten and firm up when heated. Starch in the flour absorbs liquid in the batter, swells when heated, and forms a paste (gelatinization) that stiffens and sets the cookie. The amount of protein in the flour affects the texture (tenderness or crispness) of cookies. High-protein flour like bread flour absorbs more liquid and makes cookies drier, crisper, and darker in color. Low-protein flour like cake flour soaks up less moisture and makes cookies more moist, puffy, and lighter in color. If your cookies are spreading too much, try higher-protein flour like bread flour for better structure. Higher-protein flour also makes cookies chewier. For more tender cookies, use low-protein cake flour. Keep in mind that the protein content of "all-purpose" flour in North America varies by region because of the kinds of wheat milled. The middle ground all-purpose flour (10% protein) tends to result in somewhat moist, pale brown cookies with some spread.

Fat: Butter, margarine, shortening, lard, oil, and other fats carry flavor in a cookie. They also bring along their own flavors, especially in the case of butter, the preferred fat for most cookies. The primary role of fats is that of tenderizing the cookie by coating flour proteins and preventing them from forming tough gluten. In general, the more fat in your dough, the more tender your cookies will be. Solid fats also help to aerate cookie batter when air is beaten into them during creaming. The type of fat will determine the final shape and texture of your cookies — from light, puffy, tender, and soft to heavy, flat, and crisp. Butter, shortening, margarine, and oil each produce different textures primarily because of their water content. The more water in the fat, the softer your cookies will be and the more they will puff up. For many cookies, bakers use a combination of butter for flavor and shortening for crispness and lack of spread. If you use liquid oils instead of solid fats, your cookies will be very soft, puffy, and cake-like in texture.

Sugar: Of course it makes cookies taste sweet, but it also makes them tender, browned, and crisp. Sugar tenderizes cookies by bonding with water and preventing it from hydrating flour proteins that form tough gluten. Because of sugar's tenderizing capability, applesauce, puréed prunes, corn syrup, and other sugar-rich ingredients can help tenderize cookies made with less fat. The type of sugar will affect browning and crispness, too. For instance, adding corn syrup to a cookie recipe makes the cookies browner because corn syrup browns at a lower temperature than granulated sugar. Some sugars retain more moisture than others. For crisp cookies, use plenty of granulated sugar. Brown sugar, honey, and corn syrup absorb more moisture from the air (known as hygroscopic) and make softer, less crisp cookies.

Liquid or eggs: The liquid in cookie dough — even in the form of eggs alone — activates the other ingredients. It dissolves the sugar, gelatinizes the starch in the flour, and triggers the baking powder or soda to release its leavening gas. If the liquid is fatty, like cream or egg yolks, it contributes to tenderness, too. Egg whites also hold air and can be used to puff up cookies that contain less fat (think of meringue cookies, which require no fat at all). In general, egg whites make drier, crisper cookies. The other function of eggs in cookie dough is to emulsify and bind the ingredients together, helping the cookies to set as egg proteins coagulate. Keep in mind that adding the eggs or other liquid toward the end of mixing

creates tender cookies, while adding it early develops gluten and creates tougher cookies.

Leavener: Cookies rise mostly because of air bubbles beaten into the dough. In the heat of the oven, the bubbles expand and the cookies rise. Moisture in the dough also steams and contributes some lift. The function of chemical leaveners is to help the bubbles expand even more. Most cookies include some baking powder or baking soda (about 1 teaspoon/5 mL powder or 1/4 teaspoon/1 mL soda per cup/250 mL of flour), which releases carbon dioxide that migrates to the air bubbles and increases their volume. Baking soda produces gas once, when mixed into the dough. Double-acting baking powder produces gas twice: once when mixed into the dough and later when heated in the oven. Cookie doughs that use only baking powder tend to be somewhat acidic and set more quickly with less spreading. But acidic cookie doughs made with only baking powder also don't brown as well in the oven. That's why baking soda is often included: to neutralize the acidity of the dough and help the cookies to brown. Some cookies, such as shortbread, have no chemical leavener at all. With very little lift, shortbread cookies develop a wonderfully firm, crumbly, and crunchy texture.

See Also ● Bakeware, Baking, Biscuits, Cake, Chemical Leavener, Fat, Flour, Pastry

COOKING

What It Is ● Cooking often refers broadly to any kind of food preparation. But a tossed green salad isn't really cooked. What separates the raw from the cooked is **heat**. Cooking is a process of heat transfer from a heat source to food to transform the food into something different.

What It Does ● Humans are the only species that has made such an elaborate process of cooking their food. Other species just eat it raw. We cook for many reasons. Cooking can make food:

- taste better by enhancing appearance, texture, flavor, and aroma
- more nutritious
- easier to chew and digest
- resist spoilage from harmful microorganisms

The earliest cooking method, **grilling**, used dry heat soon after the discovery of fire. The invention of clay pots led to moist-heat cooking by **boiling** food in water in the pot. With the invention of **cookware** like pots and pans, moist-heat cooking expanded beyond boiling to include poaching, simmering, and **steaming**. Pots and pans also led to more advanced dry-heat cooking methods like sautéing and **frying**. Once **ovens** were invented, dry-heat cooking evolved to include broiling, **roasting**, and **baking**. New technologies have spawned various cooking methods from pressure cooking to **microwave cooking**. Among recent avant-garde technologies are the ultrasonic water bath, the rotary evaporator (Rotovap), and the polymer box, a self-contained oven that bakes food tableside after it is heated in a larger oven.

How It Works

Regardless of cooking method, all heat causes food molecules to move, bump into each other, react with each other, and form new textures and flavors. Food molecules consist primarily of **water** (about 70% of most plant and animal cells), **protein**, **fats**, and **carbohydrates** like **starch** and **sugar**, along with smaller amounts of **minerals**, **vitamins**, and numerous chemical compounds. Heat does various things to these food molecules, such as releasing volatile aromatic compounds that make food smell delicious. The most dramatic changes occur in the water, protein, starches, sugars, and fats.

All foods contain water, and even firm foods like meat may consist of up to 75% water. As the internal temperature of foods reaches the boiling point — 212°F (100°C) — water turns to steam and evaporates, causing foods to lose weight and become drier. For instance, raw beaten eggs are very watery, but when cooked into scrambled eggs, some water evaporates and the eggs become a bit drier, losing some of their original water weight.

Proteins coagulate. Both plants and animals contain protein, large molecules that break apart and unwind, or denature, when heated to temperatures of 140 to 180°F (60 to 82°C). Once broken apart, heated protein molecules are free to reassociate and form new bonds, and they clump back together, or coagulate, throughout the food. In the scrambled egg example, the coagulation of heated egg proteins causes the eggs to firm up, which shrinks the eggs a little, squeezing out some moisture.

Starches gelatinize. Complex carbohydrates called starches are most abundant in plant foods like wheat flour, rice, corn, and potatoes. When these starches are heated in liquid in, say, a starch-thickened sauce like pan gravy, the heat breaks the bonds between starches and they absorb water that causes them to swell, soften, and form a paste or gel, which then firms up with continued heat. Depending upon the type of starch, gelatinization starts to occur between 120 and 140°F (50 to 60°C). Gelatinization causes sauces to thicken when heated with starch and cakes to stiffen and set in the oven. On cooling, starch molecules re-associate and form a gel (gelation).

Sugars caramelize and brown. Simple carbohydrates called sugars are found in all animal and plant foods. When heated, the sugars melt and eventually darken from a light straw color to deep caramel brown. This process creates hundreds of flavor compounds that we've come to associate with deliciousness. Maillard **browning**, the reaction of reducing sugars and amino groups from proteins, creates the sweet, deep flavor of caramelized onions and the dark crust on grilled steak and baked bread. Non-reducing sucrose has to be hydrolyzed into its glucose and fructose components before it can react so browns more slowly than corn syrup or honey. Foods cooked with moist-heat cooking methods, like steaming and microwave cooking, will only brown when water evaporates because water cannot be heated above 212°F (100°C).

Fats melt. Both animals and plants store fat for energy. Fats have a higher proportion of saturated fatty acids and are solid at room temperature; oils have a higher proportion of unsaturated fatty acids and are liquid at room temperature. Different fats melt at different temperatures. Butter melts at a relatively low temperature (about 85°F/30°C), and shortening melts at a higher temperature (in the range of 98 to 110°F/37 to 43°C). Many liquid oils can be heated to temperatures above 400°F (200°C) before they begin to break down and smoke, making them good fats for browning foods.

See Also • Atmospheric Pressure, Bakeware, Baking, Boiling, Braising, Cookware, Food Science, Frying, Grilling, Heat, Microwave Cooking, Molecular Gastronomy, Roasting, Smoking, Steaming

COOKWARE

What It Is • Anything that holds food and transfers heat can be considered cookware. Some of the earliest cooking vessels were clay pots, which evolved into other ceramics like earthenware, stoneware, and glass. By the Middle Ages, metal cookware became standard because it was more durable and offered much better heat control. Some plastic is now used for microwave cooking (and heat-resistant silicone is often used in **bakeware**).

What It Does • Pots and pans transfer heat to food, and ideally they would heat up quickly, distribute the heat evenly, retain the heat well, and respond quickly to changes in temperature. Unfortunately, no such material exists. Most metal cookware heats up fairly quickly and responds well to temperature changes, but because it conducts heat well, it can't retain it very well. Ceramic and glass cookware retain heat well, but for that reason they don't conduct heat very well and may crack when the temperature changes suddenly. The bottom line is that metal is best suited to cooking that requires precise temperature control and sudden temperature changes, as in frying and most stovetop cooking. Ceramic and glass are best suited to cooking that requires good heat retention and even heat distribution, as in

science wise

Seasoning Cast Iron and Carbon Steel • To keep it from rusting, cast-iron and carbon steel cookware must be seasoned, or impregnated with hot oil (if the cast iron or carbon steel is enameled, it doesn't require seasoning). When the oil heats with the metal, it polymerizes, or forms a dense plastic-like layer that keeps out oxygen and prevents rusting. It also provides a nonstick surface. Cast-iron cookware is now available preseasoned by the manufacturer. But if you need to season a cast-iron or carbon steel pan (such as a wok) at home, wash and dry the pan, then rub canola, corn, or another highly unsaturated fat all over the pan, inside and out. Bake the pan upside down in a 350°F (180°C) oven for two hours. Place a baking sheet on the oven rack below the pan to catch any oil drips. Remove the pan every 30 minutes to recoat it with oil. After two hours, turn off the oven and let the pan cool completely in the oven. If necessary, you can reseason a pan at any time.

oven-cooking and slow-cooking methods such as baking, braising, and stewing.

Reactivity is another consideration. All cookware materials can react with food, particularly acidic foods, transferring metal ions into the food and resulting in a slightly metallic taste and some discoloration. Some unglazed high-lead clay cookware can transfer lead into foods and pose a lead poisoning risk. Reactivity differs among cookware materials and isn't always harmful, but in general, nonreactive cooking materials are preferred over reactive ones.

Heat conduction, heat retention, and reactivity are the main characteristics of cookware materials. Since precise temperature control is a key factor in successful cooking, the materials below are organized by heat conductivity, from the fastest heat conductors to the slowest.

Copper: The oldest metal used for cooking, copper has a distinct advantage over all other cookware materials: it gets hot faster and cools down faster than any other metal, except for silver (but who can afford silver pots and pans!). It's the metal of choice when you want to whip up a delicate sauce in a pan that just a few seconds ago was scalding hot from browning a scallop of veal or a chicken breast. Copper is nearly twice as fast at transferring heat as aluminum and 25 times faster than stainless steel. It also has a fairly high melting point (1984°F/1084°C), making it well suited to high-heat cooking. The bad news? Copper is expensive, heavy, and a pain to keep polished. Copper's thermal conductivity is its greatest strength for temperature control but its reactivity with other chemical compounds is its greatest weakness. Exposed copper reacts with sulfur and oxygen in the air, developing a stubborn green coating on the surface. In cooking, it can also react with acidic foods, transferring copper ions into the food, so copper cookware is always lined, or clad, with stainless steel, aluminum, nickel, or tin. Inside cladding keeps copper ions away from food, and outside cladding prevents copper from oxidizing and turning green, which eliminates the need for polishing. Interior tin-lined copper cookware has traditionally been the choice of professional chefs, but tin is soft, easily scratched, and melts at about 450°F (230°C), requiring that the cookware be relined periodically. For the best heat conductivity, most modern chefs prefer copper cookware lined inside with a stainless steel cooking surface for durability and nonreactivity with acidic foods. Some clad copper cookware is lined both inside and out with stainless steel, further reducing copper's heat conductivity. Many home cooks find this to be the best compromise of quality, cost, and convenience.

fast facts

- Copper is the only metal that is found naturally in its metallic state, which is probably why it was the first metal to be used in tool making (including cookware).
- Pots and pans that aren't magnetic won't get hot on induction stoves. To check if your cookware is magnetic, put a magnet on the bottom of your pan. If it doesn't stick, the pan won't heat up by induction. This eliminates copper, aluminum, glass, earthenware, and stoneware surfaces for induction cooking. Stainless steel varies by manufacturer and must be tested with a magnet to be sure it will work. Iron cookware (even if enameled) will work.

Aluminum: Used for only about a hundred years, aluminum is the next best heat conductor after copper (about half as fast). It's moderately priced and relatively lightweight, making it the preferred material for most bakeware such as cookie sheets. The downside to aluminum is that it's reactive and easily scratched, so for cookware it's often treated like copper and clad with other metals such as stainless steel. Aluminum can also be anodized, an electrochemical process that creates a thin (about 0.03 mm) aluminum oxide coating that makes the surface harder, stick resistant, and less prone to reacting with acidic foods. Anodized aluminum loses some heat conductivity, and it isn't completely nonreactive. Some alkalis in dish detergent can react with anodized aluminum, so avoid washing anodized aluminum cookware in the dishwasher.

Cast iron: One of the least expensive metals, cast iron is only a fair heat conductor (about four times slower than aluminum), but it retains heat well and has a high melting point, making it excellent for high-heat cooking. Its excellent heat retention and even heat distribution make cast iron a good choice for frying and long-cooking dishes like stews and braises. Cast iron is alloyed with carbon to harden it, but that doesn't keep the iron from rusting. The two disadvantages of cast iron are its heavy weight and the "seasoning" required to prevent rusting (see Science Wise, page 160). Enamel, a type of glass fused onto the surface of enameled iron cookware, eliminates the need for seasoning and makes the pans easier to clean. But enamel slows down the heat conductivity, and enamel surfaces can crack or chip. Bacteria can grow in any crack, so enameled cast-iron cookware is prohibited in many commercial kitchens.

Stainless steel: Stainless steel is iron alloyed with chromium and nickel to help prevent corrosion. For cookware and kitchen utensils, 18% chromium is the standard, with either 8 or 10% nickel (labeled as 18/8 or 18/10 stainless steel). About three times slower

science wise

Foiled Again • Did you ever notice that when you cover a pan of food with aluminum foil, sometimes little holes form in the foil? You may have witnessed this phenomenon in a pan of lasagna or cornbread. What happens is that the acid in the food conducts electricity (electrons) from the aluminum foil to the metal in the pan and creates a sort of low-power battery that dissolves the foil wherever it touches the acidic food. The battery only works when two different metals are used (aluminum foil and a cast-iron or stainless steel pan, for instance). It won't happen between aluminum foil and an aluminum pan because the same metal doesn't give up electrons to itself. To prevent the reaction, only store acidic foods in a metal pan covered with the same metal, such as an aluminum pan covered with aluminum foil. Or store the food in ceramic or plastic, neither of which will create a battery when it comes in contact with foil.

kitchen wisdom

Beating Egg Whites in Copper
The reactivity of copper with food does have one unique advantage: it makes whipped egg whites more stable. Conalbumin, one of the proteins in egg whites, has the ability to bond with copper ions, forming a more stable compound, copperconalbumin. The stability of this compound creates an egg white foam that is less prone to overbeating and will rise higher during baking, creating supersized soufflés and meringues. Copperconalbumin raises the foam's coagulating temperature so that its air bubbles expand more in the oven before the egg white sets. This effect is different than that of acids, which only help to stabilize egg foams.

than iron and 25 times slower than copper, steel is a poor heat conductor. But because it's very dense and nonreactive, stainless steel is often used for the surface of cookware that is clad with a copper or aluminum core for better heat conduction. Carbon steel is manufactured without the chromium and nickel, which gives it slightly better heat conductivity, so it's sometimes used to make woks, paella pans, and crêpe pans, where high heat is desired in one part of the pan but not in another. Like cast iron, carbon steel must be seasoned to keep it from rusting. Also like iron, steel can be enameled, but that compromises steel's heat conductivity even more.

Nonstick cookware: Almost any metal can be coated with a nonstick surface such as Teflon or SilverStone. These coatings are made from polytetrafluoroethylene (PTFE), a polymer or type of plastic that's so dense it doesn't form bonds with anything. Nonstick pans allow you to use less fat for cooking, and they clean easily because food doesn't stick to them. But above 500°F (260°C), PTFE can begin to break down. Plus, truth be told, some sticking is necessary for good browning on meats and other foods. For these reasons, nonstick pans are not well suited to high-heat cooking such as **browning**. If the surface gets scratched, food will stick to the metal underneath. Use only wooden or plastic utensils on nonstick pans and avoid rough scouring.

Earthenware: Now we enter the world of ceramics, all of which conduct heat more slowly than metal cookware. But poor heat conduction means better heat retention, and ceramics like earthenware provide the even, gentle heat distribution necessary for long-cooking dishes like braises and stews.

Stoneware: Like earthenware, stoneware is made of silica (sand), but it's glazed and high-fired at about 2200°F (1200°C), making it denser, stronger, and more chip resistant. Porcelain is a type of stoneware that includes clay called kaolin. Stoneware excels at heat retention and is often used to make slow-cooker appliances. It can also be used for microwave cooking.

Glass: Made with silica and other ingredients, glass is another poor heat conductor but good heat retainer that's best suited to baking and microwave cooking. Heat-resistant glass pots made with boron oxide can withstand high temperatures, but they're still prone to cracking with extreme or sudden temperature changes.

How It Works • When cookware gets

hot, the atoms in the material vibrate more rapidly and they pass the vibrational energy to their more slowly vibrating neighbors, conducting heat through the material and to the food you're cooking. Metals conduct heat faster than ceramics, but thickness is important too. The more mass your cookware has, the more heat it can hold and, therefore, the more heat it can conduct to your food. This is why recipes often call for a heavy-bottomed pan. Thickness also allows the cookware to evenly distribute the heat. For instance, a thick sauté pan does a good job of distributing the ring of heat (uneven heat) that comes off a typical gas or electric burner. Thick metal cookware also lasts longer because it's less likely to warp or dent. When buying metal cookware, give it a rap on the bottom. Thick, heavy-gauge cookware will make a dull thud instead of a delicate ping.

See Also • Bakeware, Cooking, Heat

COPPER COOKWARE • See Cookware

CORIANDER • See Herbs, Spices

CORK

What It Is • When you want to stop the flow,

put a cork in it. Cork is the bark of an evergreen oak tree (*Quercus suber*) native to western Mediterranean regions and the world's favorite stopper. It was the standard wine bottle stopper through the 1800s and 1900s, but because of its scarcity, cork has recently given way to more plentiful alternatives such as metal screw caps and stoppers made of synthetic plastic or glass.

What It Does • Cork greatly advanced the

wine industry by preserving wine so that it could be aged and its flavor matured for several years in the bottle. It was a significant improvement over the previous stopper, an oil-soaked cloth rag, used up until the mid-1600s. Wine corks usually measure a little less than 1 inch in diameter (about 25.5 mm) compressed to about 18 mm in a wine bottle.

How It Works • Cork is a renewable

resource but can be harvested from trees only every seven to nine years. About 60% of cells in cork consist of a waxy substance called suberin that protects the cork tree

fast fact

and prolongs its life. Suberin is elastic and near impermeable, allowing cork to be squeezed into the neck of a wine bottle, where it keeps out oxygen and prevents the wine from prematurely aging or oxidizing. But suberin does let in some oxygen, which can evaporate wine, and the most obvious sign of a cork's demise is a drop in the level of liquid in the bottle. Corks are also susceptible to fungi, which can grow in the cork and produce a compound called trichloroanisole (TCA), which has a characteristic foul moldy smell like the wet fur of a dog. This type of cork taint ruins less than 10% of wines stopped with cork (such wine is said to be "corked"). But cork taint and the material's tendency to dry out give cork an estimated life expectancy of 10 to 20 years.

Many high-quality winemakers use other stoppers like plastic, metal screw tops, and glass, which may be one of the best solutions. Wine bottles stoppered with these alternative stoppers don't have to be laid on their sides, a practice that wets the cork with wine so it won't dry out, shrink, and let in air that could prematurely age or oxidize the wine.

See Also • Wine

CORN

What It Is • Outside of North America, "corn" often refers to cereal grains in general. But in North America, it refers primarily to maize (*Zea mays*), the largest of the cereal grasses. Corn was domesticated more than 7,000 years ago in Central and South America. It is the largest agricultural crop in the Americas and the third-largest human food crop worldwide, just behind wheat and rice.

A few general varieties are cultivated, each with several cultivars:

Flint corn: This Native American favorite, also known as Indian corn, has somewhat small kernels that are high in protein and lower in starch compared to other varieties.

Popcorn: Similar to flint corn, the small, high-protein kernels of popcorn have a harder outer hull that helps contain the explosive force necessary for popping.

Flour corn: Somewhat lower in protein and higher in starch compared to other varieties, flour corn is used to make some corn flours in North America.

Dent corn: Cornmeal and grits are made from dent corn, which has slightly larger, starchier kernels than other varieties and a characteristic dimple on the top of each mature kernel. Dent corn is also used for animal feed, primarily for corn-fed beef. This type contains both straight chain amylose and branched chain amylopectin starch molecules.

Waxy corn: Its starch is 100% branched chain amylopectin that thickens when gelatinized but does not form a gel when cooled.

Sweet corn: The fresh corn we eat comes from high-sugar varieties that don't convert their sugars to starch as completely as other types. It also has slightly wrinkled kernels.

What It Does • Used to make thousands of food products, corn is one of the world's most important agricultural crops. Its sugars are harvested to make **sweeteners** like corn syrup or fermented and distilled to make the grain alcohol that forms the basis of bourbon and other whiskey. The grain alcohol made from corn, also known as ethanol, has become an important biofuel that constitutes up to 10% of some gasolines. The fat in the grain is processed into corn **oil** used for frying, is the basis for many margarines, and is used to make biodiesel fuel. The starchy endosperm of the grain is dried and powdered into cornstarch that thickens **sauces**, fillings, puddings, **custards**, and other liquid mixtures (see **Starch**).

We eat corn products in hundreds of processed foods, but most cooks use either

science wise

Flavor That Pops • Popcorn is made from a variety of corn with a tough hull that dries while leaving some moisture in the center of the kernel. As it's heated to 212°F (100°C), the moisture steams and builds up inside the kernel. When the temperature reaches about 380°F (190°C), the built-up pressure (about seven times the external pressure of the atmosphere) explodes the tough hull and turns the kernel inside out as the steam puffs up the grain's mixture of protein and starch into a light, flaky exterior.

fresh sweet corn or dried, milled cornmeal. Some sweet corn varieties can lose almost 50% of their sweetness in just a few hours at room temperature. While supersweet corn hangs on to its sugar longer and tastes sweeter, it also retains more water, tastes less rich and creamy, and is slightly less flavorful than other sweet corn varieties. For the sweetest flavor, buy fresh corn in the summer months, and refrigerate it.

Fresh corn can be grilled whole in the husk or it can be husked and boiled briefly (less than three minutes is sufficient). If necessary to sweeten lackluster fresh corn, you can add sugar or honey to the cooking water. Fresh sweet corn tastes great in salads. You can also remove the kernels, then scrape the cobs to remove the sweet corn pulp, or "milk," to enrich creamed corn, corn pudding, soups, succotash, and stews. Some cooks take advantage of the starch in corn by puréeing it to add body and texture to sauces and soups.

Fresh sweet corn produces another interesting foodstuff: corn smut. Considered a defect in most corn production, corn smut (also known as huitlacoche) is a fungal disease. The fungus *Ustilago maydis* replaces corn kernels with ashen blue-gray spores that enlarge and mushroom out of the husk, making the corn look swollen and burned. In Mexico and increasingly around North America, huitlacoche is considered a delicacy for its creamy texture and its earthy, mushroom-like aroma that derives from flavor compounds like sotolon and vanillin.

The early peoples of Mexico and Central and South America made corn a cornerstone of their diet through nixtamalization. This process of soaking or cooking corn in an alkaline solution (usually limewater) loosens the tough outer hull so that it can be easily removed (along with the germ), creating

fast facts

- The U.S. leads the world in corn production, producing upwards of 300 million tons (272 million metric tons) a year, which is nearly half the world's harvest. Most of it goes into animal feed for corn-fed beef.
- In the 1950s, excavations for a new building in Mexico City uncovered pollen from the wild ancestor of corn, estimated to be 70,000 years old.
- On an ear of corn, the kernels always grow in an even number of rows.
- Baby corn is the immature ear of unpollinated corn. It was developed in Taiwan.

"nixtamal." Native North Americans treated their corn in a similar way, using alkaline ashes instead of limewater. Nixtamalization eliminates some of the aflatoxin produced by fungi that can grow on corn, makes the corn easier to grind, improves its flavor, and most important, boosts its available nutrients such as protein, calcium, iron, zinc, and niacin. Fermenting nixtamal further increases its protein and vitamin B_{12} content. These nutritional improvements prevented the debilitating disease pellagra, caused by niacin or protein deficiency, and made nixtamalized corn a crucial part of the early Latin American diet.

While it's still wet, nixtamal can be wet-milled, or ground and kneaded into fresh, moist masa dough. The masa can then be dehydrated into dried masa harina. Both types of masa are widely used to make tamales, tortillas, tortilla chips, and other corn-based foods. In North America, nixtamal is better known as hominy or samp. It is used fresh or canned to make salads, side dishes, casseroles, soups, succotash, and stews such as pozole. Dried hominy can also be coarsely ground to pieces about 0.5 to 1 mm in diameter to make hominy grits.

Other types of grits, cornmeal, and corn flour are made from dried corn that is not nixtamalized and is lower in nutrients than nixtamal or masa. In Colombia and Venezuela, for instance, thick corn tortillas or corn cakes called arepas are made from a type of coarse-ground cornmeal known as arepa flour. In North America, dry-milled corn is simply called cornmeal and is usually ground to pieces about 0.2 mm in diameter. It may be yellow, white, or blue depending on the variety of corn used. Steel-ground cornmeal found in many supermarkets lacks most of the husk and germ and consists primarily of the starchy endosperm. Stone-ground cornmeal retains more of the husk and oily germ, giving the cornmeal more flavor and a chewier texture. The oil in stone-ground cornmeal makes it more perishable, and this type should be stored in the refrigerator, where it will last a few months. Various types of cornmeal are used around the world to make corn flakes breakfast cereal, polenta, and cornbreads. Corn flour is a slightly finer grind of cornmeal (less than 0.2 mm in diameter) used often in breadings. Corn flour is different from cornstarch because it is milled from the whole kernel, whereas cornstarch is milled only from the starchy endosperm.

How It Works • The sweetness in corn comes, of course, from its sugars, which make up about 40% of some SuperSweet varieties and 16% of other sweet corn varieties. Most of corn's flavor lies beneath the tough outer hull of the kernel and comes from volatile sulfur compounds such as hydrogen sulfide and dimethyl sulfide, a flavor component it shares with cooked milk and shellfish like clams, snails, squid, and octopus. Nixtamalized corn like masa and hominy develop subtle berry-like aromas as the amino acid tryptophan is broken down into a compound called aminoacetophenone. Masa and hominy also develop distinctive floral and spicy aromas from the flavor compounds ionone and vinyl-guaiacol.

Corn's creamy texture comes from starch polysaccharides, which are about 25% by weight in a regular sweet corn and somewhat lower in SuperSweet varieties (5% by weight). Dent corn used to make cornstarch contains more than 66% starch.

Carotenoid pigments like zeaxanthin give yellow corn its sunny color, while white varieties are lower in carotenoids. Blue and red kernels are colored by anthocyanin pigments. Along with other nutrients, these pigments offer us some benefits for health. Yellow corn's carotenoids like zeaxanthin, beta-carotene, and lutein can help reduce the risk of various cancers and help prevent vision loss. An ear of corn (about 3.5 oz or 100 g of corn kernels) contains about 3 grams each of protein and fiber with only 90 calories. Corn also provides magnesium, B vitamins such as thiamin, niacin, and folate, and vitamin C.

See Also • Bread, Grains, Oil, Sweeteners

CORNICHON • See Cucumber

CORNISH GAME HEN • See Chicken

CORNMEAL • See Corn

CORN OIL • See Oil

CORNSTARCH • See Starch

CORN SYRUP • See Sweeteners

COTECHINO • See Sausage

COTTAGE CHEESE • See Cheese

COUSCOUS

What It Is • Couscous, tiny grains of moistened semolina, is popular in North Africa (Morocco, Tunisia, Algeria), France, Sicily, and the Middle East. Israeli couscous (maftoul or pearl couscous) is made with bulgur wheat and flour instead of semolina and is toasted to deepen its flavor. Other varieties of couscous are made from barley, millet, or corn, but traditional couscous is made purely from **wheat** semolina. Most North American supermarkets stock instant couscous (quick-cooking couscous), a type that is pre-steamed and dried to speed preparation.

What It Does • As a porridge, side dish, or part of a stew, couscous is a staple in parts

of North Africa. It can be cooked with milk or any other liquid and made sweet or savory. Moroccans often flavor it with saffron, while Tunisians prefer spicy harissa. In Sicily, it may be paired with trout or anchovies. In North Africa, it's typically served like rice or pasta under a meat or vegetable stew. Traditionally, couscous is steamed in a North African pot (a couscoussière), a two-part steamer with a lower pot for stewing meat, fish, and/or vegetables and a perforated upper pot that steams the couscous and infuses it with the stew's aromas. When served with the stew, the entire dish may be called couscous. If you don't have a couscoussière, you can simulate the technique by using a cheesecloth lined colander or steamer basket set over a pot. Unlike traditional couscous, instant couscous needs only to be soaked in hot water to rehydrate it.

fast fact

• In Louisiana, coush-coush is a breakfast porridge made from cornmeal, butter, cream, and sugar.

How It Works • Couscous is made by wetting and rolling coarsely ground durum wheat (semolina) into tiny balls (from 1 to 3 mm in diameter), then coating them in fine wheat flour. Traditionally, it is formed by hand in a bowl like fresh pasta. The grains are handled gently to avoid developing gluten, creating a light, fluffy texture. When cooked, the starch in couscous absorbs moisture from steam or hot water, swells, and softens, giving the wheat a tender yet chewy texture. Whole wheat couscous contains more fiber and protein and is slightly chewier.

CRAB • See Crustacean

CRACKER • See Bread

CRANBERRY • See Berries

CRAYFISH • See Crustacean

CREAM • See Milk

CREAM CHEESE • See Cheese

CREAMER, NONDAIRY • See Milk

CREAMING • See Cake

CREAM OF TARTAR • See Acid

CRÈME FRAÎCHE • See Fermentation

CRÈME LIQUEUR • See Liqueur

CRENSHAW MELON • See Melon

CRÊPES • See Pancakes

CROAKER • See Fish

CROCODILE • See Game

CROISSANT • See Bread

CRUCIFEROUS VEGETABLES

What It Is • Kids may remember them as their most loathed vegetables but many adults grow to love the slightly bitter, slightly sweet taste of cruciferous vegetables like broccoli, cauliflower, and bok choy (Chinese cabbage). Crucifers encompass a huge family of edible and inedible plants. We eat all parts of these plants, including the leaves of loose leafy greens such as kale, collards, and arugula; the tightly packed leaves of various cabbages such as green, red, napa, savoy, and Brussels sprouts; the stems of bok choy and kohlrabi; unbloomed flowers like cauliflower and broccoli; roots like radish, horseradish, turnip, and rutabaga; and even the seeds of mustard and canola. "Cruciferae" is a somewhat older name for the whole family. It means "cross-bearing" and refers to the four petals of their flowers that are reminiscent of a cross.

Today, "cruciferous vegetables" most often refers to Brassicas, the largest genus in the family. But crucifers do include a few other genera, such as *Raphanus sativus*, better known as radishes. This entry is limited to a discussion of the cruciferous vegetables in the *Brassica* genus. (For cruciferous dark leafy greens, see **Leaves**. For cruciferous root vegetables, see **Roots**.)

What It Does • Cruciferous vegetables tend to grow best and taste best in cool weather, when their starch converts to sugar for energy. They also produce fewer unpleasantly sulfurous aromas in the cold months. After harvest, keep crucifers from using up their stored sugar for energy (which would reduce sweetness) by storing them tightly wrapped in plastic in the refrigerator, where they'll last for a week or two.

The common culinary Brassicas in the crucifer family can be divided into two main types: *Brassica oleracea* and *Brassica rapa*. In the *B. oleracea* group, broccoli and cauliflower are actually immature flowers picked before the flowers bloom. Broccoli can

fast fact

- The isothiocyanates in cruciferous vegetables are goitrogens that can interfere with the proper functioning of the thyroid gland.

be eaten raw or cooked but, like all Brassicas, it is best when cooked briefly (five to seven minutes at most). Broccoli stems are slightly sweeter than the flowers (florets) and delicious when peeled and sautéed or braised. Cauliflower is sweeter still (about half the carbohydrates in cauliflower are sugars) and forms a more compact head, or curd, of immature flowers. The head may be the familiar cream color or purple, brown, yellow, or orange. Pigmented cauliflower varieties tend to have more pronounced flavors. Some cultivars include broccoflower, a green or purple cross between broccoli and cauliflower, and Romanesco broccoli, a green or purple cultivar. Cauliflower and its cultivars can be eaten raw like broccoli in salads and relishes or cooked in soups and purées. A whole head of cauliflower can be

quickly roasted in a hot oven. Cheese sauce is a popular accompaniment.

Chinese broccoli, or Chinese kale (kai-lan), also falls into the large *B. oleracea* group. It has thick green stalks, strong-flavored bluish green leaves, and white flowers, and is usually eaten whole like broccoli rabe. Broccolini (Asparation) is a hybrid of broccoli and Chinese broccoli; it has skinny stalks and flowering heads that are smaller and looser than broccoli. Broccolini is eaten whole like Chinese broccoli but has a milder flavor and its relatively tender stalks don't require peeling.

The most common cabbages in the *B. oleracea* group are green, red, and savoy types. Savoy cabbage has a somewhat looser head than green and red types, with softer, ruffled leaves. It's also milder in flavor. These types can be eaten raw in salads like coleslaw or fermented to make sauerkraut. They're often boiled, for instance with potatoes and corned beef in Irish boiled dinner. Cabbage can also be braised, steamed, or boiled, then used as a wrapping for ground meats.

Brussels sprouts, which originated in

science wise

Belgium, are like baby cabbages on a single stalk. Some varieties (such as Rubine Red) appear deep red instead of green. Brussels sprouts have a strong, nutty flavor that pairs well with chestnuts, walnuts, and other nuts. Smaller sprouts tend to be sweeter and more tender but less complex in flavor.

Kohlrabi, also called cabbage turnip, gets its name from the German words *kohl* (cabbage) and *rabi* (turnip). This cruciferous vegetable is actually a stem that swells at its base to the size of a baseball. Kohlrabi may be pale green or tinged with purple on the surface, but the flesh inside is usually pale green or white. It tastes rather mild and sweet like broccoli stems, and is wonderfully crisp when eaten raw. Cooking enhances its sweetness, and it can be hollowed out and stuffed.

Members of the *B. rapa* group include many Asian crucifers. The Chinese cabbage called bok choy has wide white stalks with relatively tight and wavy dark green leaves. The crisp, mild-flavored stalks are often stir-fried, and the leaves often turn up in soups. Choy sum, or Chinese flowering cabbage, has looser, greenish yellow leaves with small yellow flowers and delicate light green stems. Napa cabbage more closely resembles an elongated version of green or savoy cabbage. It has broad pale green leaves in a somewhat tightly packed, bullet-shaped head. Napa cabbage tends to be moister, more tender, and milder in flavor than other cabbages. Like other Chinese cabbages, it's often fermented to make Korean kimchi.

Broccoli rabe (rapini) is distinguished by its bitter flavor components. It looks similar to Chinese broccoli and broccolini, with long, skinny stalks and loose, broccoli-like heads. It's often steamed, braised, or sautéed. To remove some of the bitter flavor compounds, blanch broccoli rabe in salted water for two to three minutes before finishing cooking.

How It Works • Much of a crucifer's flavor comes from sulfur compounds. When cut and even more so when cooked, these compounds react with oxygen, moisture, and heat to form additional flavor compounds. For instance, a crucifer's pungent bite comes from isothiocyanates (mustard oils) and its bitterness comes from glucosinolates, which are precursors to additional sulfur compounds created when the vegetables are heated. That's why cabbage is rather mild when raw (as in coleslaw), more pungent when briefly cooked, and disagreeably sulfurous when trisulfides develop during extended cooking.

Soaking cruciferous vegetables in cold water can leach out some of the bitter compounds released during cutting. Fermentation into sauerkraut and kimchi also makes crucifers less bitter. When it comes to cooking, keep it brief, brief, brief — less than five minutes. Quick, high-heat cooking methods are best, especially for Brussels sprouts, which are particularly high in glucosinolates and have the most potential to develop unpleasant sulfur aromas. For the best flavor, cruciferous vegetables are often cut into florets or small pieces so they can be quickly steamed, sautéed, or stir-fried. Leave off any pan lids to allow the sulfurous compounds to escape. You can also blanch cruciferous vegetables in boiling water for 30 to 60 seconds. Blanching leaches out enough of the chemical precursors to malodorous hydrogen sulfide gas (the rotten egg smell) created during cooking so that crucifers can then be cooked for an extended period without releasing as many smelly fumes.

The tough texture of some parts of crucifers, like the lower stalks of mature broccoli, comes from a cell wall component called lignin that becomes increasingly

kitchen wisdom

Bright Idea

To preserve the white color of cauliflower, add a tablespoon (15 mL) of acid such as vinegar or lemon juice to the cooking water.

woody with age. On the other hand, cauliflower and its cultivars such as Romanesco broccoli have fairly high levels of pectins and hemicelluloses in their cell walls, which makes them taste somewhat creamy when chewed and especially when puréed because the pectin and hemicelluloses are released from the cell walls, providing a creamy texture.

Crucifer Colors

Cruciferous vegetables come in a rainbow of colors, from green and yellow to red, purple, and blue. The green of broccoli, Brussels sprouts, and green cabbages comes from chlorophyll. Broccoli florets get their dark blue-green hue from a type of pigment called chlorophyll-a, while the lighter yellow-green stalks are filled with chlorophyll-b. When cooking green crucifers, avoid acids, which will turn the chlorophyll a dull gray-green. Five to six minutes of cooking will keep most vegetables bright green, but avoid cooking much longer or the colors will dull. To brighten the green color, blanch green vegetables in boiling water for about a minute, then plunge into ice water to stop the cooking.

Cauliflower lacks the green chlorophyll found in other cruciferous vegetables because the green leaves of the plant are kept over the white curd to prevent photosynthesis. Cauliflower's pale yellow hues come from anthoxanthin pigments. These pigments can change color from yellow to blue in reaction to iron or aluminum. To prevent the color change, avoid cutting cauliflower with carbon steel knives or cooking in iron or exposed aluminum cookware. Stainless steel is the best choice for nonreactivity. Cauliflower can also discolor, turning pink or brown, when cooked in hard water. Even a small amount of metal in water can cause the cauliflower's tannins to darken. If you have hard water, consider buying a filter that removes minerals, or add ½ teaspoon (2 mL) of acid (cream of tartar, vinegar, or lemon juice) to each gallon (4 L) of water to prevent discoloration. What about the deeper sunny color of orange cauliflower? It comes from carotenoids, which also lend yellow-orange hues to other crucifers. Orange cauliflower is particularly high in carotenoids and has 25 times more vitamin A than white varieties.

The red-purple spectrum of colors in red cabbage and purple cauliflower and the purple tinge on kohlrabi comes from anthocyanin pigments. Similar to anthoxanthins, anthocyanins can turn from red-purple to blue or murky green in alkaline conditions. Cooks often prepare red or purple cruciferous vegetables with acidic ingredients to avoid the color change. Again, carbon steel knives, peelers, and cookware should also be avoided (unless you love blue vegetables!).

The many flavor and color compounds in crucifers aren't just delicious and pretty; they're healthy for us. These vegetables are best known for their antioxidants like beta-carotene and the sulfurous compound sulforaphane. Studies show that the sulfur compounds in crucifers can help the liver's ability to neutralize toxins and help prevent the development of certain cancers. In general, cruciferous vegetables are also high in fiber, vitamin C, and folic acid.

See Also • Antioxidants, Chlorophyll, Horseradish, Leaves, Mustard, Roots

CRUMPET • See Bread

CRUSTACEAN

What It Is • With more than 50,000 family members in the water, crustaceans belong to a group of animals called arthropods, which makes them relatives of landbound insects. Crustaceans live in fresh and salt water and include everything from small krill and barnacles to large king crab. These omnivorous creatures eat everything in the sea from algae and seaweed to other sea creatures.

Like other arthropods, crustaceans share a similar body structure, consisting of a hard shell, or exoskeleton, that protects the delicate muscles and organs inside. The exoskeleton has two main parts, the head (cephalothorax) and the tail or abdomen.

The meat often resides in the tail or abdomen (of shrimp, for instance) or sometimes in the claws (as in the case of lobster). To grow, crustaceans must periodically molt, or shed their shells. The crustacean forms a tough cuticle over its body, crawls from its shell, and pumps itself up with water (up to twice its original body weight) to stretch the cuticle to its maximum size. Gradually, the cuticle mineralizes and hardens, forming a new shell with enough room for growth. Molting means that the flesh of wild crustaceans varies seasonally, with large, dense muscles right before molting, and meat that is more than half water immediately afterward.

What It Does

● The sweet, briny taste of crustaceans makes them popular in all sorts of savory cakes (like crab cakes), casseroles, stews, soups, and salads. Here's a quick look at some culinary crustaceans.

All crabs have 10 legs, with pincers on two of their front legs. They range in size from tiny oyster crabs (about the size of a penny) to medium Jonah crabs (about 7 inches/17.5 cm from claw to claw) to huge king crabs (measuring up to 10 feet/3 m across). Blue crabs thrive in the Atlantic Ocean (especially in Chesapeake Bay) and the Gulf of Mexico.

They have blue claws and blue-green shells. Soft-shell blue crabs are sold when the crab molts, which occurs mostly in the summer months.

Stone crabs thrive on the Atlantic and Gulf coasts from the Carolinas to Texas, but they concentrate around Florida. Only the claw meat of these crabs is eaten, and the claws are often removed and the crab is returned to sea to grow new claws, which takes one to two years. The claws of stone crabs are sold cooked because the raw meat clings to the shell when frozen.

Dungeness crabs are most plentiful in the Pacific Ocean as far north as Alaska and as far south as Mexico. They weigh anywhere from one to four pounds (454 g to 1.8 kg) and have a slightly pink flesh. King crabs can weigh more than 15 pounds (6.8 kg). Their meat is snowy white tinged with red near the shell. Snow crabs average less than half the size of king crabs.

Male crabs are usually bigger and have more meat than females. Males are typically sold whole for boiling and pickling, while females are sold for canning or for their tasty roe (eggs), which is used in soups like she-crab soup. To tell male from female, look on the underside "apron" of the crab. Males will

have a long, narrow, T-shaped apron, while the apron of females will be wide and more rounded or triangular. Fresh crabmeat loses flavor in about a day, but crabmeat can be flash frozen to preserve its flavor. It can also be pasteurized and canned so that it lasts up to six months (although the heat of pasteurization will cause some loss of flavor). Jumbo, lump, and backfin crabmeat is best. Flake crabmeat consists of smaller bits of body meat. Claw meat is the lowest grade available. Crabs are also sold for their "mustard," a digestive gland with a strong flavor and rich texture.

Crayfish thrive in muddy waters, where they grow up to a half foot long (15 cm) and half pound (225 g) in weight. With their meat concentrated in the tail, crayfish look like small freshwater lobsters. Crayfish should always be cooked because flatworms in the raw crustacean can damage our livers and lungs.

Like crabs and crayfish, Maine, or American, lobsters have 10 pairs of legs including two front claws where a good portion of meat resides. Their shells range in color from brown to blue-black when raw. Spiny, or rock, lobsters are found in warm waters. They have no claws, but their tails are covered with sharp spines and hold most of the meat. Spiny lobsters are typically sold for their tail meat, which is firmer and slightly less sweet than the meat of Maine lobsters. We also eat lobsters for their coral, or eggs, which are light pink in color when mature, and for their green tomalley, a richly flavored digestive gland that's sometimes added to sauces. Lobsters must be purchased alive or frozen because enzymes in the tomalley begin breaking down the lobster meat within hours of death.

When buying a live lobster, pick it up. It should be feisty, or at least the tail should curl under, even if slowly because the lobster is being held at low temperatures. Store live lobsters in salt water or on ice for no more than an hour or two. If you need to keep a live lobster out of water before it will be cooked, it's most humane to kill the lobster instantly by driving a large chef's knife through the top of the head and cutting down through the front of the head in one motion. Remove the meaty claws and tail and discard the rest of the body (or at least the tomalley) to prevent spoilage. The claws and tail will last a day or two on ice.

In North America, the term "prawn" may refer to any large shrimp, but more specifically it refers to the Dublin bay prawn (scampi or langoustine), which resembles a crayfish or miniature lobster. Prawns measure about 6 to 8 inches (15 to 20 cm) in length. They have red bodies and dark red tails.

While there are only a few varieties of prawn, shrimp varieties number more than 300. Shrimp may appear black or light brown to gray-green, dark green, red, pink, or yellow. They are the most popular shellfish in North America and are classified into two main types: warm-water shrimp and cold-water shrimp. Larger shrimp tend to come from warmer waters. Most shrimp are frozen at sea, then thawed just before sale. They're often treated with bisulfites and sodium polyphosphate to prevent discoloration and moisture loss on the journey from ocean to market. If you can find them, fresh day-boat (unfrozen) shrimp will taste much more flavorful. Keep in mind that shrimp sold with the head on are more perishable and should be kept on ice and used within a day. Deveining shrimp, or removing the intestine, is a matter of choice, but it's recommended for large shrimp, which can accumulate noticeable bits of grit there. Shrimp are made into various products around the world, such as shrimp paste.

In general, crustaceans are highly perishable, spoiling within hours of harvest. When buying live crustaceans, especially lobster, check to make sure they are lively. They should have a clean, fresh scent and no ammonia odor, which indicates deterioration.

fast fact

- Imitation crab is made from surimi (washed and frozen pollock, hake, or other fish muscle tissue) mixed with starch, egg white, oil, and artificial flavors and colors to mimic the taste and texture of real crab.

How It Works • To help disguise themselves from predators, raw crustaceans appear in various colors, from brown to pink, red, yellow, gray-green, and blue-black. When frozen or cooked, these colors can change. The shells of frozen shrimp can also darken because of oxidation. Just like when a cut apple turns brown, the polyphenols in shrimp shells oxidize when they come in contact with air, darkening the shell. Shrimpers sometimes lessen this phenomenon by spraying the shrimp with citric or ascorbic acid (vitamin C). Shrimp can also be flash frozen with liquid nitrogen to help preserve color and freshness.

When cooked, shrimp, lobster, and other crustacean shells change color to red. What happens is that heat breaks down the color-binding proteins in the shell and reveals the shell's brighter orange-red pigments such as astaxanthin, canthaxanthin, and beta-carotene.

The meat of crustaceans tastes richer than most fish because of its abundance of connective-tissue collagen. But the meat of shrimp and lobster can go from succulent to mushy if kept warm for too long. When held at temperatures of 130 to 140°F (54 to 60°C), enzymes begin to digest the protein in the muscles and soften the tissues. For the moistest, firmest texture, it's best to quickly cook crustaceans well above this temperature to inactivate the protein-digesting enzymes, as when cooking lobster or shrimp until firm and opaque (about 170°F/77°C). If slowly cooking them, it's best to immediately serve crustaceans upon reaching the 130 to 140°F (54 to 60°C) temperature range.

The flavor of crustaceans comes from various flavor compounds. Their slight sweetness comes from glycine, an amino acid that balances the salt in the sea water in which they live. Remarkably, crustaceans also have some nutty, caramelized flavors even when heated to temperatures well below 340°F (170°C), the temperature at which most browning flavors develop in meat. Crustaceans taste best when cooked in the shell (or on the bone), as the shell releases some of its flavorful compounds into the meat and protects the meat from losing flavor. The shells of crustaceans such as lobster and shrimp are often simmered to extract their flavor for flavoring sauces and soups. For the most flavor, include some fat in the simmering mixture to help extract fat-soluble carotenoids from the shell.

Like other shellfish, crustaceans are low in calories and fat and high in protein, potassium, phosphorus, and vitamins A, B, and D. Crustaceans are low in saturated fat. They have a marine sterol similar to cholesterol but it is not absorbed by our bodies, so crustaceans are not considered a significant risk for developing heart disease.

See Also • Mollusks

CRYOVAC • See Vacuum

CRYSTALLIZATION • See Candy, Chocolate, Sugar

CUCUMBER

What It Is • Cucumbers are founding members of the Cucurbitaceae family that also includes hundreds of melons and squashes. While their cousins are sweeter or more fibrous, cucumbers taste more mild and watery. They were domesticated in India more than 3,000 years ago and thrive in warm climates. There are more than 100 cultivated varieties, with two primary species, *Cucumis sativus* (cucumbers) and *Cucumis anguria* (burr gherkins). The term "gherkin" has come to refer to any small cucumber from either family; particularly small ones are called cornichons in France.

Cucumis sativus provide most of our culinary varieties, such as North American slicing cucumbers, which tend to have bitter-tasting skins and only moderately moist flesh. Those sold for pickling, such as Kirby cucumbers, are shorter and fatter, with thinner skins that have bumpy white or black spines. Long, skinny English (European or Mediterranean) cucumbers, commonly grown in hothouses, tend to have very thin skins, but they have fewer seeds, moister flesh, and a

milder flavor, not least because bitter compounds have been bred out of this variety. Japanese and other Asian cucumbers are slender and deep green, and have a more complex flavor. In India, a yellow type of cucumber called dosakai may be pickled or used in chutneys, soups, and dals. Armenian cucumber (snake melon) has a long, slender, curved body with ridged light yellow to pale green razor-thin skin. It has a sweet, mildly citrus-like flavor and very crisp texture.

What It Does ● Slicing cucumbers are usually served raw in salads and condiments such as Indian raita and Greek tzatziki or in soups such as Spanish gazpacho. The thinner-skinned pickling cucumbers are more appropriate for pickling because the brine can more easily penetrate the skin, where it draws water from the cells and

creates a softer texture. Similarly, sprinkling cut cucumbers with salt draws moisture from the cells and causes them to soften.

Cucumbers are best stored at room temperature or above 50°F (10°C) since they are susceptible to chill injury. Some varieties, such as North American slicing cucumbers, are coated in wax to delay moisture loss and should be peeled before using. English (Mediterranean) cucumbers are wrapped in plastic instead of wax and need no peeling.

How It Works ● The juicy, crisp texture of cucumbers comes mostly from water, which makes up 96% of their cell walls. The mild flavor distinctive of cucumber comes from aldehydes, a group of flavor compounds similar to those of melons. Cutting or chewing is enough to release aldehydes. Cooking cucumbers greatly reduces aldehydes and therefore flavor. Cucumbers get a touch of

Cucumber Martini

While some gins would overpower the delicate flavor of cucumber, Hendrick's gin enhances it. Hendrick's has more floral and less spicy aromas than other brands. A little cucumber, some rose water, and a leaf of mint create a refreshing summertime martini.

	Crushed ice	
1	fresh mint leaf	1
1 tbsp	peeled, seeded, and finely chopped cucumber	15 mL

3 oz	gin, preferably Hendrick's	90 mL
Dash	dry French vermouth	Dash
2 to 3	drops rose water	2 to 3
	Lemon peel, for garnish	

1. Fill a shaker one-third full with crushed ice. Add mint, cucumber, gin, vermouth, and rose water. Shake hard and fast for 8 to 10 seconds. Let stand for 10 seconds, then strain into a chilled martini glass. Garnish with lemon peel.

MAKES 1 SERVING

fast fact

- China produces more than 60% of the world's cucumbers.

sweetness from sugar, which makes up about 1 to 2% of the fruit. For the most sugar, use mature, large cucumbers. The vegetable's bitterness comes from defensive compounds called cucurbitacins concentrated in the skin and meant to deter pests. Peeling cucumbers removes much of the bitterness.

See Also • Vegetables

CULATELLO • See Ham

CUMBERLAND SAUSAGE • See Sausage

CUMIN • See Spices

CURAÇAO • See Liqueur

CURD AND CURDLING • See Cheese

CURING

What It Is • Before the days of refrigeration, foods were cured with salt to preserve them. Cured foods also taste great, and today's cured meats are made mostly for flavor. **Smoking** and dehydrating (see **Drying**) are also used to cure foods such as beef jerky, but this entry deals only with salt-curing.

What It Does • Rubbing meat with salt (dry-curing) or soaking it in salted water (wet-curing) has led to a huge array of popular foods around the world, from salt cod and gravlax to bacon and ham. Curing is a simple way to flavor and prolong the useful life of meat. Dry-cured foods include most **sausages** and charcuterie. These meats were originally cured with potassium nitrate (saltpeter), which is converted to potassium nitrite during curing and helps delay spoilage and preserve color in red meat. Most cured meats are now made with sodium nitrite instead of nitrate, but curing salts can include

either one or sodium nitrate. Curing salt made with sodium nitrite may be called pink salt, a reference to its color. It contains about 94% salt and 6% nitrite. Curing salts containing sodium nitrate are used less often.

Wet-cured foods, from pickled herring and ham to corned beef and pastrami, are essentially brined, or soaked in or injected with heavily salted water. After wet-curing, many types of ham and bacon are also smoked for flavor.

How It Works • Salting changes the texture and moisture content of cured foods. All food cells are filled with water, and the water is attracted to sodium ions in the salt cure. In this way, salt draws water out of the meat, dehydrating it and reducing the availability of water for microbes that can lead to spoilage and inhibiting the growth of harmful bacteria. By inhibiting the growth of microbes and harmful bacteria, salt-curing makes some meats last without refrigeration for months. Dehydration also makes dry-cured meats denser and more concentrated but not necessarily dry. Salt also breaks down and tenderizes tough protein fibers, creating the dense yet tender texture of dry-cured prosciutto and other cured meats.

In both dry-cured and wet-cured meats, moisture exchange is a two-step process. It flows out at first and then back in. Water flows out of the cells to equilibrate with the high salt concentration of the brine. Salt is also attracted to water in the food's cells, so it enters the cells and brings with it any other flavors you have put in the salt cure, thereby flavoring the meat. Inside the cells, salt binds to meat proteins, eventually creating a higher osmotic pressure that draws water back in. This two-step exchange continues as the meat cures. Eventually the cells swell with water, increasing the juiciness of wet-cured meats such as corned beef. Cured meats average about 60% moisture and 5 to 7% salt by weight.

The sharp-edged flavor in cured meats is, in part, the taste of nitrite. Enzymes in meat also break down protein into savory peptides and amino acids like meaty-tasting glutamic acid. Fats break down into flavorful compounds that range from floral and citrusy to grassy and buttery. Wet-cured meats are not quite

Basic Dry Cure

Use this all-purpose dry cure to cure meats like Italian bresaola, an air-dried beef. Personalize the cure by adding your favorite spices like black pepper, ground chile peppers, cumin, nutmeg, and allspice. If you like, you can replace the granulated sugar with dextrose, a more fine-textured sugar refined from corn that distributes over the meat a little more evenly. It's less sweet, so use about 1½ cups (375 mL) and increase the curing salt to 5 tablespoons (75 mL).

2 cups	kosher salt	500 mL
1 cup	granulated sugar	250 mL
¼ cup	curing salt made with sodium nitrite (such as curing salt #1 or pink salt)	50 mL

1. In an airtight container, combine salt, sugar, and curing salt. Store at room temperature indefinitely.

MAKES ABOUT 3½ CUPS (875 ML)

as flavorful as dry-cured meats because their flavors are diluted with water (making the meat juicier), whereas dry-cured meats lose water, which concentrates the flavors.

Without nitrite or its precursor nitrate, salt-cured food would eventually turn an unappetizing gray or brown. Cured meats get their bright red and pink colors when nitrites are reduced to nitric oxide and then react with the red pigment myoglobin in meat to form nitrosylmyoglobin, which has a bright pink color. To ensure that cured meats have a reducing environment to convert nitrite to nitric oxide and develop good rosy color, sodium erythorbate, an isomer of sodium ascorbate, is added.

Nitrite delays rancidity, inhibits microbial growth, and stabilizes the color. But most important, it inhibits the growth of dangerous bacteria such as *Clostridium botulinum*, the cause of botulism. One drawback to these benefits is that potentially carcinogenic nitrosamines are formed when nitrites and the natural amino acids in meats interact in our stomachs or in high-heat cooking. To limit nitrosamine formation, cured meats in the U.S. must contain no more than 200 parts per million (0.02%) of residual nitrite or nitrate. Most meats fall well below this upper limit.

See Also • Bacon, Drying, Ham, Jerky, Sausage, Smoking

CURLY ENDIVE • See Chicory

CURRANT • See Berries

CURRY • See Spices

CUSK • See Fish

CUSTARD

What It Is • Zabaglione, pot de crème, pudding … almost any liquid cooked and thickened with eggs can be considered custard. The word usually refers to cooked egg mixtures made with milk or cream. But some custards, such as zabaglione, contain no dairy products. Other custards, like many puddings, may contain starch, gelatin, or alginates with or without eggs for better thickening. Typically, custards are sweet sauces or desserts, but they may be savory, as in the custard filling of a quiche. Eggs are what really define custards.

What It Does • A custard's consistency depends on its ratio of eggs to liquid and the type of liquid used. More eggs create thicker, richer, glossier custards, as do fattier liquids like cream instead of milk. Thin, delicate custards usually contain a ratio of about 1 whole egg or 2 egg yolks per cup (250 mL) of liquid. Thicker custards that are firm enough to be turned out of a mold need a higher ratio of eggs, about 2 whole eggs or 4 egg yolks per cup (250 mL) of liquid. Using egg yolks instead of whole eggs makes custards more creamy and tender. Adding starch also affects texture, making custards slightly grainier rather than silky smooth.

Orange Flan

Straining the custard makes this flan silky smooth, especially if you use whole spices instead of ground. To make the orange-scented caramel, add 2 tablespoons (25 mL) Cointreau to the recipe for Microwave Caramel on page 398.

1 cup	Microwave Caramel (page 398)	250 mL
¾ cup	granulated sugar	175 mL
1 cup	whipping (35%) cream	250 mL
1 cup	light (5%) cream	250 mL
½ tsp	ground cinnamon or 1 cinnamon stick, about 3 inches (7.5 cm) long	2 mL
½ tsp	grated nutmeg or 1 small whole nutmeg	2 mL
1 tbsp	freshly grated orange zest	15 mL
3	eggs	3
4	egg yolks	4
½ cup	freshly squeezed orange juice	125 mL
⅛ tsp	salt	0.5 mL
	Boiling water	

1. Prepare caramel as directed until it appears medium amber in color. Immediately pour into six 4- to 6-ounce (125 to 175 mL) ramekins or a 6-cup (1.5 L) shallow baking dish, quickly swirling ramekins or dish to evenly distribute liquid caramel over bottom and a little up sides. Place ramekins or dish in a baking dish large enough to hold them (or it) comfortably.

2. Preheat oven to 300°F (150°C). In a small saucepan over medium-low heat, combine sugar, whipping cream, light cream, cinnamon, nutmeg, and orange zest. Heat, stirring occasionally, until steaming, about 5 minutes.

3. Meanwhile, in a bowl, using an electric mixer or whisk, beat eggs, egg yolks, orange juice, and salt until eggs look thick and pale yellow, 2 to 4 minutes.

4. If using solid spices, remove them from cream and discard. Very gradually whisk cream mixture into eggs, stirring until thoroughly combined. Strain custard through fine-mesh strainer into prepared ramekins or dish. Put entire large baking dish on middle rack of oven and pour enough boiling water into baking dish to come at least halfway up ramekins or dish. Bake in preheated oven until custard is slightly jiggly in center and a knife inserted in center comes out almost clean, about 30 minutes (for ramekins) or 1 hour (for dish). Remove from water and let cool to room temperature. Refrigerate until cold. To serve, run a knife around the edge of custard, shake it loose, and invert flan onto plate, removing ramekin or dish.

MAKES 6 SERVINGS

There are two general types of custard: stirred and baked. Both are cooked with gentle heat to avoid scrambling the eggs (curdling the custard). Stirred custards, like zabaglione and crème anglaise, are usually made in a double boiler and have a softer, looser texture than baked custards. When a starch such as cornstarch or flour is added to stabilize a stirred custard, it's known as pastry cream and used to fill pastries.

Baked custards like flan and pot de crème get their gentle heat from the oven instead of a double boiler. To help regulate the temperature and provide even, gentle heat, they are often baked in a water bath (bain-marie), especially if the custard mixture doesn't contain starch. Baked custards tend to set more firmly than stirred custards and are often firm enough to be unmolded and sliced. Metal, porcelain, and glass custard cups all facilitate unmolding, but metal tends to work best because its temperature can be more precisely regulated. The French word for custard is *crème*, and baked custards include crème caramel and crème brûlée as well as bread puddings, quiches, and even cheesecakes and pumpkin pies, which are types of baked custard tarts.

Custard must be cooked with gentle heat to avoid scrambling the eggs, which creates a grainy texture and seeps moisture from the mixture. Traditionally, milk or cream is brought just to the boiling point (scalded), then slowly whisked into the eggs to gradually raise their temperature. But you can also cook room-temperature eggs and milk together over low heat to gently raise the temperature of both. Just watch the temperature carefully: the difference between coagulated and scrambled eggs is only 5 to 10°F (3 to 5°C). Custards made without starch should be removed from the heat when they reach 175 to 180°F (79 to 82°C). Adding starch allows you to cook custards to a higher temperature, because starch prevents the eggs from coagulating at their normal temperature of 165 to 180°F (74° to 82°C). For very smooth and creamy custard, use only egg yolks, because egg whites coagulate at a lower temperature than the yolks and will set before the yolks, creating a lumpy texture. Egg yolks also contain lecithins, natural emulsifiers that create a smooth texture in custards. For even silkier custards, strain the mixture before cooking.

When done, a stirred custard will coat the back of a spoon or if made without starch it should thicken to the point where you can draw a finger through a spoonful of custard and it will leave a line. Baked custards should be removed from the oven while still jiggly in the center. A knife inserted into the center will come out clean or moderately moist. Avoid overcooking baked custards, which can easily curdle them. Residual heat will finish coagulating the eggs in the center, and as a custard cools, it will gel even more.

When custards made with milk cool down, the milk proteins coagulate on the hot surface, forming a skin. To prevent a skin from forming, press plastic wrap or greased waxed paper over the surface before refrigerating. Or drip some melted butter or other fat over the surface of the custard to prevent the milk proteins from coagulating.

How It Works • Eggs make custards magical. When heated under normal conditions, eggs eventually clump together, or coagulate, forming the familiar texture of scrambled eggs. But in a custard, the milk, cream, or other liquid arrests the coagulating tendency of the eggs, suspending all the ingredients in a smooth and creamy network of richness. Here's how.

When heated, egg proteins unwind (denature), then reassociate by forming "crosslinks" with themselves, coagulating the eggs. In custards, the same thing happens, but the egg proteins are diluted with milk, cream, or other liquids, and the crosslinked egg proteins hold those liquids in a very delicate suspension. As the proteins coagulate, the entire mixture thickens and forms a smooth, emulsified gel. In stirred custards like lemon curd and pastry cream, the gel's consistency is typically loose like a sauce because constant stirring interrupts the egg proteins' attempts to crosslink. To prevent stirred custards from thinning once they have set, it's best to avoid any additional stirring.

Eggs are very sensitive to heat, and most custard catastrophes result from cooking the mixture too quickly at too high a heat or for too long. Eggs alone will normally coagulate, or begin to form curds, at around 145°F (63°C) and become set or scrambled between 165 and 180°F (74 and 82°C). The added milk and sugar in custards raises the coagulation temperature of the mixture above 180°F (82°C) in most cases. If custard is heated too quickly or above 180°F (82°C), the protein crosslinks develop more rapidly and can overdevelop, forming unpleasant clumps that curdle the mixture and squeeze out the moisture they once held (a process known as syneresis).

kitchen wisdom

Using a Bain-Marie

When baking custards in a water bath (bain-marie), glass or metal pans offer the best heat control. Choose an outer pan that's deep enough to bring the water a little more than halfway up the sides of the custard pan or cups placed inside. The pan should also be wide enough so that the custard cups are surrounded by 1 to 2 inches (2.5 to 5 cm) of water. To prevent uneven heat from bottom-heating ovens, line the bottom of the outer pan with a shallow rack. Avoid covering the entire bain-marie, which can raise the temperature of the water and overcook the custards, although you can poke holes in a foil cover or only cover each custard cup without raising the temperature of the water significantly.

Even, gentle heating is your best approach. Gentle heat regulates egg coagulation, causing the temperature of the custard mixture to rise slowly so that it thickens gradually. You can cook custards at a low temperature (in a 190°F/88°C oven for baked custards) for a long time to help prevent curdling. But most cooks use a water bath. The temperature of the water won't get above 212°F (100°C), and the water envelops the custard in an even source of heat that remains below the boiling point. You still have to remove baked custards from a bain-marie before they reach 180°F (82°C) or they may begin to curdle. Just above that temperature, at 185°F (85°C), egg proteins coagulate more than 500 times faster than they do at 175°F (79°C). The doneness range is very narrow. That's why custards are carefully monitored and it's safest to take their temperature. For the best insurance, bake a custard to complete doneness (175 to 180°F/79 to 82°C), then remove it from the water bath to cool on its own. If left to rest in the water bath, the custard will continue cooking from residual heat in the water and may overcook. However, if you slightly undercook the custard and monitor it carefully, you can finish cooking it in the water bath out of the oven, then remove it from the bain-marie as soon as it is set.

The Effects of Starch

Custards such as pudding and pie filling often include starch to make them firmer and more stable when set. About 1 tablespoon (15 mL) of flour or 2 teaspoons (10 mL) of cornstarch per cup (250 mL) of liquid does the trick. At approximately 175°F (79°C), that starch absorbs moisture from the custard mixture, swells, thickens, and stabilizes the custard. More importantly, adding starch like cornstarch or flour raises the coagulation temperature even higher, causing stirred custards like pastry cream to thicken near the boiling point but never really set. What happens is that the egg and milk proteins unwind when heated, but the starch prevents them from crosslinking with each other and coagulating. On cooling, starch molecules reassociate to form a gel.

Starch gives custards a grainier, less silky texture. Also, an enzyme in egg yolks called alpha-amylase can hydrolyze some of the starch into its component sugars, weakening its gelling ability. But the enzyme is denatured at about 185°F (85°C). Starch-thickened stirred custards work because they are heated close to the boiling point, which easily denatures the enzyme. Starch-thickened baked custards, however, are not stirred to prevent the eggs from coagulating. In starch-thickened baked custards like cheesecake, the coagulating temperature has to be raised high enough to denature the enzyme without scrambling the eggs, which unfortunately happens around the same temperature of 185°F (85°C). That's why these baked custards typically include a lot of sugar. Adding sugar raises the coagulation temperature high enough to denature the enzyme without scrambling the eggs (in most cases). If the custard is heated gently and there's enough starch to prevent the eggs from curdling, the enzyme will be denatured, the custard won't weep, cry, or fall apart, and your guests will rave.

The Effects of Acid

Adding an acid such as lemon juice has the opposite effect of starch: it lowers the coagulation temperature of the eggs. That's why custards made with acidic fruits and vegetables set quickly and can easily overcook. To leach out the acids from the fruit or vegetable, cooks often precook produce when making fruit and vegetable custards. It also helps to add starch to raise the coagulation temperature and help bind up any excess liquid from the fruit or vegetable. These techniques are used to make savory custards like spinach flan.

See Also • Cheesecake, Eggs

CUTTLEFISH • See Cephalopod, Mollusks

CYANIDE • See Toxin

CYNAR • See Artichoke, Bitters, Liqueur

DAIKON • See Cruciferous Vegetables

DAIRY • See Butter, Cheese, Fermentation, Ice Cream, Milk

DAL • See Legumes

DANDELION • See Leaves

DANISH BLUE • See Cheese

DASHI • See Soup

DATE

What It Is • Date gardens cultivated in oases have been part of the landscape of the desert in the Middle East and North Africa for more than 5,000 years. The fruit's precise place and time of origin has been lost to antiquity, but images of date palms appear in carvings from the earliest periods of the Egyptian and Mesopotamian civilizations.

The 600 or so varieties of named dates are drupe fruits (those with a large single stone surrounding their seed) and fall into three categories. Soft dates have a high moisture content and relatively low sugar content. They are mainly eaten fresh in the Middle East where they are grown, but they can be dried and compressed into blocks. Most of the dates produced and eaten outside of the Middle East are of the semidry type. These have firm flesh, medium moisture, and sugar content around 50%. Hard dates (aka bread dates) have dry, fibrous flesh when fresh that becomes wood hard after drying.

What It Does • The date's main food value is its high sugar content, although the fruit contains a fair amount of dietary fiber (3 medium dates, about 2 ounces/56 g, provide 10% of the RDA for fiber). Although it is far from a perfectly balanced food, desert people have been known to live healthfully on a diet of little more than dates and milk.

Date sugar made from ground dried dates contains all of the nutrition of the fruit and is therefore considered a healthy alternative to other sweeteners. However, because of its significant fiber date sugar doesn't dissolve in water and therefore can't replace sugar in all recipes. Date syrup, which is made by boiling dates until the sugar dissolves and then straining out the pulp, is used as a sweetener in the Middle East and in Indian cooking. Palm sugar is processed from the sap of the date palm.

Almost all of the dates grown in North America come from California, where the industry is centered almost exclusively on two varieties, Deglet Noor and Medjool. The Deglet Noor dominates the world market. It is very sweet and mild, with a papery shiny skin and translucent firm flesh. Medjool dates are of the soft type; their low fiber and high moisture give them a creamy consistency. They are large and lush and frequently sell for a premium price.

Date aficionados recognize four stages of fruit development, known around the world by their Arab names: immature and unripe,

when the dates are green, firm, and astringent (*kimri*); mature and unripe, when they are yellow to red and crunchy (*khalal*); ripe, when the fruit is soft, golden brown, and delicately perfumed (*rutab*); and fully ripe and dried, the point at which the dates are reddish brown, wrinkled, firm, and powerfully sweet (*tamr*). All four stages, including drying, can occur on the tree. Kimri dates are typically pickled, like olives. Khalal dates are eaten out of hand like fresh fruit. Most of the dried dates sold worldwide are picked in the rutab state. Tamr dates are usually tree dried until very firm. They are mostly used for making date sugar and syrup.

How It Works • Drying causes dates to turn brown and take on a roasted caramelized flavor as enzymatic browning causes phenolic compounds to darken, and as reducing sugars and proteins interact, developing Maillard reactions (see **Browning**). The same phenolic compounds give dates antioxidant properties. Since the amount of sugar in a date far exceeds the amount of protein and only a small amount of the sugar is used up in the Maillard reactions, the remaining sugar, which is mostly glucose and fructose, gives a dried ripe date its exceptional sweetness.

See Also • Browning, Fruit

fast facts

- In the Middle East, dates are mixed with grain for animal fodder.
- In northern Nigeria, dates and peppers added to beer before drinking are believed to make it less intoxicating.
- Date oil extracted from date seeds is used in soap and cosmetics, and as a source for oxalic acid.

DEEP-FRYING • See Frying

DEER • See Game

DEFROSTING • See Freezing

DEHYDRATION • See Drying

DEGLAZE

What It Is • When an ingredient is roasted, fried, or sautéed, juices and bits of protein and sugar cling to the bottom of the pan and brown. These flavorful bits, known as fonds in classic French cooking, are full of flavor. Deglazing is a process by which a liquid, such as stock, wine, liquor, or water, is added to the pan to dissolve the fond, thereby capturing it for use in a **sauce** or gravy.

No-Cook Date Nut Confection

The intense sweetness and meaty texture of Medjool dates makes them a sensual confection right off the tree. All a cook has to do is grind them with some walnuts and a hint of citrus for an all-natural treat that is as sweet as candy.

12	large Medjool dates (about 9 oz/270 g), pitted	12
1 cup	walnut pieces (about 4 oz/125 g), coarsely chopped, divided	250 mL
¼ cup	finely chopped orange, tangerine, or Clementine	50 mL

1. Chop dates finely.
2. In a bowl, combine dates with half the walnuts and orange. Form into a 6-inch (15 cm) log.
3. In a mini-chopper or food processor, grind remaining walnuts finely. Roll the log in the walnuts. Wrap in plastic and refrigerate for at least 1 hour or for up to 1 week.
4. Cut into ½-inch (1 cm) thick slices to serve.

MAKES ABOUT 12 PIECES

What It Does • The deglazed drippings from sautéed or roasted foods are a concentrate of browned flavors and color. Deglazing is a thrifty way of retaining these components that would otherwise be lost in cooking, and it's one of the main ways a cook has for flavoring a sauce.

To deglaze a pan:
1. Remove the cooked solid ingredients from the pan.
2. Skim or pour off excess fat. The fat can be combined with flour to make a roux for thickening the sauce or gravy.
3. Place the pan over medium-high heat. You can't do this with a glass and some nonstick roasting pans, so it is best to use a stovetop-safe pan when you know you will want the drippings for a sauce.
4. Add about 1 cup (250 mL) liquid (any kind) to the pan and vigorously scrape the bottom of the pan with a spatula or other sturdy flat-blade tool as the liquid comes to a boil. Do not use a knife, which will scratch the pan. Continue scraping and stirring until all of the browned particles are suspended in the deglazing liquid. Some will dissolve and some will just be released from the pan into the liquid. If the liquid should boil dry, add another ½ cup (125 mL) liquid.

Deglazed pan drippings can be used right away to flavor a sauce, or they can be refrigerated for later use.

How It Works • As ingredients heat in a pan, Maillard reactions (see **Browning**) transform the proteins and sugars on the surface of the ingredients into complex browning compounds. At the same time the microscopic bits of protein and sugar in the juices released by the ingredients go through the same process, but because they are dissolved in liquid and sitting on the bottom of the pan, the Maillard reactions occur more quickly and thoroughly. The water in the juices evaporates and a film of delicious roasted flavors and beautiful brown color sets across the pan.

Adding liquid returns the missing water, and the browned compounds, which are water or alcohol soluble, dissolve quickly. Scraping the pan encourages larger brown bits into suspension and helps to lift any fond that has sunk into the pores of the pan into the deglazing liquid.

See Also • Browning, Flavor, Sauces

DELICATA SQUASH • See Squash

DEMI-GLACE • See Sauces

DENATURE • See Protein

DERBY • See Cheese

DESSERT WINE • See Wine

DEWBERRY • See Berries

DEXTROSE • See Sugar

DIABETES • See Digestion

DIACYLGLYCEROL (Diglyceride) • See Emulsion

DIET

What It Is • Today, the word "diet" has two basic meanings: the food you consume or eating to achieve a certain goal.

Your diet is what you eat, and many factors influence dietary choices, most habitual or cultural and some consciously chosen. For instance, people with a medical condition may choose to avoid eating foods that aggravate their symptoms.

In affluent industrialized nations, people usually diet to lose weight but some, for instance athletes, may diet with a view toward bulking up.

What It Does • As we understand more about the relationship between diet and health, it's becoming increasingly clear that a balanced diet based on eating a wide variety of whole (not processed) foods can help to reduce the risk of illness and disease. If you are trying to lose weight, restricting certain foods or general intake is the usual route.

While there are dozens of popular weight-loss programs — some espouse restricting **carbohydrates** or **fats**, and others emphasize limiting **calories** regardless of the food source — research is showing that a weight-loss regimen that works for one person doesn't necessarily work for another, because of differences in **metabolism** and lifestyle factors.

When most people talk about weight loss, they really mean fat loss. However, it is possible to lose weight without losing any fat. For instance, taking diuretics, which cause the body to excrete water, can result in dramatic weight loss (and kidney or liver damage) but no loss of fat. Ideally, dieters want to lose fat and preserve muscle. Since muscles are denser than fat they take up less space, so losing muscle doesn't change your size much, while losing fat changes the shape of the body more dramatically. In addition, it takes more energy to maintain muscle than to maintain fat, so the higher your muscle-to-fat ratio, the higher your metabolism will be, which makes you burn more calories, even at rest.

How It Works • A balanced diet, usually based on eating a variety of whole foods, delivers the nutrition required to be healthy. Most traditional diets (the diet native to a population) are balanced, but each reaches its nutritional balance differently, guided by what foods are available, cultural preferences, and religious edicts.

For many people diet is a defining piece of their sense of self. Vegetarianism, for instance, is a dietary choice. Some cultures are vegetarian for religious reasons. Hinduism, Jainism, and Buddhism all prescribe vegetarianism. Other religions such as Judaism and Islam, kosher and halal diets respectively, use diet to reinforce religious principles by prohibiting the eating of certain meats and seafood. In Judaism, kosher law also forbids combining meat and dairy products.

At its most basic, our diet provides the energy we need to stay alive. Humans are endotherms, meaning we expend a lot of energy just keeping our bodies at a stable temperature. In addition, we use energy to keep our vital organs (particularly the heart, lungs, and brain) functioning, and except when we are in repose our skeletal muscles are working to keep us upright. When all these energy needs are combined, their measurement is the basal metabolic rate (BMR), the amount of energy you need to stay alive. For most of us the BMR is a half watt for every 1 pound (1 watt for every 908 g) of body mass, which means a 150-pound (68 kg) man doing absolutely nothing (or walking a few steps) burns about 75 watts (continuously), or about 1440 calories per day, or 1 calorie per minute.

When your body uses more energy than it takes in, your cells make up the difference from stored energy deposited in cells all over

your body. The first source your cells turn to is **glycogen**, a complex carbohydrate stored mostly in the liver and in muscle where it can be quickly converted into energy. The liver converts glycogen into glucose for energy needs throughout the body. Muscle cells store glycogen that they use internally for quick response. When your glycogen supply is nearly depleted, your body turns to its fat stores. Through lipolysis your body breaks down its fat into fatty acids and glycerol, which are then metabolized into glucose.

On the other hand, when you take in more calories than you need, your body stores the excess glucose, first as glycogen for immediate energy needs, and then as fat for long-term storage.

Significant weight loss can happen safely only over time. The minimum safe dietary intake without medical supervision is 75% of what is needed to maintain basal metabolism. At that rate it would take a moderately active person six months to lose 20 pounds (9 kg).

At the present time there is a great deal of confusion about which weight-loss programs actually work, so much so that many professionals are baffled. The safest strategy is to eat fewer calories than you burn, but even this is no guarantee. However, any expert will tell you that fad diets do not result in healthy long-term weight loss.

See Also • Animal Foods, Calorie, Carbohydrate, Fat, Glycogen, Metabolism, Protein, Starch, Sugar

DIGESTION

What It Is • A whole piece of food is useless to your body as a source of nutrients and energy, until it is broken down into its component parts. Digestion is the process by which your body transforms food into something useful. If we are what we eat, then digestion makes us who we are.

What It Does • Most of this process takes place in the digestive system, largely a one-way tube (the gastrointestinal tract or alimentary canal) consisting of the mouth, esophagus, stomach, small and large intestines, and rectum. At key points, ducts link accessory organs such as the liver and pancreas to the gastrointestinal tract, transporting digestive enzymes into the tract to help break down its nutritional contents. After being absorbed from the gastrointestinal tract, some nutrients are further digested in the liver.

How It Works • Digestion takes place in five stages:
1. Anticipation and primary ingestion — anticipating food and placing food in the mouth
2. Mechanical digestion — chewing and stomach churning that physically crush and liquefy food
3. Chemical digestion — chemicals like acids, bile, and various enzymes that are mixed with crushed food to help break down complex molecules into simpler smaller molecules that can be absorbed and metabolized
4. Absorption — the movement of nutrients from the digestive system to the circulatory and lymphatic systems
5. Elimination (evacuation) — removal of undigested material from the digestive system

Digestion starts in the mouth. Saliva contains the digestive enzyme salivary amylase that breaks down some **starches** into disaccharides (sucrose and maltose). That is why the longer you chew a piece of bread or a mouthful of cooked rice, the sweeter it tastes. Saliva is secreted in large amounts (as much as 1½ quarts/1.4 L per day), and is mixed with food by the tongue. There are two types: thin saliva wets the food, and thick saliva, which is a mucous secretion, acts as a lubricant that aids in swallowing.

The tongue forces the mixture of chewed food and saliva (called a bolus) toward the back of the mouth, where touch receptors in the pharynx trigger a series of reactions that move the food through the digestive system.

Food doesn't just fall from your mouth into your stomach — it's pushed, which is why it is possible to swallow even while standing on your head. The digestive tract is made up of two layers of smooth muscles that form a continuous movement from the esophagus to the rectum.

Digestive System

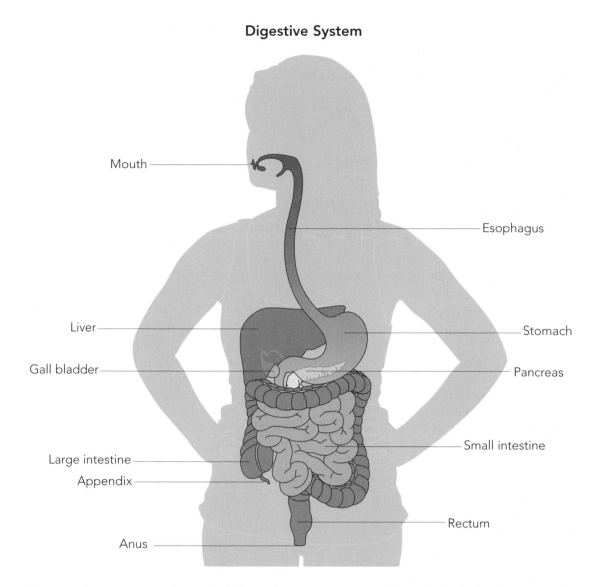

Mouth

Esophagus

Liver

Stomach

Gall bladder

Pancreas

Small intestine

Large intestine

Appendix

Rectum

Anus

The inner layer contracts above the bolus and relaxes below it, encouraging the food to move forward. At the same time the outer muscle layer contracts and expands in tandem with the circular muscles pushing the bolus along.

The stomach is a holding tank that exists mostly because we can chew and swallow faster than we can digest. In the stomach, food mixes with gastric acid and pepsin, a protein-digesting enzyme. The cardiac sphincter at the entry to the stomach controls the flow of food from the esophagus into the stomach and protects the lining of the esophagus from stomach acids that might splash back if the sphincter doesn't close completely.

Stomach acids start to dissolve chewed food, turning it into a liquid, called chyme. The acids provide an ideal pH for the action of pepsin, which separates long-chain **proteins** into shorter strings of amino acids. Very little nutrient absorption occurs in the stomach, aside from some **vitamin** B_{12}, and other small molecules, like alcohol, that are absorbed directly from the stomach into the bloodstream.

The same muscle contractions that move food along the esophagus help to churn it in the stomach and eventually pass it on to the small intestine, where most of the absorption of nutrients takes place. The stomach empties in spurts through the pyloric sphincter, taking about four hours to digest a full load.

Indigestion is a catchall diagnosis for stomach distress. It is usually caused by eating too fast or eating too much, which overloads

science wise

the stomach, causing it to work harder. Churning vigorously, the stomach produces more acid, forming gases that distend its walls, which forces the cardiac sphincter open and causes heartburn.

Most chemical digestion takes place in the duodenum, a short (about 10 to 12 inches/25 to 30 cm long) C-shaped section of intestine made up of glands that secrete mucus to protect the intestinal walls from stomach acid, and ducts that distribute bile and pancreatic enzymes to mix with the chyme.

Bile emulsifies **fat** (and fat-soluble vitamins) so it can be absorbed in watery chyme. Bile is used by the body to excrete bilirubin (a waste product that gives feces its dark color). Although bile is essential for the smooth progression of digestion, it does not contain any digestive enzymes.

Pancreatic juices contain the bulk of digestive enzymes. Trypsinogen, chymotrypsinogen, and carboxypeptidase break protein chains into individual amino acids. Pancreatic lipase breaks fats into individual fatty acids, and pancreatic amylase breaks starches into simple sugars. Other enzymes are secreted by the intestine itself. These include the sugar-digesting enzymes maltase, lactase, and sucrase.

The jejunum, the middle section of the small intestine, is covered with small projections, villi (which are in turn covered with smaller microvilli), that increase the surface area of the intestine's interior to maximize the absorption of nutrients. The total length of an adult small intestine is approximately 20 feet (6 m), and about half of that is in the jejunum. As chyme travels through the intestine its pH neutralizes, reaching between 7 and 8 in the jejunum, allowing peak activity of enzymes to activate, splitting apart the molecular structure of more nutrients so they can pass through the villi into the bloodstream, where they travel to the liver for filtering, removal of toxins, and nutrient processing.

The remaining 9 feet (2.7 m) or so of the small intestine, the ileum, has deep folds (covered with shorter villi and many more microvilli than in the jejunum) along its interior to increase surface area for absorption. Nutrient absorption continues in the ileum, as does the reabsorption of bile salts and any leftover digestive enzymes. Although there is no line of demarcation between the jejunum and ileum, there are a few distinctions. The lining of the ileum contains protein- and **carbohydrate**-digesting enzymes (gastrin, secretin, cholecystokin) that are responsible for extracting the last remnants of amino acids and sugars. Tiny lymph vessels called lacteals, present in the villi of the ileum, absorb any remaining fatty acids and glycerol molecules remaining from fat digestion. Although the entire small intestine connects to the lymph system, only the ileum has specialized lymphoid nodules (Peyer's patches) that monitor potential pathogenic material in the intestine and have the ability to fight it with large amounts of lymphocytes.

Sugars, amino acids, and short-chain fatty acids absorbed into the bloodstream travel to the liver where they are digested completely. As blood sugar levels rise after eating, the pancreas produces insulin, a hormone that causes the liver to transform glucose (blood sugar) into **glycogen**, which is stored in the liver, fat tissue, and muscle cells, thus preventing hyperglycemia (high blood sugar). Within a few hours, when glucose levels drop, the pancreas secretes glucagon, which causes stored glycogen to be converted back into glucose to prevent hypoglycemia (low blood

fast facts

- Because swallowing is activated by centers in the brain stem, damage to the brain through stroke or accident can result in an inability to swallow, a condition called dysphagia.
- The length of the intestine is 10 times longer than the length of the human body.

sugar). A breakdown of this system results in the disease diabetes.

Fatty acids and glycerol are too large to pass and are absorbed into the fatty walls of villi and reassembled into triglycerides (see **Fat**). From there they pass into the lymphatic system and are transported into the large veins that return blood to the heart.

Any food that is not absorbed passes into the large intestine, or colon. It takes 12 to 25 hours for food to travel through the colon, during which time water is absorbed back into the body, solidifying the contents of the colon into feces, largely made up of indigestible plant cellulose and the waste products of digestion. In addition, the colon is the home for a large bacterial colony, mostly *E. coli*, that produces two essential nutrients, vitamin K and biotin, which are absorbed through the colon wall.

See Also • Carbohydrate, Emulsion, Fat, Metabolism, Nutrition, Protein, Starch, Sugar, Vitamins

DIJON MUSTARD • See Mustard

DILL • See Herbs

DISINFECTANT

What It Is • Disinfectants kill microorganisms on nonliving surfaces, such as tables and sponges. They are different from **antibiotics**, which destroy microorganisms within the body, and antiseptics, which wipe out microbes on living tissue. They are stronger than sanitizers, which simply reduce the number of microorganisms to a safe level. In order to be classified as a disinfectant, a substance must be able to kill all of a specified bacterium within 30 seconds of contact (a sanitizer only has to be 99.999% lethal). Neither sanitizers nor disinfectants sterilize, which is the complete elimination of *all* microorganisms on a surface.

What It Does • The ideal disinfectant would be noncorrosive, able to obliterate all

Common Disinfectants

Type of Disinfectant	Disinfectants	Advantages	Limitations	Effective Against
Alcohol	Ethanol Isopropanol	Widespread microbiocidal activity; quick; noncorrosive; most effective diluted with water to 62% concentration	Flammable; evaporates quickly; doesn't kill bacterial spores	Bacteria, fungi, many viruses
Aldehydes	Glutaraldehyde Formaldehyde	Widespread microbiocidal activity; some residual activity	Inactivated by contact with organic matter	Bacteria, fungi, bacterial spores
Halogens	Chloramine Chlorine Hypochlorites Iodine	Widespread microbiocidal activity	Caustic to skin and eyes; strong odor; can produce toxic gas	Bacteria, fungi
Oxidizing agents	Hydrogen peroxide Peracetic acid	Widespread microbiocidal activity; quick; noncorrosive	Toxic to healthy growing cells as well as bacteria	Bacteria, fungi, molds, bacterial spores, some viruses
Phenolics	Phenol Chloroxylenol Thymol	Widespread microbiocidal activity; quick	Corrosive to skin; toxic to fish	Bacteria (including methicillin-resistant *Staphylococcus aureus*), fungi
Quats (quaternary ammonium compounds)	Benzalkonium	Very quick; noncorrosive; non-staining; safe; nontoxic	Not effective against bacterial spores	Bacteria, fungi, viruses

targeted microorganisms without harming other forms of life, and would do so inexpensively. Unfortunately, the perfect disinfectant does not exist. There are various types. Some disinfect a wide spectrum of organisms, while others kill a smaller range. Some are less or more corrosive, toxic, or both.

Most disinfectants are potentially harmful to humans and animals and come with safety precautions printed on their packaging. Most household disinfectants contain Bitrex, a bitter-tasting substance added to discourage ingestion. They should not be mixed with other cleaning agents, because dangerous chemical reactions can occur. For instance, the combination of ammonia and bleach releases toxic chlorine gas.

How It Works ● Different types of
disinfectants kill microbes in different ways. Alcohols denature the proteins of microbes and dissolve their lipids. Oxidizing agents oxidize the cell membranes of microorganisms, and quats destroy interactions between cells and deactivate enzymes.

See Also ● Ammonia, Antibiotics, Bacteria

DISPERSIONS

What It Is ● When two or more substances
are mixed together, they form a dispersion. One or more of the substances are broken into tiny pieces, and those pieces are suspended in the remaining substance. The suspended particles are called the dispersed phase. The substance that they are suspended in is known as the continuous phase.

What It Does ● Many foods are dispersions:
Emulsions are dispersions composed of two liquid phases that are immiscible (incapable of mixing) in each other, typically water and fat. They can be fat droplets suspended in water (mayonnaise, hollandaise), or water droplets suspended in fat (butter). The structure of an emulsion is not dependent on which phase is present in a greater amount. Mayonnaise and butter are both about 80% fat, but they are different types of emulsions. Mayonnaise is oil droplets suspended in a mixture of lemon juice, vinegar, and water; butter is water droplets suspended in solid butterfat. To stabilize an emulsion, the two substances are held together by an emulsifier that interacts with both phases, helping them to stay suspended. In mayonnaise and hollandaise the emulsifiers are lecithin and proteins from egg yolk. In butter it is casein and other proteins in the milk solids.

In **foams** the dispersed phase is a gas. In whipped cream or softly beaten egg white, the gas (air) is held in liquid. In a baked meringue or in peanut brittle, gas is trapped in a solid continuous phase (solid foam).

When the continuous phase is gas, the dispersion is an aerosol. Aerosols are not common in cooking. An example of a liquid aerosol (liquid dispersed in gas) would be spray oil as it sprays from the can dispersing droplets of oil in air. **Smoke** is a solid aerosol, in which lighter-than-air solid particles from burning wood travel through air to flavor a smoked ingredient.

When solid particles are involved in dispersions, the mixture is either a sol or a gel. Sols happen when the dispersed phase is solid and the continuous phase is liquid. Examples of sols are milk and cream. Chocolate and

Types of Dispersions

Continuous Phase	Dispersed Phase		
	Gas	Liquid	Solid
Gas	Not a dispersion because two gases combine evenly	Liquid aerosol (spray oil, fog, mist)	Solid aerosol (smoke, aromatic steam)
Liquid	Foam (whipped cream, beaten egg white)	Emulsion (mayonnaise, hollandaise)	Sol (milk, cream, paint)
Solid	Solid foam (peanut brittle, baked meringue)	Gel (butter, gelatin)	Solid sol (chocolate, hard cheese)

hard cheeses are culinary examples of sols in which the continuous phase is solid. Gels happen when the dispersed phase is liquid and the continuous phase is solid. Butter and **gelatin** are examples.

How It Works

The connection between the two phases of dispersions is innately unsteady. In emulsions the two phases (water and fat) are immiscible, which is why an emulsifier is added to help them stay together. Foams are generally unstable because air is hydrophobic (it lacks an affinity for water) and water is hydrophilic (it has a strong affinity for water), so the water is likely to bond with itself and fall out of dispersion. Gels and sols are sensitive to heat. The stability of these types of dispersions depends on thickening the continuous phase, which keeps the dispersed particles or droplets from moving. Because molecules move faster as they get hotter, heat tends to break sols (cream) and gels (butter, gelatin). Keeping them cold stabilizes them.

The finer the particles in the dispersed phase, the less likely they are to fall out of suspension. This is why mayonnaise made in a blender or food processor is more stable than one mixed by hand. Depending on the size of the particles in the dispersed phase, dispersions can be:

Molecular dispersions: the particle size is less than 1 nm (a nanometer, or one billionth of a meter), the size of a molecule.

Colloidal dispersions: the particle size is between 1 nm and 0.5 mcg (half a millionth of a meter). Most foods are colloidal dispersions.

Coarse dispersion: the particle size is bigger than 0.5 mcg.

See Also • Colloid, Emulsion, Foams, Gelatin, Gums

DISTILLATION • See Liquor

DISTILLED SPIRITS • See Liquor

DORADO • See Fish

DORY • See Fish

DOUGH • See Baking

DOUGHNUT

What It Is

What is a doughnut (or donut, an acceptable spelling only in the U.S., where it has been in common usage since 1930)? However you spell it, a doughnut is nothing more than a piece of yeasted dough or cake that is fried rather than baked. Fried doughs exist in almost every country and every cuisine, and though some have crossed borders (beignets are popular in both Paris and New Orleans), the doughnut is the best-known fried pastry in the world. An iconic doughnut is ring-shaped, but the original was most likely a bite-size dough ball, or dough nut, lending logic to the name. Many doughnuts lack a hole in the center, including all filled doughnuts, like the famous German doughnut, the Berliner or Bismarck, better known as a jelly doughnut.

What It Does

Ring doughnuts are formed either by joining the ends of a long rope of dough into a ring or by using a doughnut cutter, which simultaneously cuts an outside and inside circle. If you don't have a doughnut cutter, a flattened disk of dough can be made into a ring by stretching its center and pinching until the center breaks to form a hole. Batter doughnuts use a doughnut depositor that extrudes a circle of batter directly into a fryer.

Filled doughnuts are made from disks of dough that are fried before being filled. As the doughnut fries, carbon dioxide from the leavener (either yeast or a chemical leavener) expands, causing any air trapped in the dough to expand. The filling, usually some sort of fruit preserve or pastry cream, is piped into the set pastry using a pastry bag with a needle attachment, filling the larger air pockets.

Oil is absorbed into dough as it fries, making doughnuts higher in fat than either bread or cake. Yeasted doughnuts, known as raised doughnuts, are about 25% fat by weight. Cake doughnuts are only 20% fat because they fry more quickly and therefore have less time to absorb oil. Oil

fast facts

- Person for person, Canadians consume the most doughnuts in the world, and Canada has the most doughnut stores per capita.
- June 3 is National Doughnut Day in the U.S.
- In most of central Europe, the Berliner, a doughnut filled with jam or pastry cream, dominates so effectively that American-style ring doughnuts have had a hard time making headway. In Austria, where a Berliner is known as a *krapfen*, there is not a single chain doughnut store.
- In Israel, *sufganiyot*, jelly-filled doughnuts, are the traditional food for celebrating Hanukkah.

absorption varies depending on the fat content of the dough and the temperature of the frying oil. Ideal frying temperature for maximizing browning and minimizing oil absorption is about 370°F (188°C).

Some doughnut shops bake their doughnuts rather than fry them. This decreases the fat content and calories substantially, but it also changes the flavor and, for many doughnut lovers, undermines the paper-thin crunchy skin and soft interior that is the hallmark of properly fried doughnuts. Some doughnut companies parbake their doughnuts and finish them in a fryer to get the best of both worlds.

How It Works • Food-history texts like to say the ring doughnut was developed to make it easier to handle when dunking in coffee, but there is a much better culinary reason. Like its ring-shaped relative the bagel, which is boiled in water before it is baked, doughnuts need as much surface area exposed to hot fat as possible. Punching a hole in the center establishes another dimension for heat transference. The doughnut cooks through more evenly and faster, absorbs less fat because it spends less time in the fryer, and develops a greater proportion of crispy crust.

Ring doughnuts float on the surface of the frying oil and must be turned so that they brown evenly, which leaves a pale circle halfway up their sides where the dough never completely submerges. Braided doughnuts flip themselves, or flip with very slight encouragement, as do ball-shaped doughnuts. Although unsaturated fats are a healthier frying alternative, some amount of saturation is important for frying doughs, to ensure that oil clinging to the skin solidifies as the doughnut cools, giving it a dry rather than oily surface. Doughnuts used to be fried in highly saturated animal fats for that reason, but when lard and suet were identified as a cause of cardiovascular disease, most commercial doughnut makers switched to hydrogenated vegetable fats. Now that trans fats are considered even worse than

Buttermilk Doughnuts with Cinnamon Sugar

These easy cake-style doughnuts can be prepped in the time it takes to heat the frying oil. The acid from the buttermilk in the batter limits the gluten formation, which keeps the dough extraordinarily soft.

	Vegetable oil for frying	
1½ cups	granulated sugar, divided	375 mL
1 tsp	ground cinnamon	5 mL
2 cups	all-purpose flour	500 mL
¾ tsp	salt	4 mL
1½ tsp	baking powder	7 mL
½ tsp	baking soda	2 mL
Pinch	freshly grated nutmeg	Pinch
1	egg, large or extra large	1
½ cup	buttermilk	125 mL
2 tbsp	melted butter, cooled	25 mL
	Additional flour for rolling dough	

1. In a deep skillet or Dutch oven, pour oil to a depth of 3 inches (7.5 cm), and heat over medium heat to 370°F (188°C).

2. In a small bowl, mix 1 cup (250 mL) of the sugar and cinnamon together. Set aside. Set a wire rack over a rimmed baking sheet. Set aside.

3. In a large bowl, combine the remaining sugar, flour, salt, baking powder, baking soda, and nutmeg.

4. In a separate bowl, whisk together egg, buttermilk, and butter. Stir into dry ingredients just until everything is moistened. Do not overbeat.

5. On a lightly floured work surface, roll dough out to a thickness of about ¼ inch (0.5 cm) and cut with doughnut cutter or 1-inch (2.5 cm) biscuit cutter.

6. Add doughnuts to oil, 3 or 4 at a time, and fry, turning once, until deep amber brown, 2 to 3 minutes per side. Transfer with a slotted spoon to the wire rack. Allow the temperature of the oil to return to 370°F (188°C) before adding the next batch. After the doughnuts have cooled for a minute or so, roll them in the cinnamon sugar and place on a platter. Serve immediately.

MAKES ABOUT 12 DOUGHNUTS

naturally saturated fats, most doughnut companies fry in a combination of unsaturated canola and/or soy oils and naturally saturated palm oil.

See Also • Baking, Bread, Cake, Chemical Leavener, Fat

DOVE • See Game

DRAMBUIE • See Liqueur

DRESSING • See Salad, Stuffing

DRUM • See Fish

DRUPE FRUIT • See Fruit

DRY-AGING • See Beef

DRY-CURING • See Curing, Drying

DRYING

What It Is • Microorganisms need water to survive. Drying is an ancient method of preserving food (without cooking it) by removing enough water from it to make the food inhospitable to microbes. In addition, a solid skin that forms on the surface of dried food makes it harder for microorganisms to enter, allowing the food to be stored for months or years without refrigeration. Drying can be done with any moist food including meats, seafood, fruits, vegetables, and herbs.

What It Does • Before the advent of refrigeration, drying was a principal method of preserving perishable ingredients.

Removing at least 75% water was essential in order to store products for several months without spoiling. For that reason, dried foods, meats and seafood in particular, were typically salted heavily to reduce the availability of water on the surface to microbes (**curing**) and to draw out as much moisture as possible before drying began. Now that spoilage can be controlled with more consistent drying and chilling, dried meats and fish are usually salted for taste rather than preservation.

Removing moisture concentrates the flavor and nutrients of foods. Dried fruits, for example, have more sweetness than the same fruit fresh (although vitamin C is often lost in the drying process), and dried meats are higher in protein and fat than their fresh counterparts.

Drying is done with minimal heat so that cooked flavors do not develop. But even without cooking, thoroughly dried ingredients are safe to eat. However, for sensual reasons most dried ingredients go through some soaking or cooking to return moisture, soften hard textures, and remove salt before they are consumed.

Some common dried ingredients are:

Meats: Four thousand years ago meats were dried in the sun and wind, sometimes with the help of a fire, which added smoke that infused the drying meat with microbe-killing chemicals. To prevent growth of surface bacteria, heavy salting was the norm. Most traditional salumi and charcuterie products come from these rudimentary techniques. Prosciutto, speck, bresaola, and carne del sol are made from large cuts of pork or beef that are sun- and air-dried. Because their interiors are relatively moist (about 40%), they must be kept chilled once they are sliced. When meat is sliced before it is dried, it is called jerky. Jerky is much drier than hams and sausages and therefore can be stored in open air for years.

Seafood: Dried fish has a storage life of several years and has been a mainstay of seafaring cultures for 500 years. Most dried fish is heavily salted. Salt cod is the most well known dried fish. It was traditionally dried by sun and wind while hanging from scaffolding by the sea, but today it is more

typically done inside with convection heat. Dried shrimp and scallops are common ingredients in Chinese cooking, and shredded dried squid is a snack food in the South Pacific. Generic dried fish, made usually from pollock or haddock, is sold as stockfish. Gravlax, cured salmon, is partially dried to intensify its flavor and richness, but it is not preserved through drying.

Fruit and vegetables: Because of their high sugar and acid contents, fruits do not need to be salted to protect them from microbes. Dried fruits are typically treated with sulfur compounds to prevent enzymatic browning. Fruit dried without sulfur is available, although these fruits have a dark color and drier texture. While sun-drying used to be the most common method for preserving fruit, now most dried fruit is produced in hot-air dryers that work at relatively low temperatures to minimize changes in flavor and color and to prevent the surface from drying before the interior has lost most of its water. Fruit that is high in fiber and low in moisture dries best. Most vegetables do not air-dry well (with the exception of beans and tomatoes) and must be freeze-dried.

Herbs: Herbs are typically air-dried on screened racks in the dark with lots of air circulation. Because herbs are leaves, largely networks of water and air, they shrink substantially when dried. Herbs must lose at least 90% of their moisture to ensure that they do not become moldy during storage.

Noodles: Noodles are typically air-dried before storage, but unlike most dried products they are uncooked dough and must be boiled before they are eaten. Instant noodles (ramen) are precooked and then dried so they can be eaten right out of the package or briefly boiled.

How It Works • *Sun-drying:* Though
sun-drying is an effective way of preserving it is subject to the vagaries of weather. A sudden rain, a rise in humidity, or a drop in temperature can ruin a batch of dried food. Food has to be raised from the ground on noncorrosive screens to ensure proper airflow, covered to keep insects and birds away, and taken in at night to keep the cool night air

from condensing on the food and slowing down the drying. Ingredients should be cut in thin enough pieces so that they dehydrate to 25% moisture within three days.

Dehydrator drying: A food dehydrator uses gentle heat (about 140°F/60°C) and convection to evaporate moisture and wick it away from the surface of the food. Unlike sun-drying, dehydrator drying is consistent and the most common method used commercially.

Freeze-drying: First used thousands of years ago by Peruvian natives in the high altitude of the Andes for drying potatoes, freeze-drying dehydrates food not through evaporation but by sublimation, the transformation of a solid directly into a gas. At normal air pressure, water goes through three distinct states at different temperatures — solid, liquid, and gas. In freeze-drying, foods are frozen, then placed in a vacuum and gradually warmed. As the ice increases in temperature it changes from solid into gas, leaving behind a dehydrated frozen solid. The technology is commonly used for manufacturing instant soup and sauce mixes, snack foods, emergency rations, camping foods, and astronaut ice cream.

See Also • Curing, Ham, Jerky, Salt, Sausage

DRY MILK • See Milk

DUBLIN BAY PRAWN • See Crustacean

DUCK • See Poultry

DULCE DE LECHE

What It Is • Literally meaning "sweet of milk" or "milk candy" in Spanish, dulce de leche is made by slowly simmering milk with sugar until it thickens to a spreadable consistency. As the mixture concentrates, it turns ruddy brown and develops the provocative flavor combination of roasted protein and caramelized sugar. Dulce de leche is used extensively in the cuisines of South America, Latin America, the Caribbean, Spain, and Portugal as a flavoring for candies, cakes, ice creams, and custards.

Coconut Dulce de Leche

At one time, making dulce de leche was a regular task in the Spanish kitchen, and although now it is more common to purchase one of many manufactured brands, this is an easy version to try.

1	can (14 oz/396 g or 300 mL) sweetened condensed milk, regular, low fat or fat free	1
½ cup	coconut milk	125 mL
1 tsp	vanilla extract	5 mL

1. Preheat oven to 425°F (220°C).

2. In a large pie plate, combine condensed milk and coconut milk and cover with foil, crimping any foil overlap tightly around the edges of the plate. Place plate in a larger pan of water. Bake in preheated oven until the milk turns a golden brown, about 45 minutes.

3. Remove the pie pan from its water bath, add vanilla and mix with a whisk until smooth. Store in the refrigerator for up to 1 week.

MAKES ABOUT 1 CUP (250 ML), ENOUGH FOR 4 SERVINGS

What It Does • Although most dulce de leches are a spreadable consistency, there are solid products dense enough to slice that are typically cut into bars and eaten as candy. Some brands are swirled with chocolate or fruit purées. Mexican dulce de leche, called *cajeta*, is made from half goat's milk and half cow's milk. It is paler than dulce de leche made from all cow's milk and has a slight tang.

How It Works • Dulce de leche may be prepared by slowly simmering equal parts milk and sugar, or by simmering sweetened condensed milk, until Maillard reactions (see **Browning**) transform the color and flavor of the mixture. This should be done in a saucepan or open baking dish, never in the closed can, which can explode during heating. Through evaporation, the proteins and sugars concentrate as the mixture simmers. Eventually they become so concentrated that Maillard reactions happen at very low temperatures, close to the boiling temperature of water. So when making dulce de leche it may seem that little is happening for quite some time, and then all at once the mixture will darken and congeal. Especially when starting with sweetened condensed milk, the reactions can progress suddenly.

See Also • Browning, Candy, Milk

DULSE • See Seaweed

DUMPLING

What It Is • Blobs of dough dropped in boiling liquid, dumplings are often lumped together with **pasta** because the two are cooked alike, but their similarity stops there. Dumplings are more tender and lighter than pasta. They are not kneaded or intricately shaped, and they are often aerated with leaveners or beaten egg. Dumplings are irregular, evidenced by their names. In America, we call them dumplings (something "dumped"). In Germany, they're spätzle (meaning "clod" or "clump"), and in Italy they are gnocchi ("little lumps"). Other uses of the word "dumpling" include Asian dumplings, which are hand-formed stuffed pasta pockets that are steamed, fried, or both; dessert dumplings, which are a German-American form of pastry in which whole fruit is wrapped in short pastry and baked; and Asian steamed buns (sometimes called dumplings), which are soft sweet rolls that are steamed rather than baked.

What It Does • In Western cooking there are three styles of dumplings.

Soup dumplings are simple doughs. Flour, leavener, shortening, seasoning, and liquid are mixed just enough to combine, and dropped onto a stew or soup to cook. They are served with the soup or stew as a starch.

Spätzle are tiny Bavarian dumplings. The dough is more like egg pasta, but wetter and softer. It can be cut into small bits and boiled, or pushed through a spätzle press or sieve directly into boiling liquid. Spätzle are either served in their cooking broth, like soup dumplings, or eaten like pasta, tossed with a sauce or flavored butter.

The original gnocchi, *gnocchi di pane*, dating from the 1300s, were made of bread soaked in milk, mixed with eggs and flour, rolled into balls, and boiled. They were smooth and creamy but tended to be heavy. Roman gnocchi are still made in that traditional way, although the dough is more often a mixture of semolina and milk, bound with eggs and enriched with butter. It is formed into a flat cake, cut into small disks, and baked with cheese.

With the arrival of **potatoes** from the New World, Italian chefs took advantage of the starchy vegetable to fashion lighter gnocchi, *gnocchi di patate*. The fiber and starch in potato gave gnocchi substance and structure without adding heaviness from flour or toughness from egg. Mealy (starchy) potatoes are steamed or boiled, peeled, and mashed immediately to allow as much moisture to evaporate as possible. The potato pulp is cooled to firm it and then kneaded with just enough flour to make it hold a shape. The dough is then cut or hand-formed into small bits and boiled.

Even lighter gnocchi are made from ricotta cheese and egg and commonly include spinach. Ricotta gnocchi are more like a poached mousse than boiled dough, and when made properly they are ethereal, vanishing almost as soon as they enter the mouth.

Gnocchi are usually served like pasta, as a separate course, tossed with cheese, butter and herbs, or a sauce.

How It Works • The doneness of dumplings is judged by their position in the pot. Upon entering a pot of boiling liquid, raw dumplings sink toward the bottom. As they heat, air bubbles trapped in the dough, aided by steam and gases from leaveners, start

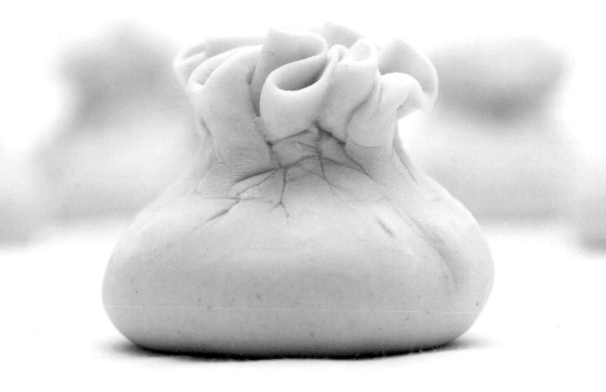

to swell. As air fills more of the dumplings' mass, they become lighter than the liquid they are cooking in, and they rise. When they break through the surface the dumplings are fully leavened and filled with steam. They're almost done cooking. A minute more will finish setting the egg in the batter or cook the remaining starch in the dough.

The gluten in flour helps to hold them together, but too much makes a dumpling tough. For that reason most dumpling doughs need a minimum of mixing. Gnocchi recipes attempt to avoid flour as much as they can. The standard potato-to-flour ratio is 8:1 by weight. Likewise, ricotta gnocchi recipes call for draining the cheese, and use flour only to coat the dumplings after they are formed. Too much flour makes all gnocchi tough, but not enough flour can make them disintegrate during cooking. The trick is to use just enough to bind the ingredients, and then to cook the gnocchi at a bare simmer, since agitation from vigorously boiling water can rip delicate dumplings apart.

See Also • Aeration, Pasta, Potatoes

DUNGENESS CRAB • See Crustacean

DURUM • See Wheat

DUTCH-PROCESS COCOA • See Chocolate

EARTHENWARE • See Cookware

EAU DE VIE • See Liquor

E. COLI • See Bacteria

EDAMAME • See Legumes

EEL • See Fish

EGGPLANT

What It Is • Eggplant, one of the more benign members of the notorious nightshade family, is neither addictive nor poisonous like its relatives tobacco leaf and deadly nightshade. Early in its history eggplant had a toxic reputation, as did other edible nightshade fruits like tomato and peppers, probably resulting from the family's characteristic of stockpiling chemical defenses, usually bitter alkaloids. Generations of breeding have reduced the alkaloids in eggplant, although the leaves can still be toxic.

There are dozens of eggplant cultivars. The **fruit** (eggplant is a fruit in the botanical sense — the fleshy part of the plant that houses the seed) are all more or less ovoid, but the size and shape can range from goose egg to human head. European and North American eggplants are typically plump, and

Asian varieties long and slender. The colors shade from creamy white, through pale green, yellow, pink, magenta, and violet, all the way to black (sometimes variegated or striped), but the color is literally skin deep. All eggplants are off-white inside.

Eggplants can develop bitterness as they mature, so younger ones are preferable for eating, although most cultivars are fairly mild regardless of age. In Southeast Asia bitter varieties of eggplant are still cultivated and usually cooked into pickles and chutneys.

What It Does • The entire fruit is edible — skin, pulp, and seeds. Eggplant has a creamy or meaty consistency, depending on the variety and cooking method. Typically eggplant is baked in a casserole (moussaka, eggplant parmigiana), stuffed (*imam bayildi*, literally "the priest fainted," a famous Turkish mezze, or antipasto, in which eggplant is stuffed with onions and garlic and simmered in olive oil), braised (ratatouille), or roasted until its flesh collapses into a smoky, creamy purée (baba ghanoush).

How It Works • Eggplant flesh is filled with thousands of tiny air pockets that give it a spongy texture when raw. During cooking the air pockets collapse, the eggplant loses volume, and the cooked pulp becomes smooth and creamy. Depending on how it's cooked and for how long, the pulp can be firm enough to hold its shape (sautéing or frying), in which case it has a meaty mouth

Baba Ghanoush

This creamy, smoky eggplant salad is traditionally served as part of a mezze plate (a Middle Eastern antipasto), but it is just as welcome as a sandwich spread, a topping for grilled meat or fish, or an instant thickener for a soup or a stew.

1	large eggplant, about 1 lb (500 g)	1
2 tsp	minced garlic	10 mL
⅓ cup	extra virgin olive oil	75 mL
2 tbsp	freshly squeezed lemon juice	2 tbsp
2	medium tomatoes, chopped	2
3 tbsp	chopped flat-leaf Italian parsley	45 mL

Salt and freshly ground black pepper to taste

1. Preheat oven to 400°F (200°C).
2. Pierce eggplant all over with a fork. Place on a baking sheet and roast until soft, about 45 minutes. Let cool.
3. Cut off stem and peel skin. In a bowl, mash eggplant with a large fork, working garlic, oil, and lemon juice into the mixture as you mash. Stir in tomatoes and parsley. Season with salt and pepper. Use immediately or cover and refrigerate for up to 1 week.

MAKES ABOUT 3 CUPS (750 ML)
OR 6 SERVINGS

feel, or it can be cooked until it completely falls apart (roasted or stewed), transforming it into a creamy sauce.

The spongy texture also makes eggplant prone to soaking up oil during frying. The best way to minimize oil absorption is to collapse the sponge before it ever comes in contact with oil. This can be done by precooking it — baking or microwaving work fine — or by salting eggplant slices to draw moisture out of the cells and into the air pockets. The traditional rationale for salting eggplant was to draw out its bitterness, and by getting rid of juices some bitter alkaloids would also be drained. But now that eggplants are bred to be mild, purging alkaloids is unnecessary.

See Also • Fruit, Vegetables

fast facts

- Eggplant contains more nicotine than any other vegetable, about 0.01%, which is negligible compared to the amount inhaled through passive smoking.
- The eggplant originated in subtropical Southeast Asia and, like most tropical fruits, it doesn't refrigerate well. Chilling causes eggplants to brown and shrivel.
- As many as 83% of the world's eggplants are produced in two countries — China and India.

EGGS

What It Is • Long before our human predecessors first climbed down from the trees, bird eggs were an important food source. Although chicken eggs dominate most cuisines, eggs from other birds are valued, if not frequently consumed. These include the eggs of ducks, turkeys, geese, quails, guinea fowl, gulls, pigeons, pheasants, emu, and ostriches (the largest bird egg). Bird eggs consist of a thin, hard shell surrounding an albumen (egg white), a vitellus (egg yolk), and various membranes holding the parts in place. Because chicken eggs are so much more common than other bird eggs, the information in this entry will center on them, unless otherwise noted.

What It Does • What makes an egg good? Take a look. The shell must be intact and clean, of uniform color and shape. An eggshell is made of calcium carbonate and **protein** secreted from the uterine lining in the last phases of the egg's development. It is riddled with thousands of pores (especially at the wide end), which allow air into the shell for the developing embryo. The surface is covered with a waxy cuticle that inhibits water loss. The color of an eggshell varies by species and breed. White eggs come from Leghorn chickens; brown eggs from Rhode Island Reds and Plymouth Rock chickens. The color of the shell has nothing to do with the nutritional quality of an egg, nor how it was processed.

Crack the egg into a dish. The shell should break cleanly and easily. The yolk should be firm, plump, and round, with a resilient membrane holding it intact. The white should be cohesive, jelly-like, and thick enough to nestle around the yolk rather than run like water across the dish.

Eggs are graded to ensure that they meet minimum safety standards (their shells are free of cracks, dirt, stains, and rough spots, and the interior is free of blood spots), and sometimes for quality (firm yolk and white, a minimum of air). In Canada, all eggs are graded, and only grade A is allowed to be sold to consumers as whole shell eggs. In the U.S., grading eggs is voluntary and is paid for by the producer. It is unusual to find grades other than AA and A sold in retail stores. In order to "see" inside an egg without cracking it open, eggs are "candled," a quaint term coming from a time when eggs were held in front of a candle to see what was going on inside the shell. Now candling is done before high-powered lights with electronic sensors looking for defects. To determine the condition of the yolk and white, the egg is twirled. If the image of the yolk remains blurred, it indicates that the contents of the egg are fresh enough to keep the yolk centered. If the yolk is easy to see, it indicates that it is mobile and is traveling close to the shell, an indication that the chalazae that hold the yolk in the center of the white have weakened.

The grade of an egg indicates its quality only at the time of packaging. Although eggs remain edible for weeks, provided they are kept whole and chilled, deterioration starts the moment an egg leaves the chicken. Both the yolk and the white become more alkaline: as carbon dioxide is lost through pores in the shell carbonic acid decreases. In the white, the resulting rise in alkalinity makes the proteins less attractive to one another, causing the white to become runny. Similarly, the proteins surrounding the yolk weaken. The

Anatomy of An Egg

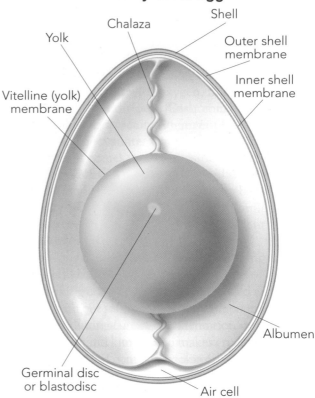

net result is that when an aged egg is cracked open, the white spreads out and the yolk is less likely to stay intact.

If eggs are used fairly soon, or if they are scrambled or mixed into a batter, age won't make much of a difference, but if eggs are to be separated, poached, or fried, a fresher egg will give noticeably better results. The one advantage of older eggs is that they are easier to peel when hard-cooked. Here's why: Egg white is surrounded by two membranes. As the egg ages, albumen shrinks, and the space between the two membranes increases. The separation of the two membranes makes older eggs easier to peel.

Although we often call eggs cooked in their shells "boiled," boiling is not a good way to cook eggs. Egg white begins to coagulate at 145°F (63°C) and finishes at 180°F (82°C). Yolks set between 150 and 158°F (66 and 70°C). Boiling water, which is 212°F (100°C), overcoagulates egg proteins, making them tough and rubbery. Soft-cooked eggs aren't cooked long enough to make much of a difference, but hard-cooked eggs should be cooked at a bare simmer, ideally around 180°F (82°C), to keep them from toughening.

An overview of different methods of cooking eggs follows.

Soft-cooked eggs are simmered in the shell until the outer white is barely solid, the inner white is milky but still fluid, and the yolk is just warm. Start the eggs in room-temperature water, cover the pot, and heat to boiling; turn down to a simmer and simmer two to three minutes. *Mollet eggs* have completely solid whites and creamy yolks, and simmer for three to four minutes.

Hard-cooked eggs are firm throughout, with completely solidified whites and moist-firm dark yellow yolks (when cooked about 10 minutes) or dry, solid pale yellow yolks (when cooked about 15 minutes). The gray-green color at the edge of hard-cooked egg yolks is a harmless (though unattractive) compound, ferrous sulfide, which forms at higher temperatures and longer cooking times. For perfect hard-cooked eggs, start the eggs in room-temperature water, cover the pot, and heat to boiling. When the water boils remove the pot from the heat and let the eggs sit for 10 to 15 minutes, depending on how cooked you want your eggs. Remove from the pot and run the eggs under cold water before peeling.

Long-cooked eggs are eggs cooked in their shells at very low temperatures (160 to 165°F/71 to 74°C) for a long time (six to

kitchen wisdom

The Fastest Foolproof Way to Peel an Egg

Crack the shell of one cooled hard-cooked egg on each end by firmly rapping it against a hard surface. There is an air bubble at the wide end of the egg that should be crushed. Place the egg on its side. Place your palm firmly on top and roll forward one revolution, cracking the shell all around. Submerge the egg in a bowl of water or hold it under running water and slip off the shell.

18 hours), resulting in exceptionally tender, almost fluid whites and creamy yolks.

Baked eggs are soft-cooked out of the shell in a baking dish in a medium-low oven. For the best results, bake eggs on the center oven rack so that neither the top nor the bottom receive more heat, set the thermostat to 325°F (160°C) or lower, and place the baking dish in a larger pan of water to control temperature at its edges.

Poached eggs are soft-cooked eggs without a shell. Because they have no container to hold their shape, caution must be taken to keep them intact. Raw eggs are slid into a pan of simmering water, where they cook until the whites set, about three minutes. Using the freshest egg available makes a big difference. Thick fresh egg white clings tightly to the yolk, forming a compact poached egg. Adding salt and vinegar to the poaching liquid, which helps to set albumin proteins more quickly, or sliding the egg into a slotted spoon and allowing the thinner white to run off before adding it to the poaching liquid, both yield tidier results. Professional chefs bring water to a simmer in a deep pot, spin the water before adding the egg, and then drop the egg into the center of the vortex. The swirling water catches the fluid egg white and spins it neatly around the yolk, trapping the yolk in a perfect pocket of albumen. "Poach" comes from *poche*, the French word for "pocket."

Fried eggs are even more liable to spread than poached eggs because heat is coming only from the bottom. Straining off any watery

Nutritional Composition of One Large Egg (2 oz/56 g)

	Whole Egg	Egg White	Egg Yolk		Whole Egg	Egg White	Egg Yolk
Weight	56 g	38 g	17 g	Vitamin D	22 mg	0 mg	22 mg
Calories	84	20	64	Vitamin E	1.3 mg	0 mg	1.3 mg
Total fat	6 g	0 g	6 g	Vitamin K	25 mg	0 mg	25 mg
Monounsaturated fat	2.5 g	0 g	2.5 g	Thiamin (B$_1$)	0.4 mg	0 mg	0.4 mg
Polyunsaturated fat	0.7 g	0 g	0.7 g	Riboflavin (B$_2$)	0.26 mg	0.15 mg	0.11 mg
Saturated fat	2 g	0 g	2 g	Pantothenic acid (B$_5$)	0.74 mg	0.05 mg	0.69 mg
Cholesterol	213 mg	0 mg	213 mg	Pyridoxine (B$_6$)	0.07 mg	0 mg	0.07 mg
Sodium	71 mg	62 mg	9 mg	Folate (B$_9$)	25 mg	1 mg	24 mg
Carbohydrate	0.6 g	0.3 g	0.3 g	Calcium	27 mg	4 mg	23 mg
Dietary fiber	0 g	0 g	0 g	Iron	0.6 mg	0.01 mg	0.6 mg
Sugar	0 g	0 g	0 g	Magnesium	6 mg	4 mg	2 mg
Protein	6.6 g	3.9 g	2.7 g	Phosphorus	87 mg	4 mg	83 mg
Vitamin A	99 mcg	0 mcg	99 mcg	Potassium	63 mg	47 mg	16 mg
Vitamin C	0 mg	0 mg	0 mg	Zinc	0.53 mg	0.002 mg	0.53 mg
				Choline	135 mg	0 mg	135 mg

white can help, but using only the freshest, highest grade egg is your best assurance. To keep the egg white tender, use medium heat and add the egg when the pan is about 275°F (135°C), the temperature at which butter is almost done sizzling and hasn't begun to brown. Using a skillet with a nonstick coating has two advantages. It ensures that the egg won't stick, and the plastic coating transfers heat more gently than a metal surface. Cook the egg until the white has set thickly across the bottom, taking care that it doesn't brown. To cook the top you can: turn the egg over for a brief period (over easy); baste it with some of the hot butter from the pan (basted); add a spoonful of water and immediately cover the pan (steam-fried); or fold the egg so that the yolk is encased in a half circle of white and flip it back and forth a few times to finish setting the white (coin-purse).

Scrambled eggs and omelets are made by beating the yolk and white together, so freshness is less of an issue. Scrambled eggs are easy to make, but making them well

(softly curded, delicately moist) takes gentle heat and patience. Use a nonstick pan and a slightly lower heat than for fried eggs. The temperature in the pan should be just hot enough to make butter begin to sizzle.

How often and how much you move the eggs as they cook determines the finished texture. For large, soft curds, allow the egg to set on the bottom of the pan before moving it. Then gently lift the set egg with a spatula or fork, allowing the looser egg on top to cover the bottom of the pan. When that sets, do it again. If the heat is properly low, each layer should take 30 seconds to a minute to set. Higher heat toughens the proteins. For the creamiest scrambled eggs, stir constantly. This keeps egg proteins on the bottom of the pan from setting, so the egg warms evenly and gradually sets into one soft, custard-like curd. If you want to add vegetables, cook them first so they don't weep liquid into the eggs. Always remove scrambled eggs from the pan when they look a little underdone, since they will continue to set from their retained heat.

Omelets are soft scrambled eggs given shape

by a thin skin of overcooked egg. The trick is to have the right amount of egg for the size of the pan (three eggs in a 10-inch/25 cm skillet) and a well-seasoned or nonstick pan to keep the egg moving freely. To get it right you need high heat and a hot pan (about 350°F/180°C, hot enough to sizzle butter as soon as it hits the pan), and you need to move quickly. Pour in beaten eggs, stir them vigorously until they set (about 30 seconds), and flatten them into a disk. Within seconds the bottom will firm. Add a filling, if desired, then fold the omelet in half or thirds and slide it onto a plate. Voilà!

Adding liquid to a scrambled egg dilutes the protein, causing it to set into softer curds; the more liquid, the more dispersed the protein, and the softer the solidified egg will be. When the ratio gets close to 4 parts liquid to 1 part egg (1 cup/250 mL to 1 large egg), the protein is so dispersed that when it coagulates the result is more like solidified liquid than a soft solid. At that ratio the mixture is said to be a **custard**.

How It Works ●
Egg yolk is the main food source for the developing embryo. It accounts for more than one-third of an egg's weight, half its protein, three-quarters of its calories (about 60 kcal), and all of its iron, thiamin, fat, cholesterol, and vitamins A, D, E, and K. Other than fatty fish or fish oils, egg yolk is the only natural food source for vitamin D.

The germ cell (the part of the egg that grows into a chicken if the egg is fertilized) is located on one side of the yolk. The germ is microscopic, but it is surrounded by a pale form of yolk (white yolk) that is visible as a white dot resting on the crown of the yolk when you crack open an egg. The white yolk is surrounded and dwarfed by yellow yolk, made of layers of fat and protein suspended in water. Some of the fat in yolk is **cholesterol** (one large yolk contains 213 mg of cholesterol; the same weight of beef has about 50 mg) and some is **lecithin**, a phospholipid that gives egg yolk its ability to bind fat and water into an **emulsion**. The color of egg yolk comes from pigments in the chickens' feed; corn and alfalfa make the yolk a deeper yellow, and the addition of marigold petals makes the color brighter. This fluid sac of protein, fat, cholesterol, phospholipid, and water is given shape by a flexible membrane (the vitelline membrane) that separates the yolk from the white.

The first layer of thick protein that coats the yolk is twisted by spiraling grooves in the oviduct to form the chalazae, two strong elastic cords that anchor the yolk to each end of the shell. These cords allow the yolk to rotate while suspending it in the middle of the egg, surrounded by cushioning layers of thin and thick albumen.

Egg white makes up two-thirds of an egg's weight, but 90% of it is water. The rest is mostly protein, with traces of minerals, glucose, and vitamins (mostly riboflavin that gives albumen its green tint). The quarter gram of glucose in egg white is not enough to make it taste sweet, but in some long cooking preparations, like the long-cooked eggs of Jewish Sabbath cooking and Chinese hundred-year eggs, it is enough to cause Maillard reactions (see **Browning**) and turn the egg white brown.

Albumen provides a trace of nutrients to the developing embryo, but its main function is protection. It cushions the embryo against knocks and bumps, and some of its proteins have chemical defense action that guards the embryo against bacteria and discourages potential predators from consuming the egg. Ovalbumin and ovomucin block digestive enzymes. Avidin prevents vitamin absorption, and ovotransferrin binds with iron, blocking its absorption. Lysozyme kills harmful bacteria that might invade the shell and also kills beneficial bacteria in the gut of a predator. Eating raw egg white causes laboratory animals to lose weight. Cooking denatures the defensive proteins, so cooked egg white is not harmful, but raw egg white should be avoided, or eaten only occasionally.

The same proteins give egg white much of its culinary prowess. Ovomucin thickens egg white, making it hold its shape during poaching and frying, and it stabilizes egg **foams** by trapping and holding on to air. Ovomucin deteriorates as an egg ages, making old egg white less viscous than fresh egg white. Ovalbumin is the most plentiful protein in egg white and accounts for its sulfur content, which gives cooked egg white its distinctive aroma and some of its color. Ovotransferrin is the first protein to coagulate in the presence of heat, so it determines the temperature that egg whites start to set. When it combines with iron in the yolk its coagulation point rises, which is part of the reason whole egg sets at a higher temperature than egg white alone.

After they're cooked, which neutralizes the defensive proteins, eggs are one of the most nutritious foods we eat. Their balance of amino acids is used as the gold standard for human protein consumption. They are abundant in linoleic acid, an essential unsaturated omega-6 fatty acid, they can be enriched with omega-3 fatty acids, and they contain a percentage of the daily value for every vitamin and mineral except vitamin C and niacin. Two plant carotenoids, lutein and zeaxanthin, valued as **antioxidants**, are

Absinthe Suissesse

Egg proteins foam up and hold their shape easily, creating an attractive "head" on cocktails. They also add great mouth feel. Now that absinthe has been scientifically disproven to be a hallucinogenic liquor and is once again available in North America (and many other countries), you can enjoy it in this classic New Orleans cocktail, often served with brunch. The "Suissesse" refers to a high grade of absinthe made in the 19th century. This cocktail is emulsified with raw egg white, so use eggs from a trusted source or liquid pasteurized egg whites (available in many supermarkets). Look for the orgeat syrup in liquor stores or gourmet and specialty coffee stores.

1½ oz	absinthe or Pernod	45 mL
1	egg white	1
¾ oz	orgeat syrup (almond syrup)	22 mL
½ oz	half-and-half (10%) cream	15 mL
¼ oz	crème de menthe liqueur	7 mL
½ cup	crushed ice	125 mL

1. In a cocktail shaker, combine absinthe, egg white, orgeat syrup, cream, crème de menthe, and crushed ice. Shake vigorously for 10 to 15 seconds, then strain into a chilled Champagne, martini, or wine glass.

MAKES 1 SERVING

plentiful in eggs. Eggs are a near-perfect food.

Egg yolks are also our richest source of cholesterol. Beginning around 1950, when it was posited that high blood cholesterol increases the risk of heart disease, many medical associations began recommending limiting the amount of egg yolk in our diets, but recent studies have shown that blood cholesterol levels are raised mostly from saturated fat, and dietary cholesterol has little influence on blood cholesterol levels. In addition, phospholipids in yolks seem to interfere with our absorption of cholesterol. Although it no longer seems necessary to count the number of weekly egg yolks in the diet, yolks should not be consumed with abandon. More than 60% of the calories in a whole egg come from fat, and a third of that is saturated fat in the yolk. Cholesterol-free egg substitutes are mostly egg white mixed with vegetable oil, milk proteins, and gums to give the mouth feel, flavor, and appearance of whole eggs.

An allergy to eggs is one of the most common food allergies in humans. Since the sensitivity often forms early on, pediatricians recommend that children not be fed any egg whites until after the age of one. Those with compromised immune systems and the elderly should avoid raw or undercooked egg white for the reasons already mentioned, but also to avoid possible salmonella contamination.

See Also • Caviar, Cholesterol, Custard, Emulsion, Fat, Foams, Lecithin, Protein

EGG SUBSTITUTE • See Eggs

ELASTIN • See Meat

ELDERBERRY • See Berries

ELECTROMAGNETIC SPECTRUM • See Heat

ELECTRONS • See Atom, Chemical Bonding

ELK • See Game

ELVER • See Fish

EMMENTAL • See Cheese

EMU • See Game

EMULSION

What It Is • Most **sauces** get their silken consistency from the dispersion of fine solid particles (starch, flour, puréed vegetables, etc.) in a watery liquid. Emulsion sauces work differently. They thicken by mixing water with something it cannot accept — fat.

Because the ingredients in emulsion sauces are innately incompatible, emulsions are always unstable. Try this: combine equal parts oil and vinegar in a jar, screw on a lid, and shake vigorously. While the ingredients combine briefly, the mixture soon disassociates. Vinegar droplets sink to the bottom, and oil rises to the top.

Emulsifiers (substances that are soluble in both water and fat) are natural diplomats. Emulsifying molecules have two regions with different affinities — one part is soluble in water, the other in fat, and they act like a bridge connecting the discordant substances and holding them in place. The melted butter and lemon juice in hollandaise or the lemon juice and oil in mayonnaise use lecithin, the emulsifier in egg yolk, to form a bond. Butter and cream sauces, usually containing vinegar or wine, rely on casein, a major protein in dairy products, for their stability. Emulsifiers are plentiful in dairy and egg yolk, because these products are emulsions themselves. Milk, cream, and butter are emulsions of milk fat and protein suspended in water (actually butter is a reverse emulsion, where water is suspended in butterfat, but we'll get to that later), and egg yolk is a combination of fat, cholesterol, and protein floating in water.

What It Does • An emulsion must be made from two liquids that don't naturally combine. One (usually water) acts as a container; the other (usually fat) becomes the contained.

Mayonnaise

Here's a recipe for mayonnaise that illustrates the basic technique for forming a cold emulsion. It is followed by several recipes for classic sauces derived from mayonnaise.

	Salt and white pepper to taste	
Pinch	cayenne pepper	Pinch
1 tbsp	boiling water	15 mL
2	egg yolks, large or extra-large, preferably pasteurized	2
2 tsp	Dijon mustard	10 mL
2 tbsp	freshly squeezed lemon juice	25 mL
1½ cups	mild vegetable oil, such as canola	375 mL

1. In a food processor or bowl, combine salt, white pepper, and cayenne in the boiling water until the salt dissolves.

2. Add egg yolks, mustard, and lemon juice, and beat with a whisk or process until well combined.

3. Add oil in a slow, steady stream, through feed tube if using food processor, mixing constantly, until thick and creamy. Adjust seasoning, if needed. Keep refrigerated and use within 4 days.

Variations

Aïoli: Follow preceding recipe, but use 2 cloves finely chopped garlic instead of the mustard, and use a mixture of 3 tbsp (45 mL) extra virgin olive oil plus 1⅓ cups (325 mL) mild vegetable oil, such as canola oil.

Note: You might like the flavor of extra virgin olive oil but don't use more than 3 tbsp (45 mL) of it. Unrefined olive oil contains its own emulsifying molecules that compete with the lecithin and undermine its ability to hold the emulsion together.

Herb Mayonnaise: Add 1 to 2 tbsp (15 to 25 mL) finely chopped fresh herbs to the finished mayonnaise.

Rémoulade: Add 1 tbsp (15 mL) each finely chopped drained capers and cornichons, 1 tsp (5 mL) each finely chopped chives, chervil, and tarragon, and ¼ tsp (1 mL) each anchovy paste and Worcestershire sauce to the finished mayonnaise. Add hot pepper sauce to taste, if desired.

MAKES ABOUT 2 CUPS (500 ML)

This is called an oil-in-water emulsion, because the oil is broken into billions of droplets that are dispersed in a continuous network of water. In technical terms, the oil is the "dispersed phase" of the emulsion and the water is the "continuous phase."

The more droplets of oil crowded into the continuous phase, the more they get in the way of the water and the thicker the sauce becomes. In a near-solid emulsion, like mayonnaise, the oil droplets take up almost 80% of the volume. (Low-fat commercial mayonnaises use starches and gels to block the water flow.) You can imagine at that density it is quite possible for oil droplets to start touching each other, and if that should happen, they are apt to bind together and fall out of suspension, causing the emulsion to break. The smaller the droplets, the less likely that is to happen, so stiff emulsions like mayonnaise are more stable when made by machine than by hand. Working with a whisk, you can break oil into pretty small droplets of about 1/3,000 of a millimeter across. Using an industrial emulsifier you can get the droplet size down to 1/10,000 of a millimeter, which is one reason why commercial mayonnaise holds together longer than mayonnaise made by hand.

Egg yolk–stabilized emulsions can be cold or warm, depending on the fat in the sauce. Mayonnaise, the prototypical cold emulsion sauce, emulsifies lemon juice or vinegar, and water (to make the emulsion more stable) with oil. In hollandaise, the main warm emulsion sauce, the oil is replaced with melted **butter**, so the sauce must be kept warm to keep the butter liquid. Structurally, the two sauces are similar, although there are differences in how they are constructed.

The first step for both sauces is to form the continuous water phase — a mixture of water and lemon juice — and mix it with the emulsifier. For both sauces the emulsifier is the lecithin and lipoproteins in egg yolk (although hollandaise uses a higher proportion, because heating yolks coagulates their protein, making them less able to coat the oil droplets and hold them in suspension). Mayonnaise may have an addition of mustard, mostly for flavor, but also because ground mustard seed releases a gum when moistened that helps to stabilize emulsions.

Once the water component, which can include vinegar or lemon juice, is mixed with the emulsifier, the oil or melted butter can be added. Sometimes recipes will add the oil directly into the egg yolk before adding any watery ingredients, and sometimes the water and egg yolk are mixed together before adding the oil. Both methods have their advantages. Waiting to add the water makes the egg and oil mixture thicker, which makes it easier to break the oil into smaller droplets, and smaller droplets mean a stronger emulsion. But mixing the watery ingredients and emulsifier together before adding oil makes bridges form between the oil and water sooner, which allows you to get more oil into the emulsion without destabilizing it.

The oil or butter must be added slowly to the water component and with constant vigorous mixing to break it into the smallest possible droplets. Too much oil going in too quickly will overwhelm the emulsifiers. The emulsifier will not be able to coat the droplets and form the appropriate connections with the water to form an emulsion. However, once the mixture begins to visibly thicken, indicating that a stable oil-in-water network has been established, it is safe to add the fat component more rapidly.

If more than a third of the oil has gone in and the mixture is not thickening, it means that an emulsion didn't happen, probably because the emulsifiers were overwhelmed. The sauce can be salvaged by mixing it into a new continuous phase. Beat a little more water-vinegar-lemon juice mixture with another egg yolk, and gradually whisk in the split sauce. If you're careful the new continuous phase and extra emulsifier will make everything thicken smoothly.

The same emulsification principles are at work in hollandaise. The only difference is that the egg yolks are partially cooked before the fat (in this case melted butter) is dispersed into the watery ingredients. The trick is to cook the yolks enough so that they become creamy and thick, but not so much that the yolk proteins coagulate into solid curds. This happens around 165°F (74°C). Heating the yolks, water, and lemon juice in the top of a double boiler set over barely simmering water provides gentle, even heat. Some recipes call for adding the lemon juice after the butter, but acidifying the yolks raises their coagulation point, making it less likely that their proteins will curdle.

Hollandaise, and sauces derived from it, such as béarnaise, have to be kept warm to prevent the butter from solidifying; 100°F (38°C) is sufficient, but safety concerns dictate holding temperatures of at least 145°F (63°C) to prevent bacteria from growing. At this temperature the egg proteins can begin to coagulate, so it is important to stir warm emulsions as they sit. If the sauce should curdle, it can be fixed the same way as a cold emulsion (see left). The only difference is that the curdled bits have to be strained out. The sauce can then gradually be beaten into a fresh base of egg yolk, water, and lemon juice, and come out as good as new. The hollandaise recipe (see below) shows the basic technique.

Egg-based emulsion sauces carry a small risk of salmonella because the egg yolks are raw or undercooked. Manufactured mayonnaise uses pasteurized egg yolks, which are also available in many supermarkets. There is a misconception that salads dressed with commercial mayonnaise can make people sick if left out of the refrigerator. Not true. The pH of commercial mayonnaise is between 3.6 and 4.0 (an acidity between yogurt and orange juice), making it acidic enough to prevent the growth of most harmful bacteria. Commercial mayonnaise can develop an unpleasant rancid aroma if left out in the sun, because of its high oil content, but it will not become dangerous.

Hollandaise

Although hollandaise (and its derivative sauces) can be kept warm over hot water or in a thermos for about an hour, it loses volume and gets denser as it sits, so it is best to serve it as quickly as possible.

¼ cup	white wine or cider vinegar	50 mL
¼ tsp	whole black peppercorns	1 mL
2 tbsp	hot water	25 mL
2 tsp	freshly squeezed lemon juice	10 mL
3	extra-large egg yolks, preferably pasteurized	3
¾ cup	melted clarified butter (see page 75), warm	175 mL
	Salt and freshly ground pepper to taste	

1. In a small saucepan, heat vinegar and peppercorns over medium heat and boil until reduced to 2 tbsp (25 mL) liquid. Strain out peppercorns.

2. In the top half of a double boiler, combine reduced vinegar, hot water, lemon juice, and egg yolks. Place over simmering water and beat with a whisk until the yolks thicken and triple in volume.

3. Remove from heat, but keep the double boiler together, and gradually whisk in the clarified butter, allowing each addition to be incorporated before adding the next. Season with salt and pepper. Keep warm in the double boiler, stirring occasionally, and use within 1 hour.

MAKES ABOUT 2 CUPS (500 ML)

Beurre Blanc

The reduction for butter emulsion sauces can be made at any time, but the butter should be added immediately before serving.

3 tbsp	white wine	45 mL
3 tbsp	white wine vinegar	45 mL
2 tsp	minced shallots	10 mL
	Kosher salt and freshly ground black pepper to taste	
¾ cup	unsalted butter, cut in small pieces	175 mL

1. In a saucepan over medium heat, combine wine, vinegar, shallots, salt, and pepper and boil until reduced by one-third.

2. Turn off the heat or keep it very low, and vigorously whisk in butter, a few pieces at a time. The sauce will thicken immediately. Watch carefully. If the sauce should become glossy, it indicates that butter is floating on the surface instead of being emulsified. If this happens, immediately remove sauce from heat, add a small spoonful of cold water, and beat vigorously before adding any more butter. Return saucepan to heat if necessary and keep stirring in butter over just enough heat to melt it until it is all incorporated. Serve immediately.

MAKES ABOUT ¾ CUP (175 ML)

Cream and butter are emulsions already, and can be turned into sauces simply by being heated. (Milk is a dispersion of milk fat in water. Whole milk is only 4% fat, so the emulsifiers coating fat droplets are too few to thicken it when heated.) Cream is a processed form of milk in which the fat has been concentrated (up to 38% in heavy or whipping cream). When cream is boiled, its water evaporates and the fat percentage rises. Heavy (whipping) cream reduced by a third is about 55% fat, giving it the thickness of a light gravy. Reduce it by half and the fat content rises to 75% (about the same as mayonnaise) and the cream reduction will become nearly solid.

Butter is a more concentrated form of milk, in which the fat content has been increased to around 80%. At that concentration the phases of the emulsion flip and the fat becomes the continuous phase, making butter one of the few emulsions that is made of water droplets suspended in fat. The suspension is stable as long as the fat is cold and solid, but when heated, the emulsion falls apart. The heavier water droplets sink to the bottom and the melted butter fat floats to the top. A butter emulsion, such as beurre blanc (see recipe, above), can be renewed by increasing the amount of water and making it the continuous phase. The process is very similar to fixing a broken mayonnaise or hollandaise. A flavorful watery liquid, such as wine, vinegar, and/or citrus juice, is heated enough to melt the butter. The butter is gradually mixed in, breaking the fat into small droplets and suspending them in the continuous water phase. Proteins in the butter act as emulsifiers, but because they are not plentiful the emulsion will not be strong. Sometimes a little cream is added to the water phase to increase the amount of emulsifier in the sauce.

The most common emulsion sauce, a simple oil-and-vinegar salad dressing (vinaigrette), typically has no emulsifier. Its standard proportions of 3 parts oil to 1 part vinegar is close to the ratio of mayonnaise, but unlike mayonnaise it has nothing to hold the oil in suspension, so like butter, the phases flip. In a vinaigrette, droplets of vinegar disperse loosely in a continuous phase of oil. Unlike thick creamy emulsions, vinaigrettes remain watery, which works perfectly for coating the delicate greens of a salad. Beating vinaigrette into an egg yolk or a dairy product, such as sour cream or buttermilk, stabilizes the emulsion, causing the dressing to thicken.

How It Works • When the molecules in two liquids aren't chemically attracted to one another, like water and oil, they arrange themselves in ways to keep their distance. By forming a single large mass (think about oil floating on top of vinegar), each exposes less surface area to the other than they would if they were broken into small droplets. The ability of liquid to minimize its surface area is dependent on the force of molecular attraction within the liquid. This force is called surface tension.

To make an emulsion, force must be exerted to overcome the natural surface tension of the players. Then something must be added to keep the surface tension from reasserting itself. Vigorous mixing provides the initial force that breaks surface tension, enabling the addition of emulsifying agents.

Two types of molecules act as natural emulsifiers. Mono- and diacylglycerol and phospholipids are relatives of fats and oils (triglycerides), having only two fatty acids, not the requisite three to qualify as a fat. The remaining position on the glycerol frame is occupied by a polar group of atoms. These atoms bind to water and the other end is attracted to fat.

Diacylglycerol (diglyceride)

When a phospholipid emulsifier is mixed with water, its water-soluble heads attach to the water molecules and the fat-loving tails float freely. As oil is mixed into the water, the tail ends bury into the oil droplets, attaching them to the water. The more the oil is mixed, the more emulsified connections get made, and the mixture thickens.

The process can be undermined in several ways. If the oil is added too quickly, the emulsifier can get overpowered and the connections never form. If the mixture is not beaten vigorously enough, the oil doesn't break into enough droplets, so that there are insufficient attachment sites for the tail ends of the phospholipids. If too much oil is added, the droplets become distorted, stress starts to cause them to

break, and in turn break the emulsion.

The other type of emulsifier is large proteins (like casein in dairy products) made up of long chains of amino acids that have different regions, some of which form bonds with fats and others that form bonds with water.

See Also ● Butter, Dispersions, Eggs, Fat, Milk, Sauces

ENAMELED COOKWARE ● See Cookware

ENDIVE ● See Chicory

ENDOSPERM ● See Grains

ENERGY

What It Is ● Cooking is about change, and energy makes change possible. Systems or objects with low energy have little possibility of changing. Those with more energy are more likely to change or more likely to exert changes on their surroundings. Energy can take many forms, and it can be converted from one form to another. The most common forms of energy in the kitchen are thermal (having to do with **heat**), kinetic (having to do with movement), radiant (having to do with energy waves), and chemical (having to do with the formation and breaking of **chemical bonds**).

What It Does ● Stoves and ovens change the characteristics of foods by bombarding them with heat and radiant energy, and refrigerators inhibit change by removing heat from food, thus slowing down the changes that result in spoilage. The kinetic energy of a whisk changes the structure of the protein in egg white, and chemical energy released when acidic and alkaline molecules combine creates the gas that makes a cake rise.

How It Works ● During cooking, chemical bonds are forming and breaking all the time, as atoms and molecules take in and release energy. When two or more atoms bond into a molecule, they're attracted to one another by an electrical force. The stronger the attraction, the faster they move toward one another and the more energy is stored in the bond that is created. The amount of energy it takes to form a chemical bond is the same amount that it takes to break it, so it takes more energy to change a molecule that is strongly bonded than one that has weak bonds.

Heat is the result of molecular movement. The more energy a food absorbs from a stove or oven, the faster its molecules move. As molecules move with greater energy, the harder it is for them to maintain their attraction to one another. When the amount of energy absorbed by the food equals the amount of energy it took to form the molecular bonds in the food, the molecular bonds break and change in relationship to one another and the food cooks.

See Also • Chemical Bonding, Heat

ENGLISH MUFFIN • See Bread

ENOKI • See Mushrooms

ENOLOGY • See Wine

ENZYME

What It Is • Not all **proteins** are important as food. Some are important because of what they do to food. These are enzymes, biological catalysts that accelerate chemical reactions that would otherwise happen much more slowly or not at all.

Enzymes catalyze reactions by reducing the amount of **energy** needed to start a reaction, and thereby greatly accelerate its speed. Most catalyzed reactions happen millions of times faster than comparable uncatalyzed reactions, and without them many of the processes in the body would happen so slowly that they would become insignificant. For example, enzymes speed the metabolism of glucose into energy. Without them your **metabolism** would not progress fast enough to be of use to your cells. A single enzyme can catalyze as many as a million reactions per second.

Some enzyme activity has undesirable effects on food. Enzymes in plant cells catalyze **browning** reactions or oxidize vitamin C. Enzymes in raw fish can turn its flesh into mush, and food spoilage is largely due to enzymes from bacteria breaking down our food for their own use. Many of the techniques used in processing food, both industrially and at home, are designed to slow down or stop enzyme action.

Some enzyme activity is very desirable in food. Yeast enzymes that convert sugars into alcohol and carbon dioxide are the basis for bread, beer, and wine production. The action of bacterial enzymes gives cheese flavor and transforms juice into vinegar. Enzymes in muscle tissues tenderize meat during aging, and are part of what gives coffee and cocoa beans their dark color and rich flavor.

What It Does • Enzymes are part of the biological processes that serve a variety of functions in our bodies. They are instrumental in most cell activities, including the transmission of signals between cells. They help to activate muscle movement and catalyze most digestive functions. Enzymes propel digestion from the moment food enters the mouth (where salivary amylase starts to turn long-chain carbohydrates into sugar) until it is completely broken down in the intestine.

Plant enzymes are used industrially in ways plants never intended them. Bromelain (from pineapple) and papain (from papaya), protein-digesting enzymes that are part of

the defense system of these plants, are the active ingredients in meat tenderizers. They are also used in topical anti-inflammatory creams used for the treatment of sports injuries and arthritis.

Other plant enzymes cause havoc in the kitchen. Some fruits and vegetables (apples, bananas, mushrooms, and potatoes) discolor when they are cut, juiced, or bruised. The discoloration, called enzymatic browning, is caused when phenolic compounds and enzymes in plant cells, which are normally kept separate from one another, mix in the presence of oxygen and copper ions. The enzymes cause the phenolics to oxidize (bond with oxygen), creating brown-tinted melanins. A similar enzyme action happens in human skin when it tans.

Enzymatic browning is easily subverted. Because an enzyme catalyzes a specific biological reaction under very specific conditions, changing those conditions slows the process. The enzyme responsible for browning is slowed or made inactive in general by exposure to heat, acid, or various sulfur compounds. Chilling slows down enzymatic activity in general, and covering the cut surface of a vegetable with oil or submerging it in water will slow oxidation. So when slicing an apple you can coat the cut surfaces with lemon juice, toss the pieces in a bowl of iced acidulated water, brush them with oil, or cook them quickly to keep them from browning.

Sometimes enzymatic browning is desirable, and food processes that take advantage of it often incorrectly refer to enzymatic browning as fermentation. Enzymatic browning is responsible for the sought-after development of rich color and flavor in the drying of tea leaves and fruit, particularly figs and raisins. Some dried fruits, like apples and apricots, can be overwhelmed by the color and flavor of enzymatic browning. These are usually treated with sulfur to counteract the effects.

How It Works • Enzymes are specific. Each one facilitates one reaction and is able to do it over and over again in quick succession. At one time it was thought that the speed and efficiency of enzyme action

came solely from that specificity. In 1894 Emil Fischer suggested that an enzyme and the substrate it acted upon possessed exact complementary geometrical shapes that fit together like a lock and key. Although it is still believed that the reactivity of an enzyme is determined by the shape of its active site, scientists no longer think the fit is that exact. The current model sees enzymes and the molecules they affect as flexible. The site where they meet is continually reshaping as the two interact, until a tight bond forms.

Most enzymes do not need any additional components to be fully active. However, some require help, which comes in the form of cofactors (compounds bound to the enzyme, such as metal ions) and coenzymes (separate molecules that act in various ways, such as transporting chemicals from one enzyme to another). Although some coenzymes are made by the body, some have to be taken in through the diet. Many are **vitamins**, including riboflavin, thiamine, and folate.

See Also • Digestion, Energy, Metabolism, Protein, Vitamins

ENZYMATIC BROWNING • See Enzyme

EPAZOTE • See Herbs

ESCAROLE • See Chicory

ESPRESSO • See Coffee

ESSENCES • See Extracts

ESTERS • See Flavor Compounds

ETHANOL • See Alcohol

ETHYLENE • See Fruit

EVAPORATED MILK • See Milk

EXTRACTS

What It Is • Since cooking began, cooks have been grinding, grating, and puréeing ingredients, sweating them in oil, steeping them in syrup, distilling them into vapors, or drying them to concentrate every drop of **flavor** they have to offer. However it is done, the goal is always the same: to extract the chemicals that give food flavor and deliver them to receptors on the tongue and in the nose before they dissipate. The process is tricky, for flavors are volatile, easy to release but difficult to capture and preserve.

What It Does ●

Natural flavors are extracted from aromatic plant parts — seeds (mostly nuts and **spices**), bark (like cinnamon), **flowers** (like rose, violet, or chamomile), fruit (citrus, peppers, and berries are most common), and **roots** or rhizomes (like **ginger** or turmeric).

Herbs (aromatic leaves) are some of the most common flavorings in recipes, but they are not typically turned into extracts, except for industrial purposes. This is partly because herb flavors are readily available fresh and dried, but it is also because aromatic oils are far less concentrated in leaves than in other parts of plants, except for mint leaves. For example, dried cinnamon bark or pepper berries might be 15% aromatic oil, while dried basil or oregano leaves would have less than 1%.

Artificial flavor extracts are made by combining chemical compounds that make up the flavors of natural ingredients. Natural flavor extracts can be drawn only from highly aromatic ingredients, but imitation flavors can be created to resemble any food, from root beer to roast beef. The ability of flavor scientists to imitate practically any flavor drives much of the product innovation in processed food, inspiring the creation of orange-flavored prunes, maple-scented oatmeal, or sour cream-and-chive potato chips.

How It Works ●

Aromatic chemicals tend to be concentrated in specialized cells near the surface of plant tissue or in channels between cells. As soon as the plant tissue is bruised, the aromatics are released. Mixing the tissue immediately with oil or another compatible medium draws the aromatic compounds from the plant into the extracting medium.

Several extraction techniques are used for making natural flavors.

Common Flavor Extracts

Flavor	Natural Source	Characterizing Chemical Species
Almond	Almond	Benzaldehyde
Anise	Aniseed	Anethole, methyl chavicol
Cinnamon	Cinnamon bark	Cinnamaldehyde, eugenol
Clove	Cloves	Eugenol
Ginger	Ginger	Gingerol, shogaol, geranial
Lemon	Lemon peel	Limonene, terpinene, pinene
Lime	Lime peel	Limonene, terpinene, pinene
Nutmeg	Nutmeg	Sabinene, myristicin
Orange	Orange peel	Limonene, linalool, decanal, pinene
Peppermint	Macerated peppermint leaves	Menthol, menthone
Rose	Macerated rose petals	Geraniol, citronellol, nerol
Spearmint	Macerated spearmint leaves	L-carvone
Vanilla	Macerated vanilla bean	Vanillin
Wintergreen	Macerated wintergreen leaves	Methyl salicylate

Essential oils are defined as aromatic, volatile flavors isolated from plant materials by steam distillation. The same basic production technique has been used since the 9th century. Plant material is loaded onto a grid and steam percolates up through the material, carrying the flavor compounds with it. The steam, along with the flavor compounds, is collected and condensed back into a liquid and recovered. Steam distillation is used to recover flavors for many herbs and spices. One disadvantage of essential oils is that they contain only the volatile flavor components of a herb or spice. Advantages are that they contain no colors or tannins. Citrus essential oils are held in sacs or glands just below the pigmented layer of the peel and are recovered by cold pressing of the peels. Lime oil can also be obtained by distillation. Undiluted, essential oils are hazardous.

Fruit flavors are obtained by concentration, using either vacuum or freeze concentration to remove water. Care must be taken to retain as many volatile compounds as possible and not damage the flavor with heat.

Enfleurage flavors are extracted by mixing macerated material with cold or warm fat. Flavors transfer to the fat and are then extracted from the fat with alcohol.

An extract is a solution obtained by passing alcohol or an alcohol-water mixture through a food material.

Oleoresins are concentrated extracts produced by removing the solvent from an extract using heat and vacuum. Oleoresins are dark and viscous and contain many of the notes that characterize a flavor.

Compound flavors used in food products are combinations of essential oils, oleoresins, and carriers produced by flavorists drawing on their experience and creativity.

See Also • Flavor, Flowers, Food Additives, Herbs, Spices

F

FAHRENHEIT • See Heat

FARINA • See Wheat

FARMER CHEESE • See Cheese

FARRO • See Wheat

FAT

What It Is • In the world of cooking, there is no ingredient more flexible than fat. Ingredients come and ingredients go, but fat remains at the core of cuisine. As author and culinary historian Waverley Root demonstrated when he divided the regional cooking of France between the provinces that rely on olive oil and those that rely on butter, our choice of fat has more to do with our expectations of flavor and texture in the foods we eat than almost any other single factor.

What It Does • In cooking, fat is the great equalizer. It collects heat gradually and maintains a constant temperature easily. Because it is fluid when hot, it can wrap around an ingredient completely, transferring its heat evenly and steadily into the tiniest crevice. Unlike other liquids made from water, which vaporize at 212°F (100°C), fats maintain their liquid states well past 400°F (200°C), giving them the ability to brown and crisp the surface of food, something steam and boiling water could never do. A thin film of fat is enough to keep most foods from sticking to a pan.

Chill a fat and it shows its other talents. Cold fats can be solid or plastic and malleable. Beaten with sugar, they capture air in millions of tiny pockets, and they hold on to it safely until the heat of the oven can use that air to send a cake aloft. Cold fat is the tenderizer in a pie crust and the melt-in-your-mouth texture of a strawberry shortcake. It makes cookies crisp and puff pastry puffed. It is the flake in a biscuit and the downy crumb of a warm muffin.

Fat is our sense of juiciness in a grilled steak or a roasted bird. It is what carries the flavors of herbs and spices in salad dressings, marinades, and sauces. Fat lubricates the flesh of a flaking fish and prevents pasta from sticking. Fat is an essential nutrient. If we delete it from our diets, we subject ourselves to nutritional deficiencies as we would lose our ability to absorb fat-soluble vitamins and valuable phytonutrients (lutein, lycopene, beta-carotene, and vitamins A, D, and E). Fats are an integral part of cell membranes and the production of hormones, and they are essential for brain development and activity and the workings of the nervous system and liver. The problem in industrialized culture is that we tend to take in too much of the wrong kinds of fat, which can have negative consequences on our health.

Though we talk of fat as a single entity, there are many different types. For culinary purposes, we categorize fats according to their physical state at a given temperature: "oils" are fats that are liquid at room temperature, and "fats" are fats that are solid at room temperature. Generally, oils come from plant sources (usually seeds, sometimes fruits), while fats generally come from animals, although through the process of hydrogenation vegetable oils can be processed to become firm enough to be solid at room temperature.

The most common culinary fats are:

Fats from Animals
Butter: The concentrated fat from milk, usually cow's milk, butter tastes of sweet, fresh dairy. It can be salted for flavor and to extend its shelf life. Butter is about 82% fat, 62% saturated. Butter is used for cooking and especially baking because of its flavor. Butter is so popular as a spread that other nondairy spreads are called "butter," such as peanut butter and apple butter. Clarified, or drawn, butter is melted butter from which all of the milk solids and most of the water have been removed, which makes is suitable for high-temperature cooking because it does not burn easily. Ghee, used primarily in Indian cooking, is similar to clarified butter except that it is cooked until all of its water has evaporated.

Lard: Rendered pig fat, lard is 100% fat, 61% unsaturated. The quality of lard depends on where on the pig the fat came from. The highest-quality lard, known as leaf lard, comes from the dense, dry fat that surrounds the

kitchen wisdom

Melting Points of Solid Fats

Solid fats remain firm at room temperature, while oils become liquid. But not all solid fats are the same. Some liquefy at lower temperatures than others. For instance, butter melts at lower temperatures than vegetable shortening. That's why butter must be kept cold when mixed into pastry dough. That's also why butter melts luxuriously in the mouth, while firmer vegetable shortening can leave behind a greasy film.

Fat	Melting Point
Butter	90 to 95°F (32 to 35°C)
Chicken fat (rendered)	75 to 95°F (24 to 35°C)
Lard (rendered pork fat)	86 to 104°F (30 to 40°C)
Margarine (stick)	94 to 109°F (34 to 43°C)
Margarine (tub)	94 to 98°F (34 to 37°C)
Suet (rendered beef fat)	113 to 122°F (45 to 50°C)
Vegetable shortening	98 to 119°F (37 to 48°C)

kidneys. The next highest grade, called fatback, is from the fat that lies along the spine right under the skin. Most lard is rendered from a mixture of fatback and lesser pig fats. Unless you buy it from a butcher who renders his own, it is typically bleached, deodorized, and emulsified to give it a longer shelf life, and likely contains harmful hydrogenated oils. Lard is less saturated than butter, and behaves similarly in baking and cooking, but has a mild meaty flavor. Its smoke point is high, and because it has a coarse crystalline structure, it makes very flaky pastry. It is still used extensively in British, central European, and Mexican cooking and is making a bit of a comeback in North America, as part of the whole food movement.

Bacon fat is the rendered fat from pork belly and is usually smoked and often flavored with spices and/or sweeteners. Bacon fat is nearly 100% fat, about 40% saturated. It is used extensively in the cooking of the southeastern U.S.

Poultry Fats: In general, rendered fat from poultry is about 98% fat, around 30% saturated, making it a healthy fat. The use of chicken and goose fat is traditional in the Jewish cooking of central Europe, because lard is not kosher and butter cannot be used with meat. Duck fat is commonly used in France and by many chefs around the world. Poultry fats are commonly used in the making of **confit**.

Suet: The hard, dry fat that surrounds the kidneys of beef and sheep is 99% fat, 52% saturated. Because of its high saturation and lack of moisture, rendered suet, called tallow, is very dense and stores extremely well, which made it a favorite fat before the advent of refrigeration. Tallow is prized for frying and soap making, and was once used for making candles. Suet is the preferred fat for making traditional steamed puddings, like plum pudding, and the pastry for meat pies, which is relatively soft because of suet's low melting point, about 70°F (21°C).

Fats from Plants

Margarine: Margarine is a generic term for butter substitute. In the past, margarines were typically made from vegetable oil hydrogenated to be solid at room temperature and flavored with skimmed milk and salt. The traditional hydrogenation method (see How It Works, page 220) produces trans fatty acids.

Because trans fats have been linked to heart disease, most margarine manufacturers have switched to manufacturing methods that do not produce trans fatty acids. Margarine can be saturated to varying degrees; generally the softer its texture, the less saturated fat it contains. Hard stick margarine is about 80% fat, almost the same as butter. Take special care when using whipped margarine and low-fat margarines in baking recipes. Whipped margarines contain up to 50% air. When the margarine heats, the air escapes, so the volume of margarine may end up being half of what the recipe called for. Low-fat margarine can be up to 58% water. When used in baking the extra water makes cookies soft and puffy (a problem if you like chewy cookies). It also thins cake batters and toughens pie crust.

Oil: Fats from plants tend to be bland and less saturated than animal fats. Soy oil, sold as vegetable oil, is the most common type, accounting for about a quarter of the world consumption. Oils are liquid at room temperature, giving them limited uses in baking, but are convenient for use in cold and uncooked foods.

Shortening: Vegetable oils are hydrogenated into shortening in order to make them look and behave more like animal fats. Compared to liquid oils, shortening is less prone to rancidity and has a higher smoke point. Although vegetable shortening is cholesterol free, it is about 40% saturated fat. Some vegetable shortenings are high in trans fats, so check the label.

How It Works ●
Unless it has been hydrogenated, the more solid a fat is, the more saturated it is. We typically speak of one fat as being saturated and another as unsaturated, but saturation is actually a continuum without clear division lines. Liquid canola oil is less saturated than more viscous olive oil, which is less saturated than chicken fat, which is less saturated than lard.

The chemical name for a fat or oil is triacylglycerol (triglyceride is an old term that is still used), meaning that these molecules are composed of three fatty acids (acyl groups) attached at one end to a glycerol molecule. Fatty acids in

triacylglycerols are chains of carbon atoms (from 4 to 28 atoms). Each carbon has the potential of bonding with two hydrogen atoms. When all of the carbons are attached to hydrogens, the fatty acid is saturated. As you can imagine, saturated fats are huge molecules and solidly packed. Because all of their bonding sites are occupied, the fatty acids can't bond with oxygen and therefore they are not as prone to rancidity as unsaturated fatty acids.

Fats made up of less-saturated fatty acids are

Saturation Ratios of Common Culinary Fats

Fats contain various ratios of saturated, monounsaturated, and polyunsaturated fatty acids. Most health experts recommend reducing your consumption of foods containing saturated fats to help lower LDL levels, reduce blood cholesterol, and reduce risk of heart disease.

Fat or Oil	% Saturated	% Monounsaturated	% Polyunsaturated
Beef tallow	50	42	4
Butter	62	29	4
Canola	7	55	33
Cocoa butter	60	35	2
Coconut	86	6	2
Corn	13	24	59
Flaxseed	9	19	72
Grapeseed	11	16	68
Hazelnut	7	78	10
Lard	40	46	12
Margarine, stick	19	59	18
Margarine, tub	17	47	31
Mustard	1	76	23
Olive	13	74	8
Palm	49	37	9
Peanut	17	46	32
Safflower	9	12	75
Sesame	18	41	41
Shortening, vegetable	31	51	14
Soy	14	23	58
Sunflower	13	24	59
Walnut	9	16	70

kitchen wisdom

Cloudy Oil
Many oils will turn cloudy in the refrigerator. All that signifies is that they are becoming cold enough to start to solidify. The change is not harmful and the oil will return to its liquid state as soon as it is heated.

Greasing Pans
The protein in batters tends to adhere to tiny scratches and microscopic openings in the surfaces of baking pans, causing cakes and cookies to stick. Greasing the pan before adding the batter fills up the openings with fat so that the batter cannot stick to the pan.

more fluid. At one time it was believed that polyunsaturated fats were the most healthful, but research has shown that fats high in monounsaturated fatty acids are optimal because they increase the desirable high-density lipoproteins and lessen the undesirable low-density lipoproteins in the bloodstream. They are also less prone to oxidation and rancidity than polyunsaturated fats, like flaxseed oil. No fat is 100% saturated or unsaturated fatty acids. The Saturation Ratios of Common Culinary Fats chart, left, gives the proportions of saturated, monounsaturated, and polyunsaturated fatty acids of common fats and oils.

The saturation level of a fat has much to do with how it is best used in cooking. Plastic or solid fats like lard, shortening, butter, and margarine are preferred for **baking**. Their thickness is essential to properly aerate cakes and to give a pastry its flake. Oil produces dense cakes, such as carrot cake, which are rich and moist but without the delicate crumb that is the sign of a cake made from butter or shortening.

When making pie crust, biscuits, or shortcakes, the solidity of the fat partially determines the size of the flake. The more completely a fat is mixed with flour in a dough, the less flaky the dough will be. Obviously, liquid fats, like oils, combine with the flour entirely, yielding a product with such a small flake that its texture is best described as sandy.

All fats will burn if heated high enough, but the smoke point for each is different, depending on its chemical composition. Saturation is the main factor influencing the smoke point. The less saturated a fat is, the higher it can be heated before it starts burning and smoking.

Fats are best stored in as cool and dark a place as possible, in tightly sealed containers that fit their contents closely. The main danger in fat storage is rancidity. Fats become rancid when they are exposed to heat, air, and light, and the less saturated they are, the more prone they are to developing rancidity.

See Also ● Bacon, Baking, Butter, Cholesterol, Frying, Oil

FATBACK • See Fat, Pork

FATTY ACID • See Fat

FAVA BEAN • See Legumes

FEIJOA • See Fruit

FENNEL

What It Is ● There is only one species of fennel, *Foeniculum vulgare*, but it comes in three forms — the herb, the seed, and the vegetable. Wild fennel has long, twiggy stems and delicate, feathery leaves. The leaves are used as a herb, and the stems are dried and used for smoking fish and meats. Cultivated fennel, known as sweet fennel, can be grown either for its seed, which tastes strongly of licorice, or as a vegetable with a milder licorice flavor. When sweet fennel is grown to be used as a vegetable it is called Florence fennel, and looks a little like celery, except the stalks fan and swell at their base to form an edible bulb. It is often mistakenly sold as anise, which is a different plant, but produces a seed that also tastes like licorice.

What It Does ● Florence fennel is popular in Italy, where it is known as finocchio. Only the bulb of Florence fennel is usable. The celery-like stalks are tough and fibrous, and the leaves are too mild to be used as a herb.

fenugreek

The flavor of fennel bulb is similar to anise although lighter and with a slight citrus note. Fennel seed delivers a stronger fennel punch than either the vegetable or herb forms. The seeds are used whole or ground and range in color from green to brown; green seeds are generally considered better. Fennel seed is a favorite flavoring in Italian sausage, a common addition to Indian spice blends, such as panch phoron, and an essential element of Chinese five-spice powder. In Eurasia it is chewed as an after-meal breath freshener. Along with aniseed, which it closely resembles, fennel seed is part of the formula for the notorious liquor absinthe, as well as Pernod and Ricard that took its place after absinthe was banned in France in 1915.

Fennel pollen has a licorice flavor with sweet floral notes. It is delicate and is generally added to dishes at the last minute.

How It Works • Fennel owes its sweet anise-like flavor to the phenolic compound anethone, which is also found in aniseed and star anise. Anethone is 13 times sweeter than table sugar. Fennel oil, which is extracted from fennel seeds, is a traditional folk medicine for the treatment of digestive problems, and fennel tea is believed to relieve bloating and gas.

See Also • Flavor Compounds, Liquor, Spices

FENUGREEK • See Herbs, Spices

FERMENTATION

What It Is • Fermentation, the action of microorganisms on food converting complex biological molecules into simple ones, is older than human history. Airborne yeasts were transforming the sugar in fruit into alcohol long before humans ever got control of the process and called the outcome wine. And bacteria had been making lactic acid from lactose in milk, causing the milk to sour and curdle, before yogurt was known. The effects of microorganisms on food can be desirable or disastrous. The art of fermentation insures that only the former happens.

What It Does • Fermentation turns

- fruit juice into wine
- grain into beer or sake
- fruit or grain into vinegar
- cacao beans into chocolate
- carbohydrates into carbon dioxide to leaven bread
- milk into buttermilk, yogurt, cheese, sour cream, and other fermented dairy products
- fresh meat into dry-aged beef and salamis
- soybeans into soy sauces and soy pastes
- fish into fish sauce
- cabbage into sauerkraut and kimchi

How It Works • *Wine:* Yeasts, either added by the winemaker or living naturally on fruit skins, convert sugar in crushed fruit into alcohol. At the same time **enzymes** create aromatic components from the decomposing sugar. White wines are generally fermented at 60°F (16°C) for four to six weeks. Hardier red wines are fermented at a slightly higher temperature, 65 to 80°F (18 to 27°C), for a shorter period. The lower the temperature, the slower the fermentation and the less the aromatic molecules accumulate. Initial wine fermentation is complete when all of the sugar has been converted into alcohol. Sweeter wines used to be made by stopping the fermentation before all of the sugar had been converted. Now it is more common to add a small amount of sweet unfermented juice after fermentation is complete. Sometimes a second fermentation is carried out to convert malic acid in the wine into less sour lactic acid. This malolactic bacterial fermentation reduces the wine's tartness and brings out several other aromatic compounds.

Beer: Enzymes in soaked, sprouted barley break down starches into sugars. Hops are then added to counter some of the sweetness, and yeasts are added to feed off the sugar and ferment it into alcohol. Ales are made with

rapid fermentation at around 70°F (21°C); lagers are made at lower temperatures with slow fermentation. Quick fermentation results in stronger-tasting, more acidic beer.

Sake: Sake is made from highly polished rice fermented similarly to beer at 50 to 64°F (10 to 18°C); the lower temperature is reserved for better grades. High-grade sake is fermented for about one month and develops many aromatic compounds, mostly esters. Sake is filtered and diluted with water to an alcohol content of about 15%.

Vinegar: Vinegar is the destiny of any alcohol (wine, beer, sake, or cider) exposed to oxygen and bacteria from the genus *Acetobacter* that have the unusual ability to use alcohol as an energy source. They metabolize alcohol into water and acetic acid, creating an extremely stable liquid, vinegar. Alcohols of 6% will produce vinegar of about 5% acetic acid. Most vinegars are 5 to 7% acetic acid.

Chocolate: Cacao beans are fermented on the farm or plantation where the cacao crop was grown. Fermentation starts when beans and the fruity pulp surrounding them are piled together in the open, and it progresses rapidly or slowly depending on the ambient temperature; typically it takes about one week. Initially, yeasts convert sugars in the pulp to alcohol, then lactic-acid-producing bacteria take over, followed by acetic acid bacteria (the same ones responsible for vinegar) that convert the alcohol to acetic acid. The beans' digestive enzymes break down proteins and sugars into aromatic molecules that will be transformed into the familiar flavors of chocolate during roasting.

Bread: Yeasts feed off sugars and starches in bread dough, producing carbon dioxide to make it rise. Lengthening the rising gives more time for the dough to develop fermented flavors, so breads that rise overnight in the refrigerator have far more flavor than breads that rise an hour at room temperature.

Fermented dairy products: Lactococcus and *Lactobacillus* bacteria feed off the sugar in milk (lactose) and produce lactic acid, which coagulates the protein in milk, causing it to thicken. The acidic environment retards the growth of competing bacteria, guarding fermented dairy products against spoilage and making them safer for human consumption than their fresh counterparts. In addition to making milk more digestible and safer, some lactic-acid-producing bacteria (*L. fermentum*, *L. casei*, *L. brevis*, and *L.acidophilus*) take up residence in the intestines, where they secrete antibacterial compounds that boost the body's immune system.

Meat: When meat is aged, whether fresh or cured, lactic-acid-producing bacteria break down its proteins and sugars into intensely savory aromatic molecules and acids. The meat becomes more flavorful, drier, richer, and less subject to the growth of harmful bacteria because of its reduced pH. Cured meats are heavily spiced and have a salt content of more than 4% and can be fermented at room temperature.

Fermented soy products: For two days, *Aspergillus oryzae* molds digest sugars, fats, and proteins in cooked soybeans and grains. Then the mixture is immersed in salt brine to kill the mold (but its enzymes remain active), and salt-tolerant lactic-acid-producing bacteria and yeasts take over the fermentation. Over several months they break down sugars, fatty acids, and amino acids into their smaller, more flavorful component parts. At the same time, enzymatic browning reactions generate deep, dark color and complex flavors.

Asian fish sauce: A mass of fish and shellfish is mixed with salt to a concentration of about 10% and packed in a sealed container with fermented grains, vegetables, and/or fruits. The high salinity keeps pathogenic bacteria from growing, and the fermented plant material provides lactic-acid-producing and malolactic bacteria that increase the mixture's acidity and generate many aromatic by-products. Fermentation usually takes two to three weeks, after which the mass is drained, filtered, and boiled to stop fermentation. Fish sauce goes by different names in different parts of Southeast Asia — nam pla in Thailand, nuoc nam in Vietnam, shottsuru in Japan.

Sauerkraut and kimchi: For sauerkraut, finely shredded cabbage is salted to a concentration of 1.5% and fermented for about a month at 70°F (21°C) until its

Fermented Dairy Products*

Product	Bacteria	Fermentation Temperature and Time	Acidity	Description
Acidophilus	*Lactobacillus acidophilus*	106 to 114°F (41 to 45°C), 2 to 5 hours	2 to 4%	Tart, semisolid, creamy, smooth, probiotic
Buttermilk	*Lactococcus lactis*, *Leuconostoc mesenteroides*	72°F (22°C), 15 hours	Around 1%	Slightly tart, lightly thickened, creamy texture
Crème fraîche	*Lactococcus lactis*, *Leuconostoc mesenteroides*	68°F (20°C), 15 hours	0.5%	Mild tartness, rich thick texture, fatty mouth feel
Kefir	*Lactobacillus kefir*, *Acetobacter*, yeasts	68°F (20°C), 24 hours	1%	Tart, lightly thickened, ropey mouth feel, effervescent, very slight alcohol
Sour cream	*Lactococcus lactis*, *Leuconostoc mesenteroides*	72°F (22°C), 15 hours	0.8%	Mild tartness, almost solid, creamy consistency
Sour milk	*Lactococcus lactis*, *Leuconostoc mesenteroides*	68°F (20°C), 15 hours	0.8%	Medium tartness, almost solid
Yogurt	*Lactobacillus delbrueckii*, *Streptococcus thermophilus*	106 to 114°F (41 to 45°C), 2 to 5 hours	2 to 4%	Tart, almost solid, smooth, creaminess depends on fat content

*Cheese starts out as a fermented dairy product, but once the curd is separated and formed into cheese most fermentation stops, except for a few specialty cheeses, like Swiss-style cheeses. (For more information, see Cheese.)

acidity is 1.5%. Kimchi, a traditional Korean dish, is made from whole cabbage leaves and pieces of stem tossed with chiles, garlic, and salt to a concentration of 3%. It ferments for about two weeks at about 50°F (10°C) and has a finished acidity of 0.6%.

See Also • Alcohol, Beer, Bread, Chocolate, Liquor, Soybeans, Vinegar, Wine

FERMENTED BEANS • See Fermentation, Soybeans

FERMENTED DAIRY • See Fermentation

FERNET-BRANCA • See Bitters

FETA CHEESE • See Cheese

FIBER

What It Is • Fiber is the only part of our diet that is essential for our health yet indigestible. Made up of the major components of plant cell walls, fiber contains insoluble components such as cellulose and lignin, which give plant cells their structural rigidity, and soluble fiber, such as hemicellulose and pectin, which form the "mortar" that helps to hold the fibers of cellulose and lignin in place. In addition to its major components, fiber includes small amounts of unusual starches (such as chitin from mushrooms and inulin from onions, chicory, and artichokes) that have far-reaching health benefits.

What It Does • Because our digestive enzymes can't break plant fibers down into absorbable components, they pass intact through the small intestine into the colon, from which they are excreted. Insoluble fiber is vital for the thorough and efficient passage of excrement through the colon, and therefore minimizes our exposure to toxins that are being excreted with our food. Soluble fiber, although not broken down in the small intestine, dissolves during digestion and forms a gelatinous material that moves quickly through the large intestine. Good

science wise

Fiber as Food Additive • Soluble fibers such as polydextrose are used as food additives in cakes, sweets, and salad dressings to replace sugar, starch, and fat. Because they are largely indigestible, their calorie content is nil, and therefore they reduce total calories in food.

sources of dietary fiber, both soluble and insoluble, include whole grains, flax, nuts, dried fruits, and hard, crunchy vegetables.

How It Works • Insoluble fiber absorbs water, which helps it add bulk to and soften stools, thus insuring rapid movement of excrement through the large intestine. It also is believed to bond with DNA-damaging chemicals and other toxins, making them less likely to be absorbed into the body during digestion.

Soluble fiber is acted upon by colonic bacteria in the large intestine and is partially broken down into short-chain fatty acids that have been shown to lower blood cholesterol and slow the rise of blood glucose after eating. These bacteria also stimulate antibodies that play a role in immune protection; increase mineral absorption; and help to strengthen the colonic walls, inhibiting inflammation and the formation of colonic polyps. Several forms of soluble fiber, including inulin and polydextrose, encourage the growth of beneficial bacteria in the gut.

See Also • Digestion, Pectin

FIG

What It Is • The fruit of the common ficus tree, figs are native to the Mediterranean and the Middle East, where they were believed to be one of the earliest cultivated crops, some 11,000 years ago. Fig fossils found near Jericho, dated to 9400 BCE, predate the cultivation of grain by several hundred years. Cretaceous fossils of fig leaves from about 70 million years ago were found in Colorado. The fig tree is one of the sacred trees of Islam, and figs are the fruit mentioned most often in the Bible.

What It Does

There are hundreds of varieties of fig, but almost all edible figs come from one species, *Ficus carica*, the common fig. The skin can be green, creamy white, purple, or practically black. The flesh is either pale green or bright red. Ripe figs are 80% water and quite perishable, which is why the vast bulk of the world's crop is dried, a process that usually starts on the tree and concludes in mechanical dryers.

Fresh figs are typically eaten raw or lightly cooked. Fresh figs are 16% sugar; after drying, the sugar content rises to nearly half the weight. Dried figs are eaten as a snack, braised with meat, or baked in pastry. Fig pastry filling became famous with the popularity of Fig Newton cookies.

How It Works

Figs are most commonly thought of as fruit, but they are much more flower than fruit. The body is a flower base turned in on itself, creating a receptacle-like core radiating female florets inwardly that develop into hundreds of tiny individual dried fruits that crunch like "seeds."

Figs come in two sexes — hermaphrodite and female — and only the female fig is edible. Inedible figs (caprifigs) are grown solely for their pollen. Small wasps lay their eggs in caprifigs, and their offspring grow inside. Upon leaving the caprifig the wasps enter the female fig through an open pore (ostiole) at the bulbous end. Once inside, they pollinate the flowers. Although many fig varieties will set fruit without being pollinated, experts say that fertilization is important for a fig to develop full flavor.

Smyrna figs (Calimyrna is the variety grown in California) do not fruit until they're fertilized. In California, fields of caprifigs grow alongside fig orchards for the sole purpose of providing pollen. Mission figs, also grown in California, do not need pollination, giving them a less crunchy interior.

Figs contain a large amount of phenolic compounds, some of which are antioxidants, which is why ripe figs have such a pronounced aroma. Fig skin can be astringent because of its high tannin content.

See Also • Fruit

FILBERT • See Nuts

FILÉ • See Herbs

FILO • See Pastry

FIRE

What It Is

Fire ignites when oxygen connects rapidly with another substance, producing flame, heat, and light. Usually oxygen bonds with other molecules steadily, and in most instances sudden rapid combustion doesn't take place. For instance, when oxygen bonds with glucose in your cells you get energy, but no flames. However, when the same union occurs with natural gas or another combustible fuel, fire happens. Antoine Lavoisier discovered the connection between oxygen and fire in the late 18th century.

What It Does

Our ability to control fire is one of the greatest human achievements. It has made it possible for

Temperature of Flames by Color

Color	Color Intensity	Temperature
Red	Barely visible	1000°F (538°C)
	Dull	1430°F (775°C)
	Bright	1650°F (900°C)
	Transparent	1830°F (1000°C)
Orange	Bright	2010°F (1100°C)
	Transparent	2190°F (1200°C)
Yellow	Transparent	2370°F (1300°C)
White	Bright	2550°F (1400°C)
	Blue white	2730°F (1500°C)

populations to inhabit colder climates and spread around the globe, and it fostered the health, longevity, and survival of our species by giving us a way to cook our food. Archaeologists have found evidence of controlled fire from about 1 million years ago.

Fire releases energy chaotically. Most common kitchen fuels — gas, wood, or the glowing electric coils — throw off at least 1000°F (538°C) of heat energy. That heat spreads everywhere and it dissipates rapidly. Cooking appliances, like stoves, broilers, and ovens, attempt to control and direct the energy from a fire to where it is needed, but none of them are completely effective. The U.S. Department of Energy estimates that only about 35 to 40% of the energy from a gas burner or wood-burning fire reaches the surface of the ingredient being cooked. Flat-top electric and induction burners, which have more contact with the surface of a pan, are more efficient, conveying about 70 to 90% of their energy to the food.

The heat of a fire is determined by how thoroughly the fuel source and oxygen combine. When a carbon-based fuel such as gas or wood burns, complete combustion produces a dull blue flame. Incomplete combustion, which is mostly the result of insufficient oxygen, produces flames that range in color from blue at the base to red and orange near the tip, with a big area of yellow-white in the center. Even under the best conditions some fuel doesn't oxidize. All fires contain noncombustible incandescent particles (soot) that suspend in the flames and change their color. In a hydrocarbon fire the particles are unoxidized carbon that change color from orange to yellow to white the hotter they get. When a fire dies down, the soot cools and turns black. If a different chemical was being burned, the color would be different. Zinc and barium, for instance, produce green soot.

The coolest part of a flame is red. As it transitions to orange, yellow, and white, the temperature increases. Within each color region, the more transparent the color becomes, the hotter that region of the flame will be.

How It Works • For fire to be sustainable, three things have to be present in enough quantity to create a chain reaction: a combustible fuel, an ignition source, and plenty of oxygen.

In cooking, the fuel is usually natural gas, which is primarily methane (CH_4), but it could also be wood or charcoal (which is partially burned wood). Natural gas ignites at 370°F (188°C) and a match head (which is mostly red phosphorus) at 464°F (240°C), so a match releases sufficient energy to ignite gas. But wood needs far more energy to ignite.

In order for a fuel to ignite, its molecules must be moving fast enough to pass into a gaseous phase and bond with oxygen, so the easier it is to turn a fuel source into a gas, the less energy it takes to start a fire. Natural gas vaporizes below room temperature, making it easy to ignite, but wood doesn't, so to start a wood fire you need something that puts out more energy than a match. The art of building a wood fire is a process of building up energy. Usually you start by igniting paper (wood pulp), which flames at 435°F (224°C). A match is hot enough to light that. Paper burns hot enough to ignite small pieces of wood (kindling), about 500°F (260°C), which in turn is hot enough to ignite branches, and so on until you get to the 800°F (427°C) needed to ignite solid wood logs.

Once the fuel is ignited, the energy it emits will form a chain reaction that will keep the fuel vaporizing and bonding with oxygen, and a fire will keep burning until the supply of either element is used up or turned off. A fire extinguisher works by covering the fuel with a coating of fine powder or foam, thus separating it from oxygen. Small fires can be extinguished with water, which cools the combusting fuel so that a chain reaction can no longer take place. Water is ineffective against large fires, unless it's under great pressure, as in a fire truck or fire extinguisher system. Water can also spread oil fires.

See Also • Cooking, Heat, Stove

FISH

What It Is • The ocean is expansive, extending over two-thirds of the earth's face and 7 miles (11 km) beneath the surface. Within those cold, dark, airless confines lives our largest source of edible wildlife. Most of the animals we eat are not wild. Over generations they have been bred away from their wild state to a standard of tenderness and flavor that we have come to expect as natural. Most fish are not like that. The quality of most fish is dependent on a number of factors — where it swam, what it ate, how and when it was caught — all of which means quality and supply can vary from season to season or even from day to day.

The fishing industry has tried to control some of the variables by farming the most popular varieties of fish, such as salmon, trout, and catfish. Aquacultured fish grow faster than their counterparts in the wild, and they are often more tender and richer tasting. They are harvested without suffering the stress and damage of being hooked or netted, and they are processed closer to the time and nearer to where they are caught. However, questions have been raised about the nutritional integrity of farmed fish and the impact of fish farming on the environment. Currently, aquaculture provides about one-third of the world's seafood supply (including shellfish), and this amount is bound to increase to meet the growing global demand for fish that cannot be met by wild fishing alone.

How fish live determines most of their culinary attributes. Savvy consumers should familiarize themselves not just with the signs of wholesomeness but with the source of their fish (farmed or wild) and the characteristics of particular families of fish before purchasing.

What It Does • Fish are categorized in a number of ways. The broadest classification is whether they live in fresh or salt water, although a number of fish are diadromous, which means they live in both fresh and salt water. These fish usually migrate to breed (spawn), during which they can travel from a few yards to thousands of miles. There are two types of diadromous fish: anadromous fish are born in fresh water, migrate to the sea, and return to fresh water to spawn (e.g., salmon, shad, steelhead, striped bass, sturgeon); catadromous fish are born at sea, migrate inland into fresh water, and return to the sea to spawn (e.g., American eel).

Fish are also classified into two groups based on body shape: roundfish and flatfish. All freshwater and diadromous fish are round, as are some saltwater fish. Saltwater fish may also fall into the flatfish category.

Roundfish, such as cod, trout, bass or salmon, are about as wide from side to side as they are from back to belly. Flatfish, such as flounder and halibut, are usually no more than an inch or two (2.5 or 5 cm) in depth from side to side, but can be several feet wide from the dorsal fin on their back to the pelvic fin on their belly side.

Roundfish can be further categorized into lean and fat fish. Lean fish have a fat content between 0 and 5% of their body weight. Since most of this fat is concentrated in the liver, which is removed when the fish is cleaned, the edible portion of fat is less than 3%. Lean fish tend to have pale, dry flesh and a subtle, nonassertive flavor. Fat fish have a body fat content from 3 to 25%. Unlike lean fish, their fat is distributed throughout the entire body. Fat fish with a fat content of less than 10%, like salmon or shad, tend to have moist, assertively flavored flesh that is pigmented. Fish with a fat content of more than 10%, like eel or pompano,

always have a rich taste, although the color of their flesh can vary from dark to very white, depending on their environment. All flatfish are lean.

Buying and Storing Fish

Unless you are purchasing from a boat at the dock, chances are the fish you buy is several days to a week old. Although fish are stored at near-freezing temperatures on board ship, fish flesh is highly perishable, so it's important to know the signs of freshness. Look for:

- *Firm flesh:* When you poke the side of a fish in its thickest portion, the imprint of your finger should spring back.
- *Clear, bulging eyes:* Reject specimens with flat, sunken, or cloudy eyes.
- *Bright gills:* Lift the gill flaps at the back of the head. The gills should be bright red or pink, without hints of brown or gray. Although the gills are not eaten, they are the best early indicators of decay.
- *Shiny scales:* If a fish has scales, they should be shiny and firmly attached. The skin color should be bright, with no blemishes or bruises under its surface.
- *No odor:* Fresh fish has no odor, except

possibly the faint aroma of seawater. Any fishy odor is an indication of decay.

Although it is best to cook and eat fish as soon as possible, sometimes it is necessary to store fish for a day or two. Here are a few tricks to prolong freshness:

- Remove the guts before storage. The organs harbor most of the bacteria and once they are removed, the degree and speed of decay are greatly diminished. In addition, the digestive enzymes are very powerful. If permitted to remain in the belly, they will eat away at the walls of the body cavity, making the interior flesh prone to decay.
- Rinse fish in salted water before it is stored. Compared to the meat of land animals, the muscle tissue of fish is weak, which makes it an easy mark for bacteria. Rinsing in lightly salted water before storage will remove any surface bacteria and inhibit more from growing. About 1 teaspoon (5 mL) of salt in a cup (250 mL) of water will help keep fish fresh without altering its flavor.
- Keep fish cold. It is best kept under refrigeration packed in ice, but only in a perforated container so water from the melting ice can drip away. Never store fish in water. If you don't have a perforated container, wrap loosely in a plastic bag and place over ice, changing the ice as needed. Even with these precautions, fish should be used within one or two days of purchase.
- Avoid freezing fish. Frozen fish has a greater chance of becoming dry during cooking, since freezing breaks down the tissue of all foods, especially if that tissue, like fish, is weak to begin with. Most fish is frozen, or kept near freezing as soon as it is caught. So when you freeze a fish there is a good chance that it is being frozen for a second time. In fact, if you know you will have to freeze a fish before you buy it, buy it already frozen. Commercially frozen fish are flash frozen to a solid state,

Farmed Fish

Freshwater	Saltwater
Carp	Char
Catfish	Mahi mahi
Eel	Salmon
Rainbow trout	Sea bass
Tilapia	Steelhead trout
	Sturgeon
	Tuna
	Turbot
	Yellowtail (amberjack; hamachi)

Fish Fat Content

Lean Fish (0 to 3% fat)	Moderately Fat Fish (3 to 10% fat)	Fat Fish (10% fat or more)
Cod	Anchovy	Carp
Croaker/drum	Catfish	Dolphinfish
Escolar*/walu*	Char	Eel
Flatfish	Pike	Herring
Monkfish	Salmon	Icefish
Mullet	Shad	Mackerel
Porgy	Shark	Pompano
Roughy	Smelts	Sablefish
Sea bass	Sprats	Wahoo
Skate	Sturgeon	
Snapper	Swordfish	
Tilefish	Tilapia	
Yellowtail	Trout	
	Tuna	
	Walleye	
	Whitefish	

*These fish contain indigestible wax esters that make them taste like fatty fish, but because the esters pass through our digestive system they do not have the calories of a fatty fish. Waxy esters cause digestive problems (see How It Works, below).

Lean fish are best suited to wet-cooking methods. Poaching and steaming delicately soften the flesh of these fish while keeping the meat moist. After cooking they are often served with buttery and creamy sauces to lend needed richness. Fatty fish are best cooked with dry-cooking techniques like grilling, broiling, roasting, or baking, where their natural oils keep the meat moist. They are typically served with strong-flavored sauces. Most moderately fat fish, particularly salmon, char, and trout, can be cooked any way. Both lean and fatty fish can be sautéed or fried.

producing better results than you can achieve at home. A new technique for improving the quality and storage life of fish is called super chilling. This industrial technique involves chilling fish at 27 to 30°F (−3 to −1°C), which extends its storage life longer than packing it in ice (another common method of storing fish), and it avoids the damage that can happen during freezing.

However, if you must freeze fish, make sure it is as fresh as possible. Clean it well and wrap it tightly in plastic, then in a layer of paper or foil. Freeze quickly; the faster it freezes solid, the less damage will be done.

Fish Products

In the centuries before refrigeration, fish had to be preserved by salting, drying, smoking, or fermenting. Although these methods are no longer necessary to preserve fish, people still appreciate the intensity of flavor and rich textures they develop. The following fish products are now valued purely for their sensuous charms:

- *Salt-cured:* gravlax, lox, lomi lomi, anchovies, sardines, caviar, salmon roe, mullet roe
- *Dried:* salt cod, akule
- *Smoked:* smoked salmon, smoked trout, smoked white fish, smoked sturgeon, smoked sable, smoked eel, kippered herring, brisling (smoked sprat), finnan haddie (smoked haddock)
- *Fermented:* nam pla (Thai fish sauce), kapi (Thai fish paste), nuoc nam (Vietnamese fish sauce), shottsuru (Japanese fish sauce)

The two reproductive cells of fish, eggs and sperm, are processed separately as luxury food products. Fish eggs can be salted lightly to become **caviar** or cooked, in their egg sac, in which case they are called roe. Milt, or fish sperm, usually from herring, is cooked and served as soft roe.

Most of the fish consumed in the U.S. comes from cans. The most commonly canned fish are tuna, salmon, herring, sardines, and anchovies. More than one billion cans of tuna are sold in the U.S. every year, making Americans the largest consumers of canned tuna in the world by far. Canned fish is typically cooked twice. Before canning it is steamed to eliminate moisture, which would contribute to a watery product. The sealed can is subsequently pressure steamed to sterilize it. The canning process is hot enough (240°F/116°C) to dissolve the bones, which increases the calcium content of the product. Four ounces (114 g) of fresh salmon contains about 5 mg of calcium; the same amount of canned salmon has 200 mg.

How It Works • Water is denser than air. Animals that live in water don't need the heavy skeletons and tough connective tissue that land animals require to support themselves against the pull of gravity. With

Common Fish

The following chart lists the most common culinary fish families, a description of each, and examples of the fish included in each family

Fish Family	Description	Examples
Carp and catfish	Freshwater; pale flesh, meaty, firm, sweet; catfish preferably from recirculated freshwater farms; carp are larger, up to 20 lbs (9 kg)	Carp, minnow, North American channel fish, U.S. farm-raised catfish, bullhead, basa and swai (Asian fish sold as catfish)
Cod	Saltwater; large, lean, firm, white meat, large flakes, mild; pollock used for frozen fish and surimi	Cod, haddock, hake, whiting, pollock, lingcod, scrod, cusk, Cape capensis, whiting
Dolphinfish (mahi mahi)	Saltwater; firm, lean, large flakes, sweet, meaty white-meat	Dorado, mahi (mahi mahi)
Drum	Saltwater; soft, finely textured, mild; a huge family of fish so-named from a muscle that contracts against the air bladder causes a drumming sound	Atlantic croaker, black drum, red drum, kingfish, ocean perch, silver perch, spot, seatrout (weakfish), white sea bass, totuava
Eel	Catadromous; fatty, rich, oily, fine-flaked flesh	American eel, anago, conger, elver (young eel)
Escolar	Saltwater; rich, firm flesh; difficult to digest (portion size should be controlled)	Escolar, snake mackerel, ruvettus (walu), "white tuna"
Flatfish, Atlantic and Pacific	Saltwater; bottom-dwellers; white, lean, delicate flake, mild; Atlantic flatfish (except for Dover sole) are more endangered than Pacific	Atlantic: flounder, fluke, plaice, Atlantic halibut, Dover (English) sole, turbot, lemon sole, gray sole, sand dab Pacific: Petrale sole, Rex sole, Pacific sand dab, Pacific halibut, California halibut
Herring	Saltwater; soft, dark meat, fatty, strong flavor; vary in size; often smoked	Anchovy, herring, sardine, sprat, shad
Icefish	Saltwater; rich, oily, firm, meaty, bright white flesh, large flake; a large order of fish from the deep cold waters under the continental shelf of Antarctica; slow to reproduce so environmentally vulnerable	Chilean sea bass (Patagonian toothfish), merluza negra, mero
Mackerel	Saltwater; rich, delicate flake, dark, assertive flavor, no scales, edible vivid skin; range in size from common mackerel to Spanish mackerel	Mackerel, Spanish mackerel, kingfish, Pacific mackerel, cero, sierra
Monkfish	Saltwater; bottom feeder; meaty, white flesh, sweet; liver a delicacy in Asia	Monkfish, goosefish, anglerfish, angler, molligut, allmouth, lotte
Mullet	Saltwater; soft, mild flesh; spoils quickly; don't confuse with European red mullet (rouget), a different species that is firm and meaty	Mullet, grey mullet, silver mullet, striped mullet, liza, jumping mullet, jumping jac
Perch	Freshwater; a market name for a number of unrelated fish (see Walleye)	Perch, white perch, tallow perch, walleye
Pike	Freshwater; finely textured, dark meat; thick, slimy skin; bony	Pike
Pompano, butterfish	Saltwater; mild, sweet, flaky, sweet-tasting	Pompano, Florida pompano, butterfish, dollarfish, skipjack, sunfish, silver pomfret
Porgy	Saltwater; mild, sweet, white flesh, firm flake; usually cooked whole	Porgy, scup, sea bream, sheepshead, white snapper
Roughy	Saltwater; mild, white meat, firm flesh, large flake	Orange roughy, red roughy, deep sea perch
Sablefish	Saltwater; oily, creamy white, meaty flesh, large firm flake; often smoked	Sable, black cod, blue cod, candlefish, Alaska cod, butterfish

continued on next page

Commom Fish (continued)

Fish Family	Description	Examples
Salmon	Anadromous; red to pink flesh, rich, assertive flavor; wild has more flavor and less fat than farm raised; typically fished when it returns to spawn, which has depleted supplies of wild, except for Alaska; roe used for caviar	Salmon, king salmon, coho salmon, sockeye salmon, Atlantic salmon, Alaskan salmon
Salmon trout, char	Anadromous; red to pink flesh, rich, mild flavor; widely farmed	Arctic char, steelhead
Sculpins	Saltwater; spiny bottom feeders, scaleless, firm white meat; large head, not much meat per fish	Cabezone (bullhead), searobin
Sea bass	Saltwater; white, large flakes, mild, sweet, lean; family includes groupers, which tend to be larger	Sea bass, striped bass, black bass, loup de mer, branzino, grouper, goliath grouper, black grouper, red grouper, rockfish, spotted cabrilla, yellowmouth grouper
Shad	Anadromous; delicate flake, dark, rich, assertive flavor; valued for roe sac	Shad, gulf shad, Atlantic shad (roe sac)
Shark	Saltwater; firm, meaty, strong tasting; can have high mercury levels; fins are valued for their gelatinous consistency	Shark, dogfish
Skate, ray	Saltwater; only wings are eaten; mild, sweet, firm, white flesh	Skate, ray, rajafish
Smelts	Anadromous; small, slender, dark flesh; cooked and eaten whole	Smelt, sparling, candlefish, rainbow smelt
Snapper	Saltwater; white meat, sweet, large flakes, mild	Snapper, red snapper, ruby snapper, gray snapper, rainbow snapper, yellowtail snapper
Sprats	Saltwater; small, slender, dark oily flesh; often smoked	Sprat, New Zealand sprat, Baltic sprat, European sprat, blue sprat
Sturgeon	Anadromous; very large, firm flesh, dark, rich, meaty; U.S. farm-raised is recommended, wild sturgeon are nearing extinction; source of sturgeon caviar (purchase farm-raised or paddlefish caviar)	Sturgeon, beluga, stellate, white sturgeon
Swordfish	Saltwater; huge; dark meat, firm, meaty; assertive flavor	Swordfish, billfish, marlin, sailfish, spearfish
Tilapia	Freshwater; native of North Africa; mild, white meat, firm-fleshed, versatile; best is U.S. farmed, avoid Asian farmed	Tilapia, St. Peter's fish, Nile perch, John Dory
Tilefish	Saltwater; mild, firm, white flesh, meaty; yellow-spotted skin	Tilefish, ocean whitefish, blanquillo, yellow-spotted tilefish
Trout	Freshwater; meaty, tender rainbow are farmed; landlocked relative of salmon	Trout, rainbow trout, brook trout, lake trout
Tuna	Saltwater; dark red, meaty, firm, assertive flavor; often canned	Tuna, albacore, ahi, bigeye, bluefin, skipjack, yellowfin
Wahoo	Saltwater; in the mackerel family, but white meated, leaner, and delicately textured	Ono, Pacific kingfish, ocean barracuda, jack mackerel
Walleye	Freshwater; white meat, mild, lean, large flake	Walleye, yellow walleye, pike-perch (zander)
Whitefish	Freshwater (mostly lakes); white, large flake, mild; frequently smoked; roe used for caviar	Whitefish, cisco, humpback, lake whitefish, inconnu, mountain whitefish
Yellowtail	Saltwater; white, meaty, mild; often farmed; favorite for serving raw	Yellowtail, Japanese amberjack, hamachi

delicate bone structure, lighter-than-water oil content, and strategically placed air bladders, fish are able to attain buoyancy that makes them practically weightless in water.

Although fish are constantly moving, because of their natural buoyancy steady cruising in water does not take much effort. More important is the ability to accelerate quickly when pursuing prey or escaping a predator. Fish need two types of muscle fibers to accomplish both kinds of movement: red muscle for slow, steady movement and white for quick response. Most fish have more than 70% white muscle and most white-fleshed fish are 90% white muscle.

Fish skin is protected by a mucus layer that gives freshly caught fish a slimy surface, which dries quickly once they are out of water. By the time fish arrive at retail their skin is dry, and any subsequent sliminess is a sign of decay. Most fish skin is about 10% fat and is high in connective tissue, which makes it tougher and richer than fish flesh. Generally, fish skin is about 30% collagen, and therefore contributes far more gelatin to fish broths than either meat or bones. Wet-cooking techniques, like poaching, turn fish skin thick and gelatinous; grilling or frying make it crisp.

Fish bones are smaller and thinner and have far less calcium than the bones of land animals. The skeleton consists of a backbone attached to the head and tail at either end, and a rib cage near the head. When boning a fish, the skeleton can be lifted out in one piece. Fish also have a small line of bones projecting from the fins, and very small pin bones that don't attach to the main skeleton. These can be removed with pliers, if necessary. (If the fish is well cooked they will dissolve.)

Unlike the muscle fibers of land animals, which are arranged in bundles, fish muscle fibers are structured in thin layers. The layers are separated from one another by collagen fibers that run from the skeleton to the skin. When fish cooks, the muscle fibers become firm and the collagen softens, resulting in "flaking" (the separation of one layer of muscle fibers from another), which is the sign that fish is cooked.

Collagen gives fish flesh a moist, rich mouth feel. Fish with less collagen, like trout, seem drier than fish with abundant collagen, like halibut. Collagen tends to be concentrated in the tail end of the fish, where stronger swimming muscles are required, so a fish steak taken from the tail is noticeably moister than one taken from closer to the head. Fat also adds to the perception of moisture, and fish with higher fat content — the herring family, for example — are perceptibly moister than leaner fish, even when well cooked.

Saltwater and freshwater fish taste very different. Because ocean fish take in salt water through their gills and digestive tract, they evolved a way to maintain the right balance of salt in their bodily fluids. Most fish and shellfish equalize sodium content in their bodies by increasing the amount of amino acids and amines in their muscle tissue. The amino acid glycine is sweet tasting and has an umami (see **Flavor**) taste. The balance of sweet, savory, and salty created by the blending of amino acids and salt water is responsible for much of the flavor appeal of seafood.

Although glycine provides desirable flavors, other amino acids and amines are responsible for undesirable fishy aromas. Marine fish contain a large amount of the trimethylamine N-oxide (TMAO). Sharks and rays build up urea (a protein waste product) to balance sodium. Both of these substances are converted to smelly trimethylamine when a fish is killed, and that breaks down to ammonia over time, which accounts for the noxious smell of old fish.

Japanese scientists have found that antioxidant-rich ingredients, such as green tea, keep TMAO from breaking down. Trimethylamine on the surface of fish can be rinsed away with water. You can also coat an over-the-hill fish with lemon juice or some other acid, which will bind trimethylamine to the fish molecules so it never escapes to your nose. This explains the traditional techniques of poaching fish in acidic liquids, or dipping fish in buttermilk before frying. Freshwater fish live in water that is less salty than their cells, so they never develop high levels of amino acids, amines, or urea.

The real challenge to cooking fish is retaining moisture because fish protein is easily overcooked. If the proteins get too hot, moisture is squeezed out and the result is dry, flaky fish. Whereas the meat of land animals begins to lose moisture between 140 and 160°F (60 and 71°C), most seafood will be completely dried out at 140°F (60°C). In most cases fish should be cooked to between 130 and 140°F (54 and 60°C). Some fish with a lot of connective tissue, like sharks, need to be cooked to the upper end of that range, because collagen will not turn to gelatin much before 140°F (60°C).

See Also • Caviar, Drying, Fat, Fermentation, Gelatin, Meat, Protein

FISH SAUCE • See Fermentation

FIVE-SPICE POWDER • See Fennel, Spices

FLATBREAD • See Bread

FLATFISH • See Fish

FLAVONES • See Pigment

FLAVONOID • See Antioxidants

FLAVOR

What It Is • Everyone thinks they know what flavor is. After all, we experience flavor every time we eat, but how often do we ever consider what those flavorful impressions mean? Is flavor more than mere sensation?

Flavor perception is a key to our survival. It leads us to make healthful food choices and steers us away from things that might harm us. Wholesome foods, like ripe fruits and fresh dairy, taste sweet. Toxins taste bitter. So we are programmed as a species to go after sweet foods and reject bitter ones. We're also attracted to saltiness because sodium is an essential nutrient that we have to take in every day, and we're repelled by sourness, the taste of underripe fruit and spoiled protein.

Those are some of the ground rules, but they hardly account for all that's going on in our heads when we take a bite of food.

What It Does • Flavor is a mixture of taste and smell. Remove either pathway and flavor diminishes.

Your mouth recognizes five tastes — sweet, salty, sour, bitter, and savory (called umami). You are probably familiar with four of the five: sweet (the taste of sugar), salty (the taste of table salt, sodium chloride), sour (the taste of white distilled vinegar), and bitter (the taste of quinine or tonic). Umami tastes savory like roasted meat, aged cheese, or sautéed mushrooms. If you want to isolate taste from flavor, hold your nostrils closed when you eat. By eliminating aroma, all you will perceive are the five mouth tastes. In reality, taste and aroma don't live in isolation, but with your nose held when you take a bite of an apple, your mouth will taste sweet sugars, tart acids, and not much else. In fact, without smelling, it's difficult to tell the difference between fruits with similar textures, like apple and pear, because almost everything that "tastes" distinctive about food isn't taste at all, it's aroma.

Our noses are more sensitive than our tongues. We have about 40 million olfactory neurons picking up odors from the air and from food vapors traveling up to the nose from the back of the mouth. In comparison to the five tastes perceived on the tongue, our perception of aromas is nearly infinite and accounts for the bulk of the sensations we call flavor.

Many foods, like fruits, are loaded with aromatic molecules and have strong aromas even when raw. Other foods have little flavor until they are cooked, or very different flavors after cooking. For example, beef is quite mild when raw, but develops rich complex aromatics from Maillard reactions (see **Browning**) that occur during roasting.

How It Works • Flavor sensations are chemical reactions. We taste and smell when receptors in our mouth and nose are stimulated by chemicals in food.

Taste

Taste receptors all over the mouth pick up all five tastes. Taste buds are concentrated over the top surface of the tongue, but taste buds also run across the back of the soft palate (the roof of the mouth) and on the epiglottis (the flap in the back of your throat that keeps swallowed food from entering your windpipe). It is a matter of debate whether individual receptors are specialized to one taste, but it is agreed that taste buds are more versatile in their taste reception than was once believed.

Taste buds sit on papillae, small projections that cover the tongue and give it a rough texture. The human tongue has about 10,000 taste buds. Each one is shaped like a little cup and has a ring of supporting cells arranged like the staves of a barrel. The gustatory cells, the ones that pick up taste, are packed in the "barrel" surrounding an opening with a hair-like filament (cilium) projecting from the center. When chewed food contacts a taste bud, the cilium picks up the taste molecules and transfers them to the gustatory cells, which react to the molecules and pass the sensation into nerve fibers that travel to the brain, where the taste is perceived.

Smell

Olfactory cells are high up in the nose and pick up aromas. They are completely covered with cilia, and those cilia are covered with olfactory receptors. It's a massive system, with millions of receptor cells packed into a very small space. The olfactory epithelium (the odor-receiving tissue in the nose) measures about 1 inch (2.5 cm) wide by 2 inches (5 cm) long. Olfactory receptors can bind to a variety of aromatic molecules with varying affinities, giving humans the ability to distinguish almost infinite combinations of aromatic chemicals.

Once a smell is captured, nerve fibers ascending from the olfactory receptor cells come together in the olfactory bulb, a structure in the front of brain that processes olfactory input. The short pathway between odor reception in the nose and odor perception in the brain is one reason why smell perception is so immediate. The olfactory bulb is close to the hippocampus, an area of the brain involved with place memory, which is why the smell of an attic or a whiff of ocean air brings back childhood adventures more vividly than any visual or auditory stimulus could.

Flavor

Aroma chemicals are volatile, which means they are small enough and light enough to float through the air. Taste chemicals are larger and typically water soluble. Aroma chemicals are more similar to oils than to water, and are therefore usually fat soluble.

When we first put food into our mouth, those flavors that are already dissolved in liquid (a sauce, for instance) hit the taste buds first. At the same time, the volatile components of the sauce travel up the back of the throat to the olfactory receptors, and we pick up the aromas in the sauce. Then, as we chew, flavor chemicals trapped in the cells of solid food like meat and vegetables are released.

Salt-sensing receptors in the taste buds react to more molecules than just sodium chloride (table salt). Most molecules that contain either sodium or chlorine will taste salty to a greater or lesser degree. Most 20-year-olds can identify saltiness in a 0.05% saline solution. People over 60 generally need twice that concentration to detect saltiness, about 1%. Most canned soups are formulated to be about 1% salt.

Women tend to have better olfactory senses than men, and many women report increased sensitivity to smells during ovulation and pregnancy. It is estimated that 4.5 million North Americans have hyposmia (reduced ability to perceive odors) or anosmia (an inability to smell), and almost everyone has experienced temporary anosmia due to congestion. Inability to smell causes loss of appetite, reduced sexual drive, and depression.

fast facts

- Dogs have 100 times more odor receptors per square centimeter of olfactory membrane than humans. Bloodhounds, the breed with the most advanced sense of smell, can perceive aromas 100 million times better than a human.
- Fish can smell in water. Salmon use their sense of smell to return to their home stream for spawning.

The variability in people's ability to perceive tastes and smells probably accounts for the wide diversity of food preferences and may account for why some people smell fermented odors, like fish sauce or truffles, as delicious while others perceive them as rotted.

Flavor perception is complex. Though we tend to think of the aroma of a particular fruit or herb as just one thing, it is always a combination of several aromatic compounds. The following entry on Flavor Compounds explains the topic in depth.

Astringency and Pungency

The dry, puckered feeling that comes across the tongue when we bite into underripe fruit or take a mouthful of strong tea is neither taste nor aroma. It's tactile, caused by tannins, phenolic compounds (see **Flavor Compounds**) that bond proteins together. They have been used for centuries to tan leather (hence their name), a process that forms bonds between the proteins in animal hides, causing them to toughen. In the mouth, tannins bond to proteins in saliva, making it lose its slippery, lubricating quality. Unlike flavor perception that tends to dull with repeated tastes, astringent reactions become stronger with each dose of tannins. In small doses astringency can be pleasant, giving an added dimension to the experience of eating, but too much becomes overpowering, so we tend to balance astringency with sweetness, adding sugar to tea, or serving melted sweet butter with artichokes.

The irritating or painful sensations caused by chiles, peppers, ginger, mustard, and radishes come from chemical defenses in these plants that cause mild damage to the sensitive membranes in our mouth and nasal passages, causing alternating sensations of burning and cooling. Thiocyanates in mustards (allyl isothiocyanate) and radishes, like horseradish (sinigrin) and wasabi (methylthiohexyl isothiocyanate), are small molecules, so they tend to affect nerves in the nose. Alkylamides in chiles (capsaicin), black pepper (piperine), and ginger (gingerol, shogaols) are heavier, and tend to stay in the mouth.

See Also ● Browning, Capsicum, Flavor Compounds, Food Additives

FLAVOR COMPOUNDS

What It Is • Flavor scientists have identified thousands of **flavor** chemicals, and have broken down complex aromas, like those of strawberries or coffee, into the individual aromatic chemicals that make up a smell in an attempt to build aromas and flavors that copy nature.

What It Does • Creating artificial flavors is not easy, and it is hardly ever completely effective. For even though scientists can capture flavor molecules in concentrations of a few parts per billion, their analyses are not fine enough to allow them to create artificial flavors that duplicate the real thing. Apparently our flavor-sensing system can respond to chemicals that even the most sophisticated piece of scientific equipment can't capture.

Give it a try. Take a bite of something, chew it, and hold it in your mouth as you try to pick apart the component flavors that form the whole. Basil is floral, sweet, minty, and anise-like, with a hint of eucalyptus and clove. Rosemary smells like mentholated pine, and vanilla is floral, sweet, and slightly spicy like nutmeg.

Sensory scientists have tools to guide them. Their main one, other than a perceptive nose and mouth and good powers of articulation, is a flavor wheel. Constructed similarly to color wheels used by painters, flavor wheels look like wagon wheels, with flavor characteristics arranged like spokes. When analyzing the flavor of a food, the researcher marks a point on each spoke. A mark near the perimeter of the wheel indicates strong intensity; a mark closer to the hub means that characteristic was more subtle. Connecting the dots creates a starburst design, called a flavor profile depicting the flavor sensations of that food.

The characteristics that make up a flavor wheel change with the food being tasted. For instance, a coffee flavor wheel would include spokes for floral and fruity flavors, but one for tasting fish would not. In general, the flavor characteristics on a flavor wheel are:

Green (Grassy), Fruity (Ester-like), Citrus, Minty (Camphoraceus), Floral (Sweet), Spicy (Herbaceous), Woody (Smoky), Roasted (Burnt), Caramel (Nutty), Bouillon (HVP), Meaty (Animal-like), Fatty (Rancid), Dairy (Buttery), Mushroom (Earthy), Celery (Soup-like), Sulfurous (Cabbage-like)

Because so much of flavor perception is aroma, we tend to use terms from the perfume industry to describe food flavors. We speak of "top notes," meaning those aromas that hit the nose quickly and then dissipate; "mid-notes," the main body of the flavor; and "bottom notes," those that develop as you hold food in the mouth and that linger long after you swallow.

How It Works • In order to effectively use the hundreds of aromatic chemicals that interplay in building the flavor of food, flavor scientists categorize them by how they function. Esters, for example, are compounds that are responsible for most of the light sweet top-note aromas of fruits. On the other hand, fatty acids are strong and pungent, making up the mid- and bottom notes in fermented cheese and gamy meats.

The classes of flavor compounds are:

Acids — Carboxylic acids have a pungent sour smell that is evident in many cheeses. This group includes common organic acids like acetic acid (the acidic flavor of vinegar) and less well known but equally recognizable compounds like propionic acid, which has a sour rancid smell, and is the dominant odor in Emmental cheese. The pungency of fatty acids disappears when they react with alcohols and become sweet fruity esters. For example, butyric acid (which accounts for the rancid smell of butter) when combined with an alcohol becomes the fruity aroma in

science wise

Chirality • In chemistry chirality refers to molecules that are not superimposable on each other — they are mirror images. In terms of aroma, chirality can make the same molecule smell different, depending on which direction it is facing in the olfactory receptor. For instance the terpene *l*-carvone, smells like spearmint but *d*-carvone (its mirror image) smells like caraway seed.

pineapples and strawberries (ethyl butyrate), in apples and pineapples (methyl butyrate), in apricots (pentyl butyrate), or in cherries (geranyl butyrate).

Alcohols — Alcohols can form floral, fruity, or fermented flavors depending on their molecular weight and what other molecules they react with. Alcohols with lower molecular weight are soluble in water and are volatile and flavorful. Ethyl maltol, the flavor of caramelized sugar and cooked fruit, is an example. As their molecular weight increases, alcohols become oily and more subtle. Decanol, the flavor of orange blossoms, and menthol are large alcohols. Alcohol molecules generate different flavors when they react with other molecules. For example, benzyl alcohol is the aroma of jasmine and hyacinth, but when it reacts with an aldehyde it becomes benzaldehyde, which is almond flavor.

Aldehydes — Aldehydes are a varied group of flavor compounds that are similar to both acids and alcohols and therefore react easily with both. Aldehydes can be floral, fruity, grassy, nutty, toasted, coffee-like, or chocolaty. One of the most commonly used aldehydes is vanillin, the flavor of vanilla. Some, like ethyl cinnamaldehyde in cinnamon, or methyl salicylate (oil of wintergreen), are so pungent they tend to dominate other flavors in a plant.

Flavor Profile for Strawberry Shortcake

This is the flavor profile of a strawberry shortcake. A sensory scientist could compare this profile to other profiles of strawberry shortcake to see how a particular product meets a standard. Another strawberry shortcake profile might be higher in fruity flavors and lower in dairy flavors. It could have more caramel flavor if the shortcake in the sample was baked more thoroughly. Or it could be higher in green flavors if the strawberries used were less ripe. All of these samples would have flavor profiles of different shapes.

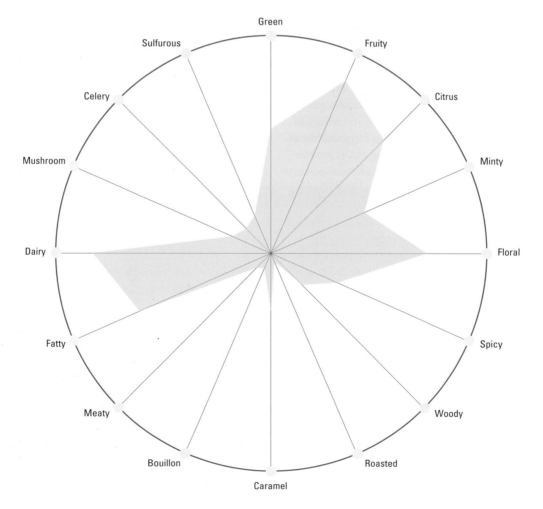

Esters — Esters are a combination of two molecules — an alcohol and an acid. Acids give vegetables and fruits tartness, and they are part of the fatty acid structure of vegetable oils. Alcohols are mostly by-products of cell metabolism in plants. Fruits in particular contain enzymes that cause acids and alcohols to combine to form aromatic esters. Apple flavor is a combination of seven esters. But banana contains just a few strong-smelling esters that give it a less complex but stronger aromatic profile.

Ketones — Ketones are polar molecules that are highly soluble in water and form bonds easily with other molecules. The acetyl-based ketones are quite subtle, giving jasmine and basmati rice their floral fragrance. Others become more pronounced from browning, giving popping corn or toasting tortillas their pleasant aroma. Some ketones produce strong dairy aromas, from the sweet, tangy aroma of cottage cheese and sour cream to the more pungent notes of blue cheese.

Iones — This subgroup of ketones produces fruit and berry flavors.

Lactones — Lactones are cyclic esters with their acid component derived from lactic acid, one of the carboxylic acids in milk. Lactones contribute to the flavors of cream, butter, honey, wine, and coconut. They are frequently added to margarine, shortening, and some baked goods to give them buttery flavors.

Phenols — Phenolic compounds account for many of the defining aromatic characteristics of spices and herbs. Eugenol, the flavor of clove, is in allspice, basil, bay leaf, cinnamon, clove, and galangal to varied degrees. Anethole is in anise, fennel, and star anise, and sotolon, a spicy caramel-tasting phenol, is in maple syrup, molasses, and tobacco. Capsaicin, the pungent part of chiles, is a phenol, as are the polyphenols in tannins.

Pyrazines — Pyrazines have the rich flavors of roasted nuts, chocolate, and browned meats. They bond easily with alcohols and acids and frequently are found in combination with them or with esters. In strong concentration they can taste musty, earthy, or fishy.

Sulfur compounds — Sulfur-containing compounds give alliums, cabbages, radishes, and mustard some of their pungency. When concentrated, sulfur compounds can be off-putting or can irritate membranes in the nose, eye, and mouth, but in small concentrations they provide an acid brightness. Much of the aromatics in roasted coffee beans come from mercaptans, which are sulfur compounds.

Terpenes – Terpenes are especially versatile, occurring in the volatile oils of many fruits and vegetables, most notably in herbs. They are volatile, which means they tend to play as top notes, providing an initial hit of light aroma, and then dissipate quickly. Most frequently terpenes have piney, woody, spicy, or citrus-like aromas. Some examples are caryophyllene, which is one of the spicy elements in allspice, black pepper, cinnamon, and clove; cineole, which gives a eucalyptus-like cooling effect to allspice, basil, bay leaf, cardamom, cubeb pepper, galangal, ginger, spearmint, and sage; citral, the citrus scent in coriander and lemongrass; and geraniol, the spicy floral quality in many tropical plants like galangal, lemongrass, and Szechwan pepper.

See Also • Extracts, Flavor

FLAVORING EXTRACTS • See Extracts

FLAVORING OILS • See Extracts

FLOUNDER • See Fish

FLOUR

What It Is • Flour is made from finely ground seeds. Most of those seeds are **grains**, the nutritious fruits from grasses, including **wheat**, barley, oats, rye, **rice**, **corn**, sorghum, and millet. Much less often flours are milled from beans (the seeds of legumes), for example mung bean or chickpea flour, or **nuts** (the seeds of a variety of plants, usually long-lived hardwood trees), like almond or walnut meal.

Non-Wheat Flours

Flour	Description	Uses
Amaranth flour	Finely ground amaranth grain, high in protein, especially the amino acid lysine.	Used in small amounts (no more than 10%) to add nutrition to any baked product or pasta
Barley flour	Barley flour can be whole grain (called dehulled barley flour) or polished (called pearled barley flour). Barley contains a relatively large quantity (about 5% by weight) of two nonstarch carbohydrates. Arabinoxylans are medium-sized sugar aggregates that can absorb large amounts of water. They remain soft during baking, giving baked goods made with barley flour a long shelf life. Glucans are similarly structured. They also absorb and hold a lot of water, which keeps baked goods moist. Glucans have been shown to lower blood cholesterol levels.	Can replace part of wheat flour (no more than 20%) in any baked product
Buckwheat flour	Buckwheat is technically a fruit and has a soft coating that is frequently ground with the starchy endosperm. The specks of hull give it a dark appearance and a nutty fragrance. Buckwheat flour is gluten free.	Japanese buckwheat noodles (soba), buckwheat pancakes, blinis
Chickpea flour	A specialty flour that is high in carbohydrate, protein, and oil. It goes by several names: gram flour, chana flour and besan in India; ceci flour in Sicily, and garbanzo flour in Spain. Chickpea flour is gluten free.	Panelle (Sicilian chickpea fritters), pappadam (Indian cracker-flatbreads), pakoras (Indian fritters), farinata (Ligurian pancakes), socca (southern French flatbread)
Corn flour	Ground dried whole-grain corn comes in a variety of colors — yellow, white, red, or blue (called atole flour). Cornmeal is more coarsely ground than corn flour. Masa harina is corn flour made from nixtamalized (lye-soaked) corn. Cornstarch is the isolated starch of corn and is used in small amounts as a thickener for sauces or as an addition in a baking recipe to make the flour mixture softer. In Britain, cornstarch is called cornflour. Corn products are gluten free.	Corn flour — corn muffins, bread, or pancakes Cornmeal — same as corn flour when mixed with wheat flour, also cornmeal mush or polenta, breading, dusting baking pans Masa harina — tortillas, tamales, pupusas Cornstarch — thickening sauces
Flaxseed flour	A nutty-tasting flour that is high in protein (30%), dietary fiber, and the omega-3 fatty acid linoleic acid. Flaxseed flour is gluten free.	Used in small amounts (no more than 10%) to add nutrition to any baked product
Nut flours	Almonds, chestnuts, hazelnuts, or walnuts ground to a fine powder. Nut flours are gluten free.	Flourless cakes (tortes) or cookies (macaroons), or added to cakes, cookies, and breads for nutrition, flavor, and texture; also breading
Oat flour	Oat flour is high in glucans, which absorb and hold water, keeping baked products moist for days. They also help to lower LDL cholesterol. Glucans are especially concentrated in oat bran. Oat flour has antioxidant properties, and although it contains a small amount of gluten-making protein it is allowed in some gluten-free diets.	Used in small to moderate amounts (no more than 5 to 20%) to add moisture to breads, cakes, and cookies
Potato flour	Potato flour is made by washing ground potato pulp to get rid of the fiber. The resulting paste is dried and ground into flour. It has some protein but is mostly starch. Not to be confused with potato starch, which is 100% starch.	Added to any baked good in small amounts (no more than 10%); used for thickening sauces and purées
Quinoa flour	Quinoa and the flour ground from it are high in protein (about 15%), and their amino-acid balance is complete. The grain is high in fiber and gluten free.	Used in any baked product in moderate amounts (no more than 20%); popular in muffins, pancakes, and bread

Rice flour	Available whole grain and white. It is mostly starch and has the smallest starch granule of all grains, so it thickens liquids smoothly. Rice flour is not very absorbent, so it makes very thin, crisp frying batter. Rice flour is gluten free.	Tempura, sauces, rice paper, neer dosa (Indian rice crêpes), roti (Indian flatbread)
Rye flour	Rye contains a high percentage (about 7% of its weight) of arabinoxylans, allowing it to absorb and hold eight times its weight in water. Arabinoxylans stay soft during baking, giving rye products a moist, plush consistency. Pumpernickel is a mixture of rye flour and coarsely ground rye meal.	Added to savory baked products, usually breads, for flavor, nutrition, and texture. Light rye flour can be 40% of the flour in a product, medium rye 30%, and dark rye no more than 25%. Due to the moisture-retention qualities of rye, rye breads stay moist.
Teff flour	Teff flour is high in dietary fiber, protein, iron, and calcium. It has a slightly sour taste. Most teff is grown in Ethiopia. Teff is gluten free.	Injera (Ethiopian flatbread)

What It Does

Seeds contain everything a plant needs to create life. They are packed with nutrition for the plant and for us. When whole seeds or grains (the entire grain, bran, germ, and endosperm) are ground into flour, all of their fiber, protein, carbohydrates, and essential lipids become readily available. However, most of the flour sold in North America today is not made from whole grains. For various reasons, the grains have been refined, which means the bran and the germ, where almost all of the vitamins and minerals reside, have been removed, leaving the largest part of the grain, the endosperm.

Before the advent of modern milling techniques, whole-grain flours were the norm, but they were peppered with debris — bits of stone, dirt, and insects. The only way to clean them was to sieve out the trash. Because the endosperm is soft, it grinds into smaller particles than the rest of the grain (and the debris). Early millers in Europe found that by passing flour through sieves of various sizes, the grain could be separated from its refuse, which made white flours the choice of privileged classes (hence the term "refined") and whole-grain flours the ingredient of peasants . However, the more fibrous parts of the grain, the bran and the germ, also stayed in bigger pieces, so they were discarded with the trash, along with their valuable nutrients. Interestingly, when white flour production was threatened during the Second World War, the British government outlawed white bread, replacing it with a rough whole-grain bread, nicknamed "the National Loaf." Surprisingly, during a time of deprivation, the mean nutrition level improved, just the opposite of what would have been expected. While whole-grain flours have all the nutrition a grain has to offer, they also have elements that can make baked goods heavy (bran) or more perishable (germ). White flours, milled from just the endosperm, make lighter, smoother baked products, and they have become the standard flours for baking in the industrialized world.

Although any grain can be ground into flour, the most common is wheat, because it has a unique ability to stretch and rise. Its **gluten**-generating properties produce aerated chewy breads, high-risen cakes with delicate, buttery crumbs, and flaky pastries. Because other grains can't compete, when we speak of how flour works in baking, we are speaking almost exclusively of the properties of wheat flours. Other flours can be added to wheat to create texture and flavor, or to boost nutrition, but usually it is in small enough amounts to ensure that the dough's raising capacity isn't damaged.

White wheat flour is made into a variety of flour products depending on the strain of wheat from which it is milled, and how its component parts — its **starch** and protein — are blended.

- *Bread flour* is milled from high-protein wheat, called hard wheat, which is why bread flour is sometimes called hard wheat flour or strong flour. Bread flour has a protein content above 12%.

- *Cake flour (aka cake-and-pastry flour or soft flour)* is milled from low-protein wheat, called soft wheat. It has a protein content between 6 and 9%.
- *Pastry flour* has 8 to 10% protein, falling between the content of hard and soft flours. In Canada, cake flour and pastry flour are often sold as cake-and-pastry flour.
- *All-purpose flour (aka plain flour)* has between 10 and 11% protein. As its name implies, it is meant to be all things to all bakers. It is the preferred choice for most home baking (professional bakers tend to use a variety of flours with different protein contents). Flour mills vary the protein content of all-purpose flour to the type of baking that is most popular in a specific sales region. For that reason, all-purpose flour in Canada and most of the U.S. is higher in protein than the all-purpose flour sold in the South and Pacific Northwest of the U.S. Whether bleached or unbleached, all-purpose flour in Canada and most of the U.S. tends to be milled from hard winter wheat and is relatively high in protein (10 to 13%). All-purpose flour in the Pacific Northwest and southern U.S. tends to be milled from soft wheat and is lower in protein (9 to 11%).
- *Self-rising flour (aka self-raising cake flour)* contains added baking powder, 1½ teaspoons (7 mL) per cup (250 mL).
- *High-gluten flour (aka pasta flour or durum semolina)* is milled from durum, a particularly hard wheat that is about 14% protein. Semolina is the name for milled durum endosperm that has a coarse particle size, similar to cornmeal. The coarseness of semolina results from the hardness of the wheat. If the flour were ground finer, the starch would get damaged.
- *Wheat gluten (aka vital wheat gluten)* is the isolated protein of the wheat endosperm. It is highly concentrated and is used to bolster the gluten content of baked products. Usually a tablespoon or two (15 to 25 mL) is added to a bread recipe to make the dough more elastic.
- *Instant or "instantized" flours* are low-protein flours designed for thickening **sauces** and

thin batters without lumping. They have been moistened and cooked until their starches gelate, then are dried and ground. It is easier for water to penetrate these porous structures, making them less likely to bond into lumps.
- *Graham flour* is white flour to which wheat bran, and sometimes wheat germ, is added back after grinding. Because the bran and germ are ground separately, they can be coarser than the rest of the flour, giving products made with graham flour a pleasantly gritty texture.

In Europe, white wheat flours are classified by ash mass, rather than protein, as in North America, although the higher the ash, the higher the protein. Ash mass measures mineral content. Since most of the minerals in wheat are in the bran, the ash mass roughly correlates with the amount of bran in the flour. White flour contains a minimum of bran, but in Europe the amount of bran that ends up in white flour is about 10% higher than in North America.

There are several varieties of whole wheat flours:
- *Whole wheat flour* is milled whole grain. It contains the bran, germ, and endosperm of the grain and has a nutty taste, brown color, and more protein, fiber, B vitamins, calcium, phosphorus, magnesium, zinc, manganese, iron (unless it is fortified) copper, selenium and potassium than white flour. Whole wheat flour is milled from hard (high-protein) red wheat.

- *White whole wheat flour (aka whole meal flour)* is milled from hard white wheat that has a little less protein than traditional red wheat. The flour has similar nutrition and baking properties to regular whole wheat flour, except it is milder and paler.
- *Whole wheat pastry flour* is milled from soft (low-protein) red wheat with a protein content of about 9%. It is designed for making delicate cookies and pastries that would be toughened by excessive gluten.

Don't compare the protein content of whole wheat flour with white flour. Whole wheat may be high in protein (about 15%), but that doesn't mean it will make chewy bread and al dente pasta. Much of the added protein comes from the bran and the germ, which do not form gluten. In addition, ground bran is rough and has a tendency to interrupt the formation of gluten in dough.

A rise in the number of cases of gluten intolerance (celiac disease) has focused attention on gluten-free baked products. Although avoiding gluten largely means avoiding wheat, other grains such as barley, rye, and (for some people) oats contain small amounts of gluten and may not be tolerated. The Non-Wheat Flours chart (see page 240) lists basic qualities of non-wheat flours, most of which are acceptable for someone on a gluten-free diet. When baking with gluten-free grains, long-chain carbohydrates, like xanthan gum or guar gum, are often added to the flour to help make the dough elastic enough so that it can be leavened.

How It Works • Freshly milled flour makes weak gluten, so millers typically age flour for a few weeks to improve its baking abilities. As flour ages, its protein oxidizes, which makes it more likely to form longer gluten chains when mixed into dough. But it is expensive to store flour, so around 1900, millers found a way to shorten the aging cycle by mixing freshly milled flour with oxidizing agents (called improving agents) like chlorine gas, ascorbic acid, and potassium bromate. Bromated flour was phased out in much of the world in the 1980s after studies showed that bromate residues in flour could be hazardous. However, bromated flour is still available in the U.S. and Japan.

In addition to improving the gluten-making properties of flour, oxidation changes xanthophyll pigments in flour, causing its color to pale from golden yellow to creamy white. To artificially whiten flours, millers treat the flour with bleaching agents, benzoyl peroxide or chlorine gas. You can assume that all flour that is not labeled "unbleached" contains bleaching agents. Although the Europeans and British avoid chlorinated flours because of health concerns, the World Health Organization considers chlorinated flour safe.

Flour mills have long supplemented white wheat flour with malted grain, which is loaded with enzymes that help break starches into sugars. These enzymes make flour sweeter and give yeast an added energy boost in bread making. Because malt flours are dark in color, some manufacturers replace them with purified enzyme extracts (fungal amylase).

See Also • Baking, Bread, Cake, Corn, Gluten, Grains, Rice, Sauces, Starch, Wheat

FLOWERS

What It Is • Flowers are attractive by design. Their vivid colors and provocative aromas exist for one reason only — sex. Flowers are a plant's sex organs. It is here where male pollen, carried on insects attracted by floral charms, meets female ovule. Many flowers are completely edible, and some are even delicious (see Edible Flowers, page 245). Some flowers are eaten fully matured, when their color and perfume are at their height. But take care: although most flowers are beautiful, some have chemical defense mechanisms that make them toxic. Azalea blossoms cause vomiting, foxglove flowers cause heart arrhythmia, and delicate hemlock blossoms are fatal. Flowers can also be cultivated as vegetables. Broccoli, cauliflower, and artichoke are examples.

What It Does • Edible blossoms are a striking salad garnish or cake decoration, but many are more than just decorative. Floral flavors add complexity to sweet dishes and delicate savories, and are popular in many cuisines. Flower waters, most often made from roses and citrus blossoms, are the water-soluble portion of floral distillation. Rose water (aka rose syrup) and orange-flower water are used heavily in Asian and Middle Eastern cooking, especially in sweets. They are added to beverages, ice creams, and candies and often flavor soaking syrups for cakes and pastries. Rose water is the distinctive flavor in *gulab jamun*, the fried dough treat of India, Pakistan, and Bangladesh.

Flower butters, a form of composed butter for topping poached seafood and poultry, are made by crushing flower petals with sweet butter and allowing the fat to absorb the flower's perfume. Flower oils and vinegars, made by steeping bruised petals in warm oil or vinegar, are used in sauces, dressings, and baking and as condiments to drizzle on food after cooking. Flower-scented sugar, made by crushing petals with sugar crystals, is an exotic flavoring for cake icing or tea, and whole flower petals frozen in ice cubes add an exotic touch to chilled drinks. Flower petal jellies are made by simmering petals in sugar syrup.

Spectacular crystallized flowers, used to adorn wedding cakes and other opulent desserts, are made by brushing petals with lightly beaten egg white, dusting them with sugar, and allowing them to dry until the egg white solidifies. Only perfect flowers can be crystallized. Even a slight amount of bruising will cause water to leach from the petals and dissolve the sugar coating. One of the most unusual edible flowers is the caper. Caper flowers are quite large, with showy white petals surrounding a heart of thread-like violet stamens. Caper flowers are usually eaten long before they bloom, when they are still immature buds. Caper buds are typically salted or brined and pickled and are used as a piquant seasoning in Mediterranean dishes. Capers are sold by size, the smallest being preferable. Sizes from small to large are: nonpareil, surfines, capucines, capotes, fines, and grusas. Caper berries, also edible, are the fruit of the bush, not the flower.

How It Works • Flower flavor is almost all fragrance, and quite volatile. Even a short period of cooking causes the flavor to vaporize and it is lost. Capturing the fragrance in butter, oil, vinegar, or syrup is a way of stabilizing it, and accounts for the popularity of floral extracts. When cooking with fresh flowers, it is best to add them at the end or use them uncooked for garnish.

A few flowers are toxic, but many cause allergic reactions. Anyone who is sensitive to pollen should probably avoid eating flowers, and whenever flowers are added to a dish the pollen sacs should be removed. Marigolds and daylilies should be eaten sparingly.

Flowers grown for display are commonly sprayed with pesticide, and they are not intended for cooking or eating, even if the flower type is edible. If you do not know the source of an edible flower, do not use it.

See Also • Extracts

Edible Flowers

Flower	Description	Flavor
Allium	Pink to purple short, firm, stick-like petals	Onion; use in salads or as soup garnish
Apple	White to pink small radiating petals (can contain cyanide precursors, so eat in moderation)	Floral; garnish or candied
Basil	White, pink, or lavender tiny petals	Basil with citrus notes
Borage	Pale blue triangular petals	Cucumber
Calendula (marigold)	Golden orange short plump petals	Peppery and tangy
Carnation	White to deep red petals	Light clove
Chamomile	Pale yellow small daisy-like petals	Sweet apple-like
Chervil	White, delicate, tiny blossoms	Light anise
Chrysanthemum	White, yellow, orange, and red spiky petals	Tangy and peppery
Citrus blossoms (orange, lemon, lime, grapefruit, kumquat)	White to golden firm, round petals; often distilled into flavor extract	Citrus
Clover	Pale purple ball-shaped flower	Sweet anise
Cornflower	Pale blue soft round petals	Sweet, slightly spicy
Daisy	White or yellow narrow petals	Mildly bitter, edible but not delicious
Dandelion	Yellow spiky petals	Sweet, honey-like
Daylilies (not other lilies)	Deep orange, white, or yellow large petals (can be a diuretic or laxative, so eat in moderation)	Mild, melon-like, slightly sweet
Gladiolus	Any color, large, cup-shaped blossom	Mild and bland
Hibiscus	White, pink, yellow, or crimson large showy trumpet-shaped blossoms	Citrus and cranberry
Honeysuckle	White to yellow tiny, cup-shaped blossoms	Honey
Jasmine	Creamy white tiny blossom	Sweet floral; very aromatic
Johnny-jump-ups	White, yellow, or purple two-tiered blossom	Mild mint
Lavender	Pale purple small blossoms	Sweet floral; very aromatic
Lemon verbena	Creamy white tiny blossoms	Citrus
Lilac	Pink to purple tiny blossoms	Slightly bitter, lemony; very aromatic
Linden	White to yellow small blossoms (frequent consumption can cause heart damage so eat in moderation)	Honey
Nasturtium	White to bright orange trumpet-shaped blossom	Sweet and peppery
Pansy	White, yellow, or purple two-tiered blossom	Sweet and mild
Peony	White to deep red soft, rose-like petals	Sweet, floral
Rose	All colors, soft, velvety petals	Highly floral and aromatic
Squash blossoms	Yellow to pale orange blossoms	Mild squash flavor; often stuffed and fried
Thyme	Pale purple tiny blossoms	Mild thyme flavor
Violet	Pale to deep purple small blossoms	Sweet, floral

FOAMS

What It Is ●
Ephemeral as air, culinary foams are there and not there. Appearing voluminous on the plate, they vanish on the palate like something imagined. Foams are simply sauces thickened with air, but that in itself can seem like magic. How can a fluid sauce gain substance from a substance that has no substance at all?

The classic edible foam, sabayon or zabaglione, an inflated amalgam of Marsala and egg yolks, has been around for centuries, as have whipped creams, and mousses and soufflés, which are both sauces made solid with aerated egg whites. Contemporary chefs continue to develop sauces foamed from a wide variety of ingredients, such as cod, squid ink, foie gras, potatoes, beets, and cheese, some of which stretch the very definition of sauce.

What It Does ●
Every time you order a latte or a hot fudge sundae with extra whipped cream, you experience the sensual charms of foam. Because of the high amount and quality of protein in milk, cream, and eggs, these products foam beautifully. The same chemistry happens with any fluid protein, and chefs have found that by adding liquid and protein, usually **gelatin**, it is possible to aerate any ingredient.

Ferran Adrià, the famous Spanish techo-cuisine chef, began experimenting with culinary foams in the late 1980s. Using a nitrous oxide whipped cream canister that had been given to him as a gift, he found he could aerate almost anything, transforming its flavor impact, as well as its texture.

Incorporating air into a sauce changes how the liquid interacts with its surroundings. A conventional sauce contacts air at its surface alone, but foams are filled with air bubbles. Since air is the vehicle for transferring aromas from food to nose, foamed sauces are more aromatic than conventional sauces. And the texture of foams can be ethereal, in delightful contrast to whatever solid ingredients they accompany.

How It Works ●
Foam sauces are structured similarly to **emulsion** sauces. In emulsions, droplets of one liquid (usually oil) are dispersed in another liquid (usually water or an acid like vinegar or lemon juice). The

Coconut Sweet Potato Foam

Sweet potatoes make ethereal foams that hold their inflation exceptionally well. This one has the perfume of honey and a lingering hot pepper hit. Serve it as a side vegetable or as sauce on pork, grilled fish, or roasted vegetables. You will need a quart-size (liter-size) nitrous oxide siphon (whipped cream siphon) and a nitrous oxide (NO_2) charger to dispense the foam.

12 oz	orange-flesh sweet potatoes, peeled and cut into large chunks	375 g
⅔ cup	full-fat coconut milk	150 mL
1 tbsp	honey	15 mL
⅛ tsp	Sriracha hot pepper sauce	0.5 mL
¼ tsp	ground aniseeds	1 mL
¼ tsp	ground cinnamon	1 mL
¼ tsp	ground ginger	1 mL
¼ tsp	kosher salt	1 mL
Pinch	ground clove	Pinch

1. In a pot of boiling water (just enough to cover), add sweet potatoes and cook until tender, about 15 minutes. Drain.

2. In a food processor, purée sweet potatoes with coconut milk, honey, hot pepper sauce, anise, cinnamon, ginger, salt, and clove. Pass through a strainer.

3. Fill the siphon, using a funnel, and charge as directed with nitrous oxide capsule. Shake well before dispensing. Foam can be kept warm in the siphon set in a pan of hot water, 150°F (66°C), for about 30 minutes. Shake well before dispensing.

MAKES 1 QUART (1 L) FOAM,
ABOUT 6 SERVINGS

droplets block the liquid's movements, causing the mixture to thicken. The same thing happens in foams, except that the dispersed droplets are air bubbles that get in the way of free-flowing liquid molecules.

Once a significant network of air has been forced into a liquid, the liquid will disperse, flowing in a thin stream around the surface of every bubble. But air and water have different densities, so quickly after a foam forms gravity takes over. The water sinks to the bottom of the bubbles. The bubble walls thin. The bubbles burst.

Anything that can slow the movement of water increases the stability of foam. The most effective materials are the proteins and phospholipids (like lecithin) that stabilize emulsions. Milk, cream, and eggs are natural emulsions and contain a ready supply of emulsifiers, which is why dairy and egg foams last the longest. But anything that blocks the flow of water — microscopic particles of vegetable purée, meat proteins, **starches**, **pectin**, or **gums** — prolongs the life of a foam.

See Also • Aeration, Dispersions, Eggs, Emulsion, Gelatin, Gums, Molecular Gastronomy, Pectin, Protein, Starch

FOCACCIA • See Bread

FOIE GRAS • See Organ Meats

FOLIC ACID • See Vitamins

FOND • See Deglaze, Sauces

FONDANT • See Candy

FONTINA • See Cheese

FOOD ADDITIVES

What It Is • If everyone grew and cooked their own food, and everything we ate could be guaranteed fresh and safe, there would be no need for food additives. But that has never been the case. Food additives have been used for millennia. Salt, which affects human cell function, and smoke, which is full of toxins, were used in meat processing by the earliest civilizations. Large amounts of empty-calorie sugar were traditionally employed to preserve fruit and milk. Volatile oils in mustards and hot peppers irritate the nervous system, yet these ingredients have been added to prepared food to reduce the growth of bacteria for thousands of years.

The idea that corporate food technologists invented additives is simply wrong, but one can still wonder what happened to get us from simply smoking meat to the point where several thousand artificial and synthesized additives are routinely used in the production of our food supply.

What It Does • Additives are put in food for a variety of reasons, some better than others. Those that prevent spoilage and keep food safe are indispensable. Others that eliminate browning of fruits and vegetables, ensure that granular ingredients stay free flowing, or keep sauces smooth and creamy make our food more pleasant to eat but not safer. Others add color and flavor to food less expensively than a fresh ingredient could, and some lengthen an ingredient's shelf life, factors that improve the profitability of a product but not necessarily its quality or safety.

One big problem with most food additives is that we usually can't be certain that they are completely safe before they go into common usage. Many are new molecules, which could be hazardous over time, and though all food additives are tested, history has shown that some have proven toxic years after they were approved. Even the most rigorous laboratory testing can't show an additive to be risk free. First of all, human testing is not possible for dangerous substances, and results of animal tests are seldom clear-cut. It is not by accident that the Food and Drug Administration (FDA) classifies approved food additives as Generally Recognized as Safe (GRAS).

In Europe, all food additives, whether approved or not, are classified by E number.

Food Additives

Coloring

Type	Name	Description
Yellows and Oranges (E100–119)	Natural: curcumin, riboflavin Artificial: FD&C Yellow 5 or 6	Natural colors have antioxidant properties, artificial can cause allergic reactions
Reds (E120–129)	Natural: amaranth, cochineal, orcein Artificial: Azorubine, FD&C Red 2, 3, and 40	From orange red to maroon; natural reds are potential carcinogens, artificial cause allergic reactions
Blue and Green (E130–149)	Natural: Brilliant Blue, chlorophyll Artificial: indigotine, FD&C Green 3	From yellow green to purple blue; no health problems
Brown and Black (150–158)	Caramel coloring	Four types: plain caramel coloring made from caramelized sugar; caustic caramel contains acids and salts; ammonia caramel (aka baker's caramel) contains ammonium compounds and is used in synthetic soy sauce; and sulfite ammonia caramel used in acidic foods like soft drinks

Preservatives

Type	Name	Description
Sorbates (E200–209)	Sorbic acid, sodium sorbate, potassium sorbate, calcium sorbate	Antimicrobials, prevent the growth of mold, yeast, fungi; salt forms more soluble than acid forms
Benzoates (E210–219	Benzoic acid, sodium benzoate, potassium benzoate, calcium benzoate	Inhibit the growth of mold, yeast, and some bacteria in acidified foods
Sulfites (E220–229)	Sulfur dioxide	Antimicrobial used to preserve appearance and moisture in dried fruits; also used in wine to prevent spoilage and oxidation
	Sodium bisulfite	Antimicrobial, kills yeasts, fungi, and bacteria in grape juice as a precursor to fermentation of wine; added to bottled wine to prevent oxidation; prevents browning in canned fruit
Phenols (E230–239)	Biphenyl, orthophenyl phenol, thiabendazole	Prevent the growth of molds, parasites, and fungi; used to preserve citrus fruits during transportation
Nitrates (E240–259)	Sodium nitrate, sodium nitrite, potassium nitrate, potassium nitrite	Used in cured meats and fish to fix color and prevent the growth of anaerobic bacteria
Acetates (E260–269)	Acetic acid, sodium acetate	Give vinegar its acidic taste; used to lower pH to control growth of bacteria, molds, and fungi; flavoring on salt-and-vinegar chips
Lactates (E270–279)	Lactic acid, potassium lactate, sodium lactate, calcium lactate	Lower pH, control bacterial growth; antioxidants

Antioxidants and Acidity Regulators

Type	Name	Description
Ascorbates (E300–305)	Ascorbic acid (vitamin C), sodium ascorbate	Used in many foods, either in acid or salt forms
Tocopherol (E306–309)	Tocopherols (alpha, delta, gamma)	Used in vegetable oils, margarines, and salad dressings

Antioxidants and Acidity Regulators

Type	Name	Description
Gallates, erythorbates, lactates, citrates, tartrates, phosphates, malates, adipates, succinates (E310–369)	Propyl gallate, sodium erythorbate, butylated hydroxyanisole (BHA), butylated hydroxytoluene (BHT)	Used in most processed foods, especially oils and meats. Listed as an acid (e.g., citric acid, tartaric acid) or as a salt (e.g., sodium citrate, potassium lactate)

Thickeners, Stabilizers, and Emulsifiers

Type	Name	Description
Alginates (E400–409)	Alginic acid, sodium alginate, potassium alginate, ammonium alginate, agar, carrageenan	Used in soups, sweets, meats, and jellies
Natural gums (E410–419)	Locust bean or carob gum, guar gum, gum arabic, xanthan gum	Stabilizers in ice cream, cream cheese, salad dressing, pastries, and candies
Other natural agents (E420–439)	Glycerol, glycerin, maltodextrins, modified starch, Polysorbate 80	Emulsifier, humectant, and sweetener in prepared foods, cookie dough, sauces, soups, dressings, and liqueurs
	Konjac	A gel from the corm of the konjac plant grown in China, Japan, and Korea; used as a vegan alternative to gelatin
Natural emulsifiers (E440–449)	Pectins, gelatin, lecithin	Gelling agent in jams and jellies, pastry fillings, yogurt drinks, candies, sauces
Phosphates (E450–459)	Di-, tri- and polyphosphates	Retain moisture in seafood; regulated by government
	Beta-cyclodextrin	A starch derivative that has the ability to retain moisture; also used to give a soft texture to fat-reduced products
Cellulose compounds (E460–469)	Methylcellulose	Thickens ice cream and whipped cream, emulsifier in dressings and sauces
Fatty acids (E470–489)	Mono- and diacylglycerals of fatty acids	Used in chewy breads to strengthen gluten, and as emulsifiers

pH Regulators and Anti-Caking Agents

Type	Name	Description
Mineral acids and bases (E500–509)	Sodium, potassium, and magnesium carbonates	Alkaline component for baking powder, jellies, pretzels; regulate acidity in water and keep salt free-flowing
Chlorides and sulfates (E510–520)	Calcium chloride	Electrolyte in sports drinks; firming agent for pickles; used for spherification techniques
	Magnesium chloride and sulfate	Coagulants for tofu
Hydroxides (E521–529)	Sodium hydroxide (lye), potassium hydroxide (caustic potash), calcium hydroxide (slacked lime)	Used in chemical peeling of fruits and vegetables, especially cocoa, processing soft drinks and hominy, thickening ice cream, soaking olives, and glazing pretzels
Silicates (E550–559)	Silicone dioxide	Used as a free-flowing agent in powdered foods
	Sodium- and Calcium silicoaluminate	Used as a free-flowing agent to prevent caking in salt

Flavor Enhancers

Type	Name	Description
Glutamates (E620–629)	Glutamic acid, monosodium glutamate (MSG), monoammonium glutamate	Provide essential flavor to savory foods, known as umami. Ajinomoto is a brand of MSG manufactured in Japan.
	Guanylic acid	Produced from dried fish or dried seaweed, an umami flavor enhancer

Miscellaneous

Type	Name	Description
Improving agents (E920–929)	Cysteine, cystine	Helps browning and softness of doughs
	Azodicarbonamide, chlorine, potassium bromate, benzoyl peroxide, calcium peroxide	Bleaching agents for flour that improve gluten formation and whiten
Sweeteners (E950–969)	Acesulfame potassium	Calorie-free synthetic sweetener that is 200 times sweeter than sugar and is stable during cooking
	Aspartame (Equal, NutraSweet, Canderel)	Calorie-free artificial sweetener derived from proteins that is 180 times sweeter than sugar; used in many commercial products; not heat stable

continued on next page

Food Additives (continued)
Miscellaneous

Type	Name	Description
Sweetener (E950–969)	Isomalt	Sugar derivative with half the calories of sugar, half as sweet as sugar; can be heated and not prone to caking
Sweeteners	Lacitol	Derived from lactose, with half the sweetness and calories of sugar; very stable to heat; a prebiotic
	Neohesperidin dihydrochalcone (NHDC)	Artificial sweetener derived from citrus that is 1,800 times sweeter than sugar; it is sensitive to pH but heat stable
	Saccharin	Calorie-free synthetic sugar that is 300 times sweeter than sugar; it is stable at cooking temperatures
	Sorbitol (aka glucitol)	Sugar substitute used in candies and diet foods
	Stevia	Natural sweetener made from a South American plant that is 300 times sweeter than sugar and heat stable; has a licorice-like aftertaste
	Sucralose (Splenda)	Derived from sugar and chlorine, it is 600 times sweeter than sugar; it is heat stable

These codes are found on ingredient and nutrition labels throughout the EU, and are used in many other countries. E numbers are uncommon in North America but are growing in popularity in Canada. In the U.S., colors are given FD&C numbers by the Food and Drug Administration. FD&C stands for the Federal Food, Drug, and Cosmetic Act, a set of laws passed in 1938 that established the FDA.

How It Works • The preceding Food Additives chart classifies food additives by what they do. Additives that have been banned or delisted in both Europe and North America are not included.

FOOD AS MEDICINE • See Antioxidants, Nutrition

FOOD POISONING • See Bacteria, Toxin

FOOD SCIENCE

What It Is • Food science is the study of how food and cooking work. Culinary studies teach us how to cook and serve, and gastronomy lets us know how to eat and drink. They are the food disciplines that teach us what to do with food, but they don't tell us *why* we're doing it, or what's happening when we do it. The study of food science invites us to look behind the curtain.

Food science is also a professional discipline that is concerned with the technical aspects of food production from the moment raw ingredients come out of the field or feedlot until they are eaten. In academia, food science is considered one of the agricultural sciences, and its practitioners are involved in all of the technical aspects of the food industry.

What It Does • Food science knowledge can move a home cook from slavish recipe follower to recipe inventor. With an understanding of the mechanics and chemistry of what is happening in the kitchen, interested home cooks can troubleshoot everything from a split hollandaise to a fallen cake. A growing public interest in food science has been fostered by, and has fostered, a growth in food science media, including Alton Brown's popular food science show *Good Eats* on the Food Network and bestselling food science books like *On Food and Cooking* by Harold McGee and *CookWise* by Shirley Corriher.

The study of **molecular gastronomy**, which blends the chefs' art with food technology, has inspired scores of professional chefs to throw away their copper sautoirs in favor of such technological gadgets as vacuum filters, ultrasonic water baths, and rotary evaporators (Rotovap). Outside of the kitchen, these chefs can expand their knowledge at the annual International Workshop on Molecular Gastronomy in Erice, Italy, or show off at the avant-garde Madrid Fusion food festival. Or if they don't want to travel they can exchange culinary concepts with like-minded chefs on one of dozens of culinary/food science blogs.

In the traditional food industry the study of food science leads to the development of new food products, food processes, types of packaging, and ways of evaluating food products.

Food science is interdisciplinary, incorporating concepts from biology, chemistry, and physics. It includes the study of:

Biotechnology — the use of biological processes in the manufacturing of new foods

Food chemistry — the chemical structure of foods and their chemical reactions

Food engineering — the industrial processes used to manufacture food

Food safety — the causes and prevention of food-borne illnesses and food contamination

Microbiology — the beneficial and detrimental interactions between microorganisms and food

Molecular gastronomy — how food science impacts fine dining

Nutrition — the connection between food and health

Packaging — how food quality is preserved through packaging

Physics — the physical aspects of food

Preservation — how to maintain food quality over time by controlling the causes of degradation

Product development — the invention of new food products and improvement of current ones

Technology — the technological and mechanical aspects of food production

How It Works • The Institute of Food Technologists (IFT), the largest food science organization in the world, promotes the advancement of food science through public awareness, spearheading programs for food safety, and helping to set education standards in university food science programs. IFT honors excellence in the field with a series of annual awards.

The Research Chefs Association (RCA), a group of food industry chefs and food scientists, certifies food professionals in culinology, an interdisciplinary approach to food preparation that involves culinary and food science training. There are several accredited university-level culinology programs. Both RCA and IFT publish food science journals.

See Also • Molecular Gastronomy

FOURME D'AMBERT • See Cheese

FRAMBOISE • See Liquor

FRANGELICO • See Liqueur

FRANKFURTER • See Sausage

FREE RADICALS • See Antioxidants

FREEZE-DRYING • See Drying

FREEZING

What It Is • When food reaches temperatures below 32°F (0°C), any water it contains becomes ice. The water is no longer available to bacteria, so spoilage is stopped while the food remains frozen. The cold temperature also slows down other chemical reactions, like enzyme activity, which helps to preserve freshness.

What It Does • While freezing stops the growth of microorganisms, it doesn't kill them. When an ingredient thaws, most of

fast fact

• Clarence Birdseye came up with the idea for frozen food while working as a field naturalist for the U.S. government in northern Canada, when he noticed that quickly frozen fish appeared fresh after thawing.

kitchen wisdom

Freezing Leftovers

Package leftovers in individual portions. They will freeze faster (which causes less damage), they will be more convenient to use, and you will never have to thaw more than you need. If possible, freeze leftovers in containers that can be heated or go into the microwave, but only use containers that can be filled completely. Air trapped next to frozen food will cause freezer burn.

the bacteria that were in the food when it was frozen will reactivate. For that reason it is inadvisable to freeze old or tainted food, and thawed ingredients should be cooked as soon as possible.

Enzyme reactions are slowed by freezing, but they are not stopped. Ingredients that could be damaged by enzymes, like fruit and vegetables, are usually blanched before freezing to prevent deterioration since boiling temperature denatures enzymes. Blanching also softens the cell walls of vegetables and fruits so that they can expand during freezing along with the water, thus keeping the cell walls from rupturing.

Frozen food will keep well for up to six months provided that the freezer maintains a constant temperature at or below 0°F (−18°C), but freezer storage time is compromised easily by fluctuations in temperature. Check freezer door seals to make sure they are tight, and avoid loading large amounts of nonfrozen food into a freezer all at once. Never put hot food into a freezer.

When freezer temperatures fluctuate or rise much above 0°F (−18°C), frozen ingredients can partially thaw or items recently put in the freezer can freeze so slowly that large ice crystals form on the surface of the food and damage its tissues. This damage, called freezer burn, appears as a discolored dry spot and indicates that water from just under the surface of the food has migrated to the surface and has frozen outside the food, leaving behind a desiccated area that appears shriveled and burned. Freezer burn occurs less in manual defrost freezers than those with an automatic thaw cycle (frost-free).

To prevent freezer burn, wrap food tightly in freezer paper, resealable freezer bags, or foil. Air contains moisture, so if ingredients are not tightly wrapped, water from the air trapped in the package will freeze on the surface of the food. Paper wrappers absorb some surface moisture, which reduces the chances of freezer burn.

There are three safe ways to thaw frozen food:

In the refrigerator — Small items, like steaks or chops, frozen in a single layer, need 24 hours to thaw in a refrigerator (if the pieces are stacked, thaw for two days). Large roasts require about 24 hours for every 5 pounds (2.5 kg) of weight. That means a 20-pound (10 kg) turkey will need four days to thaw in the refrigerator.

In cold water — Faster thawing can be done by placing food in a leak-proof plastic bag and immersing it in cold water. Check the water every 30 minutes or so to see that it remains cold, no more than 40°F (4°C), and change it if it should get warmer. Thawing time in cold water varies with the size of the item being thawed and the temperature of the water, but even large roasts will thaw using this method in less than six hours.

In a microwave — Thaw using the defrost cycle in 5-to-10-minute intervals depending

What Can I Freeze?

Not all foods freeze well. Ice takes up more space than water. If the cell walls that hold the water can expand, the ice will not cause any damage, but if they can't the cell walls will break and the water will flow out when the food thaws. Raw meats have flexible cell walls so they freeze well, as do stews and pot roasts, but in roasted meats the cooked protein cells have become rigid, leaving frozen roasted meats grainy after thawing. Do not freeze cheese or any dairy product that you want to serve fresh. Dairy products are emulsions and freezing damages emulsions. Frozen milk or cream separates during freezing, but it can be homogenized again in a blender after it thaws and used in batters and doughs.

on the size of the item until completely thawed but still cold. Cook immediately.

Provided that an ingredient was thawed safely, it is safe to refreeze it, but not necessarily advisable. Freezing, even careful freezing, breaks the cell structure of food, and subsequent freezing will weaken it more. That means if the ingredient is delicate to begin with, like a fillet of sole, it will be destroyed by multiple freezings, but a cooked casserole or soup in which all of the food fibers are already soft can be refrozen without damage.

Vegetables should be cut into serving-size pieces. Blanch them in boiling water just until barely soft, and cool them completely. Freeze them in resealable freezer bags. Spread out cooled blanched vegetables in a single layer on a baking sheet and freeze until the vegetables are solid, about one hour. Then pack in freezer bags, seal, and store. By packing vegetables after they have frozen solid you can take out as much as you want without thawing the whole bag.

Fruits, because they are more delicate, are more complicated to freeze. Because many fruits are subject to enzymatic browning, and enzymes remain active during freezing, adding a pinch of ascorbic acid (vitamin C) helps to stop enzymatic browning. Large fruits should be cut into serving-size pieces. Hard fruits, such as apples and pears, benefit from a brief blanching before sweetening. Citrus fruit cannot be frozen, although its juice freezes well.

Most foods will maintain quality for up to six months

properly wrapped and stored in a freezer. Cured meats and ground meats are a bit more perishable, and should be frozen for no more than three months.

How It Works ● As water cools, its molecules move more slowly. At its freezing point the molecules are moving so slowly that they begin to gather in loose, undefined clusters, called seed crystals. As the temperature continues to drop, molecules line up around the seed crystals in increasingly rigid formation until all of the water crystallizes. The longer it takes for crystals to form, the larger they will be.

Water is the only known nonmetallic substance to expand when it freezes. At sea level frozen water takes up about 8% more space than it did in its liquid state. Freezing liquid in a glass jar is tricky. If the jar is not specifically designed for freezing, or if you overfill the jar, the jar is apt to break. Flexible containers, like metal or plastic, expand with the ice and do not break.

When food is frozen, the same phenomenon happens to cells as the expanding ice puts pressure on cell walls. If the cells are flexible they will stretch with the ice, but if they are rigid the forming ice can break them, causing the ingredient to collapse when it thaws. The expansion of frozen water within the cells of frozen ingredients explains why meats leak juices during thawing, and why produce needs special handling before being frozen.

Make-Your-Own Frozen Dinners

Frozen meals are a staple of convenience cuisine, but almost any leftover can be arranged on a plate, frozen, and popped into a microwave to heat up for a quick meal. All you need is a plate (high-grade plastic works well), plastic wrap, and foil. The food must be fully cooked and cooled, and everything needs to be coated with something to protect it from freezer burn.

The following formula is for a standard main dish with two side dishes.

4 oz	fully cooked ready-to-eat main dish of meat, fish, or poultry	125 g
½ cup	sauce (unless meat is breaded)	125 mL
¾ cup	cooked and seasoned vegetable, such as green beans, carrots, peas, roasted peppers, etc.	175 mL
1 tsp	oil, any type	5 mL
¾ cup	cooked and seasoned starch, such as noodles, potatoes, rice, or other grains	175 mL
1 tsp	melted butter or oil	5 mL

1. Place meat on one side of plate (if sliced slightly overlap slices). Cover with sauce.
2. Toss vegetable with oil and place on plate next to meat. Make a mound of the starch in remaining open space. Drizzle with butter or oil.
3. Cover plate with plastic wrap and seal edges. Wrap tightly with foil and label with contents and date. Freeze for up to 4 months.
To reheat: Remove foil and plastic wrap. Cover with microwave-safe plastic wrap. Puncture in two places and heat in a microwave set on Defrost cycle for 5 minutes, then change to High and cook until heated through and steaming, 4 to 6 minutes. Remove plastic wrap and serve.

MAKES 1 SERVING

Animal cells are flexible, so meats can withstand freezing with limited damage, but plant cells are stiff, so vegetables and some fruits need to be blanched to soften their cell walls before being frozen.

Commercially frozen foods are flash frozen, a technique developed by Clarence Birdseye, which freezes food so quickly that ice crystals never get a chance to form and therefore cell damage is greatly reduced. Even delicate flash-frozen berries soften upon thawing, but they do not lose their shape.

See Also ● Water

FRENCH BREAD ● See Bread

FRESH CHEESE ● See Cheese

FRISÉE ● See Chicory

FROG ● See Game

FRUCTOSE ● See Sugar

FRUIT

What It Is ● To a botanist, the fruit is a plant's ovary — the part that produces the seed, protects and nourishes the seed until it is ready to grow into a new plant, and then disperses it away from the parent so that it does not compete for life-sustaining nutrients and sunlight.

To an animal, a fruit is something good to eat. Some fruits, such as burrs, are inedible, but most fruit is meant to be eaten. It serves no nutritional, structural, or vascular function for the plant. Its only purpose is to attract an animal so that it might take the fruit and seed away from the parent plant and drop it in some fertile ground. To that end, edible fruits consist entirely of storage tissue filled with delightful tasty aromatic stuff.

To cooks, a fruit is a vegetable that is prepared in a sweet manner. This differs slightly from the botanist's definition of fruit as an ovary, which would include apples, pears, peaches, cherries, tomatoes, cucumbers, squashes, eggplant, bell peppers, and avocados. The fruits that we sweeten we recognize as fruit culinarily, and all the others, we don't — we call them vegetables. Incidentally, there is one culinary fruit that's not a fruit at all. Rhubarb is a **stem**, but because we sweeten it during cooking we think of it as a fruit.

What It Does • There are hundreds of fruits in the world, and we can classify them in multiple ways. In the following charts, fruits are classified by where they grow and by botanical family. The most popular fruits in North American and European kitchens come from just a few families.

Temperate-climate fruits grow on trees, bushes, or vines. They will not grow in the tropics because they need a period of cold before they will flower (called a chilling requirement). There are two large families of temperate-climate fruits that grow principally in the Americas and in Europe (see chart below).

Rose family (*Rosaceae*) fruits include pome fruits, like apples and pears. The edible part of pome fruits develops from the flower base rather than the ovary, so it is more fibrous

than other fruits. Their high fiber content gives apples and pears a crisp snapping texture that is ruined if these fruits are allowed to ripen too much — apples become mushy and pears gritty. For that reason pome fruits are always picked underripe and either allowed to ripen off the tree or, in the case of apples, kept in cold storage to keep them from ripening.

Because of their firm fibers, pome fruits stand up well to long cooking processes like roasting, braising, and baking. Apples and pears are favorites for making sauces and butters. Fruit sauces are made by cooking fruit until it loses its shape. Fruit butters are made the same way except that they cook longer, until much of the moisture evaporates, leaving behind a thick pulp that browns from Maillard reactions.

Enzymatic browning happens to apples and pears whenever they are cut or cooked; coating them with a little citrus juice prevents the enzymatic reactions and keeps the flesh white.

Stone fruits (drupes) all come from the same genus of the rose family, *Prunus*, and are typified by soft, plush flesh surrounding a large seed encased in a hard shell. Stone fruits, including cherries, peaches, plums,

American and European Temperate-climate Fruits

Rosaceae Family			*Ericaceae* Family	Various Families
Pome Fruits	Stone Fruits	Bramble Berries	True Berries	Other Berries
Apple	Apricot	Blackberry	Bearberry	Barberry
Chokeberry	Beach plum	Boysenberry	Bilberry	Carissa
Crabapple	Black cherry	Cloudberry	Blueberry	Currant
Hawthorn	Chokecherry	Dewberry	Crowberry	Elderberry
Medlar	Japanese cherry	Loganberry	Cranberry	Feijoa
Pear	Nectarine	Marionberry	Huckleberry	Goji berry
Quince	Peach	Olallieberry	Lingonberry	Gooseberry
Rose hip	Pin cherry	Raspberry		Grape
Rowan	Plum	Salmonberry		Jujube
Saskatoon	Plumcot	Strawberry		Kiwi berry
	Prune plum	Thimbleberry		Kiwifruit
	Sour cherry	Wineberry		Mulberry
	Sweet cherry			Pawpaw
	Ume			Tamarillo

Subtropical-climate Fruits

Citrus Genus	Mulberry-Fig Family	Other Fruits
Citron	Breadfruit (jackfruit)	Avocado
Clementine	Fig	Carob
Grapefruit	Mulberry	Date
Key lime	Osage orange	Feijoa
Kumquat		Grape
Lemon		Guava
Lime		Longan
Makrut lime		Lychee
Mandarin orange		Passion fruit
Orange		Persimmon
Orangelo		Pomegranate
Persian lime		Tamarillo
Pomelo		Yangmei
Rangpur		
Tangelo		
Tangerine		
Ugli fruit		

and their cultivars, do not ripen well off the tree. Ripe stone fruit is sweet, aromatic, and pulpy. They are all delicious eaten raw, and most can be baked or simmered in a variety of ways, although they can easily become mushy when overcooked.

Some of the most popular berries are in the rose family. At face value berries seem simple enough — they're small, single fruits that can be eaten whole — but in fact the family is quite complex. Just a few berries fit that simple definition precisely. These are known as true berries, and they are all in one family, Ericaceae, and include blueberries and cranberries. The berries in the rose family, blackberries and raspberries, don't fit the definition at all. They are made up of many tiny little fruitlets, each one with its own seed, netted together. Like roses, rose-family berries grow on bramble bushes, so they are known as bramble berries. In addition to these two substantial families are a whole bunch of berries from a variety of families. Many of these fit the definition of berry, like grapes or kiwifruit, but most people don't think of those fruits as berries at all.

Bramble berries tend to be moist and soft, making them highly perishable and difficult to cook. They are best eaten raw or briefly cooked. True berries are a bit firmer and make beautiful preserves and pies. Cranberries and lingonberries must be cooked to be palatable.

Melons are a type of giant pseudoberry in which the flesh is derived not from the ovarian wall but from some other tissue. Watermelon, for example, is placental tissue rather than ovarian. Most melons, including all cantaloupes and honeydews, are from the genus *Cucumis*, which puts them in the same family as squashes. Melons generally do not heat well, and should be eaten raw. They also won't get any sweeter once they have been separated from the vine.

Subtropical fruits (see chart, left) are similar to temperate-climate fruits, but they are not hardy to extreme cold. They can tolerate a mild frost, and some have a modest chilling requirement, so they can cross over into temperate or tropical climates depending on geography. Two types of fruit dominate, **citrus** (which can be tropical or subtropical) and Moraceae, the mulberry-fig family (which can be subtropical or temperate).

Citrus fruits are full of juice and, except for their peels, they are too low in fiber to retain shape during cooking. The peel can be candied, and the colorful skin on the outside of the peel, called the zest, can be used as a seasoning. The interior of the fruit is used for juice. Citrus fruits will not ripen after harvesting, so they must develop whatever sweetness they have on the tree.

Tropical plants grow in any frost-free climate, and many can tolerate the mild end of subtropical zones. Because of the diversity of the fruits in this category, no family dominates, so the fruits in the chart on page 258 are simply listed in alphabetical order.

Superfruits

Some tropical fruits are marketed as "superfruits" promoted for containing high levels of **antioxidants**. The notion of superfruits started when wild blueberries received the highest ranking for antioxidant capacity from the U.S. Department of

kitchen wisdom

Replacing Fat with Fruit in Baking

Fat tenderizes baked goods by coating the flour proteins and keeping them from forming gluten. Sugar does the same thing. The two proteins that normally join together to make gluten first must be hydrated with water. Fat coats flour particles, keeping the water away. Sugar binds with the water so that it can't hydrate the protein. You could reduce the fat in a cake by loading a recipe with sugar (a common practice in low-fat baking recipes), but replacing up to one-third of the fat in a recipe with fruit purée does the same thing, and with much better nutrition. Use any fruit sauce or purée, as long as the flavor and color complement the recipe.

Agriculture (USDA) in 2004. Since then tropical fruits have been shown to pass blueberries in their antioxidant level, and producers of tropical juice have not been shy about promoting them. Açai, a berry from Brazil, is high in anthocyanins and other flavonoids. Goji berries, which are always dried, are touted in Chinese medicine for their ability to enhance immune system functioning. They are high in carotenoids, fatty acids, and phenols, all of which have antioxidant properties. Noni, a highly aromatic tree fruit from the South Pacific, is high in vitamins A and C (both antioxidants) and in antioxidant-active flavonoids. Guarana, sold as a super energy source, is loaded with caffeine. Miracle berry (aka Magic berry), the fruit of *Synsepalum dulcificum*, makes sour foods taste sweet. The phenomenon is attributed to miraculin, a glycoprotein that binds to taste buds on the human tongue and alters the taste perception of sourness for as long as an hour after consuming the berries. Miracle berries have little to no taste of their own.

How It Works • Once the seed is fertilized through pollination, a fruit begins to grow. The ovary wall (pericarp) may become fleshy, as it does in peaches and berries, or it may become hard, as it does in nuts and grains. A simple fruit comes from a single ovary that develops from a flower with only one pistil (the female reproductive part of a flower). Examples of simple fruits are: most nuts, legumes, stone fruits, pome fruits, bananas, cranberries, blueberries, and avocados. An aggregate fruit, such as a raspberry, develops from a flower with numerous ovaries, each with its own pistil. A miniature fruitlet develops from each ovary. They join together, yielding a fruit that looks compartmentalized. Other examples of aggregate fruits are blackberries and strawberries. Although many aggregate fruits are called berries, they technically aren't

kitchen wisdom

Pomegranates Boost Your Health

They are high in B vitamins, vitamin C, and antioxidant polyphenols. But they are a pain to eat, filled with hundreds of arils — seeds covered with a thick skin and a gelatinous fluid. The best way to get the goodness out of a pomegranate is to juice it, either by cutting it into quarters and squeezing the juice through cheesecloth or a sieve, or by puréeing the fruit in a food processor and straining out the solids.

because they come from more than one ovary. Multiple fruits are similar to aggregate fruits because they are made up of individual fruits that fuse together. The only difference is that multiple fruits develop from multiple flowers each producing one ovary. As the ovaries develop they fuse together into a single larger fruit. Pineapples and figs are examples of multiple fruits.

The pericarp has three layers that develop into different parts of the fruit: the exocarp (outer layer) usually turns into the fruit skin; the mesocarp (middle layer) becomes the center of the fruit, which is meaty and fleshy in most fruits but dry and hard in nuts and grains; and the endocarp (inner layer) becomes the seed coating. In addition, several fruits incorporate parts of the flower or stem tip into their structure.

Fruits are the only parts of plants to ripen. Ripening is the way the plant makes its fruit attractive to animals. During ripening the storage cells in the mesocarp expand, filling with water and minerals from the roots and with sugars from photosynthesis in the leaves. As the cells grow, the fruit expands, and the cell walls become reinforced with cellulose and pectin. Energy is stored in the cell vacuoles in the form of sugars, starches, and organic acids. Secondary compounds, like bitter alkaloids and astringent tannins, are synthesized to fight infections or ward off predators who might take the fruit before it is ready. These are why underripe fruit tastes astringent and bitter.

During ripening, skin color blushes from green to another color. Starch and acid content decrease. Sugar content increases.

The texture softens. Alkaloids and tannins disappear. Fruit aromas develop. All of which makes the fruit ready for consumption, which is its destiny.

Enzymes account for many of these changes. Color development, for example, happens when membranes containing chlorophyll weaken, allowing enzymes from the cell to destroy the green pigment, in turn allowing the other secondary pigments (the ripe fruit color) to shine through. Enzymes also convert starches in fruit into sugar. The starch-to-sugar ratio of unripe bananas, 25:1, switches after ripening to 1:20. On the other hand, some fruits don't store their energy as sugar, and therefore don't get sweeter during ripening. Melons, citrus, and pineapple develop sugars gradually and can't convert starch to sugar quickly during ripening. As well, enzymes break down alkaloids, but they do not affect the deactivation of tannins or the development of fruity aromatic esters.

In most fruits ripening changes are triggered by a hormone, ethylene, that

Tropical-climate Fruits

Açai	Cherimoya	Muskmelon
Acerola (West Indian cherry)	Coconut	Noni
Ackee	Custard apple	Papaya
Araza	Date	Peach-palm
Avocado	Durian	Pili nut
Babaco	Guarana	Pineapple
Bael	Guava	Plantain
Banana	Horned melon	Rambutan
Bitter gourd	Jackfruit	Rose apple (chom-phu)
Black sapote	Jujube	Salak
Breadfruit	Longan	Sapodilla
Cacao	Loquat	Soncoya
Calabash	Lychee	Soursop
Canistel (eggfruit)	Mamey sapote	Spondias (Golden apple)
Cape gooseberry	Mango	Sweetsop
Carambola (star fruit)	Mangosteen	Tamarind
	Melinjo	

develops in fruit during ripening (citrus, grapes, and strawberries are non-climacteric, which means they ripen without a burst of ethylene). Ethylene is also used by the produce industry to ripen fruit that was picked prematurely. Picked while still hard and green to prevent bruising that can happen during harvest and transport, green fruit is sprayed with ethylene gas when it arrives at its destination in preparation for sale. No one really knows how ethylene works. It probably makes cell membranes more permeable, allowing enzymes to do their jobs, but we do know that once ethylene reaches a certain concentration in a fruit, the cells switch their breathing. They switch from expelling oxygen (a by-product of photosynthesis) to expelling carbon dioxide (a by-product of cell respiration).

While growing, plants use carbon dioxide and give off oxygen during photosynthesis. But in the last stages of ripening, photosynthesis reverses, and fruit cells begin to respire — taking in oxygen and giving off carbon dioxide — about five times faster than they exchanged elements before ripening. It is believed that the switch to respiration is a key to ripening, forcing the fruit to make a last-ditch effort to attract our attention and whet our appetites.

Respiration does not stop once a fruit is ripe, and in order to control rotting, respiration has to be slowed down. Some fruits that are eaten fairly underripe, such as apples, are stored in low-oxygen/high-carbon-dioxide environments to keep their respiration rate low so that they can be stored longer.

On the other hand, ripening can be accelerated by placing underripe fruit in a loosely closed paper bag. The closed environment concentrates the ethylene and the porous paper sack continues to allow oxygen in to encourage respiration.

See Also • Apple, Apricot, Avocado, Banana, Berries, Capsicum, Carbohydrate, Cherry, Chlorophyll, Citrus, Coconut, Corn, Cucumber, Date, Eggplant, Enzyme, Fig, Grains, Grapes, Melon, Nuts, Plants, Squash, Sugar, Vanilla

FRUIT BRANDY • See Liqueur

FRUIT BUTTER • See Fruit

FRUIT LIQUEUR • See Liqueur

FRYING

What It Is • Why fry? Boiling in oil is messy, smelly, and by all accounts unhealthy, and yet we can't resist the cacophonous crunch, the spurt of juice, the whiff of unapologetic indulgence that is the glory of great fried food. No other cooking technique gives you the same sensorial satisfaction as frying, but making perfectly fried food requires precision and a thorough understanding of the process. While other cooking methods can lean on quality ingredients or inventive seasoning for success, fabulous fried food is all about technique.

Any type of cooking that uses **fat** or **oil** for heat transfer is a form of frying. They go by different names — sautéing, pan-frying, deep-frying — depending on the amount of oil used, the temperature, and what ingredient is being fried, but regardless of their differences the same scientific principles apply.

What It Does • In cooking, fat is the great equalizer. Take almost any ingredient, drop it into hot fat, and the results are delicious. Fat collects heat gradually, maintains a constant temperature easily, and most important, it stays fluid as it heats, so it can wrap around a

Frying Chart

Frying Method	Fat Temperature	Fat Depth	Ideal Ingredient Size
Deep-frying	375°F (190°C)	3 inches+ (7.5 cm+)	¼ to 1 inch (0.5 to 2.5 cm)
Pan-frying	325°F (160°C)	1 inch (2.5 cm)	1 to 2 inches (2.5 to 5 cm)
Sautéing	450°F (230°C)	1⁄16 inch (0.15 cm)	⅛ to ¼ inch (0.32 to 0.5 cm)
Stir-frying	600°F (310°C)	Less than 1⁄16 inch (0.15 cm)	¼ to ½ inch (0.5 to 1 cm)

Perfect French Fries

The high starch content of russet potatoes yields the flakiest french fries that stay crisp longer than fries made from waxy potatoes.

Soaking cut potatoes in water draws starch to the surface of the potato, creating a greater potential for a long-lasting crisp crust.

Unlike other fried ingredients, potatoes are fried twice — first to cook the interior and then to crisp the surface.

1 tbsp	salt	15 mL
4 cups	ice water	1 L
2 lbs	russet potatoes, cut into ¾-inch (2 cm) thick rods	1 kg
	Vegetable oil	
	Additional salt to taste	

1. In a large bowl, stir salt into ice water. Add the potatoes and let soak for 10 minutes.

2. In a large, heavy, deep saucepan or electric deep-fryer, heat 4 to 5 inches (10 to 12.5 cm) of oil over medium heat to 325°F (160°C).

3. Drain the potatoes and dry thoroughly with paper towels. Fry the potatoes, in batches, until tender and lightly browned at the tips, about 6 minutes per batch. Using a slotted spoon, remove potatoes from oil and drain on paper towels. Repeat with remaining potatoes, adjusting heat as necessary between batches. Let stand at room temperature for for up to 2 hours.

4. Return oil to medium heat and heat to 375°F (190°C). Fry potatoes in small batches and until golden brown and crisp, about 3 minutes per batch. Using a slotted spoon, remove potatoes from oil and drain on paper towels. Season to taste with salt and serve immediately. Repeat with remaining potatoes, adjusting heat as necessary between batches.

MAKES 4 SERVINGS

sizzling drumstick, transferring heat evenly and steadily into the tiniest crevice hidden between browning bread crumbs. Unlike water-based liquids, which vaporize at 212°F (100°C), fat can be heated well past 400°F (200°C), giving it the ability to brown and crisp food, something steam and boiling water could never do. A thin film of fat is enough to keep the gooiest batter from sticking to a griddle, and when smoking hot, it can cook through a thinly pounded chicken breast in a matter of seconds.

How It Works • At 350 to 400°F (180 to 200°C), the proper temperature for most frying, the surface of food dries almost instantaneously on contact, forming a crust. This crust acts as a barrier that separates two processes of cooking. On the outside, convecting currents of hot fat brown and crisp the surface, but once a crust forms, the oil cannot permeate any deeper than a fraction of a millimeter. In addition, steam escaping through the crust inhibits oil from being absorbed. On the inside, as heat is absorbed at the surface, water inside the

food turns to steam, causing fibers to soften, proteins to denature, and starches to gelatinize.

Although some fat is absorbed during the first few milliseconds of frying, if an ingredient is fried at the right temperature, it will have little more fat in it (once the crust is removed) than if it had been steamed. Frying at too low a temperature allows oil to be absorbed before a crust forms, and when the fat is too hot the food burns before it cooks through.

Make sure you blot excess oil from the outside of fried foods before serving. As the temperature of the food drops, a vacuum is created inside, which draws oil from the surface into the interior — a good reason to serve fried foods piping hot. There's another reason: the crunchy crisp skin of properly fried food is fleeting. After frying, moisture in the interior of the food continues to steam. As the steam travels to the surface, it cools, condensing back into juice just beneath the crust. It doesn't take long for that moisture to turn the crust from crisp to mush, which is why moist ingredients, like chicken or fish, are breaded and why french fried potatoes are fried twice (see Perfect French Fries, left). These practices create a thicker crust that can absorb moisture in the under-layer without compromising the crackling coat above.

Proper frying depends on starting out with dry ingredients. You can manually blot away excess moisture with paper towels, powder the surface with flour or starch to absorb surface moisture (in much the same way as one dusts oneself with powder after a bath), or coat the food in bread crumbs or batter to form a barrier between the frying fat and any moisture on the food.

When using a **breading** or batter, it is necessary to first lightly dust the ingredient with starch or flour to absorb any moisture that could get trapped under the coating and steam as the food fries, causing the coating to blister off. Tempura uses rice flour in the breading. Rice flour is nearly all starch, and the starch is ground super fine, which yields the thinnest, crispest crust possible.

Regardless of the frying method, the hot fat must always be kept at a constant temperature. For that reason the ingredient must be trimmed so that it cooks through in the time it takes to brown. Determine an appropriate size by the temperature of the fat and the density of the ingredient. For example, deep-fat frying is done around 375°F (190°C). A piece of chicken cooked at that temperature should be no thicker than an inch (2.5 cm) (think chicken nugget), while a carrot, which is denser, shouldn't be thicker than ¼ inch (0.5 cm).

Sautéing is used for thin ingredients that will cook through in the time they take to brown. Have the pan smoking hot before you add the oil, and always sauté in a bare glaze of oil. Pan-frying is used for thicker ingredients, like chicken parts or pork chops. The temperature is lower to give the ingredients time to cook through before they get too brown.

The smoke point of a fat is reduced every time it is heated, so frying fats cannot be reused indefinitely. Passing frying fat through a coffee filter removes fine crumbs that can shorten its useful frying life. Fat that is dark and foams or smokes at frying temperature has outlived its cooking life and should be discarded. Store viable frying fat in a cool, dark place, such as the refrigerator.

Industrial frying compounds contain antioxidants to give them a longer shelf life

What Kind of Fat Is Best for Frying?

Choose unsaturated fats (oils) for frying, because they do not burn and smoke as easily as more naturally solid fats. All fats burn if heated enough, but the smoke point for each is different, depending on its content of free fatty acids. Saturation is the main factor influencing smoke point. The less saturated a fat is, the higher it can be heated before it starts burning and smoking. For instance, lard begins to burn around 375°F (190°C), peanut oil at 450°F (230°C), and safflower oil at 510°F (265°C), which means that lard may be appropriate for deep-fat frying but not for sautéing.

and usually have a high proportion of trans fat (hydrogenated fat), to inhibit rancidity. Lawsuits and laws banning trans fat have restaurants and food manufacturers scrambling for alternatives, but suitable substitutes have been hard to come by. In 2002, McDonald's promised to reduce the trans fat in its frying oils, but delayed its plans several months later. In 2006, the company announced it was making "very good progress" but had yet to replace its oils because of worries that the change would "jeopardize the iconic nature of [their] french fry."

See Also • Antioxidants, Fat, Heat, Oil

FRYING PAN • See Cookware

FUDGE • See Candy

FUEL • See Fire

FUMARIC ACID • See Flavor

FUNGI

What It Is • Fungi are not plants. Plants have **chlorophyll** (fungi do not), and plants produce energy from sunlight. Fungi usually live underground off the energy of other living things, mostly plants and plant remains. They occupy their own biological kingdom, which they share with molds and yeasts.

What It Does • Some fungi are parasites on living plants, causing disease. Huitlacoche (corn smut) is a parasitic fungus that attacks corn. Considered a blight by most farmers, it has been a delicacy in Mexico since Aztecs first tasted it, and it has gained culinary status with growing interest in native Mexican cuisines. Now some of the farmers who once saw corn smut as a devastating disease are cultivating it for sale to the gourmet food market. Huitlacoche can grow on any part of a corn plant, but it is cultivated in the kernels, where it grows large spongy galls that are a combination of engorged plant tissue, fungal threads, and black spores. Eventually the galls dry out and become all spores, but are ideally harvested when they are about three-quarters black inside. At that point the galls on a single ear of corn can weigh about a pound (454 g).

Some fungi, most notably truffles, form a symbiosis with plants. Truffles live on the roots of various trees, mostly oak, hazelnuts, and lindens. The fungus gathers minerals from the soil and shares them with the tree. In turn the tree shares its sugars with the truffle. Due to this symbiotic relationship, truffles are nearly impossible to cultivate. One would have to grow a forest to have a truffle farm, and even then the exact conditions under which truffles generate is not completely understood.

The bulk of the fungi we eat can be cultivated. These live off the remains of dead plants, animal waste, or both. The world's most popular fungi, white button mushrooms and brown field mushrooms (genus *Agaricus*), are grown in a mixture of sterilized manure, straw, and soil.

Mushrooms are what we call the parts of fungi that have a stem, a cap, and gills on the underside of the cap. The closer a fungus resembles the classic mushroom shape, the more likely we are to call it a mushroom. Trumpet-shaped chanterelles are called mushrooms even though their caps merge

science wise

Truffle Flavor • Black truffles have a musky aroma from androstenone, a steroid that is also in male underarm sweat and in the saliva of boars, which prompts a mating response from sows. Some people find androstenone repulsive, and others don't smell it at all (which is fine because it leaves more truffles for those of us who appreciate them). Raw white truffles are more pungent than black and slightly garlicky, but their flavor is fleeting and wiped out by too much heat. For that reason white truffles are usually finely shaved (to disseminate their strong aroma) right onto hot food at the table, so that they are gently warmed and their flavor doesn't get a chance to dissipate.

seamlessly with their stems and their gills are on the outside rather than the underside, but the wavy, fleshy ear-like tree fungus, also known as wood ear (genus *Auricularia*), loved by Chinese cooks for its gelatinous texture is never called a wood ear mushroom.

How It Works • The body of a fungus, the mycelium or shiro, is composed of a fine, cottony web of fibers called hyphae that spread throughout soil gathering nutrients. Hyphae are minute and prolific. A single cubic centimeter of soil can contain as much as 2,000 yards (1,800 m) of hyphae. One of the largest mycelia ever discovered was in Malheur National Forest in Oregon. Before logging roads cut through it, it covered 2,400 acres, the equivalent of 1,665 football fields.

Hyphae excrete enzymes into the soil, breaking plant material into nutrients. They also contribute fertile organic matter to soil, providing food for many invertebrates, and they release carbon dioxide back into the atmosphere. Because fungal mycelium is so adept at decomposing organic compounds, some scientists believe that it could be used to remove organic pollutants, like petroleum products and pesticides, from contaminated soil.

When the mycelium has grown large enough and accumulated enough energy that it is ready to reproduce, it creates a dense growth of interwoven hyphae, called a pin stage mushroom, that is forced up through the surface of the soil. Water is pumped into the fruit, and it becomes visible as a button mushroom, after which its size expands rapidly until it gets large enough to open up, releasing spores into the air.

Because the mycelium is usually hidden from view, we tend to think of the fruit of a fungus, the visible mushroom, as the whole thing. But mushrooms are just a small part of the life cycle of a fungus.

Non-fruiting hyphae are the source for mycoprotein, a cultivated meat substitute made by growing a mycelium of *Fusarium venenatum*, a common fungus, in a liquid medium. When the hyphae are thick they are harvested,

Fungi Ragoût

Dried wild mushrooms are potent ingredients, packing more flavor than many times more fresh mushrooms. A little goes a long way, so don't balk at the minuscule amount in the ingredient list. Not only will they expand when soaked, their soaking liquid is a powerhouse of mushroom flavor. Serve as a condiment to roasted meats or poultry.

1 cup	beef broth, heated, approx.	250 mL
½ oz	dried wild mushrooms	14 g
2 tbsp	butter	25 mL
1	leek, white part only, thinly sliced	1
8 oz	cremini mushrooms, cleaned and sliced	250 g
1 tbsp	all-purpose flour	15 mL
1	plum tomato, peeled, seeded, and chopped	1
1 tbsp	chopped flat-leaf Italian parsley	15 mL
½ tsp	fresh thyme leaves	2 mL
½ tsp	chopped fresh rosemary leaves	2 mL
	Finely grated zest and juice of ½ lemon	

1. In a heatproof bowl, combine warm broth and mushrooms (add more stock if necessary to cover the mushrooms). Let stand for 15 minutes. When soft, strain mushrooms and soaking liquid through a coffee filter or cheesecloth, reserving both separately.

2. In a saucepan over medium heat, melt butter. Add leeks, dried mushrooms, and cremini mushrooms and sauté until leek and cremini are tender, about 5 minutes.

3. Add flour and cook, stirring, until flour browns lightly, about 2 minutes. Add tomato, parsley, thyme, rosemary, and mushroom soaking liquid. Increase heat to high and bring to a boil, and simmer for 3 minutes. Stir in lemon zest and juice. Serve immediately.

MAKES 4 SERVINGS

washed, and heated to coagulate their proteins, producing thousands of tiny protein threads about the dimension of the muscle fibers of meat. Mycoprotein can be molded into a variety of meat facsimiles. It is mostly marketed under the brand name Quorn.

The fruiting bodies of fungi are critical to their reproduction and survival, so strong chemical defenses protect them from being eaten by predators. Some fungi are poisonous or deadly. Aflatoxins are potent defense chemicals produced by some species. They most commonly colonize on grains right before harvest and during storage, but they have also been found on crops of oil seeds, spices, and tree nuts and in the milk of animals that were fed contaminated feed. High-level exposure is carcinogenic and long-term low-level exposure to aflatoxin can lead to cirrhosis and malignancies in the liver. No animal species is immune.

See Also • Corn, Mushrooms, Toxin

FUZZY GOURD • See Squash

G

GALANGAL • See Flavor, Ginger

GALIA MELON • See Melon

GAME

What It Is • The domestication of animals for food has made good-quality meat more readily available, but it has changed the diversity of animal protein on our plates from several dozen species to fewer than ten. Our image of game, the meat from wild animals, is one of succulence. In fact, game animals tend to be lean and muscular because they get more exercise than their domesticated cousins — characteristics that make their meat dry and tough.

What It Does • Game meat can be either wild or farm-raised. Wild game live a natural life, and the qualities of their meat vary depending on what they eat, where and how they live, and how they die. Their meat is prized in much of the world, but because wild meat is not inspected it is banned from commerce in North America. For that reason, "game meat" sold in stores and restaurants in North America (and increasingly in the rest of the world) refers to meat from animals raised on farms and ranches (of course hunters are perfectly free to consume animals they have hunted themselves). Game animals have been reared in captivity since ancient times. They are not intensively bred, so they are genetically similar to their wild counterparts, but farm-raised game meat is more consistent and less gamy because the animals live in confined areas protected from predators, are fed a controlled diet, and are slaughtered in the same way as domesticated farmed animals.

The popularity of game, particularly venison, buffalo, and ostrich, is on the rise because they are leaner than domestic meat and poultry. The word "venison," which comes from the Latin *venari*, "to hunt," used to mean all hunted animals, but today refers exclusively to the meat of deer, including antelope, caribou, elk, red deer, fallow deer, roe deer, gazelle, moose, and reindeer. Some exotic game animals, such as antelope and ostrich, are now farmed, which has made them more readily available and a popular low-fat alternative to domestically raised meat.

For purposes of hunting, wild game is

Types of Game Meat

The following three charts cover most game meats, both hunted and farmed. The Widespread Wild Game chart has information about hunted game animals that are not endangered (except for bison). The Exotic Wild Game chart covers hunted wild animals, some of which have conservation advisories. The Farmed Game chart gives information about game animals raised on game farms for food.

Widespread Wild Game

Animal	Meat Description	Where Found	Conservation Status*
American alligator	Cross between chicken and pork; gamy, tender, pale meat	Southern U.S.	LC
Bear (black bear and brown bear)	Like beef but dark, tough, and stringy. Harbors parasites and must be cooked thoroughly; liver can have high vitamin A levels	Northern North America	LC
Bison	Tougher, leaner, and stronger tasting than beef	Rocky Mountains	NT
Caribou (aka reindeer)	Like deer but tougher	Arctic and Subarctic	LC
Chukar	Like partridge, dark meat throughout; large breasts	Asian native, introduced into North America	LC
Deer and elk	Like beef; very lean, short tender fibers; lower in calories, fat, and cholesterol	North America	LC
Dove (pigeon)	Dark meat, very flavorful and moist, especially breast	North America	LC
Duck (mallard)	Much less fat than domestic duck; dark, flavorful meat, especially breast	North America, Europe, Asia	LC
Frog	Like chicken but slightly tougher; only leg is eaten	Southern U.S., Caribbean, Europe, and Asia	LC
Goose	Dark meat, flavorful; leaner and tougher than domestic goose	North America, Europe, Asia	LC
Grouse (willow grouse, ptarmigan)	Dark meat, very flavorful and moist, especially breast	Northern North America, Europe, and Asia	LC
Hare (jackrabbit)	Like chicken but tougher, leaner, and more flavorful	North America, Europe, Asia	LC
Moose	Like beef; tender, flavorful, very lean, and high in unsaturated fat; liver can have high cadmium levels	Northern North America, Europe, and Asia	LC
Muskrat	Like rabbit but darker; stronger flavor	North America, South America, Europe, Asia	LC
Opossum	Like chicken; fine-grained, light-colored, mild; musk glands must be removed before cooking	North America	LC
Partridge	Dark meat throughout; large breasts; similar in flavor and meatiness to squab	North America, Europe, Asia	LC
Pheasant	Bred for hunting; like turkey; very lean, pale meat, tends to be dry	Worldwide	LC
Quail (New World)	Like chicken; pale, tender meat	North America	LC
Rabbit	Like chicken or turkey; stronger-tasting, lean, pale meat; legs can be tough	Worldwide	LC
Raccoon	Like pork; very strong tasting, especially fat; can be tough	North America; mostly hunted in Southern U.S.	LC

continued on next page

Types of Game Meat (continued)

Widespread Wild Game (continued)

Conservation Animal	Meat Description	Where Found	Status*
Squirrel	Like chicken or rabbit; tender and moist	North America	LC
Wild boar	Like pork and beef; very dark sweet meat, tender and lean. Can harbor parasites and must be cooked thoroughly.	Introduced throughout North America in the 20th century; still common in Europe	LC
Wild turkey	Like turkey but smaller, leaner, tougher, more flavorful	North America	LC

Exotic Wild Game

Conservation Animal	Meat Description	Where Found	Status*
Antelope	Like beef; very lean, short tender fibers; lower in calories, fat, and cholesterol	Eurasia and Africa	NT
Crocodile	Cross between chicken and pork; gamy; tender, pale meat	Africa, Asia, Australia, South America	VU
Eland	Like beef; very lean; lower in calories, fat, and cholesterol	Africa	NT
Emu	Like beef; red meat, flavorful; fat used for cosmetics	Australia	LC
Gazelle	Like beef; very lean, short tender fibers; lower in calories, fat, and cholesterol	Africa	NT
Gemsbok	Like beef; very lean, short tender fibers; lower in calories, fat, and cholesterol	Africa	NT
Impala	Like beef; very lean, short tender fibers; lower in calories, fat, and cholesterol	Africa	NT
Kangaroo	Like beef; red, strong-tasting meat; low in fat, high in iron	Australia	LC
Wild boar	Like pork and beef; very dark sweet meat, tender and lean	Africa and Europe	LC
Zebra	Like beef; dark red, strong tasting, lean	Africa	NT

Farmed Game

Conservation Animal**	Meat Description	Where Found	Status*
Antelope, blackbuck	Like beef; very lean, short tender fibers; lower in calories, fat, and cholesterol	Western U.S.	NT
Bison	Like beef but leaner; lower in cholesterol. Also crossed with cattle to produce beefalo.	Western U.S.	LC
Deer and elk	Like beef; very lean, short tender fibers; lower in calories, fat, and cholesterol	North America and New Zealand	LC
Duck (mallard and muscovy)	Much less fat than domestic duck; dark, flavorful meat, especially breast	North America, Europe, and Asia	LC
Emu	Like beef; lean; low in fat, high in protein	North America and Australia	LC
Frog	Like chicken but slightly tougher; only leg is eaten	Southern U.S., Europe, and Asia	LC

Guinea fowl	Like chicken but leaner and more flavorful; pale meat throughout	North America and Europe	LC
Hare	Like chicken but tougher, leaner, and more flavorful	North America, Europe, and Asia	LC
Ostrich	Like beef but leaner, darker; low in fat, high in protein	Worldwide	LC
Quail	Like chicken; pale, tender meat	Throughout North America	LC
Pheasant	Like turkey; very lean, pale meat; tends to be dry	Worldwide	LC
Rabbit	Like chicken; pink to red meat; lean, flavorful	Throughout North America, Europe, and Asia	LC
Squab (young pigeon)	Dark, strong-tasting meat, especially breast	Worldwide	LC

*The World Conservation Union (IUCN) publishes the IUCN Red List, a conservation status listing that ranks the threat of extinction for all wild animals. The rankings are divided into three categories:

Lower Risk: Least Concern (LC), Near Threatened (NT)

Threatened: Vulnerable (VU), Endangered (EN), Critically Endangered (CE), Threatened (T)

Extinction: Extinct in the Wild (EW), Extinct (EX)

**Conservation status doesn't apply to the animals that are farmed, but in one case (antelope) the animal is threatened, which is why it is being farmed.

categorized by size. Small game includes small mammals (rabbit, squirrel, muskrat, etc.) and birds. Large game includes animals such as deer, bear, and elk. Although large game is sometimes called big game, big game usually refers to animals in Africa hunted for sport, or for pelts or tusks, and is not typically thought of as food. Many game animals that once were highly prized have been hunted to extinction. Most countries have laws to protect endangered species and to regulate their hunting to keep their numbers above endangered levels.

How It Works • Wild game animals get more exercise, eat a more varied diet, and are usually taken at an older age than domestically bred animals. Consequently their meat is darker, tougher, leaner, and stronger tasting. The pronounced wild taste of game is called gamy. Gaminess was appreciated in earlier times and was intensified by hanging (dry-aging) game animals after slaughter to tenderize them and increase their flavor. To the modern palate, strong gamy flavors are undesirable, and the diet and exercise of

farm-raised game are restricted to discourage gaminess. Like domestic animals, farm-raised game is usually slaughtered before it reaches sexual maturity to insure mild flavor and tenderness.

The low fat content of game meat causes it to dry out faster than the marbled meat of animals fattened in commercial farms. It cooks faster and it suffers from overcooking more overtly. For that reason, many game meats should not be cooked beyond medium-rare. If you want to cook them more, it is helpful to "bard" them with a layer of fat or fatty bacon draped over top, or "lard" them with plugs of fat inserted into the meat. Basting with

Venison Burgers with Juniper and Mustard

The mustard seeds in these hearty pungent burgers are soaked in gin, which softens their skins, giving them a resiliency that makes them pop between the teeth with every bite. The juniper in the mixture underscores the gin's flavor, and its piney fragrance connects us to the forest foliage on which deer feed.

2 tsp	brown mustard seeds	10 mL
2 tbsp	gin	25 mL
2 lbs	ground venison chuck	1 kg
2 tbsp	spicy brown mustard	25 mL
½ tsp	finely ground juniper berries	2 mL
½ tsp	kosher salt	2 mL
	Oil for coating the pan	
6	hamburger buns, split	6

1. In a small bowl, combine mustard seeds and gin and set aside to soak for about 10 minutes.

2. In a bowl, using your hands, mix venison, mustard seed/gin mixture, spicy mustard, juniper, and salt until well blended (do not overmix). Using a light touch, form into 6 patties no more than 1-inch (2.5 cm) thick.

3. Heat a large heavy skillet, preferably iron, over high heat for 5 minutes. Pour in enough oil to coat the pan with a thin film. Add burgers and cook until browned on both sides and cooked to desired doneness, about 7 minutes for medium-well done, 155°F (68°C), slightly pink. Add 2 minutes for well done, 160°F (71°C).

4. Toast buns in a toaster, if desired.

5. Just before serving, place burgers on buns (to prevent sogginess do not let stand even for a few minutes).

MAKES 6 SERVINGS

a watery liquid also helps by cooling the surface through evaporation, which slows down the heat transfer and makes the meat cook more slowly.

Food-borne illness is a concern when handling any protein, but with wild game that did not go through an inspection process, it is a greater hazard. All animals harbor bacteria, especially on their skins and in their intestinal tracts, so cleaning game properly is vitally important. Small game can be taken to a sanitary butchering facility intact, but large game, like moose or caribou, are usually partially butchered in the field to make them easier to transport. Care must be taken to clean the cutting site meticulously, and the animal parts must be kept cold until they arrive at a facility where they can be completely processed. During hunting season many commercial butchers handle wild game for hunters.

Parasites, such as *Trichinella spiralis*, which causes trichinosis, were long associated with pork, but now that feeding commercial pigs uncooked garbage is banned, the incidence of trichinosis from pork is inconsequential. There hasn't been an incidence of trichinosis from commercially raised pork in many years. However, wild game, especially bear and boar, can and do harbor parasites. They must be cooked to at least 150°F (66°C), or frozen below 5°F (–15°C) for more than 20 days before cooking.

See Also • Beef, Chicken, Meat, Pork, Poultry

GAME HEN • See Chicken

GARAM MASALA • See Spices

GARBANZO BEAN • See Legumes

GARI • See Ginger

GARLIC • See Allium

GELATIN

What It Is • Have you ever noticed that the meat drippings left in a roasting pan or the broth from a long-simmered chicken soup turn into jelly as they cool? What's happening? Collagen, the main protein in animal connective tissue, has hydrated (bonded with water), creating a gel. Gelatin is denatured collagen that has been purified and dried. It is sold in sheets or powder, and can be turned back into a gel just by mixing it with water. Except for instant products, gelatins require heat as well as water to form a sturdy gel.

What It Does • Gelatin gels are remarkable substances. Transparent, glistening with refracted light, they are beautiful on their own or as a backdrop for suspended ingredients. Gelatin melts right around body temperature, allowing it to transform into a full-bodied fluid in the heat of the mouth, bathing the mouth with flavor.

Manufactured gelatin is more predictable than the gelatin that develops when roasting meat or in a homemade stock, since meat bones vary in their collagen content and long cooking can break down gelatin chains. The best way to figure out the strength of your jellied mixture when making a homemade stock or using pan drippings and it is still liquid is to chill a spoonful in a small dish. If the gel seems fragile, you can reduce the liquid by boiling longer, thereby concentrating the gelatin content, or add a little unflavored manufactured gelatin.

Unflavored gelatin comes in the form of sheets (or leaves) and granules (or powder): 4 gelatin sheets = 1 envelope (0.25 oz/7 g) granulated gelatin = 1 tablespoon (15 mL) granulated gelatin. Sheets introduce less air

science wise

Gelatin: Poor Protein Source • For decades the Knox company touted its gelatin as a good source of protein, especially good at strengthening dry, brittle nails and hair. But our bodies produce ample amounts of all of the amino acids found in gelatin, so getting them from a dietary source is unnecessary.

Not only is there no evidence for gelatin's nutritional protein claims but gelatin provides less nutritional value as a protein than any other "protein source." Gelatin is unusually high in nonessential amino acids and unusually low in some of the essential amino acids that we have to eat in order to build high-quality protein. In fact, gelatin is one of the few foods that cause a net loss of protein if eaten exclusively. In the 1970s several people died of malnutrition while on liquid protein gelatin diets.

into the gelling liquid and therefore set into a clearer gel. Instant gelatin is manufactured so that it can dissolve in warm water without presoaking.

Aspics are natural savory gelatins usually made from clarified meat, poultry, or fish stock, but some vegetable gelatins, like tomato, are called aspic to differentiate them from sweet fruit gelatins. Classic aspic recipes often include a veal foot for added collagen to create a gel that is firm enough to cut or to coat a terrine to preserve it. Chaud-froid sauce is aspic enriched with cream, used for coating roasted chilled meats to preserve them for food-show presentations.

Gelatins are also used to make fruit desserts, set marshmallows, firm mousses, stabilize dairy products like ice cream, yogurt, and cream cheese, and provide a rich mouth feel in fat-reduced products. Gelatin is one of the secret ingredients behind the otherworldly creations of avant-garde **molecular gastronomy** chefs who use it to play with diners' expectations, forming gummy candies out of olive oil or painting a plate with beet foam.

How It Works • In order for a gel to form, the amount of gelatin in a liquid dilution has to be greater than 1% of the liquid's total weight. At that concentration there is enough hydrolyzed protein so that their long chains overlap one another, forming a continuous network. The viscosity and firmness of the gel become more solid as it becomes more concentrated and as it gets colder. A 1% gelatin gel is quivery and hard to handle, perfect for a glaze that you want to melt on contact with the warmth of the mouth. Sturdier gelatin desserts have a concentration of 3% or higher. One-quarter ounce (7 g) of gelatin in 1 cup (250 mL) water creates a 3% solution.

Natural collagen is a triple helix of long tropocollagen protein molecules. During heating in water, the bonds between the three strands break, releasing the three strands that when cooled will form a stable matrix that holds water (a gel). Gelatin can be melted and cooled countless times without disrupting its ability to form a

Chicken Noodle Soup from Leftovers

Have you ever noticed that soup made from a leftover turkey or chicken carcass isn't as good as you think it should be? You're not being picky; you're just missing the gelatin. Broth made from fresh meat and bones is loaded with gelatin that gives it a full-bodied consistency. When you start with roasted bones and meat, all the gelatin was extracted during roasting and ended up in the drippings, so your soup tastes watery. The solution is simple. Add a little powdered gelatin and the lip-smacking slightly syrupy texture of great homemade soup will be instantly renewed.

For the vegetable tops and trimmings use carrots, celery, onion, mushrooms, parsnips, turnips, leeks, tomatoes, and sweet potatoes (don't use a lot of dark leafy vegetables).

3	cooked chicken carcasses	3
1 cup	white wine	250 mL
1	envelope (¼ oz/7 g) unflavored gelatin	1
10 cups	water, divided	2.5 L
4 cups	vegetable tops and trimmings, diced, unsightly parts discarded	1 L
3 tbsp	chopped flat-leaf Italian parsley	45 mL
1 tsp	dried thyme leaves	5 mL
1	whole clove	1
	Salt and freshly ground black pepper to taste	
2 cups	cooked egg noodles	500 mL

1. In a large stockpot, combine carcasses and wine. Bring to a boil and boil for 3 minutes.
2. Meanwhile, in a small bowl, stir together gelatin with ¼ cup (50 mL) of the water to soften.
3. Add remaining water to pot. Return to a boil, skim surface, and simmer for 20 minutes.
4. Add vegetable trimmings, parsley, thyme, clove, salt, pepper, and softened gelatin. Simmer for 1 hour. Remove bones and let cool. Pick off any meat and return to the soup along with the cooked noodles. Reheat. Discard clove before serving.

MAKES 6 SERVINGS

strong, consistent gel. Gelatin will remain a gel only in a fairly narrow temperature range. Above around 212°F (100°C) (it varies slightly by manufacturer), it will melt, and if the water in the gel should freeze, it will be destroyed.

fast facts

- Salt interferes with gelatin bonding and lowers gel strength.
- Sugar attracts water away from a gel, thereby increasing its thickness.
- The protein in milk strengthens a gel.
- Alcohol makes gelatin set more firmly, although when the concentration becomes more than 30% of the total volume, the alcohol will cause the gelatin to solidify into hard particles.
- Some tropical plants, such as ginger, pineapple, and papaya, contain proteolytic enzymes that break down proteins and keep gelatin from forming a gel. Cooking (or canning) denatures the enzymes.

Most manufactured gelatin is extracted from pig skin, although some comes from cattle skin and/or bones. Industrial extraction is much more efficient than what happens on a stove. Skins are soaked in weak acid for about 24 hours to break the collagen's crosslinking bonds. Then the gelatin is gently extracted through gradual heating, starting at 130°F (54°C) and ending at 195°F (90°C). The first extraction is the clearest and strongest, and the final, which contains a greater number of broken protein chains, is slightly yellow and sets less solidly. The extractions are defatted, filtered, and purified, their pH is adjusted to 5.5, and finally they are dried into sheets or granules. Gelatin quality is graded by a Bloom number; a score of 300 indicates the best gelling power. The test is named after Oscar Bloom, the inventor of the gelling measuring device. "Bloom" also refers to the step of softening gelatin in cool water before heating it.

Gelatins for special diets specify their origin on the package. Kosher and halal gelatin comes from fish. Vegan gelatins are not protein gels but polysaccharide gels derived from **seaweeds** or **pectin**.

See Also • Colloid, Dispersions, Gums, Molecular Gastronomy

GELATINIZATION • See Starch

GELATO • See Ice Cream

GELLAN GUM • See Gums

GELS • See Gelatin

GENETICS

What It Is • Genetics explains the way living things receive traits from previous generations. Genes are units of inheritance that are passed on from parent to child and determine both physical appearance and behavior. Genes also determine the traits of a whole family or population.

What It Does • Broccoli, Brussels sprouts, and cabbage all contain a sulfur compound (and some other smelly stuff) that breaks down during cooking, causing a strong aroma that many people find distasteful. All three vegetables are members of the same botanical family, Cruciferae, which means genetically they share common traits. Because they are similarly flavored they can be substituted for one another easily, and they will have similar nutritional benefits. When a study touts the antioxidant benefits of broccoli or the high **vitamin** C content of cabbage, it's a good bet that other members of the same family will share similar benefits. Likewise, once you know that deer and moose come from the same family you can assume that their meat will have some similarity and can be cooked in similar ways.

Through artificial selection, breeders are able to develop cultivated breeds of animals and cultivars of plants that have desirable traits. The traits can be behavioral or physical, making roosters more passive, turkeys with larger breasts, or tomatoes that resist mold. Charles Darwin posited that artificial selection and natural selection were the two ways that species evolved, one determined by man's intentions, and the other by the forces of nature.

Bioengineering (aka genetic engineering or genetic modification) takes this one step further. Instead of honing genetic traits over generations of breeding, bioengineers transplant genetic material from one being to another, thereby creating specific genetic traits in a single generation. Genetically modifying plants and animals (known as GMOs, or genetically modified organisms) has been possible since the 1970s. One of the first commercial uses was in herbicide-resistant plants that revolutionized the way commercially produced soybeans and corn are grown.

Golden rice (developed in the 1990s) is genetically modified white rice implanted with a gene that synthesizes the precursors to beta-carotene in the endosperm of the grain. Golden rice was developed to help people suffering from vitamin A deficiency, which leads to blindness and death. Because rice is a staple food in the parts of the world where vitamin A deficiency is prevalent (mostly Africa and Southeast Asia), golden rice is seen as a simple, inexpensive alternative to vitamin supplements. Newer strains have increased vitamin A levels.

Controversy over genetic modification has held back its commercial applications. GMO crops are banned in many countries, partly because of the view that genetic engineering is

science wise

Origins of Genetics • Between 1856 and 1865 Gregor Mendel, an Austrian monk, cultivated and tested 29,000 pea plants and showed that one out of four plants had purebred recessive genes, two out of four were hybrid, and one out of four were purebred dominant. His study, published as "Experiments on Plant Hybridization," put forth two generalizations, which later became known as Mendel's laws of inheritance and formed the basis for later genetic studies. The paper had little impact during Mendel's lifetime.

meddling in biological processes that should be allowed to evolve naturally, and also because of suspicions that science does not fully comprehend the negative ramifications of manipulating genes. Proponents of organic farming, which forbids the use of genetically modified seed, are concerned that pollen from GMO crops can cross-pollinate with conventional crops, causing unintended genetic changes. On the other hand, planting genetically modified crops can decrease the use of pesticides and herbicides, which addresses other concerns of the organic farming movement.

Genetic transmission between species may have serious health consequences. In 1993, genes from Brazil nuts were transferred to soybeans to increase their protein quality. Unfortunately, the chosen protein gene produced allergic reactions in people with tree-nut allergies and the modification was subsequently discontinued. Some GMO opponents want cross-species modification outlawed; others want laws passed requiring products containing GMO ingredients to be labeled as such.

The controversy over genetic modification of food pales next to the reaction to the potential production of cloned food. Cloning is the process of creating an exact genetic copy of an organism asexually. In horticulture, cloning (through grafting) is a common practice. Grafting is a form of cloning, since all the shoots and branches coming from a graft are a genetic clone of an individual plant, not a mixture of genes from two parents, but plant cloning has not met the same level of ethical opposition as animal cloning.

The birth of Dolly, a Finn Dorset ewe cloned from a single adult sheep cell in 1996, focused attention — and outrage — on cloning animals. In 2008 the FDA ruled that food products from cloned animals were safe for consumption.

How It Works ● DNA (deoxyribonucleic acid) molecules store genetic information. Think of them as sets of blueprints that show an organism how to reproduce itself. They are made of long chains of genes, each one holding a piece of genetic information. Different versions of the same gene (alleles) dictate which trait will appear. For instance, the gene for eye color has two alleles, one for blue eyes and one for brown eyes. When the gene contains two copies of the same allele, that trait appears. When one of each allele is in a gene, one allele tends to dominate and is called the dominant allele; the other is called recessive. Often one allele does not have complete dominance, so the trait expressed is a combination of the two alleles. Even when one allele dominates, the recessive allele still exists in the background, and it is possible in future generations for two recessive alleles to come together and produce a trait.

Although eye color is a discrete trait, many traits, like the height or weight of an organism, are continuous features determined by many genes and their interaction with the environment. The degree to which genes contribute to these complex traits is called heritability, and that changes within a population and more dramatically across populations. (For genetic purposes a population is defined as a group of individuals belonging to the same species that share the same environment.)

The process of genetic modification has four steps:

1. The gene that will produce the desired genetic trait is identified through genetic mapping and is isolated.

2. The gene, usually within a strand of DNA, is placed in a vector, such as a bacterium or virus, that can transfer the gene into the targeted cells.

3. The targeted cells are exposed to the bacterial or viral vector, and the new genetic material transforms the targeted cells.

4. The genetically modified cells are grown in vitro, and can then be injected into the ovum of the targeted organism.

See Also ● Cells

GEODUCK ● See Mollusks

GERM ● See Grains

GHEE • See Butter

GIN • See Liquor

GINGER

What It Is • The sweet, spicy, cooling effect of ginger has been prized since prehistoric times. The underground stem (rhizome) of a tropical plant, *Zingiber officinale*, which originated in Asia, was known in classical Greece in its dried form and was one of the dominant spices in medieval European cooking. The spice cake known as gingerbread dates from that time, and ginger ale and ginger beer were popular in Victorian England. Fresh ginger is mistakenly called gingerroot even though it is not a root at all.

What It Does • The flavor of ginger is remarkably varied, giving it a wide range of uses in savory and sweet dishes. Ginger can be refreshing and light, with sparkling notes of citrus and flowers. It can have a mild peppery pungency, and a cooling effect similar to eucalyptus.

Most of the ginger in the world comes from India, China, and Africa, but Jamaican ginger is considered the finest. Depending on where it grows, ginger can have very different qualities. Chinese ginger tends to be spicy. African ginger is pungent. Indian ginger is high in lemony components, and Jamaican ginger is sweet and mild.

- A rhizome of ginger resembles a human hand, which is why a large piece of ginger is called a hand, and each digit a finger.
- Ginger stimulates the production of saliva.
- Gingerol is a chemical irritant and was used by disreputable horse traders as a suppository to make an old horse seem livelier during a sale.

Ginger is a staple in Asian cooking, and its flavor is an essential element in many European sausages and pâtés. It is the dominant flavor in ginger cookies, ginger ale, ginger tea, and ginger cakes. It is the flavor of Canton liqueur, and is a popular flavoring for coffee in the Middle East. In Yemen as much as 15% of the weight of coffee can be powdered ginger. Pickled ginger, *gari* or *beni shoga*, is a standard condiment in Japan, and fresh ginger is shredded for the Burmese salad *gyin-tho*.

In folk medicine, ginger is used to relieve nausea and gastric distress. It is also recommended to relieve inflammation, although studies of the effect of ginger on arthritis pain have had inconsistent results.

Galangal, a close relative of ginger, is more pungent and less sweet. Often called Thai ginger, it lacks the lighter citrus and floral notes of ginger and is used mostly for savory and spicy preparations. In Thailand it is frequently combined with lemongrass. Galangal is an ingredient in Chartreuse and in some bitters.

Grains of paradise are the seeds from a ginger relative and are popular in the food of North Africa. Also called alligator pepper and Guinea pepper, the spice is pungent, with a sweet piney aroma. It is a component of the Moroccan spice blend *ras el hanout*. Grains of paradise are a good substitute for black pepper.

How It Works • The characteristic compound of the essential oil in ginger, zingiberene, gives it most of its characteristic flavor, supported by several other terpenes, bisabolene, farnesene, cineol, and citral. The terpenes are intensified by phenolic compounds, particularly gingerols.

Gingerols are weak chemical relatives of the capsaicin in chiles and the piperine in black pepper. When ginger is dried its gingerol molecules are transformed into shogaols, which are twice as pungent, making dried ginger much stronger than fresh. Gingerols break down into both shogaols and zingerone during cooking. Zingerone is milder than gingerol and quite sweet. The combination of the two is why ginger flavor tempers and blossoms during baking.

See Also • Flavor, Spices, Stems

GLACE DE VIANDE • See Stocks

GLIADIN • See Gluten

GLUCOSE • See Sugar

GLUTAMIC ACID • See Protein

GLUTEN

What It Is • When two **proteins** in wheat, gliadin and glutenin, are combined with water and mixed they form the largest composite protein molecule in the world, gluten. Like all proteins in solution, gluten is viscous, but because of its size, wheat gluten forms particularly large, stretchy sheets that give wheat doughs their unique texture and their ability to rise. Other **grains**, notably rye and barley, contain some gliadin and glutenin, but not nearly as much as wheat.

What It Does • Gluten is both elastic (it stretches and bounces back) and plastic (it is malleable and holds a shape). Its elasticity (from glutenins) is what allows it to stretch, trapping gas from leaveners and raising dough. Its plasticity (from gliadins) is what causes it to resist stretching and form a sturdy round loaf of bread or flat rectangle of **pastry**. Taken together, these two properties give gluten incredible versatility.

Not all baked products profit from the development of gluten. What is delicious and chewy in bread turns out to be hard and tough

in cake. To manipulate tenderness, bakers take steps to impair the development of gluten in some recipes and encourage it in others.

High-protein bread **flours** produce strong gluten. Low-protein cake flours (and to a lesser extent medium-protein pastry flours) make weak gluten. The strongest gluten is from durum semolina wheat flour, often used for making pasta because it's more plastic and less elastic, which is exactly what you want for maintaining the delicate curve of macaroni without making the noodle tough. Oxidizing agents like bromates and ascorbic acid (often called improving agents) added to flour increase the ability of glutenin to form bonds and strengthen gluten.

A small percentage of liquid (as in pastry or shortbreads) inhibits gluten development and produces a crumbly texture. A lot of liquid (as in cake batters) dilutes the gluten and makes a soft, moist baked product.

Stirring and/or kneading a batter or dough increases gluten development.

Salt increases the crosslinking of glutenin proteins and thereby increases the elasticity of gluten. **Sugar** competes with water for the protein bonds and weakens the gluten structure.

Fats and oils coat flour particles, keeping water from hydrating gluten proteins, thereby shortening the strands of gluten (hence the name "shortening"). Solid fats layered in pastry dough create large flakes of gluten, such as in a flaky pie crust. Liquid fats disperse more finely, generating sandy-textured short doughs, such as in a shortbread cookie or a short-flake pastry.

Acids weaken gluten and tenderize doughs, which is the secret behind the softness of buttermilk pancakes, and why vinegar is added to pie crust in some recipes.

Vital gluten flour, made by washing the starch from wheat flour and drying and grinding the resulting gluten to a powder, is added to doughs to increase their elasticity, but it is also used in food processing in unexpected ways, such as a stabilizing agent in ice cream or in ketchup.

These hidden uses of gluten can be hazardous for people with celiac disease (sprue), an autoimmune intestinal disorder that causes

Seitan

Because gluten is insoluble in water, it can be isolated from wheat flour by washing a gluten-rich dough in several changes of water to remove the starch. The resulting gummy mass is 100% gluten. Its chewy texture is reminiscent of meat, and it can be flavored to taste like a variety of meats. Seitan was developed in China and is still most popular there.

To make seitan

1 cup	vital wheat gluten flour	250 mL
Pinch	active dry yeast	Pinch
¼ tsp	garlic powder	1 mL
3 tbsp	soy sauce	45 mL
1 tbsp	tomato paste	15 mL
⅔ cup	very cold water	150 mL

To cook seitan

6 cups	ice water	1.5 L
¼ cup	soy sauce	50 mL

1. To make seitan: In a bowl, stir together gluten flour, yeast, and garlic powder.

2. In a small bowl, stir together soy sauce and tomato paste until completely combined. Stir into dry ingredients just to disperse.

3. Add cold water and stir with a wooden spoon or paddle until dry ingredients come together into a ball. (Not all the liquid will be absorbed.) Using your hands, knead the ball of gluten in the bowl just until it starts to feel elastic. Remove from liquid, discarding liquid, and continue to knead the gluten for a few minutes until very bouncy. Set aside for 5 minutes.

4. To cook seitan: In a saucepan, combine ice water and soy sauce. (It is fine to include pieces of ice.)

5. Gently form gluten ball into a log about 8 inches (20 cm) long and cut into 4 pieces. Place in a saucepan, cover, and bring to a boil over medium heat. (The gluten will expand.) Immediately adjust the heat so that the liquid simmers, and simmer the gluten, covered, turning with a rubber spatula occasionally, for 1 hour. Let cool completely in the cooking liquid. Keep seitan covered and refrigerated for up to 1 week. Use in any recipe that calls for seitan.

MAKES ABOUT 1 POUND (500 G),
ABOUT 4 SERVINGS

chronic diarrhea, fatigue, and failure to thrive in infants. Celiac disease is caused by a reaction to gliadin, in which exposure to the protein causes the inflammation of the lining of the small intestine. The only treatment is a lifelong gluten-free diet. There are other forms of gluten sensitivity, some of which involve allergic reactions and others various degrees of indigestion.

How It Works • Gliadin and glutenin proteins are not soluble in water but they can form connections with water and with one another. When dry, the proteins are inert and remain separate, but when they come in contact with liquid they liven up, change shape, and start to interact.

Proteins are chains of amino acids. Gliadin and glutenin happen to be very long chains, about a thousand amino acids long each, and working together, they give wheat dough its elastic and plastic properties.

Glutenin chains are coiled like springs. A sulfur-containing amino acid sits at each end, and since sulfur molecules form strong bonds with one another, glutenin chains tend to line up end to end in super-long chains with springy midsections. Gliadin chains fold in on themselves into compact little balls that tend to stay separate, because they do not form strong bonds with one another nor with glutenins. Gluten is a combination of springy glutenin strands that stretch with kneading and roly-poly gliadin balls that act as a kind of lubricant, discouraging stretching and keeping the gluten malleable and in shape.

Kneading stretches out the gluten and aligns the protein chains. As soon as there's a pause in kneading, the glutenin recoils, causing dough to snap back. The energetic push and pull of well-kneaded glutenin can be a problem when making flatbreads, pizza, pastry, or pasta, in which maintaining a stretched-out shape is important. These products benefit from a resting period, which allows some of the weaker bonds that formed during mixing to break apart. The dough relaxes and is easier to shape.

The bonds between the coiled amino acids in the interior of glutenin chains are weak because they don't have a strong electrical attraction to one another. When you add salt to dough, the positive sodium and negative chlorine ions cluster around the amino acids and cause greater attraction, thus strengthening those bonds to create a firmer dough. Adding acid does the opposite. By increasing the number of positive ions, acid encourages repulsion between amino acids. The amount of sugar in sweet doughs (those with at least 10% sugar by weight) is concentrated enough to compete with proteins for water and block gluten formation, creating softer baked products.

See Also • Bread, Cake, Chemical Bonding, Flour, Grains, Gums, Pastry, Protein, Wheat

GLUTENIN • See Gluten

GLYCEMIC INDEX • See Carbohydrate

GLYCOGEN

What It Is • Animals store glucose in the form of glycogen for short-term energy needs. It is stored directly in muscle and organ cells so that it can be metabolized when glucose is needed for quick energy.

What It Does • All living things store energy in the form of either **starch** or **fat**. If they didn't they would have to consume energy constantly to sustain life. Plants, largely because they stay in one place, store most of their energy as starch, which is bulky and easily accessible. Fat is a more concentrated and compact form of stored energy. Plants use fats to store energy in seeds, where space is at a premium.

Active animals would be weighted down if the bulk of their energy was stored as starch, so animals use fat as their main system of energy storage. But fat takes time to be converted into energy. Glycogen, which is sometimes called animal starch, can be converted into energy quickly. Animals store glycogen in muscles and in some organs (mostly the liver) for times when a quick burst of energy is needed. The conversion of glycogen to glucose, called glycogenolysis, happens right in the cell.

Athletes rely on glycogen for quick bursts of energy during exercise and competition. Because human glycogen storage is limited, endurance athletes, who go through long periods of exertion without much energy consumption, experience glycogen depletion. This phenomenon, known as "hitting the wall" or "bonking," can be delayed by carbohydrate loading, eating extra calories before extended strenuous activity to build glycogen stores.

How It Works • Glucose absorbed into the blood during digestion travels to the liver, where some of it is converted to glycogen and stored. Up to 8% of the liver's mass can consist of stored glycogen. As blood glucose levels fall over time, the liver can metabolize its glycogen stores to meet energy needs throughout the body.

Glucose is also stored as glycogen in muscle cells, but that glycogen is only for the immediate use of that muscle. It doesn't travel through the blood the way liver glycogen does. Only about 1% of a muscle's mass can be devoted to glycogen storage, but because the mass of muscle in an animal's body is so much greater than the size of the liver, most of a body's glycogen is muscle glycogen.

See Also • Metabolism

GLYCOGENOLYSIS (Glycolysis) • See Glycogen

GMO • See Genetics

GNOCCHI • See Dumpling

GOAT

What It Is • Goats, one of the first animals to be domesticated after the dog, are able to live in rocky mountainous terrains and desert conditions unsuitable for other livestock, making them the primary source for meat and dairy in many parts of the world. Goats and sheep are closely related members of the same subfamily (Caprinae) from the family Bovidae. Sheep and goats are often grazed together in the same fields and grouped together when describing the qualities of their meat, milk, and cheese. Feta cheese is often made with a combination of sheep and goat milk. The meat from mature sheep and goat is called mutton.

What It Does • Goats are valued for almost all of their parts: meat, milk, hair, and skin. Young goat is called kid and produces pale, tender meat that is similar in quality to milk-fed veal. Mature females are does (aka nannies), males are bucks (aka billies), and castrated males are wethers. The meat of mature goats is dark, strong tasting, and stringy, but juicier than the meat from young animals. The meat from females is more flavorful than wethers' meat, which is sometimes compared to venison. Meat from bucks is very strong, and not

Milk Comparison

Milk	Protein (%)	Fat (%)	Lactose (%)	Water (%)
Human	1.1	4	6.8	88
Goat	3.4	4	4.5	88
Cattle	3.4	3.7	4.8	87

desirable for eating. Bucks are usually used only for breeding.

Unlike beef, goat meat is not marbled, which means that it does not tenderize well or retain moisture during cooking. Young goat can be roasted, but older animals need to be stewed or braised.

The main breeds of goat raised for meat are Boer and Kiko, both fast-growing, disease-resistant breeds. Although very little goat is eaten in North America, and almost all of it by Arab, Caribbean, and South Asian populations, its low fat and cholesterol content has made it one of the fastest growing sectors of the livestock industry.

Some goats are bred for **milk**. The Nubian goat is raised for meat and dairy, but because its fat content is higher than most goat's milk it is the preferred goat for large-scale dairy production. Goat's milk is more easily digested by humans than the milk of other four-legged mammals, but its strong flavor limits its popularity. In North America, most goat's milk is made into **cheese**.

Goat cheeses are produced locally all over the world. Fresh goat cheese is perfectly white and quite creamy. Unlike cow's milk cheese, goat cheese does not melt when baked. It blends easily into sauces and soups without the curdling problem of other cheeses, but heated on top of a pizza or a gratin it keeps its shape and will not flow. Goat's milk yogurt is popular in Europe and the Middle East. A small amount of goat's milk is churned into butter, which is delicious, but completely white, making it resemble rendered lard.

How It Works • Nutritionally, goat meat is lower in calories, fat, saturated fat, and cholesterol than beef, lamb, chicken, or pork. It is also higher in protein, calcium, iron, and copper.

Goat does not collect intramuscular fat (marbling), which accounts for much of its leanness. It does have thin layers of fat surrounding muscles, which is easily trimmed. Goats graze in pastures exclusively, and because they are browsers they tend to eat leaves from high-growing brush and shrubs, and large-leafed weeds rather than grass, making them ideal grazing companions for beef cattle and sheep. Goats have a particularly high need for copper, and those raised for meat are usually given supplements.

Goat's milk contains less lactose than cow's milk. Because of its low lactose content, people with lactase deficiency often tolerate goat's milk better than cow's milk.

Goat's milk does not need to be homogenized because its fat globules are so small that they do not rise like the fat in cow's milk.

The flavor of goat's milk can be intense. The flavor of most milk is mild, a blend of sweet lactose, a subtle saltiness from minerals, and a slight brightness of acid, and its mild aroma comes mostly from short-chain fatty acids (butyric and capric acids) that help keep saturated milk fat fluid at body temperature, which is why cream and butter melt in the mouth. Goat's milk contains two fatty acids (4-ethyloctanoic and 4-methyloctanoic) that are not in cow's milk, giving it a sweaty animal note; some call it barny. This aroma can become marked when the milk fats are concentrated, as they are in cheese and butter.

The color of goat dairy products is surprisingly white. The fat in dairy products carries vitamin A along with its orange-tinted precursors, the carotenes. Carotenes, which come from green leafy feed, give dairy products whatever color they have. Goats process nearly all of their carotene into colorless vitamin A, and so milk, cheese, and butter from goats, though just as nutritious as other dairy, are whiter than cow's milk products.

Sheep and goat cheeses are coagulated with acid rather than rennin (a protein coagulant from calf's stomach). In

science wise

Fainting Goat • The myotonic, or fainting, goat (aka nervous goat, wooden-leg goat, and Tennessee scare goat) is a domestic breed whose external muscles freeze when the animal is startled. The characteristic is caused by a genetic disorder called myotonia congenita. Young fainting goats fall over; older animals learn to spread their legs or lean against something when startled. The attack usually lasts about 10 seconds. In the past they were used for protecting sheep flocks by "sacrificing themselves" to predators, allowing the rest of the flock to escape.

rennin-processed products, the protein micelles that thicken the cheese are bound together by calcium atoms that hold the protein in weak suspension. When the cheese is heated, the bonds break and the cheese starts to flow. In acid-coagulated cheese, there is no calcium holding it together. Instead, the acid neutralizes the electrical repulsion between proteins, allowing them to bond together more readily. When heated, there are no calcium bonds to break, so the protein curds more tightly, becoming grainy rather than fluid. Acid-coagulated cheese freezes well, unlike other cheeses that break during freezing.

See Also • Cheese, Lamb, Meat, Milk

GOAT CHEESE • See Cheese, Goat

GOAT'S MILK • See Goat, Milk

GOOSE • See Poultry

GOOSEBERRY • See Berries

GORGONZOLA • See Cheese

GOUDA • See Cheese

GOURD • See Squash

GRAFTING • See Horticulture

GRAINS

What It Is • Grain, the edible part of a cereal grass, is a complete fruit, containing a seed and a layer of ovary that, instead of being fleshy and moist as it is in orchard and garden fruits, is thin and dry. The cultivation of many of the world's major grains — rice, wheat, barley, oats, millet, and rye — started between 12,000 and 14,000 years ago. Maize, or corn, was first cultivated about 2,000 years later. Three of these grains — barley, oats, and rice — are covered by tough hulls that need to be removed before the grain can be eaten.

What It Does • Cereal grains are one of our richest sources of calories, and in the developing world grain constitutes almost the entire diet of poor populations. Grains, even refined grains, deliver a significant amount of protein, although most are deficient in lysine, an essential amino acid, notable exceptions being buckwheat, quinoa, and amaranth. These three provide complete protein with all the essential amino acids. In many cuisines, grains that don't contain lysine are served with legumes — corn tortillas and refried beans, rice and tofu, peanut butter on bread — which contain ample supplies of lysine, because the combination provides a complete range of amino acids.

All grains are milled into flour. They are also cooked whole or cracked (to speed up cooking) and processed into ready-to-eat breakfast cereals. Ready-to-eat cereals originated as whole-grain health foods in the middle of the 19th century, a far cry from the fortified junk food many have become.

Corn (maize), **rice**, and **wheat** account for 87% of all grain grown. You can find out more about each of them in their respective entries. Other important cereal grains are:

Amaranth: A tiny seed, about 1 millimeter across, amaranth has been cultivated for 5,000 years in Central America. The Aztecs popped it like corn, and sweetened it, a recipe that lives on in modern Mexico in the festival candy *alegría. Ramdana laddu*, a boiled sweet made from amaranth, is served at family festivals in the Uttar Pradesh state of India. Amaranth is commonly used to supplement other grains to add nutrition to baked products, breakfast cereals, and healthy snacks. Amaranth is a source of complete protein.

Barley: Like all grains, barley can be highly nutritious, but the whole-grain version takes a long time to cook. To shorten cooking, almost all barley used in home kitchens is pearled, a process that removes the outer layers, most of the nutrients, and much of the flavor.

• Pearled barley is the most commonly used and least nutritious form of barley.

• Pot barley, or Scotch barley, is less polished so some of the nutritious outer layers remain. It takes about one hour to cook.

• Whole-grain barley, or whole (hulled) barley, is barley from which only the outer hull is removed, leaving the outer layers intact. It is the most nutritious form of the grain, but it needs at least an hour and up to an hour and three-quarters of cooking to make it tender enough to eat.

• Barley flakes and grits are bits of whole-grain barley and are more nutritious than pearled. They cook quickly because they are smaller than whole barley.

Most barley for human consumption is turned into **malt** and then fermented into beer. A small amount of malted barley becomes syrup for commercial baking or malt syrup. Malt syrup is made by soaking malted barley with plain cooked grains. The malted barley enzymes hydrolyze the starches in the cooked grain into a sweet slurry that is extracted with the addition of water, and boiled down to a syrup.

Barley contains a large quantity (about 5% by weight) of two nonstarch carbohydrates. Arabinoxylans (formerly called pentosans) are medium-sized sugar polymers that can absorb large amounts of water. Arabinoxylans hold on to water after being cooked and cooled, so baked goods made with barley stay fresh much longer. Glucans, water-retaining carbohydrates, are similarly structured. They also absorb and hold a lot of water, which gives barley cereal a slick, smooth consistency. Glucans keep baked goods moist and have been shown to lower blood cholesterol levels.

Buckwheat: Buckwheat is not related to wheat, and technically is not even a grain. It is the fruit of a relative of rhubarb, *Fagopyrum esculentum*. A native of Southeast Asia, it is now cultivated in cold climates all over the world, because the plant tolerates poor soil and matures in a little over 60 days, which makes it an ideal crop in areas with a short growing season.

Buckwheat kernels are a particular type of dry fruit called an achene. Achenes are frequently confused with seeds (sunflower "seeds" are achenes, as are the "seeds" on the outside of a strawberry). Buckwheat kernels have a pyramid shape and are larger than most grains, about 7 millimeters across. They are filled with a soft, starchy endosperm (80% starch, 14% protein) and encased in a thin seed coat that is dark green or tan. The hulls are removed but some hull may be present in buckwheat flour, lending it an overall brown coloring with dark brown-black specks.

Buckwheat kernels are called groats, or kasha when roasted. They are sold whole or cracked and are most often simply simmered, a dish also known as kasha. When making kasha, buckwheat is typically coated with egg and toasted before being cooked in liquid. The coating of egg protein toughens the surface of the groats, which would otherwise absorb too much liquid and become mushy because of the high starch content and the particular nature of buckwheat starch. A small percentage of buckwheat starch is structured like a **gum**. Multibranched and highly attracted to water, it gives cooked buckwheat a creamy, sticky quality. It is that quality that allows soba noodles and pancakes made from buckwheat flour (sometimes called blini) to hold together even though they have no **gluten**.

Buckwheat contains all essential amino acids and has some interesting medical properties. It contains rutin, a glycoside that strengthens capillary walls and is used to reduce the symptoms of hemophilia. It is also one of a few foods that contains D-chiro-inositol (DCI), a component of the system for insulin signaling that has been shown to be deficient in people with Type 2 diabetes and women with polycystic ovary syndrome (PCOS), an endocrine disorder that is one of the leading causes of infertility. Because buckwheat products are gluten free, they are appropriate for people with celiac disease. Buckwheat is also being malted to produce gluten-free beer.

Millets: A large group of grasses produce small round seeds that are cooked in similar ways and are therefore grouped together as millets. The most widely cultivated millet species, in order of tonnage, are pearl millet (*Pennisetum glacum*), foxtail millet (*Setaria italica*), common millet (*Panicum miliaceum*), and finger millet (*Eleusine coracana*). Millets are native to Africa and Asia, where most of the world's millet is still grown and consumed. Millets have one of the lowest water requirements for the growth of any grain. (See also Teff, page 284.)

Oats: About 95% of the world's crop of oats is animal feed. Oats are a minor grain crop worldwide because they don't tolerate hot summers well, don't contain gluten, which means they have limited use in raised baked goods, and the husk adheres to the grain, making it hard to process.

On the other hand, oats are rich in water-retaining carbohydrates, called glucans, which keeps baked products moist and chewy for weeks. The glucans are also good at reducing blood cholesterol, and since they are concentrated in the aleurone layer under the bran, they give oat bran its heart-healthy reputation. Oats are softer than other grains and don't break easily into bran, germ, and endosperm, so most oat products, including all rolled oats, are whole grain.

Oats used for oatmeal can be steel-cut (aka Irish or Scottish oatmeal), which is whole oat groats (kernels) cut in half or in quarters, or rolled, which are whole oats that are steamed to soften them and then flattened between steel rollers. The thinner they are rolled, the faster they cook, producing (from thicker to thinner) old-fashioned, quick-cooking, and instant varieties of rolled oats. Rolled oats and oat flours are a mainstay in ready-to-eat cereals.

Quinoa: Cultivated for 5,000 years in northern South America, quinoa was a staple food of the Incas, second in importance only to potatoes. A member of the spinach family, it contains a large amount (12 to 18%) of high-grade protein, is a good source of magnesium and iron, and is gluten free. It is now grown in the U.S. and milled into cereals and flours. The skin of quinoa is coated with bitter-tasting saponins. To remove the saponins, quinoa should be rinsed well in a sieve under running water and drained well before cooking. Do not soak quinoa, which drives the saponins into the interior of the grain.

Rye: An exceptionally hardy grain, rye grows as far north as the Arctic Circle and as high as 12,000 feet (3,600 m). Since its earliest cultivation in 1000 BCE, it has been a staple grain for the poor wherever it is grown, and appreciation for its flavor and its ability to make moist baked products that resist becoming stale has kept it popular in most countries in northern and eastern Europe. A large amount (about 7% of its weight) of the carbohydrate in rye is arabinoxylans, medium-chain polysaccharides that have a great potential for absorbing and holding

on to moisture. Rye flour can absorb up to eight times its weight in water (wheat can take in only twice its weight), producing a thick, sticky mass that can make rye doughs difficult to work with but which produces incredibly moist breads with a shelf life of several weeks. The ability of the arabinoxylans to cling to moisture permits bakers of traditional pumpernickel breads to bake them until the dough browns throughout without drying the bread excessively. Rye crackers are said to help control appetite by swelling in the stomach, and though not gluten free, rye contains much less gluten than wheat, which means it can be tolerated by some people who are sensitive to gluten.

Sorghum (aka milo): Although it looks like a large millet and is often grouped with millets, sorghum is a grass. Sorghum is grown mostly in arid and semi-arid parts of the world. Its protein content is similar to wheat, between 11 and 15%, but it doesn't contain gluten. In western India, millet and sorghum are combined to make *rotla*, a staple flatbread. In much of North Africa and central Asia, sorghum is eaten as simple porridges or brewed into beer. Sorghum flour is often used in gluten-free baking.

Teff: The tiniest of grains, measuring 1 millimeter across or less, teff (one of the grains classified as a millet) is mostly grown in Ethiopia and Eritrea, where it is made into a spongy, chewy, long-lasting flatbread called injera. The grain is so small that it is said you can hold enough seed in one hand to sow an entire field, an attribute that makes it important to semi-nomadic people. Its amino acid balance is good (its lysine levels are higher than either wheat or barley), and it is gluten free.

Triticale: A hybrid of wheat and rye, triticale was developed in the 19th century to produce a cereal grain with the culinary qualities of wheat and the disease-resistant qualities of rye. Depending on its cultivar, triticale can resemble either one of its parents. It is becoming an important grain in environments that are less hospitable to wheat, and though it is included in some ready-to-eat breakfast-cereal blends and health food snacks, most of the commercial harvest is currently used as animal feed.

How It Works ● All grains share a similar structure (see illustration, below).

The dry fruit layer (bran) consists of several thin layers, each a few cells thick, and coats the surface of the grain. The bran includes the pericarp, the part of the ovary wall that develops into thick flesh in other fruit. The aleurone layer lies just under the bran. Only one cell thick (except in barley), it contains protein, oil, vitamins, minerals, enzymes, fiber, and much of the grain's flavor. The aleurone is the outermost layer of the endosperm, the central and largest section of a grain. It is the only part of the endosperm that contains a significant amount of vitamins and minerals. The remainder is filled with carbohydrate in a protein matrix that will nourish the seed as it starts to grow into a new plant. The embryo lies to one end of the endosperm. It consists of two parts: the oil-rich embryo, or germ, which will grow into a new plant, and the scutellum, which projects from one side of the embryo and absorbs and conducts nutrients from the endosperm into the embryo.

Grains can be eaten whole or refined. Whole grains contain all of their parts — bran, aleurone, germ, and endosperm. After refining, just the endosperm, the least nutritious part of the grain, is left. The germ and bran, including the aleurone layer, contain most of the grain's fiber, oil, and B vitamins and about 25% of its protein.

The outer layers are removed to make grains easier and quicker to cook, to make them lighter in color, and to lengthen their storage life because oils in the germ and aleurone layer are prone to oxidation. Most refined grains are enriched with the B vitamins and iron lost in refining.

The endosperm contains storage cells, filled

Cross-Section of Grain

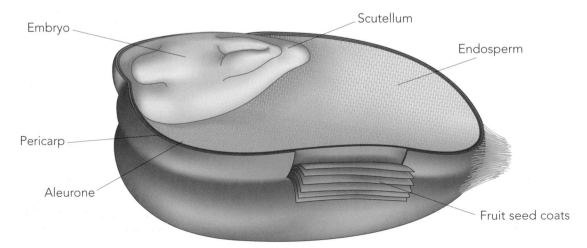

Embryo

Scutellum

Endosperm

Pericarp

Aleurone

Fruit seed coats

mostly with starch, embedded in a network of protein. There is generally more starch and less protein near the center of the grain, so the more of the exterior of a grain that is milled away, the less protein it has. Milling grinds grain into pieces. During refining the pieces are sifted. Because the outer layers are higher in fiber they are harder, and during milling break into larger pieces than the endosperm. Consequently, they can be easily removed by running the milled grain through ever finer sieves.

Because whole grains are more nutritious than refined grains many consumers are looking to increase the amount of whole grains in their diet. The Whole Grains Council, a nonprofit consumer advocacy group of millers, manufacturers, scientists, and chefs, has developed a whole-grain symbol that can be placed on packages of whole-grain products to alert interested consumers.

See Also • Bread, Corn, Flour, Rice, Wheat

The Birth of Breakfast Cereals

It might be surprising to fans of sugar-coated ready-to-eat breakfast cereals that these products were the first mass market health foods. Started by followers of Sylvester Graham, who believed in the curative power of whole grain, the first was Granula, created by James Caleb Jackson in the early 1860s. John Harvey Kellogg popularized whole-grain cereals at the Seventh-day Adventist Battle Creek Sanitarium where he became staff physician in 1875. He was joined by his brother, Will Keith Kellogg, and together they invented flaked cereal, first out of corn, and then wheat bran. C. W. Post, a patient at the sanatorium, inspired by the Kelloggs' flaked cereals, launched his version, GrapeNuts, named for its resemblance to grape seeds.

GRAINS OF PARADISE • See Ginger, Spices

GRAPEFRUIT • See Citrus

GRAPES

What It Is • Grapes are berries of a perennial woody vine of the genus *Vitis*. Most grapes come from one species, *V. vinifera*, known as Old World grapes. Native to the Mediterranean and Central Asia, vinifera grapes have spread over the globe and account for 95% of the wine and table grapes consumed worldwide. About 25 grape species are native to the New World, including *V. labrusca*, which includes the Concord cultivar of grape-jelly fame, and *V. rotundifolia*, which gives us muscadine (or scuppernong) grapes. About 10 varieties of grapes are native to Asia, none of which are important commercially, but some of which (particularly *V. amurensis*) are bred with vinifera varieties to produce frost-resistant hybrids.

What It Does • Grapes can be eaten raw, cooked into **jam and jelly**, or pressed for their juice, which is consumed fresh or fermented into **wine** or **vinegar**. About 66% of the world's grape production goes into making wine, 22% is eaten fresh, and 12% is dried into raisins. Wine grapes are explained in depth in the Wine entry. In this entry we will talk about table grapes (those that are eaten fresh) and raisins (dried grapes).

Raisin varieties have thin skins, so they remain tender after drying, a high sugar content, and a loose cluster structure that helps them to dry evenly. The most common raisin grape variety is sultana. A native of Iran and Turkey, sultanas are seedless and have a pale green skin and clear, translucent flesh. The sultana was introduced in the U.S. in the second half of the 19th century by William Thompson, a viticulturist and early grape grower in California, and it became known as the Thompson Seedless grape. In the U.S., the names Thompson Seedless and sultana are used interchangeably. Sultanas account for 95% of the raisin grapes grown in California and 33% of California's total grape output. Golden raisins are sultanas that have been treated with sulfur dioxide and specially dried to keep them from darkening.

Other raisin grape varieties include flame grapes (a cross between sultana and a red-skinned grape such as Cardinal), which are turned into large, moist, dark-colored raisins, and Black Corinth grapes. The Black Corinth story is a little confusing. A seedless Greek miniature variety, Black Corinth grapes are sold as champagne grapes in the U.S., even though they have nothing to do with the production of Champagne. Almost all Black Corinth grapes are dried into raisins, which are called Zante currants. Even though they are called currants they are not currants at all. True currants are of another genus (*Ribes*) and are never dried. Zante currants are miniature raisins that are dark colored and so tangy that they are typically used in baking rather than eaten out of hand.

Thompson Seedless is also the most popular table grape in North America. Along with flame grapes, Thompson Seedless grapes make up the majority of the table grapes grown. Because grapevines are propagated asexually, through grafting, seeds are not necessary for reproduction. Besides lacking seeds (and the **antioxidant** properties that grape seeds provide), seedless table grapes are cultivated more for looks than for flavor. Thompson Seedless and flame table grapes are both grown for size and plumpness (turgor pressure) and a large cluster size, all characteristics that impress at first sight.

Other varieties of table grapes have a wide range of attributes, but their market share is small (see Table Grapes chart, right).

Although the great majority of grape juice is fermented into wine or vinegar, a small portion is used fresh. Verjus is the juice of unripe grapes that are thinned from the vines a month or two before harvest. Used since ancient times, verjus is tart and green, similar to lemon or lime juice, and can be used in their place or as a substitute for wine vinegar.

The juice of ripe grapes can be either served as a beverage or cooked down into a syrup (*saba* in Italian). Grape syrup was an important sweetener before the ready availability of sugar. Today it is used as an embellishment for desserts and roasted meats. Grape juice, particularly pasteurized Concord grape juice, is a popular beverage because of its natural sweetness and unsurpassed level of antioxidants. Pasteurized Concord grape juice was first commercialized as nonalcoholic wine by Thomas Bramwell Welch, a supporter of the temperance movement, in 1869.

How It Works • Grapes are receiving increased recognition for their health benefits. The same benefits often reported in connection with drinking moderate amounts of red wine can be attributed to fresh grapes and grape products. Mostly they

Table Grapes

Most produce markets do not label grapes by their varietal name, so you are likely to see most of these grapes categorized generally by color (green, red, blue, or black).

Grape	Species	Description	Source
Cardinal	Vinifera	Very large red grape with mild flavor; cross between Tokay and Ribier	U.S.
Catawba	Labrusca	Large purple-red grape with musky flavor; also made into jelly and sweet wine	Eastern U.S.
Concord	Labrusca	Medium-large blue-black soft grape with strong musky flavor and sweetness; also made into juice and jelly	Northeastern U.S. and Canada
Emperor	Vinifera	Large pale red grape with sweetness and thick tannic skin	U.S.
Malaga	Vinifera	Large pink-red mild, crisp grape	U.S.
Muscadine (scuppernong)	Rotundifolia	Large round grapes ranging from bronze to purple-black; very sweet flesh and very tough skin that is usually peeled; also used for wine, juice, and jelly	Southeast U.S.
Muscat	Vinifera	A large family of grapes ranging from medium to large, yellow to almost black. They all have thick skins, lots of sugar, and strong aroma. They are also dried into Muscat raisins. They are the source of muscat wine.	Worldwide
Niagara	Labrusca	Large pale yellow-green grape with musky aroma; more acidic than most table grapes	U.S. and Canada
Ribier	Vinifera	Very large purple-black juicy sweet grape with mild flavor	U.S.
Tokay	Vinifera	Large red grape with firm texture, tough skin, and mild flavor	U.S.

come from polyphenol compounds such as resveratrol and anthocyanins in red grapes, catechins (in white grapes), elegiac acid, myricetin, quercetin, and kaempferol. Polyphenols have shown anticancer, antiviral, and anti-inflammatory properties in animal tests. They are believed to protect DNA from degradation. The largest amounts are found in muscadine (scuppernong) grapes.

See Also • Antioxidants, Fruit, Vinegar, Wine

GRAPPA • See Liquor

GRAVLAX • See Fish

GRAVY • See Sauces

GREASING • See Cake, Fat

GREEN BEAN • See Legumes

GREENS • See Chlorophyll, Leaves, Vegetables

GREEN TEA • See Tea

GRIDDLE • See Cookware

GRILLING

What It Is • There are two ways to grill: direct and indirect. In direct grilling, ingredients are placed directly over **fire** and cooked relatively quickly. Grilling directly in hot coals, as one might fire-roast a potato, is a primitive form of direct grilling. In indirect grilling, ingredients are placed beside the fire, the grill is covered to trap convection heat currents, and the food is cooked similarly to roasting. Rotisserie and spit-roasting are forms of indirect grilling.

What It Does • Direct grilling is similar to broiling, except the fire is underneath the food instead of above it, and the hot grill grate creates dark marks on the ingredient's surface. The method is best for foods that need to brown on the surface and will cook through in less than 30 minutes, which includes most everything that is typically grilled.

To set up a grill for direct grilling, the entire grilling area should be exposed to fire. On a gas grill this means turning on the required number of burners to the desired temperature. On a charcoal or wood grill it means setting up a continuous bed of hot coals. Sometimes high heat is required at first for browning the surface of a grilled ingredient and then lower, more gradual heat is needed for cooking the food through. On a gas grill this change in temperature can be accomplished by turning down the gas. For a charcoal or wood grill it is best to set up different levels of heat when you form the coal bed. Rake the coals into a thick pile on one side (for high heat) and a thinner bed on the other side (for low heat). Move ingredients from one heat level to the other as needed.

Indirect grilling is more like roasting, in that the fire is not right under the food. Rather, the ingredient, usually something large or dense that would burn over direct heat before it cooked through, is cooked by radiant heat emitting from the surrounding fire and currents of hot air rising from the fire. Typical ingredients for indirect grilling include large cuts of meat like prime rib of beef or leg of lamb; smaller cuts of tough meats like pork ribs or veal shanks; whole birds like chicken or turkey; large fish like whole salmon; and dense vegetables like beets or sweet potatoes.

When creating a fire bed for indirect grilling, leave an open space over which the food can sit without being directly exposed to

Direct-Grilled Chicken Breast with Barbecue Glaze

Boneless skinless chicken breast dries out easily. To protect it and give it extra moisture we suggest soaking it in brine for a few hours before setting it over the fire. To direct grill chicken over charcoal or wood you will need a hot bed of coals (very thin layer of ash). A gas grill should have all of the burners adjusted to medium-high, 425 to 450°F (220 to 230°C).

4	boneless skinless chicken breasts, about 1½ lbs (750 g)	4
⅓ cup	granulated sugar	75 mL
⅓ cup	kosher salt	75 mL
1 cup	hot (not boiling) water	250 mL
3 cups	ice cold water	750 mL
½ tsp	freshly ground black pepper	2 mL
1 tbsp	vegetable oil	15 mL
1¼ cups	barbecue sauce, bottled or homemade	300 mL
	Oil for coating grill grate	

1. Place one chicken breast on a sheet of plastic wrap, sprinkle with cold water, cover with another sheet of plastic wrap, and pound to an even thickness of about 1 inch (2.5 cm). Repeat with remaining chicken breasts.

2. In a large resealable plastic bag, combine sugar, salt, and hot water. Shake to dissolve salt and sugar. Add cold water and chicken breasts. Press the air out of the bag, seal, and refrigerate for 1 to 2 hours.

3. Heat the grill as directed in introduction.

4. Remove chicken from the brine and discard the brine. Pat chicken dry and sprinkle all over with pepper. Rub with oil.

5. Clean the grill grate with a wire brush and coat with oil. Place chicken on the grill, cover, and cook, turning once, until no longer pink and the juices run clear, about 160°F (71°C) on an instant-read thermometer, 4 to 5 minutes per side. Brush with barbecue sauce during the last 3 minutes (you won't use all of it). If your grill has a temperature gauge it should stay around 425°F (220°C).

6. Transfer chicken to a serving platter and serve with remaining barbecue sauce on the side.

MAKES 4 SERVINGS

the fire. On a gas grill this means turning on some burners and leaving other burners off. Typically on a two-burner grill, one side is left off; on a three-burner grill the middle burner is left off; and on a four-burner grill the middle two burners are left off. For charcoal or wood grilling, the coal bed is either split or raked to one side, depending on the size of the grill. For fatty meats or when you want to retain the meat juices dripping from a roast, a drip pan is placed in the open area of the fire bed to catch anything falling from the meat. A drip pan reduces flare-ups and gives you delicious drippings for making a sauce.

The technique of preparing a grill for direct or indirect grilling depends on the type of grill and the fuel source. Minimally, a grill is a metal grate that holds food suspended over an open fire. Campfire grills and fireplace grills are just that.

Free-standing grills have a firebox that holds the fire and supports the grate. Hibachi-style grills are the simplest form, consisting of a shallow metal box held above the ground on short legs and a detachable grate resting on top. Some hibachis have vents for regulating air flow; they typically don't have lids. A kettle grill is like a hibachi with a lid. It has a deep bowl-shaped firebox to protect the fire from wind, a domed lid to trap the heat so that it comes from all directions (not just the bottom), and vents in both the firebox and the lid to adjust air flow and regulate the heat. Gas grills work similarly to kettle grills except that the firebox is usually rectangular rather than spherical. The big difference in their operation is the type of fuel.

Any safe combustible fuel can be used for grilling. The original fuel source was wood. Wood burns hot, and because it is a natural substance, different types of wood burn at slightly different temperatures, and individual pieces of the same type of wood might burn at different rates. To even out the differences, most wood grilling is done over wood charcoal. Made from partially combusted wood, charcoal doesn't burn as hot as wood, but it burns more consistently and it is much easier to ignite. Because most of the volatile organic compounds in wood that generate smoke are burned off in the production of

Carcinogens and the Grill

When fat drips from meats being grilled over high direct heat, it flares up, sending both a sooty residue onto the surface of the meat and smoke that transfers cancer-causing molecules (called polycyclic aromatic hydrocarbons, or PAHs) into the food. At this time, according to the American Institute for Cancer Research, a safe level for PAHs has not been determined, so they advise erring on the side of caution and trying to avoid these potential carcinogens by keeping fat away from high fires. To avoid the formation of PAHs, grill lean cuts of meat and trim visible fat when direct grilling. Use indirect grilling for fattier cuts like beef brisket and pork shoulder.

Marinades seem to reduce another potential carcinogen called heterocyclic amines, or HCAs, in grilled meats. At this time it is still unclear why this happens. It may be because the oil in marinades provides a barrier between the meat and the fire, or it might be that the citrus juice, oils, and herbs in marinades provide some anticancer protection.

charcoal, charcoal fires produce far less smoke (and smoky flavor) than do wood fires. There are two types of charcoal. Natural charcoal (lump charcoal) is plain burned wood and gives similar results to natural wood. Charcoal briquettes are manufactured from wood dust and contain binders and chemicals to help them ignite faster and burn evenly. They deliver less natural-wood flavor than lump charcoal, and they are not quite as hot, but they burn longer and more evenly.

The cleanest (least smoky) grilling fuel is gas. Gas, whether propane or natural gas (primarily methane), will not burn as hot as charcoal or wood. In a gas grill the flow of air and fuel is regulated with valves and tubes, so there is no need for air vents to adjust air flow and temperature. Heat levels are changed by turning a knob.

The fuel source determines the level of heat energy in the grill, but heat retention depends on how the grill is constructed and what material it is constructed from. Most grill fireboxes are built of metal. The type of metal and its gauge (weight and thickness) determine its ability to conduct and hold heat. Unless a grill is designed for portability, heavier-gauge metals are preferred to lighter ones.

Carbon steel is the most common metal for grills because it is easy to fabricate and relatively inexpensive to manufacture. But carbon steel is not good at retaining heat, so steel grills tend to use more fuel to maintain temperature than other grills.

Stainless steel retains heat slightly better than carbon steel, but it is much more expensive to produce, and usually used in such a thin gauge that its heat retention is no better than carbon steel's.

Iron has better heat-retaining properties, but it is heavy, and because it rusts it is usually coated with enamel, which must be maintained.

Ceramic grills are excellent at retaining heat and are the most fuel efficient of all. They are heavy and have less strength (flexibility) than metal grills, so they tend to have smaller grilling areas, which limits their usefulness for direct grilling. They are ideal for roasting. Stone has similar heat-retaining abilities to ceramic. Because stone is heavy and difficult to shape, it is usually used architecturally in outdoor kitchens to house metal fireboxes to improve their heat retention.

To attain and maintain constant heat during grilling, nothing is more important than having a grill with a lid. Closing the lid traps heat (and smoke, for flavor, if using a wood fuel), which speeds the cooking and evens out fluctuations in temperature. A closed lid is essential for indirect grilling, but even for direct grilling it improves heat transfer and fuel efficiency. The one downside of using a lid is that it traps moisture, which inhibits a crusty surface from forming on meats. To get the best of both worlds, cover the grill while cooking the first side of a steak or chop to help intensify the heat, then leave the lid open after flipping the meat so that you don't soften the crust you just created.

Specialty Grilling Techniques

Rotisserie roasting and spit-roasting are forms of indirect grilling where the meat is speared and suspended far enough from the flames that the fire does not touch it as it cooks. The meat is kept constantly turning so that no part of it is in front of the heat long enough to char. The method produces beautiful crusts on roasts, because as the meat turns, its fat melts and rolls around the surface, basting the meat and keeping it moist. The only differences between rotisserie and spit cooking are the size of the meat, the size of the spear, and the size of the grill. Spit cooking is for larger cuts, generally whole animals or primal cuts.

Delicate ingredients, particularly fish and vegetables, sometimes need protection from direct flame. Primitive grill masters found that by wrapping such ingredients in leaves or placing them on a slab of wood set over the fire, the foods would cook through without being consumed by flame. They also absorb aromatic smoke from their casings. Corn is an ingredient that comes prewrapped by nature, so all you have to do to grill corn is throw it over a fire right in its husk. The husk chars and protects the vegetable inside, which gently steams and smokes in its wrapper. Likewise, when you place jacketed vegetables like potatoes directly in hot coals, the skin burns as the flesh inside softens and takes on the flavor of smoke. Steaks and chops can also be cooked directly in hot coals.

How It Works • To make fire, three things have to be present: fuel, an ignition source, and lots of oxygen. In a gas grill, these elements are mostly automated and controlled by the fuel knobs or valves, an electric igniter, and a regulated mixture of fuel and oxygen. In a charcoal grill the elements are less regulated. The fuel is some form of wood — paper, kindling, logs, or charcoal — each requiring a different amount of energy to make it ignite.

Pre-burning (charring) wood makes it easier to ignite. To make charred wood or natural lump charcoal, wood is burned without oxygen until it is reduced to carbon. At that point, a little more than half of its potential energy has been spent, so a charcoal fire will burn out faster and give off less heat than a wood fire.

The easiest way to light charcoal is to stack it up so that air can quickly and easily travel upward through the coals. To facilitate lighting, most grill aficionados recommend a charcoal chimney starter. A chimney starter looks like an oversized coffee can with a rack inside dividing the bottom quarter of the chimney from the top, some holes on the sides for air, and a heat-resistant handle. Crumpled newspaper goes in the bottom section and charcoal in the top. The newspaper is lit, and, as it burns, its heat travels up the chimney. Oxygen flowing through the holes in the sides energizes the fire and encourages it to move quickly up the chimney, igniting the coals in about 10 minutes.

Using lighter fluid or charcoal briquettes saturated with fire starter is not recommended. It's not that there's anything wrong with petroleum fire starters — once the coals are red hot, no petroleum remains — but if you happen to squirt some lighter fluid onto the side of the grill (which is pretty hard not to do) it will slowly emit petroleum fumes that will become infused in your food.

How Cooking Over Fire Works

Before an ingredient even touches a grill, the grill grate should be thoroughly heated, which ensures that the surface of the ingredient gets a blast of energy at the onset of cooking. That's why most grilled-meat recipes direct

Indirect Grill-Roasted Garlic Herb Chicken

Indirect grilling is like roasting over an open fire. If you are using a charcoal grill you will need to prepare a split bed of charcoal at least 2 inches (5 cm) thick, covered with a good layer of ash. You may also need to heat 20 to 30 more pieces of charcoal to restock the fire after the first 45 minutes of cooking. If using a 3- or 4-burner gas grill, turn the outside burners to medium and turn the middle burner(s) off. If using a 2-burner gas grill, set one burner to medium and leave the other off.

1 tsp	kosher salt	5 mL
½ tsp	freshly ground black pepper	2 mL
3	cloves garlic, minced	3
2 tsp	chopped fresh rosemary or thyme leaves	10 mL
2 tbsp	olive oil, divided	25 mL
1	chicken, about 4 lbs (2 kg)	1
	Oil for coating grill grate	

1. Heat grill as directed. Place an empty roasting pan in the empty area of the grill bed to catch drips.
2. In a small bowl, stir together salt, pepper, garlic, rosemary, and 1 tbsp (15 mL) of the oil.
3. Rinse chicken inside and out and pat dry. Gently but firmly insert your index finger under the skin at the neck end of the chicken and move it around to separate the skin from the meat. Repeat with your whole hand under the skin on the breast, legs, and drumstick. Rub the meat under the skin with the seasoned garlic mixture. Rub the outside of the chicken with the remaining olive oil.
4. Clean the grill grate with a wire brush and coat with oil. Place chicken on the grill away from the heat, cover the grill, and cook until an instant-read thermometer inserted into the thickest part of the breast registers about 165°F (74°C), about 1 hour and 20 minutes. If your grill has a temperature gauge it should stay around 350°F (180°C). If using charcoal you will probably have to replenish coals after 45 minutes.
5. Transfer chicken to a large serving platter. Let rest for 10 minutes before carving. Carve and serve.

MAKES 4 TO 6 SERVINGS

you to preheat the grill. For direct grilling, a hot grill grate is necessary to force heat deeply into the meat as quickly as possible; once the heat moves from the highly conductive metal grate into a less conductive steak, the heat transfer slows down dramatically. That's why high heat produces a thick crust on the surface of a steak but doesn't necessarily make the steak cook through any faster.

Convection, circulating air currents in a closed grill, is not a primary method of heat transfer in direct grilling (especially when there is no grill lid), but it does account for a lot of the cooking that takes place in indirect grilling. Radiant heat, the direct transfer of energy through space from fire to food, accounts for most of the heat transfer in grilling.

Although the principles of conduction, convection, and radiant heat help us to understand how grilling works, in practice pinpointing which is happening when is not clear cut. They all occur simultaneously. The flow of heat from fire to grill grate is radiation. The heating of the grate itself is conduction. The heating of the food's surface is a combination of conduction from the grill grate, radiation from the heat flowing between the bars of the grate, and convection of the air around the food (especially when the grill is covered).

See Also • Barbecue, Fire, Heat, Smoking

GRILLS • See Grilling

GRITS • See Corn

GROUPER • See Fish

GROUSE • See Game

GROWTH HORMONES • See Hormones

GRUYÈRE • See Cheese

GUANCIALE • See Bacon

GUAR GUM • See Gums

GUAVA • See Fruit

GUINEA HEN • See Game

GUM ARABIC • See Gums

GUMS

What It Is • Like **gelatin**, gums thicken liquids, but in a different way. Gelatin is protein; gums are complex carbohydrates, long chains of sugar molecules (polysaccharides) that have the ability to absorb liquid in an amount that is many times their volume. They are used as thickeners, gelling agents, emulsifiers, and stabilizers. All vegetable gums are hydrocolloids (see Science Wise, right).

What It Does • Gums come from several natural sources: seaweeds, tree sap, seeds, and bacteria.

Seaweeds adapt to the turbulence and strong currents of the ocean by filling their cells with large quantities of jelly-like carbohydrates that give them tensile strength (flexibility). In certain seaweeds, these carbohydrates become a viscous transparent jelly when heated in water and cooled.

In China and Japan, natural gums from seaweeds are used to thicken broths and prepare jellied sweets like almond jelly, and are shaped and served as a chewy textural element in composed salads and desserts. In Britain, agar, an extract of seaweed, is a popular thickener for jellied desserts. And in the Caribbean, an extract from the seaweed Irish moss is made into a popular rum drink that is rumored to have aphrodisiac properties. Industrially, seaweed gums are used to improve the viscosity of ice cream, clarify beer, and stabilize toothpaste. Gums derived from seaweeds include:

Agar (agar-agar, kanten): Obtained from the cell membrane of red algae, agar is used as a vegetarian gelatin, as a thickener in soups, jellies, and dairy desserts, and as a clarifier in brewing. Agar is sold in sheets and powdered. Like gelatin it is softened in cold water and then heated until it dissolves.

Alginates (alginic acid, algine): Extracted from brown algae, alginates are used industrially for thickening cream soups and making milk

Gluten-Free Flour

The ability of gums to form stretchy bonds can imitate the elastic qualities of gluten in a baked product without adding gluten. The gluten-free flour is made from rice flour, starch, and a touch of xanthan gum. It can be used to replace all-purpose flour in any recipe.

2 cups	rice flour	500 mL
⅔ cup	cornstarch	150 mL
⅓ cup	tapioca starch	75 mL
2 tsp	xanthan gum	10 mL

1. In a large bowl, sift together flour, cornstarch, tapioca, and xanthan gum. Use in place of flour in any recipe. Store in a tightly closed container for up to 1 year.

MAKES ABOUT 3 CUPS (750 ML)

puddings. Sodium alginate is the salt form that is used as an emulsifier in sauces. Alginates have drawn attention in the culinary world because of their use in avant-garde restaurants. Alginates form a gel in the presence of calcium. Chefs use this property to prepare a calcium-free alginate mixture of fruit juice, vegetable juice, or meat purée and algine, and then drip it into a calcium solution, where it immediately gels into miniature spheres. The technique, called spherification, is used for turning such foods as apple and beet into the "caviars" that populate molecular gastronomic menus.

Carrageenans: Their name comes from a seaweed, Irish moss or carrageen moss, that is about 55% carrageenans. Carrageenans are added to most commercial ice creams and many bottled sauces. In industry they are highly valued because they have the ability to thin under pressure and then return to their original viscosity, a quality that makes them ideal for being pumped through factory pipelines without losing their thickening abilities. There are three classes of carrageenans derived from the plant: kappa carrageenans produce firm gels, iota carrageenans produce soft gels, and lambda carrageenans form gels only when mixed with proteins, so they are used in dairy products.

The original chewing gum came from chicle, a natural polysaccharide gum tapped from a tropical evergreen. It was known by the Aztec and Maya, and was introduced to Europe by the Spanish, who liked its sweet flavor. Several other gums come from land plants, extracted from their sap or seeds. Seed gums are referred to as galactomannans because their molecular structure is made up of a mannose (a type of sugar) with galactose (a type of sugar) branches. Seed gums include:

Guar gum (guaran): Extracted from the endosperm of guar beans, guar gum has eight times the water-thickening potency of cornstarch, which makes it an inexpensive commercial thickener — very little goes a long way. It is more soluble than locust bean gum and is often used with xanthan gum for emulsifying salad dressings. Guar gum also slows the growth of ice crystals, making it a popular additive to commercial ice cream. You will see guar gum listed on many food labels.

science wise

Hydrocolloids • Hydrocolloids are water-soluble polysaccharides (large chains of sugars) from land plants, marine plants, and microorganisms that can form gels. Most hydrocolloids are gums, but some are pectins and starches. Gelatin is not technically a hydrocolloid because it comes from an animal source and it is mostly protein, not sugar, but since it behaves like a gum it is considered a hydrocolloid. The role of proteins in the behavior of hydrocolloids might be more significant than we now think. When hydrocolloids are extracted from their plant source, they often contain elements other than sugars. For example, gum arabic, although considered a polysaccharide, has amino acids attached to it. Some of its thickening ability might be attributed to these proteins. Further work in this area needs to be done.

fast facts

- Gums are loaded with water-soluble **fiber**, making them excellent laxatives.
- The Kanten diet, a fad diet made popular in Japan, employs the high-fiber content of agar to fill the stomach. Agar absorbs water in the stomach and triples in size, resulting in a full feeling with minimal calorie intake.
- Gum arabic has the ability to reduce the surface tension of liquids, thus increasing the fizzing of carbonated beverages. A little bit added to a bottle of soda causes an eruption; add a Mentos candy and create a spectacular geyser.

Gum arabic (gum acacia): Extracted from the sap of two species of sub-Saharan acacia trees, gum arabic is a thickener used in soft drink syrups, gummy candies, and chewing gum.

Gum tragacanth (astragalus gum): Obtained from the sap of several species of *Astragalus* shrubs (colloquially called goat's thorn or locoweed), gum tragacanth is viscous, odorless, and tasteless. Although it is soluble in water, it does not dissolve easily, so it is used less often in food manufacturing than other tree gums. Gum karaya, an extract from the sap of *Sterculia* trees, mostly grown in India, behaves similarly to tragacanth gum.

Locust bean gum (carob gum): Extracted from the seeds of the carob tree, locust bean gum is partially soluble in cold water, so it begins to thicken liquids on contact, and has the ability to stabilize mixtures at very low temperatures, making it a common stabilizer for ice creams. Because it gels only partially at cold temperatures, frozen products and cream cheeses containing locust bean gum do not develop a slimy mouth feel, which can be one of the unwanted side effects of other gums. Locust bean gum is often used with carrageenans in the manufacturing of gelatin-free jellied desserts.

Bacteria produce polysaccharide gums as part of their metabolic processes, so scientists began producing gums from bacteria.

Gellan gum: Gellan gum is a polysaccharide secreted by the *Sphingomonas elodea* bacterium. When combined with salts or acids, it forms a stable, clear gel that is able to withstand temperatures as high as 250°F (120°C), which makes it valuable in food processing. It is usually used as an alternative to agar, because it thickens similarly and manufacturers need only half the amount of gellan gum as agar to produce the same viscosity.

Xanthan gum: This gum is produced industrially by fermenting glucose or sucrose with the *Xanthomonas campestris* bacterium. Developed in the 1960s, not only does it thicken at very low concentrations (less than 0.5%) but it thins when agitated, which makes it ideal for nonemulsified salad dressings. In the bottle, xanthan gum keeps small bits of seasonings suspended in dressing. When the bottle is shaken, the gum thins, allowing the dressing to pour easily, and once it is dispersed on the salad it thickens again, coating each leaf perfectly. Xanthan gum is also used in gluten-free baked products and in egg substitutes, where it delivers a viscosity similar to gluten and egg yolk.

How It Works ● Like sugars, from which they are composed, gums contain lots of exposed hydrogen and oxygen atoms eager to form hydrogen bonds and absorb water, making them effective at forming hydrocolloid suspensions (see Science Wise, page 293). Because of this tendency, gums form gels at concentrations much lower than gelatin, usually less than 1%. The tendency of gums to maintain their viscosity through a wide range of temperatures allows solid gels made from gums to remain chewable in the mouth (unlike gelatin, which melts in the mouth), and it makes liquid gels stay fluid even at refrigerator temperatures, a benefit to salad dressings and sauces. Gum gels don't break down when frozen, which makes them ideal for stabilizing ice creams and reducing their melting rate.

See Also ● Dispersions, Emulsion, Food Additives, Gelatin, Sauces, Seaweed

HABANERO CHILE • See Capsicum

HADDOCK • See Fish

HAKE • See Fish

HALAL • See Diet

HALF-AND-HALF • See Milk

HALIBUT • See Fish

HALOGEN COOKTOP • See Stove

HALOUMI • See Cheese

HALVAH • See Candy

HAM

What It Is • A ham is a leg. In the 1500s, courtiers to Queen Elizabeth I would praise her nice hams, meaning her limber legs, which apparently made her a fabulous dancer. Today, ham usually refers to the cured hind leg of a pig, but it may also refer to the cured leg of other animals such as boar, venison, and goat. Ham differs from **bacon** only in that it is leg meat, while bacon is the cured meat from the belly, sides, or back of a pig (or another animal). Fresh hams are uncured raw meat, but most hams are dry- or wet-cured to help preserve and flavor them. The cure can be just salt and pepper or it can include sugar and spices such as juniper, cumin, and paprika. After **curing**, a ham can be air-dried and aged, like prosciutto, or further cured and flavored, like Smithfield ham, by being **smoked** over woods such as hickory, oak, apple, cherry, pecan, juniper, or even corncobs. You can buy a whole ham (whole hind leg) or a half ham (shank end or butt end of the leg), with the bone in, with only some of the bone in (semi-boneless), or completely boneless. Whether dry- or wet-cured, whole or in pieces, hams have wonderfully salty, meaty flavors. They are often baked for holiday celebrations, grilled, broiled, sautéed, or simmered into soups, stews, and casseroles.

What It Does • Ham gets its distinctive flavors from the breed of pig used, its diet, and age at slaughter, as well as the spices added to the salt cure and the curing time. If smoked, the smoking time and the types of wood used for smoking also have an impact on flavor. These variables produce an enormous variety of hams (see Dry-Cured Hams Around the World chart, page 298), most of which fall into two basic categories: wet-cured ham (city ham or brined ham) or dry-cured ham (country ham).

Most mass-produced hams are wet-cured, which is a faster process than dry-curing. Wet-cured hams contain 3 to 4% salt and have a mild flavor and moist texture because of **brining**.

The world's most prized hams are dry-cured. They're generally saltier than wet-cured hams (about 5 to 7% salt) because the curing process involves less water to dilute the flavor. They also have a firmer texture and much more concentrated, complex aromas. While most pigs are fed corn, those raised for dry-cured ham often eat acorns, chestnuts, beechnuts, peanuts, and other nuts indigenous to the pig's growing region. These components of the pig's diet change the flavor of the ham. Many hams, like prosciutto, Ibérico, and Bayonne, are produced under strict government regulations that dictate the pig's diet, the curing process, and the region of origin. For instance, jamón ibérico de bellota, one of the world's most expensive hams, is made from free-range black Ibérico pigs that eat only acorns (*bellota*) during the last few months of their lives as they roam the oak forests of southern Spain. Jamón ibérico de bellota must be aged for at least 36 months. Several other grades of Ibérico ham are ranked according to the pig's diet and curing. Serrano ham, a less expensive Spanish ham, is made from white pigs that are fed in captivity.

In Italy, various types of prosciutto are produced according to similar government regulations. The pigs raised for prosciutto di Parma (Parma ham from the Parma region of northern Italy) eat chestnuts and whey left over from making the region's

Parmigiano-Reggiano cheese. This diet gives prosciutto di Parma a somewhat nutty, rich flavor. Prosciutto di San Daniele, produced farther north in Italy's Friuli region, has a slightly sweeter flavor. Other prosciutti are produced throughout Italy under strict regulations to guarantee the authenticity and integrity of the ham's curing process and region of origin. Prosciutto crudo refers to all of these hams. It is the dry-cured ham often sliced thin and eaten raw (*crudo*) because it is cured. Prosciutto cotto is cooked (*cotto*) ham. Culatello is similar to dry-cured prosciutto but is packed into the pig's bladder and sometimes soaked in wine.

Whether it's prosciutto di Parma or jamón ibérico de bellota, dry-cured ham often serves as the first course of a meal, wrapped around a cube of melon or displayed on a platter of antipasti. Country hams like Smithfield are sometimes fried, the juices and fat mixed and simmered with coffee to make redeye gravy. Once a dry-cured ham is eaten, the remaining ham rinds can be used to flavor soups and stews.

Dry-cured hams don't need refrigeration and can be stored in a cool spot, sometimes for several months depending on how well they are cured. They will gradually lose moisture and concentrate further in flavor before succumbing to rancidity. Smoked hams generally last longer and don't need refrigeration or further cooking. They can be eaten raw like prosciutto. Heavily salted dry-cured hams are sometimes scrubbed to remove harmless mold and occasionally soaked in water to remove excess salt.

Wet-cured hams must be kept in the refrigerator because of their higher moisture content, which can allow bacteria to proliferate. After opening, most wet-cured ham will last about a week. If canned, the ham may be shelf stable or require refrigeration (check the can). Wet-cured ham may be sold partially or fully cooked. Partially cooked hams require further cooking, while fully cooked hams are ready to eat and need only brief heating to warm them through. Check the label to see if it's ready to eat or requires further cooking.

How It Works • To "cure" a ham originally meant to keep it from spoiling without refrigeration. Today, hams are cured primarily to add flavor. Water flows into wet-cured hams by osmosis because it is the nature of water to distribute itself evenly throughout a system. (Think of how it evenly fills a bowl.) A similar thing happens during brining. Salt in the brine binds to the meat's cellular proteins and they repel each other and swell. The water then flows into the cells with a view toward balancing its distribution throughout the system. Wet-curing is timed so that just enough water flows into the meat to make it juicy. If meat is left in a brine for too long, osmosis will eventually cause the cells to become so saturated with water that they burst, initiating the process of disintegration. But in well-timed wet-curing, the ham becomes plump and juicy, gently filling with water and the flavors in the brine such as sugar or honey.

The ham may also be injected with water, which speeds the process. Lesser-quality hams are injection-brined and spun in drums that knead and soften the meat to help the brine penetrate faster. Some boneless and most canned ham is made from pieces of ham tumbled in drums with additional phosphate salts to draw out myosin, a muscle protein that creates a gelatinous residue on the meat that helps the pieces stick together. The pieces are pressed into shapes such as rectangular blocks of deli ham used for sandwiches or the teardrop shape of canned ham. Most wet-cured hams are fully cooked or partially cooked and available bone-in, boneless, spiral-sliced, or as ham steak.

Osmosis happens in dry-cured hams, too, but the process is reversed. Dry-cured hams are rubbed with a mixture of salt and spices, which means most of the water in that system lies in the meat. The salt draws the moisture out of the meat as the system tries to equalize water distribution. By drawing moisture out, dry-curing dehydrates the meat's cells and kills the bacteria harbored there, which allows dry-cured hams to be stored without refrigeration for months. With less moisture in the meat, the texture of dry-cured ham becomes drier and firmer, and its flavor less diluted and more concentrated. But dehydration doesn't necessarily make dry-cured hams feel tough and dry in the mouth. Salt also breaks down tough protein fibers, making them more tender. Hence the deep flavor and tender texture of dry-cured hams like prosciutto and Smithfield ham.

Most curing salts for ham, whether wet-cured or dry-cured, include sodium nitrite, a curing salt that helps to preserve, flavor, and color the ham. Most important, nitrite preserves or cures the meat by inhibiting the growth of *Clostridium botulinum* bacteria and preventing botulism. Nitrite also reacts with

Dry-Cured Hams Around the World

Almost every pork-eating country in the world makes some kind of ham. Dry-curing is the traditional technique that creates the texture and flavor of many of the world's famous hams. Some hams, like Smithfield ham, are also smoked, adding more layers of flavor.

Ham	Origin	Curing, Drying, and Smoking
Ardennes	Belgium, Northern France	Air-dried or lightly smoked
Bayonne	Southwest France	Air-dried or lightly smoked
Black Forest	Southwest Germany	Smoked over fir and sawdust
Culatello	Northern Italy	Air-dried, packed in pig's bladder
Ibérico	Spain	Air-dried
Kentucky	Kentucky, U.S.	Smoked over hickory, apple wood, and corncobs
Presunto	Portugal	Smoked over oak or chestnut
Prosciutto (Parma ham)	Northern Italy	Air-dried
Serrano	Spain	Air-dried
Speck	Germany, Northern Italy	Lightly smoked over juniper
Virginia (Smithfield)	Virginia, U.S.	Smoked over hickory, oak, and/or apple wood
Westphalian	Western Germany	Smoked over beech wood and juniper
York	Northern England	Lightly smoked over sawdust
Yunnan (Xuanwei)	Southwestern China	Air-dried or lightly smoked

fast facts

myoglobin, the pigment that makes fresh meat look red, and creates nitric oxide myoglobin, which turns the meat pink. Lastly, it delivers the characteristic sharp, salty flavor in ham. Other flavors in ham come when enzymes in the meat break protein down into savory peptides and amino acids like meaty-tasting glutamic acid. Extended aging causes other reactions that give ham nutty, browned flavors similar to those found in cooked meat. Fats also break down into flavorful compounds that range from floral and citrusy to grassy and buttery. These flavors occur mostly in well-aged dry-cured hams. Wet-cured hams are not quite as flavorful because they aren't aged as long and their flavor components are diluted with water.

One downside to the use of nitrite is that potentially carcinogenic nitrosamines are formed when nitrites and the natural amino acids in ham interact in our stomachs or in high-heat cooking. To limit nitrosamine formation, hams in the U.S. must contain no more than 2 ppm residual nitrite, nitrate, or their combination, and most hams fall well below this upper limit. Some traditional hams, such as prosciutto, avoid nitrites altogether. Instead of nitrite, two specific *Staphylococcus* bacteria (*S. carnosus* and *S. caseolyticus*) help to cure the meat and develop its rosy color. Without nitrite, the fat in these hams breaks down into more flavorful compounds than those found in nitrite-cured hams, giving prosciutto and nitrite-free hams more sweet and fruity aromas.

Not only does smoking help to preserve the meat, it adds fantastic flavors to hams like Smithfield, Westphalian, and Black Forest. Hot-smoking (at 130 to 180°F/54 to 82°C) evaporates some moisture, which helps to inhibit microbial growth and slows down fat breakdown that can lead to rancidity. Hot-smoking also concentrates flavor and imbues a ham with delicious aromatic flavors. Cold-smoking (at 50 to 80°F/10 to 27°C) doesn't dehydrate the meat, so it doesn't offer much in the way of preservation, but it does add gentle smoked flavor.

See Also • Bacon, Curing, Sausage, Smoking

HAMBURGER • See Beef, Meat

HARDTACK • See Biscuits

HARE • See Game

HARICOT VERT • See Legumes

HARUSAME • See Pasta

HAVARTI • See Cheese

HAZELNUT • See Nuts

HCA (HETEROCYCLIC AMINES) • See Carcinogen

HEART • See Organ Meats

HEARTBURN • See Digestion

HEARTS OF PALM • See Coconut, Stems

HEAT

What It Is • Heat is not like the other ingredients in your kitchen. It's not made up of molecules. Instead it is a force that causes molecular motion. Heat is **energy** that makes molecules move faster. The faster the molecules move, the hotter something gets.

Think of butter in a sauté pan. Cold butter is solid, but when it hits the hot pan, that energy is transferred to the butter, and its molecules start to move. They move slowly at first, but as more energy is transferred from the pan, the butter molecules move faster, and the butter changes from a solid to a liquid, melting completely and getting increasingly hotter. The rate at which the heat travels to and through the food depends on such factors as the heat source you are using (such as burning gas, wood, or charcoal or an electric heating element), the temperature of the heat source, and the type of **cookware**, as well as the food's temperature and density, and its moisture and fat content. This entry discusses the nature of heat itself. (For details on moist-heat and dry-heat cooking methods, see **Cooking**.)

What It Does ● All heat causes molecules

to move faster, bump into each other, and react with each other. In cooking, these reactions transform food into something different from what it was in its raw, unheated state. For instance, heat releases and creates aromatic compounds that make food smell delicious. Heat melts fats and evaporates moisture from food. Even the heat generated by microwave cooking evaporates moisture as water vaporizes into steam. Heat makes

proteins in food denature, or break apart and unwind, and extended heating can make those proteins coagulate, or clump back together again, as when blended liquid eggs coagulate into scrambled eggs. Heat caramelizes sugar and promotes the Maillard reactions in foods, creating deep aromas of **browning** and new flavor compounds that we can see and taste. You can even caramelize sugar by heating it in a microwave oven (see Microwave Caramel, page 398). Heat also causes the carbohydrate starches in food to gelatinize, as the starch granules swell with moisture, soften, form a paste, and finally stiffen or set, like when the flour in a cake gelatinizes and sets when the cake is done. Different forms of heat like moist heat and dry heat are better or worse at achieving these results, but heat is the core of all cooking. It creates many of the irresistible textures and flavors we've come to love (as well as the burned aromas we've come to dislike). Heat energy can be transferred to food in three basic ways: conduction, convection and radiation.

Conduction: Imagine you are making beef stew in a pot over a gas burner. Heat is coming from the burner, and when it hits the metal pot the pot transfers the heat throughout itself in a process called conduction. All solid matter, like pots and

Electromagnetic Spectrum

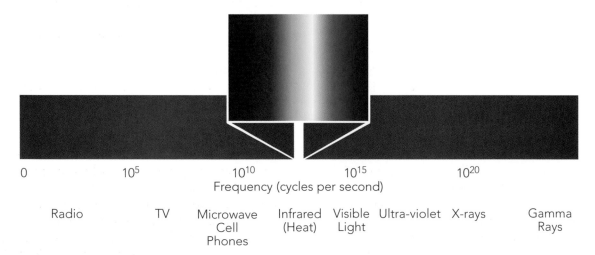

| 0 | 10^5 | 10^{10} | 10^{15} | 10^{20} |

Frequency (cycles per second)

Radio   TV   Microwave Cell Phones   Infrared (Heat)   Visible Light   Ultra-violet   X-rays   Gamma Rays

kitchen wisdom

Take Cover

To help a pot of liquid heat up faster, put a lid on it. Lids trap heat and quickly raise the temperature of the pot's contents. A covered pot of water can boil almost twice as fast as an uncovered one. This also means that braising in the oven with a tight-fitting lid — even at a low 250°F (120°C) — can raise the temperature of the liquid in the pot to the boiling point (212°F/100°C) over an extended period of braising and turn your moist, gently braised meat into dry, overcooked boiled meat. But if you leave the lid slightly ajar, heat will escape from the pot, keeping the temperature of the liquid below the boiling point yet high enough to bring the meat to a temperature range of 160 to 180°F (71 to 82°C) to gently dissolve the connective tissue and soften the meat without overcooking it. Lids trap moisture, too, which you may not want to do if you're trying to brown a piece of food in the pan. (Dry heat browns food, whereas moist heat does not because it doesn't get above 212°F/100°C and browning doesn't happen until well past 300°F/150°C.) So cover the pan when trying to quickly boil water or other liquids, but only partially cover when braising, and skip the lid altogether when browning meats.

pans and even pieces of stewing beef, transfers heat by conducting heat from one molecule to its lower-temperature neighbors. The heat is conducted more quickly when molecules are more densely packed, as in a copper pot (one of our best heat conductors). The heat is conducted more slowly when molecules are spaced farther apart, as in the beef. Either way, whenever something like beef makes direct contact with something hot like a hot stew pot, the heat is transferred by conduction. All metals are good heat conductors. Water and most foods are weak heat conductors. (See Heat Conductivity of Various Materials chart, page 303, for the approximate heat conductivity of other common cooking materials.)

Convection: The second type of heat transfer, convection, occurs when something fluid carries, or conveys, currents of heat. The fluid medium could be liquid such as water or oil, or it could be another mobile medium like air. As molecules in water, oil, or air heat up, they begin to move. Take the pot of beef stew on the stove, for example. After the heat is conducted by electrons through the pot, it hits the liquid inside the pot. The liquid molecules at the bottom of the pot begin to heat up, becoming less dense, and the more dense molecules above them fall due to gravity. As they reach the surface, the molecules cool off and fall back down. This creates currents in the liquid that convey heat throughout the stew. Convection is at work whenever a fluid medium like liquid or air moves heat around, as in boiling (and stewing), deep-frying, and baking. A convection oven exploits this form of heat transfer by using fans to speed up the heat-convecting currents, blowing hot air throughout the oven and transferring heat more quickly.

Radiation: The third type of heat transfer is the hardest to visualize. Think of the heat coming off the sun. It doesn't travel through space by conduction or convection. It radiates directly to the earth's atmosphere. Radiation is a type of invisible energy that travels through the air in electromagnetic waves. Even though you can't see them, you know about these electromagnetic waves from your radio. Radio waves are on the weakest end of the electromagnetic spectrum. Their energy is too weak to produce heat or to cook anything. On the other end of the electromagnetic spectrum are gamma rays, a very powerful form of electromagnetic energy that is strong enough to kill microbes in foods. Food manufacturers use gamma rays to sterilize meat by **irradiation**.

Infrared waves are near the middle. These waves are at work in most heat sources like the sun, a fire, or the electric heating element on your stove. It's known as radiant heat, but waves of infrared radiation themselves are not hot. They only generate heat when absorbed by another material. The sun's infrared waves don't generate heat until they hit the earth's atmosphere. A light bulb doesn't get hot until the glass absorbs the infrared radiation waves. Any food, metal pan, or other substance in proximity to a "radiant heat" source such as

science wise

a stovetop burner will begin to get hot as it absorbs infrared waves radiating from the source.

Infrared radiation is the primary form of heat transfer at work in cooking methods like broiling, spit-roasting, and grilling. But it's a rather inefficient cooking method because so much heat is lost to the air. That's why grilled and broiled foods are placed so close to the heat source (usually less than 6 inches/15 cm away). Radiation is also the primary source of heating in baking but is more efficient because the air is trapped in the oven.

Microwaves are another form of electromagnetic waves, but they are weaker than infrared waves. Microwaves are only strong enough to cause polar molecules (those with a positive charge at one end and a negative charge at the other) such as the water molecules in food to vibrate. And that's how microwave ovens work: they vibrate the water molecules in food until the vibrations generate heat, and the heat is transferred throughout the food to cook it.

Most cooking involves some combination of conduction, convection, and radiation. In the beef stew example, the stovetop burner radiates heat to the pot (radiation), the solid metal pot conducts heat throughout itself as does the stew (conduction), and the liquid in the stew develops currents that convey heat throughout the stew (convection).

Induction Heating

Induction cooktops are powered by electricity but they work a little differently than the electric heating element on an average stove. The induction heating element rests beneath a ceramic or glass surface and functions like a very powerful magnet. It carries an alternating electrical current, and when you put a magnetic metal (such as a cast-iron pan) on the cooktop, the electrons in the metal try to align with the magnet in the stove. But the stove magnet is alternating its poles. So too are the electrons in the pan and at such a rapid rate that the electrical current "induces" the pan to generate heat. The pan gets hot quickly and from that point on, the heat gets transferred from the pan to the food just as it would if a gas or electric coil burner were heating up the pan. The chief advantage of induction heat is that only 10% of the heat that's generated is lost to the air, compared with a 30% heat loss from electric coil burners and up to 65% heat loss from gas burners. Induction cooktops also offer instant heat control when you crank up or lower the heat. Plus, the ceramic or glass cooktop itself doesn't get very hot because it isn't magnetic (only residual heat from the pan will heat up the cooktop). The main disadvantage is that only magnetic metal cookware ("ferrous" high-iron cookware) will work. Cast-iron, whether enameled or not, and high-iron stainless steel will work. Pure copper, aluminum, glass, earthenware, stoneware, and some low-iron stainless steel cookware won't work. Manufacturers of stainless steel and clad metal cookware don't always say how much iron they include. The best test? Hold a magnet to the bottom of the cookware. If it sticks immediately, the cookware is "induction ready."

How It Works

• As a form of energy, heat makes molecules move and bump into each other. How hot something gets depends on how fast the molecules are moving, but also on how many molecules there are. More densely packed molecules transfer the heat quickly from molecule to molecule. Fewer molecules transfer heat more slowly because the heat has farther to go to get from molecule to molecule.

Heat Conductivity of Various Materials

Heat always seeks equilibrium. Heat (thermal energy) is transferred through matter from higher-temperature areas to lower-temperature areas until all areas are at the same temperature. Physicists call the rate at which a material transfers or conducts heat its thermal conductivity. Solid metals like silver, copper, and aluminum conduct heat the fastest, followed by liquids such as oil and water, then gases such as air. Here's a short list of the approximate thermal conductivity of various common cooking materials, ranked from the slowest heat conductors to the fastest (there is some overlap because of wide variations in materials). The figures are units of heat according to the International System of Units (SI) calculated as "k" (W/mK).

Material	Thermal Conductivity
Air, sea level	0.025
Bone	0.02 – 0.8
Hardwood (such as oak and maple)	0.1 – 0.2
Alcohol	0.1 – 0.2
Olive oil	0.17
Teflon	0.25
Muscle	0.4 – 1.4
Water, liquid	0.6
Glass	1 – 1.1
Brick	1.3
Concrete, stone	1.7
Marble	1.7 – 2.9
Granite	1.7 – 4
Ice	2.5
Stainless steel	16 – 40
Carbon steel	36 – 54
Cast iron	55
Tin	66
Aluminum	205 – 250
Copper	353 – 386
Silver	406 – 429

For instance, heat traveling through the air in a 500°F (260°C) oven makes each molecule in the air move very quickly, but the air molecules are far apart, so it takes a long time for the air to feel hot at this oven temperature. On the other hand, boiling (212°F/100°C) water molecules move more slowly (because of the lower temperature), but there are many more molecules, so it doesn't take long at all for boiling water to feel hot. This is why sticking your hand into boiling water feels much hotter faster than sticking your hand into the air of a 500°F (260°C) oven. That's also why temperature alone is not always a reliable measure of how hot a food will get. A 500°F (260°C) oven will transfer heat more slowly through its air molecules than a 212°F (100°C) stockpot will transfer heat through its boiling water. Temperature measures how fast the molecules will move. But how hot a food will get depends on how quickly the heat will be transferred to that food. To help judge how fast various cooking materials will heat up (or cool down), see Heat Conductivity of Various Materials chart, left.

Once heat travels through the cooking medium, it reaches the surface of the food and begins to cook it. The challenge of cooking is that most fresh and frozen foods consist primarily of water, which is a relatively poor heat conductor. Water conducts heat so slowly that it acts more like an insulator. Even the raging heat of a hot campfire slows down dramatically at the surface of a steak because it is very gradually transferred through the food's water molecules, which make up the majority of its mass. Plus, some of the heat is used to convert water to steam. But the fire itself is still raging against the food, so the surface of the steak tends to burn well before the heat is finally conducted through the food enough to cook the inside to the 130 to 140°F (54 to 60°C) doneness desired for most meats. To solve the problem, you have two options: use high heat to quickly brown the outside of food for flavor, then reduce the heat and slowly finish cooking the inside; or reverse the process and use low heat to gradually cook the food until it's just below the desired internal temperature, then increase the heat to quickly brown the outside for flavor. Grilling and braising often employ the first method, whereas sous vide and dishes like crème brûlée employ the second.

See Also ● Atmospheric Pressure, Calorie

science wise

The Mpemba Effect • You would think that cold water freezes faster than hot water. But many experiments have disproved this assertion. When very hot water and very cold water are placed in identical containers and frozen under identical conditions, the hot water freezes faster. Try it yourself, ideally in two separate freezers — or out in the snow — with the hot water brought to about 212°F (100°C) and the cold water brought to about 40°F (4°C). Aristotle first described the phenomenon, which was all but forgotten until 1963, when an African high school student named Erasto Mpemba rediscovered it while making ice cream and hastily put the hot ice cream mixture into the freezer. His ice cream froze faster than the cold mixture his fellow students put into the freezer. Mpemba successfully repeated the experiment several times and persistently asked why. Since then hundreds of controlled experiments have been conducted and several plausible but no definitive explanations have surfaced.

First, it's likely that the hot mixture loses its heat faster because some of the heat is carried away in the form of steam. Second, steaming causes some evaporation, reducing the total mass of the mixture, which then cools more quickly because small things cool faster than big things. Third, cold liquid is denser than hot liquid, and it takes longer for convection heat currents to develop in the denser cold liquid; but in the less dense hot liquid the heat-convecting currents develop sooner, and heat is transferred away from the hot liquid more rapidly.

These explanations don't resolve everything, so here is a fourth hypothesis. In hot liquids, ice crystals grow faster than in cold liquids because the molecules in hot liquids are moving faster than the molecules in cold liquids (remember: heat is energy in motion). Freezing, or the crystallization of liquid, starts with tiny seed crystals, which act as nucleation sites, or triggers, for bigger ice crystals to form. The seed crystals may form around impurities in the liquid or from agitation, a state of motion that characterizes hot water more so than cold water. If hot water is "on the move" or more agitated than cold water, it will more readily accept change and can more readily form seed crystals, and the crystals can grow faster, which would cause the hot water to crystallize, or freeze, faster than the cold water.

HEAVY CREAM • See Milk

HEIRLOOM PRODUCE • See Hybrid

HEMICELLULOSE • See Fiber

HERBS

What It Is • Need flavor? Add herbs. It's an easy way to heighten the aroma of a dish. Whether fresh or dried, herbs are the fragrant **leaves** of plants. Sometimes the stems and flowers are used as well, but herbs are almost always green. Most green culinary herbs come from just two plant families. The mint family (Lamiaceae) gives us basil (with varieties like Thai, cinnamon, and Indian), bergamot (bee balm), hyssop, lemon balm, lavender, marjoram, mint (spearmint, peppermint, pennyroyal, pineapple mint, and others), oregano (Greek, Turkish, Italian, Spanish, and others), rosemary, sage, savory, and thyme. The carrot family (Apiaceae) provides the herbs angelica, chervil, cicely, cilantro, dill, fennel (and fennel pollen), lovage, and parsley. Each herb has a distinct flavor but often shares some aromatic qualities with the other members of its plant family (see Flavor Components of Herbs chart, page 306).

What It Does • A herb's aromatic compounds are concentrated in its leaves. Some leaves also contain enough fibrous cell wall material to be used as thickeners. Herbs such as dried sassafras (filé powder) are sometimes used to thicken stews like gumbo.

Every region in the world has a preference for certain herbs based on its geography, climate, and history. Regions with a similar geography and climate (and those that have shared plants over the centuries) often prefer similar herbs. For instance, cilantro is widely used in India, Thailand, Vietnam, and Mexico. Thyme,

rosemary, and sage are commonly used in southern France as well as northern Italy. In the warmer climates of southern Italy, Greece, and Mexico, oregano is popular. Mint finds its way into regional dishes from North Africa to the Middle East to India. Many of these herbs have become popular in North America, but other herbs have yet to find a wide audience outside their country of origin. For example, screwpine (pandan) leaves are native to Indonesia and lend a nutty aroma to many Southeast Asian and Indian rice dishes, not least because pandan aroma comes from the same aromatic compound that flavors basmati and jasmine rice. Outside these countries, screwpine leaf is relatively obscure. Also in India, bitter-tasting fenugreek leaves are added to curries, and they form the signature flavor in Iran's popular meat-and-bean stew called *qormeh sabzi*. But North American cooks are more familiar with fenugreek seeds than the plant's fresh leaves. In Japan and in China, chrysanthemum greens lend wonderful carrot and juniper aromas to soups and stews like sukiyaki, but Europeans and North Americans have yet to look past chrysanthemum flowers and embrace the plant's leaves as a culinary herb.

Using and Storing Herbs

One of the biggest concerns among cooks is when to add fresh herbs and when to add dried herbs to a dish. But adding herbs isn't so much a matter of fresh or dried as it is whole or chopped. The fragrance of whole herbs is contained within the leaves. It takes longer to draw out the flavor from whole, uncut herbs, so they are often added at the beginning of cooking. That's why fresh whole parsley, thyme, and bay leaves are tied together and added to stocks and soups very early on. When chopped, however, the leaves' cells are broken open and the volatile aromas are free to escape.

fast facts

- Purslane contains more heart-healthy omega-3 fatty acids than any other plant on land. It also contains betalain alkaloid pigments that are antioxidants and may help prevent cancer. In Europe and Asia, cooks love purslane, but in the U.S., purslane is classified as a weed.
- Flat-leaf or Italian parsley (*Petroselinum crispum* var. *neapolitanum*) contains four times more essential oil than curly parsley (*P. crispum*). Both types contain myristicin, the same compound that gives nutmeg its characteristic aroma.

Flavor Components of Herbs

A herb's characteristic aroma comes from numerous chemical compounds in the plant. But one flavor compound often dominates. For instance, oregano and thyme get their floral and pine aromas from compounds called carvacrol and thymol, but thyme has more thymol and oregano has more carvacrol. Even within the oregano family, some types are more concentrated in one flavor compound than another. Greek oregano is higher in sharp-tasting carvacrol. Italian is higher in floral thymol. And Mexican oregano is from an entirely different plant family (verbena), which explains why it tastes stronger than other oreganos. In a similar way, California bay leaves are more potent than Mediterranean (Turkish) bay leaves because they come from a different species in the laurel family.

Herb	Flavor Components								Key Flavor Compounds
	Sweet	Fresh	Citrus	Floral	Licorice	Pine	Wood	Intensity	
Basil	•	•		•	•	•		•	Eucalyptol, linalool, citral, estragole, eugenol, methyl cinnamate
Bay (laurel)		•				•	•	•	Eucalyptol
Cilantro	•	•	•	•				•	Decenal
Dill		•	•			•			d-Carvone, limonene
Lemongrass			•	•					Citral
Lemon verbena			•	•					Citral
Marjoram	•	•	•	•			•		Terpenes, eucalyptol
Mint	•	•	•			•		•	l-Carvone, menthol
Oregano				•	•	•	•		Carvacrol, thymol
Parsley	•	•							Myristicin, limonene
Rosemary	•	•		•			•	•	Eucalyptol, pinene, camphor
Sage		•				•		•	Thujone, eucalyptol, camphor
Tarragon	•	•		•	•	•		•	Estragole, anethol
Thyme		•	•	•		•		•	Thymol, carvacrol

Chopped fresh herbs are often added to dishes just before serving. Most dried herbs are chopped, but dried herbs also need time to rehydrate. They are usually added early in the cooking to allow moisture to rehydrate them and heat to reawaken their sleeping aromas. To speed the release of aromatic compounds from dried herbs, crush them between your fingers before adding to a dish. To layer a herb's flavors, some cooks add both fresh and dried forms, such as adding dried oregano early when cooking pasta sauce, then adding fresh oregano at the end.

Most of the essential oils in herbs are volatile and evaporate during drying and storage. To prolong the aromatic life of fresh herbs, treat them like bouquets of flowers and store stems down in a tall glass of water. Loosely cover tender herbs like parsley and cilantro with a plastic produce bag and refrigerate. Woodier fresh herbs like rosemary and thyme should be stored in the refrigerator in a plastic bag, after wrapping the stems in a damp paper towel. Fresh basil is one exception to the rule of refrigerating herbs. It stores best at room temperature because cold temperatures can wither its leaves quickly.

Dried herbs are best stored in an airtight container in a cool, dark place, where they should last for about six months. Replace old herbs regularly. You can also freeze fresh and dried herbs, which delays the evaporation of their aromatic compounds. Freeze dried herbs in a resealable plastic bag after pressing out the air. To freeze fresh herbs, wash and dry them thoroughly, then lay on a mesh rack in a single layer and freeze until stiff, about two hours. Transfer to a resealable plastic bag, press out the air, and freeze for up to three months. You can also freeze the herb leaves in water in ice cube trays, then pop out the ice cubes and store those in a resealable bag. To use, thaw the ice cubes in a strainer under cool water, then chop the herb and use immediately.

How It Works • Fresh herbs contain mostly water (80 to 90%), but they also contain potent aromatic compounds and essential oils. These strongly flavored oils frequently act as natural deterrents to pests and are most concentrated when plants begin to flower. The aromas are released when the herbs are cut, chewed, or heated. And many evaporate when tender herbs such as basil are dried. Woody herbs like rosemary, oregano, and bay leaf fare better upon drying, without losing as much flavor. In general, air-drying preserves more flavor than the heat of sun-drying or oven drying. Freeze-drying (used for many commercial herbs) preserves even more aromatic compounds. For home cooks, microwave ovens work well because they evaporate water without evaporating much of the fresh herb's essential oils.

The compounds in culinary herbs not only smell good, they're often good for us,

kitchen wisdom

- To help your dried herbs last longer, keep them away from heat, moisture, and light. When adding them to cooked dishes, avoid shaking the container over the pan, because steam can enter the container. Instead, shake some of the herb into your hand away from the heat, then add it to the dish, returning the lid to the herb container as soon as possible.
- The aromatic compounds in herbs tend to be more fat soluble than water soluble. Adding a little fat or oil to food can increase our perception of the aroma in a herb.
- Dried herbs have less water and more concentrated flavor. When replacing 1 tbsp (15 mL) fresh herbs, use about ½ to 1½ tsp (2 to 7 mL) dried, depending on the dried herb's strength and how finely it is chopped or ground.

containing many polyphenolics with **antioxidant** properties that can help prevent cell damage in your body and reduce risk of cancer and heart disease. For instance, curry leaves contain antioxidant compounds called carbazoles that can help prevent the cell damage that leads to certain cancers.

Herb Pesto

Preserve the flavor of fresh herbs by making pesto. You can freeze it for months with very little flavor loss. Here's a basic recipe that you can tailor to your taste by changing the herbs, nuts, cheese, and oil.

2	cloves garlic, coarsely chopped	2
10 cups	loosely packed fresh basil, parsley, cilantro, and/or mint	2.5 L
2 cups	grated cheese, such as Parmesan, Asiago, Manchego, or dry Jack	500 mL
¾ cup	nuts, such as pine nuts, walnuts, almonds, pecans, or pistachios	175 mL
1 tsp	salt	5 mL
¼ tsp	freshly ground black pepper	1 mL
1 cup	oil, such as extra virgin olive oil, walnut oil, almond oil, hazelnut oil, pecan oil, pistachio oil, or avocado oil, divided	250 mL

1. In a food processor, combine garlic, herbs, cheese, nuts, salt, and pepper and process until finely chopped, about 30 seconds.

2. Scrape down sides, then add ¾ cup (175 mL) of oil through the feed tube in a slow, steady stream, blending pesto to a loose paste, about 20 seconds. Add additional oil as necessary to make a thick or runny paste. Scrape into airtight containers and refrigerate for up to 1 week or freeze for up to 1 year. Thaw at room temperature for 20 minutes before using.

MAKES ABOUT 2½ CUPS (625 ML)

science wise

How Menthol Cools • Menthol, the dominant flavor compound in peppermint, has a cooling effect when added to foods. It binds to receptors on nerve cells in the mouth that are responsible for sensing temperature. Menthol causes those receptors to tell the brain that they are 8 to 14°F (−13 to −10°C) cooler than they really are.

Carbazoles also have anti-inflammatory properties, relieving pain from inflammation much like aspirin does. In Mexico, the epazote that provides sharp, grassy aromas to bean dishes also contains a terpene compound called ascaridole that can help ward off intestinal worms. Culinary herbs like peppermint, cinnamon, and turmeric have also proved to be valuable in treating certain conditions. And some herbs, such as makrut leaves (wild lime), act as natural pest repellents.

Not every herb's aromatic compounds have a clean bill of health. Many of these compounds are designed to deter pests, after all. For instance, borage has a wonderful cucumber aroma, but the leaves also contain pyrrolizidine alkaloids, which can be toxic to the liver in very large amounts. (Thankfully, those amounts are much more than humans would consume with normal culinary use.) And hoja santa ("holy leaf"), widely used in southern Mexico and Central America, gets its sassafras or root-beer-like aroma from safrole, a mild **carcinogen** and the main chemical used to manufacture the recreational drug ecstasy or MDMA (methylenedioxy-methamphetamine). Safrole is currently banned as a food additive in North America.

Color in herbs comes mainly from green chlorophyll, but some herbs appear red or yellow from anthocyanins and betalains (plant pigments). For instance, the red anthocyanin pigments in perilla (shiso) give Japanese pickled plums (*umeboshi*) their deep burgundy color and flavor the plums with wonderfully floral and spicy terpene compounds.

See Also • Extracts, Flavor, Flavor Compounds, Leaves, Spices, Tea

HERBSAINT • See Liquor

HERRING • See Fish

HIBACHI • See Grilling

HIBISCUS • See Flowers

HICKORY • See Barbecue, Smoking

HIJIKI • See Seaweed

HM (HIGH-METHOXYL) PECTIN • See Pectin

HOG JOWL • See Bacon

HOISIN

What It Is • Hoisin is probably the best known of the Asian fermented bean sauces that include brown bean sauce (chee hou sauce), Thai bean sauce, and chile bean sauce. Hoisin get its thick texture, dark brown color, and sweet-spicy flavor from the **fermentation** of **soybeans** as well as added ingredients such as caramelized sugar, salt, garlic, chiles, and various spices.

What It Does • Sometimes called Chinese barbecue sauce, hoisin serves mostly as a table condiment and dipping sauce for various Chinese dishes like spring rolls, mu shu pork, barbecued pork and poultry, and Peking duck (which gave rise to its alternative name, Peking sauce). It's sometimes used as a condiment for noodle soups like Vietnamese pho.

How It Works • Like other fermented bean sauces, hoisin was developed as a by-product of fermenting soybeans to make soy sauce and miso. Its flavor develops as harmless molds like *Aspergillus* feed on soybean curd much the same way cheese is made by fermenting milk curd in the West. Enzymes from molds, bacteria, and yeasts digest sugars, fats, and proteins in the bean curd and in added grains such as rice and wheat flour. During **brining**, salt kills the molds, but the enzymes remain active and

Orange Honey Hoisin Glaze

Hoisin makes a handy concentrated flavor base that you can easily thin out to a delicious glaze. A little orange juice, honey, chili paste, and sesame oil make it a versatile glaze for slathering on roasted or grilled pork, beef, poultry, or salmon.

¼ cup	hoisin sauce	50 mL
2 tbsp	honey, preferably orange blossom	25 mL
2 tbsp	orange juice	25 mL
1 tbsp	freshly grated gingerroot	15 mL
1 tsp	crushed garlic	5 mL
1 tsp	chili-garlic paste	5 mL
1 tsp	toasted sesame oil	5 mL
¼ tsp	salt	1 mL

1. In a bowl, using a fork, combine hoisin, honey, orange juice, ginger, garlic, chili paste, oil, and salt. Use immediately or refrigerate in an airtight container for up to 3 weeks.

MAKES ABOUT ½ CUP (125 ML)

---

fermentation continues with the help of yeasts and salt-tolerant bacteria that produce lactic acid. Over several months, they break down chains of sugars, fatty acids, and amino acids into smaller, more flavorful compounds. At the same time, enzymatic browning reactions create the deep, dark color and complex flavors characteristic of hoisin.

See Also • Fermentation, Legumes, Sauces, Soybeans

HOJA SANTA • See Herbs

HOLLANDAISE • See Emulsion, Sauces

HOMINY • See Corn

HOMOGENIZATION • See Milk

HONEY

What It Is • Before the 1500s, when sugarcane emerged as the world's most popular sweetener, humans took a simpler route to sweetness. We followed the lead of bears and gathered a thick, golden liquid from beehives. Made by bees from the nectar of flowers, honey comes in as many varieties as there are plants.

Most commercial honeys are blended from honeys derived from several types of flower nectar, creating less distinctive flavors. Some honeys are unblended. When the nectar comes from unidentified flowers, unblended honey is often labeled "wildflower honey." Single-blossom, or monofloral, honeys are usually named for the primary flower from which bees have gathered nectar. Hundreds of varieties include acacia, alfalfa, buckwheat, chestnut, clover, eucalyptus, grapefruit, heather, lavender, mesquite, orange blossom, rosemary, sage, sunflower, and tupelo. Depending upon the flower nectar, the flavor of monofloral honey ranges from mild, herbal, and citrusy to strong, nutty, and salty. The color may be pale gold, caramel brown, or dark auburn.

The major forms of honey are:

Liquid honey: The most common form used in cooking is extracted from the honeycomb and is typically pasteurized to kill yeasts and help prevent crystallization.

Chunk honey: Similar to liquid honey, this form includes pieces of the honeycomb suspended in the liquid. It's often used to sweeten hot tea or any other way you would use liquid honey.

Comb honey: This type of honey is sold with liquid honey intact in the cells of the comb, which is waxy and chewy but edible. A slice of honeycomb makes a great addition to a cheese plate.

Creamed honey (aka whipped honey, honey cream, and churned honey): Crystallized honey in the form of a paste, which melts when temperatures top 80°F (27°C). Spread some on toast or muffins.

What It Does • One of the earliest uses of honey was the alcoholic beverage called mead, a fermented honey product made as far back as 1100 BCE. Mead is still made today, and honey also lends sweet caramel flavors to liqueurs like Drambuie and Benedictine. Whether you drizzle the golden liquid over biscuits, stir it into tea, or use it to glaze hams and carrots, honey has a distinctive flavor that's not easily replicated by other sweeteners.

Honey is also useful when making **candies** such as halvah and nougat because, like corn syrup, it helps to control the crystallization of sugar and create desirable textures. Bakers add it to breads and pastries for a number of reasons: sweetness, acidity, browning, and moisture. Honey undergoes Maillard reactions more readily than sugar because of its high fructose and glucose content, which is why it makes baked goods (and glazes) brown faster and more deeply than those made with sugar. Honey's main sugar, fructose, is also more hygroscopic (moisture absorbing) than granulated sugar, so it holds on to moisture longer and absorbs additional moisture from humid air, which helps to keep breads, cakes, and cookies moist, although surfaces can become sticky. The sugars in honey also delay staling and give breads and cakes a longer shelf life than those made with sugar. But honey interferes more with gluten formation in the dough, which creates less sturdy structure in breads. As a rule of thumb, for sturdy breads, use no more than 2 tablespoons (25 mL) honey per cup (250 mL) of bread flour.

For centuries, honey has been used to treat various ailments. It's often mixed into teas and cough drops to soothe sore throats with is throat-coating texture. Its relatively high acidity and low water content give honey mild antibacterial properties, which discourages the growth of microbes. When mixed with body fluids (as on a skinned knee), glucose in honey is slowly converted to antiseptic hydrogen peroxide, leading to its use as a topical ointment.

In fact, some honey can be harmful to humans and affect cooking. Because most commercial honey is pooled from many

fast facts

- To extract enough nectar to produce 1 pound (454 g) of honey, bees must visit flowers about 2 million times.
- When a bee returns to the hive with nectar, it "dances" to show the other bees where the nectar is located. The bee moves at angles relative to the sun to indicate an accurate flight pattern and intensifies its dance according to the abundance of nectar at the source.
- Honey has a pH of 3.2 to 4.5, which makes it more acidic than sour cream, yogurt, and buttermilk.
- In recent years, there have been increasing incidences of colony collapse disorder (CCD) in North America and western Europe. CCD is the name for a worldwide trend in which the number of commercially managed bee colonies drastically declined from nearly 6 million in 1940 to just over 2.5 million in 1995. CCD causes more than half of the adult bees to suddenly disappear from hives, which affects honey production and pollination of crops such as almonds, soybeans, apples, pears, melons, and berries, and other nonhybridized fruit and vegetable crops. CCD can have devastating economic effects on agriculture because honeybees pollinate about $10 billion worth of crops in the U.S. alone. The causes of CCD are unknown, but the most likely cause appears to be a virus.

sources, any potential toxicity is diluted. But honey made from bees that pollinate a limited number of certain flowers may harbor toxins. For instance, honey from bees that pollinate azaleas, rhododendrons, mountain laurels, and tutu bushes may be toxic and can produce symptoms of dizziness or nausea. Fortunately, these honeys are very uncommon. Common honey can have a negative effect in baking, however. If a common honey contains a mild toxin that's harmless to humans, the toxin may still be strong enough to kill yeast. If you have trouble with yeast doughs made with honey that don't rise well, try a different brand or type of honey. The honey may have been mildly toxic or had such strong antimicrobial activity that it killed the yeast, which kept the dough from rising.

Another caution with honey is to keep it away from infants. Honey contains the spores of *Clostridium botulinum*, the bacterium that produces the botulinum toxin. *C. botulinum* in honey isn't a big concern for older children and adults because their digestive tracts are colonized by many organisms that out-compete the botulism bacteria. But children under one year old should not be given honey because their digestive systems may not be developed enough with organisms to compete effectively, leaving them vulnerable to botulism poisoning.

Store liquid honey in an airtight container in a dark, dry place, where it will last about one year (comb and chunk honeys last about eight months). If you can, keep the humidity to less than 60% because honey will absorb moisture from the air, reducing its shelf life. For longer storage, keep honey below 50°F (10°C) or even in the refrigerator, which may cause it to get cloudy or crystallize, giving it a crunchy texture that some cooks like. If you prefer it clear and smooth, gentle heating will dissolve the crystals.

How It Works • Bees make honey as food for themselves. To make honey, honeybees (mostly *Apis mellifera*) swallow sweet nectar from flowers. In the bee's saliva, an enzyme called invertase divides the nectar's sugar (predominantly sucrose) into its two component sugars, glucose and fructose, making honey a natural invert **sugar**. Amylase, another enzyme, breaks down the nectar's starches into smaller, more flavorful compounds. The bees carry the transformed nectar back to the hive and through a complex process regurgitate it into the hexagonal wax cells of the honeycombs. At the hive, other bees cycle the nectar through themselves repeatedly, hanging droplets of it off their long proboscises until 50 to 60% of the water has evaporated. Other workers flap their wings to air-dry the nectar, further concentrating the liquid until the honey contains only 17 to 20% moisture. Each cell in the honeycomb also incubates a new bee, which feeds on the honey. To harvest the honey, beekeepers use smoke to drive away the bees, then take out the honeycombs. The bees eventually

return and continue to make honey, and the cycle repeats.

To extract honey, the combs can simply be crushed and the honey will drip out. Commercially produced liquid honey is usually separated from the waxy comb by centrifugal force. It's then pasteurized at about 155°F (68°C) to kill yeasts and filtered to remove bits of wax and other impurities. The wax is used to make beeswax candles and in cosmetics.

kitchen wisdom

Honey vs. Sugar

Desserts and candies like baklava and halvah get their distinctive sweetness from honey. But substituting honey for sugar in desserts, particularly in baked goods, can be tricky. Honey tastes different from sugar and it's about one and half times sweeter, it's higher in acid, and it contains liquid, all of which can throw off a recipe. If you must replace 1 cup (250 mL) sugar with honey, use 1 cup (250 mL) minus 2 to 3 tablespoons (25 to 45 mL) honey and reduce the liquid in the recipe by about 3 tablespoons (45 mL). To neutralize the acidity, add ¼ teaspoon (1 mL) baking soda. Watch baking times carefully or reduce the oven temperature by 25°F (10°C) to avoid overbrowning. Keep in mind that honey hangs on to moisture and absorbs it from the air, so it can make baked goods moister. Honey is sticky, too. To keep it from sticking to a measuring spoon or cup, lightly coat the utensil with oil before measuring.

Depending on the harvest season and the type of flowers from which the bees gather nectar, the flavor of honey varies considerably. In general, lighter-colored honeys like clove, orange blossom, and grapefruit taste fairly mild, while darker-colored honeys like chestnut and buckwheat taste robust, nutty, and caramelized. The primary flavors of honey come from several chemical compounds, most notably the proteins in the nectar, which provide the aroma of caramel. Fruity aromas come from chemical compounds called esters, floral aromas from aldehydes, buttery aromas from diacetyl, and dried grassy aromas from sotolon, a chemical also found in molasses (see **Flavor Compounds**). Honey's acidity comes from gluconic acid created by enzymes that oxidize the glucose. In addition to these basic flavors, monofloral honeys have other distinctive aromas such as the dark malt aroma of buckwheat honey.

Honey's exact composition changes according to the type of flower from which the bees make it. But most honey consists primarily of fructose (about 35 to 40% in commercial honey), glucose (30 to 35%), and water (17 to 20%), with a little maltose (7 to 9%) and a tiny bit of sucrose (1 to 2%). The texture of honey changes according to its fructose and glucose content. For instance, honey with a higher percentage of glucose (such as buckwheat) will crystallize more easily. Honey contains only trace proteins, enzymes, vitamins, and minerals, yet has mild antibacterial and antiseptic properties. Its color comes from pigments in the flowers, which end up in the nectar and in the honey.

See Also • Baking, Candy, Ice Cream, Sugar, Sweeteners

HONEYDEW • See Melon

HON-SHIMEJI • See Mushrooms

HOOP CHEESE • See Cheese

HOPS • See Beer

HORMONES

What It Is • Named after a Greek word meaning "impetus," a hormone is a chemical messenger that tells cells in the body what to do. Many act as neurotransmitters (compounds that transmit signals between neurons and other cells), and in mammals, the hub of hormone activity is the hypothalamus, a gland located just above the brain stem. Various hormones help to stimulate growth, control reproduction, alter mood, regulate metabolism and the immune system, and trigger changes or deterioration in the body's cells and tissues. For instance, the hormone testosterone stimulates the growth of muscles and bones. The hormone serotonin regulates hunger, mood, and sleep. Leptin reduces appetite and stimulates **metabolism** and **digestion**. Gastrin and histamine regulate the secretion of gastric juices. Epinephrine is responsible for surges in adrenaline, regulating stress (the fight-or-flight response). Hormones have wide-ranging medical uses, too. Diabetics use synthetic insulin to regulate blood sugar, and the hormone hydrocortisone (cortisol) is used as an anti-inflammatory.

What It Does • When it comes to food animals, regulating hormones has its ups and downs. Male animals have long been castrated to make them less randy. The meat of castrated steers and capons also develops more fat in its tissues, making the meat richer and more marbled. Growth hormone is perhaps the most notorious hormone in food and cooking. It stimulates cell growth and reproduction and is used primarily to bring beef cattle up to slaughter weight sooner (increasing meat production) and to increase milk production in milk cows. Beef growth hormones have been banned in the European Union since 1989. In North America, Australia, and New Zealand, however, beef cattle are treated with as many as six hormones to stimulate growth. Many studies have pointed out some potential health consequences for humans, but there's no evidence that growth hormones in meat are harmful to humans. Hormone levels in meat are strictly regulated, and the minor deposits there have not proven to be harmful to human health.

How It Works • When human growth hormone is manufactured synthetically by recombinant DNA technology (a form of genetic engineering), it's known as somatotropin or recombinant human growth hormone (rhGH). When manufactured to stimulate bovine growth, it's called recombinant bovine growth hormone (rBGH) or recombinant bovine somatotropin (rBST). Bovine growth hormone is injected into some milk cows, increasing milk production by as much as 10% over the course of 10 months. The health consequences of rBGH appear to be more severe for the cows than they are for humans. Many studies, including some meta-analysis studies, have shown that rBGH increases the risk of clinical mastitis (udder infections) by 25%, cuts fertility nearly in half, and increases the risk of lameness among milk cows. In the EU, government-appointed scientists surveyed the scientific evidence on rBGH and concluded that it increases health risks for cows to such an extent that it should be banned. In 1999, Health Canada banned its sale. Recombinant bovine growth hormone is also banned in Australia, New Zealand, Japan, and the EU. The United Nations food safety agency put a moratorium on it as well. But the growth hormone is widely used in the U.S., where roughly one-third of cattle routinely receive rBGH injections.

Recombinant bovine growth hormone has been controversial ever since the Monsanto Company introduced it in 1994. Several conjectures have been made about the effects of rBGH on human health, including reduced immune function, increased cancer risk, and increased diabetes risk, but no evidence has proven conclusive. Milk, butter, cheese, yogurt, ice cream, and other dairy products from cows given rBGH are not required to be labeled as such. Dairy products that are "rBGH-free" are often labeled, despite Monsanto's and the U.S. Food and Drug Administration's attempts to avoid such labels. Since the introduction of rBGH, demand for organic and rBGH-free milk has grown 500% and organic milk has become the fastest growing segment of the organic food market.

See Also • Antibiotics, Meat, Milk

HORSE

What It Is • Horses were domesticated in central Asia around 4500 BCE, and China still has the largest number of horses in the world (more than 8 million). They are used mostly as companion animals, for sport, and for work. However, horsemeat and milk are consumed in parts of Asia and several European countries. Slaughtering horses is highly controversial in North America, although the U.S. does export some horsemeat for human consumption.

What It Does • In the mid-1800s and during various wars, horsemeat was popular in France and parts of England because it was less expensive than beef and pork. It's now considered taboo in the U.K., the U.S.,

Ireland, and Australia. It's also forbidden by Jewish and Muslim dietary laws. However, horsemeat is enjoyed in France, Belgium, Italy, Mexico, Japan, and among the nomads of central Asia. China leads the world in horsemeat production, followed by Mexico, Kazakhstan, Italy, and Argentina. It can also be found in many supermarkets in Quebec.

Horsemeat is prepared like that of other four-legged animals, although it is fairly lean and dry, so it's best barded or cooked with additional fat. Steaks, chops, and ground meat can be grilled, broiled, sautéed, stewed, and braised. It's often cured by salting and/or smoking, especially in Germany, Switzerland, Sweden, Norway, the Netherlands, and Kazakhstan. Horsemeat is used to make Austrian *leberkäse* (meatloaf), German sauerbraten, and Italian sausages like *salsiccia di equino*. Many cultures thinly slice it and serve it raw (as in Japanese *basashi*) to highlight the meat's bold flavor.

The milk of mares is consumed by various cultures, primarily central Asian nomads such as Mongols. Mares produce more milk than goats or sheep. The milk is often fermented into a tart-tasting, slightly alcoholic beverage called koumiss, which is similar to kefir made from cow's, goat's, or sheep's milk. Fermentation converts the lactose in mares' milk (which contains about 40% more lactose than cow's milk) into lactic acid, ethanol, and carbon dioxide, making the milk easier to digest.

How It Works • Horses are herbivores that graze mostly on grasses. They're not nearly as efficient at converting grass and grain into muscle as cows, which has made the mass production of horsemeat an impractical economic pursuit. Most horsemeat comes from animals no longer suitable for riding or work. Some meat goes to zoos and wildlife centers to feed carnivorous animals. Some enters the international market for human consumption. Compared with beef, horsemeat tastes stronger, leaner, and slightly sweeter (from its higher amount of glycogen, which is broken down by enzymes into sweet-tasting glucose). It's also lower in fat and cholesterol and higher in iron, and it has a more fine-grained texture.

See Also • Meat

HORSERADISH

What It Is • Horseradish has been perking up meats and fish since the Middle Ages. Native to southeastern Europe and western Asia, this taproot of a cruciferous plant (*Armoraci rusticana*) flourishes in cool climates. The pungent white roots can grow well over a foot (30 cm) in length. Some cooks also use the horseradish greens that sprout up above ground.

fast facts

- In Sweden, horsemeat outsells lamb and mutton combined.
- In 2007, 82% of readers surveyed by London's *Time Out* magazine supported celebrity chef Gordon Ramsay's decision to serve horsemeat in his restaurants.

Lemon Horseradish Vodka

If you've got more fresh horseradish than you can use, preserve the horseradish flavor by infusing it into vodka. Freeze the lemon horseradish vodka and sip it cold or use it to make Bloody Mary drinks, marinate meats, or flavor sauces. If you're sipping the vodka straight, you may want to turn it into a liqueur by mixing in some honey or sugar syrup.

1	bottle (750 mL) vodka, preferably good-quality 100-proof potato vodka	1
2 oz	horseradish, peeled and cut into 2- by ¼-inch (5 by 1 cm) matchsticks (about ½ cup/125 mL)	60 g
	Grated zest of 1 lemon	
2 to 4 tbsp	honey or sugar syrup (optional)	25 to 60 mL

1. Empty vodka into a 1-quart (1 liter) glass container but save the vodka bottle. Add horseradish and lemon zest to container. Cover and let steep at room temperature for 6 to 8 weeks, stirring once or twice every week.

2. Strain vodka back into vodka bottle and discard solids. Add honey, if using, and shake until dissolved. Store in freezer.

MAKES ABOUT 3 CUPS (750 ML)

What It Does • Horseradish is often grated and incorporated into sauces as a condiment for roasted meats and smoked fish, especially in Denmark, Germany, eastern Europe, Russia, the U.K., and North America. Horseradish is one of the six components in the traditional Jewish Passover seder. In North America, it's a popular component of the Bloody Mary cocktail as well as cocktail sauces served with shrimp. In eastern Europe, a sweet horseradish-and-vinegar sauce called *chrain* (also available in a red version made with beets) is popular with gefilte fish during traditional Jewish holidays such as Passover. In Poland, beets and horseradish (*cwikla*) are served at Easter. When dyed green, horseradish is widely used as a less expensive alternative to wasabi, the Japanese condiment similar to horseradish.

Horseradish greens can be prepared like mustard greens and have a similar bite. When buying whole horseradish, separate the greens from the root and use both within a few days. Refrigerate fresh horseradish root tightly wrapped in plastic to keep it from losing moisture and flavor. For longer storage, it can be grated, mixed with fat to trap the pungent vapors, and refrigerated. It can also be grated and frozen in little blobs, then sealed in an airtight bag and frozen for up to six months. Once cut, fresh horseradish root loses flavor quickly. However, acid delays the release of its pungency, so horseradish has traditionally been preserved in vinegar. Commercially "prepared" horseradish preserved in vinegar is sometimes packed with grated beets, which give it a purple-red color and sweet flavor. As it loses flavor, horseradish darkens and becomes increasingly bitter, a good sign that it's time to restock your supply.

How It Works • Raw horseradish doesn't smell pungent. But like other cruciferous vegetables, as soon as its cells are broken open by cutting, chewing, or heat, sulfurous glucosinate compounds develop a sharp, penetrating aroma. These compounds are natural chemical defenses against predators. But humans love a challenge! As the horseradish cells open, they release an enzyme called myrosin, which breaks down a glucosinolate called sinigrin into allyl isothiocyanate (the same mustard oil that gives wasabi and mustard seed their bite). Isothiocyanate vaporizes immediately, carrying the pungent oil into the air, and it eventually lands on our tongues and in our

fast facts

sinuses. When isothiocyanate mixes with air and saliva, it makes our flavor perception hypersensitive, triggering nerve endings to send pain and irritation signals to the brain. We perceive this pungency as a spicy sort of "heat" that has become immensely pleasurable to cultures around the world. Another glucosinolate, gluconasturtiin, also contributes to the pungent aromas. Heat hastens the loss of these aromas, so the biggest pungency payload comes from using horseradish raw or only briefly cooked.

See Also • Cruciferous Vegetables, Roots

HORTICULTURE

What It Is • Whereas **agriculture** encompasses large-scale farming of field crops as well as animal farming, horticulture is a subset of agriculture focusing on plants used for food as well as ornamental landscaping.

What It Does • Ever since our earliest cultivation of plants for food, advances in horticulture have increased crop yields, improved disease resistance and drought tolerance, and enhanced the taste and **nutrition** of our vegetables, fruits, herbs, and flowers. These advances have generally improved the quality and quantity of our food supply. For instance, grafting, a method of propagating plants by attaching the reproducing part of one plant onto the roots of another, allowed horticulturists to accelerate the growing cycle of long-lived trees and make them exhibit more consistent and desirable traits. All orchard crops, including apples, pears, stone fruits, and grapes, are now propagated by grafting. However, some advances in controlled hybridization, genetic modification, and monocropping have led to concerns about losing the biodiversity that has become the hallmark of any thriving ecosystem. These concerns have increased interest in the great diversity of heirloom produce from plants that are open pollinated and naturally adapted to their environment as a result of years and years of growth and evolution.

How It Works • With roots in basic gardening, horticulture began as a process of saving seeds and cuttings and growing mature plants from them. Some of its greatest innovations, such as crop rotation, pesticides, and fertilizers, have advanced the field into a multidisciplinary practice that applies scientific rigor to plant breeding, **hybrids**, **genetics**, pollination, pest management, **water** and irrigation, soil health, crop management, and ecology.

See Also • Agriculture, Genetics, Hybrid

HOT DOG • See Sausage

HOT PEPPER • See Capsicum

HOT-SMOKING • See Smoking

HUBBARD SQUASH • See Squash

HUCKLEBERRY • See Berries

HUITLACOCHE • See Corn, Fungi

HYBRID

What It Is • Hybrid plants and animals are mixes of two races, breeds, varieties, species, or genera. Whereas purebred animals and plants grow from genetically similar parents, hybrids grow from genetically dissimilar parents. Think of an automobile. A "purebred" automobile is made with the familiar power source of an internal combustion engine. But a hybrid car mixes two different power sources, usually a combustion engine and a rechargeable electric battery. In a similar way, plants and animals from different races, breeds, varieties, species, and genera propagate or mate to form hybrid plants and animals.

Hybrids and crossbreeds have evolved over millions of years through natural selection. Natural hybrids occur often among plants and sometimes among animals. For instance, peppermint is a natural hybrid of spearmint and water mint. Grapefruit is a natural hybrid of pomelo and sweet orange. But the terms "hybrid" and "crossbreed" have come to refer to plants and animals propagated by humans through artificial selection (selective breeding) in which we hand-pick and reproduce desirable traits. For example, the Minneola tangelo is an artificial hybrid of the Dancy tangerine and the Duncan grapefruit that was developed in 1931 by the U.S. Department of Horticultural Research for the fruit's juiciness, sweetness, and pleasant tartness. In the animal kingdom, beefalo is a crossbreed of a cow and an American bison first developed in the mid-1800s, then perfected in 1965 by Jim Burnett, for the animal's tolerance to cold climates and the meat's relatively low fat content.

Sometimes a plant or animal will adapt both to its environment through natural selection and to the desires of humans through artificial selection. These are known as landraces rather than hybrids. Some heirloom vegetables and heritage breeds of pork are landraces because they have been allowed to develop in and adapt to their natural habitat. Agriculture experts define heirloom plants as open-pollinated plant varieties, meaning that they have been pollinated by and have developed their diverse genetic traits through relatively uncontrolled natural means, such as insects, birds, wind, and dew, as opposed to being developed through tightly controlled breeding to create hybrids with specific desirable traits. Some experts further define heirloom plants as those open-pollinated varieties that were introduced prior to 1951, when controlled hybridization greatly expanded. These heirloom plants come from old, inborn gene stock and tend to produce irregularly shaped fruits and vegetables that vary widely in size, color, and flavor. For many vegetable and fruit lovers around the world, these irregularities are desirable traits. In North America's large-scale agricultural production, however, they are considered defects.

What It Does • Purebred plants and animals will breed "true to type." That means they will produce offspring that exhibit predictable, replicable characteristics that are consistent with those of the parents. Many farm animals like cattle, sheep, goats, and pigs are purebred to ensure consistent traits among the animals. Similarly, many heirloom plants are considered purebreds because they produce vegetables and fruits that have the same general characteristics year after year.

On the other hand, hybrid plants and crossbred animals exhibit only certain traits of the parents, or they exhibit different traits. Most North American varieties of plants such as corn, beets, spinach, sunflowers, broccoli, and onions are hybrids. We intentionally propagate these hybrids to select desired traits such as improved flavor or texture, increased yield, better tolerance of climatic change, and increased resistance to viruses, fungi, bacteria, pests, and pesticides. For instance, the Russet Burbank potato was hybridized in the 1870s by Luther Burbank, an American horticulturist. Burbank also developed the plumcot, a hybrid that is half apricot and half plum. In the late 1900s, the plumcot was further hybridized by Floyd Zaiger into the aprium (one-quarter plum and three-quarters apricot) and the pluot (three-quarters plum and one-quarter apricot) in Zaiger's quest for the perfect fruit.

Some hybrids are larger, stronger, or more fertile, or exhibit genetic traits that allow them to adapt to environments in which the parent species would not survive. The development of these new traits is referred to as positive heterosis or hybrid vigor and occurs mostly when hybrids are formed between species that have similar genetics. A strong hybrid can be beneficial to a local population when it propagates with the local population, invigorating the healthy indigenous species and improving its ability to thrive in the environment.

Not all hybrids are healthy, however. When a hybrid is formed from parent plants or animals that have different genetics, the hybrid tends to be smaller, weaker, or less

fast facts

- The fictional jackalope is an imagined cross between a jackrabbit (of the *Lepus* genus) and an antelope (*Antilocapra americana*).
- Natural animal hybrids are less common than natural plant hybrids, but in 2006, DNA analysis of a bear shot by a hunter in northern Canada confirmed that the animal was a naturally occurring, fertile hybrid of a polar bear and a grizzly bear, two species that do not normally mate.

fertile (or sterile), or exhibit traits that prevent the hybrid from adapting to its environment. A weak hybrid can be detrimental when it propagates with the local population, compromising the health of indigenous species. Breeders of purebred species often consider hybrids a threat because the hybrids may be more susceptible to viruses, bacteria, and diseases. If the hybrids breed with the purebreds, they can make the purebreds more susceptible to diseases in their environment. Unintentional crossbreeding can also make the consistent traits of a purebred species less predictable, taking some of the "purity" out of the breed and compromising its identity and authenticity. For instance, purebred or wild American bison are becoming increasingly scarce because most have been intentionally or unintentionally bred with cattle, resulting in "genetic pollution" that has reduced the amount of purebreds in existence. Most "bison" sold in today's markets is actually beefalo, a hybrid of cattle and purebred bison. Today, only four genetically unmixed herds of American bison remain in the U.S. and only one of those herds is free of disease.

The threat to purebred American bison shows how hybrids can lead to a loss of genetic diversity and compromise wild, indigenous breeds. Opponents of genetically engineered plants and animals often point to this problem, as hybrids of vastly different species may not adapt well in nature. If maladapted hybrids propagate or mate with indigenous species, the hybrid could dilute the strength of the indigenous gene pool, reducing local biodiversity and threatening the health of local ecosystems.

However, whether a hybrid is viable or not depends on the combination of traits it needs to thrive in its environment or to satisfy humans enough to keep propagating the hybrid. Conservationists want to keep purebred American bison from going extinct, and beefalo breeders want to sell beefalo. If beefalo becomes more popular than purebred bison, perhaps bison will go the way of the dodo bird. The same thing could happen to seeded watermelon. Here's a case where we have decided that the sterility of a hybrid is desirable. We propagated sterile hybrid watermelon plants to prevent them from producing seeds because many consumers prefer watermelon without seeds. If seedless watermelon becomes more popular than seeded watermelon, we may stop propagating seeded watermelon and it could become extinct. These examples show how humans are a crucial part of the environment to which plants and animals adapt. That's also why growing and buying purebred animal products and heirloom produce can help keep certain animals and plants from going extinct while improving the biodiversity considered essential to thriving ecological systems. Many seed banks throughout the world store and maintain the genetic diversity of many, but not all, of the world's plants.

How It Works • Hybrids occur when genetically dissimilar parents propagate. Hybridization can happen through natural selection, artificial selection (selective breeding), or **genetic** engineering. In natural selection, similar species of plants or animals propagate or mate with each other. As generations of plants or animals evolve and adapt to their environment, hybrids form by developing genetic traits that help the organism thrive and losing traits that impede survival. In selective plant and animal breeding, humans propagate certain plants and mate certain animals. We choose which plants and animals to breed based on the genetic traits we most desire in the plant or animal, such

as improved flavor, increased yield, or even lack of seeds. Genetic engineering works in a similar way because humans also select for desired traits. But instead of propagating two plants or mating two animals, we manually move the desired genes from one organism to another.

Think of a gene in an organism as a recipe in a cookbook. Organisms are compilations of genes the same way that cookbooks are compilations of recipes. Each gene in an organism contains the instructions for a genetic trait, the equivalent of a single recipe that forms part of the whole cookbook. In natural selection, the genetic traits are selected as the organism evolves and adapts to its environment, forming hybrids over several generations. It's as though the cookbook is compiled from randomly selected recipes. In selective plant and animal breeding, we create hybrids by combining two organisms to obtain offspring with desired genetic traits: half of the genes from each parent are shared with the offspring. It's like combining two cookbooks in hopes of coming up with the desired combination of recipes. But only half of the recipes selected randomly from each parent cookbook end up in the hybrid cookbook. As you can imagine, with traditional plant and animal breeding, the results are sometimes mixed, because undesired traits are jumbled up with desired ones. That imprecision is essentially what led to genetic engineering, a more precise form of plant and animal breeding. In genetic engineering, specific desired genes and genetic traits are manually taken from one organism and inserted into another. It's like taking only select recipes from one cookbook and precisely arranging those recipes in another cookbook.

See Also • Agriculture, Genetics, Horticulture

HYDRATION • See Water

HYDROCOLLOID • See Colloid, Gelatin, Gums, Pectin, Seaweed

HYDROGEN BONDS • See Chemical Bonding

HYDROLYZED VEGETABLE PROTEIN

What It Is • Take a look at a can of soup, a tub of sauce, or a package of bouillon. Listed among the ingredients, you'll probably see hydrolyzed vegetable protein (or one of its aliases or cousins like hydrolyzed soy protein, hydrolyzed plant protein, autolyzed yeast protein, or yeast extract). Hydrolyzed vegetable protein (HVP) is the most widely used flavor enhancer in prepared foods.

What It Does • HVP and its cousins boost the flavor of countless soups, sauces, and other prepared foods like hot dogs. It's characterized by the flavor called umami, which can be generally described as savory. You can taste this distinct flavor in foods like roasted meat, sautéed mushrooms, and aged cheese.

When added to foods, HVP delivers the flavor of glutamate, which we taste as savory (also called umami). Like other flavors — sweet, salty, sour, and bitter — the flavor of umami, or savoriness, is detected by special taste receptors on our tongues. Flavor scientists are still studying exactly how HVP intensifies other flavors. But it's possible that HVP makes flavor molecules stick to our taste buds longer so the other flavors in foods taste stronger.

How It Works • HVP is made by hydrolysis, or "splitting by water," one of the fundamental processes of cooking and digestion. In hydrolysis, large molecules of protein, fat, and carbohydrates are broken down into smaller molecules. In our stomachs, gastric enzymes catalyze the hydrolysis, or breakdown of these large molecules. To make HVP, foods such as vegetables, soybeans, corn, or yeast are heated in hydrochloric acid, which hydrolyzes the food's protein into smaller, more flavorful amino acids, particularly glutamic acid. The resulting solution is usually neutralized with sodium hydroxide and dehydrated into a brown powder. Non-fermented soy sauce is made in a similar fashion.

See Also • Chemical Bonding, Flavor, Flavor Compounds, Food Additives, Soybeans

fast fact

• The U.S. Food and Drug Administration requires producers to list monosodium glutamate among the ingredients on food labels. However, foods that do not contain MSG may still contain other glutamates with a similar savory flavor. For instance, hydrolyzed vegetable protein, autolyzed yeast protein, and yeast extract all contain glutamate. If you are among the small group of people sensitive to glutamate, look out for these aliases on food labels. The FDA does not allow foods made with HVP and its cousins to be labeled as not containing MSG.

HYDROPHILIC • See Water

HYDROPHOBIC • See Water

HYGROSCOPIC • See Water

HYSSOP • See Herbs

IBÉRICO HAM • See Ham

ICE • See Freezing

ICEBERG LETTUCE • See Leaves

ICE CREAM

What It Is • Ice cream is little more than frozen sweetened cream. Manufacturers have attempted to improve its consistency and storage life with gums and milk solids, but premium ice cream is still the original, called Philadelphia-style — cream and milk, sweetened with sugar, scented with vanilla. Custom blends are flavored with fruit, or nuts, or chocolate, or whatever you want. French-style ice cream adds yolks. Soft-serve ice cream is dispensed at a warmer temperature, and Italian gelato, made with milk so it has a lower fat content than ice cream, is a dense ice cream frozen with less aeration than regular ice cream.

What It Does • Cream is a remarkable substance, a fluid flowing toward solidity. Ice cream exaggerates that quality by thickening cream through chilling. The trick is doing it without petrifying the mixture into a block of solid ice.

Cream freezes rock hard. Adding sugar makes it softer, but also reduces the freezing point below the freezing point of water, so early ice cream makers had to develop ways of getting sweetened cream to freeze. By the 13th century, the Arab world knew that if salt was added to hard ice, it formed a slush, and that slush was colder than solid ice. In other words, salt lowered the freezing point of water. The Italians were freezing sweetened fruit juice into ices by the early 17th century, and French recipes for frozen creams date from the 1680s and '90s. By the end of the 18th century, the French had learned that frequently stirring a freezing cream broke up ice crystals and yielded smoother results.

Until the mid-19th century, ice cream could be made only in small batches and was reserved for the wealthy. All of that changed with the development of the Nancy Johnson–William Young ice cream freezer, which mechanized the mixing and freezing process, allowing anyone to turn out quality ice cream. A milk dealer in Baltimore, Jacob Fussell, used the new technology to turn his excess supply of milk and cream into ice cream, which he was able to sell more affordably. By 1900, ice cream parlors were in every town in the U.S. North Americans still eat much more ice cream than any other people in the world, about 20 quarts (20 L) per person per year.

Making ice cream requires three steps:

Making the mix: The basic ingredients for ice cream are milk and cream (usually equal parts to yield about 17% milk fat), sugar (usually about 15%), and flavoring. Generally the milk and sugar are heated together to dissolve the sugar, then cooled before the cream and flavoring are added. Custard-based ice creams, which include egg yolks, have to be cooked to start to set the proteins in the egg and to kill any bacteria in the yolk.

Freezing: After cooling, the ice cream mixture is placed in a container with chilled walls. To keep ice crystals small and the ice cream smooth, the mix is frozen as quickly as possible and kept in constant motion.

As the ice cream churns, air gets incorporated into the mix. The air inflates the volume of the ice cream. The volume in excess of the volume of the original mix is called overrun. In very fluffy ice creams, the overrun can be as much as 100%, which

fast facts

- A pint of premium ice cream can weigh the same as a quart of budget-brand ice cream, because it contains so much less air.
- On December 13, 1903, Italo Marchioni received U.S. patent No. 746971 for his mold for making pastry ice cream cones. He claimed that he had been making pastry cones and selling ice cream in them since 1896. After being awarded the patent, he filed numerous lawsuits against cone manufacturers for patent infringement, but he lost every case, because his patent was for the mold for making cones, not for the cones themselves.

means the ice cream is half air. Premium ice creams and gelati tend to have less overrun than budget ice cream, usually less than 25%.

Hardening: The freezing phase is complete when about half the water in the mixture has been frozen. At that point the mixture is thick but still creamy. It is now packed into containers and frozen until firm. The faster the hardening process, the less time there is for water to grow into large, grainy crystals, so quick freezing is essential. Low-fat ice creams are particularly prone to crystallization during the hardening phase and are either modified with **gums** or hardened completely in a churn.

There are several styles of ice creams and frozen sweets. They are listed in order of popularity in North America:

Standard (Philadelphia-style) ice cream is made from cream, milk, sugar, and flavorings.

Custard (French-style) ice cream is made from cooked custard (crème anglaise).

Gelato (Italian-style) ice cream is usually made from milk or a mixture of milk and cream (rarely a custard) that is frozen to minimize aeration to produce a dense ice cream. In Italian, *gelato* can refer to any frozen dessert. Frozen sweetened fruit juice (with or without dairy) is sorbetto (sorbet). Granita (or Italian ice in the U.S.) is made by freezing a flavored mix (usually nondairy) and shaving the resulting ice block.

Reduced-fat ice creams are made with a milk-cream mixture that is less than 10% fat.

Sometimes called ice milk or frozen yogurt (even though they contain a minimal amount of yogurt), reduced-fat ice creams tend to develop large ice crystals because there is less fat to get in the way of the water droplets bonding together. Often natural gums or emulsifiers are added to increase smoothness.

Slow-churned ice creams go through a process called low-temperature extrusion where ice cream from a traditional continuous freezer is further frozen in an extruder to a very low temperature, about 5°F (−15°C) and then hardened. Double-churned ice creams go through partial aeration of the mix prior to freezing and then recirculation of some of the frozen mix back through the continuous freezer. In both cases the result is smaller ice and fat crystals and air bubbles for a smoother texture.

Another novel way of producing creamy low-fat ice creams has met with some controversy. Incorporating proteins similar to those in deep-ocean fish (such as eels) that protect them from freezing to death in deep water has met resistance in Europe. The proteins are very effective at keeping water from crystallizing, but because the ice-structuring proteins are made from genetically altered yeast proteins, EU countries do not permit their use.

Soft-serve (creemee or soft) ice cream is lower in fat (usually less than 6%). It's higher in overrun (usually over 50%) than premium ice cream, and its soft texture makes it

possible to hold it at higher temperatures than hard ice cream. Soft-serve ice cream crystallizes easily, so it is usually frozen at the point of service in a special machine from which it is dispensed.

Kulfi (Indian-style) ice cream is made from milk that has been reduced until its sugars caramelize. It is usually frozen without mixing, producing a very dense, compact ice cream with an icy texture.

Dondurma (Turkish-style) ice cream is a chewy type of ice cream made from a Turkish milk beverage, salep dondurma, that is sweetened and thickened with a vegetable gum (glucomannan) derived from the powdered tubers of wild orchids (salep). Once it is frozen enough to be malleable, salep ice cream is pounded and worked, like kneading bread, until the network of gum becomes elastic.

How It Works • Ice cream is a foam emulsion of ice, fat, and air. As an ice cream mixture chills, its water freezes into ice crystals, thickening the mixture. Through constant stirring and quick freezing, the size of the crystals is kept small, and the ice cream remains smooth.

science wise

Brain Freeze • When a part of your body experiences extreme cold, your body automatically shrinks the diameter of the blood vessels in that region to reduce blood flow and minimize heat loss. In the case of brain freeze (ice cream headache), the hard palate across the top of the mouth gets super cold, usually when ice cream is pressed against it to melt it. After the ice cream is swallowed, the blood vessels start to return to their normal size, resulting in massive dilation of the arteries that supply the palate (descending palatine arteries). The nerves surrounding the palate sense this as pain and transmit a pain sensation through the trigeminal nerve that runs across the forehead, behind the eyes, and along the jaw. Even though the syndrome is prefigured by extreme cold, it actually starts as the mouth is recovering from the cold. So slowing down the rapid warming of the area, by drinking something moderately cold, can help to keep brain freeze at bay.

Ice Cream Comparison of Fat, Calories, and Overrun

Ice Cream Type	Fat % of Weight	Calories per ½ cup (125 mL)	Overrun % of Volume
Standard (premium)	16 to 20	240 to 360	20
Standard (budget)	10	120 to 150	90
Custard	14	150 to 270	20
Gelato	6	140 to 160	0 to 10
Reduced-fat	4	100 to 110	90
Soft-serve	5	175 to 190	60
Kulfi	7	185 to 230	0 to 20
Dondurma	6	170 to 200	0 to 20

As more of the water turns into ice, the fat and dissolved sugar in the mixture become more concentrated. Even when frozen hard, about 20% of the water in ice cream remains syrupy. The resulting fluid, which is approximately equal parts water, sugar, fat, and protein, flows around the ice crystals, coating them and loosely holding them together. Air forced into the matrix during mixing (overrun) punctures the icy structure, making it less solid, lighter in texture, more voluminous, and easier to scoop.

Large ice crystals are the enemy for any ice cream, which is why pains are taken during manufacturing to keep crystals minuscule. But even the smoothest ice cream can become grainy during storage. Ice cream has to be stored at temperatures as cold as possible. In most home freezers that means 0°F (–18°C). When it thaws, even partially, the smallest ice crystals melt first, and the freed water gets deposited on the larger, and increasingly fewer, ice crystals. Eventually the ice cream becomes grainy. Adding gums, emulsifiers, and stabilizers helps to keep free water in suspension, creating a smoother, more stable product.

Ideally, ice cream should be tempered at room temperature for about 5 minutes or in a microwave on full power for 10 seconds before serving, to bring its temperature from the 0°F (–18°C) of a freezer to 8 to 10°F (–13 to –12°C), which makes it easier to scoop and serve. It also allows some of the water in the

Three Recipes for Ricotta Ice Cream

By starting an ice cream with a fresh mild sweet dairy cheese rather than cream, most of ice cream's crystallization problems disappear. Because cheese is so much lower in water than milk or cream, there is much less chance of water breaking free during freezing and forming ice. This ice cream can be made in an ice cream maker, or frozen in a pan, cut into cubes, and puréed in a food processor to crush the ice crystals. Use whole-milk ricotta cheese that is about 10% milk fat.

Vanilla Honey Ricotta Ice Cream

2	containers (each 15 oz/425 g) whole-milk ricotta cheese	2
¾ cup	honey	175 mL
1 tsp	vanilla extract	5 mL

1. In a food processor, combine ricotta cheese, honey, and vanilla and purée until completely smooth. Transfer to an ice cream maker and freeze according to manufacturer's directions.
2. Transfer to an airtight container. Press a piece of plastic wrap onto the surface, cover with a tight-fitting plastic lid, and freeze until serving, up to 2 days.

MAKES ABOUT 4 CUPS (1 L) OR 8 SERVINGS

Chocolate Chip Cannoli Ice Cream

2 cups	whipping (35%) cream	500 mL
1 cup	granulated sugar	250 mL
Pinch	salt	Pinch
1	container (15 oz/425 g) whole-milk ricotta cheese	1
1 tsp	vanilla extract	5 mL
⅛ tsp	almond extract	0.5 mL
½ cup	semisweet mini chocolate chips	125 mL

1. In a saucepan over medium heat, combine cream, sugar, and salt and heat, stirring occasionally, until sugar dissolves.
2. In a food processor, combine ricotta cheese and vanilla and almond extracts and purée until smooth and creamy. Stir in scalded cream mixture and set aside to let cool for 10 minutes. Transfer to an ice cream maker and freeze according to manufacturer's directions.
3. Stir in chocolate chips when ice cream is almost finished churning. Transfer to an airtight container. Press a piece of plastic wrap onto the surface, cover with a tight-fitting plastic lid, and freeze until serving, up to 2 days.

MAKES ABOUT 4 CUPS (1 L) OR 8 SERVINGS

Basil Ricotta Ice Cream

2 cups	whipping (35%) cream	500 mL
1 cup	granulated sugar	250 mL
1 cup	fresh basil leaves, finely chopped	250 mL
Pinch	salt	Pinch
1	container (15 oz/425 g) whole-milk ricotta cheese	1
1 tsp	vanilla extract	5 mL

1. In a saucepan over medium heat, combine cream, sugar, basil, and salt and heat, stirring occasionally, until the sugar dissolves and the mixture is simmering. Set aside for 5 minutes, then strain to remove basil.
2. In a food processor, combine the basil-infused cream, ricotta cheese, and vanilla and purée until smooth and creamy. Let cool to room temperature. Transfer to an ice cream maker and freeze according to manufacturer's directions.
3. Transfer to an airtight container. Press a piece of plastic wrap onto the surface, cover with a tight-fitting plastic lid, and freeze until serving, up to 2 days.

MAKES ABOUT 4 CUPS (1 L) OR 8 SERVINGS

ice cream to become fluid, making the ice cream flow better in the mouth. Returning ice cream to the freezer after tempering will cause it to become grainy, so you should remove from the freezer only the amount of ice cream you think you will serve.

See Also • Dispersions, Freezing, Gums, Heat

IRRADIATION

What It Is • Irradiation was developed in the 1940s to kill bacteria in food that can cause illness and to wipe out microbes that decrease the storage life of fresh food. It also kills trichina worms and inhibits sprouting of potatoes and onions.

What It Does • Irradiation kills parasites and all bacteria, including E. coli, Salmonella, and Campylobacter (the leading causes of food-borne illness). In the U.S., wheat flour and white potatoes have been irradiated since the early 1980s. In 1985, the U.S. Food and Drug Administration (FDA) approved irradiation for spices, fruits, vegetables, pork, and poultry. In 1997, irradiating beef was approved, and in 2000 eggs got the okay. Irradiation is especially valuable for treating mass-produced blended foods, such as ground meats and spices, in which a small infected part of the product can contaminate the entire batch and affect thousands of consumers. All irradiated products in the U.S. (except for spices) are labeled with a symbol called a radura.

In the U.S., the list of irradiated food continues to grow, but in much of the rest of the world there is resistance. The EU has stopped approving all irradiated foods for sale in Europe. Irradiation can leave an off flavor in some foods, especially fatty foods, that is described as metallic, sulfurous, or barn-like. Decades of testing shows that irradiated foods are safe to eat, but the process is powerful enough to alter the genetic material in cells. Initial tests done in the 1950s showed that irradiated food increased the risk of cancer in lab animals, although the process was less controlled at that time.

Irradiation is a sensible and easy solution to the serious threat of widespread food poisoning from mass-produced products like ground beef. It can also be argued that it is only a short-term fix that does not remedy the underlying food safety problems in large-scale beef production. It does not solve the problem that some mass-produced beef comes to market contaminated with bacteria from crowded cattle feedlots and improper processing in meat plants. Even though irradiation kills E. coli bacteria in meat contaminated with fecal matter, which makes the meat safe to eat, it is still meat containing fecal matter. Many consumers feel that the quality standards for our food supply should be set higher.

How It Works • Irradiation exposes food products to ionizing radiation that damages DNA in cells as it kills microbes that cause spoilage and disease. Different kinds of radiation have different levels of energy, which determines the effect they have on food (see **Heat**). Some forms of radiation are very weak. Microwaves, for instance, are only powerful enough to boil water; they can't brown proteins or affect the cell structure of foods.

The energy used for irradiation is strong enough to penetrate the cells of food and ionize molecules. With ionizing radiation, electrons are stripped from molecules, causing the formation of free radicals. In the case of delicate molecules like DNA, or in small single-celled microbes, irradiation energy is strong enough to restructure the molecules, damaging genetic material and killing pathogenic microbes.

See Also • Bacteria, Chemical Bonding, Heat

J

JACKFRUIT • See Fruit

JAM AND JELLY

What It Is • Fruits have been preserved in sugar for thousands of years. One of the earliest preserves was made by the Portuguese with quince and honey, which they called *marmelada*. In the 1600s and 1700s, as sugar became cheaper and more plentiful, it was more commonly used in preserves as it allowed the flavor of the fruit to come through better than honey did. Today, jams and jellies are usually made by boiling fruit and sugar together to evaporate water and concentrate the mixture in order to form a gel. Savory jellies like aspic and sweet jellies can also be made with **gelatin**, but this entry focuses on gels made with **pectin**.

The two main categories of fruit gels are preserves and jellies. Conserves, jams, fruit butter, and fruit pastes are all types of preserves made with whole fruit. Jellies are typically made with only fruit juice to obtain a clear product. According to U.S. Federal Standards and Definitions, commercially made jams and jellies must contain a minimum of 45% fruit and 55% sugar and be concentrated to 65% or more solids. Up to 25% can be corn syrup.

Here are descriptions of each type:

Preserves: A thick, sometimes solid gel that includes large chunks of fruit.

Jam: A thick gel with small pieces of fruit that create a smooth, soft consistency that is looser than preserves. Jams are often made from very juicy fruits like berries and include commercial pectin (a liquid or powder usually isolated from apples or citrus) to help the mixture gel. When made without sugar, jams are known as fruit spreads. When puréed fruit is mixed with pectin and minimally cooked or not cooked at all and requires freezing or chilling to set, it's known as freezer jam.

Conserves: Preserves often made with a mixture of fruits and sometimes including nuts or dried fruit.

Fruit paste or butter: Puréed fruit usually mixed with an equal weight of sugar and cooked down to a firm or solid consistency. Some fruit pastes, called fruit concentrates, are merely fruit purée that is cooked to evaporate water. Chewy fruit leather is made by using less sugar, spreading the paste thin, then drying the paste and cutting the "leather" into strips.

Jelly: A clear, gelled flavored liquid. Jellies are firmer than jam, and are typically made with fruit juice, sugar, and pectin, then gelled to the point where they will hold their shape when cut and quiver when bumped. Jellies evolved out of liquids gelled with gelatin. In that sense, a jelly can be sweet or savory, such as mint jelly and jalapeño pepper jelly.

Taken broadly, the category also includes jelly candies like jelly beans, gumdrops, and Asian konjac jelly that may be gelled with pectin, gelatin, **gums**, or **starch**.

Marmalade: Preserves or jelly made from high-pectin fruit such as citrus (often Seville oranges) and usually including some of the whole fruit or fruit rind for bitter flavor.

What It Does

Jams and jellies preserve the fruit and the flavor so it can be enjoyed later on bread, in cookies, and in pastries. Fruit jellies are also heated and used to glaze tarts and baked hams.

Making Jams and Jellies

The five main components of jams and jellies are fruit, sugar, pectin, liquid, and acid such as lemon juice. It's best to use slightly underripe fruit because it contains more high-methoxyl (HM) pectin and will gel better than overripe fruit, but ripe fruit is more flavorful, so commercial pectin is sometimes added to ripe fruit. Underripe fruit also has more acid that is necessary to form a gel. To get a firm gel, use high-pectin fruit like tart apples, blackberries, cranberries, currants, gooseberries, grapes (especially Concord), guavas, lemons, loganberries, plums, and raspberries. You can also combine these fruits with lower-pectin fruit like apricots, cherries, peaches, pears, pomegranates, and strawberries to help create a gel or simply add commercial pectin. Different pectins gel differently. Apple pectin makes an elastic gel, while citrus pectin makes a more tender, fragile gel.

Sugar makes up almost half the weight of a typical jam or jelly. Excess sugar can prevent a gel from forming because it dilutes the pectin. On the other hand, too little sugar creates a higher proportion of pectin, which can cause the mixture to set up into a tough, rubbery gel. For jam, use about 1 cup (250 mL) sugar for every 2 to 3 cups (500 to 750 mL) chopped fruit. For jelly, use about ¾ to 1 cup (175 to 250 mL) sugar for every 1 cup (250 mL) fruit juice. For jam, the sugar and fruit are usually cooked together because sugar pulls water from the fruit but leaves pectin, which causes the fruit to retain some of its shape, resulting in the chunky texture of jam. For

fast fact

- Commercial low-sugar jams are made with low-methoxyl (LM) pectin that will form a gel by forming salt bridges with calcium. Sweetness is obtained from high-intensity sweeteners such as sucralose. Commercial pectins also come in rapid-set and slow-set versions. Rapid-set pectins set a gel quickly to limit fruit pieces from floating in preserves and jams.

jelly, the whole fruit is cooked without sugar to break down the cell walls and release more pectin.

When cooking whole fruit or vegetables to extract the juice, it's best to cook briefly and gently, because extended boiling can break down the pectin and reduce its gelling ability. Cook in small batches if necessary, and use wide pans so the food heats faster. Gently boil soft fruits like berries for about 10 minutes and firm fruit like apples for about 20 minutes. If the fruit is dry, add a little water to help extract pectin from the cell walls. Then strain the fruit through a wet cloth jelly bag to isolate the pectin-rich juice. For the clearest jelly, avoid squeezing the jelly bag. After straining, you can get more pectin out of the fruit pulp by boiling it again. Of course, you can also start with fruit juice instead of whole fruit and add some commercial liquid or powdered pectin to the juice.

At this point, fruit juice (or whole fruit for jam) is mixed with sugar or corn syrup and boiled to evaporate water, concentrate the mixture, and create the gel. For the best flavor and color, boil quickly to avoid vaporizing volatile aromatic compounds. Use a wide pan to evaporate maximum moisture in minimal time. Skim the foam during boiling to remove fine solid particles and achieve a crystal clear jelly. When the mixture thickens, you can add acid such as lemon juice to adjust the acidity and balance the sweetness. Add acid at the end, because if it's added early, either it can break down the pectin before it has a chance to gel the mixture or it can cause the mixture to set before it is poured. The mixture should be about 0.5% acid by weight or have a pH between 2.8 and 3.4. Generally, that means for every pound (454 g) of low-acid fruit like strawberries, use about 2 teaspoons (10 mL) lemon juice. High-acid fruit like oranges may not need any additional acid.

When the mixture reaches about 220°F (104°C), it will set upon cooling. As the mixture boils, test how firmly it will set by dropping a spoonful of the hot mixture onto a cold surface (such as a chilled plate). Put the plate in the refrigerator for a few minutes, then tip the plate. If the mixture has set to the consistency you're after, remove the hot mixture from the heat.

Both jams and jellies typically use the **canning** method of sterilizing jars, lids, and utensils in boiling water, then pouring the hot mixture into the jars, leaving about ¼-inch (0.5 cm) headspace at the top. The sealed jars can be boiled in a boiling-water canner for 5 to 10 minutes, which creates a vacuum that forces out air, creates an airtight seal, and retards spoilage. Jars can also be sealed with melted paraffin.

kitchen wisdom

Testing for Pectin in Fruit Juice

Here's an easy way to get a rough idea of the pectin concentration of fruit juice before cooking it to make jelly. Place 1 tablespoon (15 mL) rubbing alcohol in a small glass and stir in 1 tablespoon (15 mL) of the fruit juice. How firmly it sets will tell you how much pectin is in the juice. If a strong, firm gel forms, the juice should form a good gel when you cook it to make jelly. If a weak, loose gel forms, add about 1 teaspoon (5 mL) either powdered or liquid pectin per cup (250 mL) of fruit juice. Be sure to discard your test gel before someone tries to spread it on toast. It won't taste very good!

How It Works • Sugar draws away moisture, making it hard for microbes to survive. The gel structure of jams and jellies results from complex reactions between the pectin, water, sugar, and acid that create a polymeric network that holds in the liquid.

Pectin gives the gel its internal structure.

Tomatillo Jalapeño Jam

Tomatillos are relatively high in pectin and acid, creating a fairly firm gel for jam. For a shot of spicy flavor and a whiff of citrus, the recipe includes jalapeño and lime. The jam contains a fair amount of tiny seeds but they add a pleasant crunch like that of seeded raspberry jam.

1 lb	tomatillos, husked, rinsed, and chopped	500 g
2	jalapeños, seeded and finely chopped	2
2 cups	granulated sugar	500 mL
1	lime	1

1. Sterilize four to six 8-ounce (250 mL) glass canning jars by placing them in a large saucepan, covering with water, and bringing to a boil over medium heat. Boil for 10 minutes, then remove jars and air-dry on a rack until bone dry. Time your sterilizing so jars will still be warm when spooning in hot mixture. Otherwise, jars may crack from sudden temperature change. Prepare boiling-water canner, if desired, and two-piece canning lids according to manufacturer's instructions.

2. In a wide saucepan, combine tomatillos, jalapeños, sugar, and ½ cup (125 mL) water. Bring to a boil over high heat. Boil, stirring occasionally, until tomatillos break down and mixture begins to thicken, skimming any foam from surface, 15 to 20 minutes.

3. Grate lime zest into saucepan. Then cut lime in half and squeeze in juice from one half. Boil until mixture falls in a single, heavy sheet when dripped from a spoon (about 220°F/104°C on a jelly thermometer). Pour hot mixture into sterilized jars, leaving ¼-inch (0.5 cm) headspace. Wipe rims and screw on lids. Let cool to room temperature. Refrigerate for up to 6 months. For longer storage at room temperature, process sealed jars in boiling-water bath for 5 minutes. Refrigerate any jars that do not seal.

MAKES ABOUT 4 CUPS (1 L)

A type of water-soluble fiber, this remarkable substance occurs naturally in the cell walls of plants, where it acts like mortar to hold the cell walls together. When fruits or high-pectin vegetables like carrots are cut and cooked, pectin is released from between the cell walls and becomes dispersed.

There are several types of pectin molecules. As fruits ripen, pectins change from long-chain insoluble molecules with many methoxyl groups attached (high-methoxyl HM pectin) to shorter chain soluble molecules with fewer attached methoxyl groups (low-methoxyl LM pectin). The change in pectins results in softening of fruits as they ripen. HM pectins cause juices like grape and orange to be cloudy. Removal of pectins is one step in preparing clear wines.

At the pH of ripe fruit, the pectin molecules have negative charges on them and repel each other so stay suspended in the juice. In a jam or jelly, sugar attracts water molecules away from the pectin molecules and they begin to bond together. Acid plays a key role, too. It can come from the fruit itself or be added in the form of lemon juice (or tartaric acid or citric acid in commercial jams). Acid allows the pectin molecules to continue to bond because acid neutralizes the negative charges in the pectins, allowing them to come into closer contact and form the matrix that traps water.

When the entire mixture is heated, water evaporates, which brings the pectin molecules even closer together. As the pectin molecules bond, they create a mesh-like network that cradles and supports the dissolved sugar and the liquid, holding everything in suspension as a gel. When the mixture cools below 180°F (82°C), it begins to set. Most setting occurs around 85°F (30°C), but jelly will continue to firm up for several days.

For an ideal gel, food manufacturers aim for 60 to 65% sugar concentration, 0.5 to 1% pectin, and 0.5% acid by weight (equivalent to a pH of 2.8 to 3.4). It's relatively easy to measure the sugar concentration by observing the boiling point of the mixture, which increases as the sugar concentration rises. At 218 to 220°F (103 to 104°C), the sugar concentration will be about 60 to 65%. But testing the pectin concentration and acidity requires a Bloom gelometer (to measure gel strength) and a pH meter. In the absence of these, getting a good gel is a matter of balancing high- and low-pectin fruit with added commercial pectin, and balancing high- and low-acid fruit with added acid. (For guidance, see the basic amounts listed above and page 468 in **Pectin**.) Boiling to the right sugar concentration also regulates the proportionate amount of pectin in the mixture. Fortunately, jam is very forgiving and will gel with considerable variations in the pectin and acid. Jelly, on the other hand, needs more exact proportions to create the ideal texture of a clear gel that quivers when bumped (but isn't so loose that it's sticky) and holds its shape when cut (but isn't so firm that it's gummy or rubbery).

See Also • Candy, Canning, Dispersions, Fruit, Gelatin, Pectin, Sauces, Sugar

JASMINE RICE • See Rice

JERKY

What It Is • Before salt-curing and refrigeration, meat was preserved simply by drying it out. Jerky is a type of air-dried meat that's usually cut into thin strips or slabs. It is sometimes marinated, salted, and/or smoked and can be made with everything from beef and buffalo to whale and salmon. The ancient Egyptians made various types of air-dried meat, but the word "jerky" comes from the Portuguese word *charqui*, which was a dried meat (usually horse or beef) made by Peruvians. They originally freeze-dried the meat by drying it in the sun and wind near a smoky fire during the day, then letting it freeze overnight.

Cut and dried meat is now simply called jerked meat. Here are some popular types of jerky and similar dried meat products:

Biltong: South African in origin but popular in the U.K., Australia, New Zealand, and North America, biltong is thicker than jerky and usually made with beef that is marinated, dry-rubbed, and hung to dry.

Bresaola: This large cut of salt-cured, air-dried beef, popular in northern Italy, is usually not smoked. Because it is somewhat moist and is thinly sliced, bresaola is more like beef prosciutto than beef jerky.

Bündnerfleisch (aka Bindenfleisch): This Swiss version of bresaola is beef shoulder marinated for several days in wine and seasonings, then air-dried.

Carne seca (aka carne de sol and jaba): This is a South American jerky popular in northern Brazil made by dry-salting then quickly air-drying beef.

Fenalår: Norwegian mutton or lamb leg that is marinated, dry-salted, and occasionally smoked, and air-dried.

Meat sticks: These are little sausages made with processed, chopped, and formed meat containing more fat, water, and preservatives than jerky. These less expensive food products are a type of **sausage** rather than a type of jerky.

Pemmican: Smoke-dried or sun-dried meat (usually buffalo or venison) is pulverized and mixed with dried berries and/or nuts and about 50% fat such as suet to make a paste. Native American in origin, pemmican is compressed into cakes and keeps for years. Confusingly, Pemmican is also a brand name of beef jerky widely distributed in North America, although this product bears no resemblance to traditional Native American pemmican.

What It Does •
Jerky can be made from whatever meat you'd like to preserve, although trimmed cuts of lean meat are best because fat will not dry and could become rancid. Lean cuts of venison, buffalo, and beef are commonly jerked in North America, ostrich is jerked in Australia, and salmon is jerked in the Pacific Northwest. Cutting the meat into thin strips or slabs helps it to dry faster and thus retard microbial growth. Salting helps to draw out more moisture and facilitate quick drying and reduces water activity.

Traditional jerky is heated next to a fire, in the sun, or in a low-temperature oven, because high temperatures would dry out the meat and make it brittle rather than chewy. If the meat is salted and dried in the sun, the minimum temperature should be 85°F (30°C) and the humidity should be less than 60%. Within three days, the meat should lose about 75% of its moisture. Most commercially made jerky is dried in low-heat convection ovens at or below 160°F (71°C). The warm air is blown over strips of meat on screens for good circulation, which dehydrates the meat to only 25% moisture within a few hours. If the meat isn't heavily salted to discourage microbes, jerky dried at low temperatures can still harbor potentially harmful bacteria. If you don't salt the meat, the USDA recommends heating the meat to 160°F (71°C) to destroy harmful bacteria, then maintaining a dehydrator temperature of 130 to 140°F (54 to 60°C) until the meat is thoroughly dried.

As the meat loses water, it shrinks to about three-fourths of its original weight, which concentrates the flavor and the proportion of protein to about 50% by weight. One ounce (28 g) of salted beef jerky contains 15 to 20 grams protein, roughly 1 gram fat, and about 500 milligrams sodium. Astronauts and backpackers often carry jerky because it's high in protein, lightweight, and low in bulk.

How It Works •
Air-drying meat evaporates its moisture and kills microbes, allowing the meat to be stored without refrigeration for months or even years. Salting the meat also draws out moisture, and gentle heating evaporates that moisture, both of which help to prevent microbial growth. Salt also reduces water activity so water is not available to microorganisms. Acid from any berries used in the mixture also reduces microbial activity. Smoking acts as a preservative, too, by preventing microbial growth at the surface. A typical salted, smoked, heated, and/or air-dried jerky will lose about 75% of its moisture, meaning that 16 ounces (454 g) of meat can be jerked to just 4 ounces (112 g). Jerked meat is so much drier than cured hams and sausages that it can be stored without refrigeration for years.

See Also • Curing, Drying

JERUSALEM ARTICHOKE • See Stems

JICAMA • See Roots

JOULE • See Calorie

JUICE

What It Is • Juice is primarily water and aromatic compounds extracted from the tissues of **fruit**, **vegetables**, and even **meat**. Fruit juices such as apple and grape are clarified and tend to be thin and crystal clear, while ciders are not clarified. Vegetable juices and fruit nectars are thicker and cloudier. U.S. federal regulations require juice products containing less than 100% but more than 0% fruit juice to have a qualifying term such as "drink," "beverage" or "cocktail" attached. Commercially prepared fruit nectars are diluted juice beverages that contain fruit juice or purée, sometimes water, and sweeteners. Juices of peaches, apricots, guava, and other fruits would be overly thick or tart on their own.

What It Does • For centuries, juices have been mixed with honey or sugar syrup to make drinks like lemonade. Apples, carrots, celery, cherries, cranberries, grapefruit, grapes, lemons, limes, oranges, pineapples, pomegranates, strawberries, and tomatoes have become some of the most popular fruits and vegetables to juice. These and other juices can be blended to make various juice drinks or **ice cream**, cooked with sugar to make **jam and jelly**, and fermented into alcoholic drinks like hard **cider**, **wine**, brandy, and various **liquors** and **liqueurs** and then the alcohol fermented into **vinegars** like apple cider vinegar.

In the 1940s, the technology for making frozen fruit juice concentrate without losing much flavor was developed by the Florida Department of Citrus. Frozen fruit juice concentrate greatly expanded the fruit juice industry, allowing juice to be frozen for months before being reconstituted.

Fresh juices retain some of the beneficial nutrients of fruits and

kitchen wisdom

Juicing Citrus

Rolling citrus fruit on a countertop or heating it in a microwave oven doesn't produce more juice in the fruit for you to extract. It just makes it easier to get the juice out. If you're using an electric or lever-operated press juicer or a juice extractor, the fruit's available juice will be extracted whether or not you roll or heat the fruit first. But for hand-squeezing citrus fruit like oranges and lemons, rolling the fruit on a hard surface will break the juice sacs, and heating the whole fruit for 20 to 30 seconds in a microwave oven will cause the juices to flow, allowing the juice to be extracted more quickly and easily.

vegetables such as **antioxidants** and vitamin C. For instance, açai juice, made from a Brazilian berry, is high in polyphenolic antioxidants. Pomegranate juice is high in antioxidant punicalagins. And cranberry juice contains tannins that may help prevent bladder infections. The healthfulness of juices has spawned juice bars and smoothie stands around the world, although many nutritionists recommend balancing juice consumption with eating whole fruits and vegetables to get the important benefits of fiber in the whole food. Also fruit juices are high in sugar, even natural ones.

fast facts

- V8 juice was invented by juice maker W. G. Peacock in 1933. The V8 brand and secret recipe were sold to the Campbell Soup Company in 1948 and now consists of about 87% tomato juice blended with the juices of seven other vegetables: beets, celery, carrots, lettuce, parsley, watercress, and spinach.
- Extracted meat juices and blood were used for invalid food until the early 1900s.
- In 1929, there were 100 Orange Julius juice bars in the U.S. Today, juice bars are a multibillion-dollar business worldwide.

How It Works • Juice is extracted from food in one of three main ways: pressure, blending, or cooking.

Pressure methods can be as simple as hand-squeezing or using a screw press, a ridged reamer, or a lever-operated press. All of these methods exert pressure on the food, exploding its cells and releasing the juices held within. Pressure extraction is best for very juicy fruits like citrus.

Blending tends to extract more juice but it also extracts pulp. Electric blenders and juice extractors pulverize the cell walls with cutting blades. Blenders simply mix the juice and pulp together, whereas juice extractors separate the juice from the pulp by centrifugal force. Electric juice extractors do the most efficient job of extracting the maximum amount of juice from food while leaving pulp and seeds behind. Extracted juice is essentially a filtered purée.

Briefly cooking food softens it, releasing juices from its cells. Continued cooking evaporates the juices, but brief cooking can help get juices flowing so the juice can be strained or extracted to make foods like fruit jelly. Cutting and cooking has the same effect on meat, which is how meat juices are extracted to make sauces, stocks, soups, and stews.

Heating fruits and vegetables also allows you to extract a thicker juice. Enzymes in the juice partially regulate how thick the juice will be. When cold fruits and vegetables are cut or juiced, their cell walls release enzymes that convert the food's pectic substances from insoluble to soluble. As these pectins get diluted in water, they create a thinner juice with fewer solid particles. So to get a thin, watery juice like apple juice or grape juice, it's best to keep the fruit below 140°F (60°C) before juicing, which helps the enzymes do their work. To get thicker juice, such as thick tomato juice or carrot juice, it's best to cook whole fruits or vegetables to about 180°F (82°C) before juicing. At that temperature, the enzymes are denatured and the pulp and plant cells remain intact, giving the juice a thicker texture.

The juice of fresh fruits and vegetables is best consumed immediately because it is highly unstable. Enzymatic browning can happen quickly, discoloring the juice, and oxygen-sensitive compounds can produce off flavors. For that reason, commercial juices usually undergo **pasteurization** to inactivate enzymes as well as to kill potentially harmful microbes. The process for making commercial juice typically includes extracting the juice by crushing and pressing, clarifying, pasteurizing, sometimes concentrating it, then canning, bottling, or freezing. To make crystal clear apple and grape juices, commercial juice makers add enzymes that digest the pectic substances in the juice. Filtering aids such as egg whites, gelatin, and bentonite help remove insoluble pectic substances and proteins that make the juice cloudy.

See Also • Fruits, Jam and Jelly, Vegetables

JUNIPER • See Spices

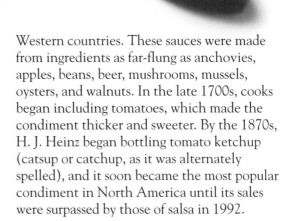

KABOCHA SQUASH • See Squash

KAFFIR LIME • See Citrus

KALE • See Leaves

KAMUT • See Wheat

KASHKAVAL • See Cheese

KASSERI • See Cheese

KEFALOTYRI • See Cheese

KELP • See Seaweed

KETCHUP

What It Is • The ubiquitous North American condiment served with hamburgers and french fries has its roots in *ke-tsiap* (pronounced ketchap), a brine of pickled fish from China, and kecap, a syrupy soy sauce condiment from Indonesia. As it evolved, ketchup became a catchall term for various runny, salty, tangy condiments popular in Western countries. These sauces were made from ingredients as far-flung as anchovies, apples, beans, beer, mushrooms, mussels, oysters, and walnuts. In the late 1700s, cooks began including tomatoes, which made the condiment thicker and sweeter. By the 1870s, H. J. Heinz began bottling tomato ketchup (catsup or catchup, as it was alternately spelled), and it soon became the most popular condiment in North America until its sales were surpassed by those of salsa in 1992.

What It Does • Commercial ketchups are made primarily from tomato paste, vinegar, corn syrup, salt, and various spices such as cloves. They're used mostly as condiments but also as the base ingredient for sauces and

fast fact

- Under U.S. regulations, products labeled "ketchup" may be thickened only with tomatoes.

Shortcut Kecap Manis

Ketchup has its roots in kecap manis, a type of Indonesian soy sauce made by cooking down the liquid of fermented soybeans along with palm sugar until it thickens into a sauce. Kecap is flavored with warming spices like star anise and makes a terrific condiment for roasted poultry and pork. Here's a shortcut version.

¾ cup	tamari or soy sauce	175 mL
⅓ cup	packed brown sugar	75 mL
3 tbsp	dark (cooking) molasses	45 mL
1	small clove garlic, finely minced	1
1	whole star anise or ⅛ tsp (0.5 mL) ground	1

1. In a small saucepan over medium-low heat, combine tamari, brown sugar, molasses, garlic, and star anise. Cook, stirring occasionally, until syrupy and smooth, about 15 minutes. Remove whole star anise, if using. Sauce can be refrigerated in an airtight container for about 3 weeks.

MAKES ABOUT 1¼ CUPS (300 ML)

dressings such as barbecue sauce and Thousand Island dressing. These ketchups can be stored at room temperature because the high proportion of vinegar and sugar keeps them from spoiling. However, they will darken and lose flavor with age.

How It Works • Ketchup stimulates five of our basic taste receptors — sweet, sour, salty, bitter, and umami — all at once. Warming spices like cloves and allspice round out the aromas and make ketchup a well-balanced sauce. While ketchup isn't generally eaten to

Tomato Ketchup

Commercial tomato ketchups get their thick consistency from tomato paste. But cooking down your own tomatoes will give you much fresher-tasting ketchup. Alter this basic recipe however you like by adding other dried spices such as coriander or adding fresh herbs such as parsley.

3 lbs	ripe red tomatoes, peeled and chopped	1.5 kg
2	onions, chopped	2
1	red bell pepper, seeded and chopped	1
1	clove garlic, chopped	1
⅓ cup	packed light brown sugar	75 mL
1 tbsp	Worcestershire sauce	15 mL
½ tsp	dry mustard	2 mL
½ tsp	celery salt	2 mL
½ tsp	ground cinnamon	2 mL
½ tsp	ground allspice	2 mL
¼ tsp	ground cloves	1 mL
⅛ tsp	cayenne pepper	0.5 mL
½ cup	cider vinegar	125 mL
	Salt and freshly ground black pepper	

1. In a deep saucepan over medium heat, combine tomatoes, onions, bell pepper, and garlic. Simmer, stirring occasionally, until vegetables are very soft, 40 to 60 minutes. Pass through a fine-meshed food mill to remove seeds (or if you don't mind the tomato seeds, purée in a food processor or blender).
2. Return tomato mixture to saucepan and add brown sugar, Worcestershire, mustard, celery salt, cinnamon, allspice, cloves, and cayenne pepper. Bring to a boil over high heat, then reduce heat and simmer, stirring often, until mixture becomes thick and is reduced in volume by about half, 15 to 20 minutes.
3. Stir in cider vinegar and simmer, stirring occasionally, until mixture is thick enough to mound on a spoon, 15 to 20 minutes. Season with salt and black pepper to taste. Spoon into jars, screw on the lids, and refrigerate for up to 4 weeks.

MAKES ABOUT 4 CUPS (1 L)

kitchen wisdom

Anticipation

What keeps ketchup from coming out of a narrow-necked bottle? Scientists call it thixotropicity. (Say "Sally sells thixotropicity by the seashore" 10 times fast!) Essentially, that means ketchup viscosity decreases under shear stress (it gets thinner as it is stirred), so once you get it moving it moves faster. To get the flow going, shake the ketchup bottle, then hold it on its side and shake gently so that air can circulate around the ketchup, allowing it to flow over itself through the small opening. Or, buy a plastic squeeze bottle instead. Once the ketchup stops moving it gets thicker over time.

boost health, the cooked tomatoes give it a fair amount of the antioxidant lycopene (about 1.5 mg per tablespoon/15 mL).

KETOSIS • See Diet

KIDNEY BEANS • See Legumes

KIDNEYS • See Organ Meats

KIELBASA • See Sausage

KIMCHI • See Fermentation

KIRSCH • See Liquor

KIWANO • See Melon

KIWIFRUIT • See Berries

KNACKWURST • See Sausage

KNIVES

What It Is • The first crude knives were invented more than two and half million years ago. These tools improved our ability to survive, and, apart from our hands, they have evolved into the single most important tools in food preparation and cooking. Early knives were made of flint, but most modern kitchen blades are made of metal or ceramic. While chef's knives can be sharp enough to cut the glaze on a dinner plate, clam, oyster, and butter knives are intentionally dull.

What It Does • A knife is an extension of a chef's hand. It is used for everything from paring, peeling, mincing, slicing, chopping, dicing, and julienning to filleting fish, boning birds, crushing spices, and transferring food from cutting board to pan. Knives range from wide-bladed stiff, heavy cleavers designed to hack through bones to thin, narrow filleting knives intended to disassemble fish to tiny curved tourne knives used to sculpt food into precise shapes.

A knife's cutting qualities are determined primarily by the material and weight of the blade, the way the blade is shaped and ground, and how the knife is constructed.

Carbon steel: Among the first metals used for making knives, carbon steel is an alloy of iron with about 0.45 to 0.5% carbon, that's inexpensive and soft enough to be easily honed to a razor-sharp edge. However, because it is soft, it tends to lose that edge more quickly than harder stainless steel. Carbon steel is also somewhat brittle and can snap under stress. Another drawback: the iron in carbon steel can discolor from acidic foods and transfer iron-like metallic flavors to foods. Carbon steel rusts easily from oxidation, so it must be kept bone dry, and it is often lubricated like cast-iron **cookware** to prevent rust. But carbon steel blades eventually develop a protective patina (similar to the "seasoning" on cast-iron cookware) that helps prevent rusting and reduce the metallic flavors transferred to food.

High-carbon stainless steel: To make steel knives harder and resistant to stains, iron is alloyed with 0.45 to 0.5% carbon (as for carbon steel blades) but with the addition of 13 to 14% chromium. A 1% combination of molybdenum and vanadium is often included to improve the blade's strength, its ability to retain an edge, and the fineness of the metal grain. It can be more difficult to get a sharp edge on a stainless steel blade, but it will last longer than that of a carbon blade.

Anatomy of a Knife

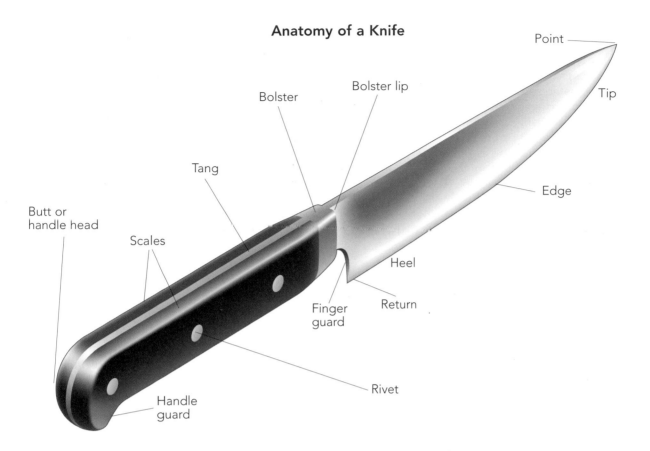

Point

Tip

Bolster lip

Bolster

Tang

Edge

Butt or
handle head

Scales

Heel

Return

Finger
guard

Rivet

Handle
guard

Very high carbon stainless steel: All stainless steel that includes at least 0.5% carbon is considered "high carbon," but very high carbon blades include more. The more carbon, the harder the metal can be made, and the finer the cutting edge can be sharpened. Very high-end chef's knives include 0.8% or more than 1% carbon to help develop a razor-sharp cutting edge. Some Japanese steels (Yasugi special steel or Hitachi super blue or white steel) used for sword making are also manufactured into exceptionally hard and sharp kitchen knives. They are made with anywhere from 0.9 to 1.5% carbon. Most very high carbon blades include about 14% chromium and 0.1 to 1% molybdenum for increased hardness and better edge holding. Super blue and white steels get hardness from the higher carbon content and about 0.2 to 0.5% chromium and 0.2 to 0.3% manganese. These knives also include 2 to 2.5% tungsten to produce a fine, dense grain structure in the metal.

Laminated steel: This type of steel, sometimes called Damascus steel, combines the advantages of two or more alloys by heating, hammering, and folding several layers into a single blade, creating beautiful wavy lines. The perceived advantage of laminated or "pattern-welded" steel is that it can be made harder through intense heat treatment, but the net carbon content is lower than if you used high-carbon steel alone. Some makers of laminated steel knives and swords use only high-carbon steel at the edge of the blade for hardness and lower-carbon steel in the spine and body of the blade for flexibility.

Titanium: Compared to steel, titanium is lighter and more flexible but not as hard, so it can't be sharpened to as fine an edge. It's also quite expensive.

Ceramic: Made from zirconium oxide, ceramic knives are extremely hard, sharp, lighter than steel, noncorrosive, and nonreactive, and hold an edge longer than most other materials (sometimes months or years without sharpening or honing).

Ceramic is very expensive and best sharpened on a special silicon carbide or diamond wheel by a professional knife sharpener. Ceramic blades can also chip or break with sudden extreme pressure or twisting.

Plastic: Some knife blades are made of hard plastic that can be resharpened and used for easily cut foods like lettuce. They're often serrated and cheap enough to be considered disposable.

Manufacturing Methods

Even the best knife material can be ruined if it's poorly manufactured. Among metals, forged knives tend to be the strongest and most durable because they are heated at extremely high temperature (upwards of 1400°F/760°C) and hammered into shape. Forged knives are typically heavy and thick, two advantages for tough chopping jobs but potential disadvantages for fine slicing. Simply cut out of a sheet of metal, stamped blades tend to be thinner and often lack a weight-balancing bolster. When made with superior cold rolled steel, a well-made, high-quality stamped knife may be stronger and more durable than a low-quality forged knife.

After forging or stamping, most knives are heat-tempered to improve their strength, then ground to create the cutting edge. Taper-ground (aka flat-ground) blades are ground from the spine down to the cutting edge in a straight or convex line to form a smooth, tapered blade with no obvious beveling. Taper-ground blades are heavier and more durable and work best in cleavers, chef's knives, and other knives needed for heavy-duty chopping. Hollow-ground blades are ground from about the middle of the blade down to the cutting edge in a concave line that forms a beveled or fluted edge. Hollow-ground blades are typically thinner, sharper, and lighter, and work best for precision slicing and dicing of easily cut foods.

The cutting edge on a kitchen knife may be curved, flat, or serrated. Curved blades allow you to rock the blade from the tip to the heel for faster chopping and mincing. Flat blades allow you to slice across food faster because the cutting edge never curves away from the food. Serrated knives have a wavy or toothed cutting edge that helps the blade saw through foods that are hard on the outside and soft on the inside, like bread and tomatoes. Serrated knives work well even when dull, but cutting straight down with a serrated blade will not make a clean cut.

Some knives are ground with oval-shaped recesses (also called kullens or granton edges) hollowed out of the side of the blade from the cutting edge about halfway up the blade. Often found on meat-carving knives and some Western versions of Japanese santoku knives, these recesses provide an air pocket between the blade and the food, reducing friction and improving the speed of slicing very sticky foods.

The cutting edge on most European and North American knives is ground to an angle of 18 to 22 degrees, and most are double-beveled. Many Chinese and Japanese knives are made of harder tempered steel, allowing the edge to be ground to a more acute cutting angle of 10 to 16 degrees. Some Japanese knives, such as usuba knives, are also ground to an edge on only one side (beveled inwards on one side only) and sold in left-handed and right-handed models.

Once the blade is shaped and ground, its opposite end, the tang, is incorporated into a handle. A full tang that's as wide as the blade and extends all the way to the opposite end of the handle creates a more durable knife that's well suited to heavy work such as hacking through bones. A tang that extends only three-quarters of the way through the handle or that is thinner and narrower than the blade (a rat-tail tang) makes the knife less durable and more difficult to balance. The point where the blade meets the handle is called the bolster, and thicker bolsters help to balance the knife and make it steadier and more durable.

The handle can be made of the same metal as the blade or of stone, bone, ivory, leather, wood, resin-impregnated wood, rubber, or plastic. Rosewood is traditional and popular because its density and fine grain are soft on the hands, provide good grip, and help prevent the wood from splitting or cracking. Woods impregnated with resin (black composite handles) improve durability and make the handle easier to keep clean. If the handle is riveted to the tang, the rivets should be flush with the surface of the handle to eliminate nooks and crannies where bacteria can grow. Plastic (polypropylene) handles are permanently molded around the tang with no seam and are often preferred (or required by law in some places) in busy professional kitchens because they are lightweight, can be easily sanitized, and don't absorb microorganisms as readily as other handles. Metal handles are the most durable and heaviest; they're often textured with dimples or ridges to provide better grip.

Sharpening

A sharp knife cuts faster and is safer because it won't slip off foods as easily as a dull knife. To keep your blades at their sharpest, avoid extreme downward pressure and concentrate on slicing across foods instead of down through them. When a blade gets dull, honing it on a butcher's steel usually improves its cutting edge. If it's still dull, the blade should be resharpened. Good-quality electric sharpeners save time, but many chefs prefer to sharpen their knives by hand on a sharpening stone (whetstone); 1,200 grit is considered sufficient to sharpen and polish a cutting edge, while 6,000 or higher grit will create a very finely sharpened, highly polished edge. Some chefs prefer diamond-impregnated stones to obtain the sharpest edge.

Whichever stone you use, place it parallel to the edge of a countertop on a wet towel to prevent slipping, and start with the coarsest grit. Spread a thin coat of mineral oil (or water) over the stone to help reduce friction and heat that could damage

the blade over time. If you're right handed, stand facing the stone with the knife in your right hand and the cutting edge facing left. Position the knife blade against the upper left-hand corner of the stone and tilt the spine of the blade up about 10 to 18 degrees (for Asian knives) or 18 to 22 degrees (for European and North American knives). Hold the knife in position with the fingertips of your left hand, providing even, gentle pressure on the entire blade. Move the blade in a gradual arc over the stone so that the heel and then the point of the knife slip off the lower right-hand corner of the stone. Repeat 10 to 20 times. Flip over the knife so that the cutting edge is facing to the right and repeat by positioning the blade against the upper left-hand corner of

the stone and tilting the spine the appropriate angle. With even, gentle pressure, arc the knife toward the lower right-hand corner so that the heel and then the point slip off the lower right-hand corner. Repeat 10 to 20 times. If your stone has more than one grit, move to the next finest grit and repeat. If you are left-handed, stand facing the stone with the knife in your left hand reverse the hands given in the directions from the beginning of the process.

Even when sharp, the edge of a knife is lined with many tiny, thin, jagged pieces like the teeth on a saw. Honing the knife on a butcher's steel keeps the teeth aligned and straight so that the edge remains sharp. Hold the steel in one hand with the point facing up and the knife in the other hand with the point facing up. Position the heel of the blade at the top of the butcher's steel at an angle of 10 to 18 degrees (for Asian knives) or 18 to 22 degrees (for European and North American knives). With even, gentle pressure, pull the blade down the length of the steel, gradually moving the knife toward you to drag the blade across the steel as it goes down. Reverse the knife and repeat the down-and-across sweeping motion. Repeat about five sweeps on each side.

To keep the blade at its sharpest, avoid extreme downward pressure and cut only on knife-friendly surfaces like wood and plastic. These materials absorb some of the knife blade and delay dulling. They also make cutting steadier, swifter, and safer. Glass, stone, and metal surfaces will dull the blade quickly.

Most knives, especially wood-handled ones, are best washed by hand to avoid discoloring the blade and damaging the handle. Store knives in slots, in racks, or on a magnetic strip to protect the cutting edges from damage and dulling.

How It Works ● The cutting edge of a knife concentrates all of the force exerted by the user on a very narrow but long area. That force delivers a fine line of pressure that's strong enough to sever tissues, slash through plant and animal cell walls, and even cut through bone. Serrated knives further concentrate the force into a smaller area on the serrations, making cutting more swift. Sharper knives require less pressure and make cleaner cuts, thus damaging fewer tissues and cells and releasing fewer compounds from the cells such as the sulfur compounds in onions that make us cry. To shed the least tears when chopping onions, use a sharp knife.

See Also ● Cookware

KOHLRABI ● See Cruciferous Vegetables

KOMBU ● See Seaweed

KOSHER ● See Diet

KNEADING ● See Baking, Bread

KUDZU ● See Leaves, Starch

KUMQUAT ● See Citrus

LACTASE • See Milk

LACTIC ACID • See Fermentation

LACTITOL • See Sweeteners

LACTOBACILLI • See Fermentation

LACTOCOCCI • See Fermentation

LACTOGLOBULIN • See Milk

LACTOSE • See Milk, Sugar, Sweeteners

LAGERING • See Beer

LAMB

What It Is • Like **goats**, which sheep are closely related to, both on the hoof (same family and subfamily, Caprinae and Bovidae) and on the plate (referred to as mutton), sheep were one of the first domesticated animals, and remain a primary livestock animal in many parts of the world. Unlike cattle, they can live on sparse ranges and rocky landscapes. Their natural tendency to flock makes them easy to herd, and they are a sensible investment due to the diversity of products they provide (wool, milk, cheese, and meat). This entry concentrates on sheep meat, particularly meat from animals one year old or less, called lamb. (See also **Milk** and **Cheese**.)

What It Does • Lamb quality is categorized by age and feed. Milk-fed lamb comes from unweaned animals, usually six to eight weeks old, called baby lamb. The carcass is tiny, weighing less than 20 pounds (9 kg), with a rack (rib section) that weighs less than a pound (500 g) and a leg that is less than 2 pounds (1 kg). True milk-fed lamb is rare in North America, where it is considered uneconomical to raise and where the tiny cuts are seen as skimpy. Along the Mediterranean coast of Europe, milk-fed lamb is highly prized, especially at Easter.

Most of the lamb in North America is slaughtered between three and five months

kitchen wisdom

Trimming Lamb

Most cuts of lamb are surrounded by a layer of fat, which is covered in a papery film called the fell. Many cooking sources advise removing lamb fell, because it is believed to be strong tasting. The fell is not nearly as strong tasting as the fat beneath it, though, and removing the fell from a leg or shoulder can cause a roast to lose its shape. It is advisable when roasting whole cuts to leave the fell intact. But trim the fell from lamb chops or steaks, because it contracts causing the meat to curl during cooking.

Lamb fat is dense and becomes quite hard as it cools. For that reason it is good practice to remove as much fat as possible from lamb that will be stewed or braised and to leave just a thin covering on roasts. Remove fat from leftover lamb before refrigerating it.

and is known as spring lamb. Sheep are seasonal breeders, and follow a similar reproductive pattern to other herd animals. The ewes of an entire flock are impregnated in a short period of time by a single ram, selected either by dominance or by the rancher. For most breeds of sheep, breeding naturally happens in the early fall so that lambs dropped in early spring have the benefit of feeding on lush spring pasturage. Today sheep are bred year round, and consequently "spring" lamb is no longer seasonal. The U.S. Department of Agriculture identifies spring lamb as lamb that is slaughtered between the first Monday in March and the first Monday in October.

Old-season lamb, also called genuine lamb, is slaughtered late in its first year. It yields larger cuts of redder, fattier, more flavorful meat than spring, or new-season, lamb. It is generally cheaper.

The meat of yearling animals, between one and two years old, is often called lamb, but is not technically lamb because the animal is older than one year. In texture and flavor, yearling lamb is more like mutton, which is the meat of fully matured sheep and goat. Mutton is from animals that are over two years old. It is strong tasting and tough. In North America, mutton is rarely sold, except by halal

Lamb Primal Cuts

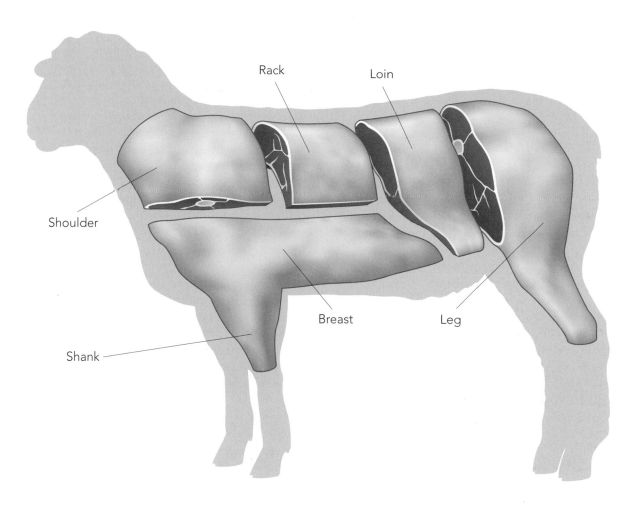

butchers serving the Islamic community.

Since almost all lamb meat comes from animals of the same age, it is most typical to see lamb identified by place of origin. The most common types are New Zealand lamb, Australian lamb, Icelandic lamb, and American lamb, in that order. These are not necessarily the largest lamb- and sheep-producing countries in the world, but they are the ones with the best marketing and distribution systems for lamb meat. The New Zealand and Australian lamb industries are the best established and export more lamb than all other countries combined. Inroads have been made by Iceland and the U.S. in recent years. Iceland produces lamb that is mild tasting and grown in a completely sustainable agricultural system that is void of feedlots, antibiotics,

and growth hormones. American lamb is also quite mild, but its real distinction is its size. American spring lamb cuts are typically twice the size of spring lamb from other countries, mostly because they spend time bulking up on grain before slaughter. Bigger cuts mean a better meat-to-bone ratio, which means more edible meat per pound.

High-quality lamb meat is light red and finely grained. It has moderately thick layers of dry white fat surrounding the meat, but not a great deal of marbling. Young lamb bones are moist and slightly pink. As lamb gets older, the color of the meat darkens to purple, the cuts of meat get larger with more pronounced marbling, the fat darkens toward yellow and becomes softer and moister, and the bones become hard, dry, and white.

lamb

How It Works • The English developed most of the modern breeds of lamb and sheep in North America. Known for a compact, blocky build that yields maximum muscle size and has early fattening characteristics that promote tenderness, the Southdown, Dorset, and Romney breeds were the basis for the eastern North American lamb industry. Lamb and sheep flocks in the west are descended from the churro, a Spanish sheep that was brought to North America in the 16th century and became the main livestock sheep of the Navajo. Branded American lamb largely comes from a cross between churro, merino (another Spanish sheep, prized for its wool), and Rambouillet, a French breed of merino sheep.

Unlike the other major meat animals (beef, veal, and pork), a lamb carcass is small and yields far fewer cuts. For the most part lambs are still delivered whole to butchers and cut in-house, so that good butcher shops will sell all parts of the animal.

As with other four-legged animals, the most tender cuts come from the rib and loin, but because lambs are fairly young and tender throughout, far more of a lamb can be roasted or grilled like the most expensive cuts of beef and veal. Still, most people want lamb ribs (either as racks or cut into chops), loin chops, and whole loins, so these cuts tend to be high priced.

Leg of lamb is more reasonably priced and can be cooked similarly to the more expensive cuts. Here are some best buys:

- Lamb riblets are great for grilling and the same cut as rib chops and rack of lamb.
- Lamb shoulder roast and lamb breast are very flavorful and tender enough to roast if the lamb is young. Lamb shoulder chops can be served like more expensive rib and loin chops, although they will take more trimming, and they will have to be cooked in sauce briefly to become fully tender.
- Lamb shanks are the richest-tasting cut of lamb, typically braised or stewed.
- Spring lamb is small enough to spit-roast whole or halved. A whole spring lamb will feed about 15 people.

Lamb has a reputation for being strongly flavored. Pasture feeding, particularly on alfalfa and clover, encourages the development of skatole, an aromatic chemical in lamb fat and meat that has a strong aroma. Skatole can be floral and sweet

Lamb "Chili" with Dal

The allure of chili and curry is in the nose, and in the intoxicating slow burn that radiates throughout the skull with every swallow. This recipe is a hybrid of the two, made like chili but replacing chili powder with garam masala, and with lentils as a stand-in for kidney beans.

3 lbs	boneless lamb cubes for stew, preferably shoulder	1.5 kg
⅓ cup	all-purpose flour	75 mL
3 tbsp	olive oil, divided	45 mL
1	medium onion, chopped	1
2	hot chile peppers, any type, seeded and stemmed, minced	2
2	cloves garlic, minced	2
¼ cup	garam masala	50 mL
2 tbsp	dried mint leaves	25 mL
1 tbsp	ground coriander	15 mL
1 tbsp	ground cumin	15 mL
Pinch	hot pepper flakes	Pinch
3 cups	beef or vegetable broth	750 mL
1 tbsp	balsamic vinegar	15 mL
	Salt and freshly ground black pepper to taste	
2 cups	dried brown or green lentils	500 mL
2 tbsp	chopped fresh cilantro	25 mL

1. Dredge lamb in flour. Heat half of the oil in a large, deep skillet over medium-high heat. Add lamb in batches and brown on all sides. Transfer each batch to a plate when finished and set aside.
2. Add remaining oil to pan and reduce heat to medium. Add onion and sauté until tender, about 3 minutes. Add hot peppers and garlic and stir for 1 minute, until aromatic.
3. Add garam masala, mint, coriander, cumin, and hot pepper flakes and cook, stirring constantly, for 30 seconds.
4. Add broth, vinegar, salt, black pepper, and lamb with any accumulated juices. Cover and simmer, stirring occasionally, until lamb is tender, about 1 hour.
5. Meanwhile, in a pot of lightly salted water, cook lentils until tender, about 40 minutes. Toss with cilantro. Serve lamb chili on a bed of cooked lentils.

MAKES 8 SERVINGS

at low levels, but turns fecal when concentrated. It is the reason that pasture-raised mutton is an acquired taste, and why feed and age are important factors for determining lamb flavor. American lamb remains mild even though it is typically slaughtered past six months, because its grain-supplemented diet discourages the development of skatole. Icelandic and New Zealand lambs are fed heavily on alfalfa and are typically slaughtered at four months.

Tougher cuts of lamb shine in stews and braised preparations where their assertive flavor beautifully complements other assertive flavors like wine, mustard, curry, anise, rosemary, citrus, and soy sauce. Lamb is a traditional braising meat for Indian curry, Moroccan tagine, Spanish asadar, Chinese red-cooking, and Irish stew.

Lamb freezes well, and some of the best buys on quality lamb are frozen products. Although lamb is becoming increasingly popular, North Americans still eat only about a pound (500 g) per person per year. Producers find it economically prudent to freeze a sizable proportion of their product in order to give it a longer marketing life. Industrially frozen lamb, if stored properly, will stay in good condition for about 12 months. If you freeze lamb at home, you can keep it for up to six months.

Lamb's nutritional profile is good. A 3-ounce (84 g) serving contains about 5 grams of fat (64% monounsaturated). It has a significant amount of B vitamins, particularly B_{12} and niacin, and it provides 48% of the daily value of protein with only 9% of the daily value of calories.

See Also • Agriculture, Cheese, Goat, Meat

LAMBICS • See Beer

LANGOUSTINE • See Crustacean

LARD • See Fat, Pork

LAUREL • See Herbs

LAVASH • See Bread

LAVENDER • See Herbs

LAVER • See Seaweed

LEAF LETTUCE • See Leaves

LEAVENING • See Baking, Chemical Leaveners

LEAVES

What It Is • Leaves are the most common and the most perishable of vegetables. They include lettuces, spinach, endives, cabbages, cresses, **herbs**, and sprouts. People eat leaves from every type of plant, including weeds (such as dandelion). Some of the vegetables we think of as roots or fruits have edible leafy counterparts. Chard is the leaf of a plant in the same species as beet roots and grape leaves are the leaves of (you guessed it) grape vines. Although most culinary leaves are for eating, some are not. The fibers of the leaves of banana, lotus, and bamboo are too tough to eat, but for millennia the leaves have been used as wrappers to protect and scent grilled or roasted fish and meat.

What It Does • All culinary leaves share some things in common. They are all thin, broad, and light in weight compared to other parts of the plant. They share a common flavor, called "green" or "grassy," that derives from the production of **chlorophyll**.

Leaves are filled with air and water that leach during cooking, which is why tough leaves like cabbages can shrink to half their volume when sautéed, and tender, leafy greens like spinach can lose 75% of their volume during cooking.

Chlorophyll, the green pigment in leaves, becomes water soluble when it is heated, so it tends to leach into cooking liquid. Green vegetables become paler the longer they cook, so maximum color (and nutrition) is attained by cooking leafy vegetables quickly and sparingly. Acid is chlorophyll's other enemy. Chlorophyll (bright green) changes to yellow-gray-green pheophytin when it is exposed to even a small amount of acid. The acid can come from an acidic ingredient, like citrus juice or vinegar, or from the vegetable itself. Because all vegetables are slightly acidic, covering the pot when cooking greens concentrates the acid and can cause discoloration. It is fine to use a lid briefly, because the acids build gradually when cooking tough greens like collard or mustard, but lift the lid occasionally to allow some steam (and acid) to escape.

Red- and purple-leaved vegetables are colored with anthocyanins, which are also sensitive to acids, but in the opposite direction — acids make anthocyanins brighter. That's why red cabbage is often pickled, and why the color of radicchio is heightened by a glaze of balsamic vinegar.

There are scores of leafy vegetables, and they are best understood when grouped by botanical family. Almost all fall into one of three families — Asteraceae (lettuces), Brassicaceae (cabbages), and Amaranthaceae (spinach and beet greens). Cabbages have their own entry (**Cruciferous Vegetables**), so the following includes just a short overview of cabbages with detailed information on other leafy vegetables.

Amaranthaceae — The Spinach Family
An extremely widespread family of leafy greens, root vegetables, and herbs, the original Amaranthaceae is amaranth, sometimes called Chinese spinach. Like all greens in this family, amaranth is high in oxalates, giving them their bitter flavor. High levels of oxalic acid makes the iron in these greens less available to the body, and can combine with calcium in the kidney, precipitating kidney stones.

Spinach has about a third of the oxalates that are in amaranth. All members of this family are nutritious, high in vitamin A, folates, and

fast facts

antioxidants such as carotenoids and lutein.

Savoy spinaches have thick crinkled leaves with fibrous stems. They have a robust flavor and lose less bulk in cooking than other spinaches. Savoy spinach is most commonly sold in bunches and needs substantial cleaning (its crevices trap dirt) and trimming (the stems are too tough to cook at the same rate as the leaves). Flat-leaf spinaches have thinner, more tender leaves and stems. They are preferred for salads because they are milder in flavor and less fibrous. Baby flat-leaf spinach is so tender that the stems do not have to be trimmed.

The family also includes chard, which is a beet grown for its greens rather than its root. Quinoa is also in this family.

Asteraceae — The Lettuce Family

Members of the daisy family, Asteraceae greens fall into two genera: *Lactuca* are mild lettuces; *Cichorium* are bitter and can be either **chicories** or endives, some of which are eaten in salads, but most are cooked. *Cichorium* lettuces are covered in depth under Chicories, so this entry deals exclusively with *Lactuca* lettuces.

There are hundreds of types of lettuce of different colors, flavors, leaf sizes, and leaf textures. Mostly they are grouped according to the leaf and head formation.

Batavian lettuces have dense, leafy, partially opened heads of crispy leaves.

Butterhead lettuces (Boston, Bibb) have soft, buttery leaves and an open head formation.

Celtuce lettuces (stem lettuce) are most popular in Asia. They are grown for their thick, crisp center rib, which is usually stripped of its small leaves.

Crisphead lettuces (iceberg) have tight, dense, spherical heads and crispy, sturdy leaves.

Loose-leaf lettuces (oak leaf, red leaf) are open headed like butterhead lettuces, but with sturdier leaves.

Romaine (cos) lettuces form closed heads of elongated leaves with crisp, wide middle ribs.

Mâche lettuce are single, small, loose-leafed peppery greens that aren't true lettuces (they are from another genus, *Valerianaceae*) but are frequently grouped with lettuces because they are used similarly.

Tender leaves are more perishable than crisp-leaved lettuce. When preparing greens for a salad, thick, crisp leaves are best torn, because they break along natural divisions between their cells but tender leaves suffer less damage when cut with a knife. Pinching the leaves for tearing bruises them.

Culinary Chlorophyll: Homemade Food Color

Renaissance chefs extracted chlorophyll from dark green leafy vegetables to use as an early form of food coloring. It is a beautiful emerald green and tastes fresh and green. A little bit in a cake icing will be overpowered by the sugar so don't worry, it won't taste like leaves.

| 4 oz | dark green leafy vegetable or herb (such as spinach, parsley, kale, etc.), coarsely chopped | 125 g |
| 1 cup | boiling water | 250 mL |

1. In a food processor fitted with a metal blade, finely chop greens. With the processor running, gradually add boiling water through the feed tube and process until greens are almost puréed. (The mixture will not become completely smooth.) Let cool for at least 20 minutes, or to room temperature.

2. In a fine sieve over a saucepan, strain purée, pushing as much through the sieve as you can, discarding solids.

3. Place saucepan over medium heat and boil until liquid simmers and dark green chlorophyll separates from the bronze-colored liquid, about 1 minute. Carefully skim off the green chlorophyll into a coffee filter set in a strainer; discard the bronze-colored layer. Strain the fluid from solids and retain the solids. Use as food coloring to color pasta, pastry fillings, icings, candy, ice cream, etc.

MAKES ABOUT 1 TABLESPOON (15 ML)

Washing and soaking lettuce in cold water can help it absorb moisture, making the leaves more turgid. Drying leaves thoroughly does not benefit their texture, but it does help oily salad dressing that would be repelled by a film of water to cling better to the leaves.

Always toss lettuce with oils (and oily dressings) at the last minute. Oil permeates the waxy, water-repellent surface of the leaf cuticle, causing the leaf to soak up oil, bloat, and sag.

Dandelion (genus *Taraxacum*) is the most prolific and least cultivated of the Asteraceae greens. It grows on every continent, and its small rosette of leaves are mildly pungent salad greens when young. As dandelion matures, the leaves become tough and strong flavored and have to be cooked. Once it bolts (flowers), the leaves become too strong to eat, but the flowers can be fermented into wine.

science wise

Keeping Leaves Green • Be careful when using citrus (or other acids) with leafy greens. Acid damages chlorophyll, which gives leaves both their deep green color and fresh vegetable flavor. So when seasoning leafy greens with lemon, do so right before serving or only use the zest of the lemon, which contains lemon oil but not citric acid.

Brassicaceae — The Cabbage Family

More than a dozen major crops have been developed from a few hardy leafy greens, similar to collard, that started out in the sandy soil on the shores of the Mediterranean, including broccoli, cauliflower, and kohlrabi. Brassicaceae greens include arugula, bok choy, broccoli rabe, Brussels sprouts, cabbage, collards, garden cress, kale, mizuna, mustard, napa cabbage, nasturtium, tatsoi, turnip, and watercress.

Other Leaves

Borage (starflower) leaves taste vaguely of cucumber and the young leaves and flowers can be used with small loose-leaf lettuces in salads. Mature borage leaves contain small amounts of liver-toxic alkaloids and should be used sparingly. Borage leaves, flowers, and the oil extracted from borage seeds are used in homeopathic medicine as a treatment for PMS and menopausal hot flashes. Borage is frequently consumed as tea.

Cresses are a diverse group of greens that technically are in the cabbage family, but they are used very differently and have flavors distinct from other cabbages. The three species of culinary cress — water, garden, and winter — are relatives of mustard greens, and like their pungent cousin they have a vibrant spiciness and meatiness that is a welcome counterpoint to mild lettuces in salads. The peppery bite of cress is also delicious paired with mild meats like poultry, veal, and fish. Cresses need to be harvested when young. Once they flower, the leaves, and especially the stems, become quite bitter. This bitterness increases during cooking, so cress stems should be meticulously trimmed when making sauces and soups. Cresses are closely related to nasturtium, with which they can be used interchangeably.

Mâche (lamb's lettuce or corn salad) is a very tender small-leafed salad green that resembles a loose-leaf lettuce and is often included in mixes of lettuce. It is sweet and fruity, without any of the bitterness associated with Asteraceae lettuces.

Nettles grow in every temperate climate and have a pronounced green flavor. The most common species is stinging nettles, which are covered with sharp hairs that secrete an irritating toxin when touched. The toxin is deactivated by boiling the greens briefly, but gloves should be worn when harvesting and washing nettles. Thick stems should be removed. Nettles should never be served raw. They are traditionally used in soups and for making medicinal teas. Nettle-stuffed ravioli are delicious.

Purslane grows in midsummer in all temperate climates. Although purslane is ubiquitous in the wild, it is cultivated only on a small scale. The cultivated varieties tend to have larger leaves that resemble small cactus paddles and contain a similar mucilaginous juice. Purslane leaves are mildly tart and slightly lemony and are typically added to salads. Purslane is high in calcium and the omega-6 fatty acid linoleic acid.

Kudzu, considered an invasive weed in North America because it can grow 12 inches (30 cm) in a day, is valued as a salad green, leaf vegetable, and medicinal herb in Eastern Asia. The flowers are battered and fried like squash blossoms, or they can be cooked into a jelly. The starchy roots can be prepared like potatoes, and are also dried, ground into powder, and used as a thickener. Young kudzu leaves can be added to salads; older ones should be cooked as you would spinach. At any age, kudzu leaves are a good source of vitamins A and C, and they contain a significant amount of protein and calcium.

Warm Spinach Salad with White Bean Vinaigrette

Dressing

1	can (14 oz/400 mL) cannellini beans or white kidney beans, drained and rinsed (1½ cups/375 mL)	1
1	clove garlic, halved	1
¼ cup	white wine vinegar	50 mL
2 tbsp	extra virgin olive oil	25 mL
1 tsp	kosher salt	5 mL
1 tsp	hot pepper sauce	5 mL
¼ cup	hot water	50 mL

Salad

1 lb	spinach leaves, stems removed	500 g
6	oil-packed sun-dried tomatoes, drained and cut into strips	6
3	green onions, trimmed and sliced	3
⅓ cup	pitted black olives, quartered	75 mL

1. Dressing: In a blender or food processor, purée beans, garlic, vinegar, oil, salt, hot pepper sauce, and hot water in a blender or food processor until smooth. Transfer to a skillet.

2. Salad: In a large salad bowl, toss together spinach, sun-dried tomatoes, green onions, and olives.

3. Heat dressing over medium-high heat until simmering, stirring often. Add more water if needed to keep it the texture of unbeaten cream. Toss dressing with salad. Serve immediately.

MAKES 6 LARGE SERVINGS

Orach (saltbush) grows well in any soil, even sand, and was one of the principal greens in medieval Europe before spinach took its place. There are hundreds of species, but the only one that is cultivated to any extent is garden orach (aka red orach, mountain spinach, French spinach), which has a gorgeous purple-red color and decorative rounded triangular leaves. Orach plants retain salts in their leaves, which makes them taste like salty spinach. They are excellent in salads, and traditionally are used for making green sauce and for flavoring and coloring pasta.

How It Works • Leaves are energy factories, producing sugar via photosynthesis. Photosynthesis uses water, carbon dioxide, and sunlight from the atmosphere to make oxygen and glucose. The oxygen is released back into the air and the glucose is used as energy by the plant. Any extra glucose is stored as starch, usually in the root or seeds.

To do their job, leaves need to be broad and flat, exposing maximum surface area to sunlight and water. Inside the leaf a network of air pockets increases the number of cells that come in contact with the air, allowing optimal transfer of carbon dioxide and oxygen through the walls of cells where photosynthesis takes place.

This unique framework makes leaves much more susceptible to dehydration and bruising than other vegetables. It also causes them to shrink dramatically during cooking. Most of a leaf is air and water. As it is heated, its cell structure collapses. The leaf wilts as all its water and air are released, which is why a gallon (4 L) of fresh spinach collapses into less than a quart (1 L) of cooked vegetable. More fibrous leaves, like those of cabbage or kale, do not shrink as much as delicate leaves like spinach. Because leaves are prone to dehydration, it is best to store them in loosely closed plastic bags and use them as soon as possible. Do not seal them too tightly, for this can cause the leaves to absorb excess water and become soggy. Wash leafy vegetables as close to serving time as possible.

See Also • Cruciferous Vegetables, Vegetables

LECITHIN

What It Is • To biochemists lecithin is the trivial name for a specific phospholipio-phosphatidyl choline. On a food label lecithin is a mixture of phospholipids that includes phosphatidyl coline. Lecithins are naturally abundant in egg yolks, soybeans, and some dairy products.

What It Does • Like all phospholipids, lecithin has the ability to stabilize **emulsions**. It is typically added to chocolate to help it stay smooth during melting. Chocolate is a **dispersion** of sugar and cocoa particles in a sea of cocoa butter. Lecithin coats the sugar and helps it bind with the cocoa butter, which increases the creaminess of chocolate. By using 1% lecithin in chocolate manufacturing, as much as 10% of the cocoa butter in a formula can be replaced. Most chocolate is between 0.3 and 0.5% lecithin by weight.

It is also used in margarine to help emulsify the water and fat and prevent spattering, and in mayonnaise to keep it from separating. Lecithin is generally regarded as safe as a food additive. Lecithin derived from egg yolk, though safe for people on low-cholesterol diets, will increase the cholesterol content of products it is added to.

How It Works • Phospholipids, like lecithin, are diacylglycerols (diglycerides). Diacylglycerols are similar to **fats** (triacylglycerols; the old term was "triglyceride") except that they have two fatty acids attached to a glycerol molecule rather than three. Phospholipids are a particular class of diacylglycerols that have a polar phosphate and nitrogen group attached to the glycerol end of the molecule, which makes the glycerol end highly attracted to water (hydrophilic). The two nonpolar fatty acids at the other end are repulsed by water (hydrophobic). Phospholipids are able to bridge between and stabilize the polar and nonpolar phases of an emulsion. When lecithin is mixed with fat, the tail ends of the molecules dissolve into the fat globules, with the water-loving heads projecting out onto the surface. When water or something water soluble like sugar is added, the water-loving heads bond with the water and hold it in suspension.

See Also ● Dispersions, Emulsion, Fat, Food Additives

LEEKS • See Allium

LEES • See Liquor, Wine

LEGUMES

What It Is ● The third-largest family of flowering plants (after orchids and daisies) and the second most important family of food plants after grains (grasses), Leguminosae bear fruit in the form of pods, each containing several seeds that are eaten as legumes. Legumes are distinctive because of their high **protein** content, which is two to three times higher than that of wheat or rice. They are known colloquially by several names — beans, peas, and lentils.

What It Does ● Legumes have provided a primary protein alternative to animal products throughout history. They are prominent in the foods of Asia, Central America, South America, and the Mediterranean basin. Although vegetables all contain protein, their balance of amino acids is not always completely usable to humans.

The human body can synthesize 11 of the 20 amino acids necessary to maintain health. The other nine must be eaten and are known as essential amino acids. Legumes contain all the essential amino acids, although some are slightly deficient in tryptophan. This lack is easily made up by eating other vegetables and grains, a complementation that is typical in vegetarian dishes throughout the world — corn tortillas and refried beans, rice and tofu, peanut butter on bread.

In addition to protein, legumes provide an adequate amount of iron, B vitamins, folate, starch, and oil. Legumes with colored seed coats are being recognized as a potent source of **antioxidants**, and **soybeans** appear to have unusual potential for improving human health.

Legumes take well to drying. Dried legumes are grouped together as pulses. Dried legume seeds are mostly starch and protein and have a hard water-resistant seed coat that helps to protect them during storage. The seed coat can be fairly thin (as in peanuts) or up to 30% of a legume's weight (such as lupine beans). Soybeans and peanuts are not usually grouped with pulses because they are commonly harvested for oil. Soybeans are 25% oil, and peanuts can be as high as 50% oil.

Because dried legumes are seeds, they can be germinated simply by being moistened, which starts their transition from seed into plants. Bean sprouts, most commonly grown from mung beans, are a staple of Asian cooking, but any legume can be sprouted. Sprouts are mostly stems, with a tiny unfurled leaf at the tip. They are universally tender, and are usually eaten raw

Common Legumes

Legume	Description and Uses
Alfalfa	Alfalfa is mostly used as fodder for livestock. The seed, which looks like a tiny white bean, is used almost exclusively for sprouts.
Alubia, Anasazi, Appaloosa	Various types of pinto bean (see right).
Azuki bean (adzuki)	Small and mahogany red, azuki is the second most popular legume in Korea and Japan, next to soybeans. It is used for sprouts and is sweetened into red bean paste for baking and candy making.
Black-eyed pea (cow pea, southernpea)	A relative of mung beans, it has a pigmented eye-shaped mark around its hilum, and a characteristic aroma. It is popular in soul food cooking in the U.S., arriving in North America from Africa via the slave trade.
Black gram (urad dal)	Similar to mung beans, these small ovoid beans are highly prized in India, where they are cooked whole or split into dal, and ground into flour for cakes and breads. White gram or lentil is the same legume peeled and split.
Calypso bean	A type of pinto bean (see right).
Chickpea (garbanzo bean, Bengal gram, channa)	Native to the Middle East, there are two types of chickpeas. Desi are small, tough, and dark in color and are used in Asia, Ethiopia, and Mexico. Kabuli are larger and beige; they are the chickpeas of the Mediterranean used for making soups, hummus, and falafel. Split chickpeas are a common form of dal in Indian cooking, where they are also ground into flour for making pappadams and pakoras.
Cranberry bean (borlotti)	A medium-large tan bean splattered with magenta streaks, it looks and tastes like pinto beans. Popular in Italian and Portuguese cuisine.
Fava bean (broad bean, English bean, horse bean, Windsor bean)	Large, meaty legumes native to the Mediterranean that are eaten both fresh and dried. Fava have a particularly tough seed coat that is removed in a separate cooking step. Fava are eaten as an antipasto or side dish or are cooked in soups and stews.
Green bean (string bean, snap beans), haricot, runner beans	These immature *Phaseolus* (common) beans can be dried but are typically eaten fresh as a vegetable. Because the whole fruit (pod) is eaten, they look different from other legumes, of which only the seed is eaten. There are 130 varieties, ranging from moist green stiletto-thin haricot vert to fat, wide, flat romano beans. Although they are usually green, fresh common beans can be speckled, streaked, purple, or golden (wax beans). They are not as starchy or as high in protein as dried legumes.
Hyacinth bean (Indian bean, Egyptian bean)	Mostly used as an ornamental plant because of its bright magenta pod. The seeds are eaten, mostly in Africa, but are often classified as poisonous because of their high level of cyanogenic glucosides. They must be well cooked to make them safe to eat.
Kidney bean (red bean)	Dark red, somewhat kidney shaped, also called red beans, but shouldn't be confused with the small red beans cooked with rice in Cajun cuisine. Kidney beans are meaty and mealy in texture and are used in soups and stews in North American cooking.
Lentil (masoor dal)	Probably the oldest cultivated legume, lentils have been grown in the Middle East and India for 5,000 years. In India, lentils are the principal source of protein for vegetarian populations. Lentils are small and flat with very thin seed coats, so they cook quickly. They come in a wide variety of kinds, with and without skins, whole and split, and in many colors. Lentils are popular for soups in Western cuisine and are a base for many dals in India.
Lima bean (butter bean)	One of the common beans, lima beans are large and fat, and are eaten both dried (when mature) and fresh (when young, tender, and pale green). Mature limas are typically white, but there are red, orange, and mottled varieties. Fresh limas are eaten as a vegetable; dried are usually used in soups and stews. Sometimes lima beans are called butter beans, but since another common bean that is larger and yellow is also called a butter bean, there can be confusion.
Lupine	Large, fat, yellow beans that resemble fava beans, lupine beans are popular in the countries of the Mediterranean basin. They are frequently salted and sold jarred. They are eaten like olives.
Mung bean (mung or moong dal, green gram)	Small dark green ovoid beans that were originally from India but have become most popular in Asian cuisine, where they are eaten in soups, cooked into a sweet paste for desserts, and most typically sprouted. The starch of mung beans is used as a jelling compound and for making transparent noodles.
Navy bean	See White bean.

Pea	Small, round, pale green pea seeds were originally dried and boiled, like other legumes. Starting in the 1700s, in France and England eating peas green (immature) became popular, and special varieties of peas called garden peas were grown for eating fresh. This is still how most peas are consumed around the world. There are several types: snow peas have flat edible pods, and snap peas have round pods that are edible when young (sugar snaps). English peas have fibrous pods that are removed before cooking. Dried peas, usually split, are called field peas. They are higher in starch and protein than garden peas.
Peanut (groundnut)	Native to South America, the pale fibrous peanut is a legume that pushes its woody fruit pod underground as it matures (hence the name groundnut). Peanuts are unique among legumes in other ways. Their high oil content, about 50% (most legumes are 1% or 2% oil), makes them more valuable as an oil crop in most of the world than a bean crop. In North America, they are thought of, and eaten like, nuts (mostly as peanut butter). Peanuts caught on as a cooking ingredient mostly in Africa, where they are ground into meal for bread and are the base ingredient for soups and sauces. Peanuts are used in stir-fries and dipping sauces in Southeast Asian recipes, most famously sambal and satay.
Pigeon pea (gandule, no-eyed pea, red gram, toor dal)	Mostly eaten in subtropical India, East Africa, and Central America, pigeon peas are split and cooked as dals, sprouted and cooked in stews, ground into flour, and eaten fresh. When dried, the seeds are pale yellow splashed with purple mottling. They are often canned in the Caribbean.
Pinto bean and other mottled beans	A member of the common bean species, pinto beans are the most popular of the mottled beans in North America, where they are the bean mostly used for making refried beans. Mottled beans have dotted skins, like a pinto horse, that blend together during cooking. Pinto beans have a creamy texture after cooking due to a high starch content.
Soybean (edamame)	Soybeans come in a variety of colors and sizes, but the most widely grown are pale, ovular, and very hard. Soybeans are the most nutritious of all legumes and the most highly cultivated legume in the world. They are eaten in every culture and are a vital ingredient in countless processed foods.
Wax bean	A form of fresh common bean (see Green bean).
White bean	This cream-colored common bean comes in various sizes identified by different names. Navy beans are small and oblong and the bean commonly used for baked beans. Great Northern beans are kidney bean size. Cannellini beans are large and fleshy and are popular in Italian cooking, where they are prepared with meats and commonly used in soups and stews.

or cooked very briefly. They contain all of the nutrition of the bean in a ready-to-eat, highly digestible form. Because sprouts are grown in warm, moist conditions, they are also prone to the growth of microbes, and raw sprouts are responsible for more than their fair share of outbreaks of food-borne illnesses. Bean sprouts should be purchased and consumed only when very fresh, and they are safest if cooked.

A limited number of legumes are eaten fresh without being sprouted (usually called green), including green beans, green garden and snap peas, lima beans, and green soybeans (edamame). Green legumes are sweeter and have a green (grassy) flavor that disappears during drying. If picked when immature, green legumes can be eaten raw, but mature legumes, whether fresh or dried, require cooking.

Most fresh legumes will cook in 30 minutes or less, but dried legumes take much longer, which has more to do with hydrating than cooking. The dried seed coat is not porous.

Water can enter a bean only through the hilum, a small pore in the center of its curved edge. However, after about an hour of soaking, the seed coat hydrates and expands, after which water can enter the interior more freely and the entire bean can become fully hydrated and expanded. Hydration generally takes about 10 hours at room temperature, and about an hour when done in boiling-hot water (see Slow-Cooked Baked Mixed Beans, page 357). Cooking time can be cut considerably by using a pressure cooker (see Kitchen Wisdom, page 356). Once beans are soaked they will cook much more quickly. Legumes with very thin seed coats, such as split peas and lentils, do not require soaking.

Soaking also alleviates another notorious legume problem — flatulence. Thousands of beneficial bacteria reside in our colons, helping us break down the food that our stomachs and small intestines have trouble digesting, and in the process they produce

kitchen wisdom

Speeding Up Beans

Salt increases the ability of dried beans to absorb water, because sodium displaces magnesium and calcium from pectins in the cell walls, making them dissolve more easily. Adding 1% salt, or 2 teaspoons (10 mL) per quart (1 L), to the soaking water or cooking water can cut cooking time in half. Salt inhibits gelatinization of the bean starch, so even though it speeds up the cooking process, the beans will tend to be grainier rather than creamy in consistency. Cooking beans in a pressure cooker can cut the cooking time even more. Cooked under pressure, presoaked medium-hard beans can reach tenderness in as little as 10 minutes.

gases, about one quart (1 L) per day. Many legumes contain hard-to-digest carbohydrates (oligosaccharides) that are held together by equally indigestible pectins and hemicelluloses. These tend to pass into the colon undigested, and as a result the colonic bacteria start to work overtime, creating a lot of gases in a short period, which causes bloating, pain, and embarrassing expulsions. Soaking legumes dissolves some of their water-soluble carbohydrates. So if you discard the soaking liquid and start cooking soaked legumes in fresh water, much of the potential discomfort and flatulence is averted. Draining the liquid and rinsing canned beans accomplishes the same thing. Most of the offending carbohydrates are consumed during sprouting and by microbes during fermentation, so bean sprouts and soy sauce don't tend to cause the same digestive problems as fresh and dried legumes.

Every cuisine that relies on beans, lentils, and peas as protein sources has developed processed products from legumes. Soy milk, tofu, tempeh, miso, bean paste, and soy sauce are produced from soybeans. Refried beans in Mexican and Tex-Mex cooking are mashed sautéed kidney beans, and hummus is a similar concoction made from chickpeas in Middle Eastern cooking. Red bean paste, a common sweet pastry filling in China, Korea, and Japan, is made from cooked sweetened puréed azuki beans. Peanuts and soybeans are oily enough to be ground into butters and pressed for their oils. In India, where legumes are called dal, they are used toasted, ground into flour (besan or gram flour), or cooked in a porridge that is also known as dal. Legumes take well to canning and are some of the most popular canned foods throughout the world.

Although boiling is the most common technique for cooking legumes, almost any legume can be roasted for a browned, crispy result. Peanuts are the most commonly roasted legume, because of their high oil content and tender texture. Harder legumes with lower oil content, notably soybeans and chickpeas, are also roasted. They need to be soaked first to soften their interiors, and are then roasted in a hot pan or 500°F (260°C) oven until crisp.

The major genera of legumes are:

Arachis — peanuts

Cajanus — pigeon pea, red gram, toor dal

Cicer — chickpeas (aka garbanzo beans, Bengal gram, Indian pea), channa dal (aka split chickpeas or split yellow peas)

Lens — lentils, including brown, small green (Eston), medium green (Richlea), large green (Laird), French green (Puy), orange/red (Red Chief), yellow, masoor dal

Lupinus — lupine (aka lupin)

Medicago — alfalfa

Phaseolus — common beans, including

science wise

Bean Disease • A toxic agent, phytohemagglutinin, found mostly in red-skinned kidney beans, is toxic, triggering vomiting, diarrhea, and abdominal pain. The syndrome is mostly associated with eating raw or undercooked kidney beans and can affect anyone. Another legume-related disease, favism, occurs in people mostly from the southern shore of the Mediterranean and the Middle East, who metabolize certain amino acids in fava beans (vicine and convicine) into forms that damage their red blood cells, causing serious, sometimes fatal anemia. Hyacinth beans and tropical strains of lima beans are high in cyanide-generating compounds that can be toxic if the beans are not cooked thoroughly.

Slow-Cooked Baked Mixed Beans

Beans take well to long, slow cooking. It helps them soften gradually and absorb the flavors of a sauce. Tending to them on a stovetop, in an oven, or over a campfire takes attention. In a slow cooker they're a snap.

1 lb	dried beans, such as white, pinto, or a combination (about 2 cups/500 mL)	500 g
½ cup	ketchup	125 mL
2 tbsp	packed brown sugar	25 mL
2 tbsp	spicy brown mustard	25 mL
2 tbsp	honey	25 mL
½ tsp	freshly ground black pepper	2 mL
1 lb	smoked ham hock or turkey leg	500 g
2 tsp	vegetable oil	10 mL
1	medium onion, diced	1
½	green bell pepper, diced	½
4 cups	chicken broth	1 L
1 tsp	spicy or hot chili powder	5 mL

1. Place beans in a large bowl. Cover with water and soak overnight. Alternatively, in a large saucepan, bring to boil, and boil for 3 minutes. Remove from heat, cover, and soak for 1 hour. Drain.

2. Meanwhile, in a bowl, combine ketchup, brown sugar, mustard, honey, and black pepper. Set aside.

3. Place smoked meat in a large slow cooker and pour soaked beans over top.

4. Heat oil in a large, heavy skillet over medium-high heat. Add onion and bell pepper and sauté until barely tender, about 3 minutes. Add broth and bring to a boil. Remove from heat and stir in half of the prepared sauce. Pour and scrape into the slow cooker. Cover and cook on Low for 10 to 12 hours, until beans are tender and sauce is lightly thickened.

5. Remove meat from beans and set aside to cool. Turn slow cooker to High. Combine chili powder and remaining prepared sauce, and stir into beans. Remove skin and bone from meat and break meat into small pieces. Stir into beans and cook for 10 minutes.

MAKES 8 TO 10 SERVINGS

black bean, cranberry bean, green bean, string bean, kidney bean (all colors), lima bean (butter bean), pinto bean (and other mottled beans), red bean, runner bean, tepary bean, white bean

Pisum — peas, including garden pea, field pea, split pea

Vicia faba — broad beans, including fava bean

Vigna — azuki, bambara groundnut, black-eyed pea, black gram (urad dal), mung bean

How It Works ● Why are legumes so protein rich? Species of Rhizobia soil bacteria form a symbiotic relationship with legumes. They enter through root hairs and establish themselves inside nodules in the roots of legumes. There they trap nitrogen from the air and convert (fix) it into a form that the plant can use (ammonium, or NH_4) to assemble amino acids, and from amino acids they build proteins. Rhizobia cannot fix nitrogen on their own. They require a plant host to provide carbohydrates and organic acids that they use for energy and sufficient oxygen.

Under most conditions, Rhizobia produce more nitrogen than a legume needs, and any extra is deposited back in the soil. Protein-rich grasses like wheat and corn draw nitrogen from the soil to build their proteins and usually leave the soil depleted of nitrogen after harvest. Nitrogen is the most commonly deficient nutrient in soils around the world. Planting legumes in rotation with grains keeps the content of nitrogen in the soil in balance, a principle of crop rotation that has been common since Roman times.

Many legume seeds are rich in defensive chemicals, particularly protease inhibitors (which block the action of protein-digesting enzymes), lectins (which bind red blood cells together and bind to intestinal walls, blocking

fast facts

• In ancient Greece and Rome, beans were
used in voting — a white bean for yes, a
black bean for no.
• The Latin word for "lentil," *lens*, gives us
the English word for a lentil-shaped
double-convex piece of glass.

nutrient absorption), and cyanogenic glucosides (cyanide precursors). At the same time, they are also potent sources of antioxidants, particularly anthocyanin pigments in the colorful seed coats of many beans. Some legumes, such as soybeans and lentils, contain phenolic compounds that resemble the human hormone estrogen and are called phytoestrogens. These compounds are not fully understood, but there is evidence that they have similar traits to human estrogen. They appear to slow bone loss and the development of prostate cancer and heart disease.

See Also • Antioxidants, Protein, Soybeans

LEICESTER • See Cheese

LEMON • See Citrus

LEMONGRASS • See Herbs

LEMON VERBENA • See Herbs

LENTILS • See Legumes

LETTUCE • See Leaves

LEUKOANTHOCYANIDINS • See Antioxidants

LIGNINS • See Fiber

LIMA BEANS • See Legumes

LIMBURGER • See Cheese

LIME • See Citrus

LINGONBERRY • See Berries

LIPOLYSIS • See Metabolism

LIQUEUR

What It Is • Liqueurs are **liquors** (distilled spirits) that have been sweetened and flavored with herbs, spices, nuts, flowers, fruit, seeds, roots, and/or bark. Liqueurs are also called cordials, a name that goes back to when liqueurs were distilled in apothecaries and prescribed to stimulate the circulation — *cordial* comes from the Latin *cor* meaning "heart." Most liqueurs use neutral grain alcohol as a base, although several are made from brandy or whiskey. Cream liqueurs are homogenized with cream. They should not be confused with crème liqueurs that have a syrupy consistency but do not contain cream.

What It Does • Liqueurs are grouped by how they are flavored. Here's an overview:

Chocolate liqueurs: Crème de cacao, a sweet chocolate-flavored liqueur, is made from grain alcohol and is usually clear, although there are dark varieties that are caramel-colored. Brands include Afrikoko (chocolate and coconut), Ashanti Gold (dark chocolate), Vandermint (mint chocolate), Mozart Amadé (dark chocolate with blood orange), and Chéri Suisse (chocolate and cherry).

Coffee liqueurs: These liqueurs can be espresso based, black-coffee flavored, or flavored with coffee and cream. Kahlúa from Mexico and Tia Maria from Jamaica are two popular brands. Tia Maria and Kona Gold are varietal coffee liqueurs made from Jamaica Blue Mountain coffee and Kona coffee, respectively. Sheridan's (made in Dublin) is a coffee-liqueur novelty packaged in a split bottle. One half is filled with a whiskey-based black-coffee liqueur, and the other with white milk-chocolate cream liqueur; the two emerge together when poured, and if you tilt the bottle the right way, the white liqueur floats on the surface of the dark.

Cream liqueurs: Mostly whiskey based, these sweet liqueurs are fortified with cream and homogenized to keep the cream in suspension. The most popular cream liqueur is Bailey's Irish Cream, a blend of Irish whiskey and cream that has spawned scores of imitators, including Carolans Irish Cream,

Fruit liqueurs: Distilled grain alcohol, brandy, or whiskey can be the base for fruit-flavored liqueurs. Fruit liqueurs are not as sweet as crème liqueurs and are more varied and more nuanced. They are sweeter and fruitier than eaux-de-vie (liquors distilled from fruit), and they are increasingly made from blends of fruits. Occasionally herbs or nuts are added. Fruit "brandies," like peach brandy or apricot brandy, are fruit liqueurs that use inexpensive brandy as their base. Fruit liqueurs include:

- Citrus liqueurs, such as Cointreau (orange), curaçao (bitter orange), Grand Marnier (brandy and orange), Gran Torres (orange peel), Grapèro (pink grapefruit), limoncello (lemon), Mandarine Napoléon (brandy and mandarin orange), triple sec (orange), and X-Rated Fusion (a blend of blood orange, mango, and passion fruit).
- Orchard fruit liqueurs, such as Apricot, Chambord (raspberry), Cherry Heering (sweet cherries), Guignolet (wild cherries), Hare Viflne (sour cherries), Kruškovac (pear), Lillehammer (lingonberry), Manzana Verde or Pucker (green apple), prunelle (plum), sloe gin (sloe berries or buckthorn plums), and Southern Comfort (whiskey, peach, and orange).
- Tropical fruit liqueurs, such as Amabili (banana), Bajtra (prickly pear), Guavaberry (guava), Hpnotiq (tropical blend), Lichido (lychee), Midori (melon), Passoã (passion fruit, mango, pineapple, and coconut), and Pisang Ambon (banana).

Herb liqueurs: Some of the most exotic liqueurs, flavored with seeds and herbs, are also some of the oldest, dating from when liqueurs were used principally as herbal medicines. The most popular are anise flavored. Anise-flavored alcohol has an unusual property of turning cloudy when mixed with water, because its terpene molecules are not water soluble. The most notorious anise-flavored liqueur, absinthe, was outlawed in most countries at the beginning of the 20th century (see Absinthe, page 360) because it was believed to promote madness, not surprising since anise-flavored liqueurs are some of the most alcoholic, many exceeding 50%

McCormick's Irish Cream, and O'Leary's Irish Cream. There are also fruit cream liqueurs, such as Amarula (made from the caramel-sweet fruit of the Marula tree in Africa), coffee cream liqueurs, and chocolate cream liqueurs that are not whiskey based.

Crème liqueurs: These highly sweetened syrupy liqueurs are made from distilled spirits flavored with extracts. They are not to be confused with cream liqueurs, which have a dairy component. Rather crème refers to a creamy, syrupy consistency coming from the high sugar content. Crème liqueurs are frequently brightly colored. They include crème de banana (bright yellow, banana flavored), crème de cassis (deep purple-red, black currant flavored), crème de menthe (bright green or colorless, mint flavored), and crème de noyaux (pale pink, almond flavored from apricot pits). Parfait d'Amour is dark purple and flavored with rose petals, vanilla, and almonds.

Absinthe

Pablo Picasso, Vincent van Gogh, Oscar Wilde, Arthur Rimbaud, and Charles Baudelaire were all fans of absinthe, a pale green, high-proof, anise-flavored spirit. In late-19th-century Europe, "the Green Fairy," or *la fée verte*, had grown so popular in France that the cocktail hour was renamed the green hour, or *l'heure verte*.

In traditional absinthe distillation recipes, anise and fennel provide the licorice-like flavor, while the green color comes from the leaves and flowers of hyssop, peppermint, and the controversial wormwood plant, *Artemisia absinthium*. Wormwood tastes extremely bitter, so sugar is typically added when serving absinthe. The iconic serving ritual begins by drizzling ice water over a sugar cube that rests on a slotted spoon placed over a glass of the green spirit. As the sweet water mixes with the absinthe (usually in a 5:1 ratio of water to absinthe), the drink turns from clear to cloudy, known as a "louche" effect. The release of water-insoluble terpene compounds in the essential oils of anise and wormwood creates the opalescent louche, which also occurs in other anise liquors.

On a summer day in 1905, the Swiss laborer Jean LaFray drank an excess of wine and hard liquor, along with a couple of glasses of absinthe. Later that day he murdered his wife and children. In media reports, absinthe was blamed for making LaFray mad and causing the murders. Over the next several years, absinthe was banned in Switzerland and many European countries as well as the U.S. and Canada.

The absinthe ban stems from concerns about one of the key ingredients, wormwood, which contains thujone ($C_{10}H_{16}O$). High concentrations of thujone were once thought to cause hallucinations among absinthe drinkers, who reported a more lucid drunkenness when compared to the effects of other alcohols. In the 1970s, thujone was even thought to function like the cannabinoid THC (tetrahydrocannabinol). But there is no evidence to support either theory.

Current studies show that thujone causes neurons to fire more easily, improving cognitive functions like thinking and memory. In extremely high doses, thujone can cause muscle spasms and convulsions. However, the strongest recipe for absinthe contains very little thujone, less than 4.3 mg per liter, much less than the allowable amount in current European Union and Canadian regulations for absinthe production. In the U.S., foods or beverages made with wormwood must be free of thujone, even though sage oil (classified by the Food and Drug Administration as "generally recognized as safe") contains as much as 50% thujone. The psychoactive effects of absinthe are more likely attributable to the spirit's high alcohol content (about 68%, or 136 proof).

alcohol. Today those laws are being reversed, and absinthe is increasing in availability. Anise liqueurs include: Aguardiente from Central America; Anis del Toro from Spain; Anisetta, sambuca, and Mistrà from Italy; absinthe, anisette, pastis, Pernod, and Ricard from France; ouzo from Greece; and Xtabentún from the Yucatán, made from honey from the nectar of morning glory (*xtabentún*) blossoms. Herbsaint is an anise-based liqueur created in New Orleans to replace absinthe after it was outlawed.

Blended herb liqueurs offer a complex layering of sweetness, savory qualities, and pungency. They are frequently considered digestive aids and are typically served after meals. Examples include Galliano (made from a blend of 30 herbs, including star anise, mint, and ginger) and Strega (made from 70 herbs, including saffron and fennel) from Italy; Bénédictine (cognac flavored with 27 herbs) and Chartreuse (flavored with 130 herbs) from France; Izarra, both yellow (made with 32 herbs and almonds) and mint-flavored green (made with 48 herbs) from the Basque country of France; Jägermeister (56 herbs) and Goldwasser (a blend of roots and herbs with flakes of 23-karat gold) from Germany; and Zen (flavored with green tea and lemongrass) from Japan.

Nut-flavored liqueurs: Sweet and slightly savory, with subtle bitter overtones, nut liqueurs are almost all from Italy. The most famous, amaretto, is almond flavored, usually from the pits of stone fruits such as apricots, peaches, or cherries. Frangelico is a hazelnut-herb liqueur. Nocello is flavored with walnuts and hazelnuts, and Nocino with unripe green walnuts. Macadamia nut liqueur, Kahana Royale, is made in Hawaii. Ratafia is a generic name for sweetened brandy infused with nut and fruit flavors, often homemade.

Whiskey liqueurs: Almost every whiskey manufacturer produces liqueurs from their core product, usually flavored with a mixture of fruit and herbs. A high percentage of them are sweetened with honey rather than sugar. They include:

- Bourbon liqueurs — Jeremiah Weed (orange and vanilla), Wild Turkey (honey and spices)
- Canadian liqueurs — Yukon Jack (honey)
- Irish liqueurs — Eblana (coffee, honey, almond, and peanut), Irish Mist (heather and clover honey and herbs)
- Rye liqueurs — Rock and Rye (citrus with rock candy)
- Scotch liqueurs — Bruadar (honey, sloe berries or Buckthorn plums), Drambuie (heather honey and herbs), Glayva (Seville oranges, honey, and herbs), Glenfiddich Malt (citrus, pear, and brown sugar), Stag's Breath (fermented comb honey)

Other liqueurs: As with any handcrafted product there are many liqueurs that do not fall into neat categories. Some popular one-of-a-kind liqueurs are advocaat, a rich, creamy eggnog-like liqueur made from eggs, sugar, and brandy; Cynar, a bittersweet liqueur flavored with artichokes and herbs; licor de oro, flavored with whey, saffron, and lemon peel; St. Germain, a clear Alpine liqueur flavored with elderflower blossoms; and Tuaca, a syrupy brandy flavored strongly with vanilla and a bit of citrus.

How It Works • The practice of infusing alcohol with other ingredients began as a way of making herbal medicines. The same chemical properties that give alcohol the ability to bind with medicinal elements in herbs and spices also make it bond flavors and aromas. Early on it was noted that the medicines that cured our ills also tasted pretty good. By the 15th century, liqueurs had moved from the pharmacy to the dining and drinking table.

Liqueurs can be flavored by soaking the flavorful ingredient in distilled alcohol or by distilling them along with the alcohol. Liqueurs made by infusion tend to be sweeter than those that are fully distilled.

The higher the proportion of sugar in a liqueur, the more viscous, or thick, it becomes. Mixologists take advantage of the various densities of distilled liquors to make layered drinks. Lighter (higher-alcohol, lower-sugar) spirits naturally float on the surface of denser (sweeter, lower-alcohol) liqueurs. The bright colors of many liqueurs can make layered drinks eye-popping.

See Also • Bitters, Liquor, Wine

LIQUOR

What It Is • Since alcohol boils at a lower temperature than water — 173°F (78°C) compared to 212°F (100°C) — when fermented fruit juice (wine) or fermented grain (beer) are heated, more alcohol than water turns into vapor. Liquor is made by capturing that vapor and cooling it until it returns to a liquid state. The resulting spirit has a higher alcohol content than the original beer or wine, and because aromatic chemicals are also highly volatile, it has a more concentrated flavor as well. The alcohol content of liquor is stated in percentage, as alcohol by volume (ABV).

What It Does • The art of distillation is ancient. Mesopotamians captured the scents of aromatic plants through distillation more than 5,000 years ago, and Aristotle noted in 4 BCE that vaporized seawater became drinkable and didn't turn back into salted water when it condensed.

Written documents suggest that the earliest distilled alcohols were made by the Chinese, who concentrated alcohol from fermented grain about 2,000 years ago. By the 10th century, privileged Chinese were drinking distilled alcohols, and by the 13th century, spirits were being sold commercially.

In 1100, alcohol distilled from wine had a reputation as a valuable medicine in Italy, and throughout Europe alchemists viewed distilled alcohol as a powerful substance that they dubbed the *quintessence*, the ethereal "fifth element" that in addition to the four basic elements — earth, water, air, and fire — made up the world.

In the early 14th century, the Valencian alchemist and physician Arnaldus de Villanova, in his medical book on wine, *Liber de Vinis* (the first mass-printed wine book), dubbed the essence of wine *aqua vitae*, "water of life." The term has given name to most distilled spirits, including Scandinavian *aquavit*, French *eau-de-vie*, and in English "whiskey," the anglicized version of the Gaelic *uisge beatha*, "water of life." Even the term "spirit" identifies alcohol as the soul of fermentation.

For several centuries *aqua vitae* remained medicinal, produced in apothecaries and monasteries and prescribed as a remedy for such ills as poor circulation and digestive difficulties. No one knows exactly when the social use of distilled alcohol started in Europe, but brandy was cited in 15th-century German laws regulating public drunkenness. Around the same time, winemakers in Armagnac, France, began distilling wine to keep it from spoiling during shipping. Gin was being made in Holland from rye that was flavored with juniper by the 16th century. Cognac brandy, made just north of Armagnac, started production around 1620, and the first rum was being distilled from molasses in the West Indies by 1630. Monastic **liqueurs** like Bénédictine and Chartreuse date from the early 1650s.

Liquor distilled from fruit has different characteristics than liquor distilled from grain. Fruit-based spirits are divided between brandy (made from grapes) and fruit alcohol (made from other fruits). Grain-based spirits are divided among single-malt whiskey (made from malted barley), whiskey and gin (made from grain and malted barley), bourbon (made from corn and malted barley plus a regulated amount of other grain), and vodka (usually made from grain but also from potato or other starches). Two types of liquor are based on neither fruit nor grain: rum is distilled from fermented molasses or sugarcane, and tequila and mezcal are distilled from fermented agave.

Brandy (grape liquors) — The word "brandy" derives from the German *bernewyne*, which means "burnt wine," a phrase that could refer either to the distillation process itself or to the flavor of charred wood absorbed by brandies as they age in fire-treated oak barrels.

Brandies are distilled from grape wine. The two most prestigious brandies are cognac and Armagnac, the first named for a town north of Bordeaux in southwest France and the second for a region south of Bordeaux. Both are made from Trebbiano (Ugni Blanc) grapes, which are used to make more wine in the world than any other grape. Trebbiano produce fresh, fruity, undistinguished wines that do not age well, but because of their full fruit and high acid, they retain full flavor throughout distillation.

Cognac is double distilled with the lees still in the juice. Lees are the sediment of dead yeast that falls to the bottom of the tank after fermentation. They are quite pungent and give cognac a savory, meaty quality that balances the sweetness of the grape. Cognac is usually distilled to an alcohol content of 70%. Armagnac is single distilled without lees to about 55% alcohol. The shorter fermentation time preserves more of the fruit's volatile acids, which makes Armagnac rougher and more assertive than cognac.

Both are aged, by law, in new French oak barrels for flavor; the oak flavors dissipate as a barrel is used for a minimum of six months, but most brandies are aged for at least two years. The best Armagnac is aged for 20 years or more; cognac can be aged for over 60 years before being bottled. Both Armagnac and cognac are diluted to about 40% alcohol, and their flavor and color may be corrected with sugar, oak extract, and caramel before bottling.

The Liquor Family Tree

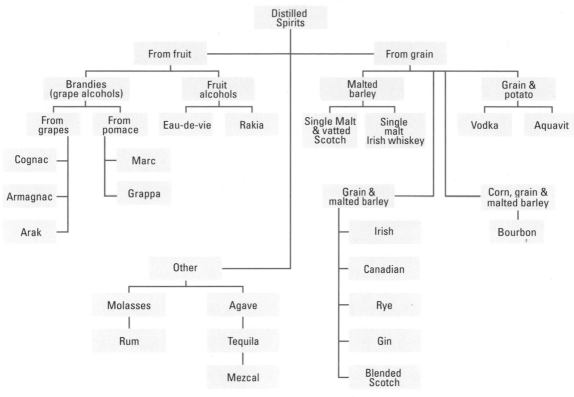

Marc and grappa are French and Italian names for single-distilled brandy made from pomace, the fermented skins, seeds, stems, and pulp left over from pressing grapes for wine. This solid debris still has some juice and a lot of sugar and tannins remaining in it, which, with the addition of water and a second period of fermentation, yield a pungent wine. Distillation concentrates the flavor, producing a brandy that is renowned for its strength and sharpness, more suitable for warming up workers after a day in the vineyards than as something to savor at the end of a fine meal.

Traditionally, marc and grappa were bottled as is, without filtering out the sharper alcohols in the distillation process, but today more refined aged products are being produced. With age, marc and grappa can develop the same flavor chemicals as those in blue cheese, a quality that is highly prized by aficionados.

Arak is a clear anise-flavored brandy from the Middle East. Its production starts out like any brandy, but aniseed is added during the second distillation. The resulting liquor is not aged in wood so it does not develop any color.

Arak looks more like an eau-de-vie and tastes a bit like pastis (anise-flavored liqueur) but is not as sweet.

Fruit Liquors — Fruit alcohols are distilled from wines that are made from fruits other than grapes. They are fermented and distilled in much the same way as brandies, but fruit alcohols are not usually aged in wood, so they tend to be colorless rather than tawny. Because they don't pick up flavor from wood, fruit alcohols have a clean, pure taste of the fruit from which they were distilled. They are called *eau-de-vie* ("water of life") in French and *schnapps* in German. The most famous fruit liquors are made mostly in France, Switzerland, Germany, and Italy from indigenous fruit. They include Poire Williams, made from Bartlett (Williams) pears; kirsch (*kirschwasser*), made from sweet black cherries; mirabelle, made from yellow plums; quetsch, made from purple plums; Reine Claude, made from greengage plums; slivovitz, a Slavic eau-de-vie made from a variety of plums and lots of plum pits; framboise, made from raspberries; apricot, made from apricots; fraise, made from wild strawberries; boukha, a syrupy spirit distilled in North Africa and the Middle East from figs; and Goldschlager, a schnapps scented with cinnamon and garnished with flecks of 23-karat gold.

The raison d'être for fruit liquor is to capture the essence of fruit in a pure crystalline liquid. To that end it takes 10 pounds (4.5 kg) of Mirabelle plums to make one bottle of eau-de-vie, or 18 pounds (8 kg) of raspberries, or 30 pounds (14 kg) of pears. Fruit liquors are never sweetened like fruit liqueurs and are always twice distilled to achieve an alcohol content between 65 and 90%, with a pronounced fruit aroma and a subtle fruit flavor. Their purity is not compromised by aging in wood except for one prominent exception.

Calvados, an apple eau-de-vie (sometimes incorrectly called apple brandy) from Brittany in France, is made from some combination of apples. Each producer has his own secret formula, but there are always some sweet varieties, some tart, and some bitter, in about equal proportions. The apples are pressed into cider, which is cold-fermented over several weeks, and then distilled. The best calvados, from the eastern end of the district (the Pays d'Auge), are typically double distilled in small batches and are given the designation *Pays d'Auge*. Other calvados may de double distilled but will not get that ranking. All calvados is aged in old French oak barrels for a minimum of two years.

Applejack is American apple liquor made from fermented sweet apple cider distilled by freeze-distillation (aka jacking). The crude process involves freezing cider until its water solidifies and then skimming off the liquid alcohol. Freeze-distillation is much less exact than heat-distilling (see How It Works, page 368) and produces liquor that tastes more of fruit and is only about 40% alcohol. Honeyjack is freeze-distilled mead (wine fermented from honey water). Like applejack, most is homemade, but Krupnik, a Polish honeyjack, is heat distilled.

Brown Grain Liquors

Whiskey — Let's clear one thing up right away: spelling. Scotch is whisky spelled without an "e"; all other whiskeys use the "e." Don't ask why. Just drink up.

Whiskey is basically distilled beer (minus the hops) that is aged in wood to develop color and flavor. Like beer, much of its primary character depends on the mix of grains used in its preparation. Whiskeys made with all malted barley are called single-**malt**. Those made with a combination of malted barley and grains are called grain whiskeys. These can be named for the type of grain used, like rye, or they can be named for their place of origin, such as Scotch, Irish, or Canadian.

Scotch whisky — Scotches, especially single-malt brands, are some of the most flavorful and nuanced (and most expensive) whiskeys in the world. One of the characteristic qualities of Scotch is a smoky aroma that comes from drying the malt over a

live fire. In the western and northern areas of Scotland, called the Islands and Highland regions, respectively, the fuel usually includes peat, a form of dried compost that gives peat-smoked Scotch a particularly earthy character.

There are five categories of Scotch:

- Single-malt whisky is made from 100% malted barley and is from a single distillery, usually in the Highland region, Speyside, or on one of the western islands, Arran, Jura, Mull, Orkney, or Skye. The Isle of Islay to the south is considered its own single-malt region. Highland single-malts include Balvenie, Cragganmore, Dalmore, Glenfiddich, McClelland, and The Glenlivet. Island single-malt distilleries include Arran, Bruichladdich, Jura, and Talisker. Laphroaig is the main Islay Scotch.
- Vatted whisky (pure-malt or blended-malt) is 100% malt whisky made from a blend of single-malt whiskies that were produced by more than one distillery located in any of the single-malt-producing regions of Scotland. They are less common than single malts. The age of the youngest whisky used in a vatted blend determines the age listed on the label: a "10-year-old" blended malt whisky could contain older whiskies in the blend.
- Single-grain whisky is a grain whisky from a single distillery. It can contain more than one grain. As of 2007 there were only seven single-grain whisky distilleries in Scotland, all in the Lowlands (south), including Auchentoshan, Bladnoch, and Glenkinchie.
- Blended grain whisky is a blend of grain whiskies from several distilleries. Very little is produced since almost all grain whiskies are used for making blended Scotch whiskies.
- Blended Scotch whisky is a blend of single-malt whiskies and grain whiskies, usually from more than one distillery. This category accounts for 90% of the whisky produced in Scotland. They usually are less than half single malt, and each brand has its own style. Popular blended whiskies include Dewar's, Johnnie Walker, Cutty Sark, and J&B.

Regardless of its type, by law all Scotch whisky must be distilled in a Scottish distillery. It cannot be distilled to an alcohol strength of more than 94.7% so that it retains the flavor of its raw materials. It must be aged in Scotland in oak barrels for at least three years. And it cannot be bottled at less than 40% alcohol by volume.

Scotch is typically aged in barrels that were previously used for aging wine or other liquors, to ensure that the most volatile elements in the wood (see How It Works, page 368) have dissipated. The most common casks are sherry or bourbon casks, most typically bourbon, since there is a near-endless supply because of U.S. regulations that bourbon must always be aged in new barrels. Scotch aged in sherry barrels tends to be darker, while bourbon barrels impart a golden honey color.

Sometimes a Scotch label will specify the type of cask used. It will also tell you if the Scotch is bottled undiluted, specified as "cask strength," which is typically between 50 and 60% ABV. If the Scotch is single malt, the name of the distillery will be specified as well as the fact that it is single malt. If it has been cask aged for any amount of time past the minimum requirement, the number of years will be listed. The age on the label is the amount of time the Scotch spent in a barrel before bottling. If there is a date on the bottle, it is the date of the bottling.

Irish whiskey — Like Scotch, Irish whiskey can be single malt, singe grain, or blended. Irish whiskey has a unique classification, "pure pot still whiskey," referring to a pot or batch method of distilling rather than column, or continuous, distilling. Many whiskeys are batch distilled, but the "pure pot" designation for Irish whiskey means that the liquor is made with 100% barley, about half of which is malted. This is different from single malt, which is also 100% barley, but all of that is malted.

Irish whiskeys are typically triple distilled, which makes them lighter in color and less flavorful than Scotch whiskies, and they are never cooked over peat, so they do not have a smoky character.

There are far fewer distilleries in Ireland than in Scotland. Bushmill makes both blended and single-malt whiskeys. Jameson is the primary distiller of pure pot still Irish whiskey; they also make a blended whiskey.

Canadian whiskey — Mostly made from a blend of grains, Canadian whiskey is known for its mild flavor and delicate aromas. Canadian whiskey often includes rye in its grain blend, and a few Canadian whiskeys are 100% rye. By law they are aged for at least three years in oak casks. The most popular brands are Canadian Club and Crown Royal. There is one boutique single-malt Canadian whiskey, Glen Breton Rare, from Nova Scotia. Canadian whiskey can include small additions of other whiskies, brandies, wine, and/or rum, up to 9% of the blend.

Bourbon whiskey — Named for a county in Kentucky that was its birthplace, bourbon is made from the New World's native grain, **corn**. By law bourbon must be at least 51% corn, but in practice the percentage is closer to 70%, with the remainder a mixture of malted barley, wheat, and/or rye. Most bourbon is double distilled to an ABV of 60 to 80%, and then aged for a minimum of two years in new charred American oak casks, which give bourbon a deep amber color and a pronounced vanilla flavor note. Unlike French brandies and Canadian whiskeys, caramel color, sugar, and other flavorings are not permitted in bourbon production. Nothing other than grain, yeast, and water goes into a bottle of bourbon. Although Kentucky continues to be the largest bourbon-producing state, Tennessee whiskey is similar, except that it is maple-charcoal filtered before aging, a step that gives it a distinctive flavor. The largest producer of Tennessee whiskey is Jack Daniel's. Popular Kentucky bourbons include Jim Beam, Knob Creek, Maker's Mark, Wild Turkey, and Woodford Reserve.

Rye whiskey — In the U.S., where most rye whiskey is distilled, it must contain at least 51% rye grain in its formula. Canadian whiskey, which usually contains some rye, is sometimes referred to as rye whiskey, although there is no Canadian regulation stipulating the amount of rye in whiskeys. Rye is harsher, less sweet, and not as syrupy as bourbon, giving it a complex, some might say harsh, flavor profile. It is sometimes compared to the Islay Scotches, which can be strongly peaty. The major producers are Jim Beam, Heaven Hill, Buffalo Trace, and Old Overholt.

Colorless Grain Liquors

Gin — Gin, a neutral spirit flavored with juniper berries, comes in two styles. The most common, English-style (or London) dry gin, is made by diluting a double-distilled 95% grain spirit with water, adding juniper berries and other flavorings, most often coriander but occasionally other spices, and distilling it a third time to flavor it and return the distillation to 95% ABV. The distillate is diluted before bottling to between 37 and 47% ABV. Brands of English-style gin include Beefeater, Bombay, Boodles, Gordon's, and Tanqueray.

The Dutch method of distilling gin is made by double- or triple-distilling a fermentation of malt, corn, and rye to a fairly low alcohol level, around 30%. At that ABV, many flavors from fermentation are still present in the spirit. Juniper and other spices are added, and the spirit is distilled one more time to an ABV of around 40%. It is then bottled without further dilution. Dutch-style gins include Bols and Hendrick's. Plymouth is a Dutch-style gin that can only be made in Plymouth, England, and Genever (called Holland gin in England) is the original Dutch gin, flavored assertively with juniper (*genièvre* is French for juniper).

The aromatics in gin, which come from terpenes in the spices, are typically piney, citrusy, and floral. They can be subtle or pronounced, with the Dutch method producing the most flavorful gins. Some distilleries flavor their gins with scores of ingredients. Hendrick's gin, made in Scotland, is distilled with cucumber and roses; Beefeater gin contains nine herbs and spices, including juniper, angelica, and coriander, as well as licorice, almonds, and Seville oranges.

Compound, or flavored, gins are made by infusing already distilled spirits with juniper and other flavorings. Sloe gin is made by steeping sloe plums from the blackthorn bush in neutral spirits. Because the aromatic components are not distilled with the alcohol, these liquors are classified as liqueurs and are not legally gins.

Vodka and aquavit — Vodka and aquavit can be distilled from a fermentation of any substance high enough in carbohydrate. In Russia, where it originated, vodka (which means "little water" in Russian) was made from the cheapest source available — commonly grain (sorghum, corn, rye, or wheat), potatoes, or sugar beets. The specific base ingredient is unimportant because vodka is distilled to rid it of all aromatics, and then filtered through charcoal to produce a smooth, neutral, pure spirit. Typically, vodka is continuously distilled to 95% ABV, and bottled without further aging at around 40% ABV.

Because the goal of vodka is purity, filtered vodkas are the norm, although small distilleries are increasingly producing unfiltered vodkas, which have more flavor and character. Vodkas are frequently flavored after distillation, infused with aromatics including chiles, ginger, fruit, flowers, vanilla, honey, or cinnamon. Smirnoff and Stolichnaya are the most well known Russian vodkas. Absolut and Finlandia are popular Scandinavian vodkas. Grey Goose is from France.

Aquavit (akavit) is Scandinavian vodka generally flavored with a blend of aromatic seeds, mostly caraway, but it can also be infused with anise, dill, fennel, coriander, and/or grains of paradise. Aquavit can be aged in old oak casks, in which case it will have a yellow to amber color and richer flavor, like whiskey.

Other Liquors

Rum — Rum contains neither fruit nor grain. It is distilled from fermented sugarcane juice or molasses, resulting in a rough alcohol that can be light or dark depending on how it is made. Traditional rums (dark or black rum), mostly from Jamaica and the French-speaking Caribbean islands, are fermented with a special yeast (*Schizosaccharomyces*) that produces a large amount of fruity-tasting esters. The fermentation is distilled in pot stills in small batches to a low alcohol concentration in order to preserve as much of the aromatic components as possible. The spirit is aged in charred American oak barrels, usually old bourbon casks, from which it gets most of its color.

Light rum is fermented with conventional yeasts and distilled industrially to about 90% ABV. The rum is matured to mollify its rough edges and usually filtered to remove residual color from the molasses. It is diluted to between 40 and 43% ABV before bottling. Golden rums are aged in oak barrels to mellow them further and to develop a light honey color. Overproof rums are diluted less before bottling and can be as high as 75% ABV. Premium rums that are aged for years in oak resemble brandies in appearance and flavor. Cachaça is Brazilian rum made exclusively from sugarcane juice. Charanda is sweet vanilla-tasting Mexican rum.

Tequila and mezcal — The agave, a succulent plant similar to cactus that grows at high altitudes mostly in the Jalisco state of Mexico, is the base for the indigenous liquors tequila and mezcal. Both are made mostly from the hearts (*piñas*) of blue agave (*Agave tequilana*), which are rich in fructose and inulin (a form of indigestible long-chain sugar). Agave for tequila is steamed to break down the sugars before fermentation. Agave for mezcal is roasted over charcoal, infusing

the *piñas* with smoke that carries into the aroma of the finished spirit. The cooked *piñas* are mashed with water and fermented with yeast. The resulting liquid is distilled. Tequila is distilled industrially. Mezcal is double distilled in small batches in pot stills made out of clay or metal.

Tequila that is bottled without any aging is called *blanco* (white) or *plata* (silver). *Oro* (gold) tequila is *blanco* tequila with added caramel coloring and flavoring to make it resemble aged tequila. *Reposado* (rested) tequila is aged between two months and one year in oak barrels. *Añejo* (aged) tequila is aged in oak between one and three years, and *maduro* (extra-aged) is held for more than three years.

All mezcal is aged. *Blanco* or *joven* (young) mezcal is aged less than two months and is colorless. *Reposado* and *añejo* mezcals are aged similarly to tequilas but in smaller barrels. For commercial purposes, worms are added to some mezcals during bottling. The famous mezcal "worm" is the larva of a moth (*Hypopta agavis*) that frequently infests agave plants. Adding larvae to bottled mezcals started after 1943, when worms became associated with an improvement in flavor. Mezcal with a worm in it is called *con gusano* ("with worm"). Today it is seen principally as a novelty, and other decorative elements such as glass figures or gold-leaf flecks might be added instead.

How It Works • Distillation

When the concentration of alcohol in a fermented beverage gets close to 20%, the alcohol will kill the yeast doing the fermenting. So it is impossible to make strong alcoholic drinks without physically concentrating the alcohol after fermentation is over. To make a concentrated alcohol:

- Fruits, grains, or other sources of carbohydrate (potatoes, rice, sugarcane, cactus) are fermented with yeasts to create a moderate 5 to 12% alcohol solution.
- The resulting liquid, a mixture of water, alcohol, and aromatic components, is heated in a closed pot. Once boiling, an azeotrope (a mixture that can't be changed by distillation) of alcohol and water containing volatile aromatic compounds rises from the surface.

Alcohol Content of Distilled Liquors

Spirit	Distilled ABV (%)	Distilled Proof	Bottled ABV (%)	Bottled Proof
Bourbon whiskey	60–70	120–140	40–54	80–108
Brandy	55–90	110–180	40	80
Canadian whiskey	80	160	40	80
Fruit alcohol	65–90	130–180	40	80
Gin	95	190	38–46	76–92
Irish whiskey	80	160	40–60	80–120
Rum	55–90	110–180	40–43	80–86
Scotch whisky	70	140	40–60	80–120
Tequila	55	110	38–46	76–92
Vodka	95–96	190–192	35–50	70–100

- The aromatic azeotrope vapor is channeled across increasingly cooler metal surfaces, where the vapors condense (become liquid) and are collected as distilled alcohol.
- The distilled alcohol can be finished in various ways, including being flavored with herbs, spices, or fruit; aged in wood; or mixed with water to adjust its alcohol level.

If all the flavors resulting from fermentation were desirable, making delicious distilled spirits would be simple — but it isn't. Yeast fermentation produces thousands of flavorful components, but some are objectionable and some (mainly methanol) are downright toxic. The distiller's art is the ability to select the best-tasting components from the vapor and get rid of the unpleasant ones. Distillers accomplish this by separating the vapor into parts that are less or more volatile and capturing the part that is richest in alcohol.

The volatile elements in alcohol vapor are divided into three tiers (called fractions):
- Heads, or foreshots, are the most volatile elements that evaporate earliest and contain toxic methanol, wood alcohol, and acetone.
- The second fraction is 95.6% ethanol and 4.4% water, which is the fraction that the distiller most wants to capture.
- Tails, or feints, are made up of components that are higher boiling than ethanol. The

lightest of these are desirable. They are called congeners and include many pleasant aromatic chemicals, such as esters, terpenes, and phenolic compounds. The tails also contain heavier compounds that are less desirable. These are called fusel (German for "rotgut") oils and are mostly long-chain alcohols that can give spirits a pleasant oily body, but they also can also contribute a harsh astringent flavor and a nasty aftertaste. A little bit of fusel components give distilled spirits character; too much turns it into rotgut.

By capturing the middle tier, a distiller is guaranteed of the purest alcohol product possible with the best neutral flavor. The congener elements in the tails are also desirable in some liquors, most notably whiskeys and brandies, to create richer flavors. Fusel oils are sometimes captured and added in small amounts to whiskeys for texture. The most volatile head fraction, which can be toxic, is forced to escape and is never included in fine distilled spirits.

There are two mechanisms for distillation: batch distillation and continuous distillation. The batch method is the oldest and is still used for making the finest liquors. It involves a closed pot (alembic) for heating the fermented liquid. An alembic, or pot still, has a large, rounded belly that sits over the heat. It tapers toward the top and connects to a series of tubes that are cooled, usually by water. As the vapors rise into the tubes they condense back into liquid, which is predominantly alcohol.

It can take 10 to 12 hours for a batch of wine or fermented grain to be heated and distilled. The initial head vapors are diverted. The alcohol vapors and some of the lighter tail vapors are captured and condensed, and the heavier fusel oil vapors are captured separately. Usually the first distillation yields a 20 to 30% alcohol solution, so two (or even three) passes through the still is common to achieve an alcohol content of 50 to 95% by volume.

Continuous distillation is done in two or more elongated chambers (columns) divided into chambers defined by plates protruding into the column from the sides. A pipe running from the top of one column to the bottom of the next traps vapors and channels them from column to column. In each column the distillate becomes purer, so there is no need to double or triple distill to achieve highly distilled alcohols. Continuous distillation is the preferred method for industrial production. The downside is that the distiller has less control over the final makeup of the distilled alcohol, which is why fine whiskeys and brandies are still made in pot stills.

In continuous distillation, the fermented liquid enters through a valve at the top of the first column and flows down toward the heat source at the bottom. As the liquid gets to the bottom, the methanol and other highly volatile elements vaporize first. Some are released, but others float up to the top of the column, where they condense and get trapped on the uppermost plates, from which they are discarded. The mid-range ethanol and congener vapors are collected on the plates in the middle of the column, and the heavier fusel vapors get trapped on the bottom plates. They are mostly discarded, although a small amount can be added during blending.

The alcohol content of a distilled spirit is a good indicator of its flavor. Highly distilled spirits have the most alcohol and the largest amount of pleasant congener flavor components.

Aging

Right out of the still, distilled spirits are colorless and harsh tasting, so all liquors are seasoned for a few weeks to a few months to permit various chemicals in the mixture to interact with one another and become mellower. After that a distilled spirit can go through various processes, depending on what kind of liquor is being produced.

White (colorless) spirits, like vodka, gin, and eaux-de-vie, are not aged further. Their flavor and alcohol level may be adjusted (by adding water) and then they are bottled. Brown liquors, like whiskeys and brandies, are aged in wood barrels for anywhere from a few months to decades. Barrel aging gives them their characteristic amber color and complex flavor.

The absorption and oxidation that happen during barrel aging result in complex changes and the development of aromatic and mellow flavors. Though several different woods are used for aging spirits, the great majority of barrels are made of oak heartwood, the inner wood that is filled with tannins and aromatic compounds like eugenol (the flavor of clove), vanillin (the flavor of vanilla), and lactones (which taste like coconut and peach).

Although both European and American oaks are made into barrels, American oak is generally preferred for spirits because it has a lower level of extractable tannins and more vanillin and lactones. For aging whiskeys, the interior of the barrel is typically charred. The carbonized surface acts as a kind of charcoal filter, accelerating the maturation of flavor. New barrels contain more aromatic compounds, and so spirits may be aged in several barrels of various ages to develop a particular flavor profile. Each time a barrel is used the spirit loses some of its volume, mostly through evaporation, which can approach half the barrel after 15 years of use.

When barrel-aged spirits are judged ready for bottling, they are usually blended to obtain a consistent flavor (single-malt Scotch is an exception) and diluted to a final alcohol content of 40 to 50%. Some are chill-filtered to remove heavy fusel oils that may cause clouding when the spirit is chilled. The filtering also removes some flavor, though, so producers of the finest whiskeys and brandies do not usually filter their products.

All distillers must state the alcohol content of their products on the label as a percentage of volume (ABV). The most common concentration is around 40%. Alcohol content is also frequently stated in terms of proof, which is about twice the ABV.

Proof developed in the 18th century when British sailors were paid partly in rum. To ensure that the rum had not been watered down, it was "proved" to be undiluted by dousing gunpowder with the liquor and testing to see if the gunpowder would ignite. If it wouldn't, the alcohol content was considered too low, or underproof. A proven solution was defined as 100 degrees proof, because it was assumed that it did not contain any water. It was later found that rum-doused gunpowder would ignite as long as the rum had more than 57% ABV. Expressed as a ratio, 57% is roughly 7:4. So 70 proof liquor had about 40% alcohol by volume. Later this was round to a ratio of 8:4, or 2:1.

As you can see, proof is only an approximate measure of liquors' alcohol content and it is not permitted as a legal measure of the amount of alcohol produced through distillation. Although a liquor label may state the proof of its contents, it must also state the alcohol content as a percentage of volume.

See Also • Alcohol, Beer, Bitters, Liqueur, Malt, Wine

LIQUID SMOKE • See Smoking

LIVER • See Organ Meats

LIVERWURST • See Sausage

LM (LOW-METHOXYL) PECTIN • See Pectin

LOBSTER • See Crustacean

LOCUST BEAN GUM • See Gums

LOMI LOMI • See Fish

LONDON BROIL • See Beef

LOVAGE • See Herbs

LOW-DENSITY LIPOPROTEINS • See Cholesterol, Fat

LOX • See Fish

LUNGS • See Organ Meats

LUTEIN • See Antioxidants, Pigment

LYCOPENE • See Antioxidants, Pigment

LYE • See Alkali

M

MACADAMIA • See Nuts

MACARONI • See Pasta

MACAROON • See Cookies, Nuts

MACE • See Spices

MACERATION • See Marinade

MÂCHE • See Leaves

MACKEREL • See Fish

MAD COW DISEASE

What It Is • First identified in 1986 among cattle raised in the United Kingdom, mad cow disease, or bovine spongiform encephalopathy (BSE), is a nervous-system disease that causes the brain and spinal cord to degenerate and become spongy in the cattle. A second strain of the disease was identified in 2004. Once BSE-contaminated meat is ingested by humans, research suggests that it can lead to a variant of Creutzfeldt-Jakob Disease (CJD), which has approximately the same neurological degenerative effects on humans as BSE has on cattle.

What It Does • The origins of BSE are still unclear, but the disease is transmitted by feeding cattle the ground meat and bones of sick, dead, or slaughtered sheep or cattle, which was once a common practice in the European beef industry. (This practice has since been halted.) In North America, the by-products of most mammals have been prohibited from cattle feed since 1997. However, according to U.S. feeding regulations, cattle and goat by-products can still be legally fed to pets or other non-ruminant livestock such as pigs and chickens. Cattle can also be fed the by-roducts of pigs and chickens. These loopholes in feeding regulations have led many consumer groups to urge stricter government controls to prevent the spread of BSE. In part, these loopholes have led to increased interest in grass-fed beef.

Worldwide, Japan has the tightest BSE controls and tests all cattle for mad cow disease at the time of slaughter. The European Union and the U.S. test fewer cattle because the only reliable test is to examine tissues during an autopsy, which is costly. Mad cow disease has a four- to six-year incubation period, so the risk of seeing symptoms of the disease increases as cattle get older. Most countries now require cattle to be slaughtered when they are less than three years old.

BSE is transmitted by prions (a kind of protein) located in the nervous-system tissue of infected cattle, especially the brain, spinal cord, vertebrae, retina, and ileum portion of the intestines. If any of this tissue ends up in the meat during slaughter, it can be transmitted to humans who eat the meat. BSE prions are not killed by normal cooking

fast facts

- The U.K. has been hit hardest by BSE, which infected about 180,000 cattle in the late 1980s. Nearly 4.5 million cattle were killed to prevent the disease from spreading, but by then more than 460,000 infected animals had entered the human food chain, leading to a little over 170 deaths worldwide as of June 2007.
- In 2003, the first mad cow in the U.S. was identified in a Washington State dairy cow, which had been purchased from a Canadian farm. The second was identified in a non-ambulatory (downer) cow in Texas in 2005. The meat from the second cow did not enter the food supply, but that of the first did and was later recalled.
- In 2006, a South Dakota biotechnology company used genetic engineering and cloning technology to produce cattle that lacked the gene necessary to make the prion protein, theoretically making the cattle immune to BSE.
- In February 2008, the USDA recalled about 143 million pounds (65 million kg) of beef, the largest recall in U.S. history. The beef was recalled because the company did not comply with government regulations and allowed the slaughter of downer cows, which are about 50 times more likely to be infected with mad cow disease than ambulatory cows. It was a Class II recall with low health risk.

temperatures, so cooking meats to well-done will not make contaminated meat safe.

Various parts of the nervous system are used in some beef sausages, so consumers have become increasingly inquisitive and cautious about sausage meats. Many countries have also cautioned against or outright banned the sale of beef brains, sweetbreads, spleen, and intestines and beef from cattle more than three years old.

A particular beef product, mechanically separated meat (MSM), has also been significantly reformed since the outbreak of mad cow disease. In the pre-BSE era, MSM was used to make some ground meat products like hot dogs, sausages, hamburgers, and frozen foods. It was produced by grinding bones and meat, then separating the meat from bone fragments under force of high pressure. This process risked contaminating ground meat with infected tissue, so MSM machines have been modified to mechanically scrape meat from intact bones. These advanced meat recovery (AMR) machines are much less likely to mix nervous-system tissue in with muscle meats. As an added measure of safety, since 2003, the U.S. Department of Agriculture (USDA) has routinely inspected beef produced by AMR for the presence of spinal cord or brain tissue.

How It Works • Mad cow disease is transmitted by prions, a type of protein that has no DNA or genes to replicate itself. Prions are not strictly "alive" and can't be "killed" by the acid or heat normally used to kill microbes and viruses. Yet prions can transmit disease in animals and humans. Prions fold healthy nervous-system proteins into themselves, a process that repeats over the four-year incubation period, increasing the amount of diseased protein molecules in the animal. As the misshapen molecules proliferate, they disrupt cell function, forming little holes in nervous-system tissue that makes it characteristically spongy. Ultimately, the prions kill healthy cells, making "downer" cattle extremely weak and unable to stand. Currently, BSE and variant CJD are untreatable and fatal, but the chances of being infected with variant CJD are remote, about one in a million.

MADEIRA • See Wine

MAGNESIUM • See Minerals

MAHI MAHI • See Fish

MAHLEB • See Spices

MAILLARD REACTIONS • See Browning

MAIZE • See Corn

MAKRUT LIME • See Citrus

MALOLACTIC FERMENTATION • See Wine

MALT

What It Is • Without malt, there would be no **beer** or whiskey. Malt is partly sprouted, or germinated, **grain**, such as barley, that has been dried in a kiln. It is used as a source of enzymes, particularly those that hydrolyze starches into sugars and proteins into amino acids. Most malt is used in **fermentation** to make various types of **alcohol**. But other products are made from malt, such as malt extract and malt syrup. Malt extract is made by mixing water with the germinated grains and with ungerminated but cooked grains, such as wheat, rice, corn, or barley, converting their starches to sugars until a sweet syrup forms. Barley malt syrup was a popular sweetener before sugar and then corn syrup usurped the lead. Malt syrup is about 60% sugar (primarily maltose with some glucose). Dehydrated extracts and syrups are available and are used in home brewing.

What It Does • Barley is malted and fermented to make beer, malt liquor, whiskey, and malt vinegar. Barley malt syrup gets used primarily in baking, brewing, and distilling and to make breakfast cereals. One form, diastatic barley malt syrup, is added to bread doughs because it contains enzymes that help with leavening and creating a good crust. Another form, nondiastatic, doesn't contain active enzymes and is used to flavor pancakes and

Malted Buttermilk Pancakes

Most commercial pancake mixes get sweetness and slightly caramelized flavors from malted milk powder, a combination of malted barley, wheat flour, and dried milk. Look for malted milk powder near the cocoa powder in most supermarkets. It will give your homemade pancakes a taste reminiscent of diner pancakes.

2	large eggs	2
1¼ cups	buttermilk	300 mL
2 tsp	vanilla extract	10 mL
3 tbsp	melted butter	45 mL
1½ cups	all-purpose flour	375 mL
⅓ cup	malted milk powder	75 mL
2 tsp	baking powder	10 mL
¾ tsp	salt	4 mL
	Butter or oil for greasing	

1. In a large bowl, whisk together eggs, buttermilk, and vanilla until foamy, about 5 minutes (or a few minutes less with a hand mixer). Stir in butter.

2. In another bowl, whisk together flour, malted milk powder, baking powder, and salt. Quickly but gently mix into wet ingredients. Let batter rest for 5 to 10 minutes to help the buttermilk tenderize the gluten in the flour and allow small clumps of flour to dissolve.

3. Preheat griddle or a nonstick skillet to medium-high. When a drop of water dances then evaporates on surface, lightly grease with butter or oil. Drop ¼-cup (50 mL) dollops of batter onto griddle and cook until bottoms are golden brown and bubbles appear on surface, 2 to 4 minutes. Flip and cook until browned on other side. Repeat with remaining batter. Serve immediately.

MAKES ABOUT FIFTEEN
3-INCH (7.5 CM) PANCAKES

biscuits as well as malted milkshakes, malt balls (Whoppers), Ovaltine, and malted milk powder, a sweetener that also includes wheat flour and dried milk. It also is brushed onto traditional versions of Peking duck to help create a browned glaze.

How It Works • The grains are typically husked, then soaked in water and allowed to germinate at about 65°F (18°C) for five to nine days to "chit," or sprout roots and stems. Germinating grains increases their enzyme activity, and amylase enzymes hydrolyze the starch and convert about 10% of it to maltose (a sugar) and dextrins, both of which help to fuel the germinating embryo's growth and make the grain taste mildly sweet. Barley contains more amylase than most grains, so it is the most widely malted grain. The longer the grain is malted, the more sugars are formed.

When the desired amount of sugars has formed, the maltster (a professional malt maker) heats the malt to varying degrees of dryness and color. Low-temperature kilning (which peaks at about 180°F/82°C after about 24 hours) creates pale, less flavorful malts but keeps enzymes more active, which benefits fermentation in brewing and baking. Low-temperature kilned malt can be made into diastatic malt. Higher-temperature kilning (300 to 360°F/150 to 182°C) creates darker-colored, more flavorful malts with less enzyme activity. High-temperature malt can be made into nondiastatic malt. After kilning, the malt can be stored for months before it is milled into a powder. The more sugars in the starting malt, the more color and flavor in the final product.

In baking, milled malt is added to flour, where it provides sugar, and amylase enzymes to break down starches in the flour to simpler sugars, which provide food for yeast. Enzymes break down proteins into amino acids, too. The sugars and amino acids contribute to the browned crust on baked breads via Maillard browning. Malt is also hygroscopic (it attracts water) and so helps keep breads moist.

When malt is lightly roasted, it tastes mildly sweet and faintly of caramel. Darker roasting creates increasingly roasted, toasted, strong, and slightly bitter, smoky flavors.

See Also • Beer, Bread, Browning, Grains, Liquor, Sugar, Vinegar

MALTODEXTRINS • See Food Additives

MALTOSE • See Sugar

MAMEY SAPOTE • See Melon

MANCHEGO • See Cheese

MANDARIN ORANGE • See Citrus

MANGO

What It Is • For more than 6,000 years, the fruit of mango trees (*Mangifera indica*) has been cultivated in India. Mangoes are so integral to Indian culture that mango leaves and the white or pale yellow flowers are used as decoration in Indian religious ceremonies such as marriage. From India and Southeast Asia, the fruit traveled widely, and mango trees are now cultivated in warm climates as diverse as Brazil, Hawaii, Florida, Mexico, the West Indies, and California.

In the same botanical family as pistachios, cashews, and mahogany, mangoes come in more than 1,000 varieties. Their size and shape range from small round fruits weighing just 4 ounces (112 g) to large oblong fruits weighing upwards of 7 pounds (3 kg). The average mango hovers around half a pound (227 g). The most widely distributed variety in North America and the U.K. is the Tommy Atkins, a fibrous but colorful good-keeping mango related to the larger Hayden (or Haden) variety developed in south Florida in 1940. Highly prized Indian cultivars such as Kesar and Alphonso are increasingly available in North America. The Alphonso has been dubbed the "king of mangoes" for its velvety flesh and strong aroma redolent of almonds, coconuts, citrus, and vanilla.

What It Does • The flesh of unripe mangoes is green, then ripens to golden yellow and finally to blush red. The thin, fibrous skin starts out green, then ripens on the tree to yellow, orange, or red. After they're picked, mangoes continue to ripen from the inside out, becoming progressively sweeter, but they change very little in color. Ripe fruits will feel firm but not rock hard and exude a sweet, resinous scent. Mangoes are often kept at room temperature to fully ripen, but after

Fruit Rojak

In the Malay language, "rojak" means "mixture," an apt description for this highly variable Southeast Asian salad. Indonesian versions include green mango. Indian renditions add cuttlefish, fried tofu, cucumbers, and turnips. Singapore versions toss in apples, pineapples, and other fruits. You could add almost anything. It is a salad after all. Apart from the tart green mango, the most distinguishing feature of this salad is its spicy, sweet, sour, and salty sauce.

1 tbsp	dried shrimp paste (belacan) or 3 tbsp (45 mL) fish sauce (nam pla)	15 mL
3 tbsp	palm sugar or light brown sugar	45 mL
2 tbsp	kecap manis (or 1 tbsp/15 mL tamari + 1 tbsp/15 mL molasses)	25 mL
2 tbsp	tamarind paste	25 mL
1 to 2 tbsp	chili paste (sambal oelek)	15 to 25 mL
1 cup	bite-size chunks of peeled green mango	250 mL
1 cup	bite-size chunks of peeled jicama	250 mL
1 cup	bite-size chunks of peeled, seeded cucumber	250 mL
1 cup	bite-size chunks of peeled pineapple	250 mL
1 cup	bite-size chunks of peeled tart apple	250 mL
½ cup	roasted peanuts, chopped	125 mL

1. In a small saucepan over medium-low heat, crumble shrimp paste and toast until fragrant, 2 to 4 minutes. If using fish sauce, simply add to pan.
2. Stir in 3 tbsp (45 mL) water, sugar, kecap, tamarind paste, and 1 tbsp (15 mL) chili paste (use 2 tbsp/25 mL if you want it extra spicy). Simmer over medium heat until sauce becomes a medium-thick syrup, 3 to 5 minutes. Let cool to room temperature, which will thicken it a bit further.
3. Place fruit in a large bowl. Pour mixture over fruit and toss gently. Top with chopped peanuts.

MAKES 4 SERVINGS

ripening, the fruits can be refrigerated like vegetables to extend their shelf life by about a week. Overripe mangoes have loose or wrinkled skin and smell sour or alcoholic.

Unripe green mangoes are twice as acidic as lemons and are used in Indian, Thai, and Malaysian cooking as a souring agent. In India, unripe mangoes are often mixed with chiles, vinegar, and spices to make a spicy mango pickle condiment. Elsewhere in Southeast Asia, green mangoes are pickled with fish sauce and rice vinegar. They're so popular that green mangoes are frequently dried and powdered to make sour-tasting amchur (amchoor), a spice commonly sold in North America as "mango powder," which provides an acidic bite to marinades, curries, chutneys, and soups. Green mango powder often turns up in marinades or as a meat tenderizer because, like papaya, it contains protein-digesting **enzymes** that break down tough connective tissue.

Ripe mangoes become nearly half as sour and develop sweet, rich juices with highly aromatic flavors. The most lush varieties are wonderfully messy to eat, with a luxuriously dripping texture like liquefied crushed velvet, which inspired the American author and cooking teacher James Beard to write that "to most enjoy a mango one should probably eat it in a bathtub, or at the very least in private." Ripe fruits are often enjoyed fresh in salads and salsas or puréed to make drinks, sauces, and desserts. In Mexico, ripe mangoes are eaten simply with a pinch of ground chiles and salt and are also cooked into salsas and chutneys. In India, mangoes turn up in everything from cereal to candies to condiments. Ripe fruits are available whole, puréed, or as nectar (a diluted purée), juice, and either fresh, frozen, or canned in syrup. They're also sold in dried pieces (*amavat*) that are chewed as is or rehydrated and incorporated into dishes.

About 60% of the fresh mangoes sold in North America come from Mexico and South Asia, but more expensive and fine-grained

Indian mangoes are increasingly available. Most mangoes on the market have been dipped in hot water to kill pests. Some fruits are now being gently irradiated, a less expensive process that delays ripening and prolongs shelf life.

To remove mango flesh from its large, flat seed, curve a knife blade around the side of the seed to cut the mango in half. Cut the seed away from the flesh. Cut the flesh in a crosshatch pattern, then push on the skin to turn the mango inside out. Cut away the cubes of flesh. If the mangoes will be puréed, you can peel and seed them like you would bell peppers. Roast or grill them until the skin becomes black all over, then seal the mangoes in a paper bag until cool enough to handle. The skin will peel off easily and the softened flesh and juice can be squeezed away from the seed.

How It Works •
Ripe, sweet mangoes contain about 14% sugar and 0.5% acid by weight. They are rich in vitamins A, C, and D as well as enzymes like magneferin and lactase that may improve digestion and intestinal health. The spicy-sweet, musky flavor of mangoes comes from more than 35 **flavor compounds** such as sulfur compounds, lactones (which provide peach and coconut aromas), and terpenes (which give mangoes their resinous, kerosene-like sharpness). Mangoes get their orange color from beta-carotene and other carotenoid pigments.

fast facts

- The U.S. market opened as exporters took advantage of a 2006 U.S. Department of Agriculture ruling that irradiation could be used to sterilize insects such as the mango seed weevil.
- Mangoes contain urushiol, a toxic phenolic compound found just under the skin. It is the same skin-irritating oil found in poison ivy, poison oak, poison sumac, and the shells of cashews, though in much lower concentration. For people sensitive to urushiol, mangoes can cause an itchy rash wherever they contact the skin. Avoid using mango wood as a cooking wood for the same reason.

See Also • Fruit

MANGOSTEEN • See Fruit

MANIOC • See Cassava

MANNITOL • See Sweeteners

MAPLE SYRUP

What It Is •
Europeans who came to North America learned about maple syrup from the Native Americans. In the late 1700s, American abolitionists who opposed the use of cane sugar produced by slaves sweetened their foods with maple syrup instead. Maple syrup comes from the sap of rock or sugar maple (*Acer saccharum*) and black maple (*A. nigrum*) trees, which are native to Canada and the northeastern U.S. and yielded the primary sweetener in the Native American diet. Boiling the sap evaporates water and concentrates it into a syrup, often labeled "100% pure maple syrup." Continued boiling evaporates more water and creates maple honey (aka maple molasses), and when nearly all of the water is boiled off, the concentrated syrup can be beaten and cooled to make maple cream. If it concentrates further, what remains is maple sugar, which is almost entirely sucrose, the same sugar in cane sugar.

Table syrup (aka pancake syrup) is a thicker, stickier, less expensive concoction of high-fructose corn syrup flavored with a small amount of pure maple syrup, maple extract, or sotolon, an aroma compound that in low concentrations is reminiscent of maple syrup. In the U.S., products must contain at least 2% pure maple syrup for the words "maple syrup" to be used on the label. In Quebec, imitation maple syrups made with corn syrup are jokingly called pole syrups because they are so different from pure maple syrup, they might as well have been produced by tapping telephone poles.

What It Does •
Beginning around mid-February, sugar and black maple trees flow with clear, thin sap. The "sugaring" season continues through April, and each tree produces an average of 12 gallons

fast facts

- Canada produces 85% of the world's maple syrup, and Quebec produces 90% of the syrup in Canada, accounting for about three-quarters of the world's average annual production of 6 million gallons (22.7 million liters). No wonder the maple leaf is a symbol of Canada.
- In the days before maple sap was boiled down to syrup, it was left out in the cold to freeze. The water would separate from maple sugar and freeze on top. The frozen water was removed, leaving behind concentrated maple sugar.

(45 L) of sap per season. The sap is taken directly from mature trees by driving metal, wooden, or plastic taps about 1 inch (2.5 cm) into the trunk. Tapping maple trees doesn't significantly harm the tree because it removes only about 10% of the tree's sap. The sap contains an average of 2% sugar and 98% water, which is then boiled off in sugarhouses to concentrate the sugar to about 65%. At the beginning of the season, the sap is more concentrated in sugar (about 3%); at the end of the season, the sap is lower in sugar (about 1%). Early in the sugar season, it takes only about

Maple Grades

Maple syrup is graded in Canada and the U.S. on flavor and color. Color is determined by comparison to colored glass standards or by measuring the transmittance of light. The more light transmittted through the syrup, the higher the grade. The highest grades tend to be taken early in the sugaring season, when the sugar content is highest and the sap is lightest in color. Lower grades are taken later in the season, when the sap is darkest, is lowest in sugar, and has a more bitter flavor. Vermont syrups tend to be slightly thicker because of higher sugar requirements.

Percentage of Light Transmitted	Canadian Label	U.S. Label	Flavor
75+	No. 1 Extra Light	Grade A Light Amber ("Fancy" in Vermont)	Delicate
61 to 74	No. 1 Light	Grade A Medium Amber	Gentle
44 to 60	No. 1 Medium	Grade A Dark Amber	Mild
27 to 43	No. 2 Amber	Grade B	Rich
Less than 26	No. 3 Dark	Grade C Commercial/ Industrial	Assertive

20 gallons (76 L) of sap to make 1 gallon (4 L) of syrup. Near the end of the season, it may take 50 gallons (190 L), and the resulting syrup develops a stronger flavor from longer boiling. Maple sugar is even more time consuming to produce, as it takes 8 gallons (30 L) of maple syrup to produce 1 pound (454 g) of maple sugar. The manual tapping and extensive boiling make pure maple syrup and maple sugar some of the most expensive sweeteners on the market.

Maple syrup preferences are similar to wine preferences (do you like white or red?). But, in general, Grade A Light and Medium Amber (No. 1 Extra Light and Light in Canada) syrups are best enjoyed uncooked on cereals, pancakes, waffles, French toast, biscuits, croissants, and cornbread and in ice cream and other dishes where maple is the sole or primary sweet flavor that you want to taste. Grade A Dark Amber (No. 1 Medium) syrup is slightly less delicate in flavor and suitable for sweetening baked beans, candying sweet potatoes, and glazing ham, pork, chicken, and salmon. Grade B (No. 2 Amber) has a more robust flavor that's best in breads and for sweetening other cooked dishes. Less delicate grades of maple syrup are also used to feed yeast in brewing. Grade C (No. 3 Dark) is generally unavailable to consumers and sometimes labeled "Industrial" because its strongly assertive aromas are used to flavor such things as tobacco.

Pure maple syrup is best stored in a refrigerator, where it will last for up to one year. Over prolonged storage, maple syrup sometimes develops a thin layer of harmless mold. You can simply scoop it off with a spoon or strain it out, then bring the syrup to a boil and store it in a clean jar or bottle. For the most pronounced maple flavor, warm maple syrup or bring it to room temperature before pouring on dishes like pancakes and waffles.

How It Works • Trees use their sugary sap for growth. Maple trees produce sweeter sap than any other tree because they are the most efficient at driving stored sugars from their trunks into the upper and outer parts of the tree each spring for growth. The sap can be simply boiled to evaporate water and concentrate the sugar, but heating also evaporates some volatile flavor compounds. For the most flavor, modern syrup producers first remove up to 80% of the water without heat using reverse osmosis technology, then quickly boil the sap until it reaches about 220°F (104°C), or 66% sugar concentration for syrup. Continued boiling to 240 to 250°F (116 to 120°C) brings the sugar concentration up to 86 to 90%, which creates crystals of moist maple sugar when cooled. To make maple cream and maple butter, the concentrated syrup is beaten and quickly cooled to about 70°F (21°C) in ice baths, then gradually reheated until it can be stirred smooth.

Maple syrup gets its sweetness from sucrose. It also has a hint of sourness from about 0.5% acids such as malic acid. Vanillin provides floral vanilla aromas, while caramel aromas come from Maillard

browning reactions that occur during boiling. Maple syrup is such an important product in Canada that researchers divide maple syrup flavors into 13 families, 39 subfamilies, and 91 flavor attributes with descriptions ranging from brown sugar and banana to sawdust and hay.

See Also • Candy, Sugar

MARBLING • See Meat

MARC • See Liquor

MARGARINE • See Fat

MARINADE

What It Is • The word "marinade" (from the Latin *marinus* meaning "of the sea") dates back to the 1600s, when **meat** or **fish** were cured in seawater to help preserve them. Today, marinades are seasoned liquids used primarily to flavor food. To help soften foods for better flavor absorption, marinades are usually somewhat acidic like vinaigrettes, many of which can double as marinades. Common **acids** in marinades include vinegar, citrus juice, pineapple juice, papaya or mango nectar or powder, tomato juice, wine, buttermilk, and yogurt. Aromatic ingredients run the gamut from onions, garlic, and ginger to chile peppers, herbs, and spices. Oil is usually included to provide additional moisture and flavor.

What It Does • Both marinades and **brines** are liquid flavoring agents. But brines add flavor and moisture to food well below the surface (through the action of salt), while marinades penetrate less than ¼ inch (0.5 cm) deep in most meats through the action of acid. Food can be soaked in marinade, or the marinade can be injected into the food. Either way, the marinade penetrates the food only a fraction of an inch from the point of contact. For this reason, marinades are not terribly effective at tenderizing food. Increasing the acid or

How Long to Marinate

Marinating times can be as short as 15 minutes or as long as several days. The appropriate time depends on the texture of the food being marinated, the size and shape of the food, the acidity and strength of the marinade, and the desired result. Mildly flavored, weakly acidic marinades are best for vegetables, seafood, and delicate meats like veal. Tougher, more strongly flavored beef and game can handle more assertive, acidic marinades.

Here's a general guide based on a medium-strength marinade of 1 part vinegar to 3 parts oil or 1 part citrus juice to 2 parts oil, about the same as a classic vinaigrette. The shortest times given below are enough to impart flavor and a little softening or tenderizing. The longest times are for tougher cuts that need more time to become even slightly more tender. If your food has finished marinating but you're not ready to cook it, remove it from the marinade, wrap it tightly, and refrigerate it until you are ready.

Food	Approximate Marinating Time
Small seafood and thin fish	15 to 30 minutes
Large seafood and thick fish	30 minutes to 1 hour
Poultry parts, skinless	1 to 3 hours
Poultry parts, skin on	4 to 6 hours
Chops and steaks	4 to 8 hours
Roasts	6 to 12 hours

the marinating time makes the food taste more astringent but does not make it much more tender. Some marinades get additional tenderizing power from enzymes such as those in papaya, pineapple, and kiwi, which digest protein and make the food softer. But the most sure-fire way to get tender meat is to buy tender meat or to cook tough cuts with low heat for a long time (until tender) as in **barbecuing**.

When marinating foods for longer than 30 minutes (especially raw meats), marinate in the refrigerator to inhibit the growth of microbes. Resealable plastic bags do the best job of enveloping food with marinating liquid. Glass, ceramic, and stainless steel are also safe marinating vessels. Avoid marinating in reactive metals like cast iron and aluminum because the acid in the marinade will leach metal ions into the marinade and food, creating off flavors and sometimes discoloration. After marinating, most marinades are discarded because they can contain harmful microorganisms from raw food. If you want to use some of the marinade for basting or as a sauce, either set some fresh marinade aside before adding the food to the rest, or boil the used marinade for 5 minutes to kill microorganisms before using it again. Keep in mind that many marinades are too salty to reduce down to a sauce.

How It Works • Marinades provide very little tenderizing or moisturizing for tough meats because they work only about $\frac{1}{8}$ to $\frac{1}{4}$ inch (0.25 to 0.5 cm) in from where the marinade contacts the food. However, within this penetration area, the acid and oil in marinades have multiple effects. The acid gradually denatures, or breaks down, the food's proteins, softening this shallow area of the food and allowing it to absorb and retain more moisture and flavor. Salt in a marinade has a similar effect. As a result of acid and salt, marinated foods taste more flavorful and slightly juicier when cooked. When raw foods are marinated for a long time, so much softening can occur that the food's texture becomes unpleasantly mushy or mealy and the taste increasingly sour.

kitchen wisdom

Faster Marinating
It appears that vacuum marinators don't speed up marinating time or absorption as advertised. A 2003 U.S. Department of Agriculture study of vacuum-marinated chicken breasts found that the vacuum did cause about 10% more marinade to be absorbed by the chicken, but that small increase was lost during cooking. Mechanical tumblers can help soften food fibers so that marinade is absorbed more easily, but the most effective way to speed up marinating time is to cut meat into smaller, flatter pieces or strips or to inject marinade deep into the interior of meat in several places. That way, the marinade contacts a greater surface area of meat and flavors a greater portion of it.

Eventually, acidic marinades will denature and then coagulate proteins much the way heat does and cause raw foods like fish and shellfish to look opaque, firm, and cooked, as in seviche.

The oil in a marinade carries flavor to the food. Most flavor compounds are fat soluble rather than water soluble, so without oil, a marinade won't be as effective at flavoring food. Oil also provides moisturizing fat to foods like lean cuts of meat and vegetables. However, oil and water don't mix, so oil-based marinades penetrate less deeply into foods (which consist primarily of water) than acid-based marinades. For better and faster flavor penetration, use oils that contain monoacylglycerols (monoglycerides), such as virgin olive oil, or oils that contain emulsifiers, because these oils mix more easily with water.

The flavor in a marinade comes primarily from aromatics such as onions, garlic, ginger, herbs, and spices as well as from flavored liquids like wine and citrus juice. Most often raw foods are marinated, but some foods are marinated after cooking to give them additional flavor, such as escabèche (a dish of poached or fried fish).

See Also • Acid, Brining, Meat

MARJORAM • See Herbs

MARMALADE • See Jam and Jelly

MARROW • See Bones

MARSALA • See Wine

MARSHMALLOW • See Candy

MARZIPAN • See Candy

MASA • See Corn

MASCARPONE • See Cheese

MATZOH • See Bread

MAYONNAISE • See Emulsion

MEAT

What It Is • Meat is essentially everything that's edible on an animal except skin and bone. This includes **organ meats** and muscle meats from **beef**, **pork**, **lamb**, **chicken**, turkey, and other **poultry**, as well as **game**. Technically, the flesh of **fish** and shellfish can also be considered meat, but their muscles are structured somewhat differently than the muscles of land animals, which is the subject of this entry.

What It Does • Meat forms an integral part of the diet in many cultures around the world. Its texture and flavor is determined by genetics, the animal's diet and activity level, how it was slaughtered, what part of the animal the meat came from, how long the meat was aged (and whether it was dry-aged or wet-aged), how it was stored and, of course, how the meat was flavored and cooked.

Meat Production and Aging

Most of our food animals are fed a diet of grain. Since the 1950s, almost all animals raised for meat in North America develop at least 30% of their weight in large feedlots 100 to 200 days before slaughter. This allows meat producers to standardize flavor (with a consistent diet) and to encourage tenderness (by discouraging exercise). Feedlots also shorten the time to market by maximizing calorie intake and minimizing energy expenditure.

In other parts of the world, raising an animal completely on grass is more common. Pasture-fed Argentinean beef is world famous, and grass feeding has gained popularity in England since the outbreak of **mad cow disease**. But in North America, the movement against grain feeding is still small. Although ruminants like cattle, goats, sheep, bison, and deer have evolved to survive solely on grass, most North American cattle are grazed on grass for less than a year, then fed grain for the rest of their lives. The opponents of this system argue that letting an animal feed on grass for its whole life gives the meat a more complex flavor, a sweeter aroma, and a meatier texture. But grass feed is much more difficult to standardize than grain feed, and although steak from a grass-fed steer can be excellent, grass-fed beef can be inconsistent in quality. Nonetheless, current demand for grass-fed beef surpasses supply. Meat producers may eventually find it more profitable to become grass growers rather than grain growers, in which case grass-fed meat could follow the path of organic produce and go from inconsistent and scarce to quality-driven and mainstream.

Organic meat is not necessarily grass fed. According to U.S. organic standards, animals that produce certified organic meat can be fed on grain in feedlots but for no more than 200 days. They cannot be given antibiotics or growth hormones, must be given access to pasture if the animals are ruminants, and must be fed exclusively 100% organic feed, whether grass or grain (vitamin and mineral supplements are allowed). Canadian regulations are similar and also specify that animals must be raised in conditions that mimic nature as much as possible.

Animals were once hunted, slaughtered, and eaten within the span of hours, but slaughtering techniques have evolved to produce the best-tasting meat. Fortunately, these techniques are also the most humane and put the least amount of stress on the animal. Animals store a small amount of **glycogen** (animal starch) in their muscle fiber, to use for quick bursts of energy, especially when an animal feels threatened. If an animal senses danger just before slaughter, it responds with fear, and its glycogen stores will be used up. Muscle cells continue to live after an animal has been killed, deriving energy from any glycogen that is present. One of the by-products of the metabolism of available glycogen is lactic acid, which reduces the activities of enzymes in muscle tissue, slows the growth of microbes that cause spoilage, and causes some moisture to migrate from within the cells out to the surface of the meat, giving it a moist appearance. If the glycogen is depleted, the accumulation of lactic acid never occurs, and the result, known as dark-cutting meat, will be dry, tough, dark colored, and easily spoiled.

To avoid "dark cutting" meat, each animal is surreptitiously stunned, usually with an electric charge to the head. Then the animal is hung by its legs, the major veins in the neck are opened, and the animal is drained of about half its blood, which decreases the risk of spoilage. After bleeding, the hide is stripped, the carcass is opened, the organs are removed, and the carcass and organs are chilled.

Within an hour or two of slaughter, the muscles clench in rigor mortis. If cut and cooked before that time, the meat will be tender, but once rigor mortis starts, the meat cannot be handled until the rigor passes, about 24 hours.

Hanging the carcass stretches the muscles to their maximum length at the time rigor mortis occurs, preventing the muscle filaments from bonding and the meat toughening. Protein-digesting enzymes continue to soften the muscle structure, and the meat texture relaxes. At this point, the carcass can be sectioned and sold as half, quarter, or primal cuts (see Land Animal Primal Cuts illustration, page 384).

Although most meat is only incidentally "wet-aged" in vacuum-packed plastic for the few days it takes to ship it from the packing plant to the butcher's counter, a small amount of high-quality beef is dry-aged for a month or more (see Aged Beef, page 48).

Land Animal Primal Cuts

Whether you're buying beef, veal, pork, or lamb, tough, flavorful cuts come from areas that move or support the body such as the shoulders, chest, legs and thighs. Tender, mild cuts come from muscle groups that get the least amount of exercise, such as those along the center of the back, the ribs, and the area between the ribs and the hips (loin). Here's how it looks on beef, but the basic parts are similar for all land animals.

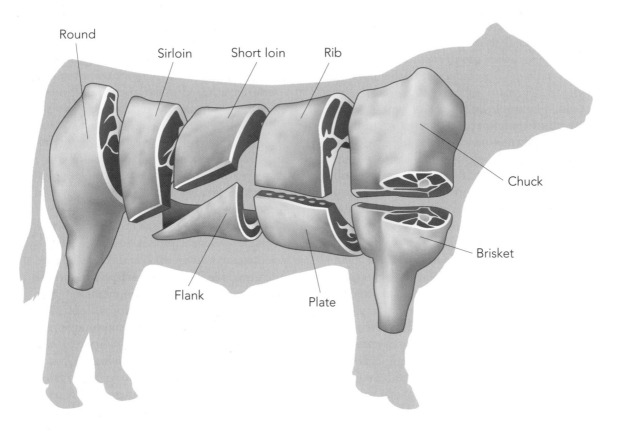

Round Sirloin Short loin Rib Chuck Brisket Flank Plate

Meat Grades, Tenderness, and Toughness

In the U.S., the meat slaughtering process undergoes mandatory inspection for sanitary handling and wholesomeness. Over 80% of the meat is also graded by the U.S. Department of Agriculture (USDA). Meat grading identifies quality but not the safety of the meat. Whether a meat producer decides to have a carcass graded or not is purely voluntary. Although any animal can be graded, beef is graded most often, followed by pork. Ironically, the qualities that many consumers say they want in their meat (less fat and more lean) are the reverse of the criteria used by the grading system.

The amount of marbling, the webbing of fat deep within the lean muscle of well-fed animals, is the primary feature that determines a high-quality grade. Other criteria, such as the age of the animal and its musculature, are considered, but they have less effect on the flavor and texture of the meat and they are given less weight in determining the final grade. (See **Beef**, page 47, for grades.)

Meat flavor and texture are also determined by exercise. As a muscle is exercised, its fibers expand, making the muscle larger, redder, and more flavorful. At the same time, its connective tissue thickens and becomes more elastic, which makes the muscle harder and tougher. Large, tough muscle fibers will make the surface of a piece of tough meat look rough, like terrycloth. On the other hand, small, undeveloped fibers are barely visible, giving tender meat a sleek, silken appearance. The thickness of the connective tissue surrounding the fibers magnifies such differences.

Tougher meat from older animals tastes more flavorful, whereas tender meat from younger animals tastes comparatively mild. All land animals have a similar muscle structure, so tough and tender meat lie in the same areas on cattle, pigs, and sheep (see Beef Primal Cuts illustration, left). In chicken and turkey, the breast meat is more tender than the legs because the breast gets less exercise.

Tenderness and toughness also tell you which cooking methods are best. As the meat cooks, the protein in the fibers becomes more firm and opaque. Then the collagen of the connective tissue turns into gelatin as it beats with moisture. Tender, lean meats with less connective tissue don't need moist-heat cooking; they are best cooked with dry-heat cooking methods that are fairly quick, such as **grilling**, broiling, and **frying**. Tough, fatty meats, on the other hand, need liquid to turn their connective-tissue collagen into gelatin and are best cooked by slower moist-heat methods such as stewing, **braising**, and **barbecuing**.

Pounding, Grinding, Marinating, and Brining

Texture and flavor of meat can be influenced before cooking by pounding, grinding, **brining**, using a **marinade**, adding tenderizing **enzymes**, larding with fat, or barding with **bacon**.

Pounding can make meat more tender, but more importantly, it makes the meat thinner so that it cooks quickly through to the center before the meat dries out and toughens. Quick cooking is essential because breaking the cells releases moisture.

Grinding is another way of tenderizing meat because it cuts the muscle fibers and connective tissue, so the meat has the flavor of a well-exercised muscle with none of its toughness. That's why tough cuts like chuck, sirloin, and round are ground most often. But grinding also destroys the structural integrity of muscle fibers, and most of the natural moisture they once held is free to drain away. The small amount that remains evaporates quickly during cooking. Once the moisture is gone, the perception of juiciness depends on the meat's fat content, which is why ground

beef with a fat content of less than 10% becomes unpalatably dry when cooked, while ground beef with more than 20% fat tastes full-flavored and mouth filling.

Marinating meat adds flavor and helps it retain some moisture but tenderizes only minimally and only about ⅛ to ¼ inch (0.25 to 0.5 cm) into the surface where the marinade contacts the meat. Brining can increase the moisture content of meats by as much as 10%. Both brines and marinades containing papaya, pineapple, kiwi, figs, and ginger have enzymes that hydrolyze the protein in meat, making the muscle fibers more tender. However, most of the tenderizing takes place during cooking, when the meat temperature reaches between 140 and 160°F (60 and 71°C). So it's most effective to inject tenderizing enzymes into meat, where they will remain during cooking. Commercial meat tenderizers are usually sold in powdered form and contain sugar, salt, and calcium stearate to prevent caking. The most common meat tenderizer is made with an extract of papaya containing the papain.

The most direct route to flavor is a spice rub or herb paste, because the flavoring agent is never removed from the meat. Seasoning meat with salt and spices before cooking also draws a small amount of meat juices to the surface, where they brown and create intense flavors. You can use any combination of tenderizing, moisturizing, and flavoring techniques, such as brining with meat tenderizers for juiciness and tenderness as well as using a spice rub for flavor.

Preserving Meat

Today, most carcasses are broken down into retail cuts right at the meatpacking plant, vacuum-packed, then shipped to supermarkets ready for sale. Vacuum-packing seals out oxygen and prolongs the shelf life of meat up to three months for beef and two months for pork and lamb.

To prolong meat's shelf life, keep it away from oxygen and light, both of which speed the breakdown of fat and cause rancidity. Block out oxygen by wrapping meat tightly in oxygen-impermeable plastic wrap (such as Saran Wrap) or use a vacuum sealer if you have one. After wrapping or vacuum-sealing in plastic, block out light by wrapping the meat again in butcher paper or foil. To reduce enzyme activity, store meat in the coldest part of the refrigerator. Refrigerated meat keeps best just above the freezing point of water (between 32 and 38°F/0 and 3°C). Meats high in unsaturated fats go rancid the fastest, so fish and poultry are the most perishable. Meats high in saturated fats last the longest, so beef keeps a bit better. Ground meat is highly perishable (especially if the meat is high in unsaturated fats) because grinding exposes more surface area to oxygen and light, so use as soon as possible. Or keep retail cuts in your own kitchen and grind them just before using.

Meat can be frozen at about 0°F (–18°C) for months or even years because freezing reduces biological activity to almost zero, but ultimately it makes it drier and less flavorful. As liquid water inside the meat freezes, it forms sharp-edged crystals and expands and punctures the meat cells. As the ice crystals melt during thawing, they open up the holes they created and allow meat juices to readily escape, resulting in dry meat. To minimize dryness, keep the ice crystals as small as possible by freezing meat quickly and at the lowest possible temperature. Quick freezing forms small ice crystals, which make smaller holes, whereas slow freezing forms large ice crystals that make bigger holes. Set your freezer to its coldest temperature and put unwrapped pieces of meat in the freezer on a rimmed baking sheet so they will chill quickly. When thoroughly frozen, double-wrap meat pieces in plastic and paper or foil as described on page 385 to block out oxygen and light.

Despite the best freezing techniques, frozen meat will still suffer from dryness and flavor loss. That's because when the moisture in meat freezes, it leaves behind the salts and metals in the muscle cells, creating a higher concentration of salts and metals in the meat, which in turn causes fats to turn rancid more rapidly. For the best-tasting frozen meat, use it as soon as possible.

Freezer burn, the whitish discoloration that forms on the surface of frozen meat, is a sign of freeze-drying. It happens when ice crystals on the surface of meat evaporate. Those evaporated crystals leave behind the little holes they created, giving freezer-burned meat a disagreeable spongy texture. If the freezer door is frequently opened, the holes also let in light, which causes the meat to appear white. It also lets in oxygen, which speeds the deterioration of fat and the development of rancid flavors.

The fastest way to safely thaw meat is in an ice bath. Water transfers heat about 20 times faster than air, so an ice bath will warm up a piece of meat faster than the air of a refrigerator will. Thawing wrapped meat in ice water is safe because it keeps the meat surface cold enough to prevent microbial growth as the meat interior thaws. You can also safely thaw meat in the refrigerator. It just takes more time (up to several days for a large roast). You can also cook unthawed meat with slow, low-heat cooking methods like slow-roasting so that the meat surface doesn't overcook before the center thaws and cooks through.

Before the days of widespread refrigeration and freezing, meat was preserved in other ways. It can be made into **confit** or preserved by **canning**, **drying**, **curing**, or **fermentation** in **sausages**. The flavor of meat can also be extracted by simmering meat to make stocks. Commercial meat extracts are made by evaporating moisture from stock in varying degrees to make liquid, gelatinous, or solid pieces of extract or bouillon.

Meat and Health

Meat has remained an important part of the human diet around the world in part because it has a complex flavor that we enjoy and because it's a more concentrated source of energy-supplying calories and growth-fueling protein than plants, but most nutrition experts agree that a well-planned meat-free diet can satisfy all human nutritional requirements. Vegetarian diets usually include alternative sources of B vitamins (such as vitamin B_{12}) and iron, which are found in especially high concentrations in meat.

Global meat consumption is expected to rise by about 2% a year, according to the United Nations, even though since the

Meat Composition: Protein, Fat, and Water

How Cooking Forces Moisture from Meat

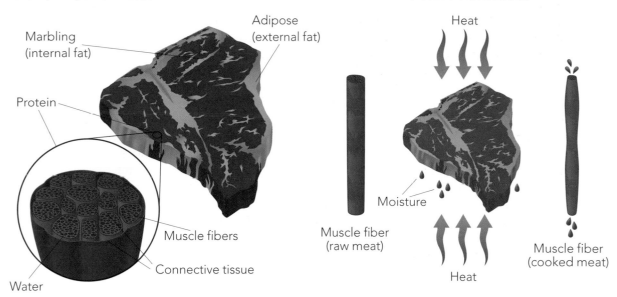

Marbling (internal fat)

Adipose (external fat)

Protein

Muscle fibers

Connective tissue

Water

Heat

Muscle fiber (raw meat)

Moisture

Muscle fiber (cooked meat)

Heat

mid- to late 1900s, excessive meat consumption has been linked to increased risk for heart disease and cancer. Apart from its protein, vitamins, and minerals, meat consists primarily of fat and water. Meat contains more saturated fat than plants do, and numerous studies show that diets high in saturated fat from meat may lead to increased heart disease risk. To lower your saturated fat consumption from meat, focus on meats higher in unsaturated fats, like fish and poultry. Game meat also tends to be less fatty because the animals get more exercise. Also, keep in mind that larger, longer-lived animals develop the most fat.

The USDA's Dietary Guidelines for Americans and Canada's Food Guide agree that eating about 5 ounces (142 g) of lean meat per day constitutes healthy adult meat consumption. However, excessive meat consumption not only displaces the vegetables and fruits linked to preventing heart disease and cancer, but when meat is prepared and cooked, potential **carcinogens** such as heterocyclic amines, polycyclic aromatic hydrocarbons, and nitrosamines are created. Meat's density of calories can also be a contributing factor to obesity and associated diseases like heart disease and Type 2 diabetes.

Mass production of meat has raised other concerns. The typical feedlot operation houses about 32,000 cattle or 100,000 chickens and contributes significantly to excess greenhouse gases and surplus nitrogen and phosphorus in rivers and lakes from waste runoff. Crowded facilities also invite the spread of such **bacteria** as *E. coli* and *Salmonella* among animals, and these sources of food-borne illness are increasingly common on mass-produced meats. Bacteria are only on the surface of meat, so when trimmed away just before serving, raw meat dishes like steak tartare and carpaccio can be safe. For the same reason, meat that is well browned on the surface but left rare in the center can be safely served. Grinding meat, on the other hand, spreads bacteria from surfaces throughout the entire mass of meat and can contaminate huge batches of meat that are mixed together.

To help prevent the spread of bacteria and to manipulate growth, most food animals are routinely given **antibiotics** and **hormones**, which has led to a sharp rise in antibiotic-resistant bacteria such as *Campylobacter*, which is now the most common source of food-borne illness. Knives, cutting boards, and work surfaces should be kept scrupulously clean of raw meat juices to avoid cross-contaminating other foods.

How It Works • Muscle meats have three main components: **protein**, **fat**, and **water**. The protein in muscle fibers consists primarily of myosin and actin. These are the proteins that cause the muscles to contract and allow animals to move. Myosin and actin are arranged in long, thin fibers (each less than 0.1 mm in diameter) that form the grain of the muscle. Think of muscle fibers as the logs that form the walls of a log cabin. What holds the "logs" or fibers together is a kind of mortar around and between the muscle fibers known as connective tissue (see illustration, page 387), a transparent protein that provides structure in meat.

For cooks, the most important component of connective tissue is collagen, which constitutes a little over 30% of the protein in animals and concentrates in the skin, tendons, and bones that accompany the muscles. When heated with water, collagen denatures into **gelatin**, a substance that gives meats, especially slow-cooked pot roasts and barbecued meats, a rich, unctuous texture. Young animals like veal have more collagen than older animals like beef. Cutting across the grain bisects the rows of muscle fibers and connective tissue, making the meat easier for our teeth to chew.

Fat supplies energy to muscles and helps them function and contains twice as many calories as the carbohydrates that plants use for energy. Animals store fat just under their skin, in body cavities that house their major organs, and throughout their muscles, where it is known as marbling. The bulk of fat is held in specialized cells called adipocytes, which are concentrated under the skin and around the outside of muscle groups. When an animal eats to excess, the adipocytes eventually become filled, and the overflow fat is rerouted directly into the organs and muscles themselves, causing the muscles to become marbled and soft.

Adipose fat is often trimmed away during butchering and has little culinary benefit. Only marbling, the barely visible veins of fat webbed throughout the lean parts of meat, significantly affects palatability. Marbling makes meat more tender, more flavorful, and perceptibly moister. It stretches the connective tissue into thin sheets so is more likely to soften during cooking. Marbling also isolates one muscle fiber from another, helping them to separate into tiny, easily chewed packets. It heightens flavor by carrying fat-soluble flavor compounds, and heightens the perception of juiciness when it melts.

Choose meat with a minimum of exterior adipose fat (about ¼ to ½ inch/0.5 to 1 cm) but a good degree of marbling. It isn't necessary to have large globs of marbled fat striated through the lean protein, but neither should you seek out fat-free pieces of meat. If fat and cholesterol are dietary concerns, the best option is to limit your quantity of meat rather than sacrificing the quality.

Water constitutes up to 70% of the weight in some meats. Held within the protein of muscle fibers, water is what makes meat taste juicy. Along with tenderness, juiciness is one of the most sought-after qualities in meat. Water remains in meat as long as the muscle fibers stay intact. But it begins to flow out of the fibers during cooking. The ratio of water to protein is what makes some meats juicy and others dry. For instance, pork has a very low ratio of water to protein, which means it dries out easily during cooking. Beef, on the other hand, has a relatively high ratio of water to protein, so it takes longer for beef to dry out during cooking. The low moisture content of pork makes it difficult to grill a juicy pork chop, but it also makes pork a good candidate for curing and smoking, because it dehydrates easily and develops very concentrated flavors. The chart on the left shows the percentages of water and protein in common meats.

Percentages of Water and Protein in Meat

Meat	Percentage of Water	Percentage of Protein
Fish	70	20
Chicken	65	30
Lamb	62	28
Beef	60	18
Turkey	58	20
Pork	52	29

fast facts

- Global meat consumption is growing by about 2% a year, according to the United Nations Food and Agriculture Organization (FAO), and the U.S. is leading the way. According to the USDA, each American ate an average of 200 pounds (91 kg) of meat (red meat, poultry, and fish) in 2005. That's 22 pounds (10 kg) more meat per person than in 1970. Since that time, annual poultry consumption has increased by about 40 pounds (18 kg) per person, and fish consumption has increased by about 4 pounds (2 kg) per person, but red meat consumption (primarily beef) has declined by about 17 pounds (8 kg) per person.
- It takes about 8 pounds (4 kg) of grain to produce 1 pound (454 g) of beef. According to the USDA, animals raised for meat consume about 70% of the U.S. grain crop, 80% of the corn crop, and 90% of the soy crop. Growing crops for meat animals also uses about half of the nation's water supply and 80% of its agricultural land.

When Meat Cooks

As meat cooks, it becomes increasingly firm and dry, and protein in the muscle fibers coagulates and toughens. When meat reaches temperatures between 100 and 110°F (38 and 43°C), the water held in its muscle fibers begins to flow and accumulate in the muscle cells. Fat begins to melt and coat the muscle fibers. Less saturated fats melt first, and the most saturated fats, like those in beef, begin melting between 110 and 115°F (43 and 46°C). Meat cooked to this stage (between 110 and 120°F/43 and 50°C) is called blue because when you cut it, you can still see the purple-blue color of the meat pigments before they turn red from exposure to oxygen. It is cooked only at the surface, is purple-red and barely warm at the center, and feels very soft to the touch.

As the meat continues to cook and reaches temperatures between 120 and 130°F (50 and 54°C), actomyosin protein in the muscle fibers denatures, or breaks down, then coagulates back together and makes the meat somewhat opaque in appearance and slightly firm in texture. Water accumulates more rapidly in the muscle cells, and fat continues to melt. Served at this temperature, meat is called rare, is warm at the center, and gives only very slight resistance to the touch. Rare meat has the maximum amount of flowing red juices (from meat pigments, not from blood) and flavor.

Between 130 and 140°F (54 and 60°C), actomyosin is mostly coagulated, making the meat more opaque and slightly firmer. In this temperature range, meat is called medium-rare and is very warm and bright red in the center. Medium-rare meat feels resilient, or somewhat springy, to the touch and is juicy, although the juices more easily escape when the meat is cut.

When the meat temperature gets above 140°F (60°C), the meat's tough connective tissue gradually shrinks, softens, and melts in a counterpoint to the toughening muscle fibers. When heated along with the moisture held in muscle fibers (or with added moisture), connective-tissue collagen begins to shrink at about 140°F (60°C) and squeezes out the water it holds. Between 140 and 150°F (60 and 66°C), the constricting connective tissue causes the entire piece of meat to shrink. Proteins in the muscle cells also continue to coagulate, making the meat increasingly opaque, firm, and dry. In this temperature range, meat is called medium, has a hot, pink center, and feels slightly firm with just a bit of resilience. Meat cooked to medium can be somewhat juicy but is slightly less flavorful because a good portion of the juices have been lost. Although it diminishes tenderness and juiciness, many people cook meat to medium because in this temperature range, most microbes are killed.

Between 150 and 160°F (66 and 71°C), meat continues to firm, dry, and shrink. Meat served in this range is called medium-well, has just a hint of pink at the center, and feels firm and springy.

As the temperature rises above 160°F (71°C), collagen bonds with any remaining water and begins to transform into gelatin, the semisolid jelly you see in meat that has cooled. Between 160 and 170°F (71 and 77°C), meat is called well-done, is brown or gray throughout, and is stiff to the touch. At this point, the flow of moisture slows down because most of it either has been squeezed from the cells or has bonded with gelatin. Brining is an effective way of increasing the moisture content of meat so that it remains somewhat juicy even when cooked to well-done.

Between 170 and 200°F (77 and 93°C), actomyosin proteins toughen the muscle fibers even more. However, collagen continues to transform into gelatin, and at 200°F (93°C) the meat fibers separate very easily from each other. As gelatin surrounds the separated and more easily chewed meat fibers, it creates the sensation of tenderness even in tough cuts of meat. For this reason, tough cuts of meat are done only when

Meat Doneness

The rate at which meat cooks depends on several factors, such as genetics, how long the meat was aged, where it comes from on the animal, the meat's temperature before cooking, its fat content, and its water content. Fat conducts heat more slowly than muscle fiber, so fatty meats cook more slowly than lean meats. Bones also slow down the heat transfer, because air within the bone structure conducts heat much more slowly than the bone material itself. Water speeds up the heat transfer, because it conducts heat more than twice as fast as fat. When meat is basted, moisture on the surface evaporates and cools the meat, slowing down the cooking. On the other hand, fat on the surface speeds cooking by preventing the evaporation of moisture.

Of course, the temperature of the heat source, such as an open flame, grill grate, frying pan, or oven, also determines how quickly meat will cook. The meat's internal temperature and visual or tactile doneness checks are the most reliable methods of testing meat doneness. The chart below is a general guide to both. The USDA defines doneness at slightly higher temperatures (about 10 to 15°F/5 to 8°C higher) than those given here. For instance, the USDA defines most meats as rare at 135°F (57°C), medium-rare at 145°F (63°C), medium at 160°F (71°C), and well-done at 170°F (77°C) and above. The USDA also recommends cooking ground meats to 160°F (71°C) to reduce risk of illness from food-borne pathogens. However, at that temperature, most of the moisture and flavor in ground meat are gone. Use the figures below in combination with the descriptions in the earlier section called "When Meat Cooks" to get a better feel for the doneness of meat. In many cases, the most reliable test is to poke it to feel how firm it is or to cut it and see how it looks in the center. Cutting releases only a minimal amount of juice from a localized area around the cut.

Meat	Blue	Rare	Medium-Rare	Medium	Medium-Well	Well-Done
	Raw red center, soft to touch	Deep red center, slight resistance to touch	Bright red center, resilient to touch	Rosy red or pink center, slightly firm to touch	Hint of pink at center, firm to touch	Tan or gray at center, stiff to touch
Beef steak or roast	120°F (50°C) (115°F/46°C for roast)	125°F (52°C)	135°F (57°C)	145°F (63°C)	155°F (68°C)	170°F (77°C)
Beef tough cuts					155°F (68°C)	170°F (77°C)
Ground beef, veal, or lamb					160°F (71°C)	
Pork chop or roast					155°F (68°C)	170°F (77°C)
Pork shoulder				165°F (74°C)	170°F (77°C)	
Ground pork					165°F (74°C)	
Lamb chop or roast	120°F (50°C) (115°F/46°C for roast)	125°F (52°C)	135°F (57°C)	145°F (63°C)	155°F (68°C)	170°F (77°C)
Lamb shoulder					155°F (68°C)	170°F (77°C)
Veal chop or roast			135°F (57°C)	145°F (63°C)	155°F (68°C)	170°F (77°C)
Veal shank					155°F (68°C)	170°F (77°C)
Poultry					170°F (77°C)	180°F (82°C)

fork-tender. Melted fats also coat the stiff and dry muscle fibers, making them taste more tender and moist. Fat, and the flavor it carries, gets our own juices flowing and makes meat taste juicier.

Resting

After meat is done to your liking, it's a good idea to let it rest off the heat. The internal temperature will continue to rise after it is removed from the heat because the meat retains some heat and conducts that heat through to the center. A small, thin steak or chop may rise only 2 to 5°F (1 to 3°C), but a large roast or whole bird may rise as much as 20°F (10°C) off the heat. Allowing meat to rest will make it taste juicier when cut. If you cut into a steaming hot steak or roast, the juices will readily escape. But as meat cools, the proteins become firmer and better able to retain precious juices. Ideally, meat should cool to about 120°F (50°C) before serving, which may take anywhere from 5 minutes (for a fairly thin steak or chop) to 15 minutes (for a thick roast or whole chicken) to 1 hour (for a whole animal like a lamb or hog).

Meat Flavor and Color

Even raw meat tastes good, because meat contains a combination of salts, minerals, sugars, amino acids, and fats that are readily released when chewed. These components activate taste receptors on our tongues, making raw meat taste flavorful in dishes like tartare and carpaccio. Well-exercised dark red meats are more flavorful than less exercised pale meats because they have developed more of these flavor compounds. Likewise, the meat of older animals is more strongly flavored than that of younger animals. Fat also has a role in the flavor of meat. Many of meat's flavor compounds are fat soluble, which explains why fatty meats taste more complex than lean meats: more flavor is stored in the fat, which then carries that flavor to our taste receptors. Meat can taste sweet, too. For instance, the sweet flavor of pork comes from lactones, the same flavor molecules in peaches and coconuts. Other flavors in meat come from the animal's diet. The meat of grain-fed animals tends to taste deep, rich, and

kitchen wisdom

Meat Cutting Made Easy

To make it easier to cut and to reduce the smearing of fat when grinding, freeze raw meat just until it begins to firm up, about 30 to 45 minutes. The protein fibers and fat in the meat will stiffen enough to make cutting, slicing, and grinding easier and more efficient.

earthy, whereas the meat of grass-fed animals tends to taste more herbal and spicy because of the conversion of chlorophyll from the green grass into terpene compounds. Grass-fed meat also gets a note of barnyardy aroma from a compound called skatole. And garlic-eating animals taste garlicky.

Though these flavors are perceptible in raw meat, most of the alluring aromas we associate with meat develop when meat is cooked. When meat is heated, the amino acids, sugars, and fats react with each other and create highly aromatic compounds such as esters, ketones, and aldehydes that give meat floral, nutty, and grassy aromas. Even when heated below the boiling point of water (212°F/100°C) during stewing, poaching, or other moist-heat cooking methods, these reactions occur and enhance the aroma of meat. However, meat cooked with moist heat will never be as flavorful or aromatic as when the surface of meat undergoes **browning**. When temperatures at the surface of meat reach 250°F (120°C) and above, hundreds of complex flavor compounds are created as a result of a special type of browning called Maillard reactions. These reactions give roasted, grilled, broiled, and fried meats the complex, savory, and "meaty" aromas that we have come to associate with good-tasting meat. This is the primary reason to sear meats. Contrary to popular belief, searing doesn't lock in juices (they still escape through the browned crust), but it does create incredible depth of flavor.

Meat color comes primarily from the protein pigment myoglobin, which makes freshly cut raw meat appear red. Lamb and veal don't contain much myoglobin (only about 0.3%) and pork contains even less, so these meats look somewhat pale. Mature beef, on the other hand, contains about four times more myoglobin than pork and has a deep red color when freshly cut. Myoglobin's function is to store oxygen in muscle cells, and it also contains atoms of iron. When oxygen is not attached to myoglobin, it appears purple, as when meat is vacuum-packed at the meat-packing plant. If you cut open a package of vacuum-packed meat it will quickly change color from purple to red as the myoglobin is flooded with oxygen in the air and changes to oxymyoglobin.

When the iron atom in a molecule of myoglobin loses an electron (becomes oxidized) and can't hold oxygen anymore, or when there is only a little oxygen available to the meat, myoglobin is known as metmyoglobin and appears brown. Beginning around 140°F (60°C), the protein part of myoglobin denatures, becoming light brown, then increasingly gray (at which point it's called hemichrome), which is why meat cooked to medium or well doneness becomes increasingly gray. Meat can also turn brown when its antioxidant enzymes become less and less active. This type of browning usually occurs when meat is stored for a long time, gets old, and starts to go bad (a sniff is the best test to check whether meat appears brown because of microbial spoilage or is just exhibiting brown myoglobin pigments). Metmyoglobin is also present in meat after it is frozen. Meat appears pink when cured because of the presence of nitrites, or when smoked from nitrogen dioxide in smoke. To find out what distinguishes dark meat from white meat in poultry, see Science Wise, page 486.

See Also • Agriculture, Antibiotics, Bacteria, Beef, Bones, Brining, Browning, Chicken, Fat, Fish, Food Additives, Game, Hormones, Irradiation, Jerky, Lamb, Mad Cow Disease, Organ Meats, Pork, Poultry, Protein, Water

MEAT TENDERIZERS • See Enzyme

MELEGUETA PEPPER • See Spices

MELON

What It Is • Humans have been enjoying melons for more than 4,000 years. These fruits most likely originated in the hot valleys of India, Iran, and Egypt. Later, they migrated to Africa and were eventually taken to South and North America in the 1500s. Melons are the sweetest members of the gourd family (Cucurbitaceae), which also includes **cucumber**, **squash**, and pumpkin. They grow best in sandy, well-watered, well-aerated soil that is free of weeds and thrive near the hives of honeybees, as melons need plenty of pollination to produce ample sweet fruits.

Melon varieties number in the thousands, including dozens of creatively named heirloom fruits such as Schoon's Hardshell and Jenny Lind muskmelons. The two main types of melons are muskmelons (*Cucumis melo*) and watermelons (*Citrullus lanatus*). Muskmelons may have netted rinds like those of North American cantaloupes and Santa Claus melons or smooth rinds like those found on casaba and honeydew melons. They all have seeds attached to a fibrous hollow center. Watermelons, on the other hand, have smooth rinds and sweeter flesh. The melon category also includes melons used as culinary vegetables, among them bitter melon (bitter gourd) and Asian winter melon (aka fuzzy melon, wax gourd, ash gourd). Some fruits, like mamey sapote, from a different botanical family (Sapotaceae), are often mistakenly called melons.

What It Does • Melons are often eaten fresh in salads and desserts. Muskmelons are also delicious with cured pork such as prosciutto. Both muskmelons and watermelons are popular puréed into drinks, smoothies, cold soups, and sorbets. Watermelons are the most popular variety worldwide: more than twice as many watermelons are produced annually than all other melons combined. All parts of the watermelon are used. The flesh is eaten fresh, puréed, candied, or infused with

science wise

Melon Gels • Melons in the *Cucumis melo* family (virtually all melons except watermelons) contain cucumisin, a protein-digesting enzyme similar to the bromelain in pineapple and the papain in papaya. Like those enzymes, cucumisin prevents gelatin gels from setting. To make a successful melon gel with gelatin, briefly cook the melon to denature the enzyme. In commercial food production, enzymes are often denatured by boiling food for 5 minutes or cooking it at 240°F (116°C) for 3 seconds.

alcohol as "hard watermelon." The rinds are commonly pickled in Japan and stir-fried in China. The seeds are roasted, seasoned, and snacked on like sunflower seeds in China. In West Africa, some varieties of watermelon seeds (*egusi*) are pressed for their oil. In Russia, pressed watermelon juice is boiled down to make watermelon syrup, which is used as a sweetener.

Watermelons are so popular that seedless varieties were developed in the early 1900s so consumers could enjoy the fruit's flesh more easily. Seedless watermelon plants are genetically modified female plants containing four sets of chromosomes. The plant bears fruit only when pollinated by a watermelon plant with two sets of chromosomes and then grows only a few soft, pale-colored seeds within the flesh. Seedless watermelons actually contain two types of seeds, smaller ones from the pollinating plant that contained two chromosomes and larger ones from the hybrid plant itself.

Melons taste best in the summer and fall, although some varieties ripen in late fall and last through winter. So-called winter melons are ready to pick in the fall and continue to ripen after picking. Winter melons generally have pale, mild-flavored flesh.

When choosing melons, pick the heaviest ones because they contain the most water and will be the juiciest. A juicy melon will produce a hollow ring rather than a dull thud as vibrations reverberate through its water. If there's a yellow patch on a slightly flattened side that's a good sign that the melon was ripened on the ground rather than picked early. Melons should show no signs of cracks, mold, or soft spots, except at the blossom end (the smooth end), which should be slightly soft when pressed and smell fragrant. The blossom ends of casabas won't soften or smell fragrant, but ripe casabas have a vibrant golden yellow rind with only a bit of green at the blossom end. If you smell arrestingly strong or alcoholic aromas, the melon is most likely past its prime. Overripe melons rattle when shaken because the seeds have loosened from the dehydrated flesh.

After they're picked, melons may change color and aroma but they won't get any sweeter. Nonetheless, you can ripen whole melons in a paper bag at room temperature. Once ripe, keep them cool. Cantaloupes, honeydews, and other *Cucumis melo* varieties

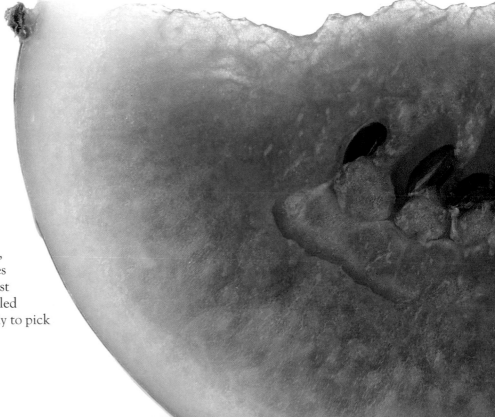

Cantaloupe Sorbet

Cantaloupes and other muskmelons make terrific sorbets. You'll need about 1 cantaloupe (2 to 2½ lbs /1 to 1.25 kg) and 1 fresh lime. You can also use frozen cantaloupe and a frozen banana if you like.

4 cups	coarsely chopped peeled cantaloupe or Charentais, Galia, or Ogen melon	1 L
1	banana, sliced	1
¼ cup	granulated sugar	50 mL
2 tbsp	corn syrup	25 mL
1 tbsp	crème de menthe liqueur	15 mL
2 tsp	grated lime zest	10 mL
1 tbsp	freshly squeezed lime juice	15 mL
¼ tsp	ground cinnamon	1 mL

1. In a food processor or blender, combine cantaloupe, banana, sugar, corn syrup, liqueur, lime zest and juice, and cinnamon. Process until smooth, then scrape into an ice cream maker and freeze according to manufacturer's directions. Or scrape into a shallow metal pan, cover, and freeze for 6 to 8 hours, then break mixture into chunks and pulse briefly in food processor just until no longer chunky and somewhat creamy in texture, 10 to 20 seconds.

MAKES 4 TO 6 SERVINGS

are best stored at about 45°F (7°C). Watermelons in the *Citrullus lanatus* family do better at slightly warmer temperatures, around 55°F (13°C). Both of these temperatures are slightly above most refrigerator temperatures, but melons can be refrigerated if you're willing to sacrifice a little flavor.

Harmful bacteria such as *Salmonella* can grow on the surface of melons and migrate to the flesh when the melon is cut. Before cutting, wash melon rinds thoroughly with warm water.

How It Works • Most melons consist of 90 to 92% water, 8 to 10% sugar, 1% protein, and 0.2% acid. Toward the end of vine ripening, melons swell with sap (primarily water and sugar) in their cell vacuoles, which are among the largest energy-storage containers in the plant kingdom and cause some melons to grow to more than 60 pounds (30 kg). Most melons are high in vitamins A and C. Orange-fleshed varieties are generally a good source of beta-carotene, potassium, and folate (which is especially high in cantaloupes). Red-fleshed varieties like watermelon are particularly high in the antioxidant lycopene, and contain more lycopene than tomatoes. Muskmelons get their musky aromas in part from sulfur compounds and their fruity aromas from esters. Green, grassy, cucumber-like scents come from aldehydes, and these aromas are more prominent in winter melons than in summer melons.

See Also • Cucumber, Squash

fast facts

- In 1941, after a worldwide search, a moldy cantaloupe in Peoria, Illinois, was identified as the best source of high-quality penicillin.
- Tsamma melons (citron melons) are higher in pectin than other melons and are often made into jams and jellies. They are also candied and used in fruitcake.
- In the early 1900s, Japanese farmers grew cube-shaped watermelons inside glass boxes. These melons could be more efficiently packed and shipped. Melons can also be grown in other geometrical shapes such as pyramids.

MENTHOL • See Flavor

MERCURY • See Minerals

MERGUEZ • See Sausage

MERINGUE • See Eggs, Foams

MESQUITE • See Smoking

METABOLISM

What It Is • Every living organism has a
metabolism. It's what makes things live and
grow. In humans, metabolism is the totality of
the chemical reactions that support our vital
functions. That encompasses the reactions
involved in breathing, blood circulation,
eating food, **digestion**, eliminating food
waste, controlling body temperature,
contracting muscles, nervous system
functions, and brain activity. Metabolism
happens on two levels. The first level,
called catabolism or destructive metabolism,
breaks apart large molecules into smaller
molecules — for example, breaking down
the carbohydrates and proteins in plant and
animal foods into smaller compounds like
sugars and amino acids so they can be used by
our bodies. The second level, called anabolism
or constructive metabolism, builds up small
molecules into larger molecules in our bodies
and includes functions like maintaining body
tissues and building muscle cells.

All metabolic functions require **energy**, the
result of **calories** taken in through the food
you eat and calories used up by activity.
The speed at which your body uses up energy
is known as your metabolic rate. It's often
measured when you're at rest and called your
resting or basal metabolic rate (BMR).

What It Does • Your metabolic rate
determines how efficiently you process food
into energy. Someone with a low BMR is like
a car that runs on very little gas. That person
requires relatively few calories (less food) for
normal body functions like breathing and
thinking. On the other hand, someone with a
high BMR, or "high metabolism," is like a gas
guzzler. That person needs more fuel (more
food) for normal body functions. Someone
with a low BMR consumes fewer calories, but
if that person takes in more calories than they
need, the excess is stored as fat, contributing
to weight gain and its associated diseases
such as heart disease and Type 2 diabetes.
Someone with a high BMR is less likely to
gain weight because that person's body burns
up many more of the calories taken in.

Metabolic rate varies from person to person
based on such things as genetics, sex, age,
height, weight, diet, lifestyle, activity level,
stress level, and lean muscle mass. Most of
these are controllable and can raise or lower
your metabolic rate. For example, studies
show that increasing your lean muscle mass
through resistance weight training can
increase your metabolism. Caffeine, nicotine,
amphetamines, ephedrine, and other central
nervous system stimulants can also
temporarily increase BMR by causing you to
burn calories more quickly. To get a rough of
idea of your current BMR, use an online
BMR calculator.

How It Works • All living organisms use
thousands of metabolic reactions every day.
But, metabolically speaking, there are just
two cornerstones to the energy that fuels all
life: photosynthesis and glycolysis.
Photosynthesis is the process by which plants
use chlorophyll and the sun to create sugar
(glucose) for energy. Glycolysis is the
opposite: it's the process by which plants,
animals, and humans break down glucose
into usable energy. Plants use that energy for
things like respiration, just as animals and
humans use it to breathe. During respiration,
molecules lose and gain electrons in a series
of reactions known as oxidation/reduction
reactions (redox). As we breathe, these
reactions generate a vital molecule called
adenosine triphosphate (ATP), which
functions as an energy carrier. ATP is
considered to be the "universal energy
currency," and the amount of ATP in any
given cell determines how much energy is
available for biological functions. With the
help of enzymes, ATP transfers energy from
cell to cell and is the main source of energy
for basic human functions like breathing and
muscle contraction. ATP also works with
hormones to send signals throughout the
body's nervous system. The faster your
metabolism, the quicker glycolysis occurs, the
more ATP is generated, and the more energy
you have to breathe and move.

When glucose is unavailable in the body,
the body abandons glycolysis and instead
burns stored fat for energy. Known as ketosis,

this process occurs in the liver, which converts stored fat into fatty acids and ketones that can be used for energy. The breakdown of fat, or lipids, is called lipolysis and creates three fatty acid chains and one glycerol molecule, each of which can be used by the body for energy.

See Also ● Diet, Digestion, Enzyme, Hormones, Nutrition, Oxygen

METAL ● See Bakeware, Cookware, Heat, Knives, Minerals

METHIONINE ● See Protein

METHYLCELLULOSE ● See Food Additives

METHYL SALICYLATE ● See Flavor, Toxin

MEZCAL ● See Liquor

MICELLE ● See Milk

MICROWAVE COOKING

What It Is ● Microwaves are a form of radiant **energy** that can generate **heat**. In 1945, an engineer named Percy Spencer was working near a magnetron (a device that generates microwaves) and noticed that the candy bar in his pocket had melted. Sensing a cooking breakthrough, Spencer grabbed another food and entered the history books as the first person to make microwave popcorn. By 1947, the first microwave ovens, called Radaranges, were sold for restaurant use. They were 6 feet (1.8 m) tall, weighed 750 pounds (340 kg), cost about $5,000, and had to be connected to water pipes for cooling. By the 1970s, smaller top-of-the line microwave ovens were available for home use and cost only about $50. Today, microwave ovens are found in more than 90% of North American homes.

What It Does ● Microwave ovens heat food faster than most other appliances. They

quickly thaw and reheat frozen foods. They handily melt butter and chocolate. They rapidly cook fish and vegetables. And they can soften the tough skins of produce like butternut squash to make peeling easier. Microwave ovens have revolutionized the popcorn industry, although many connoisseurs prefer the crisper texture of popcorn cooked in hot oil or with hot air.

Until recently, microwave ovens cooked mostly by heating up the water molecules in food, which helped food cook faster. But the resulting steam and lack of browning were big drawbacks. For instance, in older models, whole potatoes cook about 75% faster than in a conventional oven, but they cook with more steam than dry heat and consequently taste more steamed than baked. The speed also causes microwaved meat to cook so quickly that its juices tend to flow out before the lean protein is cooked through, making the meat dry. Like many foods, meats consist of 70% water or more. Even if that water reaches the boiling point (212°F/100°C), the meat won't brown because browning doesn't begin until well past 250°F (120°C). The meat has to lose its water and dry out before it can begin to brown. Browning in a microwave oven is more effective with drier foods like nuts. When put on a ceramic or glass plate, nuts will brown on the bottom after a few minutes from the heat conducted by the plate, just as nuts toasted in a metal pan will brown from the hot metal.

To circumvent the lack of browning, manufacturers of microwave ovens have added halogen lightbulbs or other broiling elements and fans to brown meats and other

fast facts

- Microwave ovens lose 30 to 40% of their heat, making them approximately 65% energy efficient. According to the American Council for an Energy-Efficient Economy, microwave ovens are two to four times more energy efficient than gas ovens, toaster ovens, electric convection ovens, and slow cookers.
- A 2006 study at Cornell University found that microwaved bacon contains significantly lower levels of carcinogenic nitrosamines than pan-fried bacon.

kitchen wisdom

Put Something Inside

Avoid operating an empty microwave oven. If there's nothing inside to absorb the microwaves, the microwaves can return to the magnetron and damage it.

foods with dry infrared heat and with convection heat blown over the food's surface. Newer combination microwave ovens may even include rotisseries, making the most of microwave, radiant, and convection cooking in one appliance. Food packaging can aid in browning as well. In some frozen foods intended for microwave cooking, thin sheets or patches of metal (called susceptors) concentrate the heat near the surfaces of food to help brown them. This packaging works well in foods like microwavable frozen french fries, which turn out fairly crisp and brown.

Newer ovens also attempt to overcome the other major weakness of microwave cooking, uneven heating. Microwave ovens cook food unevenly because the microwave energy is unevenly distributed inside the oven and because a food's components (water, fat, and protein, for example) absorb the microwave energy at different rates. Using a rotating carousel, or manually rotating the food now and then, helps to promote even heating, as does frequent stirring and cutting foods into uniform pieces. To melt chocolate evenly, break it into similar-size pieces and stir every minute or so. To evenly cook foods with both thick and thin ends, like fish fillets and chicken breasts, position the thick ends toward the walls of the microwave oven (which heat up sooner) and the thin ends toward the center (which heats up more slowly). The same goes for foods with both tough ends and delicate ends, such as broccoli florets. Avoid square containers when you can because heat collects more readily in the corners; round containers distribute the heat more evenly. Lastly, cover the container with microwave-safe plastic wrap or waxed paper to trap steam, speed heating, and help prevent foods from drying out.

Microwave Caramel

Caramelizing sugar in a microwave oven isn't any faster than doing it on a stovetop but it's easier — no stirring! As on a stovetop, monitor the color of the caramel as it cooks. Use a glass bowl so you can easily see the color and keep the caramel from getting overly browned.

1 cup	granulated sugar	250 mL
2 tbsp	light (white) corn syrup	25 mL
1/8 tsp	freshly squeezed lemon juice	0.5 mL

1. In a 4-cup (1 L) glass bowl, combine sugar, corn syrup, 2 tbsp (25 mL) water, and lemon juice, stirring until evenly moistened. Microwave on High until mixture bubbles and appears pale caramel in color, 4 to 8 minutes, depending on your oven's wattage. Remove and let cool slightly until bubbling subsides, 1 to 2 minutes (color will darken slightly from residual heat). If necessary, continue cooking in 10 to 20 second increments, removing and cooling to check the color between increments until darkened to your liking.

Variation: To heighten flavor, add 2 tbsp (25 mL) liqueur such as Cointreau or Amaretto along with the water.

MAKES ABOUT 1 CUP (250 ML)

Microwave ovens range in wattage (a measure of the microwave energy they emit) from about 500 to 2,000 watts. Combined with the volume of the oven, the watts measure the oven's cooking power, as higher watts in a smaller space cook food faster. Microwave recipes tend to be written for 700-watt models, so if your oven is a higher or lower wattage, adjust cooking times slightly down or up. For more gentle heating, cook at 50% power, which makes the oven cycle on and off so that it is emitting microwaves only 50% of the time.

Microwave Safety

Microwave ovens produce non-ionizing radiation, which doesn't have the cancer risk associated with the ionizing radiation of X-rays and ultraviolet light. Nonetheless, ovens are designed to keep the microwaves secured inside. Government regulations allow leakage of only 5 milliwatts per square centimeter when measured 5 centimeters from the surface of the oven, which is far below the exposure level that is harmful to humans.

Use only microwave-safe cooking containers made of glass, ceramic, or microwave-safe plastic (made of glass-like phenolic resin). Softer plastics like those used for food storage and takeout containers can leach adipates and phthalates into the food when heated, and these compounds have been linked to the disruption of normal hormone function. Use only microwave-safe plastic wrap and try to keep the plastic from touching the food.

When cooking whole foods with a casing or skin, such as sausages, whole potatoes, or squash, prick them with a fork to prevent steam from building up and cracking the skin or causing blowouts. Because air and steam are trapped inside, shell eggs will explode in the microwave. To melt butter, do not cut up, and melt it at 30% or 50% so it won't splatter.

Prevent sparks by keeping small or thin pieces of metal such as cutlery or aluminum foil out of the oven. These can produce high voltage at the edges and create an electric arc. Sparks are more likely with small bits of metal like the decorative edging of a plate but are less likely with large pieces of metal, such as the metal racks in some large microwave ovens.

How It Works ● Microwaves are called "micro" because the wavelengths are shorter than radio wavelengths. Shorter wavelengths have higher frequency and more energy, but microwaves are still weaker than infrared energy and carry only 1/10,000 the energy of a gas flame. Microwaves are only strong enough to cause polar molecules (those with a positive charge at one end and a negative

charge at the other), such as the water molecules in food, to move. That's why microwave cooking works best with foods that are high in water such as fish and vegetables. During microwave cooking, the oven's wave generator (magnetron) emits microwaves and creates an electromagnetic field that reverses its polarity about 4.9 billion times every second. That's a frequency of 2.45 gigahertz or 2.45 billion cycles per second. The microwaves penetrate the food about one inch (2.5 cm) from the outside in, and the polar food molecules rotate frantically (4.9 billion times per second) as they try to align themselves with the constantly alternating electric polarity, which causes the molecules to move and bump into other molecules. Moving molecules generate heat, and that heat is transferred from molecule to molecule throughout the food. Voilà! The food cooks. Air in a microwave oven remains unaffected by microwaves because it consists of nonpolar molecules. The air warms up only from heat coming off the food.

See Also • Cooking, Heat

MIDORI • See Liqueur

MILK

What It Is • Milk is baby food for mammals. Rich in protein, fat, sugar, and calcium, it helps infants grow. Since at least 7000 BCE, humans have recognized that mammals could provide us with milk as well as meat, and we began raising ruminants because they have the unique ability to convert grass into highly nutritious milk for their young. Milk has been deeply woven into the human diet in dairy products ranging from **butter**, **cheese**, yogurt, and **ice cream** to high-fat creams and low-fat powdered and condensed milks.

What It Does • Farmers discovered early on that rich, velvety cream rises from standing milk and can be skimmed off the top, and that stirring that cream churns it into butter. They also discovered that when

milk is left to stand, bacteria like *Lactococcus* attack the milk, acidify it, and cause it to coagulate, a process they manipulated to create various fermented dairy products. When acidified milk is separated into liquid whey and solid curds, the curd can be salted, cooked, pressed, and/or ripened into various kinds of fresh and aged cheese.

In the mid-1800s, railroads, new farm equipment, automated milking machines, and milk-preservation techniques all broadened the dairy industry. American businessman Gail Borden developed a process for evaporating more than 50% of the water from milk and preserving the condensed milk in cans. Swedish engineer Gustaf de Laval invented a centrifuge to quickly separate cream from milk. In France, homogenization was developed to keep cream from separating out of milk. And **pasteurization** allowed us to briefly heat milk to destroy pathogens and extend its shelf life. By the 1900s, the rich milk of Jersey and Guernsey cattle breeds gave way to the less rich milk but higher yield of Friesian or Holstein cows, which now supply about 90% of the milk in North America. Large herds are now fed hay and corn for optimal milk production, so the flavor of milk changed from fruity, barnyardy, and complex to mildly sweet and simple. About a third of North American cows are also given growth **hormones** to increase milk production and many receive antibiotics to ward off diseases associated with accelerated growth and crowded facilities. Their milk is pooled together and trucked to processing plants, so it lacks the distinctive flavors of feed from particular farms.

Some milk producers have returned to cattle breeds like Guernsey and Jersey and give the cows their natural diet of grass to make richer, more flavorful milk and dairy products. Consumer demand for "clean" milk has spurred sales of organic milk, which is produced from cows that are fed 100% organic feed and are not given antibiotics or synthetic growth hormones. Although the practice is controversial, some consumers also seek out unpasteurized "raw" milk for its complex flavor and beneficial enzymes. Although raw milk when produced by high-quality farms with healthy cows and well-regulated sanitation procedures, might have low numbers of organisms, it has been shown to contain pathogens such as *Salmonella* and *Campylobacter*.

Milk and Cream in the Kitchen

When milk or cream is added to **bread** and **pastry** dough, the additional fat tenderizes the dough and helps carry flavor. Milk's sugars and proteins help to create a browned and flavorful crust. In **candy** making, milk and cream add rich texture, moisture, and caramelized flavor. Milk and cream are essential in custards, where they dilute the egg proteins, creating a smooth and creamy **emulsion** when the eggs are gently heated and coagulated. And, of course, there would be no ice cream without milk and cream.

Milk and cream are particularly useful in sauces and soups, where the phospholipids in milk fat help to emulsify ingredients and create a smooth texture. The heat-tolerant structure of milk fat globules also makes it possible to boil down cream and use it as a thickener in luxuriously rich sauces. That's because the fat in milk is dispersed throughout the liquid (water) and surrounded by a protective layer of proteins.

Fat Content of Milk and Cream

Dairy products are sold with varying degrees of fat. Fat content is adjusted when the milk is centrifuged to separate cream from milk.

Milk or Cream	Fat Percentage by Weight
Fat-free milk (skim)	0.5 or less
Evaporated milk	0.5 or less (fat-free), 1 (low-fat), or 8 (whole)
Low-fat milk	1
Dry milk (powdered)	1 or less (low-fat), 27 (whole)
Reduced-fat milk	2
Whole milk	3.25 (minimum)
Light cream (Canada)	5 to 7
Sweetened condensed milk	8 to 10
Half-and-half (cereal)	12
Light cream (coffee cream or table cream)	18 to 30 (usually 20)
Light whipping cream	30 to 36
Heavy cream (whipping cream)	38
Double cream	42 to 48
Clotted cream (Devon cream)	55 to 60

Cooking unfolds the proteins, then they link back together and form an even stronger protective layer around the fat globules. As water is boiled away from heavy cream, its fat concentrates from its original 40% to about 55% (when reduced in volume by a third), then to 75% (when reduced by half). Cream containing at least 25% fat is less likely to curdle because it contains enough fat to get in between the proteins that would otherwise curdle into clumps. Instead, the additional fat in high-fat creams coats those few proteins in the milk with a layer of insulation. Even so, when making cream sauces with alcohol such as wine, boil the wine before adding the cream to evaporate the alcohol and other compounds that could cause curdling. If you want the thickness of boiled-down cream without the cooked flavor, at the very end add crème fraîche to taste.

Another distinct advantage of the protein in milk and cream is its ability to be whipped into **foam**. When milk is whipped, air is incorporated into it, and its proteins form a protective layer around the air bubbles. But milk foam doesn't last very long because there isn't as much protein as in, say, a foam made from egg whites. Skim and reduced-fat milks tend to foam up more easily than whole milk because fat interferes with foam formation. When foaming milk with steam such as on an espresso machine, it helps to use an ample amount (at least ¾ cup/175 mL) of very cold milk so that the steam doesn't overheat the milk, which can cause the foam to collapse, and to apply the steam near the surface of the milk.

Foamed milk isn't nearly as velvety or stable as foamed or whipped cream because cream contains more fat, which strengthens the walls around the air bubbles and prevents the bubbles from popping so easily. Only creams with at least 30% fat will create the stable foam known as whipped cream. Higher-fat cream such as double cream (48% fat) creates an even more luscious foam. The key to making whipped cream is to start with everything cold, including the cream (chilled as long as possible), the beaters or whisk, and the bowl. Cold encourages the fat globules to stick to each other around the air bubbles,

stabilizing the foam. Avoid overwhipping, which sends the cream on its way to becoming butter because the fat globules are forced to cluster together into masses of butterfat. It also helps to add sweeteners after the cream has thickened enough to form soft peaks. Superfine and confectioner's sugar are preferred because they have smaller crystals that don't deflate the foam. Unhomogenized cream whips faster than homogenized cream because the fat globules are larger, but the latter creates a more fine-textured foam. To speed the whipping of any cream, add 1 tsp (5 mL) lemon juice per cup (250 mL). The acid causes the proteins to thicken so that the fat in the cream can more easily form protective walls around the bubbles. If it's volume you're after, whip cream by hand. For greater fluffiness, whip cream with nitrous oxide capsules. To help stabilize whipped cream for mousses and soufflés, add starch, gum, egg whites, or dissolved and cooled gelatin.

Milk is so full of nutrients that bacteria readily consume it, causing it to spoil. Some milk is preserved with ultra-high temperatures (see **Pasteurization**) and sold in aseptic packaging, allowing it to be stored longer without refrigeration. But milk that

Milk Composition

The exact composition of cow's milk varies by breed and even within breed because of factors like diet, growing conditions, and season. In general, sheep and buffalo milks contain about double the fat of cow's milk, accounting for the rich texture of cheeses made from them, such as buffalo mozzarella. This chart shows the percentage of major components in milk by weight.

Milk Source	% Water	% Fat	% Protein	% Lactose
Buffalo	83	6.9	3.8	5.1
Cow, Brown Swiss	87	4	3.6	4.7
Cow, Guernsey	86	4.9	3.6	4.9
Cow, Holstein	87	3.6	3.4	4.9
Cow, Jersey	85	5.2	3.9	4.9
Cow, Zebu	86	4.7	3.3	4.9
Goat	88	4	3.4	4.5
Horse	90	1.2	2	6.3
Human	88	4	1.1	6.8
Sheep	80	7.5	6	4.8

Brandy Cream Sauce

Cream helps to round out and deliver the complex flavors of roasted and pan-seared meat. Make this basic pan sauce after cooking beef, pork, lamb, or venison and use the remaining browned bits for the sauce.

¼ cup	brandy	50 mL
1 tbsp	best-quality balsamic vinegar	15 mL
1 tbsp	tomato purée or puréed tomatoes	15 mL
½ cup	whipping (35%) cream	125 mL
1 tbsp	chopped herbs, such as fresh parsley, tarragon, rosemary, or thyme	15 mL

Salt and freshly ground black pepper

1. Remove meat from pan and pour off all but 1 tbsp (15 mL) of fat, leaving browned bits in the pan. Place pan over medium heat. Add brandy and simmer, scraping up browned bits from pan, 1 to 2 minutes.

2. Add vinegar and tomato purée and simmer, stirring until smooth, 1 to 2 minutes.

3. Increase heat to medium-high. Stir in cream and boil until slightly reduced and sauce thickens, about 1 minute. Add herbs and season with salt and pepper, to taste. Spoon over meat.

MAKES ABOUT ⅔ CUP (150 ML)

undergoes normal pasteurization is still highly perishable and should be kept refrigerated. Milk lasts longest in tightly closed opaque containers. Overexposure to light can cause unpleasant sulfur aromas, and oxygen exposure leads to increasingly rancid aromas of fish, turpentine, and vinegar. Milk also absorbs other flavors easily. Avoid freezing milk because as it thaws it tends to separate into pools of fat and clumps of protein.

Milk and Health

More calf food than human beverage, cow's milk is high in nutrients necessary for growth such as protein, fat, sugar, and calcium. In whole milk, fat accounts for about half of the calories. Lower-fat milk products are often fortified with vitamin A to make up for its loss during processing. Vitamin D is added for improved calcium absorption and metabolism.

As many as 6% of North American infants have an allergy to cow's milk caused by its high protein content, and most children outgrow milk allergy as their digestive systems develop and become stronger. The majority of adults in the world have trouble digesting lactose, the main sugar in milk. That's because the enzyme lactase is needed to digest lactose, and lactase levels are highest at birth, then steadily decline as humans age. Lack of lactase can cause gas, bloating, and diarrhea among those who are lactose intolerant. One remedy, liquid lactase derived from *Aspergillus* mold, can be added to dairy products to aid digestion. You can also buy lactose-reduced milk.

How It Works ● Milk is partly an oil-in-water emulsion, a **dispersion** of tiny butterfat globules suspended in water. The fat globules are surrounded by a membrane phospholipid that keeps the fat emulsified with the water. Milk is partly a sol, a dispersion of tiny molecules of casein protein grouped together with calcium phosphate in structures called micelles. The caseins make up about 80% of the protein in milk. The other 20% consists of water-soluble whey proteins that, rather than bundling together like casein, remain in the water when milk is separated into curds and whey. Milk also consists of lactose (milk sugar), living white blood cells, and various enzymes.

As unhomogenized cow's milk sits, cream rises to the top because the fat globules, which are lighter than water, join together and become buoyant enough to float. Homogenization creates so many small fat globules surrounded by emulsifying phospholipids that the fat globules can't join together. Pasteurization also prevents fat globules from joining together as extensively because it breaks down the proteins in milk. That's why pasteurized cow's milk, even unhomogenized, doesn't form as thick a layer of cream on top. The milk of sheep, goats, and water buffalo has fat globules that are smaller and less apt to cluster together and rise.

Milk fat's protective layer of phospholipids helps shield the fat from fat-digesting lipase enzymes that cause milk to go rancid. When milk goes sour, its acidity increases, from about 6.5 pH to 4.7 pH, which causes the casein micelles to denature and curdle into lumps. Older milk is more acidic and curdles more easily when added to acidic ingredients like coffee. When milk is intentionally "cultured" through **fermentation**, bacteria such as *Lactococcus bacillus* ferment the lactose in milk into lactic acid, inducing the casein micelles to curdle. That's the first step in making most fermented dairy products like buttermilk, yogurt, and sour cream. Acidifying milk is also the first step to making cheese, which is further coagulated by an enzyme called chymosin that occurs naturally in rennet, the stomach lining of a calf.

Milk Flavor, Texture, and Color

The flavor of milk is influenced by animal breed, diet, the environment where the animal lives, and the season. But all milk gets sweetness from lactose (milk sugar), which provides about 40% of the calories in cow's milk. Lactose is one-fifth as sweet as granulated sugar. It's also one-tenth as soluble in water, so crystals form more easily in milk, which can give some milk and cream products like ice cream a crystalline or sandy texture. Cow's milk gets its mildly salty taste from various minerals, and with a pH of 6.5, it's slightly acid. Cows raised on grass rather than grain produce sweeter milk, with fruitier aromas from esters formed by various fatty acids, and their milk exhibits some barnyardy aromas from indole compounds. Cows fed on dry feed such as grain, on the other hand, produce milk with simpler aromas because their diet lacks protein and fat. Other characteristic flavors of cow's milk come from compounds like acetaldehyde, acetone, and formaldehyde. Low-fat cow's milks also have a cooked flavor from dried milk proteins added to the milk for body. The tangier taste of sheep's and goat's milk comes from fatty acids like 4-methyloctanoic and 4-ethyloctanoic acid.

Cream has similar flavors but tastes creamy because the concentration of fat slows down the flow of the water in the mixture, allowing us to readily perceive the viscous texture of its fat globules. That's also one reason why foods to which cream is added taste so good. The fat in cream carries fat-soluble flavor compounds from the food and holds those flavors in our mouths longer, so we can perceive them more intensely.

science wise

Nondairy Creamer • Through the marvels of food science, various nondairy products imitate the flavor, texture, and color of cream and whipped cream. But they hardly come close to the real thing. Nondairy creamer is a liquid or powder that comes in various flavors. It contains no lactose and makes a good nondairy alternative for lactose-intolerant coffee drinkers. Most nondairy creamers contain sodium caseinate, a milk-protein derivative that is not considered a dairy product because it doesn't contain lactose. Some creamers are made with soy protein instead of milk protein and are suitable for vegans as well. Creamer contains artificial flavors to mimic the taste of cream, and other ingredients to simulate cream's rich texture and creamy color, such as corn syrup for sweetness and body, partially hydrogenated vegetable oils like coconut and palm kernel oils for rich smoothness, and annatto to give the product a creamy color. Mono- and diacylglycerol (diglyceride) emulsifiers are added to help the creamer mix with coffee. Similarly, nondairy whipped topping consists primarily of water, coconut and/or palm kernel oil, sweeteners like sugar and high-fructose corn syrup, modified starch for body, sodium caseinate, xanthan and locust bean gums to stabilize the mixture, emulsifiers like polysorbate 60, and various colors and flavors to mimic the look and taste of whipped cream. But without any milk fat or milk protein, it's quite a different product.

As milk is heated to increasingly higher temperatures, its flavor changes more dramatically. Pasteurization usually heats the milk to about 161°F (72°C) for 15 to 20 seconds, which blunts the subtle aromas in raw milk. At temperatures above 170°F (77°C), it undergoes some Maillard reactions and develops nutty and vanilla-like aromas characteristic of cooked milk. Just above those temperatures, as when milk is scalded or simmered in a pan, proteins at the bottom of the pan coagulate and stick to the pan. A skin forms on top of scalded milk because the proteins coagulate and dry out as water evaporates from the surface. To help prevent a skin from forming, cover the pan to retain moisture or whip the milk until a foam forms on top, which also helps prevent evaporation. At temperatures above 300°F (150°C), the sugars and proteins in milk begin to undergo further Maillard browning and develop caramel and butterscotch flavors.

The flavors and aromas of frozen milk and cream are only slightly blunted, but the texture changes drastically. In ice cream, the fat globules clump together and cover the whipped-in air bubbles and provides them with a structure that remains even after the ice has melted, giving the ice cream a "dry" appearance and reduces stickiness.

What makes milk look creamy instead of pure white? Carotenes from the animals' feed, particularly from green grass and alpine flowers. The milk of Guernsey and Jersey cows sometimes contains so many carotenes that it appears golden yellow. Sheep, goat, and water buffalo milks are whiter because their diets contain grasses with fewer carotenes. How about that greenish-blue tint in skim milk? That comes from riboflavin exposed after fat is removed from the milk. Milk is white because of light bouncing off the casein micelles.

kitchen wisdom

Need a Quick Caramel Sauce?

Empty a can of sweetened condensed milk into a pan and simmer it until thick, caramel brown, and fragrant. As an evaporated concentrate of milk plus 42% sugar, it boils at a higher temperature so browns quickly.

See Also • Butter, Cheese, Custard, Dispersions, Emulsion, Fermentation, Ice Cream, Nuts, Soybeans, Sugar, Sweeteners

MILLET • See Grains

MILLING • See Grains

MILT • See Fish

MINERALS

What It Is • Like most vitamins, minerals are essential micronutrients that can't be manufactured by our bodies. We get them from plant foods or the meat of animals that have eaten plant foods and some from the minerals in water we drink. But they serve vital body functions.

What It Does • Our bodies need dietary minerals for everything from building **bones** and regulating **metabolism** to sending nerve impulses throughout the body (see Minerals in Food chart, right). To make sure we get what we need, some foods are enriched or fortified with minerals, usually because important minerals are lost during processing. Refined wheat flour is often enriched with iron, which is lost in milling. Other foods, like breakfast cereal and iodized salt, are fortified to improve our intake of minerals.

In the kitchen, minerals have numerous effects. Water that's high in calcium or magnesium (hard water) can slow the softening of beans because the minerals strengthen the beans' cell walls. Copper in a copper bowl bonds with protein in egg whites, creating more stable egg white foams that rise higher during baking. Iodized salt dissolved in chlorinated tap water makes the water smell of the sea because of a reaction between the iodine and chlorine compounds. Hard-cooked eggs sometimes develop a greenish tint when iron in the yolk and sulfur in the white react to form harmless ferrous sulfide. (Using fresh eggs, cooking them quickly, and cooling them quickly helps to prevent the reaction.)

Minerals in Food

More than 16 dietary minerals are important for human health. About six of these are considered major minerals, or macrominerals, because we need them in fairly large amounts of more than 200 mg per day (according to U.S. Department of Agriculture recommendations). About 10 others are called trace minerals, or microminerals, because we need less than 200 mg per day. Here are 16 important minerals along with the foods highest in the mineral and the mineral's primary functions in human health.

Mineral	Food Sources	Vital Functions
Major Minerals		
Calcium	Dairy products, fish eaten with bones, canned salmon and sardines, purple broccoli, kale, spinach, watercress, okra, almonds, tofu, turnips	Maintains strength of bones and teeth, regulates nerve impulses and muscle contraction, helps blood clot
Chloride	Salt, soy sauce, milk, meat, foods processed with salt	Regulates body fluids along with sodium and potassium, helps produce hydrochloric acid in stomach for digestion
Magnesium	Whole grains, wheat germs, nuts, seeds, shrimp and other shellfish, okra, chard, soybeans, tofu, dried apricots, cocoa	Builds bone, helps enzymes produce energy during metabolism, assists in muscle contraction
Phosphorus	Meat, milk, nuts, legumes	Helps maintain strength of bones and teeth, helps the body use energy during metabolism, helps form DNA
Potassium	Meat, poultry, fish, bananas, citrus, cantaloupes, dried apricots, legumes, vegetables (especially potatoes, tomatoes, and green leafy vegetables), instant coffee	Helps regulate electrolyte and fluid balance, assists in sodium excretion, assists protein metabolism
Sodium	Salt, soy sauce, MSG, cured meat, foods processed with salt	Helps regulate electrolyte and fluid balance, regulates nerve impulses
Trace Minerals		
Chromium	Meat, liver, fish, shellfish, whole grains, legumes, nuts, oil	Helps regulate insulin, assists in fat metabolism, helps maintain structure of DNA
Copper	Meat, liver, fish, shellfish, nuts, seeds, whole grains, wheat germ, curry powder	Assists in iron absorption; component of enzymes that help release food energy
Fluoride	Fluoridated drinking water, tea, fish, shellfish, seaweed	Helps teeth resist decay
Iodine	Iodized salt, fish, shellfish, seaweed, bread	Helps thyroid produce hormones that regulate metabolism
Iron	Meat, liver, kidneys, blood sausage, game meat, oily fish (e.g., sardines), shellfish (e.g., mussels, clams, and oysters), legumes, green leafy vegetables, dried apricots, prunes, tofu	Helps enzymes release food energy; part of oxygen-carrying hemoglobin in blood
Manganese	Organ meats, tea, whole grains, nuts, green leafy vegetables, soybeans, tofu	Helps release food energy, assists in antioxidant function
Molybdenum	Liver, whole grains, kasha, wheat germ, legumes, green leafy vegetables	Helps enzymes use iron and excrete uric acid
Selenium	Meat, fish, shellfish, seaweed, eggs, whole grains, Brazil nuts, sunflower seeds	Assists in antioxidant function
Sulfur	Protein foods such as meat, eggs, and legumes	Helps enzymes function properly; a component of proteins such as cysteine
Zinc	Meat, milk, hard cheese, yogurt, fish, shellfish (particularly oysters), poultry, vegetables, legumes, nuts, pumpkin seeds	Boosts immune function, assists in wound healing, assists in taste perception; a component of insulin

fast fact

- Sodium chloride (table salt) contains about 60% chloride and 40% sodium, both essential minerals.

And sulfur compounds can help retain the natural color and flavor of dried fruits such as apples and apricots.

How It Works • Daily mineral requirements are difficult to pinpoint because minerals are bound up in compounds in food, they are absorbed in varying degrees depending on the compounds they are eaten with, and scientists are still discovering the role of minerals like chromium. We do know that some mineral deficiencies can lead to disease. Iron deficiency is a common cause of anemia, and calcium deficiency can lead to rickets (soft bones) in children and osteoporosis (porous bones) in elderly adults. An excess of some minerals, such as copper, can be toxic.

Mineral absorption is a complex process, but cooking and food combinations can improve our intake of some minerals. For instance, cooking in cast-iron **cookware** releases some iron into the food and helps us meet our daily requirements (excess iron is easily eliminated from the body). We also absorb more iron from plant foods like green leafy vegetables when they are eaten with foods rich in vitamin C, such as potatoes, whereas we don't absorb as much when we eat them with calcium-rich foods like dairy products. We can improve zinc absorption from plants and dairy products by eating these foods with meat or fish. Magnesium absorption is improved by avoiding large amounts of calcium, protein, and phosphate in the same meal. And weight-bearing exercise improves calcium absorption. Mineral absorption depends heavily on the details of personal diet and lifestyle, so most nutritionists recommend satisfying our mineral needs by eating a wide variety of foods.

See Also • Salt, Vitamins, Water

MINT • See Flavor, Herbs

MIREPOIX • See Vegetables

MISO • See Soybeans

MIZUNA • See Cruciferous Vegetables, Leaves

MOCHI • See Rice

MOLASSES • See Sugar

MOLD

What It Is • Moldy bread and fruit might be unappetizing, but molds are important for making everything from **cheese** to **wine** to soy sauce. Thousands of mold varieties grow on Earth, and they're all **fungi** that appear in a mass of soft, downy blue, green, yellow, white, gray, or black colors.

What It Does • Molds have several benefits in food production. In cheese making, white molds like *Penicillium camemberti* and *P. candidum* ripen the surface of bloomy-rind cheeses such as Camembert and Brie and help to develop their flavor. Blue molds such as *P. roqueforti* ripen the interior of blue-veined cheeses like Roquefort, Stilton, and Danish Blue, while *P. glaucum* ripens the interior of Gorgonzola. Various strains of *Mucor* mold are used to make fermented **soybean** curd, and *Botrytis cinerea* mold is allowed to grow and feed on certain grapes to dehydrate them and concentrate their sugar, so the grapes can be made into full-bodied, richly flavored wine like Sauternes and Riesling.

Most food molds are harmless and do no more than discolor the food and give off strong aromas. For instance, the white

kitchen wisdom

Keeping Mold Out

To help keep homemade breads from getting moldy, add cinnamon and chopped raisins to the dough. Professional bakers sometimes add raisin pulp or concentrated raisin juice because the propionic acid in raisins inhibits mold growth. Commercial white bread has sodium or calcium propionate added directly to inhibit mold growth.

Molds Used in Food Production

Several molds are crucial for the production of foods such as cheese, wine, and soybean products.

Mold	Color	Uses in Food Production
Aspergillus oryzae (koji mold)	White-gray	Soy sauce, miso, fermented rice (lao-chao), and alcoholic beverages like sake
Botrytis cinerea	White-gray	Sugar-rich wines like Sauternes and Riesling
Fusarium venenatum	White-gray	Meat substitutes like Quorn
Geotrichum candidum	White-gray	Fermented taro root (poi) and bantu beer
Mucor circinelloides, M. hiemalis, M. racemosus	White-gray	Fermented soybean curd (sufu)
Mucor pusillus, M. miehei	White-gray	Microbial rennet for cheese
Penicillium camemberti	White-gray	Camembert and Brie cheese
P. candidum	White-gray	Brie and Camembert cheese
P. chrysogenum	Blue-green	Penicillin antibiotic
P. glaucum	Blue-green	Gorgonzola cheese
P. roqueforti	Blue-green	Roquefort, Stilton, Danish Blue, and sometimes Gorgonzola
Rhizopus oligosporus, R. oryzae	White-gray	Tempeh

Penicillium molds that grow on the casings of fermented cured sausages contribute flavor and can be safely eaten. But some molds are harmful, and can produce deadly toxins called mycotoxins. Bread stored in a warm, moist, enclosed environment (as in a plastic bag) can develop potentially toxic blue-green *Aspergillus*, white *Penicillium*, and/or gray *Mucor* molds. In some cases, cheese stored for a long time (particularly soft cheese wrapped in plastic) can develop toxic *Aspergillus versicolor*, *Penicillium viridicatum*, and *P. cyclopium* molds that penetrate an inch or so into the cheese. Heavily molded cheese, bread, or fruit should be discarded. Likewise, mold that occasionally develops on a wine cork (cork taint) often spoils the entire bottle of wine, requiring that it be discarded.

fast fact

- *Aspergillus niger* mold is the world's foremost source of citric acid, accounting for 99% of global production.

Molds can damage food crops too. *Fusarium graminearum* mold often attacks barley crops, causing root rot and seedling blight, and has had significant economic impact on the malting and brewing industries that rely on barley. Some *Aspergillus* molds on grains and nuts produce lethal toxins or carcinogens such as aflatoxins. All moldy grains and nuts should be discarded.

How It Works • Molds thrive in warm, damp, dark conditions, but they can grow on most foods at most temperatures and under most conditions, be they dry, moist, acidic, or alkaline. As a type of fungus, molds get energy by feeding off organic matter and reproduce by spores carried through the air. They grow on the host substance in the form of long filaments called hyphae that extend beneath the surface of food and into the air, becoming visible when enough hyphae form a mold colony. Molds decompose organic matter and recycle nutrients for use by other organisms. Molds also secrete toxic substances (mycotoxins) to deter other organisms that may compete for their food. Mold can be destroyed by cooking at 140°F (60°C) for 10 minutes, but toxins secreted by the mold often survive the heat.

See Also • Bakeware, Cheese, Cookware, Cork, Fungi, Wine

MOLE • See Sauces

MOLECULAR GASTRONOMY

What It Is • Molecular gastronomy is the scientific study of fine food and cooking. While traditional food science focuses on developing food products for sale in retail markets, molecular gastronomy applies science to dishes typically served at home or in restaurants. The term was coined in 1988 by Hungarian-born Oxford-based physicist Nicholas Kurti and French chemist Hervé This to describe the first of many international workshops in Erice, Italy, that brought together (and continue to bring together) scientists and chefs to better understand how food and cooking work.

What It Does • Molecular gastronomy seeks to understand the chemical and physical properties of ingredients, equipment, and techniques that allow us to transform raw materials into fine food. For instance, why does mayonnaise become firm and creamy? What makes a soufflé rise into a delicate puff? Does searing meat really lock in its juices? As well as Kurti and This, prominent scientists who have asked these questions include Thorvald Pedersen (Belgium), Davide Cassi (Italy), Peter Barham (England), and Jorge Ruiz (Spain). Since the 1980s, the discipline has evolved as scientists investigate old recipes, question cooking assumptions, and discover new gastronomic possibilities. Their research has led to such developments as the classification of culinary **dispersions**, which are foods like **emulsions**, gels, and **foams** that include particles of one substance dispersed into and held in suspension by another substance. Similar research has debunked several old cooking myths and proved conclusively that searing meat does not lock in juices. Salting meat shortly before cooking does not dry it out. Adding an avocado pit to guacamole doesn't prevent it from browning. All the alcohol in a dish does not necessarily burn off during cooking. Washed mushrooms don't absorb a lot of water. And salting beans at the beginning of cooking doesn't keep them from softening.

How It Works • A central tenet of molecular gastronomy is that the rest of our lives have been revolutionized by science and technology, but the way we cook and eat has not. We still cook with fire, eat with sticks, and rely on cooking wisdom that may never have been subject to rigorous testing. Among its achievements, molecular gastronomy has informed us that a pan and an open flame is the least efficient cooking method because as much as 65% of the heat is lost to the air. When using pots and pans, the most efficient heat

Liquid Nitrogen Ice Cream

Liquid nitrogen (LN_2) boils at $-321°F$ ($-196°C$), which means it is super cold. Throw it in a bowl of sweetened cream and you will have ice cream in less than a minute. LN_2 is used for cryogenic freezing in industry, and for making elaborate culinary preparations in some of the most avant-garde restaurants in the world. At Moto restaurant in Chicago you can "grill" your own tuna steak on a smoked metal grid frozen in LN_2. Grilling is a bit of a misnomer. The tuna actually gets freezer-burned from the super-chilled metal. It looks grilled, but it tastes like sashimi.

Liquid nitrogen ice cream is much more popular and is a fun experiment done in many high school science labs. A recipe follows, but before you start there are some safety concerns to consider. Working with LN_2 is as dangerous as working with a deep-fat fryer filled with boiling oil. If any of the stuff gets on you it will do serious damage, so you must wear protective goggles, heavy rubber gloves, long sleeves, long pants, and closed shoes. Liquid nitrogen is available at welding supply and medical supply stores and is not expensive. However, it must be transported in either a pressurized tank or a specialized thermos, which can be pricy. It should also not be used in enclosed spaces since it can replace oxygen in the air and could cause suffocation.

1 quart	half-and-half (10%) cream	1 L
1½ cups	granulated sugar	375 mL
1 tsp	vanilla extract	5 mL
3 quarts	liquid nitrogen	3 L

1. In a large metal or plastic bowl, stir together cream, sugar, and vanilla until sugar is dissolved. (Or you can use 1 quart/1 L of your favorite ice cream base.)

2. Put on the safety goggles and gloves and slowly add a small amount of liquid nitrogen as you stir with a whisk. Nitrogen gas will rise from the bowl as you stir. Don't worry; it won't hurt you.

3. Continue stirring and adding LN_2 until the mixture thickens too much to use the whisk. Switch to a wooden spoon (or a stand mixer fitted with the paddle attachment) and mix thoroughly until the ice cream is firm, adding more LN_2 as needed. Remove the spoon (or lift the paddle) and add the remaining LN_2 to harden the mound of ice cream. Pick up a spoon and dig in, or pack into a tightly covered container and freeze for up to 48 hours. Scoop and enjoy.

MAKES 1 QUART (1 L)

transfer method is induction cooking, which loses only about 10% heat, making it 90% heat efficient.

Investigating the science behind food and cooking is nothing new. For centuries, chemists and chefs from Apicius and Antoine-Laurent de Lavoisier to Marie-Antoine Carême and Fernand Point have researched and discovered the ideal ways to prepare meat stock, thicken sauces, and brew coffee. And new technologies have always had a profound effect on food and cooking. As far back as the 1600s, the pressure cooker allowed us to raise the boiling point of water. In 1966, foam made with nitrous oxide was popularized in the form of canned Easy Cheese. But more recently molecular gastronomy has joined divergent developments in gastronomy and food science into a single scientific discipline that systematically tests the axioms and explores the undiscovered possibilities of fine food and cooking.

science wise

Whiskey Improvements • According to Hervé This, one of the founders of molecular gastronomy, you can make cheap whiskey taste more expensive. His research found that adding 5 drops of vanillin to a 750 mL bottle of inexpensive whiskey will soften its edge and round out the flavors by producing the same chemical compounds that develop in fine whiskeys aged in oak casks.

The Ripple Effects of Molecular Gastronomy

Molecular gastronomy has stimulated the development of new dishes and new technologies to expand our experience of food. That's where chefs come into the picture. Many chefs have used food science to broaden the culinary possibilities of fine dining. Ferran Adrià of El Bulli restaurant in Spain was among the first chefs to delve deeply into scientific cooking, in the 1990s. Since then several chefs have opened restaurants devoted to pushing culinary boundaries, among them Grant Achatz at Alinea (Chicago), Andoni Luis Aduriz at Mugaritz (Spain), José Andrés at Minibar (Washington, D.C.), Heston Blumenthal at The Fat Duck (England), Ettore Bocchia at the Grand Hotel Villa Serbelloni (Italy), Homaru Cantu at Moto (Chicago), Wylie Dufresne at WD-50 (New York), Pierre Gagnaire at Gagnaire in the Hôtel Balzac (Paris), and Emmanuel Stroobant at Saint Pierre (Singapore).

Many of these chefs deconstruct familiar dishes like pizza, then rearrange the dish's basic components so that diners can experience the flavors and textures in new ways. They create new sensations by making everything from watermelon foam and olive oil powder to menus printed on flavored edible paper, from smoked-bacon-and-eggs ice cream to carbonated fruit. Their favorite ingredients may be not foie gras and truffles but hydrocolloids and alginates. Their favorite equipment may be not copper pots and rotisseries but immersion circulators and rotary evaporators. Here's a look at some of the ingredients and equipment used in these chefs' kitchens.

Ingredient or Equipment	Primary Uses
Ingredients	
Agar	Thickens and gels liquids
Calcium chloride or calcium lactate	Gels liquids containing alginates into beads or spheres (spherification); used in solution
Lecithin	Emulsifies liquids like oil and water that don't normally mix; stabilizes foams
Liquid nitrogen	Cryogenically freezes (at subfreezing temperatures) liquids and fats; often used to make ice creams
Methylcellulose	Gels hot liquids that will then liquefy when cooled in your mouth
Sodium alginate	Mixed with liquid to gel it into beads (spherification) when dropped into a solution of calcium lactate
Tapioca maltodextrin	Turns liquid fats into powder that releases flavor when mixed with moisture (as in the mouth)
Transglutaminase (meat glue)	An enzyme that sticks proteins together to make foods like chicken nuggets or noodles made from shrimp
Xanthan gum	Thickens and emulsifies liquids like oil and water that don't normally mix
Equipment	
Anti-griddle	Flash freezes the exterior of foods (often liquids, creams, and gels) on a metal surface
Gastrovac	Removes air from food in a vacuum, then impregnates the food with flavored liquid when pressure is restored (cold impregnation)
Immersion circulator	Maintains precise water temperatures; used in combination with a vacuum sealer to cook food (especially meat) for a long time at low temperatures (called sous vide, or "under vacuum")
Pacojet	Turns frozen liquids into flavorful snow
Rotary evaporator (Rotovap)	Distills and recovers the flavors from food by means of a rotating flask in a hot water bath and a vacuum pump
Thermo Whip	Turns hot or cold liquid into foam with nitrous oxide (NO_2)
Vacuum sealer	Retains moisture but not air; used in combination with an immersion circulator for sous-vide cooking

This discipline is devoted to expanding and improving our experience and enjoyment of food. Molecular gastronomy often brings chefs and scientists together to collaborate on research projects or participate in workshops like those held in Erice, Italy, and by groups such as the Experimental Cuisine Collective in New York City. Similarly, the Research Chefs Association, a group formerly focused on food product development, has broadened its mission by developing Culinology, a related discipline that blends food science with culinary arts.

See Also ● Cooking, Food Science

MOLECULE

What It Is • A molecule is a stable group of two or more **atoms** held together by strong **chemical bonds**. Food consists of four basic molecules: **water**, **fats**, **carbohydrates**, and **proteins**.

What It Does • All food molecules exist in a certain state, or phase: solid, liquid, or gas. These phases help determine the texture of foods, from crunchy to creamy. Some molecules can change phase. For instance, water molecules can exist in all three states as solid (ice), liquid (water), and gas (steam). But most food molecules, like the molecules of protein in **meat**, can't change phase because they are simply too large. Yet we rarely experience single phases of matter in food. Most food consists of various molecules in the three phases. For instance, fat-free milk consists of solid milk protein casein micelles suspended in liquid water. Known as **dispersions**, these kinds of molecular mixtures create various interesting textures in food. Whipped cream and other **foams** consist of air (gas) dispersed in liquid (cream or other liquid). Jellies consist of fruit juice (liquid) dispersed in a pectin or gel network (solid). The interplay of solid, liquid, and gas phases among molecules creates the dynamic texture of food.

How It Works • All food and all matter consists of elements like carbon, hydrogen, and oxygen. A single atom of any element is made up of electrons, protons, and neutrons that carry electrical charges. Molecules form when the electrical attractivity between atoms causes them to develop chemical bonds. Molecules are stable compounds of at least two atoms. They may be held together by opposite electronic charges (ionic bonds) or may share pairs of electrons in a strong bond known as a covalent bond. Many molecules in foods are held together by weak bonds such as hydrogen bonds, salt bridges, and hydrophobic interactions.

When atoms share electrons equally, the compound is called a nonpolar molecule.

fast fact
• Molecules are invisible to the naked eye, measuring less than 1/1,000 of a millimeter across.

When atoms don't share electrons equally, the compound is called a polar molecule because it has a positive charge at one end (or pole) and a negative charge at the other. In food, triacylglycerol fat molecules are nonpolar, whereas water and sugar are polar molecules.

Electrical attractivity holds food molecules together and causes them to react with each other, break apart, and transform when various foods are mixed and cooked. The structure and reactivity of a food molecule determines how it will interact with other food molecules. Knowing how different molecules behave helps us to understand what happens during food preparation and cooking. For instance, salt is a compound of sodium and chloride held together by weak ionic bonds. When salt mixes with water, the compound breaks apart and separates into positive ions of sodium and negative ions of chloride surrounded by water molecules. This creates a brine and allows the salt water to react with other food molecules in different ways than if the water and salt didn't mix.

See Also • Atom, Chemical Bonding, Cooking, Heat

A Water Molecule

A water molecule consists of an oxygen atom with a negative charge and two hydrogen atoms, each with a slight positive charge. The opposite attraction of the charges creates surface tension.

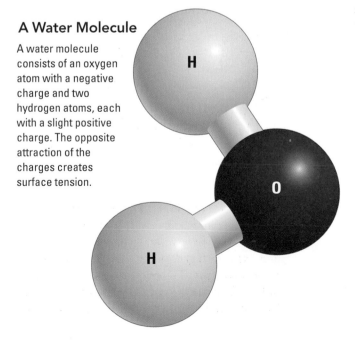

MOLLUSKS

What It Is • Including more than 250,000 species both living and extinct, mollusks are invertebrate animals with soft tissues and no internal skeleton. Most mollusks are ocean-dwelling bivalves enclosed in a pair of calcified shells, such as clams, cockles, mussels, oysters, and scallops. Abalone, conchs, snails, whelks, and periwinkles are univalve, or single-shelled, mollusks known as gastropods, some of which (such as snails) live on land. Octopuses and squids are mollusks known as **cephalopods** and have a thin internal shell called a pen or quill instead of a hard outer shell. This entry deals primarily with bivalve and gastropod mollusks.

What It Does • Mollusks are enjoyed every which way, from raw to cooked to smoked and canned. We also use the aromatic "liquor" inside their shells to make flavorings like clam juice and oyster sauce.

Most oysters and mussels are now cultivated, but clams and scallops are still harvested from the sea floor. When processed for food products, live oysters and clams are removed from the shell by hand, washed, sorted for size, then packed and shipped on ice. Sometimes they're frozen or smoked. When purchasing live oysters and clams whole, look for unbroken shells that close when tapped. Fresh scallops are typically sold out of the shell, but taste delicious in the shell if you can find them. The pale pink pouch found on some scallops is actually their roe and is considered a delicacy. When sold shelled, scallops should be ivory white or pale pink and not be clumped together. Bright white, shiny scallops that clump together have usually been soaked in a solution of sodium tripolyphosphate (STP) to help preserve them, a process that dilutes the flavor and increases the weight. Unsoaked, or "dry," scallops tend to have a more concentrated flavor and lose less liquid when cooked.

Preparing Mollusks

Fresh bivalve mollusks keep for about two days when refrigerated on ice in a single layer covered with a damp tea towel. To rid bivalves like clams and mussels of grit (cultivated mussels usually have none) before cooking, scrub the shells and soak them for 1 hour in salty water (about ⅓ cup/ 75 mL salt per gallon/4 L of water) with

Mollusks Marinière with Pernod

To capture the flavorful "liquor" of mollusks, steam them in wine or other flavored liquids like anise-scented Pernod. Butter and cream enrich the aromatic broth, which can be soaked up with crusty bread served on the side. Before cooking, rid the mussels and clams of any grit by soaking them for 1 hour in a pot filled with 1 gallon (4 L) water, ⅓ cup (75 mL) salt, and 2 tbsp (25 mL) cornmeal.

3 tbsp	butter, divided	45 mL
½ cup	chopped shallots	125 mL
¼ cup	chopped onion	50 mL
1½ cups	dry white wine	375 mL
⅓ cup	Pernod	75 mL
24	mussels, scrubbed and debearded	24
24	littleneck clams, scrubbed	24
¾ cup	whipping (35%) cream	175 mL
1 tbsp	chopped fresh tarragon	15 mL
1 tbsp	chopped fresh parsley	15 mL
	Salt and freshly ground black pepper	

1. Melt 2 tbsp (25 mL) of the butter in a deep, wide sauté pan over medium heat. Add shallots and onions and sauté until beginning to soften, 2 to 3 minutes. Add wine and Pernod and simmer for 1 minute.

2. Add mussels and clams and cover. Increase heat to high and steam, shaking pan once or twice, until the mussels and clams open, 4 to 6 minutes. Discard any unopened mollusks. Using slotted spoon, remove mollusks to serving bowl and cover with foil to keep warm.

3. Using a fine-mesh strainer or colander lined with a large coffee filter, strain cooking liquid into a bowl. Rinse out pan and pour strained liquid back into pan. Boil over high heat until liquid is reduced to about 1 cup (250 mL), 5 to 7 minutes. Add cream and boil until slightly thickened, 1 to 2 minutes. Reduce heat to low and stir in remaining 1 tbsp (15 mL) butter, tarragon, and parsley. Season with salt and pepper, to taste. Drizzle sauce over the mollusks and serve.

MAKES 4 TO 6 SERVINGS

about 2 tablespoons (25 mL) cornmeal. They will feed on the cornmeal and eject sand and debris. Using scissors, snip any remaining beards from mussels just before using; tugging can compromise quality because it tears the mussel flesh to which the beard is attached.

Clams and oysters use strong muscles to keep their shells closed. To make shucking easier, numb their muscles by freezing these mollusks for 20 minutes or so. After pressing a strong, dull knife between the hinged end of the shells, run the knife along the inside of the top shell to cut the adductor muscle, then remove the top shell and cut the other adductor muscle. The liquor from fresh oysters and clams should be fairly clear. Cloudiness indicates an older bivalve whose tissues have begun to break down (if the liquor is very cloudy give the oyster or clam a sniff to make sure it hasn't gone bad). When cooking live bivalves like oysters and clams, heat them briefly to avoid losing flavorful moisture. Cook just until they open, preferably removing them one-by-one as they open, as older, tougher ones may take longer to open. Discard any that don't open because they probably expired before cooking.

Univalves like abalone and conch are available fresh, frozen, and canned. They have a lean, sweet, and delicate flavor similar to that of clams. But their muscles are much tougher. Abalone are often tenderized with a mallet or rolling pin. Frozen abalone are slightly more tender because expanding ice crystals stretch and soften the tough cell walls. Both abalone and conch can be eaten raw, marinated in citrus juice for seviche, or gently cooked. During gentle cooking, the extensive connective tissue of abalone and conch shrinks and toughens when it reaches the

Bivalve Mollusk Varieties

There are more than 30,000 species of bivalves, among them clams, mussels, oysters, and scallops. The most common varieties are listed below. Clams fall into two basic categories: hard-shell clams, which may be eaten raw, and soft-shell clams, which are generally eaten cooked. The soft-shell varieties are named for their thin, brittle shells and long necks that they use to siphon ocean water.

Mollusk	Characteristics
Clams, Hard-Shell (Quahogs)	
Butter	3- to 5-inch (7.5 to 12.5 cm) shell
Cherrystone	2- to 3-inch (5 to 7.5 cm) shell
Chowder (large)	3- to 6-inch (7.5 to 15 cm) shell
Littleneck (Atlantic and Pacific)	1- to 2-inch (2.5 to 5 cm) shell
Manila (Japanese littleneck)	3- to 4-inch (7.5 to 10 cm) shell
Ocean quahog (mahogany)	2- to 3-inch (5 to 7.5 cm) shell
Pismo	5- to 7-inch (7.5 to 17.5 cm) shell
Surf (bar or hen clam)	4- to 8-inch (10 to 20 cm) shell
Clams, Soft-Shell (Longnecks)	
Geoduck (mirugai)	6- to 8-inch (15 to 20 cm) shell
Razor	5 to 8 inches (12.5 to 20 cm) long, ¼ to ½ inch (0.5 to 1 cm) wide
Steamer	1- to 2-inch (2.5 to 5 cm) shell
Mussels	
Blue	2- to 3-inch (5 to 7.5 cm) blue-black shell

Mollusk	Characteristics
Mussels (continued)	
New Zealand green	3- to 4-inch (7.5 to 10 cm) green shell
Prince Edward Island	2-inch (5 cm) beardless shell; farm-raised
Oysters	
Atlantic or Eastern (bluepoint)	2- to 4-inch (5 to 10 cm) gray to brown shell; native to North American Atlantic coast
European (belon or Portuguese)	1½- to 3-inch (4 to 7.5 cm) round, flat shell; native to France
Olympia	1- to 1½-inch (2.5 to 4 cm) shell; native to North American Pacific coast
Pacific Japanese	6-inch (15 cm) gray to brown shell; usually farmed
Scallops	
Bay	½-inch (1 cm) diameter; delicate, moist, sweet; available in winter in eastern North America
Calico	½-inch (1 cm) diameter; sweet but less delicate than bay scallops; best cooked briefly and gently
Sea	1½-inch (4 cm) diameter; firm texture and mildly sweet flavor

relatively low temperature of 120°F (50°C). With continued gentle cooking, the collagen melts into gelatin, creating a richer, more viscous texture.

How It Works • Bivalve mollusks live between two calcified shells made mostly from calcium carbonate absorbed from the sea. They take in oxygen and nutrients through their gills and secrete shell material through an outer fold of skin called the mantle. Their shells grow the fastest during the warm months when spawning peaks, and form growth ridges like rings on a tree stump.

The remaining anatomy of bivalves consists of muscle and digestive and reproductive organs. The adductor muscles open and close the shell. White or opaque and somewhat tender, one part of the muscle moves rapidly to expel sand and other waste. (Scallops consist primarily of this tender muscle.) The

fast facts

- The oldest mollusk fossil was found in the Burgess Shale of the Canadian Rockies and dates back more than 500 million years.
- Mussels get their orange color from algae and crustaceans, which contain carotene pigments like astaxanthin, canthaxanthin, and beta-carotene. Female and Atlantic mussels tend to ingest more.
- Scallops are among the safest mollusks to eat raw. Their filtration mechanism is discarded during processing, so only the adductor muscle, where few toxins accumulate, is eaten.

Oysters with Green Garlic Sauce

Find the freshest oysters you can for this recipe (any variety will do). A cool watercress sauce balances the sweet flavor and tender texture of the oysters.

	Ice	
12	fresh oysters, shucked	12
½	bunch (about 2 cups/500 mL) watercress	½
1	shallot	1
1	clove garlic	1
2	anchovy fillets	2
2 tbsp	sliced almonds	25 mL
2 tbsp	freshly squeezed lemon juice	25 mL
1 tbsp	olive oil	15 mL

1. Line a platter with a bed of ice and arrange oysters on top.

2. In a food processor, combine watercress, shallot, garlic, anchovies, almonds, lemon juice, and olive oil. Process to a loose paste then, spoon a bit of sauce over each oyster. Serve.

MAKES 3 TO 4 SERVINGS

other part moves very slowly but is extremely strong, and allows bivalves to clam up for hours or days to ward off predators, so it develops more tough connective tissue. This is the tough part that's cut from the shell when clams are shucked or is cut from scallops when they are trimmed.

All bivalves filter large volumes of water (as much as 10 to 15 gallons/40 to 60 L a day in mature mussels), sucking water in, filtering out nutritious plankton and algae, and excreting wastewater. For this reason, water quality affects mollusk quality. Clams, mussels, oysters, and scallops may be unsafe to eat if they have fed on toxic marine plankton and algae. They sometimes take in single-celled algae called dinoflagellates that produce defensive toxins that are poisonous to our digestive and nervous systems and can be deadly. Bivalves retain the toxins in their gills or digestive organs. Warm-water bivalves, such as Gulf Coast oysters, tend to be more susceptible to toxins like *Vibrio vulnificus*, a naturally occurring marine bacterium that can be lethal to humans. Gulf Coast clams and oysters may also harbor brevetoxins that can adversely affect our neuromuscular system. Bivalves harvested from the North American Atlantic coast sometimes contain domoic acid, which can lead to nausea and temporary amnesia, as well as saxitoxins, which can cause paralysis. Harbored within bivalves from Japanese, European, and Canadian waters, algae toxins such as okadaic acid may cause diarrhea. Because of these health risks, many countries vigilantly monitor water quality for algae bloom, or "red tide," and regularly test bivalves to ensure their safety, particularly if they will be eaten raw. Cooking offers some protection, as most bacteria and parasites are killed at 140°F (60°C). Mollusks from polluted waters can harbor *E. coli* bacteria and hepatitis viruses.

Mollusk Flavor and Texture

One of the reasons we love oysters, scallops, clams, and mussels is their delicately sweet flavor. Most of that sweetness comes from **glycogen** transformed into glucose and sugar phosphates as the mollusks age. Scallops also get sweetness from the amino acid glycine. Savory flavors in mollusks come from glutamic acid and amino acids like proline, arginine, and alanine. Clams and oysters use these amino acids to balance their salt concentration, so the most savory of these mollusks grow in very salty water.

kitchen wisdom

Buying Good Scallops

Unscrupulous fishmongers sometimes cut large fish such as skate into small pieces that resemble scallops. Be sure to buy scallops from a reputable seller.

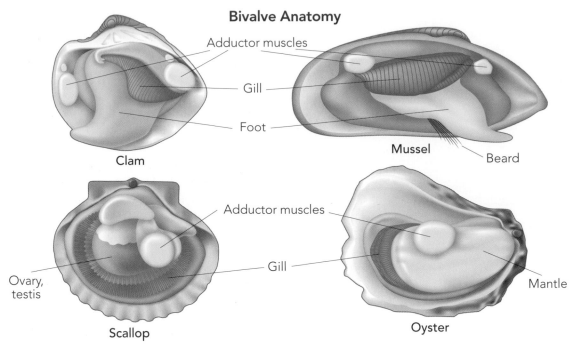

Bivalve Anatomy

Clam — Adductor muscles, Gill, Foot

Mussel — Adductor muscles, Gill, Foot, Beard

Scallop — Adductor muscles, Gill, Ovary, testis

Oyster — Gill, Mantle

Mollusks use up some of their energy to spawn in the warm months, so they tend to have richer flavor in the cold winter months. Aging them in the refrigerator for a few days causes them to accumulate succinic acid, adding more complex, savory flavors. Oysters are often enjoyed raw because as they're cooked, their protein coagulates and traps some of the flavorful amino acids. Cooking creates robust aromas in other mollusks by developing dimethyl sulfide, the same compound that gives cooked milk and canned corn their alluringly sulfurous aroma. The high levels of amino acids and sugar in scallops allows them to develop rich browned and caramelized flavors when cooked with dry heat, as on a grill or hot pan.

Apart from its sweetness, glycogen also provides some of the viscous texture of bivalves like oysters. Other textural factors depend on the species and the harvest season. Scallops taste tender because we eat the large fast-twitch portion of their adductor muscle rather than the tough part that keeps the shell closed. Bivalves are more tender in the warm summer months when they are growing (but they're more flavorful in the winter, so like other meats, simultaneously tender and flavorful bivalves don't seem to exist!). Oysters are among the most tender mollusks and abalone the toughest. When heated, all mollusks release their strong hold on their shells as their adductor muscle weakens, which causes the shells of bivalves to gradually open.

See Also • Cephalopod, Crustacean, Fish

MONKFISH • See Fish

MONOSODIUM GLUTAMATE • See Food Additives, Hydrolyzed Vegetable Protein

MORELS • See Mushrooms

MORTADELLA • See Sausage

MOUSSE • See Foams

MOZZARELLA • See Cheese

MUENSTER • See Cheese

MUFFINS • See Baking

MULLET • See Fish

MUNG BEAN • See Legumes

MUSCADET • See Wine

MUSCLE • See Meat

MUSHROOMS

What It Is • Mushrooms are the fruiting bodies of edible **fungi**. They include hundreds of species, such as *Agaricus bisporus*, which yields white, cremini, and portobello mushrooms, and the *Tuber* species, which gives us white and black truffles.

What It Does • Most edible mushrooms, including once-wild varieties like shiitake and oyster, are now cultivated in sterilized beds of nitrogen-enriched decaying plant matter and manure. Only a few varieties, such as porcini, chanterelles, hedgehogs, and truffles, are still harvested in the wild because these mushrooms are too difficult to cultivate for mass production.

Mushrooms are sold fresh, dried, canned, or freeze-dried. About a third of cultivated mushrooms are sold fresh, a third are canned, and a third are made into soup. When dried, mushrooms develop concentrated flavors (best fresh, chanterelles and oyster mushrooms are notable exceptions). In general, 2 to 3 ounces (56 to 84 g) of dried mushrooms is equivalent to 1 pound (454 g) fresh. They are reconstituted in liquid that then becomes a flavorful mushroom broth. If you want to use the broth, soak dried mushrooms in hot water to extract more flavor; when using only the reconstituted mushrooms, soak them in cold water to retain more flavor in the mushroom bodies. You can also pulverize dried mushrooms into powder in a food processor or spice mill and use the powder as a seasoning. To dry mushrooms at home, place on a rack in a convection oven set at 100°F (38°C) until dry, about 8 hours. Dried mushrooms are best stored in the freezer, for up to one year.

Tightly closed gills indicate younger, fresher mushrooms with milder flavor. Open gills indicate older mushrooms with more robust flavor but a shorter shelf life. Mushrooms decay faster than other produce because they have a higher metabolism. Slow it down with cold temperatures, and refrigerate them in a paper bag, which prevents moisture loss.

fast fact

• While the fruiting bodies of mushrooms come and go overnight, their underground fungal networks remain for years. One of the oldest, a network of honey mushrooms (*Armillariella ostoyae*) found in Oregon's Malheur National Forest, is estimated to be at least 2,400 years old.

To prepare fresh mushrooms, simply brush off any dirt or rinse briefly (they won't absorb a lot of water, but rinsing can discolor them), then trim the bottom of the stems. Mushrooms (especially white mushrooms) can discolor when cut because of enzymatic browning, but rubbing the cut surfaces with lemon juice or another acid helps prevent discoloration.

Mushrooms are best cooked slowly. That gives enzymes within the fruiting bodies time to develop new flavor compounds before they are denatured by heat. It also evaporates water, concentrating flavor and making most mushrooms pleasantly chewy. Some mushrooms, such as wood ears and

Mushroom Varieties

The diversity of mushrooms is staggering. Some are so firm they crunch between your teeth. Others seem to melt away on the tongue. White button mushrooms taste mild. But white truffles smell unmistakably strong. Here's a look at popular varieties, their parent species, and their culinary characteristics.

Mushroom	Species	Characteristics
Mushrooms with Gills		
Beech (brown clam shell, buna shimeji)	*Hypsizygus tessulatus*	White to light brown clustered caps; firm, crunchy texture; mild, nutty flavor
Blewit (blue foot)	*Clitocybe nuda*	Violet-gray cap and stem; meaty texture; earthy, somewhat spicy flavor
Cinnamon cap	*Pholiota*	Tawny-colored clustered caps; firm yet supple texture; earthy, sweet flavor
Cremini (Italian brown, immature portobello)	*Agaricus bisporus (avellanea)*	Tan to brown cap; similar to white mushrooms but with denser texture and deeper flavor
Enokitake (enoki, snow puff)	*Flammulina velutipes*	Several tiny white caps joined at the base; delicate, nearly crunchy texture; mild, aromatic flavor
Fairy ring	*Marasmius*	Smooth tawny conical cap on long beige stem; firm yet supple texture; mild, earthy flavor
Honey	*Armillariella ostoyae*	Large amber or light brown clustering caps on light brown stems; firm yet supple texture; earthy flavor
Matsutake (pine)	*Tricholoma*	Light to dark brown cap; dense, meaty texture; rich, spicy aroma
Nameko	*Pholiota*	Shiny orange-brown clustered caps; firm yet supple texture; earthy, sweet flavor
Oyster	*Pleurotus*	Light brown to gray to red flattened cap; velvety, oyster-like texture; mild flavor
Oyster (royal trumpet or king oyster)	*Pleurotus*	Light brown trumpet-shaped caps on tender white stem; delicate texture; mild flavor
Porcini (cep, king bolete, steinpilze)	*Boletus*	Smooth light to dark brown bun-shaped cap on thick barrel-shaped stem; dense, meaty texture; rich, woodsy, complex flavor
Portobello (mature cremini)	*Agaricus bisporus (avellanea)*	Dark brown cap up to 6 inches (15 cm) in diameter; meaty texture; rich, woodsy flavor
Shiitake (oak, Chinese, or black forest)	*Lentinus edodes*	Golden to dark brown umbrella-shaped caps; spongy yet meaty texture; rich, woodsy flavor
Straw	*Volvariella volvacea*	Small light brown to dark charcoal conical cap; firm yet supple texture; mild, earthy, musty flavor
White (button)	*Agaricus bisporus (alba)*	Small (button) to large (jumbo) white to light brown bun-shaped cap; firm texture; mild, earthy flavor
Mushrooms without Gills		
Cauliflower	*Sparassis crispa*	Large pale yellow-white cauliflower-like ruffled, layered lobes on a rooting stalk; firm yet supple texture; nutty, sweet flavor
Chanterelle, black trumpet	*Craterellus*	Charcoal to black trumpet-shaped cap on thick white stem; delicate texture; rich, smoky, fruity flavor
Chanterelle, golden (egg mushroom, girolle, pfifferling)	*Cantharellus*	Golden yellow funnel-shaped cap on tapered hollow yellow stem; firm yet supple texture; earthy, nutty flavor and apricot-like aroma
Chanterelle, yellow foot	*Cantharellus*	Brown funnel-shaped cap on yellow stem; firm yet supple texture; earthy flavor with plum-like aroma
Chanterelle, white	*Cantharellus*	Pale white funnel-shaped cap on pale white stem; firm yet supple texture; earthy, nutty flavor with fruity aroma

Chicken-of-the-woods	*Laetiporus sulphureus*	Yellow-orange overlapping, tiered shape; firm texture (similar to chicken); mild, earthy flavor and citrus-like aroma
Hedgehog	*Hydnum*	Creamy white slightly funnel-shaped cap on white stem; delicate texture; earthy, nutty flavor
Maitake (hen-of-the-woods)	*Grifola frondosa*	Grayish brown layered cluster of fungus petals fused to central stalk; firm yet supple texture; aromatic, woodsy flavor
Morel	*Morchella*	Beige, yellow, or black sponge-like pointed honeycomb cap on thick, hollow stem; delicate texture; rich, woodsy, nutty flavor
Pom pom (yamabushitake, bear's head)	*Hericium erinaceus*	White strands resembling the head of a mop with no stem; velvety texture; mild, sweet flavor reminiscent of seafood
Puffball	*Lycoperdaceae*	White ball-shaped cap with no stem; firm texture; mild, earthy flavor
Truffle, black	*Tuber uncinatum*	Subterranean mass of dense black tissue; stiff texture; mild earthy flavor
Truffle, white	*Tuber macrosporum*	Subterranean mass of dense white or tan tissue; stiff texture; robust earthy and garlicky flavor
Wood ear	*Auricularia*	Light brown to black ear shape; gelatinous, chewy texture; mild, earthy flavor

Mushroom Anatomy

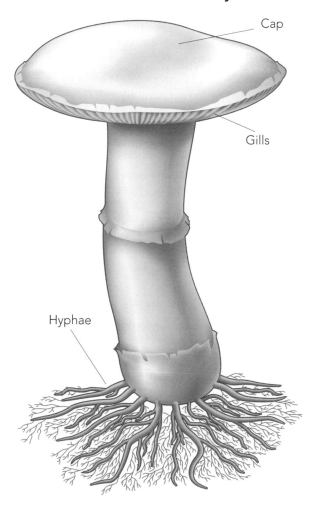

Cap

Gills

Hyphae

silver ears, become gelatinous when cooked because of their high carbohydrate content.

How It Works • Like all fungi, mushrooms are not plants that produce their own energy through photosynthesis. Instead, they live off the energy of plants and plant remains. Most of a mushroom's body lives underground in a network of filaments, called hyphae, that spreads throughout the soil, sometimes for miles, gathering nutrients. When the hyphae network has grown large enough to reproduce, it forces a fruiting body up through the soil, often overnight. As it fills with water, the mushroom quickly swells, opens up, and releases spores from its gills into the air.

To ward off predators, mushrooms harbor defensive chemical compounds that can be lethal. For instance, common button, cremini, and portobello mushrooms contain agaritine, a hydrazine compound that isn't destroyed by heat and has been shown to cause liver damage and cancer in mice. Other mushroom species contain psychoactive compounds like psilocybin and psilocin that can induce hallucinations in humans. For these reasons, avoid harvesting and eating unfamiliar mushrooms unless they have been identified as safe by an experienced mycologist (mushroom expert).

kitchen wisdom

Mushroom Stains
To keep portobello mushrooms from staining other foods, scrape away the dark gills with a spoon before using.

Mushrooms consist of nearly 90% water, but the remaining 10% is full of aromatic flavor compounds. Most mushrooms have a high concentration of amino acids such as glutamic acid, better known as the flavor of monosodium glutamate (MSG), and classified as umami. Mushrooms also contain guanosine monophosphate (GMP), which combines with MSG to enhance the flavors of other foods with which mushrooms are served. When cut, fresh mushrooms release earthy-smelling compounds like octenol, an alcohol that concentrates in the mushroom's gills and is more intense in mature mushrooms with open caps such as portobellos. Shiitake and porcini mushrooms also get meaty aromas from sulfur compounds. Other mushroom aromas range from spicy notes of cinnamon and pepper to sweet hints of butterscotch and fish.

See Also • Fungi

MUSSELS • See Mollusks

MUST • See Wine

MUSTARD

What It Is • The yellow condiment ubiquitous on North American hot dogs is but one product of the mustard plant. This huge variety of *Brassicas* also provides us with pungent mustard greens, mustard oil, mustard essence, and mustard powder. When the plants are young, their nutritious green leaves can be cooked like spinach or turnip greens. When it blooms, the plant's colorful flowers produce mustard seeds that can be pressed for oil or ground into powder to make various types of pungent prepared mustard.

What It Does • In North America, mustard seeds are rarely used whole outside of prepared mustard, but Indian cooks often sauté them in oil until they pop, which tames their pungency. Small black mustard seeds (*Brassica nigra*) are highest in the pungency-producing compound sinigrin. They make the hottest prepared mustard but are somewhat difficult to harvest.

Creamy Mushroom Soup

The richness of cream and the meatiness of mushrooms blend perfectly. Use whatever fresh mushrooms you have on hand for this recipe. It's particularly good with porcinis, chanterelles, shiitakes, or matsutakes.

2 tbsp	butter	25 mL
12 oz	fresh mushrooms, sliced	375 g
2 tbsp	all-purpose flour	25 mL
1¾ cups	chicken broth	425 mL
1 cup	light (5%) cream	250 mL
1 tbsp	cornstarch	15 mL
¼ cup	dry sherry or white wine	50 mL
½ cup	whipping (35%) cream	125 mL

Salt and freshly ground white or black pepper

1. Melt butter in a saucepan over medium-low heat. Add mushrooms and sauté until softened, about 5 minutes. Stir in flour and cook, stirring, for 30 seconds. Gradually whisk in broth and light cream. Cook, stirring constantly, until thickened and gently simmering, 2 to 3 minutes.
2. In a small bowl, dissolve cornstarch in sherry and add to pan along with whipping cream. Cook, stirring, until gently simmering, 2 to 4 minutes. Season with salt and ground pepper to taste. For extra-creamy soup, purée in a blender and force through a fine-mesh sieve. Serve hot.

MAKES 4 SERVINGS

Brown mustard seeds (*Brassica juncea*) are slightly larger and easier to harvest but are less pungent. Many German, European, and Chinese prepared mustards are made with brown seeds, which are also used to make pickles. The largest seeds, yellow or white mustard seeds (*Brassica hirta* or *Sinapis alba*), are the least pungent and used to make American-style yellow mustard.

To make prepared mustard, the seeds are ground and sieved to remove the tough seed coat. Mixing the ground mustard with liquid develops its pungency, but mustard is often made with vinegar, wine, beer, or other acidic liquids to delay the release of pungent aromas and extend the shelf life of prepared mustard. Minute changes in preparation lead to various mustard styles, such as Dijon mustard (made with brown or black seeds and white wine, wine vinegar, and/or grape must), Creole mustard (brown seeds with horseradish), and English mustard (a mix of brown and white seeds).

Mustard seeds contain about 30% oil, which is extracted by pressing the seeds much like canola oil is pressed from canola seeds. Mustard oil contains only 5% saturated fat (the lowest of all edible oils) and is a traditional cooking oil in northern India. In North America, government regulations require that imported mustard oil be labeled "for external use only" because it is high in erucic acid (which is toxic in large amounts). In Italy, a more potent mustard oil is made by distilling the essential oil (allyl isothiocyanate) from black or brown mustard seeds. This highly concentrated pure mustard essence is so powerful that it is sold in tiny vials in pharmacies. Just a few drops provide a nose-filling sharpness to preserved fruits (*mostarda di frutta*).

Culinary mustard greens come from various subspecies of brown mustard plants (*B. juncea*). They not only stimulate the olfactory system but also provide us with high amounts of important nutrients like beta-carotene and folate. Like other **cruciferous vegetables**, mustard greens tend to taste best in cool weather, when their starch converts to sugar for energy. Mustard

kitchen wisdom

How to Delay Yeast Growth
If you want to slow down the growth of yeast in bread dough, add powdered mustard. Like salt, it strongly inhibits yeast growth.

Mustard Greens with Ginger, Soy, and Sesame

Quickly sautéed greens need only a few aromatics to balance their pungency. The Asian flavors here go best with Japanese mustard greens, but southern American or curled mustard greens also work.

1 tbsp	white or black sesame seeds	15 mL
1	bunch (about 1 lb/500 g) Japanese mustard greens (or American curled)	1
1 tbsp	mustard oil or canola oil	15 mL
2	cloves garlic, minced	2
2 tsp	minced fresh gingerroot	10 mL
¼ tsp	hot pepper flakes	1 mL
1 tbsp	tamari or soy sauce	15 mL
½ tsp	toasted sesame oil	2 mL

1. Heat a deep, wide sauté pan over medium heat. Add sesame seeds and toast, shaking pan occasionally, until fragrant, 2 to 3 minutes. Transfer to a bowl and set aside.

2. Strip greens of stems, discarding stems. Cut greens crosswise into 3-inch (7.5 cm) lengths.

3. Add oil to pan over medium heat. Add garlic and ginger and sauté for 1 minute. Add greens and hot pepper flakes and cook, stirring, until greens just begin to wilt, about 1 minute. Stir in tamari and sesame oil and cook until greens are wilted, about 1 minute more. Top with toasted seeds.

MAKES 3 TO 4 SERVINGS

Mustard Greens

The mustard plant species *Brassica juncea* includes more than 18 subspecies that produce leafy greens of various appearance and pungency. These greens feature prominently in the cooking of Asia, India, Africa, and the Southern U.S. The leaves can be eaten raw when young and cooked when mature. Here are a few popular subspecies and their characteristics.

Mustard Green	Subspecies	Characteristics
Curled or American mustard	*B. juncea (crispifolia)*	Long, slender pale green stems; large bright green rippled leaves with frilly edges; sharp, hot flavor
Japanese mustard (purple, red, or giant-leafed mustard)	*B. juncea (rugosa)*	Miniature purple greens often sold for salad mixes; mature greens have long, slender pale green stems; broad, rippled leaves are green on one side and purple on the other; extremely sharp flavor when mature
Leaf mustard (juk gai choy, bamboo mustard)	*B. juncea (foliosa)*	Smaller than dai gai choy; straight narrow or slightly wide pale green stems; flat, bright green leaves; mild to slightly strong sharp flavor
Red-in-snow mustard (green-in-snow mustard)	*B. juncea (multiceps)*	Long, slender pale green stems; large teardrop-shaped leaves with jagged edges; slightly sweet and mildly peppery flavor
Wrapped heart mustard (dai gai choy, Swatow)	*B. juncea (integrifolia)*	Wide, curved pale green stems, branching toward wide bright green leaves; extremely sharp, hot flavor

greens also produce fewer unpleasantly sulfurous aromas in the cold months. As with vegetables like cabbage, it's best to cook mustard greens briefly to avoid developing malodorous trisulfides. If you cook the greens with a lid, leave it ajar to allow some steam — and the unpleasant aromas — to escape.

How It Works • Mustard plants contain

bitter-tasting chemical defenses called isothiocyanates that ward off predators. Horseradish, wasabi, and cruciferous vegetables contain the same compounds, and in mustard they create two basic flavors: bitterness and pungency. When stored in the plant, these sulfur compounds taste bitter. Sinigrin is the major bitter-tasting compound in black and brown mustard seeds; sinalbin is the compound in white or yellow mustard seeds. Cutting mustard leaves or crushing mustard seeds and mixing them with liquid releases an enzyme called myrosin that catalyzes a reaction of the sulfur compounds and transforms them into a more pungent substance called allyl isothiocyanate (mustard oil). This is the substance that irritates nerve cells in our mouth and olfactory system — a sensation many people enjoy in the same way they enjoy the spiciness of hot chile peppers.

Acidic liquids like vinegar make the enzyme transformation slower, and prepared mustard often contains vinegar to prolong its pungency. Cooked mustard loses some of its pungency because allyl isothiocyanate becomes volatile and cooks off.

Mustard powder has another important use outside of prepared condiments. It can emulsify vinaigrettes and other oil-and-water mixtures by coating the oil droplets in a gooey mucilage of powdered protein and carbohydrate particles. Powdered white (yellow) mustard seeds are highest in mucilage and make the best emulsifiers. Mustard powder also helps to thicken liquids because it's so dry that it absorbs moisture until the particles swell to be so large that they slow down the flow of liquid.

fast facts

- Canada grows about 90% of the world's supply of mustard plants. Around the world, annual consumption of prepared mustard amounts to more than 700 million pounds (318 million kg).
- Jeremiah Colman concocted his British Colman's mustard in 1804 and included wheat flour for body and turmeric for color. Today, Colman's mustard is made with only powdered white (yellow) mustard seeds.

Mustard Brown Sugar Glaze

The piney scent of rosemary blends well with sweet brown sugar and pungent prepared mustard. Slather this simple glaze on roasted pork, lamb, or chicken before cooking for complex flavor.

½ cup	Dijon or spicy brown mustard	125 mL
¼ cup	packed dark brown sugar	50 mL
1 tbsp	mustard oil or canola oil	15 mL
1 tbsp	chopped fresh rosemary	15 mL
½ tsp	freshly ground black pepper	2 mL
½ tsp	ground cinnamon	2 mL
¼ tsp	ground allspice	1 mL
¼ tsp	salt	1 mL

1. In a bowl, combine Dijon, brown sugar, oil, rosemary, pepper, cinnamon, allspice, and salt. Use immediately or cover and refrigerate for up to 2 days.

MAKES ABOUT ¾ CUP (175 ML)

Mustard greens can taste pungent like the seeds, but their bitterness tends to dominate because of glucosinolate compounds in the leaves. Cooking mustard greens actually tames their pungency by inactivating the enzymes that create the pungency. However, cooking mustard greens with alliums like onions, green onions, and/or garlic can in turn make the alliums taste more pungent: enzymes in the alliums catalyze reactions of sulfur compounds in the greens to create pungent aromas in the alliums themselves.

See Also ● Capsicum, Cruciferous Vegetables

MUSTARD OIL ● See Mustard, Oil

MUSTARD SEED ● See Mustard

MUTTON ● See Lamb

MYCOPROTEIN ● See Fungi

MYOGLOBIN ● See Meat

MYRISTICIN ● See Spices

NAAN • See Bread

NAM PLA • See Fermentation

NAPA CABBAGE • See Cruciferous Vegetables

NASTURTIUM • See Flowers

NAVEL ORANGE • See Citrus

NAVY BEAN • See Legumes

NECTARINE • See Peach

NITRATES • See Curing

NITROGEN • See Molecular Gastronomy

NIXTAMALIZATION • See Alkali, Corn

NONFAT MILK • See Milk

NONSTICK COOKWARE • See Cookware

NOODLES • See Pasta

NOPALES • See Cactus

NORI • See Seaweed

NUT FLOUR • See Flour, Nuts

NUTMEG • See Spices

NUT OILS • See Nuts, Oil

NUTRITION

What It Is • Nutrition describes what the human body needs in the form of food to support life. The nutritious parts of foods are called nutrients, and the way the body gets those nutrients is called **diet**. Nutritional science investigates the body's responses to its diet. A diet that supplies all the nutrients your body needs in the right amounts (and not much more than it needs) is considered balanced. A balanced diet supports health, and an imbalanced diet can

fast facts

- The required daily intake of minerals is minuscule, but the tiny amounts are in no way indicative of their importance to health. Your body is only 0.00004% iodine, but without that smidgen of mineral your body could not metabolize any other nutrient.
- The florets of broccoli have about 35% more beta-carotene than the stalks, and frozen broccoli has about 75% of the calcium of fresh broccoli.

lead to vitamin-deficiency diseases like scurvy or beriberi; unhealthy conditions like obesity; or chronic ailments like cardiovascular disease, Type 2 diabetes, or osteoporosis.

What It Does • The human body contains chemical compounds that are constantly being used up and need to be replaced by the chemicals in food. Through **digestion**, the body breaks down food into the basic component parts that your cells need to function. Although all humans need approximately the same basic components to maintain health, those elements can be ingested in many forms. So though all humans share similar nutritional needs, there are many balanced diets that vary according to culinary traditions, cultural and personal preferences, and individual needs.

For example, athletes have increased nutritional needs because they expend more energy and therefore need more calories. If they are in training and building muscle, their protein needs are greater than those of a sedentary person, and during exercise or competition they might have increased need for water and sodium lost through sweating.

Malnutrition, the lack of nutrients necessary for growth and maintenance of vital functions, can happen to well-fed people as well as those that are starving. Eating a wide variety of fresh food is the best way to get all of the nutrients necessary for health.

How It Works • Nutritional elements can be roughly divided into four groups:

1. Macronutrients are the ones you need in large amounts, including **carbohydrates**, **proteins**, and **fats**.

2. Micronutrients are those needed in much smaller amounts, mostly **vitamins** and **minerals**. Phytochemicals are micronutrients that come from plant sources, including **antioxidants**.

3. **Fiber** from plants is indigestible, so it is not a nutrient, but it is an essential component of a balanced diet.

4. **Water** is not usually considered a nutrient, but it is a basic component in all foods and must be replenished regularly. It is essential for life.

Each type of nutritional element has a specific function, though they all work together to build a healthy body. Most government health agencies issue dietary guidelines to help people achieve and maintain health. The U.S. Department of Agriculture and Health Canada both view a balanced diet as one that consists predominantly of vegetables, fruits, and grains, with lesser amounts of dairy, meat, and fats, although all of those foods should be eaten every day. Both government departments recommend choosing lower-fat, lower-sugar, and lower-salt alternatives whenever possible, and to consume at least half of the daily amount of grains as whole grains.

See Also • Antioxidants, Carbohydrate, Diet, Digestion, Fat, Fiber, Minerals, Protein, Vitamins, Water

NUTS

What It Is • Most nuts are the large seeds of long-lived trees. They have hard shells and store their energy as fat. By that definition acorns are nuts, as are almonds, cashews, and hazelnuts (filberts). Some nuts are gigantic (coconuts) and some look more like seeds (pine nuts). Nuts come from several plant families, which makes them difficult to classify. And then there are foods that we call nuts but that don't fit the definition at all. Peanuts are **legumes** with tender shells, only their high fat content convinces us that they are nuts. The tiger nut (chufa) is a tuber (no shell at all), but also is high in fat (it is the base for a popular Spanish nut milk, *horchata*). Chestnuts fit the definition in all ways except that they store their energy as starch rather than fat, and therefore have a mealy consistency rather than an oily one.

What It Does • Compared to other seeds, nuts are more compact nutritionally and need little or no cooking to be edible. These qualities made them an important food in prehistoric times, but since the cultivation of grains and legumes around 7000 BCE they have played a less vital role in the human diet. Except for the production of nuts for oil, nuts are mostly eaten as snacks, used as garnishes, baked into sweets, ground into nut butters, or soaked to make nut milks.

Peanut oil has a high smoke point, which makes it one of the preferred oils for stir-frying, and the most popular oil in Asia. The aromatic oil pressed from walnuts is valued in France and Italy as a flavoring for vegetables and salads. And coconut oil is commonly used as an industrial frying oil.

The best nut oils are cold-pressed, which means the nuts are crushed and pressed under mechanical pressure. Cold-pressed oils are more flavorful and richer than solvent-extracted oils, which are made by combining crushed nuts with a solvent and heating the mixture to 150°F (66°C); by that temperature all of the oil in the nut has been liquefied. The oil is then separated from the solvent and refined.

Voluptuous Coconut Macaroons

These are the biggest plumpest plushest macaroons you are likely to ever encounter. Like all macaroons they are made mostly from nuts with just enough binder to make them adhere.

1 lb	sweetened shredded coconut (about 4 cups/1 L)	500 g
1	can (14 oz or 300 mL) sweetened condensed milk	1
2 tsp	finely grated orange zest	10 mL
1 tsp	vanilla extract	5 mL
2	large egg whites	2
Pinch	salt	Pinch

1. Preheat oven to 350°F (180°C). Line one or two baking sheets with foil or parchment paper. Set aside.

2. Mix coconut with just enough condensed milk until coated. Depending on the moistness of the coconut, you might not need to use the entire can of condensed milk. Stir in orange zest and vanilla.

3. In another bowl, beat egg whites with salt until foamy. Add to coconut mixture.

4. Using a small or standard ice cream scoop or spoon, scoop mixture onto the prepared baking sheets, about 1½ inches (4 cm) apart. Bake in preheated oven until golden brown on top and well browned on the bottom, 20 minutes for small or 25 to 30 minutes for standard size. If baking two sheets at a time on separate racks, switch positions halfway through baking.

5. Slide foil or parchment with cookies onto a wire cooling rack and let cool for 5 minutes. Peel foil off of cookies and let cool on rack completely.

MAKES ABOUT 16 LARGE OR
30 SMALL COOKIES

kitchen wisdom

Skinning Nuts

Nut skins contain astringent tannins and they are often removed to make nuts taste sweeter and to separate the dark skin from the pale nut meat within. Nuts with thin skins, like peanuts and hazelnuts, can be toasted, which makes their skins brittle so that they can be peeled away just by rubbing the surface with a rough towel. The thicker skin on almonds is made firm and loosened by being boiled briefly, which blisters the skin from the nut meat, making it easy to slip off. The skin of walnuts is so thin and adheres so tightly to the nut meat that it cannot be removed. Its color can be lightened and its astringency tamed by boiling walnuts in acidified water for a few minutes. The boiling softens the nut, which can be dried and crisped by toasting.

When nuts are ground, oil from the broken cells coats the tiny particles of fiber and protein, transforming nuts instantly from crunchy morsels into creamy nut butters, pastes, and/or nut meal. The only difference between nut butters and pastes is that butters like peanut butter tend to be made out of oilier nuts and are not sweetened, whereas nut pastes, such as marzipan (almond modeling paste), are made from drier nuts and are often sweetened. Adding sugar to ground nuts makes the mixture malleable. Marzipan is frequently colored and molded into decorations. Nut pastes are also used as pastry fillings, and when combined with egg white become the batter for French macaroons.

Nut butters are used in baking, or for enriching soups and stews. Peanut butter is a popular ingredient in East African cooking, and nut butters are one of the principal thickening components in Mexican moles.

Nuts (with the exception of chestnuts and coconut) are fairly water free, and when they are ground the minuscule droplets of oil dispersed in the nut run out as pure fat. If nuts are soaked before grinding, they absorb water, and when ground the fluid that emerges is an emulsion of oil, protein, carbohydrates, and salts suspended in water, a structure that is very similar to milk. Medieval Europeans and Arabs used blanched almond milk as a replacement for dairy on fast days, just as modern vegans use it as a non-animal milk alternative. The most common nut milk is made from coconut and is used mostly in Southeast Asian cooking.

Finely ground nuts, sometimes called nut meal or nut flour, can replace flour in baking, particularly in flourless tortes and in some recipes for macaroons. Commercially produced nut flours are made from the finely ground residue from nut oil production. Because nut flours contain much less oil than nut meals, they do not clump, and they are lower in calories, although they are not as nutritious.

Praline is a nut brittle that is used as a flavoring ingredient in baking or formed into candy. Classic French praline is made with almonds and sugar and is crunchy.

fast facts

- Newly harvested nuts are moist, so producers usually dry them with low heat, about 95°F (35°C).
- Commercially salted nuts are coated with special flake-shaped salt crystals that have more surface area and therefore adhere to the surface of the nut better. Peanuts that are salted in their shells are soaked in brine in a vacuum, so that the brine is pulled through the pores of the shell onto the nuts inside. After brining they are dry-roasted, which evaporates the water from the brine and crisps the nuts.
- The flavor of almond extract comes from benzaldehyde, a by-product of the generation of cyanide compounds in bitter almonds. Pure almond extract is extracted from bitter almonds (minus the cyanide component), natural almond extract comes from cassia bark (a cinnamon relative), and imitation almond extract is synthesized chemically.
- The culinary term for a brief period of boiling, "blanch," comes from the French *blanche*, meaning white and referring to the white color of peeled almonds. It comes from blancmange, the pale pudding thickened with blanched almonds in Renaissance cooking.

Common Nuts

Nut	Description	Common Uses	Nutrition per 1 oz (28 g) edible portion
Almond, bitter and sweet	• nut of a drupe fruit • two types: bitter (wild) and sweet (cultivated) • bitter almonds contain amygdalin that when crushed form toxic hydrocyanic acid, which is toxic and illegal in North America • sweet almonds do not contain the cyanogenic glucoside component, but are not as flavorful	• bitter almonds not eaten as food (only as the base for pure almond extract); oil also flavors almond paste • sweet almonds eaten as a snack; used in baking (tortes, macaroons) and candy making (nougat, marzipan); ground into almond butter; made into almond milk; used to garnish savory dishes • both sweet and bitter are pressed for oil	Sweet Almonds Kcal: 166 Pro: 4.6 g Fat: 14.6 g Fiber: 3.9 g
Brazil nut	• large seeds of a tropical fruit grow inside a coconut-like shell on a tree native to the Amazon • contain more selenium (a potent antioxidant) than any other food	• high level of saturated fat, a good substitute for coconut or macadamias in recipes • most are eaten as a snack	Kcal: 186 Pro: 4.1 g Fat: 18.8 g Fiber: 1.5 g
Cashew	• native to Brazil, the external seeds of the cashew apple (*marañon*), the fruit of a tropical evergreen • always sold shelled because shells contain an irritating oil (relatives of poison ivy) • creamy texture, even though they have less fat than many nuts, because of a high starch content of about 12%	• ground into nut butters and added to savory dishes; eaten as a snack	Kcal: 163 Pro: 4.3 g Fat: 13.1 g Fiber: 0.9 g
Charoli (chironji)	• small, round • strong flavor similar to hazelnuts, almonds and pistachios • grown mostly in India	• used as a sweet spice in Indian cooking, often in rawa (halwa), a grain pudding • can be dried and ground into a powder used for thickening	Kcal: 160 Pro: 4.2 g Fat: 14.4 g Fiber: 2.3 g
Chestnut	• nut of various species of chestnut trees • starchy rather than oily so must be thoroughly cooked, and have a mealy, creamy texture • high in moisture (about 50%), which makes them perishable, so they must be refrigerated • frequently canned	• candied (marrons glacés); ground into flour for making cakes, pasta, and bread; puréed into soup; roasted with game meats; eaten as a snack • dried chestnuts have to be boiled	Kcal: 37 Pro: 0.2 g Fat: 0.1 g Fiber: 0 g
Coconut	• largest nut, the seed of a drupe fruit from a palm • coconut water (the thin milky liquid in the center of the nut) is high in electrolytes • coconut oil is more saturated than other nut oils, which makes it more stable	• coconut flesh, and coconut milk made from the flesh, are primary flavors in Southeast Asian cooking; in rest of the world coconut is mostly used in baking • coconut water is a common beverage and is an ingredient in some sports drinks • coconut oil is used in commercial frying	Kcal: 187 Pro: 2 g Fat: 18.3 g Fiber: 4.3 g
Hazelnut (filbert)	• seeds of the hazel bush, a tall deciduous shrub native to Europe and western Asia • 15 cultivars of hazel, but only a few produce good-quality nuts • distinctive flavorful compound is heptenone (filbertone), fairly mild when the nuts are raw, but pronounced when toasted	• ground into flour or sweetened into praline for use in cakes, breads, and pasta • flavoring in Frangelico liqueur • a popular flavoring for coffee.	Kcal: 179 Pro: 3.7 g Fat: 17.8 g Fiber: 1.7 g
Macadamia	• native to Australia, introduced to Hawaii in the 20th century • high in fat, mostly monounsaturated • cultivation remains limited, which keeps price high	• almost exclusively eaten as snacks, but can be used in baking, confections, and butters	Kcal: 199 Pro: 2.4 g Fat: 20.9 g Fiber: 2.6 g

Peanut	• seed of an underground fruit of a small legume, not nuts botanically but used like nuts • Asia is the largest producer, most are processed into oil • four varieties are produced in North America: Valencia for nuts in shells; Virginia for shelled nuts; Spanish for mixed nuts; and Runner for peanut butter and commercial baked goods because it is resistant to rancidity	• most are made into oil and butter; roasted peanuts are popular in baked goods in North America, sauces in Southeast Asia, and soups and stews in Africa	Kcal: 166 Pro: 6.7 g Fat: 14.1 g Fiber: 2.3 g
Pecan	• with 61% fat, rich, creamy, and delicately textured • shells are thin and brittle, making them prone to breakage and bruising, which can lead to the development of rancid flavors	• highly prized in pies and candies, especially pralines; used in other baked products and savory dishes	Kcal: 187 Pro: 2.3 g Fat: 18.3 g Fiber: 2.6 g
Pine nut (pignoli, piñon)	• seed kernels of pines, harvested from the scales of pine cones • hundreds of species of pines, but three produce most of the world's pine nuts: the Italian, Chinese, and single-leaf pine of the U.S. Southwest • have a piney, resinous flavor and are particularly high in fat, which can make them prone to burning	• often paired with fish, meat, and vegetable dishes; used in basil pesto and the defining element in pignoli cookies, an Italian pine nut macaroon • small amount is pressed into mildly flavored oil	Kcal: 160 Pro: 6.8 g Fat: 14.4 g Fiber: 1.3 g
Pistachio	• seeds of a tree native to the Middle East • green color results from chlorophyll that develops in seeds that grow in high altitudes	• used in baking, ice cream, sweets, and savory dishes • green color is often used as a vivid counterpoint in charcuterie products • in the Middle East used both in savory dishes and in a wide range of syrupy pastries	Kcal: 172 Pro: 4.2 g Fat: 15 g Fiber: 3.1 g
Walnut, black	• North American cousin of the more common English walnut • smaller, with a strong, acrid smoky flavor	• once used extensively in North America in breads, ice creams, sweets, and cakes, now a novelty nut and is not produced commercially	Kcal: 172 Pro: 6.9 g Fat: 16 g Fiber: 1.4 g
Walnut, English	• second only to almonds in worldwide consumption, cultivated mostly in Europe and North America • mildly astringent, the nut meat is rich in omega-3 fatty acid, which makes them nutritious but also prone to rancidity	• used in savory and sweet preparations; pressed into flavorful oil; ground into nut pastes and butters; pickled when green; preserved in syrup; ground into sauces	Kcal: 182 Pro: 4.1 g Fat: 17.5 g Fiber: 1.4 g

New Orleans praline includes dairy products that make it softer and chewier. It is usually made with pecans.

How It Works • Like legumes, most nuts are composed of two engorged storage leaves, called cotyledons, joined together with a tiny stem. The exceptions are Brazil nuts, which are just the swollen stem, and coconuts and pine nuts, which are mostly endosperm, like grains. The cell walls of nuts do not contain indigestible fibers (like the cell walls of grains and legumes) and therefore most do not need to be cooked to be edible, although their texture and flavor are improved by a brief roasting or toasting.

A protective skin covers the cotyledons that form the nut meat. The skin can be thick or thin, but almost always it is darker than the nut meat and more astringent, because of a concentration of tannins and other phenolic compounds. Like all phenolic chemicals, those in nut skin are antioxidants. Even though the skins make nuts healthier, they are sometimes acrid and are removed (see Kitchen Wisdom, page 429).

Brown Sugar Pecan Butter

Jarred nut butters are so commonplace that most of us never realize how easy they are to make fresh. And the best part is you can customize them however you like. This recipe for pecan butter is enhanced with the rich flavor of dark brown sugar.

1 lb	pecan pieces	500 g
2 tsp	dark brown sugar	10 mL
Pinch	salt	Pinch

1. In a food processor, process nuts, brown sugar, and salt, using a pulsing action until mixture is finely chopped. Process continuously until smooth, about 3 minutes, stopping periodically to scrape the bowl. Store in tightly closed jars in refrigerator for up to 1 month.

MAKES 2 CUPS (500 ML)

Nuts pack a lot of nutrition in a compact package. After pure fat, they are the richest energy source of any food, yielding at least 125 kcal per ounce (28 g). Most are between 10 and 25% protein and usually more than 50% oil. Nut oils contain a large proportion of mono- and polyunsaturated oils (except for saturated coconut oil and palm kernel oils), which are more vulnerable to oxidation and the development of rancid flavors than other vegetables oils. They should therefore be kept in a cool, dark place, and preferably refrigerated.

Unshelled nuts have an extremely long storage life, up to a year in a tightly closed container, but they are vulnerable to oxidation once they are shelled, chopped, or ground and should be used immediately, or they can be tightly wrapped and frozen for three to four months. There's usually no need to thaw nuts before cooking. They will warm up in a few minutes.

See Also • Coconut, Legumes, Oil

kitchen wisdom

Toasting Nuts

Raw nuts are slightly chewy, oily, bland, and pale. A brief period of roasting or toasting turns them into crisp, nutty, golden, delicious morsels. Nuts can be oven-roasted in a moderately hot oven, browned in oil in a skillet over medium heat, or cooked in a microwave. Judge doneness by color and aroma and stop the cooking just before you think they are done. Nuts will continue cooking after they are removed from the heat source.

To toast nuts:

In an oven: Preheat oven to 375°F (190°C). Spread nuts out on a rimmed baking sheet in a single layer. Toast for 5 to 15 minutes, checking for brownness and stirring occasionally.

In a skillet: Heat a heavy skillet over medium-high heat until hot. Leave the skillet dry or add a thin film of oil and nuts (without crowding the pan). Reduce heat to low. Stir until the nuts are browned, 2 to 4 minutes.

In a microwave: Place nuts in a shallow microwave-safe pan and microwave on High, stirring twice, until browned, 5 to 7 minutes.

OAK • See Liquor, Smoking

OATS • See Grains

OCTOPUS • See Cephalopod

OENOLOGY • See Wine

OIL

What It Is • **Fats** and oils are really the same thing — nature's vehicles for concentrated energy storage. We call them oils when they're liquid at room temperature and fats when solid at room temperature. Liquid oils, such as canola oil, tend to come from plants, whereas solid fats, like butter, tend to come from animals. Plant oils include nut oils (peanut and walnut oils), fruit oils (olive and avocado oils), and seed oils (sesame seed oil, grapeseed oil, and argan oil). Most oils are used for **frying** and **cooking** or for **salads** and raw preparations. Some oils, such as flax oil and **fish** oil, are valued primarily for their healthful compounds, such as omega-3 fatty acids. Essential oils, such as orange oil, are extracted from plants to make flavoring **extracts** and have a different chemical composition. This entry deals primarily with cooking and flavoring oils.

What It Does • Oils are vital in cooking, allowing us to sauté onions, fry potatoes, and make vinaigrettes and mayonnaise. The plant source and the way the oil is extracted determine the oil's flavor, texture, color, and smoke point (see Frying and Flavoring Oils chart, page 436). The majority of oils are extracted with solvents. The nut, seed, or fruit is ground, then mixed with a solvent, usually hexane, and heated to 150°F (66°C) or higher. The solvent is later removed by evaporation. Then the oils are usually refined with an alkaline solution to remove impurities like seed or nut fragments and trace metals, a process that also removes some flavor compounds but gives the oil a longer shelf life and a higher smoke point.

Cold-pressed and expeller-pressed oils are extracted by forcing the oil out of the ground mixture with mechanical pressure, which creates some friction. Expeller-pressing may heat the ground mixture to 140°F (60°C) or as high as 210°F (99°C), which burns off some volatile aromatic compounds. Cold-pressing keeps the extraction temperature below 120°F (50°C) to retain more flavorful compounds. Both cold-pressed and expeller-pressed oils may be refined to varying degrees to remove impurities, though cold-pressed oils are often left unrefined for maximum flavor. Some of the world's best olive oils are simply pressed from the fruit and poured into bottles with no filtering or refining. Unrefined oils tend to be used as salad and flavoring oils rather than for cooking because heat dissipates their delicate aromas.

Smoke Point and Shelf Life

The smoke point of cooking oils is determined by the level of refining and the level of saturation. More highly refined oils have higher smoke points. For example, unrefined canola oil begins to break down and smoke at a relatively low 225°F (107°C), but highly refined canola oil doesn't smoke until about 435°F (224°C). Highly saturated coconut oil begins to break down at about 350°F (180°C), but less saturated avocado oil can be heated to about 520°F (271°C) before it starts smoking. The saturation level explains why solid fats (more highly saturated) aren't as good for frying as liquid oils (less saturated). But solid fats have a longer shelf life, so some low-saturated-fat frying oils are solidified by hydrogenation (see **Fat**), which adds extra hydrogen atoms to the fatty acids.

kitchen wisdom

Silicone in Frying Oils

Some commercial frying oils include silicone to reduce foaming. Avoid using oils containing silicone in baking, as they will weaken the foam structure of cakes such as chiffon.

Spilled Oil

To easily clean up an oil spill, sprinkle it with flour. Let stand a few minutes to let the flour absorb the oil, then wipe up with paper towels.

fast facts

- Toasted sesame oil is less prone to rancidity than other oils because it is high in antioxidants, vitamin E, and other compounds created when the seeds are toasted.
- Canola oil is pressed from the seeds of a cruciferous plant developed in 1974 at the University of Manitoba. It was bred from its parent plant, rapeseed, to reduce levels of glucosinolates, which taste bitter, and erucic acid, which had been linked to increased heart disease risk. The name canola is a contraction of "Canadian oil, low acid."

Every time cooking oil is heated, its smoke point gets lower. The oil also becomes less sticky because the breakdown of fatty acids reduces the oil's surface tension. In fresh frying oil, the higher surface tension allows only a few small bubbles to gurgle up during heating. In well-used oil, lots of large bubbles come up because the oil has a lower surface tension. To help prolong the useful life of frying oil, keep it as clean as possible by filtering out crumbs or other debris through cheesecloth or a coffee filter. Frying oil that is dark and foams or smokes at frying temperatures has outlived its cooking life, tastes off, and should be discarded.

To help oils last longer, avoid heat, air, and light to help delay rancidity. Store them in as cool and dark a place as possible, preferably in tightly sealed opaque containers with very little airspace. Most oils store well at room temperature, but for the longest storage and best quality, keep all oils refrigerated (if they get cloudy, most oils will liquefy in a few minutes at room temperature), especially less saturated liquid oils, which become rancid sooner than saturated fats. Discard any oils that have a somewhat fishy or beany aroma or acrid taste.

How It Works • Chemically speaking, oils are triacylglycerols (triglycerides), meaning that their molecules are composed of three fatty acids attached at one end to a glycerol molecule. In plant oils, some of these fatty acids (such as linolenic acid) are crucial for photosynthesis and the life of the plant. A plant's oil concentrates in storage tissues in

its seeds, nuts, and fruit. Some nuts, like macadamias, contain as much as 72% oil, while others, like chestnuts, contain only 2%. Most nuts and seeds hover around 50 to 60% oil. Fruits vary widely in oil content, but those worth extracting oil from, such as olives and avocados, generally max out at about 30% oil.

Oils are exceptionally good at **browning** foods quickly because they transfer heat more quickly and get hotter than other cooking mediums like air and water, both of which can actually impede browning. Frying fish in hot oil cooks it more quickly than roasting the fish in an oven because fat transfers heat more quickly than air (in the oven). And though water can reach into the crevices of

Frying and Flavoring Oils

Most oils are used for frying or flavoring. Frying oils tend be mild in flavor but can withstand the temperatures needed for high-heat frying. For extended deep-fat frying, choose a frying oil with a high smoke point. More highly refined oils tend to have higher smoke points. Flavoring oils, on the other hand, have more pronounced flavors that tend to evaporate when exposed to heat. Choose a flavoring oil with a color and flavor that best complements the dish you are making.

Frying Oils (Refined)	Smoke Point	Characteristics
Coconut	350°F (180°C)	Mild to rich coconut flavor; light color
Corn	410°F (210°C)	Mild flavor; yellow
Mustard	410°F (210°C)	Mild to pungent mustard flavor; golden yellow
Olive	410°F (210°C)	Mild to rich olive flavor; pale yellow to deep green
Sesame (untoasted)	415°F (213°C)	Mild nutty flavor; light yellow
Canola	435°F (224°C)	Neutral flavor; light yellow
Grapeseed	445°F (229°C)	Mild flavor; light color
Palm	450°F (232°C)	Mild flavor; red-orange
Peanut	450°F (232°C)	Neutral flavor but rich texture; golden
Safflower	450°F (232°C)	Neutral flavor and light texture; light color
Soybean	450°F (232°C)	Neutral flavor; light color
Almond	495°F (257°C)	Mild nutty flavor; light color
Rice bran	500°F (260°C)	Mild flavor; light color
Avocado	520°F (271°C)	Mild to rich avocado flavor; pale yellow to deep green

Salad, Sauce, and Flavoring Oils (Unrefined)	Characteristics
Almond	Toasted almond flavor; light yellow; degrades with heat; also used in cold desserts
Avocado	Rich buttery flavor; light yellow to green
Grapeseed	Mild flavor; pale yellow to green
Hazelnut	Toasted hazelnut flavor; light golden; breaks down with heat; also used in baking
Macadamia	Mild to rich macadamia flavor; light color
Olive (extra virgin)	Mild to rich olive flavor; pale yellow to deep green; also used for baking; use extra virgin for uncooked or gently cooked dishes
Pecan	Mild to rich pecan flavor; light golden
Pistachio	Toasted pistachio flavor; deep green
Pumpkin	Toasted pumpkin seed flavor; green
Sesame (toasted)	Concentrated toasted sesame flavor; dark amber
Sunflower	Mild flavor; light yellow
Truffle	Mild (white truffle oil) to rich (black truffle oil) and complex, mushroom-like flavor; light amber
Walnut	Rich walnut flavor; amber

food to heat it, oil does a more efficient job because most cooking oils remain liquid past 400°F (200°C), whereas water vaporizes at 212°F (100°C).

Liquid oils also have advantages in **baking**. Like solid fats, they tenderize the structure of bread doughs and pancake batters and soften the gluten network. Oil can make a rich cake taste lighter and moister because the oil stays liquid at room temperature, whereas butter solidifies. Oil's liquid state also causes it to coat more of the proteins in flour than butter does, creating shorter strands of gluten and a finer texture in baked goods.

In vinaigrettes and sauces like mayonnaise, liquid oils form a crucial part of the **emulsion**. Oil and water are usually immiscible (they don't mix), but emulsifiers like mustard powder and egg yolk coat the oil droplets in a protective sheath so that they can be dispersed throughout the other ingredients without clumping back together and separating out.

Oil's single most important advantage for the diner is flavor. Most of the flavor compounds in food are fat soluble. Oil carries these flavor compounds to our mouth and makes food taste better. The viscous texture of oil also slows down the flow of liquid as we eat so that flavors remain in our mouth longer, allowing us to perceive flavors more intensely. Oil lubricates foods, too, making

Espresso Pearls

Some avante-garde chefs like to turn liquids into little gelled beads, a process known as spherification. Most chefs use sodium alginate and calcium chloride to gel the liquid, but you can also use agar and oil, ingredients that are a little easier to come by (most health food stores carry agar, which is derived from seaweed). The agar gels the liquid and the oil keeps the beads separate as they solidify. Here's a basic recipe using espresso as the liquid, but you could use tea, fruit juice, or almost any other flavored liquid. Work quickly because the liquid will start to gel as soon as it cools. Serve the pearls over ice cream or with chocolate desserts.

1 cup	extra-light olive oil or canola oil	250 mL
1 cup	brewed espresso	250 mL
2 tbsp	granulated sugar	25 mL
1½ tsp	agar powder	7 mL

1. Place oil in a saucepan and freeze until very cold but not completely solidified, about 1 hour.
2. Soak a small squeeze bottle or syringe or a turkey baster in warm water.
3. In a small saucepan, heat brewed espresso and sugar over low heat, stirring until sugar dissolves. Add agar and heat to almost boiling, 203°F (95°C). Using a whisk or an immersion blender, whisk or blend with short pulses until agar dissolves and liquid thickens to the consistency of medium syrup, 1 to 2 minutes.
4. Remove squeeze bottle, syringe or turkey baster from water. Immediately pour warm liquid in. Remove pan of oil from freezer and drop warm liquid into cold oil in separate drops (for larger pearls, use larger drops). Let pearls set, 1 to 2 minutes. Remove pearls with a slotted spoon. Or pour pearls and oil through a fine-mesh strainer. Immerse pearls in cool water to rinse. Serve immediately or chill for up to 6 hours before serving.

MAKES ABOUT 1 CUP (250 ML)

---

them less dry and more pleasant to chew. And it makes foods taste juicier by stimulating the flow of saliva and literally making our mouth water. Without oil or fat, many foods would not be mouthwatering and delicious.

The flavor-carrying ability of oils makes them popular candidates for infusion. Steep some aromatics, such as garlic, citrus, herbs, and spices, in room-temperature or gently heated oil, and the oil will extract those flavors. Commercially infused oils, like garlic oil and some truffle oil, are made by extracting aromatic oils from the flavoring component, then dissolving them in the "host" oil to create a more intensely flavored infusion. Keep in mind that infusing oils with raw ingredients like garlic and onions can add bacterial spores that can germinate and grow in the anaerobic environment. Once infused this way, flavored oils must be kept refrigerated to prevent the growth of **bacteria** such as *Clostridium botulinum*.

See Also • Butter, Coconut, Extracts, Fat, Frying, Nuts, Olive

OKRA

What It Is • A relative of cotton, okra is a pod vegetable that comes from an annual plant (*Abelmoschus esculentus*) that thrives in hot climates. The plant came to the Americas in the 1600s along with slaves and their native African foods like peanuts and sweet potatoes.

What It Does • Okra is enjoyed steamed, sautéed, fried, stewed, and pickled. The green ridged, oblong pods have glass-like fibers on the surface, so many harvesters wear gloves to protect their hands. As with most foods, small, young pods are the most tender, while older ones are tougher and more fibrous. Keep the pods in a paper bag on the upper shelves of a refrigerator (above 45°F/7°C), where they'll last a few days. If the okra is especially fuzzy, rub smooth with a kitchen towel just before using.

How It Works • Okra contains a mucilage that makes it useful for thickening soups and stews. The mucilage is a mixture of proteins and carbohydrates (resembling pectin in

Chicken Gumbo

Okra and roux are central to Louisiana gumbo (which gets its name from the Bantu name for okra, *kigombo*). After those two key ingredients, the sky's the limit. Fill the stew with whatever you like from chicken and turkey to ham and sausage to crawfish and oysters. The okra is cut crosswise and cooked slowly for maximum mucilage and thickening. Serve the gumbo in bowls with cooked rice and garnish with chopped scallions and parsley.

⅔ cup	peanut oil or vegetable oil, divided	150 mL
¾ tsp	salt, divided	4 mL
¾ tsp	freshly ground black pepper, divided	4 mL
12 oz	boneless skinless chicken thighs	375 g
12 oz	fresh or frozen okra, trimmed and sliced ¼-inch (0.5 cm) thick (about 2 cups/500 mL)	375 g
1	onion, chopped	1
1	green bell pepper, chopped	1
2	stalks celery, chopped	2
3	cloves garlic, minced	3
½ cup	all-purpose flour	125 mL
3 to 4 cups	chicken broth	750 mL to 1 L
2	cans (each 16 to 19 oz/454 to 540 mL) stewed tomatoes including juice	2
12 oz	andouille sausage, cut into slices or small cubes	375 g
2	bay leaves	2
¼ to ½ tsp	cayenne pepper	1 to 2 mL
1 lb	medium shrimp, peeled and deveined	500 g
1 lb	lump crabmeat	500 g
2 tsp	filé powder (ground sassafras leaves), optional	10 mL

1. Heat 2 tbsp (25 mL) of the oil in a large pot over medium heat. Scatter ¼ tsp (1 mL) of the salt and ¼ tsp (1 mL) of the black pepper over chicken. When oil is hot, add chicken and cook, turning once or twice, just until no longer pink inside, 5 to 10 minutes. Transfer to a cutting board. When cool, shred with a fork or cut with the grain into thin strips. Set aside.

2. Add 2 tsp (10 mL) oil to pot. When hot, add okra and sauté until tender, 5 minutes. Add onion, bell pepper, celery, and garlic and sauté until tender, about 10 more minutes. Transfer vegetables to a bowl.

3. Add remaining ½ cup (125 mL) oil to pot. Gradually whisk in flour. Reduce heat to medium-low and cook, stirring frequently, until mixture (the roux) starts to thicken and turns a nutty dark brown color, about 8 minutes. Watch carefully so the roux doesn't burn. Gradually whisk in 3 cups (750 mL) of the broth. Stir in reserved chicken and vegetables, tomatoes with juice, sausage, bay leaves, ¼ tsp (1 mL) cayenne, and remaining salt and pepper. Bring to boil over high heat. Reduce heat to medium-low and simmer gently, stirring occasionally, until flavors blend and stew is thickened to your liking, about 45 minutes. Stir in shrimp and crabmeat and cook until shrimp are bright pink, about 5 minutes. Add more broth, salt, black pepper, and cayenne pepper if needed to thin and flavor the stew. Discard bay leaves. Stir in filé, if using, just before serving.

MAKES 8 TO 10 SERVINGS

composition) that forms a protective sheath to help the plant retain water. **Cactus** pads and flaxseeds produce a similar mucilage.

fast fact

- Some varieties of okra are red instead of green and retain their red color during cooking.

Long, slow moist-heat cooking draws out the most mucilage and the greatest thickening potential, whereas quick high-heat frying or grilling minimize it. For minimal mucilage during preparation, rinse the pods just before using and trim only the stem end. Drying the pods also minimizes mucilage. In India, dried okra pods are sliced and fried into crunchy snacks.

OLALLIEBERRIES • See Berries

OLIGOSACCHARIDES • See Starch, Sugar

OLIVE

What It Is • The **fruit** of a Mediterranean evergreen tree (*Olea europaea*), olives have been cultivated at least since 3000 BCE. Olive trees may bear fruit for hundreds of years and are so revered around the world that the olive branch is widely recognized as a symbol of peace. The most extensively cultivated fruit crop in the world, olives are loved for their flavorful fruit as well as their healthful **oil**.

What It Does • It takes about four months for olives to ripen on the tree from green to purple to black. As they ripen, olives become increasingly oily, and they don't ripen further when picked. Less ripe green olives are lower in oil but have sharper, more pungent flavors than fully ripened, oil-rich black olives.

About 90% of the world's olives are pressed for their oil, and most of that oil comes from Spanish Picual olives. Slightly underripe olives (green on the verge of purple) produce the best-quality oil. The olives are ground, pits and all (sometimes with olive leaves, too), and then churned for about half an hour to help release more oil and flavor, a process known as malaxation. To preserve aromatic compounds, the best olive oils are extracted with mechanical pressure as opposed to the solvents used for other oils. Traditionally, a screw press was used, but most olive oil is now extracted by means of an expeller. Cold-pressed olive oils are typically processed at temperatures below 80°F (27°C) for maximum flavor and minimum free fatty acids (low acidity) according to criteria established by the EU and the International Olive Oil Council to measure oil quality. Extra virgin olive oil comes from the most flavorful high-quality olives and contains less than 0.8% free fatty acids. Virgin olive oil may come from slightly lower quality olives and contains less than 2% acids. Fino olive oil is a mixture of virgin and extra virgin oils generally with 2 to 3% acids. Pure and pomace olive oils are extracted with solvents, are refined, and have more than 3% acids. Light or extra light olive oil contains a mix of highly refined olive oils to lighten the color (and flavor). Light olive oil contains no fewer calories than other olive oils but it has a higher smoke point, which makes it a good choice for frying rather than flavoring.

Whole olives are preserved by **curing**. Olives may be wet-cured (brined) or dry-cured; many green olives are first cracked to allow curing salt and liquids to improve flavor penetration. After curing, olives are typically packed in 6 to 8% brine (sometimes with vinegar or wine) or oil. Brine-cured olives such as Kalamata retain more moisture and look plump and full. The salt in dry-cured olives draws out moisture, which wrinkles the olives and makes the fruit softer and drier yet more concentrated in flavor. Dry-cured olives are often packed in oil and sometimes called oil-cured olives.

For the longest storage, keep cured olives in the refrigerator in their packing liquid, where they'll last a few weeks. For the best flavor,

Black Olive Tapenade

Looking for something new to do with olives? Sure, they're great whole and coarsely chopped, but they also make a versatile pesto. Serve this olive paste on crostini, slathered over fish or chicken, or any other way you would use pesto. If you like, add a little anchovy to the mix to deepen the briny flavors.

2 cups	fresh parsley leaves	500 mL
1 cup	drained pitted black brined-cured olives (such as Kalamata, Gaeta, and/or Amphissa)	250 mL
1 cup	pine nuts	250 mL
2 tbsp	drained capers	25 mL
1 tbsp	extra virgin olive oil	15 mL
1 tbsp	freshly squeezed lemon juice	15 mL
1	clove garlic, minced	1
1 tsp	chopped fresh thyme or ½ tsp (2 mL) dried	5 mL
¼ tsp	freshly ground black pepper	1 mL

1. In a food processor fitted with a metal blade, combine parsley, olives, pine nuts, capers, oil, lemon juice, garlic, thyme, and pepper. Blend until finely minced but not completely puréed to a paste, 15 to 30 seconds. Serve at room temperature or cover and refrigerate for up to 2 days.

MAKES ABOUT 2 CUPS (500 ML)

bring them to room temperature before using. Olive oils, especially unrefined extra virgin oils, should be kept refrigerated in opaque containers to keep their chlorophyll from oxidizing in the presence of light, which speeds rancidity and the development of acrid aromas and flavors.

How It Works

• If you eat an olive off the tree, it will taste unpleasantly bitter because of the glucoside compound oleuropein. Curing olives transforms these bitter fruits into bullets of salty flavor. For table olives, the bitter compound is extracted by fermenting the olives with salt and/or by soaking them in an alkaline solution for several days. Industrial producers use a 1 to 3% solution of alkaline sodium hydroxide

science wise

Canned Olives • Canned "ripe" black olives from California start out green. The unripe green olives are treated with lye to leach out the bitter-tasting glucoside compounds, and soften the fruit. The fruit are washed to remove the lye and then aerated to darken the pigments. Ferrous gluconate is added to fix the pigments. The process also leaches out many flavor compounds. Finally the olives are canned in a 2.5 to 3.5% salt solution and sterilized.

(lye), which also softens the olives and makes brining and fermentation more efficient. During fermentation in 5 to 10% brine, bacteria convert the olive's sugars into lactic acid and, along with yeasts, create complex flavors in the olive. Olives that aren't treated with an alkali take longer to ferment (up to a year) and have more bitter tastes and fruitier flavors. This slower fermentation process is traditionally used to cure ripe black olives such Gaeta, Niçoise, and Kalamata.

Olives are rare among fruits in that their flesh contains as much as 30% oil. The oil is stored in special compartments called lipovacuoles. Crushing olives for their oil causes the glucoside compounds to naturally separate from the oil. Crushing also releases enzymes that catalyze reactions of the fatty acids in the oil and create more than a hundred aromatic compounds, which give unrefined olive oils their complex aromas. Fruity oils are high in esters, citrusy oils have more terpene compounds, and grassy oils get their green aromas from aldehydes.

The color of olives comes from chlorophyll (green) and anthocyanins (purple-black). Olive oil gets its green hues from chlorophyll and its golden ones from carotenoid pigments.

See Also • Curing, Fruit, Oil

Cured Olive Varieties

Olives are variously marketed by country of origin, curing method, and/or the varietal of the fruit. Here's a brief list of popular olives, organized by curing method.

Olive	Origin	Color and Flavor
Dry-cured Olives		
Aleppo	Middle East	Black; slightly bitter
Gaeta	Italy	Black; small; often rubbed with oil and flavored with herbs
Moroccan	Morocco	Black; shiny; slightly bitter
Niçoise	France	Black; small; oily, chewy; sometimes flavored with lemon and garlic
Nyons	France	Black-brown; shiny; salty, bitter; often packed in oil
Brine-cured Olives		
Agrinion	Greece	Green; large; soft; cracked; tart
Aleppo	Middle East	Green; salty, bitter
Alphonso	Chile	Purple-black; large; soft; tart, slightly bitter
Amphissa	Greece	Purple-black; large; soft
Arauco	Spain	Green; large; flavored with rosemary
Arbequina	Spain	Green; small; mild flavor
Atalanta	Greece	Green-brown; soft
Calabrese	Italy	Green-brown; sharp; often flavored with chile peppers and herbs
Cerignola	Italy	Green (sometimes black); very large; meaty; mildly sweet
Gaeta	Italy	Brownish purple-black; small; soft; nutty, salty
Kalamata (Calamata)	Greece	Purple-black; almond-shaped; soft; rich, fruity
Kura	Middle East	Green; cracked; bitter
Ligurian	Italy	Black-brown; small; tart and piquant; sometimes include stems
Lugano	Italy	Black; firm; salty
Manzanilla	Spain	Green; crisp; often pitted and stuffed with pimento or garlic
Mission	California	Black; soft; mild, watery flavor
Naphlion	Greece	Dark green; cracked; crisp; fruity
Niçoise	France	Black-brown; small; chewy and meaty; tart and rich
Picholine	France	Green; oblong; crisp; tart; sometimes flavored with herbes de Provence
Picual	Spain	Black; firm; nutty
Ponentine	Italy	Black; mild flavor
Royal (Victoria)	Greece	Reddish brown; large; chewy
Sevillano (Queen or super-colossal)	California	Pale green; very large; crisp
Sicilian	Sicily	Green; large; tart; meaty; often flavored with red pepper or fennel

OMEGA-3 FATTY ACIDS • See Fish

OMELET • See Eggs

ONIONS • See Allium

OOLONG TEA • See Tea

ORANGE • See Citrus

ORANGE FLOWER WATER • See Flowers

OREGANO • See Herbs

ORGANIC • See Agriculture, Beef, Meat

ORGAN MEATS

What It Is • When eaten as food, some animal organs are given quirky names like chitterlings (intestines), lights (lungs), melt (spleen), tripe (stomach), and sweetbreads (pancreas and thymus glands). With other organs, such as heart, brains, kidneys, and liver, we're comfortable telling it like it is. The term "organ meats" (aka offal or variety meats) generally includes a wide array of internal and external organs and lesser-used **meat** such as heads, ears, snouts, cheeks, tongue, feet (trotters), testicles (fries or prairie oysters), and tails. **Poultry** organ meats are often referred to as giblets.

What It Does • Thrifty cooks don't like to waste food, and organ meats have found a place in cuisines around the world. The organs of smaller, younger animals like calves and lambs are generally preferred for their softer, finer texture. In the U.K., young lamb or veal kidneys are incorporated into the pub favorite steak and kidney pie. In Italy, calves' and lamb's brains are often poached, braised, or fried. The Italians and French also make wide use of sweetbreads, either the larger, rounder, and more delicate pancreas sweetbreads or the elongated, irregularly shaped thymus sweetbreads.

Some organ meats and extremities offer advantages over muscle meats. Pork chitterlings become both filling and casing in sausages such as andouilles and andouillettes. Sheep organs become both filling and casing in Scottish haggis, made by binding the ground liver, heart, and lung meat with oats, then stuffing the mixture into the sheep's stomach. And oxtails are highly concentrated in connective-tissue collagen. When gently cooked over a long time, all that collagen melts into mouth-filling gelatin and gives dishes like oxtail soup their incomparable texture.

Of all the organ meats, duck and goose liver offer the most distinct advantage for richness. The livers of these birds have evolved to store energy for long flights in the form of voluminous fat. For centuries, ducks and geese have been overfed to fatten their liver and produce foie gras ("fat liver"). Foie gras can weigh up to 3 pounds (1.4 kg) and contain as much as 65% fat, making it incredibly rich and creamy (although higher fat percentages can actually overfatten the liver and give it an unappetizing flabby texture). Foie gras production involves

Crispy Sweetbread and Watercress Salad

Fried sweetbreads develop a crisp crust that gives way to creamy meat inside. They make a delicious lunch or snack as a warm salad drizzled with some pan drippings. If your sweetbreads are fresh, follow the directions below. Otherwise, blanch the sweetbreads in boiling water for 5 minutes, then remove the membrane, and proceed with the recipe.

12 oz	veal sweetbreads, preferably pancreas	375 g
	Kosher salt and freshly ground black pepper	
	All-purpose flour, for dusting	
2 tbsp	butter	25 mL
2 tbsp	olive oil	25 mL
2	cloves garlic, peeled	2
3	fresh sage leaves	3
2½ cups	watercress leaves	625 mL
2 tbsp	Basic Vinaigrette Salad Dressing (see recipe, page 507)	25 mL

1. Rinse sweetbreads in ice water. Remove membrane, then rinse again in ice water. Pat dry and cut sweetbreads into large bite-size pieces. Season with salt and pepper, then dust with flour.

2. Heat butter and oil in a sauté pan over medium heat. Shake off excess flour from sweetbreads, then add to pan along with garlic and sage. Cook, turning once or twice, until well browned and crisp all over, 15 to 20 minutes. Discard garlic and sage and transfer cooked sweetbreads to paper towels to drain.

3. Toss watercress with vinaigrette and divide among plates. Top with sweetbreads and drizzle with some pan drippings.

MAKES 4 SERVINGS

Stuffed Lamb's Hearts with Bacon and Mushrooms

As hard-working muscles, hearts develop more connective tissue than most other muscles. When cooked slowly, all that connective tissue melts into rich, mouth-filling collagen, the substance that gives gelatin its viscous texture. You can stuff any large heart like beef heart, but lamb's hearts have a finer, more delicate grain. Look for impeccably fresh intact lamb's hearts that have not been slit down the side. If they have been slit, simply sew them back up with string or secure them closed with toothpicks after stuffing.

4 cups	hot chicken stock, divided (approx.)	1 L
1 oz	dried porcini mushrooms	30 g
3 tbsp	butter	45 mL
2	onions, chopped	2
2	cloves garlic, chopped	2
1 lb	cremini mushrooms, chopped	500 g
1½ cups	dry red wine	375 mL
2 cups	fresh bread crumbs	500 mL
¼ cup	chopped fresh sage	50 mL
	Salt and freshly ground black pepper	
4	fresh lamb's hearts, preferably open only at the top	4
8	slices bacon	8

1. In a heatproof bowl, combine about 1½ cups (375 mL) of hot chicken stock and dried porcini mushrooms (add more stock if necessary to cover the mushrooms). Let stand for 20 minutes. When soft, pluck mushrooms from liquid and finely chop. Reserve liquid. Set aside.

2. Meanwhile, in large skillet over medium heat, melt butter. Add onions and garlic and sauté until softened, 4 minutes. Add cremini mushrooms and sauté until they release moisture and begin to shrink, 5 to 7 minutes. Add wine and simmer until liquid reduces in volume by about half, 4 to 5 minutes. Stir in bread crumbs and reserved chopped porcini mushrooms. Reduce heat to medium-low and cook, stirring occasionally, until stuffing is moist and holds together, about 15 minutes. Remove from heat and stir in sage and salt and pepper to taste.

3. Preheat oven to 350°F (180°C). Trim hearts of visible veins and tubes, but leave the fat to help baste the meat. Rinse inside and out with cold water and pat dry. Fill hearts with stuffing and cross two pieces of bacon over top of each heart to cover stuffing. Tie string over bacon to secure. Stand hearts upright in a deep 1 to 1½-quart (1 to 1.5 L) braising or baking dish. Slowly pour reserved mushroom/chicken stock over hearts, leaving any grit or sediment behind in the bowl. Add enough of remaining stock to bring liquid at least three-quarters of the way up hearts. Cover with lid or foil and bake in preheated oven until hearts are tender, about 2 hours. Transfer hearts to plates and keep warm. Strain braising liquid into a small saucepan and boil over high heat until reduced by about half. Pour over hearts.

MAKES 4 SERVINGS

force-feeding the birds and restricting their movement, a controversial practice that has led to the ban of foie gras in various countries such as Argentina, Israel, parts of Europe, and in some North American cities such as Chicago.

When buying organ meats, freshness is everything. Organs are magnets for bacterial contamination, so it's best to source the meat from small producers or local butchers. Fresh organs come from animals butchered that day and will appear plump, firm, wet, and glistening with no strong smell. As an added safety measure, organ meats are often rinsed in several changes of cold water and sometimes blanched to rinse away any microbes and off odors from the surface.

How It Works • Animal organs are vital components of the digestive, cardiovascular, nervous, and reproductive systems, assisting

fast facts

in **metabolism** and performing vital functions like breathing and digestion. Some organs perform hard work like pumping food and blood throughout the body, and the tougher organ meats, such as heart, stomach, intestines, and tongue, contain up to three times more connective tissue than muscle meats. These organs are best cooked like a tough cut of muscle meat (brisket, for instance), with long, slow cooking that includes a fair amount of liquid. The softer organ meats, like liver, brains, and sweetbreads, are more finely structured and delicate and contain very little connective tissue. These organs can be cooked like tender muscle meats with high, dry heat.

Dark organ meats, like liver and kidneys, get some of their distinctive flavor from sulfur compounds. The dark color comes from iron and carotenoid pigments. While they can be high in cholesterol, dark organ meats like liver are also high in important nutrients such as iron and folate. Liver and sweetbreads may also contain organic compounds called purines that can cause an inflammation of joints and tendons (gout) in some individuals.

See Also • Bones, Mad Cow Disease, Meat

OSTRICH • See Game

OUZO • See Liqueur

OVALBUMIN • See Eggs

OVEN

What It Is • The word "oven" comes from an Indo-European word meaning "fire-pot." The original ovens were clay pots with a lid that were placed over fire. Today's Dutch oven is a direct descendant of these early ovens. By the 1800s, ovens had evolved into more elaborate cook boxes, with a door on the side instead of a lid on top. Whereas heat previously came from wood on the bottom of the oven, the appliance transformed so that the heat source could be gas or electric and located on the bottom, top, sides, or all around. Today, an oven is any enclosure that traps heat, which includes several types of conventional (gas or electric) ovens and "combination" ovens that incorporate convection, steam, microwave, and high-watt lightbulb technology. (See also **Stove** and **Microwave Cooking**.)

What It Does • Ovens heat air in an enclosed area. Several features determine how efficiently an oven transfers heat and which foods are best cooked in it. These include size, shape, construction materials, and heat source. An oven's size determines how long it takes for the oven to heat up. Larger ovens take longer; smaller ones heat more quickly. Large ovens may also take longer to transfer heat to the food if there is a great distance from heat source to food. The shape of an oven affects heating because air currents help transfer heat. Rounded or domed ovens develop more efficient convection heat currents than square ovens and cook a bit more quickly. Most contemporary ovens, however, are square so they will easily fit into our kitchens.

Ceramic vs. Metal Ovens

Construction materials play a big role in how efficiently an oven works. Until the mid-1800s, most ovens were constructed of clay or ceramics, which retain heat better than metals do. Brick ovens, masonry ovens, adobe ovens, and clay ovens like the Indian tandoor and Japanese kamado all require less fuel to keep them hot. These ceramics also transfer heat back to the food more quickly than metals do (a process known as emissivity). That's why a brick or clay oven cooks dough so much more quickly than a metal oven. They're excellent for roasting meat and baking bread and pizza. Even if cold dough is placed directly on hot ceramics (such as a hot ceramic oven floor, a pizza stone, or the walls of a clay tandoor), the ceramic retains heat well enough to quickly heat the dough. Ceramics also absorb some of the steam from dough (and from meat), creating a dry environment that helps to brown and crisp the surface. Brick-oven pizza and clay-oven roasted meats are noticeably crisper than pizza and meats baked or roasted in conventional metal ovens. The best brick or ceramic ovens are rounded or domed inside to roll the heat around more efficiently. Their biggest drawback is that they take longer to heat up. Ceramics don't conduct heat as well as metal, so ceramic ovens also don't respond as well to temperature changes.

Most modern ovens are made of steel, which is a better heat conductor than ceramic and offers quicker, more precise temperature control. But metal ovens consume more fuel because the oven walls don't hold on to heat as well as ceramics do. Nonetheless, you can get some of the heat-retaining advantages of ceramics by using a ceramic baking stone or insert in your metal oven. The ceramic will retain its heat better than the metal and provide the steady, even heat necessary for thorough browning and crisp crusts.

Heat Sources

Around the same time that metal ovens began to replace ceramics, gas began to replace wood and coal as fuel. The chief advantage of wood

kitchen wisdom

Use an Oven Thermometer
The temperature readouts on ovens are notoriously deceptive. For the most accurate temperature readings, keep an oven thermometer in the center of the oven.

Toaster Ovens
To save time with small baking jobs like a small pan of muffins, use a toaster oven. The smaller area of toaster ovens allows them to heat up more quickly. As long as there is ample room around the bakeware, a toaster oven will perform much like a larger traditional oven. As with all ovens, it helps to rotate pans at least once during baking to promote more even heating.

is its aromatic smoke, which lends flavor to food like wood-oven pizza and roasted meats. But gas offers faster initial heating, automatic fuel replenishment, and easier heat control. Gas also burns cleaner than wood. Despite these advantages, gas ovens reigned only for about 100 years. By the mid-1900s, electric ovens took over. Today, electric ovens outsell gas by two to one. The thermostat in an electric oven allows for more precise temperature control, a big plus for heat-sensitive baking. Two-thirds to three-quarters of the heating in an electric oven is due to the infrared radiation emitted from the electric coils. Electric ovens also retain moisture better than gas ovens, which have to be vented to allow combustion gases like carbon dioxide to escape. The sealed enclosure of an electric oven is an advantage when roasting meats that may otherwise dry out in a vented gas oven.

Electric and gas aren't the only game in town. "Combination" ovens incorporate the advantages of other heating methods such as convection, steam, microwave cooking, and even high-wattage lightbulbs. Here's a quick review of each one.

Convection: A convection oven speeds up the air currents in an oven by means of one or more fans. The forced hot air speeds cooking by about 25%. By blowing hot air around, convection ovens deliver more even heat and help to dry out the surfaces of food, browning them more efficiently. They excel at creating a crisp surface on roasted meats and breads, but can blow away the delicate foam of a soufflé or meringue. Fortunately, the convection feature can be turned on or off in many ovens.

Steam: Some ovens incorporate steam to increase the rate of heat transfer and speed cooking. Water conducts heat more efficiently than air, so adding a little steam to an oven can help foods cook more quickly. For instance, at the very beginning of baking bread, steam helps the dough rise rapidly, a phenomenon known as oven spring. Continued heating without steam then dries the surface of the dough, creating a thick crust on the bread. Ovens incorporating steam can also help prevent moisture loss when baking foods prone to drying out, such as fish.

Judging Temperature

When thermometers were unreliable or nonexistent, cooks held their hands inside the oven to gauge its temperature. That told them whether the oven was running slow, moderate, or hot. Some old recipes still use these terms (and modern thermometers still measure the temperature of the air inside the oven), so here are some approximate equivalents. For temperature conversions not listed below, convert Fahrenheit to Celsius by subtracting 32 and multiplying by .56. To covert Celsius to Fahrenheit, multiply by 1.8 and add 32.

Oven Temperature Description	Fahrenheit	Celsius	British Gas Mark	French Gas Setting
Very cool	225°	110°	¼	2
Cool	250°	120°	½	2 to 3
Very slow	275°	135°	1	3
Slow	300°	150°	2	3 to 4
Low	325°	160°	3	4
Moderate	350°	180°	4	4 to 5
Moderately hot	375°	190°	5	5
Hot	400 to 425°	200 to 220°	6 to 7	5 to 6
Very hot	450 to 475°	230 to 245°	8 to 9	6 to 7
Extremely hot	500°	260°	9+	7

Microwave: A form of electromagnetic radiation, microwaves cause the water in foods to heat up, a process that cooks foods more quickly than a conventional oven can. Some combination ovens use microwaves for speed in combination with gas or electric heating elements to promote browning.

Light: Specially designed high-wattage halogen lamps produce not only visible light but also infrared radiation (see **Heat**), the same kind of heat produced by heat sources like the sun and an electric heating element. But high-wattage lamps deliver that heat more quickly than conventional gas or electric heating elements can. As well, they provide another source of dry heat that quickly browns and crisps the surface of foods.

Combination ovens: These ovens incorporate the strengths of convection, steam, microwaves, high-wattage lightbulbs, and/or traditional radiant heat (gas or electric) in a single appliance. By incorporating these alternative heat sources, combination ovens can dramatically reduce cooking times. For instance, in a combination oven incorporating all of these heat sources, a crisp and juicy roasted chicken may take 50% less time to cook because microwaves cook the bird quickly, steam keeps it moist, and convection evenly browns the skin. Restaurants have used combination ovens for years, but they are increasingly available to home cooks as well.

Uses

Regardless of materials and heat source, the enclosed area and gentle, even heat of ovens makes them ideal for baking, roasting, and oven-braising. The oven temperature makes all the difference between these cooking methods. At the relatively low temperatures (200 to 300°F/93 to 150°C) of slow-roasting and oven-braising, an oven causes foods like meat to slowly rise in temperature, helping to retain moisture, especially in large cuts of meat. At the moderate temperatures (325 to 375°F/160 to 190°C) required for general baking, an oven provides the gentle yet constant heat necessary for transforming batters and doughs into cakes and breads without creating a thick crust. At high roasting temperatures (400 to 500°F/200 to 260°C), an oven quickly heats foods and dries their surfaces, rapidly achieving a deeply brown exterior, especially in smaller or more tender cuts of meat or vegetables. Ovens with a top-heating element can also be used for broiling, which is best done with the oven door ajar to allow moisture to escape so that the surface of food browns more quickly.

Ovens can be used for another cooking method called oven-frying. The principles are the same as in frying. You use hot oil to cook food; however, you first coat the food in oil, then blast it in a hot oven (450 to 500°F/230 to 260°C). The oil crisps the food a bit more slowly than in frying, but still achieves good browning. The most efficient method is to thoroughly coat the food with oil and spread the food on a rack, then use convection heat to blow hot air around the food. Oven-frying works well for meatballs, beef chunks for beef stew, breaded fish, and even french fries.

How It Works • Ovens function by generating, trapping, and distributing heat around food. The air inside the oven heats up and slowly conducts the heat to the food, cooking it gradually. Ovens are relatively inefficient cooking appliances because air is a poor conductor of heat (see Heat Conductivity of Various Metals chart, page 303). That's why a whole potato will cook more quickly in boiling water (212°F/100°C) than it will in a 500°F (260°C) oven. Water is a faster heat conductor than air. But efficiency isn't always desirable, and that's the oven's advantage. Ovens are superior to boiling water for cooking big cuts of meat or whole birds because the relatively inefficient heat transfer in an oven gives the meat time to roast slowly, thereby retaining more interior moisture throughout the longer cooking time. Ovens also excel at drying out the surfaces of foods, a big plus because evaporating moisture concentrates flavor in food, as in oven-dried tomatoes. Cooking off moisture in ovens above 300°F (150°C) also allows oven-cooked foods to undergo browning reactions and develop crisp crusts, as on baked breads and roasted meats.

As with all appliances and cookware, a major drawback to ovens is the need to clean them. For this reason, self-cleaning ovens use extreme heat to burn off debris. The self-cleaning function is usually performed separately from cooking, and self-cleaning ovens include extra insulation to withstand the high heat. A continuous-cleaning oven works a little differently. Its interior is texturized with a nubbly material to help spread spills thinly so that they burn off more easily at normal cooking temperatures. These ovens may not get quite as clean as self-cleaning ovens but they don't require the added expense of extra insulation in the oven walls. To manually clean the interior of an oven, scrub it with a paste of baking soda and water or a commercial oven cleaner.

See Also • Baking, Braising, Cooking, Grilling, Heat, Microwave Cooking, Roasting

OVEN SPRING • See Bread, Oven

OVERRUN • See Ice Cream

OVOMUCIN • See Eggs

OVOMUCOID • See Eggs

OVOTRANSFERRIN • See Eggs

OXALATES • See Toxin

OXIDATION • See Oxygen

OXYGEN

What It Is • Discovered by chemists in the 1770s, oxygen is the third most abundant element in the universe, after hydrogen and helium. At standard atmospheric pressure and temperature, oxygen bonds with itself to form a gas (O_2). In this form, oxygen is vital for the normal breathing and functioning of all life on Earth. Air is 21% oxygen, and water (the main component of most foods) is 89% oxygen.

What It Does • Oxygen strongly attracts the electrons of other molecules to itself (see **Atom** and **Chemical Bonding**). For this reason, oxygen readily bonds with other molecules, a common chemical process known as oxidation. Because oxygen is in the air all around us (and inside us), oxidation, or oxidative damage, occurs frequently. Rusting is

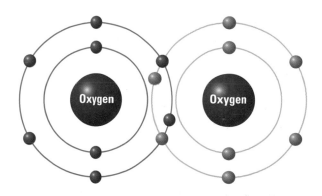

A molecule of oxygen gas (O_2) used by all living organisms for vital functions

a form of oxidation. In the presence of water, oxygen bonds with iron molecules and forms iron oxide (rust). Fire is a form of oxidation, too. When oxygen bonds rapidly with a combustible fuel like paper, the oxidation occurs so quickly that it gives off heat. That's why blowing air on a fire stokes it up. It adds oxygen and increases the rate of oxidation.

Oxidation happens all the time in food preparation and cooking. It's what makes cut apples and potatoes turn brown. The cut foods and their **enzymes** are exposed to oxygen, leading to enzymatic browning. In fact, the rancidity, rotting, and deterioration of all foods is caused, in part, by oxygen in the air stealing electrons from food molecules and breaking down those molecules. Delaying rancidity in foods is largely a matter of cutting off the air supply. That's why tightly wrapping food prolongs its shelf life. Produce growers often spray edible wax coatings on fruits and vegetables for the same reason. Fats are particularly prone to oxidation and develop rancid aromas if exposed to excess oxygen.

Keep butter, oils, meats, nuts, and other fat-rich foods tightly wrapped or sealed to prevent oxidation. Better yet, vacuum-seal meats to suck out all the air. Food manufacturers have been vacuum-sealing for years for this very reason.

Antioxidants also prevent oxidation by stopping oxygen from stealing electrons. Nature supplies these defenses as vitamin C, beta-carotene, and other polyphenols in fruits and vegetables. Sulfites are another type of antioxidant frequently added to wine and dried fruit like apricots to prevent oxidation and browning.

Oxidation isn't all bad, though. When some food molecules bond with oxygen, they are transformed into more flavorful compounds. That's why garlic releases so much aroma when it is cut and exposed to air.

Oxidation is also the principle behind aging wine. Young wines mature and develop flavor and aroma through controlled exposure to oxygen in permeable barrels or tanks. Once a wine is mature, however, it is transferred to impermeable bottles to prevent further oxidation, which could spoil it.

Milled wheat flour also benefits from a bit of oxidation. Oxygen bonds with carotenoid pigments in the flour, naturally bleaching it from yellow to pale white. Compounds like potassium bromate are sometimes added to flour to promote oxidation. These "oxidizers" improve gluten development and dough elasticity in **baking**, which is especially important for **bread**. While some bakers eschew these additives in flour, the truth is that the heat of baking converts potassium bromate in the dough to potassium bromide, a harmless salt that occurs naturally in sea salt.

How It Works • Oxygen is produced
during photosynthesis in plants. All life (and food) on Earth, from animals to plants, needs oxygen to breathe, or respire. Oxygen also forms a part of every major structural molecule in animal and plant foods, including proteins, carbohydrates, and fats. Without oxygen, life on Earth would cease to exist. But plants have produced so much of it that oxygen is the second most common element in Earth's atmosphere (after nitrogen). Even if oxygen were no longer produced by plant photosynthesis, it would take more than 5,000 years for all the oxygen-consuming processes on Earth to deplete oxygen from the atmosphere.

See Also • Antioxidants, Atom, Chemical Bonding, Enzyme, Flavor Compounds

OYSTER • See Mollusks

OYSTER PLANT • See Roots

PALM • See Coconut, Oil

PALM OIL • See Oil

PALM SUGAR • See Coconut, Sugar

PANCAKES

What It Is • One of our earliest **breads**, pancakes are little cakes cooked in a pan on the stovetop rather than baked in an oven. They're made from a thin batter of flour, eggs, and milk and may be leavened or unleavened.

What It Does • One of our universal foods, pancakes are enjoyed around the world in countless styles from sweet to savory. They're eaten flat, stacked, filled, or rolled. Additions and fillings run the gamut from nuts, fruit, and cheese to vegetables, eggs, and meat. They can be served at any meal, any time of day.

Pancakes fall into two general categories: unleavened and leavened. Unleavened tend to be thin and delicate. These include French crêpes and Italian *crespelle* (browned on both sides), blintzes (browned on one side, then filled, rolled, and browned on the other side), Mandarin or mu shu pancakes (aka *bao bing* and frequently served with Peking duck), and eastern European *palacsinta* (often stacked with sweet or savory fillings between the layers).

Leavened pancakes are thicker and fluffier. The leavening may be yeast, baking powder or baking soda, or aerated egg whites. Yeast-raised pancakes include blinis (often incorporating buckwheat flour and served with sour cream and caviar) and crumpets (cooked in rings for maximum rise). But many pancake batters are too thin and fluid to hold on to the strong leavening gases of yeast, so they are

fast facts

- The first commercial pancake mix was introduced by Chris Rutt and Charles Underwood in 1899. It was later renamed Aunt Jemima Pancake Mix. Like many commercial pancake mixes, this mix gets some of its sweetness and caramelized flavors from malted milk powder.
- Pancake Day (aka Shrove Tuesday, Fat Tuesday, and Mardi Gras) is the last day before Lent. Pancakes are traditionally eaten on that day to use up the last of the fatty foods.

Dessert Crêpes

For tender, lump-free crêpes, use instantized flour, designed for thickening sauces without lumping. The flour is made by moistening it until the flour particles stick together in a porous structure. It's then dried. This process allows the flour to readily absorb liquid in thin batters like crêpe batter and helps prevent lumping. Fill these crêpes with sweetened cream cheese and/or chopped fruit and top with maple syrup or another dessert sauce.

1 cup	instantized flour, such as Wondra or Robin Hood Best for Blending	250 mL
4	large eggs	4
1 cup	milk	250 mL
2 tsp	vegetable oil	10 mL
2 tsp	granulated sugar	10 mL
Pinch	salt	Pinch
	Vegetable oil or butter for greasing pan	

1. In a bowl, whisk together flour and eggs until thick and smooth. Whisk in milk, oil, sugar, and salt. Let stand for 10 minutes.

2. Coat a small nonstick skillet with a thin film of oil and heat over medium-high heat. When hot, add a generous 3 tbsp (45 mL) of batter, tilting pan to spread batter evenly over bottom. Cook until browned on bottom and almost set on top, about 20 seconds. Flip and brown other side, about 10 seconds. Transfer to a plate and stack (they won't stick together so there's no need for wax paper between them). Continue with remaining batter, greasing skillet and reheating as necessary.

MAKES ABOUT 20 CRÊPES

leavened with baking powder or baking soda. These include various renditions of light and fluffy North American breakfast pancakes such as flapjacks, hotcakes, flannel cakes, and other griddle cakes. Waffles are essentially a type of pancake batter cooked between embossed metal plates (waffle iron). They're often leavened with beaten egg whites, but some waffles are raised with yeast (Belgian waffles). Many waffle recipes include extra fat and/or sugar for more richness and crispness.

Mixing, Cooking, and Storing

Minimizing gluten is the key to tender, fluffy pancakes. The wet and dry ingredients are

Yeast-Raised Waffles

Waffles leavened with yeast develop a sturdy yet airy texture. These include a bit of baking soda for added lift and some sugar for crispness. Best of all, you can mix the batter the night before then cook the waffles in the morning.

½ cup	warm water	125 mL
2½ tsp	active dry yeast (¼ oz/8 g package)	12 mL
2 cups	warm milk	500 mL
⅓ cup	melted butter	75 mL
2 tbsp	granulated sugar	25 mL
1 tsp	salt	5 mL
2 cups	all-purpose flour	500 mL
2	eggs, lightly beaten	2
¼ tsp	baking soda	1 mL

Vegetable oil for greasing waffle iron

1. In a large bowl, combine water and yeast. Let stand for 5 minutes until yeast is foamy. Whisk in milk, butter, sugar, and salt. Whisk in flour until combined. Cover with plastic wrap and refrigerate for 8 to 12 hours.

2. Preheat a waffle iron. Let batter stand at room temperature for 15 minutes. Stir eggs and baking soda into batter until incorporated. Coat waffle iron with oil and pour on about ¾ cup (175 mL) of batter or amount suitable for iron, being sure not to overfill. Close lid and cook until browned and crisp, about 5 minutes. Repeat with remaining batter, oiling and heating between waffles as necessary.

MAKES ABOUT 8 WAFFLES

typically combined in separate bowls, then mixed together gently to reduce gluten development. Letting the batter stand for an hour or even overnight gives the proteins and starch time to absorb the liquid and reduce lumps. For maximum rise, leavened pancakes are usually cooked in a hot pan until bubbles rise to the top of the batter but don't break. Flipping pancakes at that point sets the batter before the bubbles burst, release their leavening gases, and deflate the batter.

Cooked and cooled pancakes freeze well. Let them cool completely and stack between sheets of waxed paper to prevent sticking. Freeze in resealable plastic bags for no more than a month. Reheat on an oven rack at 350°F (180°C) until warmed through, about 10 minutes.

How It Works • Pancake batters are fluid because they contain up to four times more liquid than doughs do. Whereas bread doughs are often kneaded, pancake batters are minimally mixed to prevent gluten development. For more tenderness, some pancake batters incorporate low-gluten flour or gluten-free flour (such as buckwheat or oat flour) and buttermilk, yogurt, beer, or other acidic ingredients to weaken the gluten structure and tenderize the batter. When pancake batter cooks, the egg proteins coagulate and the starch in the flour absorbs moisture, swells, and gelatinizes, holding the pancakes together.

See Also • Bread, Maple Syrup

PANCETTA • See Bacon

PANCH PHORON • See Spices

PANCREAS • See Organ Meats

PANEER • See Cheese

PANKO • See Breading

PAPAIN • See Enzyme

PAPAYA • See Fruit

PAPRIKA • See Capsicum, Spices

PARCHMENT • See Bakeware

PARMA HAM • See Ham

PARMESAN • See Cheese

PARSLEY • See Herbs

PARSNIP • See Roots

PARTRIDGE • See Game

PASSION FRUIT • See Fruit

PASTA

What It Is • Pasta is Italian for "paste," an unleavened dough that is shaped into small pieces and boiled. In other northern European countries, and Asian and other cultures, it goes by the name noodles, but pasta and noodles are essentially the same thing (see Asian Noodles, page 454).

What It Does • Italian pasta dough is made by mixing **flour** with **water**, **eggs**, or other liquid, kneading the dough (and often rolling it thin), then cutting and extruding it into shapes. Pasta can be cooked while the dough is fresh and pliable, or the dough can be dried before cooking. It can be flavored, sauced, and served in seemingly endless ways on its own or as part of a soup, salad, casserole, or dessert.

The pasta is typically made by adding just enough liquid for the flour to form a pliable dough that can be shaped and rolled. Sometimes oil is added for extra tenderness. The dough is also briefly kneaded to develop enough gluten so that the pasta will hold together when boiled. Pasta consists of 60 to 70% flour by weight, so the type of flour used makes a big difference in the pasta's final texture. Most dried pasta is made with water as the liquid and high-gluten flour (aka pasta flour or durum semolina). Semolina flour is milled from durum, a particularly hard wheat that is about 14%

kitchen wisdom

Pasta Wrappers

In a pinch, replace fresh pasta with store-bought egg roll wrappers or won ton skins.

protein. Semolina is less elastic and more plastic than other flours, making it harder to knead, but once it is stretched, semolina dough retains its shape without snapping back or toughening, an important trait for shaping dried pasta into elbows, cavatappi, rotini, shells, and other rounded shapes. The high protein content also means that semolina pasta stays chewy yet pleasantly firm when cooked because it doesn't absorb as much water as lower-protein all-purpose flour would.

Some dried pasta, like the egg noodles favored in northern Europe, is made with eggs instead of water as the liquid and bread flour instead of durum semolina flour. Bread flour is slightly lower in protein (about 12%), but eggs make up some of the protein difference in the dough. The yolks also enrich the yellow color and the fat content of the dough, making the noodles more tender. The added protein from the whites firms up the dough and prevents the noodles from losing too much starch and becoming mushy when boiled. Commercial egg noodles often include dried egg powder, but fresh pasta is made with fresh eggs.

Other ingredients can be added to the dough for flavor and color, including everything from alternative flours and ground nuts to fresh herbs, puréed spinach, tomato paste, and squid ink. Pasta dough can also be stuffed with any number of fillings from cheese and vegetables to meat and seafood.

Kneading, Resting, Rolling, and Shaping

Once the flour is mixed with the liquid, the dough is kneaded to force the flour and liquid together, developing **gluten**, a viscous network of protein sheets that makes the dough firm and holds it together when stretched. Gluten development contributes to the pasta's bite, or chewiness, but kneading has the drawback of making the dough more elastic, causing it to snap back into shape when stretched. To make it easier to roll out and shape, pasta dough is usually rested for 30 minutes or as long as three days. A resting period allows some of the weaker protein bonds that formed during mixing to break

Asian Noodles

Like Italian pasta, Asian wheat noodles fall into two categories: those made with egg, such as lo mein, and those made with only water, such as chow fun, soba, somen, and udon. But wheat noodles are only the beginning. Other Asian noodles are made from numerous starches and vegetables such as cornstarch, arrowroot, tapioca, rice, mung beans, soybeans, seaweed, and sweet potatoes. Whereas wheat noodles are held together by gluten, rice and starch noodles (glass or cellophane noodles) are held together by a gel of amylose starch molecules. Asian rice and starch noodles are typically made by combining starch and water to make a paste, heating the paste, sometimes kneading it, then extruding the dough into long noodles. Fresh noodles are available in many Asian markets, but the noodles are more commonly dried by briefly boiling or steaming them to gelatinize the starch, then air-drying and/or frying them in oil. This method creates firm noodles (such as ramen) that need only a brief rehydration in hot liquid rather than full cooking in boiling water. (A similar technique — with air-drying instead of frying — is used to make no-boil lasagna noodles.) Asian noodles may be formed into sheets for won ton skins and egg roll wrappers, but they are more often shaped into strands or ribbons and curled into compact nests. Most Asian noodles are served in bowls with rich hot broth, vegetables, meat, and/or seafood. Here's a brief guide to popular Asian noodles made from various ingredients.

Noodle	Characteristics
Wheat Noodles	
Chinese egg noodles	Chewy round yellowish strands or flat ribbons
Chinese wheat noodles	Tender round strands
Chow fun	Flat, wide wheat noodles
Chow mein	Thin round egg noodle strands
Chow mein, fried	Crunchy round strands
Hiyamugi	Narrow wheat ribbons
Hokkien noodles (*mee*)	Thick round yellow egg noodle strands
Kishimen	Flat, wide wheat noodle ribbons with slippery texture
Korean wheat noodles (*gook soo*)	Flat wheat ribbons
Lo mein	Round or flat egg noodle strands or ribbons
Ramen	Thin wheat noodle strands that are steamed, fried, and air-dried so they rehydrate quickly

apart so that the dough relaxes and is easier to roll and shape. It also allows the flour to thoroughly absorb the liquid and develop a stronger gluten network, adding more bite to the pasta.

After resting, fresh pasta dough is rolled several times between wooden or metal rollers in successively narrower settings to flatten the dough into a long sheet. Sheeting stretches the protein (gluten) chains and makes the dough more pliable. It also strengthens the gluten network, adding to the pasta's bite by compressing the dough and forcing out any air bubbles. After sheeting, the dough is shaped either by hand or by machine with cutters or extruders. Strips or other flat shapes can be cut with a knife, punched out with cutters, or made by running the sheet through notched metal rollers. Tubes and other shapes are made by extruding the dough through die-cut plates in a pasta machine. Traditional bronze plates create a rougher pasta surface with a matte appearance, which allows the pasta to leak more starch into the boiling water when cooked but also allows the pasta to absorb more sauce after boiling. Contemporary nonstick extruder plates create a smoother, glossier pasta surface that doesn't leak as much starch into the pasta water but also doesn't absorb as much flavorful sauce.

Once shaped, traditional homemade Italian semolina pasta is dried at room temperature for several days or for up to several weeks. Modern manufacturers speed up the drying to just a few hours by using dehydrators that heat the pasta to about 185°F (85°C), then cycle between periods of drying and resting. The heat used in the modern method helps prevent enzymatic browning in the pasta and firms up the gluten network so the noodles are less sticky when cooked. But some people claim that traditional lower-temperature methods retain more flavor.

Shanghai noodles	Thick oval wheat noodle strands
Soba	Thin wheat and buckwheat strands
Somen	Thin, delicate wheat noodle strands
Udon (*kal guksu*)	Thick, flat, slippery ribbons
Wonton noodles	Thin, wide egg noodles

Rice Noodles

Laksa noodles (*lei fun*)	Thick, round strands
Rice noodles, wide (*jantaboon, sha he fan, sen chan*)	Wide, flat ribbons
Rice sticks, medium (*banh pho, ho fun, lai fen, sen lek, kway teow*)	Medium-width, thin, flat, translucent ribbons
Rice sticks, thin (*bun, pancit palabok, sen yai*)	Very narrow, thin, round, translucent or white strands
Rice vermicelli (*sen mee, mi fen, mai fun, pancit bijon, banh hoi, bee hoon*)	Very thin delicate strands sold in nests

Starch and Other Noodles

Arrowroot vermicelli	Thin translucent strands made from arrowroot starch
Bean curd noodles (*gan si*, soybean noodles)	Thin, chewy, pale white strands made from tofu
Cellophane noodles (bean threads, *bai fun*, Chinese vermicelli)	Thin translucent gelatinous strands made from mung bean starch
Cornstarch noodles (*pancit luglug*)	Thin white gelatinous strands made from cornstarch
Harusame (Japanese vermicelli)	Thin translucent strands similar to cellophane noodles but sometimes made from potato, sweet potato, or rice starch
Korean buckwheat noodles (*naeng myun*)	Thin light brown strands made with buckwheat flour and potato starch
Korean sweet potato vermicelli (*dang myun*)	Chewy yellow strands made from sweet potato starch
Seaweed noodles	Long, thin sea-green strands made from seaweed
Tapioca sticks (*hu tieu bot loc*)	Thin pearly white strands made from tapioca starch
Yam noodles (*shirataki, ito konnyaku*)	Gelatinous yellow strands made from yams

Dried pasta can be stored in a cool, dry, dark place almost indefinitely. Homemade fresh pasta can be tightly covered and refrigerated for a few days or frozen for up to a month. Commercially made fresh pasta is briefly heated and vacuum-packed to extend its refrigerated shelf life by several weeks.

How It Works • When boiled in water, pasta cooks from the outside in, absorbing a little over one and a half times its weight in liquid. Starting at the surface of the pasta, the boiling temperature breaks down protein

fast fact

- Archaeological evidence from central Asia dates the first noodles back to about 2000 BCE. Similar types of pasta were independently developed in the Mediterranean region much later, around 500 or 600 CE, and pasta was well established in Italy before Marco Polo returned from China in 1298.

and allows the starch granules to absorb water, swell, and soften (gelatinize). Some of the gelatinized starch leaks out, making the pasta surface sticky. With continued boiling, more water penetrates to the center, and if boiled too long the pasta becomes mushy and falls apart.

To help prevent sticking, use ample water — about 5 quarts per pound (5 L per 500 g) of pasta. Bring the water to a rolling boil, and stir during the first few minutes after adding the pasta. A large volume of water returns to the boil faster because it has more hot mass than the cool mass of the pasta. A rolling boil also keeps the noodles in motion so they don't make contact and stick to each other. Salting the water helps prevent some sticking, too, as it restricts starch gelatinization. More importantly, salting the water seasons the pasta. Use about 1 tablespoon (15 mL) salt for every 2 quarts (2 L) of water. Despite common myth, this amount of salt doesn't

Fresh Fettuccine with Herb Pesto

These proportions yield soft pasta dough that's easy to work. If your kitchen is very humid, the dough will absorb more moisture and you may need to add a little extra flour to keep it from getting too wet. The amounts here make about one pound (500 g) of dough, enough for six rolled pasta sheets. This is twice as much as you'll need to serve four to six people, so the recipe directs you to freeze the other half to use at a later time.

1⅓ cups	all-purpose flour, plus more for dusting	325 mL
⅓ cup	semolina flour	75 mL
9	large egg yolks	9
⅓ cup	Herb Pesto (see recipe, page 307)	75 mL

1. In a stand mixer fitted with paddle attachment, combine all-purpose and semolina flours. With machine running on medium, add egg yolks and ¼ cup (50 mL) water, mixing just until ingredients come together. Turn dough out onto lightly floured work surface and knead until silky, smooth and somewhat elastic, about 5 minutes. (Knead in more all-purpose flour if the dough is too sticky.) Shape dough into a log, wrap in plastic, and let rest in refrigerator for 30 minutes to 1 hour.

2. Cut dough into 6 pieces and rewrap half the pieces in plastic wrap. Freeze for up to 3 weeks and use at a later date. Let remaining pieces return to room temperature. Position rollers on a pasta machine at widest setting, and roll 1 piece of dough through the rollers 2 to 3 times, lightly dusting dough with flour if necessary to prevent sticking. Reset rollers to the next narrower setting and again pass dough through rollers 2 to 3 times, lightly dusting with flour as needed and brushing off excess. Flour and pass dough 2 to 3 times through each progressively narrower setting, concluding with narrowest setting. You should have a very thin sheet of pasta about 4 to 5 feet (1 to 1.5 m) long that lets some light shine through it.

3. Lay pasta sheet on lightly floured work surface and sprinkle lightly with flour. Cut sheet crosswise into 10-inch (25 cm) lengths. Pass each piece through fettuccine rollers of pasta machine or cut lengthwise by hand into ¼-inch (0.5 cm) wide ribbons. Wrap in plastic wrap and refrigerate, then repeat rolling and cutting with remaining 2 pieces of dough. The fettuccine can be refrigerated for up to 3 days or frozen for up to 3 weeks. If frozen, thaw before using.

4. Bring a large pot of salted water to a boil. Add pasta and cook until tender yet firm, 30 to 90 seconds. Place the pesto in a pan over medium heat. Drain pasta, reserving about 2 tbsp (25 mL) cooking water, and add pasta to pesto. Gently toss pesto and pasta for a minute or two to meld pasta and sauce, adding a little of the pasta water if the sauce is too thick.

MAKES 4 TO 6 SERVINGS

Variations: *To make whole wheat pasta:* Replace ½ cup (125 mL) of the all-purpose flour with whole wheat flour and add about 1 tbsp (15 mL) more liquid.

To make tomato pasta: Add ¼ cup (50 mL) tomato paste along with the eggs and increase the all-purpose flour by 1 to 2 tbsp (15 to 25 mL).

even raise the boiling temperature of the water by 1°F (0.5°C), a negligible amount that won't cook the pasta much faster.

Other methods of reducing sticking include adding oil to the cooking water and oiling or rinsing the cooked pasta. Rinsing pasta cools it down and washes off its surface starch, reducing stickiness but also reducing the pasta's ability to absorb flavor from sauce.

Oiling creates a barrier at the pasta surface that also interferes with sauce absorption. For these reasons, pasta should generally not be rinsed or oiled. But in some food-service operations, large quantities of dried pasta are sometimes cooked, drained, oiled, portioned, and chilled until needed. The precooked pasta is then briefly reheated in boiling water just before saucing and serving.

science wise

Water Matters • If you cook pasta with hard water, consider adjusting its pH to make the pasta less sticky. Hard, or alkaline, water contains minerals such as calcium and magnesium. Pasta cooked in hard rather than soft water becomes stickier because the mineral ions accelerate the protein breakdown and the softening (gelatinization) of starch at the pasta surface. To adjust the pH of hard water, add an acid such as lemon juice. Adding 1½ tsp (7 mL) lemon juice (with a pH of 2.5) lowers the pH of 1 gallon (4 L) water by about 1 point. To lower the alkalinity of 5 gallons (20 L) of hard water with a pH of 8 to a pH of 6, add about ¼ cup (50 mL) lemon juice. It will help make the cooked pasta less sticky.

Al Dente

Fresh pasta cooks quickly — just 30 seconds to 90 seconds depending on thickness. Most dried pasta takes at least 10 minutes because it needs to absorb so much more water to become tender. Most cooks prefer to cook the pasta until "al dente," literally "to the tooth," meaning that the pasta is tender on the surface yet relatively firm in the center because less water has penetrated and softened the starch there. The term "al dente" appeared shortly after the First World War to distinguish Italian pasta, which is slightly chewy, from Asian noodles, which are soaked in water until they are soft.

You can presoak Italian pasta before boiling, but it makes the noodles softer and more mushy in texture when fully cooked. Many people who cook pasta prefer not to presoak their pasta, yet they often cook pasta in two stages. They briefly cook, or blanch, the pasta in boiling water, then finish cooking it in the sauce so that the pasta absorbs liquid and flavors from the sauce, marrying the two together. For the best flavor absorption, cook pasta until slightly underdone, then transfer it quickly to the sauce. If you let the pasta cool, the softened starch will begin to solidify and won't absorb as much sauce. If you overcook it, the pasta will become mushy when it finishes cooking in the sauce.

Another benefit of finishing the pasta in the sauce is the ready-made starch thickener left in the pasta pot. The surface of boiled pasta releases some of its dissolved starch into the pasta water, which often contains enough starch to lightly thicken the pasta sauce. Adding a little pasta water to your sauce can help it come together and meld with the pasta. In restaurants, the same water is used to cook pasta for several hours, and it becomes so rich with starch that just a tablespoon or two (15 to 25 mL) will thicken 1 to 2 cups (250 to 500 mL) of sauce

See Also • Bread, Couscous, Dumpling, Flour, Pastry

PASTA FILATA • See Cheese

PASTEURIZATION

What It Is • In the mid-1800s, French chemist Louis Pasteur developed a method of gently heating liquids like **wine** and **beer** to destroy harmful **bacteria**, **molds**, and yeasts. The process later came to be known as pasteurization and is now used to prolong the shelf life of **milk**, **juice**, beer, wine, **honey**, eggs, crabmeat, and other foods.

What It Does • When mass-produced beverages like milk are pooled together from numerous sources, pasteurization ensures that bacteria from one source don't contaminate the whole batch. Pasteurization inactivates enzymes and kills harmful bacteria, thereby extending the shelf life of the product and reducing the risk of infection. In apple juice, it also keeps the juice from fermenting into cider and protects against pathogens. In milk, it reduces some of the enzymatic activity that contributes to the ripening and flavor of traditional raw milk **cheeses** like Parmesan and Brie. For this reason, European regulations require the use of raw milk to make some traditional cheeses.

Most milk and juice sold in North America is pasteurized. Whereas raw milk may last only a few days under refrigeration,

fast fact

- The terms "cold pasteurization" and "electronic pasteurization" are euphemisms for the less accepted term "irradiation." Use of these terms remains controversial because pasteurization and **irradiation** are fundamentally different food safety processes.

pasteurized milk can be kept refrigerated for one to three weeks. (It sours eventually because pasteurization doesn't kill lactic acid bacteria.) Similarly, fresh apple juice succumbs to enzymatic browning within an hour of the juice being pressed from the apples, but pasteurized juice retains its clear golden color and keeps for weeks.

How It Works

Pasteurization methods range from fairly low temperatures and long heating times to fairly high temperatures and short heating times. The lowest-temperature method, batch pasteurization, heats milk at a minimum of 145°F (63°C) for 30 minutes. The minimum temperatures for cream are slightly higher: 155°F (68°C) for cream with 20% fat or less and 165°F (74°C) for cream with more than 20% fat. The middle-ground method used by most industrial producers is called high-temperature, short time, or HTST, pasteurization. It cycles the milk through hot metal plates or pipes, holding it at a minimum of 162°F (72°C) for 15 seconds. The highest-temperature method, called ultra-high temperature, or UHT, pasteurization, heats milk to between 265 and 300°F (130 and 150°C) for up to 3 seconds. Similarly, ultrapasteurized cream is held at 280°F (138°C) for 2 seconds. High-temperature methods are also known as flash pasteurization because the heating time is so short.

Higher temperatures extend shelf life the longest but create slightly "cooked" flavors in the milk or cream. For instance, UHT pasteurized milk can be sold in aseptic packaging and stored without refrigeration for months. But this type of pasteurization gives the milk a tan color, aromas of vanilla and almonds, and a cooked flavor from the development of eggy-smelling hydrogen sulfide. Even the HTST pasteurization method denatures enough whey proteins in milk to produce hydrogen sulfide's aromas in milk. North American consumers are so used to these aromas that some producers enhance it (and further extend shelf life) by pasteurizing milk at 177°F (80°C) instead of the minimum 162°F (72°C).

Very high temperatures have a few other effects on milk and cream. Ultrapasteurization inactivates enough enzymes and denatures enough milk protein that it prevents milk fat globules from joining together as extensively as they do in raw milk and cream. That's why ultrapasteurized cream doesn't whip as easily as raw cream or HTST pasteurized cream. It's also why pasteurized milk, even if unhomogenized, doesn't form as thick a layer of cream on top.

Sterilization is an extreme form of pasteurization that kills all bacteria by heating liquids to between 230 and 250°F (110 and 120°C) for 8 to 30 minutes. Sterilized milk can be stored without

kitchen wisdom

Pasteurized Eggs

To help prevent infection from *Salmonella* bacteria, some fresh whole eggs and liquid egg products are pasteurized at 130 to 140°F (54 to 60°C), which is enough to kill pathogenic bacteria without completely coagulating the egg proteins. Pasteurized eggs are a safe alternative for making raw and lightly cooked egg preparations like mayonnaise and Italian meringue. However, pasteurized egg yolks may not form quite as stable an emulsion, and pasteurized egg whites do take longer to whip into foam because heat denatures some of the egg proteins.

Pasteurization temperatures can be achieved at home by diluting eggs with some of the liquid and sugar from your recipe (water or cream and sugar or corn syrup, for instance), then gently heating and stirring the mixture in a metal bowl placed over a pan of simmering water. Diluted yolks will be pasteurized (and only slightly thickened) if held at 140°F (60°C) for three and a half minutes. Diluted whites will be pasteurized the second they reach 160°F (71°C).

refrigeration indefinitely but it has a very strong cooked aroma and deep tan color.

See Also • Bacteria, Cheese, Irradiation, Milk

PASTIS • See Liqueur

PASTRAMI • See Curing

PASTRY

What It Is • Both **pasta** and pastry are unleavened doughs. The major difference is that pasta is made of **flour** mixed with liquid and the dough is boiled, whereas pastry is made of flour mixed with **fat** and the dough is baked. Pastry dough may be used for sweet pies or savory tarts and turnovers. When made with **sugar**, pastries encompass a wide variety of baked goods.

What It Does • The basic ingredients of pastry are flour, fat, water or other liquid, salt for flavor, and sometimes sugar for sweetness and browning. Pastry dough differs from pasta and bread dough in that it is usually handled gently to minimize the development of **gluten**, the stretchy mix of proteins that gives dough its structure. Minimal gluten allows pastry dough to be easily shaped and remain tender when baked. Various types of pastry are made with the same basic method, but slight variations in the flour, fat, amount of liquid, and mixing method create the different dough structures that result in crumbly, flaky, or crispy pastry.

Short pastry (pâte brisée): French-style short pastry is rich, crumbly dough used for sweet or savory pies, tarts, quiches, turnovers, samosas, empanadas, and pasties, especially those with moist fillings. It's often made with lower-protein pastry flour (8 to 10% protein) to minimize gluten development and keep the pastry tender (less protein means less gluten). Instead of pastry flour (cake flour or cake-and-pastry flour in Canada), you can use about three parts all-purpose flour to one part cake flour for a similar protein content (about

9%). Proportions of flour to fat are roughly two and a half parts flour to one part fat by volume. Fat may be in the form of coarse butter pieces, shortening or rendered fat from beef, pork, chicken, duck, or goose. The fat is thoroughly cut or rubbed into the flour until the fat is barely visible and the dough resembles coarse crumbs. This fat-mixing technique makes the dough crumbly. The fat coats the flour and waterproofs it, preventing moisture from getting in and developing gluten, which keeps the dough tender. Egg yolks, cream, milk, water, or other liquids are mixed in to bind the fat-coated flour into a cohesive dough. Short pastry usually includes just a small amount of liquid because less water and more fat yields a more crumbly pastry. The dough is gently kneaded or rolled to distribute the fat throughout the flour. The resulting dough structure consists of small particles of flour separated by a coating of fat, which produces crumbly pastry. A cookie crumb crust is essentially a type of short pastry that starts with crumbs rather than mixing fat into flour to create crumbs.

Sweet short pastry (pâte sucrée): "Sugar pastry" is a *pâte brisée* sweetened for dessert pies and tarts and often enriched with egg yolks. The sugar helps to prevent gluten formation, making the dough more tender and crumbly. *Pâte sablée* (sandy pastry) contains even more sugar, which gives the pastry a super-crumbly sand-like texture.

Pie dough: Most North American pie pastry or pie dough is different from *pâte brisée* in that it's made to be more flaky than crumbly. Pie dough is usually made with slightly higher-protein all-purpose flour (10 to 12% protein), which develops a little more gluten to support the layers of fat necessary for flakiness. However, with more protein in the flour, tenderness is achieved by gently working the fat into the flour to limit gluten development. Incorporating some lower-protein pastry flour contributes to tenderness. Other ways to limit gluten and create tenderness include adding an acidic ingredient such as lemon juice, vinegar, buttermilk, or sour cream to break down and weaken the gluten protein network, and adding sugar to bind water that would otherwise hydrate the flour and develop gluten.

Flakiness is quite different from tenderness and depends mostly on the type of fat and how it is worked into the dough. Only solid fats make flaky pastry. Liquid fats like vegetable oil form rounded lumps of flour and keep them separated and crumbly as in tender short pastry. For the flakiest pastry, you need to flatten solid fat to form it into flakes. The fat is gently — not thoroughly — worked or mixed into the flour so that some of it remains in chunks (¼- to ½-inch/0.5 to 1 cm chunks are good). When rolled, these chunks flatten out into sheets of fat that you can see in the dough. The resulting dough structure consists of flattened layers of dough between fat layers that puff up into flakes when baked. The difference is that the pieces of fat are only tossed with flour rather than cut into the flour. Then they are rolled flat. Apart from the different fat-mixing method, short pastry and North American pie dough are very similar. Some pie dough recipes have a bit less fat (proportions are typically three parts flour to one part fat by volume). But a small amount of liquid and gentle kneading are the same for both pastries. As with short pastry,

the water in pie dough can be replaced with other moist ingredients such as sour cream or cream cheese, which add fat for tenderness along with protein and sugar (lactose) for good browning.

Which solid fat is best? Butter, shortening, and lard are all different. The variables are primarily flavor, melting temperature, water content, and fat-crystal size. Butter has incomparable flavor but it softens easily at room temperature and melts into liquid over a narrow range of temperatures (90 to 95°F/32 to 35°C). Ideally, butter should be kept between 58 and 68°F (14 to 20°C) during pastry making so it doesn't soften so much that it begins to melt into the flour. That's a narrow window, so pie dough recipes often call for cold butter, cold utensils, and chilling the dough between mixing and rolling. North American butter also contains 15 to 16% water, which can inhibit flakiness by providing moisture that glues together the flaky thin layers of separated dough. European-style butters contain less water (12 to 13%) and therefore create flakier pastry. Lard and shortening contain no water at all (they're 100% fat)

Crumbly or Flaky Pastry

The ingredients for crumbly and flaky pastry are the same. Cutting the fat into the flour makes the pastry more crumbly. Rolling it in makes the pastry more flaky. Rolling fats takes more effort than cutting it in with a food processor or pastry cutter, but the extra flakiness is worth the extra effort. The recipe calls for a mix of all-purpose flour and instantized flour for tenderness, but you could use pastry flour (cake flour in Canada). To keep the fat from melting and make the dough easier to roll, the dough is repeatedly chilled. If it's hot in the kitchen and the dough ever seems soft as you're working, put it in the freezer to firm up. Butter provides most of the fat, but a little shortening enhances flakiness (for an all-butter crust, replace the shortening with butter). Sour cream provides some extra fat, a little acidity for tenderness, and a little sugar (lactose) for browning. Minimal water helps bind the dough together.

1 cup	all-purpose flour	250 mL
¼ cup	instantized flour, such as Wondra or Robin Hood Best for Blending	50 mL
¼ tsp	salt	1 mL
½ cup	cold unsalted butter, cut into ½-inch (1 cm) cubes	125 mL
2 tbsp	cold vegetable shortening, cut into ½-inch (1 cm) pieces	25 mL
½ cup	cold sour cream	125 mL
1 tbsp	cold water	15 mL

1. For crumbly short pastry: In a food processor fitted with a metal blade or chilled bowl using a pastry cutter, mix all-purpose flour, instantized flour, and salt. Quickly and thoroughly cut in butter and shortening until mixture resembles coarse cornmeal. If using a food processor, transfer mixture to mixing bowl and freeze for 15 minutes. If cutting in butter by hand, freeze butter-flour mixture for 15 minutes. Remove bowl from freezer and gently fold in sour cream using a spatula until incorporated. Pinch a piece of dough and if dough isn't moist enough to hold together, add water 1 tsp (5 mL) at a time just until dough holds together. Quickly shape into a ball and flatten into a disk. Wrap in plastic and refrigerate for 30 minutes or up to 1 day.

2. For flaky pie dough: Use same ingredients as left but the following method to roll in rather than cut in the fat. Chill a mixing bowl and rolling pin until cold. In bowl, combine all-purpose flour, instantized flour, and salt. Add butter and shortening, tossing to coat, then freeze for 15 minutes. Pour mixture onto a work surface lightly dusted with flour and roll with chilled rolling pin to flatten pieces of fat into flour. Scrape back into a pile and re-roll to flatten fat. Repeat scraping and rolling one more time, then scrape mixture back into bowl and freeze for 10 minutes. Scrape mixture onto work surface again and repeat scraping and rolling three more times. Scrape back into bowl and freeze for 10 minutes. Gently fold in sour cream with a spatula until incorporated. Pinch a piece of dough and if dough isn't moist enough to hold together, add water 1 tsp (5 mL) at a time just until dough will hold together. Quickly shape into a ball and flatten into a disk. Wrap in plastic and refrigerate for 30 minutes or up to 1 day.

3. For a prebaked shell: Lightly flour a work surface and rolling pin and roll chilled dough from center outward to a circle about 12 inches (30 cm) in diameter. Roll pastry loosely around pin and transfer to a 9-inch (23 cm) tart or pie pan. Line pan with the pastry, trim and flute or crimp edges, and freeze for 20 minutes. Preheat oven to 400°F (200°C). Line pastry with foil and weight with uncooked rice, beans, or pie weights. Bake for 15 minutes, then remove foil and weights and reduce oven temperature to 375°F (190°C). Bake until fully browned, 15 to 20 minutes.

MAKES ONE 9-INCH (23 CM) CRUST OR PREBAKED SHELL

Variation: *For sweet short pastry (pâte sucrée):* Follow recipe but add ¼ cup (50 mL) powdered sugar along with the flour.

Preventing a Soggy Bottom Crust

To prevent wet fillings from making the dough soggy, pastry is sometimes crisped by prebaking it "blind" with a layer of foil or parchment and a filling of dry beans, rice, pennies, or pie weights to keep the dough from bubbling up. Other ways to prevent a soggy crust include spreading a layer of moisture-absorbing cracker or cookie crumbs across the bottom of the raw dough before adding the filling; sealing the raw dough with a glaze of coagulating protein like eggs before prebaking; or sealing the prebaked dough with a glaze of brushed-on melted jelly or chocolate (for sweet pastry) or prepared mustard (for savory pastry). When making fruit tarts or pies, it helps to cook the fruit separately and drain away extra juices to keep them from being absorbed into the crust and turning it soggy.

and yield the flakiest pastry. They're also easier to work with because they remain workable at a higher range of temperatures than butter, typically up to 75°F (24°C) for lard and up to 85°F (30°C) for shortening. The size of a solid fat's crystals also affects flakiness. Leaf lard has the largest crystals and makes the flakiest pastry. But good-quality fresh lard is hard to find because of low turnover in most markets. And shortening is flavorless. Some cooks combine butter and shortening or lard for a compromise of flavor and texture. However, if you can manage butter's low melting temperature and keep it chilled while making dough, nothing beats the taste of pure-butter pastry.

After mixing, pie dough is usually rested and chilled for 30 minutes or up to a day to keep the fat cold and to allow moisture to evenly distribute throughout the dough. Then it is rolled to continue flattening the fat-flour layers into long, thin sheets and to develop a little gluten. For even thickness and to help prevent sticking, it helps to roll

from the center outward and rotate the dough a few times. A floured surface works well but a pastry cloth is even better at preventing sticking and helps you move the pastry when rolled. When shaping the pastry or lining a pan with it, avoid stretching the dough, because gluten is elastic and will shrink back during baking. If the dough is too elastic to easily shape, let it rest in the refrigerator to relax the gluten, then reshape. Shaped dough can be tightly wrapped and frozen for about three weeks.

Puff pastry (pâte feuilletée): Here's flakiness taken to the extreme. Puff pastry is the multilayered dough used for napoleons, palmiers, and wrapped meat dishes like beef Wellington. The proportions usually consist of equal weights of flour and fat (roughly two parts flour to one part fat by volume). Traditionally, pastry flour is used for tenderness, but you can use a low-protein mixture of flours. Butter is the preferred fat for flavor, but shortening doesn't melt as easily, contains no water, and creates lighter, flakier, crisper pastry. Traditionally, puff pastry is made by mixing a preliminary dough (détrempe) of flour and liquid (such as ice water or cold cream) and a little butter so the dough can be easily worked. Then you shape the remaining butter into a flat slab and chill both the dough and butter slab so they are at the same temperature. You soften them just enough to be worked (60 to 65°F/16 to 18°C), then roll out the dough, wrap the slab of butter with the dough, and repeatedly roll and fold the dough over itself. Each folding and rolling is known as a turn, and the dough is turned four to five times and chilled between turns to keep the butter from melting. The process takes several hours but develops enough gluten to support a dough structure of long, razor-thin sheets of flour coated with long, razor-thin sheets of fat. These layers puff up dramatically during baking into brittle "leaves." For maximum puff, work quickly, use a light hand, and chill the pastry between turns to prevent the fat from melting and gluing together the separate layers of dough.

To save time, quick or rough puff pastry is

Choux Pastry (Pâte à Choux)

This pastry makes airy, crispy éclairs, cream puffs, and profiteroles. Traditionally, the pastry is made with all water but a little milk provides extra protein and sugar (lactose) for good browning. After beating in the eggs, the pastry can be chilled for 4 to 6 hours before using. After the pastry is baked, it can be frozen in an airtight container for a week before filling. Once filled, choux pastries taste best served immediately or refrigerated and served within a few hours.

½ cup	milk	125 mL
½ cup	unsalted butter, cut into ½-inch (1 cm) cubes	125 mL
¼ tsp	salt	1 mL
1 cup	all-purpose flour	250 mL
5	large eggs, divided	5

1. In a saucepan over medium-high heat, bring ½ cup (125 mL) water, milk, butter, and salt to a boil. Reduce heat to low and gradually add flour, vigorously beating with a spoon, until batter forms a ball in center of pan.

2. Transfer mixture to bowl, leaving behind any crust in pan. Let cool for 5 minutes. Beat in 4 eggs, one at a time, until mixture is thick, smooth, and glossy. Pipe through a pastry bag fitted with a wide tip or drop with a spoon onto a parchment-lined baking sheet into 5- by 1½-inch (12.5 by 4 cm) strips for éclairs or 2-inches (5 cm) in diameter for cream puffs. Beat remaining egg and brush over surface of dough and let dry for 15 to 20 minutes.

3. Preheat oven to 400°F (200°C). Bake until browned and puffed, about 15 minutes. Reduce oven temperature to 350°F (180°C), and continue baking until sides are firm, 10 to 20 minutes, depending on size of pastries. Remove from oven and poke small holes in pastry bottoms using the tip of a knife. Reduce oven temperature to 250°F (120°C) and bake until dried and crisp, 20 to 30 minutes. Let cool completely on a wire rack.

4. For cream puffs or éclairs: Fill with 2 to 3 cups (500 to 750 mL) lightly sweetened whipped cream or pastry cream.

MAKES ENOUGH FOR 12 LARGE ÉCLAIRS OR 24 CREAM PUFFS

made more like North American pie dough by skipping the preliminary dough and cutting all the fat into the flour at the beginning. Then you roll and fold the dough over itself, chilling between turns. Puff pastry freezes well, and prepared frozen puff pastry is widely available. But it often includes shortening instead of more-flavorful butter. Also, some puff pastry shortenings are formulated to remain workable up to 115°F (46°C), such a high melting temperature that the fat doesn't completely melt when it reaches our mouth (about 98.6°F/37°C), causing some products to taste a little greasy.

Puff pastry is used other ways, too. Croissants and Danish pastries are a cross between puff pastry and bread dough. The preliminary dough is made with yeast and enriched with butter or eggs and sometimes sugar. It's kneaded a little like bread dough to develop some gluten, then rolled and folded with additional fat to create layers as in puff pastry. This mixing technique creates a rich, chewy pastry that rises from yeast and gets flaky from thin layers of fat in the dough.

Phyllo (filo) and strudel dough: Another multilayered pastry, phyllo is used to make such dishes as Mediterranean baklava and spanakopita. The dough is made by mixing flour, water, and a small amount of oil or eggs, then cutting the dough into pieces and stretching each piece into extremely thin, translucent sheets. It's a painstaking, time-consuming process. The phyllo sheets are then brushed with butter and stacked. Strudel dough is a little wetter and is often made with higher-protein bread flour so that the entire volume of dough can be stretched into a thin sheet. Phyllo and strudel dough freeze well and both are commercially available.

Choux pastry (pâte à choux): Quite different

from other pastry doughs, choux pastry is a little closer to pancake batter. You combine flour, boiling water, and melted butter over low heat, then beat in eggs to make a sticky, pasty dough. The soft dough is piped into rounds, logs, or other shapes, then baked in a hot oven or fried. The water turning to steam puffs up the pastry, then the oven temperature is reduced to dry and crisp the surface. You poke a hole into the soft center of the pastry and fill the cavity with custard, whipped cream, or other fillings to make pastries like éclairs, cream puffs, profiteroles, and beignets.

How It Works • Most pastry dough is kept cold, then immediately baked at relatively high temperatures (375 to 425°F/190 to 220°C) to melt the fat, create steam, and quickly set the dough. The starch granules in the flour are coated with fat, which prevents them from absorbing moisture, so less than half of the starch gelatinizes and softens. Instead, the heat denatures the gluten chains, firming up the crust. When the fat melts, it leaves behind rounded pockets of air (in crumbly pastry) or flat layers of air (in flaky pastry). The heat of the oven expands that air, causing the dough to puff up. As moisture in the dough turns to steam, it contributes to the puff. The fat-mixing method that is used and the resulting dough structure make the pastry crumbly, flaky, or crispy in texture. The fat also makes pastry tender and taste rich.

Choux pastry is slightly different because gently cooking the fat, flour, and liquid together on the stovetop gelatinizes the starch while tenderizing the gluten network. The dough remains soft and tender. While it's baking, the extra moisture in choux pastry puffs up the dough. The egg proteins coagulate and firm up the surface, resulting in a crisp pastry that remains tender inside.

See Also • Bread, Cake, Cookies, Gluten, Fat, Flour, Pasta

PÂTÉ • See Sausage

PEACH

What It Is • The fruit of the *Prunus persica* tree, peaches have been cultivated in China since at least 1000 BCE. Other members of the *Prunus* genus include plums, cherries, apricots, and almonds. Peaches are raised from seed and came to North America with Spanish explorers. There are more than 2,000 varieties of these luscious juicy fruits, including the fuzzless varieties known as nectarines.

What It Does • Peaches and nectarines fall into two general categories: freestone and clingstone. The earliest varieties had soft, juicy flesh easily freed from the pit. These freestone varieties tend to ripen late in the season and are usually eaten fresh. Newer varieties were bred for firmness and have less juicy flesh that clings to the pit. These clingstone varieties tend to ripen earlier in the season and are often commercially canned, frozen, or processed into other products. While freestone types are juicier, clingstone varieties hold their shape better when cooked.

There is considerable overlap between the two categories, and most markets sell yellow varieties of firm-fleshed freestone peaches and nectarines. Some white peaches and nectarines are extremely soft, juicy, and sweet, but most mass-market white fruits have also been bred for firmness and transportability. Like the white varieties, flat "doughnut" peaches have long been popular

fast fact

- When peach producers adopted technology to brush excess fuzz from fruit, sales rose by nearly 50%.

in China and are relative newcomers in Western markets.

China produces about 44% of the world's peaches and nectarines. The U.S. produces about 10%, and nearly 30% of the peaches grown in the U.S. are clingstone varieties grown to be canned. Peaches are also sold frozen, as peach **juice** or nectar, or dried. Fresh varieties are enjoyed in salsas, chutneys, **jams and jellies**, pies, and pastries around the world.

Fresh peaches and nectarines taste best in warm summer months when they can fully ripen on the tree. Once picked, the fruit won't get any sweeter but will soften and develop more complex aromas. For the juiciest peaches, look for those grown locally, as mass-marketed peaches are bred to be firm and less juicy for easy shipping. Ripe fruit will yield softly to gentle pressure and smell fragrant. If the fruit is hard, it can be ripened in a loosely wrapped paper bag at room temperature for a day or two. You can speed it along by adding an apple, which will release ripening ethylene gas in the bag. Once ripe, use peaches and nectarines immediately or refrigerate them for a few days in the warmest part of your refrigerator, preferably above 45°F (7°C), as prolonged cold temperatures can mute delicate peach aromas and give the fruit a mealy texture. Bring cold peaches and nectarines to room temperature for the best flavor. If you need to peel them, slit the bottom of the skin, blanch the fruit in boiling water, then shock it in ice water to loosen the skins for easy peeling.

kitchen wisdom

Slicing Ripe Peaches
To easily slice very ripe peaches, freeze them just long enough to firm up the flesh, about 20 minutes. Cut peaches will eventually darken in the open air, but you can stop enzymatic browning by submerging the fruit in water with a little lemon juice.

How It Works • Peaches and nectarines get rich aromas of honey and cream from compounds called lactones and a whiff of almond from benzaldehyde. Some varieties have a clove-like aroma from eugenol. Ripe peaches and nectarines get their sweetness from sugar (about 10% by weight) and some puckery astringency from tannins. Yellow-flesh varieties contain about 0.4% acid; white-flesh varieties contain a bit less.

As peaches and nectarines ripen, the pectin in the cell walls is transformed and the fruit softens. Even ripe nectarines tend to be a bit firmer than peaches, but both varieties can suffer from chill injury. If the fruit is kept below 45°F (7°C) for more than two weeks, the fruit's pectin doesn't soften as it would under warmer conditions, resulting in peaches and nectarines with a dry or mealy texture.

Skin and flesh color in these fruits ranges from yellow-orange to pink to white. The yellow-spectrum fruits get their color from carotenoid pigments, while red colors come from anthocyanin pigments. In most varieties, the anthocyanins concentrate in the skin, lending the fruit a pink or red blush.

See Also • Cherry, Fruit, Plum

PEANUTS • See Legumes, Nuts, Oil

PEAR

What It Is • The fruit of the *Pyrus* tree in the rose family, pears have been cultivated in China for more than 3,000 years. They came to North America in the 1600s via British seeds and have evolved into more than 30 species and thousands of varieties. Cultivated European and North American pears (*Pyrus communis*) are typically bell shaped with soft flesh, while Asian pears (such as *P. pyrifolia* or *P. ussuriensis*) tend to be rounded with crisp flesh.

What It Does • Fresh ripe pears are often eaten out of hand, gently poached, or cooked into **jams and jellies**, pies, and cakes. Pear **juice** can be fermented to make **cider**,

North American and European Pear Varieties

Pears have a fairly wide growing season, from midsummer to early winter. Some reach peak ripeness later than others. Use the guide below to choose pear varieties at the height of the season.

Pear	Season	Characteristics	Best Uses
Anjou	Winter	Pale green-yellow skin, often russeted; velvety, juicy white flesh; mild and sweet	Eating
Bartlett (Williams)	Summer	Yellow-speckled skin blushed pink; juicy, sweet flesh	Eating, cooking
Bartlett (Williams), Red	Summer	Shiny speckled red skin; buttery-soft, sweet, and juicy flesh	Eating, cooking
Bosc	Fall	Golden or light brown russeted skin; juicy white firm yet tender flesh; sweet and mildly tart	Cooking, eating
Comice	Fall	Yellow-green speckled, russeted skin; soft, velvety, juicy white flesh; sweet, rich, and aromatic	Eating
Forelle	Fall	Red-speckled skin; firm, grainy, sweet flesh	Cooking
Packham's Triumph	Fall	Green-yellow speckled skin, sometimes russeted; soft, smooth, succulent flesh; sweet and mildly tart	Eating, cooking
Seckel	Fall	Very small rounded pear with thick green and red skin; firm (sometimes gritty) yet tender juicy flesh; sweet, spicy, and aromatic	Cooking, eating
Winter Nellis	Winter	Small rounded pear with green or red russeted skin; firm, grainy, sweet flesh	Cooking

known as perry. The juice is sometimes cooked down and concentrated into a syrup used to sweeten fruit drinks and breakfast cereals. Fresh pears also contain enough **pectin** to form a thick, cohesive sauce when cooked down, much like applesauce. Pear butter is made by slowly cooking down pears until much of the moisture evaporates, the sugars and proteins undergo Maillard browning, and the pectin thickens. Pear butter's high pectin content makes it a fair replacement for some of the fat in baked goods.

After they're picked from the tree, pears continue to ripen, becoming softer and sweeter and developing more complex aromas. Ripe pears bruise easily, so most pears are harvested and shipped underripe, then exposed to ethylene gas (a natural ripening gas emitted by fruits) to ripen them just before sale. To ripen hard, underripe pears, enclose them with a ripe apple in a paper bag at room temperature for a few days. Once ripe, pears should smell fragrant and yield to gentle pressure close to the stem. They can be stored between 35 and 40°F (2 and 4°C) for about a week.

fast fact

- The best pear brandies include a whole Bartlett (Williams) pear in the bottle. The bottles are secured over the tips of budding flower stems, and the fruit grows and ripens inside the bottle.

Like apples and apple juice, cut pears and pear juice undergo enzymatic browning. Commercial pear juice is typically **pasteurized** to inactivate **enzymes** and prevent discoloration. Pear skins also darken when cooked and are best removed before cooking.

How It Works

• Pears get their fruity aromas from esters, **flavor compounds** formed from the reaction of an acid molecule and an alcohol molecule. One of the esters in pears is hexyl acetate, which consists of a molecule of hexyl alcohol and a molecule of acetic acid. Another is ethyl decadienoate, also known as the "pear ester." Sweetness comes from about 10% sugar by weight. A small amount (about 0.5%) of pear sweetness comes from a sugar alcohol called sorbitol. Pectins are indigestible, so eating a big helping of pears, especially concentrated pear products like pear butter, can cause some stomach discomfort. A pear's acidity is relatively low and comparable to that of avocados at just 0.2%.

The creamy texture of ripe pears comes from pectins that naturally break down as the fruit ripens. The grittiness of some pears comes from an insoluble fiber called lignin in the fruit's cell walls that does not break down with ripening. All pears once had this texture, but Europeans bred pears for smoothness in the 1700s. Grittiness tends to show up in older varieties cultivated in China.

Once harvested, pears don't change color. The green or yellow sometimes blushes with red, but the flesh usually remains creamy white. However, the red anthocyanin pigments in the skin also lurk in the flesh; they're just bound up by other phenolic compounds. When some pear varieties are cooked, these phenolic compounds break down from heat and reveal the anthocyanins, giving cooked or canned pears a pink hue.

See Also • Apple, Cherry, Fruit

PEAS • See Legumes

PECAN • See Nuts

PECORINO • See Cheese

PECTIN

What It Is

• A type of fiber, pectin is a glue-like component located between plant cell walls, particularly concentrated in fruits and some vegetables. While insoluble cellulose and lignin give plant cells their structural rigidity, pectin and hemicellulose act as glue between the cells to help hold up the stiffer cellulose and lignin.

What It Does

• Pectin was first isolated from plants by French chemist Henri Braconnot in 1825. Today, more than 40,000 metric tons of pectin are produced each year worldwide. The concentrate is either a powder or a liquid made from apples and/or citrus peels. Similar to **gelatin**, pectin forms a matrix that traps water into a smooth, viscous gel. It's what makes **jams and jellies** set and provides the soft, gelled texture of gummy **candy** like jelly beans and gummy worms. The glue-like texture of pectin makes it useful as a thickener and stabilizer in food products such as low-fat yogurt and low-fat baked goods. Pectin is a useful addition to sorbets, creating a smooth texture by keeping the water from forming large ice crystals when frozen.

As forms of soluble fiber, pectin binds cholesterol in the intestine and reduces its reabsorption, thereby reducing plasma and liver cholesterol levels.

How It Works

• Think of a brick wall. Without mortar between the bricks, the wall would fall apart. Pectin is like the mortar between the cell walls of plants. It consists of long chains of sugar-like polysaccharide molecules (galacturonic acids) that bond together to form a cement-like glue that supports the plant's stiffer cellulose and lignin fibers (the bricks). In growing plants and developing fruits, pectin is known as

Pectin in Fruits and Vegetables

Fruits and vegetables high in pectin tend to gel easily. Those low in pectin are sometimes mixed with higher-pectin foods to create a good gel. Pectin content and type vary considerably, even within a single food category, especially with ripeness. Tart apples like Granny Smith are high in pectin and create good gels, but sweet apples like Red Delicious are lower in pectin and don't create good gels. Here are some common fruits and vegetables and their pectin levels:

Higher in pectin: black currants, carrots, chile peppers, citron melons, citrus skins, Concord grapes, cranberries, currants, gooseberries, guavas, lemons, loganberries, plums, quince, tart apples, tomatillos, and tomatoes.

Lower in pectin: apricots, blueberries, cherries, figs, grapefruit, melons, nectarines, oranges, peaches, pears, pineapples, pomegranates, rhubarb, raspberries, and strawberries.

protopectin, is not water soluble, and doesn't create gels. It's what gives unripe fruits and vegetables their firm texture. As fruits and vegetables mature, enzymes transform protopectin into gummy, water-soluble pectin, causing the produce to soften and ripen. Pectin levels peak as fruits and vegetables reach the height of ripeness. With continued ripening, enzymes convert the pectin to pectinic acid and then to pectic acid, which doesn't gel. That's why very ripe fruits aren't as good for making jam as just-ripe fruit.

Pectin creates a gel by trapping water in a mesh-like network. Depending on the type and amount of pectin in the mixture, the network may be stiff or supple. Apple pectin creates an elastic gel, whereas citrus pectin makes a more tender, fragile gel. Either way, in jam made with high-pectin fruit, pectin molecules flow from between the cells when the fruit is cut and cooked. The pectin dissolves in liquid from the ruptured cells (or in added liquid) and becomes diluted. The water molecules in the mixture give the pectin molecules a negative charge, causing them to repel each other. Only acid and sugar will bring the pectin molecules back together. Acid released from within the fruit (or added acid in the form of, say, lemon juice) neutralizes the negative charges, allowing the pectin molecules to repel each other less. Added sugar attracts water molecules, bringing the pectin chains closer together. And when the mixture cools, the pectin molecules bond together into a mesh-like network that cradles and supports the dissolved sugar and remaining liquid. The mixture gels into jam. It begins to set when it cools below 180°F (82°C). This type of gel is called a sugar-acid-pectin gel because sugar and acid are required for the pectin molecules to re-bond and gel. The ideal gel consists of 60 to 65% sugar concentration, 0.5 to 1% pectin, and 0.5% acid by weight (equivalent to a pH of 2.8 to 3.4).

Most jams and jellies are sugar-acid-pectin gels and contain what's known as high-methoxyl (HM) pectin. In HM pectin, more than 50% of the pectin chains are linked

science wise

Calcium and Pectin • Some plant foods, such as apples, beans, carrots, cauliflower, cherries, potatoes, sweet potatoes, and tomatoes, contain enzymes in the cell walls that can help keep the food from getting too mushy during long cooking. Precooking these foods at 130 to 140°F (54 to 60°C) for 20 to 30 minutes activates the enzyme, which catalyzes reactions of pectin in the cell walls and allows the pectin chains to more easily bond with calcium released from the fruit's or vegetable's ruptured cells. The calcium bonds with the pectin chains and makes them interact more strongly, keeping the fruit or vegetable firm even throughout extended cooking. You could also add calcium to the mixture for a similar firming effect. For instance, when making pickles, add calcium salts like calcium citrate or use unrefined sea salt (which contains calcium). The extra calcium will firm up the pectin and keep the pickles crisp even when cooked.

kitchen wisdom

Fat Replacement

High-pectin fruits and vegetables can replace some of the fat in baked goods. When puréed, apples and prunes (even carrots and tomatillos) mimic the moisturizing and tenderizing effects of fat. Water in the produce provides moisture, and pectin interrupts the development of gluten much like fat would, creating tenderness. Baked goods made with high-pectin fruit or vegetable purées can be moist and tender but are usually somewhat denser in texture than those made with all fat. For good texture in reduced-fat baked goods, use a mixture of fat and fruit purée, such as ¼ cup (50 mL) butter and ¼ cup (50 mL) fruit purée to replace ½ cup (125 mL) butter in cakes.

with methyl alcohol to form a methylester (a compound formed from the reaction of acid and alcohol molecules). But pectins come in various forms, and when less than 50% of the pectin chains are methylated, the pectin is known as low-methoxyl (LM) pectin. HM pectin sets faster than LM pectin but requires sugar and acid to form the gel. LM pectin sets more slowly but needs no sugar and less acid to form a gel. LM pectin is used to make low-sugar jams because the gel will form without sugar. Instead of sugar and acid, calcium is required to bind together the pectin molecules, and this type of gel is called a calcium-pectin gel.

Amidated pectin is a form of LM pectin in which some of the methyl groups are replaced with amide groups so that the pectin requires less calcium to form a gel. The advantage of a gel made with amidated pectin is that it can be heated after gelling and will solidify again once it cools, while an HM pectin gel remains liquid after it's heated and cooled.

See Also • Candy, Carbohydrate, Colloid, Fiber, Fruit, Gums, Jam and Jelly, Juice, Starch, Vegetables

PECTINIC ACID • See Pectin

PENICILLIUM MOLD • See Mold

PEPPERCORN • See Spices

PEPPERS • See Capsicum, Spices

PESTICIDE • See Agriculture

PESTO • See Sauces

PH • See Acid, Alkali

PHENOLS • See Flavor Compounds

PHOTOSYNTHESIS • See Chlorophyll

PHYTOCHEMICALS • See Antioxidants, Nutrition, Vegetables, Vitamins

PICKLES • See Curing, Fermentation, Vegetables

PIE CRUST • See Pastry

PIG • See Pork

PIGEON • See Game

PIGMENT

What It Is • Think of bright red apples, sunny yellow corn, and deep purple potatoes. They all get color from pigments, chemical compounds that make food appetizing. They catch our eye and induce us to eat. Only a handful of pigment families account for the color in most foods, but hundreds of pigment subtypes create the finely shaded hues of everything from yellow chard to blood-red oranges.

What It Does • Every plant on land contains **chlorophyll**, a green pigment that allows plants to produce energy through photosynthesis. Most contain a mix of other pigments, too, generating a wide spectrum of colorful fruits and vegetables. As a plant grows, its pigments and their concentration change, causing the plant's color to change. Young plants usually contain more chlorophyll and look greener than older ones. As plants mature and ripen, chlorophyll levels tend to decrease

Plant Pigments

Plants are colored by four major families of pigments: chlorophylls (green), carotenoids (yellow-orange-red), anthocyanins (red-purple-blue), and betains (deep red-purple or yellow-orange). There are more than 600 known carotenoid pigments and more than 300 known anthocyanin pigments. Various combinations of these pigments imbue our vegetables and fruits with a gorgeous rainbow of colors. Anthoxanthins are a fifth but less prominent pigment family that gives foods like cauliflower and potatoes their ivory and pale yellow hues. Here's a quick look at common plant pigments and the foods in which they are found.

Pigment	Subtypes	Colors	Common Food Sources
Anthocyanins	Cyanidin	Blue	Blueberries
	Delphinidin	Purple	Concord grape
	Pelargonidin	Red	Red cabbage, blood oranges
Betains (betalains)	Betacyanins	Red to purple	Beets
	Betaxanthins	Yellow to orange	Yellow chardChlorophyll
Carotenoids	Carotenes		
	Beta-carotene	Orange	Carrots
	Lycopene	Red	Tomatoes
	Xanthophylls		
	Lutein	Yellow	Egg yolks
	Zeaxanthin	Yellow	Corn, saffron
Chlorophyll a	Blue-green	Broccoli	
	Chlorophyll-b	Yellow-green	Leeks

because of oxidation and reveal other pigments in the plant's cells. That's why peppers and tomatoes ripen from green to red. Ripe green avocados and gooseberries are notable exceptions to this general rule.

Animals also get their color from pigments. The shells of lobster, crab, and other crustaceans contain a red pigment called astaxanthin. In raw crustaceans, astaxanthin is bound up with protein in the shell. Cooking breaks the protein-pigment bond and reveals the astaxanthin, making cooked lobster and crab shells appear bright red. Red meat gets its color from another red pigment, myoglobin. Lighter-colored meats such as pork and veal contain little myoglobin, making them appear pale pink, whereas beef contains four times more myoglobin and appears deep red. Melanin is a pigment in animals that colors human skin and gives foods like caviar their steel gray, brown, and black shades. More brightly colored animal pigments allow chameleons to blend into their surroundings and cephalopods like octopus and squid to confuse predators with blue-black or brown-black "ink."

Hundreds of plant pigments and some animal pigments serve as a natural source of color in paints, dyes, and food coloring (see **Food Additives**). But pigments also provide us with flavor and important nutrients. For instance, when saffron is crushed, heated, or exposed to oxygen, the yellow carotenoid zeaxanthin is converted to picrocrocin and safranal, two aroma compounds that give saffron its characteristic scent. Other pigments act as healthful **antioxidants**. Chlorophyll, carotenoids, and anthocyanins can all help to protect the cells in our bodies from oxidative damage and degradation. Carotenoid pigments like beta-carotene and lutein are converted to vitamin A in our bodies. They help our eyes to detect light and also help prevent the cell damage that leads to various types of cancer. Fruits and vegetables are a primary source of these healthful pigments. In general, the more deeply colored a fruit or vegetable is, the more antioxidant pigments it contains and the more health benefits it will provide. For instance, richly pigmented blueberries contain more antioxidants than most other produce.

How It Works • Most pigments, especially plant pigments, are brilliantly colored. They are contained in special cells called chromoplasts (chloroplasts for chlorophyll) in the vacuoles of plants. The color we see, such as the bright yellow of corn, is light reflecting off the pigment compound. Light is a form of electromagnetic radiation (see **Heat**) emitted over a range of wavelengths. When you shine white light through a prism, its component wavelengths are refracted, so the spectrum of red, orange, yellow, green, blue, indigo, and violet becomes visible. Each color represents a particular wavelength. Pigments in food absorb only certain wavelengths and reflect the others. The color we see is the color that is reflected, not the one that is absorbed, by the pigment compound. For instance, green peppers (and other foods colored green by chlorophyll) absorb the blue and red wavelengths, and they reflect the green wavelengths, which makes peppers appear green to our eyes.

Color Changes Caused by Heat, Acidity, and Metals

Whenever pigments are heated or react with chemical compounds, their color changes. Sometimes the colors brighten, sometimes they become dull, and sometimes their hue changes. With brief cooking, vegetables brighten in color because heat breaks open the cell walls and releases oxygen from the cells' air pockets. With oxygen no longer obscuring the pigment compounds, briefly cooked vegetables appear brighter in color. To make green vegetables appear brighter and more vibrant, blanch them in boiling water for no more than a minute to release the oxygen, then plunge the vegetables into ice water to stop the cooking.

Cooking times are especially critical with chlorophyll because this pigment is more sensitive and soluble than other pigments. Chlorophyll is fat soluble before it is heated but becomes water soluble when cooked. That's why boiled vegetables can tint the cooking water green. Overcooked green vegetables often turn a drab olive color because hydrogen ions from the cooking water (or released from the cell walls of the cooked vegetable itself) displace magnesium in the chlorophyll molecule. To prevent the drab color change, cook green vegetables tender-crisp, less than 5 or 6 minutes in most cases, and avoid acidic conditions. (See Kitchen Wisdom, page 128, for more ways to prevent the discoloration of green chlorophyll in vegetables.)

Anthocyanins and betains are water-soluble pigments. These pigments easily leach into cooking water, causing blanched red cabbage to quickly turn the water red and blanched beets to turn it purple. That's also why purple asparagus turns green during cooking: the water-soluble anthocyanins dissipate and reveal the green chlorophyll they obscured in the raw vegetable. Like other plant pigments, anthocyanins and betains are sensitive to acidic or alkaline conditions, and they can change color dramatically. For example, anthocyanins remain red in acidic conditions, but in alkaline conditions they turn blue. Betains turn purple in acidic conditions and yellow in alkaline conditions. That's why pickled red cabbage stays red (from the acidic vinegar). On the other hand, red cherries mixed into muffin batter, which is alkaline from baking powder or baking soda, develop a blue ring wherever the cherries touch the alkaline batter. Similarly, blueberries develop a green ring in alkaline quick-bread batters. To prevent these colored rings around brightly colored fruits, make the batters more acidic by adding buttermilk, sour cream, or another acidic ingredient.

science wise

Pigments That Survive Digestion • After we eat, most of the pigments in food are destroyed by stomach acids or chemical reactions in the large intestine. But some pigments can survive digestion. If you eat a lot of carrots (more than three a day), excess carotenoid pigments can build up in the fatty tissue beneath your skin and make your skin look yellow or orange. Likewise, chlorophyll from green vegetables and betains from beets can sometimes survive digestion and tint urine light green or pale red.

fast facts

- Albinistic animals and humans are born with very little to no melanin, the pigment that colors our skin, hair, and eyes.
- Black beans contain about 20 grams of anthocyanin pigments per kilogram, giving the beans such a dark purple color that they appear black.
- The yellow pigment lutein (sometimes as marigold flowers) is added to chicken feed to give some commercially produced eggs bright yellow yolks and chicken skin a richer yellow color.
- The dark yellow-orange carotenoid canthaxanthin is used in some skin-tanning formulas.

Pale anthoxanthins can also be fairly reactive. They can turn blue-gray or green when they react with certain metals such as iron and aluminum. To keep cauliflower and other pale vegetables from turning blue, avoid cutting them with a carbon steel knife or cooking them in **cookware** with exposed surfaces of iron, aluminum, or tin. Likewise, to keep the anthoxanthins in carrots from turning green, avoid cooking carrot muffins or other carrot dishes in cast-iron or aluminum baking dishes.

Carrots contain a small amount of anthoxanthins, but carotenoids provide most of their bright yellow-orange color. Carotenoids are the most stable pigments when cooked. They are more fat soluble than water soluble, so foods like carrots tend to retain their bright color even when overcooked.

The most common discoloration of fruits and vegetables is caused by enzymatic browning. Cutting an apple or potato slashes its cells and exposes the fruit or vegetable's enzymes to oxygen, which allows the formation of melanin pigments that make the apple or potato appear brown instead of white. To prevent apples, potatoes, artichokes, and other cut foods from browning, you need to slow down or inactivate the enzyme. Cold temperatures and acid slow down the enzyme's browning activity, so it helps to soak the cut food in cold water with a little lemon juice (or a crushed vitamin C tablet) or in oil. You can also inactivate the enzyme by briefly blanching vegetables like potatoes in boiling water.

Submerging them under water keeps oxygen away, as does vacuum packaging.

See Also • Antioxidants, Chlorophyll, Meat

PIKE • See Fish

PIMENTO • See Capsicum

PINEAPPLE

What It Is • Symbols of hospitality around the world, pineapples are the fruit of *Anana comosus*, a short spiky tropical plant native to dry regions of South America. A mature pineapple is actually a conglomeration of up to 200 little fruits that spiral around and bond to the central core. The individual fruits can be recognized in a pineapple's multiple thorny "eyes."

What It Does • Ripe pineapples are easily bruised, so most of the world's crop is canned or sold as juice. Excess fruit from canning is used to make food products such as pineapple vinegar. Fresh pineapple is widely used for its rich tropical flavor in salads, salsas, drinks, and desserts. The fruit holds up well during cooking and pairs well with both savory foods like pork and sweet foods like cake.

Fresh pineapples don't get sweeter or more flavorful after they're picked because the fruit does not store starch that can be broken down into sugar after harvesting. The sweetest, most flavorful pineapples are fully ripened on the plant and come from hot, dry regions right around the equator. Because ripe pineapples are too delicate for shipping, most sold in North American markets were picked less than fully ripe (at about 2 to 5 pounds/1 to 2 kg) and stored for about a month at 50°F (10°C). Fully ripened pineapples can weigh up to 20 pounds (9 kg). Ripe pineapples keep best at about 45°F (7°C). Choose heavy yellowed fruits that yield to gentle pressure, have firm green leaves, and smell fragrant at the base.

How It Works • Ripe pineapples are fairly sweet, containing about 12% sugar. About

fast facts

- Supersweet "golden" pineapples contain about four times more vitamin C than other varieties.
- The original Tupi Indian word for pineapple is *nana* or *anana*, meaning excellent or exquisite fruit. Spanish explorers called it pineapple because the fruit resembles a pine cone.
- Some wild pineapples are pollinated by nocturnal bats. To avoid infestation by weevils during the day, these varieties open their flowers at night instead.

2% acid balances the sweetness in most varieties. The acidity concentrates near the surface of the fruit, while the fruit near the core contains almost half as much acid. The aroma of a fully ripe pineapple can be overwhelmingly intense. Distinctive pineapple fragrance comes from an ester compound called ethyl butyrate, while vanilla aromas come from vanillin, clove aromas from eugenol, and some pungency from sulfur compounds. Pineapples also have a note of caramel from carbon compounds. Pineapple flavors tend to be most intense at the base, which develops first.

Pineapples contain a powerful enzyme called bromelain that catalyzes protein hydrolysis. Bromelain is particularly effective at hydrolyzing connective tissue, so it's often used in meat tenderizers and in marinades intended for tough cuts of meat like pork shoulder. In fact, bromelain is so good at hydrolyzing protein that it can ruin a **gelatin** dessert or any dish containing milk or cream. The enzyme hydrolyzes gelatin and prevents the gel from setting, and it breaks down the casein protein in milk, resulting in a bitter flavor. When making gelatin or dairy dishes with pineapple, you can avoid the problem by cooking the pineapple flesh or juice to inactivate the enzyme or by using canned pineapple, which is heated to a high enough temperature to destroy the enzyme.

See Also • Enzyme, Fruit

PINE NUTS • See Nuts

PINK PEPPERCORN • See Spices

PINOT NOIR • See Wine

PINTO BEAN • See Legumes

PISTACHIO • See Nuts

PITA BREAD • See Bread

Grilled Pineapple with Honey and Habanero

The high sugar content and firm texture of pineapple make it perfect for grilling. It also takes well to sweet, savory, and spicy flavors. Pair this easy side dish with grilled pork or serve it as a simple dessert with cajeta (caramelized goat's milk) or vanilla-flavored whipped cream.

1	small pineapple	1
¾ cup	honey, preferably orange blossom	175 mL
2 tsp	grated orange zest	10 mL
2	habanero chiles, seeded and finely chopped	2
Pinch	grated nutmeg	Pinch
Pinch	salt	Pinch

1. Heat grill to medium-high. Cut off spiky top of pineapple and about ½-inch (1 cm) from base. Stand upright and cut downward around fruit to remove rind and eyes. Cut lengthwise into quarters, then cut core from each quarter. Cut each quarter crosswise into wedges about ¾ inch (2 cm) thick.

2. In a small bowl, combine honey, orange zest, habaneros, nutmeg, and salt. Brush grill grate and coat with oil. Grill pineapple until well marked by the grill, 3 to 5 minutes per side, brushing with honey mixture during last 1 to 2 minutes of grilling.

MAKES 4 SERVINGS

PLANTAIN • See Banana

PLANTS • See Antioxidants, Carbon Dioxide, Chlorophyll, Fruit, Leaves, Nuts, Oxygen, Roots, Stems, Vegetables

PLASTIC • See Bakeware, Cookware, Storage

PLUM

What It Is • There are two main species of plums. Both come from the same genus, *Prunus*. The one from Europe (*P. domestica*) produces fruit that is fleshy rather than juicy and is usually oval, with purple skin and a pale interior. Asian plums (*P. salicina*) are larger, round, and full of sweet-tart juice. Asian plums (aka Japanese plums) have

fast fact

• In the Middle Ages, "plum" could denote any dried fruit, which explains why traditional "plum puddings" and "plum cakes" usually don't contain plums.

been cultivated in China since ancient times. It wasn't until Luther Burbank, an American horticulturist, brought them to California in 1875 (from Japan, where they arrived from China just 300 years earlier) that Asian plums came to be the dominant plums worldwide. Burbank developed more than a hundred cultivated varieties of plum, including Santa Rosa and Wickson plums, and was also the first to cross-cultivate plums and other stone fruits, developing pluots and plumcots, both plum-apricot hybrids.

Lamb Shanks Braised with Prune Plums

Through drying, plums develop many of the same flavor characteristics as roasted meats, transforming them into one of the few fruits that can make meats taste meatier. These characteristics are particularly delicious when paired with gamy meats like lamb or duck, where sorbitol in the prunes has a taming effect on pungency and bitterness.

12	pitted prunes	12
1 cup	boiling water	250 mL
4	lamb shanks	4
1/3 cup	all-purpose flour	75 mL
2 tbsp	vegetable oil	25 mL
1	medium onion, peeled and cut into eighths	1
2	cloves garlic, minced	2
1/4 cup	brandy	50 mL
2 tsp	crumbled dried rosemary	10 mL
1 tsp	dried thyme leaves	5 mL
1 cup	beef stock	250 mL
1/2 cup	prune juice	125 mL
	Finely grated zest and juice of 1 orange	
1	bay leaf	1
6	prune plums (Italian plums), quartered and pitted	6
2 tbsp	chopped Italian flat-leaf parsley	25 mL
	Salt and freshly ground black pepper to taste	

1. In a heatproof bowl, soak prunes in boiling water until plump. Drain and set aside.

2. Meanwhile, dredge lamb with flour. In a large, heavy skillet or Dutch oven, heat oil over medium-high heat. Add lamb, in batches as necessary, and brown, turning often. Transfer to a plate.

3. Add onion and sauté until starting to brown. Add garlic and brandy, and boil for 1 minute.

4. Return lamb and any accumulated juices to pan. Add soaked prunes, rosemary, thyme, stock, prune juice, orange zest and juice, and bay leaf. Reduce heat and simmer, covered, until shanks are tender, about 1½ hours. Add plums, and cook, covered, for 15 minutes more. Discard bay leaf. Stir in parsley and salt and pepper.

MAKES 4 SERVINGS

Low-Fat Brownies

The fiber and sugar in dried plums interrupt the development of gluten in a cake batter in much the same way as butter or oil do, keeping baked goods tender with a fraction of the calories and fat. Prunes are also hygroscopic (they absorb moisture from the atmosphere), so these brownies stay moist for days.

	Spray oil	
1 cup	pitted prunes	250 mL
¼ cup	hot water	50 mL
1¼ cups	granulated sugar	300 mL
¼ cup	unsweetened cocoa powder	50 mL
2 tbsp	instant coffee powder	25 mL
Pinch	salt	Pinch
2	large eggs	2
3 oz	unsweetened chocolate, melted	90 g
1 tbsp	vanilla extract	15 mL
½ cup	all-purpose flour	125 mL
½ cup	walnut pieces	125 mL

1. Preheat oven to 375°F (190°C). Grease an 8-inch (20 cm) square baking pan with spray oil.
2. In a food processor, purée prunes with water until smooth. Add sugar, cocoa, coffee powder, and salt and process until smooth.
3. Add eggs, melted chocolate, and vanilla. Process until blended, scraping the sides of the bowl with a rubber spatula as necessary. Add flour and process just enough to blend. Stir in walnuts.
4. Pour mixture into prepared pan, smoothing top, and bake in preheated oven until top is crusty, edges are set, and center feels moist when lightly pressed, about 25 minutes. Let cool in pan on a rack for 10 minutes. Remove from pan and let cool completely. Cut into 16 squares.

MAKES 16 SERVINGS

What It Does • Because European plums are meaty enough to retain their shape during cooking, they are the plum of choice for baking and cooking. The greengage plum (known as Reine Claude in France), a large green to golden variety of European plum, is one of the few that is equally good for both heating and eating fresh. Most European plums are small and purple and are typically dried into prunes, which is why they are referred to as prune plums. Today, most prune plums are produced in the San Joaquin Valley in California, which provides about 70% of the world's supply.

In order to be dried into prunes (aka dried plums), a plum needs to be at least 22% soluble fiber. Although at one time all prunes were sun-dried, today they are dried on trays in tunnel dehydrators to a moisture content of between 18 and 35%. Those with a moisture content below 24% can be stored without preservatives, but they tend to be hard and usually need to be hydrated before they can be eaten. Most prunes are dried to about 30% moisture and dipped in or sprayed with potassium sorbate to prevent the growth of molds and yeasts on the fruit. Potassium sorbate is considered a mild preservative and generally regarded as safe.

Dried prunes develop a rich flavor from the concentration of their sugars, acids, and aromatic esters during drying. Maillard **browning** reactions during drying create roasted flavor notes and a dark purple-brown-black color. They develop a meaty richness that makes them appropriate for braising with strong-tasting meats like lamb and duck.

Neither the European nor the Asian plum species are tart enough for making preserves and jellies. That distinction is reserved for damson plums, one of the most ancient European varieties, and beach plums, which are similar to damson and native to the New World. Both these plums have tart skins and dense flesh, which makes them suitable for jams and preserves. They are generally too sour to eat fresh. Another plum, known as a sloe berry, grows on blackthorn bushes and is distilled into sloe gin, a plum **liquor**. Other popular plum liquors include slivovitz and rakia. Asian plum wine is made from ume, a white Japanese plum. Ume are also salted and eaten as pickles in Japan, are the base for

Chinese plum sauce, and used in *umeboshi* vinegar.

How It Works •

Prunes are a concentrated source of phenol compounds (150 mg in 100 g) with strong antioxidant powers that prevent the development of oxidizing leftover flavors. Mixing a bit of puréed prune into meat loaf or ground beef prevents leftover flavors from developing.

Rich in soluble fiber (about 45% of their volume) and sugar, dried plums hold on to moisture and coat proteins in a batter. Because the development of protein is the principal reason baked goods become tough, adding prunes to a batter tenderizes baked products in the same way that fats do. Puréed prunes can replace as much as two-thirds of the fat in a cake recipe. The substitution works best with chocolate cakes, in which the color and flavor of prunes blend seamlessly with dark chocolate.

The laxative action of prunes comes from their fiber content and likely their natural content of the sugar alcohol sorbitol. Sugar alcohols are not digested until they get to the large intestine, which is why they are used in diatetic products that don't raise blood glucose levels, but the way they are digested also can trigger digestive disturbances like diarrhea. Prunes contain as much as 15% sorbitol by weight, which could account for their stool-loosening reputation. Products made with sugar alcohols can have the same effect.

See Also • Antioxidants, Apricot, Cake, Cherry, Liquor, Peach

PLUMCOT • See Apricot, Hybrid, Plum

POACHING • See Boiling

POBLANO • See Capsicum

POI • See Roots

POLENTA • See Corn

POLLOCK • See Fish

POLLUTANTS • See Toxin

POLYCYCLIC AROMATIC HYDROCARBONS (PAHS) • See Grilling

POLYDEXTROSE • See Fiber

POLYPHENOL • See Flavor Compounds

POLYSACCHARIDES • See Fiber, Glycogen, Gums, Pectin, Starch

POMELO • See Citrus

POMMERANZEN • See Bitters

POPCORN • See Corn

POPPY SEEDS • See Spices

PORCELAIN • See Cookware

PORGY • See Fish

PORK

What It Is • Pork is the **meat** of pigs (swine). North American domestic pigs are descended from the razorback, a free-roaming domesticated European wild boar (*Sus scrofa*), which was brought to North America by the Spanish explorer Hernando de Soto in the mid-16th century. Europeans had domesticated the pig millennia before. Images of wild pigs in Neolithic cave paintings in Lascaux, France, have led historians to believe pigs were likely domesticated in Europe from feral scavengers near Neolithic farming communities sometime between 3000 and 4000 BCE.

The genetic differences between domestic and wild pigs are minimal. The main difference in their appearance is the amount of hair. The difference in their meats is largely due to diet. Wild boar have traditionally been hunted in mid-fall after being fattened on nuts and herbs foraged in pastures and forests. Iberian pork develops its nutty flavor from a diet that is 50% acorns, and the pigs that are destined to become prosciutto di Parma get their protein-dense muscles and sweet mild flavor from feed that includes the whey left over from the curding of Parmesan cheese.

What It Does • Pork is eaten on every continent and in every cuisine except for kosher and halal diets because of religious sanctions. China is the largest consumer and producer in the world, followed by Europe and the U.S.

Although there are scores of pig breeds, only a few are raised for meat. These tend to be fast-growing muscular breeds like Landrace, the pig of Danish bacon fame, and Duroc, an American breed that is used extensively in crossbreeding. Most of the commercially raised pork in North America is a cross between Duroc, Yorkshire, and Hampshire breeds. In recent years, legendary pig breeds that were considered noncommercial because of their small size and slow growth have come to be valued for the superior quality of their meat. Once rare, the black Iberian pig, prized for its ham, and Berkshire pigs (called kurobuta in Japan), valued for their abundant fine-grained marbling, have experienced a resurgence in production, usually on smaller farms.

Swine are classified by sex and age. A pig is a young animal, between six and eight months old, usually weighing between 120 and 180 pounds (55 and 80 kg). Young pigs for roasting whole are under six months and can weigh between 20 and 60 pounds (9 and 27 kg). A hog is a mature pig over eight months, weighing over 180 pounds (80 kg), and can be either a stag or boar (male) or a gilt (female that has not borne young) or sow (female that has given birth). A castrated stag is called a barrow. Pork is graded 1 through 4 based on the ratio of lean meat to fat on the carcass, with number 1 yielding the highest proportion of lean. Almost all pork sold to consumers is number 1 grade, and all number 1 grade pork comes from gilt or barrow swine.

Because of its lower moisture content (about 52%) and ample marbling, pork has always been a good candidate for preservation through **curing**. Recipes for cured hams (hind legs) date back to Cato the Younger in 50 BCE, and Apicius mentions cured sausage in the 4th century CE. Although technically hams can be made only from the hind legs of swine, shoulder "hams" like tasso and capicola are valued for the clean, dense quality of the fat and a "porkier" flavor that takes well to heavy spicing.

There are four primal cuts of pork — shoulder, leg, loin, and belly — and all of them are small enough to be sold whole. Whole baby pigs weighing between 20 and 40 pounds (9 and 18 kg) can be roasted in most standard home ovens. Whole adult pigs weighing over 100 pounds (45 kg) need to be spit-roasted on special equipment.

How It Works • Although modern demand for lean meat has changed how all livestock are bred, raised, and fattened, pork has been changed most dramatically. Thirty years ago a full-grown pig typically weighed over 300 pounds (136 kg). Today the top weight is closer to 240 (109 kg), which yields a carcass of about 180 pounds (82 kg) and a little more than 100 pounds (45 kg) of edible meat. Today's pig has less fat (about 1 inch/2.5 cm) along the back, compared with several inches in the past, and larger, leaner muscles.

All of these changes have made lean cuts of pork very similar to chicken in overall content of fat, saturated fat, cholesterol, and calories. But it has also made cooking pork much more difficult. Pork is low in moisture. What made it juicy in the past were abundant deposits of fat dispersed within its lean parts. Now that these have been diminished through breeding and feeding, pork is unpalatably dry if cooked at too high a heat or for too long. Because of its low moisture content, pork responds well to **brining**, which can double its juiciness.

Pork can harbor trichina, the parasite responsible for trichinosis. The threat of trichinosis compelled older pork recipes to recommend cooking pork to 180°F (82°C), a temperature at which all of its moisture is long gone. Although at one time trichinosis was a concern, it has been all but eradicated from commercial pork sold today. In 1950, there were 400 recorded cases of trichinosis in the U.S. From 1997 to 2001 an average of 12 cases a year

Cuts of Pork

Primal Cuts	Retail Cuts (with alternative names)	Description	Cooking Methods and Uses
Shoulder	Blade steak (shoulder blade chops)	Lacks a distinctive eye; coarse grain; fatty; several bones; cross section of Boston butt	Braised
	Boston butt	Very flavorful; lots of fat; can be tough; top part of shoulder	Pulled pork
	Picnic ham	Flavorful; medium lean; usually boneless; lower part of shoulder	Barbecued
	Shoulder	Whole shoulder includes both butt end and picnic end	Barbecued or slow cooked
Leg	Fresh ham	Finely textured; lean; thin fat layer on one side; large roast with or without shank bone and/or hip bone	Roasted
	Ham	Cured leg; can be bone-in or boned; can be smoked	Baked
	Ham steak	Cross-cut of ham	Pan-fried or grilled
	Pig's feet	Feet from front or hind legs	Boiled or pickled; stock, gelatin
	Shank (hock)	Dark flavorful meat with lots of connective tissue; from lower section of front or rear leg	Braised or boiled
	Sirloin	Fairly lean; made of several muscles, with noticeable connective tissue; cut from upper leg	Roasted
Loin	Back ribs (baby back ribs, loin ribs)	Meaty; medium-coarse grain; little fat; cut from ribs along spine	Grilled
	Center cut chops or roast (loin chops or roast)	Large eye; pale, fine grain; fat layer on one side; T-bone (if bone-in); cross section of spine	Chops: grilled, broiled, or pan-fried; Roast: roasted or indirect grilled
	Country-style ribs	Medium-coarse grain; striated fat; several small bones; butterflied loin blade chop	Roasted, braised, indirect grilled
	Loin blade chops	Lack a distinctive eye (main muscle group); coarse grain; fatty; several bones; cut from shoulder blade area	Marinated or brined, then grilled
	Rack (crown)	Large eye; pale; fine grain; fat cap; 7 parallel rib bones	Roasted
	Tenderloin (fillet)	Fine grain; very pale; very tender; very lean	Grilled, roasted, cut into medallions and pan-fried
Belly	Pork belly	Flavorful; dark; lean; very fatty; usually boneless	Slow roasted, braised
	Slab bacon	Cured pork belly	Pan-fried
	Spare ribs (St. Louis ribs)	Striated meat and fat; coarse grain; cut from belly including part of brisket (breast); St Louis cut is trimmed of brisket and belly flap	Barbecued or braised
Other	Caul fat	Thin lacy sheet of membrane veined with fat	Wrap for sausages and pâtés
	Chitterlings	Large intestine	Simmered and fried
	Ears	Mostly skin and cartilage, very little meat; highly gelatinous	Boiled; stock, gelatin

Primal Cuts	Retail Cuts (with alternative names)	Description	Cooking Methods and Uses
	Fat back	Very white fat from back	Fat in cooking, rendered into lard
	Ground pork	Ground meat from any part of pig; sold by percentage of fat (17% lean; 20% regular)	Sausage, meat loaf, Chinese dumplings
	Head	Whole head	Boiled; head cheese
	Heart	Dark meat; very lean; very tough	Boiled; sausage
	Jowl	Fatty flavorful cut from side of head	Cured or pickled, braised or boiled
	Kidneys	Dark red; lean; can be strong tasting	Braised
	Lard	Rendered pork fat	Fat in cooking
	Liver	Dark; strong tasting	Pâté or sausage
	Neck	Mostly bone, very little but very flavorful meat; can be smoked	Boiled for soup or with greens
	Salt pork	Similar to bacon but fattier; cut from belly; cured but not smoked	Fat in cooking
	Sausage casing	Salted intestine	Stuffed for sausages
	Suckling pig	Whole cleaned infant pig, weighing less than 30 pounds (14 kg)	Roasted
	Tail	Lots of bones and cartilage, little meat; highly gelatinous	Stock
	Tongue	Small; pale; lean; mild tasting; tough	Boiled

Pork Primal Cuts

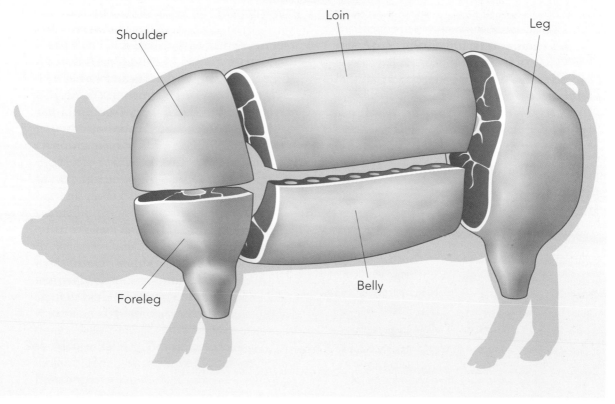

Shoulder · Loin · Leg · Foreleg · Belly

were reported, and most of these were traced to homegrown pigs that were not inspected or to hunted animals like wild boar and bear.

Trichinae are killed at 140°F (60°C). The U.S. National Pork Board and Pork Marketing Canada advise cooking pork to 160°F (71°C), and the U.S. Department of Agriculture agrees that this is the temperature required to kill microbial pathogens and make the meat safe. Most chefs recommend cooking lean, tender cuts like chops, loin, and tenderloin to between 150 and 155°F (65 and 68°C) (still slightly pink in the center), and fattier large cuts, like shoulder and fresh ham, to between 160 and 165°F (71 and 74°C).

See Also • Bacon, Brining, Curing, Game, Ham, Meat, Sausage

PORT • See Wine

PORTER • See Beer

PORT SALUT • See Cheese

POSOLE • See Alkali, Corn

POTASSIUM BICARBONATE • See Chemical Leavener

POTASSIUM BROMATE • See Flour

POTATOES

What It Is • More potatoes are eaten worldwide than any other vegetable. Known as tubers, potatoes are the underground plant **stems** of *Solanum tuberosum*, a perennial plant native to the Andes region of South America. They have been cultivated for thousands of years, and some varieties were grown as far back as 6000 BCE. Most modern

Potato Varieties

There are about 5,000 cultivated potato varieties, best categorized by starch content. High-starch potatoes, such as russets, are called baking potatoes because of their low moisture content, which makes them light and fluffy when baked. High-starch potatoes also make creamy mashed potatoes and flaky french fries. Low-starch (aka waxy) potatoes, such as round red-skinned potatoes, are called boiling potatoes because they retain their shape when boiled, which makes them a good choice for salads and stews. New potatoes (creamers) are also low-starch (and slightly sweeter) because they are harvested young, before as much starch develops. Medium-starch potatoes, such as Yukon gold, are called all-purpose potatoes because their starch content falls somewhere in between the two others. Fingerlings are named for their small, finger-like shape and may have high, medium, or low starch content. To check the starch content of a potato, cut the potato in half. If the potato sticks to the knife or leaves a creamy white residue on the blade, it's a high-starch potato. If it doesn't, it's a low-starch potato. You can also place potatoes in a brine of 1 part salt to 11 parts water. If the potatoes sink, they are high-starch and denser. If they float, they're low-starch and less dense.

Potato	Characteristics
High-Starch Potatoes	
Russet (Arcadia, Burbank, Butte, Idaho)	Oval; netted brown skin; white flesh that is mealy and fluffy when cooked
Medium-Starch Potatoes	
All Blue	Round; dense; somewhat waxy bluish purple flesh
Austrian Crescent	Fingerling shape; smooth golden skin; somewhat waxy pale yellow flesh
Banana (Russian banana)	Fingerling shape; smooth golden skin; somewhat waxy pale yellow flesh
Bintje	Long oval; golden skin; somewhat waxy creamy yellow flesh
California white (long white)	Oval; thin light tan skin; somewhat starchy, somewhat waxy white flesh
Caribe	Oval; purplish blue skin; somewhat starchy white flesh
Charlotte	Oval; thin golden skin; somewhat starchy, somewhat waxy yellow flesh
Desiree	Oval; thin red skin; somewhat waxy, creamy yellow flesh

commercial potatoes stem from a Chilean variety brought to Europe around 1700.

What It Does • Potatoes star in several culinary roles. They can be baked, mashed, boiled, roasted, or fried and incorporated into salads, soups, stews, and sauces. Because of their starch content, they can also be fermented into alcoholic drinks like vodka. They can be used like cornstarch, wheat flour, and other starchy foods to help bind together gratins, breads, and cakes. About 4 ounces (114 g) of whole potatoes (or 1½ tablespoons/ 22 mL pure potato starch) will thicken 2 cups (500 mL) of liquid in a gratin, sauce, or gravy. Potato starch has a lighter texture than grain flours, so it's also used to make light-textured potato dumplings like Italian gnocchi. Refined potato starch is widely used to thicken commercial food products, and potatoes are dehydrated to make potato flakes that can be incorporated into breads or used as breadings (see recipe for Buttermilk-Marinated Catfish with Potato Crust, page 482).

Fresh whole potatoes are often boiled to make mashed potatoes or salads. To keep boiled potatoes from becoming mushy, simmer them instead of **boiling** them. Cooking them in their skins also helps to retain starch and keep the potatoes fluffy and firm. To keep from overcooking the outer part near the skin before the interior is done, start whole potatoes in cold water and gradually raise the temperature. It also helps to use hard water or to make the cooking water slightly acidic by adding some vinegar. Avoid adding salt, which makes the outer parts soften and get mushy even sooner. Like pasta cooking water, potato cooking water is usually starchy enough to help thicken sauces. It's often added to breads to contribute flavor and a soft, moist texture.

Potato	Characteristics
German Butterball	Rounded; golden skin; somewhat starchy yellow flesh
Irish Cobbler (round white)	Tan; thin skin; somewhat starchy white flesh
Katahdin (round white)	Light brown skin; somewhat starchy white flesh
Kennebec (round white)	Light tan skin; somewhat starchy, somewhat waxy white flesh
Peruvian Blue	Oval; dark blue skin; somewhat starchy, somewhat waxy deep purple flesh with sweet, nutty flavor
Purple Peruvian	Fingerling shape; shiny, thick purple skin; somewhat waxy purple flesh
Purple Viking	Round; striking purple and pink skin; somewhat starchy white flesh
Ratte	Fingerling shape; golden skin; somewhat waxy buttery pale yellow flesh
Red Gold	Oblong; red skin; somewhat waxy creamy yellow flesh
Russian Blue	Long oval; blue skin; somewhat waxy blue flesh with white ring just inside
White rose (long white)	Oval; thin light tan skin; somewhat starchy, somewhat waxy white flesh
Yellow Finn	Oval; golden skin; somewhat starchy buttery-sweet yellow flesh
Yukon gold	Oval; golden skin; somewhat starchy, yellow flesh
Low-Starch Potatoes	
All Red	Round or oblong; thin red skin; waxy, red flesh
Anoka	Oblong; pale yellow skin; waxy, white flesh
La Soda	Small, round; smooth rosy skin; waxy, white flesh
Red Bliss (round red)	Thin red skin; waxy, white flesh
Rose Finn Apple	Fingerling shape; rosy skin; waxy, yellow fruity-sweet flesh
Ruby Crescent	Fingerling shape; rosy skin; waxy, yellow flesh
Russian Red	Fingerling shape; red skin; waxy, yellow flesh

Buttermilk-Marinated Catfish with Potato Crust

You can use potato flakes as you would other dried starchy foods such as bread crumbs. Potato flakes make terrible mashed potatoes but a terrific coating for breaded fish or chicken. The crust comes out crisp and mildly sweet from the starch in the potatoes.

1 cup	buttermilk	250 mL
1 tbsp	olive oil	15 mL
2	cloves garlic, minced	2
2 tsp	kosher salt	10 mL
1 tsp	freshly ground black pepper	5 mL
1 tsp	dried thyme leaves	5 mL
½ tsp	mustard powder	2 mL
¼ tsp	cayenne pepper (or more, if you like it spicy)	1 mL
2 lbs	skinless catfish fillets	1 kg
2 cups	dry potato flakes	500 mL

Oil, such as peanut, canola, or another vegetable oil for pan-frying

1. In a resealable plastic bag or shallow dish, combine buttermilk, olive oil, garlic, salt, pepper, thyme, mustard powder, and cayenne pepper. Add fish, seal bag or cover dish, and refrigerate for 30 to 45 minutes.

2. Remove fish from marinade, discarding marinade. Dredge fish in potato flakes. Place on a rack and let rest for 10 minutes. Heat ¼ inch (0.5 cm) of oil in a frying pan over medium heat (the oil should be about 375°F /190°C). Add breaded fish, in batches, and cook just until fish looks moist and a little filmy or slightly translucent in the center when checked, about 4 minutes per side. (Crust will brown but fish shouldn't flake easily, at which point it's overcooked.) Drain on paper towels. Add more oil to the pan and reheat as necessary between batches.

MAKES 4 SERVINGS

Mashed potatoes can be made with high-starch or low-starch potatoes, but high-starch potatoes like russets mash more easily, have a fluffier texture, and absorb more butter and cream. For light and fluffy mashed potatoes, mash them while they're still hot and let excess steam evaporate by spreading the mash thinly. To prevent a gluey mash, try not to release too much starch from the potatoes. Treat the mixture like you would quick-bread batter. Mash the potatoes firmly but briefly, preferably by hand with a potato masher, ricer, food mill, or through a sieve. Quickly stir in liquids such as hot milk or cream and fat such as butter. Avoid overmixing, which releases excess starch in the form of amylase and amylopectins that give overmashed potatoes a gluey texture. It also helps to use melted butter and hot milk to expedite the process and avoid cooling down the mash. You can mash low-starch potatoes, but it takes more work because these varieties retain their shape better. They also don't absorb as much butter and cream as high-starch potatoes.

While mashed potatoes are popular in home and restaurant kitchens, fried potatoes are among the most widely eaten commercial foods worldwide. The key to great french fries is eliminating moisture, which keeps the fries from getting too soft and soggy. The best french fries are fried twice: once at a lower temperature to eliminate excess moisture and develop a fluffy interior and a second time at a higher temperature to crisp and brown the surface (see recipe for Perfect French Fries, page 260). Most french fries are made with high-starch potatoes because they are lower in moisture. Low-starch potatoes can be fried, but the additional moisture gives them a softer, creamier texture.

fast facts

- Nearly 320 million tons of potatoes are produced each year. China, Russia, and India are the leading producers worldwide.
- Americans eat 5 to 6 ounces (142 to 170 g) of potatoes per person every day, making it the most widely consumed vegetable in the country.

Potato chips are the second most popular kind of fried potato. They, too, are made from high-starch, low-moisture potatoes such as russets. They come in two basic styles: high-fried chips and kettle-fried chips. The potatoes for both types are sliced less than 2 mm thick, but different cooking times and temperatures yield different results. High-fried chips, the most widely distributed commercial type, are cooked in three minutes or less at a constant temperature of about 350°F (180°C). The consistently high temperature produces a crisp yet fragile chip that easily crumbles. Kettle-fried chips and chips made in a deep-fryer are cooked in oil whose temperature drops to about 250°F (120°C) at the beginning of cooking because the raw potatoes cool down the oil. The oil temperature gradually rises back up to 350°F (180°C), allowing the chips to be cooked longer (about 8 to 10 minutes). The initial drop in temperature and longer cooking time produce a drier, harder, crisper, and less brittle chip. A third type of puffy, or souffléd, chip is made by slicing the potatoes a little thicker (about 3 mm) and frying them twice. The first fry is done quickly at 350°F (180°C), just until the chips begin to dry out and stiffen. The chips are drained and cooled, then fried again at about 380°F (193°C) for a few minutes until steam puffs apart the chips, creating hollow interiors.

Buying, Storing, and Preparing Potatoes

Potatoes thrive underground. When exposed to light, they manufacture increasing amounts of green chlorophyll and two bitter-tasting alkaloid compounds, solanine and chaconine. The average 4-ounce (114 g) potato contains only 5 to 6 mg of solanine, which is not considered a hazard. But very green potatoes, which have higher amounts, can give you a headache or stomachache if you eat enough of them. Intake of more than 3 mg/kg body weight can be lethal. Avoid green potatoes, or deeply cut away any green parts. Also avoid sprouted potatoes, which are high in solanine and indicate that the potato is regenerating and has probably begun to soften and decay. Choose firm potatoes free of blemishes and green spots.

kitchen wisdom

Potato Cooking Tips

For better browning of roasted and oven-fried potatoes, refrigerate the whole potatoes for a day before cutting and cooking them. Chilling converts some of the starch in the potatoes to sugar and enhances browning.

To help potatoes retain a firm texture in potato salads or during long cooking in a sauce or stew, first cook them at a fairly low temperature (130 to 140°F/54 to 60°C or about medium-low heat) for 20 to 30 minutes, then drain and let the potatoes cool. This initial low-temperature cooking activates an enzyme in the potato's cell walls that prevents the cells from weakening and making the potato mushy during longer cooking. Precooking can also help keep mashed potatoes from becoming gluey because the potatoes firm up before the final cooking and mashing.

For the longest storage, keep potatoes in a cool (45 to 50°F/7 to 10°C), dark, well-ventilated area. But avoid temperatures below 40°F (4°C) for potatoes that will be fried or cooked at high temperature. Cold storage temperatures initiate conversion of some of a potato's starch to sugar, causing excessive browning and formation of the potential **carcinogen** acrylamide when the potatoes are cooked at high temperatures, as in roasting and frying. When stored at cool temperatures, potatoes will actually "ripen" or develop more intense flavors over the course of several weeks. Potatoes will convert the sugars back to starch if returned to warmer temperatures.

When fresh potatoes are cut and exposed to the air, they turn slightly pink then brown or gray from enzymatic browning. To prevent discoloration, dip the potatoes in water containing a little lemon juice or vinegar. If your cut potatoes have already begun to brown, you can restore some whiteness by gently simmering them in milk. Even after cooking, potatoes sometimes darken near the stems because small amounts of iron in the potato are released and react with oxygen and chlorogenic acid, forming dark-colored

Shepherd's Pie

Chopped meat and mashed potatoes make a satisfying supper. Boiling the potatoes in the skin takes a little longer, but it retains more starch and keeps the potatoes more fluffy and flavorful when mashed. This recipe calls for ground lean lamb, but you can also mince or grind leftover cooked leg of lamb. If you use ground beef, the dish is known as cottage pie.

2 lbs	russet baking potatoes (4 to 6 medium)	1 kg
¾ cup	milk or half-and-half (10%) cream, warmed	175 mL
1¼ tsp	salt, divided	6 mL
¼ tsp	freshly ground black pepper, divided	1 mL
⅛ tsp	grated nutmeg	0.5 mL
1 tbsp	olive oil	15 mL
1	onion, chopped	1
2	carrots, chopped	2
1¼ lbs	lean ground lamb or beef	625 g
½ tsp	dried thyme leaves	2 mL
½ tsp	ground cumin	2 mL
2 tbsp	tomato paste	25 mL
3 tbsp	all-purpose flour	45 mL
1 cup	beef or chicken broth	250 mL
⅓ cup	dry red wine	75 mL
1 cup	frozen peas	250 mL
1 tbsp	butter, cut into pieces	15 mL
2 tbsp	grated Parmesan cheese	25 mL

1. Place potatoes in a saucepan and cover with cold water. Cover and bring to a boil over high heat. Reduce heat to medium-high and boil until tender, 20 to 30 minutes. Drain and let cool slightly. Peel, and cut into 1-inch (2.5 cm) chunks. Return to pan and add milk, ¾ tsp (4 mL) salt, ⅛ tsp (0.5 mL) black pepper, and nutmeg. Mash. Set aside and keep warm.

2. Preheat oven to 400°F (200°C). Heat oil in a large, deep skillet over medium-high heat. Add onion and carrots and cook, stirring occasionally, until tender, about 5 minutes. Add lamb and cook, breaking up into small pieces, until meat is no longer pink, 4 to 5 minutes. Stir in thyme, cumin, and tomato paste. Sprinkle flour over surface and cook, stirring to blend, for 1 minute.

3. Stir in broth and wine and bring to a boil, stirring occasionally. Remove from heat and stir in peas, remaining ½ tsp (2 mL) salt, and remaining ⅛ tsp (0.5 mL) pepper. Scrape into a deep 9-inch (23 cm) pie plate or 2-quart (2 L) baking dish, spreading evenly. Spoon potatoes over lamb, spreading to cover evenly. Drag a fork several times through topping. Dot with butter and sprinkle with Parmesan. Place a piece of foil on oven rack below to catch any drips and bake until golden brown and bubbly, 25 to 30 minutes.

MAKES 4 TO 6 SERVINGS

compounds. To prevent cooked potatoes from darkening (known as stem-end blackening), add cream of tartar, lemon juice, or another acid to the cooking water about halfway through cooking, or mix an acidic ingredient into the potatoes after they are cooked.

Potatoes are a relatively low-calorie source of nutrients. The average 4-ounce (114 g) potato contains only 90 calories and 26 grams of complex carbohydrates. If you eat a potato with the skin, you also get about 3 grams of fiber. With or without the skin, potatoes are good sources of potassium, vitamin B6, and vitamin C. To minimize nutrient losses in boiled potatoes, do not peel them; peeling results in about 30% of the nutrients leaching into the water. When boiling, keep the skins on for better flavor, too. Baking, roasting, and steaming in the skin retain the most nutrients.

How It Works • As swollen subterranean stems, potatoes store up starch for a long-lasting source of energy. When a potato is cooked, its starch granules absorb moisture, swell, and soften, forming a paste that firms up as cooking continues. This process is called gelatinization (or gelation) and occurs with all starchy foods, like wheat and rice. Potato starch gelatinizes between 156 and 158°F (69 and 70°C). When high-starch potatoes such as russets gelatinize, the starch granules absorb lots of liquid and separate from one another, producing a soft, mealy texture. The starch granules in low-starch potatoes absorb less water and stay closer together when cooked, producing a firm, waxy texture.

The structure of refined potato starch powder consists of 20 to 30% long, straight chains of amylose molecules and 70 to 80% of branched-chained amylopectin molecules. The large potato starch granules readily absorb liquid, which gives potato starch more thickening power than most other starches. However, liquids thickened with potato starch are stringy, which is a drawback. They also become thin again with continued cooking as the fragile swollen granules disintegrate. On the plus side, potato starch creates a firm, clear gel, making it wonderful in pie fillings as well as sauces. It can also be used as a gluten-free source of starch in tender cakes.

Color and Flavor

White potatoes get their ivory or pale yellow color from **pigments** called anthoxanthins. Yellow potatoes get color from carotenoids, and red or blue potatoes are tinted with anthocyanins. Potatoes taste slightly sweet, especially if stored below 40°F (4°C), which causes them to convert some starch to sugar. Their earthy flavor comes from a compound called geosmin, which was once thought to come from microbes in soil but is now believed to develop in the vegetable itself. Large mature potatoes contain the most earthy-tasting geosmin. When cooked, potato flavors intensify, and some carbohydrates react with amino groups in the Maillard reactions to form methional, a distinctive "cooked-potato" aroma compound shared with Cheddar cheese. After prolonged heating, as when mashed potatoes are kept warm for several hours, and even after prolonged chilling and reheating, cooked potatoes gradually lose their vitamin C, which allows aldehyde compounds to develop, giving the warmed-over spuds a flat, stale taste.

See Also • Frying, Roots, Starch, Sweet Potatoes

POULTRY

What It Is • There are more than 12,000 species of edible birds, but domesticated poultry production centers on far fewer species of **chicken**, turkey, duck, goose, and **game** birds like squab (pigeon), guinea fowl, pheasant, partridge, and quail. This entry deals primarily with turkey, duck, and goose.

Turkeys are members of the pheasant family of birds (*Meleagris gallopavo*). The most common commercial North American breed is the broad-breasted Bronze turkey, which produces large, mild-flavored breasts and dark, rich-flavored legs. French Bresse turkeys are slightly more flavorful, in part because they are raised nearly twice as long and fattened on corn and milk a few weeks before slaughter.

Domesticated ducks come from two primary species, mallard (*Anas boschas*) and muscovy (*Cairina moschata*). About half of the ducks produced in North America are a mallard type called Pekin (Peking) or Long Island (*Anas domesticus*). Pekin ducks have white feathers, large breasts, and dark, rich meat. Muscovy ducks, which originated in South America, are slightly larger than mallards and produce stronger-tasting meat with about 30% less fat. The moulard duck is a cross between a Pekin and a muscovy that's raised primarily for foie gras. Moulards are continually fattened, so they produce exceptionally rich breast meat (magret) that doesn't dry out as easily as other duck breasts.

While the term "goose" may refer to waterfowl like the Canada goose, most domesticated geese are descended from the European Graylag (*Anser anser*) or the Asian Swan goose (*Anser cygnoides*). Emden and Toulouse are the two most popular breeds, both of which yield dark, full-flavored meat.

What It Does • Poultry are sold by age. Among turkeys, fryer-roasters of either sex are sold at less than 12 weeks of age; young turkeys at between 13 weeks and 6 months of age; and yearlings at less than 15 months of age. Mature hens and toms are more than 15 months old. Most ducks (ducklings) are sold at less than

science wise

Dark Meat or White?

Chicken and turkey breasts are white, but duck and goose breasts are dark. Where does meat color come from? It results from pigments that develop according to how the muscle is used. Animal movements can be broadly grouped into two categories: slow, continual movements, as when cattle stand grazing in a field, and fast, sudden movements, as when a bird is startled. These two types of movement use two different types of muscles. Red meat comes from dark-pigmented muscles that control slow, prolonged movements. White meat comes from muscles that control quick, sudden movements. The difference in color comes from the different energy supply needed for these different movements.

Red muscles are fueled by fat, which needs plenty of oxygen to be metabolized. Red muscle fibers are fairly thin, allowing them easy access to oxygen and fat (in the form of fatty acids) from the blood circulating around them. They also contain their own supply of fat and the ability to convert that fat into energy. To function properly, this mechanism is dependent on myoglobin, the pigment that gives red muscle fibers their color. Myoglobin receives oxygen from the blood and passes it on to fat-oxidizing proteins in the muscle fiber, similar to the way its relative, hemoglobin, carries oxygen through the blood. Both myoglobin and hemoglobin contain iron, which provides the red color. The more exercise a red muscle fiber gets, the greater its oxygen needs will be, and the more red myoglobin it will contain.

White muscle fibers are fueled by glycogen, a small supply of starch-like carbohydrate stored directly in the muscle fiber. When an animal suddenly needs to bolt, the glycogen can be converted into energy almost instantaneously by enzymes right in the muscle cells. Normally, white muscle cells use oxygen to help metabolize glycogen, but when energy is needed sooner than oxygen can be delivered by the blood, these cells have the capability to use glycogen without the presence of oxygen. That's why white muscle fibers are used for short bursts of energy followed by a period of recuperation.

Most animal muscles perform a mixture of slow and rapid movements, so they are built from both red and white muscle fibers. The ratio of red to white depends on the muscle's genetic design and how it is used during the animal's life. Chickens and turkeys that flap their wings rapidly but briefly when agitated will have a predominance of white muscle fibers in their breasts and wings. The legs, which are used for prolonged periods of walking and standing, have a higher concentration of red muscle fibers, making the leg meat dark. Game birds that fly steadily for long distances tend to have dark breast and wing meat.

---

8 weeks of age for boiler-fryers and less than 16 weeks old for roasters. Unlike other poultry, geese are not easily raised on a commercial scale and are typically sold when mature at about 6 months old.

Birds lose about 25% of their weight after plucking and the entrails, head, and feet are removed. Before sale, poultry is typically chilled in water or with cold air. Water-chilling produces more tender meat, but the absorbed water can dilute flavor. Air-chilling has the opposite effect and removes some moisture, making the meat firmer and more concentrated in flavor.

In the U.S., all poultry is graded A, B, or C. In Canada, the grades are Canada A, Canada Utility, and Canada C. Most markets carry only the A grade, ensuring you get a thick-fleshed bird free of deformities, pinfeathers, cuts, and broken bones. Whole turkeys and geese can weigh anywhere from 5 to 20 pounds (2.5 to 9 kg) depending on age. Ducks usually weigh between 3 and 5 pounds (1.5 to 2.5 kg). As with other animals, young birds produce more tender, milder-tasting meat than older birds. Young birds can be recognized by their soft, pliable breast bones, flexible wing joints, and smooth leg skin. Whether young or old, look for plump birds with clean, unblemished skin.

Poultry is higher in unsaturated fats and spoils more easily than other meats, so it's often sold frozen. Allow plenty of time to thaw a frozen bird, especially a large one. In the refrigerator, a 4-pound (1.8 kg) bird will thaw in about a day, whereas a 20-pound bird (9 kg) can take up to four days. In cold water, a 4-pounder will thaw in just one to two hours and a 20-pound turkey takes about eight hours. When thawing in cold water, change the water every hour or so to maintain cool, safe temperatures (below 40°F/4°C).

To store fresh poultry, keep it in the coldest part of your refrigerator (32 to 36°F/0 to 2°C), where it will keep for about three days. Store the giblets separately to help extend the bird's shelf life. It also helps to wrap whole birds in a dry kitchen towel to absorb juices from the bird or that would otherwise spoil the meat. Skinless poultry lasts longer than skin-on poultry because the skin contains additional fat and harbors bacteria. Studies show that about 98% of commercial poultry is contaminated with bacteria such as *Campylobacter*, *E. coli*, and *Salmonella* because of the close confinement of large-scale production. To prevent cross-contamination and reduce food safety risks, use separate cutting surfaces and utensils for raw poultry and thoroughly cook poultry to at least 165°F (74°C).

Cooking with Poultry

According to the United Nations Food and Agriculture Organization, global poultry production has steadily increased by about 3% per year since 1980 and birds have become an important source of **meat** and **eggs** in the human diet. Poultry can be roasted or fried whole, or poultry parts can be poached, grilled, braised, sautéed, fried, or cooked in many other ways. Increasingly, the meat is ground to make burgers and sausages that are lower in calories than those made from beef and pork.

The challenge of cooking poultry is keeping it moist and cooking it evenly. Turkey is lower in moisture than other birds, containing only about 58% water. Soaking the bird in **brine** increases its moisture content by up to 10%. A self-basting turkey is essentially a sort of lightly brined turkey injected with liquid fat, water, and seasonings to flavor and moisten the meat. Brining helps whole birds cook more evenly because it allows

kitchen wisdom

Red at the Bone

When fully cooked, the meat of young poultry may appear red at the bone. The discoloration occurs because hemoglobin seeps from bone marrow through their young, porous bones. The redness is harmless, but to avoid it choose mature birds that have denser bones, or buy fresh young birds instead of frozen because freezing tends to weaken the bone structure.

the dense legs and thighs to cook before the tender breasts dry out. You can also cook whole birds more evenly by chilling the breasts with ice packs before cooking so that they don't overcook before the legs and thighs are done. For roasting, it helps to start the bird breast side down to help shield it from the heat, then turn it breast side up halfway through cooking. On a grill, a vertical roaster keeps the tender breasts farther away from the bottom heat for more even cooking. For the most even doneness using any heat source, it's easiest to cook poultry in parts rather than as a whole bird.

Keep fat content in mind when cooking ducks and geese. These birds have evolved to store large amounts of fat under their skin

fast facts

- Some electric power plants are fueled by turkey droppings. In Minnesota, a plant produces 55 megawatts of power from 700,000 tons of droppings per year.
- The global poultry industry produces an average of 3 billion pounds (1.4 billion kg) of poultry feathers every year. The feathers are used in pillows, down jackets, and other products.

as fuel for long-distance flights. To keep the skin from getting rubbery, render out the excess fat by slowly melting it before cooking the meat to doneness. With whole birds, it helps to create a channel between the fat and the meat to give the fat an escape route as it melts. A bicycle pump does a good job of blowing air between the skin and meat and creating such a channel. You can also pierce the skin near the biggest fat deposits, around the sides of each breast, and the undersides of the thighs. Then slowly pour boiling water over the skin to begin melting away the fat before cooking the bird. Goose fat is about 28% saturated and melts at about 111°F (44°C); duck fat is 33% saturated and melts at 126°F (52°C), so it will take a little longer to render out duck fat. When roasting these fatty birds, drain off the fat periodically to prevent an oven fire. Both goose and duck fat are richly flavored and can be used to make **confit** and other dishes and for frying. The fat, juices, gelled protein, and browned bits from roasted poultry make a delicious base for **sauces** and gravies.

If a bird is stuffed, the **stuffing** should reach at least 165°F (74°C) to eliminate harmful bacteria. However, by the time the stuffing reaches this temperature, poultry meat is often overcooked and dry. The safest and most flavorful approach is to cook the stuffing separately. To flavor it, spoon some of the drippings from the roasting pan over the stuffing before cooking it.

How It Works • When people taste mild-flavored meats like frog for the first time, they often say, "It tastes like chicken." What is the flavor of cooked chicken and other poultry? The distinctive aroma comes from carbon-oxygen compounds called carbonyls. Chicken, turkey, and other birds also get some meatiness and eggy aroma from sulfur compounds such as hydrogen sulfide.

Among meats, poultry is unique because we often cook it in its skin. Poultry skin consists of about 50% water, 40% fat, and 3% collagen. The skin insulates the tender meat during cooking and provides a layer of fat that melts into the meat, helping to keep it moist. For a crackling-crisp skin, eliminate as much of that 50% moisture as possible. Air-dry the skin for a day to two in the refrigerator or use the technique for Pekin duck and blow air over the bird with a fan for several hours. It also helps to grease the skin with oil or butter for more efficient heat transfer and to use high-temperature dry-heat cooking methods like roasting, grilling, and frying. Slowly cooking poultry at low temperatures tends to result in chewy, leathery skin because the heat is too low to convert the collagen into soft and mouth-filling **gelatin**.

See Also • Chicken, Confit, Meat, Organ Meats

POWDERED SUGAR • See Sugar

PRALINE • See Nuts

PRAWNS • See Crustacean

PREBIOTIC • See Fermentation

PRESERVATIVES • See Food Additives

PRESERVES • See Jam and Jelly

PRESSURE COOKING • See Atmospheric Pressure

PRICKLY PEAR • See Cactus

PROBIOTIC • See Fermentation

PROCESSED CHEESE • See Cheese

PRODUCE • See Fruit, Vegetables

PROOF • See Alcohol

PROOFING • See Bread

PROSCIUTTO • See Ham

PROTEASE • See Protein

PROTEIN

What It Is • Proteins are fundamental molecules that can take thousands of different shapes, each one capable of performing an essential biological job. Some proteins are the building blocks of cells, part of the mechanism of synthesizing molecules, as well as the agent for moving molecules within cells and between cells. Proteins make up the **hormones** and **enzymes** that precipitate change and growth in living tissue. Hemoglobin, the pigment in the blood that transfers oxygen throughout the body, is a protein, and protein largely makes up the heart muscle that pumps the hemoglobin through our arteries and veins, pathways that are largely made of protein too.

What It Does • Along with carbohydrates and fats, proteins supply us with energy, about the same amount of calories as we derive from carbohydrates (4 kcal per gram). Because proteins are structurally more complex than fats and carbohydrates they tend to be more unstable. Expose them to heat, acid, salt, or even air and their structure changes.

Raw protein is slimy and resilient. Touch a protein-rich food. It feels viscous on the surface, but with perceptible firmness underneath. Various proteins manifest these textures differently. **Egg** white is wetter than meat, so it feels slimier than the protein of a salmon fillet, and beef has thicker connective tissue than fish, so a T-bone steak feels more resilient than salmon. Yet all these proteins have the same basic slimy-resilient texture. That texture comes from the shape of the protein molecule, which is a long, strong string of amino acid molecules that twists in

on itself, forming a bouncy, resilient core that has lots of places to bond with water along its surface, which is why the outside of a protein feels moist and slimy.

When proteins are heated (or are exposed to acid or salt, or even to air bubbles in the case of beaten egg white), the bonds that hold the protein strings in a twist break, causing the strings to unravel. This process, called denaturing, sets a protein up for change.

Once denatured, the extended protein strings are more likely to bump into each other and form new bonds, especially when exposed to heat (heat causes molecules to move around). As more bonds form, the loosened strings tangle in a far more rigid pattern than they were in originally. This restructuring, called coagulation, makes proteins firmer and less springy. The process of denaturing and coagulating explains why raw meat is soft and resilient whereas well-done meat is hard and tough. It is why raw egg white is liquid and beaten egg white is stiff, and it is why cured salami is hard and firm and fresh sausage is not.

By controlling the vehicles for coagulation, the degree to which a protein firms can be adjusted. Gradual gentle heat sets the protein in custard just until it holds its shape. Cook it too quickly or too long and the proteins will tangle too much. As they do, the space on the surface of the protein where water is held will be reduced, and the moisture will get squeezed out. In the case of custard, too much coagulation makes the custard split and the water weep out. In the case of a

fast facts

It's pretty easy for most people to get enough protein. Here are three ways a person could get nearly half their recommended daily value of protein (around 30 g) in a single meal.

- 2 slices whole wheat bread (8 g protein) spread with ¼ cup (50 mL) peanut butter (15 g protein), eaten with 1 cup (250 mL) skim milk (8 g protein)
- 4 ounces (114 g) boneless and skinless chicken breast (28 g protein)
- 2-egg omelet (12 g protein) filled with ½ cup (125 mL) steamed broccoli (3 g protein) and 2 ounces (56 g) cheddar cheese (14 g protein)

Amino Acids in Food

The eight essential amino acids must be consumed in food. The 12 nonessential amino acids can be synthesized in cells from other amino or organic acids.

Amino Acid	Synthesized From	Dietary Sources	Used For
Alanine	Pyruvate, leucine, isoleucine, or valine	Cheese, eggs, gelatin, grains, legumes, meat, nuts, seafood, seeds, yeast	Metabolizes glucose, builds immune system
Arginine	Citrulline	Eggs, unripened cheese, chocolate, grains, legumes, meat, nuts, seafood, seeds, yeast, yogurt, whey protein drinks, wild game	Retards tumor growth, builds immune system, aids liver detoxification, increases sperm count, increases growth hormones, builds muscle mass
Asparagine	Oxaloacetate	Asparagus, dairy, eggs, gelatin, grains, legumes, meat, nuts, potatoes, seafood, seeds, whey	Promotes energy, detoxifies blood, helps absorption of minerals, builds DNA
Aspartic acid	Oxaloacetate	Asparagus, avocados, cured meats, oats, sprouts, wild game	Promotes energy, detoxifies blood, helps absorption of minerals, builds DNA
Cysteine	Serine, methionine	Bell peppers, broccoli, Brussels sprouts, cured meats, eggs, dairy, unripened cheese, oats, pork, poultry	Antioxidant, protects against UV damage, detoxifies alcohol, promotes healing of skin
Glutamic acid	Glutamine	Fermented soy products, meat, mushrooms, seafood	Aids sugar and fat metabolism, helps neurotransmission and brain functioning
Glutamine	Found in blood and skeletal muscle	Cabbages, meat, milk, miso, poultry, seafood, spinach	Builds and maintains muscle tissue, increases brain functioning, maintains body pH, aids digestive health
Glycine	Serine	Gelatin	Improves glycogen storage, improves nerve and immune systems, promotes healing of damaged tissue
Histidine	Supplements for newborns; in adults synthesized by intestinal microbes	Indirectly from probiotic bacteria in fermented dairy products	Protects nerve cells, builds red and white blood cells, guards against radiation damage, aids in removal of heavy metals from liver

poached fish or grilled steak, the flesh dries out. Overbeaten egg whites become stiff and dry and lose volume.

Most of the art of cooking proteins has to do with controlling and limiting coagulation, but cooks also want to encourage two other things that happen as proteins heat. **Browning** reactions change the color and flavor of proteins in beneficial ways. Known as Maillard reactions, their development is intrinsic to the characteristic flavor of chocolate, roasted coffee, bread crust, dark beer, and roasted meat. Browning starts with a chemical reaction between sugars and proteins that forms an unstable structure at temperatures over 250°F (120°C). The reaction products then continue to react to form hundreds of flavorful and colorful chemicals as temperatures increase. Some of those chemicals give browned foods their characteristic color (and the name for the reaction), but equally important to the cook is the development of hundreds of "browned" flavors.

Many of the richest flavors that develop through browning are attributable to the hydrolysis of proteins into individual amino acids (the building blocks of proteins) or peptides, protein fragments that are several amino acids long. Amino acids and peptides are smelly, flavorful molecules that not only give rich savory qualities to cooked proteins but are also the reason that aged cheeses, cured hams, and fermented soy sauces are so

Amino Acid	Synthesized From	Dietary Sources	Used For
Isoleucine	Only through diet	Cheese, eggs, legumes, meat, nuts, poultry, seafood, seeds, yeast	Helps to form hemoglobin, stabilizes blood sugar, repairs muscle, skin, and bone
Leucine	Only through diet	Unripened cheese, meat, peanuts, poultry, seafood, seeds	Repairs muscle, skin, and bone, increases level of growth hormone
Lysine	Only through diet	Cheese, eggs, legumes, meat, quinoa, sardines, spinach	Helps calcium absorption, maintains nitrogen balance, produces antibodies
Methionine	Only through diet	Meat, nuts, seeds, spinach	Antioxidant, removes heavy metals from liver, protects against free radical damage
Phenylalanine	Only through diet	Unripened cheese, legumes, meat, peanuts, poultry, seafood, seeds	Helps nerve impulses, promotes alertness, elevates mood, decreases pain
Proline	Glutamate	Dairy, eggs, gelatin, meat	Aids in collagen production, builds cartilage, strengthens joints
Serine	Glycerate 3-phosphate	Dairy, meat, peanuts, soy, wheat	Fat metabolism, muscle growth, immune system, component of myelin and DNA
Threonine	Only through diet	Fish, unripened cheese, meat, lentils, poultry, seeds	Aids in collagen and elastin production, assists metabolism
Tryptophan	Only through diet	Cheese, eggs, fish, meat, poultry, seeds	Natural relaxant, relieves nervousness, strengthens immune system
Tyrosine	Phenylalanine	Bananas, dairy, fish, legumes, nuts, poultry, seeds, soy products	Improves metabolism, helps regulate mood, suppresses appetite, improves adrenal, thyroid, and pituitary function
Valine	Only through diet	Brown rice, cheese, chickpeas, meat, mushrooms, seafood, seeds, soy flour	Helps tissue repair, improves glycogen metabolism, helps prevent liver disease

flavorful. One amino acid, glutamic aid, is especially valued for its savory quality. Better known as MSG (monosodium glutamate), it has been identified as a flavor enhancer and the element that gives some plant products, such as tomatoes and mushrooms, their flavor-enhancing qualities.

How It Works • Our bodies need a steady supply of amino acids to repair damaged cells, build new ones, replace hormones, and replenish the immune system. When you eat protein your digestive system breaks it down into individual amino acids or small peptide chains. Amino acids and peptides are absorbed through the intestinal wall and travel with the bloodstream into individual cells, where they are broken down further and recombined into new proteins that your cells can use.

All of the tens of thousands of proteins in the body are made from the same 20 amino acids. Human cells can synthesize 12 of those 20, but 8 amino acids have to be eaten in order for the body to obtain all the raw material it needs to build protein. Those eight are known as essential amino acids, and protein sources that include all eight in adequate amounts are called complete proteins.

Protein is found in most food, but we tend to categorize meat and other animal foods as "proteins" because their form of protein is particularly dense and more closely resembles the protein of our own muscles. All animal foods are complete proteins, but the protein from a

science wise

Protease: Proteins that Digest Proteins •
Enzymes are particular types of proteins that are important not as food but for what they do to food. A certain class of enzymes, proteases, work specifically on other proteins, hydrolyzing them into their amino acids during digestion and during cooking. Certain fruits, such as papaya, pineapple, and kiwifruit, produce proteases that interfere with the setting of gelatin and can irritate the protein in the mouths of sensitive individuals. Cooking these fruits deactivates the enzymes, which is why gelatin can be made with canned pineapple but not with raw pineapple. Papain (the protease in papaya) and bromelain (the protease in pineapple) are used as chemical meat tenderizers.

piece of broccoli is, to the body, essentially the same as the protein from a steak. Your cells don't distinguish between the amino acids from animal or vegetable sources, so it does not matter how you get your dietary protein, so long as you get a complete distribution of amino acids. Because most vegetable proteins are low in one or more amino acids, vegans need to be more conscientious about getting a balance of amino acids than do people who regularly eat animal products.

The Structure of Proteins Determines Their Behavior

Cells constantly collect and synthesize amino acids and assemble them into proteins. These proteins vary in size from small peptides that are only a few amino acids long to long amino acid chains. Amino acids are linked together through peptide bonding, in which the amine group (NH_2) of one amino acid links to the carboxyl group (CO) of another. Peptide bonds are very strong and form the backbone of proteins. Exposure to heat, acid, or salt won't break peptide bonds, a characteristic that allows cooks to manipulate proteins in the kitchen without destroying them. Peptide bonds are broken only under extreme conditions, or when exposed to catalytic enzymes during digestion.

Peptide bonds along a chain of amino acids form a three-dimensional zigzag pattern or spiral called a helix. The shape of the helix contributes to how a particular protein behaves. Few protein molecules form a consistent regular helix, but those that do tend to lie in closely packed fibers that have strong peptide bonds connecting the amino acids into chains, and comparatively weak bonds joining one protein to another. Collagen, the connective tissue in muscles, is such a protein. Its simple structure explains why **gelatin**, which derives from collagen, is easily denatured by heat and reassembles as soon as it cools. When gelatin is heated, the protein chains have just enough added energy to separate from one another and become soluble, but not enough energy to break into separate amino acids. As soon as the mixture cools, the chains reassemble, but this time in a random fashion trapping whatever is in between in a solid matrix — a gel.

All proteins are surrounded by water, and all proteins have side groups that can bond with water through hydrogen bonds, although the capabilities vary widely. Gluten, the protein in wheat, can bond with lots of water through hydrogen bonds along the outside of the molecule but with few in the interior of the helix. So wheat flour can absorb lots of water but doesn't dissolve. On the other hand, the proteins in milk and eggs have water-attracting sites throughout the molecules, so those proteins bond with water more thoroughly. Consequently, egg and dairy products dissolve easily in water.

See Also • Browning, Chemical Bonding, Digestion, Eggs, Enzyme, Meat

PROTONS • See Atom, Chemical Bonding

PROVOLONE • See Cheese

PRUNES • See Plum

PSORALENS • See Toxin

PUMPERNICKEL • See Bread, Flour

PUMPKIN • See Squash

PUMPKIN SEED • See Oil

PURÉES • See Juice, Sauces, Soup

PURI • See Bread

PURSLANE • See Herbs

QUAHOG • See Mollusks

QUAIL • See Game

QUESO BLANCO • See Cheese

QUICK BREADS • See Baking

QUINCE • See Fruit

QUININE • See Bitters

QUINOA • See Grains

RABBIT • See Game

RADIATION • See Heat

RADICCHIO • See Chicory

RADISH • See Cruciferous Vegetables, Roots

RAISINS • See Grapes

RAMPS • See Allium

RANCIDITY • See Fat, Oil

RASPBERRY • See Berries

REFRIED BEANS • See Legumes

REFRIGERATION • See Storage

RHIZOMES • See Stems

RHUBARB • See Stems

RIBOFLAVIN • See Vitamins

RICE

What It Is • Domestic rice is the fruit of a grass from one of two species. *Oryza sativa* is native to Asia, where it has been cultivated since 7000 BCE, and includes all commercially grown rice. *Oryza glaberrima*, from West Africa, is less ancient and has produced far fewer rice varieties. Rice is grown throughout the world, but 99% of the world's crop still comes from subtropical Asia. There, rainfall patterns benefit rice cultivation, which is simplified by a period of flooding early in the growth cycle to reduce weeding, control pests, and help fertilize the soil.

What It Does •

Rice Types and Varieties

Two subspecies of *Oryza sativa* account for most of the 40,000 rice varieties in the world. *Indica* rice is grown in lowland fields

Basic Rice Pilaf

Long-grain rice that is high in amylose starch yields separate grains of rice. This texture is enhanced by toasting the rice slightly in oil, which keeps the surface starch of individual grains from coming in contact, and thereby prevents grains from sticking to one another.

1 tbsp	oil or butter	15 mL
¼ cup	finely chopped onion	50 mL
1 cup	long-grain white rice	250 mL
2 cups	water or broth	500 mL
	Salt and freshly ground black pepper to taste	

1. Heat oil in a small saucepan over medium heat. Add onion and sauté until tender, about 2 minutes. Add rice and stir thoroughly to coat with fat. Add water, salt, and pepper. Stir briefly to moisten the rice. Bring to a boil. Reduce heat, cover, and simmer until all the liquid has been absorbed, 15 to 20 minutes. Do not stir rice when checking for doneness.

2. Remove from heat. Remove lid and cover pot with a folded kitchen towel to absorb excess steam. Cover with the lid and let rest for 5 minutes. Fluff with fork and adjust seasoning.

MAKES 4 SERVINGS

Basic Brown Rice Pilaf

Whole-grain rice is covered by tough fibrous bran that delays the absorption of liquid and requires more liquid to fully soften the grain. The bran is also full of flavorful compounds that give brown rice a sweet nutty flavor, and dietary fiber that makes each grain springy and chewy.

1 tbsp	oil or butter	15 mL
½ cup	finely chopped onion	125 mL
1 cup	long-grain brown rice	250 mL
3 cups	water or broth	750 mL
	Salt and freshly ground black pepper to taste	
1 tbsp	chopped parsley (optional)	15 mL

1. Heat oil in a saucepan over medium heat. Add onion and sauté until tender, about 2 minutes. Add rice and stir thoroughly to coat with fat. Add water and salt and pepper. Stir briefly to moisten the rice. Reduce heat and simmer, covered, until liquid has all been absorbed and rice is tender, about 45 minutes. Do not stir rice when checking for doneness.

2. Remove from heat. Remove lid and cover pot with a folded kitchen towel to absorb excess steam. Cover with the lid and let rest for 5 minutes. Fluff with a fork, and stir in parsley.

MAKES 4 SERVINGS

and yields long-grain rices. Short- and medium-grain rices that yield slightly sticky to creamy textures come from upland varieties, called japonica when grown in temperate climates and javanica when grown in tropical climates.

Long-grain rice is four to five times as long as it is wide. The grains remain separate when cooked and are springy and toothsome when hot and steamy, making long-grain the preferred rice for pilafs, where separate al dente grains is a mark of quality. Long-grain rice requires the largest proportion of water to rice for cooking (about 2:1 by volume).

Medium-grain rice is two to three times longer than it is wide. The cooked grains are

kitchen wisdom

Know Your Sake

Sake is a fermented rice beverage. There are five types of sake, mostly categorized by how highly the rice is polished before brewing begins, and modified by whether the sake is pasteurized or not. The center of a rice grain contains the bulk of the grain's starch. Since starch is the only part of the grain that is converted into fermentable sugar, the more of the outside of the rice that is removed, the purer the fermentation. The degree to which rice has been polished before brewing is labeled *seimai-buai* (for instance, "70" indicates that 30% of the rice grain has been removed).

- *Honjozo-shu* — at least 30% of the rice has been polished away, and a small amount of distilled spirits may have been added, a common practice in sake-making. It tends to be light tasting. Because the rice is milled minimally, the proteins remaining in the grains give *honjozo-shu* sake more aroma and a longer finish than sakes made with more highly milled rice.
- *Junmai-shu* — pure sake with no added distilled spirits, milled to any degree.

Junmai-shu sake is full bodied, with assertive acidity and subdued aroma, although characteristics diminish as *seimai-buai* number decreases.

- *Ginjo-shu* — at least 40% of the rice has been polished away, and a small amount of distilled spirits may have been added (if the bottle is labeled *Junmai Gingo*, no spirits were added). *Ginjo-shu* is more delicate than the previous two types of sake. It is lighter, softer, and more aromatic.
- *Daiginjo-shu* — at least 50% of the rice has been polished away, and a small amount of distilled spirits may have been added (if the bottle is labeled *Junmai Daigingo*, no spirits were added). It is the most delicate and fragrant of all sakes, often with floral and fruity notes and a short, clean finish.
- *Namazake* and/or *Nigorizake* — *Namazake* sake is unpasteurized; *nigorizake* sake is unfiltered. Any of the above sakes can be *namazake* and/or *nigorizake*, which tends to make them more flavorful and more perishable. They should be stored chilled and consumed as soon as possible.

tender and adhere slightly to one another. Varieties include arborio and carnaroli, which are preferred for risotto, and bomba, the Spanish medium-grain rice that is traditionally used in paella. The ratio of water to rice for cooking medium-grain is 1.5:1.

Short-grain rice is just slightly longer than its width. The grains become very tender and decidedly sticky when cooked. Short-grain rice is preferred for sushi, because its stickiness makes it easy to pick up with chopsticks and because it stays tender even after cooling to room temperature. The ratio of water to rice for cooking short-grain is about 1:1.

Sticky rice (aka glutinous, sweet, and waxy rice) has almost round grains that tend to disintegrate during cooking into a sticky mass. It is used in Asia for making sweet dishes, puddings, and fillings. Rice paste (mochi), made by pounding steamed sticky rice, is popular in Japan as a dessert filling and a wrapper for sweets. Sticky rice is the standard rice in Laos and northern Thailand. The proportion of water to rice for cooking is about 1:1.

Aromatic rices are long- or medium-grain varieties that have a high proportion of volatile aldehydes, giving them nutty, popcorn-like, and floral aromas. Basmati rice from India and Pakistan, Thai jasmine rice, and U.S. Della rice are popular aromatic varieties.

Pigmented rice is whole-grain rice that has a high proportion of red and purple-black anthocyanin pigments in its bran. Pigmented rice can be partially polished, which gives it a pastel color and makes it cook faster. Bhutanese red rice is an example. All pigmented rices are medium-grain.

Rice Processing

Brown rice is whole-grain unmilled rice that includes all parts of the **grain**, including the bran, aleurone layer, endosperm, and germ. Any rice can be sold in its brown form. Brown rice contains more **fiber**, **protein**, and **vitamins** than its milled counterparts. It requires a higher proportion of liquid to rice for cooking and takes two to three times longer to cook than white rice. Natural oils in the bran and germ make brown rice more prone to rancidity, which reduces its shelf life if it is not stored under refrigeration.

White rice is milled to remove the bran and germ and then "polished" with wire brushes to remove the aleurone layer and any remaining traces of oil. The resulting white grains can be stored at room temperature for months. Because most of the grain's vitamins and minerals are stripped away during polishing, white rice is frequently enriched to return some of the lost vitamins. Most of the rice eaten in the world is white rice.

Rice Varieties

Variety	Type	Origin and Description	Uses
Arborio	Short- to medium-grain	Italy; soft surface forms creamy sauce and amylose core forms al dente grains	Risotto
Basmati	Aromatic long-grain	India and Pakistan; dried to enhance aromatics; springy separate grains	Pilaf
Black	Medium-grain	China, Thailand, U.S.; purple-black bran; chewy, springy grains	Desserts, rice blends
Bomba	Medium-grain	Spain; fluffy, plump, slightly sticky al dente grains	Paella
Calrose	Medium-grain	California; tender, slightly sticky; grown without flooding	Sushi
Carnaroli	Medium-grain	Italy; similar to arborio but slightly longer grain	Risotto
Carolina	Long-grain	U.S.; firm, fluffy separate grains	All-purpose, pilaf
Della	Long-grain	U.S.; cross between Carolina and basmati	Pilaf
Jasmine	Aromatic long-grain	Thailand; floral; fluffy separate grains	All-purpose, pilaf
Red	Medium-grain	Bhutan, France, Thailand; whole grain or partially polished; chewy, nutty-tasting pale brown-red grains	All-purpose
Texmati	Aromatic long-grain	Texas; similar to Della	Pilaf
Vialone nano	Short-grain	Italy; similar to arborio but shorter grain; very creamy	Risotto
Wehani	Aromatic long-grain	U.S.; brown-red whole grain; very chewy, nutty, slightly sticky grains	All-purpose, pilaf

Parboiled (converted) rice has been steamed under pressure before the bran, aleurone layer, and germ have been milled away. The steam forces some of the vitamins from outer layers of the grain into the endosperm and makes the aleurone layer adhere to the center of the grain, so when the rice is polished some of the nutrition of the whole grain is preserved. Precooking also hardens the starch in the rice, so the surface of the cooked grain is less sticky. Parboiled rice grains stay completely separate during cooking, but because the exterior of the grain is harder than regular white rice, parboiled rice takes about 50% longer to cook, which adds seven or eight more minutes to the cooking time.

Quick-cooking (precooked or instant) rice is brown, white, or parboiled rice that has been completely cooked and dried. After drying, the surface of the rice is cracked to help it absorb water quickly. Precooked rice does not require further cooking. It just needs to be steeped in boiling water to rehydrate and heat through. Precooked rice has similar nutrition to longer-cooking types (there is a slight loss of fiber and water-soluble vitamins), but it tends to be softer and have less flavor than less processed rices.

Cooking Rice

All methods of cooking rice involve permeating the grain with liquid to hydrate it and heating it to gelatinize and soften its starch. The most straightforward ways are boiling or steaming the grains in water, which is the norm in Asian cultures, where rice is the chief staple in the diet. In the Middle East, Europe, and North America, where rice was introduced later, it is more typically cooked in broth, enriched with oil and aromatic ingredients to make rice dishes like risotto, pilaf, and paella.

Plain boiled rice can be cooked either in a large amount of water (in the same way as pasta) or in a precisely measured amount of water. The excess-water method produces grains that are completely separate and fluffy, because the rice grains don't touch much during cooking. Once the grains are cooked through, the rice is drained and shaken dry. The disadvantage of this method is that water-soluble nutrients and flavors are lost with the cooking water. Measuring the liquid results in stickier rice, which is preferred in cultures that eat rice with chopsticks, and it ensures that water-soluble vitamins and flavors that leach from the rice during cooking are reabsorbed before the rice is eaten.

Soaking or washing rice before cooking removes much of the surface starch, thus limiting stickiness. In India, basmati rice is washed to encourage separate grains and shorten the cooking time, and in Japan, the rice for sushi is typically washed and soaked until it is almost completely hydrated before it is cooked. This method produces very soft, fully puffed grains that stay intact as they cook and remain tender even as they cool.

The pilaf method of cooking rice should not be confused with pilaf the rice dish, which is a Turkish/Persian/Greek style of serving boiled rice (often flavored and colored with herbs and saffron) tossed with nuts and fruit. Pilaf method is a technique of sautéing rice in butter or oil, often with onions or other aromatic vegetables, before adding a measured amount of broth or water. The initial sautéing step enhances the flavor of the rice by toasting it lightly. As well, because the grains become coated with fat, gelatinization of the surface starch is limited, which keeps the individual grains of rice separate.

Regardless of the cooking method, plain rice benefits from a period of resting between cooking and serving to allow the grains to cool and firm slightly so that they are less likely to break when they are scooped. Stirring steamy hot cooked rice releases gelatinized starches and makes the rice gummy.

Unlike other rice preparations, risotto is stirred constantly as it cooks, which causes the starch on the surface of the grain to gradually slough into the liquid and thicken it, leaving the core of the rice intact. A large amount of liquid, about five times the amount of rice by volume, is gradually added, blending with the starch to create a creamy sauce that envelops the slightly chewy cores of the rice grains. Most risotto recipes specify serving the dish right away, and true enough, if it sits the creamy sauce will solidify into paste, but in restaurants risotto is typically cooked partway and then refrigerated, which

Basic Risotto

Risotto, the creamy rice dish of northern Italy, requires constant stirring and the right kind of rice. Risotto rice can be medium- or short-grain. The longer the grain, the less creamy and more al dente the finished risotto will be. Carnaroli makes the chewiest risotto, vialone nano yields the creamiest and softest risotto, and risotto made with Arborio rice lies somewhere in the middle.

2 tbsp	olive oil	25 mL
¼ cup	finely chopped onion	50 mL
1 cup	Arborio, carnaroli, or vialone nano rice	250 mL
½ cup	white wine	125 mL
4½ cups	chicken broth	1.125 L
¼ cup	freshly grated Parmesan cheese	50 mL
1 tbsp	butter	15 mL

1. Heat oil in a large saucepan over medium heat. Add onion and sauté until tender, about 2 minutes. Add rice and stir thoroughly to coat with oil. Add wine and cook, stirring with a wooden spoon, until wine has been absorbed.
2. Add chicken broth, ½ cup (125 mL) at a time, and stir until mostly absorbed, waiting between each addition before adding more.
3. Keep stirring in broth and simmering until rice is al dente and a creamy sauce has developed, about 20 minutes. Stir in Parmesan cheese and butter. Serve immediately.

MAKES 4 SERVINGS

Basic Aromatic Rice

Aromatic rice is high in the popcorn-like aromatic compound acetylpyrroline. This volatile flavor chemical is diminished by heat. Washing aromatic rice thoroughly until the grains turn slightly opaque reduces the amount of cooking needed to soften the grain, thereby preserving more of its aromatic quality.

1 cup	basmati or jasmine rice	250 mL
½ tsp	salt	2 mL
2 tbsp	butter	25 mL

1. Wash rice in several changes of cold water until water is clear and rice is starting to turn white and opaque.

2. In a saucepan, bring 1¾ cups (425 mL) water to a boil. Stir in rice and salt, cover tightly, and simmer over low heat until all the water has been absorbed, about 15 minutes. Do not stir rice when checking for doneness.

3. Remove from heat. Remove lid and cover pot with a folded kitchen towel to absorb excess steam. Cover with the lid and let rest for 5 minutes. Fluff with a fork and mix in butter.

MAKES 4 SERVINGS

firms the rice up. To finish the risotto, the rice is reheated with the last addition of liquid, and because the grains have become more solid in the refrigerator they withstand the stirring without breaking.

Other Rice Products

Rice flour is about 90% starch. It has the finest starch granules of any flour and makes extremely silky sauces. It is also low in protein and gluten free, which makes it unsuitable for raised breads but an alternative for those with gluten intolerance. Rice flour absorbs water poorly, which is why it yields extremely crispy results when fried, a characteristic that makes it the flour of choice for tempura.

Rice powder is a Southeast Asian condiment of ground toasted rice that is sprinkled over salads for a crunchy texture.

The starch from cooked rice can be dissolved in liquid to thicken it into rice milk, which can be used as an alternative to dairy milk. It is also fermented into a kind of kefir called amazake, or into alcoholic beverages like rice wine, such as mirin (a sweet rice wine used in Japanese cooking), and sake (see Kitchen Wisdom, page 494).

Rice noodles and rice paper are gluten-free pastas (see **Pasta**).

How It Works • Generally, the longer a rice grain, the more amylose **starch** it contains. Rice that is higher in amylose is

harder and denser and requires more water and longer cooking times to become tender. This is why long-grain rice (23 to 26% amylose) takes a higher ratio of liquid and does not become sticky the way shorter-grain (15 to 20% amylose) rice does.

Amylose has the disadvantage of remaining hard after chilling, which is why long-grain rice makes disappointing rice puddings and pastes. Short-grain rice that is higher in amylopectin starch stays tender even after refrigeration.

The outer layers of a rice grain contain the bulk of its oil, amino acids, vitamins, and minerals, all of which are flavorful. These give whole-grain rice fragrant vanilla and maple-like flavors that are missing from white rice. White rice has subtle floral, hay-like, and popcorn flavors. These are particularly pronounced in aromatic rice. Since much of this flavor dissipates during heating, aromatic rice is often soaked to decrease its cooking time and thereby diminish its flavor loss.

See Also • Grains, Starch

RICE PAPER • See Rice

RICE POWDER • See Rice

RICE WINE • See Rice

RICOTTA • See Cheese

RIESLING • See Wine

RIGOR MORTIS • See Meat

RILLETTES • See Confit

RIPENING • See Cheese, Fruit

RISOTTO • See Rice

ROASTING

What It Is • Roasting is the oldest cooking technique. Originally, roasted food was placed directly in hot coals, where it scorched by the time it cooked through. Caked with soot and ash, early roasted foods cried out for improvement. That came by impaling ingredients on a spit and cooking them suspended over the heat radiating from the flames.

Spit-roasting worked fine for haunches of game and large dense vegetables, but it was ineffective for small pieces of meat or moist foods like fruit and soft vegetables. To get these ingredients out of the coals, they had to be put in a flameproof box, which eventually morphed into the freestanding oven. Early ovens were made of heat-retaining material like stone, ceramic, or brick. A **fire** was built inside the oven and was scraped out once the interior heated. Food was placed on the oven floor where the fire had been, and since the floor of the oven was hotter than the walls, convecting currents of hot air rose from the floor and circulated around the food. In this way oven roasting (baking) heated food more by convection than radiation, the principal method of **heat** transfer when roasting over an open fire. Convection increases the rate of heat transfer, so food cooks through faster, but it doesn't develop the thick, dark crust that is the hallmark of roasting.

Although roasting over an open fire has its advantages (flame-licked flavor and rich, dark crusting), it is far less efficient than roasting in an oven. In fire roasting, most of

the heat is lost to the air, and once kitchens moved from outdoors into the house, ventilating the smoke became an issue. For these reasons, by the beginning of the 19th century the oven had replaced open fires for indoor roasting.

Rotisserie roasting is a cross between oven roasting and spit-roasting that attempts to capture the advantages of both. Food is impaled on a skewer that is turned in front of or above a heating element. Because the food is cooked by radiant heat rather than convecting air, it develops a rich crust. Crusting and browning are further enhanced by the juices that roll over the surface of the food as it rotates. Because rotisseries are closed boxes, they do not lose heat to the air, so heat transfer and fuel usage are more efficient than open-fire spit-roasting.

What It Does • To roast meat in an oven, place it fat side up on a rack. The rack can be a bed of vegetables and/or bones or a metal rack set in the roasting pan, but it is important that there be some device to raise the roast off the bottom of the pan so that hot air can circulate all the way around the meat. For the same reason, roasting pans must have low sides (3 inches/7.5 cm or less). If the walls of the pan are too high, moisture coming from the meat will be held in the pan, so the meat will steam rather than roast. Avoiding steam is also the reason roasts should never be covered. Contrary to kitchen myths, a cover does not help to keep meat moist. Rather, it traps in steam, which cooks meat much more intensely than air, with a result that more juices are squeezed from the meat fibers and the resulting roast is dryer. Unglazed clay roasters don't have this problem because the clay absorbs the steam and so the air around the meat stays drier.

Oven roasting can be done at a wide range of temperatures, although the initial temperature should be hotter than 400°F (200°C) to sterilize the surface of the food and to jump-start the development of a crisp brown crust, which is one of the marks of proper roasting. If a roast is small (less than 6 inches/15 cm thick, or about the size of a medium chicken), it can be cooked through entirely at that temperature. For large roasts, after the first 45 minutes reduce the oven temperature to 325 or 350°F (160 or 180°C) and roast until the meat reaches the desired internal temperature (see Meat Doneness chart, page 390).

Large roasts can also be slow roasted. Slow roasting starts out at a high temperature for the first 45 minutes, then the oven thermostat is turned down to the internal temperature you want the meat to reach when it is done. Because the oven temperature is no hotter than the doneness temperature, it is impossible to overcook a roast using this method. The rule of thumb is one hour per pound (454 g). Slow roasting is how prime roast beef is done in restaurants. The whole prime rib is roasted at 125°F (52°C) and held at that temperature. Rare roast beef is served directly from the oven, but if beef is ordered at medium doneness, a portion is heated in jus and cooked to desired doneness.

Because no portion of the meat ever gets hotter than its optimal doneness temperature there is very little loss of liquid. In traditional roasting, the surface of the food gets much hotter than the interior, so juices from the surface are lost into the roasting pan. These juices brown as the food cooks and are typically captured in a sauce, by adding liquid to the roasting pan. But they can also be used to enhance browning and crusting of a roast by being spooned back over the top (basting) periodically during cooking. Basting imitates the natural glazing that happens during spit-roasting or rotisserie roasting as meat juices travel over the surface of a roast as it rotates on a spit.

Specific types of meat benefit from different types of roasting. For example, because pork has a tendency to dehydrate and toughen at high temperatures, it is better to roast it slowly. On the other hand, beef and lamb, which are most typically served rare to medium, are better roasted at very high temperatures to

achieve a rich, dark crust and a rare center.

The best way to test the doneness temperature of a roast is to insert a thermometer into the thickest part of the meat. Do not rely too heavily on charts that specify a number of minutes per pound for cooking time. Unless the chart specifies individual cuts, such guidelines are too general to be of specific use. For example, heat will reach the center of a 4-pound (1.8 kg) sirloin roast that is spread out flat faster than it will reach the center of the same roast tied into a bundle. It is best to use such charts to give you a general idea of when to start checking a roast's temperature, and use temperature readings to determine doneness.

When the temperature of the meat registers 5°F (3°C) less than the desired doneness temperature, remove the roast in its pan from the oven and set it aside to rest for at least 10 minutes. In this time the temperature will rise the extra few degrees, and the roast will become much easier to slice. When meat cooks, its juices are forced out of the muscle fibers. These juices flow both toward the surface, where they evaporate, helping to form a rich, savory crust, and toward the cooler center of the roast. So by the time a roast is finished, the core of it will be saturated with meat juices, like a wet sponge. If it is sliced right away, the juices will run out, but if given a resting period they will be reabsorbed by the drier sections, and will be less likely to be lost during slicing.

Not all meats that are called roasts are appropriate for roasting. Generically, any piece of meat that is thicker than 2 inches (5 cm) is said to be a roast, but if the meat isn't fairly tender to begin with, the gentle heat of roasting will not be enough to soften its fibers. Many cuts, such as chuck roast, knuckle roast, and blade roast, need moisture to cook them through and convert their tough collagen to gelatin. To that end they are pot roasted, a technique of oven **braising** with moist heat that is as unrelated to roasting as these meats are to being roasts.

Vegetables and fruit are roasted to concentrate their flavors and brown their surfaces. Unlike meats, roasted produce does not need to reach a specific temperature; as soon as the ingredient is tender and lightly browned, it is done.

How It Works • If there is any difference between baking and roasting, it is that baking relies more on convecting air currents to circulate hot air evenly around the food, whereas roasting relies on radiant heat transfer to develop a deep, dark crust. Modern ovens often have separate baking, convection baking, and roasting settings to allow for the appropriate form of heat transfer. In baking, most of the heat comes from the bottom burner, which sets up air currents in the oven as heat rises from the oven floor. The roast setting alternates heat between the top and bottom burners, which diminishes air currents. Convection baking or roasting uses a fan to circulate air more quickly.

Radiant heat accelerates browning because most of the energy is absorbed at the surface of the roasting food. Once the heat is absorbed at the surface it is transferred internally through conduction rather than radiation, which is a much slower method of heat transfer. Although raising the roasting temperature shortens roasting time it does more to increase the level of browning at the surface.

See Also • Baking, Fire, Heat, Oven

ROCKET • See Leaves

ROCKFISH • See Fish

ROE • See Eggs, Fish

ROMAINE • See Leaves

ROMANESCO • See Cruciferous Vegetables

ROOTS

What It Is • Roots anchor plants to the ground, absorbing moisture and nutrients from the soil and conducting them into aboveground parts of the plant. Most plant roots are spindly, fibrous, and inedible, but some are engorged with storage cells that are loaded with carbohydrates and other nutrients, and these are the ones that have been cultivated as vegetables. Root storage is intended to help nourish the plant during times of deprivation, but it also provides the same nutrition (and some pleasurable flavors) to anyone who is fortunate enough to dig up a root vegetable and eat it.

What It Does ● The storage tissues in roots developed in a variety of ways. Some, like potatoes, cassava, and taro, store their energy in the form of starch. Others, such as beets, carrots, and parsnips, store energy as sugar. Technically, beets and celery root are swollen stem bases, but because they store energy, which makes them nutritious and sweet, they taste like roots and are cooked like other roots, and therefore are thought of as root vegetables.

Compared with other types of vegetables (stems, leaves, fruits, etc.), root vegetables are sturdy and relatively low in moisture, which allows them to be stored for many months without decomposing. Some anthropologists think that the discovery of starchy roots in the African savannah about 2 million years ago may have fueled human evolution. Raw starch is not easily digested, so starchy root vegetables must be cooked to be edible. Early people who learned to forage for and cook roots would have had a nutritional and evolutionary advantage over those who depended on more perishable food.

Although starchy roots have to be cooked, those that store their energy as sugar can be eaten raw, provided that they are harvested young. As sweet-tasting roots like carrots and beets, which can be as much as 5% sugar by weight, mature they get bigger, their cell walls thicken, and the vascular tissue that runs through the root becomes woody. Eventually the fibers become too tough for humans to break them down enough to get much sweetness out of the vegetable, so old carrots and beets have to be cooked to release their sugars.

How It Works ● Root vegetables that store energy as starch are drier and denser than those that contain more sugar. When starchy root vegetables are cooked, the starch granules swell, causing them to separate from one another, producing a dry, mealy texture. The cells of sweet roots, on the other hand, soften and cohere to one another as they cook. The moisture held within the cells is released, and their texture becomes soft and moist.

In general, root vegetables should be stored in the dark.

Root Vegetables

Carrots, potatoes and sweet potatoes each have their own entry, celery root is discussed in the Celery entry, chicory root in Chicory, and cassava in its entry. This chart includes less common root vegetables.

Root Vegetable	Origin and Description	Cooking Methods
Arracacha	South America; white starchy flesh; flavor of celery, parsnip, and chestnuts	Boiled
Beets	Worldwide; sweet fibrous flesh; red, orange, yellow, white, or striped; can have earthy flavor	Roasted, boiled, pickled, raw if young
Burdock	Asia; white sweet fibrous flesh; flavor similar to artichoke and parsnip	Raw in salads, pickled
Cassava (manioc, yuca)	South America, Africa, Asia; white starchy flesh; bland	Boiled, fried, processed into tapioca starch
Jicama	South America; sweet, crisp, juicy flesh; slightly nutty flavor	Raw in salads, stir-fried
Kohlrabi	Worldwide; white, round; fibrous flesh (tender-crisp when young); pungent, cabbage-like flavor	Boiled, sautéed when young
Kudzu root	Worldwide; large white root; starchy flesh; bland	Boiled, ground into starchy thickener
Lotus root	Asia; white, crisp flesh; lacy texture; mild flavor	Boiled then stir-fried, candied
Parsley root	Worldwide; cream-colored, fibrous flesh; pungent flavor similar to parsley leaf	Boiled, sautéed; used as seasoning
Parsnip	Worldwide; creamy white root; sweet, crisp flesh; mild carrot flavor	Boiled, roasted
Radish	Worldwide; multicolored; moist and crisp when young, dry and fibrous when mature; pungent flavor from mustard increases with age	Raw when young, braised when mature
Rutabaga (swede)	Worldwide; large yellow root; fibrous; strong pungent cabbage-like flavor	Boiled, roasted
Salsify (oyster plant)	Worldwide; long thin white root; fibrous; must be eaten young; mild potato-like flavor	Boiled, pickled
Taro	Asia; pale cream colored root with purple flecks; starchy, sweet flesh; potato-like flavor	Boiled, fried (poi in Hawaii)
Turnip	Worldwide; small round white root; crisp flesh; slightly sharp radish-like flavor	Boiled, roasted

Light, especially sunlight, can cause off flavors and the development of toxic defensive chemicals. White roots such as parsnips, white carrots, and turnips can generate alcohol compounds that give the vegetable a turpentine-like solvent aroma. Potatoes contain small amounts of the toxic bitter-tasting alkaloids solanine and chaconine, which accumulate when the vegetable is exposed to light. Because light also activates chlorophyll, the growth of these alkaloids is typically accompanied by a green tinge to the surface of the vegetable.

Most of the problematic compounds concentrate near the surface of the root and can largely be eliminated by deeply peeling the skin. Some roots, particularly beets and potatoes, contain an earthy (some might say dirty) flavor component, geosmin, which was once thought to come from microbes in soil but now is thought to generate in the vegetable itself. It is particularly pronounced in large mature vegetables.

See Also • Carrot, Cassava, Celery, Chicory, Potatoes, Stems, Sweet Potatoes

Roasted Root Vegetables

As root vegetables roast, their starch is converted into sugar, and the sugar combines with proteins and browns. At the same time, aromatic components in the vegetables become concentrated, resulting in richer, sweeter flavors than can't be attained by boiling or steaming the same vegetables. Serve as a side dish or in any recipe calling for roasted vegetables.

1	large onion, halved and cut into ½-inch (1 cm) thick wedges	1
1	large sweet potato, peeled, halved, and cut into wedges	1
2	carrots, peeled and cut into 1-inch (2.5 cm) chunks	2
1	medium celery root, peeled and cut into 1-inch (2.5 cm) chunks	1
1	turnip, peeled and cut into bite-size chunks	1
2 tbsp	olive oil	25 mL
	Salt and freshly ground black pepper to taste	
1 tsp	chopped garlic	5 mL

1. Preheat the oven to 425°F (220°C). On a rimmed baking sheet, toss together onion, sweet potato, carrots, celery root, and turnip. Add oil and toss to coat. Season liberally with salt and pepper. Spread out in a single layer. Roast in preheated oven for 30 minutes. Add garlic, and continue roasting until the edges of most of the vegetables have browned and they are uniformly tender but not mushy, 5 minutes more.

2. Serve immediately or cool and refrigerate in a tightly closed container for up to 1 week.

MAKES 6 SERVINGS

ROQUEFORT • See Cheese

ROSE • See Flowers

ROSEMARY • See Herbs

ROTISSERIE COOKING • See Roasting

ROUGHY • See Fish

ROUX • See Sauces

RUBS • See Meat

RUBUS • See Berries

RUM • See Liquor

RUTABAGA • See Cruciferous Vegetables, Roots, Stems

RYE • See Bread, Grains

S

SABLEFISH • See Fish

SACCHARIN • See Sweeteners

SAFFLOWER OIL • See Oil

SAFFRON • See Herbs

SAGE • See Herbs

SALAD

What It Is • No matter what you call a salad — *salade* in French or Dutch, *insalata* in Italian, *ensalada* in Spanish, *Salat* in German, *salat* in Danish or Russian, or *sallad in* Swedish — it all goes back to the same root, *sal*, Latin for "salt." The earliest salads were just that — a radish or a fresh green leaf dressed with salt — and a salad is still as natural as dining gets, just a bite away from foraging for food in the wild. Many salads include cooked elements, such as meats, grains, beans, or hard-cooked eggs, but the prototypical salad is raw.

kitchen wisdom

When to Salt

Salt draws moisture from fresh vegetables. By sprinkling shredded cabbage for coleslaw or cucumber slices with salt before tossing them with a dressing, most of the water in these vegetables can be eliminated so that it does not water down the dressing. Just toss 3 to 4 cups (750 mL to 1 L) of the cut vegetables with a small amount, ½ teaspoon (2 mL) or so, of coarse salt and set aside for 10 minutes. Wrap the vegetable in a kitchen towel and squeeze out as much water as possible; most of the salt will dissolve and drain away with the water. The vegetable pieces will shrivel, but they will be much crisper in the salad, and the dressing will cling to them beautifully.

What It Does • In North America, the most prevalent salad is the garden, or green, salad, a tumble of fresh lettuce, spinach, or cress leaves, torn or cut, casually tossed with a simple vinaigrette or mayonnaise dressing, and garnished with sliced cucumbers, mushrooms, and/or tomatoes. It is served routinely as an appetizer, palate cleanser, or low-calorie lunch. Embellished garden salads, like Caesar, Cobb, and Greek salad, are one-dish meals.

Apple and Cabbage Coleslaw

Always start coleslaws by salting the cabbage to rid it of extra moisture. The easiest way is in a colander set in a sink. That way the excess cabbage juice just runs down the drain, and doesn't dilute the dressing.

2 lbs	cabbage, any type, cored and thinly shredded	1 kg
2	large Granny Smith apples, coarsely grated	2
2 tsp	kosher salt, divided	10 mL

Dressing

¼ cup	sour cream	50 mL
3 tbsp	mayonnaise	45 mL
3 tbsp	red wine vinegar	45 mL
2 tbsp	orange marmalade	25 mL
2 tbsp	ketchup	25 mL
1 tbsp	hot pepper sauce	15 mL
¼ tsp	freshly ground black pepper	1 mL
1	bunch green onions, trimmed and thinly sliced	1

1. In a large colander set in a sink, toss cabbage and apple with 1½ tsp (7 mL) of the salt and let stand for 10 minutes.

2. Dressing: Meanwhile, in a large bowl, combine remaining salt, sour cream, mayonnaise, vinegar, marmalade, ketchup, hot pepper sauce, and pepper.

3. Squeeze excess moisture from cabbage and apples and add to the dressing along with green onions; toss to combine. Refrigerate for about 1 hour before serving.

MAKES 8 SERVINGS

Basic Vinaigrette Salad Dressing

Vinaigrette is a temporary emulsion of oil in vinegar. It will stay together only while it is in motion. The trick is to mix it and use it immediately. Its proportion of oil and vinegar (about 2 to 1) is less oily than the classic ratio of 3 to 1, which makes it better suited to modern palates that tend to prefer foods brighter and less fatty than in the past. As long as you keep the proportion of oil to vinegar the same you can season it any way you want with fresh herbs, curry spices, or basil pesto. Use to dress any salad.

⅓ cup	olive oil	75 mL
¼ cup	grapeseed oil	50 mL
¼ cup	red wine vinegar	50 mL
1	clove garlic, split	1
½ to 1 tsp	kosher salt	2 to 5 mL
¼ tsp	freshly ground black pepper	1 mL

1. In a small jar, combine olive oil, grapeseed oil, vinegar, 2 tbsp (25 mL) water, garlic, ½ tsp (2 mL) kosher salt, and pepper. Seal jar and shake vigorously until the dressing comes together just before serving. Taste and add more salt if needed. Discard garlic.

MAKES ABOUT 1 CUP (250 ML)

The popularity of fresh green salads was not conceivable before refrigeration was commonplace. In the traditional cuisines of the Mediterranean basin, salads are almost always marinated, a technique of preserving fresh or slightly cooked vegetables in dressing. Because dressings are high in salt and acid, they retard the growth of bacteria and keep fresh foods from spoiling. The mezze tradition in the Arab kitchen, antipasti in Italy, eggplant salads and stuffed grape leaves in Greece, and marinated tapas in Spain are all examples of marinated salads that are nearly as old as the cuisines themselves.

Cold meat salads like salmagundi were a way of serving up yesterday's roast in 17th-century England, and tiny pickled onions, shredded cabbage, and beets are essential garnishes for Danish smørrebrød. Aspics preserved both cooked meats and vegetables for extravagant cold presentations in 18th-century France, and eventually morphed into the 20th-century Jell-O salad.

In Asian cuisines, salads are often served as a cooling complement to something hot. A red-hot Thai curry is always served with slices of fresh cucumber or pickled onion, and a platter of fresh herbs, lettuces, cut citrus, and vegetables is as essential as a bottle of nuoc nam on the Vietnamese table. Yogurt salads (raitas) are the ubiquitous companions to curries in India, and pickled vegetables are a vast domain in the cuisines of China, Japan, and Korea.

Salad dressings can take a variety of forms. Vinaigrette, a simple mixture of two to three parts oil mixed with one part vinegar and/or citrus juice, and seasoned with salt, spices, and herbs, is popular in the countries surrounding the Mediterranean. Emulsify the same ingredients with an egg yolk and they become mayonnaise, the most common salad

dressing in northern Europe. Sour cream dressings in Russia and Scandinavia are a variation on creamy mayonnaise dressings.

How It Works • Pickled salads take on the flavors of their dressings, but in order to preserve the fresh texture of delicate vegetables, they should be dressed as lightly and as close to serving as possible. Oil-based dressings are especially damaging to tender leaves. Leaves have a waterproof waxy covering, the cuticle, that makes raindrops roll off them so they don't get sodden. Oil readily merges with the cuticle and is quickly absorbed into the empty spaces in the interior of the leaf, making it wilt and darken. Water-based dressings, or a coating of vinegar or citrus, will not do nearly as much damage.

See Also • Leaves, Salt, Vegetables

SALAMI • See Sausage

SALIVA • See Digestion

SALMON • See Fish

SALMONELLA • See Bacteria

SALSA • See Sauces

SALSIFY • See Roots

SALT

What It Is • There are dozens of salts, inorganic crystalline compounds having various colors, flavors, even aromas. But when we talk about salt in regard to eating, one dominates. Sodium chloride, the common mineral embedded in rocks that erodes into the ocean, giving it its characteristic salinity, is the standard for saltiness. And because sodium is a nutrient we cannot do without, we are programmed to go after it, and therefore destined to covet the flavor of salt.

And covet it we do. People have gathered salt from the earliest times, both by evaporating seawater and by dissolving the mineral out of rocks. It has been taxed and monopolized, has caused political rebellion, and is deeply entrenched in our language. It is the linguistic root for "salary" (from the Roman practice of paying soldiers with salt), and because it is essential to our survival we honor those we depend on most deeply as "worth their salt" and as "salt of the earth."

What It Does • Salt is the only crystal we eat regularly and one of the few foods we keep on the table to be available at every meal. We eat it every day for nutrition (sodium helps to regulate the osmotic pressure between cells), as a flavor enhancer (salt heightens the perception of aromas), and as a taste refiner (it suppresses our perception of unpleasant bitter tastes).

About half of the salt we use comes from the sea and the other half comes from land. Sea salt is produced by capturing ocean water and evaporating the water either in open-air salt pans or, more commonly, through vacuum evaporation. Rock salt is mined by pumping water into salt deposits to dissolve the salt and then evaporating the resulting brine in vacuum chambers to precipitate crystals.

There are several type of culinary salts, differentiated by their source, the size and shape of the crystals, the degree of refinement, and the additions of other elements such as flavors, colors, or nutrients.

• *Granulated table salt:* Tiny uniform cubic crystals make standard table salt one of the densest salts, and the one that takes the longest to dissolve. Its fine, regular consistency makes it prone to caking, so table salt is usually supplemented with up to 2% anticaking agents, mostly aluminum and silicone compounds. Since anticaking compounds don't dissolve as readily as salt, they tend to cloud saturated salt solutions, which is why most pickle recipes warn against using table salt. Table salt can be either sea salt or rock salt, although in North America about 95% of table salt is mined.

• *Iodized salt:* Many governments, including those in the U.S., Canada, Australia, and the EU, recommend fortifying table salt with iodine to help prevent thyroid diseases.

fast fact

- In the past, most salt was used for food, but today food-grade salt represents only 17% of production; the majority is used in manufacturing.

- *Flake salt:* Instead of crystallizing in tiny cubes, flake salt crystals are flat chips, made either by skimming the first crystals from the surface of a brine or by mechanically compacting granulated salt crystals to flatten them. Because the flakes don't pack together as well as cubic crystals, a set volume measure of flake salt weighs less than the same volume of granulated salt.

- *Kosher salt:* A coarsely ground combination of cubic crystal and flake salt, kosher salt is so named because it is used in kosher butchering where its large absorbent crystals draw out the blood on the surface of meat. Kosher salt is salt (which sometimes contains an anticaking agent), and is often the preferred salt of serious cooks because it is relatively pure and easy to sprinkle by hand.

- *Unrefined sea salt:* Made mostly by traditional methods of evaporating seawater in open-air beds, unrefined sea salts are not washed after processing, so they still contain elements of algae, clay and other sea silt, and trace minerals like magnesium and calcium sulfates that influence their flavor and aroma. Some unrefined salts have a gray cast to them and are sometimes called gray salt (*sel gris* in French).

- *Fleur de sel:* This particularly delicate salt is harvested in west-central France by skimming the surface of salt ponds. Fleur de sel ("flower of the salt") is pure sea salt. Because it is hand-harvested and the yield is small, it is expensive.

- *Flavored and colored salt:* Salt is sometimes flavored with garlic powder, onion powder, or celery seed. Salt can also be cold-smoked to make smoked salt. Some colored salt, like the black salt of India, is an unrefined salt loaded with sulfurous minerals. Red and black Hawaiian sea salts are standard sea salt colored with finely ground clay or coral for red or lava rock for black.

- *Salty condiments and other salt substitutes:* In Asian cuisines, salt is not typically used as a flavoring agent, but salty fermented sauces, such as soy sauce, fish sauce, and oyster sauce, are. For those who want to lower their intake of sodium, salt substitutes are plentiful, and include powdered seaweed, salt-free herb and spice seasoning blends, other mineral salts such as potassium salt, or a small amount of acid, which has similar flavor-enhancing properties.

How It Works • In sufficient quantity, salt acts as a preservative, such as in sausage making and curing. When dissolved in water, sodium chloride, an electrically neutral compound, dissociates into positively charged sodium atoms (NA+) and negatively charged chloride atoms (Cl–) called electrolytes. Atoms are smaller than and move faster than molecules. And because electrically charged ions are more reactive than neutral molecules, the dissolved salt ions penetrate ingredients and change their chemistry.

By concentrating in the fluids around cells, salt draws moisture out of cells and salt ions

Gravlax

A Swedish specialty, gravlax is one of the easiest cured foods to make. The salt draws the moisture out of the fish and the sugar holds on to the moisture to keep the gravlax from becoming too dry. Buy the freshest salmon you can and have your fishmonger fillet it and remove the pin bones. Once cured, it will keep refrigerated for about one week.

2	fresh salmon fillets with skin on, pin bones removed (3 to 4 lbs/1½ to 2 kg)	2
1½ cups	kosher salt	375 mL
1½ cups	granulated sugar	375 mL
¾ cup	packed brown sugar	175 mL
1 tbsp	freshly ground white or black pepper	15 mL
2	bunches fresh dill, chopped (about 2 cups/500 mL)	2
3 tbsp	aquavit, lemon vodka, brandy, or gin	45 mL

1. Line a rimmed baking sheet generously with plastic wrap. Put salmon fillets skin-side down on lined pan. In a bowl, combine salt, sugar, brown sugar, pepper, and dill. Rub salt cure into salmon flesh. Sprinkle with aquavit, then sandwich fillets together, skin sides facing out. Pack any remaining cure on top of fish, then wrap tightly with plastic wrap.

2. Place another baking sheet or large plate on top of fish and top with 3 to 5 lbs (1.5 to 2.5 kg) of weight, such as a few heavy cans. Refrigerate the weighted salmon until it becomes opaque, 2 to 4 days, unwrapping twice a day and basting with juices from bottom of pan, then rewrapping tightly.

3. To serve, scrape off any excess salt cure and discard, then thinly slice gravlax on the bias. Store covered and refrigerated for 4 to 5 days.

MAKES ABOUT 4 POUNDS (2 KG)

into cells, making foods dehydrate. Once the moisture comes out of the cells there is nothing to hold it in the food and it flows out. It cannot be reabsorbed. This is the science behind classic salt-cured fish dishes like gravlax and baccalà. It is also why salting steamed vegetables or boiled potatoes makes more of their flavors emerge. And it is how salt kills bacteria, by dehydrating the cells of harmful bacteria while allowing harmless (salt-tolerant) bacteria to flourish.

The balance of salts in bodily fluids, called the electrolyte balance, is important to sustain life. Several electrolytes work in tandem to regulate fluid pressure in the body, among them sodium, potassium, calcium, magnesium, and chloride. They mostly remain in the fluid surrounding our cells, particularly in plasma, the fluid portion of blood. Ingesting too much of one electrolyte can throw the balance off. It is estimated that we need about 1 gram of sodium chloride a day, but because of its presence in most kitchens and dining rooms and in most manufactured food, it's estimated that the average daily intake by North Americans is about 10 times that amount.

Too little sodium causes the plasma to thin, which makes the osmotic pressure inside blood cells greater than the pressure outside, and the cells take in water and can burst. Too little salt can kill you. But continually taking in excess sodium is also harmful. Too much sodium increases the density of plasma, so pressure builds up in the circulatory system, resulting over time in high blood pressure, which damages blood vessels and increases the risk of stroke and heart disease. It would seem that lower salt intake would lower blood

kitchen wisdom

The Shape of Salt

The size and shape of salt crystals make a big difference in how quickly a salt dissolves. Finely crystallized salts dissolve much faster than coarse crystals, and some large crystalline salts, like Maldon sea salt from England, have large pyramid-shaped crystals that stay crunchy even when sprinkled on moist food.

pressure, but unfortunately it's not that simple. Genetics, increasing obesity, exercise levels, and improving dietary factors like eating foods that are high in other electrolytes (potassium, calcium, magnesium, etc.) seem to have a greater benefit.

Physical activity and the corresponding sweating cause a loss of both water and electrolytes. When replacing water during strenuous exercise, it is important to take in a balance of electrolytes as well. Sports drinks are especially designed to replenish both fluids and salts. On the other side, consuming too many electrolytes, usually in the form of salty foods, which make us thirsty, requires the body to balance the onslaught with additional water.

See Also • Chemical Bonding

SALTPETER • See Curing

SALT PORK • See Pork

SALT SUBSTITUTE • See Salt

SAMBUCA • See Liqueur

SAPONINS • See Grains

SARDINES • See Fish

SASSAFRAS • See Herbs

SAUCES

What It Does • Confronted with a hunk of food that's been simply sautéed, roasted, or poached, most serious cooks want more: a flavorful nudge, a textural counterpoint, a sauce to turn what is basically nutritious into something delicious. Sauces provide cooks with a powerful tool to make what is eaten appeal to taste, scent, touch, and sight.

The word "sauce" comes from the Latin word for salt, *sal*, making a connection between the presence of a sauce and our ability to savor what we eat. The earliest sauces were just seasoned cooking juices, and may have included natural fruit juices or honeys. It wasn't long before fermented liquids were used to create the first wine and condiment sauces, including vinegars, soy sauces, and fish sauces (Worcestershire sauce is a tame version of fish sauce).

All of these sauces heighten flavor, but they do it with a thin, watery liquid (even honey loses its viscosity when warmed). For a sauce to deliver its maximum flavor potential, it must be thickened to allow it to linger on the food and in the mouth.

Flavorful liquids consist mostly of water containing suspended flavorful particles. To thicken them, you can either reduce the amount of water or increase the amount of solids. Reducing water is done by boiling the liquid until the solid particles suspended in it concentrate and thicken the resulting sauce. Since the solid particles are also the flavorful elements in the liquid, this technique, called reduction, creates intensely flavored sauces.

Adding solids can also be done by mixing in a cooked purée of fruit or vegetables, which increases a sauce's nutrition, flavor, color, and viscosity. A small amount of carbohydrate, usually a **starch** or **gum** that has the ability to absorb liquid many times its volume, may also be added. To keep sauces from lumping, carbohydrate thickeners have to be suspended in water (a slurry) or fat (a roux) before they can be incorporated smoothly into hot liquid. (See Roux: The Classic Thickener, page 516.)

Emulsion sauces and protein-thickened sauces disperse fat droplets and/or protein particles in liquid rather than use carbohydrates for thickening. Because water bonds with starches and gums better than with proteins and fats, emulsions and protein-thickened sauces tend to be less stable than carbohydrate-thickened sauces.

Every cuisine has its armory of sauces — pestos and pan sauces in Italy, salsas and moles in Latin America, raitas and curries in India, ketchup and gravy in the U.S. — but no culinary culture has done more to create a universal system of sauce making than the French. Although the roots of classic sauces in France date back to the

Classic French Sauces

Five "mother" sauces form the basis for the hundreds of sauces in French cuisine. The roux-thickened sauces were originally codified by Antonin Carême and expanded upon by chefs who followed him, most notably George Auguste Escoffier, who added emulsion sauces and tomato sauce.

Mother Sauce	Liquid	Thickener	Flavorings	Derivations
Espagnole	Brown stock	Brown roux	Browned meat; browned carrot, celery, onion; tomato, spices	Bordelaise (red wine, shallots) Périgueux (Madeira, truffles) Poivrade (vinegar, peppercorns) Robert (white wine, onion, mustard)
Velouté	Veal or chicken stock	Blond roux	Blanched meat, carrot, celery, onion, spices	Allemande (egg yolk) Chivry (white wine, herbs) Suprême (cream, butter, and usually mushroom cooking liquid)
Béchamel	Milk	White roux	Carrot, celery, onion, spices	Mornay (cheese) Nantua (cream, shellfish) Soubise (onion)
Hollandaise/ Mayonnaise	Lemon juice and vinegar	Butter/oil emulsified with egg yolk	Lemon, vinegar	Béarnaise (white wine, shallots, herbs) Dijonnaise (mustard)
Tomato	Tomatoes and stock	Tomato purée	Carrot, celery, onion, herbs	Provençale (mushrooms, garlic) Meat (ground beef, veal and/or pork)

15th century, it was largely the French chef Antonin Carême (1784–1833) who, seeking to simplify the excesses of cuisine that were popular before the French Revolution, created a family tree of sauces. By grouping sauces according to their liquid ingredient, their method of thickening, and their seasonings, he came up with three "mother" sauces, from which most other sauces derived. (See Classic French Sauces chart, above.)

Carême's system was geared to a professional kitchen. Because the sauces were cooked separately from the foods that they accompanied they could be used independently. The same roast beef could be served with a sauce Bordelaise or a sauce Périgueux.

Classic Chinese sauces are assembled from cooking liquids developed through braising or stir-frying, then seasoned and thickened with condiments like soy sauce, hoisin sauce, black bean sauce, and oyster sauce. Latin American sauces are either elaborate long-simmered stews of chiles that are thickened with ground nuts and fruits (moles) or quick raw salsas of chopped vegetables and fruits that are more like salads than sauces. Similarly, Indian sauces are either long-simmered curries or quickly prepared raw salads and yogurt sauces.

At the time of Carême, Italian sauces were much the same as they are today. They are either pulpy sauces made mostly from tomatoes, or pan sauces made from the drippings that glaze the surface of a pan after sautéing or roasting. There are two types of Italian tomato sauce. The first is all vegetables — usually a combination of onions, tomatoes, and garlic — seasoned and simmered just until the vegetables are softened; it can be chunky or smooth, and is served most often with meat, fish, or poultry. It can also be tossed with vegetables and pasta. The other tomato sauce usually contains meat and is cooked for hours with a soffritto (diced carrots, celery, and onion) until the meat and vegetables collapse into one another. This sauce, known as ragù, is almost a kind of stew, and is typically served with pasta.

Italian pan sauces, which include classic sauces like piccata and marsala, can be made only in conjunction with the preparation of the meat or fish they accompany. Pan sauces are made by dissolving (deglazing) the pan drippings with wine, stock, or fruit juice and reducing

Watercress Cream Reduction

The fresh green aroma and peppery bite of watercress is perfectly balanced by the dairy-sweet fat of heavy cream. Be careful when cooking this sauce: if the cream is less than fresh, acid from the wine can cause it to split. Once the cream is added, watch the sauce carefully and do not overcook it. Serve with seafood, poultry, vegetables, pasta, or eggs.

1 tsp	unsalted butter	5 mL
1 tbsp	minced onion	15 mL
½ cup	dry white wine	125 mL
2 tsp	finely grated lemon zest	10 mL
1 cup	whipping (35%) cream	250 mL
⅔ cup	watercress leaves, stems discarded	150 mL
	Kosher salt and ground white pepper to taste	

1. In a skillet, melt butter over medium heat. Add onion and sauté until tender, about 3 minutes.

2. Increase heat to high. Add wine and lemon zest and boil until reduced to one-third its volume.

3. Add cream and boil until reduced and thickened, stirring constantly, about 1 minute. Stir in watercress and cook just until leaves wilt. Season with salt and pepper. Serve immediately.

MAKES 4 SERVINGS

the liquid. These sauces must be served right away with the foods with which they were prepared.

The sauces that are most similar to the roux-thickened sauces of Carême are the meat gravies that are popular in England and North America. Beef gravy is akin to espagnole sauce, and chicken gravy is similar to velouté. The main difference is that gravies are made directly from the drippings of a roast, whereas the mother sauces are made independently of the food. To make gravy, flour is mixed into the drippings, and then water, milk, or stock are stirred in until the sauce is thickened.

In modern North American cuisine, flour-thickened sauces have largely been supplanted by many of the Asian, Latin, and Mediterranean sauces unknown to Carême. Today's home cooks are just as likely to sauce a sautéed chicken breast with a Thai peanut sauce or a vinaigrette salad dressing as they are to cloak it in chicken gravy. Many restaurant chefs have abandoned the French battery of classic sauces for Asian glazes, Indian raitas, and the foams and gels of **molecular gastronomy**.

How It Works • The flavor of a sauce develops from an interplay of liquid, seasoning, and thickener. Seasoning for sauces needs to be assertive. Since there is never more than a thin glaze of sauce to accompany each bite of food, if the sauce is not strong its flavor will disappear. Stocks and broths for sauce making need to be full flavored. If they are not, reduce them to concentrate their flavorful parts. To ensure full flavors in meat sauces, professional kitchens often use demi-glace (brown stock reduced to about one-third its volume or equal parts brown stock and espagnole reduced by half). Demi-glace concentrates sold for home use give cooks the potential for recreating professional results in their own kitchens.

Common Thickened Sauces

Each type of thickener adds different textural and flavor qualities. This chart explains how each thickener acts within a sauce, but in a recipe, several thickeners may be used at once. For instance, a starch-thickened broth might be flavored with a herb purée and finished with a swirl of cream.

Sauce	What's In It	How It Works	Qualities
Blood-thickened	Stock (or other liquid), blood	Proteins in blood coagulate at 167°F (75°C)	Rich and meaty, but must be heated slowly; curdles easily; can taste liver-like if overcooked
Butter sauce	Whole butter, stock, wine, or juice	Liquid is reduced to minimize water and concentrate flavors; butter is swirled in off heat	Rich, buttery, unstable; must be used immediately; splits if heated too much
Composed butter	Butter, flavoring	Dry flavorings are mixed with softened butter; melted over hot food	Buttery and rich; can be highly flavored; not cooked
Chocolate sauce	Melted chocolate, cocoa, liquid (usually cream), sugar, butter	Chocolate forms an emulsion with the liquid; starch in cocoa helps to absorb liquid	Highly flavored, smooth; used for dessert. Sometimes a small amount of chocolate is added to savory mole sauces to enrich flavor and smooth texture.
Cream reduction	Cream, flavoring	Flavoring liquid is reduced to remove water and concentrate flavors; cream added and boiled until water in cream evaporates and proteins coagulate, causing cream to thicken	Creamy and rich; high in calories; serve within 1 hour
Emulsion sauce	Melted butter or oil, egg yolk, vinegar, water, and/or lemon juice	Egg yolk and liquid are mixed together (heated for hollandaise); fat is added slowly to form an emulsion	Rich and tangy; serve within 20 minutes
Foam	Viscous liquid (purée, cream, chocolate), air	Air forced into liquid blocks water flow and thickens	Light and airy; deflates quickly
Glace	Reduced stock or broth	Protein (gelatin) in broth becomes concentrated and thickens liquid	Syrupy and meaty; clear and highly flavored; can be refrigerated for weeks and reheated
Gravy	Meat drippings, flour, broth, milk, or water	Flour is stirred into hot meat drippings and cooked to desired color; liquid is added slowly and whisked constantly to prevent lumping	Smooth; thickness easily adjusted by altering ratio of ingredients; very stable, can be refrigerated for a week
Puréed sauce	Purée of cooked vegetable, cooked fresh fruit, nuts, or dried fruit, any liquid	Pulverized food fibers disperse in liquid, causing it to thicken	Can be brightly colored and highly flavored depending on purée and liquid; can be nutritious depending on purée; water can fall out of suspension, so stir to smooth
Roux-thickened	Flour, melted fat, stock or milk	See Roux, page 516	See Roux, page 516
Slurry-thickened	Flour or starch, cold water, any liquid	Starch or flour is moistened in cold water to separate the particles without lumping; added to boiling liquid and stirred until thickened	Smooth, quick; easy to adjust thickness; starch thickens clearly; flour-thickened sauces are cloudy
Sugar-thickened	Sugar, reduced liquid or purée, fat (optional)	Fruit purée or reduced liquid (wine or fruit juice) heated with sugar until syrupy	Syrupy; very stable hot or cold; usually used for dessert
Vinaigrette	Oil, vinegar	Whisked until oil droplets are suspended in vinegar	Thickens during mixing and then immediately separates; must be remixed with each use
Yogurt (sour cream) sauce	Yogurt, flavoring	Ingredients are mixed together	Fresh dairy flavor; cannot be boiled

Troubleshooting Common Sauce-making Problems

Problem	Type of Sauce	Cause	Solution
Split sauce	Butter sauce	Butter added too quickly or too much butter	Start over
		Liquid reduced too much	Add small amount of hot water and whisk vigorously
	Cream reduction	Cream is old	Start over with fresh cream
		Acid in recipe	Find a nonacidic substitute (e.g., lemon zest for lemon juice), or reduce amount of acid, or cook briefly
	Emulsion	Too much heat	If separation is slight, whisk vigorously; if badly split, gradually whisk broken sauce into new egg yolk; if egg is curdled, start over
		Added fat too quickly	Gradually whisk broken sauce into new egg yolk
		Too much fat or not enough liquid	Stir in small amount of hot water
	Purée	Purée is too coarse	Purée more finely and reheat, or whisk in a small amount of slurry
		Sauce was refrigerated or frozen	Heat sauce, stirring often
	Roux- or slurry-thickened	Sauce was refrigerated or frozen	Heat sauce, stirring often
	Vinaigrette	Sauce sat too long	Whisk vigorously
	Yogurt	Sauce was heated	If separation is slight, add slurry over very low heat, whisking constantly. If badly split, start again
Sauce lacks flavor	Any type	Liquid is bland	Boil liquid to reduce and concentrate flavor
		Lacks seasoning	Add a little salt or a little acid (or more seasoning)
		Too much thickener	Add more liquid and seasoning
Sauce is too thin	Butter sauce	Liquid not reduced enough	If all of the butter has already been added, start again. If less than 25% of butter has been added, reduce sauce, and add remaining butter off heat
		Not enough butter	Add more butter
	Cream reduction	Not reduced enough	Reduce sauce in uncovered skillet over high heat
	Emulsion	Not enough fat	Add more melted butter or oil
	Purée	Purée too coarse	Purée more finely
		Not enough purée	Add more purée
		Sauce is undercooked	Cook longer
	Roux- or slurry-thickened	Sauce is undercooked	Cook longer
		Not enough thickener	Add more roux or slurry
Sauce is too thick	Butter sauce	Sauce is cold	Warm gradually, stirring constantly
	Cream reduction	Over-reduced	Add a small amount of water and reheat gently
	Emulsion	Too much fat	Add more liquid or water
	Purée	Purée is too thick, or too much purée, or over-reduced	Add more liquid or water
	Roux- or slurry-thickened	Too much thickener, or sauce over-reduced	Add more liquid or water

Roux: The Classic Thickener

Roux, an equal mixture of flour and melted fat, is the cornerstone of classic sauce making. Before the advent of roux in the 17th century, sauces were thickened with proteins, such as blood or egg yolks, with the starch that sloughed into cooking liquids from grains or noodles, or with crumbled toast or cake. Roux was more versatile and produced smoother sauces.

At the height of French cuisine in the 18th and 19th centuries, the earlier meat fat was replaced with clarified butter, which created a consistent roux that could be used with meat and nonmeat sauces.

Flour is a mixture of starch (the thickening component) and protein. When it is stirred directly into hot broth, its surface starch takes in water on contact, expands, and traps bits of dry flour in a casing of gelatinized starch — in other words, it forms a lump. Combining the flour with fat before it contacts the liquid separates the flour particles from each other, so when added to water the flour particles absorb the liquid individually and can't stick together; thus lumps do not form.

A roux is started by melting the fat over heat no higher than medium, because the fine grains of flour scorch easily. The flour is stirred in to combine with the fat, then cooked to varying degrees depending on the color of the sauce being made:

White roux for béchamel: cooks for about 3 minutes, just until it no longer smells of uncooked flour and before the flour colors.

Blond roux for velouté: cooks for 4 to 6 minutes, until it starts to smell like toasted nuts and turns golden to tan.

Brown roux for espagnole: cooks for 7 to 15 minutes, until it smells like toast and browns. Be careful not to splash; brown roux is very hot. In Cajun cooking, dark brown roux, which can cook for as long as 30 minutes, is used to flavor sauces, but because the starch in it toasts so much it loses its ability to thicken.

Roux can be stored in the refrigerator for several weeks and used as needed.

To complete the sauce, hot liquid is added slowly to the roux, and whisked constantly to prevent lumps. The less a roux is cooked, the more it is apt to form lumps. Roux-thickened sauces need to be cooked for a minimum of 20 minutes to fully cook the flour, and a maximum of three hours for brown sauces to clear all cloudiness from the protein in the flour.

Red Pepper Coulis

Coulis is a smooth purée thickened with vegetable pulp rather than a roux or a slurry. There is no starch to dull the brilliant red of the peppers, color or dampen their fresh vegetable flavor. This one is brilliant red and bursting with flavor. Serve with roasted, grilled, or sautéed meat, poultry, or seafood; or with vegetables, pasta, or eggs.

2	large red bell peppers, chopped	2
1	small onion, chopped	1
1	clove garlic, minced	1
½	jalapeño pepper, seeded and minced	½
1 tbsp	dark sesame oil	15 mL
2 tbsp	freshly squeezed lemon juice	25 mL
½ cup	vegetable broth	125 mL

1. In a small saucepan, combine red peppers, onion, garlic, jalapeño, sesame oil, lemon juice, and broth. Bring to a boil over medium heat. Reduce heat to medium-low. Cover and simmer until pepper is tender, about 10 minutes.

2. Add mixture to a food processor or blender and purée. Strain through a fine-mesh strainer, pushing through as much of the purée as possible. Serve hot.

MAKES 4 SERVINGS

Warm Sun-Dried Tomato Vinaigrette

Vinaigrettes are thin and tart. They usually do not heat well, but this one is held together with a purée of sun-dried tomatoes that gives it a jolt of flavor and color and a light pulpy texture. Serve with roasted, grilled, or sautéed pork, veal, poultry, or seafood; or with vegetables or eggs.

⅓ cup	extra virgin olive oil, divided	75 mL
1	clove garlic, minced	1
6	oil-packed sun-dried tomatoes, drained and puréed	6
¼ cup	red wine vinegar	50 mL
1 tbsp	chopped fresh basil	15 mL

1. In a small skillet or saucepan, heat 1 tbsp (15 mL) of the oil over medium-high heat. Add garlic and sauté until aromatic, about 20 seconds. Stir in remaining oil, sun-dried tomatoes, and vinegar and heat through, stirring constantly. Stir in basil. Serve immediately or rewarm before serving.

MAKES 4 SERVINGS

Thickeners, especially starchy thickeners, diminish flavor. Completely watery sauces taste bland because they lack the viscosity to stay on the food or palate long enough to be tasted. But as long as a sauce is thick enough to coat a surface, the thinner it is, generally the more flavor it will have.

All liquids are predominantly water. Thickeners work by limiting the movement of water in a liquid. When particles are dispersed in a liquid, they interfere with the movement of the water molecules, and the liquid becomes more solid. Coarse particles, like chopped vegetables in a salsa or a chunky tomato sauce, won't interfere much with water flow, resulting in a watery sauce. Purée the vegetables, though, and the sauce will immediately get thicker. Add a tablespoon of starch and the sauce will become smoother and more cohesive.

See Also • Dispersions, Gelatin, Gums, Milk, Soup, Starch

SAUERKRAUT • See Fermentation

SAUSAGE

What It Is • Seasonings, especially salt, have been used to preserve meats since ancient times. It helps if the meat is ground or finely chopped so that the salt combines thoroughly with the perishable protein, and also if the mixture can be encased to hinder new microbes from entering. Sausages (the root of "sausage" is *sal*, Latin for "salt") are some of the most versatile of these preparations. Spiced and stuffed into an edible skin, sausages can be fresh or cooked, cured, and/or dried.

Originally the edible casing for sausages was made from an animal's stomach lining or intestines. Depending on the animal, the dimension of the casing determined the size of the sausage, and a wide variety of shapes and sizes evolved. Today the casing is as likely to be artificial, and the filling might be soy protein rather than meat.

What It Does • As with other ancient foods (wine, cheese, and bread), there seems to be an infinite number of sausages, and each region or even village has its own versions. Italians are known for their salami (cured and dried sausages) and Germans for their wursts (creamy smooth fresh sausages). The only thing all sausages have in common is salt.

Although any meat or animal part is fair game, pork is the preferred sausage meat because it is relatively mild and therefore easy to match with a variety of flavors. Of all the domesticated meats, pork is the driest, at only 52% moisture (compared with beef at 60%), which makes it a good candidate for curing and preserving.

Pork also contains an abundance of mild-tasting fat. When meat is ground, its natural texture is destroyed and most of

kitchen wisdom

Cooking Sausages

To prepare fresh sausages ½-inch (1 cm) thick in diameter or less: Puncture in several places, then brown all over in a dry skillet over medium heat.

To prepare fresh sausages greater than ½-inch (1 cm) thick in diameter: Puncture in several places, arrange in a single layer in a dry skillet, add water until the bottom third of the sausages is immersed, then cover and cook over medium-high heat until the water has almost evaporated. Remove lid, then brown all over.

To prepare cooked sausages of any thickness: Puncture the sausages in several places. Brown in a skillet in a thin film of oil, or grill or broil, or boil in plenty of gently boiling water until plump and heated through.

To prepare dried sausages: Slice and serve at room temperature without cooking, or add to a recipe in the last 15 minutes of cooking.

its juices run out. When it is cooked, it dries and toughens. Mixing it with fat reinstates a smooth, creamy texture. Older sausage recipes can call for as much as 50% fat. Today the ratio is much leaner, with most sausages having no more than 30% fat.

The meat filling, called forcemeat, can be anywhere from coarsely chopped to finely ground. Generally, the coarser a forcemeat is, the less fat it needs to be succulent. For coarse sausages, the meat and fat are ground once and stay in separate, discernible pieces, as in salami. The mixture is seasoned and can be embedded with pieces of vegetables or fruit, whole herbs, nuts, or cheese. For finely ground sausages, the meat and fat are puréed in a blender, usually with water or milk to create a smooth "batter." Whether coarsely or finely ground, the forcemeat is filled into casings and molded into its sausage shape.

All sausages fall into one of the following styles, or a combination of two:

Fresh sausages: Soft, moist, and highly perishable, fresh sausages, such as hot or sweet Italian and breakfast sausages, should be cooked within a few days of purchase.

Cooked sausages: Fresh sausages are steamed or simmered, which coagulates the forcemeat proteins and kills microbes, making the sausages much less perishable. Usually safe to eat without further heating, nevertheless cooked sausages, such as bratwurst and liverwurst, are often cooked again before serving.

Cured (fermented) sausages: Their salt and seasoning content makes it safe to age most sausages, allowing beneficial lactic-acid-producing bacteria the time to grow and change the flavor and texture of the forcemeat. There are two types of fermented sausages. Those with a lot of salt and spice,

Sausage Overview

All sausages are seasoned with salt and all contain between 20 and 40% fat that is mixed with the meat before grinding.

Sausage	Meat	Seasonings	Type
Andouille	Pork, chitterlings (intestines)	Pepper, onion	Smoked
Andouillette	Pork, stomach, colon	Thyme, parsley, bay leaf	Cooked
Blood sausage (black pudding)	Pork, pork or beef blood	Starch, onion, cream, clove, pepper	Cooked
Boudin blanc	Pork, veal (finely ground)	Milk, eggs, starch	Fresh or cooked
Boudin noir	Pork blood	Onion, apple, chestnut	Cooked
Breakfast links	Pork	Mildly spiced; formulas vary	Fresh
Calabrese	Pork	Chiles	Dried
Cervelat	Pork (can include beef, lamb, or poultry)	Pepper, ginger, cardamom, spirits	Smoked and dried
Chaurice (Creole chorizo)	Pork	Chiles	Fresh
Chipolata	Pork (coarsely ground)	Sage, thyme, nutmeg, paprika	Fresh; small and thin
Chorizo (Mexican)	Pork	Chiles	Fresh or cooked
Chorizo (Spanish)	Pork	Paprika	Smoked and dried
Chouriço	Pork	Paprika	Smoked and dried
Cotechino	Pork, pork rind	Garlic, pepper, lots of salt	Fresh or cooked
Cumberland	Pork (coarsely ground)	Pepper	Fresh; long rope
Frankfurter (hot dog)	Pork or beef (finely ground)	Nutmeg, ginger, cumin, dill, starch, sugar	Cooked, sometimes smoked
Gelbwurst	Pork, veal (finely ground)	Nutmeg, ginger, white pepper	Cooked
Genoa salami	Pork and beef	Garlic, pepper, fennel, red wine	Cured and dried
Italian sausage	Pork	Mild (sweet): garlic and fennel; Hot: chiles	Fresh
Kielbasa	Pork	Garlic	Cooked, usually smoked
Kishka	Beef	Grain or meal, pepper	Fresh
Knackwurst	Pork or beef (finely ground)	Garlic	Cooked and smoked
Linguiça	Pork	Onion, garlic, paprika	Cured
Liver sausage (liverwurst)	Pork and pork liver	Onion	Cooked
Merguez	Lamb or beef (coarsely ground)	Paprika, sumac, harissa	Fresh
Morcilla	Pork and pork blood	Onion, rice	Cooked
Mortadella	Pork (finely ground)	Peppercorns, fat lardoons, pistachios	Cooked; wide and large
Pepperoni	Pork and beef (coarsely ground)	Ground chiles, paprika	Dried
Salami	Pork and beef (coarsely ground)	Pepper, variety of spices	Cured and dried
Scrapple	Pork offal	Sage, thyme, savory, cornmeal	Fresh; in loaves
Teewurst (Mettwurst)	Pork and pork liver	Pepper, onion	Cooked and smoked
White pudding	Pork (finely ground)	Oatmeal, onion	Fresh or cooked

such as hard salami like pepperoni, can be fermented for several days, then stored at room temperature for several months. The other type is less salty, less spicy, and moister. It is usually cured for less than 24 hours and is often smoked to further preserve it. These sausages, such as German frankfurters and knackwurst, usually need to be refrigerated, where they can be kept for up to two months.

Smoked sausages: Cured sausages are sometimes smoked (kielbasa, andouille). Before refrigeration this was mostly done to preserve them longer, but now it is mostly done for flavor. Smoked sausages can be eaten without further cooking, but they usually are cooked anyway.

Dried sausages: Dried sausages, like dried chorizo or pepperoni, tend to be the highest in salt (at least 4%) and the lowest in moisture (as low as 10%). They are firm and are shelf-stable at room temperature for months. Dried sausages are typically eaten without further cooking.

Meatless sausages: Vegan and vegetarian sausages are typically made from nonmeat proteins like tofu, seitan, nuts, and beans, supplemented with grains and vegetables. Some are flavored and shaped to look and taste like meat sausages; others are more vegetal in character. They tend to be lower in fat, and, like all vegetable products, are cholesterol free.

How It Works • Cured sausages have been made ever since people started preserving meat with salt. When salted scraps of meat are pressed into a casing, bacteria-laden surfaces get packed together into a mass that has salt-tolerant bacteria striated throughout. For the most part these are the same bacteria grown in salty anaerobic cheeses, lactobacilli and leuconostocs. They produce lactic and acetic acids, which build up in the sausage and lower its natural acidity from pH 6 to 4.5, at which point the acidity is about 1% of the sausage's volume, making the meat inhospitable to microbes that cause spoilage. As the sausage ages and dries, the acidity concentrates more. In Europe and North America, most cured sausages also contain nitrates or nitrites to keep botulism bacteria at bay and provide a characteristic flavor and color.

Pâtés

A pâté is a forcemeat that is baked in a mold, usually loaf shaped. Coarsely ground forcemeats are called country pâtés, and smooth, finely ground forcemeats are called pâtés. Pâtés served in their baking molds are sometimes called terrines. Soft pâtés, lightened with cream and egg, and often made from liver, sweetbreads, or brains, are usually referred to as mousses. Most pâtés are pork and about 30% fat, but they can be made from any meat (or fish or vegetables) and can be bound with cream or egg instead of pork fat. Pâtés are frequently studded with bits of vegetables, fruit, or nuts, or strips of meat, to reveal an attractive mosaic of color and texture when sliced.

The mold is often lined with strips of pork fat, bacon, blanched leaves, or poultry skin. The sealed mold is gently baked in a water bath to ensure gentle and thorough heating. After cooking, firm pâtés are compressed as they cool for easier slicing. Pâtés stay fresh under refrigeration for about one week.

Fermentation produces many flavorful compounds other than acids, including fruity esters and nutty aldehydes (dried salami flavor). During drying, a white powdery coating of harmless molds and yeasts can grow on the sausage casing; this adds to the flavor and discourages the growth of spoilage microorganisms.

See Also • Bacon, Curing, Ham, Salt

SAUTÉING • See Frying

SAVORY • See Herbs

SAVORY • See Flavor

SAVOY CABBAGE • See Cruciferous Vegetables

SCALLION • See Allium

SCALLOP • See Mollusks

SCHNAPPS • See Liquor

SCOTCH • See Liquor

SCRAPPLE • See Sausage

SCROD • See Fish

SCULPINS • See Fish

SEA BASS • See Fish

SEA BREAM • See Fish

SEAFOOD • See Cephalopod, Crustacean, Fish, Mollusks, Seaweed

SEA SALT • See Salt

SEASONED SALT • See Salt

SEASONING • See Capsicum, Flavor, Herbs, Salt, Spices

SEATROUT • See Fish

SEAWEED

What It Is • Seaweeds — a generic term for any plant that grows in the ocean — are mostly algae, plants that have been around for a billion years and were the predecessor to all plants on Earth.

What It Does • People have been eating and cooking seaweeds from the earliest times, and they are still a major food in Asia. The Japanese crop of nori, the seaweed used for wrapping sushi, is more valuable than all other aquaculture combined, including fish and seafood, and in Europe, the Irish mash carrageenan (Irish moss) into oatmeal and use it as a thickener for puddings.

Seaweeds are a good source of vitamins A, B, C, and E and of several minerals, most notably iodine. They also have a savory quality that enlivens other flavors (see The Birth of Umami, page 523), a characteristic that makes seaweeds a popular condiment and seasoning for soups, salads, and steamed rice in Japan.

Seaweeds are roughly classified by color:

- Green seaweeds, such as sea lettuce, which is used in seaweed salad in Japan, get their color from chlorophyll, making them nutritionally similar to the leaves of land plants. Sea beans (glasswort), succulent plants from the genus *Salicornia*, are like land-living seaweeds, with a similar chewy, gelatinous quality. They are usually steamed like asparagus and often are served with seafood.

- Red seaweeds, such as nori (laver) and dulse, get their brick-red color from a protein pigment that is soluble in water and sensitive to heat, so during cooking their color changes from red to green. Nori, the crisp wafer-like seaweed, is dark red (almost black) before toasting and then turns vivid green after being held over an open flame for a few seconds. Red algae store their energy in large polysaccharide molecules that are the bases for many **gums**, including agar agar and carrageenan, that are used in beer production and for thickening milk shakes, shampoos, and shoe polish.

Vegan "Clam" Chowder

This recipe is a rendition of a soup developed by vegetarian chef Ken Bergeron, who was the first chef to win a gold medal at the Culinary Olympics for a vegan food. The seafood flavor comes from a combination of nori and dulse, both red seaweeds. It takes very little seaweed to get a pronounced seafood flavor in this Manhattan-style "clam" chowder.

2 tsp	olive oil	10 mL
½ cup	diced onion	125 mL
½ cup	diced carrot	125 mL
½ cup	diced celery	125 mL
½ cup	diced green bell pepper	125 mL
2 tsp	minced garlic	10 mL
¼ cup	dulse flakes	50 mL
1 tbsp	crumbled nori	15 mL
1 tsp	dried oregano leaves, crumbled	5 mL
1 tsp	sea salt	5 mL
½ tsp	ground fennel seeds	2 mL
½ tsp	dried thyme leaves	2 mL
¼ tsp	freshly ground black pepper	1 mL
1	bay leaf	1
4 cups	vegetable broth	1 L
¾ cup	canned crushed tomatoes	175 mL
1 tsp	soy sauce	5 mL
½ tsp	balsamic vinegar	2 mL
1 cup	finely diced peeled boiling potatoes, boiled until tender	250 mL
	Parsley for garnish	

1. In a large heavy saucepan, heat oil over medium-high heat. Add onion, carrot, celery, and peppers and sauté until vegetables just begin to brown, about 8 minutes.

2. Add garlic and sauté for 30 seconds. Add dulse, nori, oregano, salt, fennel, thyme, pepper, and bay leaf. Then add vegetable broth, tomatoes, soy sauce, and vinegar. Reduce heat and simmer until vegetables are tender, 20 to 30 minutes. Discard bay leaf.

3. Stir in potatoes and simmer until heated through. Add parsley and serve.

MAKES 4 SERVINGS

• Brown seaweeds, such as kelp (kombu, arame), hijiki (hiziki), and wakame, are high in alginates, a family of gums that are used to thicken and stabilize products from ice cream to toothpaste. Sodium alginate, the salt form of alginic acid, is a favorite of molecular gastronomy chefs, who take advantage of one of its limitations. Alginates are quick-setting gels, but they can form gels only in the presence of calcium. By mixing a calcium-poor vegetable purée with sodium alginate, and then dripping it into a calcium-rich solution (milk, for example), chefs are able to form perfect pearls of vegetable "caviar," a process known as spherification.

How It Works • Living in the ocean has its pressures. The weight of water deep in the ocean is far greater than the air pressure that land plants must withstand, and the stress of standing up against strong currents and disturbances on the ocean floor has led seaweeds to fill their cells with large amounts of sturdy and flexible jelly-like polysaccharides (large sugar polymers). These substances are the basis for food gums.

Plant cell membranes are porous, exchanging fluids with their environment through osmosis. If the concentration of ions outside the cell becomes less than that inside, fluid will flow through the cell wall until the cell bursts. Since the salt concentration of seawater varies, seaweeds have to compensate for the changes in osmotic pressure by loading up their cells with various molecules to maintain a balance. Some of these molecules give seaweeds properties that have made them very versatile in the development of new foods. Mannitol, a sugar-alcohol found in brown seaweeds, tastes sweet, but since humans don't metabolize it until it reaches the large intestine, it doesn't raise blood glucose levels when eaten. Along with sorbitol, another sugar-alcohol, it has become a popular artificial sweetener. An amino acid in kombu seaweed, glutamatic acid, is the companion acid of monosodium glutamate (MSG), the salt that is a universal flavor enhancer.

All seaweeds have a savory flavor component resulting from concentrations of minerals and amino acids, as well as a salty flavor from living in seawater. They also share the aroma of dimethyl sulfide, which is one of the aromatic components of sea air, which is one reason seaweeds can substitute for seafood in recipes (see Vegan "Clam" Chowder, left). Prolonged cooking tends to accentuate these fishy aromas, so seaweeds are usually cooked briefly. For instance, dashi, the common Japanese soup base, is made from dried brown seaweed and dried tuna flakes. The broth is brought to a boil and the seaweed is removed immediately, leaving behind a fresh ocean flavor. Thick seaweeds are usually scored with a knife to help them release their flavors quickly.

See Also • Flavor, Gums

SEEDS • See Grains, Legumes, Oil, Nuts

SEITAN • See Gluten

SELTZER • See Carbon Dioxide

SEMOLINA • See Wheat

SERRANO CHILE • See Capsicum

SERRANO HAM • See Ham

SESAME OIL • See Oil

SESAME SEEDS • See Oil

SHALLOT • See Allium

SHARK • See Fish

SHEEP • See Lamb

SHEEP'S MILK • See Cheese, Lamb, Milk

SHELLFISH • See Crustacean, Mollusks

The Birth of Umami

Seaweed is responsible for changing the way we understand taste in the 21st century. Way back in 1908, a Japanese chemist, Kikunae Ikeda, found that kombu (brown seaweed) contained a large amount of a particularly savory amino acid derivative, monosodium glutamate (MSG), that provoked a taste sensation that could not be described by any of the four known tastes thought to be captured by taste buds — sweet, salty, sour, or bitter. He called the taste umami (roughly meaning "delicious" in Japanese) and showed that it was similar to the taste of meat and fermented foods such as cheese and soy sauce.

For most of the 20th century, Western scientists were not convinced that umami existed as a separated taste. Then in 2001, Charles Zucker, a biologist at the University of California, San Diego, isolated specific taste receptors in humans and animals for capturing savory flavors. Other umami substances have since been identified in fish and shiitake mushrooms. They have been isolated and are often used in association with MSG as flavor enhancers.

In 1968 a Chinese-American doctor, in a letter to *The New England Journal of Medicine*, described his weakness, numbness, and palpitations after eating in Chinese restaurants in the U.S. and wondered whether MSG in the food (which was rarely used in China) could be the cause. Almost immediately, MSG, a common flavor enhancer used in American homes since the early 1950s, was labeled a toxin and was removed from manufactured food products and from restaurants. Since then scores of studies have failed to show that MSG has any ill effects, and toxicologists believe it to be harmless to the great majority of people (all foods cause adverse reactions in some people).

SHERRY • See Wine

SHORTENING • See Fat

SHRIMP • See Crustacean

SILICONE • See Bakeware

SILVER • See Heat

SIMPLE SYRUP • See Sweeteners

SLAUGHTERING • See Meat

SLICING • See Knives

SLOW COOKER • See Cookware

SLURRY • See Sauces

SMOKE POINT • See Frying, Oil

SMOKING

What It Is • When organic matter, such as wood, burns it doesn't combust completely. Big pieces of incombustible material turn into ash, and those small enough to be airborne form smoke. The composition of smoke depends on the composition of the material being burned. Some of the elements in smoke are toxic to or inhibit the growth of microbes, so allowing smoke to permeate food — a process known as smoking — is an effective and time-honored way of preserving it.

What It Does • There are two methods of smoking food: hot-smoking and cold-smoking. In hot-smoking, food is placed in an enclosed space with a smoking fire. The food is surrounded by smoke as it cooks and develops smoky flavors on its surface. The cooking temperature is kept relatively low (130 to 200°F/54 to 93°C) but hot enough so that the texture of hot-smoked food is similar to gently baked or roasted food. Barbecuing in an outdoor grill with the addition of soaked wood chips is an example of hot-smoking.

In cold-smoking, food is placed in a separate chamber from the fire, and smoke is channeled into the food chamber through a flue. By separating the fire and food, the temperature around the food can be kept between 60 and 120°F (16 and 50°C), so the food can be exposed to smoke for a much longer period without overcooking, resulting in products that are tender, moist, and redolent of smoke flavors. Because smoke flavors deposit more readily on a moist surface than on a dry one, a pan of water is often placed in the food chamber to keep humidity levels high.

In addition to being antimicrobial, some particles in smoke are harmful to humans. Polycyclic aromatic hydrocarbons (PAHs), which are proven carcinogens, are formed when wood burns at high temperatures. Increasing the temperature of a fire increases the amounts of PAHs that are formed, so a hot-burning wood like mesquite produces more PAHs than an oak or hickory fire. Because PAH molecules are large and heavy, they are most concentrated near the fire source. The farther food is placed from the fire and the lower the temperature of the fire, the fewer PAHs contact the food. Commercial smokers use filters and thermostat controls to limit the amount of PAHs in commercially smoked products.

Liquid smoke, which is basically smoke-flavored water, is a convenient way to add a smoky flavor to food without ever building a fire. Smoke is composed of two phases: microscopic oily particles that appear as a haze, and an invisible gas phase, made up of aromatic water-soluble particles. Liquid smoke is largely made of trapped smoke vapor. Since many of the toxic components

Smoke Rings
Many barbecued meats develop a "smoke ring," a rosy pink area of 8 to 10 mm just beneath the surface. The ring is caused by nitrogen dioxide gas created when organic fuels are burned. The NO_2 is converted into nitric oxide in the muscle fibers of meat, where it converts the pigment in myoglobin into a stable pink molecule, the same one found in nitrite-cured hams.

Tea-Smoked Mussels with Seaweed Mignonette

The acrid smoke from tea leaves is delicious teamed with the briny flavor of shellfish. The smoke from tea is not noxious so it is safe to use for smoking inside or outside. To set up a smoker on the stove you will need a heavy metal roasting pan, heavy-duty foil, and a wire rack that fits in the pan. You can also do it outside in a covered grill. Just throw soaked tea leaves onto the hottest fire you can make and perch the shellfish on the rack above. The mussels are served with vinegary spicy mignonette dipping sauce.

¼ cup	loose tea leaves, such as oolong, black, or green	50 mL
½ cup	boiling water	125 mL

Mignonette

½ cup	rice vinegar	125 mL
1 tbsp	dulse or nori flakes	15 mL
1 tsp	cracked black pepper	5 mL
1 tsp	kosher salt	5 mL
1 tsp	finely chopped garlic	5 mL
4 lbs	mussels (about 6 dozen), scrubbed and debearded	2 kg

1. In a bowl, combine tea and boiling water. Let steep for 20 minutes. Strain through a fine-mesh sieve, reserving tea leaves and discarding liquid.

2. If smoking on a stove top, line a large roasting pan with three layers of heavy-duty foil, or if smoking outside preheat a charcoal grill to medium-high.

3. Mignonette: In a small bowl, combine vinegar, dulse, pepper, salt, and garlic. Set aside.

4. If smoking on a stove, turn on the ventilation to high. Scatter tea leaves over the bottom of the roasting pan and set a rack just large enough to fit in the pan over the tea. Cover the pan with foil and place over high heat until the tea is smoking, about 3 minutes. If smoking outside, scatter tea leaves directly on the hot coals, place the grill rack over the coals, cover the grill and wait a few minutes for the tea leaves to start smoking.

5. Tap any open mussels; discard any that do not close. Arrange mussels in a single layer on the rack. Cover and smoke until the mussels open, 10 to 15 minutes.

6. Transfer to a large serving bowl, discarding any mussels that do not open, and serve with the mignonette sauce for dipping.

MAKES 4 SERVINGS

of smoke (including most tars and PAHs) are in the oily phase, liquid smoke is relatively safe to use, but it does not preserve food. The smoke flavor in liquid smoke is quite concentrated, so it should be used judiciously.

How It Works • Wood pulp is primarily made of three elements that give smoke its character: cellulose, hemicellulose, and lignin. Cellulose and hemicellulose are polysaccharides (large sugar molecules), which oxidize into compounds that are similar to those in caramelized sugar when they burn. These elements give smoke sweet, fruity, and flowery flavor components. Lignin is made of extravagantly interlocked phenolic compounds. It is very hard and difficult to break down, so high concentrations make

wood burn hotter (mesquite is 64% lignin, hickory is 18%). When lignin breaks down it releases typical phenolic aromas of vanilla, clove, spiciness, and pungency.

The woods preferred for smoking tend to be those with a fairly equal balance of cellulose, hemicellulose, and lignin; these include most fruit woods and nut woods, such as oak. Evergreens, like pine or spruce, contain resins that produce an acrid sooty smoke, which makes them undesirable for smoking.

Keeping fire temperatures low not only reduces the amount of PAHs but it produces smoke that is more flavorful. The aromatic components in wood can be destroyed themselves if temperatures get too hot. The prime temperature for maximum flavor is around smoldering, between 570 and 750°F

(300 and 400°C). When burning wood logs, temperatures are regulated by adjusting oxygen flow through vents. When using wood chips or chunks, the wood is soaked to prolong the amount of time it takes for the wood to get to a combustible temperature of 800°F (425°C).

See Also • Barbecue

SNAPPER • See Fish

SNOW CRAB • See Crustacean

SOBA • See Pasta

SODA WATER • See Carbon Dioxide

SODIUM • See Salt

SOFFRITTO • See Sauces, Vegetables

SOFT-SHELL CLAM • See Mollusks

SOFT-SHELL CRAB • See Crustacean

SOFT WHEAT • See Wheat

SOLE • See Fish

SOMEN • See Pasta

SORBET • See Ice Cream

SORBITOL • See Sweeteners

SORGHUM • See Grains

SORREL • See Leaves

SOUFFLÉ • See Aeration, Foams

SOUP

What It Is • A basic assemblage of proteins, starches, vegetables, and broth neatly packed in a bowl, soups have been perfected into silken bisques, refined consommés, and hearty minestrones, but all soups are permutations of the same minor miracle: water transformed into a meal.

What It Does • Most soups, other than some fruit soups, start as a vegetable, fish, poultry, or meat broth.

The plainest soups, bouillons and consommés, are the most technically challenging. They are started with broth (*bouillon* is French for "broth"), strained of all

its solid ingredients. Because these soups are nothing but liquid, a strongly flavored broth is essential. It may be reduced to concentrate its flavors, or sometimes it is simmered with additional vegetables and meats and strained again. One of the principal charms of plain broth soups is the gelatinous mouth feel. If a broth is lacking in gelatin (which it gets from the collagen in meat and bones), it will be thin or watery and will not linger in the mouth long enough to deliver full flavor. The consistency of a bouillon can be adjusted by adding a pinch of unflavored gelatin to the cold broth, then heating it to dissolve the gelatin, which reinforces the broth's gelatin content.

A consommé is bouillon clarified with egg white. The egg whites are whisked into cold broth. The mixture is heated gradually and whisked continuously to keep the egg whites suspended. As it heats, the protein in the egg coagulates, making the broth appear cloudy and dirty. At a certain point the threads of egg solidify, which is the clue to stop stirring, allowing the web of egg to rise to the surface, trapping all of the minuscule elements in the broth that made it hazy. The set egg floats like a raft on the surface, and when the "raft" is removed it leaves behind a crystal clear liquid.

Additional solid ingredients are added to the broth to make most soups. Most of the time starchy ingredients, like grains, noodles, or potatoes, are cooked separately and then added to the finished soup so that their starch doesn't slough into the broth (exceptions include potato and bean soups that are thickened with the sloughed starch). Tender vegetables, fresh herbs, fish, or shellfish are usually added after the broth is fully flavored, since they would otherwise overcook. Some broth soups are lightly thickened with roux (flour mixed with fat) or a slurry (starch or flour mixed with water). Cream or milk is added to "cream of" soups to enrich the broth.

Soups can be made thicker by puréeing all or part of the solid ingredients. There are several styles of puréed soups. Bisques are rich, smooth soups (often made from seafood) that are puréed, strained, and then smoothed with some cream and sometimes starch. Puréed vegetable soups are often named for their dominant vegetable (usually something pulpy or starchy). Puréed fruit soups are more often a thinned sweetened purée that is more like a smoothie.

Chipotle Consommé

This postmodern consommé turns the soup's refined Old World image around with a smoky-spicy hit of New World chipotle peppers. If you have never clarified broth into consommé you are about to experience one of the most mind-blowing techniques of classic French cooking.

1 tbsp	gelatin (1¼ oz/7 g envelope)	15 mL
6 cups	chilled chicken broth, divided	1.5 L
¼ cup	tomato paste	50 mL
3 tbsp	minced onion	45 mL
1 tbsp	finely chopped cilantro	15 mL
1 tsp	minced canned chipotle in adobo sauce	5 mL
4	beaten egg whites	4
	Salt to taste	
12	fresh cilantro leaves, for garnish	12

1. In a bowl, combine gelatin in ½ cup (125 mL) of chicken broth. Let stand until softened, about 5 minutes. Place remaining broth in a heavy saucepan. Stir in gelatin mixture. Add tomato paste, onion, cilantro, chipotle, egg whites, and salt. Whisk until well blended and frothy.

2. Cook soup over medium heat, stirring frequently, until it becomes very cloudy. Stop stirring and bring to a boil. As soon as it does, a raft of egg white will form on the surface. Immediately reduce heat to a bare simmer. Using the handle of a wooden spoon, poke a hole about 2 inches (5 cm) in diameter in the raft, and simmer for 15 minutes without stirring.

3. Using a large slotted spoon, carefully lift out the raft and discard it. Strain soup through a sieve lined with several layers of damp cheesecloth, discarding solids. Reheat. Serve immediately, garnished with fresh cilantro leaves.

MAKES 4 SERVINGS

How It Works • Soups are almost always started by cooking flavorful ingredients — often called aromatics — lightly in a little oil. Known as sweating, the method concentrates flavorful juices and starts extracting them from the vegetables, herbs, and/or meats sweating in the pot, where they can then be captured with cold water.

Cold water is purer than water from a hot water tank (where minerals in the water tend to concentrate) and also takes longer to bring to a boil. The longer cooking time extracts more flavor. Add just enough water to cover the sweated ingredients by no more than a few inches, since more results in weak flavors, which will need to be concentrated by boiling off the excess water after the broth is finished. It's faster and easier to never add the additional water in the first place.

As soon as the liquid boils, reduce the heat so the broth barely simmers, and skim off any debris floating on the surface. This debris, known unfortunately as "scum," is not harmful or dirty. Made mostly of tiny bits of coagulated protein, it will cloud the soup and eventually coagulate. Also avoid vigorous boiling, which can break the solid ingredients apart, causing the broth to become murky.

Broths should simmer just until they are full flavored, about 45 minutes for fish broths (dashi, Japanese fish broth, is an exception; it simmers for just a few seconds), 1½ hours for vegetable broths, 2 to 3 hours for chicken broths, and 4 to 6 hours for meat broths (brown broths leaning toward longer cooking times). Simmering for too long results in an overcooked stewed flavor.

When broth is finished cooking, it can be strained or not. Inedible items like bones and whole herbs or spices are removed before finishing the broth or stock into a soup.

When making soups with fully flavored canned or boxed broths, an initial period of sweating is still important, but, once the broth is added, the soup needs to simmer only until the solid ingredients are tender.

Bouillon cubes or soup bases are broth (or stock) concentrates made by dehydrating

Broth vs. Stock
Broth and stock are made similarly and from similar ingredients — meat and/or bones, vegetables, seasonings, and water simmered into a flavorful liquid. In contemporary usage the terms are interchangeable, although classically there is a difference. Stocks are made mostly from bone, while broths are made mostly from meat. Stocks have a richer consistency from the collagen in bone, and broths a meatier flavor. In addition, stocks are always strained and broths are sometimes served with the solid ingredients that flavored them.

Chefs use stocks in a variety of dishes, including soups, sauces, braised items, and glazes. Stocks are never served as is because they are too bland, but this is a trait that makes them versatile. Broths, more common in home cooking, are made to be eaten as is or enhanced with more substantial, chunky ingredients.

broth. *Glace de viande* is the classic French version of soup base, prepared by reducing a flavorful beef or veal broth down to one-sixteenth of its original volume. *Glace de viande* gels into a solid as it chills, and can be stored in the refrigerator for up to a month. *Glace de volaille* is poultry base, and *glace de poisson* is fish soup base.

See Also • Sauces

SOUR CREAM • See Fermentation

SOURDOUGH • See Bread

SOUR MILK • See Fermentation

SOUR ORANGE • See Citrus

SOURSOP • See Fruit

SOUS VIDE • See Vacuum

SOYBEAN OIL • See Oil

SOYBEANS

What It Is • All **legumes** are good sources of **protein**, but the soybean is unusually well endowed. It has twice as much protein as other beans, with a near-perfect complement of amino acids. It provides an ample amount of mild-tasting oil that is high in polyunsaturated fatty acids. And its flesh is bland, which has made it the darling of food manufacturers, who process it into everything from highly flavored fermented sauces to imitation bacon.

What It Does • Soybeans have been cultivated in Asia for more than 3,000 years and are still a major crop in China, Korea, and Japan. The U.S. is now the largest grower of soybeans, harvesting 55% of the world's production, of which one-third is exported and most of the rest is processed for oil. Most of the defatted soy meal that remains after oil extraction is steamed (called toasting), ground, and used as livestock feed (mostly for poultry and pigs, but increasingly aquaculture-farmed fish, especially catfish). The rest is more carefully heated to minimize denaturing the soy protein (about 50% of the meal) so that it can be extruded as hydrolyzed vegetable protein (HVP) for the production of soy protein products.

Mature soybeans have a number of traits that make them unappealing as food. Unlike other legumes, they are fairly low in starch, which keeps them from developing a creamy consistency during cooking, and they tend to remain firm even after hours of boiling. They are high in indigestible sugars (oligosaccharides) and fiber, which makes us gassy, and when boiled in the usual way they have a stronger beany flavor than most other legumes, which can be minimized by cooking them in a pressure cooker.

Young soybeans are completely different. If harvested while still small and green, soybeans are sweet and tender, are lower in indigestible substances, and have a barely perceptible beany flavor. Fresh soybeans (*edamame* in Japanese, *mau dou* in Chinese) are specially grown to be eaten young, at about 80% of maturity. They are typically sold frozen and are boiled for a few minutes in salted water. They can be eaten right out of the pod as a snack, shelled and cooked in soups and stews, or served as a vegetable side dish.

There are two traditional methods for making soy milk. Both start by soaking the beans until they are soft and then grinding the resulting mash. In Japan, the mash is cooked and then strained to remove the solids. In China (where there is evidence of soy milk production in the 2nd century BCE) the mash is strained first and then the milk is cooked. Each method produces a watery liquid dispersed with droplets of protein and fat (similar to the structure of animal milk) with a strong soy flavor. Modern methods limit bean flavors by heating the soaked beans quickly before grinding and then straining. In the West, soy milk is usually seen as an alternative to cow's milk, but in China and Japan it is a raw

Spicy Lemongrass Tofu

The bland creamy personality of tofu is ignited with an intensely spicy and savory marinade. The flavor is kept high by keeping the marinade dry. There's very little liquid to water down the fragrance of lemongrass and the bite of chiles. The dryness of the marinade also helps the tofu to crisp and brown dramatically rather than steam.

¼ cup	finely chopped fresh lemongrass	50 mL
1 tbsp	minced fresh gingerroot	15 mL
1 tsp	Asian chili paste	5 mL
1½ tbsp	soy sauce	22 mL
4 tsp	granulated sugar, divided	20 mL
1 tsp	ground turmeric	5 mL
½ tsp	kosher salt	2 mL
1 lb	firm or extra-firm tofu, cut into 4 thick slices	500 g
¼ cup	rice wine vinegar	50 mL
1 tbsp	freshly squeezed lime juice	15 mL
1 tsp	Thai fish sauce (nam pla)	5 mL
2 to 3 tbsp	soybean oil	25 to 45 mL
1 cup	baby greens	250 mL

1. In a small bowl, combine lemongrass, ginger, chili paste, soy sauce, 2 tsp (10 mL) sugar, turmeric, and salt. Rub mixture all over tofu slices and let stand at room temperature to marinate for 30 minutes.

2. Meanwhile, in a small saucepan over medium heat, heat vinegar and remaining sugar, stirring, until sugar dissolves. Add lime juice and fish sauce. Set aside to cool.

3. In a large skillet, heat oil over medium heat until very hot. Add tofu and cook, turning once, until browned on both sides, about 4 minutes per side.

4. Serve a piece of tofu topped with a small mound of greens. Drizzle with some of the vinaigrette.

MAKES 4 SERVINGS

product for the manufacturing of tofu.

Tofu (bean curd) is curdled soy milk. The soy milk is heated, and salts are added to coagulate the protein in the milk, separating it from the water. As the proteins draw together they form a mass, trapping the protein-coated oil droplets with them into a curd. The remaining "whey" is drained off, and the curd is pressed to form a cohesive solid. The firmed curd is cut into blocks, packed in water, and sold as firm tofu. Firm tofu has the moist texture of raw meat. For extra-firm tofu, the drained curd is broken to release more water and then pressed. Extra-firm tofu is more resilient and denser than firm tofu, similar to semifirm cheese. Silken tofu is softer than regular tofu and is very moist and custard-like. It is made by coagulating soy milk in its packaging, so it remains almost intact, full of moisture, and very delicate. Tofu skin is the skin that develops on the surface of soy milk when it is simmered. It is a thin, mild, chewy sheet that is used as wrappers for sweet and savory fillings or folded and shaped into a variety of meat substitutes.

Tofu can be puréed into sauces, simmered in soups, baked, grilled, sautéed, or fried. Soft tofu is usually reserved for making purées and desserts, although in China it is sometimes fermented by soaking it in fish sauce. Called stinky tofu, it is quite pungent. Tofu is also pickled with chiles, or mixed with flavors during curding to produce fruit tofus, coconut tofu, or almond tofu. Freezing tofu produces a spongy aerated curd, called thousand layer tofu. During freezing, the water in the tofu (firm tofu is about 85% water) turns into ice crystals that puncture the smooth curd. When the curd thaws, the melted ice flows out, leaving behind a condensed, lightly chewy mass of protein similar in texture to cooked pork. Thousand layer tofu is especially absorbent, so it readily takes on the flavors of a sauce.

How It Works • Many of the iconic flavors identified with Asian cooking — fish sauce, soy sauce, miso, tempeh, and natto — are products of protein **fermentation**, which develops when microbes break down proteins

fast fact

- Henry Ford's interest in soybeans as a raw material for the production of industrial plastics led to the inclusion of two bushels' worth of soybeans in the plastic elements of every Ford car during the 1930s. He also helped to manufacture the first commercially produced soy milk, soy ice cream, and nondairy soy whipped topping.

into amino acids and these acids recombine into rich, savory flavors. The original fermented sauces were made from meat or fish, but by the second century BCE animal flesh had been replaced by soybeans, because they were more readily available and produced a more consistent fermentation.

Traditionally, fermented miso is started by cooking grain, usually rice or barley, or sometimes soybeans in water until soft. *Aspergillus* mold is added to the starchy mash and allowed to germinate for about two days, during which time the molds' enzymes metabolize the starch and protein for energy. The mash is then combined with freshly cooked soybeans and salt. The salt kills the mold, but the enzymes stay active, feasting on the newly added soy. At the same time, salt-resistant bacteria and yeasts start to break down the proteins and starches further, and the mixture is left to ferment for a few months to a few years. The resulting miso paste is a

science wise

Roundup Ready Soybeans • Soybeans are one of the crops that have been most effectively genetically modified. In 1995, the Monsanto Company introduced Roundup Ready (RR) soybeans containing DNA that had been altered to survive spraying with glyphosate, a nonselective herbicidal chemical. The modification allows farmers to plant RR soy in uncleared, untilled fields and then spray the fields with Roundup herbicide, which kills all other vegetation except the soybeans. In 1997, 8% of the soybeans planted in the U.S. were Roundup Ready. In 2006, 89% were. RR soybeans cannot be sold in countries that have regulations against genetically modified food.

complex amalgam of rich, savory, pungent flavors with overtones of fruity esters. Modern industrial miso products are fermented for only a few weeks and are much less complex than traditionally long-fermented miso.

Like miso, soy sauce can be made from any combination of soy and grain. Chinese soy sauce and Japanese tamari soy sauce are 100% fermented soybeans. Japanese and higher-grade North American soy sauces are usually fermented from an equal proportion of soy and wheat. The wheat provides more sugar than soybeans, which makes the soy sauce sweeter and gives it a higher alcohol content and more aromatics, like fruity esters. Shiro, or white soy sauce, is lighter in color and flavor because of a higher proportion of wheat. Budget soy sauce products are not fermented at all. They are ground soybeans that have been chemically digested with hydrochloric acid and some added salt and sugar.

Tempeh and natto are soy condiments that go through one quick fermentation without bacteria or salt, producing fresher, cleaner, less roasted flavors. Tempeh is made from a thin layer of cooked soybeans fermented at relatively warm temperatures with *Rhizopus oligosporus* mold for about 24 hours until the protein and oil are separated. It has a mushroomy aroma and a meaty texture when fried. Natto is cooked soybeans mixed with bacteria and fermented for 20 hours at about 100°F (38°C) into a fragrant sweet and savory membrane. Natto has a slimy texture that allows it to be stretched into delicate threads.

Fermented bean paste (black or red bean paste) is made from the solids left over from fermenting soy sauce. **Hoisin** sauce is fermented bean paste mixed with wheat flour, sugar, vinegar, and chiles.

See Also • Hoisin, Legumes, Protein

SOY PRODUCTS • See Soybeans

SPÄTZLE • See Dumpling, Pasta

SPEARMINT • See Herbs

SPELT • See Grains

SPICES

What It Is • Spices are the aromatic dried roots, bark, buds, fruits, and seeds of plants and have been enlivening our senses for at least 4,000 years. Unlike **herbs** (aromatic leaves and sometimes stems or flowers), which can be used fresh or dried, spices are always dried.

What It Does • Many spices develop their characteristic **flavor** as they are dried, when **enzymes** in the plant, still active after harvesting, break down the plant's cell structure, releasing volatile aromatic oils. The fact that spices benefit from drying also benefits us. Most spices are from a tropical climate, which means they must travel thousands of miles to come to market, and since spices must be harvested at specific points in their growing cycle, drying has had a profound influence on the ability of people to ship, trade, and store spices. It is the reason that Egyptians in 2000 BCE were able to import cinnamon from China (cinnamon is still an important spice in North African cooking), and why archaeologists in Syria have discovered cloves dating from 1700 BCE, when cloves were grown only on a few Indonesian islands.

Just a few spices are spicy, meaning hot. Chiles, peppercorns, and members of the mustard and ginger families all contain chemicals that irritate tissues in our mouth and nose, triggering a pain reaction that we experience as a sensation of burning. Most spices do not cause pain.

In order to be perceived, aromatic compounds must be airborne to reach the sensory receptors in our nasal passages. We take them in through olfactory sensors far up in the nose just by breathing, and more forcefully through sniffing. When food is heated, more of its aroma is released into the air, so it is important when cooking with spices to always cook them thoroughly, and to serve spiced food above 100°F (38°C) for full flavor perception.

Toasting spices before grinding them heightens their aroma. No additional fat is necessary because spices release their own oils as they heat. Just heat the pan over medium heat, add the spices, and stir until they are aromatic, which usually takes less than a minute. Remove them from the hot pan right away and grind in a spice mill, mini-chopper, or mortar and pestle. Always grind spices right before you use them. As soon as spices are ground their aromatic oils start to oxidize, which diminishes their flavor but also starts to produce rancid flavors. Avoid buying seed spices ground (bark spices, like cinnamon and cassia, or rhizomes, like ginger and turmeric, are too hard to grind with home appliances so they must be purchased ground). Store all spices in a cool, dark cabinet. Whole seeds will stay aromatic for about one year; ground spices should be used within four to six months of purchase.

The chemicals that produce aromas are fat soluble, so cooking spices in oil or fat increases their flavor more than simmering in watery liquids would. This is why when making a soup or stew, the spices are added to the sautéed ingredients rather than to the liquid ingredients.

science wise

The Preservative Power of Spices •
The defensive compounds that make up the flavor sensations of spices have antimicrobial properties. The chemicals that make peppers irritating to your tongue can be toxic enough to kill a microbe. Combined with salt, spices are used to preserve sausages and pickles. However, it takes a large amount of spice and salt to preserve ingredients effectively, and spicing should not be used at home in place of refrigeration.

The idea that spices were used in the past to mask the flavor of tainted meat is a myth. If anyone had ever tried the practice he probably wouldn't have lived long enough to pass it on. The mistaken notion probably comes from the fact that before refrigeration was commonplace, many ingredients were heavily spiced and salted for preservation. The level of spicing in historic recipes seems unpalatable to us today, so we rationalize that it could only be desirable as a way of masking flavors that are even more distasteful.

How It Works

Have you ever sucked on a cinnamon stick or gnawed a clove? The experience can be quite distasteful. That is because the aromatic chemicals that give these spices their flavor are mostly defensive compounds used by the plant to keep predators away. They are meant to irritate. However, when consumed in small amounts, what was irritating becomes stimulating. All you need is a pinch of most spices to flavor several portions of food.

When we taste a particular spice, its flavor comes through as a complex but singular sensation. In truth the flavor of most spices is a combination of several flavorful compounds. For example, the sweet floral fragrance of cardamom comes from a blend of cineole (a cinnamon-like flavor), limonene (a citrusy flavor), and linalool (floral) compounds.

See Also • Flavor, Herbs

Common Flavor Compounds in Herbs and Spices

Chemical	Flavor	Found In
Ambrettolide	Musk	Licorice
Anethole	Anise	Aniseeds, fennel seeds, star anise
Caryophyllene	Woody	Allspice, black pepper, cinnamon, clove
Cineole	Eucalyptus	Allspice, cardamom, cinnamon, cubeb pepper, galangal, ginger, nutmeg, turmeric
Cinnamaldehyde	Cinnamon	Cassia, cinnamon, cumin
Cuminaldehyde	Cumin	Cumin seeds
Citronellal	Citrus	Szechwan pepper
Cymene	Citrus	Cumin seeds
Estragole	Anise	Star anise
Eugenol	Clove	Allspice, cinnamon, clove, galangal
Geraniol	Floral	Galangal, nutmeg, Szechwan pepper
Humulene	Herbal, hoppy	Annatto, coriander seeds, grains of paradise
Limonene	Citrus	Annatto, black pepper, caraway, cardamom, celery seeds, dill seeds, nutmeg, star anise, sumac
Linalool	Floral	Cardamom, cinnamon, coriander seeds, ginger, star anise, Szechwan pepper
Myristicin	Wood	Nutmeg
Paeonol	Mint	Licorice
Phellandrene	Eucalyptus	Cumin, ginger, Szechwan pepper
Pinene	Pine	Black pepper, cardamom, coriander, cumin, juniper, mace, mint, nutmeg, Szechwan pepper, sumac
Sabinene	Spicy, woody	Cardamom, juniper, mace, nutmeg, peppercorns
Saffrole	Sassafras	Nutmeg
S-carvone	Caraway	Caraway, dill seeds
Terpineol	Floral	Cardamom, cubeb pepper
Zingiberene	Ginger	Ginger

Spice Chart

Spices are one of the elements that define a cuisine, but unlike fresh ingredients that are often native to the geography, most spices traveled halfway around the world to become an integral part of a country's food. The cayenne pepper in Southeast Asian stir-fries is a New World native, and the cinnamon in an all-American apple pie is originally from and still grows mostly in Southeast Asia. This chart lists most of the spices you will encounter in the kitchen, along with some popular spice blends that are integral to cuisines.

Spice	Other Names	Description	Uses
Ajwain (ajowan)	Carom seeds	Dried pods of bishop's weed; egg shaped; deeply creviced; tastes like thyme, cumin, caraway	Indian paratha and samosas, West African berbere spice blend, curries
Aleppo pepper	Halaby pepper	Form of mild capsaicin; similar to ancho in intensity; faint aroma of cumin	Syrian cuisine, especially with fish
Allspice	Jamaica pepper, myrtle pepper, pimento	Dried berry similar to clove, cinnamon, and nutmeg	Main part of jerk spices, moles, and pickling spices, spice cakes
Aniseeds	Anise	Small seed tastes of licorice; sweet	Sweet breads, Indian seafood
Annatto seeds	Achiote	Dimpled pyramid-shaped seeds, dark brick red	Colors butter, cheese; achiote paste used in Mexican meat dishes
Asafetida	Devil's dung	Dried gum of giant fennel; pungent fermented flavor, smells of old garlic; thickens when moistened	Cooked with lentils and in curries in Indian dishes
Ashanti pepper	West African black pepper	Similar to black pepper but more aromatic, like cubeb pepper	West Africa berbere spice blend, soups and stews
Berbere		Blend of various peppers, ginger, clove, coriander, allspice, rue berries, and ajwain	Sauces for meats, lentils, and vegetables
Caraway	Wild cumin	Elongated ridged seed tastes of eucalyptus, citrus, and fennel	Scandinavian and German cheeses, rye bread, curries, pork dishes, sauerkraut
Cardamom	Thai cardamom	Dried pale green pod containing 3 or 4 brown to black pungent seeds with sweet floral ginger-like flavor	Danish pastry, biryani rice dishes, sweet puddings
Cassia	Baker's cinnamon, false cinnamon	Bark of tropical evergreen; similar to cinnamon but coarser in flavor	Interchangeable with cinnamon
Celery seeds	Smallage	Tiny brown seeds from wild celery; astringent celery taste, similar to caraway	Pickling spice, in Bloody Mary mix and vegetable juice blends, common in seafood and poultry spice blends
Chile (chili)	Hot pepper	Widely diverse group of fiery spices (see Capsicums, page 95)	Flaked and crushed or in hot pepper blends in Latin American, Asian, African, and Caribbean cuisines
Cinnamon	Cinnamon bark	Fragrant bark of tropical tree; sweet, woody, fruity	Cakes, curries, beef dishes, teas, Moroccan tagines
Clove		Pungent dried flower bud and stem; dark brown; sweet, spicy, numbing	Cakes, stewed fruit, smoked meats, pickles, curries, mulled beverages
Coriander seeds		Beige to tan, perfect ridged spheres; taste like lemon and sage	Curries, pickling spices, harissa, berbere blends, ras el hanout
Cubeb pepper	Ashanti pepper	Dried dark red berry; pungent, slightly bitter, with terpene overtones	Moroccan pastry, West African stews, Indonesian curries
Cumin	Black cumin	Small dark brown elongated seeds; warm earthy, slightly bitter	Chili powder, Indian curries and breads, berbere spice blend
Curry		Mixture of spices, usually powdered; the most famous is Madras curry, which usually includes coriander, cumin, turmeric, ginger, mustard, fenugreek, cinnamon, clove, cardamom, chiles, and black pepper	Indian stews

Spice	Other Names	Description	Uses
Dill seeds		Pale brown oval seeds; pungent with aromas of anise and caraway	Pickles, rye bread, cabbage dishes
Fennel seeds		Small pale green seeds; licorice flavor	Breads, Italian sausages and pasta sauces, satay sauce, Malay curries
Fenugreek	Bird's foot, cow's horn, goat's horn, methi	Golden tan gravel-looking seeds; sharp tasting, slightly spicy, and leguminous in flavor; bitter and nutty when toasted	Indian curries, fresh sprouts, pickles, baked goods, extract used to make artificial maple syrup
Five-spice powder		Blend of cassia, clove, fennel, Szechwan pepper, star anise	Chinese red cooking (simmering in soy sauce)
Galangal (galingale)	Java root, Siamese ginger	Rhizome in ginger family; similar to ginger	Thai curries, ras el hanout
Garam masala		Spice blend like curry powder without warm cumin and caraway notes; contains black pepper, fennel, cinnamon, caraway, clove, cardamom	Basic Indian seasoning
Ginger		Rhizome used fresh and dried; sweet, spicy, warm, lightly floral	Cakes, cookies, and breads, curries, Chinese all-purpose flavor, tandoori blends, quatre épices
Grains of paradise	Alligator pepper, ginny grains, Guinea grains, melegueta pepper	Dark brown roundish seeds; pungent piney peppery flavor	Tunisian stews
Harissa		Blend of chiles, garlic, paprika, caraway, coriander, cumin, and mint	Basic Tunisian condiment, used in many dishes
Juniper	Juniper berries	Dried fleshy dark brown berries; piney savory flavor	Game meat, gin
Licorice root	Black sugar, sweetroot	Gray-green root; sweet anise flavor	Candies, Chinese stock, meats, and seafood
Long pepper	Indian long pepper, pipalli	Dried spike-shaped fruit; dark brown; tastes of black pepper and ancho chile	Indian pickles, Southeast Asian cooking
Mace		Red covering of nutmeg; similar flavor to nutmeg but more delicate; contains myristicin (a narcotic)	Sweet spice blends for baked products, cream sauce, sausage, garam masala
Mahleb	Mach lepi	Tan oval pits of wild black cherry; floral sweet almond flavor	Middle Eastern breads, pastries, and sweets
Mustard seeds	Brown mustard, Chinese mustard, yellow (white) mustard	Dried tiny round yellow, black, or brown seeds; becomes sharp and biting when mixed with liquid	Pickles, curries, salad dressing, panch phora blend, smoked meats
Nigella seeds	Charnushka, kalonji, devil-in-the-bush, love-in-a-mist	Small black tear-shaped seeds; nutty, sweet carrot flavor	Cheese, flatbreads, curries, panch phora blend, potato dishes
Nutmeg	Muskat	Large tan seeds; warm, pungent, slightly bitter	Pâtés, custards, spice cake and cream sauces, such as béchamel
Panch phoron (panch puran, panch phora)	Bengali five-spice powder	Blend of cumin, fennel, fenugreek, mustard seeds, nigella seeds	Indian potato, lentil, and fish dishes
Paprika	Hot paprika, Hungarian paprika, pimentón, Spanish paprika, sweet paprika, sweet pepper	Orange to red dried sweet pepper	Goulash, egg dishes, sauces, roast meats, poultry

continued on next page

Spice Chart (continued)

Spice	Other Names	Description	Uses
Peppercorn: black, green, pink, Tellicherry: white	Black peppercorns, green peppercorns, pink peppercorns, Tellicherry peppercorns, white peppercorns	Fragrant, spicy dried berry of tropical vine; black peppercorns are unripe (pungent); green are unripe and treated with brine or freeze-dried to keep the skin from darkening (fresh tasting); pink are ripe (sweet and mild); white are unripe and peeled (hotter and less fragrant); Tellicherry are high-grade black peppercorns from India (aromatic)	All-purpose wherever a mild spiciness is wanted
Quatre épices		Spice blend of white pepper, nutmeg, clove, ginger	French charcuterie seasoning
Ras el hanout		Blend of 20 spices, mainly cardamom, cassia, chiles, clove, cumin, mace, rose petals	Moroccan tagines
Saffron	Azafran	Stigma of crocus; floral and honey-like aroma; red before cooking, and turns everything it touches bright golden	Rice dishes such as paella, risotto Milanese; seafood dishes such as bouillabaisse; egg breads
Shichimi	Shichimi-togarashi	Japanese spice mixture of mandarin orange peel, sesame seeds, poppy seeds, hemp seeds, nori, sansho or Szechwan pepper	Table condiment for soups, noodle dishes, and tempura
Star anise	Badian, Chinese anise	Dried star-shaped fruit; mahogany brown; sweet anise flavor	Chinese savory dishes, especially chicken, pork, and duck
Sumac	Elm-leaves sumac, Sicilian sumac	Dried ground burgundy berries of edible sumac; tart flavor of sour apples	Middle Eastern savory dishes, garnish for flatbread
Szechwan peppercorns	Chinese pepper, Japan pepper, Sichuan pepper, Szechwan pepper	Dried red berries, split and papery; fragrant; citrus and lavender flavor	Chinese meat preparations, especially duck; Japanese soups
Turmeric	Indian saffron, yellow ginger	Dried tropical rhizome; golden yellow; warm and earthy aroma	Indian curries, Moroccan tagines, pickles
Za'atar		Middle Eastern spice blend of thyme, sumac, sesame, and salt	Middle Eastern chicken and fish dishes, flatbreads

SPINACH • See Leaves

SPINY LOBSTER • See Crustacean

SPIRITS • See Liquor

SPIT-ROASTING • See Roasting

SPLEEN • See Organ Meats

SPLENDA • See Sweeteners

SPONGE • See Bread

SPOT • See Fish

SPRATS • See Fish

SPRING WATER • See Water

SPRING WHEAT • See Wheat

SPROUTS • See Legumes

SPRUE • See Gluten

SQUAB • See Game

SQUASH

What It Is • The Cucurbitaceae family includes squash, **melons**, **cucumbers**, and gourds. All have a protective rind covering a layer of thick flesh that surrounds a soft, pulpy core containing the seeds, which are usually small and numerous. Although all members of the family have the same component parts, the proportion of moisture, fiber, sugar, and starch in each gives them widely varied characteristics.

Summer squash are picked young, when they're still mild, moist, and tender. They are fairly perishable; they are best eaten immediately after harvesting but will keep for a few weeks under refrigeration. Winter squash are sweet and starchy, and hearty enough to store for months without refrigeration. "Melon" usually refers to those family members that are super-moist and full of sugar, and cucumbers are also full of juice. Gourds are hard dried squash that are largely inedible, so they are commonly turned into utilitarian objects such as bowls and bottles.

The names of Cucurbitaceae are sometimes used interchangeably, which can be confusing. For instance, pumpkin pie is made from small, tender sugar pumpkins, which shouldn't be confused with large, tough jack-o'-lantern pumpkins that are really gourds. Bitter gourds (sometimes called bitter melons) are small immature squash that are eaten stuffed and roasted in Asia.

What It Does ● Winter squash are harvested fully mature, with hard rinds and flesh firm enough to sauté or stew without losing shape, but after simmering their flesh becomes soft enough to mash into a smooth, creamy purée. Winter squash are slightly sweet, which allows them to be equally good in savory and sweet preparations, from soups and stews to pies and cheesecake. Their tough skin and relatively hollow core are used as edible vessels.

Many winter squash are rich in beta-carotenes and can be kept for months in a cool, dry place. Although they are available year-round, they tend to be best soon after harvest in late fall. Winter squash come in a variety of shapes and sizes, but most varieties, including acorn squash, buttercup, butternut, Hubbard, and sugar pumpkin, are

fast fact
- In Africa and Asia large gourds are made into lutes and drums.

interchangeable in recipes. However, spaghetti squash is not interchangeable with others. It is low in **starch** and high in fiber, so instead of becoming creamy as it cooks, it separates into thousands of al dente strands that resemble spaghetti. Spaghetti squash has fewer calories than other winter squash, and 11 times less vitamin A.

Summer squash are harvested before they have developed a thick rind and significant fiber, starch, or sugar, so they tend to be bland and fragile. They are tender enough to eat raw, skin and all, and should be only briefly sautéed or grilled, or added to a soup or stew in the last minutes. Too much heat causes them to lose shape, and the little flavor they have evaporates.

Although any winter squash can be harvested young and cooked as a summer squash, the varieties grown for summer

Acorn Squash Filled with Pumpkin Seed Risotto

As risotto cooks, starch from the rice sloughs into the simmering liquid, thickening it into a sauce. In this elaborate side dish or vegetarian main dish, the risotto acts as a sauce and filling for the squash. Usually you need to serve risotto immediately, lest it solidify into a paste, but by baking it inside a squash the rice is kept tender and moist as it takes on the flavor of the baking vegetable.

1 tbsp	extra virgin olive oil	15 mL
¼ cup	finely chopped onion	50 mL
1 cup	Arborio rice	250 mL
½ cup	white wine	125 mL
4½ cups	vegetable broth	1.125 L
4	acorn squash	4
1 tbsp	freshly squeezed lemon juice	15 mL
1 tbsp	Worcestershire sauce	15 mL
1 cup	canned small white beans, drained and rinsed	250 mL
½ cup	toasted green pumpkin seeds (pepitas)	125 mL
1 tbsp	dark sesame oil	15 mL
¼ cup	freshly grated Parmesan cheese	50 mL

1. Preheat oven to 400°F (200°C).

2. In a large saucepan, heat oil over medium heat. Add onion and cook, stirring often, until tender, about 4 minutes.

3. Add rice and stir until coated with oil. Add wine and cook, stirring occasionally with a wooden spoon, until wine has been absorbed. Add broth, ½ cup (125 mL) at a time, and cook, stirring often, until each addition of broth is absorbed before stirring in the next addition, and rice is al dente, with a creamy sauce developed throughout, about 20 minutes.

4. Meanwhile, cut a thin slice from the pointed ends of the acorn squash so that they can stand upright, slice off about ½ inch (1 cm) stem ends and save as lids, hollow out interior cavity, and discard seeds and wet pulp. Sprinkle inside of each squash with lemon juice and Worcestershire sauce and place in a baking dish just large enough to hold the squash snuggly. Set aside.

5. Stir beans, pumpkin seeds, sesame oil, and Parmesan into rice. Fill squash with risotto, and top each with a squash "lid." Pour ¼ inch (0.5 cm) water into the dish around the squash, cover loosely with foil, and bake in preheated oven until squash are tender, about 45 minutes.

MAKES 4 MAIN-DISH SERVINGS

squash tend to be those that do not develop starch as they mature and therefore remain watery even when fully grown. Common varieties include crookneck, pattypan, and zucchini (vegetable marrow).

One squash, winter melon (wax melon), is eaten in Asia as a summer squash when young and as a winter squash when mature. The squash gets its name from a layer of wax that covers the ripe fruit so thickly that it can be scraped off and used for making candles. Thousands of wax-producing glands cover the young fruit like fine hair, hence its other name, fuzzy melon. Like other summer squash, fuzzy melons are sautéed, which makes their flesh transparent and jelly-like.

Bitter gourds, or bitter melons, are prized in Asia for a bitterness that is spurned in many Western cuisines. The bitter compounds, cucurbitacins, are the same that plague some cucumbers. Bitter gourds are pale green and warty and usually eaten young. When grown to full maturity, they are too bitter to eat. Even young fruits are blanched to remove some of the water-soluble cucurbitacins before being stuffed and roasted.

Chayote (mirliton) is an unusual squash. Grown mostly in equatorial climates, chayotes are harvested young like summer squash, but their flesh is denser and therefore takes longer to cook. Otherwise they are mild and moist like summer squash. Chayote look like large wrinkly pears, and instead of containing many small seeds, they have a large center pit similar to a mango pit.

Squash bear both male and female flowers. Only female flowers produce fruit, so the male blossoms are needed only for fertilization. Since the pollen from a single male blossom can pollinate an entire vine of female blossoms, the extra male blossoms are often fried in batter or stuffed with creamy cheese before being fried. Squash blossoms are slightly bitter and taste subtly like winter squash. Squash seeds can be toasted and eaten as a snack or used as garnish. Pumpkin seeds are particularly popular in Mexico, where they are sold as street food or ground to thicken sauces.

How It Works ● Young squash (summer squash) are mostly water. As they cook, pectin and hemicellulose in their cell walls are released, which gives their juices a slight gelatinous consistency. In contrast, mature squash (winter squash) are fibrous, starchy, and sweet. As they cook, the starch, mostly amylopectin, bonds with the water in the vegetable, causing the starch to swell and forming a soft gel that gives cooked winter squash a plush, creamy texture. With long cooking some of the starch breaks down into sugar, which is why squash simmered long enough to purée tastes sweeter than chunks of squash simmered in a soup or stew.

See Also ● Vegetables

SQUID • See Cephalopod

STACHYOSE • See Sugar

STAINLESS STEEL • See Cookware, Knives

STALING • See Starch

STALKS • See Stems

STAPHYLOCOCCUS • See Bacteria

STAR ANISE • See Spices

STARCH

What It Is ● Plants store most of their energy as starch. Starches are composed of long chains of glucose (sugar) molecules packed into the roots and tubers of plants for long-term underground storage and into the seeds of grains and legumes to provide energy for the developing embryos. They are held within plant cells in special starch-containing units called amyloplasts. During the day, when energy is being produced through photosynthesis, sugars are combined into starches and stored in the amyloplasts. At night, the amyloplasts convert the starch back into sugar to meet the plant's energy needs.

Cornstarch is the most common plant starch used in cooking. Others include rice starch, potato starch, arrowroot, tapioca, and kudzu root starch. To separate the starch from the protein, fiber, and fat that surround it, corn goes through a wet milling process. The hull and germ are removed and the endosperm is ground and centrifuged to separate the less dense protein from the denser starch granules.

Modified food starch, used in food manufacturing, is also pure starch, but it has been altered by cross-linking starches with various properties to create conjoined starch molecules specially designed to withstand the high temperatures of vacuum-packaging, the freezing temperatures of frozen foods, the shearing action of industrial pumps, or the strong acids in a salad dressing or marinade.

Hydrolyzed starch (usually corn or potato starch) is starch that has been exposed to acids and enzymes in order to hydrolyze it into individual sugars. Hydrolyzing starches rids them of grainy flavors, and if the starch is broken down enough it becomes sweet. Corn syrup and high-fructose syrup are examples of highly hydrolyzed starches that have been broken down into individual sugar molecules so that they can be used as low-cost sweeteners, mostly in candies and beverages.

What It Does ● Raw starch molecules are held together by hydrogen bonds and are tightly packed into hard granules that taste starchy when chewed. Raw starch resists

fast fact

- Sago, the powdered starch derived from the pith of the trunk of the sago palm, looks like and is interchangeable with tapioca starch in recipes. It is a staple food in New Guinea and the only starch that comes from a plant stem.

digestion and has a tendency to make us gassy. But when starch is heated in water, the hydrogen bonds are broken, water enters the granules, and they swell and the starch becomes more digestible. This is called starch gelatinization, and for most starches it occurs somewhere between 140 and 160°F (60 and 71°C). The swollen granules are large and inhibit water mobility so thicken whatever they are in. They are also quite fragile and are disrupted by agitation and so the viscosity tends to decrease as they are cooked longer, especially if severely stirred.

When a cake reaches its gelatinization point it will appear done — it will smell cooked, and the batter will be set enough so that nothing but a moist crumb will cling to a tester inserted into the center of the cake. In sauce making, it is the point at which a sauce becomes clear and thick.

In some starchy vegetables, such as baking potatoes, the swollen starch granules remain separate when cooked, giving a mealy texture. If the vegetable is also sweet, such as a sweet potato, the sugar will attract some of the moisture during cooking, keeping it away from the starch and resulting in a creamier texture. If a vegetable has sugar but no starch, like a carrot, its cooked texture will be watery.

Cornstarch is most commonly used to thicken sauces, but it also tenderizes doughs and batters. Rice starch, made from much finer starch granules, has an especially fine-grained texture.

The starch from roots and tubers form larger granules and thicken more readily. For example, potato starch becomes grainy as it thickens and tapioca becomes stringy. Potato starch will smooth eventually, but it will also become thin if overcooked. The advantage of root starches is their neutral flavor.

Pure starches cannot be smoothly integrated directly into boiling liquid. They must first be softened in cold liquid so that the starch granules absorb a small amount of water and separate from one another. Adding dry starch directly to hot sauce causes the surface of the starch to gelatinize on contact, trapping the remaining starch inside the gelatinized coating, thus forming a lump. For example, at room temperature cornstarch can absorb about 30% of its own weight in water. That is enough to turn it into a paste, which will sink to the bottom of the bowl of water as soon as you stop stirring. When the paste is whisked into boiling liquid, the softened starch

Olive Oil Crunch

Maltodextrin, partially hydrolyzed starch, is able to absorb more than twice its volume in saturated fat, like bacon fat or cocoa butter, and about half its volume in unsaturated oil. Avant-garde chefs mix tapioca maltodextrin with flavorful fats to create ethereally textured powders and savory-sweet crunchy crumbs that can be scattered over salad, sautéed seafood, or roasted fruit. Use this olive oil crumble as a garnish for salad, a crusty dusting on a plate of pasta, or mixed into gremolata to scatter over a poached fish fillet.

⅓ cup	tapioca maltodextrin	75 mL
2 tbsp	extra virgin olive oil	25 mL

1. Using an immersion blender or mini-chopper, mix maltodextrin and olive oil until the mixture is crumbly.

2. Heat a nonstick skillet over medium-high heat for 1 minute. Add mixture and cook, stirring, until the crumbs start to brown, scraping the sides and bottom of the pan if the crumbs begin to stick.

3. Spread crumbs out on a sheet of foil or a rimmed baking sheet and let cool completely. Break up any large pieces with your fingers. Use immediately or store in an airtight container in a cool, dry place for several weeks.

MAKES ½ CUP (125 mL)

granules gelatinize evenly, and they thicken the fluid into a sauce without forming lumps.

Gelatinization Temperature for Common Starches

Starch	Gelatinization Temperature
Arrowroot	174–176°F (79–80°C)
Corn	179–188°F (82–87°C)
Potato	156–158°F (69–70°C)
Rice	183–200°F (84–93°C)
Tapioca	159–179°F (71–82°C)

As gelatinized starches cool, the starch molecules start to reassemble into their original formation, and water is forced out into the interstices between the starch granules (retrogradation), which is why sauces stored in a refrigerator weep water and why baked goods dry out and go stale. When a refrigerated sauce is reheated, the water reintegrates at the starch's gelatinization point.

As a baked product cools, water forced from the retrograded starch gets pushed toward the surface. In bread, the moisture is absorbed by the crust, which changes from crisp to chewy. When you heat staling bread, water from the crust is reabsorbed back into the starch granules. It also evaporates from the surface, and the crust crisps as the interior becomes moist and light. Soft baked goods, like cakes and muffins, have no crust to trap the migrating water, so the moisture evaporates into the air, and reheating won't refresh them.

How It Works

How It Works • All starch molecules are composed of chains of glucose, but how the molecules are arranged determines how the starch behaves. There are two molecular forms of starch — amylose and amylopectin — and most starches contain both. A molecule of amylose starch is made of about 500 to 2,000 glucose molecules attached in a straight line. Each amylopectin molecule can have 10,000 to 100,000 glucose molecules arranged in hundreds of short branches. Straight and smaller, amylose starches naturally form compact, tightly bound clusters, whereas amylopectin starches settle into larger, looser structures.

The tight, dense formation of amylose starch requires higher temperature, more water, and a longer cooking time to gelatinize than the looser construction of amylopectin starch groups. Long-grain rice is about 20% amylose; short-grain rice is almost all amylopectin. This is why long-grain rice is cooked with more water than short-grain rice.

When starch is mixed with water, a small amount is immediately absorbed, mostly into the looser amylopectin portion of the granules. As the mixture heats, the hydrogen bonds between starch molecules start to break. As gelatinization begins, water rushes in, the granules swell, and viscosity increases dramatically. At that point starch-thickened sauces start to clear and thicken, a cake batter starts to set and lose its starchy aroma, and pasta begins to swell and soften.

After the initial engorgement of water, the fragile starch granules begin to disintegrate, causing sauces to decrease in viscosity as they simmer. The range of temperatures for this progression varies by type of starch and is influenced by other ingredients such as sugar or acid. Sugar increases the gelatinization temperature, so cakes have longer to rise before the structure sets.

When gelatinized starches cool, the straight-chain amylose molecules start to reassociate with each other and gel. Branched amylopectin molecules do not reassociate, so they do not form gels. Cooked long-grain rice, which is high in amylose, turns hard and chalky after refrigeration, whereas short-grain

science wise

Starch and Eggs • Starch molecules protect the egg proteins in custards from overcoagulating and curdling. The trick is that the high end of the gelatinization range of starches is similar to the temperature at which the proteins in a mixture of milk and egg start to coagulate (solidify). The starch granules swell and get in the way of protein molecules that might bond with one another into curds. The addition of starch is why pastry cream (a custard sauce containing flour or cornstarch) can be brought briefly to a boil without curdling, while a crème anglaise (a custard sauce without starch) cannot.

rice, which is mostly amylopectin, becomes firmer but stays relatively moist and tender.

See Also • Baking, Cake, Carbohydrate, Grains, Legumes, Sauces, Sugar

STAR FRUIT

What It Is • The star fruit, or carambola, is about the size of a large lemon and the color of a barely ripe banana. It has a paper-thin, waxy skin and deep ridges that give slices of the fruit a characteristic star shape.

What It Does • Cross-section slices of star fruit are quite decorative and are often used as garnish for desserts or in salads. The qualities of the fruit change dramatically with ripeness. When underripe, the tips of the ridges are tinted green, the flesh is crisp like a Bosc pear, and the flavor is decidedly tart. As the fruit ripens, the ridges brown, the texture softens to the turgid firmness of a grape, and the fruit becomes sweeter and beautifully perfumed, in between Concord grapes and quince.

How It Works • The tartness of underripe star fruit comes from oxalic acid, which also gives sorrel its tang. Its yellow color is largely beta-carotene, so star fruit has some antioxidant properties. Because its pulpy flesh is full of water, star fruit collapses when heated. For that reason it is almost always served raw.

See Also • Fruit

STARTER • See Bread

STEAMING

What It Is • Water vaporizes at 212°F (100°C). Steaming is cooking food in water vapor in a closed vessel. In most cases the food comes in direct contact with the steam, but in some recipes (steamed puddings, for example) the food is sealed in a container and the container is placed in the path of the steam. In other methods no water is used at all. Ingredients cooked in a microwave

Steamed Vegetables with Minted Yogurt

This colorful warm salad is easiest to steam in a microwave, but if you would rather, you can steam it over a pan of simmering water. Select a steaming plate and cooking vessel of the same diameter, and cover the plate with foil rather than plastic wrap. Any plate that can be placed in a microwave oven can be steamed over a pot of water. If you don't want to cover the plate with foil or wrap, you can invert another plate on top instead.

1 cup	plain full-fat yogurt	250 mL
2 tbsp	chopped mint leaves	25 mL
1 tbsp	freshly squeezed lemon juice	15 mL
1 tbsp	extra virgin olive oil	15 mL
1	small clove garlic, minced	1
	Salt and freshly ground black pepper to taste	
8	baby carrots, peeled	8
½	head broccoli, stems removed, crown cut into florets	½
¼	head cauliflower, cut into florets	¼
8	small mushrooms	8
6	cherry tomatoes	6

1. In a bowl, combine yogurt, mint, lemon juice, olive oil, garlic, salt, and pepper.

2. Select a platter large enough to hold vegetables in a single layer, and arrange them attractively on the plate. Place carrots, broccoli, and cauliflower closer to the rim, mushrooms and tomatoes more toward the center. Sprinkle with salt and pepper.

3. Cover platter with microwave-safe plastic wrap, and microwave on High until carrots are just tender, 4 to 5 minutes. Uncover, and pour any juices on the plate into the dressing.

4. Whisk dressing to make it smooth and thick, and pour over vegetables. Serve warm.

MAKES 4 SERVINGS

oven, baked in foil or parchment paper (en papillote), or buried in a pit oven (as in a luau or a clambake) are heated from the steam created when their own juices vaporize. Because steaming does not require the presence of fat for **heat** transfer, it is a low-fat cooking method.

What It Does • Steam cookers consist of a cooking vessel to hold the liquid, a perforated rack or basket to hold the food perched above the liquid in the path of the steam, and a tight-fitting lid to trap the steam. Steamers can be as simple as a rack set in a covered saucepan and as sophisticated as computerized steaming boxes that allow you to regulate steam temperature and pressure.

Regardless of the equipment, the basic technique of steaming is always the same. The liquid is heated to boiling. Flavorful ingredients like herbs, spices, aromatic vegetables, or tea leaves can be put in the liquid to scent the steam. The food is placed on the rack, the pot is covered, and the food steams until it is heated through.

Ingredients need to be cut into small enough, or thin enough, pieces that they cook through without overcooking on the surface. Because steam is hot and quick moving, it transfers heat to the outside of food rapidly, but once the surface is hot the heat transfer through the food slows down (unless the steam is under pressure), which means size matters.

Any ingredient that can be poached or simmered can be steamed. Most vegetables, seafood, and fish steam well. Spiced ground meat mixtures can be wrapped in flavorful leaves or dumpling wrappers and steamed. Low-moisture or high-fiber fruits like pears or peaches steam well, as do moist baked goods such as steamed puddings and custards.

Although cooking with steam is similar to cooking in simmering liquid, steaming has certain advantages over boiling, simmering, or poaching:
• Loss of water-soluble vitamins is less dramatic when ingredients are steamed rather than boiled or simmered.

- Ingredients are not bumped or agitated as they would be in boiling water, which makes steaming preferable for cooking delicate dumplings or a fragile fish that would break apart in boiling water.
- Liquid batters such as puddings and custards that need gentle, moist heat to cook through without curdling but which cannot be submerged in water are steamed either in a water bath or set above simmering liquid in a steamer.
- Steam flavors ingredients without submerging them in flavorful liquid. **Couscous** is traditionally steamed in the perforated top compartment of a couscoussière (a couscous steamer) over a simmering stew made from spiced broth, meat, and vegetables that is then served over the couscous.
- Whole meals can be steamed in a bamboo steaming basket or on a plate set over a pot of boiling water. The only trick is making sure all of the ingredients cook at similar rates.

How It Works ● Steam is not as dense as

water, and so its heat-transferring molecules make less contact with an ingredient than the hot molecules in a pot of boiling water. But what steam lacks in density it makes up for in energy. It takes a lot of energy to turn water into vapor, and consequently steam has a lot of energy to transfer to food when it condenses back into water.

When hot steam condenses on the surface of an ingredient placed in its path, it turns back into a film of liquid water. Provided the steam is constant, the temperature at the surface of the food will stay at the boiling point. If the ingredient is large or thick, the exterior will overcook before it is cooked through. For that reason, fish for steaming should be thin fillets, meats should be small meatballs, sausages, or dumplings, and vegetables are best cut in bite-size pieces. Wrapping ingredients in leaves moderates the heat at the surface of the food and helps it cook through more evenly.

Heat transfer is accelerated and evened out by increasing the concentration of steam or by putting the steam under pressure. This can be achieved as simply as containing the steam under a lid. As steam fills the space in a pot, it leaves less room for air, which increases the concentration of steam in the pot, forcing the steam deeper into the surface of the food. The increased air pressure also bears down on the surface of the water, which causes the boiling point to rise, making the steam hotter. If the pot is tightly sealed, pressure in the vessel increases and can greatly reduce cooking times, which is the principle behind pressure cooking.

See Also ● Atmospheric Pressure, Boiling

STEMS

What It Is ● Stems and stalks conduct

nutrients between the various parts of a plant. They transport sugars, produced in the **leaves** through photosynthesis, to the **roots** for storage as starch, and move sugars derived from the metabolism of root starch to various parts of the plants where the sugar is needed for energy. The stem also supports the above-ground parts of plants, exposing leaves to sunlight, oxygen, and water, making **flowers** accessible to insects for pollination, and lifting **fruit** off the ground where it is more likely to be seen and gathered by an animal that can spread its seed and propagate the plant's next generation. To that end stems are rigid and fibrous, and veined with vascular channels.

What It Does ● The stiff fibrous structure

and hollow vascular channels that make up most stems can pose problems for cooks. For example, the structural ridges that run the length of celery, rhubarb, and cardoon stalks are many times tougher than the vascular tissue that makes up the interior of the vegetable. They must be stripped away or the stem must be sliced thinly to shorten their length. Fennel stalks have similar problems, so only the swollen base, where the fibrous tissues are spread far apart, is eaten. The stalks, where the structural fibers concentrate, are generally not eaten (but can be used for flavoring).

How It Works ● Broccoli stems and

asparagus stems are covered in a thick

water-resistant cuticle that keeps water from evaporating out of the stem and therefore keeps it rigid without the help of tough fibers. Before cooking, the skin of mature broccoli and asparagus stalks has to be peeled or punctured to allow boiling water or steam to permeate the interior of the vegetable.

Some stems have evolved storage units at the juncture where they meet the root (hypocotyl) that swell with starch and provide a wide foundation to help support the rest of the plant. Turnips, celery root, beets, and rutabagas are all swollen hypocotyl tissue.

Some plants have developed specialized underground stem structures that reproduce asexually. These horizontal stems, called rhizomes, have the ability to grow a number of adjunct appendages that each produces roots from one side and sprouts leaves from the other, thus creating genetically identical copies of the parent plant. At the end of the growing season the parent plant dies and the rhizome offspring live on. Ginger, sunchoke, and turmeric are rhizomes. Sunchokes (Jerusalem artichokes) are a rhizome in the Asteraceae family, which also includes globe artichokes. They have a crisp texture and a pleasant sweetness because of a high concentration of inulin, a fructose polymer.

Rhizomes that can store starch in their cells are called tubers. They include potatoes, yams, chufa, and oka. Starch-storing tubers are larger and bulkier than other rhizomes. Yams can grow to be several pounds. Chufa that flourish in subtropical climates in the Northern Hemisphere are small but very dense and hard. They are used in the production of horchata, a popular drink in Hispanic cuisines. Oka are small, slightly tangy potato-like tubers native to the Andes region of South America (as is the potato).

Bamboo shoots and hearts of palm are tender parts of hard wooden stems. Bamboo shoots, the immature stems of several species of bamboo, are harvested soon after they appear above ground, before exposure to sunlight causes them to produce cyanide-generating compounds. Hearts of palm are the sprouting tips of stems from various palm trees. They are sweet and crisp.

To produce tender stem vegetables, special cultivars of celery, rhubarb, and cardoon have been developed that have very fine structural ribs. They are kept upright through growing practices that supply ample water to keep the vascular tissue turgid, and by hilling the soil or tying the stalks together to lend support.

See Also • Asparagus, Celery, Cruciferous Vegetables, Fennel, Flowers, Fruit, Leaves, Potatoes, Roots

STEVIA • See Sweeteners

STEWING • See Braising

STILTON • See Cheese

STIR-FRYING • See Frying

STOCKS • See Sauces, Soup

STONE CRAB • See Crustacean

STONEWARE • See Cookware

STORAGE

What It Is • In the best of all possible worlds, food storage would not be necessary. Corn would dive from its stalk right into a pot of boiling water, and steaks would arrive at the back door as soon as the charcoal starts to glow. But in the real world, enjoying good food is not just a matter of getting the right ingredients and cooking them correctly. Also important is storing them properly to keep them safe, nutritious, and delicious. In most kitchens a large proportion of space is devoted to food storage, which is generally divided between three areas: refrigerator, **freezer**, and pantry.

What It Does • Refrigeration retards the growth of **bacteria**, but it does not stop it, and it does not make tainted food safe. Make sure that ingredients are fresh before they are stored, and if they are not completely fresh, use them as soon as possible.

To maintain proper temperature in all parts of a refrigerator, cold air must be allowed to circulate freely. Too much food or food packed too tightly in a refrigerator can block airflow and put everything in the refrigerator at peril.

Different foods have different chilling needs, and modern refrigerators take this into account by having separate refrigerated units (separate drawers or cabinets) for particular foods or by circulating the refrigerated air and relative humidity to where it is most needed in a single-unit refrigerator. Special thermometers that hang from or sit on a shelf and register as low as –20°F (–29°C) are available to show the temperature in various parts of a refrigerator or freezer.

Meats are best stored in the coldest part of the refrigerator and they should be kept separate from other foods to avoid cross-contamination from meat juices. All meat contains potentially harmful bacteria that are killed when the meat is cooked, but if juices from meat contact other foods that will be eaten raw, the bacteria can cause problems. Eggs and dairy products are typically stored on the door of the refrigerator where it is slightly warmer, and vegetables are kept in a drawer that allows moisture to circulate around them to discourage wilting. Cooling produce slows down its metabolic processes, causing it to change less during storage, but not all produce can be kept at the same temperature. For instance, tropical fruits and vegetables suffer chill injuries from low temperatures — citrus fruits develop dark spots and bananas turn black, so it is best to store them at cool room temperatures rather than in the refrigerator. One of the critical flavor components in tomatoes is destroyed below 45°F (7°C).

Optimal Chilling Conditions for Food Groups

Food Group	Temperature	Humidity
Dairy	38 to 40°F (3 to 4°C)	75 to 85%
Eggs	38 to 40°F (3 to 4°C)	Any
Fish and seafood	30 to 34°F (–1 to 1°C)	75 to 85%
Meat and poultry	32 to 36°F (0 to 2°C)	75 to 85%
Most produce	40 to 45°F (4 to 7°C)	85 to 90%
Sauces and stocks	32 to 36°F (0 to 2°C)	75 to 85%

Freezers should be kept at an air temperature of 0°F (–18°C) or lower, and some experts recommend that the median temperature should be closer to –10°F (–23°C), since meats deteriorate more rapidly at temperatures over 0°F (–18°C). Home freezers are designed to keep frozen food frozen, not to freeze room-temperature food rapidly. For that reason make sure to place food to be frozen in a single layer in a part of the freezer with good air circulation.

Although dry food products are not as perishable as fresh food, and do not pose the same degree of food safety hazards, they can still spoil and attract insects and rodents. Dry ingredients should be stored in well-ventilated closed cabinets, preferably at 60 to 70°F (16 to 21°C) and with a humidity of less than 60%. Pay attention to use by dates and clean out pantry cabinets regularly.

How It Works • Regardless of the food being stored or where it is stored, five general principles apply to all food storage.

Rule #1 First in, first out — Use food as soon as possible. If you are getting low on mayonnaise and purchase a new jar, don't start the new jar until the old one is finished. Write the freezing date on ingredients that are intended for long-term storage, like meats or bulk items.

Rule #2 Beware of the danger zone — Potentially hazardous bacteria are always present in food. You cannot eliminate them.

science wise

Plastic Wrap • There are two types of plastic wrap: polyvinyl chloride (PVC) and low-density polyethylene (LDPE). PVC wrap, originally branded Saran, is impermeable to oxygen and aromas. It clings and stretches well and seals out oxygen for the longest storage. But it contains vinyl chloride, a potential toxin that is hard to recycle cleanly. Early PVC wraps contained plasticizers, chemicals later linked to disruption of the endocrine system, so plasticizers are no longer allowed. LDPE, originally branded Glad-Wrap, does not cling or stretch as well as PVC, and it is permeable to oxygen, which makes it less effective at preventing freezer burn and sealing out oxygen for long refrigeration. But it does not pose the same health and environmental problems as PVC so it is gaining popularity for home use. Saran also has an LDPE wrap called Saran Premium.

To increase their ability to cling and seal, LDPE wraps are coated with a film of edible adhesive gum that makes them sticky. Glad Press 'n Seal is an LDPE wrap covered with dimples, with adhesive set in the crevices between the dimples. When removed from the roll, the wrap does not feel sticky, but when it is pressed against a hard surface, such as the edge of a storage container, the dimples collapse, bringing the adhesive in contact with the container.

Most food professionals still use PVC wrap because of its better storage abilities, but oxygen-permeable LDPE wraps are used more frequently for displaying meat in supermarkets, because exposure to oxygen turns meat pigments red.

All you can do is keep them from multiplying to a level that causes problems. Bacteria don't just have the potential to make you sick; they alter the flavor and texture of foods, turning milk sour and meat slimy. Bacteria grow most rampantly on fresh, moist foods at temperatures between 45 and 140°F (7 and 60°C). The least amount of time an ingredient stays in that danger zone, the safer and higher quality it will remain.

Rule #3 Store edibles and potentially hazardous products separately — Do not store food and cleaning products in the same cabinet.

Rule #4 Package foods appropriately — All wrapping and packaging must be clean and able to protect food during storage. Do not reuse packaging. For most ingredients, storage containers and packaging should be moisture-proof and airtight.

Rule #5 Keep storage areas clean — It does no good to take good care of food and put it in a contaminated cabinet.

See Also • Bacteria, Freezing

STOUT • See Beer

STOVE

What It Is • Kitchen stoves control fire for the purpose of cooking. The first closed stoves, dating from the Qin Dynasty (221 to 206 BCE) in China, were clay or brick boxes raised from the floor to allow airflow from beneath. They were constructed with stoke holes in the front through which wood or charcoal could be added to the firebox, holes in the top to serve as burners, and holes near the floor allowing oxygen to reach the fire. They allowed the cook to direct most of the heat from a fire directly to the food. The kamado stove of Japan, developed during the Edo period (1603 to 1867), is a similar design that is still used today.

Until the mid-18th century, Europeans were still cooking in cauldrons hanging over open fires. Open fires radiate heat indiscriminately, heating the surrounding area as much as they heat the food in the pot. During the reign of Louis XIV a multi-burner closed stove was introduced to the French court. Much of the credit for the development of the closed stove in the West is given to an American, Benjamin Thompson (Count Rumford), who at the end of the 18th century, while living in Germany, improved the stove by placing baffles on the air vent. This allowed the cook to change the airflow, thereby increasing or decreasing the heat generated by a fire. Thompson also put a closed oven inside the firebox, an economy that allowed the same fire to cook food on top of the stove and to cook a roast or bake a cake in the oven. Thompson published extensively on the advantages of roasting (technically baking) meat in an oven rather than on a spit over an open fire, thereby confusing the methods of baking and roasting forevermore.

Stoves based on Thompson's designs were installed all over Europe, and they not only changed fuel efficiency in the kitchen, they changed what could be cooked. Delicate sauces that had been impossible to cook over an open fire could now be made over controlled heat that cooked the food rather than the cook. Although the use of roux was known a century before Thompson's stove, it wasn't until closed stoves were widespread that roux-thickened sauces became the norm, ushering in the age of classic French cuisine.

What It Does ● Modern kitchen stoves can be configured in a number of ways. A stovetop (aka cooktop, range top) incorporating a number of burners can be either set in a counter by itself or attached to **oven** and broiler compartments in a free-standing appliance. Free-standing stoves are the most common, but more home cooks are opting for separate stovetops and ovens, both for design flexibility and to have different fuel sources for the oven and the top.

Most cooks prefer natural gas for stovetops. Gas burners change temperature easily, moving from high to low with the turn of a knob, but natural gas is not available everywhere. It also is the least efficient of all the fuel sources at heat transference. Because a gas flame is open, much of its heat goes out into the air rather than into the pan.

Electric burners are more efficient than gas. They get hotter than gas burners, and because they are flat, the heat contacts the pan completely, so most of the energy goes into the pan rather than into the air. But electric burners are slow to respond to temperature adjustments. Once a control knob is turned, it can take several minutes for the burner to adjust. Professional chefs have developed a technique to overcome this deficiency. They turn several burners on at once, setting some on high, some on medium, and some on low. When they want to adjust the temperature under a pot, they move the pot.

Induction burners (see **Heat**) cook with electromagnetic energy and are suitable for people who want the adjustability of gas with the power of electricity. They are flat like electric burners, so most of their energy travels directly into the pan, and because they are using energy only when a pan is sitting on them, they don't waste energy. They are also safer than either gas or electric because the burner itself doesn't get hot, just the pan sitting on it. The only drawback is that they require specially made magnetic stainless steel **cookware**. Induction burners are costly, and since most people have to purchase a new set of cookware to go along with them, the investment can be daunting.

Stovetops can be made of metal or thermal glass-ceramic. Gas tops are always metal, usually steel surfaced with enamel for easy cleaning. Each burner consists of a burner assembly attached to the main gas pipe. A gas burner is just a hollow metal disk that is punctured with holes around its perimeter. The burner assembly can be a separate burner and cap or a sealed assembly in which the two are fused. Sealed assemblies are easier to keep clean. A pilot light or an electric pilot sits to one side of the burner and sends a spark or small flame to light the gas as it flows through the holes in the burner. Each burner sits above a removable drip pan, made from stainless steel or enameled steel for easy cleaning and covered by a metal grate that supports cookware above the burner.

Electric burners are generally coil style, a flattened spiral of electrical wire sheathed in metal that heats up when the control knob is turned on, triggering electricity to flow into the wire. You can see the intensity of the electrical flow in the glow of the burner. European-style electric burners look like a flat metal disk. They heat the same way as a coil burner, except that the wire is embedded in a solid disk rather than being sheathed in metal. In a smooth-top electric stove, the coil is placed under a single sheet of heat-tempered glass-ceramic material that covers the stovetop. The smooth surface allows for easy cleanup. The electric coil heats in the same way, and radiates its heat into the glass, which radiates it into a pan. Halogen stoves have rings of halogen bulbs under the glass rather than coils. When the control knob is turned on, the bulb starts to glow, immediately generating a burst of heat that starts cooking right away. Flat-bottomed pans must be used to get maximum heat transference from electric stovetops.

How It Works • Each burner on a gas stovetop has its own control knob that is attached to a small gas valve connected to the main gas line. When you turn the knob, the valve opens and gas flows through a venturi tube, a wide pipe that narrows in the middle and has a small air hole in the narrow section just before the pipe widens again. As gas passes into the narrowed section its pressure increases. That pressure releases when it moves into the wider end, sucking oxygen through the air hole. The oxygen mixes with the gas, making it combustible. The oxygen-gas mixture then flows into the burner, where a pilot flame ignites it. By turning the knob to a higher setting, the flow of gas (and air) is increased and the flame gets larger.

Electric burners are metal-encased wire coils that plug into an electrical socket in the side of the coil well. The control knob works like a rheostat, raising the heat as the flow of electricity into the wire increases. The glass-ceramic material used for smooth cooktops is a very poor heat conductor, so almost all of the heat transfer happens through radiant heat. The glass is nearly transparent, so infrared energy passes right through it. When the infrared energy hits the pan, it immediately starts to heat the metal,

but the glass surface doesn't get nearly as hot as the pan. For that reason glass tops are relatively safe to use. The area right under the pan will heat from residual heat bouncing back from the pan into the glass, but the surrounding area will stay relatively cool. Glass-ceramic scratches easily. Cooks in the habit of sliding and shaking sauté pans as they cook have to change their ways when working on a smooth-top range.

Induction burners generate an alternating current that sets up an electromagnetic field between the burner and the metal pan sitting on it. The burner is made of a coil of copper wire set under a nonconductive glass-ceramic surface. An alternating current is made to flow through the wire, creating a changing magnetic field. When a pan made out of a magnetic metal (magnetic stainless steel or iron) is placed on the burner, the magnetic field causes alternating currents in the pot. Because the copper coil is a better conductor of electricity than the steel or iron pot, the electricity flowing through the pot meets with some resistance, causing the pot to get hot, even as the copper coil stays cool.

See Also • Heat, Oven

STRAWBERRIES • See Berries

STREPTOCOCCUS • See Bacteria

STRING BEAN • See Legumes

STRING CHEESE • See Cheese

STRIPED BASS • See Fish

STRUDEL • See Pastry

STUFFING

What It Is • It seems any time there's a cavity in an ingredient, inventive cooks want to fill it with something. Stuffings (aka dressings) are most often mixtures of starch (bread, rice, whole grains, or potatoes), herbs and spices, and flavorings like fruits, nuts, or aromatic

After 1880, the term "dressing" began to replace stuffing in polite circles, a Victorian preference. Today "dressing" and "stuffing" are used interchangeably, although some people make the distinction that stuffing is cooked inside another food whereas dressing is cooked separately.

Hollow seafood like squid sacs are stuffed and roasted or braised. Large shrimp can be butterflied and filled with stuffing. Mollusks like clams are stuffed by removing the meat from its shell, making a filling, then mounding it in one of the half shells before baking or broiling. This is how clams casino is made.

The space left after the bones are removed from a meat joint is often stuffed, as are easily hollowed vegetables like tomatoes, peppers, mushrooms, and squash. Artichokes are stuffed when a filling is packed between the bracts, and cabbage leaves are said to be stuffed, although they are wrapped around a filling.

How It Works • Roasting stuffed poultry can pose food safety issues. If disease-causing bacteria are present in meat, most will be on the surface. In poultry, the surface includes both the skin covering the outside of the bird and the walls of the internal cavity. When an unstuffed bird is roasted, high heat reaches all surfaces and kills the bacteria, but when the cavity is stuffed, heat cannot easily reach the internal walls or the center of the stuffing.

The safest method is to cook stuffing separately from the bird. The only thing that will be missing is the juices dripping from the meat into the stuffing. This can be remedied by stirring some drippings from the roasting pan into the stuffing after both are finished cooking. If you want to carve the roast at the table bursting with stuffing, simply spoon the stuffing into the cavity before presenting it.

If you insist on roasting stuffed poultry, make sure that the stuffing loosely fills the cavity. This will allow some oven heat to flow inside the bird and help the interior to reach a safe temperature. When taking the internal temperature of the roast, test the temperature of the stuffing as well. It needs to be above 165°F (74°C) to be safe.

See Also • Chicken, Poultry

vegetables. Stuffings add complementary flavors and textures to otherwise plain ingredients, and without requiring a lot of extra time or money they transform a simple roast into the centerpiece for a feast.

What It Does • Because a gutted animal has a natural cavity, small animals that can be roasted whole were the first foods to be stuffed. Apicius, who wrote the first known cookbook, included recipes for stuffed chicken, hare, pig, and dormouse. Apicius called stuffing *farcire*, the Latin for "to stuff," which gave rise to the term "forcemeat," a filling for sausage (stuffed intestine) or galantine (stuffed poultry skin).

fast fact

- Turducken is a fanciful concoction in which a boned turkey is stuffed with a boned duck that is stuffed with a boned chicken that is stuffed with forcemeat. The whole is reassembled to resemble a turkey and roasted.

Traditional Bread Stuffing or Dressing

Fresh bread is like a sponge, able to absorb many times its own weight in liquid, until it practically disintegrates. That's why you must always toast bread thoroughly for stuffing. If not, the stuffing will lack texture and the amount of liquid in the recipe will never be adequate to moisten all of the ingredients. Use to stuff two medium chickens or one medium turkey.

1 tbsp	butter	15 mL
1 cup	minced onion	250 mL
2	stalks celery, sliced	2
1	Granny Smith apple, peeled and diced	1
1 tbsp	chopped fresh parsley	15 mL
1 tsp	dried sage leaves, crumbled	5 mL
½ tsp	dried thyme leaves	2 mL
½ tsp	dried rosemary leaves, crumbled	2 mL
Pinch	freshly grated nutmeg	Pinch
4 cups	toasted bread cubes, croutons, or stuffing mix	1 L
	Chopped cooked giblets from a turkey or chicken (optional)	

1 to 1½ cups chicken broth	250 to 375 mL
Salt and freshly ground black pepper	

1. In a large skillet, melt butter over medium heat. Add onion and celery and sauté until tender, but not brown, about 4 minutes. Add apple, parsley, sage, thyme, rosemary, and nutmeg and sauté for 1 minute.

2. Add bread cubes, giblets, if using, and 1 cup (250 mL) chicken broth and mix to moisten. If too dry, add remaining ½ cup (125 mL) broth. Season liberally with salt and pepper and cook, stirring, until heated through. Let cool before stuffing into bird, or bake in a casserole dish and serve hot.

MAKES ABOUT 8 SERVINGS

Variations: *Cornbread Sausage Stuffing:* Substitute an equal amount of toasted cornbread cubes for the bread and chopped fennel instead of celery. Crumble in cooked sausage.

Apple Sage Stuffing: Follow preceding recipe, deleting the rosemary, doubling the sage and apple, and using ½ cup (125 mL) apple cider in place of ½ cup (125 mL) chicken broth.

STURGEON • See Fish

SUBATOMIC PARTICLE • See Atom

SUBERIN • See Food Additives

SUCANAT • See Sugar

SUCRALOSE • See Sweeteners

SUCROSE • See Sugar

SUCROSE ESTERS • See Sugar

SUET • See Fat

SUGAR

What It Is • Sugar is the currency of energy for all living things. The simplest form, glucose (aka dextrose), is the building block for all carbohydrates and provides the sugary flavor in highly refined sweeteners like corn syrup. A chain of two glucose molecules forms a molecule of maltose, the sugar that starts the fermentation of beer and the distillation of grain-based spirits. When glucose is combined with galactose, it forms lactose, the first sweetness any mammal tastes and the one that sets us up for a lifetime of sugar attractions. In plants, glucose bonds with fructose, creating sucrose, the sweet crystal refined from the juices of sugarcane and sugar beets.

What It Does • The major source of sugar is sugarcane, a sturdy grass from 6 to 18 feet (2 to 6 m) tall with juice that is 10 to 15% sucrose by volume.

Extracting juice from sugarcane and then boiling it into a dark syrup (molasses) and a mass of crystals (sugar) was being practiced in India sometime before 500 BCE. By 100 BCE, techniques had developed for turning cane syrup into a variety of medicinal products, including one for removing the dark coating from sugar crystals to make whiter sugar. By the 6th century CE sugar-refining technology moved west to Persia, and then on to North Africa and Spain by the 7th century. After the Crusades in the 11th century, sugar trade spread throughout Europe, where sugar was used mostly for candying fruit and flowers and for sugaring medicines to make them more palatable. By the 15th century, the art of confectionery was full blown (see **Candy**).

In the 18th century, sugar became more widely available from sugarcane plantations in the West Indies. In England, the annual per capita consumption of sugar (mostly in tea and jams) rose from 4 pounds (2 kg) at the start of the century to 12 pounds (5 kg) by 1780. The Spanish and Portuguese had been growing sugarcane on Caribbean islands since the mid-16th century; by the middle of the 18th century, an estimated 13 million enslaved Africans worked in the sugar industry. By 1800 every European country had outlawed slavery in its colonies, and the West Indian sugar trade collapsed.

Another challenge came from Prussia, where a chemist, Andreas Marggraf, had developed a method for extracting sugar from white beets (sugar beets), which have a similar sucrose content to sugarcane. By the 1840s there was a flourishing sugar-beet industry in northern Europe.

Today about 30% of the sugar in the world comes from beets, grown mostly in France, Germany, Russia, and the U.S. Sugarcane is now mostly grown in Brazil and India, both accounting for 65% of world production in 2005.

Sugar Processing

Sugarcane is very perishable and must be processed immediately after harvest, so it is produced in two stages: first it is crushed, boiled, and crystallized into unrefined raw sugar near the cane plantation, and then it is shipped to factories for refining. Sugar beets, which are grown in cooler climates and are less perishable, can be stored for weeks without damage, so they can go from raw material to refined crystals in one continuous process.

The steps in sugar refinement are:

For Raw Sugar

1. Milling — The beet or cane is washed, shredded, and rolled to extract a juice of 10 to 15% sucrose.

2. Clarification — The juice is mixed with calcium hydroxide (slaked lime) to raise its pH to 7, which keeps acids in the juice from breaking the sucrose into glucose and fructose molecules, then it is heated gently to coagulate its proteins, which are removed.

3. Concentration — The clarified juice is heated gently in shallow pans until the sucrose concentration in the syrup is around 60% by weight. It is then put in a vacuum chamber to remove another 10% of the water, at which point the syrup is dark brown and supersaturated (see Candy, page 88).

4. Crystallization — The syrup is seeded with sugar crystals and cooled, causing the sucrose in the syrup to form coarse golden-hued crystals coated with thick brown syrup (molasses).

5. Centrifuging — A centrifuge draws the molasses off the crystals to produce "first" molasses (aka treacle in the U.K.) and raw sugar. First molasses can be mixed with more supersaturated sugar syrup and crystallized

kitchen wisdom

Why Is There an Apple in the Cookie Jar?
Cakes and cookies will stay moist longer if they're placed in a closed container with a piece of fruit. Because sugar is hygroscopic (water attracting), the cake or cookie, which contains more sugar than the fruit, will absorb moisture from it. Putting fruit in a bread box does just the opposite; moisture is drawn from the bread toward the sweeter fruit.

again, yielding more raw sugar and darker, less sweet "second" molasses. A third crystallization produces more raw sugar and harsh-flavored, tarry blackstrap molasses. At this point the raw sugar can be sold as is or refined into white sugar.

For Refined Sugar

6. Affination — Raw sugar is mixed with sugar syrup and centrifuged to remove any lingering bits of molasses from the surface of the crystals.

7. Clarification — The cleaned sugar is heated with water into a supersaturated solution (70% sucrose by weight), then mixed with calcium hydroxide (slaked lime) and either carbon dioxide or phosphoric acid to precipitate mineral particles that absorb microscopic impurities in the sugar and are skimmed away.

8. Decolorization — The clarified syrup is filtered through activated charcoal to remove any lingering color.

9. Crystallization — The purified syrup is heated to supersaturation, and then repeatedly crystallized and vacuum-evaporated to produce white sugar.

10. Drying — The refined crystals are air-dried to produce granulated sugar that won't clump.

White sugar is produced in several forms. From largest crystal size to smallest, they are:

- *Rock sugar (rock candy):* Large sugar crystals made by crystallizing a supersaturated sucrose solution around a large nucleation site, such as a string, to produce chunky crystals (5 mm in length).
- *Crystal sugar (coarse, decorating):* Large crystals (2 mm in length) about four times the size of regular granulated sugar, used for decorating confections and baked goods.
- *Sanding sugar:* Large, clear crystals (1 mm in length), washed with alcohol to remove dust, used for making super-clear syrups and perfectly white icings, and commonly sprinkled on cookies and doughnuts.
- *Preserving sugar:* Large crystals (1 mm in length) made from highly refined sugar treated to dissolve easily for making jams, jellies, and preserves.
- *Granulated sugar (white, table):* Medium-size crystals (0.5 mm in length); an all-purpose sugar.
- *Colored and flavored sugar:* Crystal or granulated sugar that is colored with food coloring or flavored with ground spices, flower petals, or citrus zest or infused with aromatic oils from cinnamon or vanilla, and used to decorate and flavor confections, baked goods, and beverages.

- *Superfine sugar (caster, ultra-fine, instant dissolving, fruit, berry)*: Finely ground (0.1 mm in length) granulated sugar for smooth mouth feel; dissolves without heating.
- *Confectioner's sugar (icing, powdered)*: Very finely crushed (0.01 mm in length) granulated sugar, mixed with about 3% starch to prevent clumping.

  Brown sugars can be either raw (unrefined) sugar or refined sucrose crystals that are coated with some of the dark syrup that is extracted during sugar processing. From the least refined to the most, they are:
- *Demerara sugar*: Sugar crystals taken from the first crystallization of light cane juice. The crystals are large, golden, and slightly sticky.
- *Muscovado sugar (Barbados)*: Sugar crystals taken from the final crystallization of cane syrup into blackstrap molasses. The crystals are dark brown, small, strongly flavored, and sticky.
- *Sucanat*: A trademarked raw sugar product made by evaporating cane juice to create a granular rather than a crystalline texture. (The name is a contraction of "sugarcane natural.")
- *Turbinado sugar*: Demerara sugar washed of some of its molasses so it's not sticky.
- *Brown sugar (dark brown, light brown)*: Refined white sugar that is either soaked in molasses syrup and recrystallized or thinly coated with molasses. The more molasses the darker the sugar.

  Sugars can be refined from plants other than sugarcane and sugar beets.
- *Palm sugar*: Crystallized from sugar palm sap, it can be unrefined (amber colored and with a winey taste) or refined to a more neutral-tasting white sugar. Unrefined palm sugar is called *gur* in Hindi and jaggery in English.
- *Stachyose sugar*: A complex sugar derived from any one of numerous vegetables, mostly legumes. It is about a quarter as sweet as sucrose and has some thickening abilities. It is mostly used industrially as a bulk sweetener.

  In **baking**, sugar impedes the coagulation of proteins, tenderizing doughs and pastries by interfering with gluten formation, and it protects custard and pastry cream from curdling. Sugar is hygroscopic (it absorbs water from its environment) and hydrophilic (it bonds with water and holds on to it), so it

Cooking with Sugar

Sugar dissolves easily in water and does not break down when boiled. When a sugar-water solution is concentrated sufficiently, the sugar recrystallizes, a phenomenon that is behind the production of sugar crystals from plant juices and the basis of most candy making.

At a high enough temperature, sugar caramelizes, separating into hundreds of diverse chemicals. The colorless sweet molecule melts and then unravels into deep, dark pigments and a complex flavor that combines roastedness, bitterness, tartness, and sweetness accompanied by delicious aromas of butter, milk, fruit, and flowers. The more a sugar caramelizes, the more of these new flavors develop and the less sweet it tastes. Eventually the original flavor of sugar completely disappears and all that is left is sourness and bitterness.

Caramelization Points of Various Sugars

Sugar	Caramelization Temperature
Fructose crystals	220°F (104°C)
Glucose (from corn syrup)	300°F (150°C)
Lactitol (modified lactose)	270°F (132°C)
Maltitol (modified maltose)	270°F (132°C)
Sucrose (table sugar)	340°F (171°C)

keeps sweet baked goods moist. Fructose and glucose are more hygroscopic than sucrose, so sweeteners such as honey (fructose and glucose), corn syrup (glucose), and molasses (fructose and glucose) keep baked goods moist longer.

The hydrophilic quality of molasses is also what makes brown sugar moist. Brown sugar will dry out and become hard if exposed to dry air, but wrapping it in a damp towel will soften it right up. Because the damp crystals cling to one another, they tend to trap air, so many recipes specify to pack brown sugar when measuring to force out the air.

Molasses is mildly acidic with a pH that varies between 5 and 6, so it enlivens other flavors in cooking and can upset the acid–base balance required for leavening when brown sugar is substituted for white sugar in a baking recipe.

How It Works ● There are many kinds of sugar, differentiated by the type and number of sugar molecules they contain and the

number of carbon atoms in each molecule. Basic sugar molecules and the building blocks of other sugars are monosaccharides; these include glucose, fructose, and galactose. Sugars made of two monosaccharides are called disaccharides; these include maltose, sucrose, and lactose. Sugars made of three to five monosaccharides are called oligosaccharides; these do not taste sweet until they are hydrolyzed into simpler sugars by acids, enzymes, or heat. When sugars get bigger than five monosaccharides (polysaccharides) they become starches or gums.

Sucrose, which is produced during photosynthesis in green plants, is the most common culinary sugar, mostly because it is naturally plentiful but also because it has useful properties. It is the second-sweetest sugar (after fructose) and it is the only sugar that doesn't develop an aftertaste even when highly concentrated. Almost as soluble in water as fructose, it is more viscous in solution, so it's ideal for making syrups and glazes. It has a high melting point and a high caramelization point, both of which give it flexibility in cooking.

When sucrose is heated with acids it breaks into its component monosaccharides, glucose and fructose, a process called inversion. Invert sugar, which is about 50% glucose and 50% fructose, interferes with crystal formation that can ruin the texture of candies and syrups, and so it is useful in confectionery.

The other two natural disaccharides, lactose (milk sugar) and maltose (malt sugar), are not used much in the kitchen. Both are less sweet than sucrose and less viscous in solution.

Sweetness is one of the five basic tastes, so cooks can use it as a pleasurable sensation by itself and to modify other tastes. Sugar helps to modify sour and bitter flavors, and flavor scientists have shown that it enhances aromas. The mechanism for this phenomenon is not completely understood, but it could be a signal from the brain to the nose to take special notice of a food that shows signs of being a good energy source.

The sweetness of sucrose (which is the sugar that is most familiar to us) starts slowly and

Relative Sweetness of Common Sugars Compared with Sucrose

The sweetness of sucrose is represented as 100. A sugar that has a rating of 50 is half as sweet as sucrose.

Sugar	Relative Sweetness
Fructose crystals	120
Glucose (from corn syrup)	70
Lactitol (modified lactose)	40
Maltitol (modified maltose)	45
Sucrose (table sugar)	100

The flavor of brown sugar is more complex than white because of the presence of molasses. Soft brown sugar can contain up to 2% minerals (mostly calcium, magnesium, iron, and potassium) and 4% vitamins and other materials, such as organic acids.

lingers. Fructose hits faster and fades faster, and corn syrup (which is mostly glucose) builds more slowly than sucrose, lingers longer, and is only about 70% as sweet.

See Also ● Candy, Honey, Maple Syrup, Sweeteners

SUGAR SUBSTITUTE • See Sweeteners

SULFUR COMPOUNDS • See Browning, Cruciferous Vegetables, Eggs, Flavor Compounds

SULFUR DIOXIDE • See Food Additives

SUNCHOKE • See Stems

SUN-DRYING • See Drying

SUNFISH • See Fish

SUNFLOWER SEEDS • See Oil

SURIMI • See Fish

SWEATING • See Soup

SWEETBREADS • See Organ Meats

SWEETENED CONDENSED MILK • See Milk

SWEETENERS

What It Is • Sugar is pure energy. The flavor
of sugar — sweetness — is the flavor of
energy, and humans are physiologically
programmed to find sweet-tasting, energy-
rich foods pleasing. For most of human
history this system has worked well, supplying
active hunters and gatherers with an efficient
way to obtain the maximum amount of
calories while expending the least amount of
effort, but many people in the industrialized
world consume more energy than they need,
and it has made them fat. Sweeteners are
substances that deliver the sensation of
sweetness without the calories. Some are
naturally derived from plants (natural
sweeteners) and some are manufactured in
laboratories (artificial sweeteners).

Sweeteners have been developed that
deliver other properties of sugar as well.
Isomalt, for example, is a naturally occurring
sugar alcohol that does not significantly
increase blood sugar levels, has half the
calories of sugar, and does not cause tooth
decay. It also resists humidity, and for that
property alone it has transformed the art of
pulled sugar and molded sugar sculptures,
allowing pastry chefs to store sugar
constructions for months without fear of their
collapsing in humid conditions. Other
sweeteners are used because they do not
undergo Maillard browning as easily as sugar,
so that sweet foods can be heated for shelf
stability without darkening.

What It Does • Two families of
sweeteners can substitute for sugar: sugar
alcohols and high-intensity sweeteners
that deliver greater sweetness from far
less product. Sugar alcohols are derived
by modifying one corner of a natural
sugar molecule so that the sweetener
can no longer be metabolized as sugar.
Sugar alcohols provide the bulk, mouth
feel, and appearance of sugar but with
fewer calories. Sugar alcohols are typically
combined with intensive sweeteners to
approximate the sweetness of sucrose.
In return, sugar alcohols modify the

aftertaste that is a problem with many
high-intensity sweeteners. Sugar alcohols
can also act as thickeners and humectants
(moisture-retaining agents).

Most high-intensity sweeteners are
synthesized in laboratories, but a few are
natural. Glycyrrhizin, a compound in
licorice root, is as much as 100 times sweeter
than sucrose, and stevia leaves, from a
South American shrub in the sunflower
family, have been used as a sweetener for
centuries. Stevia's active ingredient,
stevioside, is sold in the U.S. as a dietary
supplement rather than a sweetener because
stevia has not yet been approved by the
FDA for use in food products.

Sugar Alcohols

Name	Derived From	Uses	Percentage Sweetness Compared with Sucrose (100)	Calories per Gram
Erythritol	Glucose	Sweetener	80	0.2
Glycerol	Fat	Sweetener, thickener, humectant, solvent	60	4
HSH (hydrogenated starch hydrosylate)	Starch	Sweetener, humectant	40 to 90	3
Isomalt	Beets	Sweetener	50	2
Lactitol	Lactose	Sweetener, prebiotic	40	2
Mannitol	Sucrose	Sweetener, cooling agent	50	1.6
Sorbitol	Glucose	Sweetener, laxative, humectant	60	2.6
Xylitol	Sucrose	Sweetener	100	2.4
Sucrose (for comparison)		Sweetener, humectant, browning agent	100	4

High-intensity sweeteners often have flavor patterns that make them difficult to use. Saccharin, for example, has a bitter metallic aftertaste, and stevia has a woody aftertaste. Glycyrrhizin has a lingering licorice aftertaste. Oddly, their level of sweetness tends to diminish as their concentration rises, so they are often used in combination with one another or with sugar alcohols to modify their flavor impact.

Aspartame is one of the most widely used sweeteners. Marketed under the names Equal, NutraSweet, and Canderel, aspartame is currently included in the formulas of more than 6,000 commercial foods and beverages. It is 200 times sweeter than sucrose and has minimal aftertaste. Its calorie content is similar to sucrose's by weight, but because it can be used in much smaller amounts, the number of calories it contributes to foods is usually negligible. Aspartame is synthesized from two amino acids; when it is heated it breaks down into those component parts and loses its sweetness, so it can't be used for cooking. Neotame is chemically similar to aspartame but is more heat stable.

Sucralose, a chlorinated sugar sold as Splenda, is stable when heated and is now used in more than 4,500 food and beverage products. It is 600 times sweeter than sucrose, four times as sweet as aspartame, and twice as sweet as saccharine. Sucralose is not absorbed or digested so has 0 calories.

Neohesperidin dihydrochalcone (NHDC) is a derivative of citrus juice that is heat stable and 1,800 times sweeter than sucrose. It is usually used in conjunction with aspartame and saccharine (increasing its sweetness) as a flavor enhancer. It counteracts bitterness and has a light creamy mouth feel.

Tagatose and trehalose are both natural sweeteners. Tagatose is a monosaccharide that is found in dairy products. Trehalose (aka mycose) is a disaccharide that was first discovered in ergot, a parasitic fungus that grows on grains but can be found in many animals, animal products (such as honey), and plants. Neither is as sweet as sucrose, so they are usually used for their humectant properties and to bulk up more intensive sweeteners.

Cyclamate is an artificial sweetener discovered in 1937 that is about 50 times sweeter than sucrose. In 1958 it was approved for sale as an artificial sweetener and was used in conjunction with saccharin. But in 1969 a study linked cyclamate to cancerous tumors in rats and mice, and it was banned in the U.S. Follow-up studies have failed to duplicate the result, but cyclamate is still outlawed in the U.S., although it is used in place of saccharin in Canada (where saccharin is banned) and is a common sweetener in Europe.

Syrups

Sugar syrups are liquid sweeteners that do not readily form crystals. The most common, corn syrup and high-fructose corn syrup, are made by heating cornstarch in the presence of acids, which hydrolyzes the starch into individual glucose and maltose molecules. Regular corn syrup is 14% glucose, 11% maltose, 20% water, and 55% oligosaccharide chains and is only about 40% as sweet as sucrose. In the 1960s it was discovered that an enzyme added to corn syrup could convert much of the glucose into much sweeter fructose. This high-fructose corn syrup, about 75% fructose and about 1.5 times sweeter than sucrose, has become a cost-effective way to sweeten many processed foods without adding off flavors, but as the use of corn as a fuel source continues to increase the price of high fructose corn syrup, traditional cane sugar, has become more cost competitive.

Malt syrups are made the same way as corn syrups except from other grains, typically barley. Golden syrup is high-fructose syrup made from cane sugar.

Syrups can also be made from the juices of trees like maple, palm, and birch, and the cactus-like agave. Tree-sap syrups are 70 to 80% sugar (mostly sucrose), whereas agave syrup is 70% fructose and 20% glucose, so it tastes sweeter.

How It Works ● Humans don't digest or

metabolize sugar alcohols efficiently and can absorb and metabolize only a fraction of them from food through the action of microbes in the intestine, which means we obtain energy from sugar alcohols indirectly and gradually. They cause a slow rise in blood glucose levels, so they are recommended for people with diabetes. Sugar alcohols cannot be broken down by bacteria in the mouth, so they do not contribute to tooth decay.

High-fructose corn syrup is more digestible than sugar alcohols, and provides more calories than the same amount of sucrose. Most high-intensity sweeteners are not carbohydrates and are not digested or

metabolized. They therefore contribute no calories.

See Also ● Candy, Seaweed, Sugar

SWEETNESS • See Flavor, Sugar, Sweeteners

SWEET POTATOES

What It Is ● Sweet potatoes are not potatoes. Both are New World vegetables but they are from different botanical families. They aren't even the same type of vegetable. Potatoes are tubers (underground stems). Sweet potatoes are **roots** — specifically the root of a morning glory.

Crew members on Columbus's first trip to the Americas were the first Europeans to taste a sweet potato. They called it by its Haitian name, *batata*. Later European explorers started calling the white potato *batata*, leading to centuries of confusion.

The sweet potato is native to Peru, where it was cultivated before the time of the Incas. By the 13th century, it was a staple food in Central America and the Caribbean, and there is evidence that it traveled as far west as New Zealand before the Europeans ever came to the New World. Other stories attribute its movement into Asia via Europeans at the end of the 15th century. Regardless of how it got there, the sweet potato is wildly popular in Asia. Roasted sweet potatoes are sold by vendors on the streets in China and Japan, and China is the largest world producer.

It was likely slave traders who took sweet potatoes to Africa, where it was compared to a native tuber, the *nyam* or *igname*. Since then the sweet potato has grown in popularity in Africa, and the name yam has become identified with orange-fleshed sweet potatoes in North America even though the true yam is from another plant species.

What It Does ● Most sweet potatoes are eaten fresh, usually baked in their jackets or boiled and mashed. They are also fried as

fast facts

- Pale orange sweet potato noodles, made from sweet potato starch, are prized in Korea and Japan for their chewy texture.

- Sweet potatoes from the New World arrived in Spain after Columbus's first voyage but didn't travel into the rest of Europe until Catherine of Aragon, Henry VIII's first wife, took them to England as part of her dowry. The king liked them so much that he offered a prize to any gardener who could grow them in England. By the mid-16th century, sweet potatoes blossomed all over England. But their popularity was short lived. Sweet potatoes cannot thrive in a cold climate; the crops soon withered and died.

chips or wedges, and in many recipes they are candied, underscoring their natural sweetness. Sweet potatoes are higher in starch and sugar than white potatoes and lower in protein. The orange-fleshed varieties supply a good amount of vitamin A in the form of beta-carotene (one roasted medium sweet potato contains two to three times the daily value of vitamin A).

There are two types of sweet potatoes: soft and firm. Orange-fleshed sweet potatoes are of the soft type, which tend to be sweet and moist. Firm-type sweet potatoes have dry, mealy flesh when baked, and their flesh is usually white or pale yellow.

How It Works • The sweetness of sweet potatoes is intensified by slow baking, thanks to an amylytic enzyme that breaks starch down into maltose (the same sugar that makes malted grain sweet). The action of the enzyme is greatest between the temperatures of 135 and 170°F (57 and 77°C). Slow baking therefore increases the sugar content of sweet potatoes far more than boiling or quick roasting.

Sweet potatoes are fairly perishable, and like most subtropical produce they are

damaged when stored at temperatures below 50°F (10°C). Chilling injury results in a syndrome known as hardcore, in which the center of a sweet potato remains hard even after prolonged cooking.

See Also • Roots

SWISS CHEESE • See Cheese

SWORDFISH • See Fish

SYRUPS • See Sweeteners

SZECHWAN PEPPER • See Spices

T

TAFFY • See Candy

TALEGGIO • See Cheese

TALLOW • See Fat

TAMARI • See Soybeans

TANDOOR • See Oven

TANNINS • See Flavor, Fruit, Wine

TAPIOCA • See Starch

TARO • See Roots

TARRAGON • See Herbs

TASTE • See Flavor

TEA

What It Is • The evergreen tea bush (*Camellia sinensis*) has been cultivated in China for about 4,000 years. Portuguese and Dutch traders took it to Europe in the mid-1500s, and Dutch colonists brought it to North America about 100 years later. The British also cultivated it widely in India, and it is today grown in high altitudes in damp, hot regions around the world. Leaves from the tea bush are steeped in hot water to produce the world's second most widely consumed beverage (after water). A similar infused beverage, or tisane, known as herbal tea is made not from tea leaves but from other aromatic leaves, flowers, or spices.

What It Does • All tea comes from one plant species but is processed into four main types: green, black, oolong, and white. For green tea, the fresh young leaves are typically steamed to inactivate enzymes that would otherwise darken the green leaves. Then the leaves are rolled flat, dried to about 3% moisture, and sorted by size from smallest (gunpowder) to largest (hyson). The best Japanese green tea leaves are powdered to make matcha, which is used in tea ceremonies. Green tea produces a fresh-tasting brew that's light green in color. For black tea, the leaves are allowed to wither and darken, then are rolled and held for several hours undergoing enzymatic browning, during which polyphenolic tannins oxidize and develop flavor and color. The leaves are then oven-dried (fired) at about 200°F (93°C) and sorted by size from smallest (orange pekoe) to largest (souchong). Enzymatic browning intensifies the flavor of black tea and creates a brew that's reddish brown in color. For oolong tea, the leaves are rolled, partially browned, dried, and sorted. Oolong tea makes a light brown flavorful brew halfway between green and black teas. White tea is the least processed tea. It is only lightly browned, heated gently, and not rolled, producing a pale-colored faintly sweet brew. To make specialty teas such as jasmine, other herbs, spices, and/or essential oils are added to one of the four types of processed tea leaves. Instant tea is manufactured like instant coffee: tea is brewed and then water removed by spray drying (less expensive) or freeze-drying (more costly but retains more flavor).

Tea Types

More than 90% of the tea consumed in North America is black. About half of all imported tea is sold in tea bags, which are filled with broken leaves and make a slightly stronger brew than loose tea. In Asia, green tea is far more popular than black tea. Here are some popular varieties among the four main types of tea.

Tea	Source	Characteristics
Black		
Assam	Northeastern India	Full bodied, robust; malty aroma; reddish
Ceylon	Sri Lanka	Delicate citrus aroma; gold
Darjeeling	Sri Lanka	Sweet; musky aroma; gold
Earl Grey Gold	Northeastern India	Darjeeling blend with citrus aroma from oil of bergamot; pale
English Breakfast	India, Sri Lanka	Full-bodied blend of Darjeeling, Assam, and Ceylon; rich reddish brown
Keemun	China	Intense aroma; mild bitterness; rich gold
Lapsang Souchong	Fujian, China	Smoky pine aromas; rich red
Green		
Bancha	Japan	Clear; strong aroma; pale green
Gunpowder	China	Pungent; grassy aroma; pale straw color
Matcha	Japan	Delicate; sweet grassy aroma; pale straw color
Oolong		
Formosa	Taiwan	Full flavor; peach aroma; gold
Iron Goddess	Taiwan	Rich flavor; floral, toasty aroma; copper
White		
Bai Hao Yinzhen (silver needle)	Fujian, China	Full flavor; honey aroma; pale yellow
Ceylon White	Sri Lanka	Delicate flavor; pine and honey aroma; pale gold
White Pu-erh	Yunnan, China	Rich flavor; honey aroma; pale gold

Brewing and Using Tea

From Japan to Britain to North America, tea drinking has always been surrounded by ceremony, some of which involves the brewing itself. In the West, brewing usually consists of one extraction, whereas in Asia, tea leaves may be extracted several times for a single brew. The key to a high-quality extraction for black tea is maintaining the water's high temperature. It's best to begin with fresh cold water, which contains more oxygen and tastes more lively than flat standing water. Ideally, the pH will be near neutral. Most city water is alkaline, and you'll get a better brew by adding a pinch or two of cream of tartar to make city water slightly more acid. Warm your teapot or cup to prevent a sudden drop in water temperature when the tea and boiling water are mixed. Use one tea bag or about 1 teaspoon (5 mL) of loose tea per ¾ cup (175 mL) of boiling water. As soon as the water boils, pour it over the tea in the warm pot or cup. A full boil is necessary for a high temperature, but avoid letting the water boil for too long, which results in oxygen loss that results in a flat-tasting tea. When

fast facts

- The leaves of a tea plant can be harvested after about three years. The plant will continue to produce viable leaves for up to 50 years and may survive for hundreds of years.
- It takes about 6,000 leaves to make 1 pound (454 g) of tea, which yields about 200 cups.

Jasmine-Ginger Poached Rhubarb

Tea makes fabulous infusions. Use it to flavor the water for rice, pasta, or other cooked grains, to flavor milk for custards and creams, or to flavor poaching liquid as in this simple rhubarb recipe. Serve this sweet scented rhubarb with ice cream or yogurt in a parfait or other dessert.

3	jasmine tea bags or 1 tbsp (15 mL) loose jasmine tea	3
2 lbs	fresh or frozen sliced rhubarb (about 6 cups/1.5 L)	1 kg
1¼ cups	granulated sugar	300 mL
2 tbsp	freshly grated gingerroot	25 mL
Pinch	freshly ground black pepper	Pinch

1. In a large saucepan, bring 1¼ cups (300 mL) water to a boil. Remove from heat and add tea. Cover and let steep for 5 minutes, then discard tea bags or strain out loose tea.

2. Add rhubarb, sugar, and ginger and bring to a boil over medium-high heat, stirring occasionally. Reduce heat to medium-low and simmer until rhubarb is just tender, 8 to 10 minutes. Stir in pepper, then let cool slightly. Transfer to a bowl and refrigerate until well chilled, at least 3 hours or for up to 4 days.

MAKES ABOUT 5 CUPS (1.25 L)

brewing green and white teas, use water that hasn't yet reached a boil (about 140 to 170°F/60 to 77°C) to avoid extracting too much bitter flavor from the leaves. Cover the pot or cup to retain heat for the best extraction. Steep for 3 to 5 minutes, then remove the tea or strain the infusion into another warmed pot. Longer steeping times will extract more bitter tannins from any type of tea. Color is an unreliable indicator of doneness; because color is extracted before flavor, a dark color may not indicate a robust flavor. For extra flavor, press the wet tea leaves in the strainer or squeeze the tea bags before straining or removing the tea.

Iced tea dates back to the mid-1800s in North America but was popularized at the 1904 World's Fair in St. Louis, Missouri. Currently, about 80% of the tea consumed in the U.S. is iced. For the best iced tea, brew it as described above for hot tea, but use double the amount of tea: two tea bags or 2 teaspoons (10 mL) loose tea per ¾ cup (175 mL) water. The extra tea keeps the ice from diluting the tea flavor. If your iced tea turns cloudy, the tea's astringent-tasting tannins have come out of solution. To prevent cloudiness, use lower-tannin tea such as Ceylon rather than higher-tannin teas like Assam and Darjeeling. It also helps to avoid using hard water, which encourages the tannin to separate out. Start with neutral or slightly acidic water to make the tannins more soluble. Avoid pouring hot tea over ice or putting hot tea in the refrigerator; the rapid temperature change also encourages cloudiness. First cool the tea to room temperature, then chill it for 24 hours. If the tea becomes cloudy despite your efforts, add some lemon juice to help clear it.

Tea isn't only for drinking. Many cultures use the leaves like herbs to flavor liquids for marinades, sauces, desserts, and other dishes. In Japan, green tea leaves (tencha) are used to flavor ice cream, candy, cakes, and other desserts. The best Japanese green tea leaves are powdered to make matcha, which is used in tea ceremonies. In China, tea eggs are made by hard-cooking eggs, cracking the shells but leaving them on the eggs, then simmering the eggs in tea for a mottled, tea-flavored egg. Tea leaves are also used for their aromatic smoke (see recipe for Tea-Smoked Mussels with Seaweed Mignonette, page 525).

science wise

Milk in Tea • Stirring a little milk or cream into black tea balances the flavors by making it taste less astringent. The milk proteins bond with tea's puckery phenolic compounds and prevent the tannins from constricting our taste buds. To help prevent milk or cream from curdling when it hits the hot tea, warm the milk or cream in the cup first, then add the hot tea.

How It Works • Scientists have identified more than 300 **flavor compounds** in black tea. Most of these compounds are aldehydes resulting from the breakdown of amino acids during the enzymatic browning of the leaves. Leaf processing involves rolling the leaves to rupture their cells, which allows enzymes to mix with oxygen in the air (oxidize) and generate new aroma and color compounds. Some of tea's astringency and yellow or rust color come from oxidation compounds called theaflavins and thearubigins. A note of savoriness comes from the transformation of the amino acid theanine into glutamic acid. Green tea also gets some floral aromas from linalool and geraniol and some toasty aromas if the green leaves were dried in hot pans. But the primary flavors in tea are bitterness and astringency, producing a tea's "brisk" flavor.

Tea leaves harvested in the spring and early summer are more flavorful than those harvested in the late summer and autumn. The most richly flavored tea comes from the leaf buds and the first few leaves of the growing shoot. These are higher in the protective phenolic compounds that give tea its complex taste. On the tea plant, the uppermost leaves are young, soft, supple, and higher in green chlorophyll. They are used for the finest grades of green tea. Lower down the plant, the older leaves have less chlorophyll and more tannins, resulting in a stronger flavor. Tannins give tea an astringent taste, causing our palates to constrict or pucker. In general, green tea is more tannic but less bitter than black tea.

The bitter taste of tea comes primarily from **caffeine**. Dried tea leaves contain about twice as much caffeine as roasted coffee beans, but methods of brewing tea extract less caffeine than methods of brewing coffee. An 8-ounce cup of brewed black tea contains approximately 50 mg of caffeine (some green tea contains slightly less), which is about 40 to 50% less caffeine than most brewed coffee. Tea also contains trace amounts of the stimulant compounds theophylline and theobromine, which is the active compound in chocolate.

Multiple studies show that the **antioxidant** phenolic compounds in tea can help protect artery walls, prevent cell damage, and reduce risks of heart disease and cancer. Tea also contains antibacterial properties and some fluoride that can help fight tooth decay. White tea is slightly higher than other teas in antioxidants, caffeine, and antibacterial properties because it is less processed. For maximum antioxidant and flavor extraction, use tea bags or ground tea instead of loose whole tea leaves because the broken cells of ground tea leaves release more compounds into the brew.

See Also • Coffee, Herbs

TEFF • See Wheat

TELEME • See Cheese

TEMPEH • See Soybeans

TEMPERATURE • See Heat

TEMPERING • See Chocolate

TEQUILA • See Liquor

TERPENES • See Flavor Compounds

TERROIR • See Wine

THEOBROMINE • See Chocolate

THICKENERS • See Sauces

THISTLES

What It Is • Comprising more than 300 species, thistles are plants characterized by their prickly leaves or stems. Depending upon the species, most parts of the plant are edible, including the flowering heads (**artichokes**), fibrous stalks (cardoons), and firm roots (burdock).

What It Does • Artichokes and cardoons belong to the same thistle genus (*Cynara*) and share several attributes. They both discolor when cut because of enzymatic browning and

fast fact

- *Carduus*, the name of a large species of thistles, means "place with thistles" in Latin. It is the root word for cardoons as well as for Chardonnay, the famous wine grape that is believed to have originated in the thistle-rich region of Burgundy, France.

should be placed in acidulated water or oil (for artichokes) after they are cut. And they both taste bitter, astringent, and slightly sweet. Artichokes come from the plant *Cynara scolymus* and are flower buds picked before they blossom. Cardoons come from a related parent plant (*Cynara cardunculus*) and are the silvery gray stalks of the plant.

As stalks, cardoons support the thistle plant and carry nutrients from the **roots** to the **leaves**. This supporting role makes them tough with fibrous strings of cellulose similar to those found in celery. To avoid stringiness, remove the tough strings before cooking. Phenolic compounds in cardoons also contribute to the toughening of their cell walls. To soften cardoons, start them in cold water like potatoes and gradually bring them to a boil. Repeat the boiling process several times with fresh water to leach out the phenolic compounds and soften the vegetable. Repeated boiling also leaches out flavor, though, so some cooks prefer to briefly blanch cardoons, then cut the stalks crosswise in several places to sever the tough fibers and make cardoons easier to chew. In the Piedmont region of Italy, blanched cardoons are traditionally dipped in bagna cauda, the warm sauce of olive oil, butter, garlic, and anchovies.

How It Works • Thistle plants like artichokes, cardoons, and burdock all get their astringent flavors from tannic phenol compounds. To make thistles like cardoons less astringent, cook them with cream or milk. The milk proteins bind with the phenolic compounds, preventing them from constricting our taste buds and producing astringency. Depending on their age, thistles also taste slightly bitter and have a bit of celery-like sweetness.

The astringency of cardoons has a distinct advantage in cheese making: it is powerful enough to coagulate milk. In this role, cardoons serve as a vegetarian alternative to traditional rennet (calf's stomach enzyme) used for coagulation.

See Also •
Artichoke, Cheese, Roots, Stems

THYME • See Herbs

THYMUS • See Organ Meats

TILAPIA • See Fish

TILEFISH • See Fish

TIN • See Cookware

TOFFEE • See Candy

TOFU • See Soybeans

TOMALLEY • See Crustacean

TOMATILLOS • See Tomatoes

TOMATOES

What It Is • Native to South America, tomatoes are the **fruit** of the perennial plant *Lycopersicon esculentum*. They are botanical fruits but culinary vegetables because of how we use them. The plant was domesticated in Mexico, and Spanish explorers took it to Europe in the mid-1500s. Tomatoes were slow to gain popularity because they were believed to be poisonous since they are members of the nightshade family. In the 1700s, the plant was introduced to North America, and when the fruit's toxicity was dispelled as a myth, its popularity exploded. Tomatoes are now the second most popular vegetable in North America after potatoes and one of the most widely consumed vegetables in the world.

What It Does • Ripe, juicy tomatoes are often enjoyed raw in salads and sandwiches, but they're also widely used in cooked soups, sauces, and baked dishes. Tomatoes can be grilled, pickled, fried, roasted, sautéed, and stuffed. Commercially, they are processed into an array of canned, bottled, and jarred tomato juices, purées, sauces, salsas, ketchups, and pastes. Tomato purée is made by briefly cooking tomatoes, then straining them to capture a thick liquid. Tomato sauce is a thinner purée cooked with seasonings and often used as a flavor base in other dishes. Tomato paste is a thicker purée that's cooked to evaporate all but about one-fifth of the moisture, then strained to produce a dark red concentrate. Tomatoes are also dehydrated

Tomato Varieties

From green to yellow to red to purple and from small teardrops to large globes, tomatoes come in more than 4,000 varieties. Many heirloom varieties are available in farmer's markets and tend to be more flavorful but more perishable than supermarket tomatoes. Here are five basic tomato categories and some varieties in each category. Green tomatoes are unripe tomatoes in any category. They tend to be firmer, slightly more acidic, and more bitter than ripe tomatoes and are best for frying, broiling, salsas, chutneys, and relishes.

Tomato	Characteristics	Varieties
Beefsteak	Round, large; tender, juicy flesh; good raw and cooked	Amana Orange, Brandywine, Mortgage Lifter
Cherry (currant, pear)	Round or teardrop shaped, small; tender, sweet, juicy flesh; best for snacking, salads, or light sautéing	Purple Haze, Sun Gold, Tiny Tim
Globe (slicing)	Round, medium size; tender, juicy flesh; good raw and cooked	Early Girl, Green Zebra, Ida Gold
Grape	Oblong, very small; tender, sweet flesh; best for snacking and salads	Juliet, Santa F1
Paste (plum)	Oblong, medium size; thick, dry flesh with very few cavities; best for sauces or preparations requiring minimal juice	Orange Jubilee, Roma, San Marzano

into sun-dried and oven-dried tomatoes that are available in halves, slivers, or bits packed dry or in oil. Dehydrating the fruit concentrates its flavor and sweetness. Dried tomatoes can be rehydrated in hot water or in cooked dishes that contain plenty of liquid.

The best tomatoes are fully ripened on the vine, which allows the fruit to develop maximum sweetness and aroma. But ripe tomatoes are highly perishable. Most supermarket tomatoes are harvested green and unripe, then "ripened" with ethylene gas after shipping. The gas turns the tomatoes red but doesn't develop the flavor and aroma of vine-ripened tomatoes. Some supermarket tomatoes are also coated with edible wax to delay moisture loss and prolong shelf life.

When buying tomatoes, look for plump

science wise

Making Tomatoes Shape Up • Tomatoes are often cooked until they break down and thicken. But if you want them to hold their shape to create a chunky sauce or stew, an initial step of low-heat cooking does the trick. Start the tomatoes over medium-low heat (about 130 to 140°F/54 to 60°C) and hold them there for 20 to 30 minutes. This process activates an enzyme in the vegetable's cell walls that prevents the cells from weakening. Alternatively, use tomatoes that are canned with calcium salts. The calcium forms bridges between pectin molecules, strengthening them and keeping the tomatoes from disintegrating in the can, and these types of canned tomatoes resist softening.

fruit with smooth, blemish-free skin that yields to gentle pressure. Ripe tomatoes will have a rich, sweet aroma. They're best stored at room temperature (above 55°F/13°C). Avoid refrigerating tomatoes because one of the key flavor compounds, called (Z)-3-dexenal, is destroyed at temperatures below 45°F (7°C). Cold temperatures can also make tomato flesh mealy and blunt the flavor, particularly in green tomatoes. To ripen unripe tomatoes, enclose them in a paper bag with an apple at room temperature. The apple will emit the same ethylene gas that commercial wholesalers use to ripen green tomatoes after shipping.

How It Works

• Like eggplant and potatoes, tomatoes are nightshades, fruiting plants that contain a mix of bitter alkaloid compounds meant to ward off predators. Tomatoes contain tomatine, a bitter alkaloid that concentrates in green tomatoes and the green leaves. Tomatine was once considered toxic, but research shows that it can actually help reduce blood cholesterol levels. Tomatoes are also high in the **antioxidant** carotenoid lycopene, which reduces the cell damage that can lead to certain cancers such as prostate cancer. Cooked and canned tomatoes (including ketchup and tomato paste) are higher in lycopene than fresh tomatoes. High in fiber and vitamins A and C,

a medium tomato contains only 35 calories.

The taste of tomatoes is acidic, bitter, sweet, savory, and highly aromatic all at once. Acidity comes from citric acid, a weak organic acid also found in citrus fruits. Tomato acidity averages about 0.5% by weight and concentrates in the jelly and water, or "juice," that surrounds the seeds in the center of the fruit. Sweetness averages about 3% by weight but varies widely by variety, growing conditions, and ripeness when harvested. Yellow tomatoes tend to be sweeter and less acidic than red.

What tips these botanical fruits into the culinary vegetable category is a relatively high amount (up to 0.3% by weight) of glutamic acid, the savory umami flavor often associated with cooked meat. Tomatoes also have some muskiness from sulfur compounds. Elements of sweet strawberries and caramel come from furaneol, an aroma compound found in pineapples as well. Fresh grassy aromas, particularly in green tomatoes, come from the aroma molecules hexanal and hexanol. Most of a tomato's aroma compounds concentrate in the skin and flesh. For the most flavorful tomato sauce, cook tomatoes whole with the skin to capture the acidity, sweetness, and aroma in all parts of the fruit, then strain out the skin and seeds. Or peel and seed the tomatoes and cook only the tomato flesh; simmer down the skins, seeds, jelly, and juice separately, then strain the reduced liquid and stir it into the cooked tomato flesh. You can even add leaves from a

fast facts

- About 125 million tons of tomatoes are produced each year, most of them in China, the U.S., and Turkey.
- Tomatillos (*Physalis ixocarpa*) are botanically related to tomatoes but grow with thicker fruit walls, a sticky compound on the skin, and a papery husk, all of which protect the fruit and make it less perishable than tomatoes. Tomatillos remain green and are usually smaller and more tart than their tomato cousins.

tomato plant to enhance the fresh green-tomato flavor of a sauce.

While many sauces are thickened with starch, fresh tomatoes contain enough **pectin** and hemicellulose in their cell walls (about 1%) to thicken sauces on their own. When concentrated into tomato paste, the thickening power of tomatoes doubles. Tomato paste also contains enough concentrated protein (about 3%) to emulsify sauces, vinaigrettes, and other **dispersions**. Pectinic acid and hemicellulose reach their peak when tomatoes are just ripe. After that, the pectinic acid is converted to more water-soluble pectic acid and the tomatoes begin to soften and rot. For the thickest cooked tomato purée, capture the most pectin and hemicellulose by using just-ripe tomatoes. Quickly heat the tomatoes to at least 180°F (82°C) to inactivate enzymes that would otherwise break down the firm pectic substances. After an initial high temperature, you can gently simmer the tomatoes to evaporate excess moisture and concentrate flavor. By inactivating the enzymes, you will lose some fresh grassy tomato flavors created by the enzymes, but you'll get a thicker purée. To prevent bitterness, strain out the bitter seeds before puréeing.

See Also • Fruit, Juice, Ketchup, Vegetables

TONIC WATER • See Bitters

TORTILLAS • See Bread

TOXIN

What It Is • Emperors and kings sometimes employ food tasters to ensure that food isn't poisonous. These tasters offer up their lives to detect toxins, substances in food that can lead to illness or death. A food toxin is any substance in or on food that has been shown to create some degree of risk when consumed in sufficient quantity. Toxins may be inherent to the food or they may be contaminants such as microorganisms or their metabolic products.

What It Does • Toxins in food often come from plants and make their way up the food chain from there. Plants manufacture toxins as chemical defenses against predators. Most modern plants have been bred to keep toxins below harmful levels, but some foods can still cause irritation, illness, or disease in some people. The most common plant toxins belong to a chemical family called alkaloids, which manifest as a bitter taste in foods, such as in eggplant and coffee. In low doses, alkaloids are harmless and can even be pleasurable. Coffee and chocolate get their stimulating effects from the bitter-tasting alkaloids caffeine and theobromine. The only potentially harmful alkaloids in food, solanine and chaconine, are found in green patches on potatoes and are easily peeled away.

Plants as well as other foods can also carry harmful toxins from bacteria, molds, and environmental pollutants. The most deadly bacterial toxin, botulin, comes from *Clostridium botulinum*, a bacterium that grows in oxygen-free, low-acid environments, which can occur in some jarred and canned foods. The bacterial spores are killed at the high temperatures (240 to 250°F/116 to 120°C) and times used to process most canned foods. But improperly processed canned foods, and other foods such as raw garlic left to steep at room temperature in the low-acid, oxygen-free environment of oil, can allow the bacteria to produce the toxin. Botulin causes botulism, a life-threatening illness that blocks nerve function and can

Common Food Toxins

Apart from the bacteria that cause food-borne illness, plants and shellfish are the most common sources of toxins that cause food poisoning. Some toxins, such as the urushiol in mangoes and the oxalates in spinach and rhubarb, may cause irritation only in very sensitive individuals. But other toxins, such as the cyanotoxins in contaminated shellfish, can lead to more serious illness.

Plant Food	Toxin	Chemical Family	How to Avoid
Amaranth	Oxalic acid	Oxalates	Eat in moderation if you have gout or kidney disorder
Bitter almonds	Hydrocyanic acid	Cyanogenic glycoside	Eat in moderation
Bitter cassava (manioc)	Cyanide	Cyanogenic glycoside	Boil, ferment, or soak in water to leach out toxin; or use sweet cassava instead, the type most available in North American markets
Celery and celeriac	Psoralen	Furanocoumarins	Do not eat celery and celeriac exposed to extreme cold, extreme light, or mold; buy only very fresh and use within a few weeks
Fiddlehead ferns	Ptaquiloside	Glucoside	Do not eat fiddleheads from bracken ferns; instead eat fiddleheads from safer ostrich ferns
Grains	Aflatoxin	Coumarins	Do not eat moldy grains
Mangoes	Urushiol	Phenols	Do not eat if you are very sensitive to other sources of urushiol such as poison ivy
Mushrooms	Amanitin Psilocybin	Alkaloids	Do not eat unidentified wild mushrooms
	Gyromitrin	Hydrazines	Do not eat false morel mushrooms
Nuts and peanuts	Aflatoxins	Coumarins	Do not eat moldy nuts
Parsnips	Psoralen	Furanocoumarins	Do not eat parsnips exposed to extreme cold, extreme light, or mold; buy only very fresh and use within a few weeks
Pome fruits	Cyanide	Cyanogenic glycosides	Eat in moderation seeds from apples, loquats, pears, and quince
Potatoes	Solanine and chaconine	Alkaloids	Peel away green parts; do not eat bitter-tasting potatoes or potato sprouts
Rhubarb	Oxalic acid	Oxalates	Eat in moderation if you have gout or kidney disorder
Shellfish	Saxitoxin Brevetoxins Domoic acid	Steroids Polyethers Amino Acids	Do not eat raw mussels, clams, oysters, and scallops harvested from waters contaminated by red tide
Sorrel	Oxalic acid	Oxalates	Eat in moderation if you have gout or kidney disorder
Spinach	Oxalic acid	Oxalates	Eat in moderation if you have gout or kidney disorder
Stone fruits	Cyanide	Cyanogenic glycosides	Do not eat pits of apricots, cherries, nectarines, peaches, and plums

lead to respiratory and muscular paralysis. Other harmful bacteria in food include *Salmonella*, *E. coli*, and *Campylobacter jejuni*, which is the most common source of food-borne illness in the world.

Mold is another source of toxins in food. Most food molds are harmless and can be scraped away, but some produce harmful mycotoxins (fungal toxins). *Aspergillus* molds on grains and nuts produce toxins known as aflatoxins that can be lethal at high doses and are carcinogenic at low doses. *Aspergillus* can also produce harmful blue-green mycotoxins on bread and cheese.

All moldy grains and nuts and other foods that are unusually or heavily molded on the surface should be discarded.

Toxins can even enter our food supply from contaminated soil and water. Mercury, dioxins, and polychlorinated biphenyls (PCBs) enter our water supply from coal-fired power plants, the burning of industrial waste, and pollution, making their way up the food chain from plants to animals to humans. The toxic form of mercury (methylmercury) makes its way from algae to fish and builds up in the muscle tissues of long-lived fish such as tuna. Eating fish high in mercury is mostly a risk for young children and pregnant women and can lead to lower developmental IQs, impairment of motor skills, and damage to the cardiovascular, immune, and reproductive systems.

Scombroid poisoning is another food hazard from fish. Certain fish like tuna, mackerel, mahi mahi, and sardines are high in the amino acid histidine. When the fish is improperly refrigerated, bacteria convert the histidine into histamine and cause the fish to spoil. Eating spoiled fish can lead to nausea, vomiting, and other unpleasant but not life-threatening symptoms.

Shellfish can harbor four different types of toxins that can cause diarrhea, amnesia, neurological dysfunction, and even paralysis. Most of these toxins are produced by algae bloom (red tide). For this reason, water quality is closely monitored and tested by local governments to prevent contaminated mollusks from entering the food supply.

Metals are another source of toxicity. Aluminum and copper cookware are often lined with less reactive metals to prevent the leaching of potentially toxic aluminum and copper ions into food.

How It Works • Toxicology is a complex science that depends largely on dose. As Paracelsus, the 16th-century Swiss "father of toxicology" wrote, "All things are poison and nothing is without poison. Only the dose makes a thing not a poison." For instance, a small amount of alcohol induces a feeling of euphoria, but a large amount can damage our

fast fact

- Methyl salicylate is a toxic compound produced by some plants as a chemical defense against predators. It's also a flavoring agent called wintergreen that's used at concentrations below 0.04% in foods such as mints and chewing gum.

nerve cells and lead to a loss of consciousness and death. In most countries, alcohol intoxication or impairment is legally defined as a blood alcohol content of 0.05 to 0.08% (0.5 to 0.8 grams of alcohol per kilogram of blood). Even water can be fatal if consumed in huge quantities in a short time. Overexerted athletes and infants, who have especially low levels of sodium, potassium, and other electrolytes in their bodily fluids, can take in so much water that it leads to water intoxication.

Most toxins are neutralized in our bodies in the liver. We also excrete toxins as a part of normal metabolism and sweating. And many are inactivated by cooking. But some toxins can survive cooking. For instance, mycotoxins in poisonous mushrooms can survive cooking, making it extremely important to avoid eating wild-picked mushrooms that haven't been clearly identified as safe by a mushroom expert. In general, young children, the elderly, and those with compromised immune systems are most at risk for the damaging effects of toxins and food-borne illnesses.

The most common sources of food-borne illness are raw foods of animal origin, such as raw meat, poultry, eggs, shellfish, and unpasteurized milk and juice. Foods that are pooled together, such as ground beef, are particularly hazardous because a pathogen from one source can contaminate the whole batch. When processed under less than sanitary conditions, mass-produced raw vegetables and fruits can also become contaminated.

Developed countries around the world have detailed food safety regulations to prevent harmful toxins in food. In the U.S., the Department of Agriculture (USDA) and its Food Safety and Inspection Service govern the safety of meat, poultry, and eggs, the Bureau of Alcohol, Tobacco and Firearms regulates alcoholic beverages, while the Food and Drug Administration (FDA) ensures the safety of all other foods. In Canada, food safety guidelines are set by Health Canada and the Canadian Food Inspection Agency. Standards are set in the U.K. by the Food Standards Agency and in Europe by the European Food Safety Authority. These and other state and local agencies regulate food safety to control toxins in food from production, handling, processing, preparation, and storage.

Restaurants often follow a detailed system of food safety checks developed for astronauts known as Hazard Analysis and Critical Control Points (HACCP). At home, avoid toxins and food-borne illness with three basic rules of food safety:

1. *Keep it clean.* Wash your hands frequently with hot soapy water. Wash cutting boards, utensils, and work surfaces with a weak bleach-and-water solution. Rinse all produce with soapy water or commercial produce washes.

2. *Avoid cross-contamination.* Keep raw meat, poultry, seafood, and eggs away from foods that will be eaten raw. Use separate cutting boards and plates for raw and cooked food.

3. *Watch temperatures.* Cook foods, especially proteins, to safe internal temperatures (see Meat Doneness chart, page 390). Keep hot foods hot (above 140°F/60°C) and cold foods cold (below 40°F/4°C). Whenever possible, keep foods out of the danger zone, which is between 40°F (4°C) and 140°F (60°C). Use a food thermometer to test the internal temperature of foods. Marinate foods in the refrigerator and thaw them in the refrigerator, in cold water, or in a microwave oven.

See Also ● Bacteria, Canning, Carcinogen, Food Additives, Irradiation, Mad Cow Disease, Meat, Minerals, Mollusks, Pasteurization, Vitamins

TRANSGLUTAMINASE • See Colloid, Molecular Gastronomy

TRIACYLGLYCEROLS (Triglycerides) • See Fat

TRIPE • See Organ Meats

TROUT • See Fish

TRUFFLES • See Fungi

TRYPTOPHAN • See Protein

TUBER • See Stems

TUNA • See Fish

TURBINADO SUGAR • See Sugar

TURBOT • See Fish

TURKEY • See Chicken, Poultry

TURMERIC • See Spices

TURNIPS • See Cruciferous Vegetables, Leaves, Roots

UDON • See Pasta

UGLIFRUIT • See Citrus

ULTRAPASTEURIZATION • See Pasteurization

UMAMI • See Flavor

VACUUM

What It Is • A vacuum is empty space, void of everything, even air. Although near-airless spaces exist in nature (for instance, the dense interior of cured meat), total vacuums do not occur naturally. They must be manufactured.

What It Does • Vacuums are used in several areas of food processing, mostly for preservation. Because most bacteria and all fungi and molds require oxygen to live, depriving them of air kills them and therefore preserves food. Forms of vacuum packaging include cans, bottles, aseptic boxes, and heat-resistant vacuum-sealed bags such as Cryovac.

Sous vide (French for "under vacuum") is a method of placing food in vacuum-sealed bags (the technique is sometimes referred to as Cryovacking) to infuse ingredients with flavors, change their texture through compression, or heat them at an extremely low temperature, usually about 140°F (60°C), to avoid the changes that happen to proteins and fats when they are cooked at high temperatures, (such as tough protein or liquefied fat). Cryovac has been used in food packaging since the late 1960s. In 1974, Pierre Troisgros, the three-star French chef from Roanne, started to use sous vide to protect foie gras during poaching. He was able to cut weight loss to 5% from 50% — an incredible savings in ingredient, money, and flavor.

Sous vide keeps foods from drying out and allows chefs to cook foods at lower temperatures and thereby preserve quality. But its biggest advantage to restaurants is probably consistency. By preparing foods in vacuum packaging and storing them when they are perfectly cooked, all that is needed to finish the dish for a customer is to heat the food in its plastic bag. Restaurant kitchens designed for sous-vide cooking use a hot water system called a thermal circulator, basically a thermostat-regulated heater with a pump that keeps the perfectly heated water moving evenly around the package. The technology takes the guesswork out of judging doneness and allows a chef to better control food quality in multiple units.

Chefs also use the vacuum pressure of sous vide to suck the moisture from raw fruits and vegetables, transforming a juice- and air-filled slice of watermelon into something as dense and crisp as a Bosc pear or a Winesap apple. The flavor of sous-vide food is intensified but not changed. Traditional methods of intensifying flavor, such as curing and heating, change the flavor at the same time. Curing inundates an ingredient with salt, and heat causes protein to coagulate and sugars to turn brown, but sous vide dials up flavor without altering it.

Vacuums speed up marination by removing the air from an ingredient, thereby decreasing the atmospheric pressure inside it. Then the deflated food is exposed to a marinade, which is immediately drawn into the ingredient through osmosis.

Freeze-**drying** is an industrial technique that involves evaporating the moisture from a frozen ingredient without thawing it first into liquid to create perfectly preserved natural ingredients. Vacuum distillation is a way of making **liquor** without using heat by reducing the air pressure in a still enough to cause the alcohol to vaporize.

How It Works • Vacuum packaging stops the growth of aerobic bacteria in an ingredient, but it does not kill anaerobic bacteria, such as *Clostridium tetani* and *C. botulinum*, which only produce toxins when deprived of oxygen. Therefore, vacuum-packed foods have to be carefully processed. Canned foods are heated to between 240 and 265°F (116 and 130°C) for several minutes to kill bacteria and spores, and aseptic milk is brought to 275°F (135°C) for a few seconds to destroy all pathogenic microbes. Dry ingredients can't support these bacteria, so there is no danger in vacuum-packed grains, spices, or coffee. Fresh raw meat and fish that are Cryovacked to extend their storage lives are not packed under total vacuum to keep anaerobic bacteria from creating toxins. Though vacuum-sealed proteins can be stored for weeks, they must be kept under refrigeration.

Some food scientists believe that cooking sous-vide ingredients at low temperatures poses a food safety risk, even though the practice has been done safely for more than 25 years. At the boiling point at sea level — 212°F (100°C) — low-acid foods (those with a pH higher than 4.3), like vegetables and meats, have to be heated for more than five hours to ensure that anaerobic microbes are destroyed. But that amount of time decreases exponentially as temperatures rise, so traditionally, food processing has involved increasing the temperature and shortening processing time to preserve food quality. Sous-vide techniques take the opposite tack, lowering the temperature and increasing the time, sometimes to as long as 24 hours. In this way proteins can be cooked at 140°F (60°C), essentially the temperature of a hot bath. At that temperature meat fibers contract minimally, so the amount of juices they lose is a fraction of what would be excreted at higher temperatures. The juices that are expelled are retained inside the plastic packaging, and since the meat fibers remain flexible, most of those juices can be reabsorbed by the ingredient. Higher temperatures toughen protein and cause cell walls to burst, so the ingredient is no longer capable of reabsorbing lost juices.

See Also ● Atmospheric Pressure, Drying, Liquor, Meat, Molecular Gastronomy

VALINE ● See Protein

VANILLA

What It Is ● Vanilla is the most popular flavor in the world, and one of the most expensive (second only to saffron). The demand for vanilla flavoring exceeds the crop yield every year, so natural vanilla is about 100 times as expensive as artificial vanilla flavoring (mostly vanillin), which is synthesized from lignin in wood pulp.

True vanilla comes from the fruit (bean) of a climbing orchid of the genus *Vanilla*, of which there are about 100 species, native to Central and South America. Only two species (*V. fragrans* and *V. tahitenis*) are important for vanilla flavor. The first Europeans to taste vanilla were Spanish, who gave it its name, *vanilla*, which means "sheath" or "husk" in Spanish (from the Latin *vagina*). In the 19th century, techniques for hand-pollinating vanilla were developed, allowing its cultivation in areas that lack vanilla-pollinating insects. The French planted vanilla orchids off the east coast of Africa, first on the island of Réunion, then known as Île Bourbon, and later in Madagascar (which is why vanilla from Madagascar and its neighboring islands is sometimes known as bourbon vanilla). Bourbon vanilla currently accounts for about 80% of the world production.

What It Does ● The flavor of natural vanilla derives from defensive phenolic compounds in the fruit, particularly vanillin. Although the aroma of vanillin accounts for much of vanilla's flavor on its

Seared Scallops with Vanilla Mango Salsa

The floral essence of vanilla blooms when mixed with hot pepper, tart mango, and savory seared scallops. Although we think of vanilla as tasting sweet that is only because we usually sweeten the foods that include it. There is nothing intrinsically sweet about the flavor of vanilla. In fact many of its phenolic compounds are similar to those in oregano, thyme, anise, ginger, and peppers.

It is important to get sea scallops that have not been treated with sodium tripolyphosphate (STP) to force them to absorb water, called "soaked" scallops. When soaked scallops cook, the bonds that hold the water in suspension break and the soaking liquid comes pouring out, causing the scallops to steam, which makes it impossible to sear them. To make sure that they have not been treated look for scallops that are slightly gray, or beige, or pink, anything but pure white; have your pan as hot as possible; and cook the scallops quickly. They should still be a little soft in the center when they are done cooking.

1 cup	jarred mango salsa	250 mL
1 tbsp	pure vanilla extract	15 mL
1 tsp	hot pepper sauce	5 mL
1 tsp	freshly squeezed lime juice	5 mL
1½ lbs	large "dry" or "day" sea scallops	750 g
2 tsp	extra virgin olive oil	10 mL
	Coarse sea salt and freshly ground black pepper	
1 tbsp	chopped cilantro leaves	15 mL

1. In a small bowl, combine salsa, vanilla, hot pepper sauce, and lime juice. Set aside.

2. If necessary, trim off the tough strips of cartilage attached to the sides of the scallops. Flatten scallops gently, but firmly, between your palms to about ½-inch (1 cm) thickness. Rub the scallops with oil and season with salt and pepper.

3. Meanwhile, place a large cast-iron skillet over high heat for about 5 minutes. Sear the scallops in the hot skillet until crusty and lightly browned but still soft in the center, about 1½ minutes per side. Transfer to a platter, and top with half the salsa. Scatter chopped cilantro over the top, and serve with remaining salsa on the side.

MAKES 4 SERVINGS

own, it is complemented by other flavor notes in the fruit, including woodiness, floral fragrances, a tobacco-like pungency, clove-like aromas, and honey flavors reminiscent of caramel and butter. Synthetic vanilla derived from wood lignin contains mostly plain vanillin and is one-dimensional in comparison.

Various vanilla-growing regions produce beans with a range of flavors. Bourbon vanilla is considered the richest and most balanced. Indonesian vanilla has less vanillin, so it is lighter tasting, but it also has a smoky aroma that is believed to develop as the vanilla cures. Mexican vanilla contains only half the vanillin of bourbon vanilla and has a fruity, acidic, winy character. Tahitian vanilla, which is one of the rarest types, comes from a native species that is low in vanillin and high in perfumed floral notes.

The flavor of vanilla is concentrated in two parts of the fruit, the fibrous interior wall of the pod and the sticky resin that surrounds the seeds inside the pod. The resin can be scraped from the fruit, but extracting the flavor from the pod requires soaking, usually in alcohol or oil. Minimal heat must be used when extracting vanilla flavor because many of the volatile elements in vanilla are destroyed at high temperatures.

Vanilla extracts are made by chopping beans and soaking them in a mixture of alcohol and water. Because the flavor compounds in the fruit, particularly vanillin, are more soluble in alcohol than in water, the higher the alcohol content of an extract, the more flavor it has. Artificial vanilla is made the same way but from wood lignin rather than vanilla beans. About 90% of the vanilla used in North America is artificial. Half the vanilla used in North America goes into ice-cream production, and much of the remainder is used in soft drinks and chocolate.

How It Works ● Vanilla pods have to be broken down through fermentation (curing) to develop and release their flavor. Before curing, vanilla pods are green and contain thousands of tiny pale seeds embedded in a resin of sugar, fat, and amino acids. The flavorful components, largely phenol compounds, are bound to sugars, which keep them inactive. The pod walls contain enzymes that can liberate the phenolics but are kept separated from them while the vanilla bean is alive.

The first step in curing is to dip the vanilla pods in boiling water to kill them and damage both the phenol-sugar compounds and the cells in the pod walls, causing the phenolics and the enzymes to mix and thereby releasing a characteristic vanilla flavor. At the same time, other enzymes cause the pod to brown, changing its color from light green nearly to black.

The damaged pods are set in the sun for 10 to 20 days to sweat, during which time the flavors and colors mature, much of the beans' moisture evaporates (which discourages harmful microbial action), and flavorful Maillard (**browning**) reactions occur between freed proteins and sugars in the fruit.

After sweating, most vanilla pods are aged in temperature-controlled rooms to dry them even more and to further develop their flavor. Bourbon vanilla is usually aged for about a month; Mexican vanilla for three to four months. At the end of the curing process, the flavors in the fruit have evolved and concentrated. It takes between 3 and 5 pounds (1.5 and 2 kg) of green vanilla beans to produce 1 pound (454 g) of cured beans.

See Also ● Chocolate, Extracts, Flavor Compounds, Ice Cream

VANILLIN ● See Vanilla

VEAL

What It Is ● Although technically veal is baby **beef** slaughtered before nine months of age, most is from animals under four months old. Its meat is pale, tender, and lean, although these characteristics vary widely depending on how the calf was raised and what it was fed. Veal older than five months is usually classified as calf or baby beef and will have a rosy color, a firm texture, and some marbling.

What It Does ● Many cooks erroneously believe that the younger the veal, the better the **meat**. Although youth insures tenderness and mild flavor, it also means a minimum of marbling, which can cause the meat to toughen and dry as it cooks. Veal slaughtered before eight weeks will have this problem.

Because every day a calf lives it gets closer to becoming beef, traditional veal production takes measures to keep the animal from developing characteristic cattle flavor and musculature. Most veal calves are given as little exercise as possible so that meat will not darken, toughen, or develop beefy flavor. The animals are fed a low-iron diet to curtail the development of myoglobin (red muscle pigment) and to keep the fat less saturated.

Veal quality is more dependent on feed and exercise than on age (almost all veal is slaughtered before five months of age). The most tender veal (called milk-fed or white

kitchen wisdom

Veal Stock
The goal in making stock is rich flavor and a gelatinous consistency that provides a syrupy mouth feel when reduced. The bones of young animals are coated with a thick layer of collagen proteins that denature into gelatin when simmered. Although beef bones from mature cattle give richer flavor than veal bones, veal bones are almost always included in recipes for beef stock to provide a gelatinous consistency.

Cuts of Veal

Primal Cut	Retail Cuts	Description	Cooking Methods and Uses
Loin	Kidney chop	Cut from center of loin, includes a slice of kidney; very flavorful, tender meat	Grill or broil
	Loin chop (T-bone or porterhouse)	Cross-section cut of loin; flavorful and tender	Grill or broil
	Loin roast (short loin)	Whole eye of loin, usually boneless; very lean and tender	Roast
	Tenderloin	Sold whole or in two parts, the wide (butt) end and tapered (short) end; small, boneless; very mild, lean, and tender	Roast or cut in steaks and grill or pan-fry
Leg	Leg	Whole leg includes round and sirloin; usually shank is removed; overall lean and tender, but different parts can vary	Roast
	Round roast (center cut)	Usually boneless eye of leg; lean and tender	Roast or butterfly and grill
	Shank	Lower part of leg; flavorful and tough; large marrow bone in center	Braise
	Sirloin	Hip section of leg; usually boneless; fattiest and most flavorful part of leg	Roast
	Veal scallop (scaloppine)	Boneless thin-cut cross-section of leg; usually mild flavor; lean and tender; often pounded for thinness and tenderness	Sauté
Rib	Crown roast	Whole rack of ribs tied in circle; flavorful, lean eye surrounded by fat	Roast
	Rack	One side of rib cage with large meaty eye; flavorful; mix of lean and fat	Roast
	Rib chop	Cross-section of rack	Grill, broil, or pan-fry
	Rib eye	Boneless eye of rack; trimmed of fat	Roast

veal) is raised in small stalls that permit the calf to lie down and stretch, but not much else, and the calf is fed milk or soy formula. The meat is pale pink and finely grained, with good deposits of fat between the muscles, but little intramuscular marbling.

For people who object to eating veal that spends the entirety of its short life confined to a stall, grain-fed, grass-fed, and range-fed veal is an option. This veal is a deeper color than formula-fed veal and it has a beefier flavor. If you are a classicist (culinarily speaking) you might object to these qualities, but many people prefer the more assertive flavor of veal fed on grain or pasturage. Veal from animals that are between six months and one year is marketed as baby beef, and the quality of the meat is somewhere in between lean beef and grain-fed or grass-fed veal.

Special-diet veal carcasses vary greatly in size, from 50 pounds (20 kg) to over 300 (135 kg) for large formula-fed veal (aka Provimi) that yields large cuts of meat with exceptional tenderness. Grain-fed or grass-fed animals can weigh up to 600 pounds (270 kg). Because veal is immature beef, it has the same body parts, but there are fewer primal cuts. The sirloin is included with the leg, and the plate, flank, and brisket are included in the breast, which is part of the shoulder primal cut.

Primal Cut	Retail Cuts	Description	Cooking Methods and Uses
Shoulder (chuck)	Breast (brisket)	Lies between the shoulder roast and the ribs and can include some rib bones; fatty and flavorful, but tends to be tough; often sold with pocket cut for stuffing	Braise (commonly stuffed)
	Foreshank	Bottom of foreleg, between brisket and foot; flavorful, meaty, tough; small marrow bone	Braise
	Ribs	Full rack of 11 small ribs taken from underside of breast; striated with fat; flavorful	Marinate and grill or broil
	Shoulder roast (arm roast, blade roast, chuck roast)	Top of shoulder; can include blade bone or not; flavorful; striated with fat and connective tissue	Pot roast or braise
	Stew meat	Boneless or bone-in meat cut in cubes with fat and connective tissue mostly trimmed; flavorful, tough	Stew or braise
Other	Bones	Bones from any part of animal; high collagen content makes them desirable for stock; leg bones sold for marrow	Roast for marrow or boil for stock
	Cheek	Small; rich; finely grained	Roast
	Feet (calf's feet)	Lower extremity of the legs; not much meat; lots of connective tissue and collagen	Boil for jellied stock or jellied feet
	Ground veal	From trimmings of any primal cut; pale and mild; often blended with ground pork or beef to add smoothness and mildness	Use in burgers, meatballs, meat loaf, sausage
	Heart	Flavorful, lean; milder than beef, pork, or lamb heart	Braise; ground
	Kidney	Multilobed; pale, mild, and tender; must be trimmed of membrane; fat is highly prized for suet	Grill or braise
	Liver	Pale; mildest tasting of all livers; must be trimmed of tendon and ducts	Sauté
	Sweetbreads	Thymus glands; pale, rich, and creamy; highly prized	Simmer and/or sauté
	Tongue	Small; pale; mild; lean; fine grained	Simmer

How It Works • In North America, veal production is tied in to the dairy industry. For dairy cows to remain effective milk producers, they must bear calves once a year. Female calves were raised as milkers, but male offspring of dairy breeds, like Holsteins, were typically disposed of because they had little commercial use until the advent of special-diet veal. Today most male dairy cattle are raised for veal.

See Also • Beef, Meat

VEGAN • See Animal Foods

VEGETABLES

What It Is • Some vegetables are **leaves**. Some are **roots**. Some are **stems**. Some can even be **fruits**. The same vegetable can go by several names, and the same plant can produce a number of distinct vegetables. For want of a better definition, vegetables are the parts of plants that we eat. In this book each type of vegetable has a devoted entry, as do major individual vegetables such as cabbages and carrots. This entry covers vegetables in general; for more detailed information, see entries for individual vegetables.

What It Does • The flavor and nutrition of vegetables have been valued since the beginning of eating. More than a quarter of the recipes in the first known cookbook, by Apicius, are for vegetables (125 of 467 recipes), and vegetable mixtures like mirepoix (onion, carrot, and celery) and sofrito (onion, green pepper, and garlic) are so intrinsic to savory food in Europe that when they are omitted, natives can't tell you what's missing, just that there now is a hole where the flavor used to be. It would not be possible to detail all the idiosyncrasies of every vegetable in a single article, nor is it necessary. The best way to understand vegetables as a category is to look at their interconnections.

Spinach and lettuce might be unrelated, but they're both leaves and therefore show similar signs of quality. Cauliflower and mushrooms have nothing to do with one another botanically, but they require the same precautions to prevent them from browning because they're both white. New potatoes share more culinary characteristics with spring peas than they do with mature potatoes, because both are young. The part of the plant from which a vegetable comes, its color, its age, and how it has been stored are what determine a vegetable's quality.

How It Works • Roots are what plants use to absorb nutrients from the soil. They anchor the plant into the ground and they act as a storehouse of starch and sugar, which the plant or a passing animal can use for food. Like all storage units, roots need strong walls and lots of space. Hard fibers are interspersed with large starch-storing chambers (vacuoles). As the plant matures, the vacuoles get bigger, making the root sweeter, and the fibers get harder. Quality walks a tightrope between sweetness and toughness. Harvest a root vegetable too soon and it will lack size and flavor. Let it get too old and its fiber will turn to wood.

Vegetable Overview

This chart lists the most common vegetables. It includes signs of quality, storage guidelines and appropriate cooking methods and uses.

Type	Vegetable	Signs of Quality	Storage	Cooking Methods and Uses
Root	Beet	Deep color, small, smooth, no scales, crisp greens	Refrigerate 1 week	Boil, bake
	Carrot	Bright color, whole, straight, firm but not hard, smooth skin	Refrigerate 1 week	All
	Celeriac	Large, knobby, regular shape, firm, clean	Refrigerate 5 days	Boil, steam, roast, raw
	Jicama	Pale, hard, large, no blemishes, moist inside	Refrigerate 1 week	Raw, sauté, roast
	Parsnip	Cream colored, small, uniform, smooth skin	Refrigerate 1 week	All
	Sweet potato	Full color, hard, no soft spots, uniform	Refrigerate 4 days	All
Root/Stem (includes rhizomes, lower stems merged with roots, and swollen lower stems)	Ginger	Pale, firm, no mold, dry skin	Cool place 2 weeks	All
	Jerusalem artichoke (sunchoke)	Pale, firm, dry skin	Refrigerate 1 week	Boil, sauté, raw
	Kohlrabi	Pale, firm, small, uniform	Cool, dark place 2 days	Boil, roast, sauté, raw
	Potato, new and/or round	Pale, small, crisp, thin skin, uniform	Refrigerate 1 week	Steam, boil, sauté
	Potato, russet	Brown, large, long, thick skin with russeting	Cool, dark place 1 week	Bake, fry
	Turnip	Pale, small, uniform, smooth skin	Refrigerate 1 week	Boil, steam, braise, roast
Stem	Celery	Pale, crisp stalks, medium size, fresh leaves	Refrigerate 1 week	All
	Fennel	Pale, full round bulb, short stalks, fresh fronds, no scars	Refrigerate 4 days	Raw, braise, roast, sauté
Blossom	Artichoke	Heavy, closely packed, no browning	Refrigerate 4 days	Boil, bake with liquid, sauté, fry
Stem-Blossom	Asparagus	Closed buds, firm, no wrinkles, not damp	Refrigerate 2 days	Boil, steam, roast, sauté
	Broccoli	Dark, closed buds, firm stem, no yellow	Refrigerate 4 days	Boil, steam, stir-fry
	Cauliflower	Pale, tight curd, no spots, firm leaves	Refrigerate 4 days	Boil, steam, roast
Stem and Leaf	Broccoli rabe	Dark green, leafy, closed buds, no yellow, crisp stems	Refrigerate 2 days	Boil, sauté
	Chard	Large dark leaves, crisp bright red or white stalks	Wrap and refrigerate 2 days	Steam, boil, sauté

continued on next page

Vegetable Overview (continued)

Type	Vegetable	Signs of Quality	Storage	Cooking Methods and Uses
Leaf	Beet greens	Bright green, red veins, not wilted	Refrigerate 1 day	Boil, steam, sauté
	Brussels sprouts	Bright green, tight heads, round, firm	Refrigerate 4 days	Boil, steam, roast, sauté
	Cabbage	Heavy for size, tight head, fresh smell, no yellowing	Refrigerate 1 week	Boil, sauté, braise
	Collard	Dark green, firm leaves, no yellow	Wrap and refrigerate 2 days	Steam, boil, sauté
	Dandelion greens	Pale green, small, tender, thin stems	Wrap and refrigerate 2 days	Raw, steam, sauté
	Endive	Pale, firm strong leaves, no wilting	Refrigerate 2 days	Raw, grill, braise
	Leek	White part long, greens bright and crisp, no yellow, small	Refrigerate 3 days	All
	Lemongrass	Bright green stalk, moist flexible root end	Refrigerate 2 weeks	Stir-fry, sauté, boil
	Lettuce, Bibb or Boston	Pale green, fragile, loose head	Refrigerate 2 days	Raw
	Lettuce, iceberg	Pale, tight head, heavy for size, crisp	Refrigerate 5 days	Raw
	Lettuce, leaf	Full color, delicate leaves, open head	Refrigerate 2 days	Raw
	Lettuce, mesclun	Full color, small delicate leaves	Refrigerate 2 days	Raw
	Lettuce, romaine	Pale, sturdy leaves, tight head	Refrigerate 5 days	Raw, grill
	Kale	Dark green, firm leaf, crisp tender stem, no dampness	Wrap and refrigerate 2 days	Boil, steam, sauté
	Scallion	White part long, greens bright and crisp, no yellow, small	Refrigerate 3 days	All
	Spinach	Dark green, firm leaf, crisp tender stem, no dampness	Wrap and refrigerate 2 days	Sauté, steam, raw if young
	Watercress	Dark, small stems, large leaves, no yellow, no wilting	Wrap and refrigerate 2 days	Raw, steam, sauté

Judge the quality of root vegetables by their size. Smaller specimens will be milder and more tender; larger and thicker roots will be tougher and more robust. In any bunch or package of root vegetables it is likely that you will get roots of different sizes. Use the larger ones for soup and stew and save the smaller ones for shredding into a salad or for quick-cooking methods like stir-frying and sautéing.

Stems fulfill two functions for a plant. They hold the upper parts of the plant aloft, exposing leaves to sunlight, flowers to pollinating insects, and fruits to passing animals. And they contain the circulatory system through which nutrients move up from the root and sugars manufactured in the leaves descend down into the roots to be stored as starch.

To complete their dual job, stems are structured much like roots. Strong support fibers are interspersed with hollow veins, but unlike roots, the support fibers are not tough enough to do the job alone. They must be helped by a turgid flow of fluid in the veins. It is this combination of firm fiber and lots of water that gives stem vegetables their snap — a brief resistance followed by a

Type	Vegetable	Signs of Quality	Storage	Cooking Methods and Uses
Bulb (Swollen leaves)	Garlic	Pale, firm, heavy for size, dry papery skin	Cool, dark place 2 weeks	All
	Onion	Pale, heavy for size, firm, uniform, dry skin	Cool, dark place 1 week	All
	Shallot	Pale, heavy for size, firm, uniform, dry skin	Cool, dark place 1 week	All
Fruit	Beans, green	Full color, firm, crisp, dry surface	Refrigerate 4 days	Boil, steam, sauté
	Chayote (mirliton)	Pale, firm, heavy for size	Refrigerate 1 week	Steam, bake
	Corn	Full ears, heavy for size, plump kernels, dry silks	Use immediately	Boil, steam, grill
	Cucumber	Dark, firm, heavy for size, small, crisp, no yellow	Refrigerate 4 days	Raw
	Eggplant	Deep color, heavy for size, firm, medium-small	Refrigerate 2 days	Sauté, grill, roast
	Okra	Bright green, small, tender, dry skin	Refrigerate 2 days	Simmer, sauté
	Peas, garden	Bright green, small, uniform, tender	Refrigerate 3 days	Boil, steam
	Peppers, sweet or hot	Bright, firm, uniform	Refrigerate 3 days	All
	Squash, winter	Dark, hard, shiny skin, smooth, no breaks	Room temperature 2 weeks	Steam, boil, braise, bake
	Squash, yellow	Full color, resilient, tender, small	Refrigerate 3 days	All
	Tomato	Bright color, yielding, no soft spots, full aroma	Room temperature 2 to 4 days	Raw, sauté
	Zucchini	Full color, resilient, tender, small	Refrigerate 3 days	All
Other	Bean sprouts	Fresh smell, bright color, dry surface	Refrigerate 3 days	Raw, stir-fry
	Mushrooms	White to brown, button- to plate-sized, firm, dry, closed cap in milder types, open cap in stronger types	Wrap and refrigerate 2 days	All

burst of juice. If the vascular tissue dehydrates, the stem will lose its crispness, causing the vegetable to become limp.

In some stem vegetables, such as celery and fennel, crispness can be restored by submerging the stalks in ice water. This forces water back into the dehydrated veins. But other stemmed produce, such as asparagus and broccoli, needs to be peeled before it can be revived. These vegetables have a water-resistant skin that delays water loss but also inhibits the ability of the vegetable to regain crispness after it dries out.

Stem vegetables aren't usually just stems. Most often they include other plant parts. For instance, broccoli is part stem and part flower. Asparagus is both stem and bud. Chard and celery are stem and leaf. Because different plant parts differ in structure, it is important to judge each part separately. For instance, the stem of broccoli should be judged on firmness and juiciness, but the flower should be looked at for color and shape. Swollen or open buds indicate the broccoli is about to flower and yellowness means it has begun to bloom (both signs that the broccoli is past its prime).

kitchen wisdom

Vegetable Pickles

Along with **fermentation**, pickling, the process of preserving vegetables in salt brine or acid, is one of the oldest and simplest means of "cooking" vegetables. Because fermented vegetables such as olives, sauerkraut, and kimchi start out in a brine, encouraging fermenting bacteria to generate preserving acids over time, the term "pickle" can mean either fermented or unfermented preserved vegetables. Unfermented pickles, like gherkins, cornichons, okra, Japanese pickled plums, and the highly spiced pickled condiments in India, take far less time to make but are not as complex or pungent as fermented pickles. Usually, unfermented pickled vegetables are made by submerging fresh vegetables in an acidic concentration of about 2.5% (half that of vinegar); the mixture is then heat-treated at 185°F (85°C) for 30 minutes to sterilize against spoilage.

Most pickled vegetables are preferred crisp. Unrefined sea salt and pickling salt contain calcium and magnesium that help to reinforce pectins in the cell walls of vegetables and fruits, improving crispness. Alum (aluminum hydroxide) does the same thing. Pickles made with these minerals will not soften during cooking. Soft pickles are made by cooking the vegetable before pickling.

The only vegetable that is just stem ironically is considered by most of us to be a fruit. Rhubarb is the only "fruit" that's really a vegetable, but there are countless vegetables that are botanically fruits. Fruit is the pulpy part of a plant that houses the seed. Tomatoes, cucumbers, squash, eggplant, bell peppers, and avocados are all botanically fruits. As a fruit ripens, its skin blushes with color, it becomes softer and juicier, its starch is converted to sugar, making the fruit sweeter, and enzymes break down its cell walls, releasing a characteristic perfume. For fruits like tomatoes, corn, and avocados, full ripeness is the essence of quality, but for most fruit-vegetables, ripening is a process of diminishing returns.

The qualities of full ripeness are the very attributes that make a cucumber or zucchini undesirable. Ripe cucumbers are yellow and soft. Ripe zucchini are flaccid and full of seeds. Completely ripened eggplants are flabby and bitter. These fruits are judged by the opposite criteria: firmness, smallness, greenness, and a clean, fresh aroma. So you want to buy these fruit-vegetables underripe and small.

Leaves are the most common and the most perishable of vegetables. They include lettuces, spinach, endives, cabbages, cresses, herbs, rabe, and sprouts. Although leaf vegetables vary in color, firmness, and flavor, all of them are prone to wilting because of their characteristic structure. Through photosynthesis leaves convert water, carbon dioxide, and sunlight into oxygen, which is released back into the air, and sugar, which is stored in the plant. Accordingly, leaves are broad and flat to expose maximum surface area to sunlight and water. They are full of air pockets to increase the number of cells that come in contact with the air, which encourages optimal amounts of carbon dioxide and oxygen where photosynthesis takes place.

Their porous structure makes leaves prone to dehydration and bruising. It also causes them to shrink dramatically during cooking. Most of a leaf is air and water. As it is heated, its cell structure collapses and all its water and air are released.

Store leafy vegetables in loosely closed plastic bags and use them as soon as possible. Do not seal them too tightly, for this can cause the leaves to absorb excess water and become soggy. Wash leafy vegetables as close to serving time as possible.

Flowers are not typically eaten in bulk. Tea is made from chamomile, and nasturtium blossoms can highlight a salad, and stuffed squash blossoms are a seasonal treat, but when it comes to downing a hearty helping of flowers, only three vegetables come to mind, and one of those isn't really a flower. The top of broccoli is an umbrella of flower buds, which must be eaten before they bloom if the broccoli is to be any good. Cauliflower is similar to broccoli, but its "curd" is not a proper flower. Rather, it is the sterile degeneration of the stem tips, unable to perform any of the functions of a flower. Artichoke contains a flower, but we don't eat it. Artichoke is a **thistle**, harvested before it blossoms. If it were allowed to bloom, the shield of thorny leaves would splay open, revealing thousands of violet quill-like petals. We call this hairy flower "the choke" and cut it out before eating the vegetable, lest it fulfill its namesake threat.

The purple of an artichoke flower comes from the **pigment** anthocyanin. This is the same color that tints purple cabbage leaves, beets, and the skin of eggplant. Anthocyanins, along with most other vegetable pigments, are phytochemicals, biologically active trace compounds that help the body fight damage from free radicals and prevent the body from turning mildly harmful chemicals into powerful toxins. The study of trace chemicals in vegetables (*phytochemicals* means "plant chemicals") is relatively new, and though it is not known what all of these elements do for us, current nutritional wisdom says we should eat as many vegetables as possible to reap the beneficial effects of the trace chemicals they contain.

See Also • Allium, Antioxidants, Artichoke, Asparagus, Capsicum, Chicory, Corn, Cruciferous Vegetables, Cucumber, Eggplant, Fiber, Fruit, Fungi, Leaves, Legumes, Mushrooms, Potatoes, Roots, Seaweed, Squash, Stems, Thistles, Tomatoes

VEGETARIAN • See Diet, Meat

VENISON • See Game

VERJUS • See Grapes, Wine

VICINE • See Legumes, Toxin

VINAIGRETTE • See Sauces

VINEGAR

What It Is • Bacteria of the genus *Acetobacter* can use oxygen to metabolize alcohol, and produce acetic **acid** in the process. So when *Acetobacter* bacteria are added to an alcoholic liquid such as wine and exposed to air, the mixture turns sour — in French, it becomes *vin aigre*, "sour wine."

What It Does • Because fermented liquid naturally sours, ancient peoples discovered vinegar at the same time that they discovered **wine** (wine vinegar), **beer** (malt vinegar), and hard **cider** (cider vinegar). In fact, one of the breakthroughs in early wine- and beer-making practices was mastering techniques to keep oxygen away from fermenting liquid to help control its sourness.

Acetic acid is a potent preserving agent. A concentration as weak as one-tenth of 1% (1 teaspoon/5 mL 4% vinegar in

1 cup/250 mL water) is adequate to slow the growth of most microbes. Water boils more easily than acetic acid, so the acidity of vinegar becomes more concentrated as it boils, and because its chemical structure is similar to alcohol's, flavor compounds, including volatile oils, are easily dissolved in it. This is why vinegars are frequently flavored with herbs and spices and why it is a common flavor enhancer.

Though all vinegars share the common flavor of acetic acid, each retains the distinctive flavor of the alcoholic mixture from which it started, and some develop flavor and color from being fermented or aged in wood barrels. Vinegars that retain acids from their fermented base (such as tartaric acid in wine and malic acid in apple cider) have the aroma of that acid as well as acetic acid.

Types of Vinegar

Wine vinegar is fermented from grape wine and has a sweet, fruity flavor from that source. Generic wine vinegars can be red or white, and specialty wine vinegars might specify a particular grape or wine, such as Zinfandel or sherry vinegar.

Balsamic vinegar is specially aged wine vinegar. Traditional balsamic vinegar (*aceto balsamico tradizionale*) can be fermented for decades in wood casks until it becomes dark, syrupy sweet, and deliciously complex in flavor and aroma. It is made from Trebbiano or red Lambrusco grape juice that is boiled to concentrate its sugars and then fermented into wine. The wine goes through acetic acid fermentation into vinegar in a series of barrels, often made from different woods. The vinegar loses about 10% of its liquid each year, and is transferred to smaller barrels each year to maintain the ratio of liquid to oxygen. Traditional balsamic is aged for a minimum of 12 years. Inexpensive commercial balsamic vinegars are no more than facsimiles of the real stuff, made by darkening and sweetening regular wine vinegar with caramel.

Fine sherry vinegar, called solera aged, is made the same way as balsamic vinegar but derives a nuttier and floral fragrance from the sherry from which it originated.

Cider vinegar is made from fermented apple juice and contains some of the characteristic aromas of apples and apple cider. Because apples are high in malic acid, the fermentation of cider vinegar is maloacetic fermentation that yields a mellow acidity. Other fermented fruit juices can also be made into vinegar, although most fruit vinegars are generic wine vinegar flavored with fruit juice.

Malt vinegar is made from fermented malted barley, or unhopped beer, and has a sweet barley malt flavor. It is popular in Britain, where it is a traditional condiment for fish and chips.

Rice vinegars are made from rice wine and are most common in Asia. Chinese rice vinegars are generally the most flavorful because they are made from unpolished, sometimes toasted, rice. Japanese rice vinegars are less complex and usually less sweet.

Distilled white vinegar is nearly pure acetic acid fermented from pure distilled alcohol and does not develop auxiliary flavors through aging or contact with wood. It is the least sweet and least complex of all vinegars.

How It Works • For thousands of years vinegar was made by allowing partial vats of alcohol to collect *Acetobacter* bacteria from the air and sour, an erratic process that could take weeks or months. In the 17th and 18th centuries, methods of aeration over a network of wine vines increased the speed and accuracy by which alcohol could be soured into vinegar. In the 19th century, Louis Pasteur identified the connection between *Acetobacter* bacteria and oxygen, paving the way for industrial production of vinegar.

Three ingredients are needed to make vinegar: an alcoholic liquid, oxygen, and *Acetobacter* bacteria, most commonly *A. pasteurianus* and *A. aceti*. *Acetobacter* (and sometimes *Gluconobacter*) bacteria are the only microbes that are able to use alcohol as a source of energy, producing two by-products, acetic acid and water. Because acetic-acid-producing bacteria require oxygen, they tend to concentrate on the surface of the vat, where they form a film called the mother. Mother is collected from the surface of vinegar and used to begin the souring of new batches.

The percentage of alcohol in the fermented liquid base affects the acidity and stability of the finished vinegar. An alcohol concentration of 5% produces vinegar that is 4% acetic acid, which is strong enough to keep the vinegar itself from spoiling. Vinegars made from higher-proof alcohols are more acidic and more stable, but it is difficult to make vinegar from alcohol that is stronger than 5% because the high alcohol concentration inhibits the activity of the bacteria. For that reason, and to eliminate residual alcohol in the finished vinegar, wines of 10 or 12% alcohol are usually diluted with water beforehand. Some fine vinegars, particularly sherry vinegars, are fermented more slowly from full-strength alcohol.

Vinegar may be prepared in three ways. The finest vinegars are fermented in wooden barrels from wine that is inoculated with mother from previous batches of vinegar. This method is slow because the surface area of the barrels is limited, but the slow fermentation allows time for chemical reactions that make the flavor of the vinegar more complex. Barrel fermentation (called the Orleans method) takes about two months.

In the trickling method, alcohol is passed through a porous matrix impregnated with *Acetobacter* bacteria. The increased surface area and steady exposure of the alcohol to air and bacteria accelerate the production of acetic acid. This quick method can produce a batch of vinegar in a few days.

Less expensive industrially produced vinegars are made using the submerged-culture method, in which a tank of alcohol and bacteria is pumped through with air, converting the alcohol to acetic acid in about 24 hours.

After fermentation all vinegars are pasteurized to kill the remaining bacteria, and most are aged for a few months to make them mellow.

See Also • Acid, Beer, Flavor, Wine

VITAMINS

What It Is • Normally we down our nutrition by the pound, gobbling up proteins and complex carbohydrates in heaping helpings. Yet when we speak of vitamins, the scales suddenly shift. Milligrams take the place of ounces and pounds, and we begin to think in doses rather than servings.

Vitamins are found in all living things. Except for a few vitamins, our bodies cannot manufacture the amount of vitamins we need, and so they must be obtained from food or supplements. Vitamins are essential for hundreds of bodily processes, and though we need only trace amounts to sustain life, a deficiency of even one vitamin can endanger the whole body.

What It Does • There are 13 recognized vitamins, categorized by being water soluble or fat soluble. Fat-soluble vitamins (A, D, E, and K) are absorbed into the body with the help of fat in the diet or bile from the liver. The fat-soluble vitamins are stored in body fat and so they are generally available as needed even if they are not consumed daily. On the other hand, because they are stored in the body, they can accumulate to toxic levels if too much is consumed over time. Water-soluble vitamins (B-complex and C) do not need fat to be absorbed and are generally not stored in body tissue, so we need to consume these vitamins every day. What the body doesn't need it excretes through urine and perspiration, so there is no danger of toxicity. Water-soluble vitamins are more prone to damage during cooking, storage, and food processing, and therefore the amounts in fresh ingredients and preparations vary significantly.

The existence of essential elements in food that keep the body from becoming diseased has been known since ancient times. Ancient Egyptians recognized that eating liver cured night blindness (a symptom of vitamin A deficiency), and as early as 1614 doctors knew that the acid in fruit eliminated symptoms of scurvy,

The Importance of Vitamins

This chart lists the known vitamins, their solubility, functions in the body, notable food sources, their RDV, the recommended upper level intake (UL), diseases associated with deficiency of the vitamin, and diseases associated with overdose of the vitamin.

Vitamin	Chemical Name	Solubility	Functions	Food Sources (listed by amount of vitamin — most to least)
A	Retinol	Fat	Eye health, bone growth, skin health, boosts resistance to respiratory infection skin 0000dryness, weight loss, jaundice	Liver, dairy
A, provitamin	Beta-carotene	Fat	Eye health, bone growth, skin health, boosts resistance to respiratory infection skin dryness, weight loss, jaundice	Apricots, carrots, sweet potato, spinach, kale, broccoli
B_1	Thiamine	Water	Maintains muscle and nerve tissue, digestion of carbohydrates	Pork, liver, brewer's yeast, bran, whole grains
B_2	Riboflavin	Water	Metabolizes all nutrients, maintains mucous membrane (skin health), cell respiration	Liver and other organ meats, poultry, milk, eggs, brewer's yeast, whole grains, almonds legumes, dark greens
B_3	Niacin, niacinamide	Water	Health of nervous system and digestion, skin health	Tuna, liver, meat, poultry, fish, whole grains, nuts
Pantothenic acid	Same	Water	Cell building, adrenal hormones, wound healing, metabolism	Widespread in all food, especially liver, poultry, egg yolks, whole grains, nuts, greens
B_6	Pyridoxine, pyridoxamine, pyridoxal	Water	Maintains sodium–potassium balance, formation of red blood cells, metabolism, health of nervous system	Whole grains, liver, beef, avocado, cantaloupe, bananas, nuts, green vegetables
Biotin	Same	Water	Cell growth, fatty acid production, cell respiration, metabolism	Dark green leafy vegetables, tomatoes, carrots, milk, whole grains, nuts, berries
Folate, folacin	Same	Water	Forms red blood cells, maintains nervous system, promotes mental health, cell reproduction	Dark green leafy vegetables, brewer's yeast, liver, kidneys, legumes, broccoli, carrots, asparagus
B_{12}	Cyanocobalamin, hydroxocobalamin, methylcobalamin	Water	Forms red blood cells, maintains nervous system, increases energy	Liver, kidneys, beef, pork, fish, eggs, milk, cheese (only in animal products, so vegans may need supplements)
C	Ascorbic acid	Water	Production of collagen and red blood cells; maintains blood vessel strength; builds bones, teeth, and gums; helps absorption of iron; promotes healing	Fresh fruit and vegetables, especially citrus, leafy greens, tomatoes, strawberries, melon, bell peppers, cabbage, broccoli, potatoes
D	Ergocalciferol, cholecalciferol	Fat	Forms and maintains bones and teeth, helps absorption of calcium, maintains nervous system, helps blood clotting	Sunlight, cod liver oil, fortified dairy products
E	Tocopherol	Fat	Supplies oxygen to cells, forms red blood cells, maintains muscle tissue, antioxidant, promotes healing, softens scar tissue	Vegetable oil, wheat germ, whole grains, liver, seeds
K	Phylloquinone, menaquinone	Fat	Promotes proper blood clotting, aids liver function	Dark green leafy vegetables, seaweed, cruciferous vegetables, legumes

although it wasn't until 1747 that James Lind proved that eating citrus fruit cured scurvy, and not until 1928 that ascorbic acid (vitamin C) was isolated from citrus and shown to be the active agent in relieving scurvy symptoms. Although deficiency diseases were known for centuries, it was not until the 20th century that vitamins were recognized and isolated. All of the known vitamins were discovered

RDV (19 and older)	Deficiency Disease/Symptom	UL Daily	Overdose Disease/Symptom
1000 mcg	Eye disorders including night blindness	3000 mcg	Osteoporosis, skin dryness, weight loss, jaundice
6000 mcg	Eye disorders including night blindness	18000 mcg	Osteoporosis, skin dryness, weight loss, jaundice
1.5 mg	Beriberi (weakness, weight loss, pain in limbs, memory loss, heart failure)	ND*	None
1.7 mg	Ariboflavinosis (sore throat, mouth swelling, skin cracking or scaling, low red blood cell count)	ND	None
19 mg	Pellagra (skin lesions, weakness, insomnia, diarrhea, confusion, dementia)	35 mg	Liver damage
10 mg	Fatigue, abdominal pain, adrenal insufficiency, liver damage, painful nerve sensations	ND	None
1.7 mg	Anemia	100 mg	Nerve damage
30 mcg	Hair loss, intestinal distress, neuromuscular seizures and lack of coordination, skin conditions; deficiency is rare because B7 is produced by intestinal bacteria	ND	None
400 mcg	Birth defects	1000 mcg	Nerve damage
2.4 mcg	Anemia	ND	None
90 mg	Scurvy (skin lesions, tooth loss, excessive bleeding)	ND	Indigestion, diarrhea
5–10 mcg	Rickets (softening of bones)	50 mcg	Dehydration, vomiting, constipation, fatigue
15 mg	Anemia	1000 mg	None
100 mcg	Inability of blood to coagulate; deficiency is rare because K is produced by intestinal bacteria	ND	None

*Not determinable

between 1897 (thiamine) and 1941 (folic acid). In comparison to other fields of science, the initial discovery of vitamins is relatively recent, and the most recently discovered vitamins were identified only about 60 years ago. It is possible that there are more vitamins in foods that have yet to be identified.

The recommended daily allowances (RDA) of vitamins recognized in Canada and the U.S. were developed during the Second World War and have been revised every five to ten years since then. The last revision was in 2001, and at that time the RDA was changed to recommended daily value (RDV), which is what is stated currently on nutrition labels. The exact amount of vitamins needed is under constant debate, and differs for people of different ages, genetic backgrounds, and geographies. As well, the RDV is the amount of a vitamin needed to prevent symptoms of deficiency; it is not necessarily the amount needed to achieve glowing health.

How It Works • Vitamins are so diverse and perform so many functions in the body that it is impossible to say simply how they work, and in fact, the exact mechanism of how many vitamins perform their functions is still not well understood. With that caveat, the following explanations should shed some light on the workings of specific vitamins.

Vitamin A
We get vitamin A from nature in two distinct forms, retinoids (retinol) and carotenoids (carotene). Retinol is the form found in animal products, most predominantly eggs, butterfat, fish liver oils (particularly halibut and cod), and organ meats, especially liver. Retinol can be absorbed and used by our bodies immediately without conversion, and since excess is stored in the liver it is not necessary to consume the vitamin every day, except in cases where a deficiency is already present.

The nutritional hitch to retinol is that all of its primary sources are also high in cholesterol and saturated fat, dietary elements most people are trying to avoid. Fortunately, there is another form of the vitamin, which contains hardly any fat at all.

Carotenoids are known as provitamin A (beta-carotene is the most common form). They are converted into retinol in the lining of the small intestines and in the liver. Beta-carotene is a phytochemical (it comes from plants) that is found most readily in dark green leafy vegetables and in yellow and orange root vegetables and fruits. Beta-carotene does not come with the complication of cholesterol, but it does pose problems for individuals who are deficient in the enzymes and hormones necessary for its absorption and conversion to usable vitamin A.

Vitamin B Complex
The B vitamins (all the water-soluble vitamins except for vitamin C) differ widely in their chemical composition, stability, metabolic function, and distribution in foods. Many are essential to the production of energy in each cell of our bodies. Without them, we would collapse one cell at a time, until our entire physiology was destroyed. They are part of our digestive enzymes and nerve impulses. They're requisite for growth, muscle functioning, and the health of our skin, eyes, liver, and blood. They help to form our genetic structure and keep us free from mental breakdown. Their abundance enhances our appetites, increases energy, and counteracts the symptoms of stress.

B vitamins are abundant in unprocessed foods, and severe deficiencies are mostly found in areas of the world where malnutrition is endemic, but even among "well-fed" people, minor symptoms of vitamin B deficiencies are not uncommon.

The symptoms of deficiency show themselves slowly. Lack of energy, loss of memory, poor concentration, irritability, digestive problems, muscle aches, cold sores, and minor skin irritations are all early signs of a lack of B vitamins. These problems respond rapidly to a change in diet, particularly when whole grains are substituted for unenriched processed products. Many people try to counteract the loss by taking individual B vitamin supplements, but this can create its own problems if the vitamins are not taken in the correct balance.

There are eight separate vitamins in the B complex. Some work independently, but several of them work in association with one another, which means that deficiency of one B vitamin can disable the workings of several others, even though they are present in good supply. Because many deficiency symptoms are common to several of the B vitamins, accurate diagnosis to determine which of the vitamins in the complex is lacking can be done only through laboratory testing. Experimenting with supplements is hazardous, for too much of a B vitamin can cause as much harm as too little. B vitamins are not stored in the body, so the buildup of toxic levels is not the problem it can be with other vitamins. Excess amounts of B vitamins are excreted continuously through bodily fluids. Since some B vitamins work together in a complex, the disposal of a surplus of one B vitamin can trigger the removal of others working along with it. If some of these are in short supply, a deficiency can result.

The best way to insure that your vitamin B supply is balanced is to get them through food and to cook the food in ways that help to preserve the vitamin content. All B vitamins are sensitive to moist heat, so long periods of cooking in water should be avoided. Riboflavin (B_2) is destroyed quickly by light.

Vitamin C

No one challenges the importance of vitamin C. It is part of the enzymes that form and maintain collagen in our connective tissue, without which every cell in our bodies would collapse. It helps form the matrix from which bones, teeth, and blood vessels are built. It is a powerful antioxidant, and some scientists give it credit as a master infection fighter and a boon to bolster hormone flow. But ask how much to take, and watch the battle begin.

At its heart, the dispute centers on whether vitamin C (ascorbic acid) is a trace component in our system needed only to prevent specific deficiency diseases or an integral part of our biology. Two hundred years ago it was determined that its absence from the diet was responsible for scurvy. Soon after the vitamin was isolated, defined, and synthesized in laboratories in 1926, it was determined that just 10 mg taken daily eliminated all symptoms of scurvy. Since then the recommended amount of vitamin C has crept up to 90 mg for a typical adult, with the thinking that this dose not only guarded against scurvy but saturated bodily tissue to a level that eliminated the threat of further deficiency, even if the vitamin was discontinued for several weeks.

In 1970, Linus Pauling, a two-time Nobel Prize laureate, published his book *Vitamin C and the Common Cold*, recommending a minimum dose of 1,000 to 3,000 mg daily and up to 10,000 mg during times of stress or infection. Doctors and researchers disagree as to the benefits of megadosing vitamins. Excess vitamin is excreted by the body, and some believers have taken several grams a day for years without any adverse effect. Some people report minor digestive disturbances from as little as 500 mg a day.

Large doses of ascorbic acid can be attained only from vitamin supplements, but with a little planning there is no reason that anyone's diet could not supply several hundred milligrams a day without any supplementation. Natural sources also give the added advantage of bioflavonoids, substances found along with vitamin C in food but missing in most synthetic supplements. Bioflavonoids have been shown to strengthen the permeability of capillary

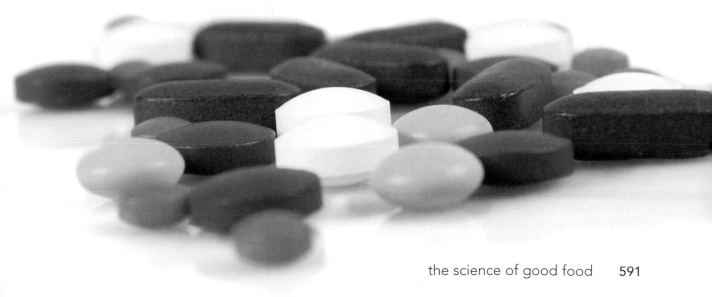

walls, thereby increasing the amount of oxygen, nutrients, and antibodies passed between the circulatory system and cells all over the body. Vitamin C and bioflavonoids are found only in fruit and vegetable products. Dairy, meats, and cereals provide negligible amounts.

Vitamin C is the most unstable of all vitamins, easily destroyed by excessive heating, long storage, and exposure to light and air. As much as 100% of the vitamin can be lost from a food source during cooking and storage. To guard against loss, cook vitamin C–rich foods quickly, in as little water as possible. Reheated or leftover foods lose vitamin C rapidly. One day in a refrigerator can slash 25% of the ascorbic acid from a food. Cooked vegetables held in a refrigerator for two to three days will retain only a third of their original vitamin C content.

Vitamin D

Food sources of vitamin D are relatively rare. Fish liver oils contain some, and dairy products are fortified with the vitamin, but most of what we need is formed using sunlight. However, no matter how much vitamin D you get from being in sunlight, its benefits are nil if adequate calcium is not also supplied, for the two nutrients work together.

Consuming adequate amounts of calcium does not guarantee that it will get to where it is needed — the bones and teeth. To absorb calcium through the intestinal wall, carry it through the blood, and deposit it in bone, a transporting agent is needed. The transporting agent for calcium through all of these processes is vitamin D.

For the skeleton to keep its strength, old calcium is constantly removed from bone and replaced by new calcium supplied by food. Because the regeneration of bone tissue is constant, calcium is needed on a regular basis throughout life. Requirements are highest for children, whose skeletons and teeth are still growing, and for the elderly, who often have problems absorbing calcium fully. The regulation of calcium metabolism is controlled in part by hormones secreted from the thyroid, adrenal, and sex glands. As hormone secretions slacken with age, the loss

of calcium from the skeleton can exceed the amount that is deposited from the blood. The result is a demineralized, weakened skeleton, conditions known as osteoporosis and osteomalacia. When severe, these ailments can cause bones to snap under the slightest stress. The problem is particularly pronounced in women past menopause. Once estrogen levels drop, the rate at which calcium is absorbed from food decreases dramatically. Mature women, therefore, should increase both calcium and vitamin D in their diets, just to maintain proper levels of calcium in the skeleton.

Calcium also helps transmit the nerve impulses and keeps the heart beating, functions of such importance that calcium and vitamin D must be available at all times — even if the body has to "steal" calcium from bone tissue. When the skeleton is already weakened, this added depletion can be disastrous. The solution for anyone prone to calcium depletion is to make sure that the blood is so well supplied with calcium and vitamin D that there is no chance that the skeleton would ever have to be used as a calcium source for other systems in the body.

Most of the vitamin D we get is synthesized whenever the skin is exposed to sunlight. Ultraviolet radiation reacts with a form of cholesterol present in skin to produce cholecalciferol (vitamin D_3), the same form of the vitamin that we get from fish oils. Once in the skin, the vitamin is carried through the blood to the liver, where it is stored until needed. Therefore, adequate supplies are not a problem in populations that get enough exposure to sunlight. However, deficiencies can occur when sunlight is scarce, as it is during winter months or when people do not get outside, as is the case with many elderly and infirm.

Vitamin E

No one can agree on exactly what vitamin E is or how it works in the body. In laboratory experiments it has restored fertility to rats, cured the symptoms of muscular dystrophy in rabbits, prevented fetal reabsorption in hamsters and guinea pigs, and prevented brain degeneration in chickens. But none of these findings have proven applicable to humans.

Here is what we do know. There are eight different forms of vitamin E, chemically named tocopherols, which are found mostly in vegetable oils. Deposits of tocopherols are present throughout the body, concentrated most heavily in glands, muscles, and fat tissue. So far, their main role seems to be to prevent oxidation of other fat-soluble vitamins, particularly vitamin A, and to prevent polyunsaturated fats from degrading into free radicals, substances that have been connected with premature aging and the development of malignancies. There is also evidence that vitamin E plays a part in the formation of red blood cells and the transfer of oxygen through the circulatory system.

The only reported cases of severe vitamin E deficiency involve newborns, who seem to receive little of the vitamin prenatally. This is remedied soon after birth from the vitamin content of breast milk or fortified infant formula. Several blood cell diseases in premature infants have been corrected with supplements of vitamin E.

Vitamin K

There are three forms of vitamin K. Vitamin K_1 is found in plants. Vitamin K_2 is produced by bacteria in the intestine in amounts that exceed the needs of most people, so deficiencies are extremely rare except in newborns or in cases where the intestine has been damaged or there is insufficient bile in the digestive system to help absorb the vitamin. Vitamin K_3 is a synthetic form that is given to individuals who can't produce or absorb the vitamin. In some countries vitamin K is routinely given to newborns that have not yet developed sufficient intestinal flora to produce the vitamin on their own.

Vitamin K is part of the mechanism that causes blood to clot and bones to form. Without it there is a risk of massive uncontrolled bleeding and malformation of developing bone.

See Also • Antioxidants, Nutrition

VODKA • See Liquor

WAFFLES • See Pancakes

WAHOO • See Fish

WAKAME • See Seaweed

WALLEYE • See Fish

WALNUT OIL • See Oil

WALNUTS • See Nuts

WALU • See Fish

WASABI • See Cruciferous Vegetables, Horseradish, Roots

WATER

What It Is • It would be difficult to exaggerate the significance of water. All of life, including human life, exists in aqueous solution. It is our principal nutrient, and we must consume more of it than any other food to maintain health. Take it away and we waste away in a matter of days. Our bodies are 70% water, and plants can be as much as 95%. And yet water is the smallest and simplest of food molecules, composed of just three atoms, two of hydrogen and one of oxygen — H_2O.

What It Does • Because water is essential for life, people have been preserving food for millennia by getting rid of it. Dehydration denies microorganisms the water they need, so ridding food of its water and keeping it dry means they cannot grow in it. Even highly perishable food, such as fish, can be dried sufficiently to be stored for a year or more without spoiling. Dried fish, like baccalà (dried salt cod), must be soaked in water to rehydrate it before it can be eaten. The molecules in the fish, having been denied their natural aqueous state, eagerly soak up the water. And the water easily bonds with the molecules in the flesh and returns about 75% of the moisture it held in the fresh state, which brings us to the next property of water that makes it essential in the kitchen.

Water is good at attaching itself to other molecules. In doughs, water connects with broken starch molecules, causing them to swell and break down further into individual sugars that become the food for yeast. At the same time, glutenin protein molecules in the flour attach to water and spread out, forming the first strands of gluten that will give the dough its structure. When dough bakes, the water attached to protein and starch molecules turns to steam, which gets trapped in the bubbles of air in the dough, causing the baked good to rise. Steam also collects on the surface of baking doughs, keeping the surface soft and moist, allowing it to expand before it forms a crust, resulting in lighter, airier breads and cakes. A cracked crust is an indication that the surface dried before the dough or batter was sufficiently risen, which means either the dough lacked water or the oven temperature was too high.

Water doesn't just attach itself to organic matter. It is attracted to minerals as well, a characteristic that can alter the composition of spring water and tap water. The two most common minerals in tap water are calcium and magnesium salts. Calcium and magnesium ions in water make water "hard" and affect how the water interacts with food. Because minerals are slightly alkaline, they actually help preserve the color of green vegetables in cooking, but they can also turn purple vegetables, like cabbage, an other-worldly turquoise color. Very hard water damages the cell walls of simmering produce, causing vegetables and fruit to turn mushy, and destroys their vitamins. In doughs, calcium and magnesium crosslink with gluten, causing doughs to become firm, which can be advantageous in bread but a problem in cake. When making coffee, magnesium and calcium salts slow flavor extraction, collect in the pipes of coffee machines, reduce the creation of espresso foam, and cloud brewed coffee. In tea, hard water creates surface scum in the cup because acid in the tea causes calcium to precipitate and float.

Water is good at transferring temperature. Because more molecules are present in a given volume of water than in the same volume of air to transfer temperature to a substance, hot or cold water feels hotter or

colder than air of the same temperature. This is why steam and boiling water are so much more effective at transferring heat than is the hot air of an oven, and why a bottle of wine submerged in a bucket of ice water chills faster than when placed in the cold air of a refrigerator or freezer.

Most substances take up less space when they change from liquid to solid because the molecules form a more compact geometric assembly, but not water. As water solidifies into ice, its molecules form a regular pattern that requires even spacing between the molecules, which causes them to spread out a bit, causing ice to take up about 11% more space than liquid water. That's why water pipes can burst in the winter if water in them freezes, and why a bottle of wine placed in the freezer for a quick chill and forgotten will pop its cork. It is also why the fibers of raw vegetables and fruits that are frozen will rupture and leak liquid when they thaw. To prevent this breakdown, frozen produce is usually blanched first to soften its cell walls so that they are able to expand with the freezing liquid rather than breaking.

How It Works • Almost all the properties of water boil down to one fact — H_2O is polar. It has a positive charge on its hydrogens and a partial negative charge on its oxygen. This electrical polarity means that the negatively charged oxygen of one water molecule is highly attracted to the positively charged hydrogen atoms of another water molecule. So the two bond together in what is called hydrogen bonds. Hydrogen bonds are weak bonds, but in water there are a lot of them so their effect is substantial.

Because heat makes molecules move faster, the temperature of water correlates to its physical state. At room temperature the molecules of water are moving quickly enough that the hydrogen bonds break easily and form new ones easily. When molecules are constantly forming and breaking bonds, the substance they make up starts to flow, which is why between its freezing and boiling points water is liquid. Below 32°F (0°C) the molecules slow down so much that the bonds stop breaking and forming, and water becomes solid ice. At 212°F (100°C) or thereabouts (depending on the altitude) water molecules start to move so quickly that they have trouble holding on to each other, and the liquid turns into a gas in the form of steam.

Water doesn't just form hydrogen bonds with itself. It easily bonds with any substance that is polar. Both proteins and carbohydrates are polar, and water molecules tend to attach to them, which is why fresh protein and carbohydrate foods are fairly moist. If enough water attaches itself to protein or carbohydrate molecules, the molecules separate and the substance dissolves in the water, which is what happens when egg white is mixed with water. Fats are nonpolar so they are not soluble in water.

When molecules have lots of sites on which hydrogen bonds can form, they are said to be hydrophilic (water loving). When they lack those sites they are hydrophobic (water fearing). When molecules are so attracted to water that they absorb moisture from the atmosphere (sugar is an example), they are said to be hygroscopic (water attracting).

See Also • Boiling, Chemical Bonding, Drying, Freezing, Heat

WATER BUFFALO MILK • See Cheese, Milk

WATERCRESS • See Leaves

WATERMELON • See Melon

WAX BEAN • See Legumes

WEAKFISH • See Fish

WESTPHALIAN HAM • See Ham

WHEAT

What It Is • Wheat is the fruit of an annual grass, *Triticum*, native to the Mediterranean. The third most widely grown grain in the world (after corn and rice), it is used to produce everything from cereal to sauces, and it is the only grain that has the appropriate balance of the proteins glidden and glutenin to make **gluten protein**, the structural basis for all leavened **baked goods**.

What It Does • About 90% of the wheat grown in the world is from the species *T. aestivum*, which has been cultivated specifically for **bread** baking. Bread wheat can be either hard, meaning it is high in protein and particularly good at making gluten, or soft, which means it is low in protein and preferred for making low-gluten baked goods like cakes and pastries. About 75% of the wheat grown in North America is hard.

In addition to being classified by protein content, wheat grains are also named for their growing patterns and color. Spring wheat is planted in the spring and harvested in the fall; winter wheat is sown in the fall, lives as a seedling through the winter, and is harvested in the summer. Red wheat is coated in a red-brown bran layer; white wheat has a pale cream bran. Most wheat is red, but white wheat is becoming increasingly popular because it can be used to produce white whole wheat flour that is milder than brown whole wheat and looks more like white flour, which is the form of wheat flour that most people prefer.

The remaining 10% of the world's wheat production is mostly durum wheat, a particularly high-protein (and therefore high-gluten) grain that is used primarily for making **pasta**. Durum gluten is less elastic than bread-wheat gluten and therefore makes doughs that are easier to roll out. Durum gluten also absorbs less water (30% as opposed to 40% in bread wheat), which helps keep pasta al dente even after boiling. Semolina is the milled endosperm (starchy core of the grain) of durum wheat. Because of the hardness of durum endosperm, and because the starch granules of semolina would be damaged by too much milling, semolina flour cannot be ground finely and therefore has a coarse gritty texture. In addition to pasta, the glutinous texture of semolina is valued in breads, puddings, and the Indian sweet *sooji halwa* (*sooji* is the Indian word for "semolina").

Small amounts of other wheat grains (often with ancient origins) are grown in pockets around the world. Most have been distributed locally for centuries, but since interest in whole grains has exploded in the industrialized world, many of them are now available globally.

Emmer wheat was one of the earliest cultivated wheat grains and is still grown in the countries that border the Mediterranean Sea. It is especially high in protein and is

Wheat Types

Wheat	Protein % by Weight	Use
Durum (semolina)	15	Pasta
Farro (emmer)	16	Grain, pasta
Hard red spring	14	Bread, grain
Hard red winter	12	All-purpose
Hard white	11	All-purpose
Soft red	10	Cake, pastry
Soft white	10	Cake, pastry
Spelt	16	Bread, grain

best known worldwide by its Italian name, farro. Farro is particularly popular in Tuscany, where it is cooked as a whole grain in soups and used for making farrotto (wheat risotto) and pasta. Sometimes farro

is erroneously labeled as "spelt." Although they are different forms of wheat, in most recipes they can be used interchangeably without ill effect.

Kamut is a relative of durum wheat characterized by a large grain size. It is mostly cooked as a whole grain. Although ancient (*kamut* is Egyptian for "wheat"), it is now a registered trademark of Kamut International Ltd.

Spelt, a particularly high-protein wheat (as much as 17%), has been grown in southern Germany since 4000 BCE, where it is used in bread making and is cooked as a whole grain.

Like all grains, most of the fiber, protein, and nutrients of wheat are held in its outer bran layer and in its germ. So eating the whole wheat kernel, called a wheat berry, provides the most complete nutrition the wheat grain has to offer. Wheat berries of any wheat variety can be boiled as grain, usually in a large amount of salted water. Red wheat takes about an hour and a half to cook through; white wheat takes about an hour. Farro is often minimally milled to remove about 25% of its bran so that it cooks faster, usually between 30 and 45 minutes.

Bulgur (cracked wheat) is an ancient form of cooked wheat native to North Africa and the Middle East. It is made by cooking whole wheat grains until tender, drying the cooked grains, and then cracking them to remove the bran and germ. Some of the nutrition from the bran and germ are absorbed into the endosperm during the initial cooking, resulting in a nutritious grain that cooks quickly. The endosperm can be cracked into coarse or fine pieces. Bulgur is cooked and served like rice or made into tabbouleh, a popular grain salad.

Farina is finely ground wheat endosperm with some germ added to it. It is most often cooked and served as hot cereal (cream of wheat), and though it is billed as being highly nutritious, it is not a whole-grain product.

How It Works • Modern wheat evolved from the chance breeding of wild grasses, which explains why there are several grains that are genetically diverse but all known as wheat. The original wild wheat, einkorn, had two sets of chromosomes (diploid), like most plants and animals, one from the male parent and one from the female parent. About a million years ago einkorn hooked up with another wild grass, producing a wheat species with four sets of chromosomes (tetraploid), which became the first modern wheat, of which two species are still grown, emmer and durum. It is believed the extra chromosomes are what gave modern wheat the ability to produce gluten.

About 8,000 years ago some of the tetraploid wheat crossed with another wild grass, and their offspring had six sets of chromosomes (hexaploid). This wheat contained gluten-making proteins that were more water absorbent, allowing it to be turned into moist, elastic, easy-to-leaven baked goods. It became our modern bread wheat and accounts for most of the wheat grown today.

See Also • Baking, Flour, Grains

WHEAT BERRIES • See Wheat

WHEAT BRAN • See Wheat

WHEY • See Cheese, Milk

WHIPPED TOPPING • See Milk

WHISKEY • See Liquor

WHITE CHOCOLATE • See Chocolate

WHITE FISH • See Fish

WHITE PEPPER • See Spices

WHITE TEA • See Tea

WHITE VINEGAR • See Vinegar

WHITE WHEAT • See Wheat

WHITING • See Fish

WHOLE WHEAT • See Wheat

WILD GAME • See Game

WINE

What It Is • Wine is grape juice fermented with yeast. Oh, if it were only that simple. Sometimes wine is fermented with its skins and seeds (and sometimes the stems are included too), and sometimes not. Sometimes it's chilled to stop bacterial (malolactic) **fermentation**, but sometimes not. Wine can be aged in barrels, or tanks, or not at all. It can be fined (clarified) and filtered, or not, before it is bottled. After bottling it can be set aside to age, for years or decades, or it can be drunk right away.

Clearly, a process that on the surface is pretty straightforward and simple — grapes + yeast = wine — is in fact inherently complex. A winemaker must make scores of decisions on the path to turning grapes into wine, and if you add the many variations in flavor, texture, and alcohol content that result from using various grapes, and the modifying influence of climate and soil (terroir), it is easy to see how we've ended up with thousands of wines, subdivided into millions of vintages, each with its own idiosyncrasies.

Many people devote a lifetime to understanding this simple, ancient process. Though it is possible to enjoy wine without knowing much about it, it is impossible to distinguish a great wine from a merely delicious one without understanding what goes into making it.

What It Does • Grapes

Grapes are berries that are about three-quarters pulp and juice by weight, the parts that will become wine. Grape pulp and juice are mostly water infused with sugar and trace amounts of acids, minerals, vitamins, and pectin. The concentration of sugar in the pulp is critical to vinification (the process of fermenting sugar in fruit juice into wine), because the sugar is what gets converted into alcohol. The minerals and vitamins contribute to the flavor of wine, and pectin affects its consistency. The remaining 25% of a grape's weight, the skin and seeds, are largely responsible for aroma and flavor, as well as color and the wine's tannic qualities (astringency).

About 5,000 varieties of wine grapes are grown worldwide and go by about 24,000 names, depending upon where they are grown. About 150 of these varieties are planted in significant enough numbers to be commercial, and of those, nine are thought of as classic. Classic wine grapes are those that have shown consistent qualities over several hundred years even though the grapes were grown in more than one location.

Classic White Grapes

Wine made from Chardonnay has big flavors — buttered toast, butterscotch, vanilla, custard, green apple, lychee, pineapple, and citrus — and a rich, creamy texture to match. It is almost always fermented and aged in oak barrels, which makes it even bigger, bolder, and creamier. If the wine stays in barrels too long, this richness will overshadow its fruit flavors, and then Chardonnay can become unfocused and flabby. Great Chardonnay always tastes mostly of fruit accompanied by a good level of acidity. The toasty vanilla flavors from oak should complement this core character and never dominate it. The principal Chardonnay-growing countries are Argentina, Australia, Chile, France (especially Burgundy and Champagne), Italy (Trentino and Tuscany), New Zealand, South Africa, and the U.S. (particularly California, Oregon, and Washington State).

Chenin Blanc wines are round and fruity with a sparkling acidity and can be anywhere from bone dry to pleasantly sweet. The most distinguished Chenin Blancs come from the Loire Valley in France; some of the more famous appellations (officially recognized wine-growing areas by which wines are recognized and labeled) are Vouvray and Savennières. Chenin Blanc from California and South Africa tend to be

fast fact

- You can earn a master's degree or Ph.D. in wine from the Department of Viticulture (the science of growing wine grapes) and Enology (the science of wine and wine making) at the University of California, Davis.

An Overview of the Wine-making Process

Most wines go through most of these steps, but the winemaker can vary the results anywhere along the line by changing the temperature, adjusting the length of time for each step, and by encouraging or discouraging natural processes, such as by letting yeasts that grow naturally on the grape do the fermenting rather than adding yeast.

White Wine	Red Wine
Harvest grapes	Harvest grapes
Crush grapes; remove stems (or not)	Crush grapes; remove stems (or not)
Press crushed grapes to extract juice; remove skins	Mix crushed grapes, juice, skins, and seeds in a tank with yeast
Add yeast	Ferment mixture (encourage or discourage malolactic fermentation, or delay until later); periodically mix skins floating on the surface in with juice to increase color and tannins
Ferment juice (encourage or discourage malolactic fermentation, or delay until later, or don't allow at all)	Press wine; remove skins and seeds
Rest wine (or not) with lees, the debris made of spent yeasts and other solid particles (or not)	Age wine in tank or barrels; rack (decant wine from sediment) several times
Strain wine, if rested with lees	Clarify and/or filter wine (or not)
Cold-stabilize wine to precipitate tartrate crystals (or not)	Bottle wine
Age wine in tank or barrels (or not) anywhere from a few weeks to several months (usually less than a year)	Age wine anywhere from a few weeks to decades
Clarify and/or filter wine (or not)	
Bottle wine	
Age wine (or not) anywhere from a few weeks to a year	

softer and fruitier. The fruit flavors in Chenin Blanc lean toward apricots, melon, pears, and peaches.

Riesling wines tend to be low in alcohol (8% as compared to most Chardonnays at 13%), which keeps them light and refreshing, and given the right climate and soil conditions they can have brilliant acidity, a clean, crisp minerality (like water from a mountain brook), and beautiful aromatic fruit, most frequently apricots, peaches, and melon. Much of Riesling's success depends on where it is planted. It needs fairly cool growing conditions. Rieslings from the mountains in the Alsace region of France, Germany, and northern Austria are considered the best in the world. Those grown in warmer climates, like California, are softer and less precise. The stony, acidic qualities of Riesling allow the wines to be made quite sweet without becoming diffuse.

German Trockenbeerenauslese Riesling (made from grapes that are left to dry, like raisins, on the vine) can have up to 30% residual sugar.

Sauvignon Blanc is tart and herbal, although in California these qualities are underplayed by aging the wine in oak, like Chardonnay, which gives California Sauvignon Blancs a fruity character (most people equate it to figs) that is uncharacteristic of Sauvignon Blanc produced in other parts of the world. When its natural character is highlighted, Sauvignon Blanc tends to have grassy, hay-like, green tea, green herb, and flinty flavors. The most famous Sauvignon Blanc wines, Sancerre and Pouilly-Fumé, come from the Loire Valley in France. In Bordeaux, Sauvignon Blanc is typically blended with Sémillon grapes, which give it an interesting honeyed character.

Sémillon, with soft, round, fresh flavors and a floral honey aroma (particularly when aged), is frequently used for blending, particularly with Sauvignon Blanc but also with Chardonnay. The sweet wines from Sauternes are made from almost all Sémillon grapes that are left on the vine until they become infected with *Botrytis cinerea* fungus (aka noble rot), which turns them into furry raisins. At that point the sugar in the juices skyrockets, producing wines with an exceptional alcohol content and incredibly concentrated fruit flavor, mostly reminiscent of apricot, peach, or melon.

Other noteworthy white grapes are Gewürztraminer, Pinot Blanc, Pinot Gris, and Viognier.

Classic Red Grapes

Cabernet Sauvignon is the most diverse red wine grape. When young or when made in a style not intended for aging, Cabernet can be soft and easy to drink, with flavors of blackberry, cassis, eucalyptus, cedar, and plum. With age the fruit flavors become lush, modified with rich leather-like notes, and the wine can become beautifully balanced and satiny. Historically the best Cabernets are from the Médoc appellations in Bordeaux, particularly Margaux, Saint-Julien, Pauillac, and Saint-Estèphe. Well-respected Cabernets are also produced in California (where more acreage is devoted to Cabernet Sauvignon than to any other red grape), Australia, and Washington State.

Merlot wines, dominated by blackberry, cassis, and plum flavors, are very similar to Cabernet, but they also have darker notes of chocolate, mocha, and leather that tend to make Merlot softer and plumper than Cabernet. Like Cabernet, it is also historically associated with the wines of Bordeaux (but mostly outside Médoc), where it is almost always blended with Cabernet Sauvignon, Cabernet Franc, and/or Malbec. When Merlot comes from a good vineyard it can have a touch of tannin to lend it complexity, but its natural softness and full fruit can give poorly made Merlot a tendency toward flabbiness.

Pinot Noir is lighter in body, more

kitchen wisdom

Cooking with Wine

All parts of the world that produce wine cook with it. Consequently their cuisines radiate the complex flavors, subtle sweetness, bright acidity, and syrupy consistency that wine can lend to food.

Even though alcohol is more volatile than water, it is not true that food cooked with wine is ever alcohol free. If wine is briefly brought to a boil, about 85% of its alcohol remains. The longer it cooks, the more alcohol evaporates, but even after an hour of simmering about 25% of the alcohol will still be there.

Don't waste great wine in cooking. You should no more add a 10-year-old Burgundy to a boeuf bourguignon than you would add beef stock, garlic, salt, and pepper to the wine in your glass. Wines that are overly tannic in the glass will tend to be more so when reduced into a sauce, but wines that might be a little too tart to drink can be wonderful in a butter sauce spooned over poached fish.

In general, try to pair the flavors of a wine to the main ingredient in the recipe. Sauvignon Blanc, which is bright and herbal, goes beautifully in a sauce for light meats and seafood. Try a fruity, floral Gewürztraminer or Viognier in a fragrant curry. Or when cooking an assertive meat like lamb or duck, rely on an equally assertive Merlot or Zinfandel.

transparent in color, and less tannic than Cabernet Sauvignon or Merlot, which leads some uninitiated Pinot imbibers to assume its character is a bit feeble as well. Not so. Great Pinots radiate the flavor of baked plums or cherries, moist earth, mushrooms, tobacco, chocolate, leather, dry leaves, and sweat. They are complex, satisfying wines, but the grape is notoriously temperamental to grow, and unstable during wine making. In Burgundy, France, all of the red wine (except Beaujolais) is made from Pinot Noir.

Syrah (Shiraz in Australia) grapes produce a robust wine with flavors that tend toward leather, damp earth, smoke, and roasted meat, with a pronounced finish of spice, notably black pepper. The flavors of Syrah tend to be exuberant and kinetic, bouncing around in the mouth. Historically the best Syrahs are from the northern Rhône valley in France, particularly Hermitage and Côte-Rôtie. Syrahs from California and Australia tend to be softer, more syrupy, and fruitier than French Syrah.

Other noteworthy red grapes are Barbera, Nebbiolo, Sangiovese, Tempranillo, and Zinfandel.

Terroir

Where and when a grape is grown modify its characteristics. Climate, soil, elevation, and exposure to wind, rain, and sun bring nuances to wine. Their combined influence, known as terroir, is why a clipping from a Pinot Noir vine in Burgundy transplanted in the Willamette Valley of Oregon produces grapes with substantially different wine-making potential, and why the same grapes grown in the same location produce different qualities every harvest. Great wine is a blend of viticulture (the science of grape growing), the art of the vintner, and terroir.

One of the most interesting aspects of terroir is how hillsides and mountains influence grape growing. The side of a mountain creased with tiny valleys, canyons, and hills forms dozens of mini microclimates. A slope can block winds that might cause grape blossoms to freeze before they set into fruit. It can trap clouds, causing them to give up their moisture on one side of a mountain, while the other side gets no rain and needs irrigation. Mountains and hills also provide a variety of elevations. A vineyard at 2,000 feet (610 m) has a much cooler climate than one at 500 feet (150 m) less than half a mile (0.8 km) away. In general, south-facing slopes in the Northern Hemisphere (or north-facing slopes in the Southern Hemisphere), which catch more sunlight, produce ripeness quicker than land on the other side of the hill, which is less exposed to the sun. In warm climates, where overexposure to the sun can cause grapes to shrivel into raisins before they ripen, the shady slope is preferable.

Soil with good drainage is essential for grape growing. Fertility is not as important. Some of the best wines in the world come from grapes grown in seemingly infertile soil. Chardonnay grapes in Champagne thrive in soil that is mostly chalk and evolve into the most celebrated beverage in the world, and the Riesling grapes in Mosel, where some of the best Rieslings are produced, thrive on sheer hillsides littered with slate.

Many viticulturists believe that a certain amount of stress is needed for vines to produce great wines, which could be why most of the great vineyards are in places where the growing conditions are challenging. Provided that climatic adversity is not so severe that it kills the fruit or the plant, a reasonable amount of stress forces plants to adapt and get stronger. They are forced to concentrate more sugar in the fruit in case energy stores run low, resulting in a wine of greater alcohol, more concentrated fruit flavors, and better body.

Making Wine

As soon as grapes are harvested, the question of quality shifts from nature to craft. There are two basic methods of making wine, one for red and one for white. Champagne (and other sparkling wines) and fortified wines (like sherry and port) are made by specific methods that will be described separately.

The first step in turning grapes into wine is to crush them, which can be done by foot, with paddles, or in a press. The resulting mass of grape pulp, juice, skin, seeds, and sometimes stems is called must. It is the raw material from which wine is fermented. Almost all must has sulfite added at this point to retard the growth of acetic-acid-producing bacteria, wild yeasts, and molds in the fermentation to follow.

The juice of all fresh grapes, regardless of the color of the grape skin, is virtually colorless. To make red wine, the fruit is fermented with its skins. Heat generated through fermentation causes the pigment in the skin to bleed into the juice. When making white wine, the skins are quickly removed after crushing, before the juice gets a chance to pick up color. Most wine grapes are red skinned, but when white wine is made from a clear-skinned grape (such as some Champagne), the skins can be kept in the must throughout fermentation. Grape skin provides more than just color to wine. It contains tannins (see page 604), which give wines nuance and structure that helps them age. Seeds and stems also contain tannins.

The must is transferred to closed tanks and mixed with yeasts, which start to metabolize the sugars in the mixture, converting them into alcohol. The yeasts also produce bubbles of carbon dioxide gas, which rise to the surface, forcing the grape skins, if present, to the surface. The skins have to be stirred or pushed back down periodically so that the wine maintains maximum contact with them. After the desired amount of sugar is converted into alcohol (a process that can take anywhere from several days to a few weeks), the wine will be between 8 and 15% alcohol, at which point it is drained from the skins and pumped into barrels or tanks to age.

Fruity wines meant to be drunk casually are usually aged for a few months before they are bottled. Serious reds will be barrel aged for several months to a few years. Wine barrels are almost always made of oak, which exchanges molecules with the wine and gradually alters its chemistry. In addition to yeast fermentation, most red wines and some white wines go through a second type of natural fermentation called malolactic fermentation, in which benign bacteria naturally present in the wine convert tart malic acid (the same acid that's in green apples) to mellower lactic acid (the acid in dairy products), which makes wine taste softer. Malolactic fermentation can occur at the same time as yeast fermentation or separately. With white wine, malolactic fermentation is sometimes avoided because the winemaker wants to preserve the tart crispness of malic acid. Rieslings, for example, do not go through malolactic fermentation. Chardonnays, on the other hand, almost always do, which is why Chardonnays are known for a rounded, soft flavor. That perception of softness is enhanced by diacetyl, a buttery flavor compound that develops only in Chardonnay

and is characteristic of that wine.

Before bottling, the wine is cleared in several steps. White wines are cold-stabilized, which produces tartaric acid crystals that might otherwise precipitate later on in the bottle, and then usually the wine is filtered to remove fine sediment. Red wines are cleared by racking the wine, a process that involves decanting, or siphoning, the liquid wine from solid sediment at the bottom of the tank or barrel several times during aging. Some wines are "fined" to remove small particles of sediment, pectins, and tannins. The process of fining wine is similar to clarifying soup. A coagulant — clay, egg protein, casein, gelatin, or isinglass (fish protein) — is mixed into the wine, where it bonds with microscopic particles, forming larger particles that fall to the bottom. The clear wine is then skimmed from the top. Some red wine is filtered after fining to further clarify it. The practice is somewhat controversial, since some experts argue that flavorful components can be removed from the wine at the same time.

Once the wine is bottled it can be drunk immediately or aged. Most modern wines are meant to be consumed soon after bottling. Only those with a particularly high tannin content can hold up to or benefit from many years of aging. Bottle aging differs from aging in barrels in several respects. For one thing, there is little evaporation from bottles, so flavors do not concentrate, and air can't enter the bottle, so there is no interplay with oxygen. Because glass bottles are inert, unlike oak barrels, the flavor changes that happen in the bottle are reactions only between tannins, sugars, acids, and aromatic compounds in the wine.

Two Unusual Wine Methods
Most of the wine made in Champagne, a wine-producing region in northern France, is sparkling wine, and only sparkling wines made in Champagne can technically be called Champagne. The method used for making Champagne and all sparkling wine is known as *méthode champenoise*. Sparkling wine is produced the same way as any wine up to the point of bottling, at which time a small amount of alcohol-tolerant yeast and sugar

are added to the wine in the bottle and the bottle is tightly capped. The yeasts metabolize the sugar, instituting a new period of fermentation. The resulting CO_2 gets trapped in the bottle and is forced into the wine in the form of thousands of little bubbles. The only problem is that the spent yeast cells (lees) are trapped in the bottle and have to be removed, lest they make the finished wine cloudy and gritty. This is done by gradually turning and tilting the bottles (a process called riddling) so that the lees slide up the neck. When the bottle is practically vertical and the plug of lees lies just under the cap, the neck of the bottle is submerged in freezing cold brine, which freezes the lees but not the alcoholic wine just behind it. The bottle is turned upright quickly, the cap is removed, and the gas pressure from the wine sends the frozen plug of lees skyward, leaving behind a crystal clear bottle of Champagne. The bottle is topped off with a bit more Champagne and recorked.

Fortified wines, such as port and sherry, are made by stopping fermentation before all of the sugar has been consumed by yeast and then adding distilled spirits. The alcohol content of the spirits kills the yeast, which can't stand an alcohol concentration greater than 16.5%. The resulting wine is sweet, usually with more than 10% sugar and an alcohol content of about 20%.

How It Works • Alcohol is an overarching element in wine quality. The riper grapes are at harvest, the more sugar they will contain, and the higher the alcohol of the finished wine will be. Why is that important? Alcohol has a perceptible viscosity that some people describe as oily or syrupy. So wines that are high in alcohol seem thicker (sometimes described as chewier) than low-alcohol wines that are wispy and lean in comparison.

Alcohol tastes somewhat sweet, so its presence helps to balance acidity in the grape. It is also a vehicle that dissolves nonpolar flavor compounds and transports them to our olfactory receptors, making wines with high alcohol content more aromatic. Too much

alcohol can be unpleasant, though, creating an irritating burning sensation in the nose and mouth. As with all elements in wine, the amount of alcohol must be in balance with everything else, although generally speaking, a wine that is higher in alcohol will tend to have more complexity than one that is lower in alcohol. This complexity comes not just from the alcohol but because high-alcohol wines are made from riper grapes with higher sugar contents and contain more of the fruity aromas and tannins that develop as the grape matures.

Acid is an important element in grapes that balances both alcohol and sugar in the pulp. As grapes ripen, their sugar content increases and their acidity decreases, and the art to harvesting is picking the fruit at an optimum point of balance. Acidity makes wine bright. Without it, dry wines are flat and sweet wines taste flabby. Low-acid wines are prone to spoilage and do not age well, but wines that are too acidic can taste harsh and sharp. The right balance is pivotal to success. In some hot, sunny wine-growing regions, especially in parts of Australia and California, where grapes ripen quickly and can lose their acidity, vintners often add a small amount (about 2 grams per liter) of malic acid to the fermenting juice.

Sweetness and dryness are opposite characteristics in wine. A dry wine is one in which all of the sugar in the grape has been used up in fermentation. The fermentation of a sweet wine is stopped while some of the natural sugar in the juice remains. A wine with 2% or less residual sugar will taste dry to most people; at 3% it will taste slightly sweet. Dessert wines contain anywhere from 5 to 30% residual sugar.

Sweetness is often confused with fruitiness (fruit-like aromas and flavors). Fruitiness is most apparent in young wines and diminishes with aging. It is possible for a wine to be fruity and sweet or fruity and dry. But it is not possible for wine to be sweet and dry.

Tannin, which comes from the skins, seeds, and stems of the grapes, is one of the more mysterious elements is wine making. Too much makes your tongue feel like it has been rubbed with sandpaper, but just the right amount ameliorates the balance of sweetness and tartness in wine, and it gives structure to the principal flavor, a backbone from which all subsidiary flavors hang. Tannin is also a potent preservative, so if everything else is in balance, wines made from grapes with lots of tannin, like Cabernet Sauvignon or Nebbiolo, age better than wines without it. And they need to.

The qualities of tannin change with aging — its astringency and bitterness mellow. Young tannic wines are tight, closed, and undrinkable, but given time those qualities can soften, and the other aromas and flavors in the wine emerge. It used to be thought that all young tannic wines eventually lose their astringency and bitterness, but since the 1980s it has been shown that some bitter young wines age into bitter old wines. It is believed that there are different types of tannin, and much of the art of wine making has centered on the ability of a vintner to parse those differences. Just what happens is not fully known, but scientists hypothesize that as grapes reach maturity, tannin molecules may bond together into tannin polymers, and these larger molecules don't taste as astringent as smaller tannins.

See Also • Alcohol, Bacteria, Fermentation

WINE VINEGAR • See Vinegar

WINTERGREEN • See Flavor

WINTER WHEAT • See Wheat

WOK • See Cookware

WOOD • See Grilling, Liquor, Smoking, Wine

WOOD ASH • See Smoking

WOOD SMOKE • See Smoking

WORCESTERSHIRE SAUCE • See Sauces

WORT • See Beer

XANTHAN GUM • See Gums

XANTHOPHYLLS • See Pigment

YAMS • See Sweet Potatoes

YARROW • See Herbs

YEAST • See Beer, Bread, Wine

YOGURT • See Fermentation, Milk, Sauces

YUCA • See Cassava

YUZU • See Citrus

ZEST • See Citrus

ZINC • See Minerals

ZINFANDEL • See Wine

ZUCCHINI • See Squash

Library and Archives Canada Cataloguing in Publication

Joachim, David
    The science of good food : the ultimate reference on how cooking
works / David Joachim, Andrew Schloss, A. Philip Handel.

Includes index.
ISBN-13: 978-0-7788-0189-4 (pbk.).   ISBN-10: 0-7788-0189-6 (pbk.).
ISBN-13: 978-0-7788-0205-1 (bound).   ISBN-10: 0-7788-0205-1 (bound)

1. Cookery. 1. Schloss, Andrew, 1951- II. Handel, A. Philip
III. Title.

TX651.J62 2008   641.5   C2008-902454-0

ACKNOWLEDGMENTS

Both of us are kitchen tinkerers, constantly testing and experimenting to see what makes food and cooking tick. We always ask *how* and *why* and always want satisfying answers. Thankfully, we've had a lot of help answering our questions over the past three years of writing this book. Scores of friends, colleagues, and near acquaintances in person, on the phone, and by e-mail helped to answer our pleas, fill in knowledge gaps, provide direction, and shape this book.

A big thank you to Phil Handel for patiently reviewing the manuscript, clarifying our explanations, and correcting inaccuracies. Thanks also to Alistair Saunders, Burton Horn, and Dana Schloss — science geeks all — who pointed the way when we were lost in the maze of enzymes, gums, and hydrogen bonds. We're also grateful for the advice of fellow food lovers Peter Flax (thanks for the subtitle!), Selene Yeager, Dave Pryor, Jeff Lockwood, Brian Fiske, and Chris Neyen. To our families, a thousand thank-yous for tolerating our endless fixations on the minutiae of food science, such as the effects of acid on coagulating protein and the mystery of why hot liquid freezes faster than cold liquid. Without your encouragement and support, this book would never have been written.

We sat down with many colleagues to discuss kitchen science and are especially grateful to Marc Vetri, Raghavan Iyer, Sharon Sanders, and Nick Malgieri for friendship and good dinner conversation.

We ate in dozens of cutting-edge restaurants and appreciate the generosity of chefs who invited us into their kitchens and the ingenuity of others who delighted us with their innovative dishes. We've learned a lot from the cooking of (in alphabetical order) Grant Achatz, Ferran Adrià, Heston Blumenthal, Homaru Cantu, Wylie Dufresne, Will Goldfarb, Thomas Keller, and Charlie Trotter.

We are also indebted to and inspired by the food science writers who came before us. They showed us the fun we could have while armed with scientific know-how and a kitchen lab to mess around in. Thank you (in alphabetical order), Alton Brown, Shirley Corriher, Howard Hillman, Harold McGee, Russ Parsons, Hervé This, and Robert Wolke.

For shepherding the book to its publisher and mastering the art of the brief phone call, thank you and hugs to our agent, Lisa Ekus-Saffer. Thanks also to publicist Trina Kaye for helping to get this book into your hands.

To everyone at Robert Rose, we deeply appreciate the late nights of editing, revising, and designing it took to fit all this information into such a tight space. Thanks to Bob Dees, Judith Finlayson, and Marian Jarkovich. Thanks especially to our editor, Carol Sherman, who handled a very difficult manuscript with aplomb and professionalism. Thanks also to Andrew Smith for his intelligent design, and to Jennifer MacKenzie and Shaun Oakey for their insightful queries and attention to detail.

What makes food so endlessly fascinating is its daily influence on our lives. But through the writing of this book, we've come to realize that there's something even more captivating than food science — namely, the people who grow, prepare, and enjoy food around the world. Without these food lovers, there would be no food to study and no tidbits to discuss. We dedicate this book to everyone who ever bit into something delicious and wanted to know what made it taste so good.

SELECTED BIBLIOGRAPHY

While writing this book, we consulted numerous journal articles, websites, blogs, forums, and books. Space restrictions prevent us from listing them all. Here are a few of the most useful books and websites we consulted.

BOOKS

Aidells, B., and D. Kelly. *The Complete Meat Cookbook*. New York: Houghton Mifflin, 1998.

Angier, N. *The Canon*. New York: Houghton Mifflin, 2007.

Atkins, P. W. *The Periodic Kingdom*. New York: Barnes and Noble, 2007.

Barham, P. *The Science of Cooking*. Berlin: Springer, 2001.

Barrett, D., et al. *Processing Fruits*. Boca Raton, FL: CRC Press, 2004.

Charley, H. *Food Science*, 2nd ed. New York: John Wiley, 1982.

Corriher, S. *CookWise*. New York: William Morrow, 1997.

Davids, K. *Espresso*. Santa Rosa, CA: Cole Group, 1993.

Davidson, A. *The Oxford Companion to Food*. Oxford: Oxford University Press, 1999.

Fox, P., et al. *Fundamentals of Cheese Science*. Gaithersburg, MD: Aspen, 2000.

Green, A. *Field Guide to Meat*. Philadelphia: Quirk Books, 2005.

———. *Field Guide to Produce*. Philadelphia: Quirk Books, 2004.

———. *Field Guide to Seafood*. Philadelphia: Quirk Books, 2007.

Grigson, J. *The Art of Making Sausages, Pâtés, and Other Charcuterie*. New York: Knopf, 1976.

Grosser, A. *The Cookbook Decoder*. New York: Beaufort Books, 1981.

Hemphill, I. *The Spice and Herb Bible*, 2nd ed. Toronto: Robert Rose, 2006.

Hillman, H. *The New Kitchen Science*. New York: Houghton Mifflin, 2003.

Joachim, D. *The Food Substitutions Bible*. Toronto: Robert Rose, 2005.

Joachim, D., et al. *Brilliant Food Tips and Cooking Tricks*. Emmaus, PA: Rodale, 2001.

Labensky, S., and J. Fitzgerald. *The Complete Idiot's Guide to Cooking Techniques and Science*. Madison, WI: CWL, 2003.

Labensky, S., and A. Hause. *On Cooking*, 3rd ed. Upper Saddle River, NJ: Prentice Hall, 2003.

Lee, F. *Basic Food Chemistry*. Westport, CT: AVI, 1975.

Levie, A. *The Meat Handbook*, 4th ed. Westport, CT: AVI, 1979.

Lister, T., and H. Blumenthal. *Kitchen Chemistry*. London: Royal Society of Chemistry, 2005.

Maarse, H., ed. *Volatile Compounds in Foods and Beverages*. Boca Raton, FL: CRC: 1991.

MacNeil, K. *The Wine Bible*. New York: Workman, 2001.

McGee, H. *The Curious Cook*. San Francisco: North Point Press, 1990.

———. *On Food and Cooking*, revised and updated edition. New York: Scribner, 2004.

North American Meat Processors Association. *The Meat Buyer's Guide*. Hoboken, NJ: John Wiley, 2006.

Parsons, R. *How to Read a French Fry*. New York: Houghton Mifflin, 2001.

Potter, N., and J. Hotchkiss. *Food Science*, 5th ed. New York: Chapman & Hall, 1995.

Rensberger, B. *Instant Biology*. New York: Fawcett Books, 1996.

Rolland, J., and C. Sherman. *The Food Encyclopedia*. Toronto: Robert Rose, 2006.

Schneider, E. *Uncommon Fruits and Vegetables*. New York: Harper & Row, 1986.

Shils, M., et al., eds. *Modern Nutrition in Health and Disease*, 10th ed. Philadelphia: Lippincott Williams and Wilkins, 2005.

This, H. *Kitchen Mysteries*. New York: Columbia University Press, 2007.

———. *Molecular Gastronomy*. New York: Columbia University Press, 2006.

Thomas, L. *The Lives of a Cell*. New York: Viking, 1974.

Wolke, R. *What Einstein Told His Cook*. New York: W. W. Norton, 2002.

———. *What Einstein Told His Cook 2*. New York: W. W. Norton, 2005.

WEBSITES

The Accidental Scientist: Science of Cooking. Exploratorium. exploratorium.edu/cooking/index.html.

Baking 911. S. Phillips. baking911.com.

Cooking For Engineers. CFE Enterprises. cookingforengineers.com.

Cook's Illustrated. America's Test Kitchen. cooksillustrated.com.

Food and Nutrition Information Center. U.S. Department of Agriculture, National Agriculture Library. nal.usda.gov/fnic.

Food Production Daily. Decision News Media. foodproductiondaily.com.

Food Resource. Oregon State University. food.oregonstate.edu.

Gernot Katzer's Spice Pages. G. Katzer. uni-graz.at/~katzer/engl.

Health Canada. Government of Canada. http://www.hc-sc.gc.ca.

How Stuff Works. How Stuff Works, Inc. howstuffworks.com.

Khymos.org. M. Lersch. khymos.org.

National Confectioners Association. ecandy.com.

Pharmacological Reviews. American Society for Pharmacology and Experimental Therapeutics. pharmrev.aspetjournals.org.

Popular Science. Bonnier Magazine Group. popsci.com.

Science of Cooking. Science of Cooking. scienceofcooking.com.

Scientific American. Scientific American. sciam.com.

Seafood Watch. Monterey Bay Aquarium. montereybayaquarium.org/cr/seafoodwatch.asp.

U.S. Food and Drug Administration (FDA). fda.gov.

PHOTOGRAPHY CREDITS

Photos by Colin Erricson and Mark T. Shapiro, © Robert Rose, except pages: 7 © iStockphoto.com/ZoneCreative; 9 © iStockphoto.com/Jarek Szymanski; 11 © iStockphoto.com/Joan Vicent Cantó Roig; 14 © iStockphoto.com/Mark Hatfield; 16 © iStockphoto.com/Dmitry Ersler; 20 © iStockphoto.com/Bertrand Collet; 27 © iStockphoto.com/Sergey Siz`kov; 31 © iStockphoto.com/Ivan Mateev; 36 © iStockphoto.com/Juan Monino; 45 © iStockphoto.com/Christine Balderas; 47 © iStockphoto.com/HannamariaH; 51 © iStockphoto.com/Juan Monino; 57 © iStockphoto.com/Cat London; 60 © iStockphoto.com/Selahattin BAYRAM; 65 © iStockphoto.com/Andres Peiro Palmer; 69 © iStockphoto.com/Gord Horne; 75 © iStockphoto.com/Pidjoe; 77 © iStockphoto.com/Christine Balderas; 79 © iStockphoto.com/Alex Sudarikov; 83 © iStockphoto.com/Marie-france Bélanger; 85 © iStockphoto.com/Yoko Bates; 89 © iStockphoto.com/Javier Fontanella; 94 © iStockphoto.com/Kristine Fletcher; 98 © iStockphoto.com/Andrew Lewis; 102 © iStockphoto.com/ranplett; 104 © iStockphoto.com/Valentyn Volkov; 108 © iStockphoto.com/YinYang; 116 © iStockphoto.com/Ivan Kmit; 123 © iStockphoto.com/Tea Potocnik; 125 © iStockphoto.com/Ievgenia Tikhonova; 127 © iStockphoto.com/YinYang; 129 © iStockphoto.com/Norman Pogson; 133 © iStockphoto.com/Trevor Fisher; 137 © iStockphoto.com/Derek Thomas; 141 © iStockphoto.com/Tarek El Sombati; 145 © iStockphoto.com/Floortje; 147 © iStockphoto.com/Andres Peiro Palmer; 153 © iStockphoto.com/Joan Vicent Cantó Roig; 161 © iStockphoto.com/Melissa King; 163 © iStockphoto.com/Loic Bernard; 165 © iStockphoto.com/mihaicalin; 167 © iStockphoto.com/Joan Vicent Cantó Roig; 168 © iStockphoto.com/Lilli Day; 172 © iStockphoto.com/Kameleon007; 175 © iStockphoto.com/Donald Erickson; 182 © iStockphoto.com/Ekaterina Ostanina; 185 © iStockphoto.com/Lane Collins; 192 © iStockphoto.com/Anna Yu; 194 © iStockphoto.com/creacart; 197 © iStockphoto.com/Alexandr Stepanov; 199 © iStockphoto.com/Roberto A Sanchez; 200 © iStockphoto.com/Graham Bedingfield Birmingham; 203 © iStockphoto.com/ranplett; 205 © iStockphoto.com/Branislav Senic; 209 © iStockphoto.com/Dirk Richter; 213 © iStockphoto.com/Olga Shelego; 215 © iStockphoto.com/Joshua Northrup; 217 © iStockphoto.com/Fredrikke Wetherilt; 219 © iStockphoto.com/Robyn Mackenzie; 222 © iStockphoto.com/Suzannah Skelton; 226 © iStockphoto.com/Pål Espen Olsen; 229 © iStockphoto.com/Eva Serrabassa; 233 © iStockphoto.com/George Peters; 235 © iStockphoto.com/Pascal Le Brun; 242 © iStockphoto.com/Virginia Hamrick; 244 © iStockphoto.com/Jowita Stachowiak; 253 © iStockphoto.com/Trevor Hunt; 257 © iStockphoto.com/Kelly Cline; 260 © iStockphoto.com/Edyta Pawlowska; 263 © iStockphoto.com/Dan Chippendale; 265 © iStockphoto.com/Mikael Damkier; 266 © iStockphoto.com/Kelly Cline; 269 © iStockphoto.com/Kevin Snair; 274 © iStockphoto.com/Ben Greer; 275 © iStockphoto.com/Norman Chan; 279 © iStockphoto.com/dra_schwartz; 283 © iStockphoto.com/Vlado Janĺekovi?; 286 © iStockphoto.com/Takács Zsolt; 290 © iStockphoto.com/Eva Serrabassa; 295 © iStockphoto.com/Christopher Badzioch; 297 © iStockphoto.com/Ivan Mateev; 305 © iStockphoto.com/Robyn Mackenzie; 311 © iStockphoto.com/Julián Rovagnati; 314 © iStockphoto.com/Elena Schweitzer; 316 © iStockphoto.com/Kelly Cline; 323 © iStockphoto.com/Monika Adamczyk; 335 © iStockphoto.com/Carmen MartÃnez BanÃºs; 336 © iStockphoto.com/Kameleon007; 341 © iStockphoto.com/Marcelo Wain; 343 © iStockphoto.com/creacart; 346 © iStockphoto.com/Kelly Cline; 349 © iStockphoto.com/Liv Friis-Larsen; 353 © iStockphoto.com/Arthur Kwiatkowski; 359 © iStockphoto.com/Monika Olszewska; 364 © iStockphoto.com/Tracy Hebden; 367 © iStockphoto.com/bluestocking; 371 © iStockphoto.com/YinYang; 375 © iStockphoto.com/Feng Yu; 378 © iStockphoto.com/Andrew Manley; 383 © iStockphoto.com/Kelly Cline; 393 © iStockphoto.com/creacart; 397 © iStockphoto.com/Bill Grove; 400 © iStockphoto.com/Stefan Klein; 407 © iStockphoto.com/Jessica Jones; 412 © iStockphoto.com/jerryhat; 417 © iStockphoto.com/Ivan Mateev; 421 © iStockphoto.com/Lars Nilsson; 422 © iStockphoto.com/Suzannah Skelton; 425 © iStockphoto.com/Anders Aagesen; 426 © iStockphoto.com/Floortje; 428 © iStockphoto.com/Ljupco Smokovski; 433 © iStockphoto.com/George Bailey; 435 © iStockphoto.com/Johan Eriksson; 439 © iStockphoto.com/Gregor Lajh; 449 © iStockphoto.com/Roman Chmiel; 451 © iStockphoto.com/bluestocking; 453 © iStockphoto.com/Ensa; 460 © iStockphoto.com/Denise Kappa; 464 © iStockphoto.com/Dmitrii; 466 © iStockphoto.com/Richard Hobson; 487 © iStockphoto.com/Eric Isselée; 495 © iStockphoto.com/Evangelos Patriarcheas; 500 © iStockphoto.com/Juan Monino; 502 © iStockphoto.com/Chiya Li; 505 © iStockphoto.com/powershot; 507 © iStockphoto.com/Robyn Mackenzie; 509 © iStockphoto.com/Andrew Johnson; 513 © iStockphoto.com/sasimoto; 518 © iStockphoto.com/Dirk Richter; 521 © iStockphoto.com/Kameleon007; 529 © iStockphoto.com/Steve Dibblee; 533 © iStockphoto.com/Elena Elisseeva; 537 © iStockphoto.com/Ekaterina Shlikhunova; 542 © iStockphoto.com/Elena Schweitzer; 545 © iStockphoto.com/FhF Greenmedia; 550 © iStockphoto.com/Kristen Johansen; 553 © iStockphoto.com/Joan Vicent Cantó Roig; 556 © iStockphoto.com/Daniel Wiedemann; 559 © iStockphoto.com/Oliver Hoffmann; 561 © iStockphoto.com/Roman Chmiel; 562 © iStockphoto.com/Joe Lena; 566 © iStockphoto.com/Doctor Bass; 568 © iStockphoto.com/Vitalina Rybakova; 573 © iStockphoto.com/Kelly Cline; 575 © iStockphoto.com/Joanna Wnuk; 580 © iStockphoto.com/kkgas; 585 © iStockphoto.com/Floortje; 591 © iStockphoto.com/Levent Ince; 594 © iStockphoto.com/Tatiana Popova; 596 © iStockphoto.com/Maria Bibikova; 603 © iStockphoto.com/Trevor Fisher

INDEX

Note: Recipe titles are listed in **red**. Page numbers followed by (t) indicate that the information can be found in a table.